Network and Distributed System Security Symposium 2012 (NDSS'12)

San Diego, California, USA
5 – 8 February 2012

ISBN: 978-1-7138-2066-6

Printed from e-media with permission by:

Curran Associates, Inc.
57 Morehouse Lane
Red Hook, NY 12571

The Internet Society
11710 Plaza America Drive, Suite 400
Reston, VA 20190
U.S.A.

Phone: (703) 439-2120
Fax: (703) 326-9881

www.internetsociety.org

Additional copies of this publication are available from:

Curran Associates, Inc.
57 Morehouse Lane
Red Hook, NY 12571 USA
Phone: 845-758-0400
Fax: 845-758-2633
Email: curran@proceedings.com
Web: www.proceedings.com

TABLE OF CONTENTS

SESSION 5: SOCIAL NETWORKS AND APPLICATION SECURITY

SESSION 6: APPLIED CRYPTO

SESSION 10: HOST SECURITY

SESSION 11: WEB

SESSION 12: NETWORKING II

SESSION 13: DISTRIBUTED SYSTEMS

SESSION 14: SOFTWARE

Plaintext-Recovery Attacks Against Datagram TLS

Nadhem J. AlFardan and Kenneth G. Paterson*
Information Security Group
Royal Holloway, University of London, Egham, Surrey TW20 0EX, UK
{Nadhem.Alfardan.2009, kenny.paterson}@rhul.ac.uk

Abstract

The Datagram Transport Layer Security (DTLS) protocol provides confidentiality and integrity of data exchanged between a client and a server. We describe an efficient and full plaintext recovery attack against the OpenSSL implementation of DTLS, and a partial plaintext recovery attack against the GnuTLS implementation of DTLS. The attack against the OpenSSL implementation is a variant of Vaudenay's padding oracle attack and exploits small timing differences arising during the cryptographic processing of DTLS packets. It would have been prevented if the OpenSSL implementation had been in accordance with the DTLS RFC. In contrast, the GnuTLS implementation does *follow the DTLS RFC closely, but is still vulnerable to attack. The attacks require new insights to overcome the lack of error messages in DTLS and to amplify the timing differences. We discuss the reasons why these implementations are insecure, drawing lessons for secure protocol design and implementation in general.*

Keywords TLS, DTLS, CBC-mode encryption, padding oracle, attack, timing, OpenSSL, GnuTLS.

1 Introduction

DTLS, OpenSSL and GnuTLS: The Datagram Transport Layer Security (DTLS) protocol was first introduced at NDSS in 2004 [10]. Two years later, the Internet Engineering Task Force (IETF) assigned Request for Comments (RFC) 4347 [11] to DTLS. The aim of DTLS is to provide a datagram-compatible variant of TLSv1.1 [6] that eliminates the dependency on the Transport Control Protocol (TCP). Since its introduction, there has been a growing interest in the security services offered by DTLS. Leading implementations of DTLS can be found in OpenSSL[1] and GnuTLS[2]. Both of these provide source toolkits that implement TLS and DTLS as well as being general purpose cryptographic libraries that software developers can use. The first release of OpenSSL to implement DTLS was 0.9.8. Since its release, DTLS has become a mainstream protocol in OpenSSL. There are also a number of commercial products that have taken advantage of DTLS. For example, DTLS is used to secure Virtual Private Networks (VPNs)[3,4] and wireless traffic[5]. Platforms such as Microsoft Windows, Microsoft .NET and Linux can also make use of DTLS[6]. In addition, the number of RFC documents that are being published on DTLS is increasing. Recent examples include RFC 5415 [1], RFC 5953 [8] and RFC 6012 [13]. A new version of DTLS is currently under development in the IETF to bring DTLS into line with TLSv1.2.

Padding oracle attacks: According to [11], the DTLS protocol is based on TLSv1.1 and provides equivalent security guarantees. In particular, then, one would expect implementations of DTLS to be resilient to attacks on TLS known prior to the development of TLSv1.1, especially those attacks explicitly mentioned in RFC 4346 [6], the specification for TLSv1.1.

One such example is the padding oracle attack introduced by Vaudenay in [15] and applied to OpenSSL by Canvel *et al.* in [2]. This attack exploits the MAC-then-Pad-then-Encrypt construction used by TLS and makes use of subtle timing differences that may arise in the cryptographic processing carried out during decryption, in order to glean information about the correctness or otherwise of the plaintext format underlying a target ciphertext. Specifically, Canvel *et al.* used timing of encrypted TLS error messages in order to distinguish whether the padding occurring

*This author's research supported by an EPSRC Leadership Fellowship, EP/H005455/1.

[1] `http://www.openssl.org`

[2] `http://www.gnu.org/software/gnutls`

[3] `http://www.cisco.com/en/US/products/ps10884/index.html`

[4] `http://campagnol.sourceforge.net`

[5] `http://www.cisco.com/en/US/docs/wireless/controller/7.0MR1/configuration/guide/cgi_lwap.html`

[6] `http://www.eldos.com/sbb/desc-ssl.php`

at the end of the plaintext was correctly formatted according to the TLS standard or not. Using Vaudenay's ideas, this *padding oracle* information can be leveraged to build a full plaintext recovery attack. However, because TLS tears down the connection in the event of any error arising during cryptographic processing, and because all the messages in the attack do provoke such errors, the attack can only recover significant amounts of plaintext if the same plaintext bytes are repeated across many TLS connections at the same location in the data stream.

OpenSSL quickly addressed the attack of [2] by modifying the code to firstly make the error messages are identical and secondly to ensure that the error messages would always appear on the network at the same time, an approach we call *uniform error reporting*. These countermeasures eventually appeared in TLSv1.1 as guidance for implementors a few years later. Since the initial work in this vein, padding oracle attacks have been generalised in various ways and applied to other network protocols such as IPsec [4, 5] and application layer protocols such as ASP.NET [12, 7], further highlighting the dangers of the MAC-then-PAD-then-Encrypt cryptographic construction coupled with non-uniform error reporting.

Our attack on DTLS: Given this history, and the fact that the DTLS specification is based on that of TLSv1.1, implementations of DTLS should be immune to padding oracle attacks and their variants. Our paper shows that this is not the case for either the OpenSSL or the GnuTLS implementations of DTLS.

We first focus on OpenSSL, showing that there is a small timing difference in OpenSSL's processing of DTLS packets having valid and invalid padding fields: just like old version of OpenSSL's implementation of TLS, if the padding is invalid, then the MAC is not checked, while if the padding is valid, the MAC check is done. This results in a timing difference for processing of packets with valid and invalid padding that is on the order of a few tens of microseconds (μs) on a modern processor.

However, one major difference between TLS and DTLS is that DTLS provides no error messages when decryption encounters an error. The detection of these error messages is essential to the attacks of [2] on TLS. Thus it would appear that this timing difference *cannot* be used to build a padding oracle. This may explain why the OpenSSL code for DTLS has not been patched to remove the known timing difference.

By bringing new techniques into play, we show that the lack of DTLS error messages is not a serious impediment to the attack – we are able to exploit the DTLS extension for Heartbeat messages [14] to ensure that the timing difference shows up in the timing of Heartbeat response messages rather than error messages. In fact, any upper layer protocol which has messages that also provoke a response message with a predictable delay can be used in place of Heartbeat messages in our attack. We also introduce new techniques which *amplify* the identified timing difference. In TLS, this is easily done by using long messages, since TLS supports messages up to roughly 2^{14} bytes in size. But this is not possible in DTLS, since the maximum message size is limited by the PMTU. To overcome this, we build trains of DTLS packets which all either have valid or invalid padding and hence which all contribute to an accumulated timing difference in the same way. These trains need to be carefully injected into the network – fast enough so as to ensure each packet arrives before the processing of the previous one has completed, but not so fast that DTLS's buffer for incoming packets gets swamped. Thus the success of the attack depends on delicate, μs-level timing of network events.

Another major difference between TLS and DTLS is that, in TLS, any error arising during cryptographic processing is treated as fatal, meaning that the TLS connection is discarded in the event of any error. TLS can afford to do this because it is built on top of a reliable transport protocol, TCP. DTLS, on the other hand, cannot afford to do so, since its underlying transport protocol is UDP. This means that DTLS does *not* discard connections in the event of errors, but merely discards error-generating packets. So, in contrast to previous attacks on TLS, our attack on OpenSSL's DTLS implementation can efficiently recover as much plaintext as the adversary desires, without having to wait for the re-establishment of DTLS connections. Our attack becomes even more efficient in the situation where DTLS's anti-replay feature is disabled, which is an option within the DTLS specification.

Our attack on OpenSSL is easily prevented, by properly implementing the countermeasures in the TLSv1.1 specification on which DTLS is based. We have informed the OpenSSL development team about our attack. They have supplied us with a potential fix that we have tested and found to be effective against the attack. We expect that the fix will be made public soon.

We then switch our focus to the GnuTLS implementation, and show that, even though it properly implements the countermeasures in TLSv1.1, it is still vulnerable to a partial plaintext recovery attack in its default configuration. We show that a small timing channel is introduced into the decryption process because a plaintext-dependent sanity check is carried out at an early stage during decryption. This introduces a detectable timing difference that, when combined with our new techniques, allows 4 or 5 bits of plaintext to be recovered per ciphertext block. In principle, the attack could also be applied to the GnuTLS implementation of TLS (but then the timing difference would be hard to amplify). We have informed the GnuTLS development team about our finding and we are working with them to identify the root cause of the timing difference.

Despite the availability of easy fixes, we argue that the attacks are still interesting and provide valuable lessons for protocol designers and implementors:

- To our knowledge, our attacks are the first of their kind against any implementations of DTLS. Our OpenSSL attack is also the first plaintext-recovering attack against a protocol implemented by OpenSSL since the work of Canvel *et al.* [2].

- Our attacks exploit the fact that DTLS has to be error-tolerant, but we had to find a novel means to circumvent the resulting lack of error messages.

- The DTLS specification is rather brief and refers to the TLSv1.1 specification for many details, particularly those relating to how packets are encrypted and decrypted. This then requires an implementor to cross-refer to other standards during implementation, which may lead to software that does not implement the known countermeasures.

- Our attack on the GnuTLS implementation of DTLS and TLS shows that, even if all the known countermeasures are carefully implemented, DTLS and TLS implementations may still be vulnerable to attack via subtle timing side channels.

We expand on these themes later in the paper.

Paper organisation: Section 2 provides further background on DTLS, TLS and padding oracle attacks, as preparation for the presentation of our basic attack against the OpenSSL implementation in Section 3. Then Section 4 discusses a number of implementation issues for this attack and discusses refinements of it. Section 5 presents our experimental results demonstrating efficient and reliable recovery of full DTLS plaintexts in the OpenSSL case. Section 6 briefly discusses how similar attacks can recover partial plaintexts in the GnuTLS case. Section 7 discusses the wider implications of our work for secure network protocol design.

2 Further Background

2.1 Encryption in DTLS

A DTLS client initiates a handshake protocol with a server to agree on a number of parameters such as the cipher suite and the keys to use for a symmetric encryption algorithm and a message authentication code (MAC). After the handshake is complete, DTLS deploys a MAC-then-PAD-then-Encrypt construction, with CBC being a commonly used mode of operation. We will assume CBC-mode encryption is in use for the remainder of the paper.

When sending a DTLS packet, the sender first calculates a MAC over the DTLS payload and other parameters including a sequence number [11]. The size of the MAC output depends on the hash function used (e.g. 160 bits in the case of HMAC-SHA-1). The MAC is appended to the DTLS message. The sender then appends padding so that the payload length is a multiple of b bytes, where b is the block-size of the selected block cipher (so $b = 8$ for 3DES and $b = 16$ for AES). As with TLS, the padding consists of $p + 1$ copies of some byte value p, where $0 \leq p \leq 255$. In particular, at least 1 byte of padding must always be added. So examples of valid padding fields are: "0x00", "$0x01, 0x01$" and "$0x02, 0x02, 0x02$". The padding may extend over multiple blocks, and receivers must support the removal of such extended padding. The concatenation of DTLS message, MAC and padding is then encrypted using CBC-mode of the selected block cipher, using an explicit IV. Thus, the ciphertext blocks are formed as:

$$C_j = E_k(P_j \oplus C_{j-1})$$

where P_i are the plaintext blocks, C_0 is the IV, and k is the key for the block cipher E. The resulting ciphertext, including the IV, is then appended to a header which includes a length field and an explicit sequence number. The decryption process reverses this sequence of steps. First the ciphertext is decrypted block by block to recover the plaintext blocks:

$$P_j = D_k(C_j) \oplus C_{j-1},$$

where D denotes the decryption algorithm of the block cipher. Then the padding is checked and removed, and finally, the MAC is checked.

2.2 DTLS versus TLS

Applications that operate over the Unreliable Datagram Protocol (UDP) can easily take advantage of the security services offered of DTLS. Such applications are generally unconcerned about the session management services that TCP provides. Simple Network Management Protocol [8] is a good example of such applications. Other examples include voice and video network streaming applications. By design, DTLS is very similar to TLSv1.1 [6]. In fact, RFC 4347 [11] presents only the changes to TLSv1.1 introduced by DTLS and refers to RFC 4346 [6] for the rest of the protocol specification. According to RFC 4347, this approach has been chosen to minimize the amount of effort needed to implement the protocol. Thus, to fully understand and be able to analyse and code DTLS, the reader of RFC 4347 is expected to be familiar with TLSv1.1.

A number of changes were introduced so that the services of TLSv1.1 could be delivered over an unreliable transport protocol like UDP. The reader can refer to [11] and [10] for the complete list of changes. We list here some of the changes relevant to our work:

- In TLS, MAC errors must result in connection termination. In DTLS, the receiving implementation may simply discard the offending record and continue with the connection. According to [11, Section 4.1.2.1], DTLS implementations should silently discard data with bad MACs, and the OpenSSL implementation takes this "discard and continue" option, with no error messages being sent on the wire. Not sending error messages clearly complicates the task of the adversary, since it is the presence of these messages (and their timings) that allowed previous attacks on TLS; however not terminating the connection in the event of an error proves to be very useful in building a reliable padding oracle that can be accessed as many times as the adversary wishes.
- Unlike TLSv1.1, fragmentation of record messages is not permitted in DTLS. Instead, a DTLS record must fit within a single lower layer datagram. Therefore, we cannot use a large size message in our attacks, a feature exploited in [2] to amplify timing differences for TLS.
- DTLS optionally supports record replay detection, whereas this is required in TLS. The technique used is the same as in IPsec's AH protocol [9], by maintaining a bitmap window of received records. Records that are too old to fit in the window and records that have previously been received are silently discarded. According to [11], the replay detection feature is optional, since packet duplication is not always malicious, but can also occur due to routing errors. In this paper, we mostly focus on the case where the DTLS anti-replay feature is disabled, but explain how to extend our attack to the case where it is enabled in Section 4.5.

2.3 Heartbeat Extension for TLS and DTLS

The Heartbeat extension [14] provides a new protocol for TLS and DTLS allowing a keep-alive functionality. This is very useful in the case of DTLS, which runs on top of unreliable transport protocols that have no concept of session management. The only mechanism available at the DTLS layer to determine if a peer is still alive is performing a costly renegotiation. The Heartbeat extension uses Heartbeat request and response messages between two entities having an established DTLS connection. A Heartbeat request message can be sent by either of the entities and is protected using the same DTLS ciphersuite and keys used for protecting other payloads. According to [14], whenever a Heartbeat request message is received, it has to be answered with a corresponding Heartbeat response message. Both messages have specific lengths that can be detected by the adversary. Although we exploit Heartbeat request messages in our attack against OpenSSL, other type of messages could also be used. The only constraint is that they should always predictably generate responses that can be detected by the adversary. We demonstrate this in our attack against GnuTLS.

2.4 Padding Oracle Attacks

The concept of a padding oracle was first introduced by Vaudenay [15]. In Vaudenay's formulation, a padding oracle is a notional algorithm which, when presented with a CBC-mode ciphertext, returns `VALID` if the underlying plaintext has padding that is correctly formatted and `INVALID` otherwise. Here, correctness is with respect to some padding scheme. For example, for TLS/DTLS padding, correctness means that the decryption of the ciphertext is a byte string ending in one of the valid padding patterns "0x00", "0x01, 0x01", etc. Vaudenay showed that, for certain padding schemes, repeated access to a padding oracle can be used to decrypt arbitrary target ciphertext blocks (and indeed complete ciphertexts in a block-by-block manner). His techniques apply to the TLS/DTLS padding scheme and, for completeness, we show in Algorithm 1 how to decrypt a complete block from a target ciphertext C^*, given access to a padding oracle. In this algorithm, for ease of presentation, we number the bytes of the target ciphertext block C_t^* from 0 to $b-1$ starting with the *rightmost* byte; we also use C_{t-1}^* to denote the ciphertext block preceding the target block in the ciphertext C^*. For any block B, we write $B[i]$, $0 \leq i < b$ to denote its bytes. The attack requires on average 128 and at most 256 queries to the padding oracle to decrypt each byte of the target block. The attack as presented uses 2-block ciphertexts, but is easily adapted to use longer ciphertexts simply by ensuring that blocks R, C_t^* are always placed at the end of the ciphertext.

In practice, to mount a padding oracle attack, an adversary must find some way of actually realizing a padding oracle for a specific implementation. In the original presentation for TLS in [15], Vaudenay posited that such an oracle could be built by sending a message to a TLS server and then waiting for a reply in the form of an error message. In TLSv1.0, a `decryption_failed` message would indicate a padding error, while a `bad_record_mac` message would indicate that padding was correct, but that MAC verification had failed. There are (at least) two challenges to building a TLS padding oracle in this way:

1. The two TLS errors, `decryption_failed` and `bad_record_mac`, are classified as fatal, causing the immediate termination of the TLS connection after *every* query to the padding oracle. Informally, we say

Algorithm 1: Decrypting a block using a padding oracle $\mathcal{PO}$ for TLS/DTLS.

Data: C^*_{t-1}, C^*_t
Result: $P^*_t = D_k(C^*_t) \oplus C^*_{t-1}$
Let R be a random b-byte block.;
for $i = 0$ **to** $b - 1$ **do**
    for $\texttt{byte} = 0$ *to* 255 **do**
        $R[i] = \texttt{byte}$;
        $C = R||C^*_t$;
        if $\mathcal{PO}(C) = \texttt{VALID}$ **then**
            $P[i] = R[i] \oplus C^*_{t-1}[i] \oplus i$;
            Break;
    for $j = 0$ *to* i **do**
        $R[j] = R[j] \oplus (i) \oplus (i + 1)$;
Output P;

that the padding oracle behaves as a *bomb oracle.* The adversary must wait for a new TLS connection to be established before making another query, but each new connection will have fresh keying material. This makes the attack impractical unless connections are re-established quickly. Moreover, unless the same plaintext is repeated in a known ciphertext block across many connections, the adversary can only efficiently recover the last byte of each block in the bomb oracle case.

2. The two error messages are encrypted, making it more difficult for the adversary to distinguish them.

The work of Canvel *et al.* [2] addressed the second issue here, by developing a different realization for the padding oracle. Their realization relies on the fact that, for a TLS implementation, the processing of a message with valid padding may take longer than the processing of a message with invalid padding. The reason for this is that the padding is checked for validity before the MAC verification is performed, and so a TLS implementation that aborts processing immediately after detecting an error (of any kind) will exhibit a timing difference in message processing for packets with valid and invalid padding: in the former case, the MAC verification will take place, while in the latter it will not. The timing difference would then show up as a difference in the time at which the error messages appear on the network. As observed in [2], this is exactly how TLS was implemented in OpenSSL.

In the attack in [2], the timing difference was amplified by working with long messages, since these take longer to pass through MAC verification. Canvel *et al.* reported timing differences of as much as 2 milliseconds for these long messages[7]. Because of noise introduced by various sources, the padding oracle so obtained is not fully reliable, so the server had to be queried a number of times for every message and a statistical model used to analyse the observed timings. Moreover, the oracle is still a bomb oracle, so only one query per TLS connection can be made. Even so, Canvel *et al.* [2] were able to use this approach to extract TLS-encrypted passwords for an IMAP e-mail server running stunnel, an application using the OpenSSL implementation of TLS. The attack was perceived as serious enough that the OpenSSL code for TLS was updated from releases 0.9.6i and 0.9.7a, to ensure that the processing time for TLS messages is essentially the same, whether or not the padding is correct, and to send the same encrypted error message, `bad_record_mac`, in both cases. Eventually, the same countermeasures appeared in the specification for TLSv1.1 [6], with the requirement that they *must* be implemented.

3 Building A Padding Oracle for the OpenSSL Implementation of DTLS

3.1 Assumptions on the Adversary

The objective of the attack is to recover DTLS-protected plaintext. We assume that the adversary:

- Has access to the ciphertext. This can be achieved by the adversary gaining access to a network device like a switch or a router, or by ARP spoofing, or by eavesdropping in a wireless environment.
- Can send arbitrary DTLS messages to the original recipient. This can be achieved by injecting packets into the network while spoofing the IP and UDP headers.
- Is aware of the encryption algorithm's block size, b. The adversary can infer this by either monitoring the connection's handshake messages, or the size of the encrypted messages over time.
- Can detect and record a number of Heartbeat request packets.

The above assumptions apply when anti-replay is deactivated. We note that anti-replay is enabled by default for both the OpenSSL and GnuTLS implementations of DTLS, and we had to modify the server source code to disable it in our experiments. When anti-replay is activated, then we also need to assume that the adversary can stop messages of his choice from reaching their final destination. For example, the adversary may achieve this by exploiting his control

[7] We measured the MAC verification time for DTLS messages with payload sizes of up to 1456 bytes and found the time to be in the tens of μs instead.

over a router or a firewall in the data path. In presenting our attack below, we assume that anti-replay is disabled, i.e. we assume that the targeted system does *not* perform sequence number checking for incoming DTLS messages. We explain how to modify the attack to handle the case where anti-replay is enabled in Section 4.5.

3.2 A Padding Oracle for the OpenSSL Implementation of DTLS

In this section, we explain how to construct a padding oracle for the OpenSSL implementation of DTLS. This oracle can then be used in the standard way to decrypt arbitrary ciphertext blocks and thence arbitrary amounts of plaintext data, as described in Section 2.4. The key observation we use is that, in the current OpenSSL implementation of DTLS, if the padding underlying a ciphertext is valid, then the MAC on the message is checked, whereas if the padding is invalid, then the MAC is not checked and the ciphertext is rejected immediately. This contravenes the requirement for equal processing times in TLSv1.1 that is inherited by reference in the DTLS specification. As a consequence of this deviation, we would expect the processing time for a DTLS packet with invalid padding to be slightly less than that of a DTLS packet with valid padding. The actual time difference depends on a number of factors including the algorithms used, the clock-speed of the target system, the size of the DTLS packet, other processes running on the target system, and the network conditions. For example, we measured the MAC verification time on our testing machine running OpenSSL with HMAC-SHA-1 and found it to be in in the order of tens of μs – see Figure 1.

So far, this is identical to the timing side channel exploited in [2]. However, DTLS does not have any error messages, so we cannot use existing methods to observe the difference in processing times. This may explain why the implementors of DTLS in OpenSSL chose not to implement the required countermeasures. Instead, we introduce an alternative means to detect the timing difference, by exploiting Heartbeat messages. The basic idea is quite simple. Suppose we send to the target system a packet train consisting of a DTLS packet P_C carrying the ciphertext C (whose padding validity we wish to test) immediately followed by a Heartbeat request message. Then this train will result in a detectable Heartbeat response message being sent back on the network, and, assuming orderly processing on the target system, the total amount of time needed to process P_C and to produce the Heartbeat response message will reflect whether or not MAC verification was carried out when processing C. From an adversary's perspective, only send and receive times of packets can be captured, so the adversary will measure the time difference between sending the initial packet train and receiving the Heartbeat response packet, which we refer to as the *round trip time (RTT)*. If this time difference is larger than some threshold T, the adversary will assume the padding was valid (and so the MAC verification was carried out), while if it is lower than this threshold, the adversary will assume the padding was invalid. The threshold can be set by doing some initial system profiling to measure the typical timing difference between packets carrying ciphertexts having valid and invalid padding. Notice also that DTLS Heartbeat packets are not essential to building the oracle: any upper layer protocol having suitably predictable and detectable response messages can be used.

In reality, the timing of packets is influenced by many factors beyond just DTLS's cryptographic processing. Moreover, as we noted above, the timing difference will be rather small for normal-sized packets. So the DTLS padding oracle as presented would be much too error-prone. To enhance the accuracy of the oracle, the adversary can:

- Choose a specific, favourable DTLS packet payload length, l.
- Send n copies of packet P_C in a train followed by a Heartbeat request instead of just one copy of P_C. Here, the idea is that each copy of P_C will be processed in the same way, so the larger the accumulated time difference will become and the easier it will become to distinguish between valid and invalid padding. This exploits the fact that DTLS does not tear-down DTLS connections in the event of errors (recall that when the padding oracle is used in a plaintext recovery attack, all the ciphertexts sent in the attack will be invalid in some way – they will either have invalid padding or invalid MACs). It also assumes that all the packets in the train can be made to arrive at the target system in such a way that no adverse delays are introduced during the processing of these packets.
- Send m packet trains (each containing n copies of P_C), and use an applicable statistical model to analyse the observed RTTs.

Algorithm 2 describes our basic DTLS padding oracle for a ciphertext C. In the algorithm, RTT_q denotes the response time in the q-th trial, T denotes the threshold for deciding on whether C has valid or invalid padding, and simple averaging is used to process the gathered RTTs. Other statistical measures could be used in place of averaging here, an idea that we discuss in more detail in the next section. There we also explore the many practical issues that arise in building this padding oracle, addressing issues such as packet timing, system profiling, parameter selection to tune the attack, and dealing with anti-replay.

Algorithm 2: Padding Oracle for OpenSSL implementation of DTLS

Data: C
Result: `VALID` or `INVALID`
for $q = 1$ **to** m **do**
  RTT_q = **Timer**(C);
RTT=Mean$(RTT_1, RTT_2, ..., RTT_m)$;
if $RTT \geq T$ **then**
  return `VALID`;
else
  return `INVALID`;

Timer(C)
Set T_s = current time;
Send n copies of P_C, a DTLS packet containing C, to the targeted system;
Send a Heartbeat request packet to the targeted system;
Set T_e = time when Heartbeat response packet is seen;
return $(T_e - T_s)$

4 Practical Considerations

In this section, we discuss a number of practical issues that arise in implementing our attack. All of our remarks are specific to the OpenSSL implementation of DTLS.

4.1 Timing and OpenSSL Cryptographic Operations

Our attack relies on detecting the time difference introduced by MAC verification that is performed for packets having valid padding but not for packets having invalid padding. Failure to detect this time difference would result in the padding oracle providing an incorrect answer. Figure 1 shows, for a variety of DTLS payload sizes, the time taken by OpenSSL in our set-up to perform decryption with 3DES or AES-256 alongside the time taken for MAC verification using HMAC-SHA-1. The hardware specifications of our set-up are listed in Section 5. We note the following features evident from this figure:

- In general, decryption is slower than MAC verification, especially in the case of 3DES.
- The MAC processing time for a single packet is on the order of a few tens of μs, which is well below that reported in [2] and below the level of jitter expected in a typical network.
- 3DES is much slower than AES-256: for a packet size of 1456 bytes, the factor is about 4. For reasons that will be explained below, using a slower decryption algorithm increases the effectiveness of the attack. Hence the attack parameters (l, m, n) may need to be tuned depending on which block cipher is in use.
- With AES-256, the processing time rapidly drops from about 50 μs to about 20 μs when the DTLS payload size reaches 512 bytes. We do not know the reason for this behaviour, but the adversary also needs to be aware of it when selecting attack parameters.

Although we have targeted HMAC-SHA-1 in our attack, the fundamentals of the attack still apply when other MAC algorithms are in use. At the time of writing, OpenSSL only supports HMAC-MD5 and HMAC-SHA-1. More detail about how packets are processed and the source of the timing difference is provided in Appendix A.

4.2 System Profiling

System profiling refers to the process by which the adversary collects information about the targeted system prior to carrying out an attack. This provides the adversary with the expected values for the RTTs (for valid and invalid padding) under some conditions such as system load, the DTLS payload length, l, and the number of packets in the train, n. This profiling in turn allows the threshold value T for the attack to be set.

Given a captured ciphertext, it is easy to construct ciphertexts having any desired length l and having either invalid or valid padding, simply by manipulating the last 2 blocks of the captured ciphertext and prepending random blocks (or truncating it if a shorter ciphertext is needed). Given such pairs of ciphertexts and a Heartbeat request message, the adversary can then construct packet trains containing the required number of packets n. These trains can then be repeatedly sent to the target system and the RTTs measured, to obtain two empirical PDFs, one for trains with validly padded packets and the other for trains with invalid padding. From these PDFs, the threshold T can be set by, for example, calculating the mean of each distribution and setting T to be the mid-point between the means. In practice, we tend to obtain small numbers of extreme outliers in such profiling experiments, and removing these before calculating the means by using a simple cut-off generally improves the performance of the attack. More sophisticated statistical methods can of course be employed, but we have found profiling followed by thresholding to be already adequate for our attacks to be successful.

4.3 An Attack Without System Profiling

System profiling is not even strictly necessary – for a given byte position i in the target block, an adversary can simply measure the RTTs for a packet train (consisting of n DTLS packets with the target ciphertext block being located

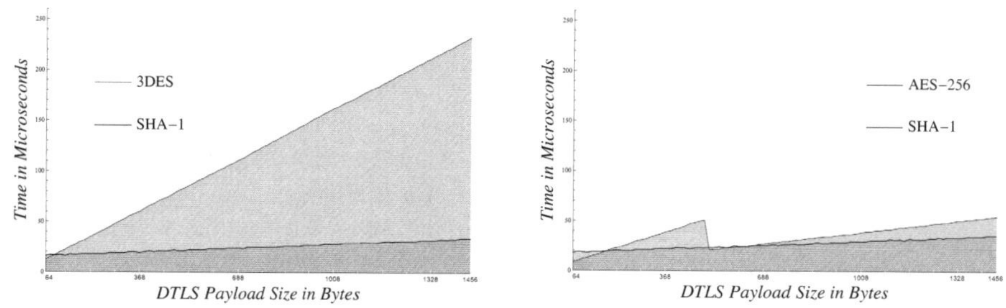

(a) 3DES and SHA-1

(b) AES-256 and SHA-1

Figure 1. Timing of cryptographic operations for DTLS payloads of sizes between 64 and 1456 bytes

at the end of each packet, followed by a Heartbeat request packet), for each of the 256 possible byte values in position i in the block preceding the target ciphertext block. Then the adversary can select as the correct byte value (i.e. the one giving valid padding) the one that maximises the RTT across the 256 measured RTT values. Accuracy can be further improved by repeating the trial for each byte m times, removing outliers, and using the maximum of the average RTTs. In fact, we have observed in our experiments that repeating the trial for each byte value m times, removing outliers, and then selecting the byte value that maximizes the *minimum* of the m measured RTTs for each byte value gives substantially higher success probabilities for the attack. We will illustrate this in Section 5 where we discuss our experimental results in more detail. This, then, is the preferred version of our attack. Note that, strictly speaking, this version of the attack does not build a padding oracle, but rather considers all possible 256 byte values simultaneously.

Even more sophisticated statistical techniques, such as sequential estimation (as in [2]) or likelihood estimation, can be used in place of averaging or selecting the minimum when processing the results of the m trials per byte. However, these more advanced approaches were not needed in order to successfully launch our attack. They could be useful in further reducing the amount of data sent or Heartbeat request messages consumed in an attack.

Finally, we note two further advantages of using an attack without profiling. Firstly, the process of profiling itself will require Heartbeat request messages to be gathered. Secondly, the attack environment may change over time during the attack itself, as varying network or server loads are experienced, for example. The attack without profiling described here automatically adjusts for such changes, at least if they do not occur within the time taken to recover a single byte of plaintext.

4.4 Measuring Success Under Budgetary Constraints

The attack is such that a byte is successfully decrypted only if all the preceding bytes in the same block are successfully decrypted. Hence, under a reasonable independence assumption, if the probability of successfully decrypting a byte is p, then the probability of successfully decrypting a block of size b will be $p_b = p^b$. For AES, $b = 16$, so for successful decryption of a whole block with a reasonable probability, we need p to be rather close to 1. For example, with $p = 0.99$ and $b = 16$ we have $p_b = 0.85$. The adversary can tune the attack parameters (l, m, n) so as to increase the success probability p of the attack and can try to find the optimal combination that results in the highest success probability. However, in practice, an adversary will have a limit on, for example, the maximum number of bytes that he wishes to send in order to recover a byte. As discussed below, when anti-replay is enabled, Heartbeat request packets (or their equivalents) will become a precious resource. Since each train consumes one such packet in this situation, it may be desirable to increase l, the packet size and n, the number of packets per train, so as to maximize the amplification effect, whilst minimizing m, the number of trains sent per byte. However, as our later experimental results will show, simply increasing l and n does not always help, especially in the case of AES-256.

4.5 Attacks with Anti-Replay Enabled

Attacking DTLS becomes slightly more complex when anti-replay is enabled. Since the OpenSSL implementation of DTLS first checks the sequence number against the anti-replay window before doing any cryptographic processing, the adversary has to take care that all packets sent in trains do not have sequence numbers that are marked as having previously arrived. Fortunately, the anti-replay window is only updated if the MAC on a packet is successfully verified, and all the packets used in the attack will fail the MAC verification (with the exception of the Heartbeat packets), so the window is not updated as a consequence of these attack packets.

With anti-replay enabled, each Heartbeat request packet can be used only once, since its sequence number will be marked in the window as having been seen once the packet arrives. Moreover, the adversary has to ensure that the sequence number for each Heartbeat request packet used does fall within (or to the right of) the current anti-replay window, otherwise the Heartbeat request will be discarded and no response generated.

Thus Heartbeat request packets become a precious resource in the situation where anti-replay is enabled: the attack can only proceed as quickly as they become available. Hence decryption in this setting may be rather slow and "opportunistic" – every time a packet is seen on the wire by the adversary, a new packet train can be launched and a byte value tested.

Given these issues, it is apparent that the adversary should try to use as few Heartbeat request packets as possible, which means minimizing m for a given target success probability p. A further enhancement arises by building packet trains that test multiple byte values *simultaneously*. For example, the adversary could build two sets of m trains, each train containing $128n$ packets, with half of the possible byte values being tested in each train n times each. This would represent the first step in a binary search for the correct byte value, requiring only 8 steps and therefore $16m$ Heartbeat request packets to extract a byte. The number of Heartbeat requests consumed could be halved again with initial system profiling. In contrast, our basic attack would consume $256m$ Heartbeat request packets for the same result. We have not tested this version of the attack, but our experience indicates that it would work well whenever using long packet trains does not degrade performance.

Finally, we recall that packets from *any* suitable application layer protocol could be used in place of Heartbeat request packets, so long as the corresponding application always sends a detectable response packet with a predictable response time. So the success of our attack does not depend completely on the availability of Heartbeat request packets in the case where anti-replay is enabled.

5 Implementation and Results for OpenSSL

5.1 Implementation

In our laboratory set-up, we have a client, the adversary and the targeted system all connected to a 100Mbps Ethernet switch on the same VLAN. The targeted system was a machine running a single core processor operating at a speed of 1.87 GHz and having 2 GByte of RAM.

We ran version 1.0.0a of OpenSSL on the client and the server. We used the built-in OpenSSL utilities for the client[8] and the server[9], `s_client` and `s_server` respectively. `s_client` implements a generic client which connects to a remote host using DTLS, while `s_server` implements a generic server which listens for connections on a given UDP port using DTLS. We implemented the Heartbeat Extension feature by installing the appropriate OpenSSL patch[10]. We deactivated anti-replay by directly modifying the OpenSSL code.

5.2 Results

The results shown in this section reflect our specific set-up. Of course, the values would change as the set-up changes – for example, the timings are heavily dependent on the clock-speed of the processor used on the target system. However, the fundamentals of the attack would remain the same.

5.2.1 Experimentally observed PDFs:

The figures we discuss hereafter show PDFs observed in our experiments for different attack parameters and encryption algorithms. In all the figures, the x-axis represents RTTs while the y-axis represents the probability of observing these RTTs. In all figures, outliers have been removed. Each figure shows two PDFs, PDF_1 (in red) and PDF_2 (in blue), that correspond to having valid and invalid padding in the packets in the trains, respectively. We recall that l denotes the DTLS payload size, m denotes the number of trials per byte, and n denotes the number of DTLS packets per trial. Figures 2 and 3 show PDFs for n equal to 10 and varying the value of l, for 3DES and AES-256 respectively. We note the following:

- It is generally easier to distinguish between the two PDFs in the case of 3DES.
- Generally, there is an increasing overlap between the two PDFs as the value of l, the DTLS payload size, increases. This is more evident in the case of AES-256.
- In the case of AES-256, increasing l makes the PDFs much harder to distinguish. The reason for this is that the adversary spends more time preparing and sending packets as the packet size increases, while the targeted system may already have finished AES decryption and

[8] `http://www.openssl.org/docs/apps/s_client.html`
[9] `http://www.openssl.org/docs/apps/s_server.html`
[10] `http://sctp.fh-muenster.de/dtls-patches.html`

MAC verification and be waiting for the next packet. Thus long packets tend to arrive "late" at the targeted system.

Figures 4 and 5 show the PDFs for $l = 1024$ and varying the value of n, for 3DES and AES respectively. We note the following:

- In the case of 3DES, increasing the value of n helps in making the two PDFs more distinguishable. This is the case with AES-256 when small DTLS payloads are used.
- With AES, increasing the value of n when using large DTLS payloads makes the PDFs harder to distinguish. Figures 6 and 5 show this effect when AES-256 is used for $l = 256$ and $l = 1024$ respectively.
- By appropriately choosing the attack parameters, it is possible to obtain PDFs that are very easy to distinguish. For example, the last graph in Figure 6 shows the PDFs for AES-256 when $l = 256$ and $n = 160$, where the peaks are separated by more than $500\mu s$ while the distributions are entirely contained within 50 μs of the peaks.

5.2.2 Success Probability:

Table 1 shows the success probability, p, of decrypting a byte under different attack parameters (l, m, n) when AES-256 is used. We recall that the success probability for a block is then given by p^b where b is the block length in bytes.

These tables were obtained using the preferred version of our attack described in Section 4.3, where no system profiling is used, outliers are removed, and, for each byte, we use the minimum RTT value from the m values available, and then select the correct byte as being the one that gives the maximum amongst these values. Each entry in the tables is calculated using 100 runs of the attack.

We can clearly see that the probability of success increases as the number of trials, m, increases. Success probabilities p equal to 0.99 or above are easily achieved for moderate values of l, m and n, making our preferred attack both efficient and highly reliable for these parameter choices.

Table 2 shows analogous success probabilities for 3DES. Note however that in these tables, we report figures for substantially larger values of l than we did for AES-256. This is indicative of the fact that our attacks are still quite successful for 3DES even with long payloads, giving an additional amplification opportunity. As further confirmation of the practicality of our attacks,Table 3 provides success probabilities for AES-256 for $l = 192$ and various values of m and n, with the probabilities being based on 1000 runs of

n \ l	**128**	**160**	**192**	**224**	**256**	**288**
1	0.00	0.15	0.41	0.32	0.00	0.01
2	0.02	0.24	0.32	0.40	0.00	0.01
5	0.05	0.08	0.49	0.02	0.00	0.01
10	0.04	0.12	0.36	0.00	0.01	0.01
20	0.01	0.13	0.34	0.05	0.02	0.01
50	0.10	0.33	0.38	0.03	0.00	0.01

$m = 1$

n \ l	**128**	**160**	**192**	**224**	**256**	**288**
1	0.99	0.99	1.00	0.99	1.00	0.99
2	0.99	1.00	0.99	1.00	1.00	0.98
5	0.99	1.00	1.00	1.00	1.00	0.98
10	0.98	1.00	0.99	1.00	1.00	0.99
20	0.99	0.99	1.00	1.00	1.00	0.99
50	0.99	0.99	1.00	1.00	0.98	0.95

$m = 5$

n \ l	**128**	**160**	**192**	**224**	**256**	**288**
1	0.99	0.99	1.00	0.99	1.00	0.99
2	0.99	1.00	0.99	1.00	1.00	0.99
5	0.99	1.00	1.00	1.00	1.00	0.98
10	0.98	1.00	0.99	1.00	1.00	0.99
20	0.99	0.99	1.00	1.00	1.00	0.99
50	0.99	0.99	1.00	1.00	0.99	0.95

$m = 10$

Table 1. Success probabilities per byte for AES, for various attack parameters.

the attack. For example, already for $m = 10$ and $n = 2$, the success probability is 0.996, meaning that an entire block of plaintext can be recovered correctly with probability 0.94, at a cost of (roughly) 7000 bytes of network traffic per byte.

6 Attacking the GnuTLS Implementation of DTLS

We have examined the GnuTLS implementation of DTLS, with the intention of finding similar attacks. However, the code for decryption[11] is such that there is no timing difference for processing of packets with valid and invalid padding: the MAC verification is carried out in either case, and only then is the packet dropped. However, the code does include the lines shown in Figure 7. These are exe-

[11] See `http://git.savannah.gnu.org/gitweb/?p=gnutls.git;a=blob;f=lib/gnutls_cipher.c`

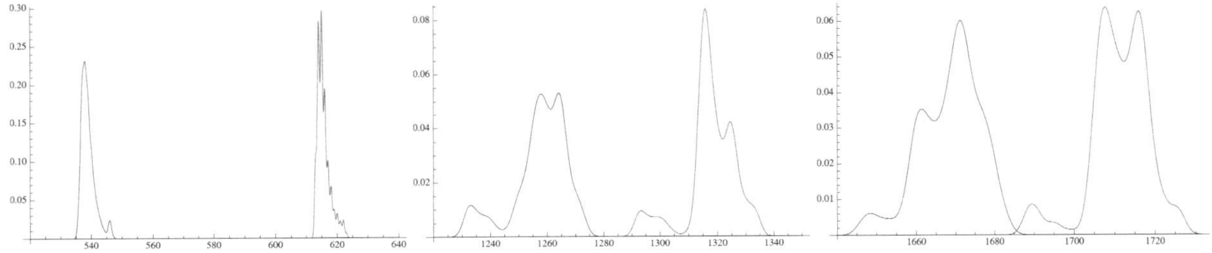

(a) $l = 256$ (b) $l = 1024$ (c) $l = 1456$

Figure 2. 3DES – PDFs for $n = 10$ and varying l.

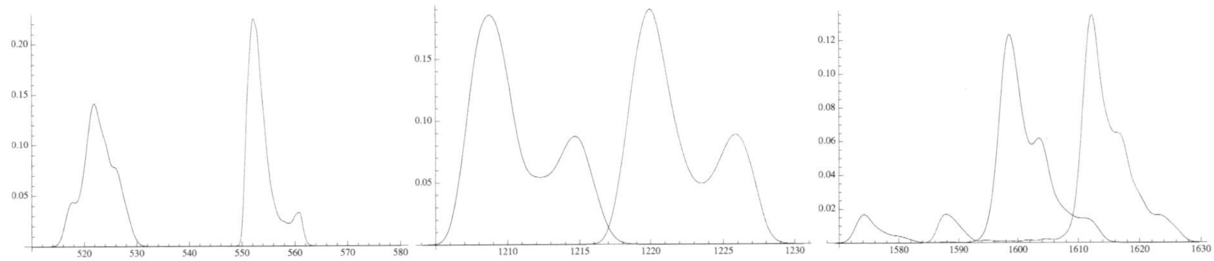

(a) $l = 256$ (b) $l = 1024$ (c) $l = 1456$

Figure 3. AES-256 – PDFs for $n = 10$ and varying l.

cuted after CBC-mode decryption, but before the full pad check and MAC verification are done.

From this code, it can be seen that if a certain test involving the padding length in `pad` and the ciphertext size fails, then `gnutls_assert` and `_gnutls_record_log` are executed. `_gnutls_record_log` logs messages to an output only if the GnuTLS program is executed with its debugging level set to 4 or higher. In our laboratory set-up, we have used the default debugging level, 0, meaning that calling `_gnutls_record_log` does not result in the server producing an error message in the case when the test fails. Whether or not error messages are output, we noticed in our tests that a small timing delay is introduced into the decryption processing when the padding length test shown in Figure 7 fails. The rest of the packet processing then proceeds as normal (but with a padding check not being performed if the padding length test has failed). Each packet that fails the padding length test or the padding check results in GnuTLS printing a "`Discarded message due to invalid decryption`" error message to the screen. Unless the debugging level is changed, no other error messages are produced.

The timing difference that we observed during testing allows a partial plaintext recovery attack against GnuTLS. We explain this next. For ease of presentation, we assume that the MAC size is 32 bytes (as would be produced by HMAC-SHA-256), but a similar attack would apply for 20-byte MACs. Now the padding length field `pad` is obtained from the last byte of the decrypted ciphertext (see line 552 in Figure 7). Consider an adversary who builds a DTLS packet whose encrypted payload (excluding the IV) is 160 bytes in length and that ends with two blocks R, C_t^*, where C_t^* is the target ciphertext block. Then, recalling our numbering convention for the bytes of a block and the CBC-mode decryption procedure, the padding length test in the GnuTLS code is triggered precisely when:

$$R[0] \oplus D_k(C_t^*)[0] > 127.$$

Thus, if the targeted system responds slowly to the adversary's packet, he can infer that the most significant bit (MSB) of $R[0] \oplus D_k(C_t^*)[0]$ is set to 1. From this, the MSB of $P_t^*[0]$, the rightmost byte of the plaintext corresponding to C_t^*, is easily deduced. The attacker can then target the second-MSB of $P_t^*[0]$, by setting $R[0]$ so that the MSB of $R[0] \oplus D_k(C_t^*)[0]$ equals 0 and then using a DTLS packet of length 96 bytes (again excluding the IV). This provides a test of the form:

$$R[0] \oplus D_k(C_t^*)[0] > 63$$

with the side information that $R[0] \oplus D_k(C_t^*)[0] \leq 127$, from which the adversary learns that the second-MSB of $R[0] \oplus D_k(C_t^*)[0]$ is set to 1. An alternative approach to this is setting $R[0]$ so that the MSB of $R[0] \oplus D_k(C_t^*)[0]$ equals 1 instead of 0 and then using a DTLS packet of length 224

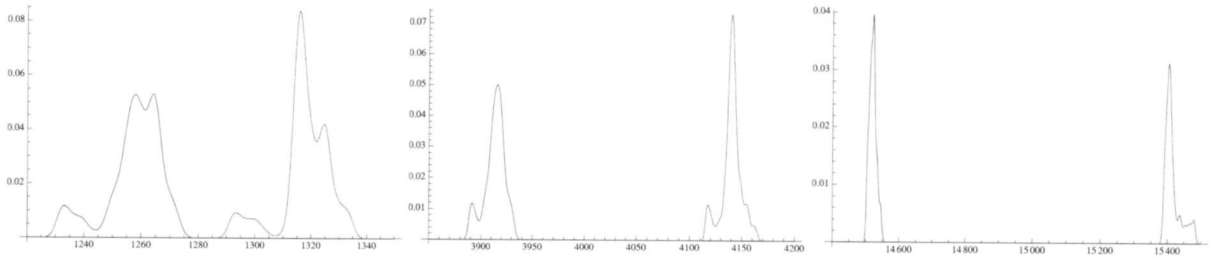

(a) $n = 10$ (b) $n = 40$ (c) $n = 160$

Figure 4. 3DES – PDFs for $l = 1024$ and varying n.

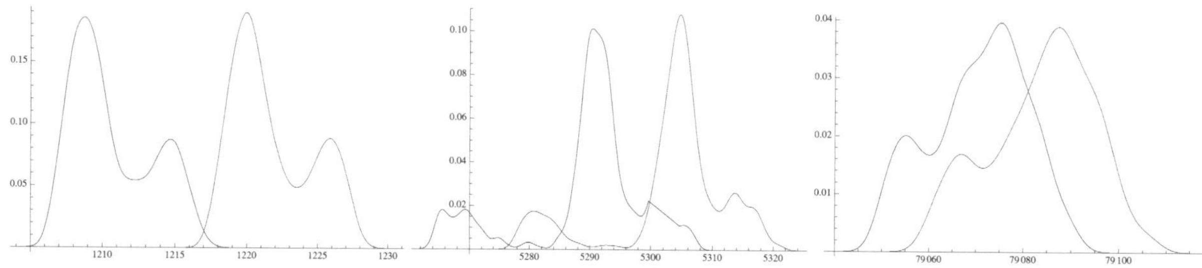

(a) $n = 10$ (b) $n = 40$ (c) $n = 160$

Figure 5. AES-256 – PDFs for $l = 1024$ and varying n.

bytes (again excluding the IV). This provides a test of the form:

$$R[0] \oplus D_k(C_t^*)[0] > 191$$

The adversary can learn that the second-MSB of $R[0] \oplus D_k(C_t^*)[0]$ is set to 1. This alternative approach gives the adversary the opportunity to use packets with sizes that result in better success probabilities as we demonstrate later, and hence is preferable. For both approaches, iterating, the attacker can extract the 4 MSBs of $P_t^*[0]$ when the block cipher is AES, and the 5 MSBs of $P_t^*[0]$ when it is 3DES. The least significant bits (LSBs) cannot be extracted using our attack because the packet size must be a multiple of the block size b.

This provides a theoretical description of our attack. Of course, the adversary can use the same techniques as worked for OpenSSL to amplify his attack: using packet trains, multiple trials, and removal of outliers. A practical issue arises because GnuTLS does not implement the Heartbeat extension, but here we can use any application layer protocol with predictable timing differences. In principal, the same attack would work against the GnuTLS implementation of TLS, with the TLS connection tear-down giving the required timing information. But, in this case, trains of packets cannot be used to amplify the timing difference, since the connection is terminated upon the first failure.

We have conducted experiments to test whether the timing difference is sufficient to allow the attack for DTLS, with experimental results being presented in Figure 8 for HMAC-SHA-256 and AES-256. Here, we see separation between the peaks of the distributions (red for packets where the inequality "`pad > ciphertext.size - hash_size`" is satisfied, blue for when it is not). In this attack, the adversary needs to adjust the payload length, l, based on the position of the bit he tries to recover. Changing the value of l to recover a bit would change the success probability of the attack.

- With the first approach, where shorter packets are used, we were able to achieve success probabilities of 1, 0.874, 0.722 and 0.724 for individually extracting the first, second, third and fourth MSB respectively, meaning that the four MSBs can be recovered correctly with probability 0.457, using (roughly) 262 Kbytes of network traffic. These probabilities were achieved with $n = 5$, $m = 200$ and were calculated over 1000 attack runs. We use the median RTT from the m values available, and then select the correct bit as being the one that gives the highest RTT. Increasing the value of m significantly increases the success probability. For example, with $m = 1000$ we were able to achieve a success probability of 0.781 for recovering the four MSBs. Using other statistical techniques can also increase the success probability. For example, using percentile filters, similar to the approach used in [3], raises the success probability from 0.781 to 0.823 for the same set

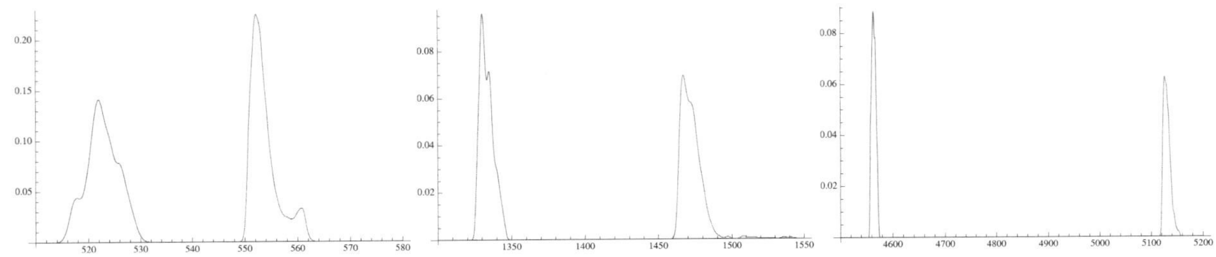

(a) $n = 10$ (b) $n = 40$ (c) $n = 160$

Figure 6. AES-256 – PDFs for $l = 256$ and varying n.

n	p
1	0.017
2	0.210
5	0.205
10	0.012
20	0.035
50	0.147

$m = 1$

n	p
1	0.961
2	0.983
5	0.983
10	0.985
20	0.989
50	0.965

$m = 5$

n	p
1	0.983
2	0.996
5	0.995
10	0.994
20	0.995
50	0.973

$m = 10$

Table 3. Success probabilities per byte for AES-256, for $l = 192$, based on 1000 trials.

of observed RTTs.

- With the second approach, where longer packets are used, we were able to achieve success probabilities of 0.797, 0.897, 0.896 and 0.917 for individually extracting the first, second, third and fourth MSB respectively, meaning that the four MSBs can be recovered correctly with probability 0.587, using (roughly) 4300 bytes of network traffic. These probabilities were achieved with $n = 5$, $m = 1$ and measured over 1000 attack runs. As expected, increasing the value of m significantly increases the success probability. For example, we were able to achieve success probabilities of 0.875 and 0.999 for recovering the four MSBs when $m = 10$ and $m = 100$ respectively.

We have shared our findings with the GnuTLS development team and are working with them to identify the root cause of the timing difference.

To implement the tests, we used the same hardware setup as the one we used for OpenSSL. We ran version 3.0.0 of GnuTLS on the client and the server. We used the built-in GnuTLS utilities for the client and the server, `gnutls_cli` and `gnutls_serv` respectively. We again disabled anti-replay by directly modifying the source code.

7 Discussion

We have demonstrated plaintext recovering attacks against the OpenSSL and GnuTLS implementations of

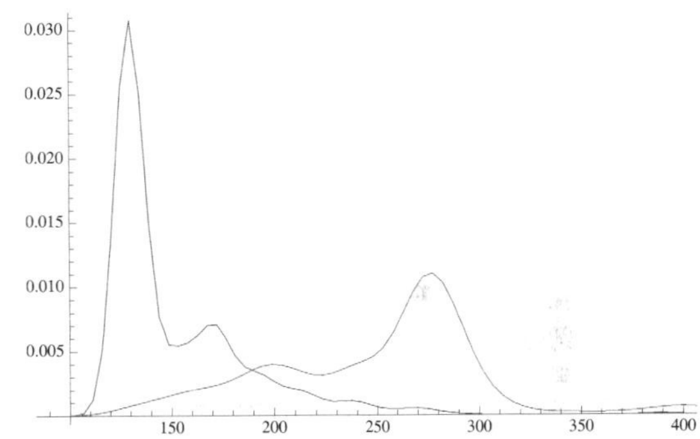

Figure 8. PDFs for AES-256 with HMAC-SHA256, $l = 176$, $n = 5$, based on 1000 trials, with outliers removed.

DTLS. These are easily prevented by modifying the code so that the receiver's cryptographic processing time is independent of how decryption fails. However, we contend that the attacks are still interesting for a number of reasons.

Firstly, the fix to prevent our OpenSSL attack is already mandated in the specification for TLSv1.1, and is implemented in OpenSSL's implementation of TLS, but not in its implementation of DTLS. Without more insight into the software development processes followed by the OpenSSL project, we can only speculate that the experience about how to securely implement TLS's MAC-then-PAD-then-Encrypt construction was not carried over to the separate

```
    pad = ciphertext.data[ciphertext.size - 1] + 1;    /* pad */

    if ((int) pad > (int) ciphertext.size - tag_size)
      {
        gnutls_assert ();
        _gnutls_record_log
          ("REC[%p]: Short record length %d > %d - %d (under attack?)\n",
           session, pad, ciphertext.size, tag_size);
        /* We do not fail here. We check below for the
         * the pad_failed. If zero means success.
         */
        pad_failed = GNUTLS_E_DECRYPTION_FAILED;
      }
```

Figure 7. GnuTLS padding length check code

n \ l	128	256	512	1024	1280	1456
1	0.00	0.12	0.39	0.06	0.01	0.13
2	0.03	0.12	0.26	0.03	0.03	0.18
5	0.03	0.20	0.23	0.30	0.07	0.02
10	0.04	0.17	0.09	0.38	0.08	0.04
20	0.14	0.10	0.08	0.22	0.09	0.07
50	0.04	0.08	0.17	0.41	0.15	0.05

$m = 1$

n \ l	128	256	512	1024	1280	1456
1	0.99	1.00	1.00	1.00	1.00	0.93
2	0.99	1.00	0.99	0.99	0.93	0.92
5	0.99	1.00	1.00	0.90	0.93	0.83
10	0.99	1.00	0.92	0.89	0.81	0.57
20	0.97	1.00	0.91	0.92	0.77	0.54
50	0.98	1.00	0.90	0.89	0.68	0.59

$m = 5$

n \ l	128	256	512	1024	1280	1456
1	0.99	1.00	1.00	0.99	1.00	0.93
2	0.99	1.00	1.00	0.99	0.93	0.92
5	0.99	1.00	1.00	0.91	0.94	0.83
10	0.98	1.00	0.93	0.89	0.81	0.57
20	0.98	1.00	0.92	0.92	0.77	0.54
50	0.99	1.00	0.91	0.89	0.68	0.59

$m = 10$

Table 2. Success probabilities per byte for 3DES, for various attack parameters.

DTLS implementation. This, then, may also indicate of a lack of truly expert code review in the OpenSSL project. This is concerning given the prominence and wide application of the OpenSSL code, but also understandable given its volunteer-led effort. By contrast, GnuTLS's implementation has common code for the TLS and DTLS packet decryption procedure, meaning that countermeasures implemented for TLS are immediately carried over to DTLS. However, as we saw, even this was not sufficient to fully protect the GnuTLS implementation against the type of attack developed in this paper.

A second reason that the obvious and mandated countermeasures were not implemented in OpenSSL may stem from DTLS's lack of error messages, which makes the previous attacks apparently impossible against DTLS. We proved otherwise, exploiting DTLS Heartbeat request and response messages to obtain the required timing information. This kind of approach may be more widely applicable than DTLS.

A third possible explanation is that the DTLS specification relies heavily on cross-references to the TLSv1.1 specification, and indeed only gives specification details at points where TLS and DTLS differ. So an implementor needs to be familiar with both specifications in order to implement DTLS properly. We suggest that "specification by `diff`" is not a good approach to specifying secure protocols, since it requires an implementor to jump back and forth between specifications and may allow important details to fall into the gap between.

Secondly, a comparison between our attacks on DTLS and previous attacks on TLS is instructive. Our attacks are in some sense more challenging because of the lack of explicit error messages, but also easier to carry out because of DTLS's tolerance of errors, meaning that DTLS connections are not torn-down whenever an error is encountered as they are in TLS. Ultimately, this error-tolerance comes from DTLS's use of an unreliable transport protocol. For similar reasons, the anti-replay feature in DTLS is made optional in the specification. In this context, our work shows how non-security features of lower layer protocols can have a major influence on security at higher layers. This phenomenon is seemingly not that well-explored in the literature, presenting an interesting challenge for future work.

References

[1] P. Calhoun, M. Montemurro, and D. Stanley. Control And Provisioning of Wireless Access Points (CAPWAP) Protocol Specification. RFC 5415, Internet Engineering Task Force, March 2009.

[2] Brice Canvel, Alain P. Hiltgen, Serge Vaudenay, and Martin Vuagnoux. Password Interception in a SSL/TLS Channel. In Dan Boneh, editor, *CRYPTO*, volume 2729 of *Lecture Notes in Computer Science*, pages 583–599. Springer, 2003.

[3] Scott A. Crosby, Dan S. Wallach, and Rudolf H. Riedi. Opportunities and Limits of Remote Timing Attacks. *ACM Trans. Inf. Syst. Secur.*, 12(3), 2009.

[4] Jean Paul Degabriele and Kenneth G. Paterson. Attacking the IPsec standards in encryption-only configurations. In *IEEE Symposium on Security and Privacy*, pages 335–349, 2007.

[5] Jean Paul Degabriele and Kenneth G. Paterson. On the (in)security of IPsec in MAC-then-encrypt configurations. In *ACM Conference on Computer and Communications Security*, pages 493–504, 2010.

[6] T. Dierks and E. Rescorla. The Transport Layer Security (TLS) Protocol Version 1.1. RFC 4346, Internet Engineering Task Force, April 2006.

[7] Thai Duong and Juliano Rizzo. Cryptography in the Web: The Case of Cryptographic Design Flaws in ASP.NET. In *IEEE Symposium on Security and Privacy*. IEEE Computer Society, May 2011.

[8] W. Hardaker. Transport Layer Security (TLS) Transport Model for the Simple Network Management Protocol (SNMP). RFC 5953, Internet Engineering Task Force, August 2010.

[9] S. Kent and R. Atkinson. IP Authentication Header. RFC 2402, Internet Engineering Task Force, November 1998.

[10] Nagendra Modadugu and Eric Rescorla. The Design and Implementation of Datagram TLS. In *NDSS*. The Internet Society, 2004.

[11] E. Rescorla and N. Modadugu. Datagram Transport Layer Security. RFC 4347, Internet Engineering Task Force, April 2006.

[12] Juliano Rizzo and Thai Duong. Practical Padding Oracle Attacks. In *4th USENIX Workshop on Offensive Technologies (WOOT'10)*, August 2010.

[13] J. Salowey, T. Petch, R. Gerhards, and H. Feng. Datagram Transport Layer Security (DTLS) Transport Mapping for Syslog. RFC 6012, Internet Engineering Task Force, October 2010.

[14] R. Seggelmann and M. Williams. Transport Layer Security (TLS) and Datagram Transport Layer Security (DTLS) Heartbeat Extension. Draft RFC, Internet Engineering Task Force. `http://tools.ietf.org/html/draft-ietf-tls-dtls-heartbeat-02`.

[15] Serge Vaudenay. Security Flaws Induced by CBC Padding - Applications to SSL, IPSEC, WTLS ... In Lars R. Knudsen, editor, *EUROCRYPT*, volume 2332 of *Lecture Notes in Computer Science*, pages 534–546. Springer, 2002.

A Timing and Packet Processing

In this appendix we look in detail at how a receiver processes a packet, with a view to building a simple model of how RTTs are affected by the attack parameters. To this end, Figure 9 shows a simplified time-line of how packet i, having valid padding, is processed by the receiver.

In the time-line we have:

- $t_{i,0}$: The time at which packet i arrives in the OpenSSL buffer. The buffer holds DTLS packets waiting to be processed.
- $t_{i,1}$: The time at which the decryption and padding check are completed for packet i.
- $t_{i,2}$: The time at which the MAC check is completed for packet i.
- $t_{i,3}$: The time at which OpenSSL is ready to process the next DTLS packet, packet $i+1$.
- OS_t: Any additional time spent by the operating system in relation to the processing of the packet. We assume this to be a constant, independent of i.

In the case of a packet with invalid padding, the MAC verification is not performed and hence we have $t_{i,2} = t_{i,1}$. Figure 10 is the analogue of Figure 9 for the case of invalid padding, and illustrates that, for a fixed DTLS packet length, the time taken to process a packet with invalid padding is less than that taken to process a packet with valid padding.

In Section 3, we defined RTT to be the time taken between sending the first packet in a train to receiving a Heartbeat response packet. Next, we analyse the different contributions to RTT. As an example, the time-line in Figure 11 shows a train made of two identical data packets (so $n = 2$), both having valid padding, followed by a Heartbeat request packet, which then provokes a Heartbeat response packet. In Figure 11 we have:

- T_s: The time at which the adversary sends the first DTLS packet, packet 1.
- T_f: The time at which the Heartbeat response packet is sent by the receiver
- T_e: The time at which the Heartbeat response packet is received by the adversary.
- $t_{1,0} - T_s$: The time it takes for packet 1 to reach the receiver.
- $T_e - T_f$: The time it takes for the Hearbeat response packet to reach the adversary after being sent by the targeted system.
- $T_e - T_s$: The RTT for the packet train.

Figure 11 shows the second data packet, packet 2, arriving **after** the completion of processing of packet 1 , i.e. so that $t_{2,0} > t_{1,3}$. The same applies to the Heartbeat request packet arriving after the completion of processing of packet 2. In this situation, the receiver enters a wait state until the next packet arrives and the arrival time of a packet and its processing start time are the same. In general, this situation results in some or all of the timing difference arising because of the MAC verification being "absorbed" into the wait state of the receiver, and hence is sub-optimal in terms of detecting the time difference.

In the opposite situation, where packet 2 arrives before processing of packet 1 is complete, packets are buffered. Then packet 2 is immediately available for processing at the receiver as soon as processing of packet 1 is complete, and none of the MAC verification time is absorbed. The buffer is managed by OpenSSL and its maximum size is 100 DTLS packets. Figures 12 and 13 illustrate this situation for packet trains having valid and invalid padding, respectively, with the white boxes representing the amount of time spent by packets in the buffer. It is evident from these figures how the time arising from MAC verification (in the case of valid padding) accumulates packet-by-packet to create an amplified time difference in the RTT for the train.

The upshot of this analysis is that, from the adversary's perspective, it is desirable to select the attack parameters so that the receiver's buffer always contains some (but not too many) packets. In this way, the receiver is never waiting for a packet to arrive and the MAC processing time accumulates across the whole packet train.

We have experimentally verified the essential basic correctness of this model for packet processing in the following way. Let RTT_1 denote the RTT for a train that uses packets having valid padding, and let RTT_2 denote the RTT for a train that uses packets having invalid padding. Let δ denote the time difference between the two RTTs, so that:

$$\delta = RTT_1 - RTT_2$$

Then, if we artificially inject delays in between packets from the train as they leave the adversary's machine, we would expect to see the value of δ steadily decrease and eventually reach zero as the size of the artificial delay increases. Figure 14 shows the results of such an experiment which confirms this behaviour. Somewhat surprisingly, Figure 14 also shows that adding small artificial delays can actually increase the time difference δ, making this difference in RTTs *easier* for the adversary to detect.

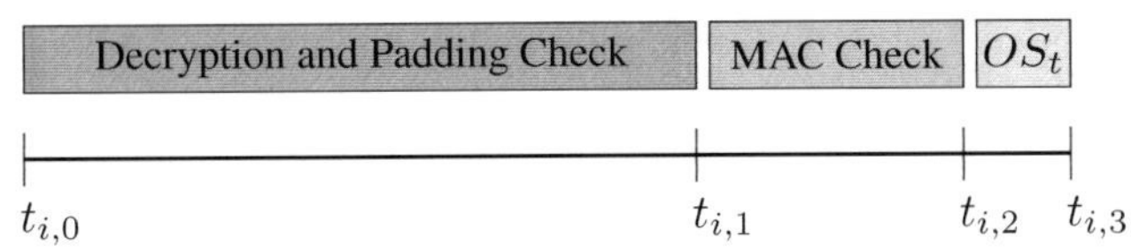

Figure 9. Packet processing time-line – valid padding

Figure 10. Packet processing time-line – invalid padding

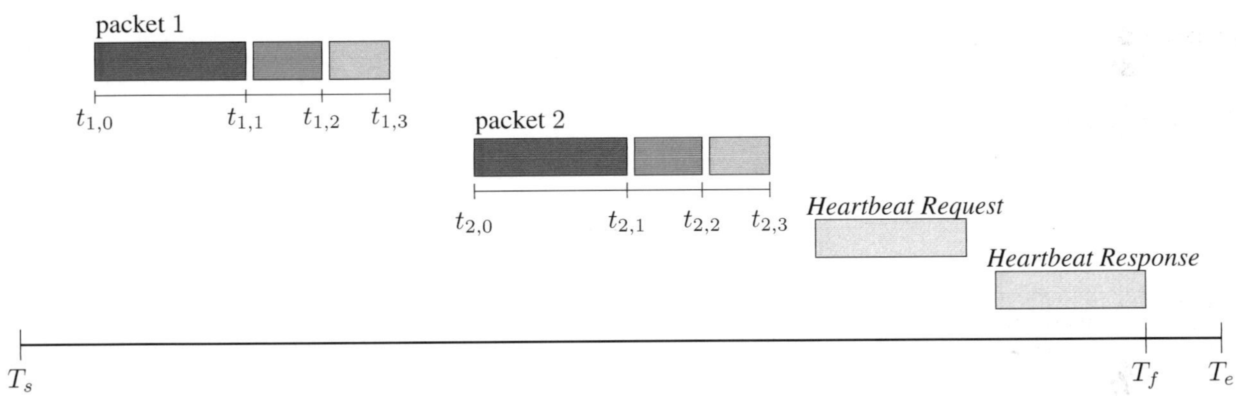

Figure 11. Time-line for a train with $n = 2$ (not to scale).

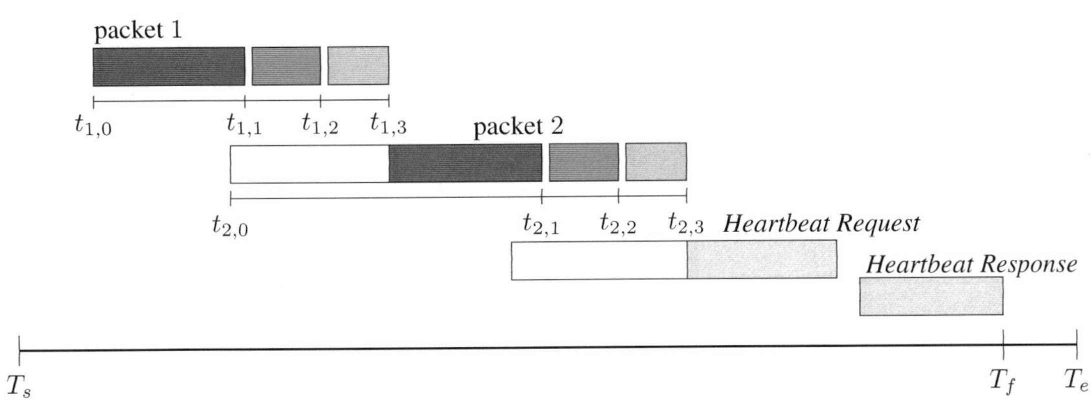

Figure 12. Time-line for packet train with valid padding and packet buffering.

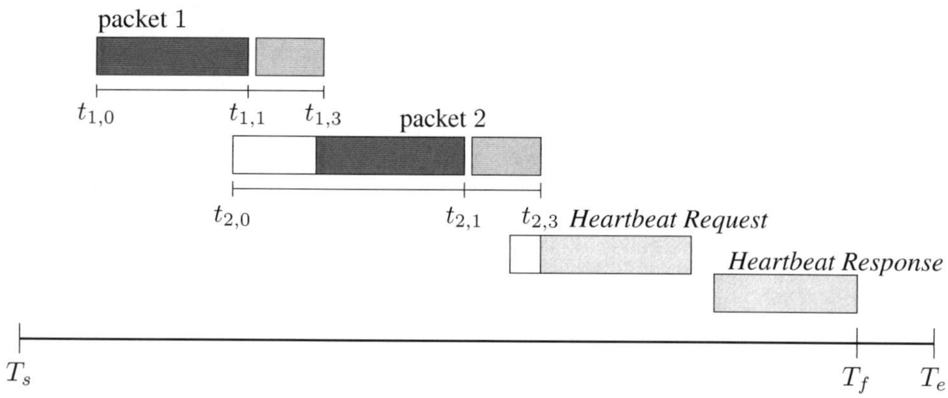

Figure 13. Time-line for packet train with invalid padding and packet buffering.

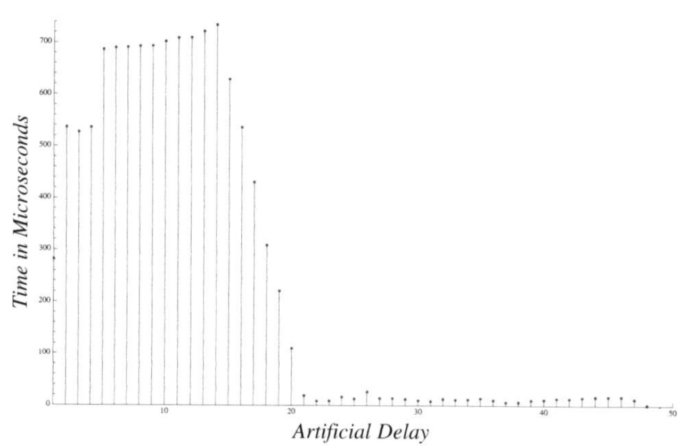

Figure 14. Value of δ, the difference in RTTs for valid and invalid padding, against artificial delay.

ANDāNA: Anonymous Named Data Networking Application

Steven DiBenedetto
Colorado State University
dibenede@cs.colostate.edu

Paolo Gasti   Gene Tsudik
University of California, Irvine
{pgasti,gtsudik}@uci.edu

Ersin Uzun
Palo Alto Research Center
ersin.uzun@parc.com

Abstract

Content-centric networking — also known as information-centric networking (ICN) — shifts emphasis from hosts and interfaces (as in today's Internet) to data. Named data becomes addressable and routable, while locations that currently store that data become irrelevant to applications.

Named Data Networking (NDN) is a large collaborative research effort that exemplifies the content-centric approach to networking. NDN has some innate privacy-friendly features, such as lack of source and destination addresses on packets. However, as discussed in this paper, NDN architecture prompts some privacy concerns mainly stemming from the semantic richness of names. We examine privacy-relevant characteristics of NDN and present an initial attempt to achieve communication privacy. Specifically, we design an NDN add-on tool, called ANDāNA, *that borrows a number of features from Tor. As we demonstrate via experiments, it provides comparable anonymity with lower relative overhead.*

1 Introduction

Although the Internet, as a whole, is a huge global success story, it is showing clear signs of age. In the 1970s, when core ideas underlying today's Internet were developed, telephony was the only example of effective global-scale communications. Thus, while the communication solution offered by the Internet's TCP/IP suite was unique and ground-breaking, the communication paradigm it focused on was similar to that of telephony: a point-to-point conversation between two entities. The communication world has changed dramatically since then and today's Internet has to accommodate: information-intensive services, exabytes of content created and consumed daily over the Web as well as a menagerie of mobile devices connected to it. To keep pace with these changes and move the Internet into the future, a number of research efforts to design new Internet architectures have taken off in the last few years.

Named-Data Networking (NDN) [32] is one such effort that exemplifies the content-centric approach [23, 27, 28] to networking. NDN names content instead of locations (i.e., hosts or interfaces) and thus transforms content into a first-class entity. NDN also stipulates that each piece of content must be signed by its producer. This allows decoupling of trust in content from trust in the entity that might store and/or disseminate that content. These NDN features facilitate automatic caching of content to optimize bandwidth use and enable effective simultaneous utilization of multiple network interfaces.

However, NDN introduces certain challenges that must be addressed in order for it to be a serious candidate for the future Internet architecture. One major argument for a new architecture is the inadequate level of security and privacy in today's Internet. We view anonymity as being a critical feature in any new network architecture. It helps people overcome communication restrictions and boundaries as well as evade censorship. In addition, some applications (e.g., e-cash or anonymous publishing) can be successfully deployed only if the underlying network allows users to hide their identity [14]. Even if end-users do not care about anonymity with respect to services they access, they might still want to hide their activities from employers, governments and ISPs, since those might censor, misuse or accidentally leak sensitive information [19].

Lack of source/destination addresses in NDN helps privacy, since NDN packets carry information only about *what* is requested but not *who* is requesting it. However, a closer look reveals that this is insufficient. In particular, NDN design introduces three important privacy challenges:

1. **Name privacy**: NDN content names are incentivized to be semantically related to the content itself. Similar to HTTP headers, names reveal significantly more information about content than IP addresses. Moreover, an observer can easily determine when two requests refer to the same (even encrypted) content.
2. **Content privacy**: NDN allows any entity that knows a name to retrieve corresponding content. Encryption in NDN is used to enforce access con-

trol and is not applied to publicly available content. Thus, consumers wanting to retrieve public content cannot rely on encryption to hide what they access.

3. **Cache privacy**: as with current web proxies, network neighbors may learn about each others' content access using timing information to identify cache hits.
4. **Signature privacy**: since digital signatures in NDN content packets are required to be publicly verifiable, identity of a content signer may leak sensitive information.

In this paper, we attempt to address these challenges. We present an initial approach, called ANDāNA that can be viewed as an adaptation of onion routing to NDN. Our approach is in-line with NDN principles. It is designed to take advantage of NDN strengths and work around its weaknesses. We optimized ANDāNA for small- to medium-size interactive communication – such as web-browsing and instant messaging – that are characterized by moderate amounts of low-latency traffic [11].

We provide a security analysis of the proposed approach under a realistic adversarial model. Specifically, we define anonymity and unlinkability under this security model and show that these properties hold for ANDāNA. Moreover, ANDāNA is secure with fewer anonymizing router hops than Tor. We prototyped ANDāNA and assessed its performance via experiments over a network testbed. Results show that ANDāNA introduces less overhead than Tor, especially, for anticipated traffic patterns.

We believe that this work is both timely and important. The former – because of the recent surge of interest in content-centric networking and NDN being a good example of this paradigm. (Also, while NDN is sufficiently mature to have a functional prototype suitable for experimental use, it is still at an early enough stage to be open to change.) The latter – because it represents the first attempt to identify and address privacy problems in a viable candidate for the future Internet architecture.

Before discussing details of our approach, we present further motivation for this work.

Why NDN? There are multiple efforts to develop new content-centric architectures and NDN is only one of those. We focus on NDN because it stands out in several aspects. First, it combines some revolutionary ideas about content-based routing that have attracted considerable attention from the networking research community. Second, it builds upon an open-source code-base called CCNx [12], that is led and continuously maintained by an industrial research lab (PARC). At the time of this writing (summer 2011), NDN is one of the very few content-centric architectural proposals with a reasonably mature prototype available to the research community.[1] Third, NDN is one of only four projects selected by NSF Future Internet Architectures (FIA) program [20].

On the other hand, NDN is an on-going research project and is thus subject to continuous change. However, we believe that it represents a good example of content-centric networking design and at least some of its concepts will influence the future of networking. More importantly, ideas, techniques and analysis discussed in this paper are not specific, or limited to, NDN; they are applicable to a wide range of designs, including host-, location- and content-addressable networks.

Approach. NDN follows the proven design principle of IP and claims to be the "thin waist" of the communications protocol stack. Thus, pushing security or privacy services (that are not critical for all types of communication) into this thin waist would contradict its design principle. Consequently, as in the case of IP, we believe that privacy tools should run on top of NDN. Looking at privacy and anonymity techniques in today's Internet, one well-established approach is an overlay anonymization network, exemplified by Tor [18]. Tor and its relatives employ layers of concentric encryption and intermediate nodes responsible for peeling off layers as packets travel through the overlay. This is commonly referred to as onion routing. Our approach falls into roughly the same category. However, as we discover and discuss in this paper, the task of adapting an anonymization overlay approach to NDN is not as simple as it might initially seem.

Scope. The primary focus of this paper is privacy. Security and other features of NDN are taken as given without justifying their existence. A number of important NDN-related security topics are out of scope of this paper, including: trust management, certification and revocation of credentials as well as routing security.

Organization. We start with NDN overview and privacy analysis in Section 2. Section 3 summarizes related work, followed by the description of ANDāNA in Section 4. Section 5 introduces a formal model for provable anonymity and security analysis of ANDāNA. Implementation details and performance evaluation results are discussed in Section 6. The paper concludes in Section 7.

2 NDN Overview

NDN [32] is a communication architecture based on named content.[2] Rather than addressing content by its location, NDN refers to it by name. Content name is composed of one or more variable-length components that are opaque to the network. Component

[1] We are aware of only two other content-centric architecture proposals – [33] and [36] – that have public prototypes.

[2] Note that we use the terms "content" and "data" interchangeably throughout this paper.

boundaries are explicitly delimited by "/". For example, the name of a CNN news content might be: /ndn/cnn/news/2011aug20. Large pieces of content can be split into fragments with predictable names: fragment 137 of a YouTube video could be named: /ndn/youtube/videos/video-749.avi/137.

Since the main abstraction is content, there is no explicit notion of "hosts" in NDN. (However, their existence is assumed.) Communication adheres to the *pull* model: content is delivered to consumers only upon explicit request. A consumer requests content by sending an *interest* packet. If an entity (a router or a host) can "satisfy" a given interest, it returns the corresponding *content* packet. Interest and content are the only types of packets in NDN. A content packet with name X in NDN is **never** forwarded or routed unless it is preceded by an interest for name X.[3]

When a router receives an interest for name X and there are no pending interests for the same name in its PIT (Pending Interests Table), it forwards this interest to the next hop according to its routing table. For each forwarded interest, a router stores some state information, including the name in the interest and the interface on which it was received. However, if an interest for X arrives while there is an entry for the same name in the PIT, the router collapses the present interest (and any subsequent ones for X) storing only the interface on which it was received. When content is returned, the router forwards it out on all interfaces where an interest for X has been received and flushes the corresponding PIT entry. Note that, since no additional information is needed to deliver content, an interest does not carry a source address. More detailed discussion of NDN routing can be found in [27].

In NDN, each network entity can provide content caching, which is limited only by resource availability. For popular content, this allows interests to be satisfied from cached copies distributed over the network, thus maximizing resource utilization. NDN deals with content authenticity and integrity by making digital signatures mandatory on all content packets. A signature binds content with its name, and provides origin authentication no matter how or from where it is retrieved. NDN calls entities that publish new content *producers*. Whereas, as follows from the above discussion, entities that request content are called *consumers*. (Consumers and producers are clearly overlapping sets.) Although content signature verification is optional in NDN, a signature must be verifiable by any NDN entity. To make this possible, content packets carry additional metadata, such as the ID of the content publisher and information on locating the public key needed for verification. Public keys are treated as regular content: since all content is signed, each public key content is effectively a "certificate". NDN does not mandate any particular certification infrastructure, relegating trust management to individual applications.

Private or restricted content in NDN is protected via encryption by the content publisher. Once content is distributed unencrypted, there is no mechanism to apply subsequent encryption. Specific applications may provide a means to explicitly request encryption of content by publishers. However, NDN does not currently allow consumers to selectively conceal content corresponding to their interests.

From the privacy perspective, lack of source and destination addresses in NDN packets is a clear advantage over IP. In practice, this means that the adversary that eavesdrops on a link close to a content producer can not immediately identify the consumer(s) who expressed interest in that content. Moreover, two features of standard NDN routers: (1) content caching and (2) collapsing of redundant interests, reduce the utility of eavesdropping near a content producer since not all interests for the same content reach its producer.

On the other hand, NDN provides no protection against an adversary that monitors local activity of a specific consumer. As most content names are expected to be semantically relevant to content itself, interests can leak a lot of information about the content they aim to retrieve. To mitigate this issue, NDN allows the use of "encrypted names", whereby a producer encrypts the tail-end (a few components) of a name [27].[4] However, this simple approach does not provide much privacy: the adversary can link multiple interests for the same content – or those sharing the same name prefix – issued by different consumers. Moreover, an adversary can always replay an interest to see what (possibly cached) content it returns, even if a name of content is not semantically relevant.

3 Related Work

The goal of anonymizing tools and techniques is to decouple actions from entities that perform them. The most basic approach to anonymity is to use a trusted anonymizing proxy. A proxy is typically interposed between a sender and a receiver in order to hide identity of the former from the latter. The Anonymizer [3] and Lucent Personalized Web Assistant [22] are examples of this approach. While relatively efficient, it is susceptible to a (local) passive adversary that monitors all proxy ac-

[3]Strictly speaking, content named $X' \neq X$ can be delivered in response to an interest for X but only if X is a prefix of X'. As an example, the full name of each content packet contains the hash of that content; however, this hash value is usually not known to consumers and is typically omitted from interests.

[4]For example, a name such as: /ndn/xerox/parc/Alice/family/photos/Hawaii might be replaced with /ndn/xerox/parc/Alice/**encrypted-part**.

tivity. Also, a centralized proxy necessitates centralized (global) trust and represents a single point of failure.

A more sophisticated decentralized approach is used in mix networks [13]. Typically, a mix network achieves anonymity by repeatedly routing a message from one proxy to another, such that the message gradually loses any relationship with its originator. Messages must be made unintelligible to potentially untrusted intermediate nodes. Chaum's initial proposal [13] defines an anonymous email system, wherein a sender envelops a message with several concentric layers of public key encryption. The resulting message is then forwarded to a sequence of *mix* servers, that gradually remove one layer of encryption at a time and forward the message to the next mix server.

Subsequent research generally falls into two classes: delay-tolerant applications (e.g. email, file sharing) and real-time or low-latency applications (e.g. web browsing, VoIP, SSH). These two classes achieve different tradeoffs between performance (in terms of latency and bandwidth) and anonymity. For example, Babel [24], Mixmaster [30] and Mixminion [16] belong to the first category. Their goal is to provide anonymity with respect to the *global eavesdropper* adversary. Each mix introduces spurious traffic and randomized traffic delays in order to inhibit correlation between input and output traffic. However, unpredictable traffic characteristics and high delays make these techniques unsuitable for many applications.

Low-latency anonymizing networks are at the other end of the spectrum. They try to minimize extra latency by forwarding traffic as fast as possible. Because of this, strategies used in anonymization of delay-tolerant traffic – batching (delaying) and re-ordering of traffic in mixes, as well as introduction of decoy traffic — are generally not applicable. For example, [40] shows how traffic patterns can be used for de-anonymization in low-latency anonymity systems. Notable low-latency tools are summarized below.

Crowds [37] is a low-latency anonymizing network for HTTP traffic. It differs from traditional mix-based approaches as it lacks layered encryption. For each message it receives, an anonymizer probabilistically chooses to either forward it to a random next hop within the Crowds network or deliver it to its final destination. Since messages are not encrypted, Crowds is vulnerable to local eavesdroppers and predecessor attacks [43].

Morphmix [38, 39] is a fully distributed peer-to-peer mix network that uses layered encryption. Unlike Crowds, it does not require a lookup service to keep track of all participating nodes. Senders selects the first anonymizer and each anonymizer along an "anonymous tunnel" picks the next hop to dynamically build tunnels. Tarzan [21] is another fully distributed peer-to-peer mix network. It builds a universally verifiable set of neighbors (called mimics) for every node to keep track of other other Tarzan participants. Every node selects its mimics pseudo-randomly.

Tor [18] is the best-known and most-used low-latency anonymizing tool. It is based on onion routing and layered encryption. Tor uses a central directory to locate participating nodes and requires users to build a three-hop anonymizing circuit by choosing three random nodes. The first is called the *guard*, the second – the *middle*, and the third — *exit* node. Once set up, each circuit in Tor lasts about 10 minutes. For better performance, bandwidth available to nodes is taken into account during circuit establishment and multiple TCP connections are multiplexed over one circuit. Communication between Tor nodes is secured via SSL. However, Tor does not introduce any decoy traffic or randomization to hide traffic patterns. Another anonymization tool, I2P [26], adopts many ideas of Tor, while using a distributed untrusted directory service to keep track of its participants. I2P also replaces Tor's circuit-switching operation with packet-switching to achieve better load balancing and fault-tolerance.

A consumer privacy technique for Information-Centric Networks (ICNs) is proposed in [4]. Instead of using encryption, it leverages cooperation from content producers and requires them to mix sensitive information with so-called "cover" content. This approach requires producers to cooperate and store a large amount of cover traffic. It also does not provide consumer-producer unlinkability or protection against malicious producers.

Telex [44] is an alternative to mix networks designed to evade state-level censorship. It uses steganographic techniques to hide messages in SSL handshakes. Users connect to innocuous-looking unblocked websites through SSL. Sympathetic ISP-s that forward user's traffic recover hidden messages and deliver them to the intended destination. While novel, this approach presents significant deployment challenges and requires support from the network infrastructure. Furthermore, the threat model in Telex is quite different from that of the other anonymizing tools presented above. Moreover, established TCP fingerprinting techniques can easily detect differences between a Telex station and a censored website. Another analogous technique – called Cirripede [25] – was recently proposed.

4 ANDāNA

ANDāNA is a onion routing overlay network, built on top of NDN, that provides privacy and anonymity to consumers. In particular, ANDāNA prevents adversaries from linking consumers with the content they are retrieving. Following the terminology introduced in [37], ANDāNA provides *beyond suspicion*[5] degree of anonymity to its users.

ANDāNA uses multiple concentric layers of encryption and routes messages from consumers through a chain of at least two onion routers. Each router removes a layer of encryption and forwards the decrypted messages to the next hop. Due to its low-latency focus, ANDāNA does not guarantee privacy in presence of a global eavesdropper. However, since it is geared for a world-wide (or at least geographically distributed) network spanning a multitude of administrative domains, the existence of such an adversary is unlikely. For this reason, we restrict the adversarial capabilities to eavesdropping on, injecting, removing or modifying messages on a subset of available links. An adversary can compromise NDN routers and ANDāNA nodes at will. Nonetheless, consumers benefit from anonymity as long as they use at least one non-compromised ANDāNA node. Details of our adversarial model and formal privacy guarantees are discussed in Section 5.

4.1 Design

We now present two techniques — *asymmetric* and *session-based* — that provide privacy and anonymity for NDN traffic. Traffic is routed through *ephemeral circuits*, that are defined as a pair of distinct anonymizing routers (ARs). An AR is a NDN node (e.g. a router or a host) that chooses to be part of ANDāNA. An ephemeral circuit transports only one (or only a few) encrypted interest(s). It disappears either when the corresponding content gets delivered, or after a short timeout (hence "*ephemeral*"). A timeout interval is needed so that the consumer can re-issue the same encrypted interest in case of packet loss. We refer to the first AR as *entry router* and the second – as *exit router*. They must not belong to the same administrative domain and must not share the same name prefix. Optionally, consumers can select ARs according to some parameters, such as advertised bandwidth, availability or average load. As pointed out in [5, 31], there is a well know natural tension between non-uniform (i.e. performance-driven) choice of routers and anonymity. Consumers should consider this when selecting ARs.

To build an ephemeral circuit, a consumer retrieves the list of ARs and corresponding public keys. Although we do not mandate any particular technique, a consumer can retrieve this list using, e.g., a directory service [18] or a decentralized (peer-to-peer) mechanism. AR public keys can be authenticated using decentralized techniques (such as web-of-trust [2]) or a PKI infrastructure.[6]

A prospective AR joins ANDāNA by advertising its public key, together with its identity defined as: namespace, organization and public key fingerprint. An AR also publishes auxiliary information, such as total bandwidth, average load, and uptime.

As mentioned earlier, both interest and content packets leak information. Even if names in interests are hidden, three components of content packets — signatures, names and content itself — contain potentially sensitive information. Of course, content producers could simply generate a new key-pair to sign each content packet. This would be impractical, since high costs of key generation and distribution would make it difficult for consumers to authenticate content. (Note that key-evolving schemes [8] do not help, since verification keys generally evolve in a way that is predictable to all parties, including the adversary.) Alternatively, the original content signature could be replaced with that generated by an AR. However, this would preclude end-to-end content verifiability and thus break the NDN trust model.

For this reason, ANDāNA implements encrypted encapsulation of original content, using two symmetric keys securely distributed by the consumer to the ARs during setup of the ephemeral circuit. Upon receiving a content packet, the exit router encrypts it, together with the original (cleartext) name and signature, under the first key provided by the consumer. Then, treating the ciphertext as payload for a new content packet, the exit router signs and sends it to the entry router. The latter strips this signature and the name and encrypts the remaining ciphertext under the second symmetric key provided by the consumer. Next, it forwards the ciphertext with the original encrypted name and a fresh (its own) signature. After decrypting the payload, the consumer discards the signature from the entry router and verifies the one from the content producer.

Because decryption is deterministic, an encrypted interest sent to an AR always produces the same output. Since ARs are a public resource, the adversary can use them to decrypt previously observed interests. It can thus observe the corresponding output and correlate incoming/outgoing interests. This is a well-known attack and there are several ways to mitigate it, such as encrypted channels between communicating parties [18] and mixing (for delay-tolerant traffic) [24]. However, such techniques tend to have significant impact on computational costs and latency. Instead, we use standard NDN features of interest aggregation and caching to prevent such attacks, as described next.

In NDN, a router (not just an AR) that receives duplicate interests collapses them. An interest is considered a *duplicate*, if it arrives while another interest referring

[5]For any packet observed by the adversary, an entity is considered *beyond suspicion* if it is as likely to be the sender of this packet as any other entity.

[6]Note that implicit replication implemented through caching allows the construction of a directory system with better resilience against denial-of-service (DoS) attacks than IP.

to the same content has not been satisfied. Also, if the original interest has been satisfied and the corresponding content is still in cache, a new interest requesting the same piece of data is satisfied with cached content. In this case, the router does not forward any interests. Therefore, the adversary must wait for the expiration of cached content.

As part of ANDāNA, the consumer includes its current timestamp within each encryption layer. ARs reject interests with timestamps outside a pre-defined time window. Thus, consumers need to be loosely synchronized with ARs that must reserve at least $(rate \times window)$ of cache, where $rate$ is the router's wire-rate and $window$ is the interval within which interests are accepted. In this way, if an interest is received multiple times by an AR (e.g. in case of loss of the corresponding data packet between the AR and the consumer), the AR is able to satisfy it using its cache.

The encryption algorithm used by consumers to conceal names in interests must be secure against adaptive chosen ciphertext (CCA) attacks.[7] CCA-security [9] implies, among other things, probabilistic encryption and non-malleability. The former prevents the adversary from determining whether two encrypted interests correspond to the same unencrypted interest. Whereas, the latter implies that the adversary cannot modify interests to defeat the mechanism described above.

We now describe two flavors of anonymization protocols: asymmetric and session-based. In order to allow efficient routing of interest packets, the encrypted component is encoded at the end of the name with both flavors.

Asymmetric: To issue an interest, a consumer selects a pair of ARs and uses their public keys to encrypt the interest, as described above and in Algorithm 1. A consumer also generates two symmetric keys: k_1 and k_2 that will be used to encrypt the content packet on the way back. We use $\mathcal{E}_{pk}(\cdot)$ and $\overline{\mathcal{E}_k}(\cdot)$ to denote (CCA-secure) public key and symmetric encryption schemes, respectively.

To account for the delay due to extra hops needed to reach the second AR (and reduce the number of discarded interests), a consumer adds half of the estimated round trip time (RTT) to the innermost timestamp. Each AR removes the outermost encryption layer, as detailed in Algorithm 2. Since $\mathcal{E}_{pk}(\cdot)$ is CCA-secure, the decryption process fails if the ciphertext has been modified in transit or was not encrypted under the AR's public key. Content corresponding to the encrypted interest is encrypted on the way back, as detailed in Algorithm 3, using $\overline{\mathcal{E}_k}(\cdot)$ and symmetric keys supplied by the consumer.

[7] Technically, in order to guarantee correctness an encryption scheme suitable for ANDāNA must also be robust [1]. However, since CCA-secure encryption schemes used in practice are also robust, we omit this requirement in the rest of the paper.

Algorithm 1: Encrypted Interest Generation

input : Interest int; Set of ℓ ARs and their keys: $\mathcal{R} = \{(\text{AR}_i, pk_i) \mid 0 < i \leq \ell, pk_i \in \mathcal{PK}\}$
output: Encrypted interest int_{pk_i,pk_j}; symmetric keys k_1, k_2

1: Select $(\text{AR}_i, pk_i), (\text{AR}_j, pk_j)$ from $\mathcal{R}$
2: **if** $\text{AR}_i = \text{AR}_j$ **or** AR_i, AR_j are from same organization **or** AR_i, AR_j share the same name prefix **then**
3:     Go to line 1
4: **end if**
5: $k_1 \leftarrow \{0,1\}^\kappa$; $k_2 \leftarrow \{0,1\}^\kappa$
6: $eint = \text{AR}_2/\mathcal{E}_{pk_j}(\text{int} \mid k_2 \mid curr\_timestamp + RTT/2)$
7: $eint = \text{AR}_1/\mathcal{E}_{pk_i}(eint \mid k_1 \mid curr\_timestamp)$
8: Output $eint, k_1, k_2$

Algorithm 2: AR Handling of Encrypted Interests

input : Encrypted Interest int_{pk_i,pk_j}, where $pk_i, pk_j \in \mathcal{PK} \cup \{\perp\}$ (where "$\perp$" denotes "no encryption")
output: Interest int_{pk_j}; symmetric key k_1

1: $(\text{int}_{pk_j}, k_1, timestamp) = \mathcal{D}_{sk_i}(\text{int}_{pk_i,pk_j})$
2: **if** Step 1 fails **or** $timestamp$ is not current **then**
3:     Discard int_{pk_i,pk_j}
4: **else**
5:     Save tuple $(\text{int}_{pk_i,pk_j}, \text{int}_{pk_j}, k_1)$ to internal state
6:     Output int_{pk_j}, k_1
7: **end if**

Algorithm 3: AR Content Routing

input : Content: $data_{k_2}$ in response to int_{pk_j}, where $pk_j \in \mathcal{PK} \cup \{\perp\}$
output: Encrypted data packet $data_{k_1,k_2}$

1: Retrieve tuple $(\text{int}_{pk_i,pk_j}, \text{int}_{pk_j}, k_1)$ from internal state where name in int_{pk_2} matches that in $data_{k_2}$
2: **if** $k_2 \neq \perp$ **then** Remove signature and name from $data_{k_2}$
3: Create new empty data packet pkt
4: Set name on pkt as the name on int_{pk_i,pk_j}
5: Set the data in pkt as $\overline{\mathcal{E}_{k_1}}(data_{k_2})$
6: Sign pkt with AR's key
7: Output pkt as $data_{k_1,k_2}$

Session-based Variant. This variant aims to reduce (amortize) the use of public key encryption thus lowering the computational cost and ciphertext size. Before sending any interests through ephemeral circuits, a consumer (Alice) establishes a shared secret key with each selected AR. This is done via a 2-packet interest/content handshake. We do not describe the details of symmetric key setup, since there are standard ways of doing it. We provide two options: one using Diffie-Hellman key exchange [17], and the other – using SSL/TLS-style protocol whereby Alice encrypts a key for AR_i. Once a symmetric key k_{ai} is shared with AR_i, Alice can establish any number of ephemeral circuits using it as either first or second AR hop. Also at setup time, Alice and AR_i agree on session identifier value – sid_{ai} – that is included (in cleartext) in subsequent interests so that AR_i

can identify the appropriate entry for Alice and k_{ai}.

The main advantage of the session-based approach is better performance: both consumers and routers only perform symmetric operations after initial key setup. However, one drawback is that, since the session identifier sid is not encrypted, packets corresponding to the same sid are easily linkable.

We note that our design neither encourages nor prevents consumers from mixing asymmetric *and* session-based variants for the same or different ephemeral circuits.

4.2 System and Security Model

In order for our discussion to relate to prior work, we use the notion of "indistinguishable configurations" from the framework introduced in [19]; the actual definitions are in Section 5.

Our security analysis considers the worst case scenario, i.e., interests being satisfied by the content producer rather than a router's cache. While, in normal conditions, encrypted interests are satisfied by caches only in case of packet loss, fully decrypted interests may not have to reach to content producers. A system secure in case of cache misses is also secure when interests are satisfied by content cached at routers along the way. (Recall that, when an interest is satisfied by a router's cache, it is not forwarded any further.) This limits the adversary's ability to observe interests in transit.

Adversary Goals and Capabilities. The goal of an adversary is to link consumers with their actions. In particular, it may want to determine what content is being requested by a particular user and/or which users are requesting specific content. A somewhat related goal is determining which cache (if any) is satisfying a consumer's requests. Our adversary is local and active: it controls only a subset of network entities and can perform any action usually allowed to such entities. Moreover, it is capable of selectively compromising additional network entities according to its local information.

Our model allows the adversary to perform the following actions:

- **Deploy compromised routers**: ANDāNA is an open network, therefore an adversary can deploy compromised anonymizers and regular routers. As such, routers may exhibit malicious behavior including injection, delay, alteration, or drop traffic.
- **Compromise existing routers**: An adversary can select any router (either ARs or regular routers) in the network and compromise it. As a result, the adversary learns all the private information (e.g. decryption keys, pending decrypted interests, cache content, etc.) of such router.
- **Control content producers**: Content producers are not part of ANDāNA. As such, the network has no control over them. An adversary can compromise existing content producers or deploy compromised ones and convince users to pull content from them. We also assume that the content providers are publicly accessible, and therefore the adversary is able to retrieve content from them.
- **Deploy compromised caches**: Similarly to compromised content producers, an adversary can compromise routers' cache or deploy its own caches. The behavior of a compromised cache includes monitoring cache requests and replying with corrupted data.
- **Observe and replay traffic**: An adversary can tap a link carrying anonymized traffic. By doing this it learns, among other things, packet contents and traffic patterns. The traffic observed by an adversary can be replayed by any compromised router.

An adversary can iteratively compromise entities of its choice, and use the information it gathers to determine what should be compromised next. In order to make our model realistic, the time required by an adversary to compromise or deploy a router, a cache or a content producer is significantly higher that the round-trip time (RTT) of an anonymized interest and corresponding data. This implies that all the state information recovered from a newly compromised router only refers to packets received *after* the adversary decides to compromise such router.

A powerful class of attacks against anonymizing networks is called fingerprinting [29, 41]. Inter-packet time intervals are usually not hidden in low latency onion routing networks because packets are dispatched as quickly as possible. This behavior can be exploited by an adversary, who can correlate inter-packet intervals on two links and use this information to determine if the observed packets belong to the same consumer [41]. This class of attacks is significantly harder to execute on ANDāNA because of the nature of ephemeral circuits and because of the use of caches on routers. Ephemeral circuits do not allow the adversary to gather enough packets with uniform delays since they are used to transport only one or a very small number of interests and corresponding data. Active adversaries who can control the communication link of a content provider can add measurable delays to some of the packets in order to identify consumers. However, consumers may be able to retrieve the same content through caches making such attack ineffective. Throughput fingerprinting consists in measuring the throughput of the circuit used by a consumer to identify the slowest anonymizer in the consumer's circuit [29]. Throughput fingerprinting is difficult to perform in ANDāNA since each ephemeral circuit does not carry enough information to mount an attack. In particular, the authors of [29] report that a successful attack requires at least a few minutes of traffic on Tor. Similarly, ephemeral circuits provide an effective protection against known attacks such as the predecessor attack [43].

Consumers, Producers and ARs. Each consumer runs several processes that generate interests. For our analysis, interests are created by a specific interface of a host, and the corresponding content is delivered back to the same interface. Interest encryption is either performed on the consumer's host, or on an entity that routes consumer's traffic. In the latter case, the channel between the user and the anonymizing entity is considered secure.

Content is generated by producers, i.e., entities that can sign data. We do not assume the correspondence between a producer and a particular host. Content can be either stored in routers' caches, at servers or dynamically generated in response to an interest.

ARs perform interests decryption and content encapsulation. Each AR advertises a public key for signature verification and one or more public keys for encryption. ARs must refresh their encryption keys frequently, discarding old keys after a short grace period. In order to simplify key distribution and allow consumer to immediately trust new public keys from routers, we use a simple key hierarchy where a long lived public key owned by the router (the signing key), is used to certify short lived encryption keys. The signing key may be certified by other entities using techniques like web-of-trust or PKI.

Denial-of-service Attacks. ANDāNA is envisioned as a public overlay network and is clearly susceptible to DoS attacks. Since anyone can join ANDāNA as an AR or use it as a consumer, we make no distinction between insider and outsider attacks. The adversary can send numerous interests to ARs or construct ephemeral circuits longer than two hops in order to maximize effectiveness of attacks. Moreover, it can consume AR resources by sending malformed encrypted interests that require ARs to perform expensive and ultimately useless public key decryption. Similar to Tor, before establishing an ephemeral circuit, an AR can ask a consumer to solve an easy-to-verify/expensive-to-solve puzzle. This and similar techniques for ANDāNA are subjects of future work. In a setting with long-lived circuits, such as Tor, disrupting a node effectively shuts down all circuits that include it. Due to the short lifespan of our ephemeral circuits, the same attack on ANDāNA only causes a very small number of interests/data packets per user to be dropped.

Abuse. Similar to any other anonymity service, ANDāNA can be abused for a variety of nefarious purposes. We do not elaborate on this topic. However, exit policies similar to those in Tor [18] can be used with ANDāNA based on content names.

5 Security Analysis

In this section we propose a formal model for evaluating the security of ANDāNA. We define consumer anonymity and unlinkability with respect to an adversary within this model. We finally provide necessary and sufficient conditions for anonymity and unlinkability. As our analysis shows, we are able to obtain a level of anonymity comparable to Tor with two — rather than Tor's three — ARs thanks to the lack of source addresses in NDN interests.

In general, efficacy of ANDāNA depends on the inability of the adversary to correlate input and output of a non-compromised AR, and its inability to observe all producer and consumers at the same time. Since ANDāNA is designed for low-latency traffic, we do not intentionally delay messages or introduce dummy packets, other than some limited padding. This is similar to how Tor and other low-latency anonymizing networks forward traffic, and implies that traffic patterns remain almost unchanged as they pass through the network [31]. It is well known that, in Tor, this allows the adversary that observes both ends of a communication flow to confirm a suspected link between them [5, 35]. For this reason, a *global passive adversary* can violate anonymity properties of both Tor and ANDāNA. However, we believe that such an adversary is unrealistic in a geographically distributed network spanning over multiple administrative domains, and designing against it would result in overkill.

We assume that any adversary monitoring all interfaces of an AR can correlate entering encrypted traffic with its exiting, decrypted counterpart using timing information. However, we believe that the short lifespan of ephemeral circuits – and therefore the limited number of related packets traveling through a single AR – severely limits the adversary's ability to carry out this attack. Unfortunately, at the time of this writing we do not have enough experimental evidence to confirm this. For the sake of safety, in the analysis below we assume that, by compromising all interfaces of an AR, the adversary also compromises the AR itself. Therefore, a non-compromised AR must have at least one non-compromised interface. To sum up, we assume that:

Assumption 5.1. *Adv cannot correlate input and output of a non-compromised AR.*

Our analysis is based on *indistinguishable configurations*. A configuration defines consumers' activity with respect to a particular network. *Adv* only controls a subset of network entities and observes only some packets. Therefore, it cannot distinguish between two configurations that vary only in the activity that it cannot directly observe or in the content of encrypted packets that it cannot decrypt. In order to provide meaningful anonymity guarantees, we identify a set of configurations that have one or more equivalent counterparts. However, unlike [19], our analysis takes into account the infrastructure underlying ANDāNA, i.e., the network topology and packets exchanged over the *actual* network. We believe that this makes our model and analysis both realistic and fine-grained, since it accounts for all adversarial advantages related to the underlying network structure. Packets sent by a non-compromised consumer u to a non-compromised AR r transit through several — possibly compromised — NDN routers that are not part of ANDāNA. The model of [19] considers r compromised even if only one link between u and r is controlled by the adversary. Whereas, in our model, r is considered to be non-compromised.

Notation and Definitions

Table 1 summarizes our notation. The intersection of P and C might not be empty, which reflects the fact that consumers can act as producers and *vice versa*. Similarly, our model does not prevent routers from being producers and/or consumers. Therefore, $\mathsf{R} \cap \mathsf{P}$ and $\mathsf{R} \cap \mathsf{C}$ might be non-empty.

The adversary is defined as a 4-tuple: $Adv = (\mathsf{P}_{Adv}, \mathsf{C}_{Adv}, \mathsf{R}_{Adv}, \mathsf{IF}_{Adv}) \subset (\mathsf{P}, \mathsf{C}, \mathsf{R}, \mathsf{IF})$ where individual components specify (respectively) sets of: compromised producers, consumers, routers and interfaces. If $r \in \mathsf{R}_{Adv}$, then Adv controls all interfaces and has access to all decryption key and state information of r. If all interfaces of r are in IF_{Adv}, then $r \in \mathsf{R}_{Adv}$. In other words, for the sake of this analysis, controlling all interfaces of a router is equivalent to learning that router's decryption/secret key. We emphasize that for $r \in \mathsf{R}$ to be non-compromised, at least one of its interfaces must be non-compromised. If $p \in \mathsf{P}_{Adv}$, Adv controls p's interfaces, monitors interests received by p and controls both content and timing of p's responses to incoming interests. If $c \in \mathsf{C}_{Adv}$, then Adv controls all fields and timing of interests. Finally, if $\mathsf{if} \in \mathsf{IF}_{Adv}$, then Adv can listen to all traffic flowing through if, as well as sending new traffic from it. IF_{Adv} includes all the interfaces of compromised consumers, producers and routers *plus* additional interfaces eavesdropped on by Adv.

For ease of notation, we do not explicitly indicate the name of the next router in interest packets nor symmetric keys chosen by consumers. We denote encrypted interests as:

$$\mathsf{int}_{pk_1,pk_2} = \mathcal{E}_{pk_1}(\mathcal{E}_{pk_2}(\mathsf{int}))$$

with $pk_1, pk_2 \in \mathcal{PK} \cup \{\perp\}$ where $\perp$ indicates a special symbol for "no encryption". If $pk_1 = \perp$ then $pk_2 = \perp$. The size of public keys is a function of the global security parameter κ. For simplicity, we denote $\mathsf{int}_{pk_1,\perp}$ as int_{pk_1}. When an AR receives int_{pk_1,pk_2} and if it is in possession of the decryption key corresponding to pk_1, it removes the outer layer of encryption. While $\mathcal{E}$ is CCA-secure (and therefore also CPA-secure), we do not require $\mathcal{E}$ to be key private [6]. Key privacy prevents an observer from learning the public key used to generate a ciphertext. In ANDāNA, knowledge of the public key used to encrypt the outer layer of an interest does not reveal any more information than the (cleartext) name on the interest.

We define the anonymity set with respect to interface if_i^r as:

$$A_{\mathsf{if}_i^r} = \{d \mid \Pr[d \rightarrow_{\mathsf{int}} r \mid \mathsf{int} \rightsquigarrow \mathsf{if}_i^r] > 0\}$$

In other words, for each interface if_i^r of router r, $A_{\mathsf{if}_i^r}$ contains all entities that could have sent int with non-zero probability. We define $\mathsf{path}^{\mathsf{int}} = \{\mathsf{if}_i^r \mid \mathsf{int} \rightsquigarrow \mathsf{if}_i^r\}$. This is the sequence of interfaces traversed by int. We use it to define the anonymity set of an interest with respect Adv:

$$A_{Adv}^{\mathsf{int}} \triangleq \bigcap_{\mathsf{path}^{\mathsf{int}} \cap \mathsf{IF}_{Adv}} A_{\mathsf{if}_i^r}$$

Intuitively, if u is far away from a compromised entity d, then all sets A_{Adv}^{int} such that $u \in A_{Adv}^{\mathsf{int}}$ are a large subset of C. Adv can rule out possible senders of an interest (i.e., determine if $u \notin A_{Adv}^{\mathsf{int}}$) only if it controls at least one entity (routers, interfaces) along each path that u does not share with other consumers. The level of anonymity of $u \in A_{Adv}^{\mathsf{int}}$ with respect to Adv is proportional to the size of A_{Adv}^{int}. In particular, if u is the only member of A_{Adv}^{int}, it has no anonymity, since int must have been issued by u.

A configuration is a description of the network activity. Each configuration maps consumers to their actions, defined as the interest they issue and the corresponding content producers. More formally, a configuration is a relation:

$$C : \mathsf{C} \rightarrow \{(r_1, r_2, p, \mathsf{int}_{pk_1,pk_2})\}$$

with $(r_1, r_2, p, \mathsf{int}_{pk_1,pk_2}) \in \mathsf{R}^2 \times \mathsf{P} \times \{0,1\}^*$, that maps a consumer to: a pair of routers defining an ephemeral circuit, an interest (encrypted for this circuit) and a producer. $C(u)$ is a 4-tuple that represents one action of u in C. C_i is the selection on the i-th component of C, i.e., if $C(u) = (r_1, r_2, p, \mathsf{int}_{pk_1,pk_2})$, then $C_1(u) = r_1$, $C_2(u) = r_2$, $C_3(u) = p$ and $C_4(u) = \mathsf{int}_{pk_1,pk_2}$.

We say that two configurations C and C' are "indistinguishable with respect to Adv" if Adv can only determine with probability at most $1/2 + \varepsilon$ which configuration corresponds to the observed network, for some ε negligible in the security parameter κ. We denote two such configurations as $C \equiv_{Adv} C'$.

We now show that assumption 5.1 holds if a passive adversary observes only input and output values of

C	set of all consumers, $u \in \mathsf{C}$	Adv	adversary
P	set of all content producers, $p \in \mathsf{P}$	d	an entity, i.e., a router or a host
R	set of all routers, $r \in \mathsf{R}$	$d \rightarrow_{\mathsf{int}} r$	entity d sends interest int to some interface of router r
IF	set of all interfaces on all network devices	$\mathsf{int} \rightsquigarrow \mathsf{if}_i^r$	router r receives interest int on interface if_i^r
$\mathsf{if}_i^r \in \mathsf{IF}$	i-th interface on router r	$\mathcal{E}_{pk}(\cdot)$	CCA-secure hybrid encryption scheme
$\mathcal{PK}$	set of all public keys	int_{pk_1,pk_2}	interest encrypted under public keys pk_1, pk_2
(pk_i, sk_i)	public/priv. encryption keypair of an AR r_i	$\perp$	no encryption

Table 1. Notation.

an AR (i.e., it cannot use timing information or other side-channels), and the underlying encryption scheme is semantically secure. Claim 5.1 below states that, for any encrypted interest, Adv cannot determine if it corresponds to an interest decrypted by a non-compromised router, by observing the two and with no additional information.

Claim 5.1. *Given any CPA-secure public key encryption scheme $\mathcal{E}$ and two same-length interests $\mathsf{int}^0, \mathsf{int}^1$ chosen by Adv, Adv has only negligible advantage over $1/2$ in determining the value of a randomly selected bit b, given $\mathsf{int}^b_{pk_1,pk_2}$, $\mathsf{int}^0_{pk_2}$ and $\mathsf{int}^1_{pk_2}$, with $pk_1 \in \mathcal{PK}$ and $pk_2 \in \mathcal{PK} \cup \{\perp\}$.*

Due to the lack of space, Claim 5.1 is formally justified in Appendix A.

Anonymity Definitions and Conditions

In this section we present formal definitions of anonymity for our model. We introduce the notions of *consumer anonymity*, *producer anonymity* and *producer and consumer unlinkability*. We show that ephemeral circuits composed of two anonymizing routers — at least one of which is not compromised — provide consumer *and* producer anonymity. This, in turn, implies consumer and producer unlinkability. Due to the lack of space, we defer formal proofs of the theorems in this section to Appendix A.

A consumer u enjoys *consumer anonymity* if Adv cannot determine whether u or a different user u' is retrieving some specific content. This notion is formalized using indistinguishable configurations: given a configuration C in which u retrieves content t, u has consumer anonymity if there exist another configuration C' in which u' retrieves t and Adv cannot determine whether he is observing C or C'. More formally:

Definition 5.1 (Consumer anonymity). *$u \in (\mathsf{C} \setminus \mathsf{C}_{Adv})$ has consumer anonymity in configuration C with respect to Adv if there exists $C' \equiv_{Adv} C$ such that $C'(u') = C(u)$ and $u' \neq u$.*

Theorem 5.1. *$u \in (\mathsf{C} \setminus \mathsf{C}_{Adv})$ has consumer anonymity in C with respect to Adv if there exists $u' \neq u$ such that any of the following conditions hold:*

1. *$u, u' \in A^{C_4(u)}_{Adv}$*
2. *$C_1(u) = C_1(u')$, $C_1(u) \notin \mathsf{R}$ and $C_1(u) \in A^{\mathsf{int}_{pk_2}}_{Adv}$ where $C_4(u) = \mathsf{int}_{pk_1,pk_2}$*
3. *$C_2(u) = C_2(u')$, $C_2(u) \notin \mathsf{R}$ and $C_2(u) \in A^{\mathsf{int}}_{Adv}$ where $C_4(u) = \mathsf{int}_{pk_1,pk_2}$*

Informally, the theorem above states that ANDāNA provides consumer anonymity with respect to Adv if: *1.* Adv cannot observe encrypted interests coming from u and u', or it cannot distinguish between the two consumers due to anonymity provided by the network layer; or *2.* u, u' share an non-compromised first router in at least one ephemeral circuit; or *3.* u, u' share an non-compromised second router in at least one ephemeral circuit.

Similarly to consumer anonymity, producer anonymity is defined in terms of indistinguishable configurations. In particular, a producer p enjoys anonymity with respect to Adv which observes int_{pk_1,pk_2} if Adv cannot distinguish between a configuration C where p produces the content corresponding to int and a configuration C' where p' and not p produces *that* content.

Definition 5.2 (Producer anonymity). *Given int_{pk_1,pk_2} for $p \in \mathsf{P}$, $u \in \mathsf{C}$ has producer anonymity in configuration C with respect to p, Adv if there exists an indistinguishable configuration C' such that int_{pk_1,pk_2} is sent by a non-compromised consumer to a producer different from p.*

Theorem 5.2. *u has producer anonymity in C with respect to p, Adv if any of the following conditions hold:*

1. *There exists $C(u)$ such that $C_1(u)$ (the first anonymizing router) is not compromised and $C_4(u) = \mathsf{int}_{pk_1,pk_2}$, $C_1(u) = C_1(u')$ and $C_3(u) = p \neq C_3(u')$ for some non-compromised $u' \in \mathsf{C}$,* or
2. *There exists $C(u)$ such that $C_2(u)$ (the second anonymizing router) is not compromised and $C_4(u) = \mathsf{int}_{pk_1,pk_2}$, $C_2(u) = C_2(u')$ and $C_3(u) = p \neq C_3(u')$ for some non-compromised $u' \in \mathsf{C}$*

Finally, we define producer and consumer unlinkability as:

Definition 5.3 (Producer and consumer unlinkability). *We say that $u \in (\mathsf{C} \setminus \mathsf{C}_{Adv})$ and $p \in \mathsf{P}$ are unlinkable in C with respect to Adv if there exists $C' \equiv_{Adv} C$ where u's interests are sent to a producer $p' \neq p$.*

Corollary 5.1. *Consumer* $u \in (\mathsf{C} \setminus \mathsf{C}_{Adv})$ *and producer* $p \in \mathsf{P}$ *are unlinkable in configuration* C *with respect to* Adv *if* p *has producer anonymity with respect to* u*'s interests* or u *has consumer anonymity and there exists a configuration* $C' \equiv_{Adv} C$ *where* $C'(u') = C(u)$ *with* $u' \neq u$ *and* u'*'s interests have a destination different from* p.

Corollary 5.2. *Consumer* $u \in (\mathsf{C} \setminus \mathsf{C}_{Adv})$ *and producer* $p \in \mathsf{P}$ *are unlinkable in configuration* C *with respect to* Adv *if both producer and consumer anonymity hold.*

We emphasize that this result also holds for ephemeral circuits with length greater than two ARs.

6 Implementation and Performance

ANDāNA is implemented as an application-level service consisting of client "stack" (used by consumers) and server program that runs on ANDāNA ARs. Both are written in C and interface to NDN through Unix domain sockets.[8] Cryptographic algorithms are implemented using OpenSSL [42]. Hybrid encryption is obtained using RSA-OAEP [10] and AES+HMAC [15, 7]. The latter is also used for symmetric encryption. We use SHA-256 for HMAC and 1024- and 128-bit keys for RSA and AES, respectively. Loose time synchronization among ANDāNA client and servers are achieved using `pool.ntp.org`, a public pool of NTP servers.

ANDāNA client encrypts interests from user applications. In order to hide all possible sources of de-anonymizing information, encryption is performed over the full interest packet, including: name, scope, exclusion filters and duplicate suppression string fields. Following NDN "rules", ANDāNA AR announces the ability to serve the root ("/") namespace and receives all traffic sent from (or to) the local NDN routing process. This allows traffic to be routed through ANDāNA by default, requiring no changes to existing applications. For more granularity, consumers can vary the default namespace, e.g., "`/andana/`". However, this would require privacy-seeking applications to explicitly direct their traffic to that namespace, similar to today's configurable proxy settings.

ANDāNA servers run as applications on NDN routers. Each server is responsible for its *relay* and *session creation* namespaces. The former is a globally routable namespace used for receiving both session-based and asymmetrically encrypted Interests. Clients using session-based encryption in ANDāNA need to first establish symmetric keys with servers. To start a new session with a server, a clients sends an interest in the `createsession` namespace, registered by the server code as a sub-prefix of the relay namespace.

[8] At the time of this writing, there is no direct function interface to NDN

We deployed our prototype and run a series of tests on the Open Network Laboratory (ONL) [34]. ONL is a testbed developed by Washington University to enable experimental evaluation of advanced networking concepts in a realistic environment. To guarantee highly reproducible results, ONL provides reservation-based exclusive access to most of its host and network resources. All our experiments used single-core Linux machines with 512 MB of RAM and gigabit switches (one machine per switch).

We compare plain NDN and ANDāNA on a simple line topology with four switches and four Linux machines, each corresponding to an NDN node. Static routing is established between nodes. The first NDN node in the line topology acts as a consumer and runs `ccngetfile` — a small tool from CCNx open-source library that retrieves data published as NDN content and stores it in a local file. We performed tests with 1, 10, and 100MB files; each file was retrieved from the NDN repository of the machine at the other end of the line topology. Results of this comparison for 10MB files are summarized in Fig. 1. Due to space constraints, we illustrate all file retrieval results in Appendix B. Results show that computational overhead introduced by ANDāNA roughly doubles download times over plain NDN. This is assuming an almost-perfect world where ARs topologically align with the best path and link bandwidths are abundant.

In order to compare ANDāNA's computational overhead with a similar anonymizing tool, we deployed Tor over ONL and measured its overhead over TCP/IP. We measured performance of TCP/IP baseline deploying five switches, connected in a line, and two Linux machines (one at each end): the first acting as client (running `curl`), the second – as server (running `lighttpd` HTTP server). Performance of Tor was measured on a topology that closely mimics that of TCP/IP baseline: five switches, connecting three Tor relays, a client and a server. To ensure "line" topology, Tor client is configured to use explicit entry and exit nodes; DNS lookups are avoided by using IP addresses in all tests.

Before discussing the results, we mention some comparison details. NDN is a research project and its code is optimized for functionality rather than performance. It provides content authentication through digital signatures – a computationally expensive feature not present in either TCP/IP or Tor. NDN stack currently runs as a user-space application, in contrast to TCP/IP that runs in kernel-space. Finally, in all our experiments, NDN had to run on top of TCP/IP (rather than at layer 2) due to limitations of the underlying ONL testbed. Consequently, we believe a fair comparison between ANDāNA and Tor can only be achieved by focusing the analysis on *relative* overhead imposed by each, over the network

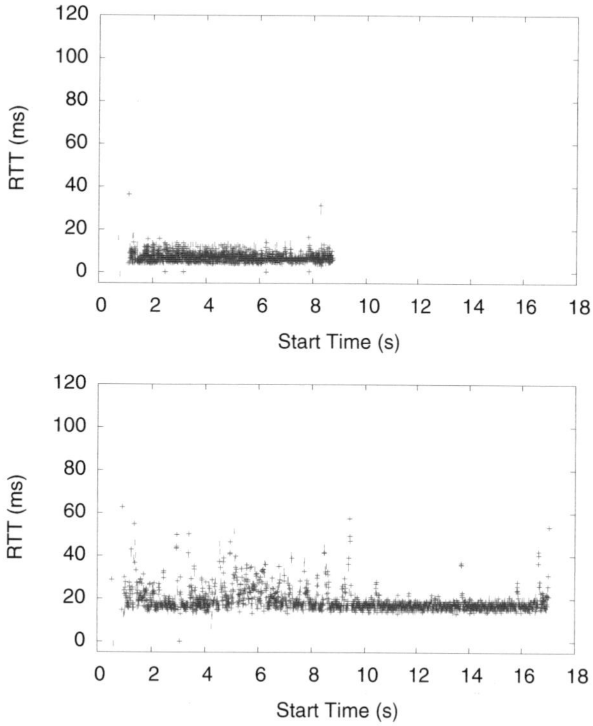

Figure 1. Left: RTT for 10MB of content over NDN (limited anonymity). Right: RTT for 10MB of content over ANDāNA (full anonymity).

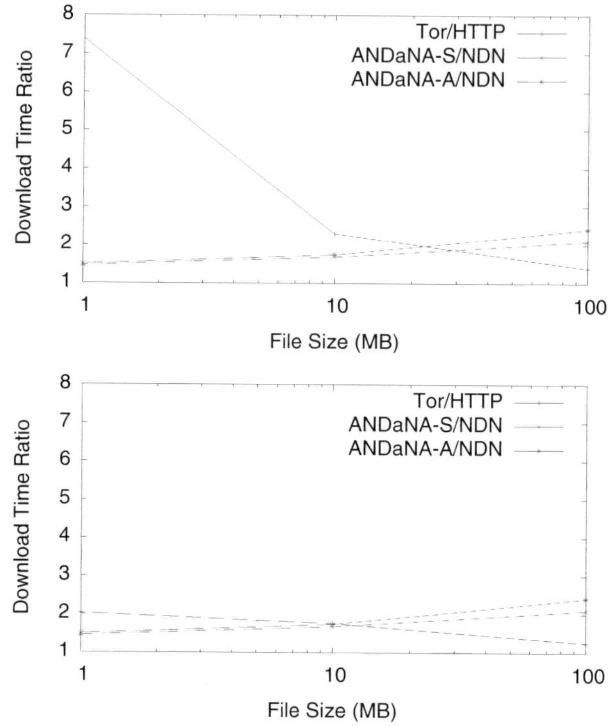

Figure 2. Comparison of 1, 10, and 100MB file download times over Tor, ANDāNA-S and ANDāNA-A with respect to respective baselines. Left: transfer time *and* circuit setup time. Right: transfer time only.

it is deployed, i.e., NDN and TCP/IP respectively.

Figure 2 shows the performance of ANDāNA and Tor with respect to their baselines. The graph on the left shows the measurements including the time required to setup a Tor circuit and all ephemeral circuits for ANDāNA. Session-based ANDāNA is denoted by ANDāNA-S, while ANDāNA with asymmetric encryption is referred to as ANDāNA-A. For small- to medium-size files (1-10MB), overhead of ANDāNA-A is between 1.5× and 1.75×. As expected, ANDāNA-S exhibits lower overhead (1.45× to 1.7×) due to more efficient symmetric encryption.

In comparison, Tor's download time for the same amount of data is between 2.3 and 7 times higher than that of TCP/IP. This imposes significant overhead for content size that fits many typical web pages. Whereas, ANDāNA is efficient in anonymizing such traffic patterns. Large file transfers are more efficient with Tor, which increases the total download time by about 1.4 times, compared to 2.4 and 2.1 of ANDāNA-A and ANDāNA-S.

The right-side graph in Figure 2 shows the relative speed of three approaches without including circuit setup time. Our measurements show that overhead of ephemeral circuit creation in ANDāNA-S is negligible. Since a new ephemeral circuit must be selected for every interest with ANDāNA-A, we simply report the same values from the previous graph. Results confirm that overhead of circuit creation in Tor is significant when retrieving small-size content. Removing this initialization phase from the measurements significantly reduces Tor's overhead. However, the overhead of ANDāNA with respect to its baseline is still smaller than that of Tor for content up to 10MB.

In absolute terms (comparing raw download times), Tor + TCP/IP performs better than ANDāNA + NDN in our testbed experiments. However, we believe that, in a realistic geographically-distributed deployment setting with limited-bandwidth links, ANDāNA + NDN would provide a significant performance advantage over Tor + TCP/IP due to its shorter (ephemeral) circuits. In other words, we anticipate that shorter circuits and content caching in ANDāNA + NDN would result in appreciably lower overall download times than Tor + TCP/IP in a global internet setting.

7 Conclusions and Future Work

Content-centric networking is a major transition from today's world that focuses on communication endpoints. NDN project represents one of the most visible current research efforts aiming to bring content-centric networking into the foreground by using it as a possible future Internet architecture. Despite some privacy-friendly features and side-effects, NDN poses some interesting privacy challenges. This work presents an initial attempt to provide anonymity in NDN. The main contribution of this work is threefold: (1) exploration of privacy issues in NDN, (2) design of an anonymization tool – ANDāNA, and (3) its security analysis and performance assessment.

At the same time, particularly because the entire NDN project (and, of course, ANDāNA) represent work-in-progress, one of the main goals of this paper is to solicit comments from the security research community. Also, since our work merely scratches the surface of privacy issues in content-centric networking and NDN, a number of issues are left for future work, including:

- More performance experimentation with ANDāNA, especially, in larger testbeds and under various traffic load / congestion scenarios. (This should lead to better code profiling and lower overhead.)
- Comprehensive directory service for effective large-scale distribution of up-to-date AR information.
- In-depth study of both privacy and performance trade-offs in the use of asymmetric vs. symmetric ANDāNA variants.
- DoS mitigation measures, such as computational puzzles for circuit establishment.
- Red-teaming experiments to assess realistic privacy attainable with ANDāNA.
- Modification of ANDāNA to support other emerging content-centric architectures and comparative experiments among them.

Acknowledgments

We thank NDSS'12 anonymous reviewers for their valuable feedback. We are also grateful to Van Jacobson, Jim Thornton, Kasper Rasmussen, Yanbin Lu, Lixia Zhang and Mark Baugher for their helpful input and comments on earlier drafts of this paper. This work was conducted in the context of the NSF project: "CNS-1040802: FIA: Collaborative Research: Named Data Networking (NDN)".

References

[1] M. Abdalla, M. Bellare, and G. Neven. Robust encryption. In *Theory of Cryptography Conference, TCC 2010*, 2010.

[2] A. Abdul-Rahman. The PGP Trust Model, 1997.

[3] Anonymizer anonymous surfing. `http://www.anonymizer.com/`.

[4] S. Arianfar, T. Koponen, S. Shenker, and B. Raghavan. On preserving privacy in content-oriented networks. In *ACM SIGCOMM Workshop on Information-Centric Networking*, 2011.

[5] K. Bauer, D. McCoy, D. Grunwald, T. Kohno, and D. Sicker. Low-resource routing attacks against anonymous systems. In *The 2007 Workshop on Privacy in the Electronic Society*, 2007.

[6] M. Bellare, B. A., D. A., and D. Pointcheval. Key-privacy in public-key encryption. In *ASIACRYPT*, 2001.

[7] M. Bellare, R. Canetti, and H. Krawczyk. Keying hash functions for message authentication. In *CRYPTO*, 1996.

[8] M. Bellare and S. Miner. A forward-secure digital signature scheme. In *CRYPTO*, 1999.

[9] M. Bellare and C. Namprempre. Authenticated encryption: Relations among notions and analysis of the generic composition paradigm. *Journal of Cryptology*, 21(4), 2008.

[10] M. Bellare and P. Rogaway. Optimal asymmetric encryption. In *EUROCRYPT*, 1994.

[11] T. Callahan, M. Allman, and V. Paxson. A longitudinal view of http traffic. In *The 11th international conference on passive and active measurement*, 2010.

[12] Content centric networking (CCNx) project. `http://www.ccnx.org`.

[13] D. Chaum. Untraceable electronic mail, return addresses, and digital pseudonyms. *Communications of the ACM*, 24(2), 1981.

[14] D. Chaum. Security without identification: Transaction systems to make big brother obsolete. *Communications of the ACM*, 28(10), 1985.

[15] J. Daemen and V. Rijmen. The design of Rijndael: AES - the advanced encryption standard. Springer, 2002.

[16] G. Danezis, R. Dingledine, and N. Mathewson. Mixminion: Design of a type III anonymous remailer protocol. In *The 2003 IEEE Symposium on Security and Privacy*, 2003.

[17] W. Diffie and M. Hellman. New directions in cryptography. *Information Theory, IEEE Transactions on*, 22(6), 1976.

[18] R. Dingledine, N. Mathewsonn, and P. Syverson. Tor: The second-generation onion router. In *The 13th USENIX Security Symposium*, 2004.

[19] J. Feigenbaum, A. Johnson, and P. Syverson. A model of onion routing with provable anonymity. In *Financial Cryptography*, 2007.

[20] National science foundation (NSF) future of internet architecture (FIA) program. `http://www.nets-fia.net/`.

[21] M. Freedman and R. Morris. Tarzan: A peer-to-peer anonymizing network layer. In *The 9th ACM Conference on Computer and Communications Security*, 2002.

[22] E. Gabber, P. Gibbons, D. Kristol, Y. Matias, and A. Mayer. Consistent, yet anonymous, web access with lpwa. *Communications of the ACM*, 42(2), 1999.

[23] M. Gritter and D. Cheriton. An architecture for content routing support in the internet. In *USENIX Symposium on Internet Technologies and Systems*. USENIX Association, 2001.

[24] C. Gülcü and G. Tsudik. Mixing e-mail with Babel. In *Network and Distributed Security Symposium*, 1996.

[25] A. Houmansadr, G. Ngyuen, M. Caesar, and N. Borisov. Cirripede: Circumvention infrastructure using router redirection with plausible deniability. In *The 18th ACM Conference on Computer and Communications Security*, 2011.

[26] I2P anonymous networking project. `http://www.i2p2.de/`.

[27] V. Jacobson, D. Smetters, J. Thornton, M. Plass, N. Briggs, and R. Braynard. Networking named content. *The 5th international conference on Emerging networking experiments and technologies*, 2009.

[28] T. Koponen, M. Chawla, B. Chun, A. Ermolinskiy, K. Kim, S. Shenker, and I. Stoica. A data-oriented (and beyond) network architecture. *ACM SIGCOMM Computer Communication Review*, 37(4):181–192, 2007.

[29] P. Mittal, A. Khurshid, J. Juen, M. Caesar, and N. Borisov. Stealthy traffic analysis of low-latency anonymous communication using throughput fingerprinting. In *The 18th ACM Conference on Computer and communications security*, 2011.

[30] U. Möller, L. Cottrell, P. Palfrader, and L. Sassaman. Mixmaster protocol — Version 2. IETF Internet Draft, 2003.

[31] S. Murdoch and R. Watson. Metrics for security and performance in low-latency anonymity systems. In *Privacy Enhancing Technologies Worshop*, 2008.

[32] Named data networking project (NDN). `http://named-data.org`.

[33] NetInf: networkd of information project. `http://www.netinf.org/`.

[34] Open network lab. `http://onl.wustl.edu`.

[35] L. Overlier and P. Syverson. Locating hidden servers. In *IEEE Symposium on Security and Privacy*. IEEE, 2006.

[36] PURSUIT - a fp7 european union project -. `http://www.fp7-pursuit.eu/PursuitWeb/`.

[37] M. Reiter and A. Rubin. Crowds: Anonymity for web transactions. *ACM Transactions on Information and System Security*, 1(1), 1998.

[38] M. Rennhard and B. Plattner. Introducing morphmix: Peer-to-peer based anonymous internet usage with collusion detection. In *Workshop on Privacy in the Electronic Society*, Washington, DC, USA, 2002.

[39] M. Rennhard and B. Plattner. Practical anonymity for the masses with morphmix. In *Financial Cryptography*, 2004.

[40] A. Serjantov and P. Sewell. Passive attack analysis for connection-based anonymity systems. *European Symposium on Research in Computer Security*, 2003.

[41] V. Shmatikov and M. Wang. Timing analysis in low-latency mix networks: Attacks and defenses. *European Symposium on Research in Computer Security*, 2006.

[42] The OpenSSL Project. OpenSSL: The open source toolkit for SSL/TLS. `www.openssl.org`.

[43] M. Wright, M. Adler, B. Levine, and C. Shields. The predecessor attack: An analysis of a threat to anonymous communications systems. *ACM Transactions on Information and System Security (TISSEC)*, 7(4), 2004.

[44] E. Wustrow, S. Wolchok, I. Goldberg, and J. A. Halderman. Telex: Anticensorship in the network infrastructure. In *The 20th USENIX Security Symposium*, 2011.

A Security Proofs

Justification of Claim 5.1: Suppose that Claim 5.1 is false. Then, Adv can be used to construct an algorithm Sim that breaks the CPA-secure encryption scheme $\mathcal{E}$ as follows: Sim plays the CPA-security game with a challenger, that selects a public key pk. Sim selects a public key pk_2 and initializes Adv, that eventually returns two interests int^0, int^1 of its choice. Sim sends $c_0 = \mathcal{E}_{pk_2}(\mathsf{int}^0)$ and $c_1 = \mathcal{E}_{pk_2}(\mathsf{int}^1)$ to the challenger, that returns $c^* = \mathcal{E}_{pk}(c_b) = \mathcal{E}_{pk}(\mathcal{E}_{pk_2}(\mathsf{int}^b))$. Sim sends (c^*, c_0, c_1) to the challenger that eventually returns its choice b'. Sim outputs b' as its choice. The output of Sim is $b' = b$ iff Adv guesses b' correctly. Since Adv guesses b' correctly with non negligible advantage over $1/2$, Sim breaks the CPA-security of $\mathcal{E}$ with non negligible advantage. This violates the hypothesis of Claim 5.1, and, therefore, such Adv cannot exist. □

Proof of Theorem 5.1 — Consumer Anonymity (sketch). We prove that each condition in Theorem 5.1 implies consumer anonymity:

1. Assume that, for each $u' \neq u$ there exists no configuration $C' \equiv_{Adv} C$ with respect to Adv such that $C'(u') = C(u)$. Adv cannot determine that $C(u) \notin C'$ using only $C_2(u)$, $C_3(u)$ and $C_4(u)$: if $C_1(u) = C'_1(u')$ for some $C' \equiv_{Adv} C$ and u' (i.e. there exist an indistinguishable configuration with respect to Adv where a consumer different from u sends an interest to $C_1(u)$ through interface $\mathsf{if}_i^{C_1(u)}$ and $u, u' \in A_{\mathsf{if}_i^{C_1(u)}}$), then there must exist a tuple $C'(u') = C(u)$ since (a possibly compromised) r cannot process interests coming from consumers in the same anonymity set differently – that would imply that they are not in the same anonymity set. Therefore, for each configuration $C' \equiv_{Adv} C$, and for each $u' \neq u$ $\exists C'_1(u') = C_1(u) \Rightarrow \exists C'(u') = C(u)$.
For this reason, $C'_1(u') \neq C_1(u)$ for all $C' \equiv_{Adv} C$ and for all $u' \neq u$, i.e. $\forall C'_1(u') = C_1(u).C(u) \notin C'$. This is true if and only if Adv controls at least one interface $\mathsf{if}_i^r \in \mathsf{path}^{C_4(u)}$ for which u' is not in the anonymity set of if_i^r, i.e., $\exists \mathsf{if}_i^r \in \mathsf{path}^{C_4(u)} \cap \mathsf{IF}_{Adv}$ s.t. $u' \notin A_{\mathsf{if}_i^r}$ Since this contradicts the hypothesis, there must exist a configuration C' indistinguishable from C with respect to Adv such that $C'(u') = C(u)$.
2. We assume that, for each $u' \neq u$, Adv can distinguish between interests from u from those from u' (i.e., condition 1 of theorem 5.1 does not hold). We show how to prove theorem 5.1 by reduction. Assume that there exists an efficient adversary Adv such that $\mathsf{C}_{Adv} = \mathsf{C} \setminus \{u, u'\}$ and $\mathsf{R}_{Adv} = \mathsf{R} \setminus \{r_1\}$ (i.e., Adv compromised all entities, except u, u' and r_1). Suppose that $C(u) = (r_1, r_2, p, \mathsf{int}^0_{pk_1,pk_2})$, $C(u') = (r_1, r'_2, p', \mathsf{int}^1_{pk_1,pk'_2})$ for some $r_2, r'_2, p, p', \mathsf{int}^0, \mathsf{int}^1$. For each C', Adv outputs: 1 on input of C and 0 on input of C' with non-negligible probability, where $C'(u) = C(u')$ and $C'(u') = C(u)$. In other words, there is no configuration for which $C \equiv_{Adv} C'$ holds. We sketch how Adv can be used as a subroutine in a simulator Sim that breaks Claim 5.1.
Sim creates a random network topology N and inputs it to Adv. Sim also inputs the information that Adv would obtain by compromising all entities in N except u, u' and r_1. As such, Sim also includes $\mathsf{int}^b_{pk_1,pk_2}$ and $\mathsf{int}^0_{pk_2}, \mathsf{int}^1_{pk_2}$ received from the challenger of Claim 5.1 to the input of Adv. Then, Sim sends to Adv configurations C and C', where C is identical to C', except that $C(u) = C'(u')$ and $C(u') = C'(u)$, and $C(u) \neq C(u')$. We have that $b = 1$ iff Adv outputs 1. Since existence of Sim violates Claim 5.1, Adv cannot exits.
3. We assume that, for each $u' \neq u$, Adv can distinguish between interests from u from those from u' (i.e., condition 1 of theorem 5.1 does not hold) and that the first router in u's and u''s paths is compromised, i.e., condition 2 of theorem 5.1 does not hold. We then prove theorem 5.1 by reduction. Assume that there exists an efficient adversary Adv such that $\mathsf{C}_{Adv} = \mathsf{C} \setminus \{u, u'\}$ and $\mathsf{R}_{Adv} = \mathsf{R} \setminus \{r_2\}$ (i.e., Adv compromised all entities, except u, u' and r_2). Suppose that $C(u) = (r_1, r_2, p, \mathsf{int}^0_{pk_1,pk_2})$, $C(u') = (r'_1, r_2, p', \mathsf{int}^1_{pk'_1,pk_2})$ for some $r_1, r'_1, p, p', \mathsf{int}^0, \mathsf{int}^1$. For each C', Adv outputs 1 on input of C, and 0 on input of C', where $C'(u) = C(u')$ and $C'(u') = C(u)$. In other words, there is no configuration where $C \equiv_{Adv} C'$ holds. We sketch how Adv can be used as a subroutine in a simulator Sim to determine, given int_{pk_2} and int'_{pk_2}, whether $\mathsf{int} = \mathsf{int}'$.
Sim creates a random network topology N and inputs it to Adv. Sim also inputs the information that Adv would obtain by compromising all enti-

ties in N except for u, u' and r_2. Sim interacts with the challenger of Claim 5.1 setting the innermost key of its challenge, denoted as $\overline{pk_2}$, to $\perp$. Sim receives $\mathsf{int}^b_{pk_1}$ for some $\mathsf{int}^0, \mathsf{int}^1$ of its choice, and adds $\mathsf{int}^b_{pk_1,\overline{pk_2}}$, $\mathsf{int}^b_{\overline{pk_2}}$ and $\mathsf{int}^b_{\overline{pk_2}}$ to the input of Adv. Then Sim sends to Adv configurations C and C', where C is identical to C' except that $C(u) = C'(u')$ and $C(u') = C'(u)$, and $C(u) \neq C(u')$. We have that $b = 1$ iff Adv outputs 1. Since the existence of Sim would violate Claim 5.1, Adv cannot exits. □

Proof of Theorem 5.2 — Producer Anonymity (sketch). We prove that each condition in Theorem 5.2 implies producer anonymity:

1. Let $C_4(u') = \mathsf{int}'_{pk_1,pk'_2}$ and let C' be identical to C except that $C'(u) = (C_1(u), C_2(u), C_3(u), C_4(u'))$ and $C'(u') = (C_1(u'), C_2(u'), C_3(u'), C_4(u))$. In other words, C' is a configuration where int_{pk_1,pk_2} is sent to a producer different from p. In this setting, Adv can only distinguish C' and C by distinguishing $C'(u)$ and $C'(u')$. Claim 5.1 guarantees that Adv that observes int_{pk_1,pk_2} and $\mathsf{int}'_{pk_1,pk'_2}$ cannot determine which corresponds to int and which – to int$'$. Moreover, Assumption 5.1 prevents Adv from linking the output of non-compromised router $C_1(u)$ with int_{pk_1,pk_2} and $\mathsf{int}'_{pk_1,pk'_2}$. Therefore, $C \equiv_{Adv} C'$.
2. Similarly, let $C_4(u') = \mathsf{int}'_{pk_1,pk'_2}$ and let C' be identical to C except that $C'(u) = (C_1(u), C_2(u), C_3(u), C_4(u'))$ and $C'(u') = (C_1(u'), C_2(u'), C_3(u'), C_4(u))$. We assume that $C_1(u)$ and $C_1(u')$ are compromised. In this setting, Adv can only distinguish between C' and C by distinguishing $C'(u)$ and $C'(u')$. Claim 5.1 guarantees that any Adv that observes int_{pk_1,pk_2} and $\mathsf{int}'_{pk_1,pk'_2}$ cannot determine which corresponds to int and which – to int$'$. Moreover, Assumption 5.1 prevents Adv from linking the output of non-compromised router $C_2(u)$ with int_{pk_2} and $\mathsf{int}'_{pk'_2}$. Therefore, $C \equiv_{Adv} C'$. □

B Performance Evaluation: Additional Results

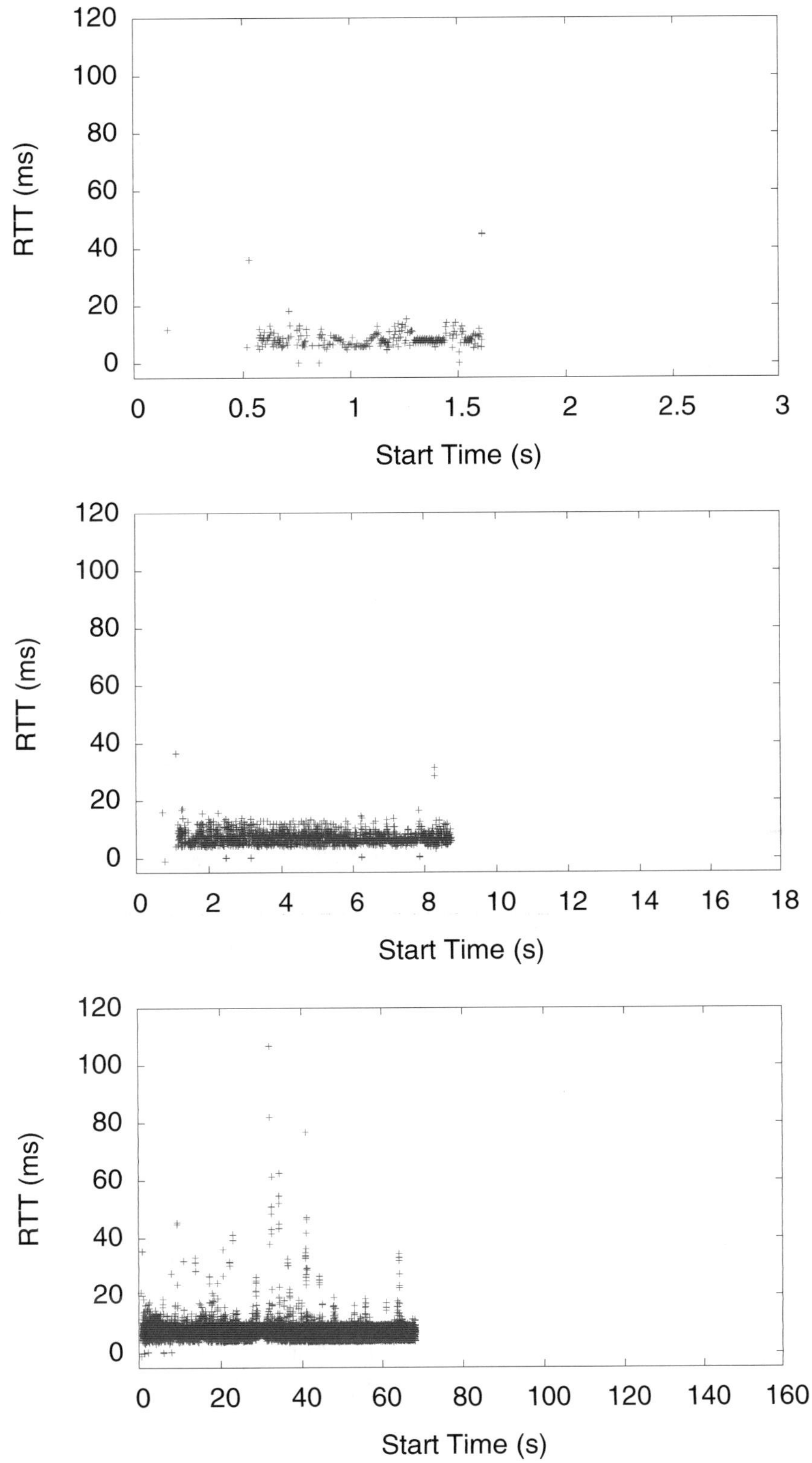

Figure 3. Round trip time for transferring 1, 10 and 100MB of content over NDN (limited anonymity)

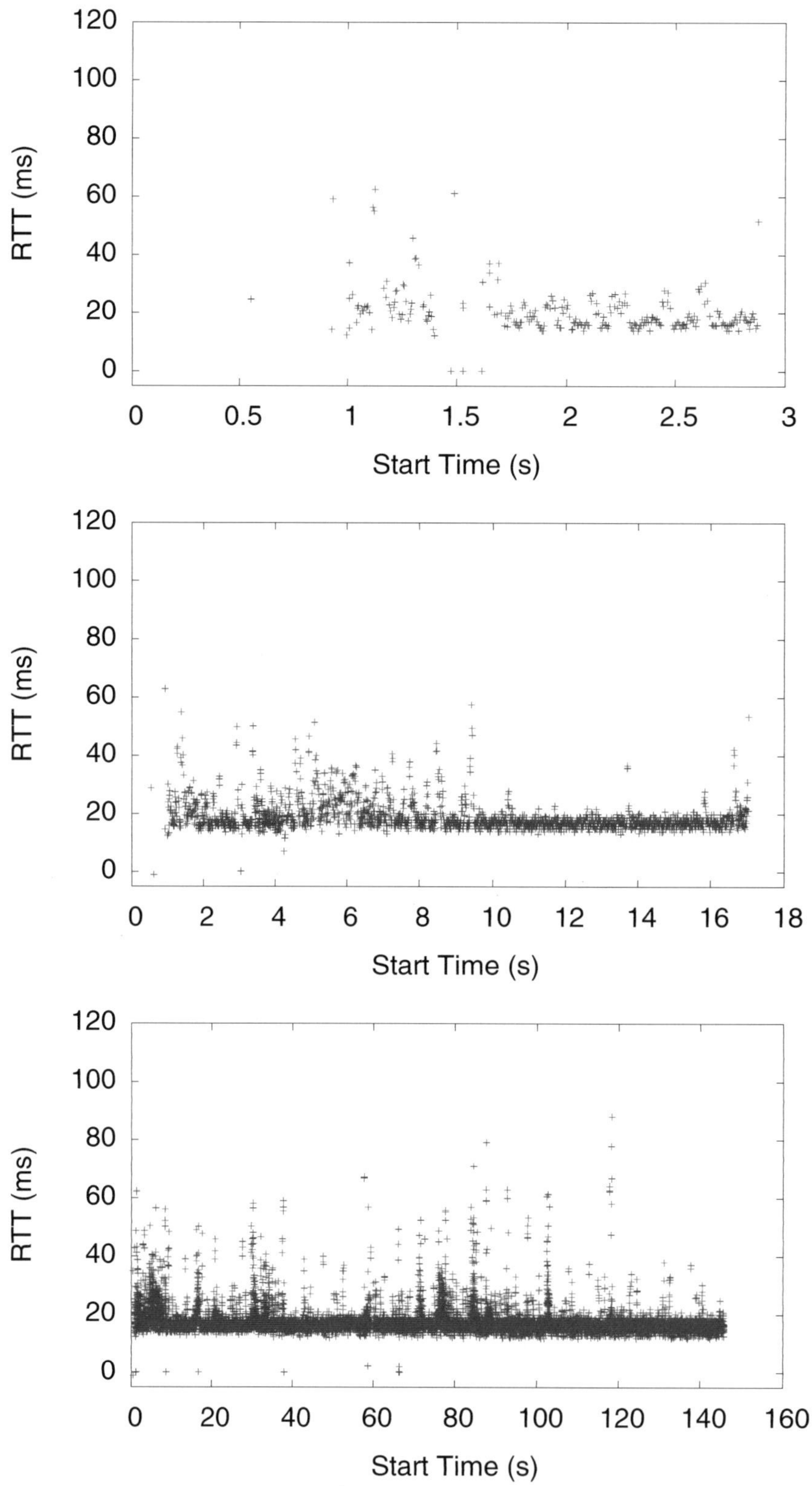

Figure 4. Round trip time for transferring 1, 10 and 100MB of content over ANDāNA (full anonymity).

RAFAEL

MANOR Advanced Defense Technologies Division
National EW Research
& Simulation Center

Persistent OSPF Attacks

Gabi Nakibly[1,2] Alex Kirshon[2] Dima Gonikman[2] Dan Boneh[3]

[1]National EW Research & Simulation Center, Israel
[2]CS department, Technion, Israel
[3]CS department, Stanford

Network & Distributed System Security 2012

1

RAFAEL

MANOR Advanced Defense Technologies Division
National EW Research
& Simulation Center

Overview

- They allow to remotely control a router's routing table without having to control the router itself.
- A single compromised router inside an AS can compromise the routing of the whole AS.
- Potentially every OSPF implementation is vulnerable.
  - The attacks were verified against Cisco's IOS.

2

Who is vulnerable?

- Potentially all commercial routers are vulnerable!
- The vulnerabilities were found in the spec of the OSPF protocol [RFC 2328].
- The attacks have been verified against Cisco IOS 15.0(1)M.
  - IOS's latest stable release

Outline

- OSPF primer
- OSPF security strengths
- The newly found vulnerabilities and attacks
- Attacks' effectiveness

Internet Routing – The Big Picture

Inter-AS routing – BGP
Intra-AS routing – OSPF, RIP, IS-IS

How OSPF works?

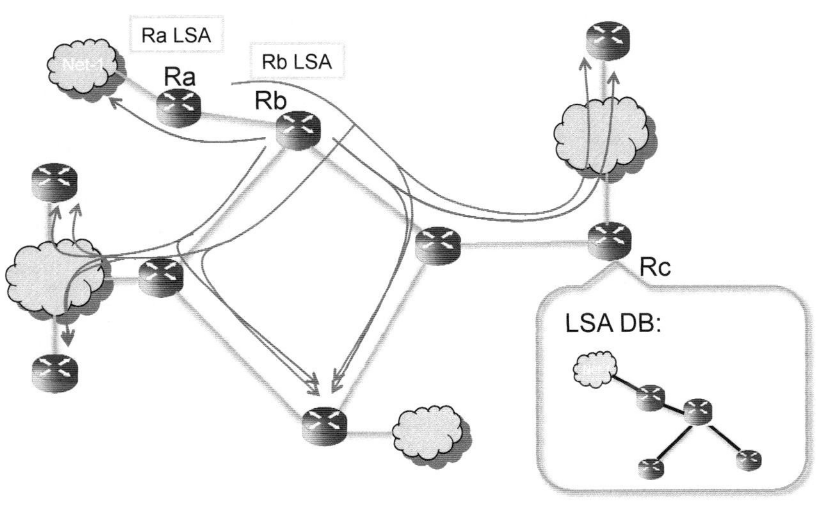

How OSPF works?

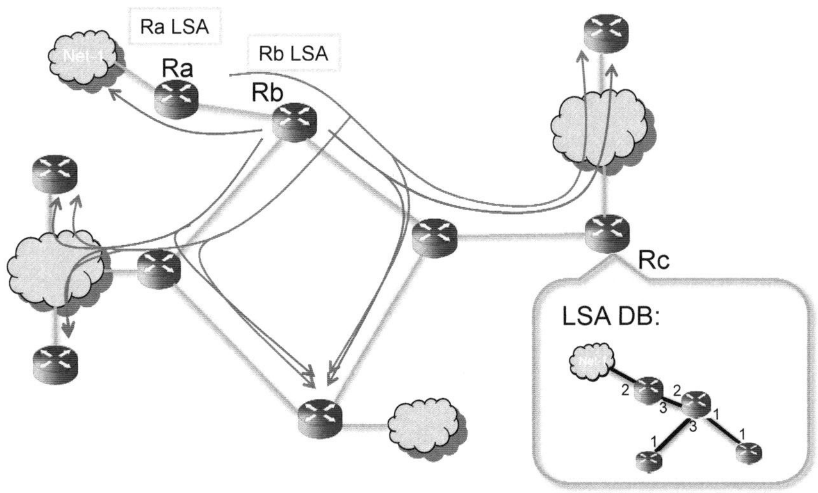

LSAs

- Each LSA is advertised periodically
  - Sequence number
    - To differentiate between instances of the same LSA
  - Age
    - To allow a specific instance of an LSA to expire

RAFAEL

MANOR Advanced Defense Technologies Division
National EW Research
& Simulation Center

The Attacker

- Location: Inside the AS
  - Controls a single router
    - Arbitrary location
- Goal:
  - Persistent control over the routing tables of other routers in the AS

RAFAEL

MANOR Advanced Defense Technologies Division
National EW Research
& Simulation Center

OSPF Security Strengths

- Per-link authentication
  - Every link has its own shared secret
- Every LSA is flooded throughout the AS
- The “fight back” mechanism

10

RAFAEL

MANOR Advanced Defense Technologies Division
National EW Research
& Simulation Center

Known Attacks

- Falsify LSAs of:
  - The attacker's router
    - Very limited
  - other routers
    - Known examples: Seq++, MaxSeq,...
    - Trigger immediate fight back
      - A non-persistent attack
  - phantom routers
    - Does not have an affect on the routing table

11

RAFAEL

MANOR Advanced Defense Technologies Division
National EW Research
& Simulation Center

Known Attacks

- In summary,
  - The common conception is that even if the attacker is an insider it can not persistently falsify the LSA of a router it does not control.
    - Hence, it can not significantly poison the routing tables of other routers.

12

RAFAEL

MANOR Advanced Defense Technologies Division
National EW Research
& Simulation Center

The New Attacks

- Attack #1 – Remote False Adjacency
  - Make a remote router include a non-existing link in its LSA
- Attack #2 – Disguised LSA
  - Falsify the entire LSA of remote router

13

RAFAEL

MANOR Advanced Defense Technologies Division
National EW Research
& Simulation Center

Attack #2 – Disguised LSA

- The vulnerability
  - Two different instances of an LSA are considered identical if they have the same [RFC 2328 Sec. 13.1]:
    - Sequence number
    - Checksum
    - Age (+/- 15 minutes)
  - The actual payload of the LSAs are not considered!
- The attack
  - Advertise a false LSA having the same values for these three fields as a valid LSA.
    - The benefit: no fight back is triggered since the victim views the false LSA as a duplicate of the LSA it just advertised.

14

RAFAEL

MANOR Advanced Defense Technologies Division
National EW Research
& Simulation Center

Attack #2 – Disguised LSA (cont.)

- The attack (cont.)
  - But, there is a problem: all other routers in the AS will also consider the false LSA as a duplicate
    - therefore, they will not install it in their LSA DB.
  - Solution: Disguise the LSA to the next valid instance of the LSA
    - While at the same time the victim originate this next valid instance
      - The trigger is done using the fight-back mechanism

15

RAFAEL

MANOR Advanced Defense Technologies Division
National EW Research
& Simulation Center

Application

- The attacker floods consecutively the trigger and then the disguised LSA.

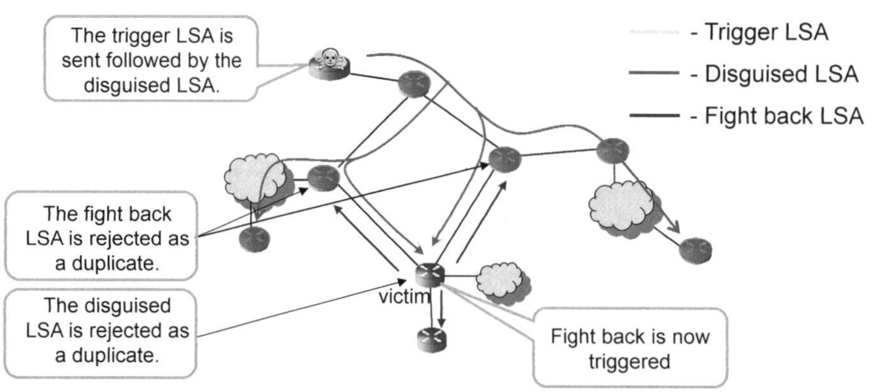

16

How the disguised LSA can be crafted?

- Age: this is the easiest one.
  - The disguised LSA will be advertised within 15 minutes of the valid (fight back) LSA.
- Sequence: the value is always incremented by one.
  - The disguised LSA will have the sequence of the trigger LSA plus 1.
- Checksum: this is the hardest feat, but not that hard.
  - The content of the next valid LSA is deterministic and predictable, hence the checksum is also predictable.
  - A dummy Link entry in added to the payload of the LSA.
  - The value of this entry is calculated such that the entire LSA will have the desired checksum.
    - This can be done since a checksum is a 16-bit result of a linear calculation on the LSA octets.

Attack Effectiveness

- We simulated the attack on real ISP topologies
  - Inferred by the RocketFuel project
- We measured for every pair of attacker-victim locations what is the percentage of poisoned routers.

Simulation Results

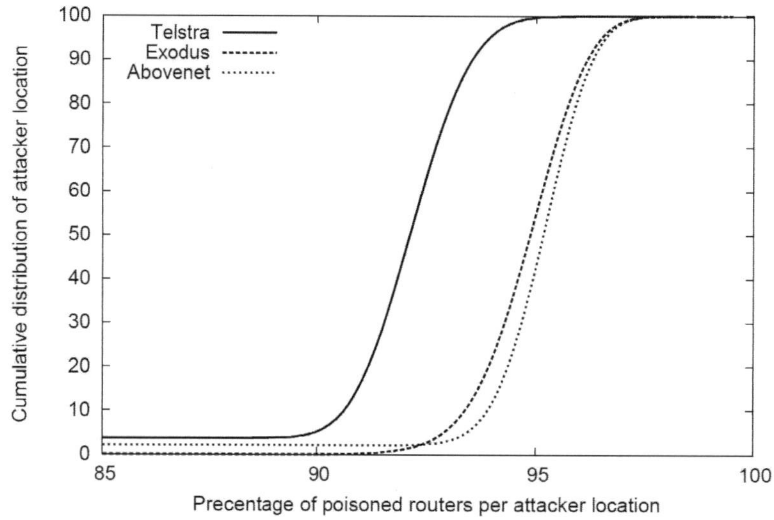

Conclusions

- Up until now the common conception was that even if the attacker is an insider it can not persistently poison the routing table of a router it does not control.
  - The new attacks shatter this misconception.
- **Using these attacks one can control the entire routing domain from a single router.**

RAFAEL

MANOR Advanced Defense Technologies Division
National EW Research
& Simulation Center

In Summary ...

Using these attacks one can control the entire routing domain from a single router.

21

NDSS Symposium 2012

YOU ARE WHAT YOU LIKE

INFORMATION LEAKAGE THROUGH USERS' INTERESTS

Abdelberi (Beri) Chaabane, Gergely Acs, Mohamed Ali Kaafar

Inria

Internet = Online Social Networks ?

- Most visited websites:
  - Facebook (2sd), YouTube (3rd), Twitter (10th)
- Facebook[1]:
  - > 800M users
  - > 350M users access through their mobile
  - > 250M photos are uploaded per day
  - > 20M application installation per day

And privacy ??

1: https://www.facebook.com/press/info.php?statistics

Identifying the threat

3

Users

rk Z. is a

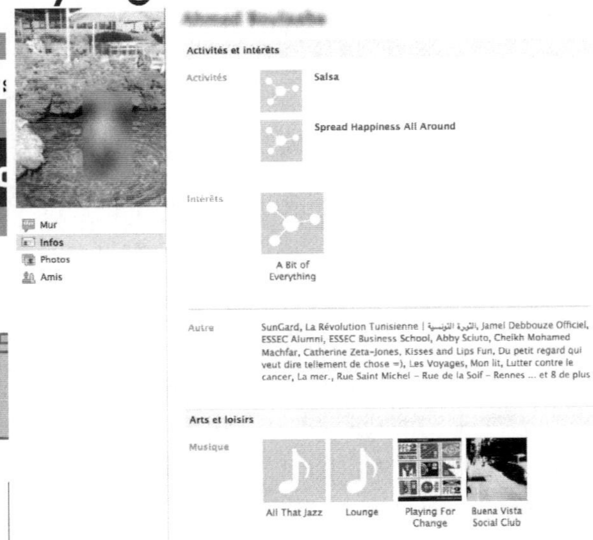

.vate Profiles

Goal

- Inferring Missing/Hidden information from a public user profile
  - ~~Using Friendship or links information~~[2,3]
  - Only using user's revealed data

*: http://13thfloorgrowingold.wordpress.com/

What people reveals ?

5

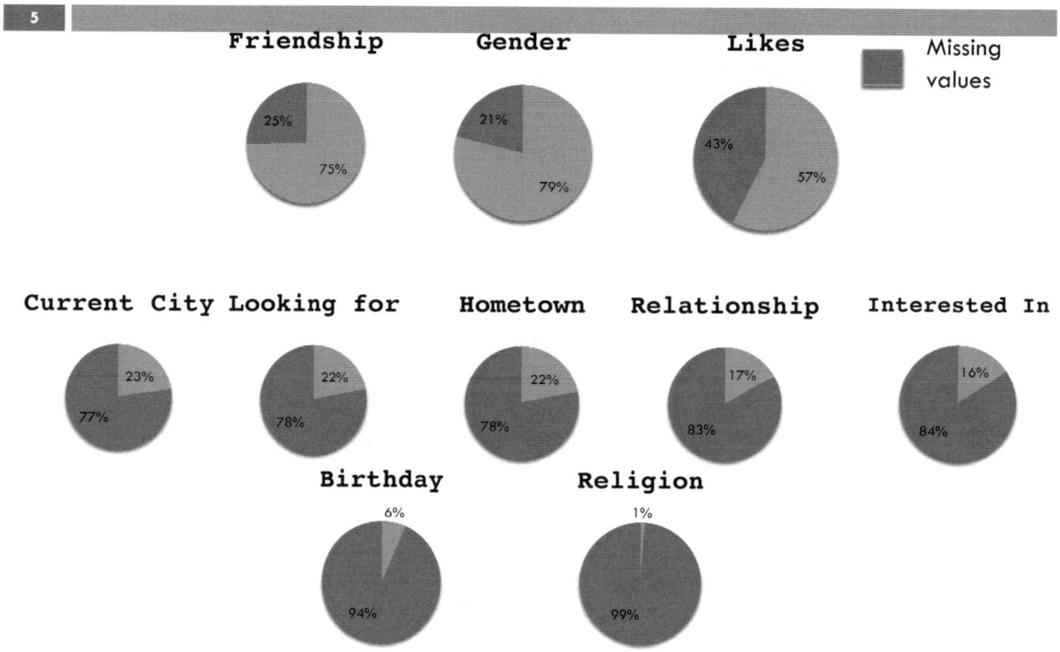

Homophily or not homophily

6

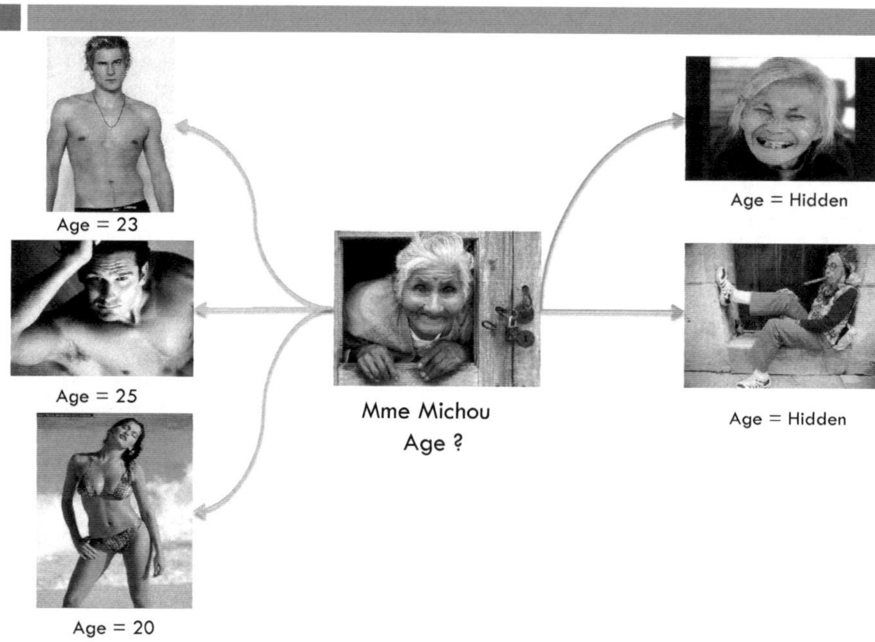

Quiz

Who is this guy ? Who likes his music ?

Music? Why would that work ?

8

- In real life, an individual interest (or lifestyle) might reveal many aspects of his personal information
  - demographics or geopolitical aspects.
- Availability
  - Seemingly harmless ;-)
  - by default settings?

Not that easy

9

- Heterogeneity
  - Too general "I like Jazz Music"
  - Too specific "Angus Young"

- Difficult to semantically link interests
  - What is the link between Angus Young, Brian Johnson and High Voltage ?

likes

10

- ✓ One of the MOST available data
- ✓ Describe users' tastes
- ✓ Can be used to derive user information
  - Gender, Location, Age, Marital status, Religion, etc.

- ✗ Very sparse (millions of likes)
- ✗ User-generated (No defined pattern)
- ✗ No "standard" granularity

A toy example

11

- Mohammad-Reza Shajarian, Nazeri, Gogosh
- What does it mean (lack of semantics)
- What can we infer ?

Semantics: a naïve example

12

- **Shajarian:** 1940 births; Living people; Iranian classical; vocalists Iranian; humanitarians Iranian; male singers; Iranian musicians
- **Nazei:** Grammy Award winners; Iranian Kurdish people; Living people; Iranian classical vocalists; Iranian humanitarians; Iranian Légion d'honneur recipients; Iranian male singers
- **Gogosh:** people of Azerbaijani; descent Iranian female; Persian-language singers; Iranian pop singers; Iranian Shi'a; Muslims People from Tehran

Btw it belongs to
http://facebook.com/kave.salamatian

Semantics: a naïve example II

- **Shajarian:** 1940 births; Living people; Iranian classical; vocalists Iranian; humanitarians Iranian; male singers; Iranian musicians
- **Nazei:** Grammy Award winners; Iranian Kurdish people; Living people; Iranian classical vocalists; Iranian humanitarians; Iranian Légion d'honneur recipients; Iranian male singers
- **Gogosh:** people of Azerbaijani; descent Iranian female; Persian-language singers; Iranian pop singers; Iranian Shi'a; Muslims People from Tehran

Topic about Iran	Topic about Islam (Religion)	Topic about classical music
Iranian classical Vocalist Iranian humanitarians Iranian Iranian Kurdish people people of Azerbaijani Persian-language ...	Iranian Shi'a Muslims People	vocalists Iranian Iranian classical vocalists

The Algorithm

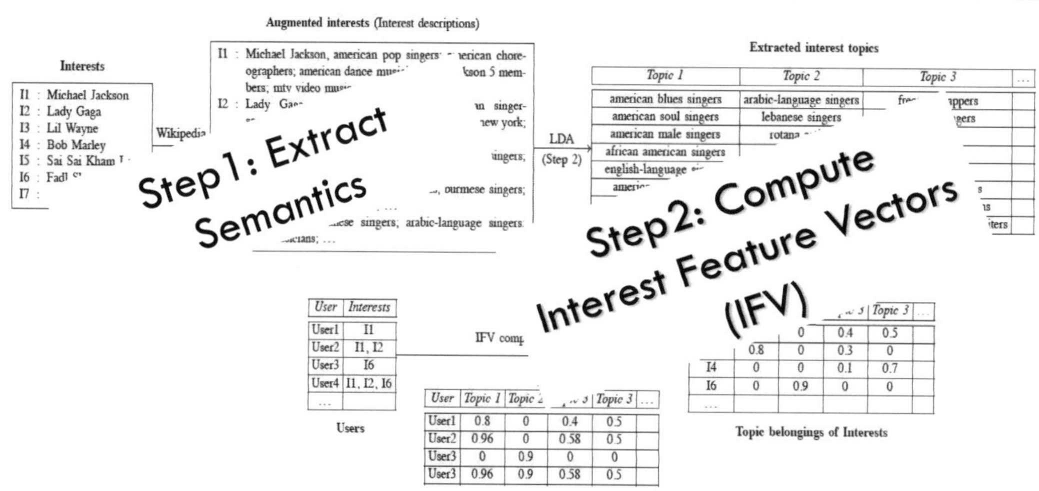

Step3: Classify Users
Infer Attributes

15

$Step1$

Tree of wikipedia

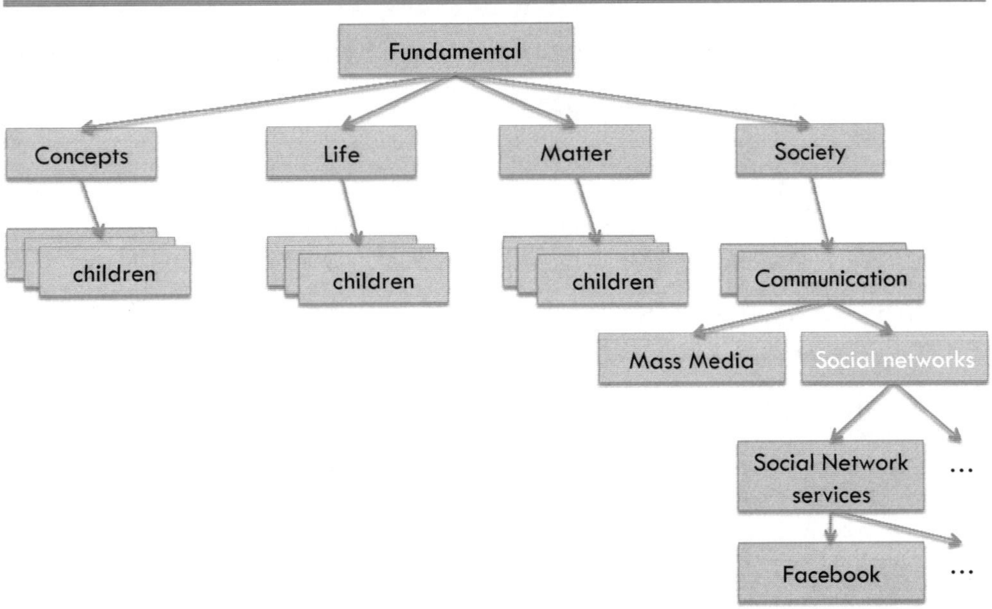

Extract semantic (Description)

17

- 'Ontologized' version of wikipedia
  - Using the "structured knowledge" of Wikipedia
    - Extract keywords from a certain 'granularity'
  - Each like is an article
  - Extract Parent Categories of the 'like' article
    - Using the same granularity

Extract semantic (Description)

- Using the same granularity allows us to semantically 'link' similar concepts

AC/DC: Australian heavy metal musical groups; Australian hard rock musical groups; Blues rock groups; Musical groups established in 1973;

Angus Young: AC/DC members; Australian blues guitarists; Australian rock guitarists; Australian heavy metal guitarists

High Voltage: AC/DC songs ; Songs written by Angus Young; 1970s rock song stubs

The Algorithm

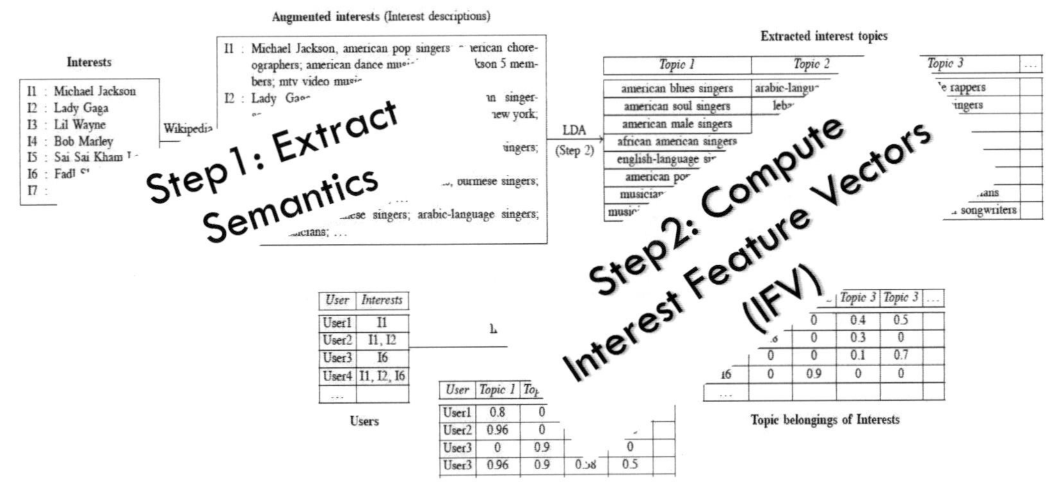

Step3: Classify Users
Infer Attributes

Step2

LDA Intuition

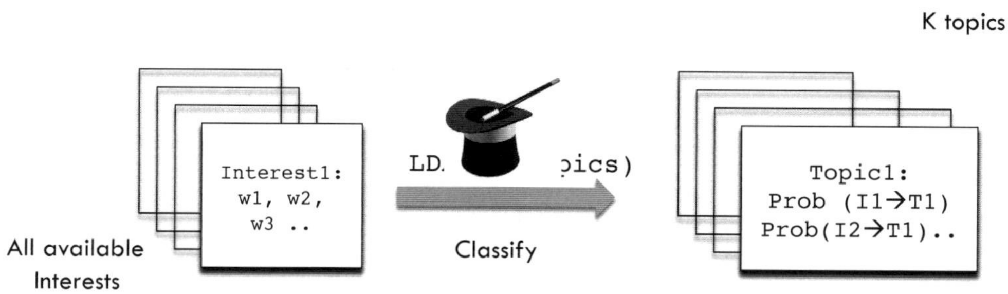

I1: Interest1
T1: Topic 1

LDA as a Probabilistic model

1. Treat data as observations that arise from a generative probabilistic process that includes hidden variables
   - For documents, the hidden variables reflect the thematic structure of the collection.

2. Infer the hidden structure using posterior inference
   - What are the topics that describe this collection?

3. Situate new data into the estimated model.
   - How does this new document fit into the estimated topic structure ?

D.Blei (MLSS'09)

LDA

23

- Words collected into documents
  - Each document is a mixture of a small number of topics
  - Each word's creation is attributable to one of the document's topics
  - Topics are not nominative
  - Input:
    - Documents (words Frequency)
    - Number of Topics (K)
  - Output
    - Word distribution per topic
    - Probability for each documents to belong to each topic

Topic example

The Algorithm

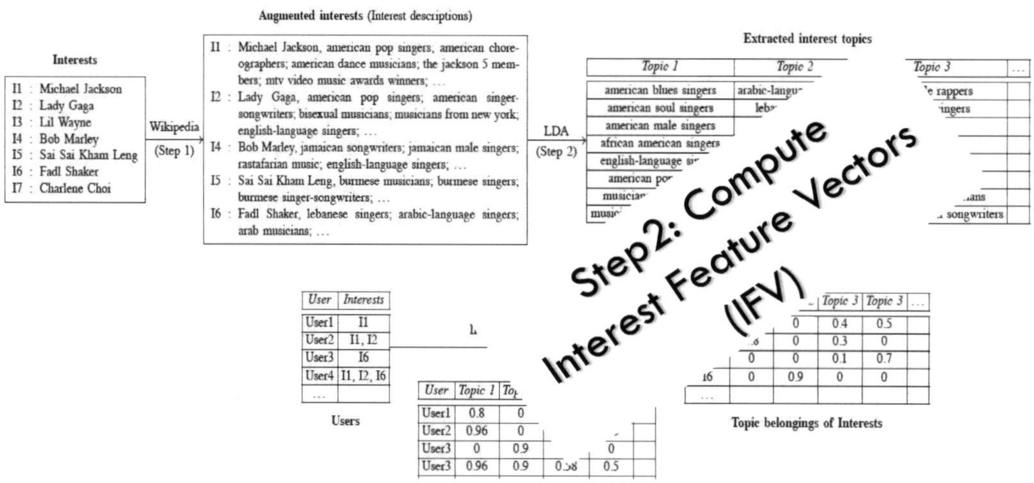

Step3: Classify Users
Infer Attributes

Step3

Inferring Hidden Attribute

27

- IFV 'uniquely' quantifies the interest of each user along topics

- Classify users based on IFV
  - Simple approach
  - Using the nearest neighbors (K-NN)

- Similar users grouped together.
  - User sharing the 'same' taste should share the same attributes

Nearest ~~Friend~~ Neighbor

28

- We define an appropriate distance measure in this space: chi-squared distance metric

$$d_{V,W} = \sum_{i=1}^{k} \frac{(V_i - W_i)^2}{(V_i + W_i)}$$

- Using Kd-tree to reduce the computation from $M^2/2$ to $O(M \log_2 M)$)

Example

	IFV				Attribute to infer
user1	0.2	0.6	0.1	0.1	Attribute=?
~~user2~~	~~0.3~~	~~0.6~~	~~0.7~~	~~0.01~~	~~Attribute=?~~
user3	0.2	0.4	0.1	0.1	Attribute=Val
...					
User *n*	0.1	0.1	0.1	0.1	Attribute=Val

$$d_{V,W} = \sum_{i=1}^{k} \frac{(V_i - W_i)^2}{(V_i + W_i)}$$

The **n** nearest users to user1 are: S={user3, user*m*, …}
The attribute is equal the the majority of the attribute in S (Majority voting)

Datasets

30

- Public Profiles
  - Crawled more than 400k profiles (Raw-Profiles)
  - More than 100k Latin-written profiles with music interests (Pub-Profiles)
- Private Profiles
  - Using a Facebook App.
  - More than 4000 Private profiles (used 2.5 K, Volunteer-Profiles)

Attribute inference

- We infer the following attributes:
  - Binary
    - Gender {Male, Female}
    - Relationship {Single, Married}
  - Multi-value
    - Country {US,PH,IN,ID,GB,GR,FR,MX,IT,BR } (top10)
    - Age group {13-17, 18-24, 25-34, 35-44, 44-54, >54}

Base-Line Inference

32

- Rely on marginal distributions
  - Maximum Likelihood of attributes

$$P(u.x = val \mid U) = \frac{|\{v \mid u.v = val \wedge v \in U\}|}{|U|}$$

- Guess the attributes' x value from its most likely value for all users

Attribute	Value
Gender	51% (Male)
Relationship status	Unknown
Age	26.1% (26-34)
Country	23% (U.S)

Inference Accuracy of PubProfiles

33

Attribute	Baseline	Random guess	IFV Inference
Gender	51%	50%	69%
Relationship	50%	50%	71%
Country	41%	10%	60%
Age	26%	16.6%	49%

TABLE IV: Inference Accuracy of PubProfiles

- More than 20% of gain in most cases

Deeper view: Gender

34

- It is clear from the results that music Interests predict Female with a high probability
- May be explained by the number of female profiles in our dataset (62%)

Attribute \ Inferred	Male	Female
Male	53%	47%
Female	14%	86%

TABLE V: Confusion Matrix of Gender

Deeper view: Relationship

35

- It is challenging since less than 17% of crawled users disclose this attributes
- Single users are more distinguishable
  - Single users share on average 9 music Interests whereas married share only 5.7

Attribute \ Inferred	Single	Married
Single	78%	22%
Married	36%	64%

TABLE VI: Confusion Matrix of Relationship

Deeper view: Country

36

- 80% of users belong to top 10 countries
- Country with specific (regional) music have better accuracy

  ➔ we clearly see the role of the **semantic**

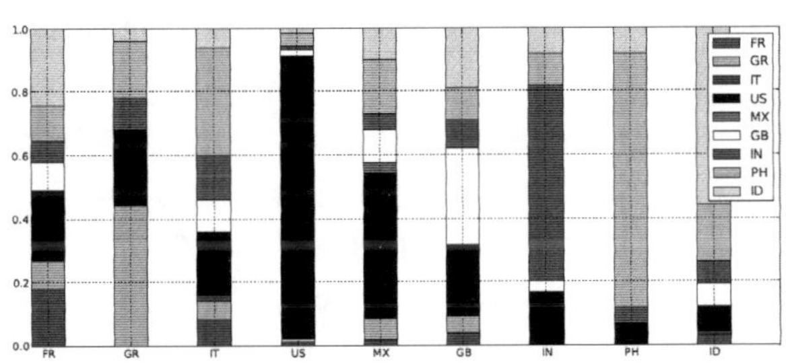

Country	% of users
US	71.9%
PH	7.80%
IN	6.21%
ID	5.08%
GB	3.62%
GR	2.32%
FR	2.12%
MX	0.41%
IT	0.40%
BR	0.01%

TABLE VII: Top 10 countries distribution in PubProfiles

Accuracy for VolunteerProfile

37

- The results are slightly the same as for PubProfile
- Our method is independent from the source of information

Attribute	Baseline	Random guess	IFV Inference
Gender	51%	50%	72.5%
Relationship	50%	50%	70.5%
Age	26%	16.6%	42%

TABLE IX: Inference Accuracy for VolunteerProfiles

Discussion ✔

38

- ✓ No need for frequent model updates
- ✓ The approach is 'rather' General
  - ✓ OSN Independent: Many other sources of Information (deezer, lastfm, blogs, forums) etc.
- ✓ Use a free, open and updated encyclopedia

Discussion ✗

Dislike

- Augment the model by analyzing more interest' category
  - Movies
  - Books
  - Sport …
- Multilanguage Wikipedia to handle foreign language
- More aggressive stemming

40

Conclusion

- Wikipedia Ontology to extract Semantics
- LDA to extract Topics
  - Socio, demographics, geo political aspects
  - "virtual" Communities
- K-NN to infer attributes
- The approach is general
  - Using seemingly harmless information
  - Efficient, inconspicuous profiling

If someday we all go to prison
for downloading music,
I just hope they split us by
the music genre.
THE BEST FUN SITE = 9GAG.COM

Facebook Questions
Get answers from the people you trust.

Crawling Facebook

43

- Crawling Facebook was challenging
  - Protection using JavaScript rendering:
    - Using a homemade lightweight browser
  - Protection using a threshold for a maximum number of request
    - Using multiple machines
- Avoiding Biased Sampling
  - Crawling Facebook public directory (100 millions users)
  - Randomly choose a user and crawl his/her profile
- Parsing HTML pages
  - It is just a mess

Availability of attributes

44

Attributes	Raw (%)	Pub(%)	Volunteer (%)
Gender	79	84	96
Interests	57	100	62
Current City	23	29	48
Looking For	22	34	-
Home Town	22	31	48
Relationship	17	24	43
Interested In	16	26	-
Birth Date	6	11	72
Religion	1	2	0

X-Vine: Secure and Pseudonymous Routing Using Social Networks

Prateek Mittal, Matthew Caesar, Nikita Borisov
University of Illinois at Urbana-Champaign
{mittal2,caesar,nikita}@illinois.edu

Abstract

Distributed hash tables suffer from several security and privacy vulnerabilities, including the problem of Sybil attacks. Existing social network-based solutions to mitigate the Sybil attacks in DHT routing have a high state requirement and do not provide an adequate level of privacy. For instance, such techniques require a user to reveal their social network contacts. We design X-Vine, a protection mechanism for distributed hash tables that operates entirely by communicating over social network links. As with traditional peer-to-peer systems, X-Vine provides robustness, scalability, and a platform for innovation. The use of social network links for communication helps protect participant privacy and adds a new dimension of trust absent from previous designs. X-Vine is resilient to denial of service via Sybil attacks, and in fact is the first Sybil defense that requires only a logarithmic amount of state per node, making it suitable for large-scale and dynamic settings. X-Vine also helps protect the privacy of users social network contacts and keeps their IP addresses hidden from those outside of their social circle, providing a basis for pseudonymous communication. We first evaluate our design with analysis and simulations, using several real world large-scale social networking topologies. We show that the constraints of X-Vine allow the insertion of only a logarithmic number of Sybil identities per attack edge; we show this mitigates the impact of malicious attacks while not affecting the performance of honest nodes. Moreover, our algorithms are efficient, maintain low stretch, and avoid hot spots in the network. We validate our design with a PlanetLab implementation and a Facebook plugin.

1 Introduction

Peer-to-peer (P2P) networks have, in a short time, revolutionized communication on the Internet. One key feature of P2P networks is their ability to scale to millions of users without requiring any centralized infrastructure support. The best scalability and performance is offered by multi-hop distributed hash tables (DHTs), which offer a structured approach to organizing peers [37, 52, 56, 59]. Multi-hop DHTs are the subject of much research and are also used in several mainstream systems [2, 7, 25].

Securing DHTs has always been a challenging task [16, 57, 63], especially in the face of a Sybil attack [22], where one node can pretend to have multiple identities and thus interfere with routing operations. Traditional solutions to this attack require participants to obtain certificates [16], prove possession of a unique IP address [43, 46], or perform some computation [12]. This creates a barrier to participation, limiting the growth of the P2P user base, and at the same time does not fully address the problem of Sybil attacks.

To address this, recent research proposes to use social network trust relationships to mitigate Sybil attacks [21, 68, 69]. However, these systems share some key shortcomings:

High control overhead: These systems rely on flooding or large numbers of repeated lookups to maintain state. For example, Whanau [34] is the state-of-art design that secures routing in DHTs, but it is built upon a *one-hop* DHT routing mechanism, and has high overheads: state and control overhead increases with $O(\sqrt{n}\log n)$, where n is the number of participants in the social network. As networked systems become increasingly deployed at scale (e.g., in the wide area, across service providers), in high-churn environments (e.g., developing regions, wireless, mobile social networks [40]), and for applications with stronger demands on correctness and availability (e.g., online storage, content voting, reputation systems) the problem of high overhead in existing works stands to become increasingly serious; multi-hop DHT routing mechanisms are going to be necessary.

Lack of privacy: These systems require a user to reveal social contact information (friend lists). Some of these schemes require global distribution of this contact information. This is unfortunate, as social contacts are considered to be private information: leading real-world systems like Facebook [3] and LiveJournal [4] provide users with a functionality to limit access to this information. Forcing users to reveal this private information could greatly hinder the adoption of these technologies.

A second privacy concern, common to both traditional DHTs and ones that use social networking information, is that users must communicate directly with random peers, revealing their IP addresses. This provides an opportunity for the attacker to perform traffic analysis and compromise user privacy [9, 35]. Prior work [42, 65]has demonstrated that a colluding adversary can associate a DHT lookup with its lookup initiator, and thus infer the activities of a user. A *pseudonymous* routing mechanism can defend against such attacks, and would be especially beneficial for privacy sensitive DHT applications [19, 43].

To address these shortcomings, we propose X-Vine, a protection mechanism for large-scale distributed systems that leverages social network trust relationships. X-Vine has several unique properties. X-Vine protects *privacy* of social relationships, by ensuring that a user's relationship information is revealed only to the user's immediate friends. At the same time, X-Vine also protects *correctness* of DHT routing, by mitigating Sybil attacks while requiring only logarithmic state and control overhead. To the best of our knowledge, X-Vine is the first system to provide both properties, which may serve to make it a useful building block in constructing the next generation of social network based distributed systems. Finally, X-Vine also provides a basis for pseudonymous communication; a user's IP address is revealed only to his/her trusted social network contacts.

X-Vine achieves these properties by incorporating social network trust relationships in the DHT design. Unlike traditional DHTs, which route directly between overlay participants (e.g., [34]), X-Vine embeds the DHT directly into the social fabric, allowing communication through the DHT to leverage trust relationships implied by social network links. This is done by using mechanisms similar to network layer DHTs like VRR [14]. We leverage this structure for two purposes. First, communication in X-Vine is carried out entirely across social-network links.The use of social network links enables pseudonymous communication; while the recipient may know the opaque identifier (pseudonym) for the source, the IP address of the source is revealed only to his/her friends. Second, recent work has shown that social networks can be used to detect Sybil attacks by identifying a bottleneck cut that connects the Sybil identities to the rest of the network [21, 68, 69]. X-Vine enables comparable Sybil resilience by bounding the number of DHT relationships that can traverse a particular edge. With this multi-hop approach, we can limit the number of Sybil identities per attack edge (attack edges illustrated in Figure 1) to logarithmic in the size of the network with logarithmic control and routing state, a dramatic reduction from previous Sybil defense approaches. This allows X-Vine to scale to large user bases and high-churn environments.

We evaluate X-Vine both analytically and experimentally using large scale real-world social network topologies. Since recent work [62, 66] has advocated the use of interaction networks as a more secure realization of social trust, we also demonstrate the performance of X-Vine on interaction graphs. From our evaluation, we find that X-Vine is able to route using 10–15 hops (comparable to other DHTs) in topologies with 100 000 nodes while using only $O(\log n)$ routing state. In particular, we show that the overhead of X-Vine is two orders of magnitude smaller than Whanau. With respect to Sybil resistance, we found that honest nodes are able to securely route to each other with probability greater than 0.98 as long as the number of attack edges is $g \in o(n/(\log n))$. Using an implementation on PlanetLab, we estimate the median lookup latency in a 100 000 node topology to be less than 1.2 seconds. Even when 20% of the nodes fail simultaneously, the lookups still succeed with a probability greater than 95%. Finally, we also implement a plugin for DHT designers that can enable them to easily integrate social network contacts with a DHT by leveraging existing online social networks like Facebook.

Our proposed techniques can be applied in a wide variety of scenarios that leverage DHTs:

- Large scale P2P networks like Vuze/Kad/Overnet are popularly used for file sharing and content distribution. However, these networks are vulnerable to attacks on the routing protocol [64] and do not protect the privacy of the user [42]. X-Vine protects against attacks that target the DHT mechanisms and provides a basis for pseudonymous communication. Moreover, X-Vine is also robust to the high churn prevalent in these networks.

- Applications like Coral [25], Adeona [54], and Vanish [27] are built on top of DHTs. The security properties of these applications can often be compromised by exploiting vulnerabilities in the DHT. As an example, the security of Vanish was recently compromised by a low-cost Sybil attack on the Vuze network [67]. Our proposed techniques protect these applications by bounding the number of Sybil identities in the DHT.

- Decentralized P2P anonymous communication systems like Tarzan [26], Salsa [46] and ShadowWalker [43] assume an external Sybil defense mechanism. X-Vine is particularly suitable for designing Sybil-resilient P2P anonymous communication systems, since it provides secure as well as pseudonymous routing.

- Freenet [19] is a widely used censorship resistant overlay network, but its routing algorithm has been shown to be extremely vulnerable in presence of even a few malicious nodes [23]. X-Vine can enable peers to resist censorship by securely and pseudonymously retrieving data objects from the Freenet network.

- Membership concealing overlay networks (MCONs) [61] hide the identities of the peers participating in a network (different from pseudonymity). Our proposed techniques can provide a substrate for designing fully decentralized membership concealing networks.

Roadmap: The rest of the paper describes and evaluates X-Vine. We start by giving a high-level overview of the problem we address and our approach (Section 2), followed by a detailed description of our routing algorithm (Section 3) and its security mechanisms (Section 4). We then describe our experimental results (Section 5). Finally, we summarize related work (Section 6), discuss X-Vine's limitations (Section 7), and conclude (Section 8).

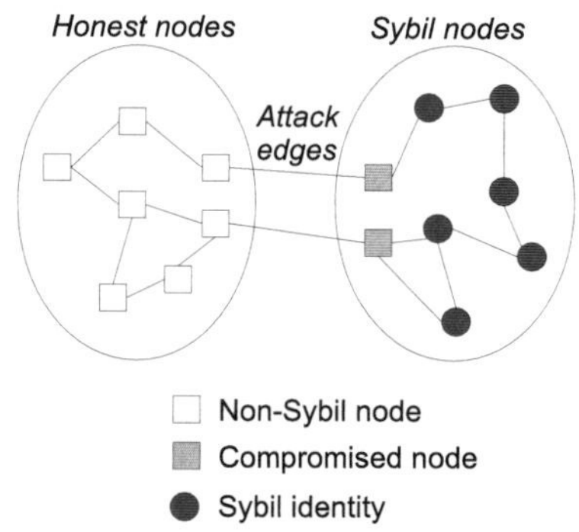

Figure 1. Illustration of honest nodes, Sybil nodes, and attack edges between them.

2 X-Vine Overview

2.1 Design Goals

We start by defining the goals for our design.

1. Secure routing: if an honest node X performs a lookup for an identifier ID, then the lookup mechanism must return the global successor of ID (present in the routing tables of honest nodes).

2. Pseudonymous communication: an adversary should not be able to determine the IP address corresponding to a user.

3. Privacy of user relationships: an adversary should not be able to infer a user's social contacts.

4. Low control overhead: the control overhead of the system should be small to enable a scalable design. This excludes flooding-based and single-hop mechanisms.

5. Low latency: the length of the path used to route to an arbitrary identifier should be small, in order to minimize lookup latency.

6. Churn resilience: even when a significant fraction of nodes fail simultaneously, lookup queries should still succeed.

7. Fully decentralized design: we target a fully decentralized architecture without any central points of trust/failure.

We note that requirements 2, 3 and 4 distinguish us from prior work—state-of-the-art approaches do not provide pseudonymous routing, do not preserve privacy of user relationships, and have high control overhead.

2.2 Threat Model and Assumptions

We assume that a fraction of real users are compromised and colluding. Recent work [21,68,69] has leveraged the insight that it is costly for an attacker to establish many trust relationships. Following this reasoning, we assume that the number of attack edges, denoted by g, is bounded. Similar to prior work, we assume that the attack edges are not specially chosen.

Recent work has challenged the assumption that it is costly for an attacker to create attack edges with honest nodes in friendship graphs [10, 13, 29, 66], and proposed the use of interaction graphs as a more secure realization of real world social trust. In this work, we will evaluate X-Vine with both traditional friendship graphs as well as topologies based on interaction graphs. Other mechanisms to infer the strength of ties between user [28] may also be helpful in creating resilient social graphs, but are not the focus of this paper.

We also assume that the set of colluding compromised nodes is a Byzantine adversary, and can deviate from the protocol in arbitrary ways by launching active attacks on the routing protocol. In particular, the set of compromised nodes can launch a Sybil attack by trying to insert multiple fake identities in the system. The key assumption we make about the adversary is that Sybil identities are distributed randomly in the DHT identifier space. We note that this assumption is a limitation of the X-Vine protocol, as discussed in Section 7. An exploration of defenses against adversaries who concentrate their nodes in a particular region of the overlay is beyond the scope of this paper.

2.3 Solution Overview

We start by describing our algorithm in the context of an abstract, static network. Suppose we have a graph G, where nodes correspond to users of the social network, and edges correspond to social relationships between them. Our approach runs a DHT-based routing scheme over the graph that embeds path information in the network. We first describe how routing is performed, and then describe how the path information it creates can be used to mitigate Sybil attackers.

Pseudonymous routing in the social network: We construct a DHT on top of the social network, using mechanisms similar to network layer DHTs [14]. Each node in the network selects a random numeric identifier, and maintains paths (*trails*) to its neighbors in the identifier space in a DHT-like fashion. To join the network, a node performs a discovery process to determine a path to its *successors* in the DHT. Then, the node embeds trails in the network that point back to the joining node's identifier. To route messages, packets are forwarded along these trails. By maintaining trails to each of the node's successors, a node can forward a message to any point in the namespace. Users that are directly connected by a social network link simply communicate via the IP layer. All communication performed by a node is done only with its friends, and this communication is done in a manner that does not reveal the node's local topology, preventing leakage of friendship list information to non-friends. Routing over social links also enables a user to communicate pseudonymous with respect to non-friends.

Protecting against Sybils: The scheme described above does not mitigate the Sybil attack, as a malicious node can repeatedly join with different identifiers, and thereby "take over" a large portion of the identifier space. Malicious nodes can in fact pretend that there is an entire network of Sybil nodes behind themselves (Figure 1). To protect against the Sybil attack, we constrain the number of paths between honest nodes and malicious nodes. Since Sybil nodes by their very nature are likely to be behind a small "cut" in the graph, by constraining the number of paths that may be set up, we can constrain the impact that a Sybil node can have on the entire network. In particular, honest nodes rate-limit the number of paths that are allowed to be constructed over their adjacent links, thereby limiting the ability of Sybil nodes to join the routing scheme, and hence participate in the network. When a joining node attempts to establish a trail over an edge that has reached its limit, the node adjacent to the full link sends the joining node a message indicating failure of the join request. This limits Sybil nodes from constructing very many paths into the network. Since Sybil nodes cannot construct many trails, they cannot place many identifiers into the DHT. Hence, an honest node can send traffic to another honest node by forwarding traffic over the DHT, as trails are unlikely to traverse Sybil-generated regions of the network.

3 X-Vine Protocol

The key feature of our design is that all DHT communication happens over social network links.[1] By ensuring that all communication takes place over social network links,

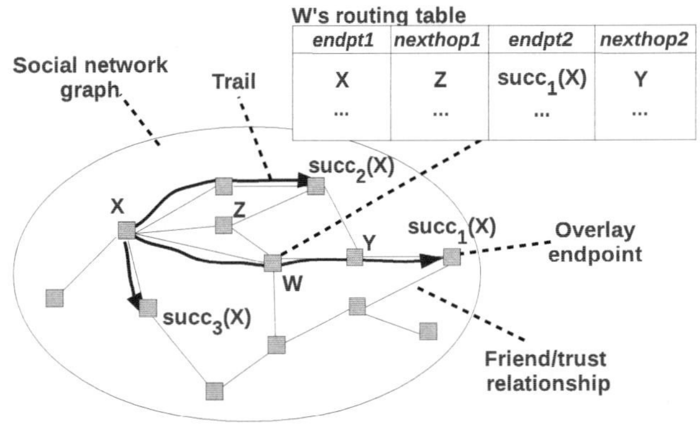

Figure 2. Overview of X-Vine.

we can leverage the trust relationships in the social network topology to enforce security properties. A trivial security property of our design is that an adversary needs to be connected to honest users via a series of social network links to communicate with them. Moreover, the IP address of the nodes only needs to be revealed to their contacts, enhancing privacy for users. Most importantly, our design is able to effectively resist Sybil attacks even when the number of attack edges is large.

3.1 Routing Over Social Networks

Figure 2 illustrates the design of X-Vine. Our design uses a VRR-like [14] protocol to construct and maintain state at the overlay layer. Here, we first describe the state maintained by each node, and then describe how that state is constructed and maintained over time.

State maintained by each node: X-Vine constructs a *social overlay* on top of the social network, where a node has direct links to friends, but also maintains "overlay links" to remote nodes. These remote nodes (*overlay endpoints*) are selected in a manner similar to Chord [59]: each node is assigned an identifier from a ring namespace, and forms overlay links to nodes that are successors (immediately adjacent in the namespace), and (optionally) fingers (spaced exponentially around the ring). Unlike Chord however, a node is not allowed to directly send packets to its overlay neighbor: for security reasons, nodes only receive packets from their social network links. Hence, to forward a packet from a node to one of its overlay endpoints, the packet will have to traverse a *path* in the social network graph. To achieve this, corresponding to each of its overlay endpoints, a node maintains a *trail* through the social network. Each node along the trail locally stores a *record* consisting of four fields: the identifiers of the two endpoints of the trail, and the IP addresses of the next and previous hops along the trail. Using this information, a node can send a packet to its endpoints,

[1]Applications such as Vuze may optionally choose to benefit only from X-Vine's Sybil resilience, and can forgo pseudonymity by directly transferring files between overlay nodes after the lookup operation.

by handing the packet off to the first node along the trail, which looks up the next hop along the trail using its trail records, and so on. Furthermore, using a Chord-like routing algorithm, a node can route to any other node in the namespace, by (upon reaching an endpoint) selecting the next overlay hop that maximizes namespace progress to the destination (without overshooting). As an optimization, instead of waiting until the endpoint is reached to determine the next overlay hop, intermediate nodes along the path may "*shortcut*" by scanning all their trail records, and choosing the endpoint that maximizes progress in the namespace (see Algorithm 1 in Appendix B). If the intermediate node discovers an endpoint that makes more namespace progress to the destination than the current next overlay hop, the intermediate node may choose to forward the packet towards this new endpoint, to speed its progress (while explicitly maintaining the next overlay hop in the packet is not strictly necessary for routing, we do so to simplify parts of our design described later).

State construction and maintenance: Since nodes can route, we can perform other DHT operations by simply performing routing atop this structure. For example, we can execute a Chord-like join: upon arriving at the network, a node can route a *join request* towards its own identifier, and the node that receives it can return back the identifiers which should be the joining node's successors. However, there are two key changes we need to make. First, when a node initially arrives, it does not yet have any trail state and hence cannot forward packets. To address this, the joining node randomly selects one of its friends in the social network to act as a *bootstrap* node. The joining node sends its join request using the bootstrap node as a proxy. Second, the joining node also needs to build trails to each of its endpoints (e.g., its successors). To do this, for each endpoint, it sends a *trail construction request* to the identifier of that endpoint. As the request is routed, each intermediate node along the path locally stores a record corresponding to the trail. Finally, when these steps are completed, the joining node can route to any node in the network (by forwarding packets through its endpoints), and it can receive packets from any node in the network (by accepting packets through its endpoints). To maintain this state, we need to achieve two things. First, we would like to correctly maintain the set of records along each trail in the presence of churn, so each node can reach the trail endpoint. This is done in a manner similar to AODV [49]: each node along the path locally probes its neighbors and removes trail records (sending *teardown* messages upstream if necessary) corresponding to failed trails. Second, we would like to make sure each trail points to the corresponding globally correct successor/finger. To do this, we leverage the stabilization mechanisms from Chord and VRR [14, 59].

3.2 Balancing Routing State

Temporal correlation: while the scheme above is correct, it performs poorly in practice. The reason for this is due to *temporal correlation*—since trails are constructed using other trails, social network links that are initially chosen to be part of a trail become increasingly likely to be part of later trails. Because of this, nodes that join the network early tend to accumulate more state over time. To illustrate this problem, we describe an example. Suppose a node X has d friends $a_1, a_2, .., a_d$. Suppose also that there is a trail from X to Y for which the next hop is node a_d. Next, suppose node X is an intermediate node in a new overlay path that is being setup from node a_1 (which is also the previous hop). With probability $2/d$, the next hop of the overlay path will be a_d. Similarly, in the future, the probability of a_d being chosen as the next hop in an overlay path increases to $3/(d+1)$, and then to $4/(d+2)$, and so on. This example illustrates that a social network link that was initially chosen as part of a trail has an increasing chance of being chosen in trails that are set up in the future. Consequently nodes that join the social network early tend to be part of many trails. This is not desirable from both a security perspective or a performance perspective.

Stabilization algorithms: To address the problem of temporal correlation, we propose two modifications to the core X-Vine algorithms: The first algorithm leverages the social connections of new users to reduce the path lengths of existing trails. When a new node joins the system, its social contacts that are already part of the X-Vine system consider all trails in their routing tables that have a path length greater than a threshold thr_1 (set to the upper quartile of trail path path lengths). Corresponding to each such trail, the social contacts check if modifying the trail via the new node would reduce the path length, and if so, a teardown message is sent to the old trail and another trail via the new node is setup. The threshold on the path length helps to avoid needless communication for trails that are already short, and are thus unlikely to benefit much from new edges in the social graph topology. The second algorithm helps to load balance the routing state at nodes, and also leads to a reduction in the path lengths of trails. This algorithm is run by all nodes whose routing state is greater than a threshold thr_2. Such nodes consider all trails in their routing tables whose path length is greater than a threshold thr_1 (similar to the previous algorithm), and send messages to the overlay end points to check if alternate trails can be established, and if their path length is shorter than the current path length. If a shorter alternate trail exists, then it replaces the existing trail. This helps reduce the routing state size at congested nodes, while simultaneously reducing the trail path lengths.

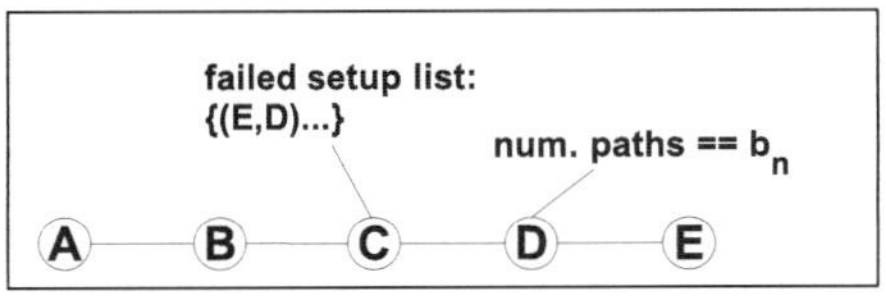

Figure 3. Example: backtracking.

3.3 Bounding State With Local Policies

We have seen that the shortcut-based routing protocol described in Section 3.1 faces the problem of temporal correlation, leading to unbounded growth in routing state. To complement our stabilization algorithms, we propose a mechanism by which nodes can set a hard bound on their routing state size using local routing policies. These policies can be set to account for heterogeneity across nodes, users' desired degree of participation in the network, and to limit the worst-case state overhead at any particular node. Our architecture allows users to set two types of policies pertaining to state maintained at their local node:*Bounding routes per link:* If the number of trails traversing an adjacent social network link reaches a threshold b_l, then the user's node refuses to set up any more trails traversing that link. *Bounding routes per node:* If the number of trails traversing the user's node reaches a threshold value b_n, then the node refuses to set up any more trails via itself. Due to these routing policies, it is possible that a request to set up a trail may be unable to make forward progress in the overlay namespace. To address this, we introduce a technique called *backtracking* that explores alternate social network paths in case an intermediate node refuses to process a path setup request. To do this, each node maintains a *failed setup list*, containing a list of trails that have failed to set up. When a node attempts to set up a trail via a next hop, and receives a *rejection* message indicating that the next hop is full, the node inserts an entry into its failed setup list. Each record in the list contains the identifier of the destination overlay endpoint that the packet was traversing towards, and the identifier of the next hop in the social network that rejected the path setup. When forwarding a message to a particular destination endpoint, a node removes from consideration next hops contained in the failed setup list corresponding to that endpoint (see Algorithm 2 in Appendix B). The failed setup list is periodically garbage collected by discarding entries after a timeout.

For example (Figure 3), suppose node A wishes to establish a path to E, and determines B is the best next overlay hop. A places E into the *next overlay hop* field in the message, and forwards the message to B. Similarly, B forwards the message to C. Suppose D is congested (has more than b_n paths traversing it). In this case, C sends the path setup message to D, but D responds back with a rejection message. C then stores the entry (E, D) in its failed setup list, to indicate that establishing a path via D to reach E was unsuccessful. C then attempts to select an alternate next hop that makes progress in the namespace (either a route to the current next overlay hop, or a "shortcut" route that makes more progress than the current next overlay hop). If C does not have such a route, it sends a rejection message back to B, which inserts the entry (E, C) in its failed setup list. This process repeats until a path is discovered, or a time-to-live (TTL) contained in the packet is exceeded. When the TTL is exceeded, the path setup fails, and the source node must attempt to rejoin to establish the path.

4 Securing X-Vine

The previous section described our approach to perform routing atop the social network. In this section, we describe how to extend and tune the design in the previous section to improve its resilience to attack. We start by providing an overview of attacks on our design(Section 4.1), and then propose extensions to improve resilience to them (Section 4.2).

4.1 Attacks on the Routing Protocol

We investigate defenses to the following attacks on DHTs:

Sybil attack [22]: The attacker can insert a large number of Sybil identities in the DHT, and set up paths with their successors and predecessors. The attack results in honest nodes' routing tables being populated by malicious Sybil identities. This increases the probability that lookup queries will traverse some malicious nodes, which can then drop or misroute the lookup queries. Observe that to minimize resources, it suffices for Sybil identities to maintain paths with only nodes in the predecessor list, since paths to the nodes in the successor list will result in a shortcut to the honest successor nodes.

Attacks on routing table maintenance: In addition to the Sybil attack, the adversary could also manipulate the routing table maintenance protocols to increase the probability of malicious nodes being present in honest nodes' routing tables. *Intercepting trails:* During churn, malicious nodes can become part of a large number of trail paths between nodes, in order to attract lookup traffic (for example, by refusing to send trail teardown messages). *Attacking trail construction:* The attacker could prevent honest nodes from finding a trail path to their correct successor. This could be done by dropping or misrouting the trail setup messages. *Attacks on message integrity:* Malicious nodes that forward control traffic could modify the content of the messages, to disrupt trail setup (for example, by creating routing loops). *Forgery attacks:* The malicious nodes could spoof source identifiers in messages sent to honest nodes (for example, to give the appearance that the message came from the honest node's friends).

Attacks on lookups: Once the attacker is able to intercept a lookup query, it can either drop the packet or misroute it. Such attacks can prevent the honest nodes from either discovering their correct successor in the ring, or discovering a malicious successor list set respectively. By advertising malicious nodes as the successors of an honest joining node, a significant fraction of the honest joining node's traffic would traverse malicious nodes. Note that attacks on both overlay construction and overlay routing are captured by this attack, since in a DHT, both bootstrap and routing are accomplished by the same operation: a lookup.

4.2 Proposed Defenses

We note that it is imperative to secure *both* the routing table maintenance and lookup forwarding. If the routing table maintenance protocol were insecure, then the adversary could manipulate the routing table entries of honest nodes to point to malicious nodes, and routing to honest nodes would not be successful. However, even if the routing table maintenance mechanisms are secure, the adversary still has the opportunity to drop lookup packets or misroute them.

Mitigating the Sybil attack: To limit the impact of the Sybil attack, we propose that nodes implement a routing policy that bounds the number of trails that traverse a social network edge. We denote the bound parameter as b_l. Since the attacker has limited attack edges, this bounds the number of overlay paths between the honest subgraph and the Sybil subgraph *regardless of the attacker strategy*. Thus, we limit the number of Sybil identities that are part of the honest node's routing table. The key challenge in this approach is to determine the bound b_l that enables most honest nodes to set up trails with each other while hindering the ability of Sybil nodes to join the DHT. Our analytic and experimental results suggest that a bound of $b_l \in \Theta(\log n)$ works quite well. Similar to Yu et al. [68], we assume that the bound b_l is a system wide constant known to all honest nodes. Honest nodes are able to set up trails with each other even though there is a bound on the number of trails per social network link because of the fast-mixing nature of the social network. On the other hand, a Sybil attack gives rise to a sparse cut in the social network topology, and we use this sparse cut to limit the impact of the Sybil identities. The number of overlay paths between the honest and Sybil subgraphs is bounded to $g \cdot b_l$. The adversary could choose to allocate each overlay path to a different Sybil identity, resulting in $g \cdot b_l$ Sybil identities in the DHT (in the routing tables of honest nodes). We can further limit the number of Sybil identities in the routing tables of honest nodes by ensuring that the adversary must allocate at least a threshold t number of overlay paths per Sybil identity. This would bound the number of Sybil identities in honest nodes routing tables to $g \cdot b_l/t$. Note that the number of overlay paths between the honest and Sybil regions does not change. We propose the following mechanism to ensure that the adversary sets up trails with at least a threshold t overlay neighbors. Nodes periodically probe their overlay neighbors to check if each successor in their routing table has set up a trail with at least t other nodes in the overlay neighborhood. Note that the check is performed by directly querying the overlay neighbors. The threshold t is set to $t < 2 \cdot num\_successors$ to account for malicious overlay nodes returning incorrect replies. If the adversary does not allocate t trails per Sybil identity (set up with its successors and predecessors), the honest nodes can detect this via probing and can teardown the trails to the malicious Sybil identity. Note that the adversary cannot game the probing mechanism unless it has a large number of Sybil identities in the overlay neighborhood of a node. Since the Sybil identities are distributed at random in the overlay namespace, this is unlikely to happen unless the adversary has a large number of attack edges ($g \in \Omega(n/(\log n))$).

Securing routing table maintenance: We provide the following defenses to attacks on routing table maintenance:

Trail interception attacks: Observe that our mechanism to defend against Sybil attacks, i.e., bounding the number of trails that traverse a social network link, also defends against malicious nodes that attempt to be a part of a large number of trails. Specifically, the adversary has a *quota* of $g \cdot b_l$ trails between honest nodes and itself, and it can choose to utilize this quota either by inserting Sybil identities in the DHT or by being part of trails between two honest nodes. Either way, the effect of this attack is limited by the bound b_l.

Trail construction attacks: Suppose that a node X is trying to set up a trail with its overlay neighbor Y. To circumvent the scenario where a malicious intermediate node M simply drops X's path set up request to Y, we propose that upon path setup the end point Y sends an acknowledgment along the reverse path back to X. If after a timeout, the node X does not receive an acknowledgment from Y, then it can retry sending the trail set up request over a different route. Again, the fast-mixing nature of the social network topology guarantees that two nodes are very likely to have multiple paths between each other.

Message integrity and forgery attacks: To provide message integrity is the use of self-certifying identifiers [8, 15, 38]. Nodes can append their public keys to the message and produce a digital signature of the message along with the appended public key. The self-certifying nature of identifiers ensures that the public key for a specified node identifier cannot be forged; this enables us to provide both message integrity as well as authentication.

Securing the lookup protocol: Even if the routing table maintenance protocol is secure, the adversary can still drop or misroute lookup requests that traverse itself. We secure the lookup protocol using redundant routing, similar to Castro et al. [16]. Instead of a single lookup, a node can choose to perform r lookups for the destination (where r is the redundancy parameter) using r diverse trusted links in the social network topology. Redundant routing increases the probability that at least one lookup will traverse only honest nodes and find the correct successor. If the lookup is performed during route table maintenance, the correct successor can be identified since it will be impossible to set up a trail to an incorrect one; if the lookup is searching for a particular node or data item, then self-certifying techniques can be used to identify incorrect responses.

4.3 Privacy Protection

All communication in X-Vine happens over social network links; while a user's IP address is revealed to his/her social contacts, it is not exposed to random peers in the network. Therefore as long as a user's social contacts are trusted, he/she can communicate pseudonymously. Moreover, observe that X-Vine's mechanisms do not require a user to expose his/her social contacts. This is in sharp contrast to prior work [34], wherein this information is revealed as part of protocol operations to everyone in the network. Note that in the absence of a mapping from a DHT ID to an IP address, the adversary cannot perform traffic analysis to infer social contacts. The only source of information leakage is when the adversary can map DHT IDs of two users to their respective IP addresses (for example, by virtue of being their trusted contacts); in this case the adversary can perform traffic analysis attacks to infer whether the two users have a trust relationship or not. In X-Vine, the privacy risk is with respect to social contacts, rather than random peers in the network. Note that in this paper, we are only concerned with overlay level adversaries; adversaries which operate at the ISP level, or have external sources of information [47] are outside the scope of our threat model.

5 Experiments and Analysis

We evaluate X-Vine with theoretical analysis, experiments using real-world social network topologies, and a prototype implementation. We measure routing state size, lookup path lengths, security against Sybil attacks, resilience against churn, and lookup latency. We also developed a Facebook application to facilitate the use of our design.

Simulation environment: We constructed an in-house event-driven simulator. As done in [14], we bootstrap X-Vine by selecting a random node in the social network as the first node, and the social network neighbors of that node then become candidates to join the X-Vine network. Next, one of these neighbors is selected to join, with a probability proportional to the number of trust relationships it has with nodes that are already a part of the X-Vine network. This process is then repeated. Note that some nodes may not be successful in joining because of the bound on number of trails per link (as discussed in detail later).

Data sets: Recent work has proposed the use of interaction graphs [62, 66] as a better indicator of real world trust than friendship graphs. Hence we consider both traditional social network graph topologies as well as interaction graph topologies in our evaluation. The datasets that we use have been summarized in Table 1.

Facebook friendship graph from the New Orleans regional network [62]: The original dataset consists of 60 290 nodes and 772 843 edges. We processed the dataset in a manner similar to the evaluation done in SybilLimit [68] and SybilInfer [21], by imposing a lower bound of 3 and an upper bound of 100 on the node degree (see [21, 68] for details) [2]. After processing, we are left with 50 150 nodes and 661 850 edges.

Facebook wall post interaction graph from the New Orleans regional network [62]: The original dataset consists of 60 290 users. After processing, we are left with 29 140 users and 161 969 edges. Note that links in this dataset are directed, and we consider an edge between users only if there were interactions in both directions.

Facebook interaction graph from a moderate-sized regional [3] network [66]: The dataset consists of millions of nodes and edges, but our experiments are memory limited and do not scale to millions of nodes. Instead, we first truncate the dataset by considering only a four hop neighborhood from a seed node. After processing, we are left with 103 840 nodes and 961 418 edges.

Synthetic scale-free graphs: Social networks exhibit a scale-free node degree topology [53]. Our network synthesis algorithm replicates this structure through preferential attachment, following the methodology of Nagaraja [45]. The use of synthetic scale free topologies enables us evaluate X-Vine while varying the number of nodes in the network.

Overhead: Figure 4 plots the routing table size for different successor list sizes. We can see the temporal correlation effect here, as the distribution of state shows super-exponential growth. Temporal correlation is highly unde-

[2] Recent work by Mohaisen et al. [44] shows that social networks may not be as fast mixing as previously believed. However, we note that their results do not directly apply to X-Vine since they did not consider node degree bounds in their analysis. X-Vine excludes users having few friends from participating in the routing protocol, though such users could use their trusted friends to lookup keys.

[3] Because of privacy reasons, the name of the regional network has been left anonymous by the authors of [66].

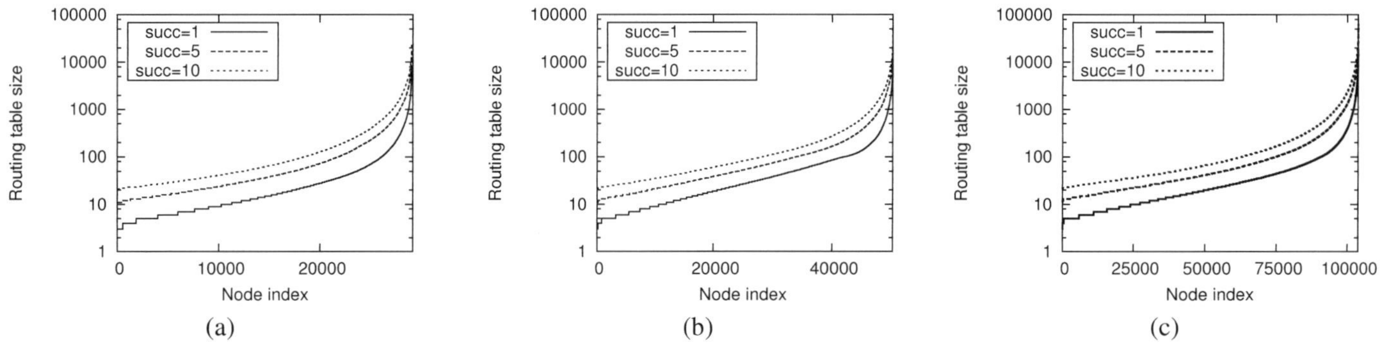

Figure 4. *Routing state, with no bounds on state:* **(a) New Orleans Interaction graph, (b) New Orleans Friendship graph, and the (c) Anonymous Interaction graph. Due to temporal correlation, some nodes exhibit high state requirements.**

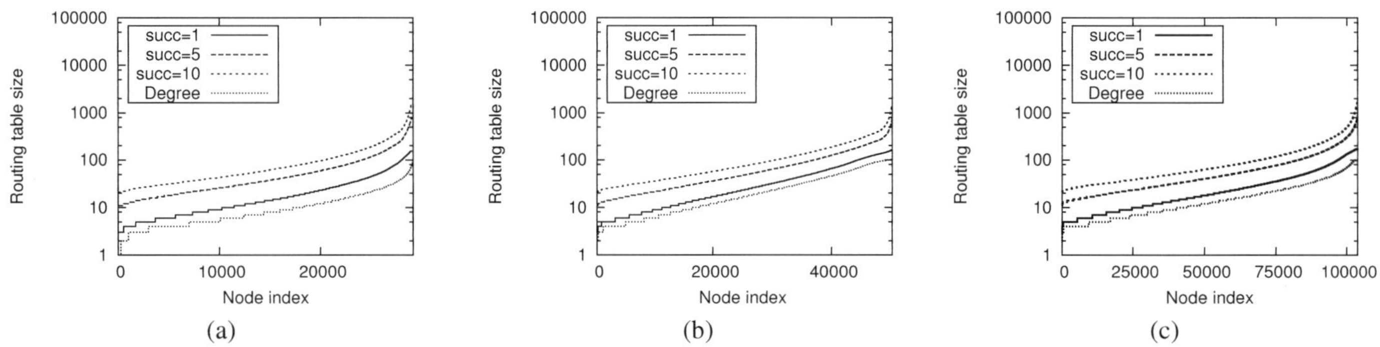

Figure 5. *Routing state, with node and edge bounds:* **(a) New Orleans Interaction graph, (b) New Orleans Friendship graph, and (c) Anonymous Interaction graph. Bounding state significantly reduces state requirements. Using a successor list of size 5, the average routing state for the three topologies is 67, 81, and 76 records respectively. X-Vine requires orders of magnitude less state than Whanau [34].**

Table 1. Topologies

Dataset	Nodes	Edges	Mean Degree
New Orleans Facebook Friendship graph	50 150	661 850	26.39
New Orleans Facebook Interaction graph	29 140	161 969	11.11
Anonymous Facebook Interaction graph	103 840	961 418	18.51

sirable both from a performance and a security standpoint. If the few nodes with very large state become unavailable due to churn, the network could get destabilized. Moreover, if one of these nodes is malicious, it could easily intercept a large number of lookups and drop them. To address this, we enable the routing policy that bounds the number of paths traversing nodes and links. Based on our analytic model in Appendix A, we propose the following bound on the number of paths per link: $b_l = \alpha \cdot 2 \cdot num\_successors \cdot \log(n)$, where α is a small fixed constant. The bound per link ensures that if a node has degree d, then its routing table size will never exceed $d \cdot b_l \in O(\log n)$. We can see that the routing state does not undergo an exponential increase as in previous plots. Moreover, routing state increases with node degrees, which is desirable. Based on these routing table sizes, we can estimate the communication overhead of X-Vine by computing the cost of sending heartbeat traffic for all records in the routing table. Considering the routing table size to be 125 records, UDP ping size to be 40 bytes, and a heartbeat interval of 1 s, the estimated mean communication overhead is only 4.8 KBps.

Comparison with Whanau [34]: Routing state in Whanau depends on the number of objects stored in the DHT. Routing tables in Whanau are of size $\Theta(\sqrt{n_o} \log n_o)$, where n_o is the number of objects in the DHT. If there are too many objects stored in the DHT, Whanau resorts to maintaining information about all the nodes and edges in the social network (increasing state/overhead to $\Theta(n)$). If there are too few objects in the DHT, Whanau resorts to flooding to find objects [34]. We note that such properties make Whanau unsuitable for many common applications. Even if we consider the case where each node in the DHT stores only tens of objects, the average routing table size in Whanau for the 103 840 node anonymous interaction graph is about 20 000 records—an increase of more than two orders of magnitude as compared with X-Vine. If we consider a heartbeat interval of 1 second in Whanau (in order to accurately maintain object states for common DHT applications), the resulting communication overhead is about 800 KBps. This difference increases further with an increase in the number of objects in the DHT or the size of the network. For instance, we scaled up our experiments to a larger 613 164 node anonymous interaction graph topology using a machine with 128 GB RAM, and found that the average routing state in X-Vine using a successor list size of 10 was only 195 records, as compared with more than 50 000 records in Whanau. (Note that routing state in X-Vine is independent of the number of objects in the DHT.)

False Positive Analysis: Next, we consider the impact of link/node path bounds on honest node's ability to join the DHT. We found that most honest nodes were able to join the DHT due to the fast mixing nature of honest social networks. In fact, for all our experimental scenarios, the false-positive rate was less than 0.5%, which is comparable to the state-of-the-art systems [21,68]. By tuning the parameter b_l, it is possible to trade off the false-positive rate for Sybil resilience: b_l will reduce the false-positive rate at the cost of increasing the number of Sybil identities in the system. For the remainder of the paper, we shall use $\alpha = 1, \beta = 5$.

Path Length Analysis: Table 2 depicts the mean lookup path lengths for the real world datasets with varying successor list sizes and varying redundancy parameter. We first observe that lookup performance improves with increasing successor list sizes. For example, in the New Orleans interaction graph, the mean lookup path length decreases from 97.9 to 15.4 when the successor list size increases from 1 to 20 (using $r = 1$). Further improvements in performance can be realized by performing redundant lookups as described in Section 4 and caching the lookup with the smallest path length. We can see that in the same dataset, mean lookup path length decreases from 15.4 to 10.3 when the redundancy parameter is increased from $r = 1$ to $r = 5$ (using successor list of size 20). Further increases in redundancy show diminishing returns. Observe that when the successor list size is at least 10, and the redundancy parameter is at least 10, then the mean lookup path lengths for all datasets are less than 15 hops. Increasing the successor list size to 20 (and keeping $r = 10$) reduces this value to less than 11.5 for all datasets.

Security under Sybil Attack: Recall that if the adversary has g attack edges, then the number of trails between the honest and the Sybil subgraph is bounded by $g \cdot b_l$ (regardless of the attacker strategy). Our attack methodology is as follows: we randomly select a set of compromised nodes until the adversary has the desired number of attack edges. The compromised nodes then launch a Sybil attack, and set up trails between Sybil identities and their overlay neighbors. If the trail set up request starting from a Sybil node gets shortcutted back to the Sybil identities, the request is backtracked. This ensures that the adversary uses only a single attack edge per trail. Node identifiers of Sybil identities are chosen at random with the adversarial goal of intercepting as many lookups as possible. All lookups traversing compromised/Sybil nodes are considered unsuccessful.

Figure 6 plots the probability of a secure lookup as a function of number of attack edges, redundancy parameter, and size of successor list. We find that the probability of secure lookup increases as the redundancy parameter is increased. This is because as the number of redundant lookups increases, there is a greater chance that a lookup will traverse only honest nodes and return the correct result. We also find that the probability of secure lookup also increases when the size of the successor list increases. This is because increasing successor list size reduces the mean lookup path length, reducing the probability that an adversary can intercept the lookup query. As long as $g \in o(n/(\log n))$, the probability of secure lookup can be made arbitrarily high by increasing the redundancy parameter and the successor list size. Finally, reducing b_l would further limit the impact of Sybil identities, at the cost of increased false positives.

Churn Analysis: Next, we evaluate the performance of X-Vine under churn. We are interested in the *static resilience* of X-Vine, i.e., the probability of lookup success after a fraction of the nodes in the system fail simultaneously. To account for churn, we modified the lookup algorithm to *backtrack* whenever it cannot make forward progress in the overlay namespace. Figure 7 depicts the mean probability of lookup success as a function of the fraction of nodes that fail simultaneously, averaged over 100 000 lookups. Similar to the analysis of lookup security, we can see that an increase in either the redundancy parameter or the successor list size result in improved resilience against churn. We can also see that as the fraction of failed nodes increases, the probability of lookup success decreases, but is still greater than 0.95 for all scenarios using $r = 4$ and $succ = 20$.

PlanetLab Implementation: To validate our design and evaluate lookup latency in real-world environments, we implemented the X-Vine lookup protocol in C++ as a single-threaded program using 3 000 LOC. We used libasync [5,6] and Tame [32] to implement non-blocking socket func-

Table 2. Mean Lookup Path Length

# Succ	New Orleans interaction graph			New Orleans friendship graph			Anonymous interaction graph		
	$r = 1$	$r = 5$	$r = 10$	$r = 1$	$r = 5$	$r = 10$	$r = 1$	$r = 5$	$r = 10$
1	97.9	57.7	51.7	103.6	57.5	48.1	166.7	96.3	81.0
5	30.0	18.2	16.8	34.8	19.3	16.7	48.9	25.5	21.7
10	20.2	13.0	12.16	23.1	13.7	12.1	29.9	16.9	14.8
20	15.4	10.3	9.6	17.0	10.7	9.45	21.0	12.8	11.3

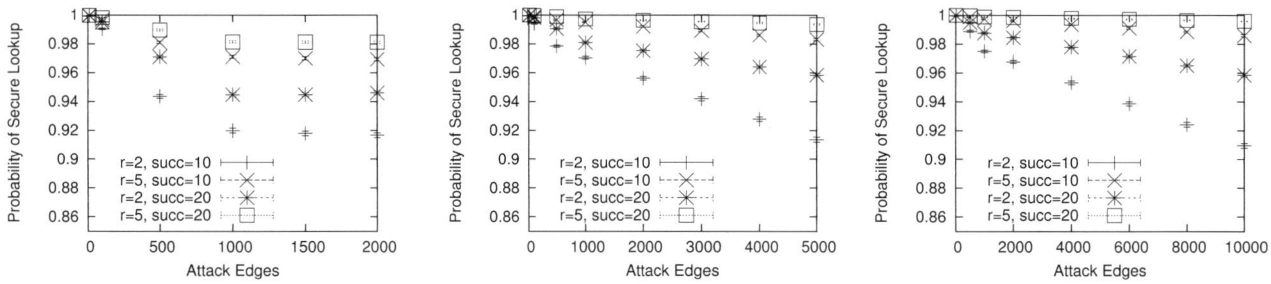

(a) (b) (c)

Figure 6. Probability of secure lookup as a function of number of attack edges for (a) New Orleans interaction graph, (b) New Orleans friendship graph, and (c) Anonymous Interaction graph.

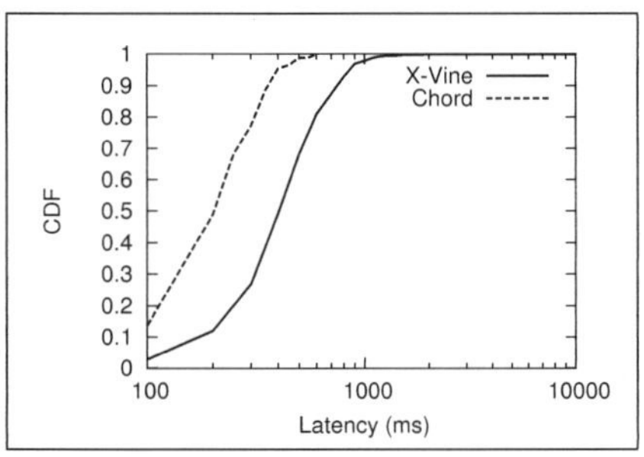

Figure 8. Lookup latency

tionality (UDP) in an event-based fashion. We ran our implementation over 100 randomly selected nodes in the PlanetLab network. We used a synthetic scale free graph as the social network topology. The duration of the experiment was set to 1 hour, and nodes performed lookups every 1 second. Figure 8 depicts the CDF of observed one-way lookup latencies. We can see that the median lookup latency was only 400 ms (as compared to 200 ms in Chord), for the mean lookup path length of 5 hops (not shown in the Figure). Using these values, we can estimate the median lookup latency for mean lookup path lengths of 10 hops and 15 hops (that were observed in our experiments over real world social network topologies in Table 2) to be about 800 ms and 1200 ms respectively. We see some outliers in Figure 8 due to the presence of a few slow/unresponsive nodes in PlanetLab. For this experiment, we mapped vertices in the social network topology to random PlanetLab nodes (possibly in different geographic locations). Thus, our analysis is conservative; accounting for locality of social network contacts would likely improve the lookup performance.

Facebook Application: To bootstrap a X-Vine node, its user needs to input the IP addresses of his/her friends. Since this can be a cumbersome for a user, we implemented a Facebook application (available at `http://apps.facebook.com/x--vine`) that automates this process and improves the usability of our design. The work flow of the application is as follows: (i) When a user visits the Facebook application URL, Facebook checks the credentials of the user, the user authorizes the application, and then the request gets redirected to the application hosting server. (ii) The application server authenticates itself, and is then able to query Facebook for user information. The application server records the user information along with the user IP address. (iii) The application server then queries Facebook for a list of user's friends, and returns their previously recorded IP addresses (if available) to the user.

This list of IP addresses could then be used by the DHT software to bootstrap its operations. Our implementation demonstrates that a user's social contacts can be integrated into the DHT protocol using only a few hundred lines of glue code. Keeping in spirit with our fully decentralized design goal, in future, our application could be implemented on a decentralized platform like Diaspora [1] such that the app server is not a central point of trust or failure.

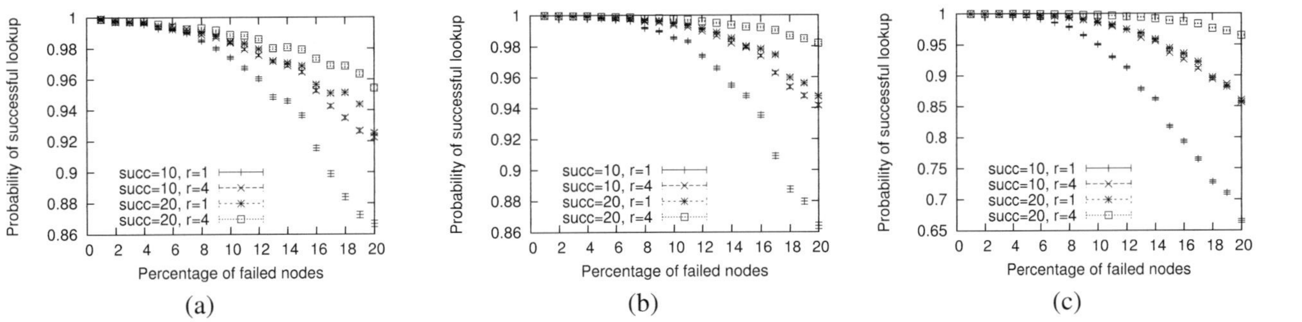

Figure 7. *Lookup resilience against churn:* **(a) New Orleans Interaction graph, (b) New Orleans Friendship graph, and (c) Anonymous Interaction graph.**

6 Related Work

X-Vine provides *multi-hop* social network routing, logarithmic state Sybil defense, protects privacy of friendship information, and enables pseudonymous communication. Our work is the first to provide these properties. However, X-Vine builds upon foundational work in several areas:

Sybil defense: Sybil defenses must fundamentally impose a cost on participation in the network [22]. One approach, advocated by Castro et al. [16], requires users to provide identity credentials and/or payment to a centralized authority, who then issues certificates allowing users to participate. This authority, of course, becomes a central point of trust. Decentralized approaches instead allow nodes to directly verify some resource expenditure by other nodes, such as CPU computation, or the possession of a unique IP address [12,55]. All these solutions face a tradeoff between creating too high a barrier for participation by honest users and making it too easy for malicious users to create Sybil identities. More recent work has recognized that it is expensive for a malicious adversary to establish trust relationships with honest users and thus social network topologies can be used to detect and mitigate social Sybil attacks. The design of X-Vine is based upon the same principle.

SybilGuard [69] and SybilLimit [68] are decentralized systems for Sybil defense. These systems use special random walks called *random routes* for Sybil defense. In SybilLimit, as long as the number of attack edges is less than a threshold ($g = o\left(\frac{n}{\log n}\right)$), then with high probability, a short random walk of $O(\log n)$ steps is likely to stay within the set of honest nodes. Nodes in SybilLimit perform $\sqrt{e}$ short random walks (where e is the number of edges amongst the honest nodes) and keep track of their last edges (tails). By the birthday paradox, two honest nodes will share a common tail with high probability. Each node allows only a certain number of random routes to traverse it, thereby limiting the number of Sybil identities that are validated by the honest nodes.

SybilInfer [21] provides an algorithm for labeling nodes in a social network as honest users or Sybils controlled by an adversary. It takes as an input a social graph G, and generates a set of traces using short random walks. Using a mathematical model of an honest social network, it performs Bayesian inference to output a set of dishonest nodes. The Bayesian inference approach can even be used to assign probabilities to nodes of being honest or dishonest. These systems are standalone Sybil defenses and do not provide a DHT functionality.

Whanau [34] is the state of art Sybil resilient DHT [20, 33] where nodes can communicate with only one intermediate hop. Each node performs $\sqrt{e}$ random walks to sample nodes for construction of their routing tables ; the Sybil resistant property of short random walks ensures that a high fraction of the sampled nodes are honest . By querying routing table entries, nodes can construct their successor lists. As compared to X-Vine, Whanau provides its properties at the cost of maintaining $\sqrt{n_o} \log n_o$ state at each node (where n_o is the number of objects). The large state requirements mean that the system has difficulty maintaining accurate state in face of object churn. Whanau also requires the entire social graph to be public, presenting significant privacy concerns. In contrast, X-Vine builds upon *network-layer* DHTs, embedding the DHT directly into the social network fabric. This enables X-Vine to provide good security while achieving improved scalability and privacy of social relationships. Moreover, X-Vine provides support for pseudonymous communication.

The concept of a bottleneck cut between a fast-mixing social network and Sybil nodes has been used in a number of other systems, such as SumUp [60], a protocol for online content rating that is resilient to Sybil attacks; Ostra [41], a system to prevent unwanted communication from nodes; and Kaleidoscope [58], a system for censorship resistance.

Security and privacy in DHTs: Other work deals with the issue of secure routing when a fraction of nodes in the DHT are compromised [16,31,46,57,63]. Sit and Morris [57], as well as Wallach [63] discuss security issues in DHTs. Castro [16] proposed the use of redundant routing to improve the lookup security. Nambiar and Wright [46] showed that redundant lookups in Chord may traverse a few common nodes, and thus a few malicious nodes could subvert all of the redundant lookups. They designed the Salsa DHT in which redundant lookups are unlikely to traverse common nodes. Kapadia and Triandopoulos [31] propose to make redundant routes diverse by making use of the observation that to perform a lookup for A, it suffices to lookup the nodes which have A as its finger, and then query them. Unlike X-Vine these systems are not concerned with the problem of Sybil attacks. Another line of research deals with the privacy of the DHT lookup. Borisov [11] as well as Ciaccio [18] proposed to incorporate anonymity into the lookup, but their algorithms do not consider active attacks. More recently, anonymous and secure lookups were considered in the designs of Salsa [46], NISAN [48], and Torsk [39]. However, recent work [42, 65] showed vulnerabilities in all the three designs. X-Vine improves the privacy of a user by enabling pseudonymous communication; the IP address of a user is revealed only to a user's trusted friends.

Social networks and routing: The benefits of using social network links for overlay routing has been recognized in a large body of academic work as well as deployed systems.

Hybrid routing using social network links: Systems in this class maintain traditional peer-to-peer structures but also make use of social network connections. Sprout [36] proposed augmenting the finger tables in traditional DHTs, such as Chord, with social network links. The authors showed that the added connections could improve the security of the routing mechanism. However, Sprout does not defend against Sybil attacks, and is not concerned with user privacy. OneSwarm [30] is a deployed peer-to-peer communication system for improving user privacy where routing is performed by combining trusted and untrusted peer relationships. Tribler [51] increases download speed in BitTorrent by discovering and downloading file chunks stored at peers. Similarly, Maze [17] leverages a social network to discover peers and cooperatively download files. These three systems leverage flooding to provide any-to-any reachability, and thus cannot scale to large networks. The hybrid systems are not resilient to Sybil attacks. Moreover, they allow direct contacts over untrusted links, exposing users' IP addresses.

Routing only using social network links: All communication in this class of systems is over social network links. This enables participants in the network to be hidden from each other, providing a high degree of privacy. Such a network is commonly known as a *darknet.* WASTE [24] is a deployed decentralized chat, instant messaging, and file sharing protocol, and is widely considered to be the first darknet. WASTE does not attempt to scale beyond small networks, and its suggested size is limited to 50 users. Turtle [50] is a deployed decentralized anonymous peer-to-peer communication protocol. Nodes in Turtle do not maintain any state information other than their trusted friend links and use controlled flooding to search for data items. Flooding methods create significant overhead as network size increases. Freenet [19] is a deployed decentralized censorship-resistant distributed storage system. Version 0.7 of Freenet nodes can be configured to run in darknet or opennet mode; the latter allows connections from untrusted nodes, and is expected to be used by less privacy-sensitive users. Freenet's routing algorithm is heuristic and does not guarantee that data will be found at all; it has also been shown to be extremely vulnerable even against a few malicious nodes [23]. Membership concealing overlay networks (MCONs) (formalized by Vasserman et al. [61]), hide the real-world identities of the participants through the use of overlay and DHT-based routing. However, their design makes use of a trusted centralized server and also requires flooding when a new user joins the network. In addition to these limitations, none of the above systems are resilient to Sybil attacks.

7 Limitations

We now discuss some limitations of our design. First, X-Vine requires a user's social contacts to be part of the overlay; the DHT needs to be bootstrapped from a single contiguous trust network. Next, X-Vine assumes that Sybil identities are distributed randomly in the DHT identifier space. We emphasize that this assumption is shared by prior systems [20], and that defending multi-hop DHTs against targeted clustering attacks is currently an open problem. In future work, we will investigate the possibility of adapting the cuckoo hashing mechanism [33] proposed by Lesniewski-Laas (for one-hop DHTs) in the context of securing multi-hop DHTs. X-Vine also does not defend against attackers who target users by compromising nodes close to them in the social network topology. Finally, applications using X-Vine experience higher than usual latencies since all communications are pseudonymous and traverse multiple social network links.

8 Conclusions

We describe X-Vine, a protection mechanism for DHTs that operates entirely by communicating over social network links. X-Vine requires $O(\log n)$ state, two orders of magnitude less in practical settings as compared with existing techniques, making it particularly suitable for large-scale and dynamic environments. X-Vine also enhances privacy by not revealing social relationship information and by providing a basis for pseudonymous communication.

References

[1] Diaspora. wwww.joindiaspora.com/.

[2] eMule. `http://www.emule-project.net/`.

[3] Facebook. www.facebook.com.

[4] Livejournal. www.livejournal.com.

[5] Sfslite. `http://www.okws.org/doku.php?id=sfslite`.

[6] Using libasync. `http://pdos.csail.mit.edu/6.824-2004/async/`.

[7] The Vuze Network. `http://www.vuze.com/`.

[8] D. G. Andersen, H. Balakrishnan, N. Feamster, T. Koponen, D. Moon, and S. Shenker. Accountable Internet protocol. In *SIGCOMM*, 2008.

[9] K. Bauer, D. Mccoy, D. Grunwald, and D. Sicker. Bitstalker: Accurately and efficiently monitoring bittorent traffic. In *Proceedings of the International Workshop on Information Forensics and Security*, 2009.

[10] L. Bilge, T. Strufe, D. Balzarotti, and E. Kirda. All your contacts are belong to us: automated identity theft attacks on social networks. In *WWW*, 2009.

[11] N. Borisov. *Anonymous routing in structured peer-to-peer overlays*. PhD thesis, UC Berkeley, 2005.

[12] N. Borisov. Computational puzzles as sybil defenses. In *IEEE P2P*, 2006.

[13] Y. Boshmaf, I. Muslukhov, K. Beznosov, and M. Ripeanu. The socialbot network: when bots socialize for fame and money. In *ACSAC*, 2011.

[14] M. Caesar, M. Castro, E. Nightingale, A. Rowstron, and G. O'Shea. Virtual Ring Routing: Network routing inspired by DHTs. In *SIGCOMM*, 2006.

[15] M. Caesar, T. Condie, J. Kannan, K. Lakshminarayanan, and I. Stoica. ROFL: Routing on Flat Labels. In *SIGCOMM*, September 2006.

[16] M. Castro, P. Druschel, A. Ganesh, A. Rowstron, and D. S. Wallach. Secure routing for structured peer-to-peer overlay networks. In *OSDI*, 2002.

[17] H. Chen, X. Li, and J. Han. Maze: a social peer-to-peer network. In *In of CEC-East*, 2004.

[18] G. Ciaccio. Improving sender anonymity in a structured overlay with imprecise routing. In *PETS*, June 2006.

[19] I. Clarke, O. Sandberg, B. Wiley, and T. W. Hong. Freenet: A distributed anonymous information storage and retrieval system. In *DPET*, July 2000.

[20] G. Danezis, C. Lesniewski-Laas, M. F. Kaashoek, and R. Anderson. Sybil-resistant DHT routing. In *ESORICS*, Milan, Italy, September 2005.

[21] G. Danezis and P. Mittal. SybilInfer: Detecting sybil nodes using social networks. In *NDSS*, 2009.

[22] J. Douceur. The Sybil Attack. In *IPTPS*, March 2002.

[23] N. S. Evans, C. GauthierDickey, and C. Grothoff. Routing in the dark: Pitch black. *ACSAC*, 2007.

[24] J. Frankel. http://waste.sourceforge.net.

[25] M. J. Freedman, E. Freudenthal, and D. Mazières. Democratizing content publication with Coral. In *NSDI*, 2004.

[26] M. J. Freedman and R. Morris. Tarzan: a peer-to-peer anonymizing network layer. In *CCS*, 2002.

[27] R. Geambasu, T. Kohno, A. A. Levy, and H. M. Levy. Vanish: increasing data privacy with self-destructing data. In *USENIX Security*, 2009.

[28] E. Gilbert and K. Karahalios. Predicting tie strength with social media. In *Computer Human Interaction*, 2009.

[29] D. Irani, M. Balduzzi, D. Balzarotti, E. Kirda, and C. Pu. Reverse social engineering attacks in online social networks. In *DIMVA*, 2011.

[30] T. Isdal, M. Piatek, A. Krishnamurthy, and T. Anderson. Privacy-preserving p2p data sharing with oneswarm. In *SIGCOMM*, 2010.

[31] A. Kapadia and N. Triandopoulos. Halo: High-assurance locate for distributed hash tables. In *NDSS*, 2008.

[32] M. Krohn, E. Kohler, and M. F. Kaashoek. Events can make sense. In *USENIX ATC*, 2007.

[33] C. Lesniewski-Laas. A Sybil-proof one-hop DHT. In *SocialNets*, pages 19–24, 2008.

[34] C. Lesniewski-Laas and M. F. Kaashoek. Whanaungatanga: A Sybil-proof distributed hash table. In *NSDI*, 2010.

[35] M. Liberatore, B. N. Levine, and C. Shields. Strengthening forensic investigations of child pornography on p2p networks. In *CONEXT*, 2010.

[36] S. Marti, P. Ganesan, and H. Garcia-Molina. SPROUT: P2P routing with social networks. In *P2P&DB*, 2004.

[37] P. Maymounkov and D. Mazières. Kademlia: A peer-to-peer information system based on the xor metric. In *IPTPS*, 2002.

[38] D. Mazieres. *Self-certifying file system*. PhD thesis, MIT, 2000. Supervisor-Kaashoek, M. Frans.

[39] J. McLachlan, A. Tran, N. Hopper, and Y. Kim. Scalable onion routing with Torsk. In *CCS*, 2009.

[40] E. Miluzzo, N. D. Lane, K. Fodor, R. Peterson, H. Lu, M. Musolesi, S. B. Eisenman, X. Zheng, and A. T. Campbell. Sensing meets mobile social networks: the design, implementation and evaluation of the cenceme application. In *SenSys*, 2008.

[41] A. Mislove, A. Post, P. Druschel, and K. P. Gummadi. Ostra: leveraging trust to thwart unwanted communication. In *NSDI*, pages 15–30, 2008.

[42] P. Mittal and N. Borisov. Information leaks in structured peer-to-peer anonymous communication systems. In *CCS*, 2008.

[43] P. Mittal and N. Borisov. Shadowwalker: peer-to-peer anonymous communication using redundant structured topologies. In *CCS*, 2009.

[44] A. Mohaisen, A. Yun, and Y. Kim. Measuring the mixing time of social graphs. In *IMC*, 2010.

[45] S. Nagaraja. Anonymity in the wild: Mixes on unstructured networks. In *PET*, pages 254–271, 2007.

[46] A. Nambiar and M. Wright. Salsa: a structured approach to large-scale anonymity. In *CCS*, pages 17–26, New York, NY, USA, 2006. ACM.

[47] A. Narayanan and V. Shmatikov. De-anonymizing social networks. In *IEEE S & P*, 2009.

[48] A. Panchenko, S. Richter, and A. Rache. NISAN: network information service for anonymization networks. In *CCS*, 2009.

[49] C. Perkins, E. Belding-Royer, and S. Das. Ad hoc on-demand distance vector (AODV) routing, 2003.

[50] B. Popescu, B. Crispo, and A. S. Tanenbaum. Safe and private data sharing with Turtle: Friends team-up and beat the system. In *12'th Cambridge International Workshop on Security Protocols*, April 2004.

[51] J. Pouwelse, P. Garbacki, J. Wang, A. Bakker, J. Yang, A. Iosup, D. Epema, M. Reinders, M. van Steen, and H. Sips. Tribler: A social-based peer-to-peer system. Technical report, Delft University of Technology, Feb 2006.

[52] S. Ratnasamy, P. Francis, M. Handley, and R. Karp. A scalable content-addressable network. In *SIGCOMM*, August 2001.

[53] M. Ripeanu, A. Iamnitchi, and I. Foster. Mapping the Gnutella network. *IEEE Internet Computing*, 2002.

[54] T. Ristenpart, G. Maganis, A. Krishnamurthy, and T. Kohno. Privacy-preserving location tracking of lost or stolen devices: cryptographic techniques and replacing trusted third parties with DHTs. In *USENIX Security*, 2008.

[55] H. Rowaihy, W. Enck, P. McDaniel, and T. L. Porta. Limiting sybil attacks in structured p2p networks. In *INFOCOM*, 2007.

[56] A. Rowstron and P. Druschel. Pastry: scalable, decentralized object location and routing for large-scale peer-to-peer systems. In *ACM Middleware*, November 2001.

[57] E. Sit and R. Morris. Security considerations for peer-to-peer distributed hash tables. In *IPTPS*, 2002.

[58] Y. Sovran, J. Li, and L. Subramanian. Unblocking the internet: Social networks foil censors. Technical report, NYU, 2008.

[59] I. Stoica, R. Morris, D. Karger, M. Kaashoek, and H. Balakrishnan. Chord: a scalable peer-to-peer lookup service for Internet applications. In *SIGCOMM*, 2001.

[60] N. Tran, B. Min, J. Li, and L. Subramanian. Sybil-resilient online content voting. In *NSDI*, pages 15–28, 2009.

[61] E. Vasserman, R. Jansen, J. Tyra, N. Hopper, and Y. Kim. Membership-concealing overlay networks. In *CCS*, pages 390–399, 2009.

[62] B. Viswanath, A. Mislove, M. Cha, and K. P. Gummadi. On the evolution of user interaction in Facebook. In *WOSN*, 2009.

[63] D. Wallach. A survey of peer-to-peer security issues. In *International Symposium on Software Security*, Tokyo, Japan, 2002.

[64] P. Wang, J. Tyra, E. Chan-Tin, T. Malchow, D. F. Kune, N. Hopper, and Y. Kim. Attacking the Kad network. In *SecureComm*, 2008.

[65] Q. Wang, P. Mittal, and N. Borisov. In search of an anonymous and secure lookup: attacks on structured peer-to-peer anonymous communication systems. In *CCS*, 2010.

[66] C. Wilson, B. Boe, A. Sala, K. P. Puttaswamy, and B. Y. Zhao. User interactions in social networks and their implications. In *EuroSys*, pages 205–218, 2009.

[67] S. Wolchok, O. S. Hofmann, N. Heninger, E. W. Felten, J. A. Halderman, C. J. Rossbach, B. Waters, and E. Witchel. Defeating vanish with low-cost sybil attacks against large DHTs. In *NDSS*, 2010.

[68] H. Yu, P. Gibbons, M. Kaminsky, and F. Xiao. SybilLimit: A near-optimal social network defense against sybil attacks. In *IEEE Security and Privacy*, 2008.

[69] H. Yu, M. Kaminsky, P. Gibbons, and A. Flaxman. SybilGuard: Defending against Sybil attacks via social networks. In *SIGCOMM*, 2006.

A Mathematical Analysis of X-Vine:

As a first step in formally modeling X-Vine security, we develop an analytic model for routing in X-Vine. The model enhances our understanding of the relationship between operational parameters of X-Vine, and can serve as a stepping stone for a complete formal model to analyze X-Vine's security against Sybil identities.

Let there be N nodes in the system with node identifiers ranging from $0..N-1$. Let $L(0, w)$ be the expected lookup path length between the node with identifier 0 and w. Let us suppose that node maintain trails with a single successor. Without loss of generality, the average lookup path length can be computed as follows:

$$E(L) = \frac{\sum_{w=0}^{w=N-1} L(0, w)}{N} \tag{1}$$

In the simplest case, $L(0,0) = 0$. Let us first compute $L(0,1)$. Note that node 0 and node 1 have a *trail* between them because they are overlay neighbors. Let d be the average node degree in the underlying topology. We assume that the length of the trail between overlay neighbors is close to their shortest path in the social network topology (approximately $\log_d(N)$). The lookup will proceed from node 0 along the trail to node 1. Thus we have that:

$$L(0,1) = \text{Expected trail length} \tag{2a}$$
$$L(0,1) = \log_d(N) \tag{2b}$$

Notice that there cannot be any shortcutting in the intermediate nodes on the trail path from node 0 to node 1 because we have assumed the trail to be the shortest path in the social network topology. Let us now compute $L(0,2)$. There are two possible scenarios. In the first case, there may be a trail with an end point at node 2 *going through* node 0. In this case, the packet is routed along the trail to node 2. Again, there cannot be any shortcutting along this trail because it is the shortest path. The mean path length in this case is $\frac{\log_d N}{2}$. In the second case, the packet will be routed towards overlay node 1 (successor of node 0). Thus we have that:

$$L(0,2) = P(\text{trail}) \cdot \frac{\log_d N}{2} + (1 - P(\text{trail})) \cdot (1 + l((\log_d N) - 1, 1, 2)) \tag{3a}$$

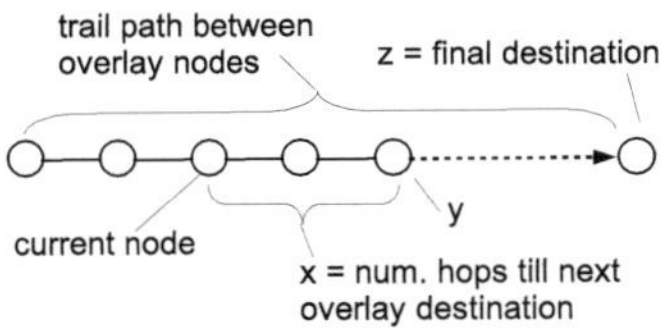

Figure 9. X-Vine lookup

where $l(x, y, z)$ is defined as the expected path length when z is the destination identifier, y is the next overlay hop in the lookup, and x is the physical distance along a trail between the current node and y (Figure 9). This means that $l((\log_d N) - 1, 1, 2)$ is the expected path length when the destination identifier is 2, the next overlay hop is 1, and the next overlay hop is $\log_d N$ hops away from the current node.

Note that each node maintains a trail to its successor, and the mean length of the trails is $\log_d(N)$. This means that the average routing state maintained by a node in the system is $\log_d(N)$. Since each routing table entry specifies two end points for a trail, the probability that a node has a trail with a particular end point going through it is $\frac{2\log_d N}{N}$. Thus:

$$L(0,2) = \frac{2\log_d N}{N} \cdot \frac{\log_d N}{2} + \left(1 - \frac{2\log_d N}{N}\right) \cdot (1 + l((log_d N) - 1, 1, 2)) \quad (3b)$$

We now need to compute $l(x, 1, 2)$. Similar to our computation of $L(0, 2)$, again, there are three possible scenarios. In the first case, the current node (say A) is a friend of node 2. Then the path length is 1. In the second case, there is a trail with an end point at node 2 going through node A. In this case, the mean path length is $\frac{\log_d(N)}{2}$. In the third case, the packet continues along the current trail to node 1.

$$l(x,1,2) = \frac{2\log_d N}{N} \cdot \left(\frac{\log_d N}{2}\right) + \left(1 - \frac{2\log_d N}{N}\right) \cdot (1 + l(x-1, 1, 2)) \quad (4)$$

Here, the boundary conditions for terminating the recursion are as follows:

$$l(x,1,1) = x \text{ if } 0 \le x \le \log_d N \quad (5a)$$

$$l(x,z,z) = x \text{ if } 0 \le x \le \log_d N, 1 \le z \le N-1 \quad (5b)$$

$$l(0,y,z) = L(y,z) = L(0,(z-y)) \text{ if } 1 \le y \le z \le N-1 \quad (5c)$$

Let us now compute $L(0, w)$. Consider the following two scenarios. In the first case, let the closest preceding node in node 0's routing table be node i (shortcut to $i \neq 1$). Now node i may either be a friend of node 0, in which case, the path length is $1 + L(i, w)$, or node i may be the end point of a trail going through node 0, in which case, the path length is $1 + l\left(\frac{\log_d N}{2} - 1, i, w\right)$. In the second case, there is no shortcutting, and the lookup proceeds towards the next overlay hop node 1. Thus, we have that:

$$L(0,w) = \sum_{i=2}^{w} P(\text{shortcut to i}) \cdot P(\text{shortcut via friend}) \cdot (1 + L(i,w)) + \sum_{i=2}^{w} P(\text{shortcut to i}) \cdot P(\text{shortcut via trail}) \cdot \left(1 + l\left(\frac{\log_d N}{2} - 1, i, w\right)\right) + P(\text{no shortcut}) \cdot (1 + l((\log_d N) - 1, 1, w)) \quad (6)$$

Let us now compute the probability of shortcutting to a node i. The probability of shortcutting to node w is simply $\frac{d + 2\log_d N}{N}$. The probability of shortcutting to node $w - 1$ can be computed as $P(\text{no shortcut to } w) \cdot P(\text{shortcut to } w - 1 | \text{ no shortcut to } w)$. This is equal to $\left(1 - \frac{d+2\log_d N}{N}\right) \cdot \frac{d+2\log_d N}{N-1}$. Similarly, we can compute the probability of shortcutting to node i as:

$$P(\text{shortcut to i}) = P(\text{no shortcut to w..i+1}) \cdot \frac{d + 2\log_d N}{N - (w - i)} \quad (7a)$$

$$P(\text{no shortcut to w..j}) = P(\text{no shortcut from w..j+1}) \cdot \left(1 - \frac{d + 2\log_d N}{N - (w - j)}\right) \quad (7b)$$

Now, given that the lookup shortcuts towards overlay hop node i, it may do so because of a friendship entry in the routing table, or a trail in the routing table. The probability that the shortcut happened via a friend entry, $P(\text{shortcut via friend}) = \frac{d}{d + 2\log_d(N)}$. The probability that the shortcut happened because of a X-Vine entry is $P(\text{shortcut via trail}) = \frac{2\log_d(N)}{d + 2\log_d(N)}$. Thus, we can rewrite equation (6) as

$$L(0,w) = \sum_{i=2}^{w} P(\text{shortcut to i}) \cdot \frac{d}{d + 2\log_d N} \cdot (1 + L(i,w)) + \sum_{i=2}^{w} P(\text{shortcut to i}) \cdot \frac{2\log_d N}{d + 2\log_d N} \cdot \left(1 + l\left(\frac{\log_d N}{2} - 1, i, w\right)\right) + P(\text{no shortcutting}) \cdot (1 + l((\log_d N) - 1, 1, w)) \quad (8)$$

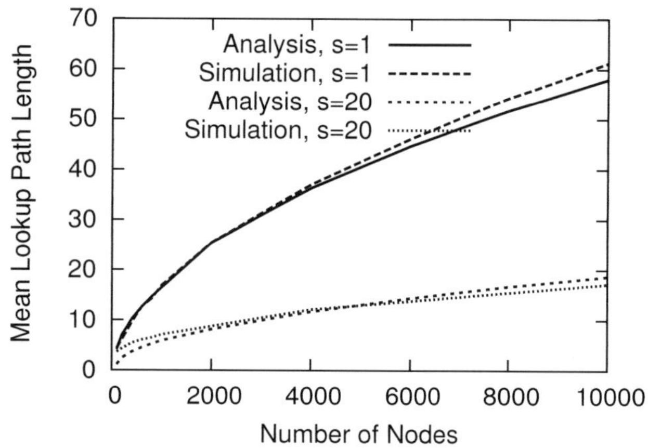

Figure 10. Validation of Analytic Model using $d = 10$

Similar to the above analysis, we can compute $l(x, i, w)$ as follows:

$$l(x,j,w) = \sum_{i=2}^{j+1} P(\text{shortcut to i}) \cdot \frac{d}{d+2\log_d N} \cdot (1+L(i,w))$$
$$+\sum_{i=2}^{j+1} P(\text{shortcut to i}) \cdot \frac{2\log_d N}{d+2\log_d(N)} \cdot \left(1+l\left(\frac{\log_d N}{2}-1,i,w\right)\right)$$
$$+ P(\text{no shortcutting}) \cdot (1+l(x-1,j,w)) \quad (9)$$

The boundary conditions for the termination of recursion are the same as in equation (5).

Validation of analytic model: Figure 10 plots the mean lookup path length as a function of number of nodes for a synthetic scale-free topology with average degree $d = 10$ using a redundancy parameter of $r = 1$. We can see that the results of simulation are a very close match with our analytic model, increasing confidence in our results. We note that our analytic model has implications for modeling network layer DHTs like VRR.

B Pseudocode

Algorithm 1 *Fwd_lookup(identifier myid, message M)*: Determines next hop for a lookup message.

```
bestroute=0
foreach element E in RoutingTable
  if distance(E.endpoint,M.dest)<
                    distance(bestroute,M.dest)
    bestroute=E
endfor
return bestroute
```

Algorithm 2 *Fwd_trailsetup(identifier myid, message M):* Determines next hop for trail path setup message.

```
bestroutes=∅
/* select all routes that make progress */
foreach element E in RoutingTable
  if distance(E.endpoint,M.dest)<distance(myid,M.dest)
    bestroutes.insert(E)
endfor
/* of these, discard (a) backtracked routes, (b) routes that
have reached bounds, (c) routes that don't make namespace
progress compared to M.nextovlhop*/
foreach element E in bestroutes
  if failed_set.contains(E.endpoint,E.nexthop) or
                (E.nexthop.numtrails > b_n) or
                (numtrailsto(E.nexthop) > b_l) or
                (distance(E.endpoint,M.dest) <
                   distance(M.nextovlhop,M.dest)
    bestroutes.remove(E)
endfor
/* if no remaining options, backtrack */
if bestroutes == ∅
  send_reject_to(M.prevhop)
  return
/* of remaining routes, select route with maximum
namespace progress */
routetouse=0
foreach element E in bestroutes
  if distance(E.endpoint,M.dest)<
                distance(routetouse,M.dest)
    routetouse=E
endfor
return routetouse
```

Towards Online Spam Filtering in Social Networks

Hongyu Gao
Northwestern University
Evanston, IL, USA
hygao@u.northwestern.edu

Yan Chen
Northwestern University
Evanston, IL, USA
ychen@northwestern.edu

Kathy Lee[†]
Northwestern University
Evanston, IL, USA
kml649@eecs.northwestern.edu

Diana Palsetia[†]
Northwestern University
Evanston, IL, USA
palsetia@u.northwestern.edu

Alok Choudhary[†]
Northwestern University
Evanston, IL, USA
choudhar@eecs.northwestern.edu

Abstract

Online social networks (OSNs) are extremely popular among Internet users. Unfortunately, in the wrong hands, they are also effective tools for executing spam campaigns. In this paper, we present an online spam filtering system that can be deployed as a component of the OSN platform to inspect messages generated by users in real-time. We propose to reconstruct spam messages into campaigns for classification rather than examine them individually. Although campaign identification has been used for offline spam analysis, we apply this technique to aid the online spam detection problem with sufficiently low overhead. Accordingly, our system adopts a set of novel features that effectively distinguish spam campaigns. It drops messages classified as "spam" before they reach the intended recipients, thus protecting them from various kinds of fraud. We evaluate the system using 187 million wall posts collected from Facebook and 17 million tweets collected from Twitter. In different parameter settings, the true positive rate reaches 80.9% while the false positive rate reaches 0.19% in the best case. In addition, it stays accurate for more than 9 months after the initial training phase. Once deployed, it can constantly secure the OSNs without the need for frequent re-training. Finally, tested on a server machine with eight cores (Xeon E5520 2.2Ghz) and 16GB memory, the system achieves an average throughput of 1580 messages/sec and an average processing latency of 21.5ms on the Facebook dataset.

1 Introduction

Online social networks (OSNs) are extremely popular collaboration and communication tools that have attracted millions of Internet users. Unfortunately, recent evidence shows that they can also be effective mechanisms for spreading attacks. Popular OSNs are increasingly becoming the target of phishing attacks launched from large botnets [1, 3]. Two recent studies [9, 10] have confirmed the existence of large-scale spam campaigns in Twitter and Facebook, respectively. Furthermore, the clickthrough rate of OSN spam is orders of magnitude higher than its email counterpart [10], indicating that users are more prone to trust spam messages from their friends in OSNs.

The OSN spam problem has already received attention from researchers. Meanwhile, email spam, a seemingly very similar problem, has been extensively studied for years. Unfortunately, the bulk of the existing solutions are not directly applicable, because of a series of distinct characteristics pertaining to the OSN spam. *i*) In any OSN, all messages, including spam, originate from accounts registered at the same site. In contrast, email spam is *not* necessarily sent from accounts registered at legitimate service providers. The widely used email server reputation based detection approaches [11, 19, 22] rely on the assumption that the spamming SMTP servers run on bot machines, and are thus inapplicable in OSNs. Realizing that this assumption is not always true , researchers have proposed to identify accounts signed up by spammers from legitimate email service providers [34]. *ii*) Spamming account identification is also the focus of the existing OSN spam detection work [14, 26, 31, 32]. However, the second characteristic of OSN spam is that the majority of spam messages come from compromised accounts [9, 10], rather than accounts created and exclusively controlled by spammers. It essentially means that spammers and legitimate users are sharing accounts. Thus, identifying spamming accounts is not sufficient to fight OSN spam. *iii*) Messages in OSNs, spam or not, are generally short. The perception that legitimate emails have variable size while spam tends to be small no longer holds in OSNs. The third characteristic, along with the previous two, obsoletes many features that used to work well in supervised machine learning based detection approaches, which we briefly discuss in Section 3.

It is worth noting that offline OSN analysis works successfully reveal OSN spam messages [9, 10], but they are not designed as online detection tools, since they either have long lag-time or limited efficiency. We offer more detailed comparison in Section 7. Meanwhile, message content based detection approaches, such as the recently proposed campaign template inference [18], are expected to perform equally well if applied to OSNs. However, they implicitly require that *all* campaigns must be present in the labeled training set in order for good detection coverage. This requirement itself is hard to satisfy, not to mention the difficulty of fighting campaigns that emerge in the future. In addition, approaches based on malicious URL detection are also applicable [27]. Nonetheless, URL obfuscation techniques (*e.g.* , using "nevasubevu\t. blogs pot\t.\tco\tm (take out spaces)" instead of "nevasubevu.blogspot.com") make it difficult for any automated tool to recognize the embedded URLs in the first place.

In this paper, we present an online spam filtering system specifically designed for OSNs and can be deployed as a component of the OSN platform. After the initial training phase, it efficiently inspects the stream of user generated messages, immediately dropping those classified as spam before they reach the intended recipients. The system owns four desirable properties as an online filtering tool, which are: i) high accuracy, ii) no need for all campaigns to be present in the training set, iii) no need for frequent re-training , and iv) low latency.

The key insight is that we always seek to uncover the connection among all the messages by performing clustering on them, instead of directly inspecting each individual message without correlating it with others. The correlated spam messages form spam campaigns. Although the clustering approach has been used for offline spam analysis [4, 35], it is never used for online spam filtering due to its computational overhead. We leverage incremental clustering and parallelization to address this challenge. When a new message is generated, the system organizes it, along with all the previously observed messages, into clusters. The new message is then classified according to whether or not the cluster it resides in is a spam cluster, which is determined by all the messages in the same cluster collectively.

Accordingly, the classifier is trained on a set of features associated with message clusters instead of individual messages. We identified six such distinguishing features. They all stem from the spammers' need to push spam messages to as many recipients as possible. Meanwhile, these features grasp the *commonality* among spam campaigns, *e.g.* , they generate spam messages fast while lasting, rather than the speciality of any individual campaign, *e.g.* , word distribution or underlying templates. Hence, spam campaigns can still be detected even if they do not have any instance included in the training set. In addition, the features pertaining to campaigns cannot be easily maneuvered. For example, if the spammer slows down the speed of spam message generation, he has to pay the price of the reduced ability to affect potential victims. As a result, these features are persistent over time. After the initial training, the system can work online for a long period of time without the need for re-training. For the same reason, it is also harder for the spammers to craft their sending pattern to evade detection. We evaluate the system using 187 million wall posts collected from Facebook and 17 million tweets collected from Twitter. Experimental results show that the system yields 80.9% true positive rate and 0.19% false positive rate in the best parameter settings. It stays accurate for more than 9 months after the initial training phase, and achieves an average throughput of 1580 messages/sec and an average processing latency of 21.5ms on the Facebook dataset.

In summary, we frame our contributions as:

- We propose to use spam campaigns, instead of individual spam messages, as the objects for spam classification.
- We solve the challenge of reconstructing campaigns in real-time by adopting incremental clustering and parallelization.
- We identify six features that distinguish spam campaigns from legitimate message clusters in OSNs.
- We develop and evaluate an accurate and efficient system that can be easily deployed at the OSN server side to provide online spam filtering.

The rest of the paper is organized as follows. We first provide necessary background information and clarify what will be achieved in Section 2. After that, we present the six features to distinguish spam clusters in Section 3, illustrate the detailed system design in Section 4, and thoroughly evaluate its performance in Section 5. Next, we discuss possible attempts to evade the system in Section 6 and the related work in Section 7. Finally, we conclude the paper in Section 8.

2 Background and Goal

In this section, we provide necessary background information and how our system can be incorporated into the current OSN architecture. We also describe the dataset used in this study.

2.1 Background

All current OSNs adopt the client-server architecture. The OSN service provider acts as the controlling entity. It stores and manages all the content in the system. On the other hand, the content is generated by users spontaneously from the client side. The OSN service provider offers a rich set of well-defined interfaces through which the users can interact with others. Currently two popular ways of interaction exist. Facebook is representative of OSNs that adopt the interaction between a pair of sender and recipient as their primary way of interaction, although they also support other ways. Twitter is representative of OSNs that adopt broadcasting as their primary way of interaction.

Figure 1(a) illustrates a simplified OSN architecture. It only depicts the components that are related to message exchanging, while all other functionalities, *e.g.* , user authentication, video sharing and 3rd party applications, are omitted. In this simplified example, multiple users are interacting via the message posting and viewing interface. In Facebook-like OSNs, it represents the case that user A and B are posting messages to user C and D, respectively. In Twitter-like OSNs, it represents the case that user A and B are broadcasting messages to all the followers including user C and D, respectively, while other possible recipients are omitted for simplicity. In both cases, the service provider mediates all the interactions. The generated messages are first stored at the service provider's side, and will be relayed when the corresponding recipient signs in.

Unfortunately, all the content in OSNs is generated by users and is not necessarily legitimate. The posted messages could be spam. Note that although spam traditionally refers to massive, unsolicited campaigns trying to promote products or services, we do not restrict ourselves to this behavior alone. Rather, we use the term "spam" to refer to unsolicited campaigns that attempt to execute a variety of attacks, including but not restricted to: i) product advertisements, ii) phishing and iii) malware spreading. In the example of Figure 1(a), user A's account is compromised and sends a spam message to user C, trying to direct user C to some malicious website. Once user C signs in, the spam message will be displayed to him, exposing him to potential threats.

2.2 Goal

Our goal is to design an online spam filtering system that is deployed at the OSN service provider side, as Figure 1(b) shows. Once deployed, it inspects every message before rendering the message to the intended recipients and makes immediate decision on whether or not the message under inspection should be dropped. In this particular example, the message generated by user A is classified as spam and is thus dropped instantly. The message from user B is legitimate and is stored by the service provider. Later when user C and D sign in to the system, C will not see the dropped spam message.

We assume the spam message originates from a compromised account in the above example. We stress that this is *not* an assumption that our system relies on. Rather, our system can detect spam messages originating from both compromised accounts and spamming bots.

2.3 Dataset

Facebook and Twitter are two representative OSNs. We use data collected from both sites in the study. The Facebook dataset contains 187 million wall posts generated by roughly 3.5 million users in total, between January of 2008 and June of 2009 [29]. For the Twitter data collection, we first download trending topics, *i.e.* , popular topics, from the website *What the Trend* [2], which provides a regularly updated list of trending topics. We then download from Twitter all public tweets that contain the trending topics while the topics are still popular via Twitter APIs. For example, while the topic "MLB" is trending, we keep downloading all tweets that contain the word "MLB" from Twitter. For each tweet we also obtain the userID that generates it along with its friend number, *i.e.* , the number of users it follows. the Twitter dataset contains over 17 million tweets related to trending topics that were generated between June 1, 2011 and July 21, 2011. The primary form of communication in Facebook and Twitter is called "wall post" and "tweet", respectively. From now on, we use the term "message" to refer to both of them for the ease of description.

We need labeled spam and legitimate messages to train and evaluate the system. For the Facebook dataset, we use the result of one previous study [9], where 199,782 wall posts are confirmed as spam. We further scan through the entire dataset looking for additional wall posts that share either identical textual description or URL with the confirmed spam wall posts. We label the newly found wall posts as spam, too. At last we have 217,802 wall posts labeled as spam. For the Twitter dataset, we visit all the embedded links. In Twitter, all the embedded links sit behind a URL shortening service. We label a URL as malicious if the URL shortening service stops serving the URL due to a policy violation. All Tweets containing the malicious URLs are labeled as spam. In total 467,390 tweets are labeled as spam. Note that in general, we lack comprehensive ground truth. Although all the messages labeled as spam are truly spam, some spam might be missed and labeled as legitimate message. Thus, we may somewhat underestimate false negative rate (spam that the system fails to report) during the evaluation, and overestimate false positive rate (legitimate messages misclassified as spam).

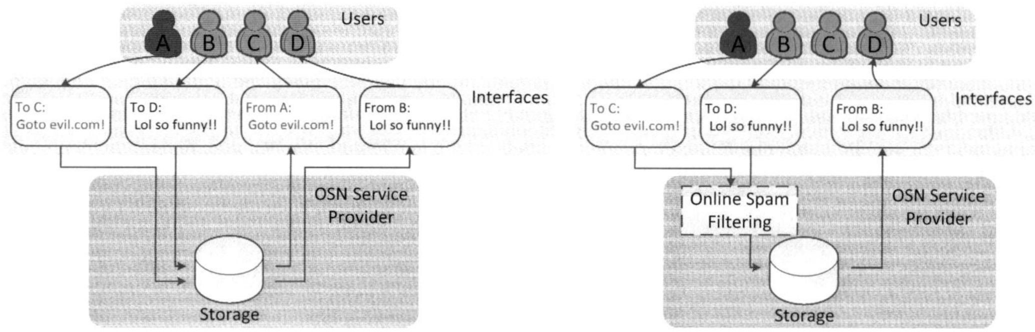

(a) The scenario without the deployment of our system. (b) The scenario with the deployment of our system.

Figure 1: A simplified OSN architecture, only illustrating the components related to the message exchanging functionality. User A represents the account controlled by spammers.

3 Features

We first briefly review some features used in existing spam detection work but are not suitable for the OSN environment. After that, we investigate various features that can potentially differentiate between spam and legitimate clusters. Note that *not* all features have never been used before. For each feature, we conduct experiment with the labeled Facebook dataset to show their effectiveness. In this section, we cluster the spam and legitimate messages separately to obtain the "pure" clusters, using the approach that is given out in Section 4, which provides the system design detail.

We organize the features into two categories. *OSN specific features* are those that need social network information to compute. *General features* are those that could also be used to detect spam outside OSNs. No single feature is perfectly discriminative between spam and legitimate clusters. Each single feature is likely to fail in some scenario. Instead, these features are used in combination to train the best classifier.

3.1 Obsolete Features

Supervised machine learning has been a popular tool for spam detection. Numerous features have been proposed and work particularly well. However, OSN is a different context where the features' effectiveness needs a reevaluation. Note that we do not review *all* the previously proposed features. Instead, we cover the features used in two state-of-the-art works that detect spam in email [11] and forum [23], believing those features are the most advanced ones. Next, we present the ones found to be problematic.

Message size is a popularly used feature, because legitimate emails have variable sizes while spams tend to be small. We measure the size of the spam and legitimate messages in our dataset, and present the distribution in Figure 2. Apparently both types of messages in OSNs are small. Their distribution heavily overlaps in the area of less than 200 bytes. Consequently, for the majority of messages the size is not a distinguishing feature. Two similar features are the number of words and the average word length in each message. We present their distribution in Figure 3 and Figure 4, respectively. The observation is consistent with the message size feature. Neither of them would remain effective in OSNs.

A series of network based features, which are sender IP neighborhood density, sender AS number and status of sender's service ports, have also been proposed. Although we cannot measure them straightforwardly due to the lack of such information in our dataset, we still find it problematic to use them to detect OSN spam, because the underlying assumption is violated. The assumption is that spam emails are sent out using SMTP servers running on large number of infected ordinary end hosts, whereas legitimate emails originate from a set of dedicated SMTP servers. As a result, the spam senders' IP neighborhood will be crowded due to the botnet infection, but the IP addresses of legitimate SMTP servers are far apart. Also because of the infection pattern of botnet, spamming hosts tend to aggregate into a small number of ASes, which makes sender AS number a promising feature. At last, the spamming bots may not listen to other service ports, but legitimate SMTP servers will do so. Unfortunately, in OSNs both spam and legitimate messages are sent from ordinary end hosts. Given the large number of OSN users, the sender's IP neighborhood is expected to be dense for both spam and legitimate messages. In addition, there would be no difference in the status of sender's service ports for the two cases. At last, spam senders may still be aggregated into a small number of ASes. However, legitimate message senders will be mixed

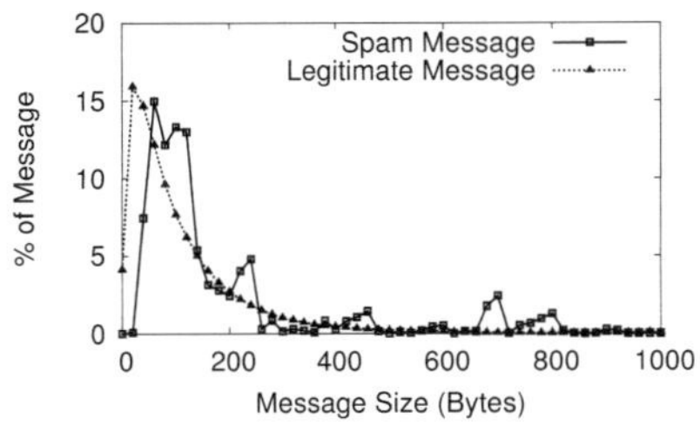

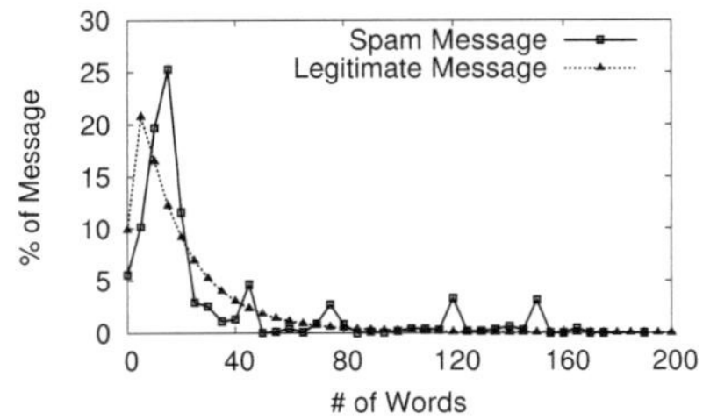

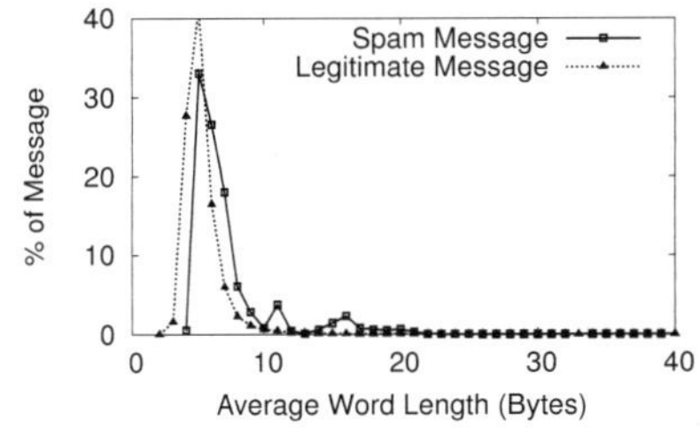

Figure 2: Distribution of spam and legitimate message size, respectively. Each bin is 20 bytes.

Figure 3: Distribution of spam and legitimate message word count, respectively. Each bin is 5 words.

Figure 4: Distribution of average word length of spam and legitimate messages, respectively. Each bin is 1 byte.

into the same ASes and the effectiveness of sender AS number as a feature would be seriously degraded.

3.2 OSN Specific Features

OSN users form a huge social graph, where each node represents an individual user. In Facebook-like OSNs, a social link would connect two nodes if the two corresponding users have mutually agreed to establish a social connection. Two users without a social link between them cannot directly interact with each other. Twitter-like OSNs impose looser restrictions, where a user can "follow" anyone to establish a directed social link, so that he can receive all the updates. Similarly, the interaction history among users forms an interaction graph.

Sender Social Degree Recent studies suggest that the majority of spamming accounts in OSNs are compromised accounts [9, 10]. Meanwhile, research on modeling epidemics in topological networks indicates that the more edges a node has, with a higher probability it will be infected quickly by an epidemic [6, 36]. On the other hand, the accounts created by spammers also have an incentive to make large number of friends to open up communication channels. Consequently, we hypothesize that spamming accounts have higher degree in the social graph than legitimate accounts. In Twitter-like OSNs, we define the social degree of one node as the number of other nodes it "follows", since this number is controlled by the account itself. In Facebook-like OSNs, there is no ambiguity as edges are not directed.

Figure 5 shows that our intuition is roughly correct. The average social degree of spamming accounts is 59.2. It is about 50% higher than that of legitimate accounts, which is 40.8. Given such an observation, it is tempting to use the message sender's social degree as one feature. Unfortunately, the compromised spamming account will send a mixture of spam and legitimate messages. Hence in many cases spam and legitimate messages share the same sender and will naturally have exactly the same value of the sender's social degree. However, after being organized into

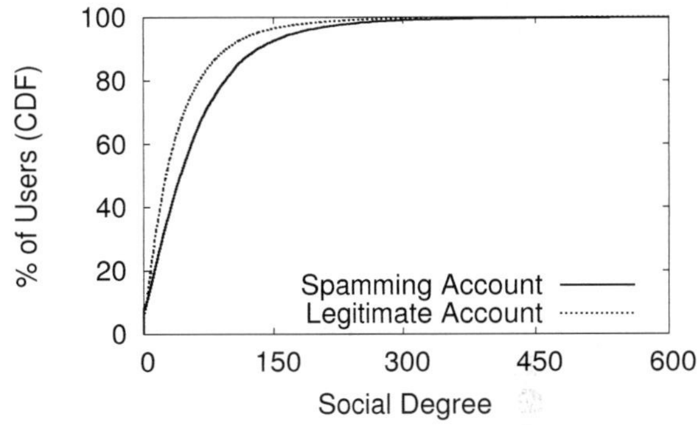

Figure 5: Cumulative distribution of the social degree of spamming and legitimate accounts, respectively.

clusters, the average senders' social degree of the clusters becomes an effective feature. The main reason is that *all* senders in spam clusters are spamming accounts, while this is very unlikely to be true for legitimate clusters. As a result, spam clusters are expected to exhibit higher average senders' social degree. Figure 6 confirms this expectation. It does not depict the clusters whose senders' social degree is not available in the dataset. Despite some overlapping in the lower left region, the solid curve representing spam clusters is to the right of the dashed curve representing legitimate clusters. About 80% of legitimate clusters have an average senders' social degree of less than 400. In contrast, this value is larger than 400 for about 50% of spam clusters.

Interaction History Although one account may establish a large number of social links in the social graph, it only interacts with a small subset of its friends [29]. However, its behavior is expected to deviate from this pattern once the account is compromised and under the control of spammers, since the spammers desire to push spam messages to as many recipients as possible. Consequently, a sudden burst that the accounts start to interact with the friends that they do not, or rarely, interact with before becomes a strong signal indicating spamming activities. Note that this intuition

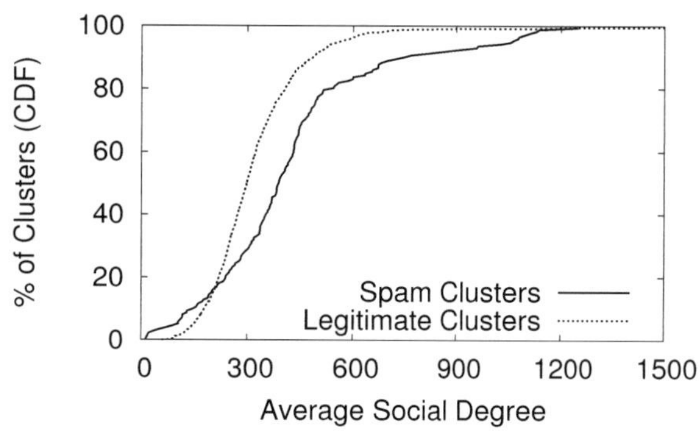

Figure 6: Cumulative distribution of average senders' social degree of spam and legitimate clusters, respectively.

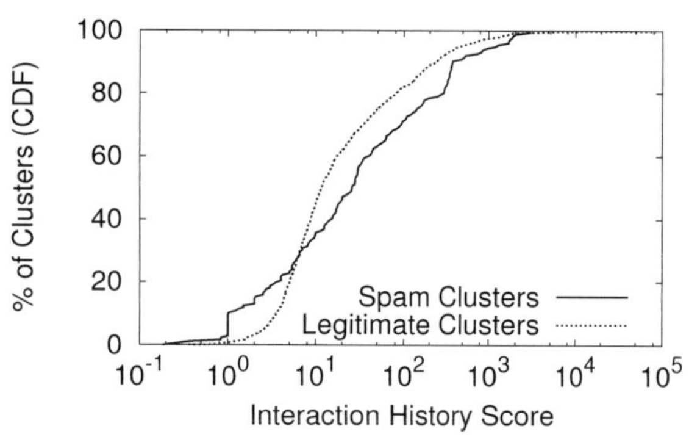

Figure 7: Cumulative distribution of interaction history score of spam and legitimate clusters, respectively.

applies specifically to Facebook-like OSNs, since messages are always broadcast to all followers in Twitter-like OSNs.

We use the notion of "interaction history score" to quantify this intuition. The k_{th} interaction between a user pair is weighted $1/k$, so that messages sent between user pairs that rarely interact are given heavier weight values. As k increases, the message weight between frequently interacting user pairs decreases. We define the interaction history score of a cluster as the sum of the message weight within the cluster. Naturally, the spam clusters are expected to have higher score because larger number of less frequently interacting user pairs is contained. Figure 7 plots the CDFs of this score for spam and legitimate clusters, respectively. For the 20% clusters with the lowest scores, the expectation is not always true. However, spam clusters indeed exhibit higher score for the rest of the cases. Note that the x-axis is in log scale. The score of spam clusters is usually several times higher.

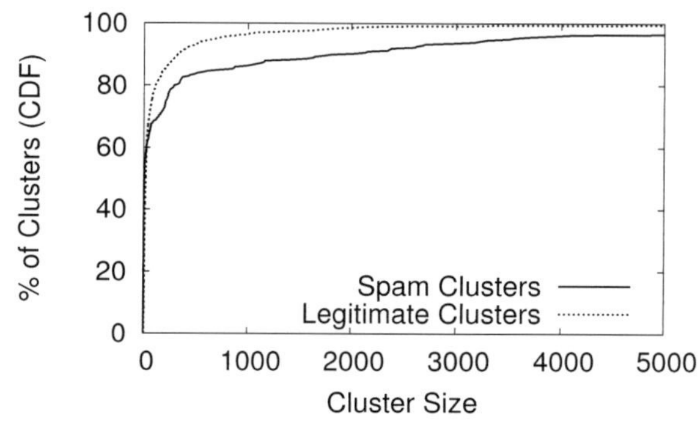

Figure 8: Cumulative distribution of spam and legitimate cluster size, respectively.

3.3 General Features

We find four additional features effective to discriminate between spam and legitimate clusters. These features do not need the social graph or the interaction graph to compute, and could also apply to spam detection problems outside OSNs. They are denoted as the general features.

Cluster Size Although each spamming account might not generate large number of spam messages, the spam campaign as a whole must contain large number of spam messages in order to be prosperous. Figure 8 plots the CDFs of the size, measured as the number of message contained, for spam and legitimate clusters, respectively. We observe that about 50% of spam clusters' size is less than 10, which causes the overlapping part of the two curves. On the other hand, large spam clusters exhibit a big difference in size comparing with legitimate clusters. The overlapping of size of small clusters does not make this feature invalid. The reason is that small spam clusters only have minor impact on the system's detection performance. Instead, the big clusters are those that matter. As an extreme example, it is still acceptable even if the system correctly identifies 10% of spam clusters of size 1,000 while missing the remaining 90% of spam clusters of size 10.

Average Time Interval Known as the "bursty" property, most spam campaigns involve coordinated action by many accounts within short periods of time [30]. The effect is that messages from the same campaign are densely populated in the time period when the campaign is active. Consequently, if we compute the intervals between the generation time of consecutive messages in each cluster, the spam clusters are expected have shorter intervals than the legitimate clusters. From a statistical prospective, the median interval would nicely quantify the "bursty" property, and is robust to outlier values. However, it is expensive to maintain during runtime, as the complete list of intervals must be recorded and

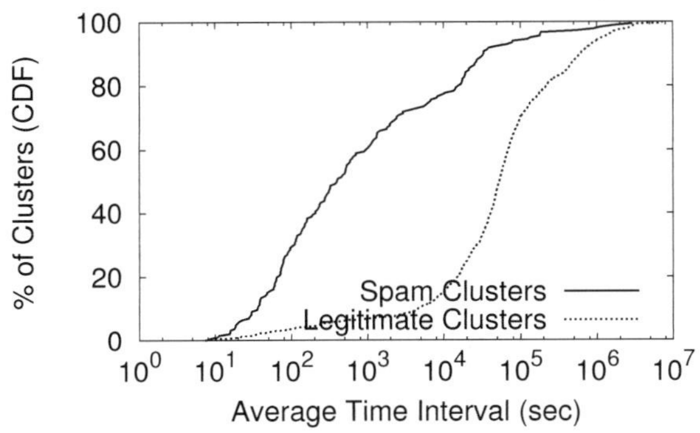

Figure 9: Cumulative distribution of average time interval of spam and legitimate clusters, respectively.

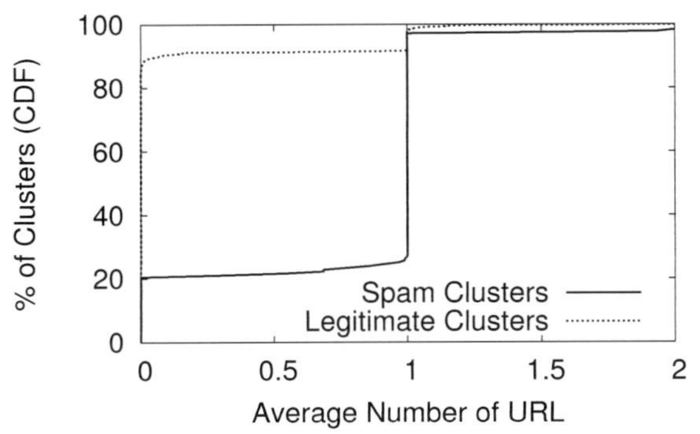

Figure 10: Cumulative distribution of average number of URLs per message of spam and legitimate clusters, respectively.

sorted. Alternatively, we quantify this property using the average time interval, which is much more "lightweight", since only the starting time, ending time and the total number of messages in the cluster are needed to calculate its value. Figure 9 plots the CDFs of average time interval of spam and legitimate clusters, respectively. The x axis is in log scale so that the figure is readable. It shows that the average time interval of legitimate clusters is orders of magnitude larger than that of spam clusters.

Average URL Number per Message Spammers always solicit some action from the recipients, *e.g.* , to click a link, in order for economic benefit ultimately. As the most commonly adopted practice, spam messages are embedded with URLs that the spammers want to advertise. In contrast, legitimate messages do not contain URLs in most of the case. Hence, we use the average number of URLs per message in each cluster as one feature. Figure 10 plots the CDFs of this feature for spam and legitimate clusters, respectively. It shows that more than 80% of benign clusters do not contain any URL. Only about 2% benign clusters contain more than

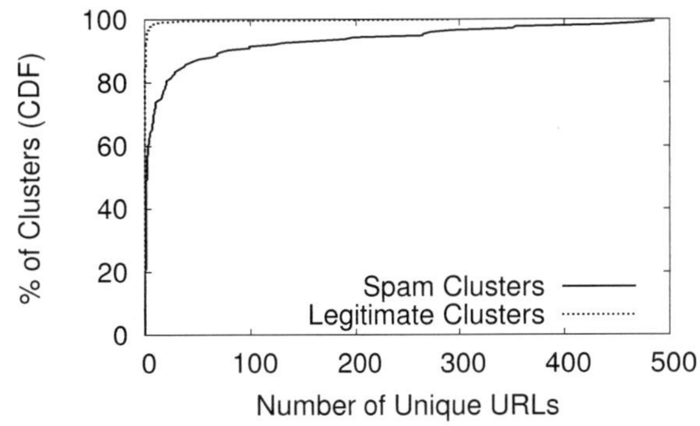

Figure 11: Cumulative distribution of number of unique URLs contained in spam and legitimate clusters, respectively.

one URL in each message on average. In comparison, about 80% of malicious clusters contain at least one URL in each message on average.

Unique URL Number URL blacklist has been extensively used nowadays. As an attempt to evade blacklist based detection, spammers have evolved to embed different URLs in messages from the same campaign, with each URL being used less frequently, so that some, if not all, of the spam URLs will not be blacklisted. This type of spam campaigns will inevitably contain large number of unique URLs. On the other hand, legitimate clusters are not likely to exhibit the same behavior. Figure 11 plots the CDFs of the number of unique URLs contained in spam and legitimate clusters, respectively. The curve representing legitimate clusters embraces the y axis, which is consistent with the fact that many legitimate messages do not contain URL. On the contrary, about a half of the spam clusters have multiple URLs. The most diverse cluster uses 486 different URLs.

4 System Design

In this section, we present the detailed design of the online spam filtering system. Section 4.1 first introduces the system overview. After that, Section 4.2 and Section 4.3 present the incremental clustering module and the supervised machine learning module, respectively. Finally, Section 4.4 illustrates an extension on the basic design that exploits parallelism to boost the system throughput.

4.1 Overview

Figure 12 shows the system design overview. The intuition is that spam campaigns are generated using templates and that messages in the same campaign shall retain certain similarity among them. After a clustering process, spam

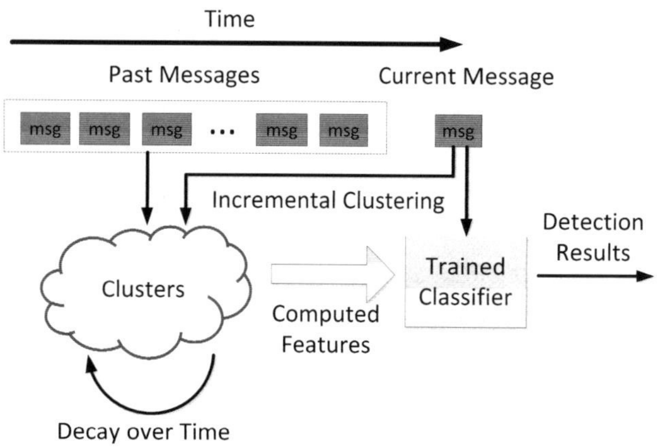

Figure 12: The system design overview.

messages in the same campaign will reside in the same cluster or only a small number of clusters. Note that we do not depend on the system to agglomerate an entire campaign into one single cluster, which is impractical due to the variation brought by the spam template. However, because the total number of messages in a spam campaign is very large, each spam cluster will still contain significant number of messages. In addition, the clusters formed by the spam messages will exhibit different characteristics comparing to the legitimate clusters as Section 3 shows. Hence, they can be differentiated using supervised machine learning.

Accordingly, the two major components in the system are the *incremental clustering module* and the *supervised machine learning module*. The first module maintains a collection of disjoint clusters such that each message that has been processed in the past is present. The second module is essentially a trained classifier that makes binary decisions. When the system receives a new message, it first incrementally updates the clustering result with minimal computational overhead. The new message may form a new cluster by itself, be incorporated into one existing cluster or even trigger the merge of multiple existing clusters. In the first case, the system directly marks the message as "legitimate" without invoking the classifier, because the average time interval feature cannot be calculated with only 1 message. This implicit limitation will cause a false negative only when the new message is the first one in a spam cluster, which happens very rarely. In any other case, the values of the six features of the cluster that the new message resides in are (re-)calculated. The other clusters are intact. After that, the trained classifier accepts these values and decides whether these values represent a spam cluster. Note that if the classifier outputs "spam", it will only trigger a spam alarm on the current message, rather than all the messages in the cluster. Since it is an online system, the decision on the previous messages in the same cluster has already been made and is not changed.

A practical concern is that the hardware resource is always limited. It is not affordable to keep track of all the messages observed in the past. In addition, recent messages should be given heavier weight that influences the clusters' feature values. To address these two concerns, the clusters that the system maintains decays exponentially over time. More specifically, once after the system has processed w messages, it shrinks the six feature values associated with each cluster by a factor of a, where w and a are two important system parameters to determine the decaying speed. If a cluster's size is shrunk to a value below a threshold t, it is permanently removed and all the resources it takes up are freed.

4.2 Incremental Clustering

The ability to do incremental clustering is the key to the system. The first design choice we must make is to define the distance between two messages. Naturally, using semantic similarity will result in more accurate clustering result as messages in the same campaign are more likely to have small distance. However, semantic analysis involves heavier computational overhead that is not acceptable for a real-time system. Alternatively, we choose text shingling [7] as the basic tool to calculate the distance between messages. Text shingling is initially proposed to analyze web page similarity in huge volume and is sufficiently lightweight. In the shingling process, the original message is disassembled into fixed-length substrings, each of which is called a "shingle". We sort the hashed shingle and use the first 20 of them to represent each message. For the messages with less than 20 shingles, the system does not cluster them and directly marks them as legitimate if they do not contain any URL, since they are too short to carry out attacks. The similarity between a message pair is estimated by its *resemblance* score, defined as the ratio of shared shingles to all unique shingles. Two messages are deemed as "similar" if their resemblance score surpasses a predefined threshold.

We augment the original text shingling with URL comparison as an adaptation to the specific application of spam detection. URLs embedded in the spam messages represent the spammers' goal. Hence two spam messages sharing the same embedded URL shall come from the same campaign, although their textual description might be quite different judged by text shingling due to the usage of templates. To sum up, two messages are considered as "similar" if their resemblance score is sufficiently large *or* their embedded URLs are identical. They will reside in the same cluster if either condition is satisfied. A similar method was also used by Zhuang *et al.* [35] to analyze email spam traces offline.

We use a hash table to store the text shingling result, indexed by the shingles. It keeps track of all the messages that contain the corresponding shingle. Meanwhile, we use another hash table to store the result of URL comparison. It is indexed by the URLs and each element is a list of messages that contain the corresponding URL. When a new message arrives, it is disassembled into shingles and all the previously observed messages with identical shingles can be conveniently identified. The same holds for the URL comparison. In this way, the system does not need to compare the new message with all observed messages sequentially. Instead, it directly looks up the hash tables at the location of matching shingles and URLs, thus minimizing the overhead.

For the purpose of incremental clustering, our system maintains a set of disjoint clusters. Upon the arrival of a new message, it first creates a cluster containing a single element, the new message itself. Next, all clusters that contain a message that is "similar" to the new message must be found and merged with the new cluster, while the other clusters stay intact. We build a Union-Find data structure to accommodate this need. A Union-Find data structure supports three operations very efficiently, which are $i)$ creating a new set, $ii)$ finding the set containing a given element and $iii)$ merging two sets. In addition, the system needs to eliminate clusters from time to time because of the exponential decaying. This operation is not supported by the standard Union-Find data structure. As a result, we enhance it to provide the functionality to return all the elements of a given cluster.

4.3 Supervised Machine Learning

While clustering provides a division of the observed messages, our system needs to make decision on each incoming message that flags it as either a spam or a legitimate message. The supervised machine learning module is essentially a trained classifier that makes this binary decision.

Two classifier candidates, support vector machine (SVM) [8] and decision tree [21], are widely used in the literature. Decision tree has the advantage that the trained classifier is simple to understand and fast. The time complexity to make a prediction on a new test point is $O(log(N))$, where N is the number of nodes in the trained tree. Such efficiency is a desirable property for an online system. On the other hand, SVM is reported to achieve good accuracy on a wide variety of problems such as handwriting recognition, face detection, text categorization, *etc.* However, the classification process of new data points gets slower if the training set is large. We test both classifiers on our dataset and decision tree yields better accuracy, *i.e.* , higher true positive rate and lower false positive rate. Consequently, we pick decision tree as the classifying module in the system.

4.4 Parallelization

Our system needs to achieve high throughput as an online spam filtering tool. The basic design shown in Figure 12 spends the majority of running time on incremental clustering. Consequently, accelerating the clustering process can greatly enhance the throughput.

Parallelization is a natural choice to achieve such a goal, but it seems to be counterintuitive in our specific case at the first glance, since incremental clustering is a sequential process, in the sense that the clustering process of the $n + 1_{th}$ message is based on the clustering result of the first n_{th} messages. Our solution is to compute the incremental clustering result for the next k messages, instead of the next one message, simultaneously. For each one of the next k messages, we compare its similarity to the observed messages and decide which existing clusters it should be merged into. The computation for one message is independent from others. Accordingly, k threads are executed at the same time with each thread handling one message. Note that only the message similarity comparison is parallelized. All other operations, such as cluster merging, remain sequential to avoid conflict among threads.

The parallel design might slightly alter the clustering result comparing to the sequential case, but it will not noticeably affect the detection result. Without loss of generality, we analyze the potential alteration under the scenario of two threads, t_1 and t_2, processing two messages, m_1 and m_2, in parallel. The only situation when the clustering result differs must satisfy two conditions: $i)$ m_1 and m_2 are similar, $ii)$ there does *not* exist a previously observed message m_0, such that m_0 is similar to both m_1 and m_2. In this situation, a sequential execution will cluster m_1 and m_2 together immediately, but a parallel execution will not do so. The reason is that t_1 is unaware of m_2 and cannot find any previously observed message that is similar to m_1. Hence m_1 is left in a separate cluster containing only itself. The same applies to m_2. However, their corresponding clusters will be merged once a third message, m_3, which is similar to both m_1 and m_2, has been processed. In the context of spam message detection, the above scenario maps to the case that the first two spam messages from the same campaign are handled by the system in parallel. Given the limited number of spam campaigns, this scenario shall happen very rarely. For legitimate messages, such inconsistency in the clustering process will not affect the detection result at all since any clusters with size of 1 will be assumed to be legitimate.

5 Experiment

5.1 Methodology

We evaluate the system on a server machine that has eight cores (Xeon E5520 2.2Ghz) with Hyper-Threading and 16GB memory. We sort all the messages according to their timestamps and divide them into the training set and the testing set. The training set includes the first 25% of spam messages and all the legitimate messages in the same time period. The testing set contains the remaining messages.

The system has multiple tunable parameters (Section 4.1). W and a control the speed of cluster decay. The choice of their value is mainly constrained by the hardware resource, as lower decaying speed results in more resource consumption and slower processing speed. We pick 100,000 and 0.2 as the value of w and a in the experiments, respectively, according to our hardware resource limit. We also tested faster decaying speed by setting a as 0.5, but only found very slight change in the detection result. We pick 3 as the value of t, the size threshold to eliminate a cluster, since a small value reduces the risk of removing a live spam cluster from the system.

In the training phase, we first feed the incremental clustering module with the training set, and record the feature values for all spam and legitimate clusters. We use all 6 features for the Facebook dataset. We use the 5 features other than interaction history score for the Twitter dataset, since interaction history score is not applicable for the broadcast interaction in Twitter. Next, We use the extracted feature values to train the classifier. We only use the clusters whose size is at least 5 for training. After that, the system is fed with the testing set. We conduct all the experiments obeying the time order, so that the experimental results can resemble the system performance in real-world deployment accurately.

5.2 Clustering Resemblance Threshold

The detection is based on the clustering of spam messages. Hence, the resemblance threshold used in the clustering process could potentially affect the detection result. Recall that the resemblance of a message pair is the ratio of shared shingles to the total number of distinct shingles, which represents the "similarity" between the message pair. In order to understand how to pick the best threshold, we study the resemblance value among spam and legitimate message pairs, respectively.

We first divide the Facebook dataset into the spam set and the legitimate message set. The division is trivial using the label of each message. After that, we compute the resemblance value of all the spam message pairs and the legitimate message pairs, respectively, by repeating the clustering process. Figure 13 shows the cumulative distribution of such value. The curve for legitimate message pairs embraces the y axis. For both types of message pairs, most of them have a very small resemblance value, meaning that they are almost totally dissimilar. This is expected because legitimate messages are spontaneously generated and are different to others naturally. For spam messages, many campaigns exist in our dataset and the message pairs across different campaigns are also very different. However, the curve for spam message pairs exhibits a sudden rise at the right most part, showing that some message pairs are very similar, which are those belonging to the same spam campaigns. The legitimate message pairs do not exhibit such a pattern due to the spontaneous nature. Despite this difference, it is apparent that both curves are flat in the middle. It suggests that comparably very few message pairs have the resemblance value falling in the middle area. Consequently, the system is insensitive to the threshold value as long as the value is not too small or too large, since varying the threshold would not significantly affect the clustering result. At last we pick 0.5 as the threshold used in all the experiments.

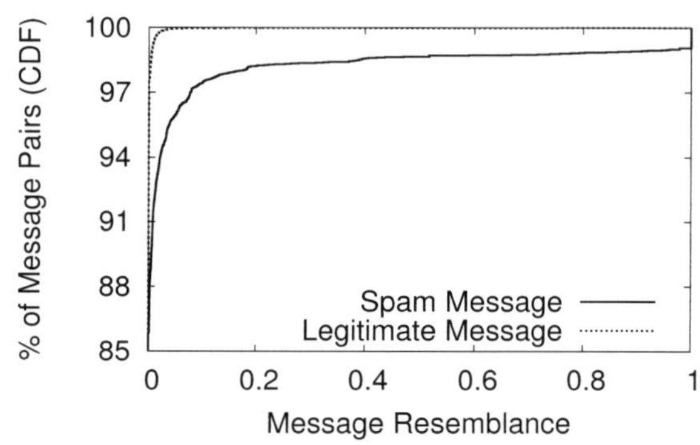

Figure 13: The distribution of resemblance value among spam and legitimate message pairs in the Facebook dataset, respectively.

5.3 Accuracy

The accuracy of a detection system is characterized by two metrics, *true positive rate* (TPR) and *false positive rate* (FPR). True positive rate shows the detection completeness. It is defined as the number of instances correctly classified as spam divided by the total number of spam instances. False positive rate reflects the detection error on the legitimate messages. It is defined as the number of instances incorrectly classified as spam divided by the total number of legitimate instances. In this section we evaluate the overall accuracy (Section 5.3.1), the accuracy of different fea-

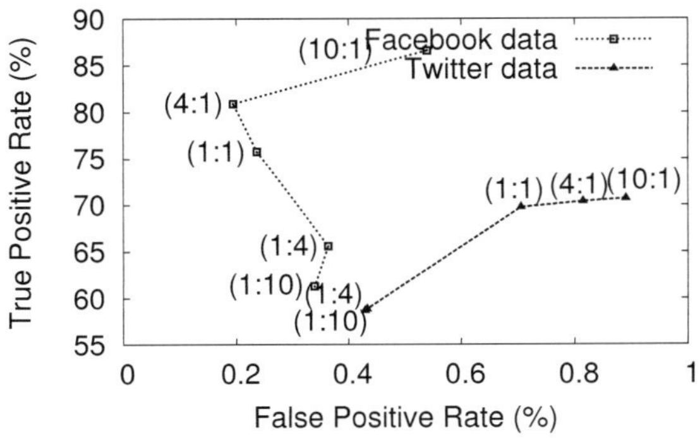

Figure 14: The overall detection accuracy subjecting to the varying spam to legitimate message ratio in the training set.

ture sets (Section 5.3.2) and the accuracy over time (Section 5.3.3) to show that our system can indeed provide satisfactory accuracy guarantee.

We use the C4.5 decision tree library provided by Quinlan [20].

5.3.1 Overall Accuracy

We first test the overall detection accuracy, using all applicable features and the complete dataset. An accurate detection system desires high true positive rate and low false positive rate simultaneously. Unfortunately, parameter tuning usually causes these two metrics to increase or decrease at the same time. We are forced to face the trade-off between them. We decided to tune the classifier to emphasize low false positive rate while maintaining a reasonably high true positive rate.

As suggested by Zadrozny *et al.* [33] and used by Thomas *et al.* [27], we adjust the ratio of spam to legitimate message in the training set by random sampling to tailor the performance, where a larger ratio indicates a stronger tendency to classify a message as spam. We use the ratios of 10:1, 4:1, 1:1, 1:4 and 1:10. Regardless of the ratio in the training set, the full testing set is used. Figure 14 shows the detection accuracy. For the Twitter dataset, the two rates grow in consistency with the ratio in the training set. Both rates minimize when the ratio is 1:10, and maximize when the ratio is 10:1. A 1:1 ratio in the training set results in a reduction of false positive rate by about 20%, comparing to a 10:1 ratio. On the other hand, the true positive rate decreases very slightly and reaches 69.8% at this ratio. A 1:4 ratio or a 1:10 ratio results in a substantial drop in both true positive rate and false positive rate. After all, we still favor the 1:1 ratio for the twitter data. The detection accuracy of the Facebook dataset exhibits irregularity. A 4:1 ratio yields the lowest false positive rate (0.19%) and a relatively high true positive rate (80.9%). For the remainder of the evaluation, we conduct all experiments over the Facebook dataset at a 4:1 ratio in the training set and all experiments over the Twitter dataset at a 1:1 ratio.

Feature Set	Features Contained	TPR	FPR
OSN Specific	Social Degree Interaction History	38.3%	0.30%
General	Cluster Size Average Time Interval Average URL Number Unique URL Number	80.8%	0.32%

Table 1: The detection accuracy using each of the two feature sets with the Facebook dataset.

5.3.2 Accuracy of Different Feature Sets

As stated in Section 3, we divide our features into two sets: the OSN specific features and the general features. To understand their significance to the system, we train the classifier exclusively using each feature set, test the detection accuracy and present the result in Table 1. The ratio of spam to legitimate message in the training set is 4:1. Since the Facebook dataset uses the complete 6 features, we conduct this experiment using the Facebook dataset. The general features achieve a true positive rate of 80.8%, which is similar to the result of using all features. Unfortunately, the false positive rate increases by more than 50%. On the other hand, the OSN specific features lead to a lower true positive rate (38.3%). We do not mean to compare between these two sets and decide which one gives better performance. Rather, the result shows that the detection accuracy would be significantly degraded in the absence of either feature set. Using their combination keeps the high true positive rate while reducing the false positive rate.

5.3.3 Accuracy Over Time

Spam campaigns are not persistent. Criminals will promote new campaigns on a continuous basis. As a result, it is important to evaluate how much time it takes before the classifier becomes out of date and needs to be re-trained. We carry out the evaluation using the Facebook dataset, because it contains messages generated throughout a time period of one year and a half. In comparison, the Twitter dataset is collected in a much shorter period of time and is not suitable for this type of evaluation. We use 4:1 as the ratio of spam to legitimate message in the training set. We dissect the testing set into 3-month time periods and study how the detection accuracy changes over time. We use the same trained classifier on the first 9 months of testing data, and measure the true positive rate as well as the false positive rate in each period. We only present the result in the first

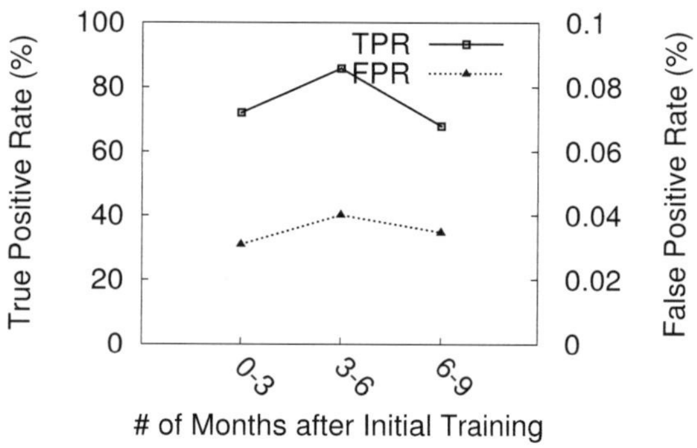

Figure 15: The detection accuracy on the Facebook dataset over time.

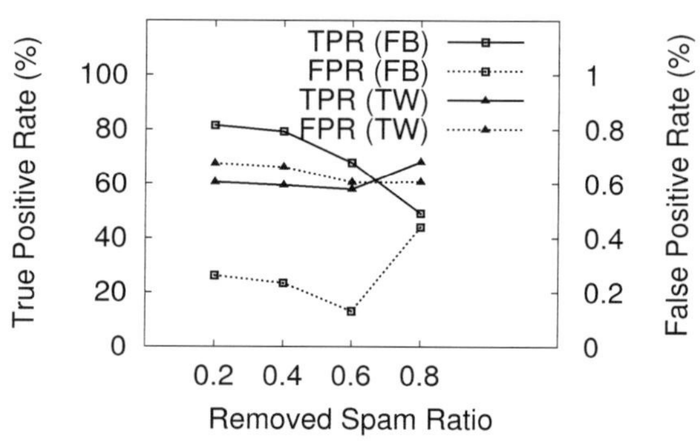

Figure 16: The detection accuracy on the Twitter dataset under stealthy attack.

9 months, because after 9 months the spam becomes very sparse in our dataset and the true positive rate is not representative. However, we do observe a significant rise in the false positive rate after 9 months, suggesting that our system may need re-training after such a long time to further reduce the false positive rate. Figure 15 shows the experimental result.

The false positive rate remains extremely low for all 3 periods. The period between 3 and 6 months after training incurs the highest false positive rate, which is about 0.04%. It shows that our system misclassifies very few legitimate messages as spam, even if the training takes place up to 9 months before the time of classification. The true positive rate in the first period and the third is a bit lower. We find that it is caused by campaigns heavily adopting obfuscation that results in large number of small clusters instead of small number of big ones. This type of campaign does not appear in the second period. It demonstrates that the features we select indeed capture the commonality among spam campaigns, so that they remains effective even if the campaigns being classified do not present in the training data. These findings indicate that our system can remain accurate without the need for re-training for a long period of time, which minimizes the maintenance cost after deployment.

5.4 Resilience against Stealthy Attack

One of the spammers' common attempts to evade detection is to carry out stealthy attack. Under stealthy attack, the speed of spam generation is reduced so that the anti-spam system cannot acquire sufficient instances to learn the spam pattern. To simulate such an attack, we randomly remove certain proportion of spam messages , ranging from 20% to 80%, from both dataset. The effect is the same as if the spammers generate spam messages at a reduced speed. The legitimate messages are untouched. After that, we repeat the overall accuracy test on the modified dataset, choosing 4:1 and 1:1 as the ratio of spam to legitimate messages in the training set for Facebook and Twitter dataset , respectively. Figure 16 illustrates the result. In the Twitter experiment, the true positive rate and the false positive rate exhibit very slight difference comparing with the experiment using the original dataset in all test cases. In the Facebook experiment, the true positive rate and the false positive rate decrease moderately when we remove 20%, 40% and 60% of spam messages. The reason is that as spam becomes more sparse in the dataset, more spam clusters become indistinguishable from legitimate message clusters. When we remove 80% of spam messages, the system does not handle it gracefully as the true positive rate drops to 49% and the false positive rate rises to 0.44%. The results show that except for the Facebook experiment when we remove 80% of spam messages, stealthy attack slightly decreases the system's the true positive rate. Nonetheless, the false positive rate does not increase, which means that the system is still "safe" against legitimate messages under such attack.

5.5 Run Time Performance

The run time performance is critical, since our system must not be the bottleneck that slows down the OSN platform if deployed. The training time is only a few seconds in all the experiments. In addition, we measure the latency and throughput to demonstrate that our system can respond to an incoming message very quickly and that it can inspect large number of messages per second.

Latency The latency is measured as the time between when the system receives a message and when the system outputs the inspection result. We process all the messages sequentially in this experiment. Figure 17 shows the cumulative distribution of the system latency, measured in milliseconds. The average and median latency for the Face-

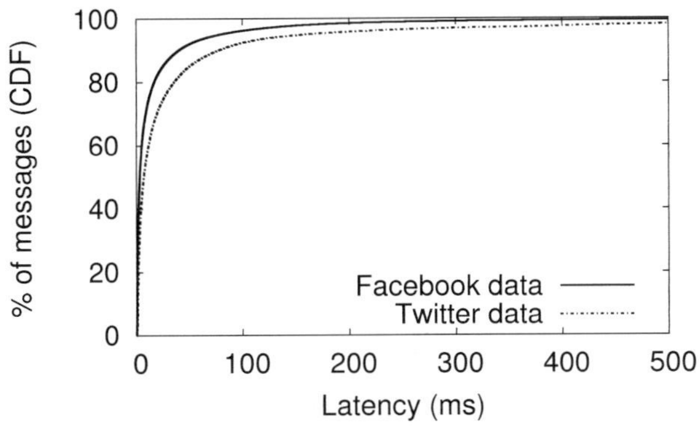

Figure 17: The cumulative distribution of the system latency, measured in milliseconds.

book dataset is 21.5ms and 3.1ms, respectively. The average and median latency for the Twitter dataset is 42.6ms and 7.0ms, respectively. Even for the Twitter dataset that results in comparatively longer processing delay, the whole inspection process for over 90% of messages is completed within 100ms. Given that modern browsers spend several hundred milliseconds before they start to render ordinary webpages [17], the system latency is sufficiently low. An OSN user would not feel any noticeable additional delay due to the deployment of our system.

Throughput In order to test the throughput, we feed the system with the testing set as fast as possible. Due to the hardware limitation (8 physical cores with Hyper-Threading), we execute 16 threads simultaneously. We divide the total number of messages processed by the system by the total running time to calculate the average throughput. The throughput on the Facebook and the Twitter dataset is 1580 messages/sec and 464 messages/sec, respectively.

6 Discussion

Spammers continuously rival anti-spam solutions. Although our system is demonstrated to be robust against stealthy attacks, other approaches might be adopted to evade it. One possible way is to tamper with the clustering process by reducing the syntactic similarity among messages from the same campaign. We have observed such attempts in both of our datasets. In the Facebook dataset, spam campaigns start to include obfuscation in the textual message, *e.g.* , using "profil imaage" instead of "profile image". In the Twitter dataset, almost all spam tweets contain random meaningless words, which we suspect to be obtained from a collection of popular words. Nonetheless, our system defeats these attempts and yields good detection accuracy. Meanwhile, obfuscation and embedded random chunks decrease the message readability as well as trigger the recipients' suspicion, which lowers the underlying conversion rate. Another way to evade the system would be to manipulate the features of spam clusters, for the purpose of making them indistinguishable from legitimate clusters. It is not too difficult to do this for each individual feature. For example, spammers may use fake accounts with lower social degree to tamper with the "sender social degree" feature. In addition, they may only send spam to the friends that the compromised accounts frequently interact with to tamper with the "interaction history" feature. They may also send spam with longer time interval to tamper with the "average time interval" feature. However, manipulating any individual feature is likely to have very limited effect, since our system uses all six features in combination. Even though deliberate spammers in theory may manipulate all the features simultaneously, they have to pay a heavy price for doing so. In the previous three examples, the spam recipient population becomes much smaller, and the speed of spam generation becomes slower by orders of magnitude. If we can force spammers to do that, it is already a victory. The third evasion technique is to produce image-based spam. Our current design does not work for image-based spam.

7 Related Work

We discuss prior related work by organizing them into two general categories: studies of spamming problem in OSNs and in other environments.

Spam Studies in OSNs. Stein *et al.* present the framework of the adversarial learning system that performs real-time classification on read and write action in Facebook [25]. However, the lack of details, *e.g.* , the features and policies used, and performance results prevent us from further comparison. Two offline studies have revealed large-scale spam campaigns in Twitter and Facebook, respectively [9, 10]. Designed as offline analysis tools, none of them can be directly used for online spam detection. [10] is based on URL blacklists which have too long lag-time to protect a significant number of users. [9] uses a similar clustering technique. However, it needs to operate on the complete set of messages, and its efficiency limits the clustering to be performed on the 2 million messages with URLs. In comparison, we adopt incremental clustering and parallelization to enable the system to inspect messages only based on other messages observed in the past, as well as to increase the scalability. Also, we develop the feature set to distinguish spam cluster that can be efficiently computed online. Thomas *et al.* [27] propose to filter malicious URLs in OSNs in real-time, which can be used to identify malicious messages later. While their approach does deep analysis of the URLs' landing pages, our approach uses an alternative information source for the investigation, *i.e.* , the message content. Song *et al.* propose to use sender-receiver relationship to classify twitter messages [24]. Stringhini *et al.* [26] , Lee *et al.* [14] and Yang *et al.* [31] use machine learning techniques to detect spamming bots in OSNs, which are accounts created by spammers and used exclusively for spamming. Yardi *et al.* use a collection of ad-hoc criteria to identify spamming bots on Twitter [32]. In comparison, our detection focuses on spam messages instead of accounts, so that we can secure OSNs from spams generated by both spamming bots and previously legitimate accounts that have been compromised. Additionally, Benevenuto *et al.* [5] and Markines *et al.* [16] apply supervised machine learning to detect spammers in Youtube and social bookmarking sites, respectively. These websites do not focus on communications among users. Instead, their key functionality is video and bookmark sharing. Hence, the feature set used for machine learning is very different.

Other Spam Studies. There is a large body of prior work studying the characteristics of email spam [4, 12, 13, 35]. However, few of them can potentially be used as online detection tools. Researchers propose to enhance IP blacklists by correlating IP addresses according to their email sending history, network-level information, blacklisting history and so on, in order to discover spamming IP addresses that are not yet blacklisted [19, 22, 28]. As discussed previously, sender reputation based approaches are not suitable for OSN spam detection. Pitsillidis *et al.* extract the underlying templates to match future spams [18]. Li *et al.* propose to enhance Bayesian filter by adjusting the weight of spam keywords using personal social network information [15]. Both approaches detect campaigns that have been contained in the training set. Our approach does not have such a restriction. Xie *et al.* generate regular expression signatures for spamming URLs [30]. In addition, Thomas *et al.* use a comprehensive list of features to determine whether a given URL directs to spam in real-time [27]. The above two approaches essentially detect spamming URLs. In comparison, our approach can detect spam messages even if no URL can be recognized in them due to the obfuscation techniques.

8 Conclusions

In this paper, we describe our work to provide online spam filtering for social networks. We use text shingling and URL comparison to incrementally reconstruct spam messages into campaigns, which are then identified by a trained classifier. We evaluate the system on two large datasets composed of over 187 million Facebook wall messages and 17 million tweets, respectively. The experimental results demonstrate that the system achieves high accuracy, low latency and high throughput, which are the crucial properties required for an online system. In addition, the system is able to remain accurate for more than 9 months after the training phase, which shows its very low maintenance cost after deployment. For more information, please refer to the project web page at http://list.cs.northwestern.edu/.

Acknowledgments

We express our sincere thanks to the anonymous reviewers for their valuable feedback. The authors denoted with † are supported by NSF award numbers CCF-0621443, OCI-0724599, CCF-0833131, CNS-0830927, IIS-0905205, OCI-0956311, CCF-0938000, CCF-1043085, CCF-1029166 , and OCI-1144061.

References

[1] Users of social networking websites face malware and phishing attacks. Symantec.com Blog.

[2] What the trend. `http://www.whatthetrend.com/`.

[3] Zeus botnet targets facebook. `http://blog.appriver.com/2009/10/zeus-botnet-targets-facebook.html`.

[4] ANDERSON, D. S., FLEIZACH, C., SAVAGE, S., AND VOELKER, G. M. Spamscatter: characterizing internet scam hosting infrastructure. In *Proceedings of 16th USENIX Security Symposium on USENIX Security Symposium* (Berkeley, CA, USA, 2007), USENIX Association, pp. 10:1–10:14.

[5] BENEVENUTO, F., RODRIGUES, T., AND ALMEIDA, V. Detecting spammers and content promoters in online video social networks. In *Proc. of SIGIR* (Boston, Massachusetts, USA, July 2009).

[6] BOGUÑÁ, M., PASTOR-SATORRAS, R., AND VESPIGNANI, A. Epidemic spreading in complex networks with degree correlations.

[7] BRODER, A. Z., GLASSMAN, S. C., MANASSE, M. S., AND ZWEIG, G. Syntactic clustering of the web. *Comput. Netw. ISDN Syst. 29* (September 1997), 1157–1166.

[8] BURGES, C. J. C. A tutorial on support vector machines for pattern recognition. *Data Min. Knowl. Discov. 2* (June 1998), 121–167.

[9] GAO, H., HU, J., WILSON, C., LI, Z., CHEN, Y., AND ZHAO, B. Y. Detecting and characterizing social

spam campaigns. In *Proceedings of the 10th annual conference on Internet measurement* (New York, NY, USA, 2010), IMC '10, ACM, pp. 35–47.

[10] GRIER, C., THOMAS, K., PAXSON, V., AND ZHANG, M. @spam: the underground on 140 characters or less. In *Proceedings of the 17th ACM conference on Computer and communications security* (New York, NY, USA, 2010), CCS '10, ACM, pp. 27–37.

[11] HAO, S., SYED, N. A., FEAMSTER, N., GRAY, A. G., AND KRASSER, S. Detecting spammers with snare: spatio-temporal network-level automatic reputation engine. In *Proceedings of the 18th conference on USENIX security symposium* (Berkeley, CA, USA, 2009), SSYM'09, USENIX Association, pp. 101–118.

[12] KANICH, C., KREIBICH, C., LEVCHENKO, K., ENRIGHT, B., VOELKER, G. M., PAXSON, V., AND SAVAGE, S. Spamalytics: An empirical analysis of spam marketing conversion. In *Proc. of the ACM Conference on Computer and Communications Security* (October 2008).

[13] KREIBICH, C., KANICH, C., LEVCHENKO, K., ENRIGHT, B., VOELKER, G., PAXSON, V., AND SAVAGE, S. Spamcraft: An inside look at spam campaign orchestration. In *Proc. of LEET* (2009).

[14] LEE, K., CAVERLEE, J., AND WEBB, S. Uncovering social spammers: social honeypots + machine learning. In *Proceeding of the 33rd international ACM SIGIR conference on Research and development in information retrieval* (New York, NY, USA, 2010), SIGIR '10, ACM, pp. 435–442.

[15] LI, Z., AND SHEN, H. SOAP: A Social Network Aided Personalized and Effective Spam Filter to Clean Your E-mail Box. In *Proceedings of the IEEE INFOCOM* (April 2011).

[16] MARKINES, B., CATTUTO, C., AND MENCZER, F. Social spam detection. In *Proc. of AIRWeb* (2009).

[17] MOSHCHUK, A., BRAGIN, T., DEVILLE, D., GRIBBLE, S. D., AND LEVY, H. M. Spyproxy: execution-based detection of malicious web content. In *Proceedings of 16th USENIX Security Symposium on USENIX Security Symposium* (Berkeley, CA, USA, 2007), USENIX Association, pp. 3:1–3:16.

[18] PITSILLIDIS, A., LEVCHENKO, K., KREIBICH, C., KANICH, C., VOELKER, G., PAXSON, V., WEAVER, N., AND SAVAGE, S. Botnet Judo: Fighting Spam with Itself . In *Proceedings of the 17th Annual Network and Distributed System Security Symposium (NDSS)* (San Diego, CA, USA, March 2010).

[19] QIAN, Z., MAO, Z. M., XIE, Y., AND YU, F. On Network-level Clusters for Spam Detection . In *Proceedings of the 17th Annual Network and Distributed System Security Symposium (NDSS)* (San Diego, CA, USA, March 2010).

[20] QUINLAN, J. R. Ross quinlan's personal homepage. `http://www.rulequest.com/Personal/`.

[21] QUINLAN, J. R. Induction of decision trees. *Mach. Learn. 1* (March 1986), 81–106.

[22] RAMACHANDRAN, A., FEAMSTER, N., AND VEMPALA, S. Filtering spam with behavioral blacklisting. In *Proceedings of the 14th ACM conference on Computer and communications security* (New York, NY, USA, 2007), CCS '07, ACM, pp. 342–351.

[23] SHIN, Y., GUPTA, M., AND MYERS, S. Prevalence and mitigation of forum spamming. In *Proceedings of IEEE International Conference on Computer Communicationi (INFOCOM)* (Shanghai, China, 2011), IEEE Computer Society.

[24] SONG, J., LEE, S., AND KIM, J. Spam filtering in twitter using sender-receiver relationship. In *Proceedings of the 14th International Symposium on Recent Advances in Intrusion Detection (RAID'11))* (September 2011).

[25] STEIN, T., CHEN, E., AND MANGLA, K. Facebook immune system. In *Proceedings of the 4th Workshop on Social Network Systems (SNS'11)* (New York, NY, USA, 2011), ACM.

[26] STRINGHINI, G., KRUEGEL, C., AND VIGNA, G. Detecting spammers on social networks. In *Proceedings of the 26th Annual Computer Security Applications Conference* (New York, NY, USA, 2010), ACSAC '10, ACM, pp. 1–9.

[27] THOMAS, K., GRIER, C., MA, J., PAXSON, V., AND SONG, D. Design and Evaluation of a Real-Time URL Spam Filtering Service. In *Proceedings of the IEEE Symposium on Security and Privacy* (May 2011).

[28] WEST, A. G., AVIV, A. J., CHANG, J., AND LEE, I. Spam mitigation using spatio-temporal reputations from blacklist history. In *Proceedings of the 26th Annual Computer Security Applications Conference* (New York, NY, USA, 2010), ACSAC '10, ACM, pp. 161–170.

[29] WILSON, C., BOE, B., SALA, A., PUTTASWAMY, K. P., AND ZHAO, B. Y. User interactions in social networks and their implications. In *Proceedings of the ACM European conference on Computer systems* (2009).

[30] XIE, Y., YU, F., ACHAN, K., PANIGRAHY, R., HULTEN, G., AND OSIPKOV, I. Spamming botnets: signatures and characteristics. In *Proc. of SIGCOMM* (2008).

[31] YANG, C., HARKREADER, R., AND GU, G. Die free or live hard? empirical evaluation and new design for fighting evolving twitter spammers. In *Proceedings of the 14th International Symposium on Recent Advances in Intrusion Detection (RAID'11))* (September 2011).

[32] YARDI, S., ROMERO, D., SCHOENEBECK, G., AND BOYD, D. Detecting spam in a twitter network. *First Monday 15*, 1 (2010).

[33] ZADROZNY, B., LANGFORD, J., AND ABE, N. Cost-sensitive learning by cost-proportionate example weighting. In *Proceedings of the Third IEEE International Conference on Data Mining* (Washington, DC, USA, 2003), ICDM '03, IEEE Computer Society, pp. 435–.

[34] ZHAO, Y., XIE, Y., YU, F., KE, Q., YU, Y., CHEN, Y., AND GILLUM, E. Botgraph: large scale spamming botnet detection. In *Proceedings of the 6th USENIX symposium on Networked systems design and implementation* (Berkeley, CA, USA, 2009), USENIX Association, pp. 321–334.

[35] ZHUANG, L., DUNAGAN, J., SIMON, D. R., WANG, H. J., AND TYGAR, J. D. Characterizing botnets from email spam records. In *Proceedings of the 1st Usenix Workshop on Large-Scale Exploits and Emergent Threats* (Berkeley, CA, USA, 2008), USENIX Association, pp. 2:1–2:9.

[36] ZOU, C. C., TOWSLEY, D., AND GONG, W. Modeling and simulation study of the propagation and defense of internet e-mail worms. *IEEE Trans. Dependable Secur. Comput. 4* (April 2007), 105–118.

Location Leaks on the GSM Air Interface

Denis Foo Kune,
John Koelndorfer, Nick Hopper, Yongdae Kim

UNIVERSITY OF MINNESOTA

Problem definition

- Large array of towers broadcasting messages
  - Can those messages reveal a phone's location?
- Given a person's phone number
  - can we locate the tower they are attached to in a GSM network?
- GSM: dominant protocol worldwide
  - Analysis of layer 2/3 messages only.
- No collaboration from the service provider.
- No support from apps.

UNIVERSITY OF MINNESOTA
Driven to Discover℠

Cellular network architecture

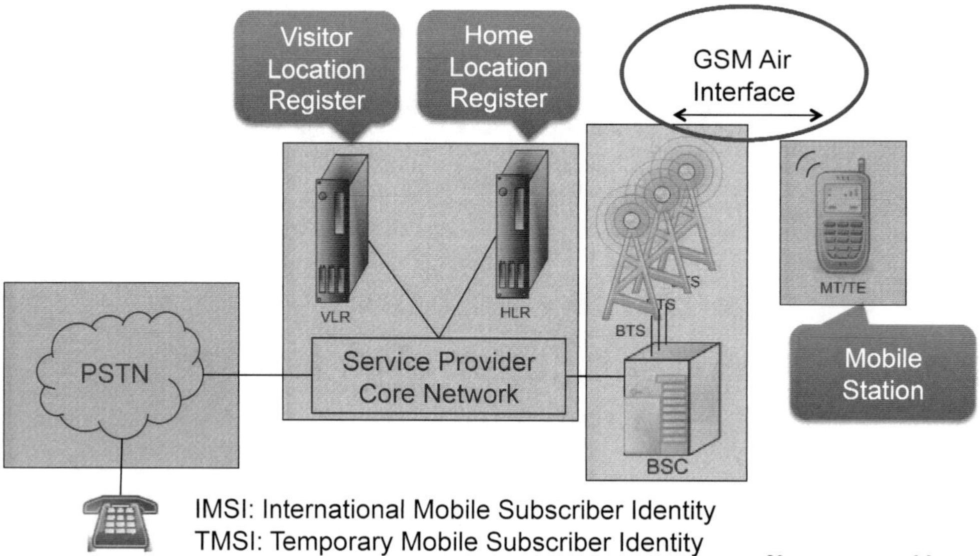

IMSI: International Mobile Subscriber Identity
TMSI: Temporary Mobile Subscriber Identity

UNIVERSITY OF MINNESOTA
Driven to Discover℠

The GSM paging procedure

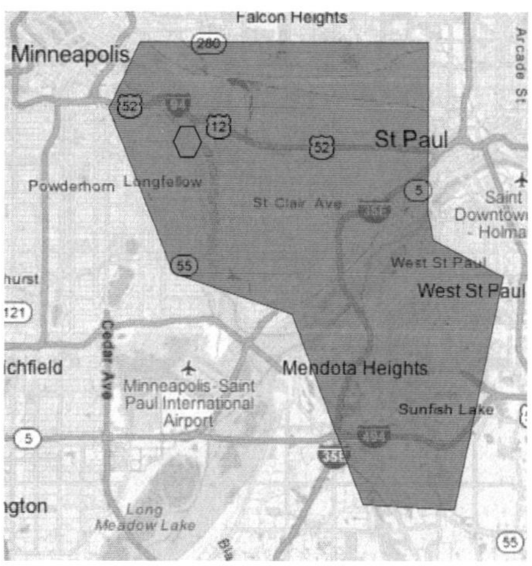

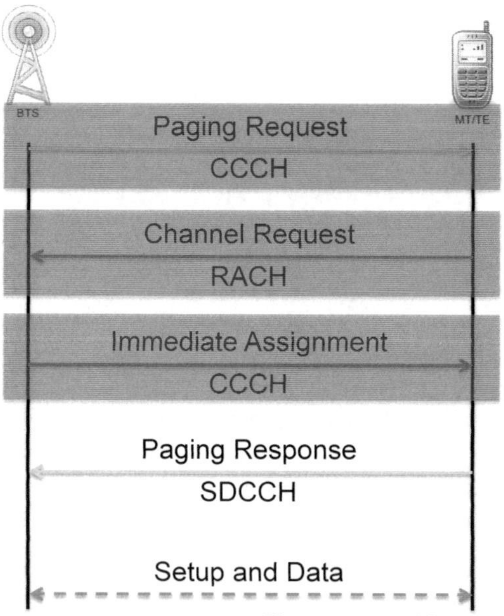

UNIVERSITY OF MINNESOTA
Driven to Discover℠

Measurement platform

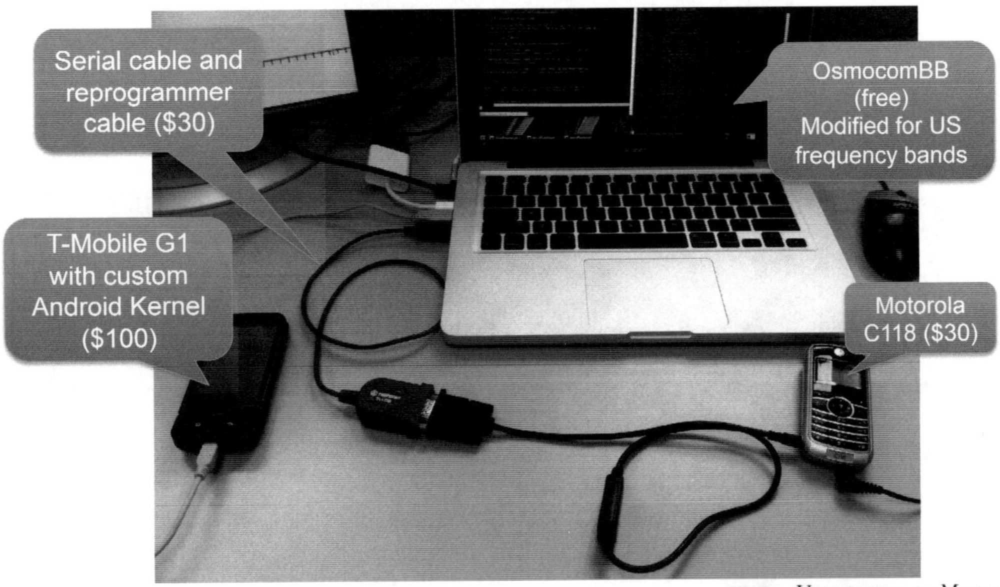

UNIVERSITY OF MINNESOTA
Driven to Discover℠

GSM paging channel observations

	T-Mobile LAC 747b	AT&T LAC 7d11
Paging Requests – IMSI	27,120	8,897
Paging Requests – TMSI	257,159	84,526
Paging Requests Type 1	284,279	91,539
Paging Requests Type 2	1,635	26
Paging Requests Type 3	0	1
Observation period	24 hours	24 hours

UNIVERSITY OF MINNESOTA
Driven to Discover℠

Pages and human activity

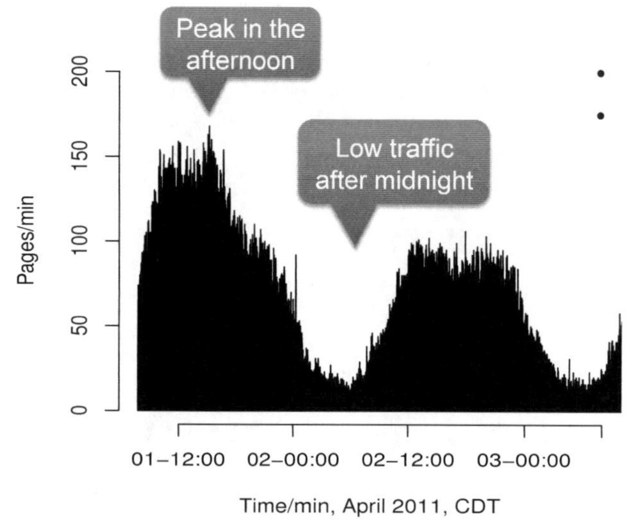

- University campus
- Day of the week during the semester

UNIVERSITY OF MINNESOTA
Driven to Discover℠

Phone number-TMSI mapping

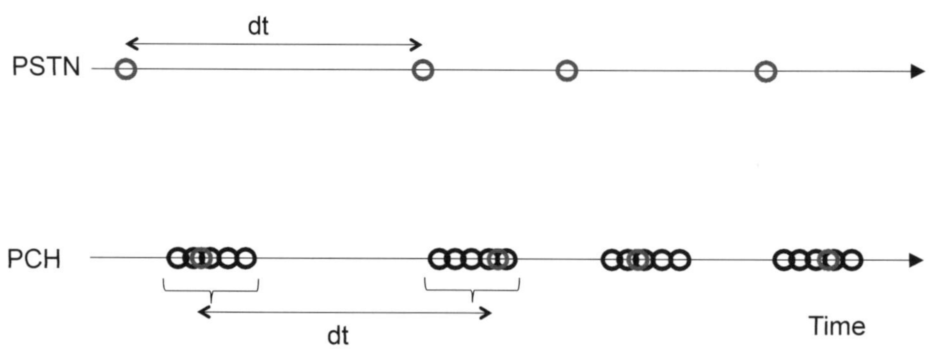

UNIVERSITY OF MINNESOTA
Driven to Discover℠

No recovered TMSI

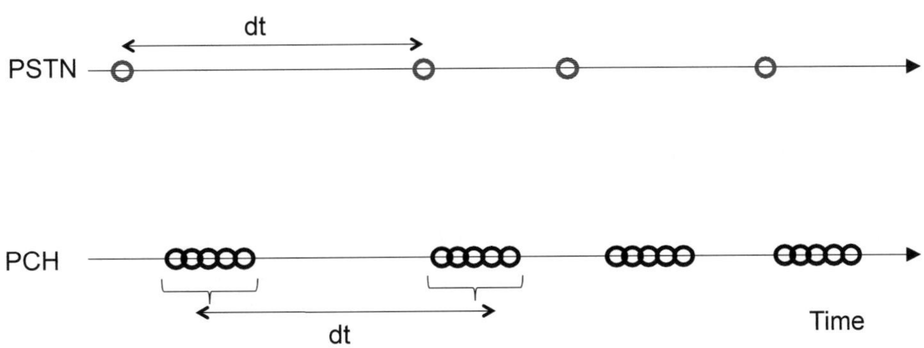

UNIVERSITY OF MINNESOTA
Driven to Discover℠

Silent paging

- Delay between the call initiation and the paging request
  - 3 seconds

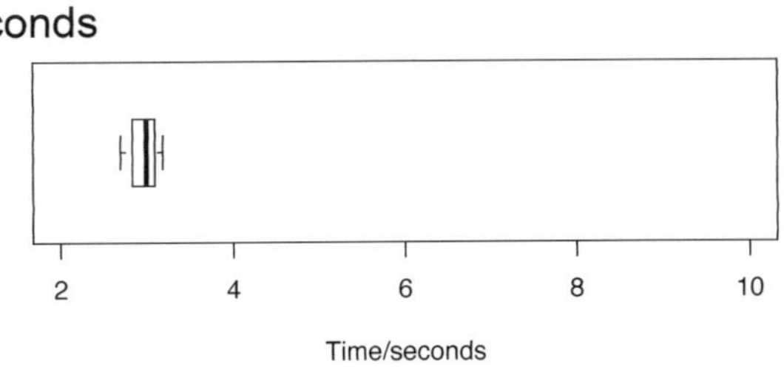

- Median delay between call initiation and ring
  - 6 seconds

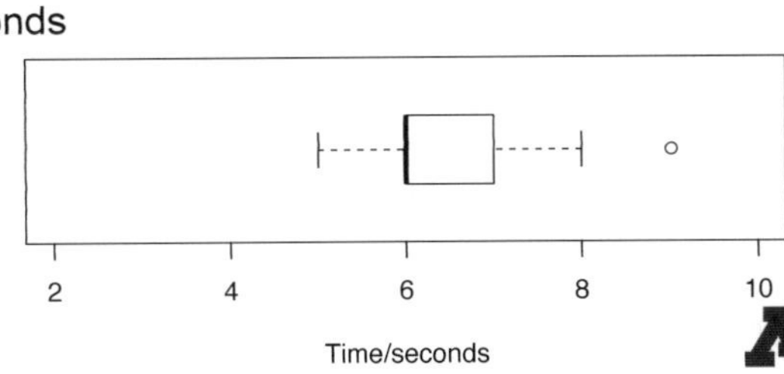

UNIVERSITY OF MINNESOTA
Driven to Discover℠

Bounding the LAC

- LACs can be very large.
  - T-Mobile LAC 747d: 100km^2
- Used a wall-following algorithm, road permitting.

- Call to MS on NW corner.
- Observed paging request on SE corner.

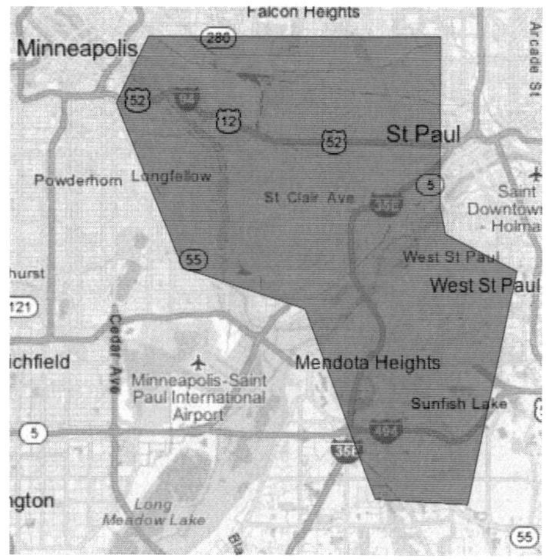

UNIVERSITY OF MINNESOTA
Driven to Discover℠

The GSM paging procedure

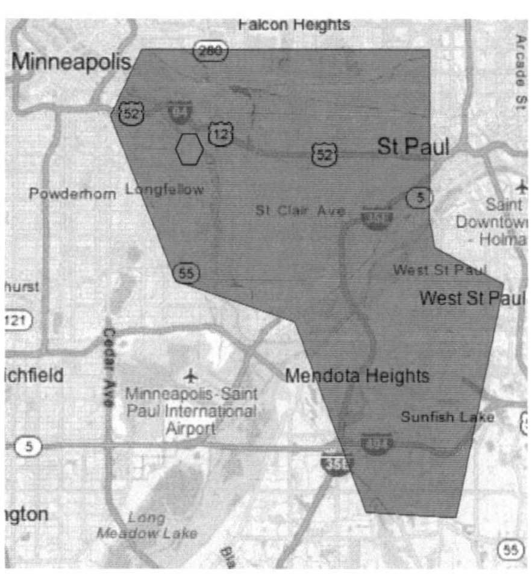

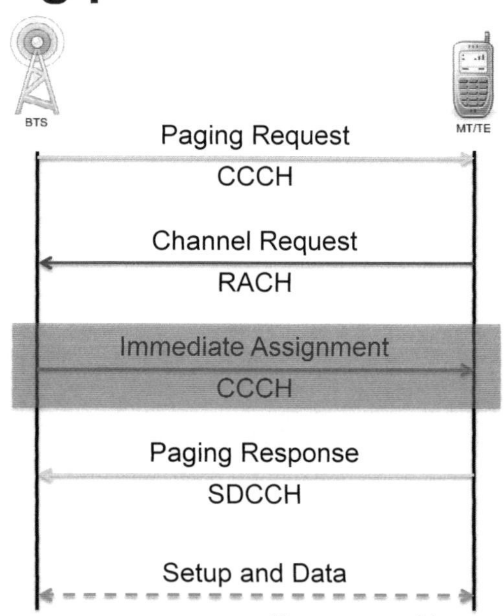

UNIVERSITY OF MINNESOTA
Driven to Discover℠

Same tower test

- Delay between the paging request and the immediate assignment message.

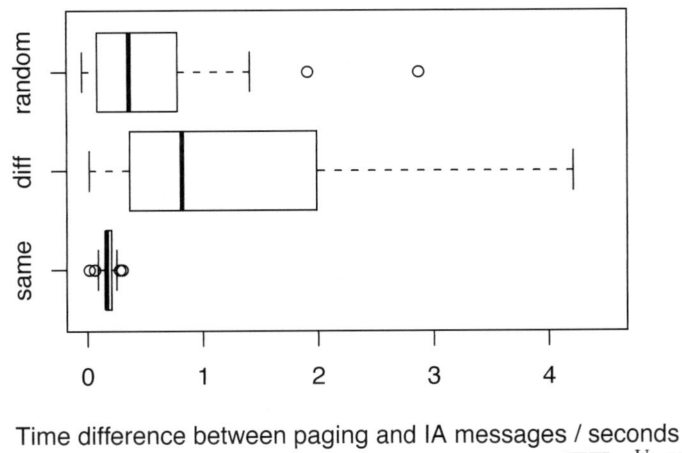

University of Minnesota
Driven to Discover℠

Finding individual towers

- Find individual towers with a hill-climbing algorithm.
  - Non-uniform RF attenuation.
  - Overshoot by 50m to avoid local maximum.

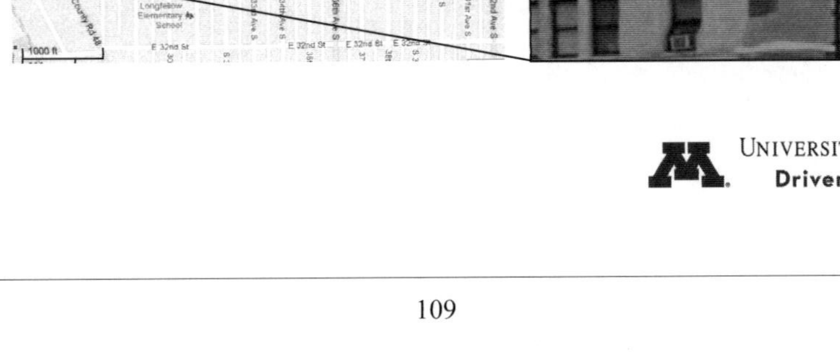

University of Minnesota
Driven to Discover℠

ARFCN a phone is likely to camp on

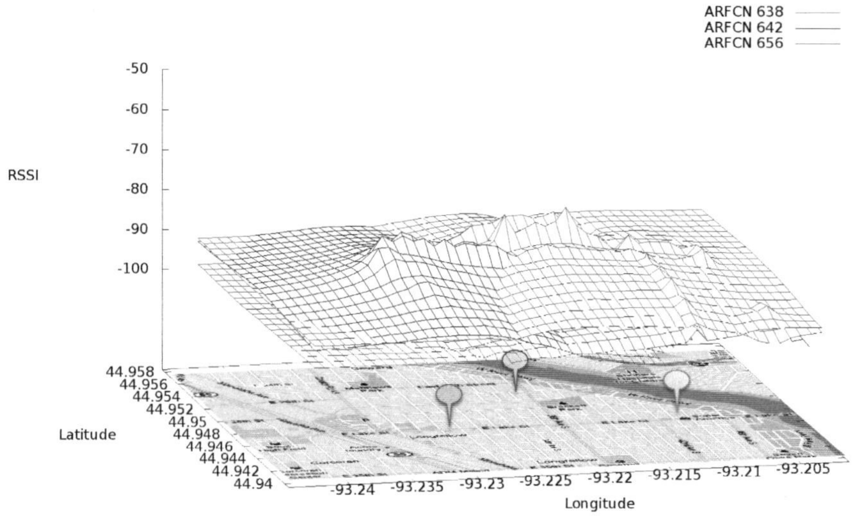

UNIVERSITY OF MINNESOTA
Driven to Discover℠

Tracking users in motion

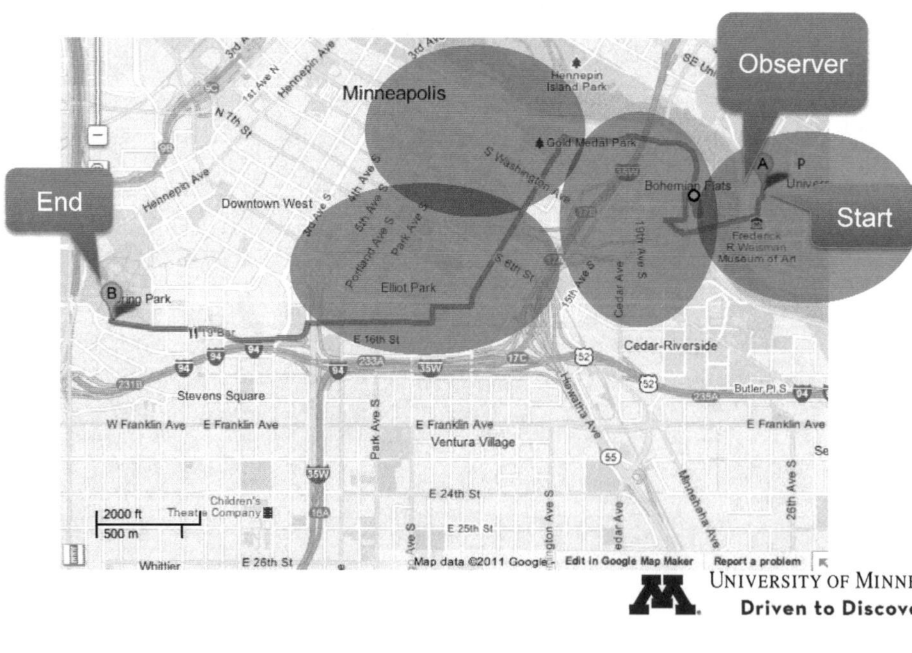

UNIVERSITY OF MINNESOTA
Driven to Discover℠

Defenses

- Page multiple areas.
  - Less than 0.6% of paging requests are not type 1.
  - Available bandwidth for additional pages.
  - Human trajectories are predictable.
- Continuous time mixes.
  - Switch TMSI at least once per page.
    - phone/TMSI bitwise unlinkable.
  - Prevent traffic analysis.
    - Cover traffic.
    - Add exponential delay to paging requests.

UNIVERSITY OF MINNESOTA
Driven to Discover℠

Conclusion

- Systems with broadcast paging protocols could leak location information.
- Leaks observable with
  - readily available equipment equipment,
  - no (direct) help from the service provider.
- Proposed low cost fixes.
- Responsible disclosures.
  - 3GPP, Nokia, AT&T research

UNIVERSITY OF MINNESOTA
Driven to Discover℠

Thank you

- Questions

UNIVERSITY OF MINNESOTA
Driven to Discover℠

Track Me If You Can: On the Effectiveness of Context-based Identifier Changes in Deployed Mobile Networks

Laurent Bindschaedler[1,*] Murtuza Jadliwala[2,*] Igor Bilogrevic[1] Imad Aad[3]
Philip Ginzboorg[3] Valtteri Niemi[3]
Jean-Pierre Hubaux[1]
[1]EPFL, Switzerland. [2]Wichita State University, USA. [3]Nokia Research Center.

E-mail: firstname.lastname@{[1]epfl.ch, [2]wichita.edu, [3]nokia.com}

Abstract

Location privacy is a major concern in an increasingly connected and highly pervasive network of mobile users. Novel location-based applications and device-to-device services (on these mobile devices) are gaining popularity, but at the same time, these services allow curious service providers and eavesdroppers to track users and their movements. Earlier research efforts on location-privacy preservation, which were mostly based on identifier-change mechanisms in spatio-temporal de-correlation regions called mix-zones, *show that coordinated identifier-change techniques are reasonably effective in a simulation setting, although some smart attacks are still possible. However, a thorough analysis of these mechanisms that takes into consideration communication patterns and mobility from a real-life deployment is missing from these results. In this paper, we evaluate in a real-life setting the effectiveness of standard mix-zone-based privacy protection mechanisms against probabilistic tracking attacks. Our experiments involved 80 volunteers carrying smartphones for 4 months and being constantly eavesdropped on an adversarial mesh network of standard wireless Access Points (APs). To the best of our knowledge, this is the first study that provides empirical evidence about the effectiveness of mix-zone-based privacy-preserving mechanisms against practical adversaries in upcoming wireless and mobile systems.*

1. Introduction

Over the last few years, smartphones and mobile devices have replaced traditional personal computers as the main means to access web and other context-based services. A wide variety of applications are available on these devices, including applications for friend-finding [1], dating [2, 3], micro-blogging [27], localized advertisement [16], gaming, entertainment [49] and localized social networking [4, 7]; they take advantage of both infrastructure-based and device-to-device communications. Novel data-sharing applications have also emerged in societies that enforce strict censorship and data-regulation. For example, device-to-device messaging applications are being used in Iran to exchange sexually-explicit messages [39] and by anti-governmental insurgents in order to coordinate their actions [22]. New infrastructure-less systems for wireless device-to-device communications have been recently announced by Nokia [43], Qualcomm [17], Peep Wireless [30], and NEC [46].

In such pervasive communication systems, privacy, specifically location privacy, is always a critical issue. Eavesdroppers can constantly track users based on device identifiers in the broadcasted wireless messages. This information can be used by curious service providers in order to de-anonymize users and their availabilities [29], to track their preferences [26], to identify their social networks [23], or it can be used by malicious parties for nefarious activities [5, 20]. Infrastructure owners and third-party service providers who track user communications and location information in order to improve the offered service can inadvertently harm users' privacy if the collected data is leaked to unauthorized parties or improperly shared with corporate partners.

The location privacy problem in pervasive and mobile communication networks has recently received much attention. Inspired by Chaum's seminal work on mix networks [14, 15], Beresford and Stajano [9, 10] propose the concept of *mix-zones*, which are spatio-temporally defined regions where users can mix [41] or change [34, 13] their device identifiers, such as IP and MAC addresses. Application layer identities are generally encrypted by using session keys and are not visible. While in the mix-zone, users remain silent after this identifier change operation. They re-

*Equally contributing authors; ordered alphabetically. Murtuza was with EPFL when this work was accomplished.

sume communication with a new identifier (or pseudonym) after exiting the mix-zone. By providing de-correlation between users and their device identifiers, mix-zones make it difficult for an adversary to continuously track users simply by linking messages containing the same identifier. In cellular networks, location privacy is supported by changing a subscriber's Temporary Mobile Subscriber Identity, or TMSI [21], upon moving to a new geographical area.

The effectiveness of mix-zone-based identifier-change mechanisms has been studied in some of the recent research efforts [12, 28, 48], where authors proposed new location-privacy attacks in such systems. Buttyán et al. [13] and Freudiger et al. [24] focus on mix-zone schemes that consider specific network characteristics, whereas, Palanisamy et al. [42] propose schemes that guarantee a lower-bound on the level of achieved anonymity. Freudiger et al. [25] and Jadliwala et al. [36] address the problem of optimal mix-zone deployment by minimizing the probabilistic advantage of the adversary in tracking users. More recently, the mix-zone placement problem was also addressed from a game-theoretic perspective [35, 8] by deriving optimal attack and defense strategies for both eavesdroppers and users. However, a majority of these efforts consider only vehicular networking scenarios, which have significantly different network characteristics and mobility patterns compared to networking scenarios involving mobile humans. Moreover, due to the difficulty in conducting large-scale field trials, these results are based solely on simulations with rather restrictive parameters. Additionally, most of these studies assume a global passive adversary, which is a highly unrealistic assumption. Before this contribution, there did not exist a single field-study that evaluated context-based identifier-change mechanisms under a practical adversary model both on real mobile devices and in real communication scenarios. In our opinion, such a study is crucial in order to realistically evaluate the effectiveness of coordinated identifier-change mechanisms.

In this paper, we evaluate mix-zones and context-based identifier-change mechanisms by means of a real on-campus mobile network deployment consisting of 80 state-of-the-art Nokia N900 smartphones. These smartphones, carried and used by EPFL students and staff for a period of four months, were enabled with both standard infrastructure-based communications, such as cellular and WiFi, as well as a novel WiFi-based wireless peer-to-peer technology by Nokia, called Nokia Instant Community or NIC. We deployed an adversarial wireless mesh network of Access Points (APs) over a target region of the campus in order to eavesdrop on user communications in that region. In addition to developing a variety of custom applications to stimulate usage and participation, we implemented and deployed a context-based identifier-change service on all the deployed smartphones. This service performs a device identifier change operation based on the device context such as the number of neighborhood devices obtained from the wireless peer-to-peer channel. Setting up a real deployment is a challenging exercise with several non-trivial tasks such as volunteer recruitment, providing usage incentives, device configurations, application development and deploying regular updates. More details can be found in [6].

Given the data collected, during four month, from the adversarial mesh network, we first reconstruct the groundtruth of user movements and device identifiers. We then outline a Markov chain-based tracking framework for user tracking and propose two straightforward tracking strategies. By using well-established privacy metrics, we evaluate the effectiveness and cost of the deployed context-based identifier-change mechanism against the proposed tracking strategies for various adversarial strengths and parameters.

2. System Model

In this section, we outline the setup of our experimental mobile network and the deployed adversarial mesh network. We also describe the context-based identifier-change mechanism deployed on the mobile devices.

2.1. Mobile Network Model and Deployment

In order to conduct our experiments, we deployed a real mobile network testbed on the EPFL campus in Lausanne, Switzerland. The network model corresponding to the deployment is depicted in Fig. 1 (leftmost). We recruited 80 volunteers (mostly students and a few instructors) to participate in our four month-long experiments from March to June 2011. Each participant was equipped with, and was expected to use, a Nokia N900 smartphone for the duration of the experiment. In addition to accessing web services using the standard WLAN and cellular interfaces, participants also exchanged information with other co-located users by using an experimental wireless peer-to-peer messaging platform from Nokia called *Nokia Instant Community* or *NIC* [43]. NIC uses WiFi-based ad-hoc connections to seamlessly carry small-sized data between devices without any infrastructure requirement. The NIC wireless peer-to-peer interface not only provides a novel and inexpensive means for participants to seamlessly communicate with each other, but it is also useful in determining context such as device neighborhood. We stress that any other non-WiFi-based short-range wireless peer-to-peer communication interface, such as Bluetooth, could also be used for the purpose of context determination.

As mentioned earlier, participants used the NIC interface to exchange information with other colocated participants based on relationship, interests, affiliations and context. NIC communications are either *non-interactive*, where

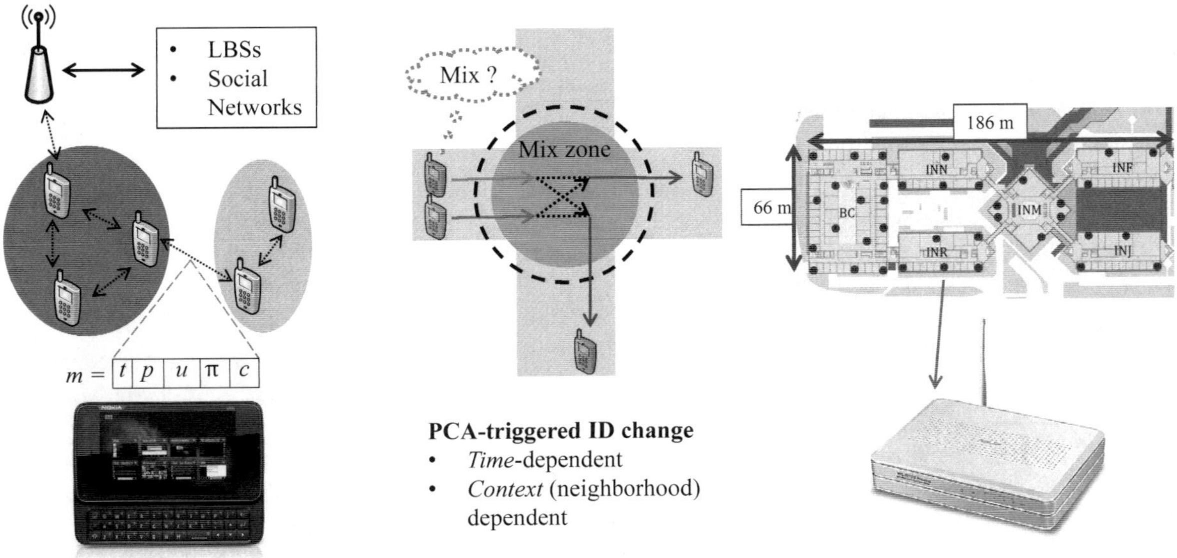

Figure 1. Left: System and network model with communities shown as shaded regions. Nokia N900 smart phone shown at bottom used in actual deployment. Middle: Mix-zone showing silent period and identifier changes. Right: Adversarial wireless mesh network of Asus routers.

users broadcast information without any specific request from others, or *interactive*, where users multi-cast relevant information only in response to specific queries. In order to stimulate information exchange, participants were recruited from closely-knitted groups, such as people in the same course or study group. To support both forms of communications, we developed seven custom NIC-based applications including a "*Classforum*" application for students to interact with the lecturer, a simple chat application, a restaurant application and a friend-finding application. These applications were either pre-loaded on the devices or remotely installed after deployment. Users could also dynamically create and organize themselves into communities using NIC. All users belonged to one large *public* community. *Private* communities could also be formed locally by users based on interest, preferences and affiliations. In adddition to this, participants also accessed Internet-based services, such as email, web browsing, etc., using these smartphones by connecting to the campus WiFi network. We note that, unlike Bluetooth, NIC-enabled smartphones seamlessly switch to the wireless peer-to-peer mode when NIC applications are running or other NIC devices appear in the neighborhood.

NIC messages are multi-hop and valid up to a certain maximum hop count. NIC messages carry limited data ($\approx$ 100 bytes) for efficiency and timing purposes (considering the short encounter period between devices). NIC implements an adaptive beaconing mechanism for *neighborhood discovery*. In order to prevent trivial linking of user messages from beacons, provisions are made in the beaconing mechanism, which allows a group of devices in the vicinity of each other to efficiently distribute the beaconing task uniformly within the group. Thus, the probability of the same device sending a beacon message regularly is low.

All NIC messages, similar to UDP/TCP segments, consist of (1) an unencrypted identifier or pseudonym (such as MAC and IP address) that belongs to the message originator and (2) the message itself in either encrypted or unencrypted form, depending on whether the message is private or public, respectively. If the message is not public, identifying information of the target user(s) or community is also included. Link-layer encryption [38, 50] could be used to encrypt MAC addresses, but the performance degradation due to the additional message size and cryptographic operations makes it infeasible for use in NIC. Each device runs (in the background) an identifier-change service, called Pseudonym-Change Algorithm (PCA), which conditionally changes the device MAC address. In this work, we assume that only the MAC address is changed, but the PCA can be easily extended to change application and network layer identifiers as well. For notational purposes, we denote an *actual message* sent by a user u as a five-tuple $m = (t, p, u, \pi, c)$, where t, p and π are the device time (in seconds), location (as a 2-D coordinate) and device identifier, respectively, when m was sent and c is the message content. Note that u is shown here only to associate a message to a particular user and may not actually be sent with the message on the network. M is the set of all actual messages (sent by all users) and $t(m)$, $p(m)$, $\pi(m)$ refer to the time, position and identifier associated with m. A symbol table can be found in the Appendix.

2.2. Adversary Model and Deployment

In this work, we assume a passive adversary that eavesdrops on the messages sent by the devices and that is localized in a certain part of the network. We implement such an adversary by means of a mesh network of IEEE 802.11 wireless routers or APs (Asus WL-500gP APs running OpenWRT Linux), as shown in Fig. 1 (rightmost). This wireless mesh network of 37 APs is located on the same floor-level of six interconnected buildings, where there is high student activity because of the presence of various classrooms, study-areas and a cafeteria. Beyond this area, the adversary has no information on sent messages. The adversary has no direct access to any device, and all devices are assumed to be honest (i.e., non-colluding with the adversary).

Within the coverage area, the adversary is not be able to capture all possible messages due to hardware-related limitations, such as radio interference and hidden terminals, and AP software failures. The amount of data that the adversary can sniff or collect, i.e., adversary's strength, depends on the total number of APs used by her for sniffing. Each of these APs run a "tcpdump" background process to capture all communications on the specified channel and periodically upload the sniffed messages to a central server. The adversary is limited by the constraints of the cryptographic methods, i.e., she is not able to obtain/break the required cryptographic keys to decrypt private messages between devices. The adversary is not able to replay old messages or to inject or synthesize false messages into the network. Our adversary is weaker compared to the standard Dolev-Yao [19] model where the adversary is global, is able to overhear and intercept all messages, and is able to synthesize fake messages in the network. Our weaker, local eavesdropper adversary model is practical, given the current state of the art in monitoring technology, and it is sufficient for launching localized user-tracking attacks.

Let us represent a message observed by the adversary as a five-tuple $\hat{m} = (\hat{t}, \hat{\pi}, \hat{c}, \hat{o}, \hat{s})$, where $\hat{o}$ is the adversary AP observing the message, and $\hat{t}, \hat{\pi}, \hat{c}$ are the reception time (at the AP), device identifier or pseudonym and message content, respectively, and $\hat{s}$ is the received signal strength (in dB) measured by $\hat{o}$. Note that an observed message, obviously, does not contain the identity of the user u who sent the message, but only the device pseudonym $\hat{\pi} = \pi$. Let $\hat{M}$ be the set of all the messages observed by the adversary. The adversary attempts to link all pseudonyms (hence, the messages) belonging to a given user from the set of all observed pseudonymous messages, and thus to reconstruct the path taken by him (over the area observed by the adversary). We refer to this as a *reconstruction attack*, defined as follows:

Definition 1. *A reconstruction attack attempts to construct a temporal sequence or trace* $\tilde{r} = (\hat{\pi}_0, \hat{\pi}_1, \ldots, \hat{\pi}_k)$ *of pseudonyms belonging to the same user, where* Π *is the set of all user pseudonyms and* $\hat{\pi}_i \in \Pi, \forall i$. *The corresponding true sequence, also called* ground-truth, *is denoted by* r.

The adversary's goal is to maximize the success of her reconstruction attack. We measure the success of the adversary by using well-established metrics, as described in Section 5.1. After all the traces belonging to a given user have been reconstructed, the adversary can attempt to deanonymize the actual identity of the user. Such re-identification attacks are beyond the scope of this paper; they could be carried out using several existing strategies in the literature [29, 26].

2.3. Pseudonym Change Algorithm (PCA)

In this work, our main aim is to evaluate context-based location-privacy protection mechanisms against passive adversaries as outlined in the earlier section. For this purpose, we implement a standard context-based identifier-change mechanism, referred to as Pseudonym Change Algorithm or PCA, which uses the concept of *mix-zones* [9, 10]. Mix-zones, as shown in Fig. 1 (middle), are dynamically formed regions (in our case, device neighborhoods) where users' devices stop transmitting and synchronously change their identifiers to achieve communication unlinkability. After exiting the mix-zone, the devices resume communication with new identifiers. It has been shown [10] that such coordinated identifier-changes provide sufficient spatio-temporal de-correlation between devices and their communications. But in order to be effective, identifier-changes should be reflected across all communication layers, including link, network and application layers. As application-layer identifiers can be encrypted and network addresses are dynamically assigned (at least in NIC), we focus on changing only the link layer or MAC address in our PCA.

We now briefly describe our PCA implementation (see Algorithm 1). Using a *context-check* timer t_c, the PCA periodically checks whether its current neighborhood is favorable (enough devices in the neighborhood) for an identifier-change operation. If there are enough devices in the neighborhood and if the total number (*num_context_changes*) of context-based identifier changes on the device, so far, is below some system-defined threshold Q_c, then the PCA initiates the MAC address change operation on the host device by calling the CHANGE_PSEUDONYM() function. It

Algorithm 1 Pseudonym Change Algorithm (PCA)

Define $Q_c \rightarrow$ context quota, $Q_f \rightarrow$ forced quota, $radio\_off\_time \rightarrow$ min. radio silence after identifier change, *change_time_threshold* $\rightarrow$ required min. time threshold and *neighbor_threshold* $\rightarrow$ required min. neighbor threshold for identifier change.

```
on t_f expired do                                ▷ Forced timer expiration
    if num_forced_changes < Q_f then
        BROADCAST(mix_request)
        CHANGE_PSEUDONYM( )
        RADIO_SILENCE(radio_off_time)
        num_forced_changes + +
    end if
end on

on t_c expired do                                ▷ Context timer expiration
    if current neighborhood > neighbor_threshold and num_context_changes < Q_c then
        BROADCAST(mix_request)
        CHANGE_PSEUDONYM( )
        RADIO_SILENCE(radio_off_time)
        num_context_changes + +
    end if
end on

on mix_request received do                       ▷ Incoming mixing request
    Let d_t ← last_change_timestamp − current_timestamp
    if d_t > change_time_threshold and num_context_changes < Q_c then
        CHANGE_PSEUDONYM( )
        RADIO_SILENCE(radio_off_time)
        num_context_changes + +
    end if
end on
```

also initiates a *mix attempt* by sending a *mix-request* to the neighboring devices. After the identifier-change operation, PCA switches off the wireless interface for a random time period and increments the counter for context-based identifier changes. Random timers are used to prevent trivial timing-based linking attacks.

Upon receiving a mix-request, the neighboring devices follow a similar procedure for changing their MAC addresses; they perform an additional check before the identifier-change operation in order to prevent frequent changes that are ineffective and expensive. If the identifier-changes were solely based on device context, it would be possible that devices do not have a favorable context or neighborhood for a long period of time, thus making them trivially trackable. In order to overcome this issue, PCA makes use of another timer, called the *forced-change* timer or t_f. When t_f expires, the device, independently of its neighborhood, changes its MAC and enters a radio silence period if the number of forced identifier changes ($num\_forced\_changes$) is below the system-defined forced-change threshold Q_f. In order to prevent trivial timing attacks, both t_f and t_c are not fixed values but are chosen from a normal distribution (with appropriately chosen mean and variation) independently by each device. Note that the thresholds Q_c and Q_f are maximum *daily* thresholds and the counters $num\_context\_changes$ and $num\_forced\_changes$ are reset *daily* at 00:00 on each device.

In order to evaluate PCA under different privacy settings, we select three sets of parameter values, as shown in Table 1. The first set focuses on *cost-effectiveness* by requiring a comparatively lower number of overall identifier-changes and a larger time-gap between changes, which leads to fewer mixing attempts. Due to relaxed neighborhood requirements per change, the probability that the mixing attempt will be successful for this set of parameters is high. The third set of parameters has provisions for a large number of identifier-changes and a smaller time-gap requirement between changes, thus representing a *privacy-sensitive* behavior. The higher neighborhood requirement per change, in this case, is aimed at improving the unlinkability per change, i.e., each change is more effective than in the earlier case. Finally, the second parameter set represents an *intermediate* behavior.

Before the actual deployment, we divide the devices into three *groups*, each running PCA with a different parameter setting. In order to achieve a uniform distribution of parameters across all devices, the device parameters were shuffled across the groups remotely, once a month. In order to determine an appropriate value for the neighborhood threshold, we refer to the analysis by Kiukkonen et al. [40] who studied real user mobility based on mobile phone data (GPS locations and Bluetooth encounters) of 200 users collected over a period of 2 years. The authors observed that the average probability of any device having a Bluetooth encounter with more than 3 other devices was less than 0.2. WiFi-based peer-to-peer and Bluetooth communications differ in many aspects, but as WiFi-based peer-to-peer networks, such as NIC, are not commonplace, we rely on the above results to select initial values for the neighborhood thresholds. As NIC devices, unlike Bluetooth, are context-sensitive and may be switched-on all the time, the selected threshold values are a bit pessimistic, but they serve as a good starting point. Due to the limited duration of our deployment, we could not test a large variety of parameter configurations in real experiments. Later, as discussed in Section 5.6, we will perform simulation experiments with other PCA parameters and configurations by using the mobility patterns and data flows from the real deployment.

Table 1. PCA parameter values used in the real deployment.

Parameter	Mean t_f	Mean t_c	$Q = Q_c + Q_f$	*change_time_threshold*	*neighbor_threshold*
Cost-effective	14400 sec	3600 sec	5	7200 sec	1
Intermediate	7200 sec	1200 sec	20	1800 sec	2
Privacy-sensitive	3600 sec	300 sec	60	600 sec	3

3. Data Collection and Processing

In order to accurately measure the adversary's success, it is important to compare the results of her tracking attacks to the *groundtruth* (or actual user traces); the groundtruth acts as a reference for evaluating the success of the tracking attacks. The adversary wants to be as close to the groundtruth as possible. In this work, our first task is to reconstruct the groundtruth by adding extra information in the observed data. We assume that this extra information will not be available to the adversary, and as a result she will not be able to reconstruct the groundtruth as outlined in Section 3.1. Nevertheless, the adversary has to perform some basic processing on the observed data, as outlined in Section 3.2, before using it in her tracking attacks.

3.1. Groundtruth Reconstruction

The groundtruth reconstruction step provides the *true* mapping between each observed message and the device that sent it. This mapping will be used later to verify the correctness of the mapping created by the adversary's tracking algorithm. The source MAC address in the messages cannot be used for groundtruth reconstruction because it is regularly updated by the PCA. Thus, in order to obtain the groundtruth, we need to include some *fixed* device identifier in the observed messages. We achieve this by embedding the device *International Mobile Equipment Identity (IMEI)* number in the messages generated by a few user applications. The IMEI contained in the messages from these applications can be used to match different MAC addresses to the same device. For instance, two sets of messages, each with a different MAC address, can be linked to the same device (or user) if there is at least one message containing the IMEI for each MAC used. Even messages that do not contain the IMEI, such as system messages, can be linked together if there is at least one IMEI containing message with the same MAC address. In this way, we are able to reconstruct approximately 99% of the groundtruth from the observed messages.

3.2. Adversary Post-Processing

The adversary faces two main challenges while processing the observed or sniffed data: First, for any message m there may exist multiple copies of observed messages $\hat{m}$ (from different APs or sniffing stations), possibly with different values of $\hat{t}$, $\hat{o}$ and $\hat{s}$ (but obviously, with identical $\hat{\pi}$ and $\hat{c}$). Second, the position of the original message m is not directly available from the observed messages $\hat{m}$; it must be derived from the position of the sniffing stations ($\hat{o}$) and the Received Signal Strength Indicator (RSSI) ($\hat{s}$). For any message m, let $\tilde{m}$ be the re-construction of m by the adversary from the observed messages $\hat{m}$. The objective of the adversary is to reconstruct $\tilde{m}$ as close to m as possible. In order to do this, she has to first gather all observed messages $\hat{m}$ corresponding to the same sent message m. We refer to such a collection of identical observed messages as an *event* that can be represented as a five-tuple $e = (\hat{\pi}, \hat{c}, \hat{T}, \hat{O})$, where $\hat{\pi}$ is the pseudonym the device used while sending the message with content $\hat{c}$, $\hat{T}$ is the set of time-stamps corresponding to the times observed in each of the $\hat{m}$ forming e and $\hat{O}$ is the set of sniffing-station identifiers and corresponding RSSIs associated with each $\hat{m}$ forming e. The set of all events is denoted by E. The construction of E, referred to as *event identification*, can be accomplished by the adversary by matching the pseudonyms ($\hat{\pi}$) and contents ($\hat{c}$) of observed messages. After E is constructed, the adversary can use each event e in E to reconstruct the corresponding $\tilde{m}$ by aggregating all the information in that event. In other words, given an event e, the reconstructed message $\tilde{m}$ can be represented as $\tilde{m}(e) = (u, \tilde{t}, \tilde{p}, \tilde{\pi}, \tilde{c})$, where u is the user that sent the message m, $\tilde{\pi} = \hat{\pi}(e)$, $\tilde{c} = \hat{c}(e)$ and $\tilde{t}, \tilde{p}$ are aggregated values of time and position from $\hat{T}$ and $\hat{O}$ in e. The user u is not known to the adversary after the aggregation phase and it can be determined by using re-identification techniques [29, 26] after executing the tracking algorithms. We now outline the post-processing that the adversary does to construct $\tilde{m}$ (except user information) for each message m from a set of observed messages $\hat{m}$.

3.2.1 Time-stamp Synchronization

In order to accurately aggregate and order time-stamps during event identification, the adversarial sniffing stations or APs should be synchronized with each other. In our deployment, the APs suffer from synchronization problems due to large clock drifts (sometimes in several minutes) and random clock resets (in some rare cases) to the Unix Epoch, i.e., *1970-1-1 00:00:00*. Due to the unavailability of NTP-based solutions on these APs, we employ a *best-effort* synchronization technique. We first divide time into discrete intervals of two hours. For each interval, we construct a graph where the (observed) APs represent the vertices of the graph and there is an edge between two vertices if a clock skew is detected between them. The clock skew gives the edge weight. Then, by means of a standard all-pairs shortest path algorithm such as Floyd-Warshall algorithm, we build a set of *least cost paths* between all pairs of sniffing stations. By starting from the node with the smallest cost path to all other nodes, we correct the clock skews step-by-step, until all clocks are resynchronized. The Nokia N900s are time-synchronized by using the NTP implementation on the devices.

3.2.2 Event Identification

Event identification consists of aggregating identical messages observed by different sniffing stations at (or approximately) the same time. A naive approach that searches the entire message space is infeasible. We use the following two heuristics, which significantly reduce the search space, and thus the event identification time.

- *Temporal proximity-based search*: Typically, any message broadcast by a device arrives at the neighboring sniffing stations within a delay of a few milliseconds of each other. Thus, we define an appropriate time threshold for each observed message and limit our search for identical messages to only those messages that have reception times within this threshold.
- *Spatial proximity-based search*: Assuming that all sniffing stations have the same range, any message sent by a device can be seen by sniffing stations only within a certain distance from the device. As defining distance thresholds is not practical, we define a neighborhood for each sniffing station and limit our search to messages observed by the station and its neighborhood.

We further reduce the processing time for message comparison by comparing the message content hashes (obtained using a cryptographic hash function such as SHA-2) rather than the actual content. This improves the comparison speed because of the reduced length and absence of long common prefixes in the compared strings.

3.2.3 Time-stamp Aggregation

After the event identification step, the adversary needs to reconstruct individual messages $\tilde{m}$ from their corresponding events. For each such message, she needs to first estimate the time at which it may have been sent by the source device. For a reconstructed message $\tilde{m}$ of the original message m, we assume that the adversary chooses the time-stamp $\tilde{t}$ as $min(\hat{T})$, where $\hat{T}$ is the set of time-stamps of the corresponding event. In other words, she chooses the lowest observed time-stamp for each event because it will be closest to the time instant at which the message was actually sent. The goal of aggregating time-stamps in such a fashion is to obtain an accurate ordering for reconstructed messages.

3.2.4 Coordinate Mapping

After assigning time-stamps to each reconstructed message $\tilde{m}$, the adversary needs to estimate its position, i.e., the position of the device when the corresponding m was sent. The adversary does this by aggregating the sniffing station and RSSI information present in each observed message of the event. The location of devices (hence, the messages) and sniffing stations can be represented as two-dimensional coordinates (x, y), where $0 \le x \in \mathbb{R} \le 200$, $0 \le y \in \mathbb{R} \le 100$. Note that the message (or device) positions can be slightly beyond the $186m \times 66m$ sniffing station deployment area. As the adversarial sniffing network is deployed on the same floor level, we do not consider the third dimension. For each reconstructed message $\tilde{m}$, the adversary first computes its distance to each sniffing station (observing that message) from the corresponding RSSI value in the event by using a standard radio propagation model [47] (Eqn. 1).

$$P_r = P_t + 20\log\left(\frac{\lambda}{4\pi}\right) + 10n\log\left(\frac{1}{d}\right) \quad (1)$$

In (1), P_t and P_r are the transmitted and received power [dBm], λ is the wavelength of the radio signal [m], n is the path-loss exponent and d is the distance between the transmitter and receiver [m]. In our deployment, we have $P_t = 20dBm$, $\lambda = 0.125m$ and $n = 4.8$ (considered suitable for indoor environments).

In Algorithm 2, we outline the procedure for computing the message position once the distances have been estimated. There can be four cases, depending on the distinct number of RSSIs available for the event, which in turn depends on the number of distinct observations (by sniffing stations) per message. In case only one observation is available, the position of the reconstructed message is chosen as the location of the sniffing station observing the message. If two observations are available, then a position weighted on the distance to each sniffing station is chosen. In the case three or more distinct distances to non-collinear sniffing stations are available, a straightforward trilateration procedure [37] is used by choosing an appropriate bound on the distance-error .

4. Tracking Framework and Algorithms

We now outline our probabilistic tracking framework and two tracking algorithms within this framework.

Algorithm 2 Position Estimation

Input: $P[]$ is the list of positions of sniffing stations observing the message. $P[i] = (P_x[i], P_y[i])$ are the x and y coordinates of the ith sniffing station observing the message

Input: $\tilde{D}[]$ is the list of distances (computed from signal strength indicator) from each sniffing station observing the message

Output: $\tilde{p}$, the estimated position of the message

$n = |P|$, the number of sniffing stations
$m = |\tilde{D}|$, the number of distances
if not $(n = m)$ OR $n = 0$ **then**
  return ERROR
else if $n = 1$ **then** ▷ Only sniffing station i observes the message
  return $P[i]$
else if $n = 2$ **then** ▷ Only sniffing stations i and j observe the message
  return $\left(P_x[i] + \frac{P_x[j] - P_x[i]}{(\tilde{D}[i] + \tilde{D}[j])/\tilde{D}[i]}, P_y[i] + \frac{P_y[j] - P_y[i]}{(\tilde{D}[i] + \tilde{D}[j])/\tilde{D}[i]}\right)$
else if $n = 3$ **then** ▷ Only sniffing stations i, j and k observe the message
  return TRILATERATION($P[i]$, $\tilde{D}[i]$, $P[j]$, $\tilde{D}[j]$, $P[k]$, $\tilde{D}[k]$)
else
  Let l, m, n be the three sniffing stations in $P[]$ with the smallest distances
  return TRILATERATION($P[l]$, $\tilde{D}[l]$, $P[m]$, $\tilde{D}[m]$, $P[n]$, $\tilde{D}[n]$)
end if

4.1. Probabilistic Tracking Framework

We model the daily observations by the adversarial AP mesh network by using a Markov chain, where a state of the system is defined as the set of ordered observations with the same pseudonym and the transition probability gives the probability of going from one set of observations to the next. As the total number of observations is finite and the transitions probabilities are time-invariant (as discussed below) with a fixed probability distribution on the initial states, the proposed model can be characterized as a *finite state first order Markov chain*.

Let S be the state space and each state $s \in S$ be represented as a triple of the form $s = (\pi, e_{start}, e_{end})$, where $\pi \in \Pi$ is a pseudonym and e_{start}, e_{end} are temporally[1] the first and last event respectively using the pseudonym π. Here, $t_{start}(s) = \tilde{t}(e_{start}(s))$ and $t_{end}(s) = \tilde{t}(e_{end}(s))$ are the corresponding start and end times of the state s, respectively. A similar notation is used for the observers and received signal strengths of the state. The transition probability matrix is defined by a transition function $P : S \times S \rightarrow [0, 1]$ that satisfies the following two constraints: 1) *Validity*: $\sum_{s_j \in S} P(s_i, s_j) = 1 \; \forall s_i \in S$ and 2) *Time monotonicity*: $P(s_i, s_j) = 0 \; \forall s_i, s_j \in S$ such that $t_{end}(s_i) > t_{start}(s_j)$. Each entry in the transition probability matrix $P[i, j]$ represents how likely the adversary considers state s_j to follow s_i; it gives the likelihood of the adversary to observe events in s_j immediately after observing events in s_i for any user. The transition probability matrix is user-invariant, i.e., the adversary's transition function is the same for all users. The tracking success of the adversary depends on how well the transition function is defined and how close it is to the actual transitions. In this work, we estimate the transition function by using two heuristics that intuitively capture the likelihood of observing a set of events from some previous events.

1. *Common sniffing stations*: The probability that a state s' is the next state of state s is proportional to the number of common sniffing stations in the events observed in s and in s'. The higher the number of common sniffing stations between s and s', the higher the probability of transitioning from s to s'.

2. *Speed matching*: As each event has position and time information, a notion of *speed between two events* can be defined as the Euclidean distance between the (position of) two events divided by the time difference between the events. Then, according to our speed-matching heuristic, the probability that a state s' follows state s is $1 - |v(s) - v(s')|/v_{max}$, where $v(s)$ is the speed of state s and v_{max} is the maximum speed ($5m/s$ in our case).

The tracking framework and the transition probabilities described above are for a single user, given his initial state (or some probability distribution on it). In this case, the attacker wants to determine a single (most probable) path in the state space corresponding to the user in the initial state. It is also possible to track multiple users simultaneously using the above model, i.e., the attacker will attempt to find several non-overlapping paths in the state space, given the initial states of multiple users. As the transitions in this case are between *sets* of states or *multi-states* (one state for each user being tracked), the transition probability function needs to be accordingly modified. The transition probability of one multi-state to the next can be estimated by normalizing the sum of the individual transition probabilities in the multi-set. Specific details of the single user and multi-user transition probability matrix computations can be found in [11].

[1] An implicit assumption here is that no pseudonym is reused.

4.2. Tracking Strategies

We propose two straightforward adversarial tracking strategies based on the above tracking framework.

4.2.1 Locally Optimal Walk (L-WALK)

The L-WALK algorithm (Alg. 3) reconstructs the user trace by performing a locally-optimal walk in the state space. In other words, at each state (of the walk), starting from the initial state, the next state candidate with the highest probability is selected, until there are no further candidates. L-WALK produces an ordered sequence of states $T = (s_0, s_1, ..., s_k)$ $(k > 0)$ such that $P(s_i, s_{i+1}) > P(s_i, s') \ \forall\ s' \in S \setminus s_{i+1} \ \forall\ i = 0, 1, ..., k$.

Algorithm 3 Locally optimal walk (L-WALK)

Input: Initial state s_0, heuristic function P
Output: Trace $T = (s_0, ..., s_k)$

$T \leftarrow (s_0)$, $continue \leftarrow True$
repeat
  Let c be the next state candidate with the highest probability
  Append c to T
until no more candidates
return T

From Alg. 3, we can see that L-WALK iteratively builds a walk by selecting the probabilistically best next state at each iteration and stops when no more states are available. It is possible to improve L-WALK by using additional reference points along the walk. For instance, if the adversary is able to ascertain that some state s_j is associated to a given user, she can use s_j to better direct her search in cases where multiple next states are equally probable at a given state. Due to this additional knowledge, paths that do not pass through s_j can also be discarded by the adversary. More than one such reference point will further improve the accuracy of the adversary's walk.

4.2.2 Globally Optimal Walk (G-WALK)

The G-WALK algorithm (Alg. 4) reconstructs the user trace by performing a walk in the state space such that the probability over the entire walk is maximized over all walks. In other words, G-WALK produces an ordered sequence of states $T = (s_0, s_1, ..., s_k)$ $(k > 0)$ such that $\Pi_{i=0}^{k-1} P(s_i, s_{i+1}) > \Pi_{j=0}^{l-1} P(s'_j, s'_{j+1}) \ : \ \forall T' = (s'_0, s'_1, ..., s'_l)$ with $T' \neq T$ and $s_0 = s'_0$. Unlike L-WALK, G-WALK does not rely on locally optimal choices but makes a globally optimal choice.

An exhaustive search for a globally optimal path is infeasible due to the large number of paths in the state space. In order to obtain a fairly good approximation of the global optimum, we use a randomized search heuristic called Simulated Annealing (SA) [33]. In G-WALK, the current solution in each iteration is replaced by a random "nearby" solution chosen with a probability that depends both on the difference between the values of those solutions and a global parameter t, called the temperature, which is gradually decreased in each iteration. The "nearby" solution or path is chosen by the MUTATE function, which replaces one of the state transitions in the current solution by an alternate one. The temperature parameter enables the algorithm to escape local optima throughout the simulation, while slowly converging to a near-optimal solution.

Algorithm 4 Globally optimal walk (G-WALK)

Input: Initial state s_0, transition function P, maximum evaluation count c_{max}, initial temperature $t_{initial}$ and temperature decrease factor $k \in [0, 1]$
Output: Trace $T = (s_0, ..., s_k)$

$T \leftarrow$ L-WALK(s_0), $v \leftarrow \Pi_{i=0}^{k-1} P(s_i, s_{i+1})$ ▷ Initial solution and likelihood
$T_{best} \leftarrow T$, $v_{best} \leftarrow v$ ▷ Best solution and likelihood
$c \leftarrow 0$ ▷ Initial evaluation count
while $c < c_{max}$ **do**
  $T_{new} \leftarrow$ MUTATE(T), $v_{new} \leftarrow \Pi_{i=0}^{k-1} P(s_{new,i}, s_{new,i+1})$
  $t \leftarrow$ TEMPERATURE(c), $c \leftarrow c + 1$
  if RANDOM( ) $<$ ACCEPT_PROBABILITY(v, v_{new}, t) **then** ▷ Randomly move to a new state
    $T \leftarrow T_{new}$, $v \leftarrow v_{new}$
  end if
  if $v_{new} > v_{best}$ **then**
    $T_{best} \leftarrow T_{new}$, $v_{best} \leftarrow v_{new}$
  end if
end while
return T_{best}

function MUTATE(T)
  Let T' be a random mutation of T.
  return T'
end function

function TEMPERATURE(c)
  return $t_{initial} \cdot (k)^c$
end function

function ACCEPT_PROBABILITY(v, v_{new}, t)
  return $min(1, e^{(v_{new}-v)/t})$
end function

5. Empirical Results and Evaluation

We evaluate the success of the L-WALK and G-WALK algorithms in tracking users by using well-known metrics for location privacy.

5.1. Privacy Metrics

We use four metrics in our evaluation; each uniquely captures the extent to which users can be tracked.

5.1.1 Traceability Metrics (τ-metrics)

Traceability metrics, originally proposed by Hoh et al. [32], capture the extent to which the user can be tracked in time or distance. In our setting, we define two traceability metrics: the percentage of time τ_t and the percentage of space τ_d during which tracking is successful. Formally, these metrics are defined as follows:

Definition 2 (Traceability metrics). *Let $\tilde{r} = (\tilde{\pi_0}, \tilde{\pi}_1, ..., \tilde{\pi}_l)$ denote the reconstruction of user pseudonyms as obtained by a reconstruction attack and $r = (\pi_0, \pi_1, ..., \pi_k)$ be the real sequence (groundtruth) of pseudonyms. The time- and distance-traceability metrics are:*

$$\tau_t(r, \tilde{r}) = \frac{\sum_{i=0}^{min(k,l)} t_{match}(\pi_i, \tilde{\pi}_i)}{\sum_{i=0}^{k} t_{used}(\pi_i)}$$

$$\tau_d(r, \tilde{r}) = \frac{\sum_{i=0}^{min(k,l)} d_{match}(\pi_i, \tilde{\pi}_i)}{\sum_{i=0}^{k} d_{used}(\pi_i)}$$

where $t_{used}(\pi)$ and $d_{used}(\pi)$ are the actual time and distance that pseudonym π was used by the user being tracked, and $t_{match}(\pi, \tilde{\pi})$ and $d_{match}(\pi, \tilde{\pi})$ are the time and distance during which pseudonym $\tilde{\pi}$ is correctly matched to π in the reconstructed trace by the adversary for that user.

5.1.2 Uncertainty Metrics (u-metrics)

Uncertainty metrics, originally proposed by Diaz et al. [18], capture the uncertainty of the adversary to correctly predict the next pseudonym used by the user. We define three uncertainty metrics as follows.

Definition 3 (Uncertainty metrics). *Let $\tilde{r} = (\tilde{\pi_0}, \tilde{\pi}_1, ..., \tilde{\pi}_l)$ denote the reconstruction of user pseudonyms obtained by a reconstruction attack. Let $Y(\overline{\pi})$ be the random variable denoting the next possible pseudonym (selected by the adversary) of pseudonym $\overline{\pi}$ and $\mathcal{H}$ denote the entropy operator. Then, we have the following uncertainty metrics that give the average, maximum and minimum entropy for all pseudonym changes:*

$$u_{avg}(\tilde{r}) = \frac{1}{l} \cdot \sum_{i=0}^{l-1} \mathcal{H}(Y(\pi_i))$$

$$u_{max}(\tilde{r}) = \max\{\mathcal{H}(Y(\pi_i)) \mid \pi_i \in \tilde{r} \setminus \tilde{\pi}_l\}$$

$$u_{min}(\tilde{r}) = \min\{\mathcal{H}(Y(\pi_i)) \mid \pi_i \in \tilde{r} \setminus \tilde{\pi}_l\}$$

5.1.3 Traceability-Uncertainty Metrics (μ-metrics)

Traceability-Uncertainty metrics combine the advantages of the traceability and uncertainty metrics by capturing both the extent to which the user can be tracked, as well as the difficulty (or uncertainty) in tracking. They can be defined as follows.

Definition 4 (Traceability-uncertainty metric). *Let $\tilde{r} = (\tilde{\pi_0}, \tilde{\pi}_1, ..., \tilde{\pi}_l)$, $r = (\pi_0, \pi_1, ..., \pi_k)$, $Y(\overline{\pi})$ be defined as above. Let $\mathcal{H}_{max}(Y(\overline{\pi})) = \log_2 |Y(\overline{\pi})|$ denote the maximum achievable entropy for pseudonym $\overline{\pi}$. Then, the corresponding time- (μ_t) and distance-traceability-uncertainty (μ_d) metrics are:*

$$\mu_t(r, \tilde{r}) = \frac{\sum_{i=1}^{min(k,l)} \frac{\mathcal{H}(Y(\pi_{i-1}))}{\mathcal{H}_{max}(Y(\pi_{i-1}))} \cdot t_{match}(\pi_i, \tilde{\pi}_i)}{\sum_{i=1}^{min(k,l)} t_{used}(\pi_i)}$$

$$\mu_d(r, \tilde{r}) = \frac{\sum_{i=1}^{min(k,l)} \frac{\mathcal{H}(Y(\pi_{i-1}))}{\mathcal{H}_{max}(Y(\pi_{i-1}))} \cdot d_{match}(\pi_i, \tilde{\pi}_i)}{\sum_{i=1}^{min(k,l)} d_{used}(\pi_i)}$$

5.1.4 Clustering Metrics (c-metrics)

Clustering c-metrics, as proposed by Hoh et al. [31], capture the extent to which one user was confused with another in the context of multiple user tracking. We define the clustering error metric as a measure of the average distance-error between the reconstructed and real sequence of pseudonym over all users. We first define the clustering error for a single user as follows:

Definition 5 (Clustering error for single user). *For any user u, let $\tilde{r} = (\tilde{\pi_0}, ..., \tilde{\pi}_l)$ and $r = (\pi_0, ..., \pi_k)$ be defined as above and $p_{start}(\overline{\pi})$ be the position of the start event of the subtrace with pseudonym $\overline{\pi}$. Then, the clustering error c_u for user u is the average distance between the start events in the reconstruction and in the groundtruth:*

$$c_u(r, \tilde{r}) = \frac{1}{min(k, l) - 1} \cdot \sum_{i=0}^{min(k,l)} \|p_{start}(\tilde{\pi}_i) - p_{start}(\pi_i)\|$$

Then, the multi-user clustering error metric can be defined as follows.

Definition 6 (Clustering error metric). *Let $\tilde{R}$ be the set of reconstructed sequences of user pseudonyms as obtained*

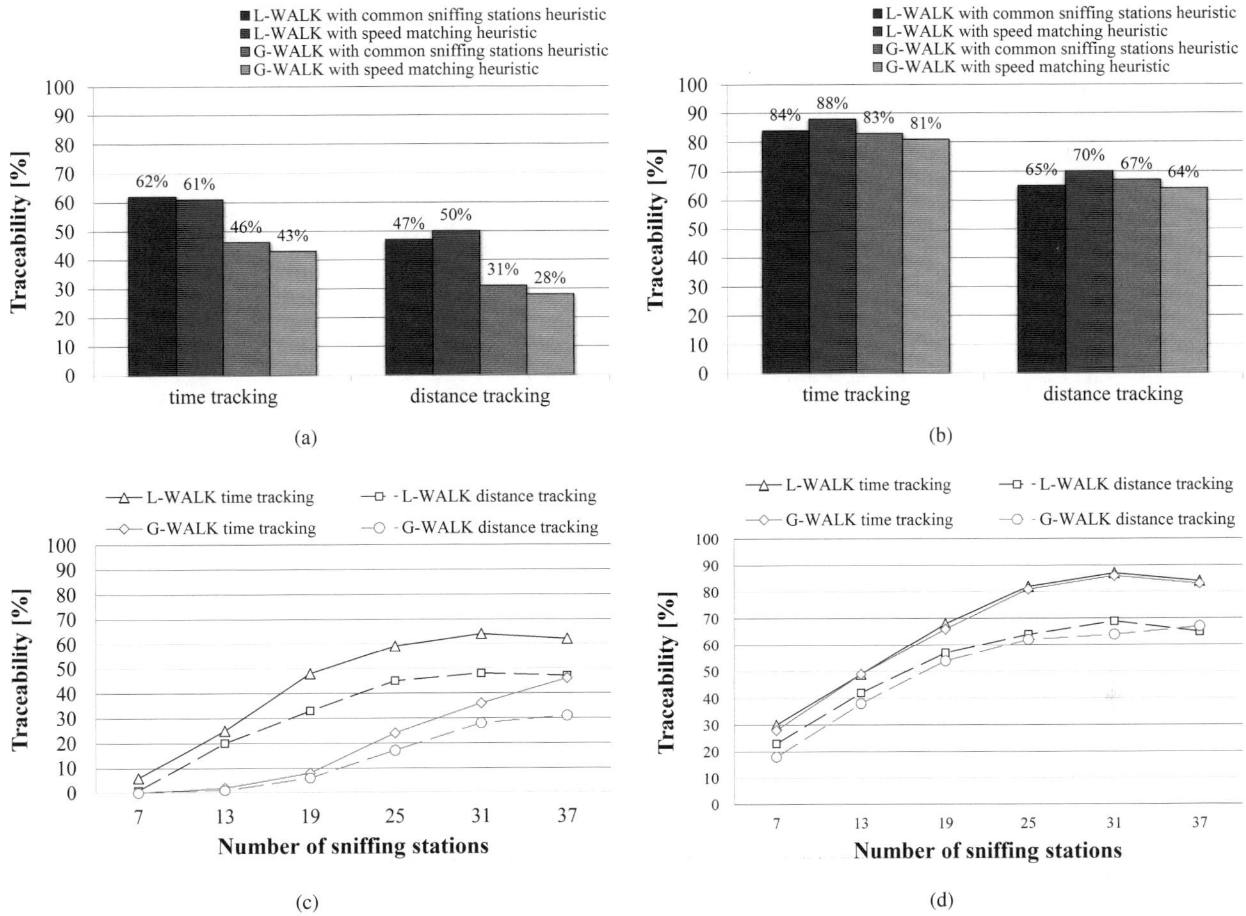

Figure 2. Traceability success: 2(a) single user tracking results; 2(b) multiple user tracking results. Adversary strengths using `L-WALK` and `G-WALK`: 2(c) single user; 2(d) multiple users.

by a multi-user reconstruction attack, R be the set of real sequences (groundtruth) of pseudonyms for the same users and U be the set of all users. Then, the the clustering error metric C is defined as the average clustering error over all users:

$$C(R, \tilde{R}) = \frac{1}{|U|} \cdot \sum_{u \in U, r \in R, \tilde{r} \in \tilde{R}} c_u(r, \tilde{r})$$

The evaluation of the proposed tracking algorithms with more sophisticated privacy metrics, such as the one by Shokri et al. [45, 44], is left as part of future work.

5.2. Results Overview

Fig. 2(a) shows the results for the single-user tracking using time and distance traceability metrics, which are averaged across all users and all tracking attempts over the entire 4-month duration. We can observe that the success ratio of `L-WALK` is around 60% with the time traceability metric and roughly 50% with the distance traceability metric. Also, both the speed and common station heuristics fared more or less equally well. The high success ratio of the simple `L-WALK` algorithm shows that the current PCA parameters (Table 1), althought realistic, do not perform very well in networking scenarios with slow or limited mobility, such as a network of smartphone users. In our setting, it is indeed rare to observe users move significantly during a mixing attempt. Consequently, even simple algorithms, such as `L-WALK`, are very effective in providing a correct ordering on candidates for the next state, despite the fact that transition probability estimates are not extremely precise.

In order to have an equivalent performance comparison of the `G-WALK` with `L-WALK` for the single user case, we need to slightly adapt `G-WALK`'s maximization criterion. In the single-user case, simply maximizing the product of probabilities for each complete walk is inherently prone to selecting shorter walks (as their products tend to be larger than those of longer walks). In our implementation, rather than simply maximizing the product of probabilities, G-WALK selects the walk that maximizes the geometric average of its probabilities, i.e., $\sqrt[k]{\Pi_{i=0}^{k-1} P(s_i, s_{i+1})} > \sqrt[l]{\Pi_{i=0}^{l-1} P(s'_i, s'_{i+1})}$ $\forall T' = (s'_0, s'_1, ..., s'_l)$ with $T' \neq T, s'_i \in S$ $\forall\ i = 0, 1, ..., k$. Thus, by taking into account the length of each walk, we avoid the previous bias towards selecting shorter walks.

Experimental results show that the success rate of G-WALK in tracking individual users is just over 43% with the time traceability metric and around 30% with the distance traceability metric, which is obviously lower than that of L-WALK. This fact can be explained based on the probability assignment done by the common sniffing stations and speed-matching heuristics. Both these heuristics are static and memoryless, i.e., they do not consider the probability of reaching a particular state (from the initial state) in order to estimate transition probabilities from that state. As a result, the transition probabilities assigned by these heuristics would suggest a good ordering rather than an accurate overall probability estimate, which explains why L-WALK performs better as it attempts to determine the most likely order of states by making locally optimal decisions. Figure 3 shows a (partial) snapshot of the single-user tracking algorithm execution on the data collected from our experiments. In this figure, the blue color shows the groundtruth, the green color indicates the path chosen by the L-WALK algorithm and the red color indicates the path chosen by the G-WALK algorithm. We can clearly see that G-WALK attempts to choose a globally optimal path, which is not the correct one, and thus results in a lower traceability. Moreover, a manual examination of a few tens of sample paths also reveals that the percentage of situations, where the overall most likely path in the graph was truly the correct path, was less than 20%, thus explaining the discrepancy between L-WALK and G-WALK. Further improvements of the likelihood heuristics and G-WALK are left as future work. L-WALK could be further improved by using reference points in order to guide the state search. Only one extra reference point suffices to increase L-WALK's average traceability by 20%. With two more reference points, the traceability nears 95%.

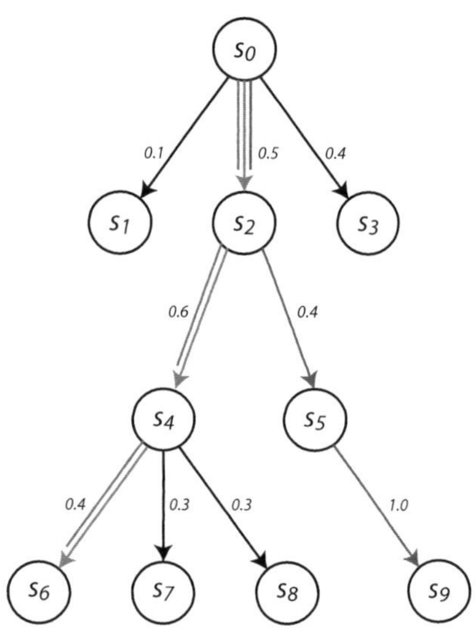

Figure 3. L-WALK **versus** G-WALK.

Fig. 2(b) presents multiple user time- and distance-traceability results. Both L-WALK and G-WALK methods yield approximately the same results: over 80% time traceability and over 60% distance traceability. The main advantage of multiple user tracking over single user tracking is that the former leads to no collisions: as all users are being tracked simultaneously, no two users can have the same next state. Another advantage is that multiple user tracking algorithms can handle the users' leaving the experiment area, and their coming back, because they have a global picture of all users. These advantages lead to a higher tracking success.

Table 2 summarizes all tracking results for the previously defined metrics. In particular, we observe that the uncertainty (u_{avg}) depends both on the data and the heuristic used and that the μ-metrics (traceability-uncertainty combined) roughly follow the τ-metrics (traceability only). Finally, the c-metric, which is defined only in the multiple user scenario, indicates a clustering error of about 8 meters. Although this is not enough to precisely track a single user, in most cases it is enough to identify the room in which the user is.

5.3. Adversary Strength

Hereafter, we evaluate the success of the proposed tracking algorithms under varying adversarial strengths. We vary adversarial strengths by systematically reducing the adversary's sniffing capabilities (see Table 3) at each step of the evaluation. At each step, we reduce the number of sniffing stations (specifically, by six additional stations), and thus the corresponding sniffed data, available for tracking. These sniffing stations are selected based on the coverage provided by each of them such that the overal coverage after their removal is maximized.

Fig. 2(c) shows the success rate of single user tracking under varying adversarial strengths. We can observe that the traceability success increases with the number of adversarial sniffing stations, which is intuitive. Interestingly, the traceability success stabilizes after a given point (31 sniffing stations), where the adversary's coverage can be considered as optimal and additional stations are not very useful.

Similarly, Fig. 2(d) shows the success rate of multiple user tracking for varying values of adversary strength. The traceability success trends for the multiple user track-

Table 2. Complete tracking results using the time, distance and clustering privacy metrics.

Users	Method	Heuristic	τ_t	τ_d	u_{avg}	μ_t	μ_d	c_{avg}
Single User	L-WALK	common stations	62%	47%	0.69	40%	37%	-
		speed matching	61%	51%	1.21	59%	41%	-
	G-WALK	common stations	46%	31%	0.33	23%	17%	-
		speed matching	43%	28%	0.80	36%	25%	-
Multiple Users	L-WALK	common stations	84%	65%	0.47	-	-	8.32
		speed matching	88%	70%	0.63	-	-	7.86
	G-WALK	common stations	83%	67%	0.52	-	-	8.78
		speed matching	81%	64%	0.56	-	-	8.10

ing case are very similar to those in single user tracking, except that in multiple user tracking, the success rate is around 20% higher compared to single user tracking over all the adversary strengths. In fact, by processing multiple users at the same time, we observe that the algorithms perform better even with significant inaccuracies in the user positions.

Table 3. Adversary strengths.

# stations	Density [$/1000m^2$]	Strength
37	1.9	100%
31	1.6	84%
25	1.3	68%
19	1.0	51%
13	0.7	35%
7	0.4	19%

There might be other adversary models for tracking that are significantly weaker than (even the passive version of) the omni-potent Dolev-Yao model but relevant from the practical point of view. To be more widely useful, such an adversary model should, of course, be applicable to many different kinds of scenarios. Finding such a model is an interesting research challenge.

5.4. Impact on Network Efficiency

While providing privacy protection, one major concern for pseudonym change mechanisms is the effect it can have on the network performance. We analyze the effect of our pseudonym change mechanism on the network performance by computing the average time spent by devices in a mix-zone and the resulting packet loss rate. We estimate the average time of a device in a mix-zone by computing the ratio of the average mixing time to the average time between two mixings for that device. We estimate the packet loss between two mix attempts by computing the ratio of the average number of packets that would be sent during a mix attempt to the average number of packets sent between two mix attempts. In our experiments, we observe that between two mixing attempts, devices spend an average of 1.5% of their network time in mix-zones, resulting in a packet loss rate of approximately 2.4%. These results show that PCA with the current parameters does not have a major effect on the network performance. However, these values do not consider the costs involved in re-establishing connections or the effect on transport protocols with congestion control mechanisms.

5.5. Traceability in Large User Clusters

Intuitively, when users organize themselves in large clusters (each cluster consisting of many mix-zones close to each other), user density within individual mix-zones also increases, thus leading to larger anonymity sets. Technically, this should result in better protection against trace reconstruction or tracking attacks. To verify this intuition, we measure the traceability of users on some selected days when the user-density is comparatively higher, for example, around the time when participants have lectures. Specifically, we define two tracking intervals, each of approximately 10 minutes, one at the beginning and the other at the end of the monitored lecture.

We plot (Fig. 4) the average time traceability, as defined in Section 5.1, and the *picked-up* ratio during these two tracking intervals. The picked-up ratio is the ratio of the number of users for which the subtraces in the first and the second tracking interval match the ground truth to the total number of users in both the intervals. The horizontal axis in the plot denotes the number of users, during a particular lecture, that can be followed by our multiple target tracking algorithm. This number is also indicative of the size of the user cluster on that particular day, although it does not directly represent the size of each mix-zone within that cluster. We plot tracking results for 9 different lectures of the same course. We can see from the results that an increase in the number of users present in the cluster decreases both the traceability and the picked-up ratio. In other words, large clusters enable users to hide from the adversary. Note that these results include users (not necessarily in equal num-

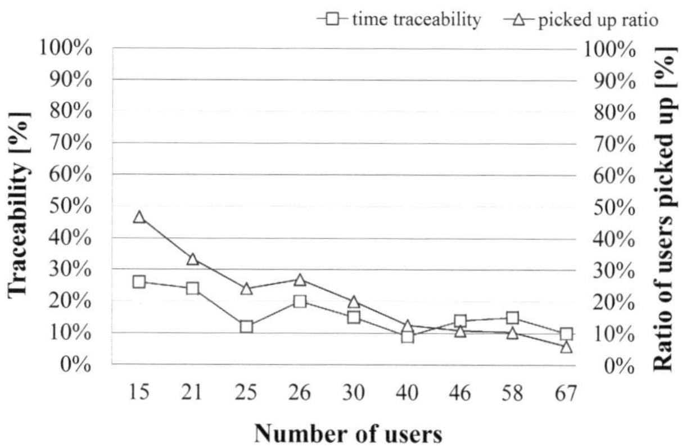

Figure 4. Traceability and picked-up ratio versus the number of users in large clusters.

bers) from all the three parameter values outlined in Table 1 and that non-deterministic factors, such as user movements, speed etc., can have an influence on the traceability, as visible from the slight irregularities in the plots.

5.6. PCA Improvements

The experimental results with the current set of PCA parameters (Table 1) show that even mobile users deploying identifier-changes are highly traceable and are prone to location privacy-related attacks. The question remains: Is it possible to choose better values (from the privacy perspective) for PCA parameters or to improve the PCA in general? In this section, we attempt to answer these questions by selecting two new sets of PCA parameters, which we consider to be significantly more aggressive with respect to privacy preservation. These parameters are outlined in Table 4. We performed simulations to verify the effectiveness of these aggressive parameter values in preventing user traceability.

Table 4. Aggressive PCA parameters.

Parameter	Aggressive	V. aggressive
Mean t_f	1200 sec	600 sec
Mean t_c	120 sec	60 sec
$Q = Q_c + Q_f$	200	500
change_time_threshold	300 sec	120 sec
neighbor_threshold	3	3

We simulated PCA with these new parameters, while retaining all original user communication and mobility patterns. These simulations build a new set of traces from the original traces and from the groundtruth (obtained during the real experiments) by correctly simulating coordinated identifier-changes or mixing on the devices at the appropriate times and locations.

Fig. 5(a) and 5(b) show the traceability results of the `L-WALK` and `G-WALK` algorithms on the simulation-based traces. These plots show that, although aggressive parameters result in better location privacy for users in general, multiple-user tracking still performs sufficiently well and is a concern to location privacy. Furthermore, both the new sets of parameters result in a significant network performance degradation, which makes it harder to implement them in practice. Network performance will only worsen for more aggressive parameter values.

Overall, the traceability results indicate that the current PCA specification, regardless of the chosen parameter values, is not very successful in preventing tracking attacks against users in mobile and pervasive networking systems. As a result, we propose three improvements to our original PCA specification, as outlined below, and evaluate each of them in a simulation setting.

1. *PCA with radio silence randomized over a larger time interval*: each device implements a radio silence delay (t_{silent}) that is randomly selected between 0 and 30 seconds, as opposed to the original specification, where it was randomly selected between 10 and 20 seconds.

2. *PCA with longer radio silence*: radio silence (t_{silent}) is observed for a longer time period (30-90 seconds).

3. *PCA with radio silence until movement detected*: radio silence is observed until the user has traveled a distance of at least d (randomly selected in the interval $[0, 20]$) meters since the mixing decision.

As before, we simulate these PCA improvements over the original experimental traces and the groundtruth obtained from the real experiments. Tracking is performed on the resulting simulated traces and the traceability results are outlined in Fig. 5(c) and 5(d). We can see that all the PCA improvements discussed above are successful against the speed matching heuristic. However, solely randomizing the radio silence, as proposed in the first two cases, is not enough to defeat the common sniffing stations heuristic due to the lower mobility and speed of users. Determining the length of the radio silence period by making use of the user's mobility (third improvement) provides protection against this heuristic. In this case, radio silence periods can sometimes be extremely long, e.g., 30 minutes or more, which could result in poor network performance and QoS.

6. Conclusion

In this paper, we have evaluated the effectiveness of mix-zone-based identifier-change mechanisms in upcoming

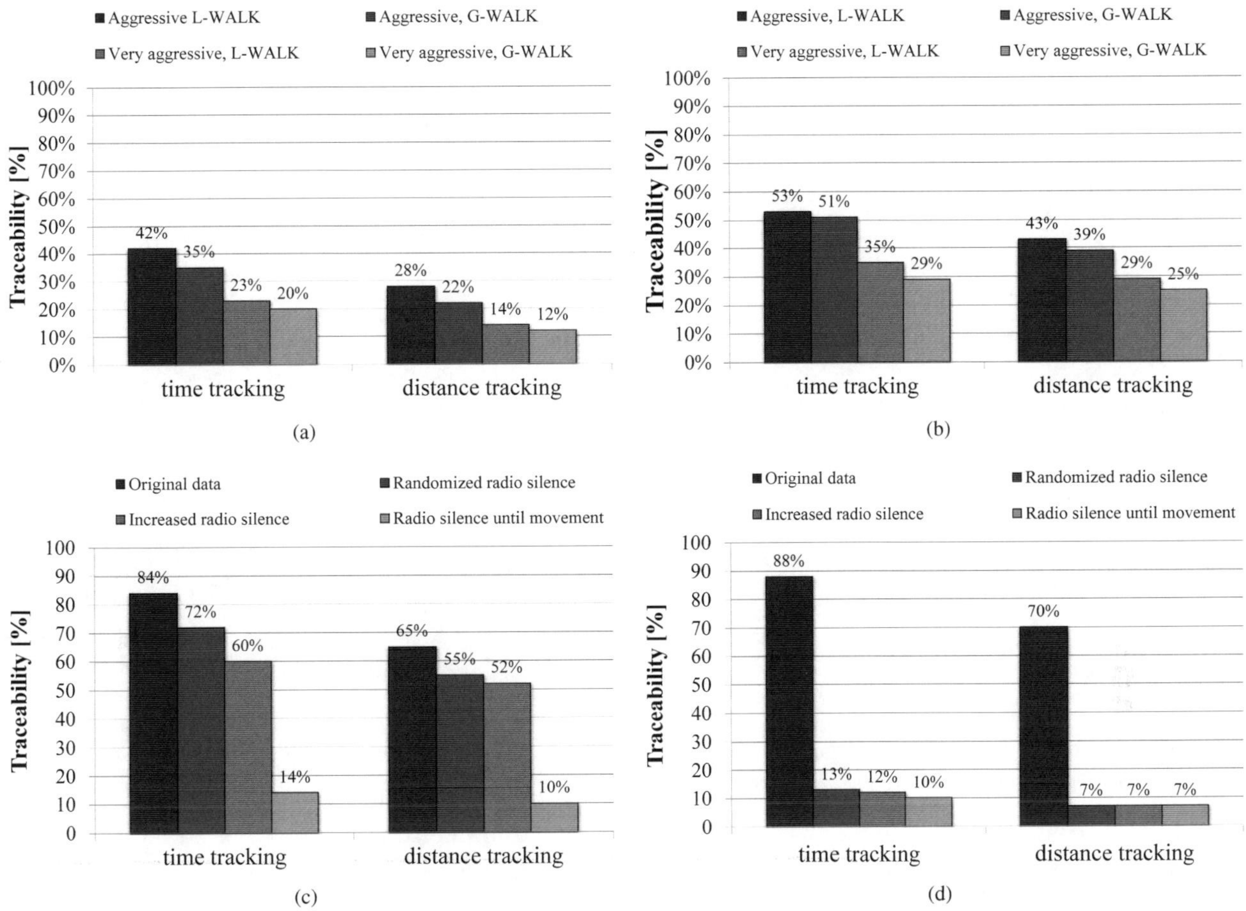

Figure 5. Results for aggressive parameters: 5(a) single user; 5(b) multiple users. Results with modified PCA in multiple user tracking: 5(c) common sniffing stations; 5(d) speed matching.

wireless and mobile systems by means of a real deployment of 80 Nokia N900 smartphones on the EPFL campus. The local passive adversary, in our case, is comprised of a wireless mesh network of 37 access points covering a $200m x 100m$ rectangular area of the campus. Our adversary's goal was to reconstruct an accurate ordering of identifiers that belong to the same device in order to learn the path taken by users. For this purpose, the adversary constructed a probabilisitc tracking (Markov) model by employing intuitive heuristics on the observations from the adversarial access points. Two strategies were used to determine the most likely path taken by the users, (1) a local greedy strategy (`L-WALK`) and (2) a globally optimal strategy (`G-WALK`).

Our results have shown that, in real settings, even simple tracking strategies achieve high traceability success. By changing identifiers in an aggressive fashion, we have observed that the tracking success of the adversary reduces considerably, albeit with a significant decrease in the network performance. We have observed that a decrease in the number of adversary sniffing stations results in lower traceability. There is still a need to find a generic adversary model that is weaker than the standard Dolev-Yao model but stronger than our localized and stationary eavesdropper. Finally, we have also shown that randomizing silence periods within a mix-zone, based on time-of-change or distance travelled post-change, can vastly imrove the effectiveness of mixing in real systems.

Acknowledgments

We would like to thank Adel Aziz, Julien Herzen and Patrick Thiran for their support and guidance during the setup of the adversarial wireless mesh network. Special thanks to Andreea Anghel for implementing the PCA and to all the EPFL students who participated in the trial. Finally, we are grateful to Nokia Research Center for funding this project.

References

[1] https://foursquare.com/.
[2] http://en.wikipedia.org/wiki/Lovegetty.
[3] http://en.wikipedia.org/wiki/Bluedating.
[4] https://facebook.com/.
[5] http://pleaserobme.com/.
[6] I. Aad, M. Jadliwala, I. Bilogrevic, V. Niemi, L. Bindschaedler, J.-P. Hubaux, P. Ginzboorg, and K. Leppänen. Nokia Instant Community at EPFL: a Real-world Large-scale Wireless Peer-to-Peer Trial. Technical Report EPFL-REPORT-170421, EPFL, Lausanne, Switzerland, 2011.
[7] A. Ahtiainen, K. Kalliojarvi, M. Kasslin, K. Leppanen, A. Richter, P. Ruuska, and C. Wijting. Awareness networking in wireless environments: Means of exchanging information. *IEEE Vehicular Technology Magazine*, September 2009.
[8] T. Alpcan and S. Buchegger. Security games for vehicular networks. *IEEE Transactions on Mobile Computing*, 2011.
[9] A. R. Beresford and F. Stajano. Location privacy in pervasive computing. *Pervasive Computing*, 2003.
[10] A. R. Beresford and F. Stajano. Mix zones: User privacy in location-aware services. In *PerCom Workshop*, 2004.
[11] L. Bindschaedler. Track me if you can. Master's thesis, School of Computer and Communication Sciences, EPFL, 2011.
[12] L. Buttyán, T. Holczer, and I. Vajda. On the effectiveness of changing pseudonyms to provide location privacy in VANETs. In *ESAS*, 2007.
[13] L. Buttyán, T. Holczer, A. Weimerskirch, and W. Whyte. Slow: A practical pseudonym changing scheme for location privacy in VANETs. In *IEEE VNC*, 2009.
[14] D. Chaum. Untraceable electronic mail, return addresses and digital pseudonyms. *Comm. ACM*, 1981.
[15] D. Chaum. The dining cryptographers problem: Unconditional sender and recipient untraceability. *J. Cryptology*, 1988.
[16] Z. Chen, H. Shen, Q. Xu, and X. Zhou. Instant Advertising in Mobile Peer-to-Peer Networks. In *ICDE*, 2009.
[17] M. Corson, R. Laroia, J. Li, V. Park, T. Richardson, and G. Tsirtsis. Toward Proximity-aware Internetworking. *Wireless Communications*, 2010.
[18] C. Diaz, S. Seys, J. Claessens, and B. Preneel. Towards measuring anonymity. In *PETS*, 2002.
[19] D. Dolev and A. C. Yao. On the security of public key protocols. *IEEE trans. on Information Theory*, 1983.
[20] B. M. East. Iranian opposition activists hanged for protest footage. *http://www.bbc.co.uk/news/world-middle-east-12272067*, 2011.
[21] J. Eberspächer, H.-J. Vögel, C. Bettstetter, and C. Hartmann. *GSM - Architecture, Protocols and Services*. Wiley, 2008.
[22] M. Follman. "Bluetoothing" Iran's revolution. *Markfollman.com*, 2010.
[23] J. Freudiger, M. Jadliwala, J.-P. Hubaux, V. Niemi, P. Ginzboorg, and I. Aad. Privacy of community pseudonyms in wireless peer-to-peer networks. Technical Report EPFL-REPORT-170392, EPFL, Lausanne, Switzerland, 2011.
[24] J. Freudiger, M. Raya, M. Felegyhazi, P. Papadimitratos, and J.-P. Hubaux. Mix zones for location privacy in vehicular networks. In *Win-ITS*, 2007.
[25] J. Freudiger, R. Shokri, and J.-P. Hubaux. On the optimal placement of mix zones. In *PETS*, 2009.
[26] J. Freudiger, R. Shokri, and J.-P. Hubaux. Evaluating the privacy risk of location-based services. In *Financial Cryptography*, 2011.
[27] S. Gaonkar, J. Li, R. R. Choudhury, L. P. Cox, and A. Schmidt. Micro-blog: sharing and querying content through mobile phones and social participation. In *MobiSys*, 2008.
[28] M. Gerlach and F. Guttler. Privacy in VANETs using changing pseudonyms - ideal and real. In *IEEE VTC-Spring*, 2007.
[29] P. Golle and K. Partridge. On the anonymity of home/work location pairs. In *Pervasive*, 2009.
[30] M. Hachman. Peep Proposes Wireless P2P System. *PC Magazine*, 2011.
[31] B. Hoh and M. Gruteser. Protecting location privacy through path confusion. In *SecureComm*, 2005.
[32] B. Hoh, M. Gruteser, H. Xiong, and A. Alrabady. Preserving privacy in GPS traces via uncertainty-aware path cloaking. In *ACM CCS*, 2007.
[33] J. Hromkovič. *Algorithms for Hard Problems*. Springer-Verlag, 2004.
[34] L. Huang, K. Matsuura, H. Yamane, and K. Sezaki. Enhancing wireless location privacy using silent period. In *IEEE WCNC*, 2005.
[35] M. Humbert, M. H. Manshaei, J. Freudiger, and J.-P. Hubaux. Tracking games in mobile networks. In *GameSec*, 2010.
[36] M. Jadliwala, I. Bilogrevic, and J.-P. Hubaux. Optimizing mixing in pervasive networks: A graph-theoretic perspective. In *ESORICS*, 2011.
[37] M. Jadliwala, S. Zhong, S. Upadhyaya, C. Qiao, and J.-P. Hubaux. Secure distance-based localization in the presence of cheating beacon nodes. *IEEE Transactions on Mobile Computing*, 2010.
[38] C. Karlof, N. Sastry, and D. Wagner. Tinysec: a link layer security architecture for wireless sensor networks. In *SenSys*, 2004.
[39] M. Khiabani. Metro-sexual. http://bit.ly/theranMetroSexual, 2009.
[40] N. Kiukkonen, J. Blom, O. Dousse, D. Gatica-Perez, and J. Laurila. Towards rich mobile phone datasets: Lausanne data collection campaign. In *ICPS*, 2010.
[41] M. Li, K. Sampigethaya, L. Huang, and R. Poovendran. Swing & swap: user-centric approaches towards maximizing location privacy. In *WPES*, 2006.
[42] B. Palanisamy and L. Liu. Mobimix: Protecting location privacy with mix zones over road networks. In *ICDE*, 2011.
[43] Rhiain. Nokia instant community gets you social. http://conversations.nokia.com/ 2010/05/25/nokia-instant-community-gets-you-social/.
[44] R. Shokri, G. Theodorakopoulos, G. Danezis, J.-P. Hubaux, and J.-Y. Le Boudec. Quantifying location privacy: The case of sporadic location exposure. In *PETS*, 2011.
[45] R. Shokri, G. Theodorakopoulos, J.-Y. Le Boudec, and J.-P. Hubaux. Quantifying location privacy. In *IEEE Security & Privacy Symposium*, 2011.
[46] M. Stiemerling and S. Kiesel. A system for peer-to-peer video streaming in resource constrained mobile environments. In *U-NET*, 2009.

[47] Theodore S. Rappaport. *Wireless Communications: Principles and Practice, 2nd Edition*, chapter Mobile Radio Propagation: Large-Scale Path Loss. Pearson Education, Inc., 2003.

[48] B. Wiedersheim, Z. Ma, F. Kargl, and P. Papadimitratos. Privacy in Inter-Vehicular Networks: Why simple pseudonym change is not enough. In *IEEE/IFIP WONS*, 2010.

[49] H. Yoon, J. Kim, F. Tan, and R. Hsieh. On-demand video streaming in mobile opportunistic networks. In *PERCOM*, 2008.

[50] X. Zhang, H. Heys, and C. Li. An analysis of link layer encryption schemes in wireless sensor networks. In *ICC*, 2010.

Appendix

Table 5. Symbol Table.

Symbol	Definition
m	User's actual message
$t(m)$	Device time when the message m is sent
$p(m)$	Device position when message m is sent
$\pi(m)$	Device identifier when message m is sent
c	Message content
M	Set of all actual messages (sent by all users)
Q_f	Quota for forced identifier changes
t_f	Forced timer
Q_c	Quota for context-based identifier changes
t_c	Context check timer
t_{silent}	Radio silence period
Q	Total identifier-change quota
$\hat{m}$	Copy of the m observed by the adversary
$\hat{o}(\hat{m})$	Adversary AP observing $\hat{m}$
$\hat{s}(\hat{m})$	Received signal strength of $\hat{m}$
r	Actual sequence of pseudonyms
$\tilde{e}$	Event constructed from observed messages
$\hat{T}$	Set of time-stamps in the event
$\hat{O}$	Set of observing APs in the event
$\tilde{r}$	Reconstructed sequence of pseudonyms
$\tilde{m}$	Message reconstructed from an event $\tilde{e}$
S	State space
P	State transition function
$v(s)$	Speed associated with the state s
τ	Traceability metric
u	Uncertainty metric
μ	Traceability-uncertainty metric
C	Clustering metric

You Can Run, but You Can't Hide: Exposing Network Location for Targeted DoS Attacks in Cellular Networks

Zhiyun Qian[1] Zhaoguang Wang[1] Qiang Xu[1] Z. Morley Mao[1] Ming Zhang[2] Yi-Min Wang[2]
[1] *University of Michigan* [2] *Microsoft Research*

Abstract

An important class of attacks against cellular network infrastructures, i.e., *signaling DoS attack, paging channel overload, and channel exhaustion attack, operates by sending low rate data traffic to a large number of mobile devices* at a particular location *to exhaust bottleneck resources such as radio resource and radio resource controller. We term this class of attack* targeted DoS attack *on cellular networks, given the focus on a specific location. The success of such attacks depends on an important but unvalidated assumption that it is possible to create a relatively accurate hit list of mobile devices associated with the target network location to which attackers can direct traffic. In this study, we take an important first step to validate this assumption by performing a large-scale study on the feasibility of these attacks. In addition, we propose accurate and efficient techniques for generating IP address to network location association in real time for existing commercial UMTS networks.*

Our technique relies on developing and measuring network signatures consisting of both static and dynamic features of key network elements such as Radio Network Controllers (RNCs) that are stable within the same location but distinct across locations. We find that a single feature in some cases is unique enough to locate a city such as NYC. With as little as 800kbps probe rate, we can identify a sufficient number of IPs to accurately target a network location, after scanning millions of IPs within 1.2 hours to effectively impose 2.5 to 3.5 times the normal load on the network.

1 Introduction

Data cellular networks are perennially constrained by limited radio resources due to ever-increasing user demand. To enable efficient resource reuse, there exists built-in support for intelligently allocating radio resources among multiple users and releasing them when they are perceived no longer actively in use. However, the mechanism for implementing the radio resource management primitives requires complex and heavy signaling procedures, rendering cellular networks vulnerable to a variety of low-rate *targeted DoS attacks* [25, 35, 32]. Due to the low bandwidth property, they can be launched from merely one or more external Internet hosts and can deny service to a large number of legitimate users in a particular area. In Figure 1, this class of attacks is illustrated at the bottom left side. Different from another class of attacks such as HLR attack [34] (on the top right of the figure) that requires access to cellular botnets, the low-rate targeted DoS attacks are considered much more realistic given the weaker requirements.

Although targeted DoS attacks are seemingly serious threats, they are still hypothetical. In particular, an important requirement, *i.e.,* locating a sufficient number of mobile devices in the same area (the so-called hit-list) is not fully investigated. Previous work [19] on exploiting SMS functionality to overload cellular voice service proposed using phone numbers under specific area codes to generate the hit-list. However, phone numbers cannot be directly translated into IP addresses needed for launching targeted DoS attacks on cellular data services and have limited location accuracy (detailed in §5.3).

To bridge this gap, we develop localization techniques to identify IP addresses under a given area via active probing and fingerprinting. It works by controlling a probe phone under the target area to measure the baseline signature of that location, then searching for other devices with sufficiently similar signature to the baseline. Our observation is that it is possible to actively measure characteristics and configuration parameters associated with network elements that are similar at the same location and distinct across locations. We empirically evaluate this approach on two large UMTS carriers in the U.S. (anonymized as Carrier 1 and Carrier 2 for privacy concerns). We find the approach promising in identifying a set of near-by mobile IPs with high accuracy. This is particularly true for big cities that often have unique configurations or features to satisfy their load requirement. In certain cases, it is even possible to uniquely identify a big city such as NYC with only a single feature. Thus, our work demonstrates that the threat of targeted DoS attacks is real.

Besides exposing the potential abuse of network information to enable this class of targeted attack against cellular networks, our technique can also support legitimate privacy-preserving applications that rely to the knowledge of the number of nearby users to determine whether a user should send his location information while ensuring k-anonymous properties [21]. More generally, our technique opens up a new direction in understanding how critical infrastructures like cellular networks can leak information about their networks which leads to privacy implications, *e.g.,* in the form of location exposure.

In this work, we make the following contributions:

- We conduct the first large-scale empirical study on the feasibility of targeted DoS attack against commercial cellular data networks (with overview shown in Table 1), using data collected through our deployed mobile app on major smartphone platforms (with details of the app covered in §3). We show that 80% of the devices keep their device IPs for more than 4 hours, leaving ample time for attack reconnaissance.
- We develop novel techniques to map IP addresses of mobile devices to a geographic area, using a combination of network features including static configuration settings, topological properties, and dynamic features.
- Using the proposed network signatures, we empirically validate the evidence of diverse network signatures across Radio Network Controllers (RNCs). We show that in big cities, the signature is typically unique enough to allow an attacker to locate enough IPs to impose 2.5 to 3.5 times the normal load on the network.

The rest of the paper is organized as follows. §2 presents the background on UMTS network as well as the attack overview, followed by the IP-related feasibility analysis in §3. §4 describes the methodology for localization, and §5 discusses the evaluation results. Possible defense solutions are described in §6. Finally we cover the related work in §7 and conclude in §8.

2 Background and Overview

In this section, we first describe the UMTS background with a focus on the measurable parameters which can be configured differently across network locations. We then discuss the intuition of the technique and the detailed steps of the attack.

2.1 UMTS Background

UMTS architecture. A UMTS network consists of three subsystems: Devices, Radio Access Network and Core Network [24]. They form a hierarchical structure where the lowest layer is the device, followed by radio access network consisting of base-stations and Radio Network Controllers (RNCs). At the highest level is the Core Network which has Serving GPRS Support Node (SGSN) and Gateway GPRS Support Node (GGSN). The latter connects to the Internet. Our focus is on the radio access network—the DoS target.

Radio Resource Control and State Machine. In UMTS, to efficiently utilize the limited radio resources (*i.e.,* physical communication channels), the radio resource control (RRC) protocol uses a state machine (shown in Figure 2) associated with each device typically with three RRC states—**IDLE**, **CELL_DCH** (or DCH) and **CELL_FACH** (or FACH). Different states have different amount of radio resource assigned. **IDLE** has no radio resource allocated. To send or receive any traffic, it has to promote to **DCH** where a dedicated channel is assigned to the device. In **FACH**, devices are assigned a shared channel which only provides limited throughput (less than 20kbps). It is designed for applications requiring a very low data rate. There are several configurable static parameters associated with state transitions. For example, Downlink/Uplink (DL/UL) Radio Link Controller (RLC) buffer size is used to determine when the FACH $\rightarrow$ DCH transition occurs (we refer to it as **queue size threshold** thereafter). If the number of bytes sent or received exceeds the threshold, the state transition will be triggered. Another example is the **inactivity timer** which determines when the DCH $\rightarrow$ FACH transition occurs. They are all configured at the RNC and may differ across RNCs in different locations, making them good candidates to construct the network signatures. Note that different RNC implementations may also employ slightly different state machines due to vendor differences. For instance, there could be a IDLE $\rightarrow$ FACH transition instead of IDLE $\rightarrow$ DCH. In some cases, new states (*e.g.,* CELL_PCH) are introduced to further optimize radio resource. These differences can also be part of the signatures.

It is worth mentioning that in the next generation LTE networks, similar resource control mechanism and control parameters also exist [5].

2.2 Attack Outline

RNC-level Localization. At a high level, our intuition is that network elements (*e.g.,* RNC) in different locations may be configured differently,

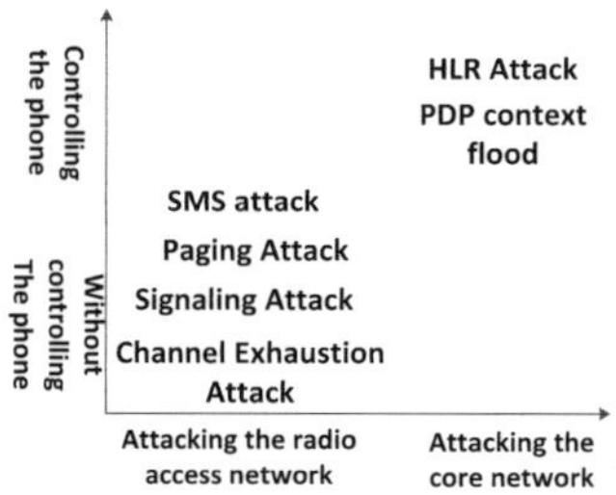

Figure 1. Cellular attacks

Category	Measurement target
MobileApp	Cellular IP reachability analysis (§3.1)
MobileApp	IP duration analysis (§3.2)
Probing	Active vs. Idle IPs (§3.3)
MobileApp	IP locality analysis (§4.1)
MobileApp	Phone-number-based localization accuracy (§5.3)

Table 1. Attack feasibility analysis

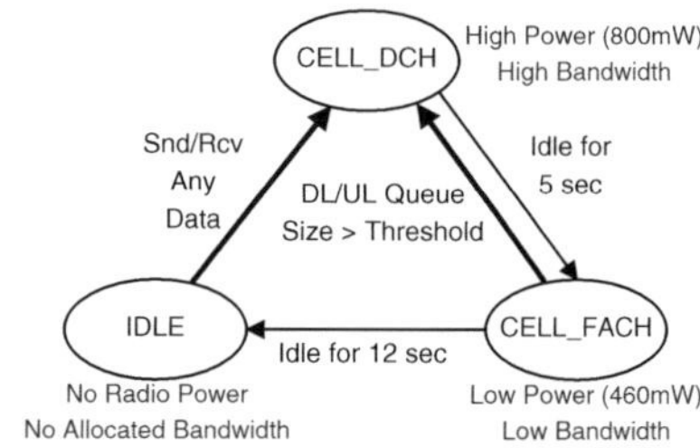

Figure 2. State machine for Carrier 1

therefore exhibit distinct network signature. Since geographically close-by devices are governed by the same RNC, they also share the same signature. We discuss a more complete list of features of our proposed network signature in §4.2.1. Since most features identified are associated with the RNC, the localization granularity is naturally at the RNC level. Typically, a big city such as NYC has multiple RNCs, while a few small cities may share the same RNC. To clearly illustrate the attack, we outline the steps.

1. The attacker has access to a *probe phone* in the target location. This phone measures the network signature of that location and uses it as the baseline to match against signatures of other probed phones. The probe phone could either be compromised or owned by the attacker. Note that we do not assume access to a cellular botnet. Otherwise, it is trivial to obtain the location information (*e.g.,* GPS) from the phone.

2. The attacker first exclude IPs that are unlikely under the target area through a coarse-grained localization step. For instance, the attacker can exploit the approximate IP locality in cellular networks, *i.e.,* each GGSN responsible for a geographic region assigns distinct IP blocks to phones (See §4.1).

3. The attacker probes the remaining IPs to measure their associated signatures (as a fine-grained localization step) with certain time and resource constraint. The signatures are matched against the baseline signature. The ones that are sufficiently similar are considered to be under the same RNC.

4. After identifying enough IP addresses for the target network location, the attacker can launch the targeted DoS attack.

3 IP-related Feasibility Analysis

In this section, we investigate the feasibility of our localization technique and the targeted DoS attack in general. First (§3.1), we study how many carriers allow cellular IPs to be probed directly (a requirement for scanning/fingerprinting and the DoS attack itself). Second (§3.2), we quantify how long a device keeps its cellular IP address (to ensure IPs are still valid after fingerprinting). Third (§3.3), we measure how many devices are online versus active (to estimate the additional attack load that can be introduced).

MobileApp. To answer the above questions, we collect empirical data using a mobile app we deployed on major platforms (referred to as *MobileApp* thereafter) which measures various aspects of any cellular network including throughput and port blocking behavior. It also reports additional information such as Carrier, GPS, IP address, timestamp, Signal Strength, and 7-digit phone number prefix (with user's consent). As of March, 2011, there are 100,223 users who have voluntarily downloaded and run our app all over the world. There is a small subset consisting of 1,683 users who opted to run the periodic test that report the device's IP address every one hour and allow the signature measurement to be conducted from our server. We focus on the data set collected over a 2-week duration from Nov 7th to 21th, 2010. The complete list of analysis based on the *MobileApp* is summarized in Table 1.

3.1 IP Reachability

Some carriers deploy NAT or firewall to ensure traffic originated from the Internet cannot reach the mobile devices directly. They affect signature-based localization as well as the set of existing attacks assuming direct reachability to the phones. Based on the MobileApp data set, we collected reachability information of 180 UMTS carriers in different continents as summarized in Table 2. Among them, 77 of them assign public IP addresses to devices, 52 of which are directly reachable from the Internet; 103 carriers assign private IP addresses to devices (with NAT), 40 of which are reachable because they allow either device-to-device probing within the same network or one device to spoof other device's IP address (4 out of the 40 allow IP spoofing). In summary, regardless of public or private IP carriers, the percentage of carriers that allow direct reachability is $\frac{40+52}{180} = 51\%$. This result motivates our localization technique.

In those cases where carriers do not allow phones to be probed in any way, existing attacks discussed

Carrier count	Private IP		Public IP	
	Reachable[1]	Not	Reachable	Not
180	40	63	52	25

[1] In-NAT device-to-device probe allowed

Table 2. Reachability for 180 UMTS carriers.

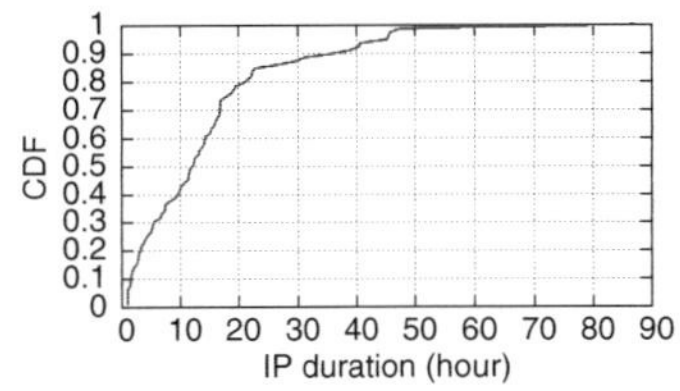

Figure 3. CDF of IP duration

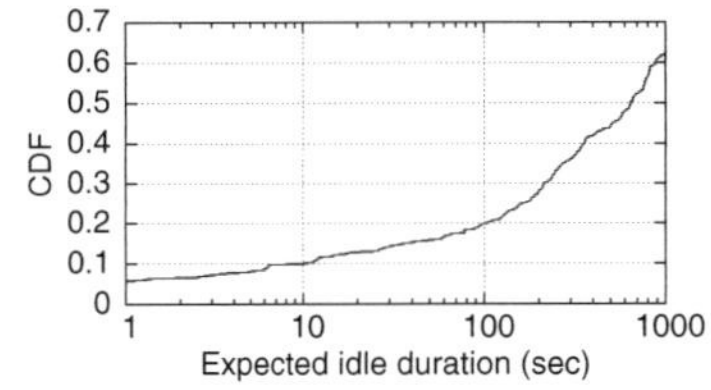

Figure 4. CDF of idle duration

in [25, 35, 32] will also be deterred. However, denying reachability is not without any cost. For instance, it may hurt peer to peer applications as well as applications that require running servers on the phones.

3.2 IP Duration

It is critical to understand how long a device keeps the same IP address as it takes time to measure the signature and identify the location of an IP. Previous work has shown that when NAT boxes are deployed, the public IPs assigned by NAT can change frequently in cellular networks [15]. For instance, they show that with the same private IP address, the public IP address can change on the order of tens of seconds. However, device IPs (IPs directly assigned to devices) often change much less frequently in contrast to NAT-assigned IPs. Typically such IPs only change when the device reboots or the network interface is switched (*e.g.,* WiFi to 3G). Carriers do not have incentives to frequently reassign new device IPs as it incurs overhead.

Indeed, from the *MobileApp*'s periodic test data consisting of (deviceID, timestamp, deviceIP) tuples, we quantify the expected IP duration of each device as shown in Figure 3 and find the duration of the device IP is fairly long, with more than 80% devices keep their IP addresses longer than 4 hours.

3.3 Online Devices vs. Active Devices

We define *online* devices as the ones reachable but may or may not be actively using the network. *Active* devices as the ones reachable and also actively using the network. The ratio of active to online devices determines the upper bound of additional load an attacker can impose on the network.

To quantify the number of online and active devices, we conduct a TCP SYN probing experiment on 12 sampled /24 IP prefixes used in the cellular network operated by Carrier 1 in the U.S. in March, 2011 for two hours at different time-of-day (one hour at noon, one hour after midnight). We probe all IP addresses in the range every 30 seconds. Though the analysis does not cover all the IP ranges, we believe the result is still representative based on randomly sampled IP prefixes.

For validation, we confirm that TCP SYN packets can indeed elicit response from the phone instead of the firewall with spoofed responses. We verify this by launching two different "TCP traceroutes" from the server to the phone – if the probing packet is non-SYN packet, the traceroute will discontinue at the firewall hop (the firewall drops out-of-state TCP packets) while SYN packet can move forward until it reaches the phone and elicit response. To infer if a phone is actively using the network, we exploit the IP ID field in the IP header in the response packets [31]. In practice, many operating systems (such as Windows family) increment a system-wide IP ID counter for every outgoing IP packet. If two consecutive response packets have IP ID values X and $X+1$, it means the phone is **idle** for the 30-second probing interval. Otherwise, it is **active**.

On average, there are 22% of the probed IPs respond (other IPs are likely unassigned at the moment we probe). Out of the responsive/online devices, the active ratio is 20% during day time and 13% at midnight, showing some time-of-day pattern. The ratio indicates that an attacker can introduce at most 5 times the normal load at day time, assuming all IPs can be correctly located. Even if the attacker finds only half of the online phones, he can still impose 3 times the normal load on average, or $\frac{50\%}{20\%} = 2.5$ to $\frac{50\%+20\%}{20\%} = 3.5$, depending on how many identified IPs are overlapping with the ones that are already active. Either way, the attack load is significant enough to cause damage assuming a common over-provisioning factor of 1:2 [20].

From the probing, we can also infer the average idle duration for each IP address. This information helps us understand how likely there will be background traffic interfering with the feature measurement described in §4.2.2. Figure 4 shows that 85% of the IP addresses have an idle duration of 100 seconds, which are long enough for most measurements.

In summary, we have studied various aspects of real networks and collected evidence demonstrating that the localization scheme and the targeted DoS attack are indeed feasible.

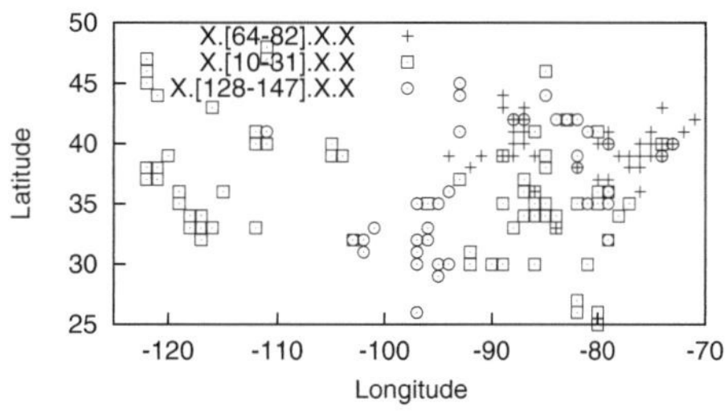

Figure 5. IP address locality

Feature	Type	Measurement cost
Min-RTT	Dynamic	Medium
DCH tail time	Static	Medium
FACH DL queue size threshold	Static	Medium
FACH UL queue size threshold	Static	Medium
FACH queue consumption rate	Static	High
Avg promotion delay	Dynamic	Low
RRC State machine	Static	Low
Max number of RLC retransmission	Static	High

Table 3. Features of the network signature.

4 Localization Methodology

4.1 Coarse-grained Localization using IP Locality

IP address is known to have locality on the Internet – close-by IPs in the address space tend to share geographic proximity. However, as pointed out by previous work [36], a large geographic area may share the same set of IP pools managed at a GGSN location. We verify this using 13,784 samples of GPS-IP pairs of Carrier 1 and 17,589 pairs of Carrier 2 from the MobileApp data, during the time period from Sep 2009 to Nov, 2010.

Figure 5 shows Carrier 1's private IP address locality. We observe the same private IP range is indeed shared by a large geographic area. For example, X.64.X.X – X.82.X.X are always allocated to devices from the East Coast, while IPs in X.128.X.X – X.147.X.X are mostly assigned to devices on the Central or Northeast. In total, we find 4 such disjoint IP ranges which likely correspond to different GGSNs [36]. Similar results are found for Carrier 2. In summary, device IPs only show coarse-grained geographic locality. Nevertheless, it allows the attacker to exclude a large range of IPs without ever probing them.

For an attacker without prior knowledge about which IP range corresponds to the target area, we devise a simple technique to obtain such knowledge — one can reset the network interface programmatically to continuously obtain new IP addresses. It takes about 30 seconds to get a new IP address every time. In our experiment, this technique allows us to obtain the IP pool of X.128.X.X – X.147.X.X within about an hour.

4.2 Fine-grained Localization using Network Signatures

From coarse-grained IP locality, the attacker can obtain a set of candidate IPs only knowing their rough location at the granularity of several states in the U.S. To narrow down to a more fine-grained target location, the next step is probe these IPs directly to obtain their network signatures.

4.2.1 Network Signature Definition

Here we define network signature as a set of measurable features that are potentially distinct across different locations. We discuss why the signature exists and how we select them:

- **Incremental changes**: different hardware components are purchased and upgraded at different time to improve capacity of the network or to introduce new technologies [4, 3], thus likely introducing heterogeneity in the RNC hardware. For example, min-RTTs are reduced when HSUPA are deployed on top of HSDPA compared to when HSDPA deployed alone [23]. Also, different RNC products can have slightly different state machine behavior as explained before. As 4G LTE network technology is gradually deployed, we expect even more heterogeneity across network locations.
- **Connectivity between RNC and base-stations**: this may vary across locations. The network delay variation may be due to either RNC processing delay difference or base-station-to-RNC link delay difference (*e.g.,* link congestion) [25, 7], thus affecting the observed state promotion delay.
- **Configurations**: Different RNCs have different static parameter settings to accommodate the load at different locations. For instance, big cities often configure resource-recycling parameters (*e.g.,* inactivity timer) more aggressively to accommodate more users.

The general criteria for selecting features is that any *measurable properties* associated with RNC can be considered. We list the potential set of features in Table 3, most of which have been introduced in §2.1. Although it may not be complete, it is a good starting point. These features can be classified as static or dynamic. Static features are configured statically on the RNC. They are thus very stable and relatively easy to measure. Dynamic features, on the other hand, are likely to vary over time thus harder to measure. Also, some features are more expensive to characterize.

For example, the maximum number of allowed RLC retransmission [26] and the FACH queue consumption rate may take many measurements to correctly identify.

In our current study, we pick the 5 features highlighted in Table 3 (and described in §2.1) that are relatively easy to measure. The methodology for measuring them is described in the next section. We did not include the RRC state machine feature because we did not find a corresponding ground truth RNC to test our measurement methodology. The local RNC on which we rely for testing did not implement the CELL_PCH state. A dedicated attacker can however spend more effort and take advantage of the remaining features to refine the signature.

4.2.2 Measurement Methodology

Our probing methodology assumes control at only one end (*i.e.,* the server side). It is different from a previous study [29] that devised a methodology to measure similar features but with complete control on both ends. In our case, we have to overcome additional challenges such as background traffic on the device which may distort the measured result. Moreover, when state promotion delay is measured from the server, there is an additional variable, *i.e.,* paging delay that needs to be factored out. Finally, without controlling the device, it is hard to control the size of the packet responded by the device (thus hard to measure the UL queue size threshold). For instance, we can use a large TCP SYN packet to probe a device, but the size of the response packet is fixed (40 bytes TCP RST). To control the uplink size, we use UDP probing where the response packet is 24 bytes larger than the original probing packet because the triggered *ICMP port unreachable* packet embed the original UDP packet and wrap it with a new ICMP and IP header. The ICMP response packet is limited to at most 576 bytes as per RFC [6]. We will discuss how to use TCP and UDP probing by adjusting the probing packet size to measure DL and UL queue size threshold respectively.

DCH inactivity timer. As described in §2.1, this parameter determines when to release radio resource (after N seconds of inactivity). The procedure to measure inactivity timer is as follows: (1). The attacker first sends a large probe packet (*i.e.,* 1200 bytes). If the phone is in IDLE or FACH, it will trigger a state promotion to DCH; otherwise, it will reset the inactivity timer [30]. (2). Then the attacker waits for some interval, X seconds before he sends the next large packet. (3). If the next packet incurs an RTT sufficiently large to include the state promotion, this indicates the power state has changed from DCH to FACH after X seconds of inactivity, and therefore the inactivity timer is X seconds. (4). Else, if the next large packet experiences a small RTT, indicating that the power state is still in DCH, it then set $X = X + \Delta$ and go back to step (2). We set the initial X to be 2.5s which is small enough to catch all the known values of inactivity timer. We use a measurement granularity of 0.2s (Δ = 0.2s). It is not useful to increase the granularity further since the variation of normal cellular RTT will prevent us from getting more fine-grained results.

As mentioned, one challenge is background traffic, which may prematurely reset the timer, inflating the measured inactivity timer. The counter strategy is to continue the measurement only when the initial state is in IDLE. The assumption is that if the phone is not using network now, it is likely to continue to stay idle in the near future (demonstrated in Figure 4). After all in a real attack, the timer inference can finish much more quickly given the attacker can profile the timer value in the target RNC offline using his attack phone. Specifically, instead of measuring all possible timer values, he only needs to make a binary inference – whether the tested IP has a target timer or not. Nevertheless, the above general methodology assumes no prior knowledge of the timer value; we use it to understand how diverse they can be across locations.

The other source of noise is fast dormancy [13], a mechanism implemented on some devices to release radio resource before the timer expires and save battery life on the phone, causing early transition from DCH to IDLE. However, since the power state transitions directly from DCH to IDLE instead of to FACH, the next observed RTT is much larger and thus distinguishable from the non-fast-dormancy case. More importantly, it is not always implemented or triggered every time. Thus, we can repeat the measurements several times and discard the fast dormancy cases. In practice, we find UDP probing rarely encountered fast dormancy (compared to TCP probing), likely due to more bytes being exchanged in the UDP case.

FACH $\rightarrow$ DCH DL/UL queue size threshold. As described before, there exists a queue size threshold for DL and UL respectively. Using TCP probing, the size of the TCP RST response is fixed, allowing DL packet size adjusted independently without affecting the UL packet size (ensuring UL threshold is not exceeded first). The following depicts the procedures on the server side to measure DL queue size threshold: (1) send a large packet to make sure the state will be in DCH; (2) wait for $T = Timer$ seconds to let the power state enter FACH; (3) send a packet with size Y; (4) If a state promotion is triggered (identified by a large RTT), then record Y as the queue size threshold and exit; (5) else, try a larger packet size $Y = Y + \xi$ and go back to (3). We set the initial $Y = 20$ and $\xi = 30$ in the MobileApp

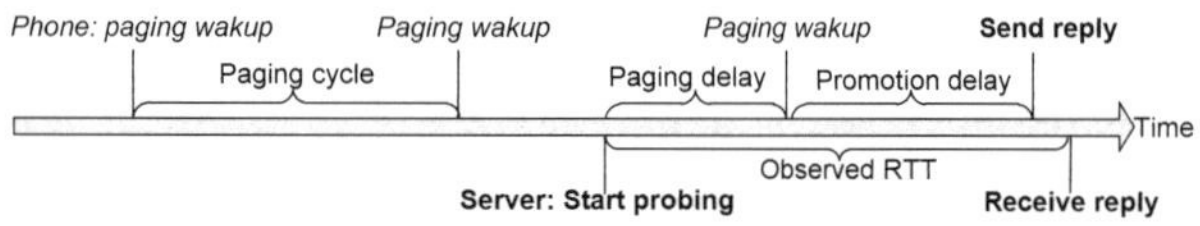

Figure 6. An example of paging delay.

experiment. In the later large-scale probing experiment, we change $\xi = 10$ bytes in an attempt to measure more fine-grained queue size threshold. Nevertheless, the later experiment confirms that the results with $\xi = 30$ are still valid (without missing any values in between).

Measuring UL queue size threshold is more difficult, because distinguishing between DL threshold and UL threshold being exceeded is hard — in both cases we just observe a large RTT indicating that state promotion is triggered. Fortunately, since we now already know the DL queue size threshold via TCP probing, we can send UDP packets with size smaller than the DL threshold so that they are guaranteed not to exceed the DL queue threshold. If there is still a state promotion triggered, then it has to be the UL packet that exceeds the UL queue size threshold. This is why we have to measure the DL threshold before the UL threshold. There are two constraints in the results: 1). The UL response packet is always 24 bytes larger than the DL probe packet (as described earlier), therefore, we can measure the UL threshold up to 24 bytes larger than the DL queue threshold. 2). The max size of the UL response packet is 576 bytes (as discussed earlier). As a result, the UDP probing can only measure up to 576 bytes for the UL threshold.

IDLE → DCH Promotion delay. Although it is easy to measure promotion delay from the phone, it is much more difficult to do so from the other end. This is because when a downlink packet is to be received in **IDLE** state, it may get delayed significantly due to a process called paging [2].

Figure 6 shows an example where the phone is in **IDLE** state, only periodically wakes up to listen for incoming packets. If a packet happens to arrive between two paging occasions, it will be delayed until the next paging occasion. In the worst case, the delay can be as large as a full paging cycle length. The paging cycle length is determined by Core Network and is stable across RNCs [2]. According to the 3GPP specification [1], the protocol should support several values: 0.64s, 1.28s, 2.56s, *etc.* In practice, we observe it to be 2.56s for Carrier 1 and 1.28s for Carrier 2. It is stable and validated through a hardware power-meter: every 2.56s a power spike is seen, and we can observe that the promotion process must wait after the spike.

To overcome the effect due to paging delays, we design a probing technique using binary search that can distinguish the paging delay from the estimated promotion delay. It requires several rounds of probing (the exact number of rounds depends on the accuracy desired). The high-level idea is that we gradually narrow down the exact paging occasion. The more we probe, the closer to the paging occasion the probing will be. We validated the inferred promotion delays match the duration of power spikes using power-meter. Below is the detailed methodology:

We use the following notations: we denote C as the paging cycle, S_i as the start time of ith probe mod by C ($0 \leq S_i \leq C$), P_i as the paging delay of the ith probing, and T_i to be the RTT of the ith round.

Initially, without any knowledge of the paging occasion, we conduct the initial two probes spaced out with an offset of $\frac{C}{2}$. More specially, $S_2 - S_1 = \frac{C}{2}$. An example outcome is shown in Figure 7.(a). We can infer $P_1 < P_2$ based on the fact that $T_1 < T_2$, and paging occasion should be somewhere between $S1$ and $S2$. Despite potential variation in promotion delay (on the order of hundreds of milliseconds), the spacing between P_1 and P_2 of $\frac{C}{2}$=1.28s should be large enough to overcome the noise.

We select the next S_i to bound the paging occasion further. For example, in Figure 7.(b), the start time is selected to be $S_3 = \frac{S_1+S_2}{2}$ given $T_1 < T_2$. Note that here the difference between P_3 and P_2 is even bigger than the difference of P_1 and P_2, making each step of the algorithm robust to the noise of promotion delay variation.

The process is repeated until we are able to bound the S_i to be very close to the paging occasion. We pick i to be 8 since it is able to bound the distance to be less than $\frac{2.56s}{2^8} = 10$ms. Even though each individual promotion delay may vary significantly, the average is expected to be stable, thus collecting multiple samples of promotion delay is useful. After inferring the paging occasion, we are able to recover each previous paging delay P_i, and the corresponding promotion delay can then be computed simply as $T_i - P_i$.

Note that it is possible there are background traffic during the 8 rounds of probing since it spans $8 \times 30 = 240$ seconds. However, such background traffic only matters when the measured promotion delay is very small, indicating the device is already in DCH instead of IDLE. Such cases can be easily excluded and the attacker can simply try again in the next round.

Minimum RTT in DCH. Although it has been shown that cellular network RTT is highly variable, we find the minimum (over 40 measurements) is surprisingly stable within the same area (See Figure 10). It is also diverse in different geographic areas. Our local experiment shows that the standard deviation of 100 min-RTTs (each is computed over 40 RTT measurements) measured in

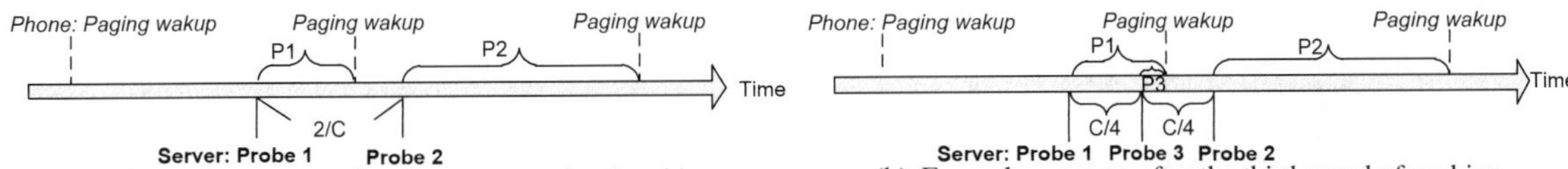

(a) Example outcome after first two rounds of probing

(b) Example outcome after the third round of probing

Figure 7. Illustration of our proposed paging delay elimination method to measure promotion delay.

6 hours is only 2.003. In fact, computing min-RTT over 30 measurements is also acceptable as its standard deviation is 2.07. 10 measurements will however increase the standard deviation to 3.46.

Validation. We thoroughly validate the proposed methodology using local experiments over two different UMTS carriers across several types of phones. The results are consistent and match with those collected assuming direct access to the phone. For instance, we verified that the UL/DL queue size threshold measurements are consistent with or without direct access to the phone.

5 Evaluation

In this section, we evaluate the effectiveness of the signature-based localization through empirical data collected from the MobileApp as well as a large-scale probing experiment. We focus on three main evaluations.

1. We quantify the distribution and entropy of each feature.

2. We compare the signature-based localization with the state-of-the-art phone-number-based approach.

3. We evaluate the scalability, *i.e.,* time requirement, to locate enough number IP addresses.

Data collection. We collect data from two main sources. One is from the periodic test of the MobileApp, which allows us to obtain ground truth RNC, timestamp, and signature to evaluate two major UMTS carriers in the U.S. covering 20 RNCs in Carrier 1 (shown in Figure 10) and 43 RNCs in Carrier 2 from Nov 8th to Nov 19, 2010. In this dataset, we collect all five features except the UL queue size threshold, which can be measured in the actual attack via UDP probing as discussed in §4.2.2. The other dataset is from large-scale probing on Carrier 1 in March 2011, the goal of which is to understand the signature distribution more comprehensively without knowing where each IP is located. The two datasets jointly allow us to evaluate the accuracy of our localization technique.

RNC ground truth. Even though we run our MobileApp on the phone, there is still no direct way to obtain the current RNC the phone is connected to. As an approximation, we obtain "location area code" (LAC) — an identifier that covers an area that is usually

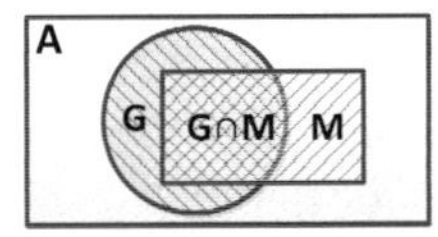

Figure 8. Illustration of coverage and accuracy

comparable to an RNC [9] through standard platform APIs.

RNC/LAC coverage estimation. To understand the challenge to distinguish different RNCs, we first need to estimate the number of RNCs and their coverage. To do so, we leverage the OpenCellID project [11], an open source project aimed to create a complete database of LAC number and Cell IDs worldwide. The data shows 1596 unique LAC numbers for Carrier 1 with about 3/4 of the U.S. covered. A rough estimate based on area uncovered leads to about 2000 LACs in the entire U.S. Since the number of GGSN locations is estimated to be 4 (See §4.1), a single GGSN should cover about 500 LACs/RNCs. Typically, a big city such as NYC has multiple RNCs (to accommodate the load), while a few small cities may share the same RNC (verified by LAC and location data from OpenCellID).

Evaluation methodology. As described in §2.2, in the actual attack, an attacker measures the baseline signature from his controlled probe phone and then compare it against signatures of other probed devices in real time. We simulate this process by considering each signature sample in the MobileApp as a baseline (where we know its ground truth RNC) and compare it with other samples for a similarity match. Static features should have exactly the same value to be considered a match. For dynamic features, *e.g.,* average promotion delay and min-RTT, we allow a **signature distance threshold parameter** (**SD-threshold** in short) to tolerate some variation. For example, if we set the min-RTT SD-threshold to 5ms, then all samples within +/- 5ms of the baseline sample are considered to match the baseline. For min-RTT and promotion delay SD-threshold, we select a large range of them from (5ms, 50ms) to (20ms, 400ms). We discuss later how set the SD-threshold to balance between the coverage and accuracy metrics.

Coverage and Accuracy metrics. As illustrated in Figure 8, the sets A, G, and M represent different signature samples. A represents signature samples for

Figure 9. Carrier 1's queue threshold

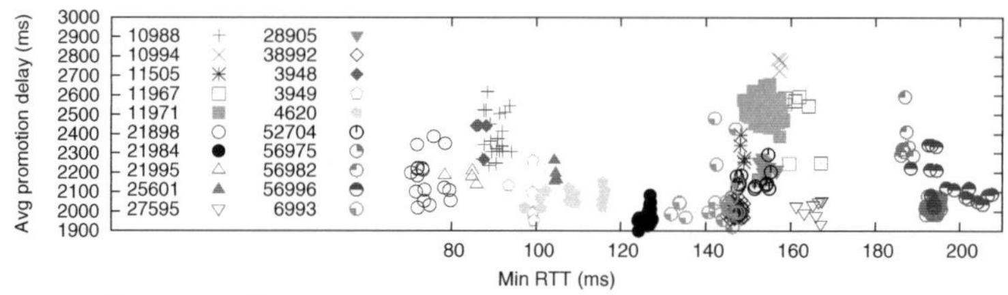

Figure 10. Carrier 1's 20 different RNCs' dynamic features

all RNCs. G denotes all the signature samples under the target RNC. M corresponds to the signature samples inferred to be under the same target RNC (using the localization technique). Ideally, localization should output an M that is equivalent to G. However, in reality, M and G may only partially overlap. Based on the notations, we define two metrics to evaluate the performance of the localization: $Coverage = \frac{|G \bigcap M|}{|G|}$ and $Accuracy = \frac{|G \bigcap M|}{|M|}$. Intuitively, coverage quantifies the fraction of phones that can be successfully identified under the target RNC. Higher coverage implies that the attack can impose higher load on the network. Accuracy quantifies the fraction of targeted phones that are indeed under the target RNC. Higher accuracy implies less wasted attack traffic.

5.1 Evaluation using the MobileApp Data

In this section, we mainly discuss the findings about the characteristics of the features and city-level properties (*e.g.,* big cities usually have distinct values). We also briefly discuss how we can compute the localization coverage metric using just the MobileApp data.

Static features. We find that although inactivity timer and queue size threshold do not have many distinct values, they already show some interesting diversity patterns even from the limited samples.

For Carrier 1, we observe two main inactivity timer values: around 3s and 5s. For the queue size threshold, we also observe two main values: around 480 and 510 bytes. 480 tends to correlate with the 5s inactivity timer, while 510 tends to correlate with the 3s one. Besides these, there is one exceptionally large queue size threshold at around 1000 bytes observed at three places – Bay Area, Dallas, and Chicago Area (*i.e.,* big cities). In Figure 9, we can clearly see the distribution of different queue size threshold values. Marker 1, 2, and 3 represent 480, 510, and 1000 bytes respectively. It is interesting that Marker 2 and 3 are always at big cities while Marker 1 is often present in small cities. In the cases where two Markers are closely located (*e.g.,* Marker 1 and 3 in Dallas), we observe that Marker 1 is in fact at a nearby small city.

For Carrier 2, we observe similar patterns. Two main values of inactivity timer: 3s and 8s, and two main values for queue threshold: around 110 and 300 bytes. However, there is also an exception of 1000 bytes which is only observed in New York City (multiple LACs in the city and different users consistently show this value), likely due to its higher load requirement. We also observe interesting patterns around big cities, *e.g.,* Los Angeles is configured with 300 bytes while near-by California cities are configured with 110 bytes.

Despite the limitations of the small number of observed values, we note that the features are promising in distinguish big cities which often have bigger queue size threshold than their near-by cities. Coupled with dynamic features, the signatures will be even more unique.

Dynamic features. Figure 10 shows the distribution of Carrier 1's two dynamic features – promotion delay and min-RTT. Each data point is an average over 8 measurements of promotion delay (after subtracting the normal RTTs) and 40 measurements of RTT. We employ 95th percentile filtering to exclude outliers of promotion delay due to measurement noise. Data points with the same shape indicate that they are from the same LAC. We can see from Figure 10 that min-RTT is very stable in most cases, even though a user can move around in nearby locations connecting to different base-stations with varying signal strength.

For promotion delay, it is still reasonably stable but less stable than min-RTT. In Figure 10, we aggregate enough data points during off-peak hours (3AM - 6AM where promotion delays should be stable), which have relatively stable range of values and do show diversity across different LACs. In the cases where two different RNCs have similar signatures (*e.g.,* at min-RTTs close to 150ms in the figure), we may need to combine static features to distinguish them.

Coverage calculation. Coverage is relatively simple to calculate using only the MobileApp data. As defined in §5, $Coverage = \frac{|G \bigcap M|}{|G|}$. G denotes all the signature samples under the target RNC. We use the samples collected in MobileApp data (where we know the ground truth RNCs) to serve as G. $G \bigcap M$ is the signature samples correctly inferred to be under the target RNC. They both can be derived from the MobileApp data.

Inact.	queue threshold		Prob.	Inact.	queue threshold		Prob.	Inact.	queue threshold		Prob.	Inact.	queue threshold		Prob.
timer	DL	UL		timer	DL	UL		timer	DL	UL		timer	DL	UL	
5s	480	484	41.1%	3s	510	>=534	4.3%	3s	480	244	1.7%	3s	1010	244	1.4%
3s	510	244	28.8%	3s	480	>=504	2.7%	3s	<=340	244	1.6%	3s	1010	>=576	1%
5s	480	>=504	6.9%	3s	480	484	2.6%	5s	<=340	244	1.5%	Others			6.4%

Table 4. Static feature probability distribution from large-scale probing

For accuracy, however, using the MobileApp data alone is not sufficient because it is possible there are other unknown RNCs which have similar signatures, *i.e.,* collisions. This motivates our subsequent measurement on the general distribution of the signatures in an entire GGSN.

5.2 Evaluation via Large-Scale Probing

In this section, we focus on two results. First, we characterize the signature distribution of all five features via large-scale probing. Next, based on the distribution, we calculate the localization accuracy for the MobileApp data where we have the ground truth RNC.

Evaluation methodology. In our large-scale probing data, we measure all 5 features but only 4 features are measured in the MobileApp data (UL threshold was not included). When we join two datasets together, we need to make up for the missing feature in the MobileApp data. We choose a very conservative way to do this – we fill in a UL threshold such that the (DL,UL) threshold combination is the least unique possible. This way, the signature is never more unique than it should be, thus the resulting localization accuracy can only be worse.

Signature distribution measurement for Carrier 1. Previous results only provide a limited view on the signature distribution. To get a more comprehensive view, we sample $\frac{1}{10}$ of an entire GGSN IP range in Carrier 1 comprising 20 /16 IP prefixes to measure all five features.

First, we use *Shannon entropy* – a metric measuring the uncertainty associated with a random variable, to measure how "random" the network signature variable is and how many RNCs can be distinguished on average in our context. Entropy is defined as $H(X) = -\sum_x p(x)\log_2 p(x)$, where X is the signature variable and x is a possible value for X. Here we break X into S and D representing static and dynamic features respectively. Thus $H(X) = H(S,D) = H(S) + H(D|S)$, by the law of entropy.

For $H(S) = -\sum_s p(s)\log_2 p(s)$, we need the s and $p(s)$ which are both shown in Table 4. There are in total 11 different static feature s with at least 1% probability (appearance). Plugging in the probability $p(s)$, entropy $H(S)$ is calculated to be 2.3 bits, indicating that we can distinguish on average $2^{2.3} = 5$ different groups of RNCs, using static features alone.

A closer examination of the table shows that, despite the inactivity timer taking on only two distinct values of 3s and 5s, the queue size threshold values are much more diverse than those from the MobileApp dataset (especially when combined with inactivity timer values). The distribution is biased towards the top two combinations where DL threshold values are 510 and 480, which match the values observed in our MobileApp dataset. This means that some RNCs will be harder to distinguish than others. Specifically, big cities with smaller inactivity timer and bigger queue size threshold are typically more distinct, considering that 41.1% of the static features contain 5s inactivity timer and 480 DL threshold (likely in small cities). The results indicate that big cities are more easily identified and targeted.

For $H(D|S)$, it can be computed as $\Sigma p(s) \times H(D|S=s)$ by enumerating different static feature s. To compute $H(D|S=s)$, we slice the two-dimensional dynamic feature space into equal-sized bins using various threshold choice of min-RTT and promotion delay (as described in §5). Plugging in the probability associated with each bin, the computed $H(D|S)$ varies from 2.5 to 5 bits. This means the combined entropy $H(S,D)$ is between 4.8 and 7.3 bits, which can distinguish 28 – 158 different groups of RNCs on average. Remember this is without including other potential features in Table 3 which can provide additional entropy. Using the calculated entropy number and the estimated RNC number (500 per GGSN), we know on average there are $500/158 = 3.2$ to $500/28 = 17.9$ RNCs left indistinguishable to the attacker. Again, given the distribution is nonuniform, the actual accuracy will depend on which RNC is targeted.

Accuracy calculation using both the MobileApp and probing data. We already discussed how to compute coverage in §5.1. Now we discuss how to calculate $Accuracy = \frac{|G \bigcap M|}{|M|}$. First, accuracy calculation requires knowing M — the signature samples inferred to be under the target RNC. We perform the following procedure to output M — for each RNC's signature sample in MobileApp (termed as **baseline sample**), we go through all the probed signature samples (without knowing their ground truth RNCs), and compare them against the baseline sample. The signatures that match

LAC	Signature		Location	Phone-number	
	Coverage	Accuracy		Coverage	Accuracy
11956	52%	41%	Queens, NY	N/A[1]	
11974	50%	83%	Newton, NJ	N/A[1]	
26507	50%	3%	Ann Arbor, MI	N/A[1]	
52704	54%	88%	Arlington, TX	15.5%	6%
52818	50%	75%	Arlington, TX		
52903	51%	77%	Fort Worth, TX	0%	0%

[1] No such phone number data from MobileApp

Table 5. Coverage and accuracy comparison

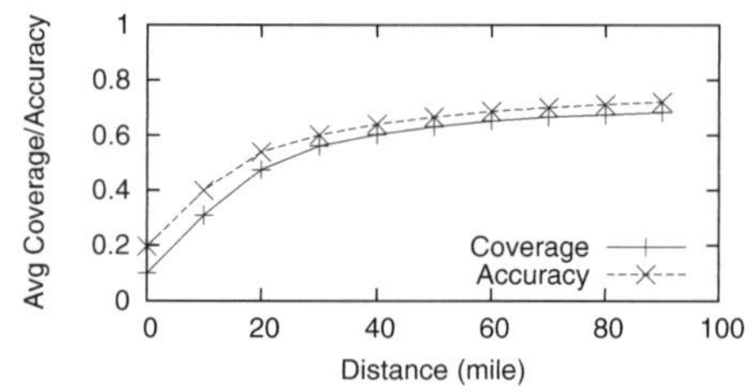

Figure 11. Phone-number-based coverage and accuracy in small cities

the baseline close enough are then included in M. Now the only unsolved part is $|G \bigcap M|$ — the number of correctly inferred signature samples, which is in fact semantically equivalent to $|G| \times coverage$ — out of all the signature samples that are under the target RNC, the covered ones are effectively the ones correctly inferred. Since we already know $coverage$, all we need is $|G|$ at this point. We can estimate $|G|$ based on the population distribution observed in our MobileApp. Specifically, if we know the fraction of users that are under a particular RNC out of all the users, then we can rewrite $|G|$ into $|N| \times p$ where $|N|$ is total number of signature samples in the GGSN, and p is the fraction of population that are under the target RNC. Therefore, $Accuracy = \frac{|G| \times coverage}{|M|} = \frac{|N| \times p \times coverage}{M}$. Since our dataset is not complete enough to calculate p that is representative, we resort to the uniform population distribution where every p is equal only for the purpose of evaluation.

Coverage and accuracy results. As described in §5, the SD-threshold for deciding if two samples are close enough can be tuned according to the desired attack impact and the resource constraint. The more relaxed the SD-threshold, the more samples are considered under the target RNC and thus likely to include more correct samples (and better coverage and higher attack impact). However, this is at the cost of lower accuracy (*i.e.,* other non-related signature samples will be mistakenly inferred to be under the RNC). As an example, we tune the SD-threshold to achieve 50% coverage (which is equivalent to 2.5 to 3.5 times the normal load), the corresponding accuracy is shown in Table 5 for the 6 RNCs that are under the probed GGSN from the MobileApp data.

Here LAC 52704 and 52818 (Arlington) both belong to the "Dallas-Fort Worth-Arlington" metropolitan area that has a large population. The accuracy is high because their DL queue size threshold of 1010 is very unique. LAC 52903 (Fort Worth) also belongs to the same metropolitan area. However, its DL threshold is only 510 bytes. The reason why its accuracy is high is that its min-RTT is also very unique to distinguish it from most other LACs. LAC 26507 has a very bad accuracy because the promotion delay is unstable and requires a large threshold value to maintain the coverage rate. Further, its static features are also the most commonly observed ones, further decreasing the accuracy. From the attacker's perspective, he can also perform such signature distribution sampling offline regularly to estimate how distinct the target RNC's signature is before the attack. To further improve the accuracy, we discuss an optional step to further filter IPs that are in other RNCs (in §6). Finally, the last two columns in Table 5 are the results of the phone-number-based approach described in the next section.

5.3 Comparison with Phone-Number-Based Localization

In the state-of-the-art phone-number-based localization [19, 35], the first seven digits of the phone number (area code) are used to map out its corresponding physical location (and carrier name) using the public NPA/NXX database [8]. The fundamental difference between signature- and phone-number-based approach is that phone number is a static property — users carry the same phone number to different places, even when they switch network providers. In contrast, network signature is dynamic and up-to-date, thus robust to user mobility. Based on the data we collected (described later), we find 75.4% of the carrier names returned from NPA/NXX database are incorrect, leading to extra effort for correction, assuming there is a way to do so.

Data & evaluation methodology. From our deployed MobileApp, with user's permission we collected 15,395 entries consisting of first 7 digits of phone number, carrier name, GPS location from users all across the U.S. as ground truth. We use the data to calculate coverage and accuracy and compare them directly with the signature-based approach. Ideally we want to map each GPS location to its RNC and do an RNC-level comparison on the coverage and accuracy. However, the NPA/NXX database returns only city-level location. Thus, we approximate the RNC-level

Category	Signature-based localization/IP traffic	Phone-number-based localization/MMS
Localization overhead	× Scanning large range of IPs	✓ Crawl database, correct carrier name
Localization accuracy	– Better in large cities	– Better in small cities
Localization technique extensibility	✓ More features to improve accuracy	× Difficult to extend
Stealthiness in actual attack	✓ Hard for users to notice	× Easy for users to notice or disable
Feedback in actual attack	✓ Immediate feedback	× No feedback
Timing control in actual attack	✓ Easy to control	× Can get queued and delayed
Current defense effectiveness	– Can be hard to traverse NAT	– MMS blocked or rate limited
Detectability in actual attack	– Probing traffic can be detected	– MMS flooding can be detected

Figure 12. Comparison between signature-based and Phone-number-based attacks

comparison through city-level comparison instead. To begin, we map each GPS location to its corresponding city via a city-to-GPS database, and map the phone number prefix to its city via the NPA/NXX database. We term them *GPS-city* and *queried-city* respectively.

We treat big cities and small cities differently. For each big city big, which is defined to have multiple RNCs (or LACs from OpenCellID), we compute its city-level coverage as $\frac{X}{Y1}$ where X is the number of cases where *GPS-city* = *queried-city* = big, and $Y1$ is the number of cases where *GPS-city* = big. Similarly, we compute accuracy as $\frac{X}{Y2}$ where X is the same as before, and $Y2$ is the number of cases where *queried-city* = big. Note that since a phone number can only map to a city-level location, its RNC-level coverage and accuracy need to be divided further by n — the number of RNCs in that city. The coverage and accuracy are then $\frac{X}{Y1 \times n}$ and $\frac{X}{Y2 \times n}$. Here we conservatively use $n = 2$ to account for any inaccuracy when mapping from LAC to RNC. In reality, n is likely bigger and makes their results even worse. For small cities that may share a single RNC with other cities, we need a different method. Specifically, if the *GPS-city* and *queried-city* are within a certain physical distance, we consider them to be under the same RNC.

Coverage and accuracy results. For big cities, the average coverage and accuracy are 18.8% and 18.4% respectively for phone-number-based approach. Both values are much lower than the signature-based results in Table 5. In comparison with our signature-based localization, if we set the SD-threshold to allow the same accuracy, the coverage of the two big cities in Table 5 can increase to 60% – 80%, which is equivalent to 3 to 4 times the normal load. For small cities, Figure 11 illustrates how average coverage and accuracy over all cities change with different distance threshold. At 10 miles, which is our locally observed distance to observe two different RNCs in small-city area, the coverage and accuracy are about 30% and 40% respectively. At 30 miles, they are around 56% and 60%, indicating that the phone-number-based approach can perform better in the small city case as the signature-based approach has less distinct signatures in small cities.

As a more direct comparison, we look at the intersection between the phone-number-based results and signature-based results from MobileApp, arriving at these following cities: Arlington and Fort Worth. As we can see in Table 5, the phone-number-based coverage and accuracy are much worse than the the signature-based approach. For Arlington, $coverage = \frac{X}{Y1 \times 2} = \frac{11}{46 \times 2}$; $accuracy = \frac{X}{Y2 \times 2} = \frac{11}{92 \times 2}$. For Fort Worth, $coverage = \frac{X}{Y1 \times 2} = \frac{0}{30 \times 2}$; $accuracy = \frac{X}{Y2 \times 2} = \frac{0}{3 \times 2}$ ($X, Y1, Y2$ are defined earlier). Surprisingly for city "Fort Worth", both metrics are 0%, showing how ineffective phone-number-based approach can be. Other cities do not have enough phone number data points in MobileApp, thus are marked as N/A.

Other aspects.

Note that NPA/NXX database does not provide mappings from phone numbers to IPs. Therefore, the only way to attack the data channel using phone numbers is through MMS messages, as SMS uses control channel instead. To launch the attack, a large number of MMS messages must be sent regularly.

Different from sending direct IP traffic, sending MMS has a number of short-comings (shown in Table 12). We illustrate a few of them: 1). Repeated MMS messages are easy for users to notice and disable or even report to their carriers as abuse. In contrast, sending direct IP traffic is much less noticeable to users. 2). We find that sending MMS through the email interface (*e.g.*, 123456789@mms.att.net) provides no feedback on the success of message delivery, thus potentially wasting significant effort by attacking phones that received no MMS at all (*e.g.*, no MMS capability). 3). The timing of MMS delivery is very unpredictable, making the attack coordination difficult. In our local experiment, we sent MMS messages repeatedly every 30 seconds over 4 hours at night, which presumably should incur little delay. In contrast, we observe significant delays, causing the phone 22.7% of the time to be idle and making the attack significantly less effective. In a real attack where the MMS gateway/server is more loaded, it is expected to observe even longer delays. In fact, since MMS still uses SMS to push the notification [10], it is likely that the control channel is overloaded first.

5.4 Attack Scalability Analysis

An important question is how fast the attacker can scan a sufficient number of IPs. If it takes too long, the collected IP address may change (*e.g.,* users may power off the phone). With a simple analysis, we estimate that it takes 1.2 hours to scan enough IPs with 800kbps of bandwidth. The duration can be significantly shortened using more attack machines and bandwidth.

Input. The prefix ranges found to be allocated for a target location under a GGSN: X.128.X.X – X.147.X.X.(§4.1) are used as input. This corresponds to 1,300,500 IPs.

Min-RTT probing. The attacker can first use min-RTT measurements to filter irrelevant IPs as min-RTT has the smallest probing bandwidth requirement and the highest entropy. Although in total we need 30 – 40 probes (as described in §4.2.2) to determine the min-RTT, we need only 1 probe to first check if the IP is assigned or not. Probing one IP with one probe requires bandwidth of $\frac{40byte*8bit}{RTT} = 1kps$ (assuming $RTT = 0.3s$). Probing 800 IPs simultaneously requires $1kbps \times 800 = 800kbps$. Probing each IP once takes about $\frac{1{,}300{,}500}{800} \times 0.3s = 8min$.

Since many IPs are not allocated at run time, they can be dropped easily upon the first probe. Considering the online IP ratio of 22% (§3.3), around 286,110 IPs are left. Probing the remaining IPs with additional 29 back-to-back measurements will take $\frac{286{,}110}{800} \times (0.3s \times 29) = 51min$. In total, it takes roughly 59 minutes to scan the entire GGSN IP range.

Static feature probing. After min-RTT probing, on average $\frac{1}{8}$ of IPs (around 35,763) remain since the entropy of min-RTT is 3 bits. The attacker can then measure the static features to further narrow down IPs to probe. Given that the attacker knows the exact inactivity timer and the queue size threshold in the target location from the probe phone in that area, it can directly look for these values during scanning. Depending on the timer and queue size threshold, a complete round to measure both values takes a large packet (1200 bytes) to trigger state promotion to DCH, a small packet (40 bytes) to test the inactivity timer, and a packet with size matching the queue size threshold (suppose it is 500 bytes) to see if it forces the state to go back to DCH. The time to finish such a round would be the $promotion\ delay(2s) + inactivity\ timer(5s) = 7s$. The throughput requirement is then $\frac{(1200+40+500)*8bits}{7} = 1.94kbps$. Scanning 412 IPs simultaneously would require $1.94kbps \times 412 = 800kbps$ bandwidth and $\frac{35{,}763}{412} \times 7s = 10min$ to finish.

Promotion delay probing. After the static feature probing, there are on average $\frac{1}{5}$ IPs (around 7,152) remaining for entropy of 2.3 bits. Then the promotion delay can be measured. It takes only 10.7bps uplink on the server side, since it only needs to send and receive one 40-byte packet every 30 second. It takes 4min to complete 8 rounds of probing (8 rounds is selected in §4.2.2). The attacker can easily target the rest simultaneously using $7,152 \times 10.7bps = 76kbps$ bandwidth. The estimated time to finish probing should be 4min since all of them can be done in parallel.

In total, the time to complete the measuring of all features is $59 + 10 + 4 = 73min$. Considering 80% of IPs keep their IPs for more than 4 hours (Figure 3), the attacker has enough time to launch the attack thereafter for at least several hours.

6 Discussion and Defense

Impact of device difference on dynamic features. Ideally, end-devices should have little impact on the dynamic features such as RTT and promotion delays. However, we do realize that different phones supporting different technologies may co-exist. For instance, some phones may support only HSDPA while their network supports both HSUPA and HSDPA (*i.e.,* HSPA). This means that these "older" phones may experience slower network performance (*e.g.,* longer RTT and promotion delay) thus exhibiting different network signatures. In practice, however, it is likely that there will always be one or two "dominating" technologies that are most widely used in the end-devices and can be considered as the target for an attacker. For instance, devices are frequently updated given that smartphones are becoming cheaper and quickly out-dated. Regardless, such phone differences do not impact the static features such as queue length threshold and inactivity timer.

Impact of base-station difference on dynamic features. Besides device differences, different base-stations can also impact the measured RTTs or promotion delays, with bounded noise. Indeed, from the MobileApp data, we find that in a short duration (*e.g.,* peak hours), the measured promotion delays do not vary significantly under the same RNC considering the samples are collected across multiple base-stations already. We do find one instance where the promotion delay can vary more significantly in different base-stations. This means that we either have to relax the SD-threshold to cover enough signature samples, or need some way to account for it. As a preliminary investigation, we find that the difference could be caused by different base-stations under different load, indicated by significantly differing average RTTs (min-RTTs are still the same) which can be used for calibration. We leave for future work to systematically address this.

Optional final step to narrow down RNCs. In cases where the attacker wants to ensure that the inferred IPs indeed belong to the target RNC, an optional step that the attacker can take is to actually try these IPs out. More specifically, the attacker can choose a subset of the total IPs and launch a mini-attack against the RNCs (which should increase the processing delay on the RNC) and observe the changed baseline promotion delay from his probe phone. If the promotion delays of the tested IPs match the perturbed baseline promotion delay, it is likely that they indeed belong to the same RNC. The attacker can repeat this step multiple times to perform more fine-grained filtering.

Next generation LTE networks. As discussed earlier, LTE networks still have the built-in radio resource control mechanism with associated configurable parameters [5]. For instance, they allow various timers such as inactivity timer, discontinuous reception (DRX) cycle timer to be configured [5]. Fundamentally, due to the scarce nature of the radio resource, the corresponding radio resource control protocol has to provide mechanisms for sharing the resource smartly and flexibly among a large number of users. It is conceivable that network signatures exist for LTE networks as well since different network locations may again use a different set of configurations to accommodate the load difference.

Defense. The network signatures can be considered as a type of side channel that leaks information about the network location. A common defense is to eliminate such side channel. For instance, instead of using the fixed configuration parameter for all devices at all times, carriers can assign parameters probabilistically within a range, which makes it significantly harder for an attacker to infer the actual parameter. However, this may reduce the effectiveness of the parameter for accommodating workload and still requires scrutinization. As network defenses, the carrier can disallow direct probing from the Internet or other phones. However, it also has negative impact as discussed. As host-based defenses, one simple solution is to use host firewall that drops unsolicited probing packets to prevent information leakage. This could be an effective solution in the short term. As smartphones evolve, however, they may open more ports to accept incoming connections, making host firewall protection less effective. We leave for future work to systematically study how to defend against such information leakage in critical infrastructures such as cellular networks.

7 Related work

The wide adoption of cellular networks increasingly draws attention to study their vulnerabilities. Various forms of attacks have been revealed in the past few years. Serror *et al.* [32] found malicious traffic from the Internet can overload the paging channel in CDMA2000 networks. Traynor *et al.* [35] presented two attacks on GPRS/EDGE networks by abusing the radio resource setup and teardown process. Lee *et al.* [25] showed well-timed attack traffic can trigger excessive radio resource control messages, which in turn overburden RNCs in UMTS networks. The success of all these attacks hinges on the ability to identify many target devices in a particular cellular network region, *e.g.,* under a RNC (which is the focus of this paper).

Our work draws on earlier cellular network measurement studies. Balakrishnan *et al.* [15] found IP address alone cannot be used to determine the geographic location of mobile phone in AT&T's 3G network. Latency measurement appears to be more informative. However, their observations are drawn from latency samples of only three locations.

Prior work leveraged phone numbers to create a hit list for the purpose of launching targeted attacks. Enck *et al.* [19] generated a hit list of phone numbers through a combination of sources such as NPA/NXX database and web scraping. However, its effectiveness is not thoroughly evaluated. Moreover, sending SMS or MMS has a number of limitations compared to sending IP traffic directly to phones.

There have been extensive studies on geolocating IP addresses in the Internet. Most of them assume a list of landmarks with well-known geographic location, extracted from manually-maintained sources like DNS names [28, 33, 12]. They then use latency constraints to multiple landmarks to geolocate an IP address [22]. Unfortunately, these techniques are ill-suited for geolocation in cellular networks because a phone is often far from its first IP hop (*e.g.,* GGSN) not only in terms of geographic distance but also in terms of network latency. Given this, instead of attempting to infer the exact location of a phone, we solve a slightly different (but easier) problem, *i.e.,* determining if two phones are under the same RNC.

There are also studies for localizing mobile devices such as Escort [18], VOR [27], Virtual Compass [16], PlaceLab [17], and Radar [14]. The key difference is that they all require participation and cooperation from the phone, which is not assumed in the attack.

8 Conclusion

Motivated by the recent attacks against cellular network infrastructure at a particular target region (*e.g.*, signaling attack), we focus on a simple but important question of how to create a hit-list of reachable mobile IP addresses associated with the target location to facilitate such targeted DoS attacks. Our approach uses network signatures through active probing and is applicable for a large set of current cellular networks we studied. This exposes a new attack vector that cannot be easily eliminated. From a thorough empirical analysis, we offer suggestions on how to defend against such reconnaissance effort by attackers.

References

[1] 3GPP TS 25.133: "Requirements for support of radio resource management".

[2] 3GPP TS 25.331: "RRC Protocol Specification".

[3] AT&T: 80 percent of network now upgraded to HSPA+. `http://www.engadget.com/2010/11/17/atandt-80-percent-of-network-now-upgraded-to-hspa/`.

[4] AT&T: wireless capacity upgrades complete in Hillsborough, Pasco. `http://www.bizjournals.com/tampabay/stories/2010/10/11/daily38.html`.

[5] Evolved universal terrestrial radio access (e-utra); radio resource control (rrc); protocol specification. `http://www.3gpp.org/ftp/Specs/html-info/36331.htm`.

[6] Extended icmp to support multi-part messages. `http://tools.ietf.org/html/rfc4884`.

[7] iPhone Troubles Might Go Beyond Signaling. `http://www.lightreading.com/document.asp?doc_id=190764&piddl_msgid=226225#msg_226225`.

[8] Local Calling Guide. `http://www.localcallingguide.com/index.php`.

[9] Mobility management. `http://en.wikipedia.org/wiki/Mobility_management`.

[10] Multimedia Messaging Service. `http://en.wikipedia.org/wiki/Multimedia_Messaging_Service`.

[11] OpenCellID. `http://www.opencellid.org/`.

[12] Whois ip address/domain name lookup. `http://whois.domaintools.com`.

[13] UE "Fast Dormancy" behavior. 3GPP discussion and decision notes R2-075251, 2007.

[14] P. Bahl and V. N. Padmanabhan. Radar: an in-building rf-based user location and tracking system. In *Proc. of INFOCOM*, 2000.

[15] M. Balakrishnan, I. Mohomed, and V. Ramasubramanian. Where's That Phone?: Geolocating IP Addresses on 3G Networks. In *Proc. of IMC*, 2009.

[16] N. Banerjee, S. Agarwal, P. Bahl, R. Chandra, A. Wolman, , and M. Corner. Virtual Compass: relative positioning to sense mobile social interactions. In *IEEE Pervasive Computing*, 2010.

[17] Y. Chen, Y. Chawathe, A. LaMarca, and J. Krumm. Accuracy characterization for metropolitan-scale wi-fi localization. In *Proc. of Mobisys*, 2005.

[18] I. Constandache, X. Bao, M. Azizyan, and R. R. Choudhury. Did You See Bob?: Human Localization using Mobile Phones. In *Proc. of MobiCom*, 2010.

[19] W. Enck, P. Traynor, P. McDaniel, and T. La Porta. Exploiting open functionality in SMS-capable cellular networks. In *Proc. of CCS*, 2005.

[20] H. Galeana, R. Ferrus, and J. Olmos. Transport capacity estimations for over-provisioned utran ip-based networks. In *WCNC*, 2007.

[21] M. Gruteser, D. Grunwalddepartment, and C. Science. Anonymous usage of location-based services through spatial and temporal cloaking. In *Proc. of Mobisys*, 2003.

[22] B. Gueye, A. Ziviani, M. Crovella, and S. Fdida. Constraint-based Geolocation of Internet Hosts. In *Proc. of IMC*, 2004.

[23] H. Holma and A. Toskala. HSDPA/HSUPA for UMTS: High Speed Radio Access for Mobile Communications. John Wiley and Sons, 2006.

[24] H. Kaaranen, A. Ahtiainen, L. Laitinen, S. Naghian, and V. Niemi. UMTS Networks: Architecture, Mobility and Services (2E). John Wiley & Sons, 2005.

[25] P. P. C. Lee, T. Bu, and T. Woo. On the Detection of Signaling DoS Attacks on 3G Wireless Networks. In *Proc. of INFOCOM*, 2007.

[26] O. D. Mey, L. Schumacher, and X. Dubois. Optimum Number of RLC Retransmissions for Best TCP Performance in UTRAN. In *Proc. of Annual IEEE International Symposium on Personal Indoor and Mobile Radio Communications (PIMRC)*, 2005.

[27] D. Niculescu and B. Nath. VOR base stations for indoor 802.11 positioning. In *Proc. of MobiCom*, 2004.

[28] V. Padmanabhan and L. Subramanian. An Investigation of Geographic Mapping Techniques for Internet Hosts. In *Proc. of SIGCOMM*, 2001.

[29] F. Qian, Z. Wang, A. Gerber, Z. M. Mao, S. Sen, and O. Spatscheck. Characterizing radio resource allocation for 3G networks. In *Proc. of IMC*, 2010.

[30] F. Qian, Z. Wang, A. Gerber, Z. M. Mao, S. Sen, and O. Spatscheck. TOP: Tail Optimization Protocol for Cellular Radio Resource Allocation. In *Proc. International Conference on Network Protocols*, 2010.

[31] Z. Qian, Z. M. Mao, Y. Xie, and F. Yu. Investigation of triangular spamming: a stealthy and efficient spamming technique. In *In Proc. of IEEE Security and Privacy*, 2010.

[32] J. Serror, H. Zang, and J. C. Bolot. Impact of Paging Channel Overloads or Attacks on a Cellular Network. In *WiSe*, 2006.

[33] N. Spring, R. Mahajan, and D. Wetherall. Measuring ISP Topologies with Rocketfuel. In *Proc. of SIGCOMM*, 2002.

[34] P. Traynor, M. Lin, M. Ongtang, V. Rao, T. Jaeger, P. McDaniel, and T. La Porta. On Cellular Botnets: Measuring the Impact of Malicious Devices on a Cellular Network Core. In *Proc. of CCS*, 2009.

[35] P. Traynor, P. McDaniel, and T. La Porta. On Attack Causality in Internet-connected Cellular Networks. In *Proc. of USENIX Security*, 2007.

[36] Q. Xu, J. Huang, Z. Wang, F. Qian, A. Gerber, and Z. M. Mao. Cellular data network infrastructure characterization and implication on mobile content placement. In Proc. of SIGMETRICS, 2011.

Weaponizing Femtocells: The Effect of Rogue Devices on Mobile Telecommunication

Nico Golde, Kévin Redon, Ravishankar Borgaonkar

Berlin Institute of Technology, Security in Telecommunications
femtocell@sec.t-labs.tu-berlin.de

NDSS 2012, San Diego, 6th February 2012

Introduction

- Mobile data traffic is rapidly increasing (3G, 4G), but coverage often bad
- Operators seek for solutions to offload traffic to other networks
- Introduction of small/cheap cells in residential environments (home)
- As of Q2 2011, 31 operators in 20 countries adopted femtocell technology (Vodafone, AT&T, SFR, NTT DoCoMo, ...)

What is a femtocell (HNB or FAP)?

- Small and cheap base station, small coverage (around 50m)
- Deployed in home environment (no tamper resistance)
- Connected to operator backend via Internet

- Reduce expenditure by offloading traffic from public infrastructure
- Low maintenance and installation costs
- Improved 3G coverage in buildings
- Location based services

Contributions

- End-User risk assessment
  - Demonstrate attacks violating confidentiality, integrity and availability of subscriber traffic

- Femtocell/Infrastructure weakness analysis
  - Network attacks originating from a femtocell and design shortcomings in current architectures

⇒ Implementation and evaluation in a real network

Assumption

We assume a rooted device!

More information on the rooting process is available in:
Ravishankar Borgaonkar, Kevin Redon and Jean-Pierre Seifert. "Security Analysis of a Femtocell device". 4th ACM International Conference on Security of Information and Networks (SIN)

Home Node B Subsystem (HNS)

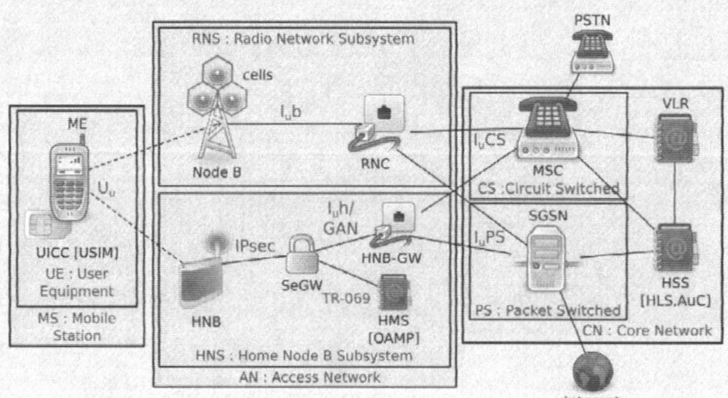

IMSI-Catching

- IMSI-Catching in GSM easy by just configuring the BTS with correct MCC/MNC
- In 3G subscribers are protected from IMSI-Catching by mutual authentication
- Authentication performed with the home network, not the actual cell
  ⇒ Femtocells by design provide network authenticity!

- Given device access it is possible to:
  - Reconfigure MCC/MNC
  - Open access for all subscribers (roaming allowed by SFR)

Voice recording (Confidentiality)

- Over-the-Air traffic encrypted but **decrypted** on the femtocell

- All traffic between femtocell and network is plaintext and only protected by IPsec

- Hijacking control flow of IPSec tunnel software
  ⇒ Decode IPsec traffic, extract voice/SMS
  ⇒ Femtocells can be a very cheap IMSI-Catcher

Traffic MitM (Integrity/Authenticity)

- What if we change the HNB-GW?
  ⇒ Full control over all communication

- Modify traffic, impersonating subscribers
- Relay messages to subscriber whenever authentication is required
- Demo implementation based on SMS:
  Modify messages or inject SMS on behalf of subscriber (will be billed)

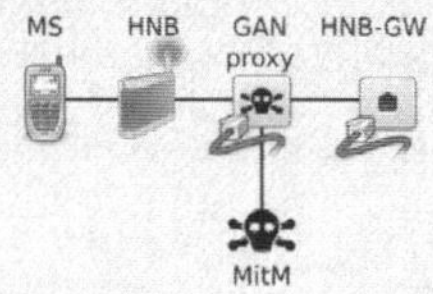

Detach subscribers (Availability)

- Disconnecting subscribers in GSM via IMSI DETACH message (unauthenticated!)
- Limited to a certain geographical location!

- Femtocell networks have one dedicated VLR
  ⇒ Limitation vanishes
  ⇒ DoS against subscribers by detaching the complete femtocell network

Datamining subscriber information

- Femtocells store various subscriber and location information (registered users, neighbour cells, ...)
- 3GPP specifications require Node-B's to submit measurement reports to a central entity

- Our device exposed a hidden technician web interface with broken authentication
  ⇒ Subscriber and femtocell data exposed!
  ⇒ No filtering for HNB⇔HNB communication
- Measurement reports are pushed to an FTP server, with a **shared account**!

Mapping femtocells

- Using neighbour cell list, you could, e.g., map femtocells

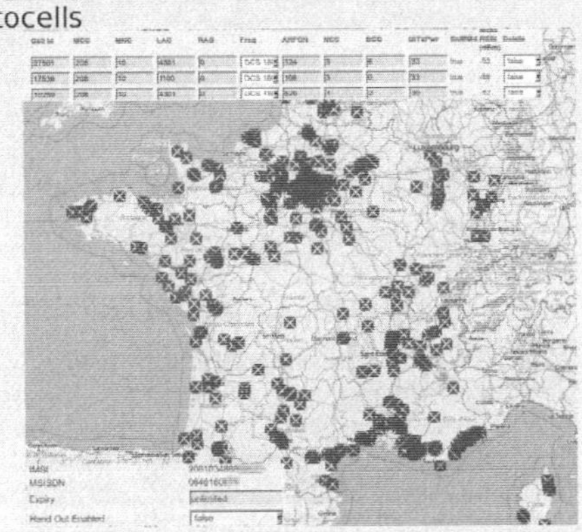

Femtocell attack surface

- Attack surface limited:
  - Network protocols: NTP, DNS spoofing (not tested)
  - Services: webserver, TR-069 provisioning (feasible)
  - TR-069 is the de-facto standard for femtocell remote provisioning
- Both HTTP; TR-069 is based on SOAP and XML
  ⇒ Great potential for software vulnerabilities
- All services run as root
- Eventually we found a remote root vulnerability in the webserver (CVE-2011-2900)
  ⇒ Take over femtocell network
  ⇒ End-user threats become a global problem!

Possible infrastructure impact

- Signaling attacks a well known problem, e.g. HLR overload [1]
- TCP/IP based communication allows for easy signaling traffic generation at a high rate
  ⇒ Given a remote root bug this can be amplified with a femtocell botnet
- Connect to femtocell network without femtocell!
- Act as femtocell by using network protocols

[1] Traynor et al., On Cellular Botnets: Measuring the impact of Malicious Devices on a Cellular Core Network

Conclusion

- This is a big mess
- Given the history of rooted femtocells (Vodafone SureSignal, Samsung, SFR) security poorly implemented in practice
- Inherent trust in the physical security of these low cost devices may be wrong
- Femtocell security strongly affects subscriber privacy, authenticity, availability and operator network

Acknowledgements (in no particular order) & Questions

- Jean-Pierre Seifert
- Collin Mulliner
- Benjamin Michéle
- Dieter Spaar
- K2
- Nicholas Weaver

Thanks for the attention!
Questions?

PRIVACY-PRESERVING LOGARITHMIC-TIME SEARCH ON ENCRYPTED DATA IN CLOUD

1

Yanbin Lu
University of California, Irvine
(NDSS'11, Feb 6)

CLOUD DATABASE ENVIRONMENT

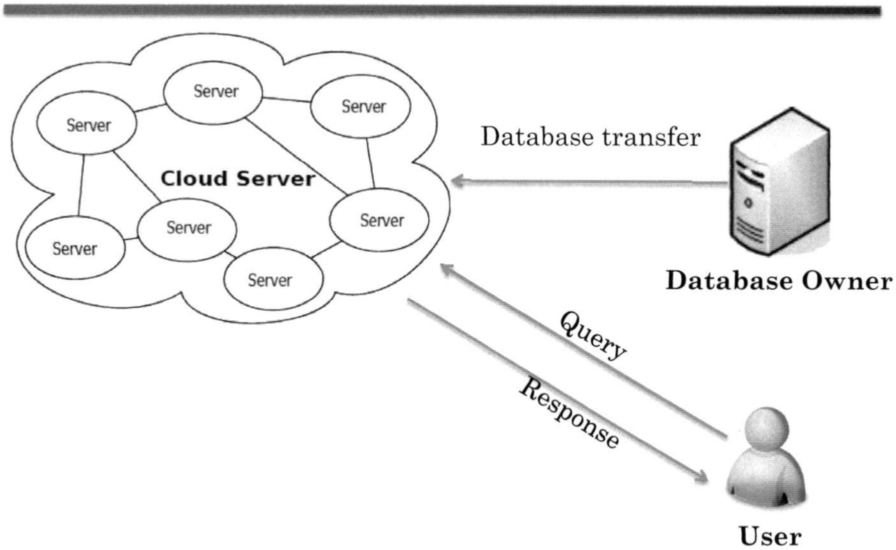

2

PRIVACY REQUIREMENTS

- Privacy requirements:
  - Cloud server learns no information about database
  - Cloud server learns no information about user query
  - Owner can exercise access control over user query
- Personal data vault example:
  - Owner: Patient
  - Database: Heart beat rate
  - Cloud server: Amazon RDS
  - User: Cardiologist

3

PRIVACY-PRESERVING SOLUTION

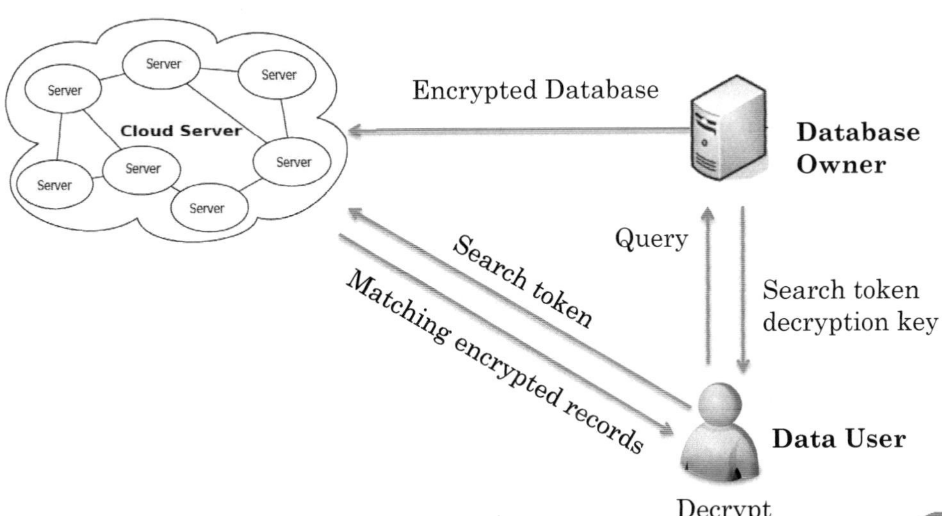

4

Requirements

- Sublinear search
  - Linear search is untolerable in massive data
- Query result integrity
  - Prevent cloud server from cheating user
- Provable database update
  - Prevent cloud server from cheating database owner

5

Related work

- Order preserving encryption
  - Deterministic and not IND-CPA secure
  - Domain distribution is fixed
- Bellare et al. [crypto'07]
  - Deterministic and not IND-CPA secure
  - Only equality search is supported
- Predicate encryption
  - Useful in privacy-preserving cloud database
  - Linear complexity

6

Predicate encryption

- Setup(1^k): output secret key *SK*.
- Encrypt(SK, I, m): encrypt message m under attributes I with key *SK*.
- Key-extraction(g): outputs key k_g
- Decrypt(k_g, C_I): decrypts iff $g(I) = 1$

7

Building blocks

- Range predicate encryption (RPE)
  - Ciphertext associated with point t
  - Decryption key associated with a range Q
  - Decryption works if $t \in Q$
- Inner-product predicate encryption (IPE)
  - Ciphertext associated with vector $\vec{x}$
  - Decryption key associated with vector $\vec{v}$
  - Decryption works if $\langle \vec{v}, \vec{x} \rangle = 0$

8

STRAWMAN RPE BUILDING FROM IPE

- Encrypt(t): create $\vec{x} = (x_1, \ldots, x_i, \ldots, x_T)$ where
  $x_i = 1$ if $i = t$ and $x_i = 0$ otherwise.
  Run IPE encryption.

- Extract(Q): create $\vec{y} = (y_1, \ldots, y_i, \ldots, y_T)$ where
  $y_i = 0$ if $i \in Q$ and $y_1 = 1$ otherwise.
  Run IPE key extraction.

- Decrypt(e_t, k_Q): Run IPE decryption.

9

EFFICIENT RANGE REPRESENTATION

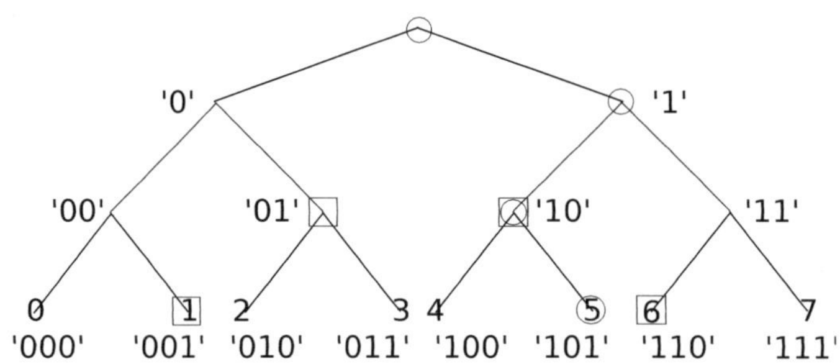

- Any range can be covered by $2 \cdot (\log T - 1)$ nodes.
- Point path intersects with range representation

10

EFFICIENT RANGE PREDICATE ENCRYPTION

- Encrypting point t:
  - $P(X) = \prod_{v \in \mathcal{CP}(t)} (X - v) = \sum_{i=0}^{\log T} \alpha_i X^i$
  - $\vec{A} = (\alpha_0, \ldots, \alpha_{\log T})$
- Key extraction for range Q:
  - $\vec{K}_x = (x^0, \ldots, x^{\log T}), \forall x \in \mathcal{MCS}(Q)$
- Observation:
  - $\vec{A} \cdot \vec{K}_x = \alpha_0 \cdot x^0 + \alpha_1 \cdot x^1 + \cdots + \alpha_{\log T} \cdot x^{\log T} = P(x)$

11

LOGARITHMIC-TIME SEARCH

- Encrypting each node of B-tree
  - One RPE for search token
  - One RPE for real message
- Search token extraction involves two rounds
  - One for left range
  - One for right range
  - Example:
    - Domain size [0-100]
    - Query range [10-20]
    - Left range [0-9], right range [21-100]

12

QUERY AUTHENTICATION

- Authenticated data structure
  - Encrypted B-tree
  - Authenticated root
- Query result verification
  - Left and right boundary to query range
  - Verification without leaking records out of range
- Provable data update
  - Owner first verifies change path
  - Reconstructs and authenticates root

13

PERFORMANCE

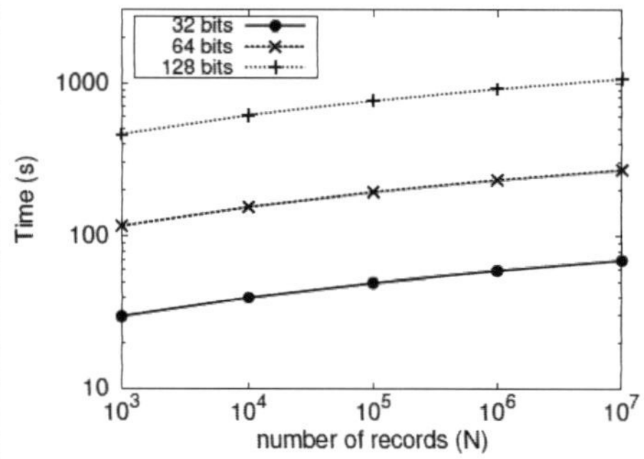

Total search time

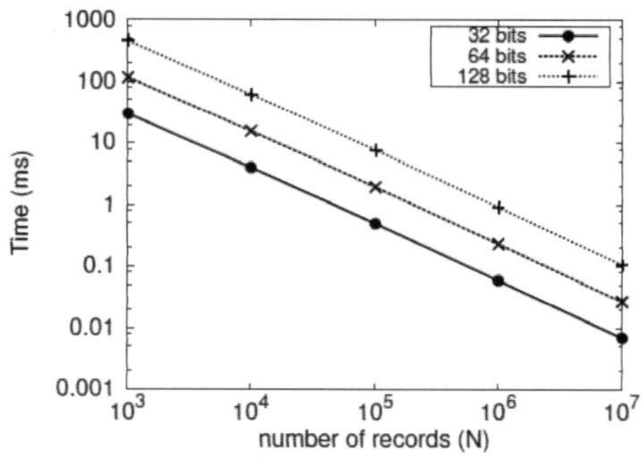

Search time per record

14

Thank you!

15

Large-Scale Privacy-Preserving Mapping of Human Genomic Sequences on Hybrid Clouds

Yangyi Chen, Bo Peng, XiaoFeng Wang, Haixu Tang
School of Informatics and Computing
Indiana University Bloomington, IN, USA
{yangchen, pengbo, xw7, hatang}@indiana.edu

Abstract

An operation preceding most human DNA analyses is read mapping, which aligns millions of short sequences (called reads) to a reference genome. This step involves an enormous amount of computation (evaluating edit distances for millions upon billions of sequence pairs) and thus needs to be outsourced to low-cost commercial clouds. This asks for scalable techniques to protect sensitive DNA information, a demand that cannot be met by any existing techniques (e.g., homomorphic encryption, secure multi-party computation). In this paper, we report a new step towards secure and scalable read mapping on the hybrid cloud, which includes both the public commercial cloud and the private cloud within an organization. Inspired by the famous "seed-and-extend" method, our approach strategically splits a mapping task: the public cloud seeks exact matches between the keyed hash values of short read substrings (called seeds) and those of reference sequences to roughly position reads on the genome; the private cloud extends the seeds from these positions to find right alignments. Our novel seed-combination technique further moves most workload of this task to the public cloud. The new approach is found to work effectively against known inference attacks, and also easily scale to millions of reads.

1 Introduction

The rapid advance of human genomics technologies has not only revolutionized life science but also profoundly impacted the development of computing technologies. At the core of this scientific revolution is the emergence of the high-throughput Next Generation Sequencing (NGS) technologies: today, a single sequencer can generate millions of short DNA sequences (called *reads*) with 35 to 250 base-pairs (bp) long over one billion nucleotides [40]. To interpret these sequences, the most important step is to align them to a public human DNA sequence (called *reference genome*) to identify their genetic positions and other features, e.g., whether they belong to human or human microbes. This operation, known as *read mapping*, is a *prerequisite* for most DNA sequence analyses [54] (e.g., SNP discovery, genotyping, personal genomics, etc. [49]). It is also a step involving intensive computation, given the huge size of the reference genome - 6 billion nucleotides, and the complexity of the mapping operation - calculating *edit distances* between reads and all the substrings on the reference genome. With the fast-growing sequence data produced by NGS, the demands for mapping such data are increasingly hard to be met by the computing power within organizations [52]. A trend widely believed to be inevitable is outsourcing this computation to low-cost commercial clouds [52]. For example, Amazon Elastic Compute Cloud (EC2) provides different types of computing instances at a price as low as 0.015 dollar per hour [2]. This development, however, brings in privacy risks: on the one hand, NGS reads can be used to identify sequence donors [39], a serious privacy threat that can lead to denying their access to health/life/disability insurance and educational/employment opportunities; on the other hand, today's cloud providers do not offer high security assurance and tend to avoid any liability [3]. To protect donors and avoid legal troubles, the NIH so far disallows any datasets involving human DNA to be handed over to the public cloud.

Secure computation outsourcing. Addressing this urgent demand requires the techniques capable of sustaining large-scale secure computation outsourcing. Unfortunately, none of the existing approaches are designed for the computation of such an enormous scale. Particularly, homomorphic encryption, secret sharing and secure multi-party computation (SMC) are far too heavyweight to handle read mapping. For example, a privacy-preserving protocol [17] takes about 5 minutes to calculate the edit distance between two 25-element sequences through homomorphic encryption and oblivious transfers. Such a task can be computed much more efficiently by SMC techniques, thanks to the recent progress in this area [33, 35]. However, even the state-of-the-art SMC implementation needs about 4 seconds to process two 100-element sequences [33]. Also, secret-sharing based approaches [17, 18] all incur data exchanges between share holders when aligning a single sequence pair. Given that a mapping task routinely evaluates the edit distances for 10^{15} sequence pairs, all these approaches are simply not up to this job. Alternatively, one may consider anonymizing the sequence data by aggregating the reads from multiple individuals or adding noise. These approaches are known to be vulnerable to statistical re-identification attacks [32, 34, 46, 56], a threat that prompted the NIH to remove all aggregated DNA data [12] from the public domain.

Special features of the problem. We feel that existing generic approaches all fail to appreciate the special features of the problem, which can be leveraged to build a practical solution. Actually, the edit distance considered in read mapping is small, typically no more than 6 for standard 100-bp reads [29]. This is because human genetic variation is believed to be small, below 0.5%. In practice, the differences between a read and its counterpart on the reference genome mainly come from sequencing errors, whose rate is typically 2-3%. Therefore, a privacy-preserving technique that works on small edit distances (caused by the variations and the errors) should be enough for handling most sequence-analysis tasks.

The cloud also has distinctive features. It is extremely good at performing simple operations over a large amount of data, as evidenced by the pervasiveness of *MapReduce*-based computing services [23]. Also interesting is the way that commercial clouds are used in practice: they often serve as a receiving end of the computation "spill-over" from an organization's internal system when its computing resources are about to deplete. This way of computing, which involves both the private cloud within an organization and the public commercial cloud, is called *hybrid cloud computing* [26]. The hybrid cloud has already been adopted by most organizational cloud users and is still undergoing rapid development. It also presents a new opportunity that makes practical, secure outsourcing of computation tasks to untrusted environments possible: for example, we can split a task, delegating to a commercial cloud a large amount of relatively simple computation over encrypted data, like exact string matching, while letting the user's private cloud work on a small amount of relatively complicated computation such as calculating edit distances.

Our approach. Given that read mapping is one of the most important and pervasive operations in DNA sequence analysis [54], we believe that a special solution is justified here to enable secure and practical outsourcing of this computation to the low-cost commercial cloud. In this paper, we show how the aforementioned features can be used to serve this purpose. Our idea is based upon the observation that the edit distance of two sequences can actually be evaluated by checking the exact matches between some of their substrings, an operation easy to secure on the public cloud, when all we care about is whether the distance is below a small threshold. This is described by the well-known *seed-and-extend* strategy [19], which first matches a *seed*, a segment of a read with one-$(d+1)$th of the read's length given an edit distance d, to the substrings on the reference genome[1], and then *extends* from these substrings to align the whole read. Our approach splits the mapping task along these two stages, delegating them to public and private clouds respectively: the public cloud searches for the exact matches between the keyed hash values of seeds and those of substrings (called *l-mers* for a substring of length l) on the reference genome to determine the possible positions of reads, while the private cloud extends from these positions to find the right alignments of these reads (which involves calculating edit distances under a threshold [28]).

However, this simple approach cannot guarantee to offload most of the mapping workload to the public cloud. This is because the traditional seed-and-extend approach used in computational genomics [38] has always considered the situation when seeding and extension happen on the same system: there has never been a need to move the workload from one stage to the other. Particularly, when seeds are too short, due to a relatively large edit distance (e.g., 6 for 100-bp reads), they randomly match a large number of genetic locations on the reference genome. As a result, a lot of extensions have to be done on the private cloud. In our research, we come up with a novel solution, which transforms the computation workload of the private cloud to the spatial cost for the public cloud. More specifically, our approach uses *seed combinations* to ensure that only a relatively small number of extensions happen to each read.

We conducted a security analysis of our technique over the reference genome, particularly on the threat of frequency analysis. This risk is found to be minimum by our experimental analysis over the whole genome, due to the special structure of human genome: most of its l-mers become unique when l grows over 20. Our performance evaluation on a cross-the-country cloud testbed with real human microbiome data indicates that the technique is sufficiently practical for real-world use: it mapped 10 million reads to the whole reference genome in a few hours, outsourced over 97% of the workload to the public cloud and maintained an acceptable level of overall computational, communication and spatial overheads.

Contributions. Here we summarize the contributions of the paper:

- *Practical privacy-preserving mapping technique*. We

[1] At least one seed will match a substring on the region within d edits from the read.

propose a new technique that makes an important step towards secure and scalable DNA sequence mapping. Running on the hybrid-cloud platform, our approach works effectively against inference attacks and has the capacity to process millions of reads with most of the workload being outsourced to the public cloud. This opens the great potential to use the cheap computing resources of the commercial cloud to meet the urgent demand of analyzing a large amount of NGS data. Although the technique was designed for read mapping, lessons drawn from this study can have broader implications: the idea like combining lightweight cryptography/aggregation and transforming complicated computation to easy-to-protect but data intensive computation for the cloud could find other applications in the domains that need practical privacy protection.

• *Implementation and evaluation*. We implemented our technique over *Hadoop*, and evaluated the privacy and the performance of our prototype using real human microbiome data, on a large-scale, across-the-country cloud testbed.

The focus of our research is confidentiality, as it is the main hurdle to outsourcing read-mapping computation to the public cloud and therefore urgently needs practical solutions. Although integrity of cloud computing is no doubt important, so far people are willing to live with the risk that their tasks may not be handled correctly by the cloud. This is evidenced by the fact that mapping of non-human reads already happened on EC2 [47], while the tasks involving human data are not allowed to be given to the public cloud.

Roadmap. The rest of this paper is organized as follows. Section 2 describes security challenges in outsouring anonymized read data; Section 3 presents our secure mapping techniques and analyzes the privacy protection they offer; Section 4 reports an evaluation on the performance of our approach; Section 5 surveys related prior research and Section 6 concludes the paper.

2 Backgrounds

2.1 Read Mapping

The DNA data produced by a next generation DNA sequencer consists of millions of reads, each typically including 35-250 nucleotides. These reads are randomly sampled from a human genome. To interpret them, their genetic locations must be found, which is achieved through read mapping. Specifically, given a set of reads, a reference genome (i.e., a long DNA sequence) and a threshold, the mapping operation aims at aligning each read to a substring on the reference genome such that the edit distance between the read and the substring does not exceed a threshold. This operation positions each read to its genetic location, which is necessary for most human DNA analyses, including SNP discovery, genotyping, gene expression profiling (e.g. RNA-seq), comparative genomics, personal genomics and others [49]. It is also a critical step for analyzing the DNA data of human microbes [8], serving to sanitize such data by removing the DNA contamination from human hosts.

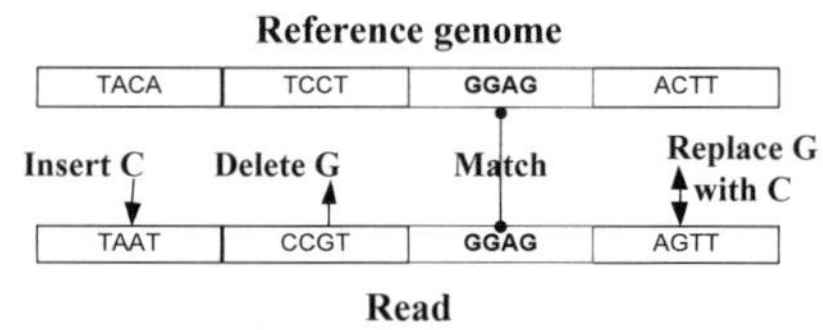

Figure 1. An Example (two sequences with edit distance 3)

Seed-and-extend. As discussed before, a prominent feature of read mapping is that the edit distance is small between a read and the reference substring it should be aligned to: since the genetic variation between different humans is typically below 0.5% and sequencing errors are about 2-3%, almost all the mapping tasks look at a distance threshold no more than 6 for standard 100-bp reads [29], which is sufficient for tolerating both the variations and the errors. For such a small edit distance, alignments can be efficiently found through *seed-and-extend* [19], a method that has been extensively used in high-performance mapping systems like BLAST [15], BLAT [36], Bowtie [37], RMAP [50, 51] and CloudBurst [47]. The method is based upon the observation that for a sequencing read partitioned into $d+1$ segments (seeds) of length l, if it has at most d errors, then at least one of its $d+1$ segments must match a substring at the genetic location (on the reference genome) the read should be mapped onto [19]. Therefore, one can use the segment to roughly locate the read on the reference (the seeding stage), and then extend from these possible locations to determine where it indeed belongs (the extension stage). Figure 1 gives an example: one of the 4 seeds of a 16-bp read matches a 4-mer on a reference substring when the edit distance between them is 3; once this match is found, we can align these two strings to check whether the distance is indeed no more than 3. Our idea is to let the public cloud take care of the seeding, roughly locating reads, which enables the private cloud to quickly extend each read at a relatively small set of positions (rather than at each of the 6 billion positions on the reference genome). The extension is done by a linear algorithm that calculates the edit distances no more than a threshold [28].

2.2 Privacy threat

Threat. The main threat to human genomic data is identification of the individual the DNA comes from. Since such data is often produced by clinic studies, its donor, once identified, could be linked to the disease under the study, which can have serious consequences such as denial of access to health/life insurance, education, and employment. The Health Insurance Portability and Accountability Act (HIPAA) requires removal of explicit identifiers (such as name, social security number, etc.) before health data can be released [11]. This protection, however, was found to be insufficient for genomic data, as re-identification can still happen through examining the genetic markers related to the donor's observable features (i.e., phenotypes) after the genetic locations of reads are recovered, a concern shared by the NIH [12].

The genetic variation most widely-used for such identification is single-nucleotide polymorphism (SNP). SNP occurs when a single nucleotide (`A`, `T`, `C` or `G`) differs between the members of a species. It can take one of two *alleles*, either 0 (major) or 1 (minor). This variation has been employed by all existing re-identification techniques [32, 34, 46, 56]. Theoretically, other variations, including rare alleles [48] and copy number variation (variations over sections of DNA) [13], could also be used to identify an individual. However, a critical barrier for the identification based on rare variations is that they are not mapped at the whole genome scale in any reference population. Also note that to pose the same level of the threat, those variations need a larger population: given that rare-allele frequencies are much lower than those of SNPs, a population 100 or even 1000 times larger than the HapMap population (about 270 people in Phase I and II) may need to publish their whole genomes for accurate estimate of the frequencies, which may not be likely given the increasing awareness of the privacy implication of DNA data. Note that under the protection of our technique, an adversary cannot infer the rare alleles from the data on the public cloud (i.e. the keyed-hash values of l-mers, not their content), because without known rare allele frequencies in a reference population, the hash values of these l-mers are indistinguishable from those not belonging to human, such as those of microbes. For copy-number variations, a recent study [22] shows that their identification power is way lower than SNPs, due to their small numbers, much lower density in comparison to SNPs, and continuous distributions [42]. Therefore, it is commonly believed that the threat can be easily mitigated by simple approaches like data aggregation. *So far, no known re-identification techniques use such variations.*

Challenges in outsourcing read mapping. To enable read mapping to happen on the public cloud, we need to either encrypt the data or anonymize it, making it unidentifiable. Unfortunately, only a few cryptographic approaches [17, 18, 20, 33, 35, 55] support secure calculation of edit distances, and all of them are too expensive to sustain a large-scale computation like read mapping (Section 5). Less clear is the efficacy of simple data anonymization techniques such as aggregation, noise adding and data partition. These techniques have long been used to protect genomic data. As a prominent example, Genome-Wide Association Studies (GWAS) typically use DNA microarrays to profile a set of pre-determined SNPs from a group of patients (called *case*) to study the genetic traits of their common disease. The SNPs from different case individuals were often aggregated into a mixture, from which nothing but the counts (or equivalently, the frequencies) of different SNP values (alleles) can be observed and used for statistical analysis. Such aggregate data was deemed safe to release. However, recent studies show that the data is actually vulnerable to a type of re-identification attacks [32, 34, 46, 56]: given the allele frequencies of a *reference* population, which can be acquired from public sources such as the International HapMap Project [9], and a DNA sample from an individual, her presence in the case population can be determined from the aggregate data through a statistical test.

Different from the microarray data studied in the prior work [32,34,46,56], the SNP sets covered by the reads from two persons often differ significantly, due to the randomness in sequencing. In our research, we systematically evaluated the effects of these anonymization techniques on read data using a near-optimal test statistic proposed in the prior research [32]. Our findings show that such data is equally vulnerable to the re-identification attack. For example, to ensure that no more than 10% of a case group can be identified at a confidence of 0.99, we found that the reads from about 38000 individuals, with 10 million reads each, need to be aggregated. The details of this study is presented in Appendix 7.1.

3 Secure Read Mapping

3.1 Overview

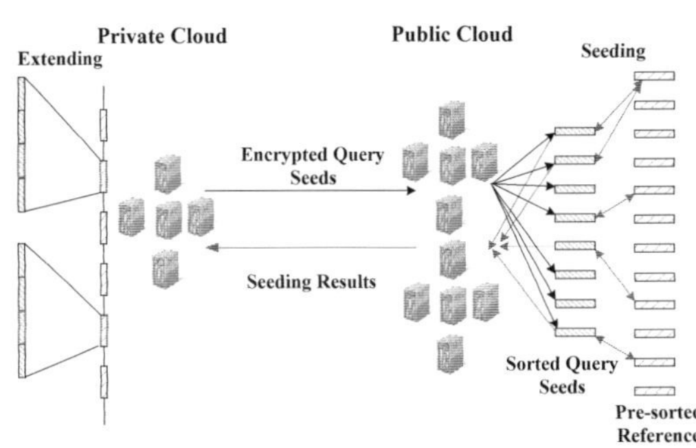

Figure 2. High-level design of our system.

Our design. The high-level design of our techniques is illustrated in Figure 2. Our approach is built upon a hybrid cloud: the public commercial cloud is delegated the computation over the keyed hash values of read data, while the private cloud directly works on the data. Our idea is to let the private cloud undertake a small amount of the workload to reduce the complexity of the secure computation that needs to be performed on the public cloud, while still having the public cloud shoulder the major portion of a mapping task. To this end, we divided the task according to the seed-and-extend strategy [19]. The seeding part roughly locates a read on the reference genome by matching a small segment of it to the substrings on the genome. For example, given an edit distance of 3 and reads of 100 bps, we can partition each read into 4 segments (seeds), each of 25 bps. At least one of these seeds will match a 25-mer on the read's counterpart on the reference genome. Searching for this position is done over the keyed-hash values of the seeds and 25-mers: we first extract all 25-mers from the reference genome, remove repeated sequences and fingerprint the *distinctive* ones with a cryptographic hash function and a secret key; these reference hash values are compared with the hash values of the seeds on the public cloud; all the matches found are reported to the private cloud, which extends the reads from the genetic positions (on the reference genome) indicated by these matches to find an optimal alignment for each read, using a threshold edit-distance algorithm (Section 3.2).

This basic approach works when the seeds are long enough to suppress random matches: for example, most 25-mers are unique across the genome, so a 25-bp seed often locates a read at a small set of positions, which reduces the workload of calculating edit distances between millions of reads and billions of reference 25-mers to the extensions that just need to happen at millions of positions. However, the seeds can be short in practice. For example, given an edit distance of 6, the seed for an 100-bp read has only 14 bps and often matches thousands of positions. To address this problem, we improve the basic approach to perform the seeding over keyed-hash values for 2-combinations of 12-bp seeds, which significantly reduces the workload of the private cloud at a spatial cost easily affordable by modern clouds (Section 3.3).

The privacy assurance of our techniques is evaluated by the amount of information the public cloud can infer from the data it observes. To achieve an ultra-fast mapping, we adopted keyed hash, which allow the public cloud to unilaterally determine whether a match happens. This, however, brings in the concern about a frequency analysis that infers the content of l-mers by counting the matches their hashes receive. To assess this risk, we conducted a whole genome study, which demonstrates that the adversary actually cannot achieve any re-identification power through such an analysis (Section 3.4).

Adversary model. We consider an adversary who aims at re-identifying the individuals related to read data. As discussed before, we focus on this re-identification threat because it is the main privacy concern for releasing protected health information [32, 34, 46, 56], which includes sequencing reads, and therefore the major barrier to moving read mapping to the public cloud. We assume that the private cloud is trustworthy while the nodes on the public cloud can be compromised and controlled by the adversary. Also, we assume that the adversary has a DNA sample of a *testee*, the person she wants to identify from a read dataset, and a reference population genetically similar to those whose reads are inside the dataset. Access to such knowledge is widely considered to be a very strong assumption [30] that gives the adversary advantages. It serves as the standard background information in all studies on re-identification threats to genomic data [32,34,46,56], and the foundation for evaluating whether such data can be safely released [10, 46]. Finally, note that all we care about here is to prevent the adversary from identifying read donors, rather than to ensure the success of the computation, which may not be achieved when the adversary controls the public cloud.

3.2 Computation Split

In this section, we elaborate the basic design of our technique, which is also summarized in Table 1.

Data preprocessing. To perform the seeding on the public cloud, we need to compute the keyed-hash values for both the reference genome and individual seeds. Specifically, given a keyed hash function $H_K()$ with a secret key K, our approach first fingerprints all *distinctive* l-mers α_i on the reference genome: $H_K(\alpha_1), H_K(\alpha_2), \cdots$ and then sends their hash values (in a random order) to the public cloud. We remove all repeats here to mitigate the risk of a frequency analysis. Depending on the length l, l-mers have different levels of repetitions on a human genome: for example, we found that more than 80% of 24-mers are unique on the reference genome. Note that such data processing and transfer only need to be done once to enable the public cloud to map a large number of read datasets using the hashed reference. For each dataset, we compute keyed hashes for the seeds s_j extracted from each read, $H_K(s_1)$, $H_K(s_2), \cdots, H_K(s_{d+1})$, randomly permutate this list and then deliver it to the public cloud for the seeding operation. Our implementation adopts SHA-1 and a 256-bit secret key, and only uses the first 10 bytes of an l-mer's hash as its fingerprint for the comparison. The following 6 bytes are XORed with the information for locating the l-mer on the reference genome (we only use 16 bytes of 20-byte output).

Computing on the public cloud. The seeding task delegated to the public cloud is as simple as comparing all the hashes of the seeds with those of the reference l-mers and reporting the indices of the matched sequence pairs (i, j)

Table 1. Privacy-Preserving Read Mapping: the Basic Approach

- *Generating keyed hashes for reference l-mers (one-time cost).* Given an edit-distance threshold d and a read length λ, set $l = \frac{\lambda}{d+1}$. For each distinctive l-mer α_j on the reference genome, compute $H_K(\alpha_j)$ (j is unrelated to the l-mer's position). Remove all the repeats and send the distinctive hash values to the public cloud.
- *Generating keyed hashes for seeds.* On the private cloud, for each read in a given read dataset, break it into $d+1$ seeds with a length of l each. Compute $H_K(s_i)$ for every seed s_i and send all these hash values to the public cloud.
- *Seeding.* On the public cloud, compare the hashed seeds to the hashed references. For all $H_K(\alpha_j) = H_K(s_i)$, send (i, j) to the private cloud.
- *Extension.* On the private cloud, for every matched pair (i, j), extend the read including s_i from the genetic location pinpointed by α_j on the reference genome to check whether the edit distance (between the read and the substring on that location) is no more than d.

to the private cloud. The only problem here is the scale of this computation, which involves millions upon billions of string comparisons. One way to achieve a fast seeding is to build an index for the reference genome, as typically done by the fast-mapping software designed to work on standalone systems. This approach, however, needs a huge amount of memory and cannot be easily parallelized. Our implementation uses ultra-fast sorting, which the cloud is good at, to do the seeding. Specifically, the public cloud pre-sorts the reference l-mers according to their hash values. For every batch of seed hashes, the cloud first sorts them and then merges them with the sorted l-mer hashes to find matches. This strategy has also been adopted by CloudBurst [47], a famous cloud-based (yet insecure) mapping system. Today's cloud can already support high-performance sorting: for example, Terasort [44] running on Hadoop attained a sorting speed of 0.578 terabytes per minute.

Computing on the private cloud. The private cloud extends the seeds at the locations where matches happen. These locations are recovered from the indices of seed hashes and the l-mer hashes they match, as reported by the public cloud. For this purpose, two look-up tables are needed: one maps the hash of an l-mer to its occurrences on the reference genome, and the other maps that of a seed to its read. The first table is relatively large, at least 10 GB. We reduced the size of the table using the features of human genomes. When l goes above 20, most l-mers are unique across the reference genome. Particularly, only a small portion (below 20%) of 24, 25-mers repeat. For every unique l-mer α_i, our approach keeps its location information directly on the last 6 bytes of $H_K(\alpha_i)$. Specifically, let θ_i be these bytes; we XOR the location of α_i, L_i, onto θ_i: $\pi_i = \theta_i \oplus (I_i || L_i)$, where I_i is a one-byte indicator for the uniqueness of the l-mer. Once this l-mer is matched by a seed (that is, the first 10 bytes of the seed's hash matching the first 10 bytes on the l-mer's hash), L_i is recovered from π_i using θ_i, which comes from the hash of the seed and is kept on the private cloud. For those still in the table, we organize them according to the indices of their hashes to ensure that only sequential access happens when searching the table.

When the read dataset is relatively small (10 million reads or less), its look-up table, which does not go above 1.2 GB, can often be accommodated in the memory. In the table, we also keep the last 6 bytes of seed hashes for decrypting the location information of the l-mers they matched. To handle a large dataset, our design encrypts the read information R_j for a seed s_j using a simple stream cipher such as AES CTR. Specifically, we first compute the key-stream $\sigma_j = E_{K'}(V||j)$, where $E()$ is an encryption algorithm, V is an initial vector and K' is another secret key, and then use the first 10 bytes of the stream to do the encryption: $\tau_j = \sigma_j \oplus (R_j || \theta_j)$, where θ_j is the last 6 bytes of $H_K(s_j)$. This ciphertext is concatenated with the first 10 bytes of the seed's hash, and given to the public cloud. Once a match is found between the hashes of α_i and s_j, it sends (π_i, τ_j, j) to the private cloud for recovering L_i and R_j.

The workload of the private cloud is determined by the number of extensions it needs to perform for each read. As discussed before, when l is no smaller than 20, most l-mers are unique and thus the reads whose seeds match them often need to be extended only a few times. Among the rest of l-mers that reoccur on the genome, some of them are actually part of longer repetitive substrings, and only need to be extended once for all these reoccurrences. This can be achieved by compressing the reference genome according to its 100-mers: we can identify all distinctive 100-mers and extend the reads on them instead of the whole genome. Also important here is an efficient extension algorithm. Our implementation utilizes a threshold dynamic programming algorithm [28] to compute the edit distance no more than a threshold d. This algorithm's complexity is only $O(d\lambda)$, where λ is the length of the read.

Discussion. This application of seed-and-extend works well when the seeds are at least 20 bps. Given standard 100-

Table 2. Privacy-Preserving Read Mapping: Seed Combinations

- *Generating keyed hashes for combined l-mers (one-time cost).* Set $l = \frac{\lambda}{d+2}$, with a distance threshold d and a read length λ. For every λ-mer (substrings of λ long) on the reference genome, compute the keyed hash values for all the 2-combinations of the l-mers it contains: $H_K(\alpha_1||\alpha_2)$, $H_K(\alpha_1||\alpha_3)$, $\cdots$, $H_K(\alpha_{\lambda-l}||\alpha_{\lambda-l+1})$. Remove all the repeats and send the distinctive hash values to the public cloud.
- *Generating keyed hashes for seed combinations.* On the private cloud, break each read into $d+2$ equal-length seeds. Compute the keyed hashes for all 2 combinations of the $d+2$ seeds: $H_K(s_1||s_2)$, $\cdots$, $H_K(s_{d+1}||s_{d+2})$. Send the hashes for all the reads to the public cloud.
- *Seeding.* On the public cloud, compare the hashes of combined seeds to those of combined l-mers. For any two hashes that match, send their indices (i, j) (i for the hash of the combined seed and j for that of the combined l-mer) to the private cloud.
- *Extension.* On the private cloud, for every matched pair (i, j), extend the read associated with the combined seed from the genetic location identified by the combined l-mer to check whether the edit distance is no more than d.

bp reads, this means that the edit distance we are looking at should not go above 4. Our research shows that less than 20% of 24-mers re-occur. To prepare for a mapping task, the private cloud must compute the keyed hashes for reference l-mers, which only needs to be done once, and seed hashes for every dataset. Using a high-end desktop (2.93 GHz Intel Xeon), we found that SHA-1 achieved a throughput of 100 million 25-mers per minute using a single core. In other words, a typical dataset with 10 million reads can be proceeded around a minute. Fingerprinting the whole reference genome took longer time, about 1 hour using 1 core. However, this only needs to be done once. Note that SHA-1 is not known for its speed. We chose it in our implementation just for simplicity. Many other cryptographic hash functions perform much better [7]. Our evaluations (Section 4) show that this approach moved the vast majority of the workload to the public cloud, compared with the situation when the whole computation is done within the private cloud.

3.3 Combined Seeds

Short seeds. When edit distance goes up to 6, the 7 14-bp seeds of a read often align it to hundreds or even thousands of possible positions for extensions. For example, in a microbiome filtering task described in Section 4, our experiment shows that on average 895 extensions need to be made before an alignment within the edit distance of 6 could be found for one read. To reduce the number of matches, our idea is to use multiple seeds: given an edit distance d, we can partition a read into $d+2$ seeds, of which at least 2 will have exact matches on the region the read should be aligned to. For example, a 100-bp read, once partitioned into 8 12-bp seeds, can use 2 seeds (totally 24 bps long) to find out the 100-mers to which its distance may not exceed 6. Given the total length of such combined seeds, most reads can be located at a few genetic positions: in the microbiome filtering task mentioned above, the 2-combination of 12-bp seeds successfully aligns a read within 28 extensions on average. A straightforward implementation of this idea, however, forces the private cloud to intersect a large number of positions randomly matched by the short seeds for each read before the reference substrings including both seeds can be identified. This intersection operation often incurs a significant overhead, which sometimes even exceeds the cost for simply running the whole task locally. As a result, the private cloud often has to shoulder most of the mapping workload.

Mapping 2-combinations. Our answer to this challenge is a novel design built upon the special features of the cloud. Today's clouds are designed for data intensive computations, and can easily store and process terabytes of data at a low cost, as long as the operations on such data are simple and parallelizable. This property allows us to trade the spatial cost on the public cloud for the reduction in the computing workload on the private cloud, converting the intersection operation to the string matching that happens between the keyed-hash values of 2-seed combinations and those of l-mer combinations. Specifically, for every 100-mer on the reference genome, we save to the public cloud *distinctive* hashes for all the 2-combinations of its l-mers α_i: $H_K(\alpha_1||\alpha_2)$, $H_K(\alpha_1||\alpha_3)$, $\cdots$, $H_K(\alpha_2||\alpha_3)$, $\cdots$, $H_K(\alpha_{100-l}||\alpha_{101-l})$. Given a read dataset, the private cloud also fingerprints all the 2-combinations of $d+2$ seeds s_j for each read: $H_K(s_1||s_2)$, $\cdots$, $H_K(s_{d+1}||s_{d+2})$. These combined-seed hashes are compared to those of the l-mer combinations on the public cloud to help locate the reads on the reference genome. This approach is summarized in Table 2.

To perform this seeding operation, the public cloud needs to accommodate the keyed hashes for both reference l-mer combinations and combined seeds. Each 100-mer

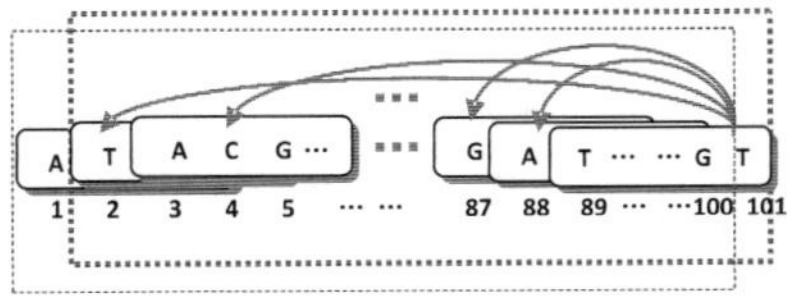

Figure 3. 12-mer Combinations in 100-bp Windows on the Genome

contains $101 - l$ different l-mers and totally $\frac{(101-l)(100-l)}{2}$ combinations. For example, there are 3916 combinations of 12-mers within a 100-bp window. However, the total size of the reference will not grow that much, as the seeds within two overlapping 100-mers are also heavily overlapped: from Figure 3, we can see that whenever the window right shift by one bp, only one new l-mer has been created, which brings in an additional $100 - l$ combinations. Therefore, the total size of the reference actually increases by roughly $100 - l$ times. In the above example, 12-mer combinations are about 88 times of the total size of all reference 12-mers. Using the 16 bytes of the 20-byte output of SHA-1, the keyed hashes for the reference sequences have about 6.8 TB. *Storing, transferring and processing this amount of data are extremely economic for today's commercial clouds.* For example, to keep such data at Amazon Simple Storage Service (S3), the NIH only needs to spend $890 per month [4]. Transferring the data to the EC2 is completely free [4]. In practice, a typical approach is simply to mail a hard drive, a standard service adopted by the S3 when bandwidth is low [5]. Note that this is just a one-time cost, and data storage and transfer at that scale are quite common for today's cloud users. Operations on this reference include sorting and merging with the hashes of combined seeds, which can also be efficiently done through ultra-fast sorting algorithms [44]. On the other hand, the seed combinations cause a much smaller rise in the spatial cost: the number of 2-combinations of $d+2$ seeds is $\frac{(d+1)(d+2)}{2}$, just $\frac{d+1}{2}$ times the number of the seeds. For example, the keyed hash data of 12-bp seed combinations for 10 million 100-bp reads has about 5 GB, roughly 20 times the size of the read dataset.

The private cloud needs to compute the hashes and deliver them to the public cloud for each mapping task. Given merely $\frac{d+1}{2}$ times of the increase in the number of the seeds, the overheads for computing and transferring those hashes can be easily afforded. Since the combined seeds often are sufficiently long ($\geq$ 20 bps), most of them are distinctive across the reference genome: as an example, our research shows that nearly 70% of combined 12-mers (24 bps long) are unique. This helps reduce the number of extensions performed on the private cloud. To further avoid unnecessary extensions, our approach uses a strategy that for each read, we first extend the combined seed with a unique match. This works particularly well for the task like microbiome filtering, which stops to remove a read as soon as it is found similar to a human 100-mer. A major engineering challenge on the private cloud side is the sizes of the look-up tables. The one for finding reads (from the combined seeds) is still okay, and can always be replaced with the encoding technique as described in Section 3.2. The other one, which maps l-mer combinations to their positions on the reference genome, needs to be expanded by nearly 40 folds, and has a size of roughly 400 GB. To work on this table efficiently, we can partition it into a set of sub-tables and distributed them to multiple nodes on the private cloud. As discussed in Section 3.2, the content of the original table is organized according to the index order of the hashes for l-mer combinations on the public cloud, for the purpose of sequential data access from the hard drive. Here, we further ask the public cloud to group the matches it found into several bins with regard to the index ranges of the sub-tables, and then dispatch these bins to different nodes for distributed table look-ups and extensions on the private cloud. Another approach is simply encrypting the genetic locations for the l-mer combinations that repeat less than 10 times on the reference genome, and saving them on the public cloud. Whenever the hash value of one such combination is matched, the ciphertext of its locations is sent back to the private cloud. This strategy trades bandwidth consumption for the saving of data processing time on the private cloud.

Discussion. Using combined seeds, we essentially outsource the computing burden of intersecting the matches produced by short seeds to the public cloud, which further reduces the proportion of the overall workload the private cloud needs to undertake. This has been justified by our experimental study (Section 4). Also, although computing the hash values for all 12-mer combinations takes about 11 hours and a half using 8 cores (2.93 GHz Intel Xeon), the operation only needs to be performed once. The cost for processing each dataset is still very low: for example, 280 million seeds for 10 million reads took 6 minutes to hash.

3.4 Privacy Analysis

Our study. Our approach exposes nothing but keyed hash values of seeds and l-mers to the public cloud, from which the adversary cannot directly recover reads. We further ensure that only the hashes of distinctive l-mers are disclosed, making them hard to distinguish by an observer. Under such protection, what is left to the public cloud is just the counts of the exact matches that individual reference hashes (those of l-mers or combinations) receive from the hashes of seeds or combined seeds. Therefore, the adversary's best chance is leveraging such information and the background knowledge at her disposal, i.e., the genomes of a reference population and a DNA sample from the testee, to determine the presence of the testee's DNA in the read dataset she cannot directly access. We analyze the threat in this section.

As discussed in Section 2.2 and 3.1, we made two assumptions in our study. First, we assume the aforementioned background knowledge for the adversary. This would not be necessary if we wanted to achieve differential privacy [25], a privacy goal that does not rely on any assumption of background knowledge. However, such a privacy guarantee is often too strong to attain in practice, particularly in the case of read mapping where the genetic locations of reads and the distributions of their hashes are not known in advance and expensive to get. Also, the background information we used has been assumed in all prior studies on re-identification risks in human genomic data [32, 34, 46, 56], as it reflects the special features of the data, and serves as the foundation for evaluating when it can be released [10]. Actually, even this assumption has already been complained of as being overpessimistic [30] by the genomics community, because the knowledge it assumed often cannot easily come by in practice. Our objective is to show that even under such an assumption, which is strongly in favor of the adversary, she still cannot acquire identifiable information from the public cloud. Second, our analysis focuses on SNPs, as for the time being, other genetic variations cannot be effectively used for re-identification during read mapping (see Section 2.2).

l-mer based re-identification. The public cloud only observes the frequency with which the keyed hash value of each reference l-mer has been matched. This frequency is actually the l-mer's average rate of occurrence across genome datasets. The only thing the adversary can do is trying to map each hash value to its plaintext l-mer, according to their frequencies (i.e., the average rate of occurrence) calculated from seed-hash datasets and public genome data (e.g., the HapMap population and the reference genome) respectively. In most situations, however, this attempt will not yield unique answers, as many l-mers share same frequencies: for example, roughly 5 billion 24-mers on the reference genome are unique; many of them have same average rates of occurrence (e.g., those carrying single SNPs with identical allele frequencies) in a population. In the end, what the adversary can get is just a mapping between a set of hash values and a set of plaintext l-mers with the same average rate of occurrence, assuming that she learnt the rate from her long-term observations. Within a pair of such sets, the adversary cannot determine which hash indeed belongs to a given l-mer through the frequency analysis, as each of such hash values and l-mers has an identical frequency. Here, we use *bin* to describe this set pair, i.e., a set of l-mers grouped by the frequency they share and their corresponding set of hash values. Note that this is the best the adversary can achieve without considering the relations among the hash values. Such relations are actually very difficult to establish in practice, as elaborated in Appendix 7.3.

Consider the h bins $B_{k\in[1,h]}$ the adversary is able to identify from all the seed-hash datasets she sees. Given a specific seed-hash set (the *case* group) that involves the seeds from multiple individuals, these bins are the only attributes at the adversary's disposal for a re-identification attack. Specifically, what she can do is to find out the aggregated frequency of all the hash values within B_k for the case group. For example, suppose that only two hash values η_1 and η_2 are in B_k and they totally show up 1000 times in the 1-million-seed case group; the frequency of B_k becomes $\bar{f}_k = 0.001$ for the case. Then, the adversary figures out the aggregated frequency of the l-mers in the bin for a *reference* population (e.g., the Hapmap group), $\bar{F}_k$, and that for a DNA sample from the testee, ρ_k. In the example, $\bar{F}_k = 0.0012$ if the two l-mers in B_k, l_1 and l_2, occur totally 1200 times in 1 million l-mers of the reference population[2]. In this case, the best the adversary can do is to run the most powerful statistical test over $\bar{f}_k$, $\bar{F}_k$ and ρ_k for all h bins to determine whether the testee is present in the *case* group: i.e., whether the hash values of the testee's seeds (which the adversary cannot see) are included in the seed-hash dataset. If we treat these bins as a set of attributes like SNPs, this re-identification problem does not fundamentally differ from that studied in prior research [32, 46]. Therefore, the test statistic reported by the prior work also works here:

$$\bar{D} = \sum_{k=1}^{h} \bar{D}_k = \sum_{k}[|\rho_k - \bar{F}_k| - |\rho_k - \bar{f}_k|] \quad (1)$$

$\bar{D}$ is called *Homer-like test*, as it is a direct application of Homer's test [32], which works on the allele frequencies of SNPs, to the re-identification over the frequencies of bins ($\bar{f}_k$, $\bar{F}_k$ and ρ_k). This test is known to be close to optimal [46] in re-identifying the testee from the case group given the aforementioned background knowledge. The truly optimal test is the famous log likelihood ratio test [46], according to the Neyman-Pearson lemma:

$$\bar{T} = \sum_{k=1}^{h} \bar{T}_k = \sum_{k}[log(Pr_k^C(\rho_k)) - log(Pr_k^R(\rho_k))] \quad (2)$$

Let $\bar{\rho}_k^C$ be the aggregated rate of occurrence for a case individual's seeds (l-mers) in B_k over all her seeds. In Equation 2, $Pr_k^C(\rho_k)$ represents the cumulative probability for seeing case members whose $\bar{\rho}_k^C$ are even less likely to observe than ρ_k (the frequency of the testee's B_k) according to the distribution of $\bar{\rho}_k^C$ in the case group, which we

[2]It is meaningless to check the frequencies of η_1, η_2, l_1 and l_2 for the case/reference/DNA sample, as the hashes cannot be linked to the l-mers.

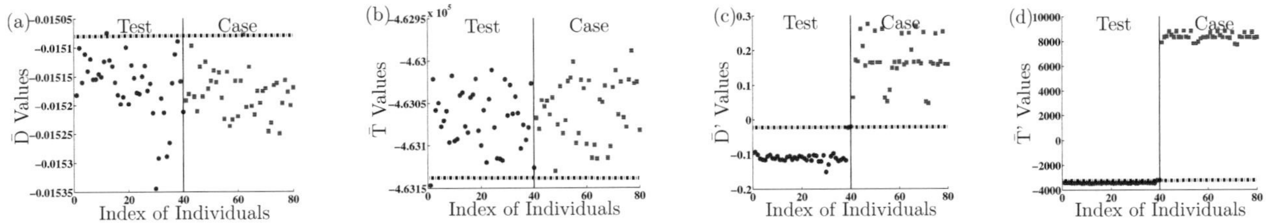

Figure 4. Power Analysis and Comparison. On bin aggregated l-mer frequencies: (a) the Homer-like statistic test $\bar{D}$ (Equation 1) (b) the likelihood ratio test $\bar{T}$ (Equation 2). On SNP allele frequencies: (c) Homer's test [32] $\bar{D}' = \sum_{k=1}^{h} \bar{D}'_k = \sum_k [|\rho'_k - \bar{F}'_k| - |\rho'_k - \bar{f}'_k|]$, where ρ'_k is the testee's allele for SNP k, and $\bar{F}'_k$ and $\bar{f}'_k$ are the major allele frequencies for the SNP on the reference and the case populations respectively. (d) the likelihood ratio test [46] $\bar{T}' = \sum_{k=1}^{h} \bar{T}'_k = \sum_k [log(\bar{P}_k^C(\rho'_k)) - log(\bar{P}_k^R(\rho'_k))]$, where $\bar{P}_k^R = \bar{F}'_k$ if ρ'_k is major allele and $\bar{P}_k^R = 1 - \bar{F}'_k$ otherwise, and $\bar{P}_k^C = \bar{f}'_k$ if ρ'_k is a major allele and $\bar{P}_k^C = 1 - \bar{f}'_k$ otherwise. All the statistics were computed for each of 40 case individuals (blue dots) and 40 test individuals (red squares). The distributions of $\bar{D}$ and $\bar{T}$ in these two groups are indistinguishable in (a) and (b), while those of $\bar{D}'$ and $\bar{T}'$ are completely separated in (c) and (d). The dash lines represent the 1% false positive rate level. The individuals identified at this rate are *above* the lines for all statistics except for $\bar{T}$, where the identified are *below* the line.

pessimistically assume that the adversary knows. Similarly, $Pr_k^R(\rho_k)$ is the cumulative probability for the reference individuals with regards to ρ_k. Note that to avoid computing complicated joint distributions, Equation 2 treats bins as being independent from each other. In practice, the correlations among the vast majority of bins are indeed weak, given the fact that each of them typically covers many SNPs and only in rare cases, a small portion of the SNPs in one bin also appear on the l-mers in other bins. Even when strongly correlated bins are found, the adversary still cannot build a stronger log likelihood ratio test (the most powerful test) over them, simply because identifying related hash values is very difficult (Appendix 7.3), not to mention determining the joint distributions over these values in different case bins, a prerequisite for the test.

Power analysis. Given the background knowledge, the two test statistics are the *most powerful* identification tools available to the adversary. Here we report a study that evaluated the identification powers of these statistics over real DNA data from the largest population available in the public domain. In this study, we compressed the whole reference genome into 372,869,332 distinctive 24-mers that involve SNPs. The selected 24-mers were further classified into 7,260,607 bins according to their frequencies. For simplicity, this was done in a way that gives advantage to the adversary. Specifically, the 24-mers involving a single SNP were grouped into bins according to their frequencies, which depended not only on their rates of occurrence across the reference genome but also on the allele frequencies (3 digits of precision) of their SNPs. For those associated with more than one SNP, we just created a unique bin for each of them, assuming that they were identified by the adversary.

The reference individuals in our study were acquired from the reference human genome. To produce realistic human genome sequences for multiple individuals, we randomly set the alleles for the SNP sites on the reference genome according to their allele frequencies reported by the HapMap. $\bar{F}_k$ in the Homer-like test (Equation 1) and the distribution in the likelihood ratio test (Equation 2) were estimated from 100 such sequences, which constituted the reference group. We used the YRI population (80 individuals) on the HapMap [9], the largest population whose DNA data is available in the public domain, to construct a case group and a *test group* (a population including neither case nor reference individuals). Each of these two groups had about 40 individuals. We sampled 10 million reads from each individual in the case group to compute $\bar{f}_k$ and the distribution of B_k frequencies. Then, we repeatedly ran $\bar{D}$ (Equation 1) and $\bar{T}$ (Equation 2) for 40 times over randomly selected case/test groups with individual group members as testees, and found that each time the case and the test individuals were completely indistinguishable. An example is presented in Figure 4 (a) and (b), which illustrates the power of $\bar{D}$ and $\bar{T}$ in one experiment. For $\bar{D}$, at 1% false positive level (denoted by the dash line), one in the case and one in the test group (i.e., a false positive) were identified (above that line), indicating equal true positive and false positive rates, so no statistical power was achieved. For $\bar{T}$, only a test individual was identified (below the line), which is a false positive.

We further compared this outcome with the identification powers the adversary can get in the absence of the new protection we propose here, i.e., when the DNA data of the case individuals was just aggregated, the standard protection the

NIH took. Over the aggregated data, the adversary observes the allele frequencies of different SNPs and can therefore run both tests over these frequencies [32,46] using the same background knowledge (the reference and the DNA sample from the testee). In our experiment, we ran these tests on the SNPs of the same populations. The results, as presented in Figure 4 (c) and (d), show that both tests easily separated the case and test populations. In contrast, these tests were completely ineffective upon the keyed hashes our approach exposes to the public cloud (Figure 4 (a) and (b)). This strongly indicates that our techniques offer effective protection against the most powerful known re-identification attacks. In Appendix 7.2, we show that $\bar{D}$ and $\bar{T}$ also cannot achieve a higher power on the combined seeds.

4 Performance Evaluation

4.1 Experiment Setting

Our evaluation was performed over a microbial filtering task [8]. The sequences extracted from human microbes include the DNA information of their hosts, which, if not taken out, will not only contaminate the outcome of a microbiome analysis but also disclose the identities of the donors the microbes come from. Therefore, one of the most important read-mapping tasks is to compare the reads from microbiome datasets to the reference genome, to identify and remove those belonging to humans. For the time being, this task is still undertaken by the NIH internal servers, but there are strong demands to move the computation to the low-cost public cloud given the privacy of the donors is protected [52].

Data. We utilized a real microbiome dataset collected from a fecal sample of a human individual [45]. The dataset contains 10 million reads, totally 250 MB, a data scale typical in today's microbe projects. In our research, we added to the dataset 500,000 human reads collected from the reference genome, a typical level of human contamination (5%) in microbiome data, as the original dataset was already sanitized, being removed of human sequences. These human reads were randomly sampled from Chromosome 1 (*Chr1*), the largest chromosome with 252.4 million bps, Chromosome 22 (*Chr22*), the smallest one with 52.3 million bps, and the whole genome with 6 billion bps respectively. They were further randomly adjusted to simulate the sequencing error and mixed with the microbiome dataset to build three test datasets (with human reads from Chr1, Chr22 and the whole genome respectively). Over these datasets, we ran our prototype under three scenarios, mapping these 10 million reads to Chr1, Chr22 or the whole genome.

Clouds. These datasets were mapped on *FutureGrid* [43], an NSF-sponsored large-scale, cross-the-country cloud testbed. The public cloud we used includes 30 nodes with 8-core 2.93 GHz Intel Xeon, 24 GB memory, 862 GB local disk and Linux 2.6.18. Our private cloud is a single node with the same software/hardware settings. We also evaluated the bandwidth use of our prototype on the 40 MBps link between the private cloud and the public cloud.

4.2 Results

In the experiments, we ran our prototype to filter the reads on the hybrid cloud, using edit distances of 3 and 6. The overheads incurred during each step of the computation was measured and compared with those of *CloudBurst*[3] [47], the most famous cloud-based mapping system, which is also a standard service of Amazon MapReduce [6]. The results are presented in Table 3 and 4.

Data preparation (one-time cost). When the distance was 3, we extracted from our "reference genome" (Chr1, Chr22 or the whole genome) distinctive 24-mers for each of the experiment scenarios, and generated keyed hash values for these references using SHA-1 with a 32-byte secret key on the private cloud. It took 29 seconds to work on Chr22, 213 seconds on Chr1 and a little more than one hour on the whole genome using a single core. For the distance of 6, we first identified 12-mers, which were further combined within 100-bp windows, as described in Section 3.3. The combined 12-mers (24 bps long in total) were then fingerprinted. This time, all 8 cores were put in use to generate the hash values. The overall time to have this job done was estimated to be 11 hours when it came to the whole genome. All these reference hashes were delivered to the public cloud, which further sorted them for preparing the mapping jobs. This sorting time varied over the scales of the computation. When processing the whole genome with a distance of 6, the public cloud took about 29 hours to complete the job on the 6.8 TB reference hash values. Note that this data preprocessing only incurs a *one-time cost*[4]. Such overheads are completely affordable. For example, Amazon routinely receives terabytes or even a larger amount of data through its Import/Outport service [5].

Seeding performance (every dataset). Preparing the hash values for the 10 million reads turned out to be highly efficient. Even for the edit distance of 6, the keyed hash values for the combined seeds, about 5 GB, were computed from those reads within 7 minutes using a single core. Seeding on such data was also fast. When the distance was 3, the time our prototype took to process all the seeds over the

[3]CloudBurst extends a seed at every genetic location it matches, rather than drops its read as soon as the read is successfully aligned to a reference substring (within the distance threshold). For the fairness of comparison, our prototype also did all extensions. Note that this is not necessary for the filtering and our approach can achieve a much faster speed when doing the filtering alone.

[4]The reference hashes can be replaced after they are used to process a large amount of data, e.g., 10,000 read datasets (Appendix 7.3).

Table 3. Performance of Preprocessing and Seeding

Reference (# of errors)	Reference data perparation (One-time cost)			Seeding (Every dataset) (h:min:sec) (8 cores/node)
	Hash Reference (h:min:sec)	Sort hashed l-mers (h:min:sec) (8 cores/node)	Reference Generated (GB)	
Chr1 (3)	0:3:33 (1 core)	0:6:54 (5 nodes)	5.7	0:5:29 (5 nodes)
Chr22 (3)	0:0:29 (1 core)	0:2:12 (5 nodes)	0.9	0:5:22 (5 nodes)
Whole Genome (3)	1:1:13 (1 core)	0:23:53 (20 nodes)	79.6	0:6:12 (20 nodes)
Chr1 (6)	0:51:48 (8 cores)	2:39:2 (20 nodes)	558.9	0:13:1 (20 nodes)
Chr22 (6)	0:10:11 (8 cores)	0:17:31 (20 nodes)	88.11	0:5:39 (20 nodes)
Whole Genome (6)	11:20:7 (8 cores)	29:4:43 (30 nodes)	6997.8	1:32:53 (30 nodes)

Table 4. Outsourced Computation

Reference (# of errors)	Workload of Our Private Cloud					Full Workload of CloudBurst			Outsource ratio (%) (*Estimate)
	Hash seeds (h:m:s) (**1 core**)	Extension (**1 core**)		Bandwidth		Workload (h:m:s) (**8 cores/node**)	Bandwidth		
		Time (h:m:s)	Mem (GB)	Up (GB)	Down (MB)		Up (GB)	Down (MB)	
Chr1 (3)	0:1:3	0:1:16	1.85	0.72	11.18	0:31:10 (1node)	0.81	11.32	99.1
Chr22 (3)	0:1:4	0:0:38	1.47	0.72	11.11	0:3:52 (1node)	0.81	11.52	94.5
Whole Genome (3)	0:1:8	0:10:41	6.92	0.72	17.83	0:14:1 (20nodes)	0.81	15.16	99.5 *
Chr1 (6)	0:6:33	0:12:22	3.71	5.07	74.93	0:59:23 (1node)	0.81	998.06	96.1
Chr22 (6)	0:5:26	0:4:9	3.13	5.07	74.96	0:13:29 (1node)	0.81	402.46	91.1
Whole Genome (6)	0:6:1	2:37:27	8.97	5.07	120.71	0:26:43 (30nodes)	0.81	1456.14	97.5 *

whole genome was merely a little more than 6 minutes, using 20 nodes. When the distance became 6, our approach understandably ran slower (one hour and a half), given the protection it offers and the seed-combination strategy that moves the cost from the extension to the seeding. In the experiment, we set Java virtual machine's maximum memory heap size to 1.6GB both for the cloud instances running CloudBurst and those working on the seeding tasks in our approach. We found that our approach consumed much less memory than CloudBurst, which kept additional information for extensions.

Extension performance (every dataset). The extension tasks, based upon matched seeds or combinations, were so small that they were all comfortably handled by the single core: even in the case of the whole genome and the distance of 6, our desktop used about two hours and a half to complete the extension. To understand the amount of the workload our approach outsourced to the public cloud, we tried to run CloudBurst on the desktop (using 8 cores). This attempt succeeded when the references were Chr1 and Chr22: in all these cases, at least 91% of the computation were outsourced, even considering the time for preparing the hash values of the seeds. However, running CloudBurst on the whole genome within a single machine turned out to be impossible, which forced us to look at its performance on the public cloud. Specifically, for the distance of 6, CloudBurst spent about 26 minutes on 30 8-core nodes to map all the 10 million reads, whereas our cost on the private cloud were merely 163 minutes using 1 node 1 core, including the time for hashing the seeds. Therefore, we estimated that over 97% workload was offloaded to the public cloud.

Communication overheads (every dataset). We found that the communication overheads of our approach was rather small. The maximum amount of data needed to be uploaded to the public cloud was 5.07 GB (including the hashes of the combined seeds for the 10 million reads), which took only a couple of minutes to transfer on our 40 MBps link. The data downloaded from the public cloud was much smaller, merely 120.71 MB. We can compare this level of overheads with those incurred by having the whole map job done by CloudBurst on the public cloud without any privacy protection: about 0.81 GB data was uploaded in this case and 1.42 GB data needed to be downloaded. Note that our approach only needs to download a relatively small amount of data for matched seed combinations[5] rather than the outcome of the whole computation.

Discussion. The overall computation time (the time spent on the public cloud and the private cloud combined) of our prototype was about 372 CPU hours for the mapping task

[5]Only 5% of the reads belong to human hosts.

on the whole genome with an edit distance of 6, which is about 3.5 times as much as that for performing the whole computation by CloudBurst, without privacy protection at all. Note that all existing privacy-preserving techniques [17, 18, 20, 33, 35] are not even remotely close to achieving this level of performance on the read-mapping problem. On the EC2, this computation only costs $26 (estimated based on the price for reserved Cluster Compute EC2 instance [1], whose computing power is comparable to the cloud nodes we used) . At this expense, one does not need to purchase and maintain a 240-core cluster: a single desktop is sufficient to do the whole work.

5 Related Work

Secure outsourcing of genomic computations. Most of the proposed techniques for secure outsourcing of genomic computations focus on new cryptographic primitives [17,21,35]. For example, a protocol for computing edit distances [17] shares a matrix for dynamic programming to multiple servers, which need to collaborate with each other through homomorphic encryptions and oblivious transfers to calculate each matrix element. This approach was found to need 5 and a half minutes to compute an instance of the size (25, 25) [35]. Another example is the work on optimized SMC for DNA sequence alignment [35], which is designed to leverage the special features of dynamic programming to improve the performance of SMC. Compared with [17], the approach is much more efficient, taking about 14 seconds to complete the above task. Further improvement on SMC [33] can align 2 100-element sequences in 4 seconds. Still, this overhead makes it hard to scale up to the bar of comparing millions of reads with millions to billions of l-mers. Recent developments on this line of research include oblivious automata evaluation [20], which only needs $O(n)$ modular exponentiations to work on the sequences with n elements. This performance, however, still cannot sustain the scale of read mapping. Another recent proposal [14] attempts to "disguise" DNA sequences by scrambling some of its nucleotides to produce multiple versions of the sequence and let multiple servers compute on them. The outcomes of these computations are then analyzed by the client to restore the edit distance between the sequence and an l-mer. The problem with this approach is that the server needs to communicate with the client for every alignment attempt, making its scalability questionable. Fundamentally, those approaches all fail to take advantage of the special features of human genomes, which were utilized in our research to build a simple and practical solution.

Secret-sharing based approaches may bring in new policy challenges: once the data has been shared to multiple parties, the NIH completely loses the control of it, since these parties can work together to restore the data; it is still unclear whether the NIH needs to sign an agreement with each of them, which these parties may want to avoid for liability concerns [3], and if so, what the agreement will look like. This concern is also applied to the approaches such as distributed Smith-Waterman algorithm [53] that decomposes a computation problem into small sub-problems and allocates them to multiple problem solvers, under the assumption that these parties will not collude. Another related approach [57] lets the provider of genomic data replace SNP values with symbols, which allows an untrusted party to perform a program specialization on the sanitized data. The approach assumes that the data provider knows the locations of SNPs in its data, whereas reads do not carry such information before they are mapped onto the reference genome. Also remotely related to our work is the study on the information leaks caused by aligning a query sequence to those in a genomic database [27]. In our research, a similar problem occurs when the public cloud analyzes the frequencies of the hash values of l-mers. This threat, however, was found to be very limited (Section 3.4).

Other secure outsourcing techniques. Early research on secure outsourcing is mainly on delegating cryptographic operations (e.g., modular exponentiations) to a set of untrusted helpers [31,41]. More recent studies, in addition to secure computing of edit distance, also include the computations such as linear algebra operations [16] and machine-learning tasks [24]. For example, Peer-for-Privacy decomposes a category of data mining algorithms into vector addition steps and distributes them to multiple nodes on a cloud, which can be securely evaluated through a special secret sharing scheme [24]. All these approaches, however, may not be suitable for computing edit distances and also incur a large amount of communication during the computation.

6 Conclusion

In this paper, we propose a suite of new techniques that achieve secure and scalable read mapping on hybrid clouds. Our approach leverages the special features of the read mapping task, which only cares about small edit distances, and of the Cloud, which is good at handling a large amount of simple computation. These features enable us to split the mapping computation according to the seed-and-extend strategy: the seeding stage performs simple computation (exact matching) on a large amount of ciphertext, which is undertaken by the public cloud, and the extension stage involves a very small amount of relatively complicated computation (edit-distance calculation) at the genetic locations found by the matches, which is shouldered by the private cloud. We carefully designed these techniques to move the workload from the private cloud to the public cloud, and thoroughly evaluated their privacy protection and performance. The study shows that the approach, though simple, offers a high privacy assurance and can easily handle the computation of a practical scale.

Acknowledgements

This work is supported in part by the National Science Foundation under Grant CNS-0716292 and CNS-1017782. Also, the FutureGrid testbed used to evaluate our approach is supported in part by the NSF Grant No. 0910812.

References

[1] Amazon EC2 Pricing. http://aws.amazon.com/ec2/pricing/.

[2] Amazon Elastic MapReduce Pricing. http://aws.amazon.com/elasticmapreduce/#pricing.

[3] Amazon Web Services Customer Agreement. http://aws.amazon.com/agreement/.

[4] Amazon Web Services Simple Monthly Calculator. http://calculator.s3.amazonaws.com/calc5.html.

[5] AWS Import/Export. http://aws.amazon.com/importexport/.

[6] CloudBurst on Amazon Web Services. http://aws.amazon.com/articles/2272?_encoding=UTF8&jiveRedirect=1.

[7] Crypto++ 5.6.0 Benchmarks. http://www.cryptopp.com/benchmarks.html.

[8] Human Microbiome Project. http://nihroadmap.nih.gov/hmp/.

[9] International HapMap Project. http://www.hapmap.org/.

[10] SecureGenome. http://securegenome.icsi.berkeley.edu/securegenome/.

[11] The Health Insurance Portability and Accountability Act. http://www.hhs.gov/ocr/privacy/, 1996.

[12] Policy for sharing of data obtained in nih supported or conducted genome-wide association studies (gwas). http://grants.nih.gov/grants/guide/notice-files/NOT-OD-07-088.html#principles, 2007.

[13] Copy Number Variation. http://www.nature.com/scitable/topicpage/copy-number-variation-445, 2008.

[14] R. Akimana, O. Markowitch, Y. Roggeman, and U. L. De. Secure outsourcing of dna sequences comparisons in a grid environment. 2008.

[15] S. F. Altschul, W. Gish, W. Miller, E. W. Myers, and D. J. Lipman. Basic local alignment search tool. *Journal of molecular biology*, 215(3):403–410, October 1990.

[16] M. J. Atallah and K. B. Frikken. Securely outsourcing linear algebra computations. In *Proceedings of the 5th ACM Symposium on Information, Computer and Communications Security*, ASIACCS '10, pages 48–59, New York, NY, USA, 2010. ACM.

[17] M. J. Atallah, F. Kerschbaum, and W. Du. Secure and private sequence comparisons. In *Proceedings of the 2003 ACM workshop on Privacy in the electronic society*, WPES '03, pages 39–44, New York, NY, USA, 2003. ACM.

[18] M. J. Atallah and J. Li. Secure outsourcing of sequence comparisons. *Int. J. Inf. Secur.*, 4:277–287, October 2005.

[19] R. A. Baeza-Yates and C. H. Perleberg. Fast and practical approximate string matching. In *Proceedings of the Third Annual Symposium on Combinatorial Pattern Matching*, CPM '92, pages 185–192, London, UK, 1992. Springer-Verlag.

[20] M. Blanton and M. Aliasgari. Secure outsourcing of dna searching via finite automata. In S. Foresti and S. Jajodia, editors, *DBSec*, volume 6166 of *Lecture Notes in Computer Science*, pages 49–64. Springer, 2010.

[21] F. Bruekers, S. Katzenbeisser, K. Kursawe, and P. Tuyls. Privacy-preserving matching of dna profiles. Technical Report Report 2008/203, ACR Cryptology ePrint Archive, 2008.

[22] D. F. Conrad, D. Pinto, R. Redon, L. Feuk, O. Gokcumen, Y. Zhang, J. Aerts, T. D. Andrews, C. Barnes, P. Campbell, T. Fitzgerald, M. Hu, C. H. Ihm, K. Kristiansson, D. G. MacArthur, J. R. MacDonald, I. Onyiah, A. W. Pang, S. Robson, K. Stirrups, A. Valsesia, K. Walter, J. Wei, C. Tyler-Smith, N. P. Carter, C. Lee, S. W. Scherer, and M. E. Hurles. Origins and functional impact of copy number variation in the human genome. *Nature*, 464(7289):704–712, Oct. 2009.

[23] J. Dean and S. Ghemawat. Mapreduce: simplified data processing on large clusters. *Commun. ACM*, 51:107–113, January 2008.

[24] Y. Duan, N. Youdao, J. Canny, and J. Zhan. P4p: Practical large-scale privacy-preserving distributed computation robust against malicious users abstract. In *Proceedings of the 19th USENIX Security Symposium*, Washington, DC, August 2010.

[25] C. Dwork. Differential privacy. In *in ICALP*, pages 1–12. Springer, 2006.

[26] B. Furht. Cloud computing fundamentals. In B. Furht and A. Escalante, editors, *Handbook of Cloud Computing*, pages 3–19. Springer US, 2010.

[27] M. T. Goodrich. The mastermind attack on genomic data. *Security and Privacy, IEEE Symposium on*, 0:204–218, 2009.

[28] D. Gusfield. *Algorithms on strings, trees, and sequences : computer science and computational biology*. Cambridge Univ. Press, January 2007.

[29] F. Hach, F. Hormozdiari, C. Alkan, F. Hormozdiari, I. Birol, E. E. Eichler, and S. C. Sahinalp. mrsFAST: a cache-oblivious algorithm for short-read mapping. *Nature Methods*, 7(8):576–577, Aug. 2010.

[30] Heeney C, Hawkins N, de Vries J, Boddington, and P, Kaye J. Assessing the Privacy Risks of Data Sharing in Genomics. . *Public Health Genomics*, 2010.

[31] S. Hohenberger and A. Lysyanskaya. How to securely outsource cryptographic computations. In J. Kilian, editor, *Theory of Cryptography*, volume 3378 of *Lecture Notes in Computer Science*, pages 264–282. Springer Berlin / Heidelberg, 2005.

[32] N. Homer, S. Szelinger, M. Redman, D. Duggan, W. Tembe, J. Muehling, J. V. Pearson, D. A. Stephan, S. F. Nelson, and D. W. Craig. Resolving individuals contributing trace amounts of dna to highly complex mixtures using high-density snp genotyping microarrays. *PLoS Genet*, 4(8):e1000167+, 2008.

[33] Y. Huang, D. Evans, J. Katz, and L. Malka. Faster secure two-party computation using garbled circuits. In *Proceedings of the 20th USENIX Security Symposium*, San Francisco, CA, August 2011.

[34] K. B. Jacobs, M. Yeager, S. Wacholder, D. Craig, P. Kraft, D. J. Hunter, J. Paschal, T. A. Manolio, M. Tucker, R. N. Hoover, G. D. Thomas, S. J. Chanock, and N. Chatterjee. A new statistic and its power to infer membership in a genome-wide association study using genotype frequencies. *Nature Genetics*, 41(11):1253 – 1257, 2009.

[35] S. Jha, L. Kruger, and V. Shmatikov. Towards practical privacy for genomic computation. *Security and Privacy, IEEE Symposium on*, 0:216–230, 2008.

[36] W. J. Kent. BLAT: The BLAST-Like Alignment Tool. *Genome Research*, 12(4):656–664, April 2002.

[37] B. Langmead, C. Trapnell, M. Pop, and S. Salzberg. Ultrafast and memory-efficient alignment of short dna sequences to the human genome. *Genome Biology*, 10(3):R25, 2009.

[38] H. Li and N. Homer. A survey of sequence alignment algorithms for next-generation sequencing. *Briefings in Bioinformatics*, 11(5):473–483, September 2010.

[39] J. E. Lunshof, R. Chadwick, D. B. Vorhaus, and G. M. Church. From genetic privacy to open consent. *Nature reviews. Genetics*, 9(5):406–411, May 2008.

[40] E. R. Mardis. The impact of next-generation sequencing technology on genetics. *Trends in Genetics*, 24(3):133 – 141, 2008.

[41] T. Matsumoto, K. Kato, and H. Imai. Speeding up secret computations with insecure auxiliary devices. In *Proceedings of the 8th Annual International Cryptology Conference on Advances in Cryptology*, pages 497–506, London, UK, 1990. Springer-Verlag.

[42] S. A. McCarroll and D. M. Altshuler. Copy-number variation and association studies of human disease. *Nature genetics*, 39(7 Suppl), July 2007.

[43] NSF. Award abstract #091081 - futuregrid: An experimental, high-performance grid test-bed, 2009.

[44] O. OMalley and A. C. Murthy. Winning a 60 second dash with a yellow elephant. Technical report, Yahoo! Inc., 2009.

[45] J. e. a. Qin. A human gut microbial gene catalogue established by metagenomic sequencing. *Nature*, 464(7285):59–65, March 2010.

[46] S. Sankararaman, G. Obozinski, M. I. Jordan, and E. Halperin. Genomic privacy and limits of individual detection in a pool. *Nat Genet*, 41(9):965–7, 2009.

[47] M. C. Schatz. CloudBurst: highly sensitive read mapping with MapReduce. *Bioinformatics*, 25(11):1363–1369, 2009.

[48] N. J. Schork, S. S. Murray, K. A. Frazer, and E. J. Topol. Common vs. rare allele hypotheses for complex diseases. *Current opinion in genetics & development*, 19(3):212–219, June 2009.

[49] S. C. Schuster. Next-generation sequencing transforms today's biology. *Nature Methods*, 5(1):16–18, December 2007.

[50] A. Smith, Z. Xuan, and M. Zhang. Using quality scores and longer reads improves accuracy of solexa read mapping. *BMC Bioinformatics*, 9(1):128, 2008.

[51] A. D. Smith, W.-Y. Chung, E. Hodges, J. Kendall, G. Hannon, J. Hicks, Z. Xuan, and M. Q. Zhang. Updates to the RMAP short-read mapping software. *Bioinformatics*, 25(21):2841–2842, 2009.

[52] L. Stein. The case for cloud computing in genome informatics. *Genome Biology*, 11(5):207+, May 2010.

[53] D. Szajda, M. Pohl, J. Owen, and B. G. Lawson. Toward a practical data privacy scheme for a distributed implementation of the smith-waterman genome sequence comparison algorithm. In *NDSS*. The Internet Society, 2006.

[54] C. Trapnell and S. L. Salzberg. How to map billions of short reads onto genomes. *Nature biotechnology*, 27(5):455–457, May 2009.

[55] J. R. Troncoso-Pastoriza, S. Katzenbeisser, and M. Celik. Privacy preserving error resilient dna searching through oblivious automata. In *Proceedings of the 14th ACM conference on Computer and communications security*, CCS '07, pages 519–528, New York, NY, USA, 2007. ACM.

[56] R. Wang, Y. F. Li, X. Wang, H. Tang, and X. Zhou. Learning your identity and disease from research papers: Information leaks in genome wide association study. In *CCS '09: Proceedings of the 15th ACM conference on Computer and communications security*, pages 534–544, New York, NY, USA, 2009. ACM.

[57] R. Wang, X. Wang, Z. Li, H. Tang, M. K. Reiter, and Z. Dong. Privacy-preserving genomic computation through program specialization. In *CCS '09: Proceedings of the 16th ACM conference on Computer and communications security*, pages 338–347, New York, NY, USA, 2009. ACM.

7 Appendix

7.1 Read Anonymization and Re-Identification

Anonymizing read data. Different from the microarray data that targets a specific set of SNPs, sequencing reads are randomly drawn from a human genome, which consists of 6 billion nucleotides. In a dataset with 1 million sequences of 100-bp long, about 40% of these reads carry SNPs, typically, one on each of them. These SNPs, roughly 0.03 of the total 14 million SNPs, can be viewed as randomly picked out from the whole SNP set. This ratio can become even lower when it comes to human microbiome sequencing data [8], which has about 1-8% of the reads contaminated from the respective human host. Given that each random sample (all SNPs on the reads from one individual) is small relative to the total number of SNPs, the overlapping between two different persons' sequence datasets, in terms of the SNPs they share, is often not significant. Therefore, the question becomes that once we aggregate multiple persons' read datasets, each carrying a different set of SNPs, whether the resulting mixture can still be used

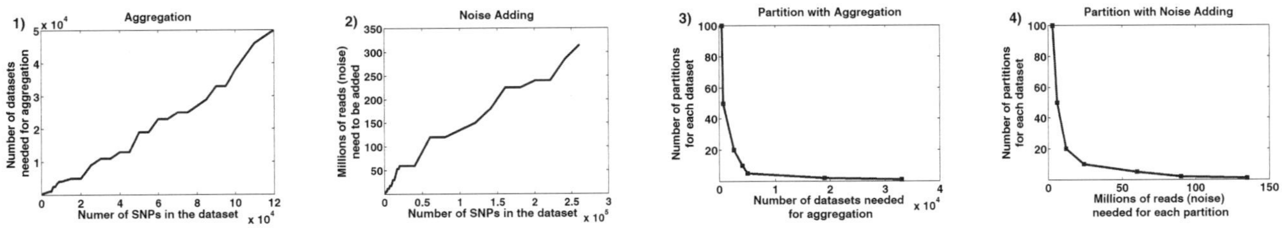

Figure 5. Effectiveness of simple mitigation techniques: 1)aggregation, 2)noise adding, 3)data partition after aggregation, and 4)data partition after noise adding.

to re-identify these individuals. We can make this identification attempt even more difficult to succeed by randomly adding to the mixture *noise* reads, which are randomly sampled from the reference genome with its SNP sites randomly set to major/minor alleles according to the known allele frequencies in human population (e.g. taken from the HapMap project [9]), and/or by partitioning an individual's dataset into multiple subsets to let the public cloud process them separately.

The re-identification threat. Our research shows that these techniques are still insufficient for protecting the read data from the adversary with access to a reference population and a DNA sample from the victim. Specifically, consider a dataset whose reads are sampled from a population (referred to as the case group). We first estimate the allele frequencies in the case group by aligning these reads to the reference genome: if a SNP site k has been covered by m reads, and i of them have the major allele and the rest carry the minor allele, the major allele frequency is calculated as $f_k = \frac{i}{m}$. Note that this frequency often deviates from the SNP's real major-allele frequency in the population, simply because not everyone's SNP k has been sampled. Actually, it might well be that many SNP sites are not covered by any read and therefore have frequencies of zero. The case group here describes a group of human subjects whose reads are aggregated into the sequence dataset, as well as a mixture of real and fake humans, when artificial reads are added to the dataset as noise. In either case, our objective is to determine whether or not an individual (the testee) is present in the case group from the allele frequencies we observe. To this end, we also need a *reference group*, for example, the HapMap population [9] whose allele frequency for each SNP k, F_k, is public knowledge, and a sequence of allele pairs[6] from the testee, one pair for each of the SNP site k whose major-allele frequency Y_k can be 0 (two minor alleles), 0.5 (one major and one minor) or 1 (two major). Based upon such information, we analyzed anonymized read data using a statistic proposed by Homer, et al. [32]:

$$D_k = |Y_k - F_k| - |Y_k - f_k| \qquad (3)$$

Assuming that the distributions of SNPs' allele frequencies in the case and reference populations are identical, the sum of D_k across all independent SNP k will have a normal distribution, whose mean becomes zero when the testee is not in the case/reference groups, and significantly larger than zero when she is a case. By testing this statistic on the null hypothesis: "the testee is not within the case group", we assessed the level of privacy protection that different anonymization techniques are able to offer. Note that although this statistic is well-known to be effective on the aggregated microarray data [12, 32], the vulnerability of the anonymized sequence data to such a re-identification attack has not been investigated before.

The setting of our study. To evaluate the re-identification risk in outsourcing anonymized read data, we performed a series of hypothesis tests on such data under four scenarios: 1) aggregation only, 2) noise-adding only, 3) aggregation and then data partition and 4) noise-adding and then data partition. All the genomic sequences used in our study were randomly sampled from the reference genome: when a sampled read covered a SNP site, its allele was randomly picked according to the major allele frequency of the site in the YRI population, as provided by the HapMap [9]. In this way, we acquired the realistic sequencing reads from a large group of simulated people. Our research utilized published 3,138,397 SNP sites of the YRI population in the HapMap dataset. We consider an anonymized dataset with 100-bp reads to be not secure if a sequence donor for the dataset has a probability of at least 0.1 to be identified with a confidence level no less than 0.99 (i.e. a false positive rate no more than 0.01). Our analysis aims at determining the necessary condition, e.g, the minimum number of the *personal datasets* (the dataset of an individual's reads) needed to be aggregated or the noise reads needed to be added, to protect the person from being re-identified through her N SNPs in the dataset.

Our findings. The outcomes of our evaluation study are presented in Figure 5. In the leftmost panel of the figure,

[6] A human inherits genes from both of his/her parents and therefore has two alleles at each SNP site. For a case individual, his/her two alleles appear on two different reads.

we show the cost for the aggregation strategy. The simple test statistic in Equation 3 was found to be able to pose an alarming level of threat to the DNA donors, exactly as it does to the GWAS participants through their aggregated allele frequencies derived from microarray data: as illustrated in the panel, to cover the identity information disclosed by the N SNPs from each donor (x-axis), a large number of personal datasets (each with N SNPs) have to be aggregated (y-axis). As an example, consider a human microbiome sequencing dataset that contains 10 million reads with 3% of human contamination. These human reads cover about 100,000 SNPs, and therefore, according to the figure, need an aggregation of at least 38000 personal datasets of the same size to secure, which. This amount of data cannot be afforded by even the largest microbiome project.

Noise adding is another way to reduce the privacy risks in outsourcing read data. In our study, we generated noise reads covering major/minor alleles at randomly-chosen SNP sites and evaluated the re-identification power achievable over the personal dataset including these reads. The middle-left panel in Figure 5 shows the minimum number of noise reads (y-axis) that are required to secure the dataset with N SNPs from a donor (x-axis). Our study shows that the number of the required noise reads grows linearly with regards to N. For example, at least 140 million noise reads need to be added in order to secure a human microbiome sequencing dataset with 10 million reads covering about 100,000 SNPs.

We further studied the strategies that partition the datasets after they were anonymized through aggregation or noise adding. All our analyses were performed on the personal dataset that contained 10 million reads and covered about 100,000 human SNP sites, a large case in human microbiome sequencing. The middle-right panel in Figure 5 shows the number of partitions needed (y-axis) to secure a dataset aggregated over different numbers of personal datasets (x-axis), and the rightmost panel demonstrates the number of required partitions (y-axis) vs. the number of noise reads being added (x-axis). As illustrated by the figure, when it is possible to partition an aggregated dataset into 100 subsets for the public cloud to process independently, the dataset should be built from at least 500 personal datasets, or carry at least 100 million noise reads (1 million noise reads per subset) to stay safe, which are better than aggregation or noise adding alone, though the overheads are still significant (particularly when it comes to other read datasets with higher levels of SNPs). Moreover, data partition could bring in large communication overheads, because each subset needs to be transferred to the public cloud separately. It is also less clear how to prevent the public cloud from linking different subsets together (e.g. based on the those who submit the jobs): when this happens, the cloud can aggregate the subsets for the re-identification.

7.2 Identification Attacks on Combined Seeds

We demonstrate that the l-mer based near-optimal statistics have no power at all, which indicates that the frequency analysis on the keyed-hash values of l-mers does not offer sufficient information for a re-identification attack. Below, we show that the Homer-like statistic cannot achieve a higher power on the combined seeds than on the continuous seeds. The similar analysis can be applied to the log likelihood ratio test. Consider a continuous seed (24 bps) consisting of two consecutive 12-mers, one of which contains a SNP site (denoted by α_1). Because most of the 100-bp windows in the human genome contain at most one SNP site, totally there are $100 - 12 = 88$ combined seeds within the same 100-bp window that contain the SNP site. All of them include α_1, thus can be denoted as $\alpha_1 || \alpha_i$ $(i = 2, ..., 89)$, and one of them is the continuous seed (denoted as $\alpha_1 || \alpha_2$). Let $B_{k(i)}$ $(i = 2, ..., 89)$ be the bins for combined seeds $\alpha_1 || \alpha_i$ when α_1 carries a major allele, and $B_{k'(i)}$ be the bins for $\alpha_1 || \alpha_i$ when α_1 carries a minor allele. Because all these seeds involve the same SNP site on the 12-mer α_1, all the related seeds from the testee's genome must all carry the same allele, major or minor. Then, the numbers of l-mers in the bins $B_{k(i)}$ and $B_{k'(i)}$ ($\bar{f}_{k(i)}$ and $\bar{f}_{k'(i)}$, respectively) are equally deviated from their expected counts ($\bar{F}_{k(i)}$ and $\bar{F}_{k'(i)}$, respectively) as compared to the numbers of l-mers in the bins of the continuous seeds ($\bar{f}_{k(2)}$ and $\bar{f}_{k'(2)}$) deviated from their expected counts ($\bar{F}_{k(2)}$ and $\bar{F}_{k'(2)}$). Hence, we have $\sum_i (|\rho_{k(i)} - \bar{F}_{k(i)}| + |\rho_{k'(i)} - \bar{F}_{k'(i)}|) \approx 88 \times (|\rho_{k(2)} - \bar{F}_{k(2)}| + |\rho_{k'(2)} - \bar{F}_{k'(2)}|)$, and $\sum_i (|\rho_{k(i)} - \bar{f}_{k(i)}| + |\rho_{k'(i)} - \bar{f}_{k'(i)}|) \approx 88 \times (|\rho_{k(2)} - \bar{f}_{k(2)}| + |\rho_{k'(2)} - \bar{f}_{k'(2)}|)$. Therefore, the Homer-like statistic on the bins of all combined seeds will become: $\bar{T}_{com} \approx 88 \times \bar{T}$ where $\bar{T}$ is the Homer-like statistic on the bins of continuous 24-bp seeds (as defined in Equation 1). This implies that, no matter the testee is a case individual or not, the test statistic on all combined 12-bp seeds ($\bar{T}_{com}$) is a constant (88) times larger than the test statistic on the continuous 24-bp seeds $\bar{T}$. As a result, at the same confidence level, $\bar{T}_{com}$ cannot achieve higher power than $\bar{T}$. Since we have shown $\bar{T}$ has little re-identification power, $\bar{T}_{com}$ should not either.

7.3 Correlation Analysis

Here we show that identification of correlated hash values is very hard in practice[7] and attempts to do so can be easily defeated. This challenge (to the adversary) comes from the fact that she only observes the hash values for a small portion of a donor's genome: by far the largest dataset from an individual contains no more than 10 million reads

[7] Remember that each hash value in a bin cannot be uniquely linked to an l-mer and therefore, the correlations among hashes cannot be identified through l-mers.

(of 100 bps long each), only $\gamma = 1/150$ of all the 24-mers on her genome. To understand what the adversary can do, let us first consider the simplest case, when two 24-mers are completely correlated. This happens when they contain alleles of the same SNP: if both share the same allele, they are positively correlated; otherwise, if one contains the major allele and the other contains the minor allele, they are negatively correlated. To detect such correlations, the adversary needs to conduct a co-occurrence statistical test to find out whether the hash values of these 24-mers always appear or disappear together in different donors' seed-hash datasets. To defeat this attack, we can aggregate the reads from 20 individuals (sampled from 40 DNA sequences, 2 from each) in one read-mapping task. After the aggregation, in a single aggregated dataset, no SNP site likely contains only minor alleles: the probability for this to happen is below $2^{-40} \approx 10^{-12}$, since the minor allele frequency is below 0.5. In other words, l-mers with major alleles are always carried by some case individuals, regardless of the presence or absence of related l-mers in the seed-hash dataset the adversary sees. As a result, the test will fail on the pairs of 24-mers that both contain major alleles or contain one major and one minor allele. For the pair of 24-mers both containing a minor allele, the adversary can confidently conjecture they are correlated only if she observes both 24-mers in multiple aggregated datasets, because the probability of observing a pair of minor-allele-containing 24-mers in a specific dataset by chance is not small. Assuming there are N SNP sites in the human genome ($N > 10^6$), the random probability of observing a pair of minor-allele-containing 24-mers in n aggregated datasets is approximately $P \sim N^2 \times l^2 \times (\gamma^2 \times t)^n$ (where t is the minor allele frequency and $t < 0.5$), indicating it requires $n \geq 4$ for $P \ll 1$. On the other hand, the probability of observing a highly correlated pair of minor-containing 24-mers in 4 aggregated datasets is very small, unless there are many aggregated datasets to be analyzed. For example, if $M = 500$ aggregated datasets (i.e., $20 \times 500 = 10,000$ human genome reads datasets) are analyzed, the probability of observing 4 aggregated datasets that contain both minor-allele-containing 24-mers can be estimated by a binomial distribution: $P < 500^4 \times (\gamma^2/2)^4 \approx 10^{-8} \ll 1$. Even considering there are many potentially correlated SNP pairs (e.g., close to the total number of SNPs, $N \approx 10^7$), the expected number of confidently assigned l-mer pairs is very small. Therefore, the test will also fail on the pairs of 24-mers containing the same minor allele.

Alternatively, the adversary may attempt to correlate two hashed 24-mers (which can be only partially correlated) at two specific genetic locations through their *relative frequencies* across multiple samples. In other words, she wants to know whether the frequency of one of these two hashes changes with that of the other over different *samples*. Here a sample we refer to includes one individual's read data that indeed contains the substrings at the locations of these two 24-mers, and the frequency of the 24-mer is calculated over multiple such samples. What we want to understand here is whether the adversary can acquire enough samples to establish a reliable correlation between the 24-mers. Remember that the probability a read dataset includes the substring at a specific location is only $\gamma = 1/150$. The adversary needs a set of 10 such samples to calculate the frequency of the 24-mer (at the location) at the precision of one decimal digit and multiple such sets to correlate two 24-mers. Due to the presence of 2% sequencing errors, the best correlation coefficient the adversary can get between a pair of completely correlated 24-mers (at two specific locations) is within ± 0.5 because 40% of the instances of the 24-mers contain an error at 2% error rate per nucleotide, and therefore their hash values will become incorrect and their presences will not be observed in the seed-hash datasets. As a result, the adversary has to carry out a correlation test on at least 15 sets (i.e. 150 samples) to obtain a confidence level (P-value) of 0.05 based on the table of critical values for Pearson's correlation coefficient (other statistics yield similar results). Note that the confidence level becomes even lower when those 24-mers are *not* completely correlated. Therefore, assume the adversary has collected M samples, the probability for a pair of completely correlated 24-mers to be both observed in at least 150 (out of M) samples can be estimated by a normal approximation of the binomial distribution with $\mu = \sigma^2 = \gamma \times M$. When $M = 10,000$ (that is, $10,000$ read datasets), the probability of getting those 150 samples from those datasets is negligible ($\approx 10^{-28}$) even when we consider that a total of $24 \times 14 \times 10^6 = 3.4 \times 10^8$ 24-mers are subject to this correlation analysis (there are 14 million SNP sites in the human genome, each associated with 24 24-mers). For the 24-mers not completely correlated, for example, those containing different SNPs, the probability to get 150 samples in 10,000 datasets is even lower, because the chance to have both 24-mers in one sample becomes $(0.6\gamma)^2$. Therefore, even when we consider the 2-combinations of all 3.4×10^8 24-mers, the probability to correlate any two of them using 10,000 read datasets is well below 10^{-12}. This is the best chance that the adversary can correlate a single pair of 24-mers (which is not enough for a re-identification). If such a risk is acceptable to the data owner, what she can do is re-hashing the reference genome with a new secret key every 10,000 datasets. The cost for this update is small: SHA-1 took about 5,440 minutes of CPU time to hash the whole genome on a 8-core desktop (2.93 GHz Interl Xeon) used in our study and produced about 6.8 TB data; the average overheads are merely 40 seconds CPU time and 700 MB data transfer for each of the 10,000 datasets.

Making Argument Systems for Outsourced Computation Practical (Sometimes)

Srinath Setty, Richard McPherson, Andrew J. Blumberg, and Michael Walfish
The University of Texas at Austin

Abstract

This paper describes the design, implementation, and evaluation of a system for performing verifiable outsourced computation. It has long been known that (1) this problem can be solved in theory using probabilistically checkable proofs (PCPs) coupled with modern cryptographic tools, and (2) these solutions have wholly impractical performance, according to the conventional (and well-founded) wisdom. Our goal is to challenge (2), with a built system that implements an *argument system* based on PCPs. We describe a general-purpose system that builds on work of Ishai et al. (CCC '07) and incorporates new theoretical work to improve performance by 20 orders of magnitude. The system is (arguably) practical in some cases, suggesting that, as a tool for building secure systems, PCPs are not a lost cause.

1 Introduction

This paper describes progress toward the goal of practical and general-purpose verifiable outsourced computation. This broad area has seen renewed interest, owing to cloud computing (a computationally limited device offloads processing to the cloud but does not assume the cloud's correctness [36]), volunteer computing (some 30 projects on the BOINC [1] software platform use volunteers' spare cycles, but some "volunteers" return wrong answers [6]), peer-to-peer computing, and high assurance computing (in the latter cases, remote peers or components are likely to be untrusted). Research has resulted in practical solutions, which depend on various conditions particular to the operating regime (e.g., they require trusted hardware [27, 62], or assume independent failures and replicate [6, 25, 42, 52, 56]), and theoretical solutions, which tend toward specialized algorithms for the computation at hand. There is, however, a strand of theory that is *unconditional* and *general-purpose*. Unfortunately, this theory has so far been totally impractical, which leads to the question: can we incorporate this powerful and enticing theory into a built system?

Our focus is on *argument systems*, which are interactive protocols with two actors, a *prover* and a *verifier*. Assuming that the prover is computationally bounded, such protocols can convince the verifier that the prover executed a given computation correctly and that the prover holds a proof to that effect. This theory dates to the 1980s [24, 39], and starting with Kilian [48, 49] *efficient* argument systems [45] have been based on probabilistically checkable proofs (PCPs)—which themselves are astonishing. Informally, the central result is that a verifier can—with a suitably encoded proof and with a negligible chance of regarding a wrong answer as correct—check an answer's correctness by probing a constant number of locations in a proof [8, 9]. Unfortunately, PCPs and hence arguments are wildly impractical: traditional PCPs are too expensive to instantiate at the prover or query from the verifier. While state-of-the-art PCP schemes are asymptotically efficient [15–17, 30], the constants on their running times are large, and they seem too intricate to be implemented easily.

This brings us to our animating question: can we construct an argument system for outsourced computation that has practical performance and is simple? Specifically, we require, first, that the verifier do less work than if it executed the outsourced computation locally. Some of the theoretical schemes meet this requirement asymptotically, but we want to meet it for reasonable computation sizes. Second, we require that the prover not do much more work than it would without verification. Last, we strongly favor protocols that are simple for both verifier and prover: a simple protocol is easier to implement, check for correctness, and optimize for performance.

Our starting point in answering the above question is a powerful and elegant insight of Ishai, Kushilevitz, and Ostrovsky [45]: some PCPs, though hopelessly impractical to materialize explicitly, are linear functions for which evaluation at any given point is inexpensive. Ishai et al. use such *linear PCPs* to build argument systems, via a novel *linear commitment* protocol: the prover commits to a linear function (the PCP), after which the verifier can inexpensively "query the proof" by asking the prover to evaluate the linear function at a verifier-chosen point. Since linear PCPs are simple (as PCPs go), the resulting argument systems are too. Nonetheless, they are still not practical. For example, for $m \times m$ matrix multiplication, the verifier would have to do $10^9 \cdot m^6$ work—a factor of $10^9 \cdot m^3$ more than executing the computation locally. This overhead comes from the encoding of the computation, a large number of cryptographic commitments, and substantial setup costs.

This paper describes a built system, called PEPPER, that goes a long way toward making argument systems practical. PEPPER refines the protocol of Ishai et al. to shrink program encoding (via a concise representation that generalizes arithmetic circuits), reduce the cost of commitment (via a stronger and streamlined commitment primitive), and amortize the verifier's costs (via batching). We prove the soundness of these refinements. The result is a simple constant-round protocol that gains a factor of over 10^{17} (no joke) versus a naive implementation of [45].

Much (but not all) of PEPPER's remaining costs stem from the computational complexity of the prover's work. This problem is shared by all PCP schemes, so a protocol in which the prover's total work is not much greater than the cost of executing the computation would be a major improvement. In fact, a key innovation in PEPPER is to meet this goal for computations of real interest (matrix multiplication, polynomial evaluation, etc.) by tailoring the PCP encoding to reduce overhead. The result is roughly three more orders of magnitude saved, for a total of 20. We note that the tailoring is systematic, and we believe that it will lend itself to automation (see §3.6, §4.2, and §6).

The tailored protocols for our examples are close to practical: at problem sizes of $m = 500$ variables, for instance, the verifier benefits from outsourcing degree-2 polynomial evaluation when working over 25,000 batched computations, and the verification takes minutes. And with two heuristic optimizations, we can get these numbers down to a batch size of 118 and sub-second verification time.

Of course, PEPPER is not yet ready for production deployment, but its remaining obstacles, while significant, do not seem insurmountable. Modular exponentiation is a bottleneck, but this primitive occurs in many cryptographic protocols and will benefit as researchers optimize it. Another obstacle is the computation encoding. One might guess that arithmetic circuits are too inefficient to be useful, but we discovered that we could tailor circuits until they imposed no overhead above a C++ program (§3.3). Of course, in the real world, people perform computations besides self-contained numerical functions. However, our work suggests that it will be possible to build a compiler that transforms a broader class of computations to efficient tailored protocols. Also, we had to start somewhere, to move PCPs from theory to technology. Our hope now is that PEPPER opens the door to an exciting area of systems research.

To explain this paper's organization, we note that there is a contrast between the "what" and the "why" of PEPPER. The "what" is surprisingly simple: the verifier submits vectors to the prover and expects dot products in return. The "why", however, requires some notation and time to explain, as PEPPER builds on the theory of PCPs, which is subtle and counter-intuitive. For this reason, Section 2 is a fairly technical overview of the underlying machinery. While this background is necessary for the precise specification of our protocols, the trusting reader can probably skip to Section 3, where we discuss the innovations and details of PEPPER. We experimentally evaluate PEPPER in Section 4. We survey related work in Section 5. Here, we just note that while there has been much theoretical work on unconditional, general-purpose verifiable computation, these works are not yet practical, and there have been few concerted efforts to make them so.

We originally proposed this research program in a position paper [64]. However, that paper gave only a high-level sketch that we have since heavily modified; it did not give a concrete protocol, proofs, an implementation, or an evaluation. The specific contributions of this paper are (1) a built PCP-based system that is near practical; (2) a series of refinements, with proofs, to the protocol of Ishai et al. [45] that save 20 orders of magnitude; (3) tailored PCP protocols that result in a prover whose overhead is only a constant factor; and (4) the implementation and experimental evaluation of our system, PEPPER.

2 Preliminaries and base protocol

2.1 A crash course in PCPs

Consider a *verifier* V that wishes to be convinced that a given problem instance X (e.g., a given 3-CNF logical formula) is in an NP language L (e.g., the set of satisfiable 3-CNF formulas). By definition of NP, if X is in L, then there is some witness z that V can check in polynomial time to be convinced of X's membership in L. Remarkably, there also exists a proof π that convinces V of X's membership but only needs to be inspected in a *constant number* of places—yet if X is not in L, then for any purported proof, the probability that V is wrongly convinced of X's membership can be arbitrarily close to zero. This remarkable statement is the rough content of the PCP theorem [8, 9], and the rest of this subsection describes the machinery from this theorem that is relevant to PEPPER.

Following [8], we take L to be Boolean circuit satisfiability: the question of whether the input wires of a given Boolean circuit $\mathcal{C}$ can be set to make $\mathcal{C}$ evaluate to 1.[1] It suffices to consider this problem because L is NP-complete; any other problem in NP can be reduced to it. Of course, a satisfying assignment z—a setting of all wires in $\mathcal{C}$ such that $\mathcal{C}$ evaluates to 1—constitutes an (obvious) proof that $\mathcal{C}$ is satisfiable: V could check z against every gate in $\mathcal{C}$. Note that this check requires inspecting all of z. In contrast, the PCP theorem yields a V that makes only a *constant number* of queries to an oracle π and satisfies:

- **Completeness.** If $\mathcal{C}$ is satisfiable, then there exists a linear function π (called a proof oracle) such that, after V queries π, $\Pr\{V \text{ accepts } \mathcal{C} \text{ as satisfiable}\} = 1$, where the probability is over V's random choices.
- **Soundness.** If $\mathcal{C}$ is not satisfiable, then $\Pr\{V \text{ accepts } \mathcal{C} \text{ as satisfiable}\} < \epsilon$ for *all* purported proof functions $\tilde{\pi}$. Here, ϵ is a constant that can be driven arbitrarily low.

[1] A Boolean circuit is a set of interconnected gates, each with input wires and an output wire, with wires taking 0/1 values.

Note that we are requiring a correct proof π to be a linear function over finite fields.[2] Following [45], we call such proofs *linear PCPs*. By linear function, we mean that $\pi(q_1+q_2)=\pi(q_1)+\pi(q_2)$. A linear function $\pi\colon \mathbb{F}^n \mapsto \mathbb{F}^b$ can be regarded as a $b \times n$ matrix M, where $\pi(q)=M\cdot q$; in the case $b=1$, π returns a dot product with the input. Below we describe a linear PCP that is used by [8] as a building block; this linear PCP is also presented in [16, 45], and we borrow some of our notation from these three sources.

To motivate this linear PCP—that is, the encoding of π, and how V interacts with it—recall that we must avoid V's having to check a purported assignment, z, against every gate, as that would be equivalent to the polynomial-time check of membership. Instead, V will construct a polynomial $P(Z)$ that represents $\mathcal{C}$, and π will be carefully constructed to allow evaluation of this polynomial. For each of the s gates, V creates a variable $Z_i \in \{0,1\}$ that represents the output of gate i. V also creates a set of arithmetic constraints, as follows. If gate i is the AND of Z_j and Z_k, then V adds the constraint $Z_i - Z_j \cdot Z_k = 0$; if gate i is the NOT of Z_j, then V adds the constraint $1-(Z_i+Z_j)=0$; if gate i is an input gate for the jth input, V adds the constraint $Z_i - in_j = 0$; and finally, for the last gate, representing the output of the circuit, we also have $Z_s - 1 = 0$. V then obtains the polynomial $P(Z)$ by combining all of the constraints: $P(Z)=\sum_i v_i \cdot Q_i(Z)$, where $Z=(Z_1,\ldots,Z_s)$, each $Q_i(Z)$ is given by a constraint (e.g., $Z_i - Z_jZ_k$), and V chooses each v_i uniformly and independently at random from a finite field $\mathbb{F}$. The reason for the randomness is given immediately below.

Notice that $P(z)$ detects whether z is a satisfying assignment: (1) if z is a satisfying assignment to the circuit, then it also satisfies all of the $\{Q_i(Z)\}$, yielding $P(z)=0$; but (2) if z is not a satisfying assignment to the circuit, then the randomness of the $\{v_i\}$ makes $P(z)$ unlikely to equal 0 (as illustrated in the next paragraph). Thus, the proof oracle π must encode a purported assignment z in such a way that V can quickly evaluate $P(z)$ by making a few queries to π. To explain the encoding, let $\langle x,y\rangle$ represent the inner (dot) product between two vectors x and y, and $x \otimes y$ represent the outer product $x \cdot y^T$ (that is, all pairs of components from the two vectors). Observe that V can write

$$P(Z)=\langle \gamma_2, Z\otimes Z\rangle + \langle \gamma_1, Z\rangle + \gamma_0.$$

The $\{\gamma_0,\gamma_1,\gamma_2\}$ are determined by the $\{Q_i(Z)\}$ and the choice of $\{v_i\}$, with $\gamma_2 \in \mathbb{F}^{s^2}$, $\gamma_1 \in \mathbb{F}^s$, and $\gamma_0 \in \mathbb{F}$. The reason that V can write $P(Z)$ this way is that all of the $\{Q_i(Z)\}$ are degree-2 functions.

Given this representation of $P(Z)$, V can compute $P(z)$ by asking for $\langle \gamma_2, z\otimes z\rangle$ and $\langle \gamma_1, z\rangle$. This motivates the form of a correct proof, π. We write $\pi=(z, z\otimes z)$, by which we mean $\pi=(\pi^{(1)},\pi^{(2)})$, where $\pi^{(1)}(\cdot)=\langle \cdot, z\rangle$ and $\pi^{(2)}(\cdot)=\langle \cdot, z\otimes z\rangle$. At this point, we have our first set of queries: V checks whether $\pi^{(2)}(\gamma_2)+\pi^{(1)}(\gamma_1)+\gamma_0=0$. If z is a satisfying assignment and π is correctly computed, the check passes. Just as important, if z' is *not* a satisfying assignment—which is always the case if $\mathcal{C}$ is not satisfiable—then V is not likely to be convinced. To see this, first assume that V is given a syntactically correct but non-satisfying π'; that is, $\pi'=(z', z'\otimes z')$, where z' is a non-satisfying assignment. The test above—that is, checking whether $\pi'^{(2)}(\gamma_2)+\pi'^{(1)}(\gamma_1)+\gamma_0=0$—checks whether $P(z')=0$. However, there must be at least one i' for which $Q_{i'}(z')$ is not 0, which means that the test passes if and only if $v_{i'}\cdot Q_{i'}(z') = -\sum_{i\neq i'} v_i \cdot Q_i(z')$. But the $\{v_i\}$ are conceptually chosen *after* z', so the probability of this event is upper-bounded by $1/|\mathbb{F}|$.

The above test is called the *circuit test*, and it has so far been based on an assumption: that if π' is invalid, it encodes *some* (non-satisfying) assignment. In other words, we have been assuming that $\pi'^{(1)}$ and $\pi'^{(2)}$ are linear functions that are consistent with each other. But of course a malevolently constructed oracle might not adhere to this requirement. To relax the assumption, we need two other checks. First, with *linearity tests* [12, 21], V makes three queries to $\pi^{(1)}$ and three to $\pi^{(2)}$, and checks the responses. If the checks pass, V develops a reasonable confidence that $\pi^{(1)}$ and $\pi^{(2)}$ are linear functions, which is another way of saying that $\pi^{(1)}(\cdot)$ is returning $\langle \cdot, z\rangle$ for some z and that $\pi^{(2)}(\cdot)$ is returning $\langle \cdot, u\rangle$ for some $u \in \mathbb{F}^{s^2}$. In the second test, the *quadratic correction test*, V makes four queries total and checks their responses; if the checks pass, V develops reasonable confidence that these two linear functions have the required relationship, meaning that $u = z\otimes z$. Once these tests have passed, the circuit test above is valid.

In all, V makes $\ell = 14$ queries. The details of the queries and tests, and a formal statement of their completeness and soundness, are in [8] and Appendix A. Here, we just informally state that if $\mathcal{C}$ is satisfiable, then V will always be convinced by π, and if $\mathcal{C}$ is not satisfiable, then V's probability of passing the tests is upper bounded by a constant κ (for any $\tilde{\pi}$). If the scheme is repeated ρ times, for $\mu=\ell\cdot\rho$ total queries, the error probability ϵ becomes $\epsilon=\kappa^\rho$.

2.2 Arguments

The theory above says that V can be convinced of a circuit's satisfiability by making only a constant number of queries to the proof oracle π. But how does V query π? Clearly, π cannot be available for direct inspection by V because it is tremendous: written out, π would be a list of the function's values at every point in an exponentially-sized domain. The idea of an efficient argument (due to Kilian [48, 49]) is to use a PCP in an interactive protocol: a separate *prover* P computes a PCP and responds to V's queries. However, P

[2] The PCP theorem permits, but does not impose, this restriction; we need it for reasons elucidated in the next subsection.

must be forced to "act like" a fixed proof—P must be prevented from adjusting answers to later queries based on earlier answers. Kilian's observation is that this can be done with cryptographic commitments.

In the sections ahead, we build on an elegant scheme by Ishai, Kushilevitz, and Ostrovsky [45]. They (1) observe that π is a linear function (determined by z and $z \otimes z$) and (2) develop a *commitment to a linear function* primitive. In this primitive, P commits to a linear function by pre-evaluating the function at a point chosen by V and hidden from P; then, V submits one query, and the response must be consistent with the pre-evaluation. Roughly speaking, V can now proceed as if P's responses are given by an oracle π. (More accurately, V can proceed as if P's responses are given by a set of non-colluding oracles, one per PCP query.)

In more detail, V obtains a commitment from P by homomorphically encrypting a random vector r and asking P to compute $\mathsf{Enc}(\pi(r))$; P can do this without seeing r, by the linearity of π and the homomorphic properties of the encryption function (we do not need or assume fully homomorphic encryption [37]). V can then apply the decryption function to recover $\pi(r)$. To submit a PCP query q and obtain $\pi(q)$, V asks P for $\pi(q)$ and $\pi(r + \alpha q)$, for α randomly chosen from $\mathbb{F}$. V then requires that $\pi(r + \alpha q) = \pi(r) + \alpha\pi(q)$, or else V rejects $\pi(q)$. By running parallel instances of the commitment protocol (one for each time that V wants to inspect π), Ishai et al. convert any PCP protocol that uses linear functions into an *argument system* [24, 39].

Arguments are defined as follows; we borrow some of our notation and phrasing from [45], and we restrict the definition to Boolean circuits. An *argument* (P, V) *with soundness error* ϵ comprises two probabilistic polynomial time entities, P and V, that take a Boolean circuit $\mathcal{C}$ as input and meet two properties:

- **Completeness.** If $\mathcal{C}$ is satisfiable and P has access to the satisfying assignment z, then the interaction of $V(\mathcal{C})$ and $P(\mathcal{C}, z)$ always makes $V(\mathcal{C})$ accept $\mathcal{C}$'s satisfiability.
- **Soundness.** If $\mathcal{C}$ is not satisfiable, then for every efficient malicious P^*, the probability (over V's random choices) that the interaction of $V(\mathcal{C})$ and $P^*(\mathcal{C})$ makes $V(\mathcal{C})$ accept $\mathcal{C}$ as satisfiable is $< \epsilon$.

3 Design and details of PEPPER

Problem statement and threat model. We wish to implement the following protocol. A computer that we control, the *verifier*, sends a program Ψ and an input x to a remote computer, the *prover*. The prover returns a result y, and the verifier issues queries over a small number of interaction rounds to the prover, whose responses either establish for the verifier that Ψ was run correctly and that y is the result of running Ψ on x, or else cause the verifier to reject. If y is incorrect, the verifier should reject with high probability. We do not provide the converse; that is, rejection in our context implies only that the prover has not given a correct proof, not that $y \neq \Psi(x)$. We require the following: (1) this protocol should be cheaper for the verifier, in computational resources, than computing y locally, and (2) the guarantee that the protocol provides to the verifier should make no assumptions about the prover, other than standard cryptographic ones. That is, the prover can subvert the protocol, can choose not to follow it, can return wrong answers, etc.

3.1 The promise and perils of PCPs

In principle, the problem above can be solved with PCPs. In practice, a number of severe obstacles arise, as can be seen by the following attempt to use PCPs. There is a Boolean circuit $\mathcal{C}$ (which depends on Ψ, x, and y) such that $\mathcal{C}$ is satisfiable (that is, evaluates to 1) if and only if y is the correct output of Ψ run on x. Assume that the prover and verifier can efficiently derive $\mathcal{C}$, given Ψ, x, and y. Then, the prover can issue a PCP (as in §2.1) of $\mathcal{C}$'s satisfiability. At that point, if y is the correct output, the verifier can efficiently inspect the PCP to be convinced both that Ψ was executed correctly and that Ψ produces y when run on x; if y is not the correct output, the probability that the verifier accepts $\mathcal{C}$ as satisfiable is upper-bounded by a negligible constant—for *any* purported PCP. This approach sounds promising; unfortunately, it is totally impractical:

- *The proof is too long.* It is much too large for the verifier to handle or for the prover to write out in full.
- *The protocol is too complicated.* State-of-the-art PCP protocols [15–17, 30] partially address the concern about proof length, but they are intricate to the point of making a bug-free implementation difficult. Unfortunately, in this context, even small bugs can be security-critical. Complexity also hinders optimization.
- *The phrasing of the computation is too primitive.* Even if they have simple control flow, most general-purpose computations are far longer when expressed as Boolean circuits than in, say, C++.
- *The preparatory work is too high for the verifier.* Deriving $\mathcal{C}$ and generating queries to the proof take at least as much work for the verifier as executing the computation.
- *The prover's overhead is too high.* In the base PCP protocol (§2.1), the prover's work is at least quadratic in the number of circuit wires. While this overhead can be reduced to a polylogarithmic factor [15–17, 30] (at the cost of intricacy, as noted above), we ideally want to limit the prover's overhead to a small constant factor.

The first two obstacles above can be addressed by the argument system of Ishai et al. [45]. As discussed in Section 2.2, their approach addresses proof length (since the proof is not materialized) and proof complexity (since the proof is sim-

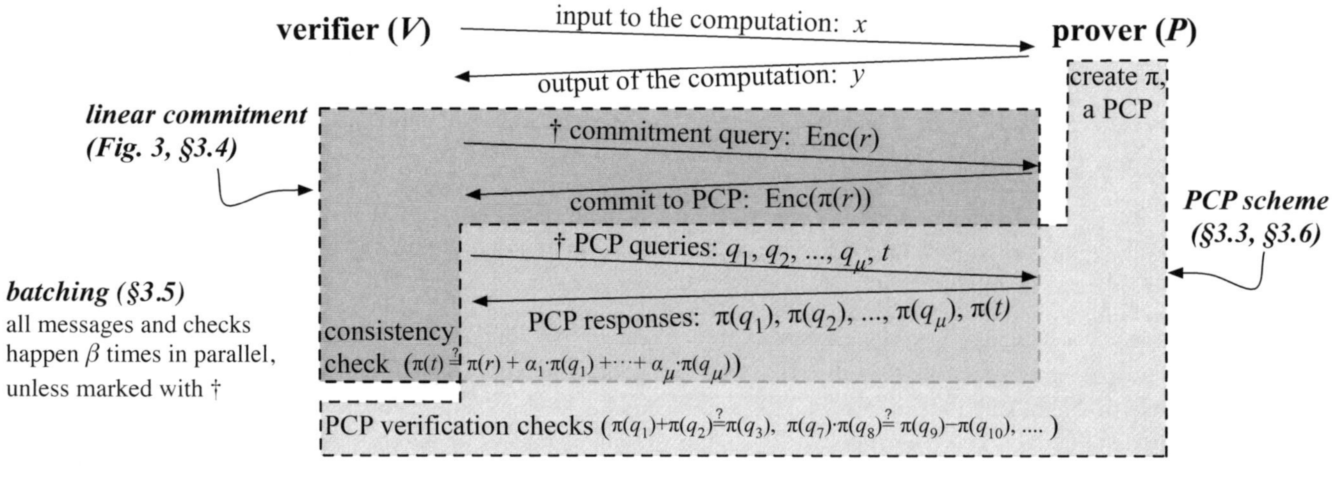

FIGURE 1—High-level depiction of PEPPER, a PCP-based argument system for verified outsourced computation between a verifier and a prover. We formalize this picture and prove its soundness in the appendices.

ply a linear function to which the prover commits). Proof length and proof complexity in exchange for commitment: this is a great trade! However, it brings another obstacle:

- *The parallel commitments are too expensive.* Commitment requires cryptographic operations and hence multiprecision arithmetic, and the scheme of [45] invokes these operations far too much (by several orders of magnitude) to be practical.

We now turn to our system, PEPPER, which builds on [45] and addresses all of the items above.

3.2 Overview of PEPPER

Figure 1 depicts PEPPER. In the computation phase, V selects a computation[3] Ψ and different inputs $x_1, \ldots, x_\beta$, and P returns outputs $y_1, \ldots, y_\beta$. These computations can happen iteratively or in a batch. For each computation, P creates and stores a proof oracle π_i establishing that $\Psi(x_i) = y_i$. In the proof commitment phase, V asks P to commit to all of its proofs. Then V moves to the proof verification phase and issues PCP queries to P, whose responses must be consistent with the commitment phase. Then, V runs the PCP verification checks on P's responses. At that point, V outputs `accept` or `reject` for each computation. An output of `accept` on y_i means that $y_i = \Psi(x_i)$, with high probability.

The rest of this section describes how PEPPER overcomes the obstacles mentioned in Section 3.1. PEPPER addresses proof length and complexity by inheriting from [45]; it shrinks the program encoding by using arithmetic circuits instead of Boolean circuits (§3.3); it reduces commitment costs by requiring fewer commitments while offering better security (§3.4); it uses batching to reduce V's costs (§3.5); and it reduces P's overhead for some problems by reducing redundancy in the PCP encoding (§3.6). Figure 2 summarizes the costs under these refinements; we explain this figure over the course of the section.

[3]Our implementation supports both preconfiguring computations and uploading binaries online for P to execute.

3.3 Arithmetic circuits and concise gates

To address the concern about the encoding of the computation, PEPPER uses *arithmetic circuits*, instead of Boolean circuits. In a traditional arithmetic circuit, the input and output wires take values from a large set (e.g., a finite field or the integers). This extension is a natural one, as the PCP machinery is already expressed as arithmetic versions of Boolean circuits. However, we observe that the machinery also works with what we call *concise gates*, each of which encapsulates a function of many inputs (e.g., a dot product between two large vectors). Note that a gate here does not represent a low-level hardware element but rather a modular piece of the computation that enters the verification algorithm as an algebraic constraint.

This simple refinement is critical to practicality. First, it is vastly more compact to represent, say, multiplication with a single gate than as a Boolean circuit. Beyond that, for certain computations (e.g., parallelizable numerical ones, such as matrix multiplication), the circuit model imposes no overhead; that is, the "circuit" is the same as a C++ program, so the only overhead comes from proving and verifying (as demonstrated in §4.3). However, this model has known limitations; for example, comparison operations require relatively large circuits. Future work is to address this problem, perhaps using tailored PCP encodings (§3.6).

Details and an example. Using arithmetic circuits requires only minor modifications to the PCP scheme described in Section 2.1. Here, V produces a set of constraints (there, V

	op	naive impl. of [45]	batching (§3.5)	arith. circ. (§3.3)	new commit (§3.4)	new PCPs (§3.6)
PCP encoding size ($\|\pi\|$)		$10^9 m^6$	$10^9 m^6$	$4m^4$	$4m^4$	m^3
V's per-instance work (compare to local, naive computation: $f \cdot m^3$)						
Issue commit queries	$e + 2c$	$10^9 m^6 \cdot \mu'$	$10^9 m^6 \cdot \mu'/\beta$	$4m^4 \cdot \mu'/\beta$	$4m^4/\beta$	m^3/β
Process commit responses	d	μ'	μ'	μ'	1	1
Issue PCP queries	c	$10^9 m^6 \cdot \mu'$	$10^9 m^6 \cdot \mu'/\beta$	$4m^4 \cdot \mu'/\beta$	$4m^4 \cdot \mu/\beta$	$m^3 \cdot \mu/\beta$
Process PCP responses	f	$(2\mu' + 96m^2 \cdot \rho)$	$(2\mu' + 96m^2 \cdot \rho)$	$(2\mu' + 3m^2 \cdot \rho)$	$(2\mu + 3m^2 \cdot \rho)$	$(2\mu + 3m^2 \cdot \rho)$
P's per-instance work (compare to local, naive computation: $f \cdot m^3$)						
Issue commit responses	h	$10^9 m^6 \cdot \mu'$	$10^9 m^6 \cdot \mu'$	$4m^4 \cdot \mu'$	$4m^4$	m^3
Issue PCP responses	f	$10^9 m^6 \cdot \mu'$	$10^9 m^6 \cdot \mu'$	$4m^4 \cdot \mu'$	$4m^4 \cdot \mu$	$m^3 \cdot \mu$

$\ell = 14$: # of PCP queries per repetition (Appendix A)
$\rho = 70$: # of repetitions to drive error low (Appendix A)
$\mu = \ell \cdot \rho \approx 1000$: # of PCP queries per instance
$\mu' \approx 3\mu$: # of PCP queries pre-commit-refinement (§3.4)
β: # of computation instances batch verified (§3.2, §3.5)
$|\pi|$: # of components in matrix associated to linear function π (§2.1)
e: cost of homomorphic encryption of a single field element (Fig. 3, step 1)
d: cost of homomorphic decryption of a single field element (Fig. 3, step 3)
f: cost of field multiplication (Fig. 3, steps 4–6)
h: cost of ciphertext addition plus multiplication (Fig. 3, step 2)
c: cost of generating a pseudorandom # between 0 and a 192-bit prime (§4.1)

FIGURE 2—High-order costs under our refinements, cumulatively applied, compared to naive local execution and a naive implementation of [45], for our running example of $m \times m$ matrix multiplication. Rows for V and P contain operation counts, except for the "op" field, which includes a parameter denoting the cost of the operations in that row. Section 4.5 quantifies d, e, f, h and c; Section 4.6 quantifies β. The "PCP" rows include the consistency queries and checks (Fig. 3, steps 4–6).

transforms a Boolean circuit into a set of constraints) over s variables from a finite field $\mathbb{F}$ (there, over binary variables) that can be satisfied if and only if y is the correct output of $\Psi(x)$ (there, if and only if the circuit is satisfiable); V then combines those constraints to form a polynomial over s values in the field $\mathbb{F}$ (there, in the field $GF(2)$). One way to look at this use of arithmetic circuits is that it represents the computation as a set of constraints directly.

To illustrate the above, we use the example of $m \times m$ matrix multiplication. We choose this example because it is both a good initial test (it is efficiently encodable as an arithmetic circuit) and a core primitive in many applications: image processing (e.g., filtering, rotation, scaling), signal processing (e.g., Kalman filtering), data mining, etc.

In this example computation, let A, B, C be $m \times m$ matrices over a finite field $\mathbb{F}$, with subscripts denoting entries, so $A = (A_{1,1}, \ldots, A_{m,m}) \in \mathbb{F}^{m^2}$ (for $\mathbb{F}$ sufficiently large we can represent negative numbers and integer arithmetic; see §4.1). The verifier V sends A and B to the prover P, who returns C; V wants to check that $A \cdot B = C$. Matrix C equals $A \cdot B$ if and only if the following constraints over variables $Z = (Z^a_{1,1}, \ldots, Z^a_{m,m}, Z^b_{1,1}, \ldots, Z^b_{m,m}) \in \mathbb{F}^{2m^2}$ can be satisfied:

$$Z^a_{i,j} - A_{i,j} = 0, \text{ for } i,j \in [m] \,; \quad Z^b_{i,j} - B_{i,j} = 0, \text{ for } i,j \in [m] \,;$$

$$C_{i,j} - \sum_{k=1}^{m} Z^a_{i,k} \cdot Z^b_{k,j} = 0, \text{ for } i,j \in [m].$$

Note that the third type of constraint, which captures the dot product, is an example of a concise gate.

V is interested in whether the above constraints can be met for some setting $Z = z$ (if so, the output of the computation is correct; if not, it is not). Thus, V proceeds as in Section 2.1 and Appendix A. V constructs a polynomial $P(Z)$ by combining the constraints: $P(Z) = \sum_{i,j} v^a_{i,j} \cdot (Z^a_{i,j} - A_{i,j}) + \sum_{i,j} v^b_{i,j} \cdot (Z^b_{i,j} - B_{i,j}) + \sum_{i,j} v^c_{i,j} \cdot (C_{i,j} - \sum_{k=1}^{m} Z^a_{i,k} \cdot Z^b_{k,j})$, where V chooses the variables $\{v\}$ randomly from $\mathbb{F}$. As before, V regards the prover P as holding linear proof oracles $\pi = (\pi^{(1)}, \pi^{(2)})$, where $\pi^{(1)}(\cdot) = \langle \cdot, z \rangle$ and $\pi^{(2)}(\cdot) = \langle \cdot, z \otimes z \rangle$ for some $z \in \mathbb{F}^{2m^2}$. And as before, V issues linearity test queries, quadratic correction test queries, and circuit test queries (the randomly chosen $\{v\}$ feed into this latter test), repeating the tests ρ times. We address V's cost of constructing $P(Z)$ and issuing queries in Section 3.5.

The completeness and soundness of the above scheme follows from the completeness and soundness of the base protocol. Thus, if $C = A \cdot B$ (more generally, if the claimed output y equals $\Psi(x)$), then V can be convinced of that fact; if the output is not correct, P has no more than $\epsilon = \kappa^\rho$ probability of passing verification.

Savings. Moving from a Boolean to a non-concise arithmetic circuit saves, for a fixed m, an estimated four orders of magnitude in the number of circuit "wires" (the "wires" being $\{Z\}$) and thus eight orders of magnitude in the query size and the prover's work (which are quadratic in the number of wires). The dot product gates decrease these quantities by another factor of m^2 (since they reduce the number of "wires" from $m^3 + 2m^2$ to $2m^2$). In Figure 2, the arithmetic circuit column reflects these two reductions, the first being reflected in the elimination of the 10^9 factor and the second in the move from the m^6 to the m^4 term.

Commit+Multidecommit

The protocol assumes an additive homomorphic encryption scheme (Gen, Enc, Dec) over a finite field, $\mathbb{F}$.

Commit phase

Input: Prover holds a vector $w \in \mathbb{F}^n$, which defines a linear function $\pi\colon \mathbb{F}^n \to \mathbb{F}$, where $\pi(q) = \langle w, q \rangle$.

1. Verifier does the following:
   - Generates public and secret keys $(pk, sk) \leftarrow \mathsf{Gen}(1^k)$, where k is a security parameter.
   - Generates vector $r \in_R \mathbb{F}^n$ and encrypts r component-wise, so $\mathsf{Enc}(pk, r) = (\mathsf{Enc}(pk, r_1), \ldots, \mathsf{Enc}(pk, r_n))$.
   - Sends $\mathsf{Enc}(pk, r)$ and pk to the prover.
2. Using the homomorphism in the encryption scheme, the prover computes $e \leftarrow \mathsf{Enc}(pk, \pi(r))$ without learning r. The prover sends e to the verifier.
3. The verifier computes $s \leftarrow \mathsf{Dec}(sk, e)$, retaining s and r.

Decommit phase

Input: the verifier holds $q_1, \ldots, q_\mu \in \mathbb{F}^n$ and wants to obtain $\pi(q_1), \ldots, \pi(q_\mu)$.

4. The verifier picks μ secrets $\alpha_1, \ldots, \alpha_\mu \in_R \mathbb{F}$ and sends to the prover $(q_1, \ldots, q_\mu, t)$, where $t = r + \alpha_1 q_1 + \cdots + \alpha_\mu q_\mu \in \mathbb{F}^n$.
5. The prover returns $(a_1, a_2, \ldots, a_\mu, b)$, where $a_i, b \in \mathbb{F}$. If the prover behaved, then $a_i = \pi(q_i)$ for all $i \in [\mu]$, and $b = \pi(t)$.
6. The verifier checks: $b \stackrel{?}{=} s + \alpha_1 a_1 + \cdots + \alpha_\mu a_\mu)$. If so, it outputs $(a_1, a_2, \ldots, a_\mu)$. If not, it rejects, outputting $\perp$.

FIGURE 3—PEPPER's commitment protocol. V decommits queries $q_1, \ldots, q_\mu$ for the price of a single commitment query, $\mathsf{Enc}(r)$. This protocol strengthens one by Ishai et al. [45] and makes only minor changes to their notation and phrasing. The intent is that the μ queries be the PCP queries and that n be the size of the proof encoding ($s^2 + s$, until §3.6). The protocol assumes an additive homomorphic encryption scheme but can be modified to work with a multiplicative homomorphic scheme (such as ElGamal [32]); see Appendix E.

3.4 Strengthening linear commitment

The commitment protocol in the base scheme of Ishai et al. [45] relies on an additive homomorphic encryption operation.[4] If executed once, this operation is reasonably efficient (hundreds of microseconds; see Section 4.5); however, the number of times that the base scheme invokes it is proportional to at least the *square* of the input size *times* μ, the number of PCP queries (roughly 1000). For the example of $m \times m$ matrix multiplication with $m = 1000$, the base scheme would thus require at least $(1000)^4 \cdot 1000 \cdot 100\ \mu$s: over 3000 years, and that's after the concise representation given by the previous refinement!

While we would be thrilled to eliminate homomorphic encryptions, we think that doing so is unlikely to work in this context. Instead, in this section we modify the commitment protocol to perform three orders of magnitude fewer encryptions; Appendix B proves the soundness of this modification by reducing its security to the semantic security of the homomorphic encryption scheme. Moreover, our reduction is more direct than in the base scheme, which translates into further cost reductions.

Details. In the base scheme [45], each PCP query by V (meaning each of the μ queries, as described in §2.1, §3.3, and Appendix A) requires V and P to run a separate instance of commitment. Thus, to check one computation Ψ, V homomorphically encrypts $\mu \approx 1000$ (see Figure 2) vectors, and P works over all of these ciphertexts. This factor of 1000 is an issue because the vectors are encrypted componentwise, and they have many components! (In the example above, they are elements of $\mathbb{F}^{s^2}$ or $\mathbb{F}^s$, where $s = 2 \cdot 10^6$.)

Figure 3 presents our modified commitment protocol. It homomorphically encrypts only one vector $r \in \mathbb{F}^{s^2+s}$, called the *commitment query*, with the encryption work amortizing over many queries $(q_1, \ldots, q_\mu)$. This new protocol leads to a more direct security reduction than in the base scheme. In their central reduction, Ishai et al. establish that commitment allows V to treat P as a *set* of non-colluding but possibly malicious oracles. In each repetition, their V must therefore issue extra queries (beyond the ℓ PCP queries) to ensure that the oracles match. With our commitment protocol, V can treat P as a *single* (possibly cheating) oracle and submit *only* the PCP queries. Stated more formally, Ishai et al. reduce linear PCP to linear MIP (multiprover interactive proof [14]) to the argument model, whereas we reduce linear PCP directly to the argument model. We prove the reduction in Appendix B.

Savings. This refinement reduces the homomorphic encryptions and other commitment-related work by three orders of magnitude, as depicted in Figure 2 by the elimination of the μ' term from the "commit" rows in the "new commit" column. As a second-order benefit, we save another factor of three (depicted in Figure 2 as a move from μ' to μ queries), as follows. The queries to establish the consistency of multiple oracles have error $(\ell - 1)/\ell = 13/14$. However, the soundness error of our base PCP protocol is $\kappa = 7/9$. Since $(13/14)^{\rho'} = (7/9)^{\rho}$ when $\rho' \approx 3\rho$, it takes roughly three times as many repetitions of the protocol to contend with this extra error. Finally, the direct reduction yields a qualitative benefit: it simplifies PEPPER.

[4] Note that we do not require fully homomorphic encryption [37]; as we discuss in Section 5, the costs of such schemes are still prohibitive.

3.5 Amortizing query costs through batching

Despite the optimizations so far, the verifier's work remains unacceptable. First, V must materialize a set of constraints that represent the computation, yet writing these down is as much work as executing the computation. Second, V must generate queries that are *larger* than the circuit. For example, for $m \times m$ matrix multiplication (§3.3), the commitment query has $4m^4 + 2m^2$ components (matching the number of components in the vector representation of the proof), in contrast to the $O(m^3)$ operations needed to execute the computation. A similar obstacle holds for many of the PCP queries. To amortize these costs, we modify the protocols to work over multiple computation instances and to verify computations in batch; we also rigorously justify these modifications. Note that the modifications do not reduce V's checking work, only V's cost to issue queries; however, this is acceptable since checking is fast.

Details. We assume that the computation Ψ (or equivalently, $\mathcal{C}$) is fixed; V and P will work over β instances of Ψ, with each instance having distinct input. We refer to β as the *batch size*. The prover P formulates β proof oracles (linear functions): $\pi_1, \ldots, \pi_\beta$. Note that the prover can stack these to create a linear function $\boldsymbol{\pi} : \mathbb{F}^{s^2+s} \rightarrow \mathbb{F}^\beta$ (one can visualize this as a matrix whose rows are $\pi_1, \ldots, \pi_\beta$).

To summarize the protocol, V now generates *one* set of commitment and PCP queries, and submits them to *all* of the oracles in the batch.[5] The prover now responds to queries q with $\boldsymbol{\pi}(q) \in \mathbb{F}^\beta$, instead of with $\pi(q) \in \mathbb{F}$. By way of comparison, the previous refinement (§3.4) encrypts a single r for a set of queries $q_1, \ldots, q_\mu$ to a proof π. This one issues a single r and a single set of queries $q_1, \ldots, q_\mu$ to multiple proofs $\pi_1, \ldots, \pi_\beta$.

Appendix C details the protocol and proof-sketches its soundness. We note that each of the β PCPs has the same soundness error (ϵ) as if it were queried individually. However, the errors for the β PCPs in a batch are correlated.

Savings. The most significant benefit is qualitative: without batching, V cannot gain from outsourcing, as the query costs are roughly the same as executing the computation. The quantitative benefit of this refinement is, as depicted in Figure 2, to reduce the per-instance cost of commitment and PCP queries by a factor of β.

3.6 Optimizing the PCP encoding

In some cases, we can address the obstacle of prover overhead by tailoring the PCP encoding. The key observations are that (1) the basic protocol *does not require a particular PCP encoding, as long as the encoding is a linear function*, and (2) some circuits permit a much more streamlined encoding. Specifically, we can tailor the prover's linear function so that it contains only terms that the prover had to compute anyway to return the result of the computation. (In essence, we are reducing the redundancy in the PCP.) The result for some computations, such as the examples given below, is protocols in which the prover's work is only a constant factor above simply executing the computation.

Details and examples. Under the linear PCPs in Sections 2.1 and 3.3, the prover computes $z \otimes z$, where z is a satisfying assignment to the circuit (or constraint set). However, for some computations V's circuit test (§2.1) interrogates only a subset of $z \otimes z$. Loosely speaking, P thus needs to compute only that subset to produce the proof oracle.

Matrix multiplication. As in Section 3.3, V again combines constraints that represent the computation, again picks random $\{v\}$ to be coefficients of those constraints, again obtains a polynomial (which we will write as $P'(Z)$), and again submits queries to the prover's oracle to get $P'(Z)$ evaluated and to test that the prover is holding an oracle of the correct form. There are two modifications to the approach presented in Section 3.3. First, in combining the constraints to construct $P'(Z)$, V does not include the degree-1 constraints (meaning $Z^a_{i,j} - A_{i,j} = 0$, etc.). Thus, V obtains $P'(Z) = \sum_{i,j} v^c_{i,j} \cdot (C_{i,j} - \sum_{k=1}^m Z^a_{i,k} \cdot Z^b_{k,j})$, which, using our notation from before, can be written $P'(Z) = \langle \gamma_2, Z \otimes Z \rangle + \gamma'_0$.

However, we will write $P'(Z)$ differently. In Sections 2.1 and 3.3, the form above motivated the definition of $\pi^{(2)}(q)$ as $\langle q, z \otimes z \rangle$, for $q \in \mathbb{F}^{s^2} = \mathbb{F}^{m^4}$. There, answering queries to $\pi^{(2)}$ required the prover to do work proportional to m^4. This is not only more than we would like to pay, given the $O(m^3)$ naive algorithm, but also more than we *have* to pay: $P'(Z)$ includes only a subset of $Z \otimes Z$. Specifically, observe that the degree-2 terms in $P'(Z)$ all have the form $Z^a_{i,k} \cdot Z^b_{k,j}$.

The above suggests the following notation: for $x, y \in \mathbb{F}^{m^2}$, $x \oslash y$ consists of $\{x_{i,k} \cdot y_{k,j}\}$ for all i, j, k. The cardinality of $x \oslash y$ is m^3. Thus, letting $Z^a = (Z^a_{1,1}, \ldots, Z^a_{m,m})$ and $Z^b = (Z^b_{1,1}, \ldots, Z^b_{m,m})$, we write:

$$P'(Z) = \langle \gamma'_2, Z^a \oslash Z^b \rangle + \gamma'_0,$$

where $\gamma'_2 \in \mathbb{F}^{m^3}$ has the same non-zero components as γ_2. As in the base protocols, V wants to evaluate $P'(z)$ since $P'(z)$ is a bellwhether that indicates whether $Z = z$ meets all constraints (here, z is the satisfying assignment that is purportedly encoded in the oracle π).

This brings us to the second modification: the PCP encoding is now $\pi = \pi^{(c)}(\cdot) \triangleq \langle \cdot, z^a \oslash z^b \rangle$, where $z^a = A$ and $z^b = B$. To evaluate $P'(z)$, then, V asks for $\pi^{(c)}(\gamma'_2)$, and V tests whether $\pi^{(c)}(\gamma'_2) + \gamma_0 = 0$. This is our new circuit test; observe that it is $O(m^3)$ for the prover to answer, and for V to formulate a query. Like the base PCP protocols, this one requires two other types of tests. The first is again a linearity test, to ensure that $\pi^{(c)}$ is (nearly) linear. The second is

[5] Early in their paper Ishai et al. briefly mention such an approach, but they do not specify it. Later in their paper [45, §6.1], in a more general context, they reuse PCP queries but not commitment queries.

again a consistency test, to ensure that $\pi^{(c)}$ indeed represents $A \oslash B$; this test is modified from the base scheme. The details of the queries and tests, and proofs of their correctness, are in Appendix D. Finally, note that $\pi^{(c)}$ is a linear function, so it fits into the commit protocol (§3.4).

Low-degree polynomial evaluation. Suppose that we wish to evaluate a degree-D polynomial A over the variables $X = \{X_1, X_2, \ldots, X_m\}$. If we let A_k denote the vector of coefficients for the degree-k terms in A, then the evaluation of A at $X = x$ can be written $A(x) = \langle A_D, \bigotimes_{i=1}^{D} x \rangle + \cdots + \langle A_2, x \otimes x \rangle + \langle A_1, x \rangle + A_0$. For $D = 2$, we can represent the evaluation of A with a single degree-2 concise gate (§3.3), where the "assignment" z is simply x itself; then, computing $\pi^{(2)}$ in the base PCP encoding requires computing $x \otimes x$. Thus, if A is dense (meaning that it has $\Omega(m^2)$ monomials), the PCP encoding adds little prover overhead over computing $A(x)$. However, for $D = 3$, a naive application of the base protocol would include only degree-2 and degree-1 constraints, requiring prover work and query size of $O(m^4)$—higher complexity than the $O(m^3)$ computation.

We can remove this overhead, if A is dense. We modify the encoding so that the prover holds not only $\pi^{(1)}$ and $\pi^{(2)}$ (as in §2.1 and §3.3) but also $\pi^{(3)} : \mathbb{F}^{m^3} \to \mathbb{F}$, where $\pi^{(3)}(\cdot) \triangleq \langle \cdot, z \otimes z \otimes z \rangle$. As above, the "assignment" z is simply x itself. At this point, V must add several PCP queries to establish the (near) linearity of $\pi^{(3)}$ and the consistency of $\pi^{(3)}$ with $(\pi^{(1)}, \pi^{(2)})$. For details of the queries and tests, see [58, §7.8], which describes a similar construction. An analogous approach applies for $D > 3$ when D is odd; if D is even, there are "circuits" that add no overhead.

Savings and discussion. For matrix multiplication and degree-3 polynomial evaluation, the tailored PCP encoding reduces the prover's work and the query size from $O(m^4)$ to $O(m^3)$. In our domain of interest, m is hundreds or thousands, so the savings in V's querying costs are two or three orders of magnitude. The same factor is saved in the prover's costs. In fact, if the relevant objects (the matrices or polynomials) are dense, the prover's work to create the PCP is the same complexity as executing the computation.

There is a caveat, however. Though the prover is linear, the constant is not ideal. With matrix multiplication, for example, the prover's work is roughly $(h + f \cdot \mu) \cdot m^3$ (as depicted in the prover's rows in Figure 2). Meanwhile, there is an approach that costs the prover $f \cdot m^3$, namely Freivalds's randomized algorithm for verifying matrix multiplication [58, §7.1]: this algorithm requires $O(m^2)$ time for the verifier and no overhead for the "prover". More generally, we know that many computations admit special-purpose verification protocols (see §5). However, we believe that the work of this subsection is interesting because it refines the general-purpose PCP encodings and so might work for a broad class of other circuits.

4 Implementation and evaluation

We assess our work by answering three high-level questions, which correspond to the three goals for PEPPER that we stated in the introduction: (1) Is PEPPER simple enough to be easily implementable and optimizable? (2) For what values of the batch size, β, and the input size does PEPPER's verifier gain from outsourcing? (3) At these values, how much does PEPPER cost the prover? We answer these questions in the context of three model computations: matrix multiplication, degree-2 polynomial evaluation, and degree-3 polynomial evaluation. We chose these because they are self-contained test cases and core primitives in many applications. The rest of this section describes our implementation, parameter choices, and further optimizations (§4.1); then addresses the first question (§4.2); and then answers the latter two with experiments and analysis (§4.3–§4.7).

4.1 Implementation and optimizations

Implementation. Although PEPPER requires that computations be expressed over a finite field $\mathbb{F}$, we want to simulate computations over the integers (which requires simulating signed values and unbounded magnitudes). To that end, we use the standard technique of working in $\mathbb{F}_p$ (the integers modulo p), where p is a prime far larger than the actual input domain of the computation (e.g., see [22, 70]). In particular, we require the inputs (e.g., the matrix entries) to be 32-bit quantities and choose p to be either a 128-bit prime (for matrix multiplication and degree-2 polynomial evaluation) or a 192-bit prime (for degree-3 polynomial evaluation). To implement field operations (as needed for verification and the computations themselves), PEPPER uses multiprecision arithmetic, as implemented by the GNU MP library.

The core of the verifier and prover are implemented in C++. The prover can run as a Web service, with its interfaces exposed via HTTP URLs: we run the C++ prover core and helper PHP utilities as persistent FastCGI processes [2] to which the Apache Web server delegates HTTP requests.

Currently, our implementation parallelizes only the prover's commit phase, using OpenMP [3]. Parallelizing the verifier and the rest of the prover, and distributing the prover over multiple machines, are works in progress.

We implemented both Paillier [59] and ElGamal [32] homomorphic encryption. Because the ElGamal homomorphism is multiplicative, not additive, ElGamal requires minor modifications to the commitment protocol (Figure 3); these are described in Appendix E. Where the algorithms call for random numbers, we use pseudorandom numbers, as generated by the ChaCha/8 stream cipher [19], specifically the `amd64-xmm6` variant in its default configuration.

Parameter choices. PEPPER has three security parameters, which drive its total error of $\epsilon' < \epsilon + \epsilon^c$ (as given by Theorem B.1). The first parameter is ρ, the number of PCP repetitions, which determines the PCP soundness error through the bound $\epsilon < \kappa^{\rho}$. (Per Appendix A, $\kappa = 7/9$.) We usually take $\rho = 70$, yielding $\epsilon < 2.3 \cdot 10^{-8}$ for the PCP error. The second two parameters determine ϵ^c, the commitment soundness error. They are (a) $|\mathbb{F}|$, the size of the field for the PCP and commitment machinery, and (b) the homomorphic encryption scheme's key size, which determines ϵ_S, the error from encryption. From Appendix B, we have $\epsilon^c < 2^{14} \cdot (1/|\mathbb{F}| + \epsilon_S)^{1/3}$. We take $|\mathbb{F}| \approx 2^{128}$ (we discussed field size above) and disregard ϵ_S (we discuss key size below), yielding $\epsilon^c < 2^{-28}$.

We performed all of our experiments with both encryption schemes but report results only from ElGamal because its performance is better by almost a factor of 10 (as others have also observed [35]). By default, we take the prime modulus to be 704 bits, though we experiment with other sizes. Of course, 704 bits is not industrial strength for usual cryptographic applications. However, homomorphic encryptions (Figure 3) are a bottleneck for PEPPER, so we make a considered choice to use this key size. We believe that this choice is acceptable in our context, as the key need hold up only for one run of the protocol. Our choice is based on the RSA factoring challenge.[6]

Further optimizations: HABANERO. We report results from both PEPPER, whose design we have treated rigorously, and HABANERO, a PEPPER variant that has two performance improvements. First, under HABANERO, V *precomputes* and installs on P the commitment query, $\mathsf{Enc}(pk, r)$. Under this modification, we use an industrial-strength key length—1280 bits—as we intend to amortize this offline step over a long time. The soundness of this modification is counterintuitive; since we don't have space for a proof, we call it a heuristic. For intuition, we note that this modification generalizes the way that a single r is used for the entire batch (Appendix C). The second modification is to lower ρ from 70 to 1. This allows a prover to cheat with probability as high as $\kappa = 7/9$. However, if V and P interact repeatedly, a cheating prover would be detected.

4.2 Is PEPPER simple to implement and apply?

PEPPER is built on PCP theory, which requires a lot of detail to explain. At the same time, that theory results in a system whose mechanics are surprisingly simple. The verifier doesn't do much more than generate and encrypt some pseudorandomness (Section 3.4), ask the prover to multiply some vectors with a matrix that it holds (Sections 3.3 and 3.6), and perform basic operations on the returned vectors (Appendices A and D). Likewise, the prover doesn't need to do much more than determine the assignment z to "gates" (which it does anyway as a result of executing the algorithm), and return dot products.

component	language	lines of code
Crypto library	C++	549
Core library	C++	323
Prover library	C++	174
Verifier library	C++	280
Data exchange module	PHP	43
Helper utilities	C++	388
Computation-independent total		**1727**
matrix multiplication	C++	394
degree-2 polynomial evaluation	C++	462
degree-3 polynomial evaluation	C++	608

FIGURE 4—PEPPER's components and their lines of code.

Our sense of PEPPER's simplicity is buttressed by three things. The first is its small code size. Figure 4 tabulates the lines of code in our implementation (using [71]); the computation-independent modules require only 1727 lines.

Second, applying PEPPER to new computations has proved easy, in part because the "circuit" model of the computation is not very far from an imperative statement of the computation in C++ (§3.3). In fact, once our software architecture was in place, a single graduate student was able to implement new computations in less than an hour per computation. While this is obviously longer than it would take to code the computation with no verification, it is not a ridiculous amount of time. Moreover, a compiler could perform this step automatically.

Third, optimizing the implementation has so far been relatively easy. For example, parallelizing the prover's commitment phase required only three compiler directives and one C++ statement; this simple change gives a substantial speedup on multi-core hardware (as quantified below).

4.3 Experimental evaluation: method and setup

In the sections ahead, we will determine the input sizes (which we loosely refer to as m) and batch sizes (β) at which V gains from outsourcing versus computing locally, and we will report CPU and network costs at these points. We first run experiments to illuminate the prototype's performance (§4.4); then use this performance plus microbenchmarks to calibrate our CPU cost model from Figure 2 (§4.5); and then use the model to estimate break-even points under PEPPER, under HABANERO, and under the refinements that lead to them (§4.6). We treat network costs in §4.7.

Our baseline is local computation, which we assume uses multiprecision arithmetic. While this assumption deprives the baseline of native operations and hence may be an overly optimistic comparison for PEPPER, we note that it is not totally ridiculous: multiprecision arithmetic is a standard approach for avoiding overflow and roundoff concerns when multiplying and adding many large numbers.

To measure CPU usage at prover and verifier, we use

[6]In Nov. 2005 a 640-bit key was factored using "approximately 30 2.2GHz-Opteron-CPU years" and in Dec. 2009 a 768-bit key was factored using "almost 2000 2.2GHz-Opteron-CPU years" [4].

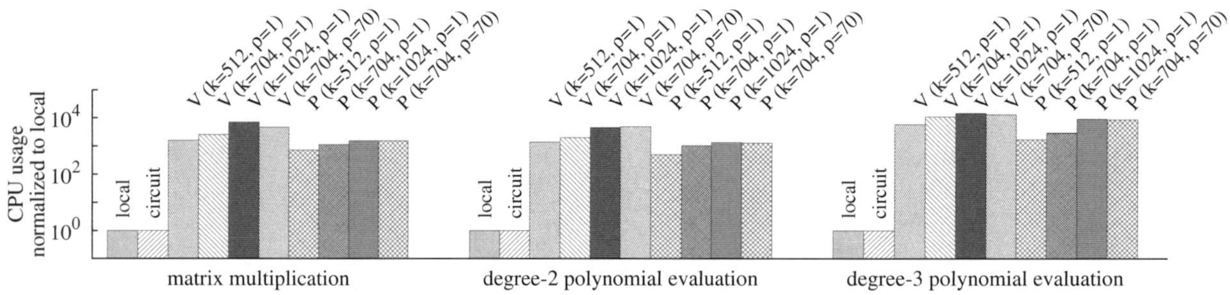

FIGURE 5—Measured CPU cost of one instance ($\beta = 1$) of PEPPER, compared to local execution, circuit execution, and under different security parameters (k is the key size, and ρ is the number of PCP repetitions), for verifier (V) and prover (P). For all computations, $m = 100$. Much of PEPPER's overhead is fixed-cost, so it amortizes under batching (see Figure 6).

getrusage(); to measure network costs, we record the amount of application-level data (not including network headers) exchanged between the prover and the verifier. We run our experiments on Utah Emulab's [72] d710s, which are 2.4 GHz 64-bit Intel Quad Core Xeon E5530 with 12 GB of memory; they run 64-bit Ubuntu 11.04 Linux.

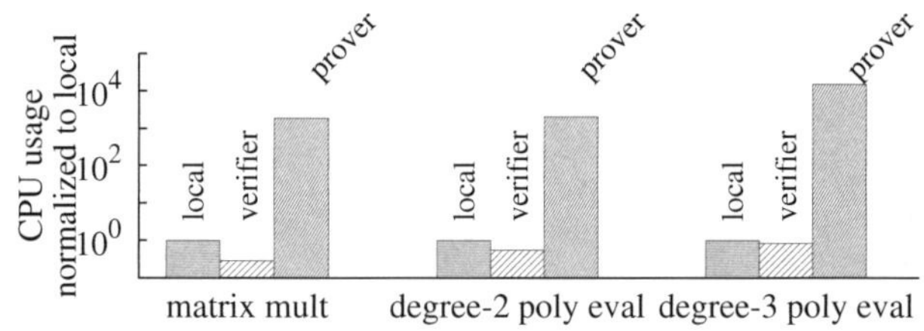

FIGURE 6—Measured CPU cost of the verifier and the prover in HABANERO, compared to local execution, for matrix multiplication ($m = 200$) under a batch size of $\beta = 100$, degree-2 polynomial evaluation ($m = 500$) under a batch size of $\beta = 200$, and degree-3 polynomial evaluation ($m = 200$) under a batch size of $\beta = 350$. At these batch sizes, the verifier gains from outsourcing.

4.4 What is PEPPER's end-to-end performance?

Beyond illustrating PEPPER's overhead, the experiments in this section are intended to assess the cost of the circuit representation; to indicate how the security parameters (§4.1) affect costs; and to illustrate how PEPPER's overhead can be mitigated by batching and parallelizing.

In the first set of experiments, our baseline is the CPU cost of local execution for matrix multiplication and polynomial evaluation (degrees 2 and 3), with $m = 100$ in all cases. We compare these baselines to executing the computation as a "circuit" but without verification. We also measure PEPPER, configured with smaller (512 bits) and larger (1024 bits) key sizes than our target (704 bits); these keys are not suitable for PEPPER (owing to insecurity and inefficiency, respectively), but they give a sense of what PEPPER pays for its cryptographic guarantees. Finally, we configure PEPPER to run with a single repetition ($\rho = 1$) and with multiple ones ($\rho = 70$). We do not depict HABANERO here.

We measure the CPU time at the verifier and prover consumed by PEPPER, end-to-end; this includes originating the queries, transferring them through the HTTP interface, handling responses, etc. The prover runs with one thread. For each configuration, we run 5 experiments, reporting average CPU time in seconds; standard deviations are within 5% of the means.

Figure 5 depicts the results. As shown in the figure, the circuit representation imposes no overhead. (Verification and proving are another matter—more on that soon.) The effect of PEPPER's security parameters is as follows. For matrix multiplication, PEPPER with 512-bit keys and 1024-bit keys costs, respectively, 1.7 times less and 1.9 times more than PEPPER with 704-bit keys (this holds for both prover and verifier); results for the other computations are similar. Interestingly, ρ has far less effect, since the cryptographic commitment amortizes over the ρ repetitions (§3.4).

Verification and proving clearly impose high overhead: for example, with degree-2 polynomial evaluation, the overhead over local computation is a factor of $3 \cdot 10^4$ for V and 10^4 for P. However, much of this cost is fixed and amortizes under batching (§3.5), as we demonstrate next.

Batching. We run HABANERO with multiple instances. We run 3 experiments for each computation, reporting mean CPU time (standard deviations are again within 5% of means). The prover runs with four threads; we report its cost as the sum of the CPU times taken by all four cores.

Figure 6 depicts the results. In these experiments, the verifier's cost is below the cost of local computation. (We will investigate break-even points systematically in Section 4.6.) The prover's cost is still high, but as we show next, parallelizing mitigates its latency.

Parallelizing. Here, we experiment with HABANERO, varying the number of threads (and hence cores) used. In each of the prover's two phases, we measure the wall clock time taken by the phase. We report the speedup with N cores as the ratio of total time taken (the sum of the two phases, over three trials) when one core is active to the time taken when N cores are active (again, over three trials).

	computation (Ψ)	batching (§3.5)	arith. circ. (§3.3)	new commit (§3.4)	new PCPs (§3.6)	HABANERO (§4.1)
β^* (break-even batch size)	matrix multiplication, $m = 400$	Never	$2.8 \cdot 10^{11}$	$7.1 \cdot 10^{7}$	$4.5 \cdot 10^{4}$	111
	matrix multiplication, $m = 1000$	Never	$2.0 \cdot 10^{11}$	$1.1 \cdot 10^{8}$	$2.7 \cdot 10^{4}$	111
	degree-2 polynomial eval, $m = 200$	Never	Never	$4.5 \cdot 10^{4}$	$4.5 \cdot 10^{4}$	180
	degree-2 polynomial eval, $m = 500$	Never	Never	$2.5 \cdot 10^{4}$	$2.5 \cdot 10^{4}$	118
	degree-3 polynomial eval, $m = 200$	Never	Never	$9.3 \cdot 10^{6}$	$4.6 \cdot 10^{4}$	221
	degree-3 polynomial eval, $m = 500$	$1.6 \cdot 10^{25}$	$6.0 \cdot 10^{10}$	$2.3 \cdot 10^{7}$	$4.6 \cdot 10^{4}$	220
V's computation time at β^*	matrix multiplication, $m = 400$	Never	9900 yr	2.5 yr	14 hr	2.1 min
	matrix multiplication, $m = 1000$	Never	$1.1 \cdot 10^{5}$ yr	61 yr	5.4 days	32 min
	degree-2 polynomial eval, $m = 200$	Never	Never	32 s	32 s	0.13 s
	degree-2 polynomial eval, $m = 500$	Never	Never	110 s	110 s	0.5 s
	degree-3 polynomial eval, $m = 200$	Never	Never	7.5 days	55 min	15 s
	degree-3 polynomial eval, $m = 500$	$5.6 \cdot 10^{17}$ yr	2100 yr	290 days	14 hr	4.0 min
P's computation time at β^*	matrix multiplication, $m = 400$	Never	$1.9 \cdot 10^{14}$ yr	$2.1 \cdot 10^{7}$ yr	8.1 yr	17 days
	matrix multiplication, $m = 1000$	Never	$5.4 \cdot 10^{15}$ yr	$1.3 \cdot 10^{9}$ yr	76 yr	260 days
	degree-2 polynomial eval, $m = 200$	Never	Never	45 hr	45 hr	24 min
	degree-2 polynomial eval, $m = 500$	Never	Never	6.2 days	6.2 days	1.6 hr
	degree-3 polynomial eval, $m = 200$	Never	Never	$7.1 \cdot 10^{4}$ yr	1.7 yr	5.8 days
	degree-3 polynomial eval, $m = 500$	$2.5 \cdot 10^{42}$ yr	$3.7 \cdot 10^{13}$ yr	$6.8 \cdot 10^{6}$ yr	27 yr	92 days

FIGURE 8—Estimated break-even points (β^*) and running times at those points under PEPPER's refinements, to two significant figures, obtained by (1) setting V's cost in Figure 2 equal to the cost of computing locally (also in Figure 2) and then (2) using the estimates of e, d, h, f, c (from Figure 7) to solve for β^*. Batching is required to make outsourcing profitable for V; without our refinements, the batch size is astronomical. Solving for m^* using more reasonable values of β also yields extremely large results. Our refinements bring these numbers into the realm of the conceivable. Both V and P can be parallelized to reduce latency; Section 4.4 describes the effect of parallelizing P.

key size	field size	e	d	h	f	c
704 bits (PEPPER)	128 bits	240 μs	95 μs	72 μs	18 ns	120 ns
704 bits (PEPPER)	192 bits	270 μs	95 μs	110 μs	45 ns	140 ns
1280 bits (HABANERO)	128 bits	660 μs	260 μs	200 μs	18 ns	120 ns
1280 bits (HABANERO)	192 bits	760 μs	260 μs	290 μs	45 ns	140 ns

FIGURE 7—Estimated parameters in our cost model (Figure 2), for the field and key sizes in our experiments.

For $N = 2$, the speedups are 1.99 in all three cases (the ideal is 2). For $N = 4$, the prover's end-to-end latency reduces by a factor of 3.7 for matrix multiplication, a factor of 3.7 for degree-3 polynomial evaluation, and a factor of 3.1 for degree-2 polynomial evaluation (the ideal is 4). We hypothesize that the latter computation sees smaller speedup because the computation is far smaller, so fixed setup costs are comparatively larger. These results suggest that there is profit in distributing the prover over multiple machines.

4.5 Calibrating the cost models

We use a cost model for each of our computations; Figure 2 depicts the one for matrix multiplication.[7] When making predictions about HABANERO (versus PEPPER), we adjust the models to remove the cost of issuing commit queries and to set $\rho = 1$. Note that, for simplicity, the models include field multiplication (f) but not field addition. Nevertheless, for the purposes of estimating break-even points, the models are pessimistic for PEPPER. First, not counting additions underestimates the number of operations in the baseline computation. Second, the models overestimate PEPPER's operations. Specifically, the models more than compensate for the omitted field additions (which PEPPER performs in equal number to field multiplications) by double-counting field multiplications (which are more expensive).[8]

To estimate the parameters, we run a program that executes each operation at least 5000 times, using 704-bit and 1280-bit keys. Figure 7 shows the means (standard deviations are within 5% of the means). The two field sizes yield different parameter values because in the cryptographic operations, field entries appear in exponents.

How well do our models predict the end-to-end empirical results (§4.4)? The prover's costs are at most 8% above the model's prediction. The verifier's costs are at most 50% above what the model predicts. However, much of this difference can be explained by the cost of I/O operations (to files and the network); subtracting this cost from the verifier's measured performance yields an estimate that is at most 10% above the model's prediction. Finally, the base-

computation (Ψ)	network costs
matrix multiplication, $m = 400$	17.1 GB
matrix multiplication, $m = 1000$	263 GB
degree-2 polynomial eval, $m = 200$	11.4 MB
degree-2 polynomial eval, $m = 500$	68.4 MB
degree-3 polynomial eval, $m = 200$	2.93 GB
degree-3 polynomial eval, $m = 500$	45.8 GB

FIGURE 9—Estimated network costs under HABANERO for the computations and break-even points (β^*) in Figure 8. These costs are significant but amortize under batching.

[7]Not depicted is an additive $2e$ term in the "Process PCP responses" row, from the modified check under ElGamal (see §4.1 and Appendix E).

[8]The reason for the double-counting is that we take ℓ, the number of PCP queries per repetition, as equal to 14, but in reality only *seven* of those 14 queries are submitted to the high-order proof (see Appendix A).

line's empirical costs range between 20% and 100% more than the model's predictions. We hypothesize that this divergence results from the model's omitting field additions (as discussed above) and from adverse caching behavior.

4.6 What are the break-even points?

Given the model's rough accuracy, it can systematically (if roughly) make predictions about break-even points—that is, about PEPPER's regime of applicability. We set V's costs in the (now parameterized) models equal to the cost of local computation, and solve for β^*, the batch size at which V gains from outsourcing under PEPPER. We do not account for the cost of serialization (this part of our implementation is unoptimized) so may slightly underestimate β^* (by a factor nearly equal to the overhead of serialization).

Figure 8 depicts the estimated break-even points. Under PEPPER (the column marked "new PCPs"), the numbers are sometimes reasonable for V. The latency from P is, ahem, somewhat larger. However, we would ask the reader to look leftward on this table to see what the numbers *used* to look like. Under HABANERO, we do not need to appeal to relativism quite as much: V gains from outsourcing at reasonable batch sizes, and while P's latency is surely high, the work can be parallelized and distributed (see §4.4). For example, if P used 128 cores, we would expect its latency to be on the order of hours or less for all but one of the rows.

4.7 What are the network costs?

The main network expense is from issuing queries (see Figure 3). To assess this cost, we estimate the sizes of the queries and responses, applying this simple model to the computations at the break-even points in Figure 8. (For HABANERO, we count only PCP queries; commitment queries are assumed to be pre-installed.) We separately validate by comparing to predictions with various experimental runs, finding that the model is within 3% of the measured traffic.

Figure 9 depicts the estimates, under HABANERO. These costs are obviously significant. However, compared to the prover's running time, the latency from network costs is not high. Moreover, PEPPER's network overhead amortizes, as the query cost stays fixed with increasing β. By contrast, some plausible baselines (for example, replicating the computation to multiple workers) have network overhead in proportion to β.

5 Related work

There has been a lot of work on verified computation, and the motivation of outsourcing to the cloud has given a new impetus to this area. In this section we try to situate our work in this landscape. We note that our work is concerned only with verifying computations, not hiding their content or input; thus, even though some of the works that we cite below achieve such hiding, our comparison will be silent about this property. Also, we do not summarize work that adopts a different threat model, such as multiple provers [10, 43] or assumptions about the difficulty of mimicking valid program counter values [67].

General-purpose approaches intended for practice. Perhaps the most basic technique, replication [6, 25, 42, 52, 56], relies on assumptions about the independence of the workers, in contrast to our goal of unconditional verification. Trusted computing [27, 62] assumes that the hardware or a hypervisor works properly. Some attestation work, though powerful, gives assurance that a remote application has desired properties but not that it is implemented correctly [26, 53, 63, 66]. Other attestation work requires a trusted base [5, 54]. Auditing and spot-checking [31, 42, 46, 50, 57] focus directly on the output, but unless the audit coverage is nearly perfect (which degenerates to executing the computation), a worker that alters a key bit (e.g., in an intermediate step) is unlikely to be detected, in contrast to the properties of PCPs (§2.1).

Special-purpose approaches from theory and practice. Recent work by Benabbas et al. [18] and Boneh and Freeman [22] outsources polynomial evaluation, which inspired our use of this computation (§3.6, §4). Ergun et al. [33] study efficient approximate property testing protocols for polynomials and related computations. Golle [40] outsources the inversion of one-way functions, and Karame et al. [47] apply this to detect cheating in a distributed sequential computation. Sion [65] and Thompson et al. [68] outsource database operations. Wang et al. outsource linear programming [69] and approximating systems of linear equations [70]. Atallah has protocols for linear algebra (see [10] and citations therein). Other work [34, 61] handles aggregate statistics computed from distributed sensors. While some of these works inspired our choice of particular computations, our focus is on general-purpose approaches.

Homomorphic encryption and secure multiparty protocols. Homomorphic encryption is a powerful building block, as it lets the prover compute over ciphertext. Groth uses homomorphic encryption to produce a zero-knowledge argument protocol [41]; unfortunately, a preliminary feasibility study that we performed indicated that this was not efficient enough for our purposes. Gentry's recent breakthrough construction of a fully homomorphic encryption scheme [37] has led to new protocols for verifiable non-interactive computation [28, 36] with input hiding. However, fully homomorphic encryption is completely infeasible on today's computers.

Closely related are secure multi-party protocols. In such protocols, parties compute an agreed-upon function of private data, revealing only the result [73]. In fact, the scheme of [36] builds such a protocol based on fully homomorphic encryption. Other general-purpose protocols for computation on hidden data using homomorphic encryption include the work of [7] and the circuit application of the Boneh-Goh-Nissim cryptosystem [23]. However, in general, because of the input hiding requirements, the costs for the verifier are proportional to the size of the circuit; such protocols are not really suitable in our context. Moreover, while general-purpose compilers for such protocols exist [13, 44, 51], they are not yet practical, despite the striking improvements reported in [44].

PCPs, argument systems, and efficient interactive protocols. The potential of PCPs and efficient arguments to serve as a foundation for verified computations has long been known to theorists [8, 9, 11, 14, 20, 39, 48, 49, 55]. We borrow from this theory, guided by our goals. We turn to argument systems because advances in short (non-interactive) PCPs [15–17, 30, 60] seem too intricate to be implemented easily; e.g., they require recursive application of their own machinery. And among interactive approaches, we build upon the scheme of [45], which is simple, instead of upon an interactive protocol that is asymptotically more efficient but far more intricate [38]. We now review recent work that makes the opposite decision.

Following our position paper [64], Cormode, Mitzenmacher, and Thaler have a recent publication [29] with similar positioning. As with our system, they obtain a lot of mileage from the observation that arithmetic circuits and concise gates are compatible with the protocols and result in substantially more efficient encodings. Some of their focus is on specialized algorithms for linear problems in the streaming model. However, they also describe a general-purpose implementation, based on [38] instead of [45]. On the one hand, the protocol of [38] does not require public-key cryptography and has better asymptotic overhead than that of [45]. On the other hand, the protocol of [45] has better round complexity and does not require uniformity assumptions on the circuit families in question. A more detailed comparison using measurements on benchmark problems is work in progress.

6 Discussion, next steps, and outlook

This work began from the intuition that the protocol of Ishai et al. [45] might lead to a simple and potentially practical built system, and PEPPER appears to have fulfilled that promise: the verifier is relatively inexpensive, the prover is much better than we expected, the protocol is simple, and the tailored scheme is not so far from true practicality. A deployable system is plausibly within view.

Nonetheless, there is still much work to do to get PEPPER ready for prime time. Its protocols are still not cheap enough, particularly for the prover. Its model of computation is restrictive: we studied problems that admit concise expressions with arithmetic circuits performing multi-precision arithmetic (§3.3, §4.1), with a focus on problems that allow decomposition into identical parallel modules (§3.5) or permit tailored PCPs (§3.6). And while for arbitrary computations, one can theoretically apply PEPPER—by compiling the computation to a circuit with, say, the compiler developed as part of the Fairplay system [13, 44, 51]—our estimates indicate that this approach is unlikely to achieve acceptable performance and that a more specialized compiler is necessary.

The good news is that substantial further improvements seem possible. In the short term, there is much to be gained from engineering: a move to elliptic curve cryptography will allow us to improve the security parameters while decreasing overhead, and we plan to explore special-purpose hardware for modular exponentiation. We are working on compilers to automate the manual process described in Section 4.2; the goal is to output our non-tailored protocol for suitable computations and (when applicable) to generate the tailored PCPs that produce the most practical scheme (§3.6).

More broadly, the key challenge for this area is to expand the approach beyond computations that are naturally specified as arithmetic circuits over finite fields. For instance, a basic issue is handling floating point numerics efficiently. More generally, handling computations with interesting control flow is a central problem. Satisfactory answers to these questions will help realize the vision of making efficient arguments (and PCPs) truly practical.

Acknowledgments

Nikhil Panpalia created the parallel prover implementation. For helpful comments, we thank Lorenzo Alvisi, Dan Boneh, Allen Clement, Mike Freedman, Maxwell Krohn, Josh Leners, Antonio Nicolosi, Bryan Parno, Raluca Popa, Victor Vu, Shabsi Walfish, Ed Wong, Hao Wu, and the anonymous reviewers. Emulab was helpful as always. The research was supported by AFOSR grant FA9550-10-1-0073 and by NSF grants 1055057 and 1040083.

Our implementation and experimental configurations are available at: `http://www.cs.utexas.edu/pepper`

References

[1] Berkeley Open Infrastructure for Network Computing (BOINC). `http://boinc.berkeley.edu`.

[2] FastCGI. `http://www.fastcgi.com/`.

[3] OpenMP. `http://openmp.org/`.

[4] The RSA Challenge Numbers. `http://www.rsa.com/rsalabs/node.asp?id=2093`.

[5] S. Alsouri, Ö. Dagdelen, and S. Katzenbeisser. Group-based attestation: Enhancing privacy and management in remote attestation. In *TRUST*, 2010.

[6] D. P. Anderson, J. Cobb, E. Korpela, M. Lebofsky, and D. Werthimer. SETI@home: An experiment in public-resource computing. *CACM*, 45(11):56–61, Nov. 2002.

[7] B. Applebaum, Y. Ishai, and E. Kushilevitz. From secrecy to soundness: efficient verification via secure computation. In *ICALP*, 2010.

[8] S. Arora, C. Lund, R. Motwani, M. Sudan, and M. Szegedy. Proof verification and the hardness of approximation problems. *J. of the ACM*, 45(3):501–555, May 1998.
[9] S. Arora and S. Safra. Probabilistic checking of proofs: a new characterization of NP. *J. of the ACM*, 45(1):70–122, Jan. 1998.
[10] M. J. Atallah and K. B. Frikken. Securely outsourcing linear algebra computations. In *ASIACCS*, 2010.
[11] L. Babai, L. Fortnow, L. A. Levin, and M. Szegedy. Checking computations in polylogarithmic time. In *STOC*, 1991.
[12] M. Bellare, D. Coppersmith, J. Håstad, M. Kiwi, and M. Sudan. Linearity testing in characteristic two. *IEEE Transactions on Information Theory*, 42(6):1781–1795, Nov. 1996.
[13] A. Ben-David, N. Nisan, and B. Pinkas. FairplayMP: A system for secure multi-party computation. In *ACM CCS*, 2008.
[14] M. Ben-Or, S. Goldwasser, J. Kilian, and A. Wigderson. Multi-prover interactive proofs: how to remove intractability assumptions. In *STOC*, 1988.
[15] E. Ben-Sasson, O. Goldreich, P. Harsha, M. Sudan, and S. Vadhan. Short PCPs verifiable in polylogarithmic time. In *Conference on Computational Complexity (CCC)*, 2005.
[16] E. Ben-Sasson, O. Goldreich, P. Harsha, M. Sudan, and S. Vadhan. Robust PCPs of proximity, shorter PCPs and applications to coding. *SIAM J. on Comp.*, 36(4):889–974, Dec. 2006.
[17] E. Ben-Sasson and M. Sudan. Short PCPs with polylog query complexity. *SIAM J. on Comp.*, 38(2):551–607, May 2008.
[18] S. Benabbas, R. Gennaro, and Y. Vahlis. Verifiable delegation of computation over large datasets. In *CRYPTO*, 2011.
[19] D. J. Bernstein. ChaCha, a variant of Salsa20. `http://cr.yp.to/chacha.html`.
[20] M. Blum and S. Kannan. Designing programs that check their work. *J. of the ACM*, 42(1):269–291, 1995.
[21] M. Blum, M. Luby, and R. Rubinfeld. Self-testing/correcting with applications to numerical problems. *J. of Comp. and Sys. Sciences*, 47(3):549–595, Dec. 1993.
[22] D. Boneh and D. M. Freeman. Homomorphic signatures for polynomial functions. In *EUROCRYPT*, 2011.
[23] D. Boneh, E. J. Goh, and K. Nissim. Evaluating 2-DNF formulas on ciphertexts. In *TCC*, 2005.
[24] G. Brassard, D. Chaum, and C. Crépeau. Minimum disclosure proofs of knowledge. *J. of Comp. and Sys. Sciences*, 37(2):156–189, 1988.
[25] M. Castro and B. Liskov. Practical Byzantine fault tolerance and proactive recovery. *ACM Trans. on Computer Sys.*, 20(4):398–461, 2002.
[26] L. Chen, R. Landfermann, H. Löhr, M. Rohe, A.-R. Sadeghi, C. Stüble, and H. Görtz. A protocol for property-based attestation. In *ACM Workshop on Scalable Trusted Computing*, 2006.
[27] A. Chiesa and E. Tromer. Proof-carrying data and hearsay arguments from signature cards. In *ICS*, 2010.
[28] K.-M. Chung, Y. Kalai, and S. Vadhan. Improved delegation of computation using fully homomorphic encryption. In *CRYPTO*, 2010.
[29] G. Cormode, M. Mitzenmacher, and J. Thaler. Practical verified computation with streaming interactive proofs. In *ITCS*, 2012.
[30] I. Dinur. The PCP theorem by gap amplification. *J. of the ACM*, 54(3), June 2007.
[31] W. Du, J. Jia, M. Mangal, and M. Murugesan. Uncheatable grid computing. In *IEEE Intl. Conf. on Dist. Computing Sys. (ICDCS)*, 2004.
[32] T. ElGamal. A public key cryptosystem and a signature scheme based on discrete logarithms. *IEEE Transactions on Information Theory*, 31:469–472, 1985.
[33] F. Ergun, R. Kumar, and R. Rubinfeld. Approximate checking of polynomials and functional equations. In *FOCS*, 1996.
[34] M. Garofalakis, J. M. Hellerstein, and P. Maniatis. Proof sketches: Verifiable in-network aggregation. In *ICDE*, 2007.
[35] S. Garriss, M. Kaminsky, M. J. Freedman, B. Karp, D. Mazières, and H. Yu. RE: Reliable Email. In *NSDI*, 2006.
[36] R. Gennaro, C. Gentry, and B. Parno. Non-interactive verifiable computing: Outsourcing computation to untrusted workers. In *CRYPTO*, 2010.
[37] C. Gentry. *A fully homomorphic encryption scheme*. PhD thesis, Stanford University, 2009.
[38] S. Goldwasser, Y. T. Kalai, and G. N. Rothblum. Delegating computation: Interactive proofs for muggles. In *STOC*, 2008.
[39] S. Goldwasser, S. Micali, and C. Rackoff. The knowledge complexity of interactive proof systems. *SIAM J. on Comp.*, 18(1):186–208, 1989.
[40] P. Golle and I. Mironov. Uncheatable distributed computations. In *RSA Conference*, 2001.
[41] J. Groth. Linear algebra with sub-linear zero-knowledge arguments. In *CRYPTO*, 2009.
[42] A. Haeberlen, P. Kouznetsov, and P. Druschel. PeerReview: Practical accountability for distributed systems. In *SOSP*, 2007.
[43] S. Hohenberger and A. Lysyanskaya. How to securely outsource crytographic computations. In *TCC*, 2005.
[44] Y. Huang, D. Evans, J. Katz, and L. Malka. Faster secure two-party computation using garbled circuits. In *USENIX Security*, 2011.
[45] Y. Ishai, E. Kushilevitz, and R. Ostrovsky. Efficient arguments without short PCPs. In *Conference on Computational Complexity (CCC)*, 2007.
[46] S. Jha, S. Katzenbeisser, C. Schallhart, H. Veith, and S. Chenney. Semantic integrity in large-scale online simulations. *ACM Transactions on Internet Technology (TOIT)*, 10(1), Feb. 2010.
[47] G. O. Karame, M. Strasser, and S. Capkun. Secure remote execution of sequential computations. In *International Conference on Information and Communications Security (ICICS)*, 2009.
[48] J. Kilian. A note on efficient zero-knowledge proofs and arguments (extended abstract). In *STOC*, 1992.
[49] J. Kilian. Improved efficient arguments (preliminary version). In *CRYPTO*, 1995.
[50] L. Kissner and D. Song. Verifying server computations. In *ACNS*, 2004.
[51] D. Malkhi, N. Nisan, B. Pinkas, and Y. Sella. Fairplay: A secure two-party computation system. In *USENIX Security*, 2004.
[52] D. Malkhi and M. Reiter. Byzantine quorum systems. *Distributed Computing*, 11(4):203–213, 1998.
[53] J. M. McCune, Y. Li, N. Qu, Z. Zhou, A. Datta, V. Gligor, and A. Perrig. TrustVisor: Efficient TCB reduction and attestation. In *IEEE Symposium on Security and Privacy*, 2010.
[54] J. M. McCune, B. J. Parno, A. Perrig, M. K. Reiter, and H. Isozaki. Flicker: An execution infrastructure for TCB minimization. In *EuroSys*, 2008.
[55] S. Micali. Computationally sound proofs. *SIAM J. on Comp.*, 30(4):1253–1298, 2000.
[56] N. Michalakis, R. Soulé, and R. Grimm. Ensuring content integrity for untrusted peer-to-peer content distribution networks. In *NSDI*, 2007.
[57] F. Monrose, P. Wycko, and A. D. Rubin. Distributed execution with remote audit. In *NDSS*, 1999.
[58] R. Motwani and P. Raghavan. *Randomized Algorithms*. Cambridge University Press, 1995.
[59] P. Paillier. Public-key cryptosystems based on composite degree residuosity classes. In *EUROCRYPT*. Springer-Verlag, 1999.
[60] A. Polishchuk and D. A. Spielman. Nearly-linear size holographic proofs. In *STOC*, 1994.
[61] B. Przydatek, D. Song, and A. Perrig. SIA: Secure information aggregation in sensor networks. In *ACM Sensys*, 2003.
[62] A.-R. Sadeghi, T. Schneider, and M. Winandy. Token-based cloud computing: secure outsourcing of data and arbitrary computations with lower latency. In *TRUST*, June 2010.
[63] A. Seshadri, M. Luk, E. Shi, A. Perrig, L. van Doorn, and P. Khosla.

Pioneer: Verifying integrity and guaranteeing execution of code on legacy platforms. In *SOSP*, 2005.
[64] S. Setty, A. J. Blumberg, and M. Walfish. Toward practical and unconditional verification of remote computations. In *Proc. Workshop on Hot Topics in Operating Systems (HotOS)*, 2011.
[65] R. Sion. Query execution assurance for outsourced databases. In *VLDB*, 2005.
[66] F. Stumpf, A. Fuchs, S. Katzenbeisser, and C. Eckert. Improving the scalability of platform attestation. In *ACM Workshop on Scalable Trusted Computing*, 2008.
[67] S. Tang, A. R. Butt, Y. C. Hu, and S. P. Midkiff. Lightweight monitoring of the progress of remotely executing computations. In *International Workshop on Languages and Compilers for Parallel Computing*, 2005.
[68] B. Thompson, S. Haber, W. G. Horne, T. Sander, and D. Yao. Privacy-preserving computation and verification of aggregate queries on outsourced databases. In *PET*, 2009.
[69] C. Wang, K. Ren, and J. Wang. Secure and practical outsourcing of linear programming in cloud computing. In *INFOCOM*, Apr. 2011.
[70] C. Wang, K. Ren, J. Wang, and K. M. R. Urs. Harnessing the cloud for securely outsourcing large-scale systems of linear equations. In *IEEE Intl. Conf. on Dist. Computing Sys. (ICDCS)*, 2011.
[71] D. A. Wheeler. SLOCCount. `http://www.dwheeler.com/sloccount/`.
[72] B. White, J. Lepreau, L. Stoller, R. Ricci, S. Guruprasad, M. Newbold, M. Hibler, C. Barb, and A. Joglekar. An integrated experimental environment for distributed systems and networks. In *OSDI*, Dec. 2002.
[73] A. C.-C. Yao. How to generate and exchange secrets. In *FOCS*, 1986.

A A linear PCP

We state the queries, then the tests, then the statement of correctness of the PCP in [8, §5–6]. We use $\in_R$ to mean a uniformly random selection. The purpose of q_{10}, q_{12}, q_{14} below is *self-correction*; see [8, §5] or [58, §7.8.3] for details.

- Generate linearity queries: Select $q_1, q_2 \in_R \mathbb{F}^s$ and $q_4, q_5 \in_R \mathbb{F}^{s^2}$. Take $q_3 \leftarrow q_1 + q_2$ and $q_6 \leftarrow q_4 + q_5$.
- Generate quadratic correction queries: Select $q_7, q_8 \in_R \mathbb{F}^s$ and $q_{10} \in_R \mathbb{F}^{s^2}$. Take $q_9 \leftarrow (q_7 \otimes q_8 + q_{10})$.
- Generate circuit queries: Select $q_{12} \in_R \mathbb{F}^s$ and $q_{14} \in_R \mathbb{F}^{s^2}$. Take $q_{11} \leftarrow \gamma_1 + q_{12}$ and $q_{13} \leftarrow \gamma_2 + q_{14}$.
- Issue queries. Send queries $q_1, \ldots, q_{14}$ to oracle π, getting back $\pi(q_1), \ldots, \pi(q_{14})$.
- Linearity tests: Check that $\pi(q_1) + \pi(q_2) = \pi(q_3)$ and that $\pi(q_4) + \pi(q_5) = \pi(q_6)$. If not, `reject`.
- Quadratic correction test: Check that $\pi(q_7) \cdot \pi(q_8) = \pi(q_9) - \pi(q_{10})$. If not, `reject`.
- Circuit test: Check that $(\pi(q_{11}) - \pi(q_{12})) + (\pi(q_{13}) - \pi(q_{14})) = -\gamma_0$. If so, `accept`.

The $\gamma_0, \gamma_1, \gamma_2$ above are described in §2.1. The following lemmas rephrase Lemmas 6.2 and 6.3 from [8]:

Lemma A.1 (Completeness [8]). Assume V is given a satisfiable circuit $\mathcal{C}$. If π is constructed as in Section 2.1, and if V proceeds as above, then $\Pr\{V \text{ accepts } \mathcal{C}\} = 1$. The probability is over V's random choices.

Lemma A.2 (Soundness [8]). There exists a constant $\kappa < 1$ such that if some proof oracle π passes all of the tests above on $\mathcal{C}$ with probability $> \kappa$, then $\mathcal{C}$ is satisfiable.

Applying the analysis in [8], we can take $\kappa > \max\{7/9, 4\delta + 2/|\mathbb{F}|, 4\delta + 1/|\mathbb{F}|\}$ for some δ such that $3\delta - 6\delta^2 > 2/9$. This ensures soundness for all three tests. Here, δ relates to linearity testing [21]; to justify the constraint on δ and its connection to the $7/9$ floor on κ, see [12] and citations therein. Taking $\delta = \frac{1}{10}$, we can take $\kappa = 7/9 + \text{neg}$, where neg can be ignored; thus, for convenience, we assume $\kappa = 7/9$. Applying the lemma, we have that if the protocol is run $\rho = 70$ times and $\mathcal{C}$ is not satisfiable, V wrongly accepts with probability $\epsilon < \kappa^\rho < 2.3 \cdot 10^{-8}$.

B Reducing linear PCPs to arguments

This section first reduces PCPs to arguments directly, using Commit+Multidecommit (Figure 3); this will formalize Figure 1. The soundness of the reduction relies on Commit+Multidecommit actually binding the prover after the commit phase. Thus, the second (bulkier) part of the section defines a new and strengthened commitment protocol (Defn. B.1), proves that Commit+Multidecommit implements this protocol (Lemma B.1), and proves that any such protocol binds the prover in the way required by the reduction (Lemma B.2).

The reduction composes a PCP (such as the one in Appendix A) with Commit+Multidecommit. The protocol, theorem, and proof immediately below are almost entirely a syntactic substitution in [45, §4], replacing "MIP" with "PCP".

Given a linear PCP with soundness ϵ, the following is an argument system (P', V'). Assume that (P', V') get a Boolean circuit $\mathcal{C}$ and that P' has a satisfying assignment.

1. P' and V' run Commit+Multidecommit's commit phase, causing P' to commit to a function, π.
2. V' runs the PCP verifier V on $\mathcal{C}$ to obtain $\mu = \ell \cdot \rho$ queries $q_1, \ldots, q_\mu$.
3. P' and V' run the decommit phase of Commit+Multidecommit. V' uses $q_1, \ldots, q_\mu$ as the queries. V' either rejects the decommitted output, or it treats the output as $\pi(q_1), \ldots, \pi(q_\mu)$. To these outputs, V' applies the PCP verifier V. V' outputs `accept` or `reject` depending on what V would do.

Theorem B.1. Suppose (P, V) is a linear PCP with soundness ϵ. Then (P', V') described above is an argument protocol with soundness $\epsilon' \leq \epsilon + \epsilon^c$. ($\epsilon^c$ represents the error from the commitment protocol and will be filled in by Lemma B.2.)

Proof. Completeness follows from the PCP and the definition of Commit+Multidecommit. For soundness, Lemma B.2 below states that at the end of step 1 above, there is an extractor function that defines a single (possibly incorrect) oracle function $\tilde{\pi}$ such that, if V' didn't reject during decommit, then with all but probability ϵ^c, the answers that V' gets in step 3 are $\tilde{\pi}(q_1), \ldots, \tilde{\pi}(q_\mu)$. But (P, V) has soundness ϵ, so the probability that V' accepts a non-satisfiable $\mathcal{C}$ is bounded by $\epsilon + \epsilon^c$. □

We now strengthen the commitment primitive in Ishai et al. [45], borrowing their framework. We define a protocol: *commitment to a function with multiple decommitments* (CFMD). The sender is assumed to have a linear function, π, given by a vector, $w \in \mathbb{F}^n$; that is, $\pi(q) = \langle w, q \rangle$. In our context, w is normally $(z, z \otimes z)$. The receiver has μ queries, $q_1, q_2, \ldots, q_\mu \in \mathbb{F}^n$. For each query q_i, the receiver expects $\pi(q_i) = \langle w, q_i \rangle \in \mathbb{F}$.

Definition B.1 (Commitment to a function with multiple decommitments (CFMD)). Define a two-phase experiment between two probabilistic polynomial time actors (S, R) (a sender and receiver, which correspond to our prover and verifier) in an environment $\mathcal{E}$ that generates $\mathbb{F}$, w and $Q = (q_1, \ldots, q_\mu)$. In the first phase, the *commit phase*, S has w, and S and R interact, based on their random inputs. In the *decommit phase*, $\mathcal{E}$ gives Q to R, and S and R interact again, based on further random inputs. At the end of this second phase, R outputs $A = (a_1, \ldots, a_\mu) \in \mathbb{F}^\mu$ or $\perp$. A CFMD meets the following properties:

- **Correctness**. At the end of the decommit phase, R outputs $\pi(q_i) = \langle w, q_i \rangle$ (for all i), if S is honest.
- **ϵ_B-Binding**. Consider the following experiment. The environment $\mathcal{E}$ produces two (possibly) distinct μ-tuples of queries: $Q = (q_1, \ldots, q_\mu)$ and $\hat{Q} = (\hat{q}_1, \ldots, \hat{q}_\mu)$. R and a cheating S^* run the commit phase once and two independent instances of the decommit phase. In the two instances R presents the queries as Q and $\hat{Q}$, respectively. We say that S^* *wins* if R's outputs at the end of the respective decommit phases are $A = (a_1, \ldots, a_\mu)$ and $\hat{A} = (\hat{a}_1, \ldots, \hat{a}_\mu)$, and for some i, j, we have $q_i = \hat{q}_j$ but $a_i \neq \hat{a}_j$. We say that the protocol meets the ϵ_B-Binding property if for all $\mathcal{E}$ and for all efficient S^*, the probability of S^* winning is less than ϵ_B. The probability is taken over three sets of independent randomness: the commit phase and the two runnings of the decommit phase.

Informally, binding means that after the sender commits, it is very likely bound to a function from queries to answers.

Lemma B.1. Commit+Multidecommit (Figure 3, Section 3.4) is a CFMD protocol with $\epsilon_B = 1/|\mathbb{F}| + \epsilon_S$, where ϵ_S comes from the semantic security of the homomorphic encryption scheme.

Proof. Correctness: for an honest sender, $b = \pi(t) = \pi(r) + \sum_{i=1}^{\mu} \pi(\alpha_i \cdot q_i) = s + \sum_{i=1}^{\mu} \alpha_i \cdot \pi(q_i) = s + \sum_{i=1}^{\mu} \alpha_i \cdot a_i$, which implies that $b = s + \sum_{i=1}^{\mu} \alpha_i \cdot a_i$, and so verification passes, with the receiver outputting $\pi(q_1), \ldots, \pi(q_\mu)$.

To show ϵ_B-binding, we will show that if S^* *can* systematically cheat, then an adversary $\mathcal{A}$ could use S^* to break the semantic security of the encryption scheme. Assume that Commit+Multidecommit does not meet ϵ_B-binding. Then there exists an efficient cheating sender S^* and an environment $\mathcal{E}$ producing $Q, \hat{Q}, i, j$ such that $q \triangleq q_i = \hat{q}_j$ and S^* can make R output $a_i \neq \hat{a}_j$ with probability $> \epsilon_B$.

We will construct an algorithm $\mathcal{A}$ that differentiates between $\alpha, \alpha' \in_R \mathbb{F}$ with probability more than $1/|\mathbb{F}| + \epsilon_S$ when given as input the following: a public key, pk; the encryption, $\mathsf{Enc}(pk, r)$, of r for a random vector $r \in \mathbb{F}^n$; $r + \alpha q$; and $r + \alpha' q$. This will contradict the semantic security of the encryption scheme. $\mathcal{A}$ has Q, q, i, j hard-wired (because $\mathcal{A}$ is working under environment $\mathcal{E}$) and works as follows:

(a) $\mathcal{A}$ gives S^* the input $(pk, \mathsf{Enc}(pk, r))$; $\mathcal{A}$ gets back e from S^* and ignores it.

(b) $\mathcal{A}$ randomly chooses $\alpha_1, \ldots, \alpha_{i-1}, \alpha_{i+1}, \ldots, \alpha_\mu$. It also randomly chooses $\hat{\alpha}_1, \ldots, \hat{\alpha}_{j-1}, \hat{\alpha}_{j+1}, \ldots, \hat{\alpha}_\mu$.

(c) $\mathcal{A}$ now leverages Q, q, i, j. $\mathcal{A}$ was given $r + \alpha q$, so it can construct $r + \alpha q + \sum_{k \in [\mu] \setminus i} \alpha_k q_k = r + Q \cdot \boldsymbol{\alpha}$, where $\boldsymbol{\alpha} = (\alpha_1, \ldots, \alpha_{i-1}, \alpha, \alpha_{i+1}, \ldots, \alpha_\mu)$. $\mathcal{A}$ gives S^* the input $(Q, r + Q \cdot \boldsymbol{\alpha})$; that is, $\mathcal{A}$ invokes S^* in the decommit phase. $\mathcal{A}$ gets back (A, b).

(d) Likewise, $\mathcal{A}$ constructs $r + \alpha' q + \sum_{k \in [\mu] \setminus j} \hat{\alpha}_k \hat{q}_k = r + \hat{Q} \cdot \hat{\boldsymbol{\alpha}}$, where $\hat{\boldsymbol{\alpha}} = (\hat{\alpha}_1, \ldots, \hat{\alpha}_{j-1}, \alpha', \hat{\alpha}_{j+1}, \ldots, \hat{\alpha}_\mu)$. $\mathcal{A}$ gives S^* $(\hat{Q}, r + \hat{Q} \cdot \hat{\boldsymbol{\alpha}})$, invoking S^* in the decommit phase again. $\mathcal{A}$ gets back $(\hat{A}, \hat{b})$.

When S^* wins (which it does with probability greater than $\epsilon_B = 1/|\mathbb{F}| + \epsilon_S$), $b = s + \boldsymbol{\alpha} \cdot A$ and $\hat{b} = s + \hat{\boldsymbol{\alpha}} \cdot \hat{A}$, but $a_i \neq \hat{a}_j$ (here, $\cdot$ represents the dot product). Now we will get two linear equations in two unknowns. The first is $\hat{b} - b = \hat{\boldsymbol{\alpha}} \cdot \hat{A} - \boldsymbol{\alpha} \cdot A$, which can be rewritten as: $\boxed{K_1 = \alpha' \hat{a}_j - \alpha a_i}$, where $\mathcal{A}$ can derive $K_1 = \hat{b} - b - \sum_{k \neq j} \hat{\alpha}_k \hat{a}_k + \sum_{k \neq i} \alpha_k a_k$. Now, let $t = r + Q \cdot \boldsymbol{\alpha}$ and let $\hat{t} = r + \hat{Q} \cdot \hat{\boldsymbol{\alpha}}$. To get the second equation, we start with $\hat{t} - t = \sum_{k \in [\mu] \setminus j} \hat{\alpha}_k \hat{q}_k - \sum_{k \in [\mu] \setminus i} \alpha_k q_k + \alpha' q - \alpha q$. This equation concerns a vector. We choose an index ℓ in the vector where q is not zero (if q is zero everywhere, then r is revealed). At that index, we have the following equation in scalars: $\boxed{K_2 = \alpha' - \alpha}$, where $\mathcal{A}$ can derive $K_2 = (\hat{t}^{(\ell)} - t^{(\ell)} - \sum_{k \neq j} \hat{\alpha}_k \hat{q}_k^{(\ell)} + \sum_{k \neq i} \alpha_k q_k^{(\ell)}) / q^{(\ell)}$. Now $\mathcal{A}$ can solve for α (since the contrary hypothesis gave $a_i \neq \hat{a}_j$). □

We now prove that after the commit phase, the prover is effectively bound to a *single* function. Our articulation again follows [45], specifically their Lemmas 3.2 and 3.6.

Lemma B.2 (Existence of an extractor function). Let (S, R) be a CFMD protocol with binding error ϵ_B. Let $\epsilon^c = \mu \cdot 2 \cdot (2\sqrt[3]{9/2} + 1) \cdot \sqrt[3]{\epsilon_B}$. Let $v = (v_{S^*}, v_R)$ represent the views of S^* and R after the commit phase (v captures the randomness of the commit phase). For every efficient S^* and for every v, there exists a function $\tilde{f}_v : \mathbb{F}^n \to \mathbb{F}$ such that the following holds. For any environment $\mathcal{E}$, the output of R at the end of the decommit phase is, except with probability ϵ^c, either $\perp$ or satisfies $a_i = \tilde{f}_v(q_i)$ for all $i \in [\mu]$, where $(q_1, \ldots, q_\mu)$ are the decommitment queries generated by $\mathcal{E}$, and the probability is over the random inputs of S^* and R in both phases.

Proof. We will reuse the ideas in the proof of Lemma 3.2 in [45], but we must also ensure that q yields the same answer independent of its position and the other queries in the tuple. We begin with a definition: let $\mathsf{Ext}(v, q, i, \vec{q}) \triangleq \text{argmax}_a A_v(q, i, \vec{q}, a)$, where $A_v(q, i, \vec{q}, a)$ equals, in view $v = (v_{S^*}, v_R)$, the probability over the randomness of the decommit phase that R's ith output is a when the query tuple is $\vec{q}$; note that q is the ith component of $\vec{q}$ and is included in $\mathsf{Ext}(\cdot)$ and $A_v(\cdot)$ for convenience. In other words, $\mathsf{Ext}(\cdot)$ is the most likely a_i value to be output by R, if the full tuple of queries is $\vec{q}$ and if q appears in the ith position. Note that, after the commit phase, $\mathsf{Ext}(\cdot)$ is given deterministically.

Claim B.3. Define $\epsilon_2 = (\sqrt[3]{9/2} + 1) \cdot \sqrt[3]{\epsilon_B}$. For all $\mathcal{E}$ producing $(q, i, j, \vec{q}_1, \vec{q}_2)$, where $\vec{q}_1$'s ith component is q and $\vec{q}_2$'s jth component is also q, we have the following with probability $> 1 - \epsilon_2$ over the commit phase: either $\mathsf{Ext}(v, q, i, \vec{q}_1) = \mathsf{Ext}(v, q, j, \vec{q}_2)$, or else the probability over the decommit phase of outputting $\perp$ is greater than $1 - \epsilon_2$.

Proof. Assume otherwise. Then there is an environment $\mathcal{E}$ producing $(q, i, j, \vec{q}_1, \vec{q}_2)$ such that with probability $> \epsilon_2$ over the commit phase, $\mathsf{Ext}(v, q, i, \vec{q}_1) \neq \mathsf{Ext}(v, q, j, \vec{q}_2)$ and with probability $> \epsilon_2$ over the decommit phase, R outputs something other than $\perp$. Define $\epsilon_1 = \sqrt[3]{\epsilon_B 9/2}$. We will show below that with probability $> 1 - \epsilon_1$ over the commit phase, $\sum_{a \in \mathbb{F} \setminus \mathsf{Ext}(v,q,i,\vec{q}_1)} A_v(q, i, \vec{q}_1, a)$ is $< \epsilon_1$. Thus, with probability $> \epsilon_2 - \epsilon_1$ over the commit phase, we have (1) the probability over the decommit phase is $> \epsilon_2 - \epsilon_1$ that R outputs $\mathsf{Ext}(v, q, i, \vec{q}_1)$ in the ith position (since R outputs *something* other than $\perp$ with probability $> \epsilon_2$, yet the probability of outputting anything *other* than $\mathsf{Ext}(v, q, i, \vec{q}_1)$ is $< \epsilon_1$); and (2) likewise, the probability of outputting $\mathsf{Ext}(v, q, j, \vec{q}_2)$ in the jth position is $> \epsilon_2 - \epsilon_1$. If we now take $Q = \vec{q}_1$ and $\hat{Q} = \vec{q}_2$, we have a contradiction to the definition of CFMD because with probability $> (\epsilon_2 - \epsilon_1)^3 = \epsilon_B$ over all three phases, $a_i \neq \hat{a}_j$, which generates a contradiction because the definition of ϵ_B-Binding says that this was supposed to happen with probability $< \epsilon_B$.

We must now show that, with probability $> 1 - \epsilon_1$ over the commit phase, $\sum_{a \in \mathbb{F} \setminus \mathsf{Ext}(v,q,i,\vec{q}_1)} A_v(q, i, \vec{q}_1, a)$ is $< \epsilon_1$. If not, then with probability $> \epsilon_1$ over the commit phase, $\sum_{a \in \mathbb{F} \setminus \mathsf{Ext}(v,q,i,\vec{q}_1)} A_v(q, i, \vec{q}_1, a) \geq \epsilon_1$. Now, following Lemma 3.2 in [45], we can partition $\mathbb{F}$ into two sets T_1, T_2 such that $\sum_{a \in T_1} A_v(q, i, \vec{q}_1, a)$ and $\sum_{a \in T_2} A_v(q, i, \vec{q}_1, a)$ are each greater than $\epsilon_1/3$. (There are two cases; consider $a^* = \mathsf{Ext}(v, q, i, \vec{q}_1)$. Either $A_v(q, i, \vec{q}_1, a^*)$ is greater than $\epsilon_1/3$, or it is not. If so, then the partition is $(a^*, \mathbb{F} \setminus a^*)$. If not, then there is still a partition because the sum of the $A_v(\cdot)$ is greater than $\epsilon_1/3$.) This implies that, in the binding experiment, R outputs values from the two partitions with probability $> (2/9) \cdot (\epsilon_1)^3 = \epsilon_B$ over all three phases, which contradicts the definition of a CFMD protocol. □

Now define $\mathsf{Ext}(v, q) = \mathsf{Ext}(v, q, i^*, \vec{q}^*)$, where i^* and $\vec{q}^*$ are designated (any choice with q in the i^* position of $\vec{q}^*$ will do). The next claim says that the response to q is independent of its position and the other queries.

Claim B.4. Let $\epsilon_3 = \epsilon_2 + \epsilon_1$. For all $\vec{q}, i$, where q is in the ith position of $\vec{q}$, we have that with probability $> 1 - \epsilon_3$ over the commit phase, either R's ith output is $\mathsf{Ext}(v, q)$, or else the probability over the decommit phase of outputting $\perp$ is $> 1 - \epsilon_3$.

Proof. Assume otherwise. Then there are $\vec{q}, i$ such that with probability $> \epsilon_3$ over the commit phase, the probability of outputting something (non-$\perp$) besides $\mathsf{Ext}(v, q, i^*, \vec{q}^*)$ is $> \epsilon_3$. But with probability $> 1 - \epsilon_1$ over the commit phase, $\sum_{a \in \mathbb{F} \setminus \mathsf{Ext}(v,q,i,\vec{q})} A_v(q, i, \vec{q}, a) < \epsilon_1$ (by the partitioning argument given in the proof of Claim B.3). Thus, with probability $> \epsilon_3 - \epsilon_1$ over the commit phase, the probability of outputting something (non-$\perp$) besides $\mathsf{Ext}(v, q, i^*, \vec{q}^*)$ is $> \epsilon_3$ and $\sum_{a \in \mathbb{F} \setminus \mathsf{Ext}(v,q,i,\vec{q})} A_v(q, i, \vec{q}, a) < \epsilon_1$. Thus, with probability $> \epsilon_3 - \epsilon_1 = \epsilon_2$ over the commit phase, $\mathsf{Ext}(v, q, i^*, \vec{q}^*) \neq \mathsf{Ext}(v, q, i, \vec{q})$ and R has $> \epsilon_3 > \epsilon_2$ probability of outputting something other than $\perp$. This contradicts Claim B.3. □

To complete the proof of the lemma, define $\tilde{f}_v(q) \triangleq \mathsf{Ext}(v, q)$. Consider the probability ϵ^c, over both phases, that the output $A \neq (\tilde{f}_v(q_1), \ldots, \tilde{f}_v(q_\mu))$, i.e., that at least one of $a_i \neq \tilde{f}_v(q_i)$. By the union bound, $\epsilon^c < \sum_{i=1}^{\mu} \Pr\{a_i \neq \tilde{f}_v(q_i)\}$. By Claim B.4, $\Pr\{a_i \neq \tilde{f}_v(q_i)\} < \epsilon_3 + \epsilon_3$, since this bounds the probability that either of the two phases goes badly. Thus, $\epsilon^c < \mu \cdot 2 \cdot \epsilon_3$, as was to be shown. □

To compute ϵ^c, we ignore ϵ_S (the homomorphic encryption error); i.e., we set $\epsilon_B = 1/|\mathbb{F}|$. We then get $\epsilon^c < 2000 \cdot (7\sqrt[3]{\epsilon_B}) < 2^{14} \cdot \sqrt[3]{1/|\mathbb{F}|}$. For $|\mathbb{F}| = 2^{128}$, $\epsilon^c < 2^{-28}$.

C Batching

Under batching, V submits the same queries to β different proofs. Below, we sketch the mechanics and then proofs of correctness. First, we modify Commit+Multidecommit (Figure 3) to obtain a new protocol, called BatchedCommit+Multidecommit. The changes are as follows:

- P is regarded as holding a linear function $\pi : \mathbb{F}^n \to \mathbb{F}^\beta$, so $\pi(q) = (\pi_1(q), \ldots, \pi_\beta(q))$. One can visualize π as an $\beta \times n$ matrix, each of whose rows is an oracle, π_i. Thus, P returns vectors instead of scalars.

- Commit phase, steps 2 and 3: instead of receiving from P the scalar $\mathsf{Enc}(pk, \pi(r))$, V in fact receives a vector $\mathbf{e} = (\mathsf{Enc}(pk, \pi_1(r)), \ldots, \mathsf{Enc}(pk, \pi_\beta(r)))$ and decrypts to get $\mathbf{s} = (\pi_1(r), \ldots, \pi_\beta(r))$.
- Decommit phase, steps 5 and 6: P returns $\mathbf{a}_1, \ldots, \mathbf{a}_\mu, \mathbf{b}$, where $\mathbf{a}_i$ is supposed to equal $(\pi_1(q_i), \ldots, \pi_\beta(q_i))$ and $\mathbf{b}$ is supposed to equal $(\pi_1(t), \ldots, \pi_\beta(t))$; V checks that $\mathbf{b} = \mathbf{s} + \alpha_1 \mathbf{a}_1 + \cdots + \alpha_\mu \mathbf{a}_\mu$.

Second, we modify the compilation in Appendix B as follows. P' creates β linear proof oracles, and V' and P' run BatchedCommit+Multidecommit, causing P' to commit to a linear function $\boldsymbol{\pi}\colon \mathbb{F}^n \to \mathbb{F}^\beta$. V' then submits the μ PCP queries and receives vectors $\boldsymbol{\pi}(q_1), \ldots, \boldsymbol{\pi}(q_\mu)$ in response. Then V' runs the PCP verifier on each instance separately (e.g., for the kth instance, V' looks at the kth component of each of $\boldsymbol{\pi}(q_1), \ldots, \boldsymbol{\pi}(q_\mu)$). V' thus returns a vector of β `accept` or `reject` outputs. To argue correctness, we use a theorem analogous to Theorem B.1:

Theorem C.1. Under (P', V') as described above, each of the β instances is an argument protocol with soundness $\epsilon' \leq \epsilon + \epsilon^c$. ($\epsilon^c$ is defined in Appendix B.)

Proof. (Sketch.) Nearly the same as for Theorem B.1. We need an analog of Lemma B.2, described below. □

This theorem says that if any of the β instances tries to encode a "proof" for an incorrect output, the probability that V outputs `accept` for that instance is bounded by ϵ'. This makes intuitive sense because if we fix a given instance, the probabilities should be unaffected by "extra" instances.

To formalize this intuition, we need BatchedCommit+Multidecommit to yield an extractor function for each of the β instances. To get there, we define a general protocol: *batch-CFMD*. This protocol has a binding property modified from the one in Definition B.1. In the new one, R gives stacked output $\mathbf{A} = (\mathbf{a}_1, \ldots, \mathbf{a}_\mu)$ and $\hat{\mathbf{A}} = (\hat{\mathbf{a}}_1, \ldots, \hat{\mathbf{a}}_\mu)$. The entries of $\mathbf{A}$ are denoted a_i^k; that is, $\mathbf{a}_i = (a_i^1, \ldots, a_i^\beta)$. We allow $a_i^k \in \{\mathbb{F} \cup \perp\}$ but require that $(a_1^k, \ldots, a_\mu^k) \in \mathbb{F}^\mu$ or $a_i^k = \perp$ for all $i \in [\mu]$. We now say that S^* wins if for some i, j, k, we have $q_i = \hat{q}_j$ and $a_i^k, \hat{a}_j^k \in \mathbb{F}$ but $a_i^k \neq \hat{a}_j^k$. We again say that the protocol meets ϵ_B-Binding if for all $\mathcal{E}$ and efficient S^*, S^* has less than ϵ_B probability of winning.

We can show that BatchedCommit+Multidecommit is a batch-CFMD protocol by rerunning Lemma B.1, nearly unmodified. To complete the argument, we can establish an analog of Lemma B.2. The analog replaces a single extractor function $\tilde{f}_v$ with β functions $\tilde{f}_v^1, \ldots, \tilde{f}_v^\beta$, one per instance. The analog says that, viewing each instance k separately, we have with probability $> 1 - \epsilon^c$ that either R's output for that instance is $\perp$ or else $a_i^k = \tilde{f}_v^k(q_i)$ for all $i \in [\mu]$. The proof is nearly the same as for Lemma B.2; the main difference is that $\mathsf{Ext}(\cdot)$ and $A_v(\cdot)$ receive a per-instance parameter k.

D Tailored PCP for matrix multiplication

This section expands on the tailored PCP construction for matrix multiplication, introduced in Section 3.6. Recall that V wants to verify that C equals $A \cdot B$, where $A, B, C \in \mathbb{F}^{m^2}$. Further recall that V constructs a polynomial $P'(Z)$ from the constraints in Section 3.3, but V drops the degree-1 constraints. Loosely speaking, V is justified in doing so because (a) V knows what $z_{i,j}^a$ and $z_{i,j}^b$ should be, namely the values of A and B; and (b) the resulting circuit test is still likely to catch an incorrect output C. Further recall that the modified PCP encoding is $\pi = \pi^{(c)}(\cdot) \triangleq \langle \cdot, A \oslash B \rangle$, where $x \oslash y = \{x_{i,k} \cdot y_{k,j}\}$ for all i, j, k.

After stating the queries and tests below, we give proofs of correctness and estimate costs.

- Generate linearity queries: Select $q_1, q_2 \in_R \mathbb{F}^{m^3}$. Take $q_3 \leftarrow q_1 + q_2$.
- Generate quadratic correction queries: select $q_4, q_5 \in_R \mathbb{F}^{m^2}$ and $q_7 \in_R \mathbb{F}^{m^3}$. Take $q_6 \leftarrow (q_4 \oslash q_5 + q_7)$
- Generate circuit test queries: select $q_9 \in_R \mathbb{F}^{m^3}$ and $q_8 \leftarrow \gamma_2' + q_9$. ($\gamma_2'$ is defined in Section 3.6.)
- Issue queries. Send q_1, q_2, q_3 and $q_6, \ldots, q_9$ to π, getting back $\pi(q_1), \pi(q_2), \pi(q_3), \pi(q_6), \pi(q_7), \pi(q_8), \pi(q_9)$.
- Linearity test: Check that $\pi(q_1) + \pi(q_2) = \pi(q_3)$. If not, `reject`.
- Quadratic correction test: Check that $\pi(q_6) - \pi(q_7) = \sum_{k=1}^m \langle A_{*,k}, q_{4_{*,k}} \rangle \cdot \langle B_{k,*}, q_{5_{k,*}} \rangle$, where $M_{*,k} \in \mathbb{F}^m$ denotes the kth column of matrix M, and $M_{k,*} \in \mathbb{F}^m$ denotes the kth row of matrix M. If not, `reject`.
- Circuit test: Check that $\pi(q_8) - \pi(q_9) = -\gamma_0$. ($\gamma_0'$ is defined in Section 3.6.) If so, `accept`.

Lemma D.1 (Completeness). If V is given $C = A \cdot B$, if $\pi = \pi^{(c)}$ is constructed as above, and if V proceeds as above, then $\Pr\{V \text{ accepts}\} = 1$. The probability is over V's random choices.

Proof. If $\pi = \pi^{(c)}$ is constructed as above, then the linearity test passes because $\pi^{(c)}$ is a linear function. The quadratic correction test also passes because $\pi^{(c)}(q_6) - \pi^{(c)}(q_7) = \pi^{(c)}(q_4 \oslash q_5) = \langle q_4 \oslash q_5, A \oslash B \rangle$, which indeed equals $\sum_{k=1}^m \langle A_{*,k}, q_{4_{*,k}} \rangle \cdot \langle B_{k,*}, q_{5_{k,*}} \rangle$. Finally, the circuit test passes because $\pi^{(c)}(q_8) - \pi^{(c)}(q_9) = \pi^{(c)}(\gamma_2') = \langle \gamma_2', A \oslash B \rangle$, and γ_2' and γ_0' are constructed so that if $C = A \cdot B$, then $\langle \gamma_2', A \oslash B \rangle + \gamma_0' = 0$. □

Lemma D.2 (Soundness). There exists a constant $\kappa < 1$ such that if some proof oracle π passes all of the tests above with probability $> \kappa$, then $C = A \cdot B$.

Proof. Choose δ such that $3\delta - 6\delta^2 > 2/9$, and take $\kappa > \max\{\frac{7}{9}, 2\delta + 2/|\mathbb{F}|, 2\delta + 1/|\mathbb{F}|\}$; with $\delta = 0.1$, we can take any $\kappa > 7/9$. We establish soundness by going through each of the tests in turn. (This is the same proof flow as in [8] though the details differ for the quadratic correction test and circuit test.) First, from the given, we have that $\Pr\{\pi \text{ passes the linearity test}\} > 7/9$. This, together with our choice of δ, implies (see [12]) that $\pi^{(c)}$ is δ-close to some linear function $\phi(\cdot)$ (meaning that the fraction of inputs on which $\pi^{(c)}$ and $\phi(\cdot)$ disagree is $< \delta$). Second, we also have from the given that the probability of passing both the quadratic correction test and the linearity test is $> 2\delta + 2/|\mathbb{F}|$, so we can apply the following claim:

Claim D.3. If $\pi^{(c)}$ is δ-close to some linear function $\phi(\cdot)$ and if $\Pr\{\pi^{(c)} \text{ passes the quadratic correction test}\} > 2\delta + 2/|\mathbb{F}|$, then $\phi(\cdot)$ is exactly $\langle \cdot, A \oslash B\rangle$.

Proof. We begin with notation. Let $N_{A,B}(x,y) = \sum_{k=1}^{m} \langle A_{*,k}, x_{*,k}\rangle \cdot \langle B_{k,*}, y_{k,*}\rangle$, where $x, y \in \mathbb{F}^{m^3}$. We write the (i,k) element of q_4 and the (k,j) element of q_5 as q^4_{ik} and q^5_{kj} respectively. Let ϕ_{ijk} refer to the (i,j,k) element of the vector that corresponds to ϕ. Let $\sigma_{ijk} = \phi_{ijk} - A_{i,k}B_{k,j}$. Finally, let η be the event $\{\phi(q_4 \oslash q_5) = N_{A,B}(q_4, q_5)\}$.

Now, assume toward a contradiction that $\phi(\cdot) \neq \langle \cdot, A \oslash B\rangle$. Then $\exists i', j', k'$ such that $\sigma_{i'j'k'} \neq 0$. Let ν be the event $\{q^5_{k'j'} \neq 0\}$. We can write $\Pr\{\eta\} < \Pr\{\eta|\nu\} + \Pr\{\neg\nu\} = \Pr\{\eta|\nu\} + 1/|\mathbb{F}|$. To get an expression for $\Pr\{\eta|\nu\}$, note that if ν occurs, then $(q^5_{k'j'})^{-1}$ is defined. Also, $(\sigma_{i'j'k'})^{-1}$ is defined, by contrary assumption. Noting that η can be written $\{\sum_{i,j,k} q^4_{ik} q^5_{kj} \sigma_{ijk} = 0\}$, we have $\Pr\{\eta|\nu\} = \Pr\{q^4_{i'k'} = -(\sum_{i,j,k\setminus(i',j',k')} q^4_{ik} q^5_{kj} \sigma_{ijk}) \cdot (q^5_{k'j'})^{-1} \cdot \sigma^{-1}_{i'j'k'}\} = 1/|\mathbb{F}|$, since we can regard $q^4_{i'k'}$ as being chosen after the right-hand side of the equality. Thus, $\Pr\{\eta\} < 2/|\mathbb{F}|$. We now use the given, to derive a contradiction:

$$\begin{aligned} 2\delta + 2/|\mathbb{F}| &< \Pr\{\pi(q_6) + \pi(q_7) = N_{A,B}(q_4, q_5)\} \\ &< \Pr\{\phi(q_6) + \phi(q_7) = N_{A,B}(q_4, q_5)\} \\ &\quad + \Pr\{\pi(q_6) \neq \phi(q_6)\} + \Pr\{\pi(q_7) \neq \phi(q_7)\} \\ &< \Pr\{\phi(q_4 \oslash q_5) = N_{A,B}(q_4, q_5)\} + 2\delta, \end{aligned}$$

so $\Pr\{\eta\} > 2/|\mathbb{F}|$. Contradiction. □

Third, the probability of passing all three tests is $> 2\delta + 1/|\mathbb{F}|$ (again from the given), so we can apply the following claim to complete the lemma. □

Claim D.4. If $\pi^{(c)}(\cdot)$ is δ-close to $\phi(\cdot) = \langle \cdot, A \oslash B\rangle$ and if $\Pr\{\pi^{(c)} \text{ passes the circuit test}\} > 2\delta + 1/|\mathbb{F}|$, then $C = A \cdot B$.

Proof. Assume toward a contradiction that $C \neq A \cdot B$. Then there exists i', j' such that $C_{i',j'} \neq \sum_{k=1}^{m} A_{i',k} B_{k,j'}$, which implies that $P'(A,B) \triangleq \sum_{i,j} v^c_{i,j} \cdot (C_{i,j} - \sum_{k=1}^{m} A_{i,j} \cdot B_{i,j}) = 0$ with probability $\leq 1/|\mathbb{F}|$ (see Section 2.1). But

$$\begin{aligned} P'(A,B) &= \langle \gamma'_2, A \oslash B\rangle + \gamma'_0 && \text{(by choice of } \gamma'_2, \gamma'_0) \\ &= \phi(\gamma'_2) + \gamma'_0 && \text{(by definition of } \phi), \end{aligned}$$

so $\Pr\{\phi(\gamma'_2) + \gamma'_0 = 0\} \leq 1/|\mathbb{F}|$. We now use the given:

$$\begin{aligned} 2\delta + 1/|\mathbb{F}| &< \Pr\{\pi(q_8) - \pi(q_9) = -\gamma'_0\} \\ &< \Pr\{\phi(q_8) - \phi(q_9) = -\gamma'_0\} \\ &\quad + \Pr\{\pi(q_8) \neq \phi(q_8) \text{ or } \pi(q_9) \neq \phi(q_9)\} \\ &< \Pr\{\phi(\gamma'_2) = -\gamma'_0\} + 2\delta, \end{aligned}$$

so $\Pr\{\phi(\gamma'_2) + \gamma'_0 = 0\} > 1/|\mathbb{F}|$, giving a contradiction. □

We now briefly cover the costs; upper bounds are in Figure 2. The PCP encoding is m^3 work to produce. V constructs 8 queries and submits 7 of them to π; this is the same as the number of queries to $\pi^{(2)}$ in the baseline PCP (Appendix A). V requires $2m^2$ field multiplications for the quadratic correction test plus m^2 multiplications in the circuit test (to construct γ'_0), for a total of $3m^2$ per repetition. By comparison, the baseline PCP requires 2 operations for the quadratic correction test and $3m^2$ for the circuit test.

E Modifications for ElGamal

Since ElGamal encryption is multiplicatively homomorphic (rather than additively homomorphic), small modifications to Commit+Multidecommit (Figure 3) and the soundness arguments are necessary. Below, we describe these modifications and establish that the results of Appendix B still hold.

Fix the ElGamal group G, choose a generator g (known to both parties), and assume for now that $|\mathbb{F}_p| = |G|$ (we revisit this assumption below). Define the map $\psi : \mathbb{F}_p \to G$ by $x \mapsto g^x$. The map ψ is a group homomorphism and in fact an isomorphism; furthermore, ψ induces a ring structure on G. By composing ψ with ElGamal encryption, we get an additive homomorphism: $\mathsf{Enc}(pk, g^x)\mathsf{Enc}(pk, g^y) = \mathsf{Enc}(pk, g^{x+y})$. Of course, the verifier cannot recover $x + y$ explicitly from g^{x+y}, but this does not matter for Commit+Multidecommit. Also, given $\mathsf{Enc}(pk, g^x)$ and $a \in \mathbb{F}_p$, the properties of the ElGamal protocol imply that one can compute $\mathsf{Enc}(pk, g^{ax})$. Thus, given $(\mathsf{Enc}(pk, g^{r_1}), \ldots, \mathsf{Enc}(pk, g^{r_n}))$, one can compute $\mathsf{Enc}(pk, g^{\pi((r_1,\ldots,r_n))})$, where π is a linear function.

Therefore, we can modify Figure 3 as follows. First, during step 1, the verifier componentwise sends $\mathsf{Enc}(pk, g^r)$ rather than $\mathsf{Enc}(pk, r)$ to the prover. Next, in step 2, the prover computes $\mathsf{Enc}(pk, g^{\pi(r)})$ (without learning g^r), as described above. Then in step 3, V decrypts to get g^s. Finally, in step 6, the verifier checks that $g^b = g^{s+\alpha_1 a_1 + \cdots + \alpha_\mu a_\mu}$.

We now need to check that Lemma B.1 still holds. Correctness applies, by inspection. Binding applies because the semantic security of the encryption scheme can be formulated in terms of $\mathcal{A}(pk, \mathsf{Enc}(pk, g^r), r + \alpha q, r + \alpha' q)$ and because $g^x = g^y$ if and only if $x = y$ (since ψ is injective).

Note that when $|G| > |\mathbb{F}_p|$, the same approach works, via modular arithmetic. Specifically, although ψ is no longer a group isomorphism, it is injective. Provided that the computations never overflow, i.e., result in values in the exponent larger than $|G|$, the protocol remains correct.

Towards Practical Oblivious RAM

Emil Stefanov
UC Berkeley
emil@cs.berkeley.edu

Elaine Shi
UC Berkeley/PARC
elaines@cs.berkeley.edu

Dawn Song
UC Berkeley
dawnsong@cs.berkeley.edu

Abstract

We take an important step forward in making Oblivious RAM (O-RAM) practical. We propose an O-RAM construction achieving an amortized overhead of $20 \sim 35$*X (for an O-RAM roughly* 1 *terabyte in size), about* 63 *times faster than the best existing scheme. On the theoretic front, we propose a fundamentally novel technique for constructing Oblivious RAMs: specifically, we partition a bigger O-RAM into smaller O-RAMs, and employ a background eviction technique to obliviously evict blocks from the client-side cache into a randomly assigned server-side partition. This novel technique is the key to achieving the gains in practical performance.*

1 Introduction

As cloud computing gains momentum, an increasing amount of data is outsourced to cloud storage, and data privacy has become an important concern for many businesses and individuals alike. Encryption alone may not suffice for ensuring data privacy, as data access patterns can leak a considerable amount of information about the data as well. Pinkas *et al.* gave an example [13]: if a sequence of data access requests q_1, q_2, q_3 is always followed by a stock exchange operation, the server can gain sensitive information even when the data is encrypted.

Oblivious RAM (or O-RAM) [3, 4, 11], first investigated by Goldreich and Ostrovsky, is a primitive intended for hiding storage access patterns. The problem was initially studied in the context of software protection, i.e., hiding a program's memory access patterns to prevent reverse engineering.

With the trend of cloud computing, O-RAM also has important applications in privacy-preserving storage outsourcing applications. In this paper, we consider the setting where a client wishes to store N blocks each of size B bytes at an untrusted server.

The community's interest in O-RAM has recently rekindled, partly due to its potential high impact in privacy-preserving storage outsourcing applications. One of the best schemes known to date is a novel construction recently proposed by Goodrich and Mitzenmacher [5]. Specifically, let N denotes the total storage capacity of the O-RAM in terms of the number of blocks. The Goodrich-Mitzenmacher construction achieves $O((\log N)^2)$ amortized cost when parametrized with $O(1)$ client-side storage; or it achieves $O(\log N)$ amortized cost when parametrized with $O(N^a)$ client-side storage where $0 < a < 1$. In this context, an amortized cost of $f(N)$ means that each data request will generate $f(N)$ read or write operations on the server.

Despite elegant asymptotic guarantees, the practical performance of existing O-RAM constructions are still unsatisfactory. As shown in Table 1, one of the most practical schemes known to date is the construction by Goodrich and Mitzenmacher [5] when parametrized with N^a ($a < 1$) client-side storage. This scheme has more than $1,400X$ overhead compared to non-oblivious storage under reasonable parametrization, which is prohibitive in practice. In summary, although it has been nearly two decades since O-RAM was first invented, so far, it has mostly remained a theoretical concept.

1.1 Results and Contributions

Our main goal is to make Oblivious RAM practical for cloud outsourcing applications.

Practical construction. We propose an O-RAM construction geared towards optimal practical performance. The practical construction achieves an amortized overhead of **20** $\sim$ **35X** (Tables 1 and 2), about **63 times faster** than the best known construction. In addition, this practical construction also achieves *sub-linear* $O(\log N)$ *worst-case cost*, and *constant round-trip latency* per operation. Although our practical construction requires asymptotically linear amount of client-side storage, the constant is so small (0.01% to 0.3% of the O-RAM capacity) that in realistic settings, the amount of client-side storage is comparable to $\sqrt{N}$.

Theoretical construction. By applying recursion to the practical construction, we can reduce the client-side

Scheme	Amortized Cost	Worst-case Cost	Client Storage	Server Storage	Practical Performance
Goldreich-Ostrovsky [4]	$O((\log N)^3)$	$\Omega(N)$	O(1)	$O(N \log N)$	$> 120,000$X
Pinkas-Reinman [13]	$O((\log N)^2)$	$O(N \log N)$	$O(1)$	$8N$	$60,000 \sim 80,000$X
Goodrich-Mitzenmacher [5]	$O(\log N)$	$O(N \log N)$	$O(N^a)$ $(0 < a < 1)$	$8N$	$> 1,400$X
This paper:					
Practical, Non-Concurrent	$O(\log N)$	$< 3\sqrt{N} + o(\sqrt{N})$	cN (c very small)	$< 4N + o(N)$	$20 \sim 35$X
Practical, Concurrent	$O(\log N)$	$O(\log N)$	cN (c very small)	$< 4N + o(N)$	$20 \sim 35$X
Theoretic, Non-Concurrent	$O((\log N)^2)$	$O(\sqrt{N})$	$O(\sqrt{N})$	$O(N)$	—
Theoretic, Concurrent	$O((\log N)^2)$	$O((\log N)^2)$	$O(\sqrt{N})$	$O(N)$	—

Table 1: Our contributions. The practical performance is the number of client-server operations per O-RAM operation for typical realistic parameters, e.g., when the server stores terabytes of data, and the client has several hundred megabytes to gigabytes of local storage, and $N \geq 2^{20}$. For our theoretic constructions, the same asymptotic bounds also work for the more general case where client-side storage is N^a for some constant $0 < a < 1$.

O-RAM Capacity	# Blocks	Block Size	Client Storage	Server Storage	Client Storage / O-RAM Capacity	Practical Performance
64 GB	2^{20}	64 KB	204 MB	205 GB	0.297%	22.5X
256 GB	2^{22}	64 KB	415 MB	819 GB	0.151%	24.1X
1 TB	2^{24}	64 KB	858 MB	3.2 TB	0.078%	25.9X
16 TB	2^{28}	64 KB	4.2 GB	51 TB	0.024%	29.5X
256 TB	2^{32}	64 KB	31 GB	819 TB	0.011%	32.7X
1024 TB	2^{34}	64 KB	101 GB	3072 TB	0.009%	34.4X

Table 2: Suggested parametrizations of our practical construction. The practical performance is the number of client-server operations per O-RAM operation as measured by our simulation experiments.

storage to a sublinear amount, and obtain a novel construction of theoretic interest, achieving $O((\log N)^2)$ amortized and *worst-case* cost, and requires $O(\sqrt{N})$ client-side storage, and $O(N)$ server-side storage. Note that in the $O((\log N)^2)$ asymptotic notation, one of the $\log N$ factors stems from the the depth of the recursion; and in realistic settings (see Table 2), the depth of the recursion is typically 2 or 3.

Table 1 summarizes our contributions in the context of related work. Table 2 provides suggested parametrizations for our practical construction.

1.2 Main Technique: Partitioning

We propose a novel *partitioning* technique, which is the key to achieving the claimed theoretical bounds as well as major practical savings. The basic idea is to partition a single O-RAM of size N blocks into P different O-RAMs of size roughly $\frac{N}{P}$ blocks each. This allows us to break down a bigger O-RAM into multiple smaller O-RAMs.

The idea of partitioning is motivated by the fact that the major source of overhead in existing O-RAM constructions arises from an expensive *remote oblivious sorting* protocol performed between the client and the server. Because the oblivious sorting protocol can take up to $O(N)$ time, existing O-RAM schemes require $\Omega(N)$ time in the worst-case or have unreasonable $O(\sqrt{N})$ amortized cost.

We partition the O-RAM into roughly $P = \sqrt{N}$ partitions, each having $\sqrt{N}$ blocks approximately. This way, the client can use $\sqrt{N}$ blocks of storage to sort/reshuffle the data blocks locally, and then simply transfer the reshuffled data blocks to the server. This not only circumvents the need for the expensive oblivious sorting protocol, but also allows us to achieve $O(\sqrt{N})$ worst-case cost. Furthermore, by allowing reshuffling to happen concurrently with reads, we can further reduce the worst-case cost of the practical construction to $O(\log N)$.

While the idea of partitioning is attractive, it also brings along an important challenge in terms of security. Partitioning creates an extra channel through which the data access pattern can potentially be inferred by observing the sequence of partitions accessed. Therefore, we must take care to ensure that *the sequence of partitions accessed does not leak information about the identities of blocks being accessed.* Specifically, our construction ensures that the sequence of partitions accessed appears pseudo-random to an untrusted server.

It is worth noting that Ostrovsky and Shoup [12] also came up with a technique to spread the reshuffling work of the hierarchical solution [4] over time, thereby achieving poly-logarithmic worst-case cost. However, our technique of achieving poly-logarithmic worst-case cost is fundamentally from Ostrovsky and Shoup [12].

Moreover, our partitioning and background eviction techniques are also key to the practical performance gain that we can achieve.

1.3 Related Work

Oblivious RAM was first investigated by Goldreich and Ostrovsky [3, 4, 11]. Since their original work, several seminal improvements have been proposed [5, 13, 15, 16]. These approaches mainly fall into two broad categories: constructions that use $O(1)$ client-side storage, and constructions that use $O(N^a)$ client-side storage where $0 < a < 1$.

Williams and Sion [15] propose an O-RAM construction that requires $O(\sqrt{N})$ client-side storage, and achieves an amortized cost of $O((\log N)^2)$. Williams *et al.* propose another construction that uses $O(\sqrt{N})$ client-side storage, and achieves $O(\log N \log\log N)$ amortized cost [16]; however, researchers have expressed concerns over the assumptions used in their original analysis [5, 13]. A corrected analysis of this construction can be found in an appendix in a recent work by Pinkas and Reinman [13].

Pinkas and Reinman [13] discovered an O-RAM construction that achieves $O((\log N)^2)$ overhead with $O(1)$ client-side storage. However, some researchers have observed a security flaw of the Pinkas-Reinman construction, due to the fact that the lookups can reveal, with considerable probability, whether the client is searching for blocks that exist in the hash table [5]. The authors of that paper will fix this issue in a future journal version. While Table 1 shows the overhead of the Pinkas-Reinman scheme as is, the overhead of the scheme is likely to increase after fixing this security flaw.

In an elegant work by Goodrich and Mitzenmacher [5], they proposed a novel O-RAM construction which achieves $O((\log N)^2)$ amortized cost with $O(1)$ client-side storage; or $O(\log N)$ amortized cost with $O(N^a)$ client-side storage where $0 < a < 1$. The Goodrich-Mitzenmacher construction achieves the best asymptotic performance among all known constructions. However, their practical performance is still prohibitive. For example, with $O(\sqrt{N})$ client-side storage, their amortized cost is $> 1,400$X from a very conservative estimate. In reality, their overhead could be higher.

In an independent and concurrent work by Boneh, Mazieres, and Popa [2], they propose a construction that can support up to $O(\sqrt{N})$ reads while shuffling (using $O(\sqrt{N})$ client-side storage). The scheme achieves $O(\log N)$ online cost, and $O(\sqrt{N})$ amortized cost.

Almost all prior constructions have $\Omega(N)$ worst-case cost, except the seminal work by Ostrovsky and Shoup [12], in which they demonstrate how to spread the reshuffling operations of the hierarchical construction [4] across time to achieve poly-logarithmic worst-case cost. While the aforementioned concurrent work by Boneh *et al.* [2] alleviates this problem by separating the cost into an online part for reading and writing data, and an offline part for reshuffling, they do so at an increased amortized cost of $O(\sqrt{N})$ (when their scheme is configured with $O(\sqrt{N})$ client-side storage). In addition, if $\Omega(\sqrt{N})$ consecutive requests take place within a small time window (e.g., during peak usage times), their scheme can still block on a reshuffling operation of $\Omega(N)$ cost.

Concurrent and subsequent work. In concurrent/subsequent work, Goodrich *et al.* [6] invented an O-RAM scheme achieving $O((\log N)^2)$ worst-case cost with $O(1)$ memory; and and Kushilevitz *et al.* [9] invented a scheme with $O(\frac{(\log N)^2}{\log\log N})$ worst-case cost. Goodrich *et al.* also came up with a stateless Oblivious RAM [7] scheme, with $O(\log N)$ amortized cost and $O(N^a)$ ($0 < a < 1$) client-side transient (as opposed to permanent) buffers. Due to larger constants in their constructions, our construction is two to three orders of magnitude more efficient in realistic settings.

2 Problem Definition

As shown in Figure 1, we consider a client that wishes to store data at a remote untrusted server while preserving its privacy. While traditional encryption schemes can provide confidentiality, they do not hide the data access pattern which can reveal very sensitive information to the untrusted server. We assume that the server is untrusted, and the client is trusted, including the client's CPU and memory hierarchy (including RAM and disk).

The goal of O-RAM is to completely hide the data access pattern (which blocks were read/written) from the server. In other words, each data read or write request will generate a completely random sequence of data accesses from the server's perspective.

Notations. We assume that data is fetched and stored in atomic units, referred to as *blocks*, of size B bytes each. For example, a typical value for B for cloud storage is 64 KB to 256 KB. Throughout the paper, we use the notation N to denote total number of data blocks that the O-RAM can support, also referred to as the capacity of the O-RAM.

Practical considerations. One of our goals is to design a *practical* O-RAM scheme in realistic settings. We observe that *bandwidth is much more costly than computation and storage* in real-world scenarios. For example, typical off-the-shelf PCs and laptops today have gigabytes of RAM, and several hundred gigabytes of disk storage. When deploying O-RAM in a realistic setting, it is very likely that the bottleneck is network bandwidth and latency.

As a result, our practical O-RAM construction leverages available client-side storage as a working buffer, and this allows us to drastically optimize the bandwidth consumption between the server and the client. As a typical scenario, we assume that the client wishes to store *terabytes* of data on the remote server, and the client has *megabytes* to *gigabytes* of storage (in the form of RAM or disk). We wish to design a scheme in which the client can maximally leverage its local storage to reduce the overhead of O-RAM.

Security definitions. We adopt the standard security definition for O-RAMs. Intuitively, the security definition requires that the server learns nothing about the access pattern. In other words, no information should be leaked about: 1) which data is being accessed; 2) how old it is (when it was last accessed); 3) whether the same data is being accessed (linkability); 4) access pattern (sequential, random, etc); or 5) whether the access is a read or a write. Like previous work, our O-RAM constructions do not consider information leakage through the timing channel, such as when or how frequently the client makes data requests.

Definition 1 (Security definition). *Let* $\vec{y} := ((\mathsf{op}_1, \mathsf{u}_1, \mathsf{data}_1), (\mathsf{op}_2, \mathsf{u}_2, \mathsf{data}_2), ..., (\mathsf{op}_M, \mathsf{u}_M, \mathsf{data}_M))$ *denote a data request sequence of length* M*, where each* op_i *denotes a* $\mathsf{read}(\mathsf{u}_i)$ *or a* $\mathsf{write}(\mathsf{u}_i, \mathsf{data})$ *operation. Specifically,* u_i *denotes the identifier of the block being read or written, and* data_i *denotes the data being written. Let* $A(\vec{y})$ *denote the (possibly randomized) sequence of accesses to the remote storage given the sequence of data requests* $\vec{y}$*. An O-RAM construction is said to be secure if for any two data request sequences* $\vec{y}$ *and* $\vec{z}$ *of the same length, their access patterns* $A(\vec{y})$ *and* $A(\vec{z})$ *are computationally indistinguishable by anyone but the client.*

3 The Partitioning Framework

In this section, we describe our main technique, *partitioning*, as a framework. At a high level, the goal of partitioning is to subdivide the O-RAM into much smaller partitions, so that the operations performed on the partitions can be handled much more efficiently than if the O-RAM was not partitioned.

The main challenge of partitioning the O-RAM is to ensure that the sequence of partitions accessed during the lifetime of the O-RAM appears random to the untrusted server while keeping the client-side storage small. In this way, no information about data access pattern is revealed.

3.1 Server Storage

We divide the server's storage into P fully functional *partition O-RAM's*, each containing N/P blocks on average. For now, we can think of each partition O-RAM as a black box, exporting a read and a write operation, while hiding the access patterns within that partition.

At any point of time, each block is randomly assigned to any of the P partitions. Whenever a block is accessed, the block is logically removed from its current partition (although a stale copy of the block may remain), and logically assigned to a fresh random partition selected from all P partitions. Thus, the client needs to keep track of which partition each block is associated with at any point of time, as specified in Section 3.2.

The maximum amount of blocks that an O-RAM can contain is referred to as the *capacity* of the O-RAM. In our partitioning framework, blocks are randomly assigned to partitions, so the capacity of an O-RAM partition has to be slightly more than N/P blocks to accommodate the variance of assignments. Due to the standard balls and bins analysis, for $P = \sqrt{N}$, each partition needs to have capacity $\sqrt{N} + o(\sqrt{N})$ to have a sufficiently small failure probability $\frac{1}{\text{poly}(N)}$.

3.2 Client Storage

The client storage is divided into the following components.

Data cache with P **slots.** The data cache is a cache for temporarily storing data blocks fetched from the server. There are exactly P cache slots, equal to the number of partitions on the server. Logically, the P cache slots can be thought of an extension to the server-side partitions. Each slot can store 0, 1, or multiple blocks. In the full version of this paper [1], we prove that each cache slot will have a constant number of data blocks in expectation, and that the total number of data blocks in all cache slots will be bounded by $O(P)$ with high probability . In both our theoretic and practical constructions, we will let $P = \sqrt{N}$. In this case, the client's data cache capacity is $O(\sqrt{N})$.

Position map. As mentioned earlier, the client needs to keep track of which partition (or cache slot) each block resides in. The position map serves exactly this purpose. We use the notation $\mathsf{position}[\mathsf{u}]$ for the partition number where block u currently resides. In our practical construction described in Section 4, the position map is extended to also contain the exact location (level number and index within the level) of block u within its current partition.

Intuitively, each block's position (i.e., partition number) requires about $c \log N$ bits to describe. In our prac-

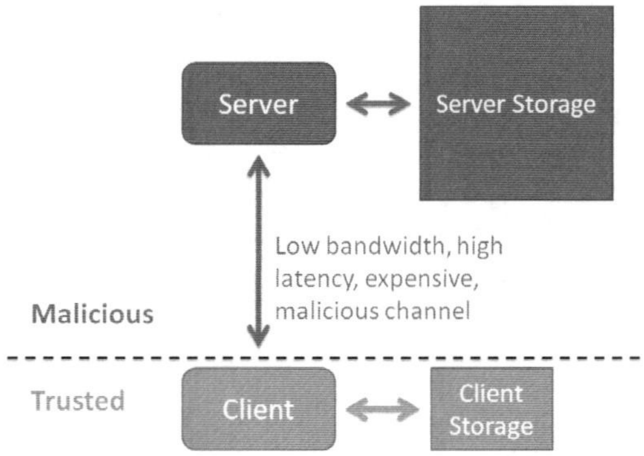

Figure 1: Oblivious RAM system architecture.

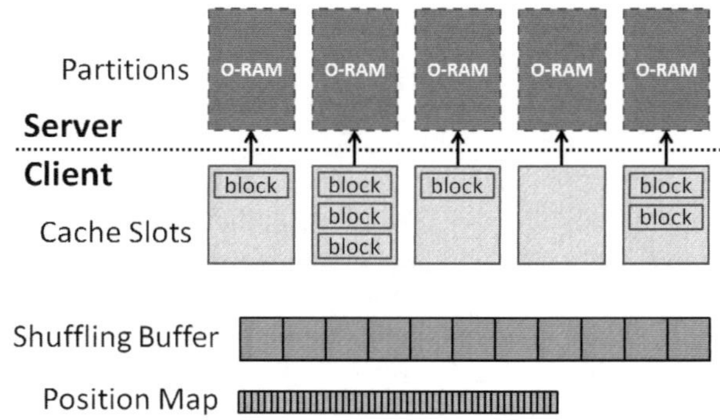

Figure 2: The partitioning framework.

tical construction, $c \leq 1.1$, since the practical construction also stores the block's exact location inside a partition. Hence, the position map requires at most $cN \log N$ bits of storage, or $\frac{c}{8} N \log N$ bytes, which is $\frac{cN \log N}{8 \cdot B}$ blocks. Since in practice the block size $B > \frac{c}{8} \log N$, the size of the position map is a constant fraction of the original capacity of the O-RAM (with a very small constant).

Shuffling buffer. The shuffling buffer is used for the shuffling operation when two or more levels inside a partition O-RAM need to be merged into the next level. For this paper, we assume that the shuffling buffer has size $O(\sqrt{N})$.

Miscellaneous. Finally, we need some client-side storage to store miscellaneous states and information, such as cryptographic keys for authentication, encryption, and pseudo-random permutations.

3.3 Intuition

In our construction, *regardless of whether a block is found in the client's data cache, the client always performs a read and a write operation to the server upon every data request* – with a dummy read operation in case of a cache hit. Otherwise, the server might be able to infer the age of the blocks being accessed. Therefore, the client data cache is required for security rather than for efficiency.

In some sense, the data cache acts like a holding buffer. When the client fetches a block from the server, it cannot immediately write the block back to a some partition, since this would result in linkability attacks the next the this block is read. Instead, the fetched block is associated with a fresh randomly chosen cache slot, but the block resides in the client data cache until a background eviction process writes it back to the server partition corresponding to its cache slot.

Another crucial observation is that the eviction process should not reveal which client cache slots are filled and which are not, as this can lead to linkability attacks as well. To achieve this, we use an eviction process that is independent of the load of each cache slot. Therefore we sometimes have to write back a dummy block to the server. For example, one possible eviction algorithm is to sequentially scan the cache slots at a fixed rate and evict a block from it or evict a dummy block if the cache slot is empty.

To aid the understanding of the partitioning framework, it helps to think of each client cache slot i as an extension of the i-th server partition. At any point of time, a data block is associated with a random partition (or slot), and the client has a position map to keep track of the location of each block. If a block is associated with partition (or slot) $i \in [P]$, it means that an up-to-date version of a block currently resides in partition i (or cache slot i). However, it is possible that other partitions (or even the same partition) may still carry a stale version of block i, which will be removed during a future reshuffling operation.

Every time a read or write operation is performed on a block, the block is re-assigned to a partition (or slot) *selected independently at random from all P partitions (or slots).* This ensures that two operations on the same block cannot be linked to each other.

3.4 Setup

When the construction is initialized, we first assign each block to an independently random partition. Since initially all blocks are zeroed, their values are implicit and we don't write them to the server. The position map stores an additional bit per block to indicate if it has never been accessed and is hence zeroed. In the practical construction, this bit can be implicitly calculated from other metadata that the client stores. Additionally, the data cache is initially empty.

3.5 Partition O-RAM Semantics and Notations

Before we present the main operations of our partitioning-based O-RAM, we first need to define the operations supported by each partition O-RAM.

Recall that each partition is a fully functional O-RAM by itself. To understand our partitioning framework, it helps to think of each partition as a blackbox O-RAM. For example, for each partition, we can plug in the Goodrich-Mitzenmacher O-RAM [5] (with either $O(1)$ or $O(\sqrt{N})$ client-side storage) or our own partition O-RAM construction described in Section 4.

We make a few small assumptions about the partition O-RAM, and use slightly different semantics to refer to the partition O-RAM operations than existing work. Existing O-RAM constructions [3, 5, 13] always perform both a read and a write operation upon any data access request. For the purpose of the partitioning framework, it helps to separate the reads from the writes. In particular, we require that a ReadPartition operation "logically remove" the fetched block from the corresponding partition. Many existing constructions [3,5,13] can be easily modified to support this operation, simply by writing back a dummy block to the first level of the hierarchy after reading.

Formally, we think of each partition O-RAM as a blackbox O-RAM exporting two operations, ReadPartition and WritePartition, as explained below.

- $\mathsf{ReadPartition}(p, \mathsf{u})$ reads a block identified by its unique identifier $\mathsf{u} \in \{\perp, 1, 2, \ldots, N-1\}$ from partition p. In case $\mathsf{u} = \perp$, the read operation is called a dummy read. We assume that the ReadPartition operation will *logically* remove the fetched block from the corresponding partition.
- $\mathsf{WritePartition}(p, \mathsf{u}, \mathsf{data})$ writes back a block identified by its unique identifier $\mathsf{u} \in \{\perp, 1, 2, \ldots, N-1\}$ to partition p. In case $\mathsf{u} = \perp$, the write operation is called a dummy write. The parameter data denotes the block's data.

Remark 1 (About the dummy block identifier $\perp$). *The dummy block identifier $\perp$ represents a meaningless data block. It is used as a substitute for a real block when the client does not want the server to know that there is no real block for some operation.*

Remark 2 (Block identifier space). *Another weak assumption we make is that each partition O-RAM needs to support non-contiguous block identifiers. In other words, the block identifiers need not be a number within $[1, N]$, where N is the O-RAM capacity. Most existing schemes [3, 5, 13] satisfy this property.*

3.6 Reading a Block

Let $\mathsf{read}(\mathsf{u})$ denote a read operation for a block identified by u. The client looks it up in the position map, and finds out which partition block u is associated with. Suppose that block u is associated with partition p. The client then performs the following steps:

Step 1: Read a block from partition p.

- If block u is found in cache slot p, the client performs a dummy read from partition p of the server, i.e., call $\mathsf{ReadPartition}(p, \perp)$ where $\perp$ denotes a reading a dummy block.
- Otherwise, the client reads block u from partition p of the server by calling $\mathsf{ReadPartition}(p, \mathsf{u})$.

Step 2: Place block u that was fetched in Step 1 into the client's cache, and update the position map.

- Pick a fresh random slot number s, and place block u into cache slot s. This means that block u is scheduled to be evicted to partition s in the future, unless another $\mathsf{read}(\mathsf{u})$ preempts the eviction of this block.
- Update the position map, and associate block u with partition s. In this way, the next $\mathsf{read}(\mathsf{u})$ will cause partition s to be read and written.

Afterwards, a background eviction takes place as described in Section 3.8.

3.7 Writing a Block

Let $\mathsf{write}(\mathsf{u}, \mathsf{data}^*)$ denote writing data^* to the block identified by u. This operation is implemented as a $\mathsf{read}(\mathsf{u})$ operation with the following exception: when block u is placed in the cache during the $\mathsf{read}(\mathsf{u})$ operation, its data is set to data^*.

Observation 1. *Each* read *or* write *operation will cause an independent, random partition to be accessed.*

Proof. (sketch.) Consider each client cache slot as an extension of the corresponding server partition. Every time a block u is read or written, it is placed into a fresh random cache slot s, i.e., associated with partition s. Note that every time s is chosen at random, and independent of operations to the O-RAM. The next time block u is accessed, regardless of whether block u has been evicted from the cache slot before this access, the corresponding partition s is read and written. As the value of the random variable s has not been revealed to the server before this, from the server's perspective s is independently and uniformly at random. □

3.8 Background Eviction

To prevent the client data cache from building up, blocks need to be evicted to the server at some point.

```
Access(op, u, data*):
1: r ← UniformRandom(1 . . . P)
2: p ← position[u], position[u] ← r
3: if block u is in slot[p] then
4:     data ← slot[p].read_and_del(u)
5:     ReadPartition(p, ⊥)
6: else
7:     data ← ReadPartition(p, u)
8: end if
9: if op = write then
10:    data ← data*
11: end if
12: slot[r] ← slot[r] ∪ {(u, data)}
13: Call Evict(p)    /*Optional eviction piggy-backed on normal data access requests. Can improve performance by a constant factor.*/
14: Call SequentialEvict(ν) or RandomEvict(ν)
15: return data
```

Figure 3: Algorithm for data access. Read or write a data block identified by u. If op = read, the input parameter data* = None, and the Access operation returns the newly fetched block. If op = write, the Access operation writes the specified data* to the block identified by u, and returns the old value of the block u.

There are two eviction processes:

1. *Piggy-backed evictions* are those that take place on regular O-RAM read or write operations (see Line 13 of Figure 3). Basically, if the data access request operates on a block currently associated with partition p, we can piggy-back a write-back to partition p at that time. The piggy-backed evictions are optional, but their existence can improve performance by a constant factor.

2. *Background evictions* take place at a rate proportional to the data access rate (see Line 14 of Figure 3). The background evictions are completely independent of the data access requests, and therefore can be equivalently thought of as taking place in a separate background thread. Our construction uses an eviction rate of $\nu > 0$, meaning that in expectation, ν number of background evictions are attempted with every data access request. Below are two potential algorithms for background eviction:

   (a) Sequentially scan the cache slots at a fixed rate ν (see the SequentialEvict algorithm in Figure 4);

   (b) At a fixed rate ν, randomly select a slot from all P slots to evict from. (a modified version of the random eviction algorithm is presented as RandomEvict in Figure 4);

Our eviction algorithm is designed to deal with two main challenges:

- **Bounding the cache size.** To avoid the client's data cache from building up indefinitely, the above two eviction processes combined evict blocks at least as fast as blocks are placed into the cache. The actual size of the client's data cache depends on the choice of the background eviction rate ν. We choose $\nu > 0$ to be a constant factor of the actual data request rate. For our practical construction, in Section 5.1 we empirically demonstrate the relationship of ν and the cache size. In the full version of this paper [1], we prove that our background eviction algorithm results in a cache size of $O(P)$.

- **Privacy.** It is important to ensure that the background eviction process does not reveal whether a cache slot is filled or the number of blocks in a slot. For this reason, if an empty slot is selected for eviction, a dummy block is evicted to hide the fact that the cache slot does not contain any real blocks.

Observation 2. *By design, the background eviction process generates a partition access sequence independent of the data access pattern.*

Lemma 1 (Partition access sequence reveals nothing about the data request sequence.). *Let $\vec{y}$ denote a data request sequence. Let $f(\vec{y})$ denote the sequence of partition numbers accessed given data request sequence $\vec{y}$. Then, for any two data request sequences of the same length $\vec{y}$ and $\vec{z}$, $f(\vec{y})$ and $f(\vec{z})$ are identically distributed. In other words, the sequence of partition numbers accessed during the life-time of the O-RAM does not leak any information about the data access pattern.*

```
Evict(p):
if len(slot[p]) = 0 then
    WritePartition(p, ⊥, None)
else
    (u, data) ← slot[cnt].pop()
    WritePartition(cnt, u, data)
end if
```

```
RandomEvict(ν):
for i = 1 to ν do    //Assume integer ν
    r ← UniformRandom(1 ... P)
    Evict(r)
end for
```

```
SequentialEvict(ν):
num ← D(ν)    //Pick the number of blocks to evict according to distribution D
for i = 1 to num do
    cnt ← cnt + 1    //cnt is a global counter for the sequential scan
    Evict(cnt)
end for
```

Figure 4: Background evicition algorithms with eviction rate ν. Here we provide two candidate eviction algorithms SequentialEvict and RandomEvict. SequentialEvict determines the number of blocks to evict num based on a prescribed distribution $\mathcal{D}(\nu)$ and sequentially scans num slots to evict from. RandomEvict samples $\nu \in \mathbb{N}$ random slots (with replacement) to evict from. **In both SequentialEvict and RandomEvict, if a slot selected for eviction is empty, evict a dummy block for the sake of security.**

Proof. The sequence of partition numbers are generated in two ways 1) the regular read or write operations, and 2) the background eviction processes. Due to Observations 1 and 2, both of the above processes generate a sequence of partition numbers completely independent of the data access pattern. □

Theorem 1. *Suppose that each partition uses a secure O-RAM construction, then the new O-RAM construction obtained by applying the partitioning framework over P partition O-RAMs is also secure.*

Proof. Straightforward conclusion from Lemma 1 and the security of the partition O-RAM. □

3.9 Algorithm Pseudo-code

Figures 3 and 4 describe in formal pseudo-code our O-RAM operations based on the partitioning framework. For ease of presentation, in Figure 3, we unify read and write operations into an Access(op, u, data*) operation.

4 Practical Construction

In this section, we apply the partitioning techniques mentioned in the previous section to obtain a practical construction with an amortized cost of $20 \sim 35$X overhead under typical settings, about 63 times faster than the best known construction. The client storage is typically 0.01% to 0.3% of the O-RAM capacity. The worst-case cost of this construction is $O(\sqrt{N})$, and we will later show how to allow concurrent shuffling and reads to reduce the worst-case cost to $O(\log N)$ (Section 6).

While the practical construction require cN client-side storage, the constant c is so small that our cN is smaller than or comparable to $\sqrt{N}$ for typical storage sizes ranging from gigabytes to terabytes. For the sake of theoretic interest, in Appendix A, we show how to recursively apply our O-RAM construction to part of the client-side storage, and reduce the client-side storage to $O(\sqrt{N})$, while incurring only a logarithmic factor in the amortized cost.

4.1 Overview

Our practical construction uses the partitioning framework (Section 3). For the partitions, we use our own highly optimized O-RAM construction resembling the Pinkas-Reinman O-RAM at a very high level [13].

Choice of parameters. In this practical construction, we choose $P = \sqrt{N}$ partitions, each with $\sqrt{N}$ blocks on average. We use the SequentialEvict algorithm as the background eviction algorithm. Every time SequentialEvict is invoked with an eviction rate of ν, it decides the number of blocks to evict numbased on a bounded geometric distribution with mean ν, i.e., let c be a constant representing the maximum number of evictions per data access operation, then $\Pr[\mathsf{num} = k] \propto p^k$ for $0 \leq k \leq c$, and $\Pr[\mathsf{num} = k] = 0$ for $k > c$. Here is $0 < p < 1$ is a probability dependent on ν and c.

As mentioned earlier, the piggybacked evictions enable practical savings up to a constant factor, so we use

```
ReadPartition(p, u):
L ← number of levels
for ℓ = 0, 1, ..., L − 1   (in parallel) do
    if level ℓ of partition p is not filled then
        continue   // skip empty levels
    end if
    if block u is in partition p, level ℓ then
        i = position[u].index
    else
        i = nextDummy[p, ℓ]
        nextDummy[p, ℓ] ← nextDummy[p, ℓ] + 1
    end if
    i' = PRP (K[p, ℓ], i)
    Fetch from the server the block in partition p, level ℓ, and offset i'.
    Decrypt the block with the key K[p, ℓ].
end for
```

Figure 5: The ReadPartition operation of our practical construction that reads the block with id u from partition p.

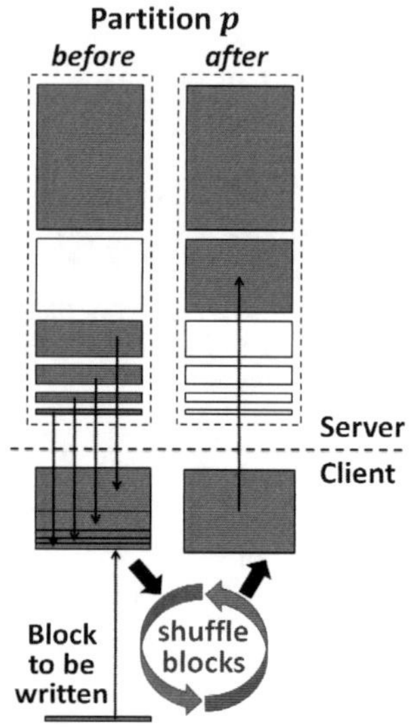

Figure 6: WritePartition leads to the shuffling of consecutively filled levels into the first empty level.

piggybacked evictions in this construction.

Optimized partition O-RAM construction. While any existing O-RAM construction satisfying the modified ReadPartition and WritePartition semantics can be used as a partition O-RAM, we propose our own highly optimized partition O-RAM. Our partition O-RAM construction resembles the Pinkas-Reinman O-RAM at a very high level [13], but with several optimizations to gain practical savings. The practical savings come from at least three sources, in comparison with the Pinkas-Reinman construction:

- *Local sorting.* Due our partitioning framework, each partition is now of size $O(\sqrt{N})$ blocks. This allows us to use a client shuffling buffer of size $O(\sqrt{N})$ blocks to reshuffle the partition locally, thereby eliminating the need for extremely expensive oblivious sorting procedures during a reshuffling operation. This is our most significant source of saving in comparison with all other existing schemes.
- *No Cuckoo hashing.* Second, since we use a position map to save the locations of all blocks, we no longer need Cuckoo hashing, thereby saving a 2X factor for lookups.
- *Compressed data transfer during reshuffling.* Third, during the reshuffling operation, the client only reads blocks from each level that have not been previously read. Also, when the client writes back a set of shuffled blocks to the server (at least half of which are dummy blocks), it uses a compression algorithm to compress the shuffling buffer down to half its size. These two optimizations save about another 2X factor.
- *Latency reduction.* In the practical construction, the client saves a position map which records the locations of each block on the server. This allows the client to query the $O(\log N)$ levels in each partition in a single round-trip, thereby reducing the latency to $O(1)$.

4.2 Partition Layout

As mentioned earlier, we choose $P = \sqrt{N}$ partitions for the practical construction. Each partition consists of $L = \log_2(\sqrt{N}) + 1 = \frac{1}{2}\log_2 N + 1$ levels, indexed by $0, 1, \ldots, \frac{1}{2}\log_2 N$ respectively. Except for the top level, each level ℓ has $2 \cdot 2^\ell$ blocks, among which at most half are real blocks, and the rest (at least half) are dummy blocks.

The top level where $\ell = \frac{1}{2}\log_2 N$ has $2 \cdot 2^\ell + \epsilon = 2\sqrt{N} + \epsilon$ blocks, where the surplus ϵ is due to the fact that some partition may have more blocks than others when the blocks are assigned in a random fashion to the partitions. Due to a standard balls and bins argument [14], each partition's maximum size (including real and dummy blocks) should be $4\sqrt{N} + o(\sqrt{N})$ such that the failure probability $\frac{1}{\text{poly}(N)}$. In Appendix 5.3, we empirically demonstrate that in practice, the maximum number of real blocks in each partition is not more than $1.15\sqrt{N}$ for $N \geq 20$, hence the partition capacity is no more than $4 \cdot 1.15\sqrt{N} = 4.6\sqrt{N}$ blocks, and the total server storage is no more than $4.6N$ blocks. In Appendix B.2, we propose an optimization to reduce the server storage to less than $3.2N$ blocks.

At any given time, a partition on the server might have some of its levels *filled* with blocks and others *unfilled*. The top partition is always filled. Also, a data block can be located in any partition, any filled level, and any offset within the level. In the practical construction, we extend the position map of the partition framework to also keep track of the level number and offset of each block.

From the perspective of the server, all blocks within a level are pseudo-randomly arranged. Because the blocks are encrypted, the server cannot even tell which blocks are real and which ones are dummy. We use keyed pseudo-random permutation (PRP) function for permuting blocks within a level in our construction. When the context is clear, we omit the range or the PRP function in the pseudo-code.

4.3 Setup

The initial set of filled levels that contain the blocks depends on the partition number p. In order to better amortize the reshuffling costs of our scheme, the client randomly chooses which levels of each partition will be initially filled (with the restriction that the top level is always filled). Note that there are 2^{L-1} such possible *fillings* of a partition where L is the number of levels in the partition. The client notifies the server which levels are filled but does not write the actual blocks to the server because the blocks are initially zeroed and their values can be calculated implicitly by storing one bit for each level of each partition. This bit indicates if the entire level has never been reshuffled and is hence zeroed.

4.4 Reading from a Partition

The ReadPartition operation reads the block with id u from partition p as described in Figure 5. If $\mathsf{u} = \perp$, then the ReadPartition operation is a dummy read and a dummy block is read from each filled level. If $\mathsf{u} \neq \perp$, block u is read from the level that contains it, and a dummy block is read from from each of the other filled levels. Note that all of the fetches from the server are performed in parallel and hence this operation has single round trip latency unlike existing schemes [3, 4, 11] which take $\Omega(\log N)$ round trips.

4.5 Writing to a Partition

Each write to a partition is essentially a reshuffling operation performed on consecutively filled levels in a partition. Therefore, we sometimes use the terms "write" and "shuffling" interchangeably. First, unread blocks from consecutively filled levels of the partition are read from the server into the client's shuffling buffer. Then, the client permutes the shuffling buffer according to a pseudo-random permutation (PRP) function. Finally, the client uploads its shuffling buffer into the first unfilled level and marks all of the levels below it as unfilled. The detailed pseudo-code for the WritePartition operation is given in Figure 7.

There is an exception when all levels of a partition are filled. In that case, the reshuffling operation is performed on all levels, but at the end, the top level (which was already filled) is overwritten with the contents of the shuffling buffer and the remaining levels are marked as unfilled. Note that the shuffling buffer is never bigger than the top level because only *unread real (not dummy)* blocks are placed into the shuffling buffer before it is padded with dummy blocks. Since the top level is big enough to contain all of the real items inside a partition, it can hold the entire shuffling buffer.

During a reshuffling operation, the client uses the pseudo-random permutation PRP to determine the offset of all blocks (real and dummy) within a level on the server. Every time blocks are shuffled and written into the next level, the client generates a fresh random PRP key $K[p, \ell]$ so that blocks end up at random offsets every time that level is constructed. The client remembers the keys for all levels of all partitions in its local cache.

Reading levels during shuffling. When the client reads a partition's levels into the shuffling buffer (Line 5 of Figure 7), it reads exactly 2^ℓ previously unread blocks. Unread blocks are those that were written during a WritePartition operation when the level was last constructed, but have not been read by a ReadPartition operation since then. The client only needs to read the unread blocks because the read blocks were already logically removed from the partition when they were read. There is a further restriction that among those 2^ℓ blocks must be all of the *unread real (non-dummy)* blocks. Since a level contains up to 2^ℓ real blocks, and there are always at least 2^ℓ unread blocks in a level, this is always possible.

The client can compute which blocks have been read/unread for each level. It does this by first fetching from the server a small amount of metadata for the level that contains the list of all blocks (read and unread) that were in the level when it was last filled. Then the client looks up each of those blocks in the position map to determine if the most recent version of that block is still in this level. Hence, the client can obtain the list of unread real blocks. The offsets of the of unread dummy blocks can be easily obtained by repeatedly applying the PRP function to nextDummy and incrementing nextDummy. Note that for security, the offsets of the 2^ℓ unread blocks must be first computed and then the blocks must be read in order of their offset (or some other order independent

WritePartition(p, u*, data*):

// Read consecutively filled levels into the client's shuffling buffer denoted sbuffer*.*
$\ell_0 \leftarrow$ last consecutively filled level
for $\ell = 0$ to ℓ_0 **do**
  Fetch the metadata (list of block ID's) for level ℓ in partition p. Decrypt with key $K[p, \ell]$.
  Fetch exactly 2^ℓ previously unread blocks from level ℓ into sbuffer such that all unread real blocks are among them. Decrypt everything with the key $K[p, \ell]$. Ignore dummy blocks when they arrive.
  Mark level ℓ in partition p as *unfilled*.
end for
$\ell = \min(\ell_0, L - 1)$ *// Don't spill above the top level.*
Add the (u*, data*) to sbuffer.
$k \leftarrow$ number of real blocks in sbuffer.
for $i = 1$ to k **do**
  Let (u, data) = sbuffer[i]
  position[u] $\leftarrow \{p, \ell, i\}$ *// update position map*
end for
$K[p, \ell] \leftarrow_R \mathcal{K}$ *// generate fresh key for level ℓ in partition p*
Pad the shuffling buffer with dummy blocks up to length $2 \cdot 2^\ell$. *// The first k blocks are real and the rest are dummy.*
Permute sbuffer with $\mathsf{PRP}_\ell(K[p, \ell], \cdot)$. A block originally at index i in the shuffling buffer is now located at offset i' in the shuffling buffer, where $i' = \mathsf{PRP}_\ell(K[p, \ell], i)$
Write the shuffling buffer into level ℓ in partition p on the server, encrypted with key $K[p, \ell]$.
Write the metadata (list of block ID's) of level ℓ in partition p to the server, encrypted with key $K[p, \ell]$.
Mark level ℓ in partition p as *filled*.
nextDummy[p, ℓ] $\leftarrow k + 1$ *// initialize counter to first dummy block.*

Notations:

$K[p, \ell]$	Secret key for partition p, level ℓ. (PRP or symmetric encryption key depending on context)
nextDummy[p, ℓ]	Index of next unread dummy block for partition p, level ℓ.
$\{p, \ell, i\} \leftarrow$ position[u]	Position information for block u (partition p, level ℓ, index i within the level).

Figure 7: The WritePartition operation of our practical construction that writes block u* with data* to partition p.

of which blocks are real/dummy).

4.6 Security

Our practical construction has the following security guarantees: **obliviousness (privacy), confidentiality, and authentication (with freshness)**.

Theorem 2. *The practical construction is oblivious according to Definition 1.*

Proof. The proof is presented in the full version of the paper [1]. □

Theorem 3. *The practical construction provides confidentiality and authentication (with freshness) of all data stored on the server.*

Proof. The proof is presented in the full version of the paper [1]. □

It should be noted that although our partition O-RAM construction resembles the Pinkas-Reinman construction, it does not have the security flaw discovered by Goodrich and Mitzenmacher [5] because it does not use Cuckoo hash tables.

5 Experimental Results

For our experiments, we implemented a simulator of our construction. Each read/write operation is simulated and the simulator keeps track of exactly where each block is located, the amount of client side storage used, and the total bytes transferred for all communication between the client and server. We also implemented a simulator for the best previously known O-RAM scheme for comparison.

For each parametrization of our O-RAM construction, we simulated exactly $3N$ read/write operations. For example, for each O-RAM instances with $N = 2^{28}$ blocks, we simulated about 800 million operations. We used a round-robin access pattern which maximizes the size of the client's data cache of our construction by maximizing the probability of a cache miss. Therefore our results always show the worst case cache size. Also, because our construction is oblivious, our amortized cost measurements are independent of the simulated access pattern. We used the level compression, server storage reduction, and piggy-backed eviction optimizations described in Appendix B.

5.1 Client Storage and Bandwidth

In this experiment, we measure the performance overhead (or *bandwidth overhead*) of our O-RAM. An O-RAM scheme with a bandwidth overhead of w performs w times the data transfer as an unsecured remote storage protocol. In the experiments we ignore the metadata needed to store and fetch blocks because in practice it is much smaller than the block size. For example, we may have 256 KB blocks, but the metadata will be only a few bytes.

In our scheme, the bandwidth overhead depends on the background eviction rate, and the background eviction rate determines the client's cache size. The client is free to choose its cache size by using the appropriate eviction rate. Figure 8 shows the correlation between the background eviction and cache size as measured in our simulation.

Once the client chooses its cache size it has determined the total amount of client storage. As previously mentioned, our scheme requires $O(\sqrt{NB})$ bytes of client storage plus an extra cNB bytes of client storage for the position map with a very small constant. For most practical values of N and B, the position map is much smaller than the remaining $O(\sqrt{NB})$ bytes of client storage, so the client storage approximately scales like $O(\sqrt{NB})$ bytes. We therefore express the total client storage as $k\sqrt{NB}$ bytes. Then, we ask the question: How does the client's choice of k affect the bandwidth overhead of our entire O-RAM construction? Figure 9 shows this trade-off between the total client storage and the bandwidth overhead.

5.2 Comparison with Previous Work

To the best of our knowledge, the most practical existing O-RAM construction was developed by Goodrich *et al.* [5]. It works by constructing a hierarchy of Cuckoo hash tables via Map-Reduce jobs and an efficient sorting algorithm which utilizes N^a $(a < 1)$ blocks of client-side storage. We implemented a simulator that estimates a lower bound on the performance of their construction. Then we compared it to the simulation of our construction.

To be fair, we parametrized both our and their construction to use the exact same amount of client storage: $4\sqrt{NB}$ bytes. The client storage includes all of our client data structures, including our position map (stored uncompressed). We parametrized both constructions for exactly 1 TB O-RAM capacity (meaning that each construction could store a total of 1 TB of blocks). We varied the number of blocks from $N = 2^{16}$ to $N = 2^{24}$. Since the O-RAM size was fixed to 1 TB, the blocks size varied between $B = 2^{24}$ bytes and $B = 2^{16}$ bytes. Table 11 shows the results. As it can be clearly seen, our construction uses *63 to 66 times less bandwidth* than the best previously known scheme for the exact same parameters.

5.3 Partition Capacity

Finally, we examine the effects of splitting up the O-RAM into partitions. Recall that in our practical construction with N blocks, we have split up the server storage into $\sqrt{N}$ partitions each containing about $\sqrt{N}$ blocks. Since the blocks are placed into partitions uniformly *randomly* rather than uniformly, a partition might end up with slightly more or less than $\sqrt{N}$ blocks. For security reasons, we want to hide from the server how many blocks are in each partition at any given time, so a partition must be large enough to contain (with high probability) the maximum number of blocks that could end up in a single partition.

Figure 10 shows how many times more blocks a partition contains than the expected number: $\sqrt{N}$. Note that as the size of the O-RAM grows, the maximum size of a partition approaches its expected size. In fact, one can formally show that the maximum number of real data blocks in each partition over time is $\sqrt{N} + o(\sqrt{N})$ [14]. Hence, for large enough N, the partition capacity is less than 5% larger than $\sqrt{N}$ blocks.

6 Reducing the Worst-Case Cost With Concurrency

The constructions described thus far have a worst-case cost $O(\sqrt{N})$ because a WritePartition operation sometimes causes a reshuffling of $O(\sqrt{N})$ blocks. We reduce the worst-case cost by spreading out expensive WritePartition operations of $O(\sqrt{N})$ cost over a long period of time, and at each time step performing $O(\log N)$ work.

To achieve this, we allow reads and writes (i.e., reshuffling) to a partition to happen concurrently. This way, an operation does not have to wait for previous long-running operations to complete before executing. We introduce an *amortizer* which keeps track of which partitions need to be reshuffled, and schedules $O(\log N)$ work (or $O((\log N)^2)$ for the theoretic recursive construction) per time step. There is a slight storage cost of allowing these operations to be done in parallel, but we will later show that concurrency does not increase the

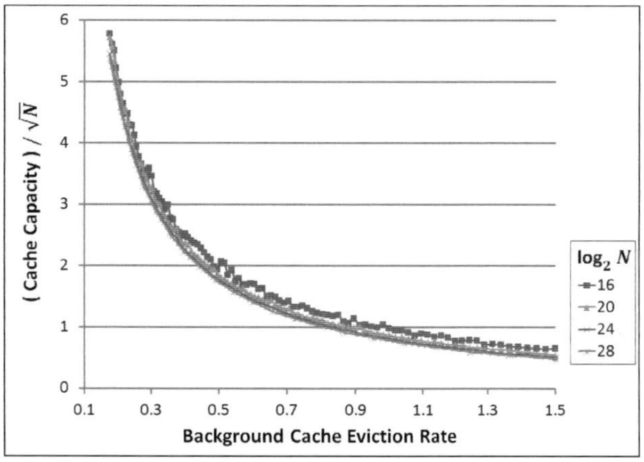

Figure 8: Background Eviction Rate vs. Cache Capacity. The x-axis is the eviction rate, defined as the ratio of background evictions over real data requests. For example, an eviction rate of 1 suggests an equal rate of data requests and background evictions. The y-axis is the quantity (cache capacity)$/\sqrt{N}$, where cache capacity is the maximum number of data blocks in the cache over the course of time.

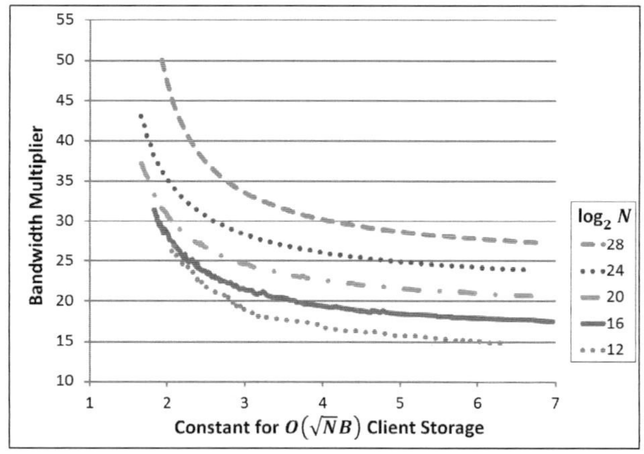

Figure 9: Trade-off between Client Storage and Bandwidth. The plot shows what bandwidth overhead a client can achieve by using exactly $k\sqrt{NB}$ bytes of client storage for different values of k (horizontal axis). The client storage includes the cache, sorting buffer, and an uncompressed position map. A block size of 256 KB was assumed.

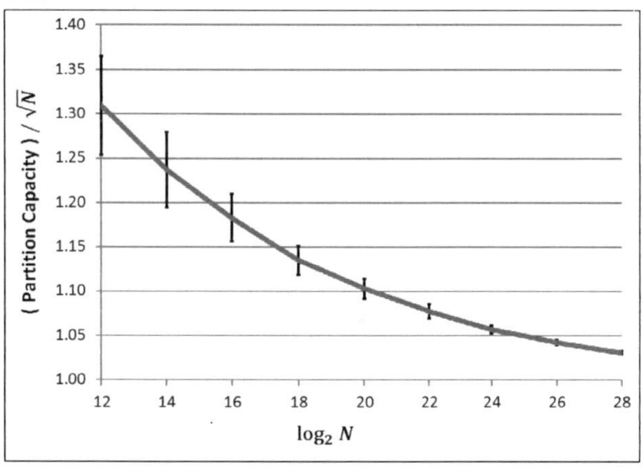

Figure 10: Partition capacity. The y-axis is the quantity (partition capacity)$/\sqrt{N}$, where partition capacity is the maximum number of real data blocks that the partition must be able to hold, i.e., the maximum number of real data blocks inside a partition over time.

# Blocks	Block Size	Practical Performance	
		Ours	Best Known [5]
2^{16}	16 MB	18.4X	> 1165X
2^{18}	4 MB	19.9X	> 1288X
2^{20}	1 MB	21.5X	> 1408X
2^{22}	256 KB	23.2X	> 1529X
2^{24}	64 KB	25.0X	> 1651X

Figure 11: Comparison between our construction and the best known previous O-RAM construction. A 1 TB O-RAM is considered with both constructions using exactly $4\sqrt{NB}$ client storage. The practical performance is the number of client-server operations per O-RAM operation. Our construction has a *63 to 66 times better performance* than the best previously known scheme for the exact same parameters.

asymptotic storage and amortized costs of our constructions.

By performing operations concurrently, we decrease the worst-case cost of the practical construction from $O(\sqrt{N})$ to $O(\log N)$ and we reduce the worst-case cost of the recursive construction from $O(\sqrt{N})$ to $O((\log N)^2)$. Our concurrent constructions preserve the same amortized cost as their non-concurrent counterparts; however, in the concurrent constructions, the *worst-case cost is the same as the amortized cost.* Furthermore, in the concurrent practical construction, the latency is $O(1)$ just like the non-concurrent practical construction, as each data request requires only a single round-trip to complete.

6.1 Overview

We reduce the worst case cost of our constructions by inserting an Amortizer component into our system which explicitly amortizes ReadPartition and WritePartition operations as described in Figure 12. Specifically, the Amortizer schedules a ReadPartition operation as a ConcurrentReadPartition operation, so the read can occur while shuffling. A ReadPartition al-

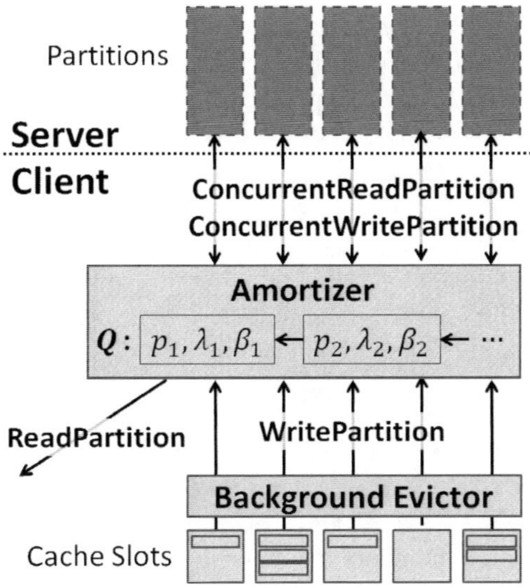


```
TimeStep(op):
if op is ReadPartition(p, u) then
    Call ConcurrentReadPartition(p, u)
else if op is WritePartition(p, u, data) then
    λ ← max i for which C_p = 0 mod 2^i.
    β ← {(u, data)}
    if (p, λ', β') ∈ Q for some λ' and β' then
        Q ← Q − {(p, λ', β')}
        λ ← max(λ, λ'), β ← β' ∪ β
    end if
    Q ← Q ∪ {(p, λ, β)}
    C_p ← C_p + 1
end if
Perform O(log N) work from job queue Q in the form of
    ConcurrentWritePartition operations.
```

Figure 12: The Amortizer component helps reduce the worst case costs of our constructions. It is inserted between the background eviction process and the server-side partitions as shown on the left. The component executes one operation per time step as defined on the right.

ways finishes in $O(\log N)$ time. Upon a WritePartition operation (which invokes the shuffling of a partition), the Amortizer creates a new shuffling "job", and appends it to a queue Q of jobs. The Amortizer schedules $O(\log N)$ amount of work to be done per *time step* for jobs in the shuffling queue.

If reads are taking place concurrently with shuffling, special care needs to be taken to avoid leakages through the access pattern. This will be explained in the detailed scheme description below.

Terminology. To aid understanding, it helps to define the following terminology.

- **Job.** A job (p, λ, β) denotes a reshuffling of levels $0, \ldots, \lambda$ of partition p and then writing the blocks in β to partition p on the server.
- **Job Queue** Q**.** The *job queue* Q is a FIFO list of jobs. It is also possible to remove jobs that are not necessarily at the head of the queue for the purpose of merging them with other jobs, however jobs are always added at the tail.
- **Partition counter.** Let $C_p \in \mathbb{Z}_s$ denote a counter for partition p, where s is the maximum capacity of partition p. All operations on C_p are modulus s.
- **Work.** The *work* of an operation is measured in terms of the number of blocks that it reads and writes to partitions on the server.

Handling ReadPartition **operations.** The amortizer performs a ReadPartition(p, u) operation as a ConcurrentReadPartition(p, u) operation as defined in Sections 6.1.1 for the practical and recursive constructions respectively. If block u is cached by a previous ConcurrentReadPartition operation, then it is instead read from β where $(p, \lambda, \beta) \in Q$ for some λ and β.

Handling WritePartition **operations.** The amortizer component handles a WritePartition operation by adding it to the job queue Q. The job is later dequeued in some time step and processed (possibly across multiple time steps). If the queue already has a job involving the same partition, the existing job is merged with the new job for the current WritePartition operation. Specifically, if one job requires shuffling levels $0, \ldots, \lambda$ and the other job requires shuffling levels $0, \ldots, \lambda'$, we merge the two jobs into a job that requires shuffling levels $0, \ldots, \max(\lambda, \lambda')$. We also merge the blocks to be written by both jobs.

Processing jobs from the job queue. For each time step, the reshuffling component perform $w \log N$ work for a predetermined constant w such that $w \log N$ is greater than or equal to the amortized cost of the construction. Part of that work may be consumed by a ConcurrentReadPartition operation executing at the beginning of the time step as described in Figure 12. The remaining work is performed in the form of jobs obtained from Q.

Definition 2 (Processing a job)**.** *A job (p, λ, β) is performed as a* ConcurrentWritePartition(p, λ, β) *operation that reshuffles levels $0, \ldots, \lambda$ of partition p and writes the blocks in β to partition p. The* ConcurrentWritePartition *operation is described in Sections 6.1.2 for the practical and recursive constructions respectively. Additionally, every block read and* *written to the server is counted to calculate the amount of work performed as the job is running. A job may be paused after having completed part of its work.*

Jobs are always dequeued from the head of Q. At any point only a single job called the *current job* is being processed unless the queue is empty (then there are no jobs to process). Each job starts after the previous job has completed, hence multiple jobs are never processed at the same time.

If the current job does not consume all of the remaining work of the time step, the the next job in Q becomes the current job, and so on. the current job is *paused* when the total amount of work performed in the time step is exactly $w \log N$. In the next time step, the current job is resumed from where it was paused.

We now explain how to perform ConcurrentReadPartition and ConcurrentWritePartition operations in the practical construction to achieve an $O(\log N)$ worst-case cost with high probability.

6.1.1 Concurrent Reads

The client performs the ConcurrentReadPartition(p, u) operation by reading 0 or 1 blocks from each filled level ℓ of partition p on the server as follows:

- If level ℓ in partition p contains block u, then
  - Read block u from level ℓ in partition p on the server like in the ReadPartition operation.
- If level ℓ in partition p does not contain block u and this level is not being reshuffled, then
  - Read the next dummy block from level ℓ in partition p on the server like in the ReadPartition operation.
- If level ℓ in partition p does not contain block u and this level is being reshuffled, then
  - Recall that when level ℓ is being reshuffled, 2^ℓ previously unread blocks are chosen to be read. Let S be the identifiers of that set of blocks for level ℓ in partition p.
  - Let $S' \subseteq S$ be the IDs of blocks in S that were not read by a previous ConcurrentReadPartition operation after the level started being reshuffled. The client keeps track of S' for each level by first setting it to S when a ConcurrentWritePartition operation begins and then removing u from S' after every ConcurrentReadPartition(p, u) operation.
  - If S' is not empty, the client reads a random block in S' from the server.
  - If S' is empty, then the client doesn't read anything from level ℓ in partition p. Revealing this fact to the server does not affect the security of the construction because the server already knows that the client has the entire level stored in its reshuffling buffer.

When $\mathsf{u} = \perp$, block u is treated as not being contained in any level. Due to concurrency, it is possible that a level of a partition needs to be read during reshuffling. In that case, blocks may be read directly from the client's shuffling buffer containing the level.

6.1.2 Concurrent Writes

A ConcurrentWritePartition(p, λ, β) operation is performed like the non-concurrent WritePartition operation described in Figure 7, except for three differences.

The first difference is that the client does not shuffle based on the last consecutively filled level. Instead it shuffles the levels 0, ..., λ which may include a few more levels than the WritePartition operation would shuffle.

The second difference is that at Line 9 of Figure 7, the client adds all of the blocks in β to the buffer.

The third difference is at Line 4 of Figure 7. In the non-concurrent construction, client fetches the list of 2^ℓ blocks ID's in a level that is about to be reshuffled. It then uses this list to determine which blocks have already been read as described in Section 4.5). Because 2^ℓ is $O(\sqrt{N})$ fetching this metadata in the non-concurrent construction takes $O(\sqrt{N})$ work in the worst case.

To ensure the worst case cost of the concurrent construction is $O(\log N)$, the metadata is stored as a bit array by the client. This bit array indicates which real blocks in that level have already been read. The client also knows which dummy blocks have been read because it already stores the nextDummy counter and it can apply the PRP function for all dummy blocks between $k + 1$ and nextDummy where k is the number of real blocks in a level. Observe that the client only needs to store a single bit for each real block on the server. Hence this only increases the client storage by $2N + \epsilon\sqrt{N}$ bits, which is significantly smaller than the size of index structure that the client already stores.

Theorem 4 (Practical concurrent construction)**.** *With $1 - \frac{1}{poly(N)}$ probability, the concurrent practical construction described above has $O(\log N)$ worst-case and amortized cost, and requires cN client-side storage with a very small c, and $O(N)$ server-side storage.*

The formal proof of the above theorem is in the full version of the paper [1].

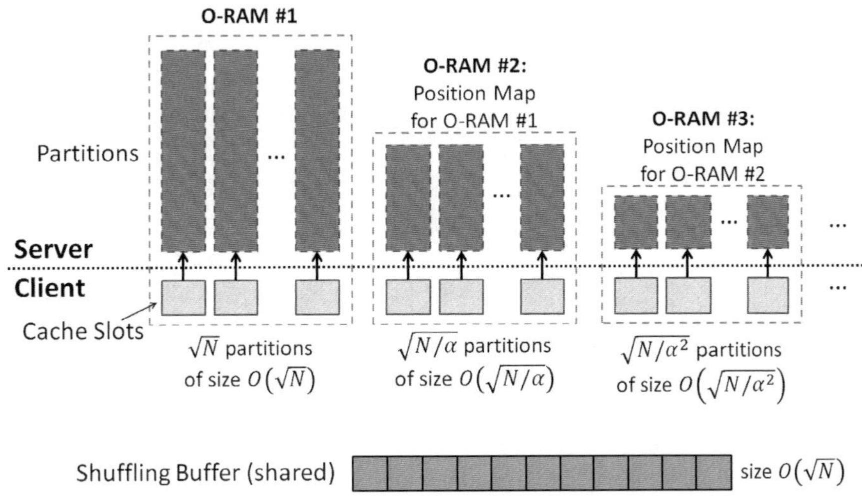

Figure 13: The recursive construction.

Appendices

A Recursive Construction

The practical (non-current and concurrent) constructions described so far are geared towards optimal practical performance. However, they are arguably not ideal in terms of asymptotic performance, since they require a linear fraction of client-side storage for storing a position map of linear size.

For theoretic interest, we describe in this section how to recursively apply our O-RAM constructions to store the position map on the server, thereby obtaining O-RAM constructions with $O(\sqrt{N})$ client-side storage, while incurring only a logarithmic factor in terms of amortized and worst-case cost.

We first describe the recursive, non-concurrent construction which achieves $O((\log N)^2)$ amortized cost, and $O(\sqrt{N})$ worst-case cost. We then describe how to apply the concurrency techniques to further reduce the worst-case cost to $O((\log N)^2)$, such that the worst-case cost and amortized cost will be the same.

A.1 Recursive Non-Concurrent Construction

Intuition. Instead of storing the linearly sized position map locally, the client stores it in a separate O-RAM on the server. Furthermore, the O-RAM for the position map is guaranteed to be a constant factor smaller than the original O-RAM. In other words, each level of recursion reduces the O-RAM capacity by a constant factor. After a logarithmic number of recursions, the size of the position map stored on the client is reduced to $O(1)$. The total size of all data caches is $O(\sqrt{N})$, hence the construction uses $O(\sqrt{N})$ client storage.

For the recursive construction, we employ the Goodrich-Mitzenmacher O-RAM scheme as the partition O-RAM. Specifically, we employ their O-RAM scheme which for an O-RAM of capacity N, achieves $O(\log N)$ amortized cost and $O(N)$ worst-case cost, while using $O(\sqrt{N})$ client-side storage, and $O(N)$ server-side storage.

Definition 3 (O-RAM$_{GM}$). *Let O-RAM$_{GM}$ denote the Goodrich-Mitzenmacher O-RAM scheme [5]: for an O-RAM of capacity N, the O-RAM$_{GM}$ scheme achieves $O(\log N)$ amortized cost, and $O(N)$ worst-case cost, while using $O(\sqrt{N})$ client-side storage, and $O(N)$ server-side storage.*

Definition 4 (O-RAM$_{base}$). *Let O-RAM$_{base}$ denote the O-RAM scheme derived through the partitioning framework with the following parameterizations: (1) we set $P = \sqrt{N}$ denote the number of partitions, where each partition has approximately $\sqrt{N}$ blocks, and (2) we use the O-RAM$_{GM}$ construction as the partition O-RAM.*

Notice that in O-RAM$_{base}$, the client requires a data cache of size $O(\sqrt{N})$ and a position map of size less than $\frac{2N\log N}{B}$ blocks. If we assume that the data block size $B > 2\log N$, then the client needs to store at most $\frac{2N\log N}{B} + \sqrt{N}\log N = \frac{N}{\alpha} + o(N)$ blocks of data, where the compression rate $\alpha = \frac{B}{2\log N} > 1$. To reduce the client-side storage, we can recursively apply the O-RAM construction to store the position map on the server side.

Definition 5 (Recursive construction: O-RAM*). *Let O-RAM* denote a recursive O-RAM scheme constructed* *as below. In O-RAM$_{base}$, the client needs to store a position map of size $cN(c < 1)$. Now, instead of storing the position map locally on the client, store it in a recursive O-RAM on the server side. The pseudocode of the O-RAM* scheme would be otherwise be the same as in Figure 3 except that Line 2 is modified to the the following recursive O-RAM lookup and update operation:*

The position position[u] *is stored in block* u$/\alpha$ *of the smaller O-RAM. The client looks up this block, updates the corresponding entry* position[u] *with the new value r, and writes the new block back. Note that the read and update can be achieved in* **a single O-RAM operation** *to the smaller O-RAM.*

Theorem 5 (Recursive O-RAM construction)**.** *Suppose that the block size $B > 2\log N$, and that the number of data accesses $M < N^k$ for some $k = O(\frac{\sqrt{N}}{\log N})$. Our recursive O-RAM construction achieves $O((\log N)^2)$ amortized cost, $O(\sqrt{N})$ worst-case cost, and requires $O(N)$ server-side storage, and $O(\sqrt{N})$ client-side storage.*

The proof of the above theorem is presented in in the full version of the paper [1].

A.2 Recursive Concurrent Construction

Using similar concurrency techniques as in Section 6, we can further reduce the worst-case cost of the recursive construction to $O((\log N)^2)$. Recall that the recursive construction differs from the practical construction in two ways: (1) it uses the O-RAM$_{GM}$ (Goodrich-Mitzenmacher [5]) scheme as the partition O-RAM and (2) it recurses on its position map. We explain how to to perform concurrent operations in the O-RAM$_{GM}$ scheme to reduce the worst case cost of the base construction to $O(\log N)$ with high probability. Then when the recursion is applied, the recursive construction achieves a worst case cost of $O((\log N)^2)$ with high probability.

A.2.1 Concurrent Reads

As concurrency allows reshuffles to be queued for later, it is possible that a level ℓ is read more than 2^ℓ times in between reshufflings. The O-RAM$_{GM}$ scheme imposes a restriction that at most 2^ℓ blocks can be read from a level before it must be reshuffled by using a set of 2^ℓ dummy blocks. We observe that it is possible to perform a *dummy read* operation instead of using a dummy block and performing a *normal read* on it. This essentially eliminates the use of dummy blocks. Note that the same idea was suggested in the work by Goodrich *et al.* [8].

A dummy read operation ConcurrentReadPartition$(p, \perp)$ is performed by reading two random blocks within a level instead of applying a Cuckoo hash on a element from small domain. Observe that the Cuckoo hashes for real read operations output uniformly random block positions. Because the blocks read by dummy read operation are also chosen from a uniformly random distribution, dummy reads are indistinguishable from real reads.

This observation allows the client to securely perform a ConcurrentReadPartition(p, u) operation as follows. For each level (from smaller to larger) of partition p, as usual the client performs a Cuckoo hash of the block identifier u to determine which two blocks to read within the level. Once the block is found in some level, the client performs dummy reads on subsequent levels. The client always first checks the local storage to see if the block is in the job queue. If so, then the client performs dummy reads of all levels.

In summary, instead of reading specific dummy blocks (which can be exhausted since there are only 2^ℓ dummy blocks in level ℓ), the client performs dummy reads by choosing two random positions in the level.

A.2.2 Concurrent Writes

In the concurrent recursive construction, the ConcurrentWritePartition(p, λ, β) operation is performed by first reshuffling levels $0, ..., \lambda$ along with the blocks in β using the oblivious shuffling protocol of the O-RAM$_{GM}$ scheme. After the reshuffling has completed, the updated Cuckoo hash tables have been formed.

Theorem 6 (Recursive concurrent O-RAM)**.** *Assume that the block size $B > 2\log N$. With $1 - \frac{1}{poly(N)}$ probability, the concurrent recursive construction described above has $O((\log N)^2)$ worst-case and amortized cost, and requires $O(\sqrt{N})$ client-side storage, and $O(N)$ server-side storage.*

The formal proof of the above theorem will be included in the full version of the paper [1].

B Optimizations and Extensions

B.1 Compressing the Position Map

The position map is *highly* compressible under realistic workloads due to the natural sequentiality of data accesses. Overall we can compress the position map to about 0.255 bytes per block. Hence its compressed size is $0.225N$ bytes. Even for an extremely large, 1024 TB O-RAM with $N = 2^{32}$ blocks, the position map will be under 1 GB in size. We now explain how to compress the position map.

Compressing partition numbers. In [10], Oprea *et al.* showed that real-world file systems induce almost entirely sequential access patterns. They used this observation to compress a data structure that stores a counter of how many times each block has been accessed. Their experimental results on real-world traces show that the compressed data structure stores about 0.13 bytes per block. Every time a block is accessed, their data structure stores a unique value (specifically, a counter) for that block. In our construction, instead of placing newly read blocks in a random cache slot, we can place them in a pseudo-random cache slot determined by the block id and counter. Specifically, when block i is accessed for the j'th time (i.e., it's counter is j), it is placed in cache slot $\mathsf{PRF}(i.j)$. $\mathsf{PRF}(\cdot)$ is a pseudo-random function that outputs a cache slot (or partition) number.

Compressing level numbers. Recall that each partition contains L levels such that level ℓ contains at most 2^ℓ real blocks. We can represent the level number of each block by using only 1 bit per block on average, regardless of the number of levels. This can be easily shown by computing the entropy of the level number as follows. If all levels are filled, each block has probability $2^{\ell-L}$ of being in level ℓ. Then the entropy of the level number is

$$-\sum_{\ell=0}^{L-1} 2^{\ell-L}\log_2(2^{\ell-L}) = \sum_{i=1}^{L} i\cdot 2^{-i} < 1$$

If not all levels in a partition are filled, then the entropy is even less, but for the sake of simplicity let's still use 1 bit to represent a level number within that partition. Note that since the top level is slightly larger (it contains ϵ extra blocks), the entropy might be slightly larger than 1 bit, but only by a negligible amount.

Using the compressed position map. These two compression tricks allow us to compress our position map immensely. On average, we can use 0.13 bytes for the partition number and 0.125 bytes (1 bit) for the level number, for a total of 0.255 bytes per block.

Once we have located a block's partition p and level ℓ, retrieving it is easy. When each level is constructed, each real block can be assigned a fresh alias $\mathsf{PRF}(K[p,\ell],\text{"real-alias"},\mathsf{u})$ where u is the ID of the block and PRF is a pseudo-random function. Each dummy block can be assigned the alias $\mathsf{PRF}(K[p,\ell],\text{"dummy-alias"},i)$ where i is the index of the dummy block in partition p, level ℓ. Then during retrieval, the client fetches blocks from the server by their alias.

B.2 Reducing Server Storage

Each partition's capacity is $\sqrt{N}+\epsilon$ blocks, where the surplus ϵ is due to the fact that some partitions may have more blocks than others when the blocks are assigned in a random fashion to the partitions. A partition has levels $\ell = 0,\ldots,\log_2\sqrt{N}$. Each level contains $2\cdot 2^\ell$ blocks (real and dummy blocks), except for the top level that contains 2ϵ additional blocks. Then, the maximum size of a partition on the server is $4\sqrt{N}+2\epsilon$ blocks. Therefore, the maximum server storage is $4N+2\epsilon\sqrt{N}$.

However, the maximum amount of server storage required is less than that, due to several reasons:

1. Levels of partitions are sometimes not filled. It is extremely unlikely that at some point in time, all levels of all partitions are simultaneously filled.
2. As soon as a block is read from a level, it can be deleted by the server because its value is no longer needed.

In our simulation experiments, we calculated that the server never needs to store more than $3.2N$ blocks at any point in time. Hence, in practice, the server storage can be regarded as being less than $3.2N$ blocks.

B.3 Compressing Levels During Uploading

In Line 18 of the $\mathsf{WritePartition}$ algorithm in Figure 7, the client needs to write back up to $2\sqrt{N}+o(\sqrt{N})$ blocks to the server, at least half of which are dummy blocks. Since the values of the dummy blocks are irrelevant (since the server cannot differentiate between real and dummy blocks), it is possible to use a matrix compression algorithm to save a 2X factor in terms of bandwidth.

Suppose that the client wishes to transfer $2k$ blocks $b := (b_1, b_2, \ldots b_{2k})$. Let $S \subseteq \{1,2,\ldots,2k\}$ denote the offsets of the real blocks, let b_S denote the vector of real blocks. We consider the case when exactly k of the blocks are real, i.e., b_S is of length k (if less than k blocks are real, simply select some dummy blocks to fill in). To achieve the 2X compression, the server and client share a Vandermonde matrix $M_{2k\times k}$ during an initial setup phase. Now to transfer the blocks b, the client solves the linear equation:

$$M_S \cdot x = b_S$$

where M_S denotes the matrix formed by rows of M indexed by the set S, and b_S denote the vector B indexed by the set S, i.e., the list of real blocks.

The client can simply transfer x (length k) to the server in place of b (length $2k$). The server decompresses it by computing $y \leftarrow Mx$, and it is not hard to see that $y_S = b_S$. The server is unable to distinguish which blocks are real and which ones are dummy, since the Vandermonde matrix ensures that any subset of k values of y are a predetermined linear combination of the remaining k values of y.

Acknowledgments

We would like to thank Hubert Chan, Yinian Qi, and Alina Oprea for insightful feedback, helpful discussions, and proofreading.

This material is partially supported by the National Science Foundation Graduate Research Fellowship under Grant No. DGE-0946797, the National Science Foundation under Grants No. CCF-0424422, 0311808, 0832943, 0448452, 0842694, 0627511, 0842695, 0808617, 0831501 CT-L, by the Air Force Office of Scientific Research under MURI Award No. FA9550-09-1-0539, by the Air Force Research Laboratory under grant No. P010071555, by the Office of Naval Research under MURI Grant No. N000140911081, by the MURI program under AFOSR Grant No. FA9550-08-1-0352, and by a grant from the Amazon Web Services in Education program. Any opinions, findings, and conclusions or recommendations expressed in this material are those of the author(s) and do not necessarily reflect the views of the funding agencies.

References

[1] Towards practical oblivious ram. Techinical Report, `http://arxiv.org/abs/1106.3652`, 2011.

[2] D. Boneh, D. Mazieres, and R. A. Popa. Remote oblivious storage: Making oblivious ram practical. Manuscript, `http://dspace.mit.edu/bitstream/handle/1721.1/62006/MIT-CSAIL-TR-2011-018.pdf`, 2011.

[3] O. Goldreich. Towards a theory of software protection and simulation by oblivious rams. In *STOC*, 1987.

[4] O. Goldreich and R. Ostrovsky. Software protection and simulation on oblivious rams. *J. ACM*, 1996.

[5] M. T. Goodrich and M. Mitzenmacher. Privacy-preserving access of outsourced data via oblivious ram simulation. *CoRR*, abs/1007.1259, 2010.

[6] M. T. Goodrich, M. Mitzenmacher, O. Ohrimenko, and R. Tamassia. Oblivious ram simulation with efficient worst-case access overhead. In *CCSW*, 2011.

[7] M. T. Goodrich, M. Mitzenmacher, O. Ohrimenko, and R. Tamassia. Privacy-preserving group data access via stateless oblivious ram simulation. In *SODA*, 2012.

[8] M. T. Goodrich, O. Ohrimenko, M. Mitzenmacher, and R. Tamassia. Privacy-preserving group data access via stateless oblivious ram simulation. `http://arxiv.org/abs/1105.4125`, 2011.

[9] E. Kushilevitz, S. Lu, and R. Ostrovsky. On the (in)security of hash-based oblivious ram and a new balancing scheme. In *SODA*, 2012.

[10] A. Oprea and M. K. Reiter. Integrity checking in cryptographic file systems with constant trusted storage. In *USENIX Security*, 2007.

[11] R. Ostrovsky. Efficient computation on oblivious rams. In *STOC*, 1990.

[12] R. Ostrovsky and V. Shoup. Private information storage (extended abstract). In *STOC*, pages 294–303, 1997.

[13] B. Pinkas and T. Reinman. Oblivious ram revisited. In *CRYPTO*, 2010.

[14] M. Raab and A. Steger. Balls into bins – a simple and tight analysis, 1998.

[15] P. Williams and R. Sion. Usable PIR. In *NDSS*, 2008.

[16] P. Williams, R. Sion, and B. Carbunar. Building castles out of mud: practical access pattern privacy and correctness on untrusted storage. In *CCS*, 2008.

Transparent and Extensible Malware Analysis by Combining Hardware Virtualization and Software Emulation

Lok Kwong Yan [†‡] Manjukumar Jayachandra[†] Mu Zhang[†] Heng Yin[†]
[†]Syracuse University [‡]Air Force Research Laboratory
{loyan, mjayacha, muzhang, heyin}@syr.edu

Malware is actively making efforts to evade analysis. In particular, anti-emulation techniques have been deployed to defeat fine-grained dynamic analysis. Our evaluation of 150 real world malware samples revealed that 14 could not be analyze by any of three popular emulation based analysis tools, Anubis [1], CWSandbox [3] and TEMU [5]. While these samples operated normally in KVM using hardware virtualization, they either crashed or exhibited no malicious behaviors on these three analysis platforms. Apparently, emulation-based malware analysis is extensible to provide good instrumentation support, but its downside is lack of transparency.

In contrast, leveraging hardware virtualization, Ether [4] achieves ideal transparency because the malicious code is executed on bare metal hardware and the in-guest changes caused by analysis can be intercepted and hidden by the hypervisor. However, Ether is not extensible, because it incurs a prohibitive performance penalty to conduct instruction-level analysis. Our experiment shows an approximately 3000 times slowdown by enabling single-step, not to mention the extra heavy instrumentation needed by in-depth malware analysis. Moreover, it is far more challenging to implement the code instrumentation tools within a hypervisor (i.e. Ring -1) than an emulator (i.e. Ring 3).

Therefore, it is still an unresolved problem to build an extensible and transparent malware analysis platform. We aim to tackle this problem by combining hardware virtualization and software emulation. The essence is *precise heterogeneous replay*. That is, we record malware execution using hardware virtualization for transparency, and then replay and analyze the malware's execution using dynamic binary translation for flexibility and efficiency of in-depth analysis.

The idea of heterogeneous replay was first proposed and implemented in Aftersight [2], which records the virtual machine execution from VMWare and replays it in QEMU, for heavyweight analyses (such as bug detection) on production workloads. In contrast to Aftersight, our platform needs to work under the malicious context: the emulator should exactly replay the execution recorded from the hardware virtualization platform in spite of the fact that malware is trying to detect every possible heterogeneous property in these two systems.

We carefully classify various operations and instructions into several categories and handle them properly to ensure precise replay. More specifically, we choose to emulate basic integer-based instructions for efficiency, directly pass floating point instructions to the FPU, and record and replay the remaining complex instructions, exceptions, interrupts and device I/O. With the assumption that integer-based instructions are easy to emulate correctly, this design choice achieves transparency, analysis efficiency, and extensibility.

We have implemented a prototype in KVM and TEMU. KVM has been modified to transparently record malware execution using hardware virtualization, and TEMU has been enhanced to precisely replay the execution via dynamic binary translation. With minimum changes, the existing analysis plugins (such as taint analysis, unpacker, and tracing) work properly, achieving the advantages of transparency and greater analysis efficiency. Our experiment on the 14 real world emulation-resistant malware samples has demonstrated that our prototype is able to defeat emulation-resistant malware and conduct in-depth analysis with acceptable performance overhead.

References

[1] Anubis: Analyzing Unknown Binaries. `http://anubis.iseclab.org/`.

[2] J. Chow, T. Garfinkel, and P. Chen. Decoupling dynamic program analysis from execution in virtual environments. In *Proceedings of 2008 Usenix Annual Technical Conference*, June 2008.

[3] CWSandbox::Behavior-based Malware Analysis. `http://mwanalysis.org/`.

[4] A. Dinaburg, P. Royal, M. Sharif, and W. Lee. Ether: malware analysis via hardware virtualization extensions. In *Proceedings of the 15th ACM Conference on Computer and Communications Security*, pages 51–62, 2008.

[5] H. Yin and D. Song. Temu: Binary code analysis via whole-system layered annotative execution. Technical Report UCB/EECS-2010-3, EECS Department, University of California, Berkeley, Jan 2010.

FreeMarket: Shopping for free in Android applications*

Daniel Reynaud, Eui Chul Richard Shin, Thomas R. Magrino, Edward X. Wu, Dawn Song
University of California, Berkeley

Google recently launched Android Market In-app Billing (IAB), a service that allows developers to sell digital content in their Android applications by delegating the billing responsibilities to Google. This feature has already gained immense popularity with developers—16 of the top 20 grossing apps in the Android Market rely on IAB for generating revenue. However, despite Google's recommendations for preventing attacks on IAB applications,[1] the majority of applications do not use adequate security measures to authenticate IAB purchases.

In this work we present the *FreeMarket attack*, which automatically identifies and exploits such insecure IAB coding practices. Our attack produces a rewritten application for which all in-app purchases succeed without any payment. The rewritten application retains the full functionality of the original and can be executed on unmodified Android devices. We show that at least 174 applications in the Android Market (more than 50% of the applications we tested) are vulnerable to this attack.

As part of this work, we develop a translation tool named Deja, which converts the proprietary Dalvik bytecode used by Android applications to standard Java bytecode, enabling the use of the ASM bytecode rewriting library.[2] Deja uses SSA-based dataflow analysis to infer the operand types, which must be explicitly specified in Java bytecode, and correctly reasons about important differences between the two formats (e.g., the bytecode verification process).[3]

In the IAB protocol, Google digitally signs the message notifying an application of a successful purchase. Although Google advises developers to verify this signature on a remote server before acknowledging the purchase, many applications either do not perform any verification or perform the verification on the device using the `java.security.Signature.verify` API.

The FreeMarket attack exploits this behavior by rewriting all calls to `java.security.Signature.verify` with a method that always returns true. To enable this rewriting, it first translates the application to Java bytecode using Deja, then invokes the ASM rewriting library on the Java bytecode. The rewritten application is translated back to Dalvik bytecode, then repackaged and signed so that it can be installed and executed on unmodified Android devices.

To evaluate the effectiveness of the FreeMarket attack, we perform the attack on 295 IAB applications from the Android Market: 126 applications on Android Market's top-2000 grossing list and 169 additional randomly-selected applications. We manually exercise the IAB functionality of each rewritten application to check whether the attack succeeded.

Our results indicate that 58.98% (174 applications) are vulnerable to the attack, and 22.03% (65 applications) are not vulnerable (i.e., the rewritten applications correctly refused to acknowledge the purchases). We were unable to evaluate the remaining 18.98% (56 applications), which were inoperable after the rewriting. Applications with greater revenue were less likely to be vulnerable to our attack, which is not surprising given the greater incentives for developers of higher-revenue applications to implement IAB securely despite the increased development costs.

Upon manual inspection, we find that most of the applications unaffected by this attack perform server-side verification, in accordance with Google's recommendations. Several applications perform validation in native code (which our rewriting tool does not handle) or use third-party cryptographic libraries to verify the signature locally.

Given the increasing popularity of IAB, we expect it will become an increasingly attractive target for attackers. We strongly recommend that developers use server-side verification of cryptographic signatures and techniques to prevent unauthorized modification of code in order to prevent automated attacks such as FreeMarket.

Acknowledgements. This material is based upon work supported by the National Science Foundation under Grant No. 0842695, and the MURI program under Air Force Office of Scientific Research Grant Nos. FA9550-08-1-0352 and FA9550-09-1-0539.

*The full version of this paper is available at `http://droidblaze.cs.berkeley.edu/freemarket.pdf`.

[1] `http://developer.android.com/guide/market/billing/billing_best_practices.html`

[2] `http://asm.ow2.org`

[3] Existing tools for this translation do not properly reason about some of these differences and consequently produce output that cannot be translated back to Dalvik bytecode.

Distance Hijacking Attacks on Distance Bounding Protocols – Abstract

Cas Cremers
ETH Zurich
Information Security group
Zurich, Switzerland
cas.cremers@inf.ethz.ch

Kasper B. Rasmussen
University of California, Irvine
Computer Science Dept.
Irvine, California
kbrasmus@ics.uci.edu

Srdjan Čapkun
ETH Zurich
Systems Security group
Zurich, Switzerland
capkuns@inf.ethz.ch

Using a *distance bounding protocol*, a device (the verifier) can securely obtain an upper bound on its distance to another device (the prover) [1]. A number of distance bounding protocols were proposed in recent years, which provide different performance and security guarantees. So far, several distance-bounding protocols were implemented, some using digital processing and short symbols, whereas others rely on analog processing and use signal streams [4].

The security of distance-bounding protocols was so far mainly evaluated by analyzing their resilience to three attack types: *Distance Fraud*, *Mafia Fraud* and *Terrorist Fraud*. In Distance Fraud, a sole dishonest prover convinces the verifier that he is at a different distance than he really is. In Mafia Fraud, the prover is honest, but an external attacker tries to modify the measured distance by interfering with the communication. In Terrorist Fraud, a dishonest prover colludes with an attacker that is closer to the verifier, to convince the verifier of a wrong distance to the prover. So far, it was assumed that distance bounding protocols that are resilient against these three attack types, are indeed secure.

However, we show that many of these protocols, irrespective of their physical-layer implementation, are vulnerable to a fourth type of attack, which we coin *Distance Hijacking*. In Distance Hijacking attacks a dishonest prover P convinces the verifier V that P is at a distance at which some other honest prover P' resides, which differs from the actual distance from V to P. For example, one of the ways in which P can achieve this is by hijacking the distance measurement phase of a distance bounding protocol from an honest (closer or further) prover P' and inserting his own identity into messages that are not time-critical. This type of attack can pose a serious threat in many practical scenarios, including in situations where other attacks, e.g. Terrorist Fraud, may not be a concern. In Table 1 we list protocols that are vulnerable to Distance Hijacking attacks.

We propose two classes of effective and generic countermeasures that make Brands and Chaum and related protocols secure against Distance Hijacking. Our countermeasures are inexpensive, i.e., they do not require introducing additional messages or cryptographic operations.

Additionally, we show that all distance bounding protocols, including those based on the Hancke and Kuhn protocol [2], are vulnerable to Distance Hijacking if run alongside another distance bounding protocol. This can occur if more than one distance bounding protocol is used in the same environment. This result can be seen as an extension of the Chosen Protocol Attack [3]. We also generalize Distance Hijacking to Location Hijacking, and show that it is possible to hijack locations at which no other provers reside.

Protocol	Year
Brands and Chaum (Fiat-Shamir) [1]	1994
Brands and Chaum (Schnorr) [1]	1994
Brands and Chaum (signature) [1]	1994
MAD	2003
Meadows et al. for $\langle NV, NP \oplus P \rangle$	2007
Noise resilient MAD	2007
WSBC+DB	2010
WSBC+DB Noent	2010
Kuhn, Luecken, Tippenhauer	2010
CRCS [4]	2010

Table 1. Vulnerable protocols

References

[1] S. Brands and D. Chaum. Distance-bounding protocols. In *EUROCRYPT '93*, volume 765 of *LNCS*, pages 344–359. Springer, 1994.

[2] G. Hancke and M. Kuhn. An RFID distance bounding protocol. In *Proc. of IEEE/CreatNet SecureComm*, pages 67–73, 2005.

[3] J. Kelsey, B. Schneier, and D. Wagner. Protocol interactions and the chosen protocol attack. In *Proc. 5th International Workshop on Security Protocols*, volume 1361 of *LNCS*, pages 91–104. Springer, 1997.

[4] K. Rasmussen and S. Čapkun. Realization of RF distance bounding. In *USENIX Security 2010*, 2010.

Throttling Tor Bandwidth Parasites

Rob Jansen Paul Syverson
U.S. Naval Research Laboratory
{rob.g.jansen, paul.syverson}@nrl.navy.mil

Nicholas Hopper
University of Minnesota
hopper@cs.umn.edu

Tor's network congestion and performance problems stem from a small percentage of users that consume a large fraction of available network capacity. These users continuously drain relays of excess bandwidth, creating new network bottlenecks and exacerbating the effects of existing ones. This may currently be a performance issue due to unfair resource consumption, but it also shows that the network is vulnerable to malicious service degradation by a relatively low-resource adversary using similar techniques.

There are three general approaches to alleviate Tor's performance problems: optimizing scheduling strategies, increasing network capacity, and reducing network load. Improved path selection and circuit scheduling may shift network load to better utilize the available bandwidth, but do not increase the capacity of the network or provide any defense against DoS. Organizations such as The Tor Project may increase network capacity by joining new relays to the network, however this approach is a short-term solution that does not scale: the bulk users attracted to the faster network will continue to leech the additional bandwidth.

In this work, we present the design of three new algorithms that throttle clients to reduce network congestion and increase web client performance. Unlike existing techniques, our new adaptive throttling algorithms use information local to a relay to dynamically select which connections get throttled and to adjust the rate at which those connections are throttled. Adaptively tuned throttling mechanisms are paramount to our algorithm designs in order to avoid the need to re-evaluate parameter choices as network capacity and load changes. Our *bit-splitting* algorithm adaptively throttles each connection at its fair share of bandwidth, our *flagging* algorithm adaptively throttles only connections whose throughput exceeds the statistically fair throughput, and our *threshold* algorithm adaptively throttles connections above a throughput quantile at a rate represented by that quantile.

We implement our algorithms in Tor and compare significant client performance benefits using network-wide deployments of our algorithms under a range of light to heavy network loads. We test various configurations of our algorithms and compare our results to static throttling under a

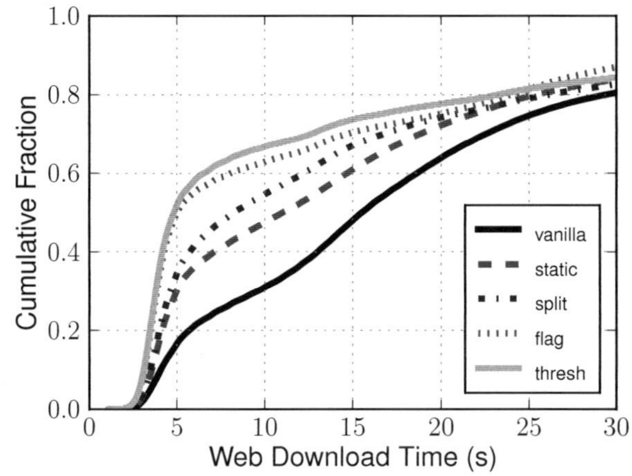

Figure 1: Throttling improves web client performance for each throttling algorithm over vanilla Tor, using 50 relays and a load of 950 web clients and 50 bulk clients.

varied range of network loads. We find that the effectiveness of the existing static throttling approach is highly dependent on network load and configuration whereas our adaptive algorithms work well under various loads with no configuration changes or parameter maintenence: web client performance was improved for every parameter setting we tested. Figure 1 shows that each of our new algorithms provides a significant improvement in web client performance over vanilla Tor.

We also analyze the security of our algorithms under adversarial attack, discussing several realistic attacks on anonymity while comparing the information leaked by each algorithm relative to unthrottled Tor. We find that throttling clients reduces information leakage and improves network anonymity against realistic adversaries, and is an effective defense against practical bulk traffic DoS attacks while minimizing the false positive impact on honest users.

For a more detailed discussion of this work, please see our technical report [1].

References

[1] Rob Jansen, Paul Syverson, and Nicholas Hopper, *Throttling Tor Bandwidth Parasites*. University of Minnesota TR 11-019, 2011.

Taking Routers Off Their Meds: Why Assumptions Of Router Stability Are Dangerous

Max Schuchard, Christopher Thompson, Nicholas Hopper, Yongdae Kim
University of Minnesota
{schuch, cthomp, hopper, kyd} @ cs.umn.edu

In this work, we examine how an adversary in control of a BGP speaker in a transit AS can cause a victim router in an *arbitrary* location on the Internet to become unstable. Through experimentation with both hardware and software routers, we look at the behavior of routers under *abnormal* conditions and come to four conclusions. First, routers placed in certain states behave in anything but a stable manner. Second, unexpected but *perfectly legal* BGP messages can place routers into those states with disconcerting ease. Third, an adversary can use these messages to disrupt a victim router to which he is not directly connected. Fourth, modern best practices do little to prevent these attacks.

Through experiments on hardware and software routers, we observed what happens when routers find themselves starved for CPU cycles or memory. We witnessed a variety of failure modes, ranging from severe performance degradation to the unrecoverable failure of all active routing sessions. We also observed that a router placed into one of these states would more than likely cause its peers to enter one or more of these states as well. An example of this is a CPU starved router was the exhausting its *peer's* memory. When the rate of incoming BGP updates exceeds a router's computational capacity, the receiving router only buffers a fixed number of incoming BGP messages. When those limits are reached it is up to the sender to buffer all future updates until the CPU starved router can accept them. We term this behavior *back pressure*. Figure 1 opposite shows the increase in memory usage over time for a router that is attempting to exchange routing tables with a CPU starved peer versus a peer with sufficient processing power.

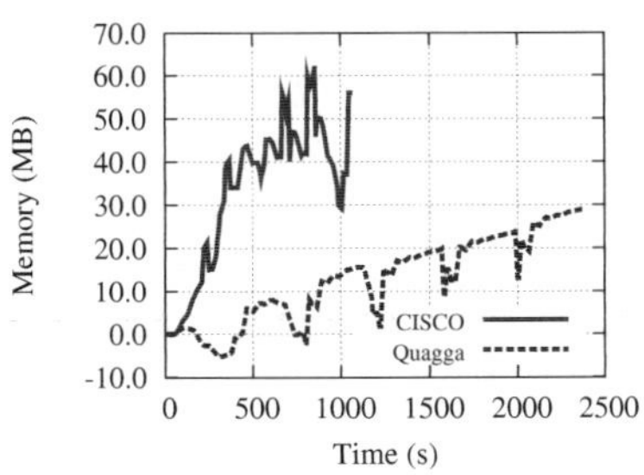

Figure 1.

We found it surprisingly easy to force a router into one of these unstable states. The majority of the methods we found are the result of taking commonly held assumptions about path attributes and invalidating those assumptions. Routers fail to handle these "corner cases" in a reasonable fashion. For example, in the software router Quagga uses a small, fixed size hash map with a predictable hashing function. This is acceptable so long as the assumption that AS paths will be spread evenly over all of the buckets holds. However, an adversary can violate this assumption, advertising AS paths that hash to the same value. Plots of the time to process updates with colliding AS paths compared to random AS paths can be seen in the figure opposite.

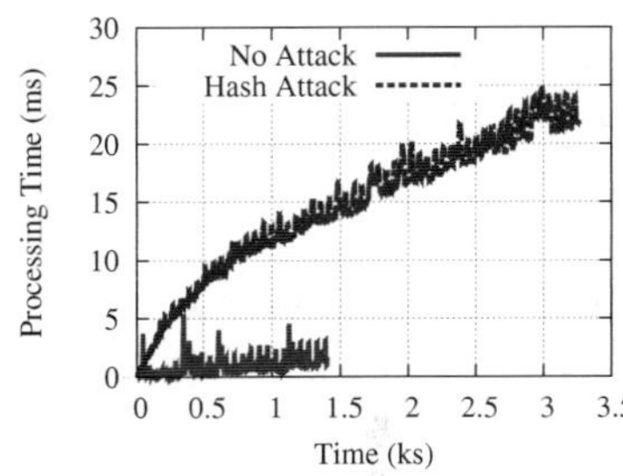

Figure 2.

An adversary in control of a BGP speaker can take advantage of these assumptions to attack other honest routers. By convincing legitimate BGP speakers to propagate these messages, an adversary can push a target in an arbitrary network location into unstable operation. A table below briefly highlights some current best practices, observations about how an adversary avoids them, and experimental evidence to support our observations. Details of how our adversary launches such an attack, along with how best practice fail to stop this can be found in our tech report [1].

Best Practice	Limitation	Experimental Evidence
Prefix Filters	Limits still allow millions of prefixes	/24s advertised by 88.5% of transit ASes
Prefix Aggregation	Not applied to routes from transit ASes	Hole punches and non-aggregated IP blocks
Prefix Limits	Malicious updates based on sum of victim prefix limits	Prefix limits applied on a per connection basis
AS Path Limits	Weakened by generous limits and memory allocation	Patsy allocates memory in fixed size blocks

[1] `http://www.cs.umn.edu/research/technical_reports.php`

Newton Meets Vivaldi: Using Physical Laws to Secure Virtual Coordinate Systems

Jeff Seibert, Cristina Nita-Rotaru
Purdue University
{jcseiber, crisn}@cs.purdue.edu

Sheila Becker, Radu State
University of Luxembourg - SnT
{sheila.becker, radu.state}@uni.lu

1 Introduction

Virtual Coordinate Systems (VCS) have been proposed as an efficient and low cost service to provide network locality estimations by accurately predicting round-trip times (RTT) between arbitrary nodes in a network. Each node measures the RTT to a small number of other nodes and then can estimate the RTT between any two nodes. VCSs assign a set of coordinates to each node based on the estimated RTTs and a distance function. In a distributed and decentralized VCS, like Vivaldi [2], each node maintains and updates its own coordinate by relying on information received from other nodes.

Distributed VCSs have been shown [3] to be extremely vulnerable to insider attacks, where compromised nodes delay measurement probes and lie about their coordinates with the motivation to decrease system performance. As many applications rely on a VCS to build robust services, there have been several proposals to secure them using anomaly detection. However, these schemes are vulnerable to attacks where through small changes attackers make the defense mechanisms to learn malicious behavior as being good behavior. One such attack is the well-known frog-boiling attack where attackers lie by small amounts that accumulate over time and gradually lead to large changes in system performance [1].

2 Description of Newton

A classical approach in designing distributed systems is to use *safety invariants* in order to ensure system correctness. These safety invariants specify states into which the distributed system should never enter. At first glance, VCS do not appear to have such invariants as minimal constraints are imposed. We make the key observation that Vivaldi [2] is built upon an abstraction of a mass-spring system and therefore all nodes must follow physical laws. These laws are universal truths so they represent invariants that all nodes in Vivaldi should globally follow. In particular, we derive three invariants (**IN1**, **IN2**, and **IN3**) that are based on Newton's three laws of motion.

IN1: *If the centroid is not at the origin, then an attacker, has introduced an unbalanced force that has the same direction as a force vector from the origin to the centroid ($\vec{c}$).*

IN2: *Nodes i and k are physically close and if node i experiences a force $\vec{f_{ij}}$ from node j, then node i would expect node k to experience a force from j similar to the vector projection of $\vec{f_{ij}}$ onto the vector $u(x_j - x_k)$.*

IN3: *As the springs in the physical system stabilize and come closer to their rest position, nodes should decelerate and thus also the forces that are applied to them should decrease over time.*

3 Results

We implement Newton, a decentralized VCS which extends Vivaldi to withstand a wide class of insider attacks. When an update sent by a node violates an invariant, the recipient simply discards the update. We run experiments on Planetlab with 500 nodes. In Fig. 1(a) we find that Newton performs 25% better than Vivaldi in benign settings. We also find that Newton is able to mitigate the advanced frog-boiling attack in Fig. 1(b) even under 30% of attackers.

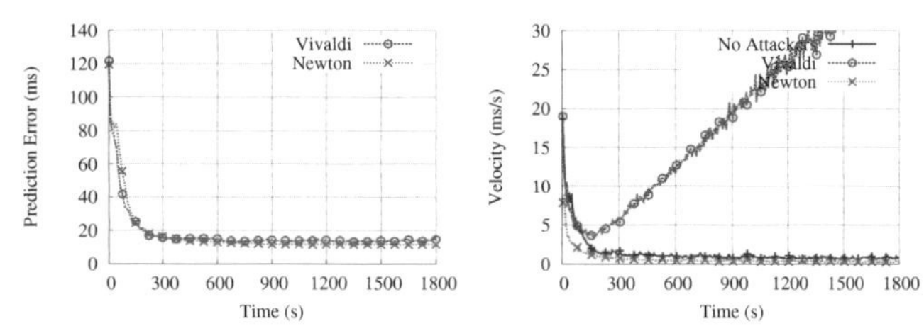

(a) No attack (b) Frog-boiling 30% attackers

Figure 1: PlanetLab results

References

[1] E. Chan-tin, D. Feldman, and Y. Kim. The frog-boiling attack: Limitations of anomaly detection for secure network coordinate systems. In *SecureComm*, 2009.

[2] F. Dabek, R. Cox, F. Kaashoek, and R. Morris. Vivaldi: a decentralized network coordinate system. In *Proc. of ACM SIGCOMM*, 2004.

[3] M. A. Kaafar, L. Mathy, T. Turletti, and W. Dabbous. Virtual networks under attack: Disrupting internet coordinate systems. In *Proc. of CoNext*, 2006.

Charm: A Framework for Rapidly Prototyping Cryptosystems

Joseph A. Akinyele, Matthew D. Green, and Aviel D. Rubin
Johns Hopkins University
{akinyele1j, mgreen, rubin}@cs.jhu.edu

1 Abstract

We present Charm, an extensible Python-based framework for rapidly prototyping cryptographic systems. Charm was designed from the ground up to support the development of advanced cryptographic schemes and protocols. It includes support for multiple cryptographic settings such as integer and elliptic curve groups. Moreover, we provide an extensive library of re-usable routines such as secret sharing and hash functions, and the infrastructure necessary to quickly implement interactive protocols.

Our framework, shown in Figure 1, utilizes a developer-friendly high-level language with operator overloading so that algorithms can be expressed as mathematical expressions. In addition, we take advantage of automatic memory management and typing features to reduce programmer errors. Our goal is to provide a tool that allows developers and researchers to quickly implement advanced cryptographic algorithms while alleviating them of low-level implementation details such as with C or C++.

Charm provides a series of message space conversion routines that enable different cryptosystems to interoperate. In addition, we provide support for embedding cryptosystems in existing applications. This includes support for automatically handling serialization of public/private keys and ciphertexts. We have implemented several cryptographic algorithms in the research literature. We also implemented the first (to the best of our knowledge) implementations of new cryptographic schemes such as multi-authority ciphertext-policy attribute-based encryption, a stateful hash-and-sign RSA digital signature, and anonymous ring/group signatures. Our techniques result in an order of magnitude reduction in code size with only a negligible impact to performance.

The Charm framework is modular with low-level native modules implementing performance critical details and high-level modules providing advanced features. Computationally intensive operations are encapsulated in C math libraries and exposed in Charm via the Python/C extensions API. We provide a benchmarking module for schemes and protocols to measure efficiency. Furthermore, we provide a protocol engine that handles arbitrary data serialization and network transmission between interactive parties. This allows developers to focus on the details of their protocol rather than on low-level network implementation specifics.

Charm is in its 3rd alpha release, and the first beta release is planned for mid-February 2012. The code and a full paper describing the system are available at http://charm-crypto.com.

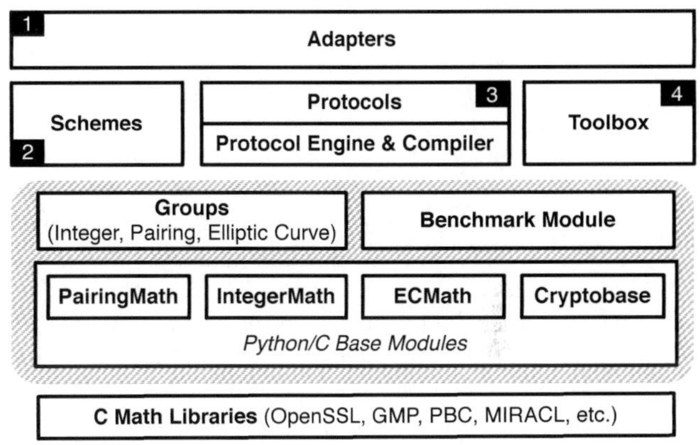

Figure 1: Charm architecture overview. There are four major components built on top of Charm: adapters, schemes, a protocol engine, and a toolbox. 1) An adapter interface that alters the input/output or security properties of a scheme. This promotes code re-use by removing incompatibilities between implementations. 2) A library of implemented cryptosystems accessed via standard APIs. 3) Protocols infrastructure to support the development of interactive protocols via a dedicated protocol engine. 4) An extensible library of common routines, including secret sharing, X.509 certificate handling, parameter generation, policy parsing and hash functions.

This work was sponsored by NSF Award CNS1010928 and HHS Grant Number 90TR0003/01.

Abuse Detection and Prevention Systems at a Large Scale Video Sharing Website [Extended Abstract]

Yu-To Chen, Pierre Grinspan, Blake Livingston, Palash Nandy, Brian Palmer
YouTube, Inc.

1. Overview

Abuse on a large-scale website such as YouTube comes in various forms — scraping, email spam, hate speech, or "black-hat" search engine optimization to name a few — and must be fought accordingly. The detection of abusive behaviors uses supervised (machine learning) as well as unsupervised algorithms to mine billions of requests and predict the likelihood of abuse of each. We describe here an unsupervised system scoring incoming traffic for spam, more specifically bot activity, through some simple statistical anomaly detection rules we found to be quite effective.

Each incoming record includes a number of characteristics or *entities*, such as user id or IP address, used to group the traffic into *slices*; for each entity type we have a number of metrics known to correlate with anomalous behavior in that large values, observed over large slices, reliably indicate anomalous behaviour. Each metric, for each slice, produces a score $\beta \in [0, 1]$ which represents a conservative estimate (0 for most slices), based on that metric alone, of the proportion of undesirable (automated) traffic.

We map metric values to scores using the key fact that each metric is a log-ratio; thus the most standard outlier detection method — flagging as suspicious any value x of metric X more than α standard deviations σ above the mean μ_X — naturally extends into a scoring method by yielding a *goodness* score $\gamma = \exp(-\max(0, x - \mu_X - \alpha\sigma))$, then a *badness* (or spam) score $\beta = 1 - \gamma$. The quantity $\sigma = \sqrt{\sigma_X^2 + \sigma_x^2}$ combines two very different sources of noise : the (weighted) standard deviation σ_X of the metric across entities, and the sampling error σ_x on its measurement x.

2. Metric types

These metrics are implemented using Sawzall [3].

2.1. Ratio and Unique metrics

Assume we have a binary feature such that given a slice of N records, the ratio $q = C/N$ of records with that feature on is cause for suspicion if well below its average p; the associated *ratio* metric is $R_C = \log(p/\tilde{q})$, where the sample estimate $\tilde{q}$ of q and its standard error σ_{r_C} can be obtained by standard methods [2]. The resulting spam score is quite intuitive : say that ratio turns out 10 times smaller than it should be, even taking into account the error margin, i.e. $r_C = \mu_{R_C} + \alpha\sigma + \log(10)$; this will result in $\beta = 0.9$.

If we break this slice's traffic by another entity type or *dimension* D (e.g. a user's comments broken down by target video), an interesting extension using the "novelty" feature ("Is this a new video within this slice?") replaces the counter C with the number U of unique items along this dimension, producing the associated *unique* metric U_D.

2.2. Divergence and Concentration metrics

Assume the distribution $\mathcal{P} = \{p_d\}_{d \in D}$ along a certain dimension is largely stationary (at least across its most common values); an extension of the ratio metric idea measures, given the distribution $\mathcal{Q} = \{q_d = \frac{n_d}{N}\}$ within a slice, the divergence from that reference distribution : $KL_D^{(1)} = \sum_{p_d > q_d} p_d \log \frac{p_d}{q_d}$. Of course one can also look for the predominance of usually rare items, leading to $KL_D^{(2)} = \sum_{q_d > p_d} q_d \log \frac{q_d}{p_d}$. In cases (think of the "user" dimension) of an extremely spread out reference distribution ($p_d \ll 1$) we can, in practice, dispense with it entirely and use absolute, rather than relative, entropy, leading to the *concentration* metric $C_D = \frac{\sum_k n_k \log(n_k)}{N} = \log N - H(D)$, for which [1] for example provides useful variance estimates.

References

[1] A. Antos and I. Kontoyiannis. Convergence properties of functional estimates for discrete distributions. *Random Structures & Algorithms*, 19(3-4):163–193, 2001.

[2] L. D. Brown, T. T. Cai, and A. DasGupta. Interval estimation for a binomial proportion. *Statistical Science*, 16(2):pp. 101–117, 2001.

[3] R. Pike, S. Dorward, R. Griesemer, and S. Quinlan. Interpreting the data: Parallel analysis with sawzall. *Sci. Program.*, 13:277–298, October 2005.

Access Pattern disclosure on Searchable Encryption: Ramification, Attack and Mitigation

Mohammad Saiful Islam, Mehmet Kuzu, Murat Kantarcioglu
Jonsson School of Engineering
and Computer Science
The University of Texas at Dallas
{saiful, mehmet.kuzu, muratk}@utdallas.edu

Abstract

The advent of cloud computing has ushered in an era of mass data storage in remote servers. Remote data storage offers reduced data management overhead for data owners in a cost effective manner. Sensitive documents, however, need to be stored in encrypted format due to security concerns. But, encrypted storage makes it difficult to search on the stored documents. Therefore, this poses a major barrier towards selective retrieval of encrypted documents from the remote servers. Various protocols have been proposed for keyword search over encrypted data to address this issue. Most of the available protocols leak data access patterns due to efficiency reasons. Although, oblivious RAM based protocols can be used to hide data access patterns, such protocols are computationally intensive and do not scale well for real world datasets. In this paper, we introduce a novel attack that exploits data access pattern leakage to disclose significant amount of sensitive information using a modicum of prior knowledge. Our empirical analysis with a real world dataset shows that the proposed attack is able to disclose sensitive information with a very high accuracy. Additionally, we propose a simple technique to mitigate the risk against the proposed attack at the expense of a slight increment in computational resources and communication cost. Furthermore, our proposed mitigation technique is generic enough to be used in conjunction with any searchable encryption scheme that reveals data access pattern.

1. Introduction

Searching over remote encrypted data (commonly referred to as Searchable Encryption) has been an active area of research for the last few years. Due to increased popularity of cloud based services, more and more sensitive data (e.g., health care records, personal emails etc.) are stored encrypted in the cloud. But, the advantage of cloud data storage is lost if the user can not selectively retrieve segments of their data. Therefore, we need secure and efficient search schemes to selectively retrieve sensitive data from the cloud. The need for such protocols are also recognized by researchers from major IT companies such as Microsoft [14].

Although, there are quite a few proposed solutions for searchable encryption schemes, the basic settings remains the same. There is a set of clients and an untrusted server. A client, (e.g., *Alice*), has a set of sensitive documents which she wants to store in a remote server owned by *Bob*. Due to the sensitive nature of the documents, *Alice* does not want *Bob* to learn the content of any of her documents. Since, *Bob* cannot learn the content of the documents, storing the documents in the server in plaintext is unacceptable. Therefore, the document set is stored encrypted using a secure encryption scheme. To facilitate search on encrypted data, an encrypted index structure is stored in the server along with the encrypted data. Authorized users in this setting have access to a trapdoor generation function. Therefore, they can generate valid trapdoors for any arbitrary keyword. This trapdoor is used in the server to search for the intended keyword. It is assumed that the server does not have access to the trapdoor generation function, and therefore, can not ascertain the keyword searched for. However, it is imperative to hide the corresponding keyword of a given query[1] from an adversary. Otherwise, the adversary learns the set of documents that contains the given keyword and the set of documents that does not. In the context of the search over remote encrypted data, it is generally assumed that *Bob* is 'honest but curious', i.e., *Bob* tries to learn as much knowledge as he can without deviating from the protocol.

A 'Searchable Encryption scheme' is qualified as secure, if it satisfies the following necessary conditions.

[1]We use the term 'query' to refer to a trapdoor sent by a user to the remote server as a search request.

1. Query generation function is only known to the authorized data users.

2. The search mechanism works only in conjunction with a valid query generation function.

The first condition specifies that only *Alice* is able to generate a valid query for a given keyword. Furthermore, for a given $\langle keyword, query \rangle$ pair, no entity other than *Alice* has a mechanism to predict the validity of the pair with non-negligible advantage. The second condition guarantees that the search mechanism only works for a given query only if the valid query generation mechanism has been used.

There are many proposed solutions to date that satisfies the conditions outlined earlier. Some models like that of Oblivious ram (e.g., [11]) do not leak any information to the attacker, but are too expensive to be practical on large datasets. Other symmetric key encryption based models, such as [7, 8, 10, 20] proposes efficient solutions to the problem, but leaks data access pattern. That is, in all of those search schemes, given a query x of keyword w, an attacker does not learn w, but she knows which are the documents that contains w. Although, this fact has been noted in the literature (e.g., [8, 10]), none of the previous works systematically analyzed the implications of revealing data access pattern. In this paper, we identify the potential risks of access pattern disclosure via a novel attack. Our empirical analysis with a real world email dataset shows that significant amount of sensitive information can be compromised by the proposed attack. Finally, we propose a simple noise addition technique to mitigate risk against this type of attacks.

We summarize the contributions of this paper as follows.

1. To the best of our knowledge, this is the first study that investigates the implications of data access pattern disclosure in searchable encryption schemes.

2. We formalize a query identity inference attack model based on access pattern disclosure.

3. We prove that such an inference attack is $\mathcal{NP}-complete$ in general and give a heuristic solution that can identify approximately 80% of the queries with minimal background knowledge.

4. Finally, we propose a simple noise addition technique to limit the effect of inference attacks due to access pattern disclosures and empirically show the efficiency of our proposed model.

2. Related Work

In [11], Goldreich et. al. presented their oblivious RAM model, where a user can securely perform search over encrypted data without revealing their access patterns. Although, their technique is theoretically sound, it incurs polylogarithmic overhead on all parameters. They also proposed a lighter version of the Oblivious RAM protocol which works in 2 rounds, but this protocol comes with a very high square root overhead [8]. Therefore, even this lighter version is computationally very expensive for large datasets. Boneh et. al. proposed a public key encryption based keyword search in [4], where data access pattern is revealed. Later, Boneh et. al. presented a public key solution that can hide access patterns in [5]. Again, these public key encryption based solutions are computationally expensive and not always practical for large datasets.

Song et. al. proposed a special symmetric key based searchable encryption technique in [20]. The authors themselves acknowledged the fact that certain statistical analysis can be performed to successfully leak valuable knowledge over the encrypted documents but did not provide a detailed analysis of such attacks.

In [10], Goh et. al. proposed a security definition to formalize the security requirements of *Searchable Symmetric Encryption* (SSE), and proposed a search technique based on Bloom Filters. Unfortunately, Bloom Filters can lead to false positives, a fact the authors themselves pointed out in [10]. Also, since this technique requires separate indexes for each of the documents, it is not very space (or time) efficient.

At the same time as [10] , Chang et. al. proposed a simulation based definition of SSE in [7]. But, their proposed definition does not take into account how an adversary can generate queries adaptively, i.e. an adversary can choose his subsequent queries after seeing the outcome of all the queries he has submitted so far. This shortcoming have been addressed by Curtmola et. al. in [8]. Furthermore, they also proposed SSE techniques that satisfy their improved definitions. We remark that although their security definition allows adversaries to generate queries adaptively, it does not guarantee hiding of access pattens of any particular user. It has been mentioned in [8, 10] that none of these symmetric key based SSE hides access pattern from the server.

In [17], Kumar et. al. used statistical techniques to compromise the anonymization of query logs using token-based hashing. The authors used a reference query log to infer statistical properties of words in the log-file. They used these properties to process an anonymized query log and tried to invert the underlying hash values to their respective tokens. Although, both their methods and ours employ statistical properties of words, the inference method is quite different. Again, the context of these attacks and even the attack themselves are quite different.

Again, access pattern is a fundamental issue in the context of *Steganographic File Systems*. The concept of a steganographic file system was first proposed by Anderson et. al. in [1]. The main goal of such a system is to hide the very existence of the files it stores from an attacker so that the users can be protected from compulsion attacks[2]. Xuan et. al. presented a steganographic system in [23] that can hide data access from an attacker who has continuous access to the underlying storage system. Unfortunately, it has been later shown by Troncoso et. al. in [21] that the proposed file system is susceptible to traffic analysis attacks. Although, the attack presented in [21] may seem related to our work, the fundamental objective of these two models is quite different. In [21], the authors proposed a pattern recognition model which tries to identify *block access patterns* in the midst of a seemingly random sequence of block accesses. That is, their attack model tries to identify the block access patterns during the repeated access of a given file. Once a pattern is identified, the model successfully extracts the blocks of that file, and thus proves the existence of that file. Therefore, the scope of this attack model is significantly different from ours. Their attack model tries to discover the data access pattern from a sequence of seemingly random data accesses. Our model, on the other hand, discovers additional sensitive information using the data access patterns. Quite naturally, the attack methodologies are also quite different for these two attack models.

Therefore, to our best of knowledge, none of the previous works in the literature analyzed the potential security risks due to access pattern disclosure in **searchable encryption schemes**. We show that an attacker can gain significant advantage by utilizing access patterns with the help of some background knowledge on the document set. We further elaborate this point in the following section with an example.

A preliminary version of this work has appeared in the $18th$ *ACM Conference on Computer and Communications Security* (CCS '11) as a 3-page poster abstract [12]. Compared to the CCS paper, we provide a generalized version of the attack model, a complete mitigation scheme, formal proofs and additional experiments in this final version of the paper.

3. Motivation

Let us assume *Alice* stores a set of sensitive documents regarding *Major League Baseball* to a remote server (e.g., *Bob*) using a searchable encryption technique that leaks data access pattern. Furthermore, an attacker *Mallory* can intercept data access pattern of *Alice* for an arbitrarily unbounded amount of time. Let us also assume that the underlying searchable encryption protocol is safe in the sense that it does not reveal any information about the document contents other than the user access patterns. We argue that *Mallory* can infer some valuable knowledge about query identities using these access patterns with the help of some background knowledge on the keyword distribution of the underlying document set.

Considering the type of the documents stored, let us assume an highly likely scenario, where the words 'New', 'York' and 'Yankees' appear in any given document with a higher probability than any other subset of words of length 3 in the document set. Now, let us assume *Alice* sends search request for these three words interspersed among a set of other keywords in a particular period of time. After all the communication rounds are finished, *Mallory* sees a list of trapdoors and the set of documents they appear in. Quite naturally, *Mallory* can calculate the probability of any two of these queried words appearing together in a document by noticing the number of documents the corresponding trapdoors appear together. Now, by observing these probabilities, *Mallory* can easily isolate the three trapdoors representing the keyword set {'New', 'York', 'Yankees'} because of their high probabilities. Furthermore, it is likely that the pair of words 'New' and 'York' appear together in some documents to refer to the state or the city, not the baseball team. Therefore, the probability of both 'New' and 'York' appearing in a document will be higher than that of 'New' and 'Yankees' or 'York' and 'Yankees'. This important observation enables *Mallory* to uniquely identify the trapdoor for the word 'Yankees'. Furthermore, if *Mallory* learns the identity of the trapdoor for 'New', she will also be able to infer the trapdoor for 'York'. Therefore, it is quite evident that a modicum of prior knowledge can lead to the revelation of many encrypted queries and thus lead to significant document contents disclosure.

The above mentioned trivial motivating example considers the information revealed by only a few number of queries. But, an attacker with significantly large computing power can intercept hundreds of $\langle query, response \rangle$ pairs and combine these access patterns with every piece of information she has about the document contents to launch a very successful attack.

In this paper, we show a practical demonstration of such an attack where an attacker can build a model to identify a significant portion of the queries by combining access patterns with some known background knowledge. Furthermore, we show that conceptually very simple noise addition techniques can successfully thwart such attacks from happening.

4. Simplified Model

To explain the attack concept described in this paper, we present a simple model to simulate 'search over remote encrypted data'. A similar type of model was briefly mentioned in [20]. Before describing the model, we like

[2]In compulsion attack, the users are forced to hand over the decryption keys of an encrypted file.

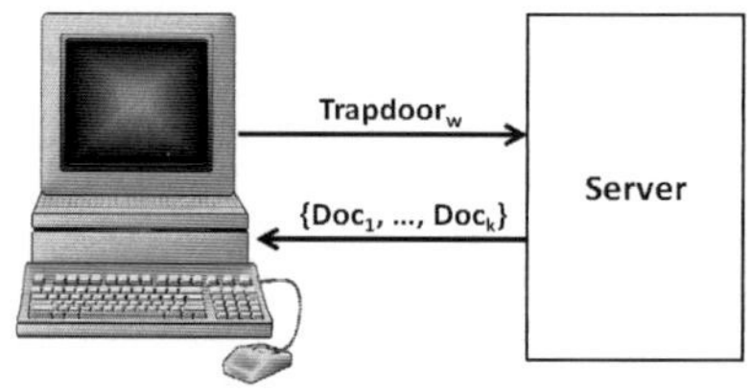

Figure 1. Simplified model of search over remote encrypted data from Mallory's point of view.

to elaborate one very important fact. Our attack model **does not depend on the underlying searchable encryption scheme**. Our attack model succeeds as long as the searchable encryption scheme reveals data access patterns to the attacker. Therefore, the model we describe in the next paragraph is internal to us, and hence should not be interpreted as a necessary condition for the attack to be successful.

In our simplified model, *Alice* has a set of keywords she wishes to search over the document set. At first, *Alice* builds a modified *Inverted Matrix* over the set of documents. That is, *Alice* builds a binary matrix, where the rows are indexed by the keyword set, while the columns are indexed by the document set. Throughout this paper, we refer to this binary matrix for an particular instance of 'search over encrypted data' as *Index Map* (ID). The $(i,j)^{th}$ entry of this Index Map is 1 iff the ith keyword appears in the jth document, and 0 otherwise. In our model, the server *Bob* performs searches for different keywords based on this $Index\ Map$. Since, sending the Index Map in plaintext reveals document contents, *Alice* encrypts the rows of this matrix independently. Furthermore, she also applies a trapdoor function on the set of keywords. Finally, *Alice* sends each of the encrypted rows of the matrix along with the trapdoor value of the corresponding keyword.

When *Alice* wants to search for a particular keyword, she applies the keyword to the trapdoor function and sends *Bob* the result. *Bob* performs a simple text matching and sends *Alice* the encrypted row of the Index Map. *Alice* decrypts the row, and asks for the appropriate set of documents. The search concludes by *Bob* sending back the requested documents.

We like to underscore the statement that we **do not propose a new search scheme** by the above discussion. Almost identical schemes like this one has been outlined by various papers including [20] and [10]. Rather, we simply outline a simple scheme that can simulate the access pattern disclosures of **existing solutions** to the 'search over remote encrypted data' so that we may use this scheme to explain our attack concept.

Now, we can visualize the above scheme as a two step process. *Alice* wants to search a keyword w on an encrypted document set stored in the server. She evaluates $Trapdoor_w$ and sends it to the server. The server sends her the document set that contains the word w. It is worth noting that we purposefully omitted some intermediate communication steps between *Alice* and *Bob*. The rationale behind this omission is, any third party attacker who has access to the communication channel, can omit those intermediate communication steps and see the whole protocol as described in Fig. 1. Furthermore, we argue that any solution to the 'search over encrypted text' that does not hide the access pattern of the client, can be viewed as the protocol shown in Fig. 1. To see why, please note that an attacker, during keyword search process, can record the documents accessed to answer the query. Of course, protocols will have different processes inside the black box, but when viewed from a third party attacker, their interaction with *Alice* will be the same as Fig. 1.

Hence, we assume that *Mallory* intercepts messages of the form $\langle Trapdoor_w, \{Doc_1, \cdots Doc_k\}\rangle$. As we will show next, Malory can infer the underlying keyword w of the query $Trapdoor_w$ that appears in each of the documents in the set $\{Doc_1, \cdots, Doc_k\}$ with the help of some background knowledge.

5. Notations

Table 1 summarizes a short list of notations we use in this paper.

In this paper, we informally treat a document as a set of keywords. So, notations like $x \in d$ are extensively used to mean that keyword x appears in the document d. Furthermore, we assume $\mathcal{D}$ and $\mathcal{K}$ are a total ordering on the document set and keyword set respectively. That is why, we uniquely identify a document by $\mathcal{D}_i$ for $i \in [1,n]$. Similarly, we can uniquely identify a keyword by specifying $\mathcal{K}_i$ for $i \in [1,m]$.

We mathematically denote the ith keyword $\mathcal{K}_i$ as an m bit row vector $[\mathcal{K}_i^1, \mathcal{K}_i^2, ..., \mathcal{K}_i^m]$, such that $\mathcal{K}_i^i = 1$ and $\mathcal{K}_i^j = 0$ for $\forall j \neq i$. Again, we denote $\mathcal{Q} = \langle \mathcal{Q}_1, \cdots \mathcal{Q}_l\rangle$ be the ordered sequence of queries submitted by *Alice* for a given period of time. Here, $\forall i\ \exists j, \mathcal{Q}_i = Trapdoor_{\mathcal{K}_j}$. We refer $R_q = \langle d_1, \cdots, d_n\rangle$ as the result sent by the server in response to a query $q = Trapdoor_{\mathcal{K}_j}$ such that $d_i = 1$ iff the ith document contains the keyword corresponding to the query q and $d_i = 0$ otherwise. That is, if $R_q = \langle d_1, \cdots, d_n\rangle$ be the response for query q and

Table 1. Notations

Notation	Meaning
$\|x\|$	The cardinality of the set x.
x^T	The transpose of the matrix x.
$\mathcal{D}$	An ordered sequence of all the documents stored in the server.
n	The number of documents in $\mathcal{D}$. That is, $n = \|\mathcal{D}\|$.
$\mathcal{K}$	An ordered sequence of all the keywords.
m	The number of keywords in $\mathcal{K}$. That is, $m = \|\mathcal{K}\|$.
$\mathcal{D}_i$	The ith document in $\mathcal{D}$.
$\mathcal{K}_i$	The ith keyword in $\mathcal{K}$.
$Trapdoor_w$	The output of the trapdoor function with argument $w \in \mathcal{K}$.
R_q	The result sent by the server in response to a query q.
$\mathcal{Q}$	A sequence of queries in a given time.

$q = Trapdoor_{\mathcal{K}_j}$, then each d_i is defined by the following function.

$$d_i = \begin{cases} 0 & : \text{if } \mathcal{K}_j \notin Doc_i \\ 1 & : \text{if } \mathcal{K}_j \in Doc_i \end{cases}$$

Since, $\mathcal{Q} = \langle \mathcal{Q}_1, \cdots \mathcal{Q}_l \rangle$ is the sequence of queries the client poses to the server at some given interval, the server sends the corresponding documents as the query answer in response to each of these queries. It should be noted that in our settings, the attacker can intercept the queries $\mathcal{Q}_i$, can uniquely identify them, but do not know which keywords they are associated with. Similarly, he/she can intercept the documents, but is not able to learn the contents of the documents.

6. Threat Model

In our model, the attacker, *Mallory* observes a sequence of l queries $\mathcal{Q} = \langle \mathcal{Q}_1, \cdots \mathcal{Q}_l \rangle$ submitted by the client to the server. Naturally, *Mallory* has also access to the sequence of query responses $R_{\mathcal{Q}_i}$, $\forall i \in [1, l]$, since he has full access to the communication channel. The goal of *Mallory* is to successfully ascertain the sequence of keywords $\mathcal{K}_A = \langle \mathcal{K}_{a_1}, \cdots \mathcal{K}_{a_l} \rangle$, where $\mathcal{K}_A \subset \mathcal{K}$ and $\forall i \in [1, l]$, $Trapdoor_{\mathcal{K}_{a_i}} = \mathcal{Q}_i$. That is, *Mallory* wishes to uniquely identify the underlying keywords of each of the queries $\mathcal{Q}_i$. In this paper, we show that *Mallory* has a very high probability of succeeding if she has access to the following background knowledge on the document set.

- *Mallory* knows the underlying keywords for k of the queries in the sequence $\mathcal{Q}$. That is, *Mallory* has access to the set $K_Q \subset \mathcal{K}_A \times \mathcal{Q}$, where $K_Q = \{\langle x, y \rangle \mid (x \in \mathcal{K}_A) \wedge (y \in \mathcal{Q}) \wedge (y = Trapdoor_x)\}$ and $k = |K_Q|$. We later show that *Mallory* can be successful with very high probability even when $k << l$. Furthermore, we empirically show that *Mallory* has high probability of being successful even when she does not know the identity of any of the queries in $\mathcal{Q}$, i.e., $k = 0$.
- *Mallory* has an $m \times m$ matrix M. Please recall that m is the number of possible keywords in our model. Each $(i, j)^{th}$ cell in matrix M contains the expected probability of both i^{th} and j^{th} keywords appearing in any random document $d \in \mathcal{D}$. That is, $M_{i,j} = Pr\left[(\mathcal{K}_i \in d) \wedge (\mathcal{K}_j \in d)\right]$, where d is a document sampled uniformly from the set $\mathcal{D}$.

An attacker can simulate the matrix M by carrying out a probabilistic analysis over the large publicly available online datasets. Sophisticated frequency analysis techniques can also be used to approximate M. Again, an inside attacker may already have access to a sizable subset of the original dataset in his/her disposal. Therefore, he can create the background matrix from this subset. In this case, there is a significant probability that this matrix is a reasonable approximation of the background matrix M our model requires. We later empirically show that our model works reasonably well for a noisy background knowledge matrix. Therefore, we argue that the background matrix M does not have to be completely accurate. Rather, any close approximation of M is sufficient for an successful attack. For example, there are quite a substantial number of `WikiLeaks` documents in public domain now. An adversary can use a related subset of documents to come up with a matrix that can approximate a background matrix M for a dataset that involves dimplomatic affairs. We plan to explore the ways to build the background matrix and their effects on our model in further details in the future.

Again, obtaining a set of known queries might prove to be a difficult task for an attacker under some scenario. But, we still find it appropriate to add it as a background knowledge in our model for the following reasons. First, we empirically show that our model performs quite well even when the adversary does not have access to a set of known queries. Therefore, an attacker only uses this known query set when he has access to it. He still does quite well when he does not have access to this set. Second, under some scenario, it is quite possible for an inside attacker to know a known query set. And finally, we believe that any secure searchable encryption scheme should not reveal any additional query content given a set of known queries. The Oblivious RAM [11] is one such secure protocol. Therefore, we find it justified to consider the set of known queries as a part of the background knowledge the adversary has in our model.

To best explain our proposed model, we introduce the attack concept with a simplified but effective version of the model in the following section. Later, we proceed to present a more generalized attack model in the subsequent section of this paper.

7. Simplified Attack Model

In this section, we describe how *Mallory* can formulate an attack to identify query identities as an optimization problem with constraints. Here, *Mallory* has access to the communication channel, and thus intercepts a set of l queries $\mathcal{Q} = \langle \mathcal{Q}_1, \cdots, \mathcal{Q}_l \rangle$ and has access to K_Q and M as defined earlier. Let us assume that *Mallory* already knows the corresponding keywords for each of the queries in the set $\mathcal{S} \subset \mathcal{Q}$. That is, $\mathcal{S} = \{y | \exists x \langle x, y \rangle \in K_Q\}$. Now, the goal for *Mallory* is to assign keywords to all the queries $q \in (\mathcal{Q} - \mathcal{S})$ such that the joint keyword distribution as seen by the message responses R_q fits our prior knowledge, namely the background knowledge matrix, M.

Hence, *Mallory* tries to find a sequence of l indices $\langle a_1, \cdots, a_l \rangle$ s.t. *Mallory* believes that $\forall j : \mathcal{Q}_j = Trapdoor_{\mathcal{K}_{a_j}}$, given the matrix M. We present the simplified attack model as an optimization problem by Eq. 1.

$$\underset{\langle a_1, \cdots, a_l \rangle}{\text{argmin}} \sum_{\mathcal{Q}_i, \mathcal{Q}_j \in \mathcal{Q}} \left(\frac{R_{\mathcal{Q}_i} \cdot R_{\mathcal{Q}_j}^T}{n} - \left(\mathcal{K}_{a_i} \cdot M \cdot \mathcal{K}_{a_j}^T \right) \right)^2 \tag{1}$$

$$Constraints: \quad \forall j \text{ s.t. } \mathcal{Q}_j \in \mathcal{S}, a_j = x_j \text{ s.t. } \langle \mathcal{K}_{x_j}, \mathcal{Q}_j \rangle \in K_Q$$
$$\forall j, \parallel \mathcal{Q}_j \parallel = 1$$

The first constraint in $Eq.$ (1) guarantees that the known queries will be assigned to their correct known keywords. While the second one makes sure that all the queries in the set has an assignment of a valid keyword format, i.e., each query $\mathcal{Q}_j$ conforms to the query format outlined in section 5.

The result of this constraint satisfying optimization problem is an assignment of keywords to the queries that achieves minimum distance from our background knowledge matrix M.

To explain the model described in $Eq.$ (1), let us consider the following example. Suppose, $\mathcal{Q}_s$ and $\mathcal{Q}_t$ are two encrypted queries. Therefore, *Mallory* can calculate the probability of the underlying keywords appearing together in a given document by $\beta = \frac{R_{\mathcal{Q}_s} \cdot R_{\mathcal{Q}_t}}{n}$, here $\cdot$ operation denotes the "dot" product between two vectors. Now, for any two given keywords $\mathcal{K}_f$ and $\mathcal{K}_g$, *Mallory* can calculate the probability of these two keyword appearing together by $\gamma = M_{f,g}$. When, the keywords K_f and K_g are presented by their proper bit-vector representation, γ can be equivalently written as $\gamma = (\mathcal{K}_f \cdot M \cdot \mathcal{K}_g^T)$. Here, $\cdot$ operation denotes matrix multiplication. Naturally, *Mallory* will assign $\mathcal{K}_f$, $\mathcal{K}_g$ to the queries $\mathcal{Q}_s$, $\mathcal{Q}_t$ iff the observed probability from the query response β is close to the known probability γ. This closeness can be measured by a simple arithmetic distance function $(\beta - \gamma)^2$, where a lower value of this function is preferred over a higher value. So, the aim of *Mallory* will be to assign keywords to queries such that this distance function is minimized. Our model given by $Eq.$ (1) is just a formalization of this objective function.

8. Generalized Model

In this section, we outline the generalized version of the proposed attack model. Here, instead of taking the joint probability distribution of keyword pairs, we consider joint probability distributions up to r keywords. In this model, instead of the background matrix M, *Mallory* has access to a family of r functions $F = \{F_i\}$. The ith function in the family F, denoted as $F_i : \mathcal{K}^i \rightarrow [0, 1]$ takes i keywords as arguments and returns the probability of all of these i keywords appearing in a document d sampled uniformly from the document set $\mathcal{D}$. That is, F_i can be defined by the following equation.

$$F_i(\mathcal{K}_1, \cdots, \mathcal{K}_i) = Pr\left[(\mathcal{K}_1 \in d) \wedge \cdots \wedge (\mathcal{K}_i \in d)\right] \tag{2}$$

Before we present our generalized attack model, let us define a crude version of "*dot*" product for p equal length vectors[3].

Definition The MSP (Multi Scalar Product) function, denoted by $\odot$, takes as argument p equal length binary vectors $V_1, \cdots, V_p$ and returns a positive integer. Let us assume that each vector V_i is a q bit vector s.t. $V_i = \langle V_i^1 \cdots V_i^q \rangle$. Then, $\odot$ is defined as follows.

$$\odot(V_1, \cdots V_p) = \sum_{i=1}^{q} \prod_{j=1}^{p} (V_j^i) \tag{3}$$

[3]The value of p can be arbitrarily greater than 2.

It should be noted that the MSP function defined above degenerates to the conventional "dot" product operation for the limiting case of $p = 2$.

Also in this generalized model, *Mallory* aims to find a sequence of l indices $\langle a_1, \cdots, a_l \rangle$ s.t. *Mallory* believes that $\forall j : Q_j = Trapdoor_{\mathcal{K}_{a_j}}$, given the function family F.

Let us define c_i for $i \in [1, k]$ for a given sequence of indices $\langle a_1, \cdots, a_l \rangle$ in the following way.

$$c_i = \sum_{\mathcal{Q}_1, \cdots \mathcal{Q}_i \in \mathcal{Q}} \left(\frac{\odot(R_{\mathcal{Q}_1} \cdots R_{\mathcal{Q}_i})}{n} - (F_i(\mathcal{K}_{a_1}, \cdots, \mathcal{K}_{ai})) \right)^2 \quad (4)$$

Here, $\odot(R_{\mathcal{Q}_1} \cdots R_{\mathcal{Q}_i})$ returns the number of documents where all of the underlying keywords corresponding to the query response sequence $R_{\mathcal{Q}_1} \cdots R_{\mathcal{Q}_i}$ appear in. Again, let us define $w = (w_1, w_2 ..., w_k)$ be a real-valued weight vector. Our model can be expressed in terms of $Eq.$ (4) in the following way.

$$\underset{\langle a_1, \cdots, a_l \rangle}{\text{argmin}} \sum_{i=1}^{k} w_i \cdot c_i \quad (5)$$

Subject to: $\forall_i \forall j$ s.t. $\mathcal{Q}_j \in \mathcal{S}, a_j = x_j$ s.t. $\langle \mathcal{K}_{x_j}, \mathcal{Q}_j \rangle \in K_Q$
$\forall_i \forall_j, \| \mathcal{Q}_j \| = 1$

Unfortunately, the optimization problem presented in our generalized model is $\mathcal{NP} - Complete$. In fact, we show in $Theorem$ 1 that even a smaller subset of the given problem, i.e., the optimization problem given for the simplified model in $Eq.$ (1), is $\mathcal{NP} - Complete$.

Theorem 1. *Finding an optimal assignment of keywords to a given set of queries w.r.t. the objective function defined by Eq. (1) is* $\mathcal{NP} - Complete$.

For interested readers, the proof of $Theorem$ 1 is presented in Appendix A.

Therefore, it is quite evident that solving the optimization problem outlined earlier is computationally infeasible for large dataset. Quite naturally, we propose an efficient approximation of this problem that uses *Simulated Annealing* [15]. Simulated Annealing is a probabilistic metaheurestic which is frequently used to find good approximation to the global optimum of some given function when the search space is large. It turns out that if we run the optimization problem long enough, a significant subset of the query set $\mathcal{Q}$ can be successfully revealed. A detailed description of the algorithm of our optimizer for the simplified attack model is given in Fig. 2 at page 8.

9. Experiment Results

In this section, we present an empirical evaluation of our proposed simplified attack model on various instances of 'search over remote encrypted data'. In our experiments, we use a real world dataset, namely, the Enron dataset as our corpus [16]. We also use a well known stemming technique such as *Porter Stemming Algorithm* [19] to ascertain the root of every keyword. Our experimental results suggest that even the simplified model can predict the identity of over 80% queries for large datasets. On the other hand, the execution time of the implemented model suggests that the proposed approximation of the model is quite efficient. Rest of this section is organized as follows. We describe our methodology first, then describe various experiments and explain their results.

9.1. Experimental Setup

9.1.1 Dataset Used

As we have already mentioned, we use *Enron* dataset as our corpus [16]. This dataset was originally prepared by the CALO Project (A Cognitive Assistant that Learns and Organizes). This dataset has already been extensively used in various study in the past [3, 6, 9]. *Enron* dataset contains emails of about 150 different users. The dataset is organized into various folders. We have chosen all the 30109 emails contained in the $\_sent\_mail$ folder of all the users as our experimental dataset. This dataset was made public by the Federal Energy Regulatory Commission during its investigation.

The most important characteristic of this dataset is that each of the documents is a real email sent by a person. One of the motivations [20] behind 'search over encrypted data' is to store emails to a remote server in encrypted format and search the emails from time to time. Therefore, we find it appropriate to run our experiments on real email dataset like that of enron. The first few lines for each of the emails contains some metadata about that mail. Since, these lines are not part of the original email, we strip these lines off the email documents as a preprocessing step.

9.1.2 Stemming Algorithm

Since, most of the emails are personal in nature, they capture informal communication made between two individuals. Therefore, we use a stemming algorithm, namely the *Porter Stemming Algorithm* [19] to find the root of each of the words in the document set. Throughout this section, it will be implicitly assumed that all the processing step on the keywords have been done after the keywords have gone through the porter stemming algorithm. It should

Algorithm 1 Optimizer

```
Require: V : variable List
         D : domain List
         K : known assignments
         Mp, Mc : pair similarity matrices

valList ← copy D
for all cipher var_i ∈ V do
   val_i ← select random member of valList
   add { vari = vali} to initState
   remove val_i fom valList
end for
add K to initState
return ANNEAL (initState, D, Mp, Mc)
```

- V, D: V and D contains the cipher and plain keywords respectively that are not part of the background.
- K: K contains the background knowledge in the form of known cipher-plain keyword pairs.
- Mp, Mc: Mp, Mc contains the joint frequency distrubition of plain and cipher keyword pairs respectively.
- valList ... add K to initState: Any state of the problem contains cipher-plain keyword pairs such that each cipher keyword is assigned to a unique plain keyword. Initial state is constructed by the union of mappings in backgrund and random mapping between cipher and plain keywords that are not part of the background.
- return ANNEAL: Simulated annealing is applied to find an approximate solution to the formulated optimization problem.

Algorithm 2 ANNEAL

```
Require: initState, D, Mp, Mc
         initTempareture, coolingRate. rejectThreshold

currentState ← initState
succReject ← 0
currT ← initTempareture
while (temp ≠ 0 and succReject < rejectThreshold) do
   currentCost ← 0, nextCost ← 0
   nextState ← copy currentState
   (x, y) ← select random pair from nextState
   y' ← select random member of D different from y
   remove {x = y} from nextState
   add {x = y'} to nextState
   if (z,y') is a member of initState then
      remove {z = y'} from nextState
      add {z = y} to nextState
   endif
   for all cells i,j in Mc
      (i,k) ← currentState.get(i), (i,k') ← nextState.get(i)
      (j, l) ← currentState.get(j), (j, l') ← nextState.get(j)
      currentcost += (Mc[i,j] - Mp[k,l])^2
      nextcost += (Mc[i,j] - Mp[k',l'])^2
   end for
   E =nextCost – currentCost
   if (E < 0) then
      accept new state
   else
      accept new state with probability exp(-E/currT)
   end if
   if new state is accepted then
      succReject ← 0, currentState ← nextState
   else
      succReject++
   end if
   currT= coolingRate*currT
end while
return currentState
```

- initTempareture, coolingRate, rejectThreshold: Simulated annealing parameters
- while: Search continues until tempreature reaches zero or the system is frozen (i.e. no new state is being accepted for a large period of time).
- nextState ... add {x = y'}: Next state is generated by choosing a random cipher-plain keyword pair from the current state and assigning a new plain keyword to the selected cipher keyword
- if (z,y') ... endif: If plain keyword y' that is assigned to selected cipher x is previously assigned to another cipher z, old plain keyword y that was assigned to x is assigned to z
- for all cells ... end for: Cost of the current and neighbor states are evaluated against the formulated evaluation function. state.get(i) returns the cipher,plain pair corresponding to cipher i. k,k' are the plain keywords assingned to cipher i in current and next states respectively. l,l' are plain keywords for cipher j in current and next states
- E ... end if: Standard step for simulated annealing approaches. If next state is better than the current, accept new state. Even if new state is worse than the current state, accept new state with some probability to get rid of local minimums
- currT= coolingRate*currT: Decrement temparature according to exponential cooling scheme, coolingRate is a constant close to but smaller than 1

Figure 2. Algorithm for Optimizer.

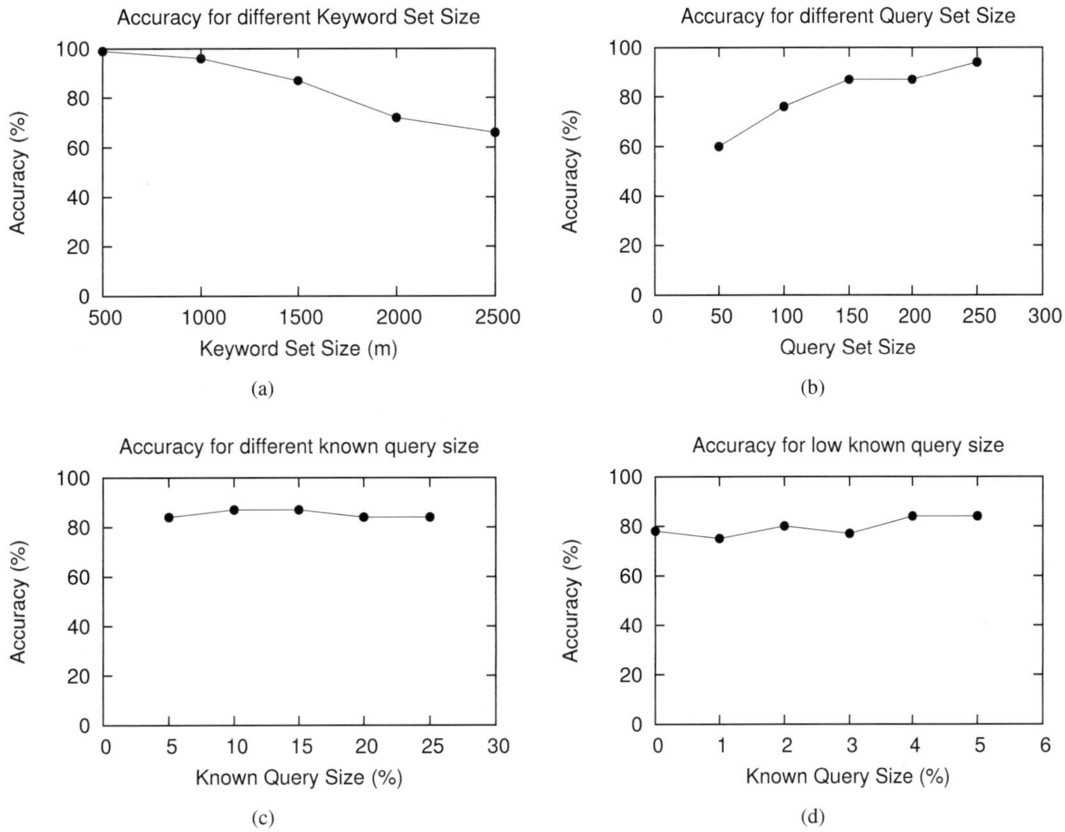

Figure 3. Accuracy for various (a) Keyword Set Size. (b) Query Set Size. (c) Known Query Set Size. (d) Low Known Query Set Size.

be noted that we have used an implementation of Porter's Stemming [19] written by its author Martin Porter.

9.1.3 Keyword Generation

Our whole corpus of 30109 documents contains 77000 unique keywords after getting rid of most common 200 words like 'the', 'a', 'from' etc. We sort these keywords based on the decreasing number of their occurrences and always use the first x number of words as our keywords. We refer to this x as the keyword set size. It should be noted that the value of x differs from experiment to experiment. But, unless noted otherwise, the keyword set size are always chosen as the most frequent x words out of the 77000 unique words.

9.1.4 Query Generation

Query patterns of individual users are expected to vary quite significantly. Therefore, it is hard to adopt a methodology that is able to capture the idiosyncratic behaviors of all the users. To make matter worse, we did not find any real-world query set on the *Enron* dataset. Therefore, we use *Zipfian Distribution* to create synthetic query sets from our keyword set. Fortunately, our attack scheme does not use query frequency. Therefore, our attack can be equally applicable to any other query distribution. Furthermore, we suppress query repetition from the attack model to undermine the effects of our query generation process on the model accuracy. That is, we generate the query set in such a way that no keyword is chosen as a query more than once. It should be noted that such suppression does not limit the applicability of our model in anyway. This is because, an attacker can always identify the duplicate queries and discard them before applying to the attack model.

To generate the query set, we sort the keyword set in non-increasing order of occurrences. If a particular keyword appears in the jth position in this list, we call the rank of this keyword j. According to the *Zipfian distribution*, the probability of this keyword being chosen as query (Pr_j) is given by the following[4].

[4]If the keyword chosen is already in the query set, we discard it to suppress query repetition.

$$Pr_j = \frac{\frac{1}{j}}{N_x} = \frac{1}{j \times N_x}.$$

Here, the denominator $N_x = \sum_{i=1}^{x} \frac{1}{j}$ is the normalization factor. According to the Zipf's law, in a corpus of natural language utterances, the frequency of appearance of an individual word is inversely proportional to its rank [24]. Since, we run our experiments on natural language corpus, we argue that the queries might follow *z*ipfian distribution. But, we like to stress that our attack scheme **does not use query frequency**. Therefore, our attack can be applicable to **any other query distribution**.

9.1.5 Execution Time

We use a serial implementation of our model for all the experiments mentioned in this paper. This implementation took no more than 14 hours to finish for any of the experiments in a AMD Phenom II $X6$ $1045T$ Windows 7 machine clocked at 2.70 GHz with 8 GB of system memory. Our model is supposed to run even faster if we allow parallel computation. Therefore, we argue that the attack model we present in this paper is quite efficient.

9.2. Experiment & Results

9.2.1 Accuracy over varying Keyword Set Size

Fig. $3(a)$ in *page* 9 shows the accuracy (%) for various keyword set size. Here, we have chosen the keyword set size to be multiples of 500 with the maximum value of 2500. Keywords were generated according to the *Keyword Generation* step described earlier. The number of queries for this experiment was set at 150 and 15% of the queries were known beforehand. It is quite evident that for relatively smaller keyword set size, the attack model can correctly identify almost all the queries. But, as the keyword set size increases, the identification accuracy is decreased. But, even for keyword set size of 2500, the model can successfully identify most of the queries.

9.2.2 Accuracy over varying Query Set Size

Fig. $3(b)$ in *page* 9 shows the accuracy (%) for various query set size. Here, we have chosen query set size to the multiples of 50 with the maximum being 250. Queries were generated using the *Zipifian* distribution as described earlier. Our model works fairly well for a small query set size of 50. But, as the query set size goes up, the accuracy of the model goes higher as well. This is due to the fact that higher query set size indicates that higher portion of the background matrix M is used to predict the query identity.

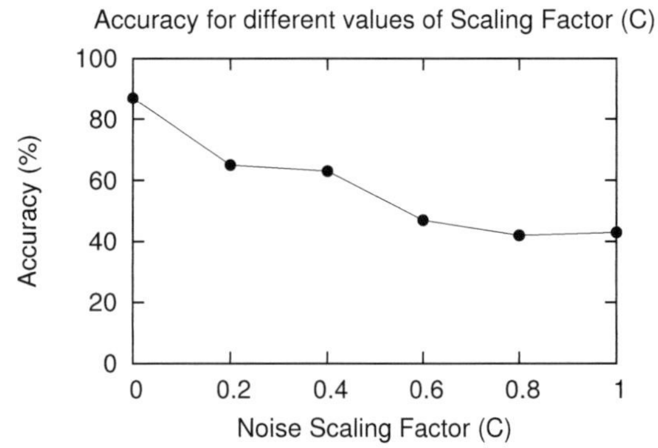

Figure 4. Accuracy (%) for different Noise Scaling Factor C.

x, the keyword set size is chosen to be 1500 for this experiment and 15% of the queries were assumed to be known beforehand.

9.2.3 Accuracy for varying Known Query (%)

In this experiment, we have run experiments for varying known query (% of Query set size). We start off with 5% known query and increase it upto 25%. It is quite apparent from Fig. 3-(c) in *page* 9 that increasing the known query size does not improve accuracy that much. Rather, the accuracy measurement are almost similar for different known query sizes. Fig. 3-(d) in *page* 9 shows the accuracy for very low known query percentage. We can see that the model can successfully identify nearly 80% of the queries correctly even if there are no known queries. This proves that the model is quite useful even without the knowledge of known queries. For this experiment, we fix the keyword set size to 1500 and the query set size to 150.

9.2.4 Accuracy for Noisy Matrix

All the experiments described up to this point has an implicit assumption that the attacker has access to a perfect background matrix M. But, getting a perfect matrix M may proved to be difficult under some scenario, even impossible under others. That's why, we have investigated the accuracy of our model under a noisy matrix M. Let, $\sigma^2 = Var\{M_{i,j}\}$. That is, σ^2 is the variance of the set of elements in the matrix M. We modeled the noise for the elements of the matrix M as a $Normal\ Distribution$ with mean 0 and variance $C \times \sigma^2$. Here, C is a constant, which we refer to as 'noise scaling factor'. That is, the noise will increase as C increases. We added noise to the element of the matrix M according to the distribution $\mathcal{N}(0, C \cdot \sigma^2)$. For this experiment, we fixed our keyword set size to be 1500,

Query set size to be 150 and (%) known query to be 15%. We varied noise scaling factor C and present the result in Fig. 4. It can be deduced from Fig. 4 that our model works fairly well for low values of C. Even when the noise scaling factor is 1.0, our model predicts a reasonable number of query identities accurately.

10. Preventing Inference Attack

In this section, we develop a framework to thwart 'Inference Attacks' described earlier. Our proposed framework aims to make query responses as similar as possible at the expense of a few false positives. We assume, even a very small false negative rate is unacceptable in the context of search over remote encrypted text. But, a few false positives, on the other hand, is acceptable in the sense that the client can easily detect these false positives and discard them upon decrypting the documents.

It should be noted that our proposed mitigation scheme only aims to thwart the inference type of attacks described earlier. It does not guarantee the overall security of a searchable encryption scheme. For example, even with our mitigation scheme in place, an attacker may still be able to extract some sensitive information by applying a different attack model that uses query frequencies and some other useful domain knowledge. Guarantee of the overall security requires rigorous study of all the vulnerable aspects of a searchable encryption schemes. We leave such a study as a possible future work. Therefore, in the following sections, we propose a mitigation scheme that provides security only against the inference attack described earlier in this paper.

10.1. Our Framework

To explain our framework, we like to use the simplified model we have described in *Section* 4. But, it worths noting that the framework, does not depend on the underlying model in anyway. That is, our concept can be **easily applied to any searchable encryption scheme**.

In our simplified model, we assume that the server holds a bitmap for each of the query words. Of course, these bitmaps are stored encrypted for the sake of privacy. Once a query is serviced by a server, the client decrypts the bitmap and request the relevant documents. Thus, the server has a mechanism to relate a particular encrypted keyword and the list of documents that contain the keyword. Our approach formulates a mechanism to add fake documents in the bitmaps so as to prevent attacks described above by the server, or any third party eavesdropper.

Let us assume $ID \in m \times \{0,1\}^n$ be an index matrix s.t. each $(i,j)^{th}$ entry $ID_{i,j}$ is defined in the following way.

$$ID_{i,j} = \begin{cases} 0 & : \text{if } \mathcal{K}_i \notin \mathcal{D}_j \\ 1 & : \text{if } \mathcal{K}_i \in \mathcal{D}_j \end{cases}$$

Here, $\mathcal{K}_i$ is the ith keyword and $\mathcal{D}_j$ is the jth document. Again, we denote the ith row of the matrix ID by ID_i. Given two bit strings A and B of same length k, we define the function $d_H : \{0,1\}^k \times \{0,1\}^k \rightarrow \mathcal{N}$ to be the function that returns the $Hamming\ Distance$ between its arguments.

11. Privacy Definition

Definition $(\alpha, t) - secure\ index$. We say an $m \times n$ binary index matrix ID is $(\alpha, t) - secure$ for a given $\alpha \in [1, m]$ and $t \in \mathcal{N}$, if there exists a set of partitions $\{S_i\}$ s.t. the following holds.

1. The partition set is complete. That is, $\bigcup_i S_i = [1, m]$.
2. The partitions in the set are non-overlapping. That is, $\forall i, j, S_i \cap S_j = \emptyset$.
3. Each partition has at least α rows. That is, $\forall j, |S_j| \geq \alpha$.
4. Finally, the hamming distance between any two rows of a given partition j is at most t. That is, $\forall i_1, i_2 \in S_j$, $d_H(ID_{i_1}, ID_{i_2}) \leq t$.

It should be noted that an $m \times n$ matrix ID is $(m, 0) - secure$ if all the rows of the matrix ID is identical to each other. On the other extreme, any matrix ID is $(\alpha, n) - secure$ for any value of $\alpha \leq m$. Informally speaking, an $(\alpha, 0) - secure$ index matrix guarantees that for each keyword, there are at least $\alpha - 1$ keywords which appear exactly in the same set of documents. Therefore, it's hard for an attacker to distinguish a keyword given the query response of that particular keyword.

Theorem 2. *Let ID be an $m \times n$ $(\alpha, 0) - secure$ index for some $0 < \alpha \leq m$. Given the response of a query $q_i = Trapdoor_w$ for some keyword w and the complete ID matrix, an attacker can successfully identify the keyword w with probability at most $\frac{1}{\alpha}$ by just using background information related to ID matrix.*

Proof The attacker has the complete ID matrix and the query response of q_i. Now, the query response of q_i is a row of ID matrix. Let's assume, without loss of generality, the response of q_i is the jth row of the ID matrix for some unique j s.t. $1 \leq j \leq m$. Since, the matrix ID is $(\alpha, 0) - secure$, there are at least $\alpha - 1$ rows of ID which are exactly identical to each other. Hence, the attacker can find this set S of at least α rows that are exactly similar to ID_j. Since, we assume that our trapdoor function is secure, the attacker can at best select an element from the set S randomly. Therefore, the attacker can successfully identify w with probability at most $\frac{1}{\alpha}$. ∎

$Theorem$ 2 states that an attacker can successfully identify a keyword from a query response with probability at most $\frac{1}{\alpha}$ even in the unlikely case of having full access to the index matrix. Here, we assume that the query repetition is visible to the attacker. Naturally, the attacker has significantly smaller chance of success when he does not have full access to the complete index matrix, rather has access to some partial information, for example, the background knowledge matrix used in previous sections. Therefore, we argue that making an index matrix $(\alpha, 0) - secure$ can make keyword frequency based attack significantly harder.

12. Securing Index Matrix

In this section, we outline our approach to transform a given $m \times n$ index matrix into a $(\alpha, 0) - secure$ matrix. It should be noted that an existing index matrix may not be modified by putting $0's$ in place of $1's$ for any row indexed by a keyword w. Otherwise, search results for this keyword w will be incomplete. That is, the resultset will not contain some documents in which the keyword belongs to, namely, the documents corresponding to those $1's$ which has been made $0's$. Furthermore, the user may well be unaware of these documents. Therefore, we assume that $false$ $negatives$ are not allowed, which in turn prohibits replacing $1's$ with $0's$ in any row of the matrix. On the other hand, replacing $0's$ with $1's$ may induce some false positives in the resultset, which can be detected later by the user upon decrypting the documents. Therefore, the user can safely discard these $false\ positives$. Hence, introducing some false positives in the resultset will only affect performance, not accuracy.

Definition The function $t_\alpha : \{0,1\}^{m \times n} \rightarrow \{0,1\}^{m \times n}$ takes an $m \times n$ binary index matrix ID and returns a $(\alpha, t) - secure$ matrix ID' s.t. the function $(\sum_{i=1}^{m} w_i \cdot d_H(ID_i, ID'_i))$ is minimized for a given weight vector w, and if $\forall i, j, (ID_{i,j} = 1) \implies (ID'_{i,j} = 1)$ holds.

It should be noted that in the process of making rows of the index matrix similar, we are adding false positives. This will result in increased communication overhead as well as processing overhead. The function t_α is defined in a way so that it converts a given ID matrix to the closest $(\alpha, t) - secure$ matrix. We define the cost of an transformation as follows.

Definition If an $m \times n$ index matrix ID is transformed into an $m \times n$ $(\alpha, 0) - secure$ index matrix ID' by applying the

Input : A index matrix ID
Output: A $(\alpha, 0) - secure$ index matrix ID'

Run clustering algorithm on the rows of ID to get p clusters.;
while *Any cluster* C_p *have less than* α *elements* **do**
  combine the cluster C_p to the nearest cluster.
end
for *each of the cluster* C_p **do**
  Feed the set of elements of C_p to the t_α function to obtain a new set of elements S ;
  Replace the set C_p by S in ID ;
end
return ID;

Algorithm 1: Approximation algorithm to transform a index matrix into a $(\alpha, 0) - secure$ matrix

function t_α, the cost of such a transformation is denoted by the function c_t, defined as follows.

$$c_t(ID, ID') = \sum_{i=1}^{m} d_H(ID_i, ID_i').$$

Informally speaking, the function c_t returns the total number of elements $ID_{i,j}$ where a 0 bit has been changed to a 1 bit to obtain the matrix ID'. Thus, minimizing the c_t function will ultimately result in a less number of false positives to be injected into the $(\alpha, 0) - secure$ matrix ID'. It can be easily showed that t_α function converts a given ID matrix to a $(\alpha, 0) - secure$ matrix s.t. the cost function c_t is minimized.

Based on this observation, we can convert a given index matrix ID to a $(\alpha, 0) - secure$ matrix ID' by applying the t_α function on the matrix ID.

The main hurdle of finding an optimal conversion of a given matrix to a $(\alpha, 0) - secure$ matrix is that finding an optimal partitioning of rows is hard. It turns out, the problem of finding such optimal partitioning belongs to $\mathcal{NP} - hard$ [13]. Therefore, we propose an approximation algorithm given in $Algorithm$ 1 to convert an index matrix ID to a $(\alpha, 0) - secure$ index matrix.

Although, $Algorithm$ 1 returns a $(\alpha, 0) - secure$ index matrix, the c_t measure is not optimally minimized. But, since the optimal reduction of c_t is computationally infeasible, $Algorithm$ 1 is a very good approximation of the optimal conversion. To test the efficiency of our approach, we have implemented $Algorithm$ 1 and present our results in the following section. We use agglomerative hierarchical clustering algorithm [2] with average distance. Furthermore, we use $cosine$ distance as our distance measure.

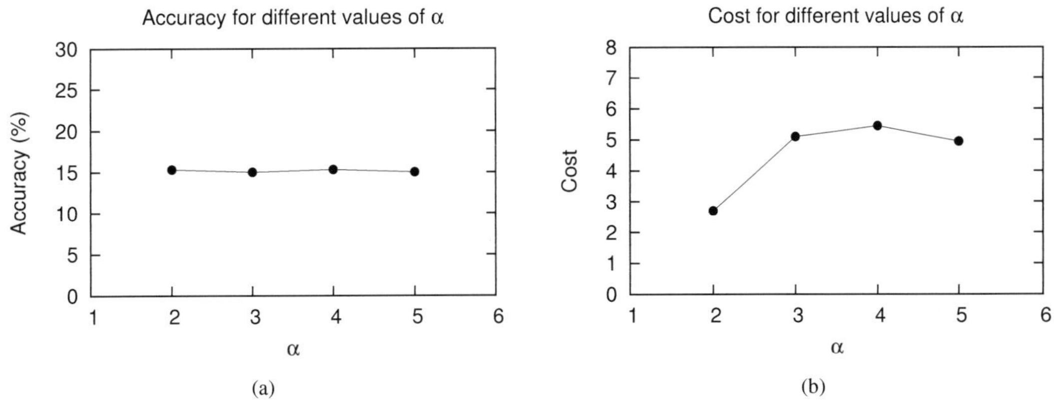

Figure 5. Accuracy and cost for different α values.

13. Experiment & Results

In this section we present the efficiency of our approach of evading attack model described in the earlier sections for different values of α. We run the experiments for $\alpha \in \{2,3,4,5\}$. Fig. $5(a)$ shows the accuracy for different values of α. For these experiments, we have fixed the keyword set size to be 1500, query set size to be 150 and the $(\%)$ known query to be 15% (i.e., best possible scenario for attacker as identified by previous experimental results). Furthermore, we assume the background matrix M to be perfect, that is, no element of M contains any noise (again, this is optimal from attackers point of view). From Fig. 5-(a), it is evident that the accuracy is almost equal to that of the $(\%)$ known query. That is, the attacker failed to successfully identify queries any other than the known queries. Fig. 5-(b) presents the increased cost because of the converted ID' matrix. We define cost as the ratio of increase in number of documents retrieved by the new ID matrix to the number of documents retrieved by the old matrix. That is, Let, $p =$ (number of documents returned for the old matrix ID), and $q =$ (number of documents returned for the new matrix ID'). Then, the cost is defined as, $cost = \frac{q-p}{p}$. It is apparent from Fig. 5-(b), that the percent increase in the cost is increased as the value of α is goes up.

To compare the cost of our proposed mitigation strategy with ORAM based solutions, we analyzed the ORAM construction given in [22]. To our knowledge, the ORAM solution proposed by Williams et. al. in [22] is one of the most efficient ORAM constructions available in the literature.

The protocol in [22] has a computational overhead of $O(\log n \log\log n)$ per request for n data items. This overhead includes the constant factor of $1.44c$ for an allowed error probability of 2^{-c} along [5] with other constant factors in the big O [18]. Based on this analysis, we can accurately approximate the value of the constant associated with this overhead to be around 100. Now, let us assume the number of data items to be 1024 or (2^{10}). That is, $n = 1024$. Therefore, $\log n = 10$. Then, even the most efficient ORAM presented in [22] requires more than $100 \times 10 = 1000$ data items to be retrieved for a single data access. Furthermore, this overhead grows much larger when the number of data items (n) increases. In our approach, on the other hand, the required overhead is only $3-5$ accesses per request and does not change as n increases. Therefore, our approach is more efficient than the ORAM constructions. But, unlike our case, ORAM approach hides all the access pattern disclosure.

Therefore, it is evident from the above discussion that adding noise to the index matrix is quite efficient in thwarting *Inference Attacks*. But, this approach incurs some additional computational overhead. However, this overhead is still quite negligible when compared to that of the most efficient ORAM constructions. Therefore, we argue that noise-addition based mitigation scheme is quite useful where efficiency is a major concern. However, if an user is only concerned about privacy, efficient versions of ORAM is perhaps a better choice.

14. Conclusions

In this paper, we investigate the potential vulnerability posed by the disclosure of data access patterns during 'search over encrypted text'. We formalize a model that can be used to launch an inference attack utilizing this vulnerability and empirically show their efficiency in successfully predicting query identities. Furthermore, we present a simple noise addition scheme to thwart such attacks with the expense of retrieving a slightly more documents than needed. We conclude that 'hiding access pattern' is extremely im-

[5] If we assume, $c = 64$, then the constant 1.44c is 92 itself. Please see [18] for more details.

portant in encrypted keyword search and therefore is a necessary characteristics of a secure encrypted search scheme.

15. Acknowledgements

This work was partially supported by Air Force Office of Scientific Research MURI Grant FA9550-08-1-0265, National Institutes of Health Grant 1R01LM009989, National Science Foundation (NSF) Career Grant CNS-0845803, NSF Grants CNS-0964350,CNS-1016343.

References

[1] Anderson, Needham, and Shamir. The steganographic file system. In *IWIH: International Workshop on Information Hiding*, 1998.

[2] P. Berkhin. Survey of clustering data mining techniques. Technical report, Accrue Software, San Jose, CA, 2002.

[3] M. Berry and M. Browne. Email surveillance using non-negative matrix factorization. *Computational & Mathematical Organization Theory*, 11(3), 2005.

[4] D. Boneh, G. Crescenzo, R. Ostrovsky, and G. Persiano. Public key encryption with keyword search. In *proc. of EUROCRYPT*, 2004.

[5] D. Boneh, E. Kushilevitz, and R. Ostrovsky. Public key encryption that allows PIR queries. In *proc. of CRYPTO*, 2007.

[6] K. Borgwardt, H. Kriegel, and P. Wackersreuther. Pattern mining in frequent dynamic subgraph. In *ICDM*, pages 818–822. IEEE Computer Society, 2006.

[7] Y. Chang and M. Mitzenmacher. Privacy preserving keyword searches on remote encrypted data. In *International Conference on Applied Cryptography and Network Security (ACNS), LNCS*, volume 3, 2005.

[8] R. Curtmola, J. Garay, S. Kamara, and R. Ostrovsky. Searchable symmetric encryption: improved definitions and efficient constructions. In *proc. of the 13th ACM Conference on Computer and Communications Security, CCS 2006*, pages 79–88. ACM, 2006.

[9] J. Diesner, T. Frantz, and M. Carley. Communication networks from the enron email corpus. *Computational & Mathematical Organization Theory*, 11(3), 2005.

[10] E. Goh. Secure indexes. *Cryptology ePrint Archive*, (Report 2003/216), 2003.

[11] O. Goldreich and R. Ostrovsky. Software protection and simulation on oblivious RAMs. *JACM: Journal of the ACM*, 43, 1996.

[12] M. S. Islam, M. Kuzu, and M. Kantarcioglu. Poster: Inference attacks against searchable encryption protocols. In *CCS*, pages 845–847. ACM, 2011.

[13] B. Jackson, J. Scargle, C. Cusanza, D. Barnes, D. Kanygin, R. Sarmiento, S. Subramaniam, and T. Chuang. Optimal partitions of data in higher dimensions. In *proc. of the Conference on Intelligent Data Understanding*, pages 98–108. NASA Ames Research Center, 2010.

[14] S. Kamara and K. Lauter. Cryptographic cloud storage. In *Financial Cryptography Workshops*, volume 6054, pages 136–149. Springer, 2010.

[15] S. Kirkpatrick, C. Gelatt, and M. Vecchi. Optimization by simulated annealing. *Science*, 220(4598):671–679, May 1983.

[16] B. Klimt and Y. Yang. Introducing the enron corpus. In *CEAS*, 2004.

[17] R. Kumar, J. Novak, B. Pang, and A. Tomkins. On anonymizing query logs via token-based hashing. In *Proceedings of the 16th International Conference on World Wide Web, WWW*, pages 629–638. ACM, 2007.

[18] B. Pinkas and T. Reinman. Oblivious RAM revisited. *IACR Cryptology ePrint Archive*, 2010:366, 2010.

[19] M. Porter. An algorithm for suffix striping. *Program*, 14(3):130–137, 1980.

[20] D. Song, D. Wagner, and A. Perrig. Practical techniques for searches on encrypted data. In *IEEE Symposium on Security and Privacy*, 2000.

[21] C. Troncoso, C. Díaz, O. Dunkelman, and B. Preneel. Traffic analysis attacks on a continuously-observable steganographic file system. In *Information Hiding*, volume 4567, pages 220–236. Springer, 2007.

[22] P. Williams, R. Sion, and B. Carbunar. Building castles out of mud: practical access pattern privacy and correctness on untrusted storage. In *Proceedings of the 2008 ACM Conference on Computer and Communications Security, Alexandria, Virginia, USA, October 27-31, 2008*, pages 139–148. ACM, 2008.

[23] X. Zhou, H. Pang, and K.-L. Tan. Hiding data accesses in steganographic file system. In *ICDE*, pages 572–583. IEEE Computer Society, 2004.

[24] G. Zipf. *Selected studies of the Principle of Relative Frequency in Language*. Harvard U.P., 1932.

Appendix A

Proof of Theorem 1 Let $C = \{e_1, e_2, ..., e_n\}$, $P = \{p_1, p_2, ..., p_m\}$ be the encrypted and plain keyword lists and M_C, M_P be the pair similarity matrices for E and P respectively such that $n \leq m$. Let $B = \{(i,j)|f(e_i) = p_j, 1 \leq n, 1 \leq j\}$ be a set of pairs where f is a bijection from E to P and $cost : B \mapsto Integer$ be the evaluation function which is defined as follows:

$$\begin{aligned} cost(B) &= \sum_{i=1}^{n}\sum_{j=i}^{n}(M_C[i,j] - M_P[k,l])^2 \\ s.t. & \quad (i,k) \in B, (j,l) \in B \end{aligned}$$

Notice that constructed setting is equivalent to formulated optimization problem. We can formulate the decision version of the problem as follows: Given C, P along with M_C and M_P, does there exist any B such that $cost(B) \leq k$?

It is easy to see that the problem is in NP. The certificate is the mapping set (B) and a certifier can check if the cost(B) is at most the given bound (k) in polynomial time.

We now show that the problem is NP-Hard by a reduction from the Hamiltonian path problem. Given an instance of Hamiltonian path problem specified by graph G(V, E), we can construct an input $< C, P, M_C, M_P, k >$ for decision version of the optimization problem as follows.

$$C = V \tag{6}$$

$$P = \{1, 2, ..., n\}, n = |V| \tag{7}$$

$$M_C[i,j] = \left\{ \begin{array}{ll} w & \text{if } (v_i, v_j) \in E \text{ and } i < j \\ 0 & \text{otherwise} \end{array} \right\} \tag{8}$$

$$where, 1 \le i \le n, 1 \le j \le n \tag{9}$$

$$M_P[i,j] = \left\{ \begin{array}{ll} w & \text{if } j = i+1 \\ 0 & \text{otherwise} \end{array} \right\} 1 \le i \le n, 1 \le j \le n \tag{10}$$

$$k = \left\{ \begin{array}{ll} 0 & \text{if } |E| < |V| - 1 \\ w^2(|E| - |V-1|) & \text{otherwise} \end{array} \right\} \tag{11}$$

We claim that there is a mapping set B for the input $< C, P, M_C, M_P, k >$ such that $cost(B) \le k$ if and only if G has a Hamiltonian path.

Without loss of generality, suppose G has a Hamiltonian path v_1, v_2, ..., v_n. Since G has an Hamiltonian path, it should have at least $|V| - 1$ edges. Thus, $k = w^2(|E| - |V-1|)$. In this case, cost of assignment set $\{(1,1), ...(i,i), ..., (n,n)\}$ is bounded by k. In such a case,

$$cost(B) = \sum_{i=1}^{n}\sum_{j=i}^{n}(M_C[i,j] - M_P[k,l])^2 \quad s.t. \quad i = j$$

case i : $j = i + 1$
By the construction of M_P, $M_P[i,j] = w$, similarly $M_C[i,j] = w$ for this case since there exists an edge between (v_i, v_{i+1}). Therefore, $\sum_{i=1}^{n}\sum_{j=i}^{n}(M_C[i,j] - M_P[i,j])^2 = 0$ for this case.

case ii : $j \neq i + 1$
By the construction of M_P, $M_P[i,j] = 0$, $M_C[i,j] = w$ if $(v_i, v_j) \in E$ and $i < j$, $M_C[i,j] = 0$ otherwise for this case. There exist $|V| - 1$ edges (v_i, v_j) such that $j = i + 1$ which implies the existence of $(|E| - |V - 1|)$ edges such that $i \neq j+1$. Hence, $M_C[i,j] = w$ for $(|E| - |V-1|)(i,j)$ pairs. Therefore $\sum_{i=1}^{n}\sum_{j=i}^{n}(M_C[i,j] - M_P[i,j])^2 = w^2(|E| - |V-1|)$ for this case.

Cases i and ii covers all possible (i,j) pairs. Therefore $cost(B) = w^2(|E| - |V-1|) = k$

Conversely, suppose $cost(B) \le k$ for some B, then G has a Hamiltonian path. For the sake of contradiction, suppose G has no Hamiltonian path, then

case i : $|E| < |V| - 1 \rightarrow k = 0$
By the construction of M_P, $M_P[i, i+1] = w$ for each (i, i+1) pair for $i, i+1 \in P$. If v_k is matched with i and v_l is matched with $i+1$ for $v_k, v_l \in C$, then $(M_C[k,l] - M_P[i,i+1])^2 = 0$ if and only if $(v_k, v_l) \in E$. Since there exist $|V|-1$ (i, i+1) pairs, we need $(|V-1|)$ edges to satisfy $cost(B) = 0$ for any B. However, $|E| < |V| - 1$ for this case and $cost(B) > 0$

case ii : $|E| \ge |V| - 1 \rightarrow k = w^2(|E| - |V-1|)$
Notice that cost(B) becomes smaller if consecutive elements $(i, i+1)$ of P is matched with some $v_k, v_l \in C$ such that $(v_k, v_l) \in E$. However, there exist at least one $(i, i+1)$ pair for $i, i+1 \in C$, such that i is matched with v_k and $(i+1)$ is matched with v_l for $v_k, v_l \in C$ and $(v_k, v_l) \notin E$. Otherwise G has a Hamiltonian path which is not the case. Therefore, at most $|V| - 2$ consecutive pairs in P can be matched with some v_k, v_l for $v_k, v_l \in C$ such that $(v_k, v_l) \notin E$. Notice that $cost(B) \ge w^2(|E| - |V-1| + 2)$ in such a case. Hence $cost(B) > w^2(|E| - |V-1|) = k$ for this case.

Both case i and ii shows that $cost(B) > k$ for any B if G has no Hamiltonian path. Therefore, we can conclude that G should have a Hamiltonian path if there exist some assignment set B such that $cost(B) \le k$. ∎

On Limitations of Designing Leakage-Resilient Password Systems: Attacks, Principles and Usability

Qiang Yan, Jin Han, Yingjiu Li, Robert H. Deng
School of Information Systems, Singapore Management University
{qiang.yan.2008, jin.han.2007, yjli, robertdeng}@smu.edu.sg

Abstract

The design of leakage-resilient password systems (LRPSes) in the absence of trusted devices remains a challenging problem today despite two decades of intensive research in the security community. In this paper, we investigate the inherent tradeoff between security and usability in designing LRPS. First, we demonstrate that most of the existing LRPS systems are subject to two types of generic attacks - brute force and statistical attacks, whose power has been underestimated in the literature. Second, in order to defend against these two generic attacks, we introduce five design principles that are necessary to achieve leakage resilience in the absence of trusted devices. We also show that these attacks cannot be effectively mitigated without significantly sacrificing the usability of LRPS systems. Third, to better understand the tradeoff between security and usability of LRPS, we propose for the first time a quantitative analysis framework on usability costs of password systems. By decomposing the authentication process of existing LRPS systems into atomic cognitive operations in psychology, we show that a secure LRPS in practical settings always imposes a considerable amount of cognitive workload on its users, which indicates the inherent limitations of such systems and in turn implies that an LRPS has to incorporate certain trusted devices in order to be both secure and usable.

1 Introduction

Password has been the most pervasive means for user authentication since the advent of computers. Compared to its alternatives, such as biometrics and smartcard which are cumbersome to use and require the existence of an underlying infrastructure, password is much easier and cheaper to create, update, and revoke. However, the use of password has intrinsic problems. Among them, secret leakage is one of the most common security threats [21], in which an adversary steals the password by capturing (e.g. by shoulder-surfing or key logging) and analyzing a user's inputs during an authentication session. Traditional password systems ask a user to directly input his entire plaintext password recalled from the user's memory so that an observation of a single authentication session is sufficient to capture the password. In order to prevent secret leakage during password entry, a user needs to input the password indirectly, which imposes an extra burden on the user. How to design a password system that *minimizes secret leakage and is still easy to use* is the fundamental problem in the design of leakage resilient password systems (LRPSes).

An ideal LRPS allows a user to generate a *one-time password* (OTP) for each authentication session based on an easy-to-remember secret. This can be easily achieved when a secure channel is available between user and authentication service. The secure channel blinds the adversary by decoupling a user input from the underlying secret, when the message delivered over the secure channel is not revealed to the adversary. However, the prerequisite of a secure channel may be infeasible or introduces other vulnerabilities in practical settings. For example, when the secure channel is formed by a trusted device such as secure token or mobile phone, that device is subject to theft or loss. This motivates the existing research on usable and secure LRPS systems with only the support of human cognitive capabilities [22, 15, 26, 20, 31, 32, 35, 4, 27, 2]. A few representative systems include Convex Hull Click (CHC) [32], Cognitive Authentication Scheme (CAS) [31], and Predicate-based Authentication Service (PAS) [4].

The difficulty in designing an LRPS system stems from the *capability asymmetry* between user and strong adversary. A strong adversary may use a hidden camera or malicious software to record complete interactions between user and his computer and then analyze the data with powerful machines. Many LRPS systems [15, 20, 31, 32, 35, 4, 27, 2] have been proposed to defend against this type of secret-leakage attacks. However, as we will demonstrate later in the paper, all the existing proposals with acceptable usability are vulnerable to either or both types of generic attacks: brute force attack and statistical attack.

Brute force attack is a pruning process for the entire candidate password set, whose strength has often being underestimated in prior research. Our experiments show that brute force attack is able to recover the secrets of certain existing LRPS systems from a small number of observations of authentication sessions. Statistical attack, on the other hand, represents a learning process to extract a user's secret due to statistical significance of the secret. We introduce two types of statistical attack, probabilistic decision tree and multi-dimensional counting. Rigorous experiments are conducted to show the effectiveness of these two attacks in breaking existing schemes.

We note that these two generic attacks are different from other specific attacks that have been systematically studied in the literature, including SAT [13] and Gaussian elimination [19]. SAT attacks can be efficiently prevented by asking a user to select only one of the correct responses while multiple correct responses can be derived from each challenge, since this would increase the size of the SAT expression exponentially with the number of observations. On the other hand, Gaussian elimination-based algebraic attacks can be efficiently prevented by using a non-linear response function [20] or introducing noises from user's intentional mistakes [15]. Unlike these specific attacks, brute force and statistical attacks cannot be easily defended without significantly sacrificing the system's usability, which implies inherent limitations of LRPS without using trusted devices. In order to defend against these attacks, we introduced five design principles which should be followed to achieve leakage resilience. Using counterexamples, we show that an LRPS system can be easily broken when these principles are violated.

To further understand the tradeoff between security and usability in the design of LRPS systems, we propose for the first time a quantitative analysis framework on usability costs of LRPS systems. This framework decomposes the process of human-computer authentication into atomic cognitive operations. Performance data of average human-beings reported in psychology literatures [28, 12, 9, 30, 10, 23, 25, 7, 33, 34, 16, 6, 14] are used to estimate usability costs of existing LRPS systems [15, 20, 31, 32, 35, 4, 27, 2]. Our analysis results are consistent with the experimental results reported in the original literatures, while the hidden costs previously not addressed are identified. Our results show that a secure LRPS in practical settings [15, 2] always leads to a considerable amount of cognitive workload, which explains why some of the existing LRPS systems require extremely long authentication time and have high authentication error rate. This limitation has not been, and will not be easily solved in the design of LRPS in the absence of trusted device.

In a nutshell, the contributions of this paper are three-fold:

- We analyze and demonstrate the effectiveness of two types of generic attacks, brute force and statistical attacks, against LRPS systems. We propose two statistical attack techniques, probabilistic decision tree and multi-dimensional counting, and show their effectiveness against existing schemes.
- We introduce five principles that are necessary to mitigate brute force and statistical attacks. We use typical existing LRPS proposals as counterexamples to show that an adversary can easily obtain user secrets in the schemes violating our principles.
- We establish the first quantitative analysis framework on usability costs of the existing LRPS systems. This framework utilizes the performance models of atomic cognitive operations in authentication to estimate usability costs. Our analysis result shows that there is a strong tradeoff between security and usability in the existing LRPS systems. It implies that an unaided human may not be competent enough to effectively use a secure LRPS system in practical settings; in other words, it is inevitable to incorporate certain trusted device in LRPS design.

2 Definitions and Threat Model

In this section, we introduce related notions and our threat model. We focus on the fundamental problem of designing LRPSes for unaided humans, i.e. *when a secure channel or trusted device is unavailable.* We exclude LRPSes using secure channel or trusted device in our discussion unless explicitly mentioned.

2.1 Leakage-Resilient Password System

An LRPS is essentially a challenge-response protocol between human and computer. We refer to human as *user*, and computer as *server*. During registration, a user and a server agree on a *root secret*, usually referred to as a password. The user later uses the root secret to generate *responses* to *challenges* issued by the server to prove his identity. Unlike traditional password systems, a response in LRPS is an obfuscated message derived from the root secret, rather than the plaintext of the root secret itself. Considering the limited cognitive capabilities of unaided humans, a usable obfuscation function F is usually a many-to-one mapping from a large candidate set to a small answer set. The small size of the answer set increases the success rate of *guessing attack* where an adversary attempts to pass the authentication by randomly picking an answer from the answer set. For this reason, an *authentication session* of LRPS often requires executing multiple rounds of the challenge-response procedure in order to reach an expected authentication strength D (specifically, the resistance against random guessing, e.g. $D = 10^{-6}$ for 6-digit PIN), where each round is referred to as an *authentication round*. We use d to denote the average success rate of guessing attack per authentication round. Given d and D, the minimum number m of authentication rounds for an authentication session is $\lceil \log_d D \rceil$.

To imbue the server with a high flexibility in challenge generation, the *k-out-of-n paradigm* [15] has been adopted for secret agreement in most existing LRPS systems [15, 20, 31, 32, 35, 27, 2]. In this paradigm, the root secret consists of k independent elements randomly drawn from a pool of n elements. An element can be an image, a text character, or any symbol in a notational scheme. The set of k secret elements is called the *secret set* (and forms the root secret of the user), and the complementary set is called the *decoy set*. The server knows the secret set chosen by the user, and uses a subset or all of these k elements to generate the challenge in each round. We refer to the chosen portion of the root secret for an authentication round as a *round secret*.

Based on the above notions, the common system parameters of the most existing LRPS systems [15, 20, 31, 32, 35, 4, 27, 2] can be described by a tuple (D, k, n, d, w, s), where D is the expected authentication strength of an authentication session, k is the number of secret elements drawn from an alphabet of n candidate elements, d is the average success rate of guessing attack in a single round, w is the average window size which is the number of elements appearing on the screen for an authentication round, and s is the average length of user's decision path which is the number of decisions that a user has to make before producing the correct response for an authentication round. The total round number m can be derived from D and d. The parameters m, w, and s are required for usability evaluation. More details will be given in Sections 5 and 6.

2.2 Threat Model and Experimental Setting

There are two types of passive adversary models for secret leakage attacks used in prior research. The weaker passive adversary model (e.g. *cognitive shoulder-surfing* [26]) assumes that the adversary is not able to capture the complete interaction between a user and the server [26]. Such an assumption actually forms a secure channel between user and server, which transforms the secret leakage problem to the protection of the secure channel. However, this assumption may not hold for a prepared adversary who deploys a *hidden camera, key logger, or phishing web site* to capture the whole password entry process. To address such realistic concerns, recent efforts [20, 31, 32, 35, 4, 27, 2] have focused on the strong passive adversary model, where the adversary is allowed to record the complete interaction between the user and the server.

In the strong passive adversary model, secret leakage during human-computer authentication is unavoidable. The user's response is based on his knowledge of the secret, which distinguishes it from a random choice as required for the authentication purpose. This difference leaks information about the secret. After recording a sufficient number of authentication rounds, the adversary may use any reasonable computation resources to analyze and recover the underlying secret. The research problem under such a threat model is to lower the secret leakage rate while maintaining acceptable usability for unaided humans.

In this paper, we consider both brute force attack and statistical attack under this strong passive adversary model. The security strength of an LRPS is defined as *the resistance against these two generic attacks given the same success rate of random guessing* (i.e. the same authentication strength for a legitimate user). We will use simulation experiments to evaluate the security strength of existing schemes, whose process is summarized as follow: 1) Generate a random password as the root secret; 2) Generate a challenge for an authentication round; 3) Generate a response based on the password and the underlying system design; 4) Analyze the collected challenge-response pairs after each authentication round assuming that the adversary has full knowledge of the system design except the password; 5) Repeat steps 2, 3, and 4 until the exact password is recovered. The final findings shown in the following sections are the average results of 20 runs for each system.

3 Brute Force Attack and Its Defense Principles

3.1 Attack Strategy

Brute force attack is a general pruning-based learning process, where the adversary keeps removing irrelevant candidates when more and more cues are available. Its procedure can be described as follows: 1) List all possible candidates for the password in the target system; 2) For each independent observation of a challenge-response round, check the validity of each candidate in the current candidate set by running the verification algorithm used by the server, and remove invalid candidates from the candidate set; 3) Repeat the above step until the size of candidate set reaches a small threshold.

The above procedure shows that the efficiency of brute force attack in the leakage resilience setting is *design-independent*, and is only limited by the size of the candidate set. We introduce two statements to further describe the power of brute force attack. These statements apply not only to root secret, but also to round secrets when the adversary is able to reliably group the observations for individual round secret.

Statement 1: *The verification algorithm used in brute force attack for candidate verification is at least as efficient as the verification algorithm used by server for response verification.*

The proof is trivial as the verification process for candidate pruning is essentially the same as the verification process for the server to check correct response. It is also possible for the adversary to design a more efficient algorithm if there are correlations between candidates.

Statement 2: *The average shrinking rate for the size of valid candidate set is the same as one minus the average success rate of guessing attack.*

The average success rate of guessing attack is defined as the probability of generating correct response by randomly picking a candidate from the candidate set. This is an equivalent definition of average shrinking rate of the valid candidate set. Given X as the size of the candidate set, and d as the average success rate of guessing attack, the average number of rounds to recover the exact secret is $m = \lceil \log_{1/d} X \rceil$, assuming that each candidate is independent of each other. If each candidate is not independent, the average number of rounds to recover the exact secret will be smaller than m. This statement can be used to estimate the average success rate of guessing attack, $d = X^{-\frac{1}{m}}$, when the precise analysis is difficult to perform (see later examples). The statement also explains why most password systems [26] reveal the entire secret after one or two authentication sessions recorded by the adversary, as their expected success rates of guessing attack are sufficiently low so that the whole candidate set rapidly collapse to the exact secret. This implies that, when brute force attack is feasible, enhancing strength against guessing attack is strictly at the cost of sacrificing leakage resilience.

3.2 P1: Large Root Secret Space Principle

Principle 1: *An LRPS system with secret leakage should have a large candidate set for the* **root secret**.

The first principle requires a large password space as the basic defense against brute force attack, where large means that it is computational infeasible for the adversary to enumerate all candidates in a practical setting (the same meaning of *large* will be used in the following discussion). This principle seems trivial but actually not, as the necessity of involving a large password space depends on whether an LRPS system has secret leakage under a given threat model, which is not straightforward to decide. In general, there are three possible leakage sources in an LRPS system: *the response alone*, *the challenge-response pair*, and *the challenge alone*. Among them, the last source has not been well recognized. We use Undercover [27] as a counterexample to show that secret leakage could happen even when a secure channel is present.

Undercover is a typical scheme based on the k-out-of-n paradigm. During registration, a user is assigned k images as his secret from a pool of n images. In each authentication round, the user is asked to recognize if there is a secret image from w candidate images and report the position of that image if the secret image is shown in the current window; otherwise the user reports the position of the "none" symbol. Before the user reports the position, a haptics-based secure channel is deployed to map the real position to a random position decided by the hidden message delivered via the secure channel.

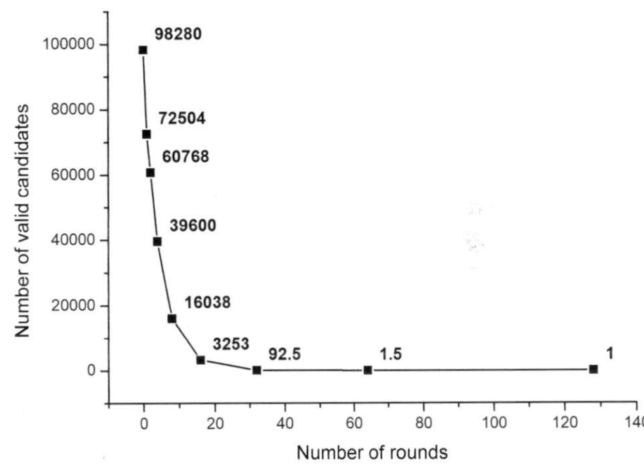

Figure 1. The average number of valid candidates shrinks for Undercover.

The hidden mapping blinds the adversary from learning any information from the response. The authors suggested a small password space is sufficient so that the default parameters are $k = 5$, $n = 28$, and $w = 4+1$ (i.e. four images and a "none" symbol). The number of candidate root secrets is $C_{28}^{5} = 98280$. However, this scheme does not prevent the challenge alone from becoming a source of leakage. *In Undercover, there is at most one secret image among the w candidate images for each authentication round. This implies a candidate of the root secret is invalid if two images in this candidate appeared in an authentication round.* Since it has a small candidate space, we can use brute force to recover the secret with the information from the challenge alone. Figure 1 shows how the size of the candidates shrinks as the number of observed authentication rounds increases. On average, 53.06 rounds (6 sessions) are sufficient to recover the exact secret, and the size of the candidate set can be reduced to less than 10 after 43.55 rounds (5 sessions). This result shows that *a secure channel alone is not sufficient to prevent secret leakage.*

The same problem also appears in the Convex Hull Click (CHC) scheme [32], where the default parameters are $k = 5$, $n = 112$, $w = 83$. The size of the candidate set for its root secret is $C_{112}^{5} = 1.34 \times 10^{8}$. In our simulation, we are able to recover the exact secret within 12.28 rounds (2 sessions). Another interesting finding for CHC is that we can now estimate the average success rate of guessing attack from the results of brute force attack, though a precise analysis is difficult [32]. According to *Statement 2*, the average success rate is $21.78\% = (C_{112}^{5})^{-\frac{1}{12.28}}$. This technique can also be applied to other complex LRPS systems to determine their security strength when the other analysis techniques are infeasible.

3.3 P2: Large Round Secret Space Principle

Principle 2: *An LRPS system with secret leakage should have a large candidate set for the* **round secret**.

This principle emphasizes that a large candidate set for the *root secret* is necessary but not sufficient to defend against brute force attack. The large candidate set for the root secret can be *broken down* based on the attack to the round secrets. We use Predicate-based Authentication Services (PAS) [4] as a counterexample to show that a round secret with a small candidate set can be easily recovered and later used to reveal the root secret.

During registration of PAS, a user is asked to remember p secret pairs, each of which includes a secret position and a secret word. At the beginning of each authentication session, the server prompts for an integer index I. Then the user uses I to calculate p predicates as follows: For each pair, the corresponding predicate is the secret position and a secret character. The secret character is the xth character in the secret word (1-based indexing), where $x = 1 + ((I-1) \mod len)$, and len is the length of the secret word. For example, given two secret pairs (⟨2,3⟩, sente), (⟨4,1⟩, logig) and $I = 15$, the predicates are (⟨2,3⟩, e) and (⟨4,1⟩, g), where $x = 5 = 1 + ((15-1) \mod 5)$, and the secret position $\langle a, b\rangle$ means "at row a and column b". Given these p predicates, the user examines the cells at secret positions in l challenge tables to check whether a secret character is present in its corresponding cell. It yields an answer vector that consists of $p \cdot l$ "present" or "absent" answers with a candidate space of 2^{pl}. This vector is then used to lookup another response table, which provides a many-to-one mapping from 2^{pl} elements to 2^{l} elements. Finally, the user inputs one of those 2^{l} elements indexed by the answer vector to finish an authentication round.

The above many-to-one mapping is used in PAS to confuse the adversary. However, when the round secret only has a small candidate set, many mappings will have the same pre-image and the effective mapping space collapses to the candidate set of the round secret. In PAS, the size

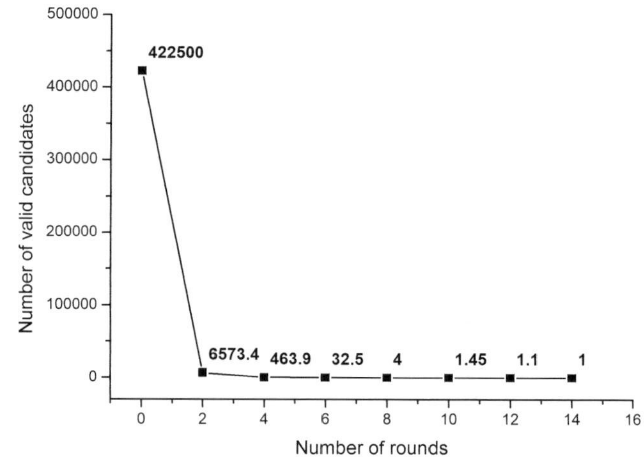

Figure 2. The average number of valid candidates shrinks for PAS.

of the candidate set for the round secret is $422500 = (25 \times 26)^2$ for the default parameters, where $p = 2$, and there are 25 cells in each challenge table and 26 possible letters for the secret character. It is not difficult to use brute force to recover the round secret of PAS. Figure 2 shows the shrinking of the candidate set size as the number of observed authentication rounds increases. On average, 9.4 rounds are sufficient to recover the exact round secret (1 session). Since all the predicates generated from the same secret pair share the same secret position, after recovering the first round secret, it is easy for the adversary to recover the other round secrets and finally the root secret. A similar attack technique has been used in [18]. The same problem also appears in the S3PAS scheme [35], which is a variant of the CHC scheme [32]. In our experiments, we are able to discover the exact root secret in 8 sessions.

4 Statistical Attack and Its Defense Principles

4.1 Attack Strategy

Statistical attack is an accumulation-based learning process, where an adversary gradually increases its confidence on relevant targets when more and more cues are available. Compared to brute force attack, statistical attack has fewer limitations as it can be applied to schemes with a large password space. Recall that a user response is statistically biased towards his knowledge of the secret. Theoretically there exists a specific statistical attack for any password system. The efficiency of statistical attack is *design-dependent* and varies with different schemes and different analysis techniques. Here we introduce two general statistical analysis techniques that are able to efficiently extract the root secret of most existing schemes.

The first technique is *probabilistic decision tree*. It works efficiently for the existing schemes based on simple challenges [31, 32, 35, 4]. The procedure is described as follows: 1) Create a score table for each possible individual element or affordable-sized element group in the alphabet of the root secret, where *affordable* means computational feasible to maintain. We refer to a score table whose entry contains t individual elements as an *t-element score table*. 2) For each independent observation of a challenge-response pair, the adversary enumerates every *consistent* decision path that leads to the current response. Each possible decision path is assigned a probability calculated based on the uniform distribution. For the k-out-of-n paradigm, the probability is $p1 = k/n$ for a decision event in which the corresponding individual element belongs to the secret set, and $p0 = 1 - p1$ for the complementary event. For the example decision path X given in Figure 3, its probability is $p(X) = p1 \cdot (p0 \cdot p1)$. After enumerating all consistent decision paths, the adversary sums up the probabilities of these paths and uses the sum p_c to normalize the probability $p(X)$ for each decision path to its conditional probability $p(X|C) = p(X)/p_c$. The conditional probability represents the probability that a decision path is the path chosen by the user when the current response C is observed. After the normalization, the adversary updates the score table using $p(X|C)$. For an entry that appears in a consistent decision path X, its score will be added by $p(X|C)$ if the corresponding event is that the entry belongs to the secret set, otherwise its score will be deducted by $p(X|C)$. 3) Repeat the above step until the number of entries with different score levels reaches a threshold (e.g. finding out k entries with the highest/lowest scores when each entry represents a single element).

The second technique is *counting-based statistical analysis*. The basic idea is to simply maintain a counting table for the occurrences of elements. Multiple counting tables can be maintained simultaneously according to different response groups. The procedure proceeds as follows: 1) Create l counting tables for l response groups. The adversary creates a counting table for each possible response if affordable. "Any response" is still a useful response group if the secret elements appear more or less frequently than the decoy elements *in the challenge*. An entry in a counting table can be an individual element or affordable-sized element group. We refer to a counting table whose entry contains t individual elements as an *t-element counting table*. When $t \geq 2$, we call this type of statistical analysis as *multi-dimensional counting*. 2) For each independent observation of a challenge-response pair, the adversary first decides which counting table is updated according to the observed response. Then each entry in the chosen counting table is incremented by the number of occurrences of the corresponding individual element or element group. If the group of "any response" is used, its counting table is always updated for each observation. 3) Repeat the above step until the number of entries with different score levels reaches a threshold (e.g. finding out k entries with the highest/lowest scores when each entry represents a single element). The score for an entry is a weighted sum of the count values for the same entry in different tables. The weight function is dependent on the specific target scheme and the response grouping strategy.

> A *decision path* is an emulation of the user's decision process that consists of multiple decision nodes. Each *decision node* represents a decision event decided by the membership relation of a corresponding entry in the score table, whether or not it belongs to the secret set.
>
> Consider a scheme which shows a four-element window $\langle S_1{:}1,\ S_2{:}2,\ S_3{:}1,\ D_1{:}1\rangle$ and asks the user to report the sum of the numbers associated with the *first* and *last* secret elements displayed in the window, where $S_i{:}x$ represents a secret element associated with number x, and $D_i{:}y$ represents a decoy element associated with number y. Since the correct response for this challenge is 2 by adding the numbers associated with the first and third elements, its decision path is $X = \langle S_1{:}1\rangle|\langle D_1{:}1;\ S_3{:}1\rangle$. There are two segments in this decision path. The first segment implies that S_1 is a secret element, and the second segment implies that D_1 is a decoy element and S_3 is a secret element. There usually exist other decision paths leading to the same response, such as $\langle S_1{:}1\rangle|\langle D_1{:}1\rangle$.

Figure 3. Definition and example for decision path

4.2 P3: Uniform Distributed Challenge Principle

Principle 3: *An LRPS system with secret leakage should make the distribution of the elements in each* **challenge** *as uniformly distributed as possible.*

This principle requires that an LRPS system should be able to generate the challenges without knowing the secret[1]. For example, if there is a *structural requirement* in the challenge generation, secret leakage is very likely to happen. Non-uniformly distributed elements in a challenge leave cues for the adversary to recover the secret even without knowing the response. Undercover [27] is a typical counterexample to show secret leakage from biased challenges.

[1] Even if server knows the secret, the secret (or its alternative form, e.g. hash value) should be only used to verify the response.

Undercover ensures that the distribution for each image is unbiased by showing every candidate image exactly once for each authentication session. However, its 2-dimensional distribution is biased in each authentication round, as secret-secret pairs cannot appear in the challenge (at most 1 secret image appearing). We use *2-element counting table* to recover the secret from the challenge. For each pair of candidate images, the count value is zero only if both of them belong to the secret set after a sufficient number of observations. On average, it is sufficient to recover the exact secret within 172.7 rounds (20 sessions), and recover 80% secret elements (five secret images in total) after 126.9 rounds (15 sessions).

The same problem also appears in the CHC scheme [32] and in the low-complexity CAS scheme [31]. Both of them require that at least k secret elements appear in the challenge window, while the challenge window only holds a subset of candidate elements. These structural requirements make the distribution of the elements in each challenge deviate from the uniform distribution. Under default parameters, we are able to recover the exact root secret within 18.18 rounds (2 sessions) for CHC. For the low-complexity CAS scheme, we can recover the exact root secret (i.e. 60 independent secret images) within 2087.2 rounds (105 sessions), and recover 90% secret elements within 870.4 rounds (44 sessions).

The above discussion shows that the consequence of the distribution bias caused by structural requirements in the challenge is subtle to identify and has not been well recognized. In order to prevent leakage from biased challenges, the distribution of the elements in each challenge should be indistinguishable from the uniform distribution. If a structural requirement is *compulsory* in a password system (e.g. at least k secret elements being displayed) but the element distribution in each challenge is not uniform when the challenge window only shows a subset of candidate elements, the scheme should display *all* the candidate elements in each challenge.

4.3 P4: Large Decision Space or Indistinguishable Individual Principle

Principle 4: *An LRPS system with secret leakage should make each individual element* **indistinguishable** *in the probabilistic decision tree if the candidate set for decision paths is* **enumerable**.

This principle is critical to limit the feasibility of probabilistic decision tree attack. The power of probabilistic decision tree stems from its emulation of all possible decision processes leading to the observed response. The emulation creates a tight binding between each challenge and its response, from which the adversary is able to extract the subtle statistical difference during the user's decision if individual elements are distinguishable on consistent decision paths. It is not easy to make each individual element indistinguishable, especially when weight or order information is used in the challenge design. We use the high-complexity CAS scheme [31] as a counterexample to show how probabilistic decision tree efficiently discovers the root secret even when a number of decision paths lead to the same answer.

The high-complexity CAS scheme is another typical scheme based on the k-out-of-n paradigm. During registration, a user is assigned $k = 30$ images as his secret from a pool of $n = 80$ images. In each authentication round, a challenge is an 8×10 grid consists of all the images, one image for each cell. The user is asked to mentally compute a path starting from the cell in the upper-left corner. The computation rule is described as follows: Initially the current cell is the cell in the upper-left corner. If the image in the current cell belongs to the secret set, move down by one cell, otherwise move right by one cell; if the next moving position is out of the grid, it is referred to as an *exit position*. The path computation ends with an exit position. The user reports the answer associated with that exit position to finish an authentication round. The answer is an integer from $[0, 3]$, and is randomly assigned to each exit position. Since the same answer is assigned to multiple exit positions (i.e. 4 answers assigned to 18 exit positions), the adversary cannot easily tell which the exact exit position is. For each exit position, there are also many possible paths leading to it, which further increases the difficulty for the adversary.

Since the default parameters are large ($k = 30$, $n = 80$), brute force attack is infeasible for this scheme. The scheme also follows *Principle 3* to display all the candidate images in each challenge so that the adversary cannot extract the secret only by analyzing the challenges. However, each individual element is distinguishable in this scheme during the decision process, as each element has different impact on the transition of decision paths. One can use probabilistic decision tree to recover the secret from the observations of challenge-response pairs.

Each possible path leading to the observed response forms a decision path in the probabilistic decision tree. The probability of a decision path is decided by the movements on this path. For example, a path $X = \langle$*DOWN*, *RIGHT*, *RIGHT*, *DOWN*$\rangle$ means the first and the fourth images belong to the secret set, while the second and third images do not. The probability $p(X)$ is $p1 \cdot p0 \cdot p0 \cdot p1$, where $p1 = k/n$ and $p0 = 1 - p1$. Initially, we create a *1-element score table*. Given a response with the answer i, we enumerate all consistent decision paths leading to this answer, and update the score table according to the conditional probability $p(X|\text{response} = i)$.

For an 8×10 grid specified by the default parameters, there are 43758 possible decision paths in total, with aver-

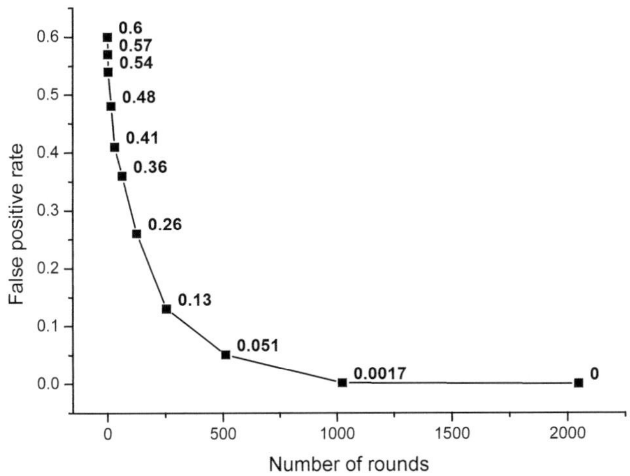

Figure 4. The average false positive rate decreases for the high-complexity CAS scheme.

age path length of 14.5539. For each candidate image, its score is at a significantly high level if it belongs to the secret set after a sufficient number of observations. Figure 4 shows the false positive rate decreasing along with the increasing number of observed authentication rounds. On average, it is sufficient to discover the exact secret within 640.8 rounds (65 sessions), and discover 90% secret elements after 264.7 rounds (27 sessions). Although the required number of session observations is larger, it is still possible for the adversary to collect them using a key logger, and such security strength is achieved only when the user is able to remember 30 independent secret images.

Probabilistic decision tree can also be applied to the low-complexity CAS scheme [31], the CHC scheme [32], the S3PAS scheme [35], and the PAS scheme [4]. All of them are based on simple challenges with an enumerable candidate space for decision paths and the individual element has different impact on the transition of decision paths.

From these counterexamples, we can see that *it is necessary to increase the number of candidate decision paths if it is infeasible to make each individual element indistinguishable in the probabilistic decision tree.* The only known designs that satisfy this indistinguishability requirement are the counting-based schemes [15, 20]. In those schemes, there is no order or weight information associated with each candidate element, which usually distinguishes the elements in decision paths. The user is asked to count their secret elements appearing in the challenge. The final response is based on the count value. For these schemes, probabilistic decision tree attack does not apply, but they may still subject to counting-based statistical analysis attack.

4.4 P5: Indistinguishable Correlation Principle

Principle 5: *An LRPS system with secret leakage should minimize the statistical difference in low-dimensional correlations among each possible* **response**.

This principle is complementary to *Principle 4* to limit the efficiency of counting-based statistical analysis. Although counting-based statistical analysis is straightforward, it cannot be completely prevented without a secure channel, as the user's response is always statistically biased towards his knowledge of the secret. In the extreme case, the adversary is able to maintain a counting table to hold every candidate for the root secret, and update the table according to every available observation. Using these counting tables, the statistical difference caused by the knowledge of the secret is always identifiable even when the user is asked to make intentional mistakes at a predefined probability only known by the server. Its informal proof is given in Appendix B. In this sense, the counting-based statistical analysis is more powerful than brute force attack if sufficient resources are available to the adversary.

In reality, the resources available to the adversary are not unbounded. The cost of maintaining *t-element counting tables* is $O(n^t)$, which increases exponentially with the number of elements t contained in a table entry, where n is the number of total individual elements. If the adversary fails to maintain a high-dimensional counting table, the correlation information in these tables is safe from the adversary. However, it is still possible for the adversary to exploit the low-dimensional correlation to recover the secret. We use SecHCI [20] as a counterexample to show how it works while brute force and probabilistic decision tree are infeasible.

During registration of SecHCI, a user is assigned k icons as his secret from a pool of n icons. In each authentication round, the challenge is a window consisting of w icons. The user is asked to count how many secret icons appearing in the window. After getting the count value x, the user calculates $r = \lfloor (x \mod 4)/2 \rfloor$. The final response r is either 0 or 1. The challenge is designed so that each individual candidate has the same probability to appear in the window for either response. Hence, it is impossible for the adversary to extract useful information based on *1-element statistical analysis*.

Since the default parameters are large, $k = 14$, $n = 140$, brute force attack is not applicable. Also because it is a counting-based scheme, it is not subject to probabilistic decision tree attack according to *Principle 4*. However, 2-dimensional counting attack is still applicable. Compared to decoy icons, there are 0.599 more pairs on average among secret icons for response 0, and 0.599 less pairs on average among secret icons for response 1. So we can use two *2-element counting tables* to recover its secret, one table

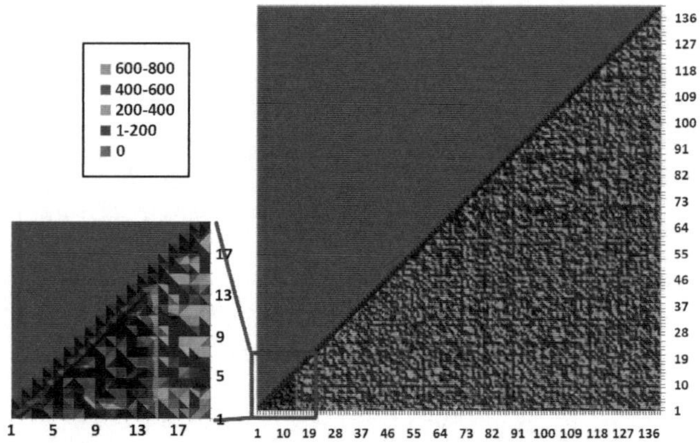

Figure 5. The pair-based score distribution is distorted for SecHCI. The first 14 elements are the secret icons, whose pair-based scores are distinguishable from the scores of other icons.

for each response. We update the count value for each pair displayed in each challenge and each response. The score for each entry is calculated as the value difference between these two tables. For each pair of candidate icons, the score is at a significantly high level if both of them belong to the secret set after a sufficient number of observations. Figure 5 shows the pair-based score distribution after 20000 authentication rounds, from which the secret icons can be easily distinguished. On average, it is sufficient to recover the exact secret with 14219.4 rounds (711 sessions), and recover 90% secret elements after 10799.8 rounds (540 sessions). Since SecHCI follows most of our principles, these numbers are much larger than the schemes we analyzed previously, but it is still far less secure than it is claimed to be [20]. Its security strength is achieved by imposing a high cognitive workload where the user is asked to correctly examine 600 icons (30 icons per round $\times$ 20 rounds) one by one for each authentication session.

The secret leakage on pair-based statistics for SecHCI can be fixed by changing its response function from $r = \lfloor (x \bmod 4)/2 \rfloor$ to $r = x \bmod 2$, where x is the number of secret icons in the challenge window, but this fix will make SecHCI subjects to algebraic attack based on Gaussian elimination [20]. This is also the original motivation of the scheme to use its current function. To further defend against this algebraic attack, a user has to produce incorrect answers with a fixed error probability to create noises as suggested in [15]. This certainly further decreases the scheme's usability. Another design limitation on counting-based scheme is that the response function cannot be in the form of $r = x \bmod q$, where q is an integer larger than 2. The detailed explanation for this limitation is given in Appendix C.

5 Usability Costs of Defense Principles

In this section, we provide a qualitative analysis for usability costs of our defense principles. We show the relation and tradeoff among the constraints imposed by our principles and the requirements on human capabilities. This section aims to provide a high level understanding of the quantitative tradeoff analysis to be presented in the next section.

As defined in Section 2, the common parameters of an LRPS system is a tuple (D, k, n, d, w, s). All of the parameters except D (the expected authentication strength) are affected by our principles. The principles related to brute force attack mainly dictates the memory demand for the secret, and the principles related to statistical attack mainly increase the computation workload for each authentication session. Their impacts are also interrelated.

Principles 1 and 2 require a large candidate set for the root secret and the round secret. This implies that either k increases or n increases. An increase in k requires the user to memorize more elements as his secret. An increase in n will not raise the memory demand, but will increase statistical significance of the secret in the whole candidate set, which indirectly increases the computation workload as analyzed later. Principle 2 also directly raises the computation workload, as it indicates a challenge is not safe against brute force attack if it can be solved by using a small number of possible secret elements. In order to increase the candidate space of the round secret, the round secret must be either randomly selected from the root secret [20, 31, 32] or use all elements in the root secret [15, 2]. The former choice requires the user to recognize the current displayed secret elements that change in every round; the latter requires the user to recall a large number of secret elements that would be difficult when k is large. Finally, more elements appearing in a challenge means more computation workload to aggregate them into the correct response. This demands much more effort compared to using a fixed short round secret in a traditional password system.

Principles 3, 4, and 5 have more impact on (d, w, s). Principle 3 requires that the elements in the challenge should be uniformly drawn from the candidate set. Due to previous requirements of large secret space and our preference of minimizing the memory demand for the secret, the value of k is to be small and the value of n is to be large. The consequence of this is that the average number of secret elements displayed in a challenge window, $w \cdot k/n$, cannot be large enough if the window size w is not large. This restricts the number of possible responses to a small value, which raises the success rate d of guessing attack and increases the round number required to achieve an expected authentication strength D. On the other hand, if the window size is large, the LRPS system is limited only for large screen devices and it also increases the difficulty for the user to examine the elements in the challenge window. Regardless of the window size, this principle imposes increased computation workload and the error rate for the user. Principles 4 and 5 further rule out most schemes based on simple challenges. Principle 4 states if a leakage-resistant challenge design is not complex enough to aggregate a large number of secret elements into a response, it leads to a counting problem. Principle 5 further states that only 0 and 1 can be safely used as the response for a counting problem if the modular operation is the only operation used to generate the final response. Hence, the three possible choices for a challenge are: 1) a complex challenge using many secret elements - the round number will be small but the challenge will be very difficult for the user to respond (the average length s of decision paths significantly increased); 2) a counting-based challenge using the modular operation - the round number will be large and the challenge will be relatively easier to respond; and 3) a counting-based challenge using a specially designed response function that has a large number of possible responses and satisfies the correlation indistinguishability condition; however, it will be a challenge to design such a function with acceptable usability. All of the three choices impose a considerable burden on the user.

6 Quantitative Tradeoff Analysis

In this section, we establish a quantitative analysis framework for evaluating the usability cost of typical existing LRPS systems. This framework decomposes the process of human-computer authentication into atomic cognitive operations in psychology. There are four types of atomic cognitive operations commonly used: single/parallel recognition, free/cued recall, single-target/multi-target visual search and simple cognitive arithmetic. Their definitions and performance models are given in Appendix A, which characterizes the relation between experiment parameters and reaction time of an average human. These performance models are used to evaluate the cognitive workload for typical existing LRPS systems. The result in this section provides quantitative assessment of the tradeoff between security and usability of LRPS systems. According to conventions in psychology literature, we will refer user as *subject* in this section.

6.1 Quantitative Analysis Framework

There are two components in our quantitative analysis framework, *Cognitive Workload* (C) and *Memory Demand* (M). Cognitive workload is measured by the total reaction time required by the involved cognitive operations. Long reaction time for each *authentication round* implies that it is difficult for the subject to answer each challenge and the overall error rate is also high. Long reaction time for each *authentication session* implies that the overall cognitive workload is high and the involvement of attention and patience is also high. Memory demand is measured by the number of elements that must be memorized by the subject, which is the prerequisite of any password system. Since this prerequisite process is independent from the authentication process, we consider it as a separate component. Since the precise relation between overall error rate and total reaction time is difficult to measure in controlled psychology experiments, our framework provides *lower bound* estimation for the usability of a human-computer authentication system. The detailed calculation for both components is described as follows.

For cognitive workload, the cost for each authentication round is the sum of average reaction time for all involved atomic cognitive operations. This cost represents the average thinking time of a subject required to answer a challenge. A typical authentication round consists of at least a memory retrieval operation and a simple arithmetic operation. For the graphic-based scheme, visual search is also common. According to the working memory capability theory [25, 9, 30, 29], the average reaction time is not shortened by repetitive rehearsal, when the subject has to maintain more than $4(\pm1)$ items in his working memory. The rehearsal only improves the accuracy, which represents an inherent limitation of human capabilities. This limitation is also applied to other non-memory operations such as visual search when the item positions are shuffled in each challenge [33]. Overall, the cognitive workload of an authentication session is calculated as the product of the cognitive workload of an authentication round and the round number when the number of the secret items is larger than 5. For the schemes [4, 32] with no more than 5 secret items, we only count once for their memory retrieval operations, assuming that the secret will not be flushed out due to the limitation of working memory capacity.

Besides the reaction time, other usability measurements for cognitive workload (such as user frustration level, concentration load, and motivational effort) are usually collected from standardized testing questionnaires. However, these measurements are susceptible to many implementation and environmental factors, such as screen size, graphic or text-based interface design, and the education background of subjects. In contrast, the influence of those unstable factors has been minimized in more than a century's development of experimental psychology. So the advantage of using performance models of atomic cognitive operations is that they are *implementation-independent*. This property is necessary for a fair comparison between different LRPS designs. Consequently, our estimation of cognitive workload is very consistent with the time costs reported in the

	k	n	Win size	Password space	Guess Rate /round	No. of rounds /login	Reported Time /round(sec)	HP (C) /round (sec)	HP (C) /login (sec)	HP (M)	HP Total =M×C ($\times 10^2$)
LPN[15]	15	200	200	1.463×10^{22}	0.50	20	**23.71**	**33.423**	668.45	50.68	**338.74**
APW[2]	16	200	200	8.369×10^{24}	0.10	6	**35.50**	**57.928**	347.57	54.05	**187.87**
CAS Low[31]	60	240	20	2.433×10^{57}	0.50	20	**5.00**	**6.073**	121.46	70.75	**85.94**
CAS High[31]	30	80	80	8.871×10^{21}	0.25	10	**20.00**	**22.099**	220.99	35.38	**78.18**
SecHCI[20]	14	140	30	6.510×10^{18}	0.50	20	**9.00**	**10.638**	212.76	16.51	**35.13**
CHC[32]	5	112	83	1.341×10^{8}	0.22	10	**10.97**	**9.326**	93.26	16.89	**15.75**
PAS[4]	4	N/A	13	4.225×10^{5}	0.25	10	**8.37**	**6.837**	68.37	13.51	**9.24**

Table 1. Tradeoff comparison of representative leakage-resilient password systems for their default parameters.

original papers [20, 31, 32, 4].

For memory demand, the cost for each scheme is a ratio k/λ_{op} between the number of secret items, k, and the *accuracy rate* of corresponding memory retrieval operation within a fixed memorization time, λ_{op}. Since recognition is much easier than recall [14, 25, 29, 23, 10], it is necessary to distinguish the difficulty for different memory retrieval operations. According to [14], λ_{op} is 29.6% for recall and 84.8% for recognition. A better estimation for the memory demand could be the minimum time for the subject to remember all the secrets. However, the lower bound of memorization time is difficult to measure in experimental psychology, as the subject may not realize the precise time point when he just remembers all the secrets. An unconfident subject may take more time to rehearsal than that actually required. Other memory factors, like password interference and recall accuracy over extended periods, may also be considered but are not integrated in our current analysis framework.

Finally, an overall score, HP (standing for *Human Power*), is calculated as the product of cognitive workload score HP(C) and memory demand score HP(M). This score (HP) indicates the expected human capability requirement for a human-computer authentication system.

6.2 High Security at Cost of Heavy Cognitive Demand

Table 1 shows the security strength and HP for the representative LRPS systems based on our quantitative analysis framework. Those systems are listed in the descend order of their HP. All the schemes use their default parameter values except that the round number is adjusted to make the successful rate of random guessing to reach the same level (i.e. the authentication strength of 6-digit PIN). This adjustment is necessary to make a fair comparison as they now have the same strength to defend against an adversary without prior knowledge. The other two points in this table which need explanation are about PAS [4] and CHC [32]. In PAS, we consider the root secret for each authentication session as the predicates instead of the complete secret pairs, due to that the same predicates are used for all the rounds in an authentication. The predicates are the actual root secret of each authentication session. In CHC, the expected successful rate of guessing attack is not reported in the original paper. We estimate it based on *Statement* 2, which is 21.78% derived from our simulation results. The detailed computation of the cognitive workload for those schemes is given in Table 2 of Appendix A.

The column "HP(C)/round" in this table shows the cognitive workload required to solve the challenge in each authentication round. It shows the average thinking time. All of them except LPN [15] and APW [2] are very close to the average time cost reported in the original literatures [20, 31, 32, 4]. For LPN, there is no report on a controlled user study. The scheme is implemented as a public web page, to which the subjects can freely access and get a reward for each successful login. There is no evidence showing that the subjects were asked to memorize their root secret (which are 15 secret positions), and then recall them in each authentication round. Thus, the average time cost reported for each round is very likely to be underestimated, as the recall operations are probably replaced by directly reading their written-down secrets. For APW, its time cost is directly estimated based on the results of LPN (with no actual user study conducted), which implies it could also be underestimated.

This table shows three tiers in these representative schemes. From bottom to top, the schemes in an upper tier have better security against secret leakage at the cost of lower usability. The schemes at the bottom are PAS [4] and CHC [32], which are susceptible to both brute force and statistical attacks. When moving to the middle tier (consisting of CAS [31] and SecHCI [20]), the memory demand increases to make brute force attack infeasible. However, they are still susceptible to statistical attack as the simple challenge used in these schemes is not sufficient to hide the statistical significance of the secret. More cognitive workload is required to mix the secret items with the other items. The top tier consists of LPN [15] and APW [2], which follow all of our design principles. They are immune to both brute force and statistical attacks in practical settings, but impose significantly high usability cost.

There is an interesting finding when looking at the two schemes in the top tier. In our quantitative analysis framework, LPN has a higher HP score but a smaller password space compared to APW. This is because our security measurement is limited to brute force and two generic statistical attacks. It is still possible to find out other more efficient attacks that lower the security strength of APW. The tradeoff relation under our quantitative analysis framework may not strictly follow the order of HP, as it is always feasible to design a scheme with a lower usability for a given security strength. But it is required that the human capability should reach a *lower bound* so as to achieve a high security strength.

The above results provide quantitative evidence for the inherent limitations in the design of LRPS. They indicate the incompetence of human cognitive capabilities in using secure LRPS systems without a secure channel in practical settings. This may also explain why the problem is still open since its first proposal [22] twenty years ago.

7 Related Work

As one of the most important security tools of modern society, the design problem of a secure and usable password system has been extensively investigated. We summarize the closely related research work from the following aspects: attacks, principles, and tradeoff analysis for LRPS systems.

Most of proposed LRPSes have been broken. The recent works on representative attack and analysis include: Golle and Wagner proposed the SAT attack [13] against the CAS schemes [31]; Li et al. demonstrated the brute-force attack [18] against the PAS scheme [4]; they later presented a Gaussian elimination-based algebraic attack [19] against the virtual password system [17]; Asghar et al. introduced a statistical attack [1] against the CHC scheme [32]; Dunphy et al. analyzed a replay-based shoulder surfing attack for recognition-based graphical password systems under a weaker threat model [11]. Compared to them, our paper provides security analysis in a more generic setting, which presents two types of generic attacks that can be used to analyze any LRPS systems. Furthermore, we introduce a new statistical attack, probabilistic decision tree, and a generalized version of existing statistical attacks, multi-dimensional counting. We analyze and re-examine the existing LRPS systems with these new attack tools. Thereby, we discover the vulnerabilities of Undercover [27] and SecHCI [20] that have not been reported before. We notice that a recent work by Perkovic et al. [24] also identified the design flaw of Undercover independently.

Some other design principles have been proposed for LRPS systems. Roth et al. [26] proposed the basic principle of using cognitive trapdoor game, where the knowledge of secret should not be directly revealed during password entry. Li and Shum [20] later suggested another three principles that require time-variant responses, randomness in challenges and responses, and indistinguishability against the statistical analysis. Our principles further extend the coverage by including the defense principles against brute force attack, and provide more concrete guidelines against two generic statistical attacks introduced in our paper.

Until now it is still a challenge to provide a quantitative tradeoff analysis among multiple LRPS systems [5]. As pointed out by Biddle et al. [5], the usability evaluation in prior research lacks consistency, which makes it is difficult to compare those results. Our quantitative analysis framework is the first attempt to provide a uniform usability measurement based on experimental psychology. Based on this framework and our security analysis, we discover that the tradeoff between security and usability is strong, which indicates the inherent limitation in the design of LRPS systems. This limitation was first addressed by Hopper and Blum [15], where they hoped the future research could find out practical solutions for unaided humans that satisfy both security and usability requirements. Unfortunately, from our results, such solution may not exist. Coskun and Herley [8] also reached a similar conclusion by analyzing the efficiency of brute force attack with regards to response entropy. Their conclusion is based on the assumption that a user has to make a large number of sequential binary decisions so as to increase response entropy. However, this assumption may not be valid as humans have a strong parallel processing capability when performing certain visual tasks (e.g. visual search). Other prior research related to LRPS systems can be found in a recent survey paper [5], which summarized the development of new password systems in the past decade.

We remark that our quantitative analysis framework is still in its preliminary stage. We would like to point out two limitations in our current work: 1) Since the cognitive workload is not totally independent with the memory demand, it is possible to improve the overall score calculation instead of using the product operation (i.e. HP= M$\times$C); 2) Error rate is currently not included in our analysis framework as it is difficult for experimental psychology to provide the general relation between thinking time and error rate. Certain approximation can be added to improve the precision of this framework in the future.

8 Conclusion

In this paper, we provided a comprehensive analysis for the inherent tradeoff between security and usability in designing a leakage-resilient password system. We analyzed the impacts of two types of generic attacks, brute force and statistical attacks, on the existing schemes designed for unaided humans. Unlike the specific attacks proposed before (such as SAT [13] and Gaussian elimination [19]), these two generic attacks, as demonstrated in our paper, cannot be mitigated without involving considerable demand on human capabilities. We introduced five principles that are necessary to achieve leakage resilience when a secure channel is unavailable. Usability costs for these principles are analyzed. Our findings indicate that either high memory demand or high cognitive workload is unavoidable in the design of secure LRPS for unaided humans. To further understand the tradeoff between security and usability, we established the first quantitative analysis framework on usability costs. Our result shows that there is a strong tradeoff between security and usability, indicating that an unaided human may not be competent enough to use a secure leakage-resilient password system in practical settings.

References

[1] H. J. Asghar, S. Li, J. Pieprzyk, and H. Wang. Cryptanalysis of the convex hull click human identification protocol. In *Proceedings of the 13th international conference on Information security*, pages 24–30, 2010.

[2] H. J. Asghar, J. Pieprzyk, and H. Wang. A new human identification protocol and coppersmith's baby-step giant-step algorithm. In *Proceedings of the 8th international conference on Applied cryptography and network security*, pages 349–366, 2010.

[3] A. D. Baddeley. *The Essential Handbook of Memory Disorders for Clinicians*, chapter 1, pages 1–13. John Wiley & Sons, 2004.

[4] X. Bai, W. Gu, S. Chellappan, X. Wang, D. Xuan, and B. Ma. Pas: Predicate-based authentication services against powerful passive adversaries. In *Proceedings of the 2008 Annual Computer Security Applications Conference*, pages 433–442, 2008.

[5] R. Biddle, S. Chiasson, and P. C. van Oorschot. Graphical passwords: Learning from the first twelve years. In *Technical Report TR-11-01*, 2011.

[6] J. I. D. Campbell and Q. Xue. Cognitive arithmetic across cultures. *Journal of Experimental Psychology: General*, 130(2):299–315, 2001.

[7] L. Corbina and J. Marquer. Effect of a simple experimental control: The recall constraint in sternberg's memory scanning task. *European Journal of Cognitive Psychology*, 20(5):913–935, 2008.

[8] B. Coskun and C. Herley. Can "something you know" be saved? In *Proceedings of the 11th international conference on Information Security*, pages 421–440, 2008.

[9] N. Cowan. The magical number 4 in short-term memory: a reconsideration of mental storage capacity. *Behavioral and Brain Sciences*, 24(1):87–114, 2001.

[10] F. I. Craik and J. M. McDowd. Age differences in recall and recognition. *Journal of Experimental Psychology: Learning, Memory, and Cognition*, 13(3):474–479, 1987.

[11] P. Dunphy, A. P. Heiner, and N. Asokan. A closer look at recognition-based graphical passwords on mobile devices. In *Proceedings of the Sixth Symposium on Usable Privacy and Security*, pages 3:1–3:12, 2010.

[12] D. L. Fisher. Central capacity limits in consistent mapping, visual search tasks: Four channels or more? *Cognitive Psychology*, 16(4):449–484, 1984.

[13] P. Golle and D. Wagner. Cryptanalysis of a cognitive authentication scheme (extended abstract). In *Proceedings of the 2007 IEEE Symposium on Security and Privacy*, pages 66–70, 2007.

[14] R. M. Hogan and W. Kintsch. Differential effects of study and test trials on long-term recognition and recall. *Journal of Verbal Learning and Verbal Behavior*, 10(5):562–567, 1971.

[15] N. J. Hopper and M. Blum. Secure human identification protocols. In *Proceedings of the 7th International Conference on the Theory and Application of Cryptology and Information Security: Advances in Cryptology*, pages 52–66, 2001.

[16] T. S. Horowitz and J. M. Wolfe. Search for multiple targets: Remember the targets, forget the search. *Perception & Psychophysics*, 63(2):272–285, 2001.

[17] M. Lei, Y. Xiao, S. Vrbsky, C.-C. Li, and L. Liu. A virtual password scheme to protect passwords. In *Proceedings of IEEE International Conference on Communications*, pages 1536–1540, 2008.

[18] S. Li, H. Asghar, J. Pieprzyk, A.-R. Sadeghi, R. Schmitz, and H. Wang. On the security of pas (predicate-based authentication service). In *Proceedings of the 2009 Annual Computer Security Applications Conference*, pages 209–218, 2009.

[19] S. Li, S. A. Khayam, A.-R. Sadeghi, and R. Schmitz. Breaking randomized linear generation functions based virtual password system. In *Proceedings of the 2010 IEEE International Conference on Communications*, pages 23–27, 2010.

[20] S. Li and H. yeung Shum. Secure human-computer identification (interface) systems against peeping attacks: SecHCI. In *Cryptology ePrint Archive, Report 2005/268*, 2005.

[21] J. Long and J. Wiles. *No Tech Hacking: A Guide to Social Engineering, Dumpster Diving, and Shoulder Surfing*. Syngress, 2008.

[22] T. Matsumoto and H. Imai. Human identification through insecure channel. In *Proceedings of the 10th annual international conference on Theory and application of cryptographic techniques*, pages 409–421, 1991.

[23] P. A. Nobel and R. M. Shiffrin. Retrieval processes in recognition and cued recall. *Journal of Experimental Psychology: Learning, Memory, and Cognition*, 27(2):384–413, 2001.

[24] T. Perkovic, A. Mumtaz, Y. Javed, S. Li, S. A. Khayam, and M. Cagalj. Breaking undercover: Exploiting design flaws and nonuniform human behavior. In *Proceedings of the Seventh Symposium on Usable Privacy and Security*, 2011.

[25] D. Rohrer and J. Wixted. An analysis of latency and interresponse time in free recall. *Memory. & Cognition*, 22(5):511–524, 1994.

[26] V. Roth, K. Richter, and R. Freidinger. A pin-entry method resilient against shoulder surfing. In *Proceedings of the 11th ACM conference on Computer and communications security*, pages 236–245, 2004.
[27] H. Sasamoto, N. Christin, and E. Hayashi. Undercover: authentication usable in front of prying eyes. In *Proceeding of the twenty-sixth annual SIGCHI conference on Human factors in computing systems*, pages 183–192, 2008.
[28] S. Sternberg. Memory-scanning: Mental processes revealed by reaction-time experiments. *American Scientist*, 57:421–457, 1969.
[29] N. Unsworth and R. W. Engle. The nature of individual differences in working memory capacity: Active maintenance in primary memory and controlled search from secondary memory. *Psychological Review*, 114(1):104–132, 2007.
[30] E. Vogel and M. Machizawa. Neural activity predicts individual differences in visual working memory capacity. *Nature*, 428(6984):748–751, 2004.
[31] D. Weinshall. Cognitive authentication schemes safe against spyware (short paper). In *Proceedings of the 2006 IEEE Symposium on Security and Privacy*, pages 295–300, 2006.
[32] S. Wiedenbeck, J. Waters, L. Sobrado, and J.-C. Birget. Design and evaluation of a shoulder-surfing resistant graphical password scheme. In *Proceedings of the working conference on Advanced visual interfaces*, pages 177–184, 2006.
[33] G. F. Woodman and M. M. Chun. The role of working memory and long-term memory in visual search. *Visual Cognition*, 14(4-8):808–830, 2006.
[34] G. F. Woodman and S. J. Luck. Visual search is slowed when visuospatial working memory is occupied. *Psychonomic Bulletin and Review*, 11(2):269–274, 2004.
[35] H. Zhao and X. Li. S3pas: A scalable shoulder-surfing resistant textual-graphical password authentication scheme. In *Proceedings of the 21st International Conference on Advanced Information Networking and Applications Workshops - Volume 02*, pages 467–472, 2007.

A Atomic Cognitive Operations and HP(C) Calculation

There are four types of atomic cognitive operations commonly used in human-computer authentication systems. Their definitions and performance models are introduced in this section, which characterize the relation between experiment parameters and reaction time (RT) of an average human. These performance models are utilized to evaluate the cognitive workload for the existing LRPS systems, as shown in Table 2.

A.1 (Single/Parallel) Recognition

Recognition is the process to correctly judge whether a presented item have been encountered before. Recognition can be considered as a matching process of comparing presented items with those stored in memory. The reaction time of a recognition operation depends on the number of items which a subject memorizes. The item set in the subject's memory is referred to as a *positive set*. For single item recognition, that is, only one item is shown to the subject each time, one of the most well-known recognition models [28] evaluates the reaction time as $RT = 0.3964 + 0.0383 \cdot k$, where k is the size of the positive set. When multiple items are present simultaneously, the subject is able to perform recognition in parallel. According to the working memory capacity theory [12, 9, 30], the maximum number of parallel recognition channels is limited to 4 for an average subject. The reaction time of recognizing x items displayed simultaneously can be estimated as $RT = (0.3964 + 0.0383 \cdot k) \cdot \lceil x/4 \rceil$.

Recognition is a common operation in LRPS, which is used by the subject to judge whether an element appearing in the challenge belongs to the positive set. The high-complexity CAS scheme [31] is an example for single item recognition, where the subject is asked to recognize an image in the current position before deciding which image will be recognized in the next move. The low-complexity CAS scheme [31] and SecHCI [20] are examples of parallel recognition. In the low-complexity CAS scheme, the subject needs to find out the first and the last secret image appearing in a window consisting of 20 images; while in SecHCI, the subject needs to identify all his secret images among 30 candidate images.

A.2 (Free/Cued) Recall

Recall is the other principal method of memory retrieval [3], which is defined as reproducing the stimulus items. Compared to recognition, the recall process is much slower [10, 23]. The common interpretation of this is that recall is associated with greater resource costs than recognition [10]. Recall might be carried out as a slow process of serial search while recognition as a fast process of parallel retrieval [23].

Free recall and cued recall are two basic recall types. In free recall, the subject is given a list of items to remember and then is tested by recalling them in any order [25]. In cued recall, the subject is given a list of items with cues to remember, and cues are given in the test. Cues act as guides to what the person is supposed to remember. For example, given "a body of water", the phrase is the cue for the word "pond" [10]. Many psychological experiments have shown that the reaction time of free recall increases *exponential* as the size of positive set increases [25, 29]. In contrast, the reaction time for cued recall is much shorter and only increases *linearly* [10, 23].

Some LRPS systems require subjects to recall all his secret items during the authentication. The LPN scheme [15] and the APW scheme [2] are two examples, where the subject has to recall all the secret items and their corresponding locations in order to read the challenge digit associated with

	Atomic Cognitive Operations	Calculation of HP (C) per round
LPN[15]	Cued-recall with position, counting, mod	$(0.3964 + 0.0383 \cdot k \cdot \varphi \cdot \gamma) \cdot k + (k/2 - 1) \cdot \alpha_0 + 1 \cdot \alpha_0$
APW[2]	Cued-recall with position, large addition, mod	$((0.3694 + 0.0383 \cdot k \cdot \varphi \cdot \gamma) + 1 \cdot \alpha_3 + 1 \cdot \alpha_0) \cdot k$
CAS Low[31]	Parallel recognition, xor	$(0.3694 + 0.0383 \cdot k) \cdot \lceil 7.4038/4 \rceil + 1 \cdot \alpha_0$
CAS High[31]	Recognition	$(0.3694 + 0.0383 \cdot k) \cdot 14.5539$
SecHCI[20]	Parallel Recognition, counting, mod, small division	$(0.3694 + 0.0383 \cdot k) \cdot (\lceil 30/4 \rceil) + 2 \cdot \alpha_0 + 1 \cdot \alpha_0 + 1 \cdot \alpha_2$
CHC[32]	Cued-recall, Multi-target visual search (3-based)	$((0.3694 + 0.0383 \cdot k \cdot \varphi) \cdot 5/10) + (0.583 + 0.0529 \cdot 83) \cdot 1.8$
PAS[4]	Cued-recall, single-target visual search, small addition	$(0.3694 + 0.0383 \cdot 2 \cdot \varphi) \cdot 4/10 + (0.583 + 0.0529 \cdot 13) \cdot 4 + 2 \cdot \alpha_1$

Table 2. Detailed computation of cognitive workload for representative leakage-resilient password systems. $\alpha_0 = 0.738$, $\alpha_1 = 0.773$, $\alpha_2 = 0.959$, $\alpha_3 = 0.924$ **are the average reaction time for arithmetic problems involving 0 or 1, small addition, small division, and large addition correspondingly.** $\varphi = 1.969$ **is the ratio of cued recall compared to single item recognition, while** $\gamma = 1.317$ **is the additional penalty caused by simultaneously recalling the position of an item. For CAS Low and High,** 7.4038 **and** 14.5539 **are the average lengths of their decision paths, respectively.**

each secret item. These recall processes should be classified as free recall as cues are not presented. However, no experimental data have been provided in psychology literatures for a large positive set consisted of 15 items required by these schemes, while the common size for a positive set is 8 for free recall. Since it is difficult to decide whether the exponential trend still holds when the positive set is large, we use the reaction time of cued recall as a conservative estimation for free recall used in those schemes. According to the experimental results in [23, 7], the formula for the reaction time of cued recall is $RT = (0.3964 + 0.0383 \cdot \varphi \cdot \gamma \cdot k)$, where φ is the ratio of cued recall compared to single item recognition ($\varphi = 1.969$ in [23]), while γ is the additional penalty if subjects are required to simultaneously recalling the position of an item ($\gamma = 1.317$ in [7]).

A.3 (Single-target/Multi-target) Visual Search

Visual search is a perceptual task that involves an active scan of the visual environment for particular targets among other distractors. The measure of the involvement of attention in visual search is often manifested as a slope of the response time function over the number of items displayed (referred to as *window size*) [33]. For single-target visual search, searching a single target among a set of items, its reaction time is believed to be linear as the window size increases [34, 33] and can be estimated as $RT = 0.583 + 0.0529 \cdot w$ [34], where w is the window size. For multi-target visual search, the reaction time is accelerated instead of increasing linearly as the number of targets increases in a fixed-sized window [16].

Visual search is usually used in LRPS systems based on simple challenges. PAS [4] and CHC [32] are examples of using single-target visual search and multi-target visual search, respectively. In PAS, the subject is asked to scan a table cell containing 13 random letters to check whether a secret letter is present or not. In CHC, the subject needs to locate 3 secret elements in a window to form a triangle. According to the results from [16], the reaction time of 3-targets visual search in CHC is approximately 1.8 times longer than that of single-target visual search in the same window.

A.4 Simple Cognitive Arithmetic

Simple cognitive arithmetic is a mental task to solve simple problems involving basic arithmetic operations (e.g., $3+4$, $7-3$, 3×4, $12 \div 3$). The simple arithmetic problems can be further divided into three subsets, small, large and zero-and-one problems [6]. For both addition and multiplication, small problems are defined as those with the product of two operands smaller than or equal to 25, and large problems are defined as those with the product of two operands larger than 25. The small and large problems in subtraction and division are defined on the basis of the inverse relationships between addition and subtraction and between multiplication and division. Zero-and-one problem is defined as involving 0 or 1 as an operand or answer. The common instances of zero-and-one problems include counting, exclusive-or, and mod 2. As reported in the experiments of [6], the average reaction time is 0.773 seconds for small addition, 0.959 seconds for small division, 0.924 seconds for large addition, and 0.738 seconds for zero-and-one problems.

Simple cognitive arithmetic is usually used in LRPS systems based on algebra problems. The counting-based schemes [15, 20] are examples, where the subject is asked to count the number of secret icons appearing in the challenge, and use the count value to calculate a response based on a simple algebraic function.

B Strength of Multi-dimensional Counting

Assuming the user makes mistakes in the responses with a fixed error probability ρ, the average success rate of guessing attack on the "correct" response for each authentication round is d, the number of candidate root secrets is N, the adversary cannot distinguish the true secret only when the equation $\frac{1-\rho}{(1-\rho)(Nd-1)+\rho \cdot Nd} = \frac{1}{N-1}$ holds, which means the decoys get the same count value as that of the secret. Solving the equation gives $\rho = 1 - d$. Therefore, the user should make the correct response with probability $1 - \rho = d$. This implies that the user's decision process is similar to a random guessing, which defeats the purpose of the authentication.

C Design Limitation of Counting-Based LRPSes

In our simulation experiments, we discover that pair-based statistical difference in Counting-based LRPSes appears when q is larger than 2, and increases with the value of $|r - w \cdot k/n|$, where r is the response value, w is the window size, k is the number of secret elements, and n is the total number of elements. This can be explained as follows: For a response, if the expected number of secret elements in a window is less than the expected number $w \cdot k/n$ derived from the uniform distribution, the number of pairs among secret elements is also less than the expected number $C^2_{wk/n}$, and the number of pairs among decoy elements is larger than the expected number derived from the uniform distribution, and vice versa. The adversary is then able to distinguish the secret elements from the other elements by grouping the observations of different responses. Such attack restricts a counting-based scheme from using a larger q and thus reducing the number of rounds of an authentication session without using a more complex response function.

Adaptive Password-Strength Meters from Markov Models

Claude Castelluccia
INRIA
claude.castelluccia@inria.fr

Markus Dürmuth
Ruhr-University Bochum
markus.duermuth@rub.de

Daniele Perito
INRIA
daniele.perito@inria.fr

Abstract

Measuring the strength of passwords is crucial to ensure the security of password-based authentication. However, current methods to measure password strength have limited accuracy, first, because they use rules that are too simple to capture the complexity of passwords, and second, because password frequencies widely differ from one application to another. In this paper, we present the concept of adaptive password strength meters *that estimate password strength using Markov-models. We propose a* secure *implementation that greatly improves on the accuracy of current techniques.*

1 Introduction

Passwords are a traditional and widespread method of authentication, both on the Internet and off-line. Passwords are portable, easy to understand for laypersons, and easy to implement for the operator. Thus, password-based authentication is likely to stay for the foreseeable future. Most sites let users choose their password, as the usability of automatically generated passwords is low [32]. However, users tend to choose weak passwords, for instance, many users choose passwords from a rather small set of passwords, and hence, these passwords can easily be guessed.[1]

To ensure an acceptable level of security of user-chosen passwords, sites often use mechanisms to test the strength of a password (often called *pro-active password checkers*) and then reject weak passwords. Hopefully this ensures that passwords are reasonably strong on average and makes guessing passwords infeasible or at least too expensive for the adversary. Commonly used password checkers rely on rules such as requiring a number and a special character to be used. However, as we will show and also has been observed in previous work [28], the accuracy of such password checkers is low, which means that often insecure passwords are accepted and secure passwords are rejected. This adversely affects both security and usability. The commonly used rule-sets are too simple to capture the complexity of passwords, and users confronted with them often choose the same modifications to fulfil the rules (like the sadly famous `password1`). Furthermore, password distributions differ from site to site (for example due to language differences) and no password checker is equally suitable for all sites.

We propose to use password strength meters based on Markov-models, which estimate the true strength of a password more accurately than rule-based strength meters. Roughly speaking, the Markov-model estimates the strength of a password by estimating the probability of the n-grams that compose said password. Best results can be obtained when the Markov-models are trained on the actual password database. We show, in this paper, how to do so without sacrificing the security of the password database, even when the n-gram database is leaked. We call these *Adaptive* Password Strength Meters (APSMs), as they can react dynamically to changes in how users choose passwords. Previous work [6, 19] has already shown that Markov-model based password *crackers* outperform existing cracking techniques, and conjectured that they could be used to create better proactive password strength meters. However, before our work it was unclear how this could be implemented securely, and how accurate it would be be.

In this paper, we show how to build secure adaptive password strength meters, where security should hold even when the n-gram database leaks. This is similar to traditional password databases, where one tries to minimize the effects of a database breach by hashing and salting the stored passwords. This is not a trivial task. One potential problem is that, particularly strong passwords, can be leaked entirely by an n-gram database (without noise added). This is best illustrated with an example: If the password "`!*(%$.&`" is used, then from the 5-grams "`!*(%$`", "`*(%$.`", and "`(%$.&`" one can reconstruct the password with high probability by searching for the overlapping segments. By adding a carefully chosen amount of noise we can eliminate this kind of attack, and

[1] From leaked password lists we learn that 20% of passwords are covered by a list of only 5,000 common passwords [27].

in fact we can prove that the noisy n-gram database leaks very limited information about the actually stored password database. By varying the amount of noise added we can balance our system between security and privacy, and we show parameters that strike a reasonable balance between the two for large password databases.

The attacker model makes the following two assumptions: First we make the common assumption that the adversary does not attack one specific user, but is interested in guessing *any* password correctly in the system. This means that the attacker does not use information about a specific user such as his date of birth, children's names, and so on.

Second, we argue that a reasonable analysis of password strength needs to assume that the adversary knows the distribution of the passwords. This is a necessary assumption, as a number of password databases have leaked over the past years and are available to everybody. An attacker might be able to obtain a very accurate distribution for a given site by correlating user statistics. Consequently, assuming that the exact distribution is known to the attacker is the only way to conservatively estimate his knowledge.

1.1 Contributions

This paper makes the following contributions:

- We propose the first adaptive password strength meter (APSM). Our password meter, based on n-gram models, is both accurate in gauging password strength and secure against the strong attacker model described above.
- The need for adaptive password strength meters is motivated in Section 3 by showing that the way users choose passwords is greatly influenced by the type of service (among other factors), which reduces the accuracy of heuristic password checkers that are widely in use today.
- Since our construction needs to store additional (non hashed) information about passwords, we formally prove the security of our scheme, by proving an upper bound on the information that leaks per passwords if a data breach occurs and the actual n-gram database is leaked. We show a bound of 1.3 (per password) bits for reasonable parameters. This leakage only occurs if the password database is breached.
- We evaluate the accuracy of our scheme by performing extensive experiments. More specifically, we show that our scheme outperforms existing schemes, such as NIST, Microsoft, and Google schemes. We also show that the noise added on n-grams, necessary to provide security in case of leakage of the n-gram dataset, does *not* significantly affect performance. We discover that traditional password meters are inaccurate, and perform only slightly better than a scheme that would output random values. On the contrary, our construction can distinguish between strong and weak passwords with high accuracy.

1.2 Related Work

We review relevant previous work on password metrics as well as work in the closely related field of password guessing.

Password metrics: Estimating the strength of passwords as a measure to defend against guessing attacks has a long history. In [18], password checking was done by attempting to crack the hashed passwords. The ones successfully cracked were marked as weak and the users notified.

Later, one started to estimate the strength of a password before it is accepted by a system by what are called *pro-active password checkers* or *password strength meters (PSM)*, using certain rules-sets that aim at excluding weak passwords [24, 11, 2, 20]. An influential PSM was proposed by the NIST [4] (see Section 2.2 for a comparison of rule-sets that are used in practice). Recently, the NIST rule-set was shown [28] to be a rather weak measure for the actual password strength (see also [12] for more results on such a comparison). We reach a similar conclusion in Section 6, showing a low correlation of this measure and the actual password strength.

Schechter et al. [23] classify passwords as weak by counting the number of times a certain password is present in the password database. This password meter, however, cannot generalize on common variations of weak passwords, e.g., `password1`. These variations have to become *popular* before the system can mark them as weak. Our construction, instead, can easily meter those password by leveraging on the capabilities of Markov-models.

Several papers study user behaviour regarding (in-)secure passwords [22, 9, 26, 30]. Some more work on estimating password strength or related ways to increase the security of password-based authentication can be found in [21, 31, 13].

Password cracking: Password cracking is a problem in many ways similar to estimating a password's strength. [18, 5, 15]. To protect passwords they are usually stored in hashed form, and under the common assumption that an attacker cannot invert this hash function, his optimal strategy is to test passwords in decreasing likelihood, i.e., most frequent passwords first. This means the attacker needs a method to enumerate passwords with decreasing likelihood, in other words, with increasing strength.

While most previous attacks use large (external) dictionaries and ad-hoc mangling rules to modify these, Narayanan and Shmatikov [19] proposed Markov-models to overcome some of the problems of dictionary-based attacks, by training Markov-models to general rules that passwords follow. This work also is the first to hint that Markov-models might yield useful password strength meters; however, they neither considered accuracy nor security of such a construction. While [19] uses ad-hoc "templates" on password structures, i.e., on the proportion and position of numbers and letters, subsequent work [29] learns these structures from sets of leaked passwords. An empirical study on the effectiveness of different attacks including those based on Markov-models can be found in [6]. A study also taking into account password re-use is [7].

1.3 Organization

The rest of the paper is organized as follows: We review password strength meters in Section 2. We motivate and define adaptive password strength meters in Section 3 and give the construction of such a scheme in Section 4. Next, we prove its security in Section 5, demonstrate its accuracy in Section 6, and discuss some implementation details in Section 7 . Finally, Section 8 concludes the paper.

2 Password Strength Meters

A password strength meter is a function $f\colon \Sigma^* \to \mathbb{R}$, that takes as input a string (or password) x over an alphabet Σ and outputs a number s, a *score*, which is a measure of the strength of string x as a password. The output is, in general, a real number indicating the passwords strength. The strength s provides an estimation of the effort an attacker is required to invest to guess the password x and can be used either to advise the users on the strength of the passwords or to enforce mandatory password strength policies. Both approaches have their merits and problems.

The strength of a password is the amount of work an adversary needs to break the password. In the context of password guessing, the adversary has a way to check if a (guessed) password is the correct one, usually by a hash-value representing the hash of the correct password, by an online-login, or similar means. Consequently, the optimal strategy for an attacker is to guess passwords in increasing order of strength and decreasing order of probability, i.e., more likely passwords are tried before less likely ones. This also motivates the definition of guessing entropy, which gives the average number of passwords an attacker has to guess before finding the correct one. Let X be a random variable with finite domain D and $P(X = d_i) = p_i$, ordered with decreasing probabilities $p_i < p_j$ for $i < j$. The *guessing entropy* $G(X)$ is defined as

$$G(X) = \sum_{i=1}^{|D|} i \cdot Pr(X = i). \quad (1)$$

2.1 An Ideal Password-Strength Meter

Definition 1 *Let us fix probabilities $P\colon \Sigma^* \to [0,1]$ on the space of passwords (i.e., strings over a certain alphabet). An* ideal password checker *$f(x)$ is given by the function $f(x) = -\log(P(x))$.*

We denote this password strength meter as "ideal", as the order which is given by this function is the same as the order with which passwords are guessed in an optimal guessing attack. Consequently, the following two functions $f'(x) = 1/P(x)$ and $f''(x) = R_P(x)$ also constitute ideal password checkers, where $R_P(x)$ is the rank of x according to the distribution P, i.e., if the probabilities $p_i = P(x_i)$ are ordered with $p_i < p_j$ for $i < j$, then $R_P(x_i) = i$.

Any password checker or password strength meter can be seen as an approximation to this function, often clustered in few buckets such as "insecure/secure", or "insecure/medium/high". We will survey some commonly used approximations in the next section.

2.2 Common Approximations

The commonly used (rule-based) password checkers can be seen as ad-hoc approximations to an ideal strength meter as described above, where passwords with strength over a certain threshold should be accepted, and otherwise rejected. There is a large number of password checkers employed today. Many web-services implement their own password checker using a combination of educated guessing and craft. However, as we will show, these approximations perform poorly in the task of gauging the strength of a password. As a consequence, both usability (by scoring strong passwords as weak) and security (by scoring weak passwords as strong) are affected.

We compare our work to three different password checkers that are widely used today: the NIST, Google and Microsoft password checkers. They were chosen because of their popularity and because they are representative for the techniques employed currently for password strength meters.

The *NIST password meter* tries to estimate the entropy of a password mainly based on their length. Special bonuses (in bits) are given if the password matches particular conditions, like containing special characters or a combination of upper case and numbers. The NIST also optionally suggests to give a bonus for a dictionary check. We did not implement this feature as it would have been bound to a specific dictionary, and it affects a small number of passwords only.

The *Microsoft password meter* [17] (employed, e.g., in Hotmail, Windows Live) outputs an integer in the range $[0, 4]$. The strongest score 4 is given to passwords that match all the "good" conditions: passing a dictionary test (included in the JavaScript), minimum length of 14, using at least three types of characters (upper, lower, number, special). The tool is implemented as a JavaScript routine that measures the strength of passwords entered in a text box. For our tests we downloaded the JavaScript code and ran it inside SpiderMonkey [25], a Perl interface to the Mozilla JavaScript Engine. This allowed us to use the tool unchanged for our experiments.

The *Google password meter* also outputs an integer between 0 and 4. We do not know the inner workings of this meter, that is implemented on the server-side and not in JavaScript. This design choice is probably affected by security concerns, as it "hides", to possible attackers, how passwords are metered. Based on our observations, however, this password checker seems to be based on a set of fixed rules like the others. We used the server as an oracle to measure the password strength.

3 Adaptive Password Strength Meters

A password strength meter is a fixed function, and cannot take into account site-specific aspects of the password distribution. This is why we propose using adaptive password strength meters, which can additionally base their score on specifics of the site. To our knowledge this has not been defined before, even though the motivation is similar to [23].

Definition 2 *An* adaptive password strength meter (APSM) *$f(x, L)$ is a function $f: \Sigma^* \times (\Sigma^*)^k \rightarrow \mathbb{R}$, that takes a string (or password) x over an alphabet Σ and a password file L containing a number of passwords as input and outputs a* score *S.*

Intuitively, the password database L contains a number of passwords sampled from the same distribution, and the task of the password strength meter is to estimate the strength of the password x based on his estimation of P. Alternatively, as in our scheme, a *noisy* model of L is stored to preserve the secrecy of the password database. The amount of noise added to the model of L needs to strike a balance between accuracy and secrecy.

We note that the adaptive password strength meter f does not need to have a-priory knowledge of the distribution P, whereas a (non-adaptive) password strength meter does.

3.1 The Need for Adaptive Password Meters

The main motivation for adaptive password meters is the observation that password distributions are different for different sites. This is illustrated by Figure 1(b), which shows the ten most frequent passwords from three leaked password sets (more information about these datasets can be found in Section 6). At a glance it can be seen that the passwords in each service have distinctive characteristics. For example the password `rockyou` is only popular in the RockYou service. While this password and possible variations have a very low guessing entropy on RockYou, this is not the case on different web services. The MySpace passwords, at some point, have been influenced by a rule-based password checker that requires number to be included in the passwords.

The results of a more comprehensive analysis are shown in Figure 1(a). These graphs show the fraction of frequent passwords that are shared by two or more password lists, considering varying thresholds. While RockYou and PhpBB share 50% of the most common passwords, other services share substantially less passwords, with as few as 10% shared between RockYou and MySpace.[2]

We believe these differences are caused by different languages spoken and cultural backgrounds of the users, different perceived importance of the password, different password checkers in place, and so on. This variety of different influences makes it very hard for a site to estimate the actual distribution in advance, without accessing the actual passwords. Furthermore, the password checkers influence the distribution of passwords, as exemplified by the MySpace passwords. This means that no static set of rules can capture the dynamic changes in password creation habits by the users.

3.2 Challenges

Security: While adaptive password meters have the potential for a better and more robust estimation of password strength, computing the strength of a given password based on the actual password database (and outputting this value to the user) prompts a few security concerns. Our main contribution is to devise an adaptive password meter that is secure even when the n-gram database is leaked, while still providing high accuracy.

Accuracy: A password strength meter needs to correctly gauge the strength of a password as wrong estimations can affect both the usability and guessing entropy of the passwords: if strong passwords are marked as weak then users might get frustrated, reducing usability; if weak password are marked as strong, security is decreased. For example, users might "circumvent" rule-based password meters by modifying weak passwords to match the required minimum strength. For example, `password` is frequently "strengthened" by the addition of upper cases and numbers, leading to `Password1`.

[2]Further details on the datasets are given in Section 6.

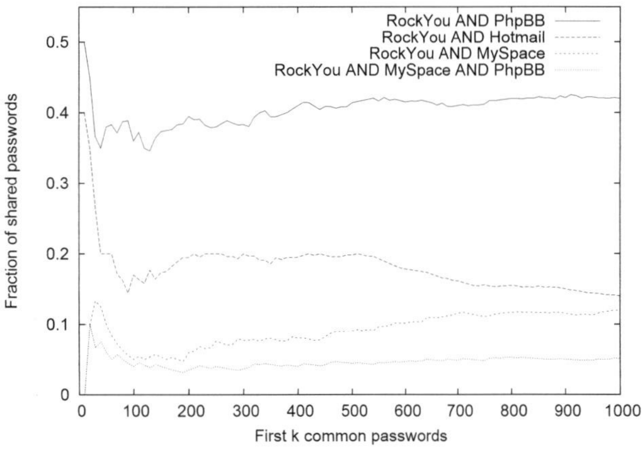

(a) Fraction of passwords that are used in common by different sites

RockYou	Faithwriters	MySpace
123456	123456	password1
12345	writer	abc123
123456789	jesus1	fuckyou
password	christ	monkey1
iloveyou	blessed	iloveyou1
princess	john316	myspace1
1234567	jesuschrist	fuckyou1
rockyou	password	number1
12345678	heaven	football1
abc123	faithwriters	nicole1

(b) Ten most frequent passwords for different sites. Passwords underlined are shared by at least two services. The wide difference likely depend on background (e.g., Faithwriters) or password rules (e.g., MySpace).

Figure 1. Password Distributions for Different Sites

4 Constructing an Adaptive Password Meter

We use techniques from statistical language processing, namely Markov-Models [14], to implement an adaptive password strength meter that both *accurately estimates* the probabilities from a relatively small sample, and is *secure against leakage* of the locally stored data. Basically, for every password x which is added to the password list, we store the hashed (and possibly salted) value $Hash(x)$ as commonly done. In addition, we determine the n-gram counts for the password (i.e., frequencies of n consecutive characters in the password), merge this information with previously stored n-grams, to obtain the frequencies over the entire password database, and add some noise to this data. These n-gram frequencies can then be used to compute an estimate on the probability of a fresh password.

4.1 Markov Models

Over the last years, Markov models have proven very useful for computer security in general and for password security in particular. For example, Narayanan et al. [19] showed the effectiveness of Markov models to password cracking.

The idea is that adjacent letters in human-generated passwords are not independently chosen, but follow certain regularities (e.g., the 2-gram `th` is much more likely than `tq` and the letter `e` is very likely to follow `th`). In an n-gram Markov model, one models the probability of the next character in a string based on a prefix of length n. Hence for a given string $c_1, \ldots, c_m$ we can write

$$P(c_1, \ldots, c_m) = \prod_{i=1}^{m} P(c_i | c_{i-n+1}, \ldots, c_{i-1}).$$

Our construction only keeps track of the n-gram counts $count(x_1, \ldots, x_n)$, and the conditional probabilities can easily computed from these by the following formula:

$$P(c_i | c_{i-n+1}, \ldots, c_{i-1}) = \frac{count(c_{i-n+1}, \ldots, c_{i-1}, c_i)}{\sum_{x \in \Sigma} count(c_{i-n+1}, \ldots, c_{i-1}, x)}$$

Also note that the size of the password's alphabet (Σ) is quite important. We initially used an alphabet of size 96 to estimate the password strength. However, we observed that most of the characters are rarely used, leading to sparseness problems. In the final version of our scheme, we choose to use the following alphabet composed of 38 distinct characters $[a-z][0-9][U][S]$, where U and S are two symbols representing all upper-case letters and all special characters, respectively. This leads to reduce sparseness in the dataset and better probability estimations.

4.2 Our Construction

Our construction uses Markov Models [14] from the previous section to estimate the strength of passwords. What makes this construction interesting is that, by adding some fine-dosed amount of noise, we can actually prove that the construction is secure against leakage of the n-gram database. (For notational simplicity, we assume that all passwords have length $m = l + n - 1$, thus the total number of n-grams is ln.)

4.2.1 N-gram Database Construction and Update (`DCU` algorithm)

The n-gram database is constructed and updated as follows:

1. The algorithm keeps as state the n-gram counts, $count(x_1, \ldots, x_n)$, for all $x_1, \ldots, x_n \in \Sigma$. All these counts are initialized to 0.

2. Whenever a password $c = c_1, \ldots, c_{l+n-1}$ is added, it is decomposed into n-grams. The database is then updated by incrementing the counts corresponding to each of the password's n-grams by 1, as follows:

$$count(c_i, \ldots, c_{i+n-1}) = count(c_i, \ldots, c_{i+n-1}) + 1,$$

   for each $i = 1, \ldots, l$.

3. Additionally, noise is added to the database by increasing each individual n-gram's count, by one, with probability γ each (independently):

$$\forall x_1, \ldots, x_n : \\ count(x_1, \ldots, x_n) = count(x_1, \ldots, x_n) + 1$$

   with probability γ.

4. Finally, the password is stored hashed with salt as usual, e.g., choose $salt \leftarrow^R \{0,1\}^{16}$ and store

$$hash(x \parallel salt) \parallel salt.$$

4.2.2 Password Strength Estimation (`PSE` algorithm)

The strength of a password $c = c_1, \ldots, c_m$, where each character c_i is chosen from alphabet Σ, is estimated as follows:

1. For $i = 1, \ldots, m$, the following conditional probabilities are computed:

$$P(c_i | c_{i-n+1}, \ldots, c_{i-1}) \\ = \frac{count(c_{i-n+1}, \ldots, c_i)}{count(c_{i-n+1}, \ldots, c_{i-1})} \\ = \frac{count(c_{i-n+1}, \ldots, c_i)}{\sum_{x \in \Sigma} count(c_{i-n+1}, \ldots, c_{i-1}, x)}.$$

   (If the numerator equals zero we use a small out-of-dictionary probability, to account for unseen n-grams. However, this will almost never happen, due to the added noise.)

2. Finally, the strength estimate $f(c)$ for the password c is:

$$f(c) = -log_2(\prod_{i=0}^{m} P(c_i | c_{i-n+1}, \ldots, c_{i-1}))$$

Example: The probability of the string `password` (with $n = 5$) is computed as follows

$$P(password) = P(p)P(a|p)P(s|pa)\ldots P(d|swor)$$

Picking one of the elements as an example: $p(o|assw) = \frac{count(asswo)}{count(assw)} = \frac{98450}{101485} = 0.97$. This results in the overall estimation $P(password) = 0.0016$, where the actual frequency of this password in the RockYou database is 0.0018. A short list of passwords as scored by our markov model is included in Table 1. The example shows that the markov meter is able to correctly recognize weak passwords and, in fact, closely approximate the actual probability of the passwords. Furthermore, more complex and random passwords are correctly estimated as stronger.

On the other hand, the NIST, Microsoft and Google password checkers fail to correctly gauge password strength. For example, the Google meter gives a 0 score to a random password (`dkriouh`) only because it does not match the minimum length of 8 characters. The Microsoft checker gives a very high score to `P4ssw0rd` and `Password1`, while giving a lower score to the randomly generated password `dkriouh`. The NIST checker assigns a higher score to `Password1` than to `2GWapWis`. Mistakes of this type are mostly inevitable in heuristic password checkers and are reflected in the poor accuracy of these as shown in the next sections.

5 Security of our Construction

Under normal operation, the n-gram database will be secret and not accessible to an attacker. However, best practices mandate that even when an adversary gets access to the n-gram database (e.g., by breaking into the server), little information about the plain-text passwords should be leaked. In this section we will show that our system has this property, by proving a strong bound on the (Shannon) entropy that leaks when the n-gram database leaks. Consequently, the remaining guessing entropy of the passwords in the database remains high by the results from [16].

5.1 Security Definition

When defining the security of an adaptive password checker, it is necessary to consider the adversary's prior knowledge on the password distribution. An adversary can

Password	Ideal	Markov	NIST	MS	Google
`password`	9.09	9.25	21	1	1
`password1`	11.52	11.83	22.5	2	1
`Password1`	16.15	17.08	28.5	3	1
`P4ssw0rd`	22.37	21.67	27	3	1
`naeemha`	21.96	28.42	19.5	1	0
`dkriouh`	N/A	42.64	19.5	1	0
`2GWapWis`	N/A	63.67	21	3	4
`Wp8E&NCc`	N/A	67.15	27	3	4

Table 1. Scores (in bits) as computed by the markov model and the ideal password meter from Section 2.1. For the ideal meter the probability is the empirical frequency in the RockYou dataset. The last three passwords were generated at random using, respectively, the following rules `[a-z]{7}`, `[a-zA-Z0-9]{8}` and `[a-zA-Z0-9\special]{8}`.

have access to statistics from lists such as language dictionaries and leaked password lists, and knowledge about common mangling rules (i.e., rules to derive more passwords from such lists by appending numbers and special characters). However, there are many more sources of information an adversary has access to: their technical background, the password policies enforced by the site, theme of the site, etc.

It is hard, if not impossible, to come up with a comprehensive list of sources that the adversary is using. Therefore, in this paper, we consider an adversary who knows the distribution of the service's passwords. This automatically considers all the above sources of information, and protects us against any future improvements of password cracking software, such as John the Ripper.

We explicitly note that in normal operation our password strength meter hardly leaks information. (An exception is the unavoidable leakage from the password strength meter itself; as we cannot prevent the attacker from accessing the password strength meter f, we cannot prevent him from learning a limited number of data points of this distribution.) Only when the n-gram database is leaked, then the distribution, as well as some bits of additional distribution about the actual passwords in the database, leak.

One might argue that while the password distribution is generally known, it is not known for very unlikely passwords, and the n-gram database might leak these passwords. This is incorrect since we are adding noise to all n-grams, including rare ones. In addition, as explained previously, knowing the n-gram frequencies does not help the adversary to break unlikely, i.e., strong passwords.

The assumption that the password distribution is known can be seen as an extension of Kerckhoffs' principle [10]. We do not assume that the distribution is secret, but only the password chosen with this distribution are. It also underlies the definition of guessing entropy (see Equation (1)), which also considers the optimal guessing strategy.

Finally, we argue that this assumption does not weaken security since by enforcing a minimum password strength (similar to [23]) we can still guarantee a minimal guessing entropy of the passwords. In fact, if we assume that X is a distribution on passwords with $Pr(x) \leq t$ for all passwords x, then the Shannon entropy of X is bounded by

$$H(X) \geq -\log(t). \tag{2}$$

By using the results from [16] we can compute a lower bound on guessing entropy as

$$G(X) \geq \frac{1}{4}2^{H(X)} \geq \frac{1}{4t}. \tag{3}$$

Enforcing, e.g., a maximum probability of 2^{-20} yields a lower bound on the guessing entropy of 2^{18}. In other words, a strong password will remain strong, even if the password distribution is known. The adversary will be able to compute its guessing entropy from the distribution, but not more. On the other hand, weak passwords might be easier to break since the adversary will be able to optimize his guessing strategy. However, such passwords should be prohibited in most services.

5.2 Information and Entropy

The (noisy) n-gram database, when leaked to an adversary, constitutes a noisy channel that transports information about the stored passwords in the database. In this section we introduce the notion of entropy and mutual information, including some basic properties.

The information content of a random variable is measured in terms of entropy. For two discrete random variables X, Y with finite domain $D = \{d_1, \dots, d_n\}$, *Conditional Shannon entropy* is defined as

$$H(Y|X=x) \stackrel{\text{def}}{=} -\sum_{i=1}^{n} Pr(Y=d_i|X=x)\log(Pr(Y=d_i|X=x)) \tag{4}$$

and

$$H(Y|X) \stackrel{\text{def}}{=} \sum_{x \in X} Pr(X=x)H(Y|X=x).$$

For independent random variables X, Y, a simple calculation shows

$$H(X+Y|X) = H(Y). \tag{5}$$

A central notion used to define the transport of information on a (noisy) channel is the notion of mutual information. The *mutual information* between the input X and the output

Y, where both X and Y are discrete random variables with finite domain, is given by

$$I(X,Y) \stackrel{\text{def}}{=} H(Y) - H(Y|X). \qquad (6)$$

When defining channel capacity, one takes the maximum of the mutual information over input distributions; in our application the input distribution is fixed by the construction, so the information flow is given directly by the mutual information $I(X,Y)$.

Computing a closed formula for the entropy of a given distribution can be hard. However, for some distributions such as the binomial distribution the literature gives closed formulas. Let $Bin(m,p)$ denote the binomial distribution with m trials that follow a Bernoulli distribution with parameter p each, and write $q = 1-p$. From [1] we obtain the following estimates on the entropy of binomial variables:

$$\begin{aligned} H(Bin(m,p)) \quad &\geq \qquad (7)\\ \frac{1}{2} + \frac{1}{2}\log(2\pi mpq) + \frac{C_1^{(p)}}{m} &+ \frac{C_2^{(p)}}{m^2} + \frac{C_3^{(p)}}{m^3} \end{aligned}$$

and

$$\begin{aligned} H(Bin(m,p)) &\leq \qquad (8)\\ \frac{1}{2} + \frac{1}{2}\log(2\pi mpq) &+ \frac{C_4^{(p)}}{m} \end{aligned}$$

for $C_1^{(p)} = \frac{13}{12} - \frac{3\log(pq)}{2} - \frac{5}{6pq}$, $C_2^{(p)} = -\frac{7}{3} + 4\log(pq) + \frac{8}{3pq} - \frac{1}{6(pq)^2}$, $C_3^{(p)} = -\frac{1}{360}$, and $C_4^{(p)} = \frac{1}{12} + \frac{\log(pq)}{2} + \frac{1}{6pq}$.

From [33] we learn that the entropy of the sum of two binomially distributed random variables with the same number of trials can be estimated by the the entropy of a binomial variable with double the number of trials and the average parameter:

$$H\Big(Bin(m,a) + Bin(m,b)\Big) \leq H\Big(Bin(2m, \frac{a+b}{2})\Big). \qquad (9)$$

5.3 Leakage Estimation

To prove the security of the scheme we prove that the total amount of information leaked (in terms of Shannon entropy) is limited (A detailed version of this section can be found in Appendix A).

In this section we use the following variable names: n denotes the length of the n-grams, $N = |\Sigma|^n$ is the total number of n-grams, l the number of n-grams per password, k the number of passwords in the database, $m \stackrel{\text{def}}{=} k \cdot l$ the total number of N-grams in the database, γ is the probability of adding noise used in the construction, and L is the information leaked from the database.

First, we consider the leakage of an individual n-gram with index j (where $1 \leq j \leq N$) with expected frequency t_j, and we consider n-grams at the i-th position of the passwords only (thus $1 \leq i \leq l$). Define the random variables $S_h^{i,j} := \chi_j(P_h^i)$, where $\chi_j(P_h^i)$ is the indicator function for the j-th n-gram on the i-th position in the h-th password. The random variables $S_h^{i,j}$ all have $Pr(S_h^{i,j} = 1) = t_j$ and $Pr(S_{i,j}^h = 0) = 1 - t_j$.

For $1 \leq i \leq l$ and $1 \leq j \leq N$, we define the empirical frequency obtained from a password database with k passwords as $T_k^{i,j} = \frac{1}{k}\sum_{h=1,\ldots,k} S_h^{i,j}$. $T_k^{i,j}$ follows a binomial distribution $Bin(k, t_j)$ with k trials with success probability t_j each.

Let $R^{i,j} \sim Bin(k,\gamma)$ be random variables describing the noise added to the i-th n-gram in our construction, where $1 \leq i \leq l$ ranges over the n-grams per password, and $1 \leq j \leq N$ ranges over all n-grams, and let $O_k^{i,j} \stackrel{\text{def}}{=} T_k^{i,j} + R^{i,j}$ be the observed noisy value. The information that can leak by publishing a single noisy n-grams is the mutual information between $T_k^{i,j}$ and $O_k^{i,j}$, i.e., the quantity $I(T_k^{i,j}; O_k^{i,j})$:

$$\begin{aligned} & I(T_k^{i,j}; O_k^{i,j}) && (10)\\ &\quad = H(O_k^{i,j}) - H(O_k^{i,j}|T_k^{i,j}) \\ &\quad = H(O_k^{i,j}) - H(R^{i,j}), \end{aligned}$$

where the first equality is the definition of mutual information (Eq. (6)), and the second equality follows from Equation (5).

Using first Equation (9) and then Equations (7) and (8) we can evaluate this further as follows:

$$\begin{aligned} & H(O^{i,j}) - H(R^{i,j}) && (11)\\ &\quad = H(Bin(k,\gamma) + Bin(k,t_j)) - H(Bin(k,\gamma)) \\ &\quad \leq \gamma + \frac{t_j}{2\gamma} + \frac{C_4^{(\gamma+t_j)/2}}{2k} - \frac{C_1^{\gamma}}{k} - \frac{C_2^{\gamma}}{k^2} - \frac{C_3^{\gamma}}{k^3} \end{aligned}$$

The full n-gram database which is leaked is the concatenation of the sums of the individual n-gram counts, i.e., the actual information leakage is[3]:

$$\begin{aligned} L &= I\big((\sum_{i=1}^{l} T_k^{i,j})_{1\leq j\leq N}; (\sum_{i=1}^{l} O_k^{i,j})_{1\leq j\leq N}\big) \\ &\leq 4k\gamma + \frac{1}{\gamma}\left(6.1 + \frac{1}{5k\gamma}\right) \qquad (12) \end{aligned}$$

for $l = 4$. For a reasonable choice of parameters $\gamma = \frac{1}{1.000.000}$ and $k = 5.000.000$ this means that overall, the n-gram database can leak at most 6.2 million bits, or on "average" about 1.3 bits per password. Values for different parameters are given in Table 2.

[3] Appendix A presents in details how the results presented in this section were derived.

	$k = 1 \cdot 10^6$	$k = 5 \cdot 10^6$	$k = 1 \cdot 10^7$
$\gamma = 5 \cdot 10^{-7}$	$13.1 \cdot 10^6$ (13.1)	$12.4 \cdot 10^6$ (2.5)	$12.4 \cdot 10^6$ (**1.24**)
$\gamma = 1 \cdot 10^{-6}$	$6.4 \cdot 10^6$ (6.4)	$6.2 \cdot 10^6$ (**1.24**)	$6.2 \cdot 10^6$ (**0.62**)
$\gamma = 5 \cdot 10^{-6}$	$1.3 \cdot 10^6$ (**1.3**)	$1.3 \cdot 10^6$ (**0.3**)	$1.3 \cdot 10^6$ (**0.13**)

Table 2. Total leakage (and average leakage per password) in bits for different parameters of k and γ, bold numbers indicate parameters that strike a good balance between accuracy and security.

6 Accuracy of our Construction

We now evaluate the accuracy of our scheme and compare it with other password strength meters.

Datasets: In order to evaluate the accuracy of our scheme, we use the RockYou password list. This list consists of over 32.6 million passwords that were released to the public after a breach occurred in December 2009 to the website `www.rockyou.com`.[4] The dataset is valuable for different reasons. First, it was the result of an SQL injection attack against the password database that was successful because passwords were stored in clear and not hashed. This means that all the passwords were collected, not only weak ones. A number of other, smaller password lists exist, e.g., the MySpace list which was obtained by a phishing attack and thus might include weaker passwords as well as fake input by users that realized the phishing attempt. Also, RockYou did not enforce any password rules, yielding a "plain" password set that provides a clear insight of how users choose passwords.

We also used the MySpace list of $37,000$ passwords leaked from MySpace by a phishing attack in 2006, $184,389$ leaked by PhpBB in 2009, and a list of 8347 passwords from the religious forum Faithwriters. Note that these passwords were not used to train our model for the experiments, but only to assess the need of adaptive password strength meters as shown in Figure 1(a).

6.1 Measuring Accuracy Using Rank Correlation

First, we analyse the accuracy of our Markov-based password meter (with and without adding noise) as well as the NIST, Google, and Microsoft password meters, by comparing their score to the ideal password strength meter (see Section 2.1). The ideal password meter is built upon the knowledge of the most common passwords in the RockYou dataset. This comparison only makes sense if there are enough data-points to keep the approximation error for the probability low. The estimation is reasonable for the 10000 most frequent passwords; see Appendix B for a derivation of this bound.

[4]One can remark the irony in the fact that a failure in password storing best-practices led to a deeper understanding of user chosen passwords.

For comparing the different password meters we use Spearman's rank correlation. It describes how well the relationship between two vectors can be described using a monotonic function. The coefficient lies between $[-1, 1]$, with 0 indicating no correlation, $+1$ indicating perfect positive correlation and -1 indicating perfect negative correlation (i.e., given two sets of values X and Y, the Spearman correlation coefficient becomes 1 when X and Y are perfectly monotonically related, i.e., $\forall i, j \; x_i > x_j$ implies $y_i > y_j$). All the password meters under examination where measured by computing the rank correlation of their scores against the scores of the ideal meters. (The intuition is that if the ideal score of password p_1 is higher than the ideal score of password p_2, then an approximation of the ideal meter should rate these two passwords in the same order.) To obtain a more fine-grained comparison, we plotted the correlation at different intervals, using the first 10, 20, ..., 10000 passwords in the set. The results are shown in Figure 2(a).

First, we can see that our Markov-based password meter outperforms the other checkers, even when noise is added. Second, the noise added to establish the security of the scheme only slightly decreases the accuracy of the meter. Third, the NIST, Microsoft and Google checker perform equally badly and are not much better than random guessing the password strength, as their correlation with the ideal meter is close to zero.

Training and Testing using Different Datasets: In order to quantify the importance of using the correct password database, in an additional experiment we included data from the PhpBB password list. We computed the optimal score for the 1000 most frequent passwords of the PhpBB list from their empirical frequency, let us call the resulting vector X. Then we scored the same 1000 passwords using the Markov 5-gram Model trained on the RockYou password dataset, we call the resulting vector Y. The correlation between the two vectors X and Y is 0.27 only, much lower than 0.55, the result we obtained by training and testing on the same password list.

This test shows that training a Markov Model on a web service (in this case RockYou) and using it to score passwords on a second service (in our case PhpBB) potentially significantly lowers accuracy, which further strengthens the previous findings in Section 3.1. This serves as justification for our APSM to be trained on the same web service where

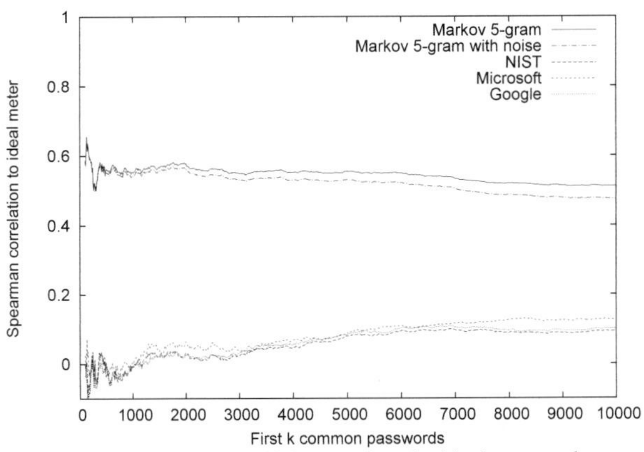

(a) Spearman correlation coefficient against the ideal password meter.

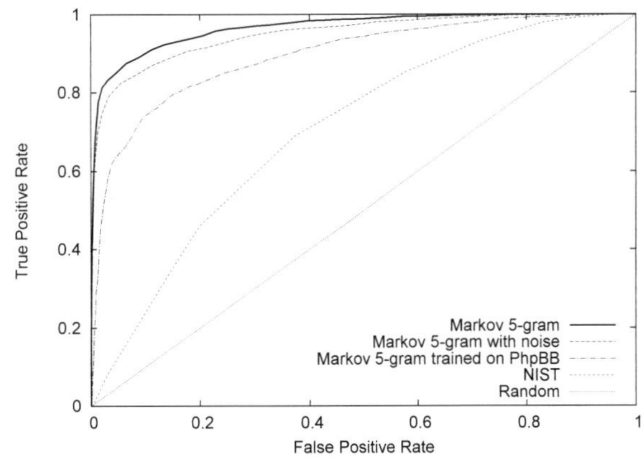

(b) ROC Curve comparing the performance of our password meter (with and without noise) to the NIST password checker. $\gamma = 5 \cdot 10^{-6}$ was chosen for the noise.

Figure 2. Accuracy Analysis

it is used to score passwords.

6.2 Measuring Accuracy based on Binary Classification

Next, we compare the accuracy of the password meters in terms of binary classification accuracy, i.e., we establish the accuracy of distinguishing between "strong" and "weak" passwords. The security of a password is the inverse of its probability. In this experiment we set a probability threshold of 2^{-20} to distinguish between strong and weak passwords. For guessing attacks, this threshold guarantees that in order to correctly guess one *single* password the attacker has to guess 2^{18} different passwords. This number should be sufficiently high to prevent online guessing attack if the server uses simple rate limiting on the password guesses. We refer the interested reader to [8] for an analysis of rate limiting policies on passwords.

This threshold was chosen because, given our dataset of 32 million password, we can divide the password in "strong" and "weak" using their frequency and build a *ground truth* set. Roughly, all the passwords that appear with frequency higher than 2^{-20} are marked as weak, the others are marked as strong. However, special caution must be taken when dealing with this probability estimation. In fact, a small estimation error near the threshold can mean that a password is incorrectly labelled. Thus we excluded the passwords with frequency too close to the threshold using Wilson interval estimation for the binomial probability estimation [3], with z-value $z_{1-\alpha/2} = 2.58$.

Using this estimation we can find the passwords above and below the threshold probability with 99% confidence. We divided our testing dataset of 600000 passwords in 4163 surely weak password, called W, and 142205 strong passwords, called S. In this experiment too, we built an ideal ground-truth using the RockYou dataset and sound probability estimations.

We test the accuracy of our Markov-based password meter (with and without noise) in distinguishing between these two sets. We also test the NIST meter alongside as a comparison. The Microsoft and Google meter were not tested in this experiment, as we cannot map the threshold t to the scoring given by those meters. We computed the score of all the passwords in the sets W and S using both the Markov method and NIST. For different thresholds, we measured true positives ratio (passwords correctly marked as weak) and false positive ratio (strong password incorrectly marked as weak). The results can be seen in the ROC curve showed in Figure 2(b). The diagonal line gives the performance of a random password meter, which scores the passwords as weak or strong at random (this is a inherent property of ROC curves). The closer a curve is to the top-left corner (false positive rate of zero and true positive rate of one) the better the classification is. An ideal meter would be a perfect classifier of strong and weak passwords. Again, we can see that our password strength meter (with and without noise) clearly outperforms the NIST meter. Also, the introduction of noise affects performance only slightly. The Markov based meter performs close to optimal with a success rate of 93.4%.

7 Implementation Considerations

7.1 Bootstrapping

One remaining question is how to bootstrap our system. In fact, when only few passwords are stored in the system, those might be particularly vulnerable to leakage as the adversary can easily learn what passwords are *not* present, by checking what n-grams are not present in the database. We notice, however, that both these problems can be easily addressed. The solution lies in inserting the noise in batches of size k rather than every time a password is inserted. In practice we execute step 3 of the `DCU` algorithm, (described in Section 4.2.1) k times in advance. The value k should be high enough to provide a balance between usability and security and a reasonable value of k could be 1.000.000 (Section 5.3 details how k should be selected in order to provide security). Then, for the first k passwords entered in the system, only step 2 and step 4 of the `DCU` algorithm are executed (i.e., no noise is added as it was added in advance). After the first k passwords, the full `DCU` algorithm (step 2, step 3 and step 4) is then executed.

Note that our system cannot be used to estimate the strength of the first k passwords (the noise would introduce too much error in the estimations). For these passwords, we suggest to use our scheme with a n-gram database configured with n-grams extracted from a public source such as the RockYou database, and then switch back to our database when the number of passwords exceeds k.

One additional remark is that our password meter is better suited for large web services, that can leverage on password databases of several thousand passwords and larger. In our tests we observed that the accuracy of the Markov model increases rapidly with small training sets and then achieves only marginal better performance with larger training sets. For example, the Markov model trained with only 100.000 passwords achieved an accuracy of 90.3%, when trained with 50.000 passwords an accuracy of 92.9%, and when trained with 32 million passwords an accuracy of 93.4%. This is most likely due to the fact that the most common n-grams are quickly learned, while there is a very long tail of uncommon n-grams. Services that do not have access to tens of thousands of passwords (e.g., smaller web services or local services) must either rely on training the markov model on dictionaries [19] or leaked password databases like RockYou.

7.2 Usability

Our password meter returns real numbers between 0 and 1. However, these values might not be easy for users to interpret. We envision three ways in which the output of our password strength meter can be presented to the users. First, the user can be given the score computed by the Markov model, but converted to a discrete value, e.g., too weak, weak, medium, strong, instead of a real number. The probability could be translated into a sliding "strength bar" that reflects the score computed. This approach would look exactly like current password strength meters, albeit with the higher accuracy given by our construction.

However, we notice that the fine-grained score given by our meter enables us to do more. We could translate the score of the password strength meter into a more concrete metric such as the effort required by an adversary to break the password in terms of time. This could be done, for example, by using the guessing entropy bound derived from the Shannon entropy. In this context, the user could be given a message of the type, "your password can be guessed – on average – in x attempts, that can be tried automatically in about y hours".

Third, the score could be used to compute an estimation of the strength of the password relative to their peers, which might provide an incentive for users to choose better passwords. Users could be prompted with a message that says, for example, "your password is amongst the 5% weakest passwords on our web site", which might encourage them to choose a better password. Conversely, having a password in the top 5% might be an incentive for users to choose stronger passwords.

8 Conclusion

In this work, we proposed a novel way to measure the strength of user-selected passwords. The construction is based on Markov-models and achieves much higher accuracy than commonly used password meters. The fine-grained measurement of the password strength provided by our strength meter allows for a very precise feedback to users.

We have formally proven that this construction is secure even when the local data storage is compromised by an attacker, thus, meeting best practices in securing password storage. We evaluated the accuracy of our scheme by performing extensive experiments and showed that it outperforms existing schemes.

References

[1] J. Adell, A. Lekuona, and Y. Yu. Sharp bounds on the entropy of the poisson law and related quantities. *Information Theory, IEEE Transactions on*, 56(5):2299–2306, 2010.

[2] M. Bishop and D. V. Klein. Improving system security via proactive password checking. *Computers & Security*, 14(3):233–249, 1995.

[3] L. D. Brown, T. T. Cai, and A. DasGupta. Interval estimation for a binomial proportion. *Statistical Science*, 16(2):101–133, 2001.

[4] W. E. Burr, D. F. Dodson, and W. T. Polk. Electronic authentication guideline: NIST special publication 800-63, 2006.

[5] J. A. Cazier and D. B. Medlin. Password security: An empirical investigation into e-commerce passwords and their crack times. *Information Security Journal: A Global Perspective*, 15(6):45–55, 2006.

[6] M. Dell'Amico, M. Pietro, and Y. Roudier. Password strength: An empirical analysis. In *INFOCOM '10: Proceedings of 29th Conference on Computer Communications*. IEEE, 2010.

[7] D. Florencio and C. Herley. A large-scale study of web password habits. In *WWW '07: Proceedings of the 16th international conference on World Wide Web*, pages 657–666. ACM, 2007.

[8] D. Florêncio, C. Herley, and B. Coskun. Do strong web passwords accomplish anything? In *Proceedings of the 2nd USENIX workshop on Hot topics in security*, Berkeley, CA, USA, 2007. USENIX Association.

[9] C. Herley. So long and no thanks for the externalities: The rational rejection of security advice by users. In *Proceedings of the 2009 Workshop on New security paradigms*, pages 133–144. ACM, 2009.

[10] A. Kerckhoffs. La cryptographie militaire. *Journal des sciences militaires*, IX:5–38, January 1883.

[11] D. V. Klein. Foiling the cracker: A survey of, and improvements to, password security. In *Proc. USENIX UNIX Security Workshop*, 1990.

[12] S. Komanduri, R. Shay, P. G. Kelley, M. L. Mazurek, L. Bauer, N. Christin, L. F. Cranor, and S. Egelman. Of passwords and people: Measuring the effect of password-composition policies. In *CHI 2011: Conference on Human Factors in Computing Systems*, 2011.

[13] C. Kuo, S. Romanosky, and L. F. Cranor. Human selection of mnemonic phrase-based passwords. In *Proc. Symposium on Usable Privacy and Security (SOUPS)*, pages 67–78, 2006.

[14] C. D. Manning and H. Schütze. *Foundations of statistical natural language processing*. MIT Press, Cambridge, MA, USA, 1999.

[15] S. Marechal. Advances in password cracking. *Journal in Computer Virology*, 4(1):73–81, 2008.

[16] J. Massey. Guessing and entropy. In *IEEE International Symposium on Information Theory*, page 204, 1994.

[17] Microsoft password strength meter. Online at `https://www.microsoft.com/security/pc-security/password-checker.aspx`.

[18] R. Morris and K. Thompson. Password security: a case history. *Communications. ACM*, 22(11):594 – 597, 1979.

[19] A. Narayanan and V. Shmatikov. Fast dictionary attacks on passwords using time-space tradeoff. In *CCS '05: Proceedings of the 12th ACM conference on Computer and communications security*, pages 364–372, New York, NY, USA, 2005. ACM.

[20] The password meter. Online at `http://www.passwordmeter.com/`.

[21] B. Pinkas and T. Sander. Securing passwords against dictionary attacks. In *Proc. CCS '02*, pages 161–170, 2002.

[22] S. Riley. Password security: What users know and what they actually do. *Usability News*, 8(1), 2006.

[23] S. Schechter, C. Herley, and M. Mitzenmacher. Popularity is everything: a new approach to protecting passwords from statistical-guessing attacks. In *Proceedings of the 5th USENIX conference on Hot topics in security*, pages 1–8. USENIX Association, 2010.

[24] E. H. Spafford. Observing reusable password choices. In *Proceedings of the 3rd Security Symposium*, pages 299–312. USENIX, 1992.

[25] SpiderMonkey. Online at `http://search.cpan.org/~mschilli/JavaScript-SpiderMonkey`.

[26] J. M. Stanton, K. R. Stam, P. Mastrangelo, and J. Jolton. Analysis of end user security behaviors. *Comp. & Security*, 24(2):124–133, 2005.

[27] A. Vance. If your password is 123456, just make it hackme. New York Times, oneline at `http://www.nytimes.com/2010/01/21/technology/21password.html`, retrieved May 2011, January 2010.

[28] M. Weir, S. Aggarwal, M. Collins, and H. Stern. Testing metrics for password creation policies by attacking large sets of revealed passwords. In *Proceedings of the 17th ACM conference on Computer and communications security (CCS 2010)*, pages 162–175. ACM, 2010.

[29] M. Weir, S. Aggarwal, B. de Medeiros, and B. Glodek. Password cracking using probabilistic context-free grammars. In *IEEE Symposium on Security and Privacy*, pages 391–405. IEEE Computer Society, 2009.

[30] J. Yan, A. Blackwell, R. Anderson, and A. Grant. Password memorability and security: Empirical results. *IEEE Security and Privacy Magazine*, 2(5):25–31, 2004.

[31] J. J. Yan. A note on proactive password checking. In *Proc. NSPW '01*, pages 127–135. ACM, 2001.

[32] J. J. Yan, A. F. Blackwell, and R. J. Anderson. Password memorability and security: Empirical results. *IEEE Security & Privacy*, 2:25–31, 2004.

[33] Y. Yu. On the entropy of compound distributions on non-negative integers. *IEEE Trans. Inf. Theor.*, 55:3645–3650, 2009.

A Details of the Leakage Estimation

To prove the security of the scheme we prove that the total amount of information (in terms of Shannon entropy) is limited. In this section we use the following variable names: n denotes the length of the n-grams, $N = |\Sigma|^n$ is the total number of n-grams, l the number of n-grams per password, k the number of passwords in the database, $m \stackrel{\text{def}}{=} k \cdot l$ the total number of N-grams in the database, γ is the probability of adding noise used in the construction, and L is the information leaked from the database.

First, we consider the leakage of an individual n-gram with index j (where $1 \leq j \leq N$) with expected frequency t_j, and we consider n-grams at the i-th position of the passwords only (thus $1 \leq i \leq l$). Define the random variables $S_h^{i,j} := \chi_j(P_h^i)$, where $\chi_j(P_h^i)$ is the indicator function for the j-th $n$gram on the i-th position in the h-th password. The random variables $S_h^{i,j}$ all have $Pr(S_h^{i,j} = 1) = t_j$ and $Pr(S_{i,j}^h = 0) = 1 - t_j$.

For $1 \leq i \leq l$ and $1 \leq j \leq N$, we define the empirical frequency obtained from a password database with k passwords as $T_k^{i,j} = \frac{1}{k} \sum_{h=1,\dots,k} S_h^{i,j}$. $T_k^{i,j}$ follows a binomial distribution $Bin(k, t_j)$ with k trials with success probability t_j each.

Let $R^{i,j} \sim Bin(k, \gamma)$ be random variables describing the noise added to the i-th n-gram in our construction, where

$1 \leq i \leq l$ ranges over the n-grams per password, and $1 \leq j \leq N$ ranges over all n-grams, and let $O_k^{i,j} \stackrel{\text{def}}{=} T_k^{i,j} + R^{i,j}$ be the observed noisy value. The information that can leak by publishing a single noisy n-grams is the mutual information between $T_k^{i,j}$ and $O_k^{i,j}$, i.e., the quantity $I(T_k^{i,j}; O_k^{i,j})$:

$$\begin{aligned} I(T_k^{i,j}; O_k^{i,j}) &= H(O_k^{i,j}) - H(O_k^{i,j} | T_k^{i,j}) \quad (13) \\ &= H(O_k^{i,j}) - H(R^{i,j}), \end{aligned}$$

where the first equality is the definition of mutual information (Eq. (6)), and the second equality follows from Equation (5).

Using first Equation (9) and then Equations (7) and (8) we can evaluate this further as follows:

$$\begin{aligned} &H(O^{i,j}) - H(R^{i,j}) \quad (14) \\ &= H(Bin(k,\gamma) + Bin(k,t_j)) - H(Bin(k,\gamma)) \\ &\leq H(Bin(2k, \frac{\gamma + t_j}{2})) - H(Bin(k,\gamma)) \\ &\leq \frac{1}{2} \ln\left(\frac{1}{1-\gamma}\right) + \frac{1}{2} \ln\left(1 + \frac{t_j}{\gamma}\right) \\ &\quad + \frac{C_4^{(\gamma+t)/2}}{2k} - \frac{C_1^\gamma}{k} - \frac{C_2^\gamma}{k^2} - \frac{C_3^\gamma}{k^3} \\ &\leq \gamma + \frac{t_j}{2\gamma} + \frac{C_4^{(\gamma+t_j)/2}}{2k} - \frac{C_1^\gamma}{k} - \frac{C_2^\gamma}{k^2} - \frac{C_3^\gamma}{k^3} \end{aligned}$$

where the last inequality uses $\gamma \leq \frac{1}{2}$ In addition to this estimation, for at most $k \cdot l$ n-grams can this difference be different from 0: if an n-gram never appeared, then the observed value $O_k^{i,j}$ is identical to the randomness $R^{i,j}$, and thus the entropy of both is the same. (*)

The full n-gram database which is leaked is the concatenation of the sums of the individual n-gram counts, i.e., the actual information leakage is

$$\begin{aligned} L &= I((\sum_{i=1}^{l} T_k^{i,j})_{1\leq j\leq N}; (\sum_{i=1}^{l} O_k^{i,j})_{1\leq j\leq N}) \\ &= H((\sum_{i=1}^{l} O_k^{i,j})_{1\leq j\leq N}) - H((\sum_{i=1}^{l} R_k^{i,j})_{1\leq j\leq N}) \\ &\leq \sum_{j=1}^{N}\sum_{i=1}^{l} \left(H(O_k^{i,j}) - H(R_k^{i,j})\right) \quad (15) \end{aligned}$$

Now we estimate the constants from Equation (15) using that $\gamma, t \leq 0.01$ and get:

$$\frac{l \cdot C_4^{(\gamma+t)/2}}{2k} \leq \frac{1}{5.8\gamma \cdot k}, \qquad \frac{l \cdot C_1^\gamma}{k} \geq -\frac{5}{5.95\gamma \cdot k},$$

$$\frac{l \cdot C_2^\gamma}{k^2} \geq -\frac{1}{5lk^2\gamma^2}, \qquad \frac{l \cdot C_3^\gamma}{k^3} = -\frac{1}{360k^3l^2}.$$

Finally, from these estimations, from remark (*), and Equations (15) and (15) we get

$$\begin{aligned} L &\leq \sum_{j=1}^{N}\sum_{i=1}^{l}\left(\gamma + \frac{t_j}{2\gamma} + \frac{C_4^{(\gamma+t_j)/2}}{2k} - \frac{C_1^\gamma}{k} - \frac{C_2^\gamma}{k^2} - \frac{C_3^\gamma}{k^3}\right) \\ &\stackrel{(*)}{\leq} \frac{l}{2\gamma} + lk \cdot \left(\gamma + \frac{C_4^{(\gamma+t_j)/2}}{2k} - \frac{C_1^\gamma}{k} - \frac{C_2^\gamma}{k^2} - \frac{C_3^\gamma}{k^3}\right) \\ &\leq 4k\gamma + \frac{1}{\gamma}\left(6.1 + \frac{1}{5k\gamma}\right) \end{aligned}$$

for $l = 4$. For a reasonable choice of parameters $\gamma = \frac{1}{1'000'000}$ and $k = 5'000'000$ this means that overall, the n-gram database can leak at most 6.2 million bits, or on "average" about 1.3 bits per password.

B Interval Estimation for Password Frequencies

As explained in Section 2.1, given the *true* probability of each password, we can easily build an ideal password meter by applying any monotonically increasing function to these probabilities. Furthermore, even if we only have an estimation of these probabilities the we could build an ideal password checker, as long as the relative ranking of the passwords remains unchanged.

Unfortunately, we do not in general the *true* probability of a password thus rendering this approach impractical. However, there exist certain classes of passwords for which it is possible to give a good probability estimation that can be used as a ground truth for measuring the accuracy of our construction in measuring password strength.

One such class is the most common passwords in the RockYou dataset. Intuitively, with a large dataset of 32.6 million passwords, we should be able to obtain a good probability estimation of, at least, the most common passwords. This probability estimation could then be used to be an ideal password meter for these common passwords. For example, the most common password in the dataset (`123456`) has been chosen 290729 times, while the second most common (`12345`) has been chosen 79076.

If we estimate the probability of `123456` using the empirical frequency we might introduce some small error (the mathematical treatment is explained later), however, we can be confident that `123456` will remain the most common password. This is not true for passwords with much lower counts though. For example, the password `zxcvbnmp` has been chosen 3 times in the dataset and it is the $288078th$ most common password together with almost $400'000$ other passwords, due to ties. However, if `zxcvbnmp` had been chosen only 2 times, it would be the $1136277th$ most common password. In this case a small difference in the probability estimation can make a big difference in the guessing entropy of a password.

In order to measure the accuracy of a password meters we would like to find a subset of common passwords for which we can estimate, with high confidence, the probability and therefore the ranking. By assuming that each passwords x binomially distributed, with *unknown* probability $p(x)$. With this interpretation, each password x in our dataset is binomially distributed with N number of trials and unknown probability $p(x)$. In our case, N is the number of times a password in our RockYou dataset was chosen, i.e., 32.6 million. Given the counts of each password x in our dataset, we can estimate its probability as $\hat{p}_x = \frac{count(x)}{N}$. However, this is only an estimation of the *true* probability mentioned above. The error of this estimation depends on $\hat{p}_x$ and N and, for example, larger N lead to better estimations. The sampling error of $\hat{p}_x$ can be estimated using Wilson score interval:

$$W(\hat{p}_x, N) = \frac{\hat{p}_x + \frac{z^2_{1-\alpha/2}}{2n} \pm z_{1-\alpha/2}\sqrt{\frac{\hat{p}_x(1-\hat{p}_x)}{N} + \frac{z^2_{1-\alpha/2}}{4N^2}}}{1 + \frac{1}{n}z^2_{1-\alpha/2}}$$

The relative ranking of two passwords x and x', with estimated probability $\hat{p}_x > \hat{p}'_x$, remains unchanged as long as $W(\hat{p}_x, N) > W(\hat{p}'_x, N)$. The confidence level depends on the z-score $z_{1-\alpha/2}$, for example if $z_{1-\alpha/2} = 2.58$ than the ordering is correct with 99 $\%$ probability.

Private Set Intersection:
Are Garbled Circuits Better than Custom Protocols?

Yan Huang, David Evans, Jonathan Katz

University of Virginia, University of Maryland

www.MightBeEvil.org

Motivation --- Common Acquaintances

http://www.mightbeevil.com/mobile/

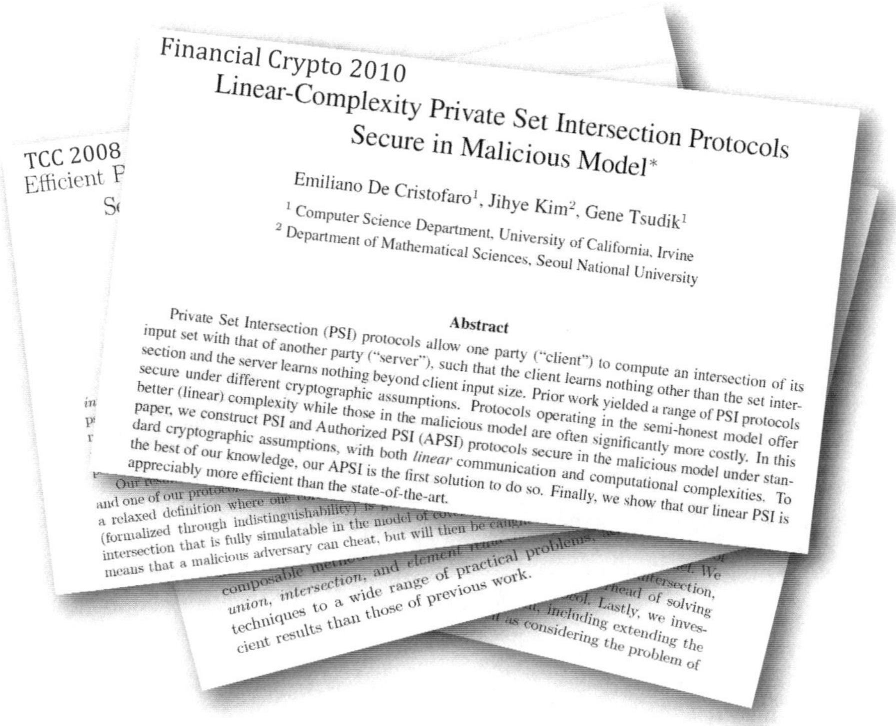
TCC 2008
Efficient P
Financial Crypto 2010
Linear-Complexity Private Set Intersection Protocols
Secure in Malicious Model*
Emiliano De Cristofaro[1], Jihye Kim[2], Gene Tsudik[1]
[1] Computer Science Department, University of California, Irvine
[2] Department of Mathematical Sciences, Seoul National University
Abstract
Private Set Intersection (PSI) protocols allow one party ("client") to compute an intersection of its input set with that of another party ("server"), such that the client learns nothing other than the set intersection and the server learns nothing beyond client input size. Prior work yielded a range of PSI protocols secure under different cryptographic assumptions. Protocols operating in the semi-honest model offer better (linear) complexity while those in the malicious model are often significantly more costly. In this paper, we construct PSI and Authorized PSI (APSI) protocols secure in the malicious model under standard cryptographic assumptions, with both linear communication and computational complexities. To the best of our knowledge, our APSI is the first solution to do so. Finally, we show that our linear PSI is appreciably more efficient than the state-of-the-art.

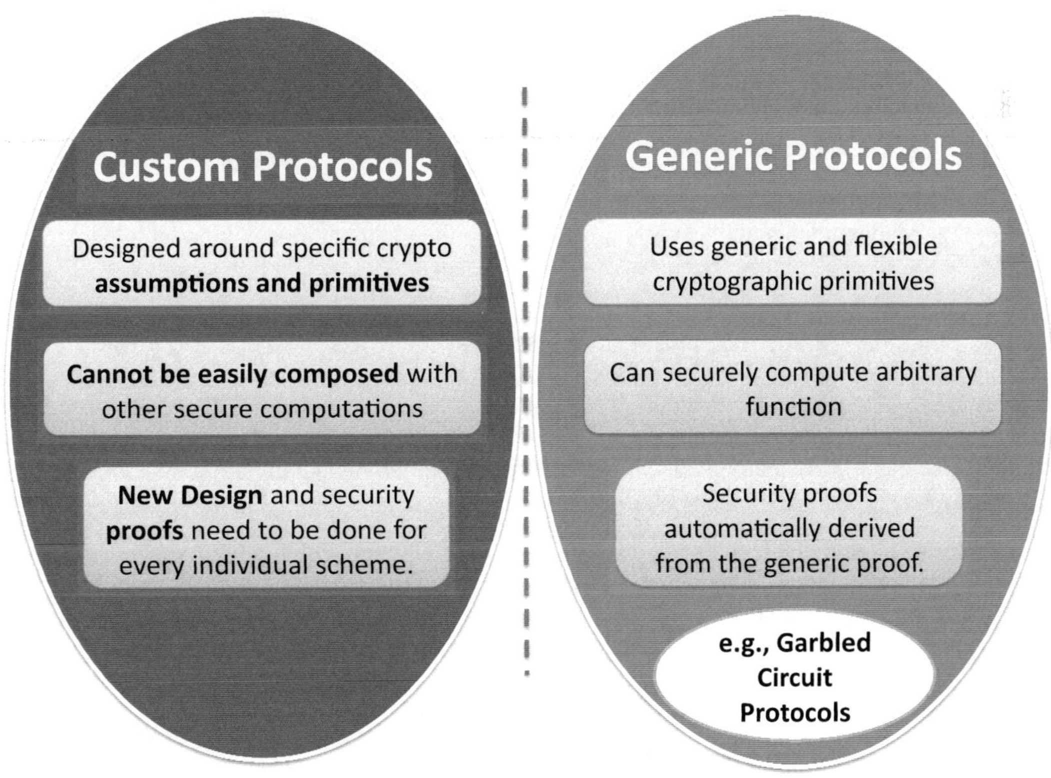
Custom Protocols
Designed around specific crypto assumptions and primitives
Cannot be easily composed with other secure computations
New Design and security proofs need to be done for every individual scheme.
Generic Protocols
Uses generic and flexible cryptographic primitives
Can securely compute arbitrary function
Security proofs automatically derived from the generic proof.
e.g., Garbled Circuit Protocols

Garbled Circuits & Oblivious Transfers

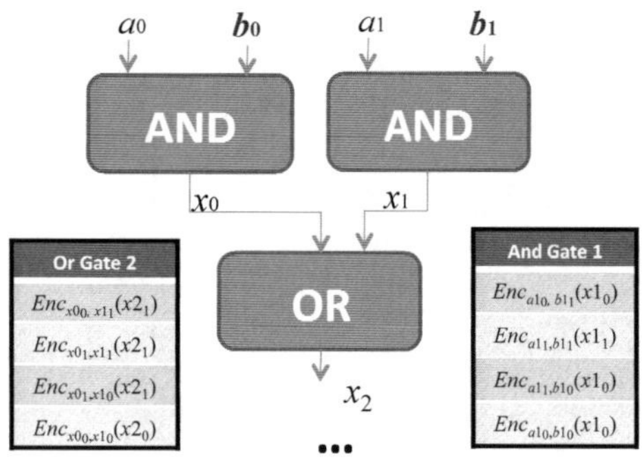

Andrew Yao, 1982/1986

***Free-XOR** technique*, Kolesnikov and Shneider, 2008

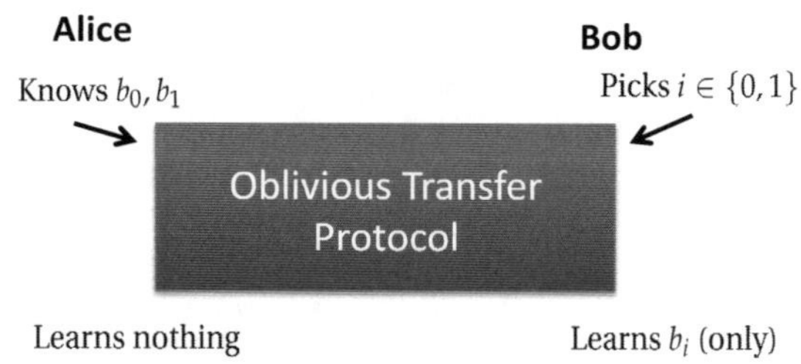

Rabin, 1981; Even, Goldreich, and Lempel, 1985; Naor and Pinkas 2001, Ishai et al., 2003

Y. Huang, D. Evans, J. Katz, L. Malka, Faster Secure Computation Using Garbled Circuits, USENIX Security 2011.

Threat Model

Semi-Honest Adversary: **follows the protocol as specified**, but tries to learn more from the protocol execution transcript

Generic PSI Protocols Overview

Protocols	Cost in non-XOR gates	Best for
Bitwise-AND (BWA)	2^σ	Small element space
Pairwise-Comparison (PWC)	$O(\sigma n^2)$	
Sort-Compare-Shuffle-WN (SCS-WN)	$O(\sigma n \log n)$	Large element space

σ – the number of bits used to denote a set element
n – the size of the sets

Generic PSI Protocols Overview

Protocols	Cost in non-XOR gates	Best for
Bitwise-AND (BWA)	2^σ	Small element space
Pairwise-Comparison (PWC)	$O(\sigma n^2)$	
Sort-Compare-Shuffle-WN (SCS-WN)	$O(\sigma n \log n)$	Large element space

σ – the number of bits used to denote a set element
n – the size of the sets

PSI: Needn't be Complex

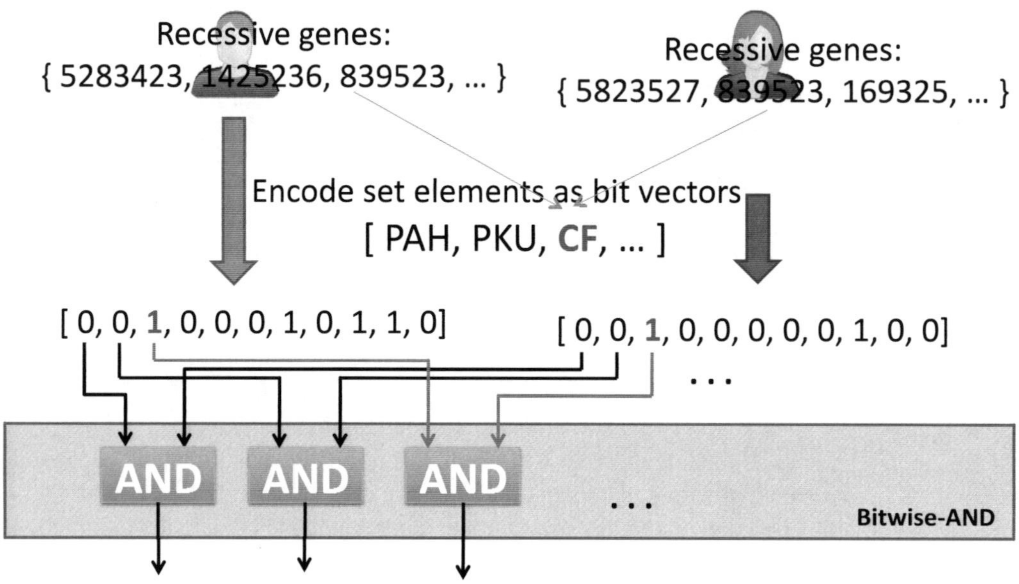

BWA Performance

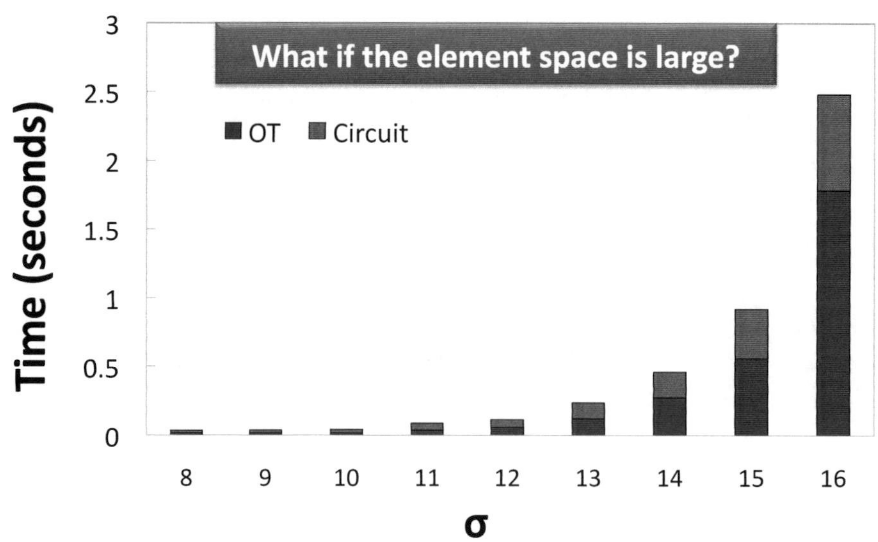

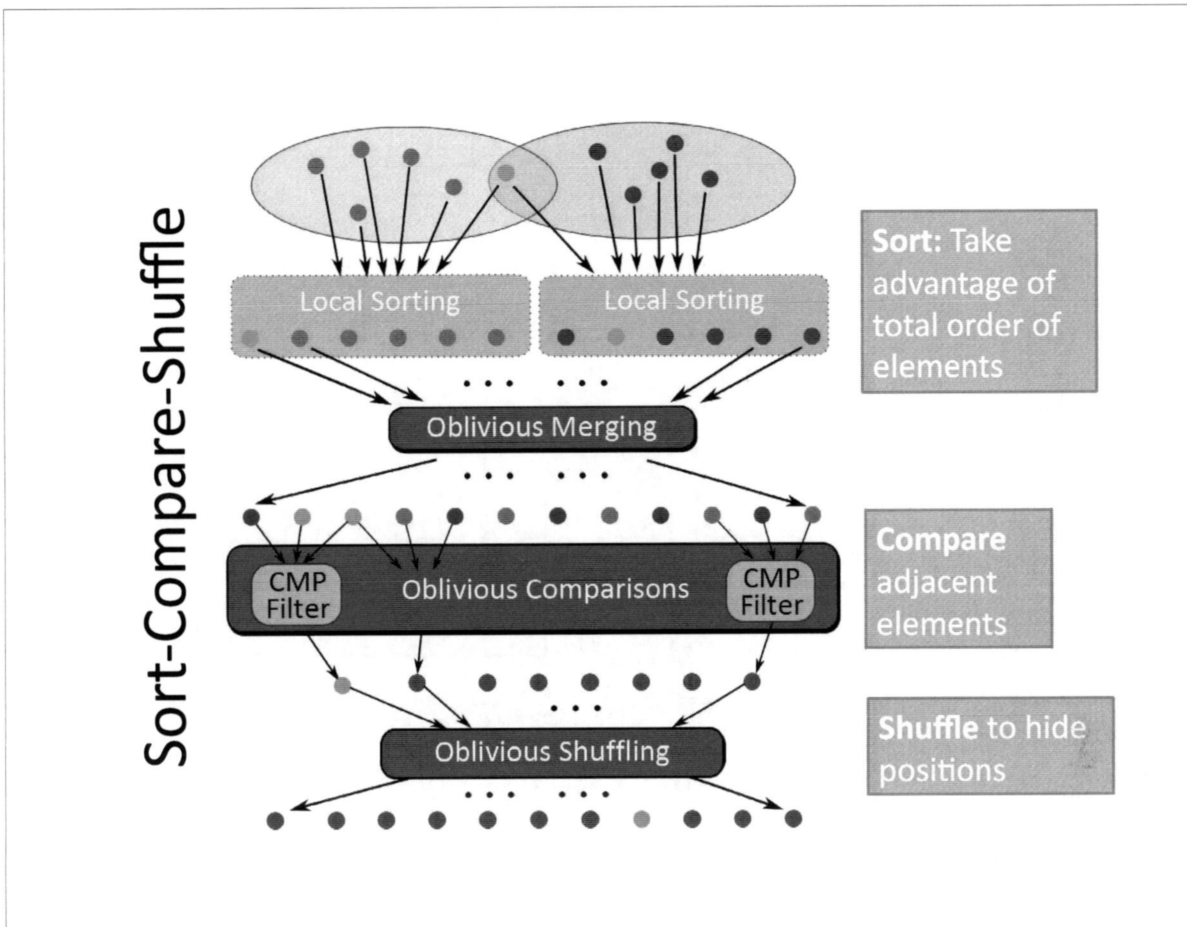
Sort-Compare-Shuffle
Local Sorting
Local Sorting
Oblivious Merging
CMP Filter
Oblivious Comparisons
CMP Filter
Oblivious Shuffling
Sort: Take advantage of total order of elements
Compare adjacent elements
Shuffle to hide positions

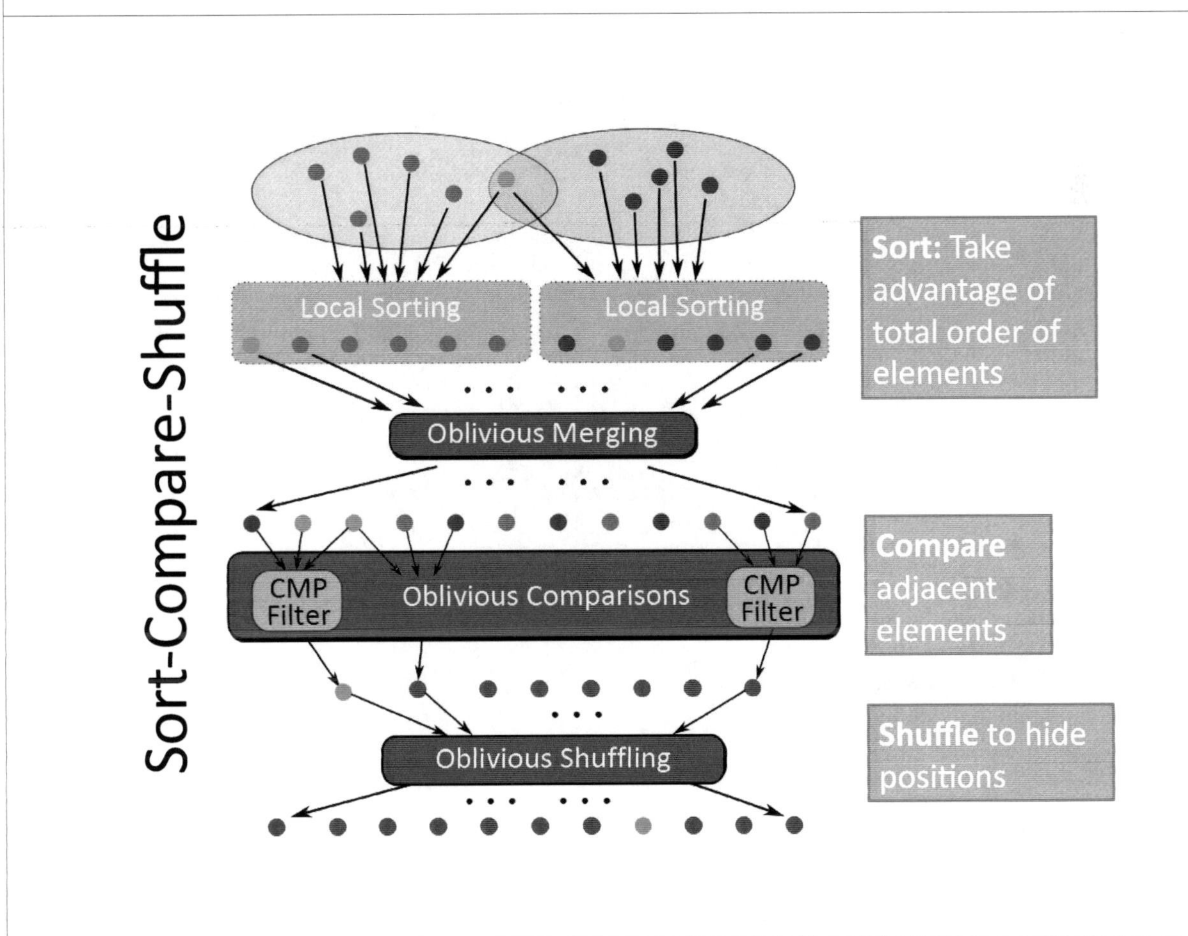
Sort-Compare-Shuffle
Local Sorting
Local Sorting
Oblivious Merging
CMP Filter
Oblivious Comparisons
CMP Filter
Oblivious Shuffling
Sort: Take advantage of total order of elements
Compare adjacent elements
Shuffle to hide positions

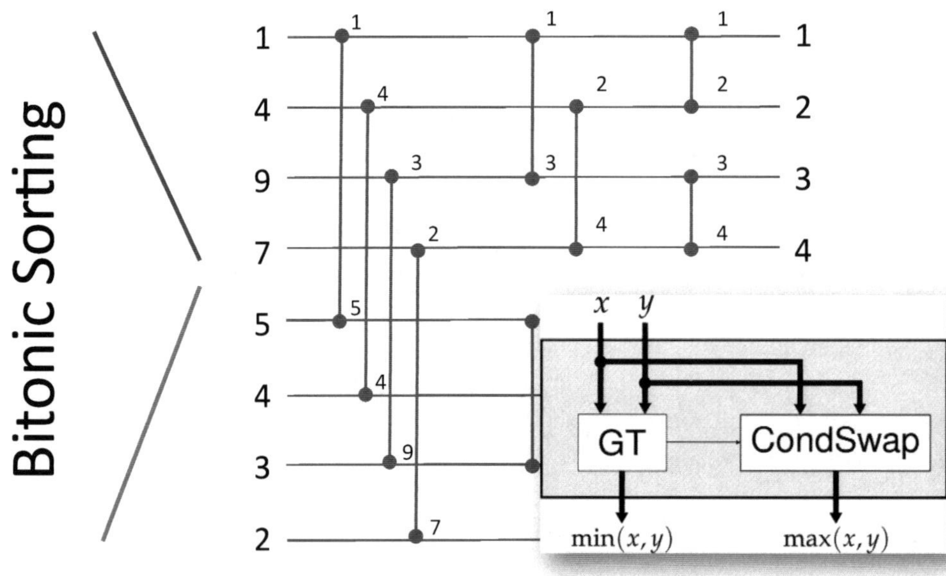

Sort $2n$ bitonic inputs with $n\log(2n)$ CompareSwap circuits.

Sorting Networks and their Applications, Ken Batcher, 1968

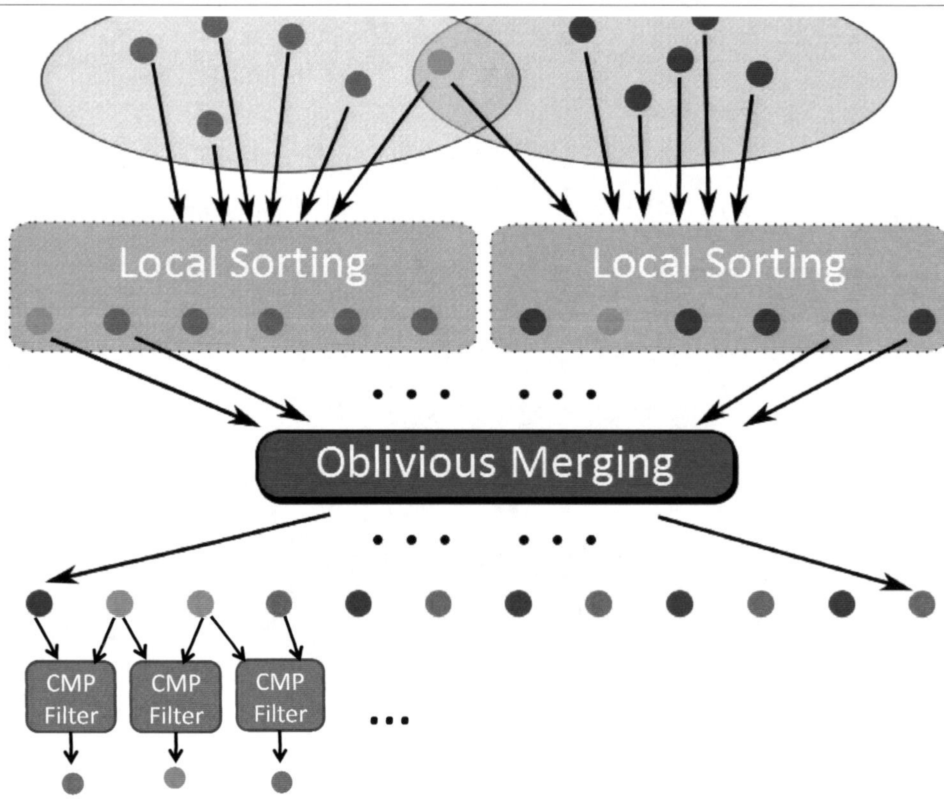

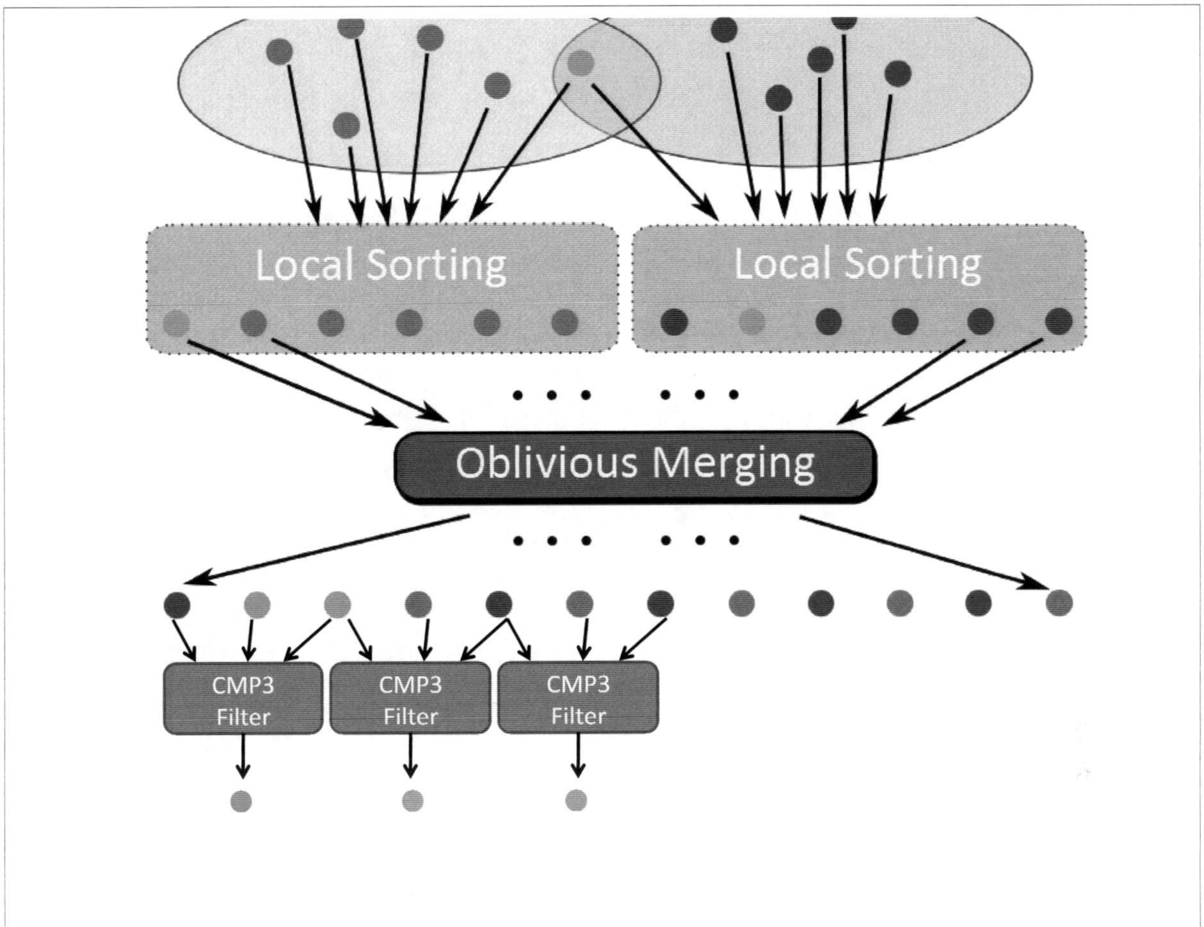
Local Sorting
Local Sorting
Oblivious Merging
CMP3 Filter
CMP3 Filter
CMP3 Filter

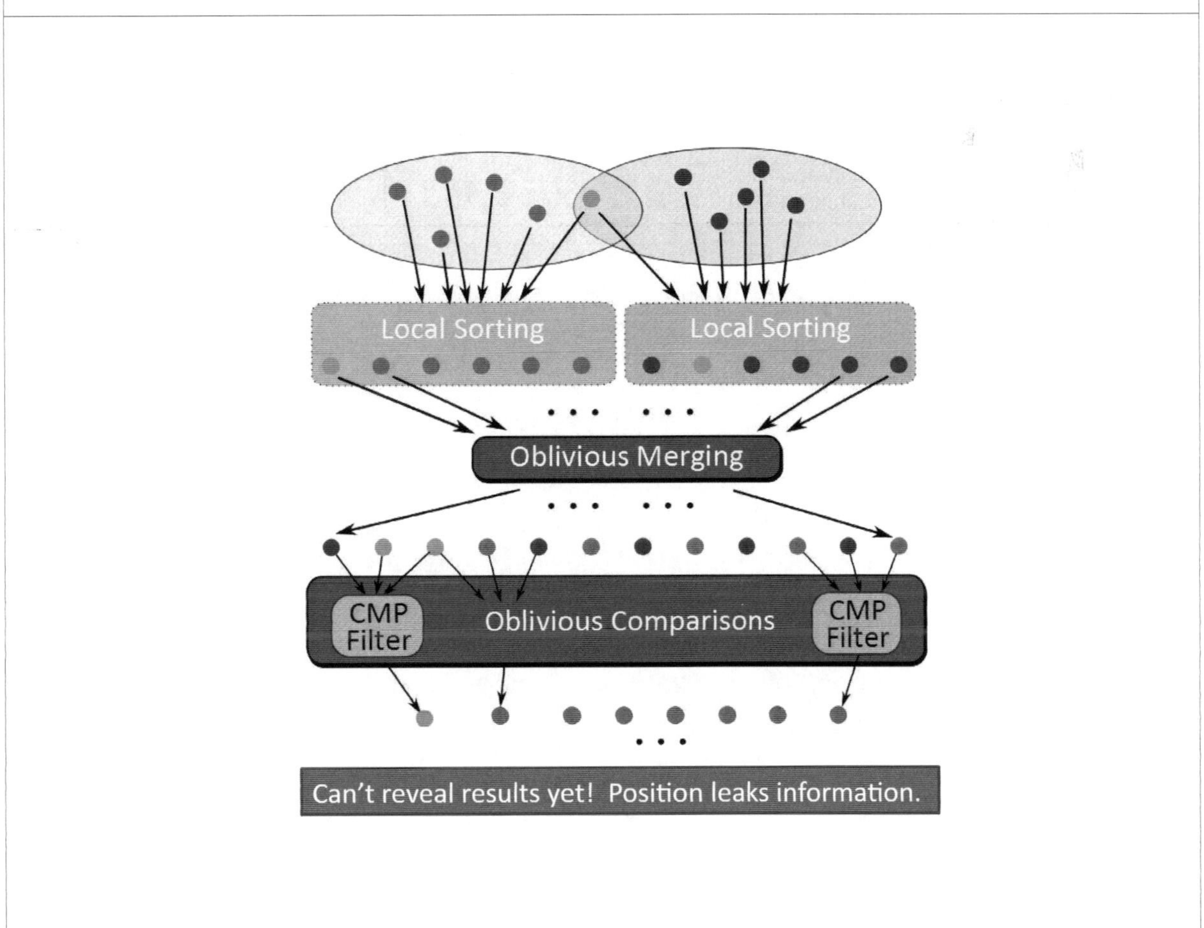
Local Sorting
Local Sorting
Oblivious Merging
CMP Filter
Oblivious Comparisons
CMP Filter
Can't reveal results yet! Position leaks information.

A Permutation Network

ABRAHAM WAKSMAN

Stanford Research Institute, Menlo Park, California

ABSTRACT. In this paper the construction of a switching network capable of $n!$-permutation of its n input terminals to its n output terminals is described. The building blocks for this network are binary cells capable of permuting their two input terminals to their two output terminals.

The number of cells used by the network is $\langle n \cdot \log_2 n - n + 1 \rangle = \sum_{k=1}^{n} \langle \log_2 k \rangle$. It could be argued that for such a network this number of cells is a lower bound, by noting that binary decision trees in the network can resolve individual terminal assignments only and not the rtitioning of the permutation set itself which requires only $\langle \log_2 n! \rangle = \langle \sum_{k=1}^{n} \log_2 k \rangle$ binary ions.

Journal of the ACM, January 1968

Waksman Network

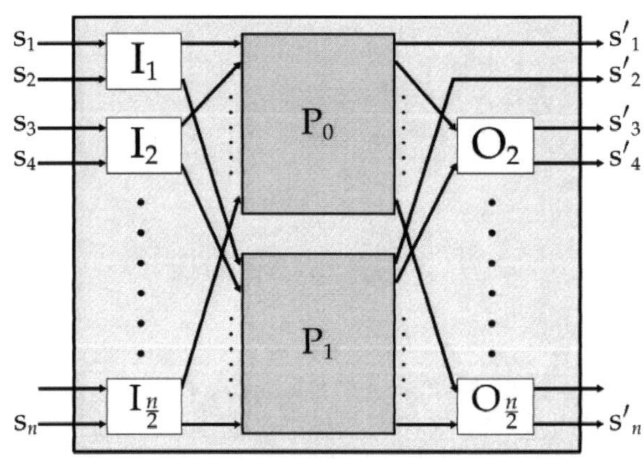

Same circuit can generate any permutation: select a random permutation, and pick swaps

$$\frac{\sigma(n \log n - n + 1)}{3} \text{ gates}$$

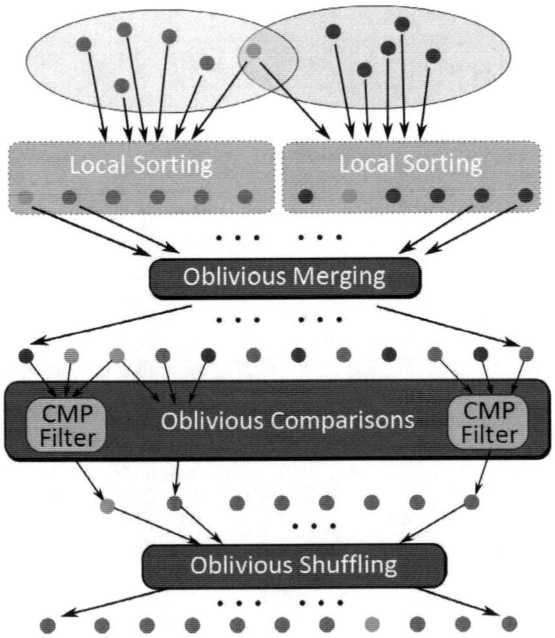

Private Set Intersection Protocol

Gates to generate and evaluate

Free

$$n\log(2n) \times 2\sigma$$

$$(3\sigma - 1)(n-1) + (2\sigma - 1)$$

$$\frac{\sigma(n\log n - n + 1)}{3}$$

σ – the number of bits used to denote a set element
n – the size of the sets

SCS-WN Protocol Results

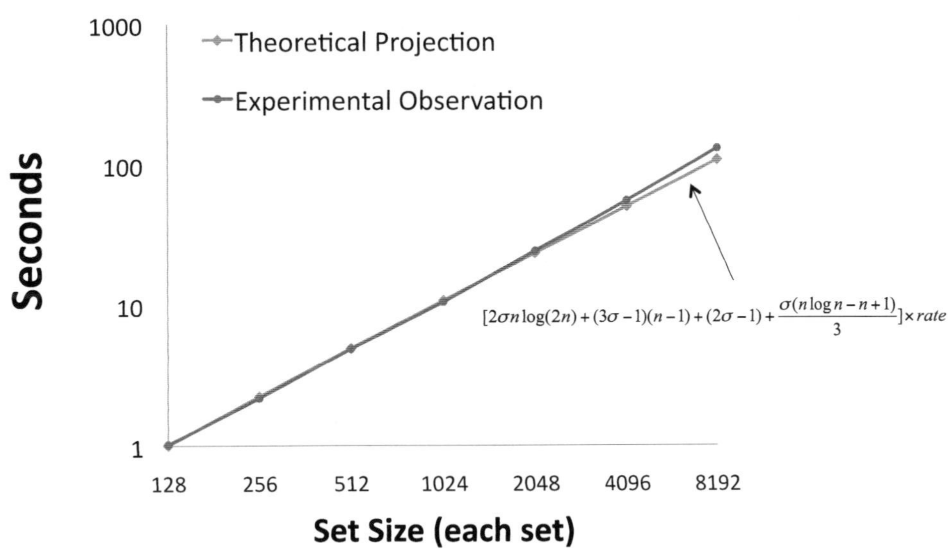

32-bit values

Relating Performance to Security

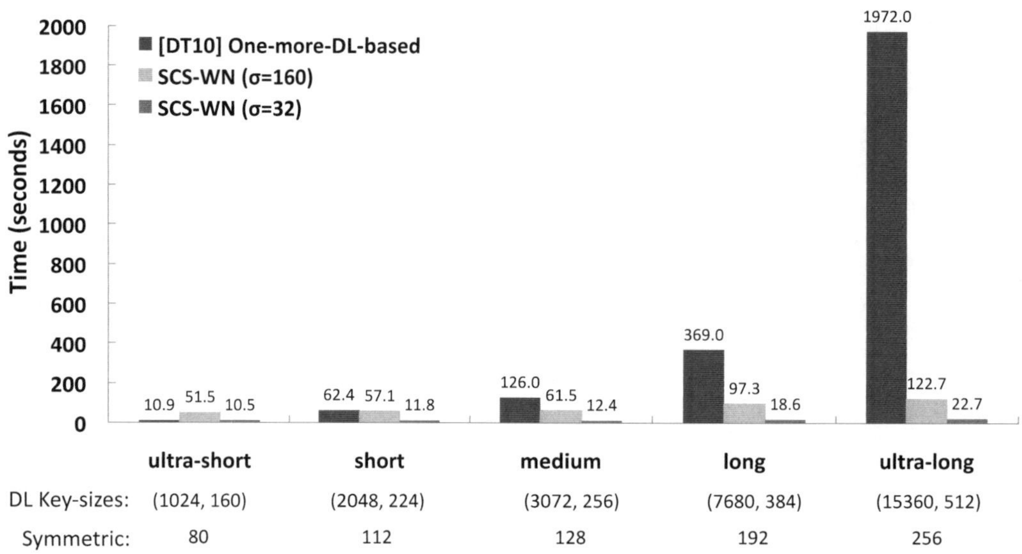

Conclusion

Generic protocols offer many advantages

- Composability
- Flexibility on hardness assumptions
- Design cost
- Performance

Q & A?

Guess Who's Texting You? Evaluating the Security of Smartphone Messaging Applications

Sebastian Schrittwieser, Peter Frühwirt, Peter Kieseberg, Manuel Leithner,
Martin Mulazzani, Markus Huber, Edgar Weippl
SBA Research gGmbH
Vienna, Austria
(1stletterfirstname)(lastname)@sba-research.org

Abstract

In recent months a new generation of mobile messaging and VoIP applications for smartphones was introduced. These services offer free calls and text messages to other subscribers, providing an Internet-based alternative to the traditional communication methods managed by cellular network carriers such as SMS, MMS and voice calls. While user numbers are estimated in the millions, very little attention has so far been paid to the security measures (or lack thereof) implemented by these providers.

In this paper we analyze nine popular mobile messaging and VoIP applications and evaluate their security models with a focus on authentication mechanisms. We find that a majority of the examined applications use the user's phone number as a unique token to identify accounts, which further encumbers the implementation of security barriers. Finally, experimental results show that major security flaws exist in most of the tested applications, allowing attackers to hijack accounts, spoof sender-IDs or enumerate subscribers.

1 Introduction

In the past few months, several new smartphone messaging and VoIP services with a novel user authentication concept were introduced. These new-generation communication applications aim at replacing traditional text messaging (SMS) and only require the user's phone number for registration. Contrary to well-known instant messaging services, no additional authentication mechanisms other than the phone number are used by these applications. In this paper we focus on the security of applications that are using this novel authentication concept. Due to this limitation, services such as Skype, Facebook Chat and Google Chat were regarded as out of scope. Note that these services have been the subject of an ample amount of past research.

The common advantages of the tools we examined lie in very simple and fast setup routines combined with the possibility to incorporate existing on-device address books. Additionally these services offer communication free of charge and thus pose a low entry barrier to potential customers. However, we find that the very design of most of these messaging systems thwarts their security measures, leading to issues such as the possibility for communication without proper sender authentication.

The main contribution of our paper is an evaluation of the security of mobile messaging applications with the aforementioned properties and the possibilities of abuse in real-world scenarios. Additionally, we draw attention to a number of suitable security mechanisms to prevent the misuse of these systems. The rest of the paper is organized as follows: Section 2 gives an overview of related work. Section 3 outlines the basic functionalities of the examined communications services, while Section 4 introduces our threat assessment for these applications. Section 5 documents our findings and explains how the flaws we identified might pose threats to users. We conclude in Section 6 and give a brief overview of approaches for future research.

2 Related Work

In this paper we document our findings on weak user authentication in messaging applications on smartphones. User authentication is a popular field of research in information security [16, 2], especially applied to distributed systems [13] or for web services [11, 18]. A vast number of protocols has been designed to provide secure user authentication, for example based on Kerberos [15] or public key cryptography and the usage of a PKI [4].

Due to the steadily increasing pervasiveness of smartphones these platforms have sparked the interest of the security community. The security features and properties of

Android [9, 8, 3, 10] as well as iOS [5] have been widely studied. Furthermore, smartphone application security has been evaluated in the past [6, 7]. To the best of our knowledge no evaluation of novel smartphone messaging services analyzed in this paper has been published at the time of writing. Recently, cloud storage services have attracted the interest of security researchers [12] analyzing the implications of faulty authentication in that area. There are numerous applications for Android that promise encrypted, secure communication, such as RedPhone and TextSecure [17].

3 Mobile Messaging Applications

General Characteristics All applications analyzed in this paper have one thing in common: They use the user's phone number as the basis for identification. During the setup process, the software asks the user to enter the phone number of the device. Although Android can grant direct access to the user's phone number to applications, this mechanism is currently not in use. Apple's iOS App Store guidelines on the other hand do not allow applications to access the phone number, making manual input necessary. One major, if unintentional, benefit of this approach is that even devices without a phone module (e.g. a WiFi-only tablet) can be activated using the phone number of another device. It should be noted that these messaging applications use the phone number for user identification only and do not attempt to communicate over the regular mobile phone network. The main problem with this approach is naturally that the system has to verify the user's input, seeing as a malicious user could enter someone else's phone number and therefore hijack or create an account with false credentials.

All the messengers we analyzed implement measures to prevent users from impersonating others by trying to authenticate a number they do not control. Still, several of these approaches display fundamental design flaws. Section 5 analyzes the shortcomings of several messengers.

WhatsApp The most popular tested application (judging by its widespread distribution among various smartphone platforms) is the WhatsApp messenger. It is a cross-platform messaging application for Android, BlackBerry, iOS and Symbian. The vendor has not released any information on its user base, however, based on the Android Market sales, it can be estimated to have at least a few million users[1]. Recently, the vendor reported that in one single day over one billion messages were sent over Whatsapp[2]. In contrast to other comparable messengers, this piece of software does not support calls via VoIP.

[1] https://market.android.com/details?id=com.whatsapp, retrieved on August 23rd, 2011

[2] http://blog.whatsapp.com/index.php/2011/10/one-billion-messages, retrieved on November 2nd, 2011

4 Evaluation

In this section we detail the methodology and the experimental setup of our evaluation.

4.1 Methodology

For our evaluation, we selected nine popular messaging and VoIP applications for both Android and iOS. We estimated the user base of the applications by accumulating data available from the Android Market[3] and Xyologic[4], a company providing download estimations for iOS applications. Table 1 gives an overview of the applications and their features. The great majority of our selected smartphone messaging applications support Voice over Internet Protocol (VoIP) calls and text messages. Furthermore, all tested applications used the user's phone number as the unique user ID for initial authentication, with the Short Message Service (SMS) being the preferred method to verify the user's control over a given phone number. We then identified five possible attack vectors exploiting the insufficient authentication methods employed in these applications. Lastly, we systematically examined the software packages for the presence of these flaws. This section describes the five common attack vectors we identified amongst popular smartphone messaging applications.

Authentication Mechanism and Account Hijacking We analyzed the initial setup mechanisms of the applications during which a phone number is linked to a device. None of the tested applications retrieve the device's phone number automatically but instead ask the user to input it manually during the setup phase. The common method to verify the entered number is sending a SMS message to the specified number containing a verification PIN that the user has to enter in the application's user interface. We analyzed the communication between phone and server during the initial setup and tested if an attacker could hijack accounts by passing another user's phone number as his/her own.

Sender ID Spoofing / Message Manipulation In the second part of our evaluation, we analyzed the communication between the phone and the server during message sending and receiving. The attack scenarios for this part are a malicious user that wants to send a message with a spoofed sender ID. In contrast to the scenario outlined in the previous paragraph, the attacker may do this without hijacking the entire account.

The manipulation of a message during transfer is another possible threat, however, as most tested application use en-

[3] https://market.android.com, retrieved on November 2nd, 2011

[4] http://search.xyologic.com, retrieved on November 2nd, 2011

	VoIP	Text Messages	Number Verification	Uploads Address Book
WhatsApp 2.6.4	no	yes	SMS, active SMS	yes
Viber 2.0.3	yes	yes	SMS and passive phone call	yes
eBuddy XMS 1.15.2	no	yes	SMS	yes
Tango 1.6.9568	yes	no	SMS	yes
Voypi 1.2	yes	yes	SMS	yes
Forfone 1.5.6	yes	yes	SMS	yes
HeyTell 2.3.0	yes	no	no	no
EasyTalk 2.0.1	yes	yes	SMS	yes
Wowtalk 1.0.3	yes	yes	SMS	yes

	Status Messages	Platforms	Estimated User Base
WhatsApp 2.6.4	yes	Android, iOS, BlackBerry, Symbian	23-63M
Viber 2.0.3	no	Android, iOS	10-15M
eBuddy XMS 1.15.2	no	Android, iOS	1-1.5M
Tango 1.6.9568	no	Android, iOS	10-15M
Voypi 1.2	no	Android, iOS	0.1-0.15M
Forfone 1.5.6	no	Android, iOS	0.2-0.25M
HeyTell 2.3.0	no	Android, iOS	5-9M
EasyTalk 2.0.1	no	iOS	0.25-0.3M
Wowtalk 1.0.3	yes	iOS	0.06M

Table 1. Overview of selected smartphone messaging applications, their features, supported platforms, and estimated user base.

cryption for communication with the server, such an attack would usually not be practical in real life scenarios.

Unrequested SMS/phone calls Most services emit SMS messages or even phone calls throughout the phone number verification process. A malicious user could use another user's number in the setup process to generate annoying messages or phone calls on the victim's phone without revealing his identity.

Another scenario in this class is eavesdropping and replaying a message.

Enumeration Most applications upload the user's address book to the server and compare the entries to a list of registered users (only EasyTalk utilizes a slightly different mechanism and only transmits the number as it is dialed). The server then returns the subset of the user's contacts that are using the service. We analyzed how this mechanism could be used to enumerate users of the service, e.g. by uploading an address book containing a large amount of phone numbers.

The main problem resulting from this functionality is that an attacker can derive useful information about the user's device such as the operating system, if a specific application only runs on one specific system (for instance a certain OS/version combination). This enables the attacker to perform system specific attacks.

Modifying Status Messages Two out of the nine applications allow the user to set a status message that is shared with people that have this user in their address book. In this part of the evaluation, we considered two threats. The first one is the modification of a user's status message by an attacker. We analyzed the protocol for setting the status message and explore possible vulnerabilities that could result in unauthorized modification of status messages.

The second threat is a privacy-related design error. Not only is it possible to determine whether the owner of a given phone number has installed the messenger application (as outlined above), but also the status message of a user is visible to people that have stored this user in their address book. Since no user confirmation is required to store a number in the address book, an attacker can very easily get access to the status messages of all subscribers to services vulnerable to this attack. In practice, this approach would likely be combined with some sort of enumeration attack.

4.2 Experimental Setup

For our security evaluation we used a Samsung Nexus S running Android 2.3.3 and an Apple iPhone 4 running iOS 4.3.3. Applications that are available for both platforms were tested on both the Nexus S and the iPhone. To be able to read encrypted HTTPS traffic from and to the tested applications, we set up a SSL proxy that acted as a man-in-the-middle and intercepted requests to HTTPS servers. We further used SSLsniff [14] by Moxie Marlinspike to read SSL-protected traffic that is not sent over HTTPS (e.g. XMPP).

Figure 1 explains our approach for the experimental setup. The SSL proxy was used to analyze HTTPS connections and allowed us to read as well as modify HTTPS traffic on the fly. Other protocols were observed with SSLsniff.

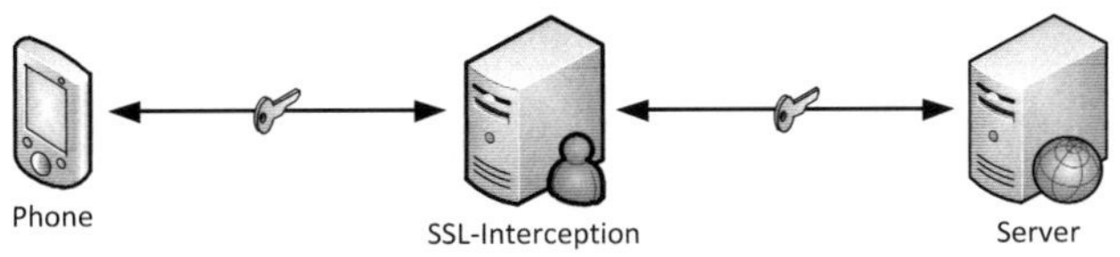

Figure 1. Experimental setup for intercepting SSL.

5 Results

In this section we present the results of our security evaluation of the application discussed in Section 3 with respect to the different attacks outlined in section 4.

5.1 Overview

Table 2 gives a compact overview of the vulnerabilities found in the tested applications. It is notable that almost all applications were vulnerable to SMS flooding and enumeration attacks, but only very few to sender spoofing or message manipulation.

5.2 Authentication Mechanism and Account Hijacking

In this section we describe successful attacks against the authentication mechanisms of the tested applications. The general idea is that an attacker tries to hijack accounts to be able to spoof the sender ID and receive messages targeted to a victim. In essence, the attacker aims at linking his mobile device to the phone number of the victim.

WhatsApp To prevent malicious users to impersonate somebody else using the victim's number, a verification SMS containing a 4-digit PIN is sent to the phone. The user then has to copy that code into the WhatsApp application's GUI. This process binds a WhatsApp user account (represented by the phone number) to a physical device.

Figure 2 shows the authentication process of WhatsApp. We discovered that the verification process of WhatsApp is fatally broken. The PIN for the verification SMS message is generated on the phone and then sent to the server via a HTTPS connection. The server then initiates the SMS message via a SMS proxy to the phone, where the app then

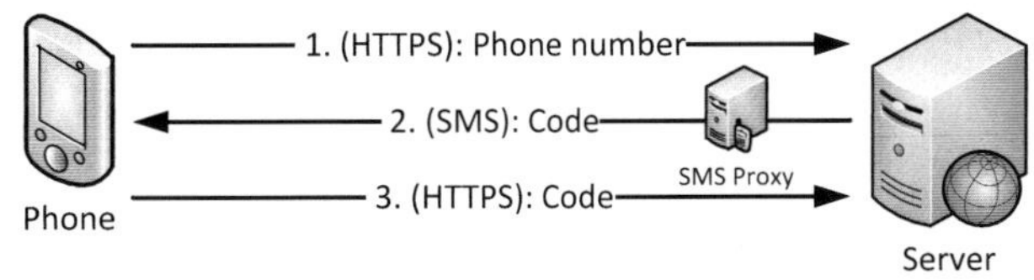

Figure 2. Authentication process of WhatsApp

checks if the PIN entered by the user matches the previously generated PIN. An attacker could exploit this mechanism to hijack any WhatsApp account. This can be done by typing the victim's phone number during the verification phase and then intercepting the communication between the phone and the server to eavesdrop the PIN. This communication is SSL-protected; however, the attacker has to intercept only the connection between his own phone and the WhatsApp server. To exploit this vulnerability, it is possible set up a SSL proxy and install the proxy's certificates as described in Section 4 on the phone in order to get access to the encrypted communication transparent to the application.

Once the attacker has entered the PIN into his phone, the victim's WhatsApp account is linked to the attacker's phone. This enables the attacker to send and retrieve messages from the victim's account. This process also unlinks the victim's device, causing it to not receive messages from WhatsApp anymore.

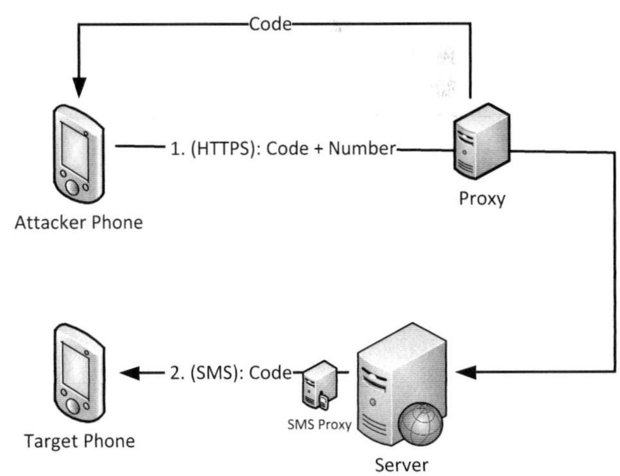

Figure 3. MitM-Attack against WhatsApp authentication

Figure 3 shows a possible attack on the authentication process of WhatsApp. A man-in-the-middle attack on the communication between the phone and the client makes it possible to eavesdrop the secret SMS verification code be-

	Account Hijacking	Spoofing / Manipulation	Unrequested SMS	Enumeration	Other Vulnerabilities
WhatsApp	yes	no	yes	yes	yes
Viber	no	no	yes	yes	
eBuddy XMS	no	no	yes	yes	
Tango	yes	no	yes	yes	
Voypi	yes	yes	yes	yes	yes
Forfone	no	yes	yes	yes	
HeyTell	yes	no	no	limited	
EasyTalk	yes	no	yes	yes	
WowTalk	yes	no	yes	yes	yes

Table 2. Overview on attacks.

fore it was even delivered to the spoofed phone number.

Tango and Voypi The applications Tango and Voypi share a very similar approach for device registration. Like WhatsApp, both applications ask the user to enter the device's phone number. If the number is not registered for the service yet, no verification is done. Only if the number is already known to the system, a verification process via SMS (similar to WhatsApp) is performed.

While this registration schema is not vulnerable to account hijacking, an attacker can impersonate users that are not yet registered for that service. As long as a number is not registered for Tango or Voypi, an attacker can use it without SMS verification.

HeyTell HeyTell does not have any kind of verification. During the setup process the user has to select his or her own cellphone number from the address book (or create a new entry if it does not exist). The device is then linked to the chosen number without verification.

WowTalk WowTalk's registration mechanism is based on SMS-verification. The user has to enter his phone number into the application which transmits it to the server. The server generates a random verification code and sends it back to the phone via SMS. The problem, however, is that the server also sends the verification code via HTTPS to the phone so that it can compare the user's input to the correct code. We used the SSL proxy to intercept the server's reply and so retrieve the verification code. An attacker can use this technique to hijack any WowTalk account. Figure 4 explains our attack against WowTalk's client authentication.

EasyTalk EasyTalk uses SMS for phone number verification. After a device's registration request, the server generates a verification code that is sent to the device via SMS. After receiving the SMS the user has to enter the code into the application that forwards it to the server for verification. The server then replies to the device with either "OK" if the device sent the correct code or "ERROR" if the user entered

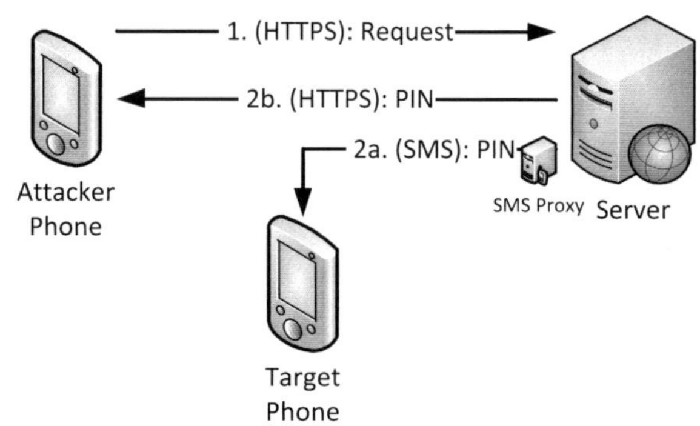

Figure 4. MitM-attack against WowTalk application

an incorrect code into the application. We were able to successfully authenticate a client by modifying this message from "ERROR" to "OK". The server does not detect this message manipulation and keeps the device authenticated.

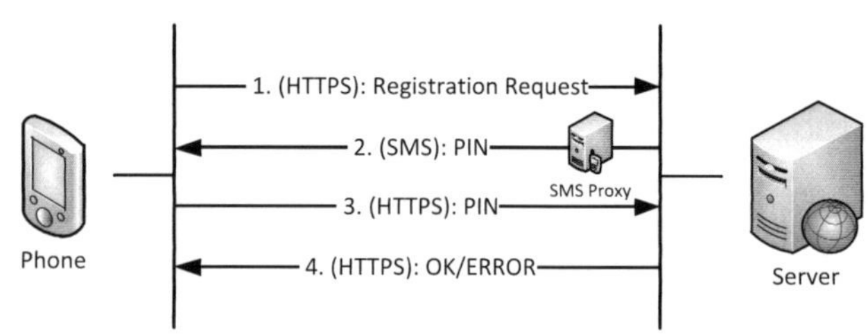

Figure 5. Device authentication in EasyTalk.

Figure 5 shows the authentication mechanism of EasyTalk.

Viber Compared to the other introduced applications, Viber's authentication mechanism is well designed and properly implemented. The application asks the user for the phone number and sends an authentication request to the server. The server generates a verification code and sends it via SMS message to the user's phone. Alternatively, the user can request a phone call from Viber. In that case, a speech synthesizer voice speaks the code on the phone call. The user has to the enter the received code in the Viber application that forwards it to the server, which in turn checks the input. At no time does the server trust the client (i.e. the application on the user's phone) and no sensitive authentication data is transmitted between phone and server. Figure 6 explains the authentication mechanism of Viber.

Forfone and eBuddy XMS The authentication mechanisms of Forfone and eBuddy XMS are similar to Viber's and thus not susceptible to attacks that are based on intercepting the communication between the device and the server.

Conclusion We do not propose our own authentication schema, as some of the tested applications already have secure protocols. While a secure implementation seems trivial, our evaluation showed that the majority of the tested applications are susceptible to even basic attacks.

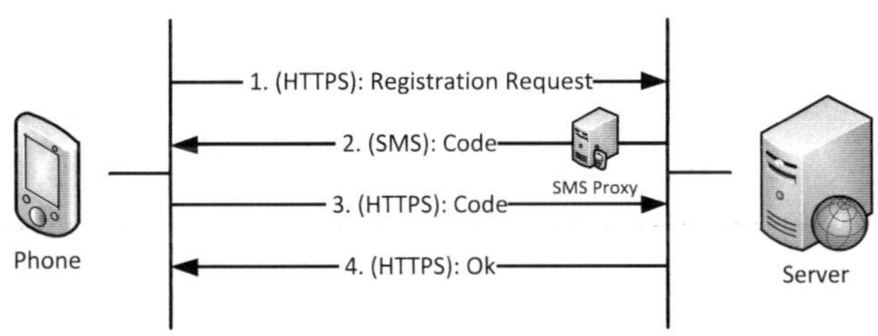

Figure 6. Authentication in Viber.

5.3 Sender ID Spoofing

This section introduces the results of our evaluation of messaging protocols in the tested applications. We analyzed the protocols and attempted to send messages with spoofed sender IDs without hijacking the entire account. Most of the tested applications use the Extensible Messaging and Presence Protocol (XMPP) [19] for messaging and can therefore rely on the security features present in the XMPP server that prevent sender ID spoofing. However, Voypi and Forefone have their own implementations for messaging that are based on HTTP(S) requests.

Voypi The unencrypted HTTP request that is used by Voypi to generate messages has four GET parameters: both the sender's and the receiver's phone number, the message, and a time stamp. There is no authentication required to send a message, therefore, an attacker can spoof the sender ID.

Forfone In Forfone's messaging protocol an additional identifier of the sender is required for sending messages. In Android the IMSI of the phone and in iOS the UDID (Unique Device Identifier) are used for sender authentication. While this additional parameter raises the difficulty of sender ID spoofing, it cannot be considered as a secure authentication mechanism as these two identifiers can be accessed by any third party application on the phone.

Table 3 summarizes the layout of the messaging protocols used by Voypi and Forfone.

	Voypi	Forfone
HTTP-Method	GET	POST
Parameters	sender phone number receiver phone number receiver country code message timestamp	sender phone number receiver phone number message sender UDID

Table 3. Messaging protocols of Voypi and Forfone.

5.4 Unrequested SMS

When taking a look at the authentication mechanisms, several applications use an SMS sent to the (assumed) requesting handset in order to verify the validity of the request and to thwart account hijacking (see Section 5.2). However, several implementations of this mechanism can be misused in order to send these verification-messages to the arbitrary users. In one application (WhatsApp) we were even able to modify the messages sent, thus being able to communicate via SMS worldwide free of charge.

General Approach The general approach consists of spamming an arbitrary user with text messages containing validation requests from a messaging service. Since we are able to do this in an automated fashion, this can be frustrating to a victim constantly receiving authorization requests. Unfortunately for the attacker (and fortunately for potential victims) all examined applications had some kind of timeout that thwarted real mass spamming. Still, an attacker is able to send messages at a regular interval. The adversary could also target certain numbers used for emergencies such as those used by system administrators in high-availability data centers, potentially causing the victim to switch off her device. The idea behind the attack can be seen in Figure 7

This approach works for the following messengers: WhatsApp, Viber, Tango, eBuddy XMS, WowTalk, Voypi, Forfone and easyTalk. However, no application other than WhatsApp allow for the injection of content into the verification SMS, thus making it rather useless for actual spamming (as used for marketing purposes).

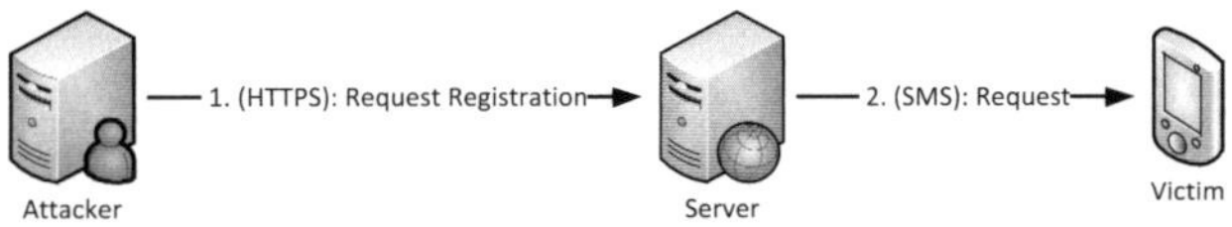

Figure 7. General approach.

Viber The messaging application Viber allows for an even more annoying attack. In case the SMS message for authentication was not answered by the target, the attacker can choose to set up an authentication request using a phone call (Figure 8 shows the relevant parts of the authentication mechanism in Viber).

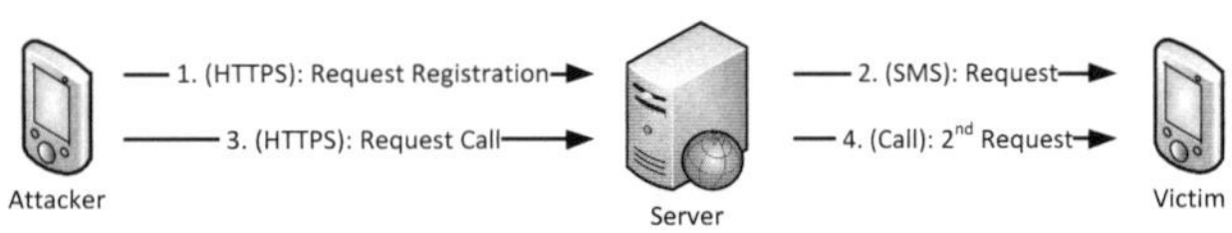

Figure 8. Sending SMS and requesting phone calls with Viber.

WhatsApp Finally, WhatsApp offers an intriguing feature (or rather design error) that can be (mis-)used for sending free text messages worldwide. When looking at the authentication mechanism, we discussed that the authentication code is chosen by the handset that is requesting authentication and the WhatsApp-server simply echoes it back to the handset by a SMS. This authentication code consists of the string "WhatsApp code" followed by a PIN generated by the phone. In our analysis, we were able to intercept and modify the transmission of the PIN from the phone to the server. The modified SMS was even delivered when the PIN was replaced by any alphanumerical string, allowing an attacker to send SMS messages with nearly arbitrary content to the target handset. These techniques can either be used for free communication, or for sending spam. In fact, the verification messages can be sent by requesting the URL

```
https://s.whatsapp.net/client/iphone/
    smsproxy.php?to=\<receiver\>
    &auth=\<text message\>.
```

Figure 9 details the relevant parts of the authentication protocol that are abused in this attack.

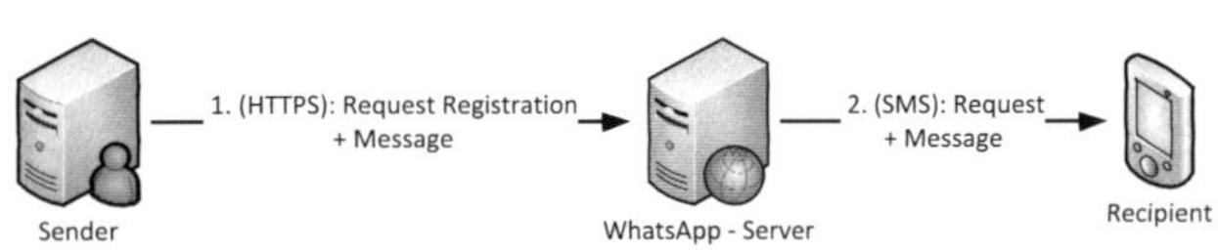

Figure 9. Free SMS with WhatsApp

5.5 Enumeration

Another security-relevant aspect of this type of messaging applications is their ability to automatically import the user's contacts. All tested applications except HeyTell allow the user to upload the entire address book to the system's server and compare the contained phone numbers to already registered phone numbers stored on the server. The server returns a subset of the user's contact list containing only phone numbers that are registered.

A possible threat resulting from a user account enumeration is the identification of active phone numbers. Furthermore, an attacker could try to identify the operating system of the user, based on the applications installed on the phone and their availability for a certain operating system. This enables an attacker to target a system with OS-specific exploits.

We tested the feasibility of such an enumeration attack with WhatsApp. To this end, we selected the US area code 619, which covers the southern half of the city of San Diego, CA and enumerated the entire number range from 000-0000 to 999-9999. A similar approach for Facebook is described by Balduzzi et al. [1]. In their paper, the authors tested the validity of mail addresses by uploading them to the friend-finder feature of Facebook. Based on the return value of Facebook, they were able to determine the status of a mail address.

In our evaluation, we split the entire number range of the San Diego area code 619 into chunks of 5000 phone numbers each and simulated a standard address book upload as performed by WhatsApp during device registration. While we noticed some slowdowns in server response time during our evaluation, the WhatsApp server did not prevent us from uploading ten million phone numbers and returned 21095 valid phone numbers that are using the WhatsApp application as well as their status messages. The entire process finished in less than 2.5 hours.

Figure 10 shows the distribution of phone numbers that are linked to a WhatsApp account over the entire number range. As the figure indicates, active phone numbers of the area code 619 start at 200000. We believe that the mobile number range starts above this value, but have not independently confirmed that.

A simple countermeasure would be the introduction of a rate limit. Clearly, no regular user would upload ten million phone numbers and such an attempt could be easily detected and blocked by the server.

HeyTell HeyTell does not support upload of a whole address book for enumeration, but enumeration can be done number by number by requesting to send a voice message for every single number in the address book. This, however, is restricted by a privacy setting that allows users to

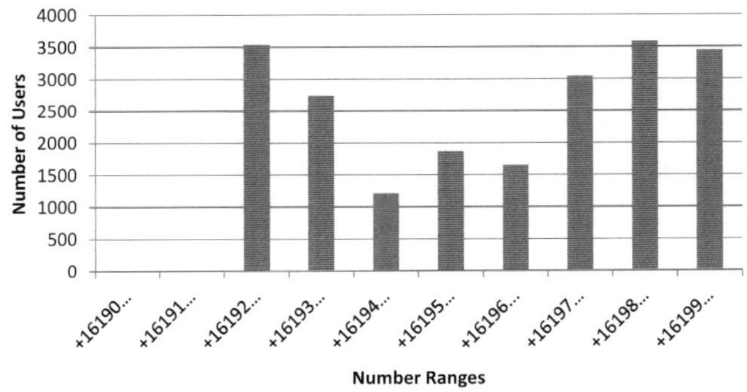

Figure 10. Distribution of phone numbers in area code 619 that are registered with WhatsApp.

limit their visibility.

5.6 Other Vulnerabilities

WhatsApp An additional feature of WhatsApp is the possibility to set a status message, similar to instant messaging clients like Skype, that can be read by the user's contacts. Changing this status message does not require any authentication. In fact, everyone can change anyone else's status message by sending an HTTPS request to

```
https://s.whatsapp.net/client/iphone/u.php?
    cc=<country code>&me=<phone number>
    &s=<status message>.
```

WowTalk Like WhatsApp, WowTalk offers the feature of setting a status message. A user can change the status message for an arbitrary user by issuing a POST-request to `https://sip.wowtalk.org/wowtalk_srv.php` containing

```
action=user_status_update&username=<user id>
    &status=<New Status>
```

Voypi We were able to identify two other vulnerabilities in Voypi. It is possible to request Voypi users in the address book of other users. To this end, a simple HTTP request with the phone number of the victim is sent to the server:

```
http://msg.voypi.com/myphone_v1/getusers.php?
    phone=<phone number>&version=1.2
```

No further authentication is required to perform this query. The server responds with the subset of Voypi users from the victim's address book containing names and phone numbers.

The second vulnerability allows an attacker to request messages of other users without authentication. The Voypi client has to be running in order to be able to receive messages. When active, Voypi pulls new messages in an interval of seven seconds from the server:

```
http://msg.voypi.com/myphone_v1/getmsg.php?
    dbname=<phone number>8&version=1.2
```

As long as the client has not pulled messages, an attacker can do so and thus steal another user's messages. The term "stealing" fits this scenario, because the victim is not able to retrieve the messages from the server once the attacker has done so.

6 Conclusion

In this paper, we assessed nine mobile messaging and VoIP applications for smartphones. Our evaluation showed that many applications have broken authentication mechanisms and thus are vulnerable to account hijacking attacks. Most applications also suffer from other vulnerabilities such as account enumeration. We practically demonstrated an attacker's capability to enumerate any number of active WhatsApp accounts with a given area code (US area code 619 in our example, which corresponds to Southern San Diego, CA). All identified flaws stem from well-known software design and implementation errors. Although these vulnerabilities may not endanger human lives, they might have a severe impact on the privacy of millions of users.

Future work might include security assessments of upcoming solutions slated for mass adoption such as Apple's iMessage. Furthermore, research towards an authentication scheme suitable as a best practice template for newly developed applications would be a welcome addition.

7 Acknowledgements

This work has been supported by the Austrian Research Promotion Agency under grant 824709 (Kiras) and the Austrian COMET Program (FFG).

References

[1] M. Balduzzi, C. Platzer, T. Holz, E. Kirda, D. Balzarotti, and C. Kruegel. Abusing social networks for automated user profiling. In *Recent Advances in Intrusion Detection: 13th International Symposium, RAID 2010, Ottawa, Ontario, Canada, September 15-17, 2010, Proceedings*, volume 6307, page 422. Springer-Verlag New York Inc, 2010.

[2] M. Bishop. *Computer Security: Art and Science*. Addison-Wesley, 2002.

[3] L. Davi, A. Dmitrienko, A. Sadeghi, and M. Winandy. Privilege escalation attacks on android. *Information Security*, pages 346–360, 2011.

[4] W. Diffie and M. Hellman. New directions in cryptography. *Information Theory, IEEE Transactions on*, 22(6):644–654, 1976.

[5] M. Egele, C. Kruegel, E. Kirda, and G. Vigna. Pios: Detecting privacy leaks in ios applications. In *Network and Distributed System Security Symposium (NDSS)*, 2011.

[6] W. Enck, P. Gilbert, B. Chun, L. Cox, J. Jung, P. McDaniel, and A. Sheth. Taintdroid: An information-flow tracking system for realtime privacy monitoring on smartphones. In *Proceedings of the 9th USENIX conference on Operating systems design and implementation*, pages 1–6. USENIX Association, 2010.

[7] W. Enck, D. Octeau, P. McDaniel, and S. Chaudhuri. A study of android application security. In *Proc. of the 20th USENIX Security Symposium*, 2011.

[8] W. Enck, M. Ongtang, and P. McDaniel. On lightweight mobile phone application certification. In *Proceedings of the 16th ACM conference on Computer and communications security*, pages 235–245. ACM, 2009.

[9] W. Enck, M. Ongtang, and P. McDaniel. Understanding Android Security. *Security & Privacy, IEEE*, 7(1):50–57, 2009.

[10] A. Felt, H. Wang, A. Moshchuk, S. Hanna, E. Chin, K. Greenwood, D. Wagner, D. Song, M. Finifter, J. Weinberger, et al. Permission re-delegation: Attacks and defenses. In *20th Usenix Security Symposium, San Fansisco, CA*, 2011.

[11] K. Fu, E. Sit, K. Smith, and N. Feamster. Dos and Don'ts of Client Authentication on the Web. In *Proceedings of the 10th conference on USENIX Security Symposium-Volume 10*, pages 19–19. USENIX Association, 2001.

[12] Intrepidus Group. Intrepidus group, 2011. [Online; retrieved Aug 21st, 2011], `http://intrepidusgroup.com/insight/2011/08/dropbox-for-android-vulnerability-breakdown/`.

[13] B. Lampson, M. Abadi, M. Burrows, and E. Wobber. Authentication in distributed systems: Theory and practice. *ACM Transactions on Computer Systems (TOCS)*, 10(4):265–310, 1992.

[14] M. Marlinspike. Website of sslsniff tool, 2011. [Online; retrieved Jun 21st, 2011], Online at `http://www.thoughtcrime.org/software/sslsniff`.

[15] B. Neuman and T. Ts'o. Kerberos: An authentication service for computer networks. *Communications Magazine, IEEE*, 32(9):33–38, 1994.

[16] W. Stallings. *Cryptography and network security: principles and practice*. Prentice Hall Press, 2010.

[17] Whisper Systems. Whisper systems, 2011. [Online; retrieved Aug 21st, 2011], `http://www.whispersys.com/`.

[18] A. Whitten and J. Tygar. Why Johnny can't encrypt: A usability evaluation of PGP 5.0. In *Proceedings of the 8th USENIX Security Symposium*, pages 169–184, 1999.

[19] XMPP Foundation. XMPP Standard, 2011. [Online; retrieved Jun 21st, 2011], `http://xmpp.org/l`.

MoCFI: A Framework to Mitigate Control-Flow Attacks on Smartphones

Lucas Davi[1], Alexandra Dmitrienko[2], Manuel Egele[3], Thomas Fischer[4], Thorsten Holz[4], Ralf Hund[4], Stefan Nürnberger[1], Ahmad-Reza Sadeghi[1,2]

[1]CASED/Technische Universität Darmstadt, Germany
{lucas.davi,stefan.nuernberger,ahmad.sadeghi}@trust.cased.de

[2]Fraunhofer SIT, Darmstadt, Germany
{alexandra.dmitrienko,ahmad.sadeghi}@sit.fraunhofer.de

[3]University of California, Santa Barbara, USA
maeg@cs.ucsb.edu

[4]Ruhr-Universität Bochum, Germany
{thomas.fischer,thorsten.holz,ralf.hund}@rub.de

Abstract

Runtime and control-flow attacks (such as code injection or return-oriented programming) constitute one of the most severe threats to software programs. These attacks are prevalent and have been recently applied to smartphone applications as well, of which hundreds of thousands are downloaded by users every day. While a framework for control-flow integrity (CFI) enforcement, an approach to prohibit this kind of attacks, exists for the Intel x86 platform, there is no such a solution for smartphones.

In this paper, we present a novel framework, MoCFI (Mobile CFI), that provides a general countermeasure against control-flow attacks on smartphone platforms by enforcing CFI. We show that CFI on typical smartphone platforms powered by an ARM processor is technically involved due to architectural differences between ARM and Intel x86, as well as the specifics of smartphone OSes. Our framework performs CFI on-the-fly during runtime without requiring the application's source code. For our reference implementation we chose Apple's iOS, because it has been an attractive target for control-flow attacks. Nevertheless, our framework is also applicable to other ARM-based devices such as Google's Android. Our performance evaluation demonstrates that MoCFI is efficient and does not induce notable overhead when applied to popular iOS applications.

1. Introduction

Although control-flow (or runtime) attacks on software are known for about two decades, they are still one of the major threats to software today. Such attacks compromise the control-flow of a vulnerable application during runtime based on diverse techniques (e.g., stack- or heap-based buffer overflows [4, 5], uncontrolled format strings vulnerabilities [23], or integer overflows [9]). Many current systems offer a large attack surface, because they still use software programs implemented in unsafe languages such as C or C++. In particular, modern smartphone platforms like Apple's iPhone and Google's Android have recently become appealing attack targets (e.g., [25, 33, 26, 27, 43]) and increasingly leak sensitive information to remote adversaries (e.g., the SMS database [26]).

A general approach to mitigate control-flow attacks is the enforcement of *control-flow integrity* (CFI) [1]. This technique asserts the basic safety property that the control-flow of a program follows only the legitimate paths determined in advance. If an adversary hijacks the control-flow, CFI enforcement can detect this divagation and prevent the attack. In contrast to a variety of ad-hoc solutions, CFI provides a general solution against control-flow attacks. For instance, to detect conventional return-oriented programming attacks one can check every return instruction the program is executing [12, 21, 16], but recent results show that return-oriented programming without returns is feasible on both x86 and ARM [11]. Moreover, CFI provides stronger protection than recent ASLR (address space layout randomization) mainly due to the fact that existing randomization realizations are often vulnerable to brute-forcing [38] or leak sensitive information about the memory layout [40]. Surprisingly, and to the best of our knowledge, there exist no CFI framework for smartphone platforms.

In this paper, we present the design and implementation of *MoCFI* (Mobile CFI), a CFI enforcement framework for smartphone platforms. Specifically, we focus on the ARM architecture since it is the standard platform for smartphones, and there is currently no smartphone available deploying an x86-based processor [28]. The implementation of CFI on ARM is often more involved than on desktop PCs due to several subtle architectural differences that highly influence and often significantly complicate a CFI solution: (1) the program counter is a general-purpose register, (2) the processor may switch the instruction set at runtime, (3) there are no dedicated return instructions, and (4) control-flow instructions may load several registers as a side-effect.

Although our solution can be deployed to any ARM based smartphone, we chose Apple's iPhone for our reference implementation because of three challenging issues: First, the iPhone platform is a popular target of control-flow attacks due to its use of the Objective-C programming language. In contrast, Android is not as prone to control-flow attacks because applications are mainly written in the type-safe Java programming language. Second, iOS is closed-source meaning that we can neither change the operating system nor can we access the application's source code. Third, applications are encrypted and signed by default.

Contribution. To the best of our knowledge, *MoCFI* is the first general CFI enforcement framework for smartphone platforms. Solutions like NativeClient (NaCl) for ARM [36] only provide a compiler-generated sandbox and are unsuitable for smartphones. NaCl needs access to source code and currently does not support 16-Bit THUMB code which is typically used in modern smartphone apps. In contrast, our solution operates on binaries and can be transparently enabled for individual applications. *MoCFI* allows us to retrofit CFI onto smartphone applications with commonly unavailable source code. Note that a compile-time solution would be specific to a single compiler, and Apple currently supports two compilers (LLVM and GCC). Hence, compiler-solutions are typically not suitable in practice, since neither the end-user nor the App store maintainer can recompile the application.

To this end, we first implemented a system to recover the *control-flow graph (CFG)* of a given iOS application in binary format. In particular, we extend PiOS [19] (a data-flow analysis framework) to generate the CFG. Based on this information, we perform control-flow validation routines that are used during *runtime* to check if instructions that change the control-flow are valid. Our prototype is based on library injection and in-memory patching of code which is compatible to memory randomization, static code signing, and encryption. Finally, our approach only requires a jailbreak for setting a single environment variable, installing a shared library, and allowing our library to rewrite the application code during load-time.

For performance evaluation, we measured the overhead *MoCFI* introduces as well the average overhead for typical applications and worst-case scenarios. The evaluation shows that our implementation is efficient. Moreover, we proved the effectiveness by constructing a control-flow attack that uses return-oriented programming [37, 10, 20, 24, 30, 11] and techniques similar to GOT (Global Offset Table) dereferencing [45, 22], which our tool can successfully prohibit.

Outline. The remainder of this paper is organized as follows: after briefly recalling the ARM architecture and the iOS smartphone operating system in Section 2, we present the problem of modern control-flow attacks, the original concept of CFI, and technical challenges when applying CFI to smartphones in Section 3. Afterwards, we present the design and implementation of *MoCFI* in Section 4 and 5. In Section 6 we discuss the security of *MoCFI* and current limitations. We present performance measurements in Section 7, summarize related work in Section 8, and conclude the paper in Section 9.

2. Background

In this section, we present a brief overview of the relevant aspects of the ARM processor architecture and the iOS operating system that are closely related to our work.

2.1. ARM Architecture

ARM features a 32 bit processor and sixteen general-purpose registers `r0` to `r15`, where `r13` is used as stack pointer (`sp`) and `r15` as program counter (`pc`). Furthermore, ARM maintains the so-called *current program status register* (`cpsr`) to reflect the current state of the system (e.g., condition flags, interrupt flags, etc.). In contrast to Intel x86, machine instructions are allowed to directly operate on the program counter `pc` (`EIP` on x86).

In general, ARM follows the *Reduced Instruction Set Computer* (RISC) design philosophy, e.g., it features dedicated load and store instructions, enforces aligned memory access, and offers instructions with a fixed length of 32 bits. However, since the introduction of the ARM7TDMI microprocessor, ARM provides a second instruction set called THUMB which usually has 16 bit instructions, and hence, is suitable for embedded systems with limited memory space.

The *ARM architecture procedure call standard* (AAPCS) document specifies the ARM calling convention for function calls [8]. In general, a function can be called by a `BL` (**B**ranch with **L**ink) or `BLX` (**B**ranch with **L**ink and e**X**change) instruction. `BLX` additionally allows indirect calls (i.e., the branch target is stored in a register), and the exchange ("*interworking*") from ARM to THUMB code and vice versa. Both instructions have in common that they store the return address (which is simply the instruction succeeding the `BLX/BL`) in the link register `lr` (`r14`). In order to allow nested function calls, the value of `lr` is usually pushed on the stack when the called function is entered.

Function returns are simply accomplished by loading the return address to `pc`. *Any* instruction capable of loading values from the stack or moving `lr` to `pc` can be used as return instruction. In particular, ARM compilers often use "load multiple" instructions as returns meaning that the instruction does not only enforce the return, but also loads several registers, e.g., `POP {R4-R7,PC}` loads `R4` to `R7` and the program counter with new values from the stack.

2.2. Selected Security Features of Apple iOS

Apple iOS is a closed and proprietary operating system designed for mobile Apple devices such as iPhone, iPad, and iPod Touch. A remarkable security feature of iOS is that only binaries and libraries signed by Apple are allowed to execute, which reduces the attack surface for malicious software. Furthermore, Apple only signs applications after inspecting the code. However, Apple provides no information how code inspection is enforced. Further, Apple only has access to the application binary (and not to the actual source code).

Since iOS v2.0, Apple enables the $W \oplus X$ (**W**ritable **xor** e**X**ecutable) security model, which basically marks a memory page either writable or executable. $W \oplus X$ prevents an adversary from launching a code injection attack, e.g., the conventional stack buffer overflow attack [4]. Furthermore, iOS deploys dynamic code signing enforcement (CSE) at runtime [48] to prevent the injection of new (malicious) code. In contrast to systems that only enable $W \oplus X$ (e.g., Windows or Linux), CSE on iOS prevents an application from allocating new memory (e.g., via `mprotect`) marked as executable. On the other hand, CSE at runtime in conjunction with $W \oplus X$ has practical drawbacks because it does not support self-modifying code and code generated by just-in-time (JIT) compilers. Therefore, iOS provides the so-called *dynamic-codesigning* entitlement that allows applications to generate code at runtime. At the time of writing, only the Mobile Safari Browser and full-screen web applications are granted the *dynamic-codesigning* entitlement. However, a very recent attack demonstrates that the current CSE implementation is vulnerable allowing an adversary to apply the *dynamic-codesigning* to arbitrary market applications [35]. Moreover, neither CSE at runtime nor $W \oplus X$ can prevent return-oriented programming attacks that only leverage existing and signed code pieces.

To detect stack-based buffer overflow attacks, iOS deploys the Stack-Smashing Protector (SSP). Basically, SSP uses *canaries*, i.e., guard values that are placed between local variables and control-flow information to detect simple stack smashing attacks. Moreover, SSP features bounds-checking for selected critical functions (like `memcpy` and `strcpy`) to ensure that their arguments will not lead to stack overflows. However, bounds-checking is only performed for a limited set of functions and SSP cannot detect heap overflows or any other control-flow attack beyond stack smashing.

A very recent feature of iOS (since iOS v4.3) is *address space layout randomization* (ASLR). Basically, ASLR randomizes the base addresses of libraries and dynamic areas (such as stack and heap) thereby preventing an adversary from guessing the location of injected code (or useful library sequences). However, it has been shown that existing randomization realizations are vulnerable to various attacks [38, 40, 13]. In addition, we present an own developed iOS exploit (see Appendix B) that successfully circumvents ASLR on iOS.

3. Problem Description

In the following, we discuss the problem of modern control-flow (runtime) attacks, present the basic idea of control-flow integrity (CFI), and finally elaborate on the technical obstacles to overcome when designing CFI enforcement for smartphone platforms.

3.1. Control-Flow Attacks

Figure 1 depicts a sample *control-flow graph* (CFG) of an application. Basically, the CFG represents valid execution paths the program may follow while it is executing. It consists of *basic blocks* (BBLs), instruction sequences with a single entry, and exit instruction (e.g., return, call, or jump), where the exit instruction enables the transition from one BBL to another. Any attempt of the adversary to subvert the valid execution path can be represented as a deviation from the CFG, which results in a so-called *control-flow* or *runtime* attack.

In particular, Figure 1 illustrates two typical control-flow attacks at BBL3: (i) a *code injection attack* (transition 2a), and (ii) a *code reuse attack* (transition 2b). Both attacks have in common that the control-flow is not transferred to BBL 5, but instead to a piece of code not originally covered by the CFG. A conventional control-flow attack is based on the injection of malicious code into the program's memory space. For instance, the adversary may overflow a buffer on the stack by first injecting his own malicious code and then overwriting a function's return address with the start address of the injected code [4]. However, modern operating systems (such as iOS) enforce the $W \oplus X$ security model that prevents an adversary from executing injected code. On the other hand, code-reuse attacks such as return-into-libc [34, 39] and modern return-oriented programming (ROP) [37, 10, 20, 24, 30, 11] bypass $W \oplus X$ by redirecting execution to code already residing in the program's memory space. In particular, ROP allows an adversary to induce

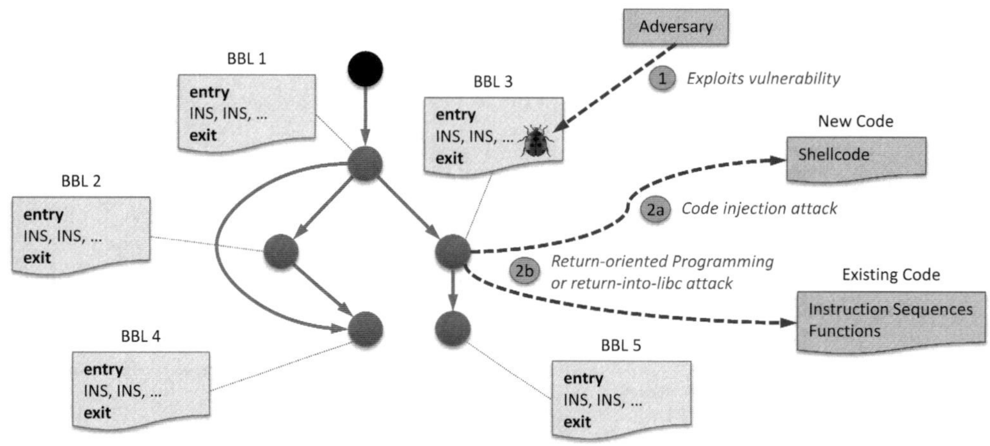

Figure 1. Schematic overview of control-flow attacks

arbitrary program behavior by only combining small code pieces from different parts of linked libraries.

Recent news underline that control-flow attacks are a severe problem on smartphones. In particular, control-flow attacks can be utilized to steal the user's SMS database [26], to open a remote reverse shell [27], or to launch a jailbreak [13]. Unfortunately, there is no general countermeasure to defeat such attacks on smartphones.

3.2. Control-Flow Integrity (CFI) on x86

A general approach to defeat control-flow attacks is the enforcement of control-flow integrity (CFI) [1]. Basically, CFI guarantees that a program *always* follows a valid execution path in the CFG, where the CFG is created ahead of time by means of static analysis. This is achieved by checking branch instructions of the BBLs: such instructions are overwritten with a new block of instructions that validates if the branch instruction targets a valid execution path in the CFG. For instance, in Figure 1, CFI would check if the exit instruction of BBL3 targets BBL5. In particular, the CFI prototype implementation presented by Abadi et al. [1] inserts unique labels just above each entry instruction. Hence, the CFI validation routine only has to check whether the branch address targets an instruction that is preceded by a valid label. However, the adoption and adaption of CFI (as presented in [1]) to smartphone platforms involves several difficulties and challenges.

3.3. Technical Challenges on Smartphone Platforms

The technical challenges are due to the architectural differences between ARM (RISC design) and Intel x86 (CISC design), and because of the specifics of smartphone operating systems. These highly influence and often complicate a CFI solution as we argue in the following.

No Dedicated Return Instruction. As mentionend in Section 2.1, ARM does not provide dedicated return instructions. Instead, any branch instruction can be used as a return. Moreover, returns may have side-effects, meaning that the return does not only enforce the return to the caller, but also loads several registers within a single instruction. Hence, in contrast to Intel x86, a CFI solution for ARM has to handle all different kinds of returns, and has to ensure that all side effects of the return are properly handled.

Multiple Instruction Sets. CFI on ARM is further complicated by the presence of two instruction sets (ARM and THUMB), which can even be interleaved. Hence, it is necessary to distinguish between both cases during the analysis and enforcement phase, and to ensure the correct switching between the two instruction sets at runtime.

Direct Access to the Program Counter. Another difference is that the ARM program counter `pc` is a general-purpose register which can be directly accessed by a number of instructions, e.g., arithmetic instructions are allowed to load the result of an arithmetic operation directly into `pc`. Furthermore, a load instruction may use the current value of `pc` as base address to load a pointer into another register. This complicates a CFI solution on ARM, since we have to consider and correctly handle all possible control-flow changes, and also preserve the accurate execution of load instruction that use `pc` as base register.

Application Signing and Encryption. Smartphone operating systems typically feature application encryption and signing. Since the traditional CFI approach [1] performs changes on the stored binary, the signature of the application cannot be verified anymore.

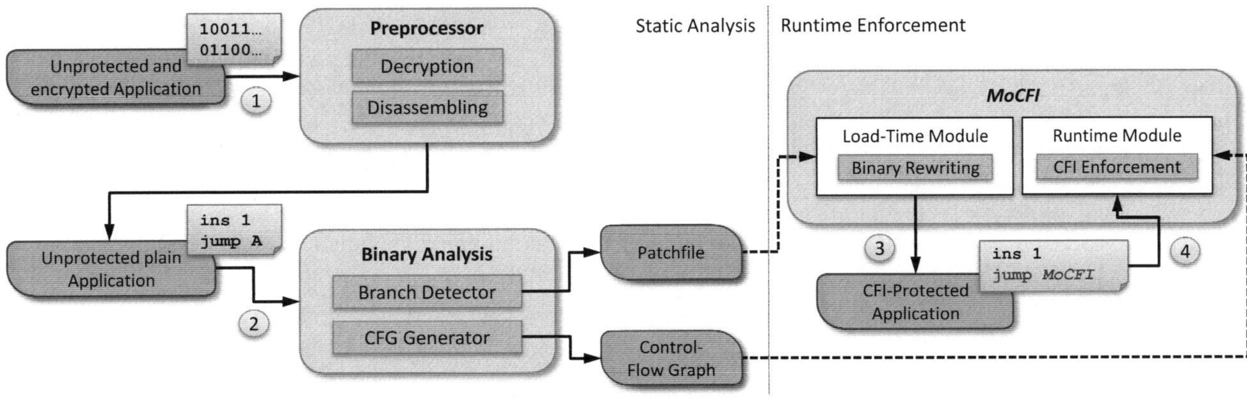

Figure 2. Control-flow integrity for smartphone applications

Closed-Source OS. Several smartphone OSes (such as iOS) are closed-source. Hence, we cannot change the actual OS to deploy CFI on smartphones. Moreover, end-users and even App Store maintainers (e.g., Apple's App Store) have no access to the application source code. Hence, a compiler-based CFI solution is not practicable from the end-user's perspective.

4. Design of our CFI Framework

Our general architecture is shown in Figure 2. From a high-level point of view, our system is separated in two different phases: static analysis and runtime enforcement. The *static* tools perform the initial analysis of the compiled application binary file. In the preprocessing phase, we first decrypt and disassemble the binary (step 1). Afterwards, we thoroughly analyze the application binary and its structure (step 2): In particular, we generate the control-flow graph (CFG) of the application and employ a branch detector to identify all branches contained in the binary and extract all information that is necessary to enforce CFI at runtime. Note that these steps have to be performed only *once* after compilation and can be integrated as an additional step in the deployment phase of a typical smartphone application. Finally, we monitor the application at *runtime* by applying our *MoCFI* shared library that rewrites the binary at load-time (step 3) and enforces control-flow restrictions while the application executes (step 4).

Although the depicted design applies in general to all CFI solutions, our design requires a number of changes, mainly due to (i) the architectural differences between ARM and Intel x86, (ii) the missing binary rewriter and automatic graph generation for ARM, and (iii) the specifics of smartphone operating systems. In the following we describe each involved system component and our approach in more detail.

Preprocessor. The first step of our static analysis phase is performed within the preprocessor component, which has mainly two tasks: (1) decrypting, and (2) disassembling the target application binary. In particular, we faced the challenge that smartphone applications are often encrypted by default (e.g., iOS applications). We thus obtain the unencrypted code of a binary through *process dumping* [19]. For disassembling the application binary we deploy standard disassembler tools that support the ARM architecture.

Binary Analysis. The original CFI work for Intel x86 [1] employs the binary instrumentation framework Vulcan [18] to automatically derive the CFG and to statically rewrite an application binary. However, such a framework does not exist for ARM. Hence, we developed own techniques to accurately generate the CFG. After our preprocessor decrypted and disassembled the application binary, we identify all relevant branches contained in the binary. By relevant branches, we refer to branch instructions that an adversary may exploit for a control-flow attack. These mainly comprise indirect branches, such as indirect jumps and calls, and function returns. Moreover, we include direct function calls to correctly validate function returns, i.e., to be able to check if a function return targets the original caller. We do not instrument direct jump instructions for obvious reasons: the target address for these are fixed (hard-coded), and hence cannot be manipulated by an adversary. Finally, we store meta information for each indirect branch and function call (e.g., instruction address, length, type, etc.) in a separate patchfile.

Based on the result of the branch detector, we generate the CFG by static tools that we developed ourselves. In particular, our static tools calculate possible target addresses for each indirect branch. Finally, a binary representation of the CFG is stored in a separate file (denoted as Control-Flow Graph), which is linked to the smartphone application at runtime.

***MoCFI* Load-Time Module: Binary Rewriting.** The binary rewriting engine is responsible for binding additional code to the binary that checks if the application follows a valid path of the CFG. Typically, one replaces all branch instructions in the binary with a number of new instructions that enforce the control-flow checks [1]. However, replacing one instruction with multiple instructions requires memory adjustments, because all instructions behind the new instructions are moved downwards. The Intel x86 approach uses the Vulcan binary instrumentation framework [18] which automatically accomplishes this task. However, memory adjustment without a full binary rewriting framework requires high implementation efforts.

Due to the limited possibilities to change smartphone binaries (due to code signing) and the missing full binary rewriter, we opted for the following rewriting approach (which has been originally proposed by Winwood et al. [44]). At *load-time* we replace all relevant branches (based on the extracted rewriting) with a single instruction: the so-called *dispatcher instruction*. The dispatcher instruction redirects the control-flow to a code section where the CFI checks reside, namely to the runtime module of our *MoCFI* shared library.

This approach also raises several problems: First, accurate branch instructions have to be implemented that are able to jump to the correct CFI check. Second, the CFI checks require information from where the dispatch originated. As we will demonstrate in the rest of the paper, our solution efficiently tackles the above mentioned problems.

***MoCFI* Runtime Module: Control-Flow Integrity Enforcement.** The key insight of CFI is the realization of control-flow validation routines. These routines have to validate the target of every branch to prevent the application from targeting a BBL beyond the scope of the CFG and the current execution path. Obviously, each branch target requires a different type of validation. While the target address of an indirect jump or call can be validated against a list of valid targets, the validation of function returns requires special handling because return addresses are dynamic and cannot be predicted ahead of time. To address this issue, *MoCFI* reuses the concept of shadow stacks that hold valid copies of return addresses [12], while the return addresses are pushed onto the shadow stacks when a function call occurs.

5. Implementation Details

Our prototype implementation targets iOS 4.3.1, and we successfully applied to 4.3.2 as well. We developed the static analysis tools (842 lines of code) with the IDC scripting language featured by the well-known disassembler IDA Pro 6.0. Moreover, we used Xcode 4 to develop the *MoCFI* library (1,430 lines of code). Our prototype implementation currently protects the application's main code, but no dynamic libraries that are loaded into the process. Hence, an adversary may launch a control-flow attack by exploiting a shared library. We leave support for shared libraries open to future work. However, it is straightforward to extend *MoCFI* accordingly, there are no new conceptional obstacles to overcome. We now describe how we generate the CFG and the patchfile of an iOS binary, and in particular present implementation details of our *MoCFI* library.

5.1. Static Analysis

Since iOS restricts access to source code, we apply our static analysis techniques directly on iOS binaries to generate the CFG and to identify all branches in the binary. We need the former one to validate if a branch follows a valid execution path, while the latter one is used to guarantee accurate binary rewriting. To perform this task, we use the IDA Pro v6.0 Disassembler that enables us to accurately disassemble ARM and THUMB code. Specifically, we implemented IDA scripts to automate the analysis and extract the necessary information from a given binary.

Patchfile Generation. As shown in Figure 2 in Section 4, step 2 involves the generation of rewriting information for each individual binary. This information is required by the load-time module of *MoCFI* to replace each branch instruction with a new instruction that redirects execution to the accurate CFI validation routine. In order to identify all relevant branch instructions, we evaluate each instruction belonging to the text segment and check if the instruction is relevant in the context of CFI. Afterwards, we perform a fine-grained instruction analysis and store the derived meta information (e.g. instruction address, mode, length, type, etc.) in the patchfile. By bundling the patchfile with the application, we can protect its integrity, as all application bundle contents are code-signed.

Generation of the Control-Flow Graph. In order to generate the CFG, we utilize IDA Pro to divide the binary into basic blocks (BBLs, see Section 3) and gather all assembly instructions that divert the control-flow. These instructions can be divided in two categories: (1) instructions that contain their possible control-flow destination as an immediate value, (2) instructions that continue control-flow based on the value of a register. While the first type is trivial in a $W \oplus X$ environment (i.e., the destination cannot be changed), the latter case can only be checked during runtime. Hence, as an optimization step and as argued in Section 4, we remove type (1) branches from the CFG. Type (2) branches are more challenging as the value they depend on needs to be calculated during static analysis. If this is not possible, heuristics have to be applied at runtime to narrow the possible control-flow destinations. Therefore, it is impossible to construct the CFG in all cases. Note that this is a general shortcoming of all CFG generation methods and not specific to our approach.

Indirect Branches and Heuristics.

To calculate the target address of an indirect branch (e.g., `LDR pc, [r2,r3,LSL #2]`), the registers have to be tracked backwards and all of their possible values must be calculated. In the above example, the target (`pc`) is calculated as $pc \leftarrow r2 + r3 \cdot 4$. If `r2` and `r3` can be tracked, the correct value can be extracted.

```
0x1000: MOV     r2, 0x2000
0x1004: ADD.W   r2, r2, r3, LSL#2
0x1008: MOV     pc, r2

0x2000: B.W     0x3000
0x2004: B.W     0x3100
0x2008: B.W     0x3200
```

Listing 1. Indirect Jump with jump table

Listing 1 is a common compiler-generated pattern to optimize `switch`-statements. Depending on `r3`, the possible control-flow targets (`pc`) are `0x3000`, `0x3100`, and `0x3200` and our analysis can recover these possibilities.

In case an indirect branch cannot be resolved (e.g. hand-written assembler code), it is possible to apply a heuristic in order to constrain the control-flow. A general constraint on ARM is that the target address must be a multiple of the instruction length. For indirect calls this constraint can be narrowed down to the beginning of functions. Even though it is still possible to call arbitrary functions, the target control-flow cannot land inside a function body.

Indirect jumps (`BX`) can be constrained to only take place inside one function body, i.e., not crossing function boundaries. Despite there is no technical need for this restriction, the `C`, `C++` and `Objective-C` languages restrict control-flow to the scope of one function, with the exception of function calls. Hence, we can assume that the scope of indirect jumps is limited by the boundary of a function body.

Objective-C Peculiarities. Traditional CFG generation techniques also need to be extended for iOS applications due to a peculiarity of Objective-C. Internally, any method call of an Objective-C object is resolved to a call to the generic message handling function `objc_msgSend`. The name of the actual method (called *selector*) is given as a parameter. Consequently, we must track these parameters in the CFG generation phase and include them in the CFG. Otherwise, an adversary might mount an attack by modifying the method parameters of `objc_msgSend`, thus diverting the control-flow to an invalid method. We built upon PiOS [19] and former reverse-engineering work on iOS [17, 32] to generate CFG information for `objc_msgSend` calls.

5.2. Control-Flow Integrity Checking with *MoCFI*

Most UNIX-based operating systems support the injection of libraries by providing the environment variable `LD_PRELOAD` that is checked by the OS loader upon initialization of each new process. The loader ensures that the library is loaded before any other dependency of the actual program binary. iOS provides an analogous method through the `DYLD_INSERT_ LIBRARIES` environment variable [6]. Setting this variable to point to *MoCFI* enables us to transparently instrument arbitrary applications. To force loading *MoCFI* into every application started though the touchscreen, we only need to set this environment variable for the *SpringBoard* process.

We stress that *MoCFI* is initialized *before* any other dependency of the program and *after* the signature of the application was verified (i.e., the program binary itself is unaltered). Subsequently, *MoCFI* implements the CFI enforcement by rewriting the code of the application in memory. We call this part of *MoCFI* the *load-time module* in contrast to the *runtime* module, which holds the actual validation checks. The load-time module makes sure that all relevant control-flow instructions are diverted to a corresponding validation routines in *MoCFI*. If validation succeeds, execution continues at the desired branch location.

5.2.1. Load-Time Module: Binary Rewriting

Upon initialization of *MoCFI*, the load-time module first locates the correct patchfile. Afterwards, it rewrites the binary according to the information stored in the patchfile. Since Apple iOS enforces $W \oplus X$, code cannot be writable in memory. Therefore, the code pages must be set to writable (but not executable) first. This is usually accomplished using the POSIX-compliant `mprotect` system call. Our experiments revealed that iOS does not allow the code pages to be changed at all (`mprotect` returns a permission denied error). However, this problem can be overcome by re-mapping the corresponding memory areas with `mmap` [7] first. When all relevant instructions of a page are patched, the page permissions are set back to executable but not writable. Note that the presence of `mmap` does not give an adversary the opportunity to subvert *MoCFI* by overwriting code. In order to do so, he would have to mount an attack beforehand that would inherently violate CFI at some point, which in turn would be detected by *MoCFI*.

Trampolines. Our binary rewriting engine overwrites the relevant control-flow instructions with the so-called *dis-*

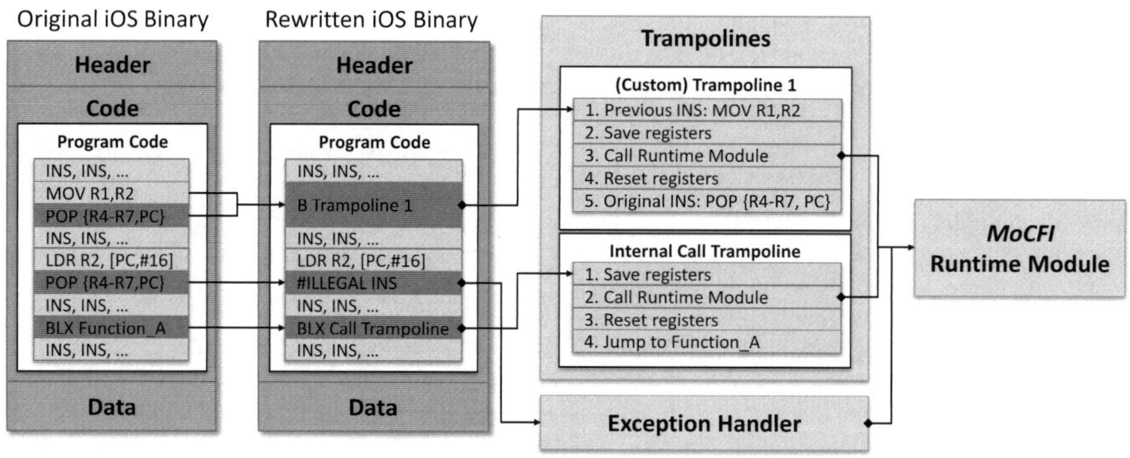

Figure 3. Trampoline approach

patcher instructions. The dispatcher redirects the program flow to a short piece of assembler code, namely to the *trampoline*, which in turn transfers the execution to our *MoCFI* library (see Figure 3). Hence, the trampolines are used as bridges between the application we aim to protect and our *MoCFI* library.

Specifically, we allocate dedicated trampolines for each indirect branch (i.e., indirect jumps / calls and returns), one generic trampoline for direct internal function calls (i.e., calls within the same code segment), and one generic trampoline for external function calls. Two example trampolines are shown in Figure 3: the first one (Trampoline 1) is used for a return instruction, while the second one (Internal Call Trampoline) handles a (direct) internal function call. In general, each trampoline saves the current execution state, invokes the appropriate *MoCFI* validation routine, resets the execution state, and issues the original branch. Due to the last step, we ensure that all registers are loaded correctly, even if the branch loads several registers as a side-effect, e.g., the replaced return `POP {R4-R7,PC}` is copied by our load-time module at the end of Trampoline 1. Hence, we ensure that `r4` to `r7` are correctly loaded with values from the stack before the return address is loaded to `pc`.

Note that, depending on the replaced branch instruction, we allocate a THUMB or ARM trampoline to ensure the correct interworking between the two instruction sets. In the following, we present the different kinds of dispatcher instructions our solution utilizes. The specific implementation of the different ARM/THUMB trampolines is described in Appendix A.

ARM (32 bit) dispatcher instruction. Since each ARM instruction is 32 bit long, we can use the default branch (`B`) instruction as a generic dispatcher instruction, which yields a possible target range from -2^{24} to $2^{24}-1$ bytes (32MB). As a consequence, the dispatcher target cannot lie within arbitrary memory address ranges. We address this problem by jumping to the mentioned *trampolines* rather than directly to the validation routine. The trampolines are small in size and are allocated near the code section of the application using `mmap`. Note that, theoretically, an application's memory image could be too large to find a free memory page for the trampolines. However, the application image would have to be larger than 16MB in order to break this approach. In practice, this is very unlikely. Even if this would be the case, one could search for memory regions within the code section that are unused (e.g., due to alignment) and use them as trampolines.

Note that for direct function calls, we use the `BLX` instruction instead, which provides the same target range as the `B` instruction. Using `BLX` ensures that the return address of the call is moved into the `lr` (link) register[1]. Further, *MoCFI* can easily lookup the original call target (stored in our patchfile) by inspecting the link register.

THUMB (16 bit and 32 bit) dispatcher instructions. For THUMB instructions, the situation is more complicated. While immediate branches are typically 32 bits in size (i.e., one can use the same approach as discussed previously), many control-flow instructions exist that are only 16 bits long. As a consequence, the reduced range for a branch target (only -2^{11} to $2^{11}-1$, i.e., 1KB) demands for a different solution. *MoCFI* addresses this issue by replacing a 16 Bit indirect branch with a 32 Bit dispatcher instruction. However, this has the effect that we overwrite 2 Thumb in-

[1]Note that for indirect calls *MoCFI* uses `B` as dispatcher instruction and correctly sets `lr` within the validation routine, because the value of `lr` for indirect calls is dependent on whether the call is an external or internal call. For external calls we let `lr` point to a specialized code piece of *MoCFI* to recognize when external (indirect) library calls returned (see also Appendix A).

structions: the original branch (`POP {R4-R7,PC}`) and the instruction preceding the branch (`MOV R1,R2`). To preserve the program's semantics, we execute the latter one at the beginning of our trampolines (step 1 in Trampoline 1).

Dispatching through exception handling. However, replacing 2 THUMB instructions is not possible if the instruction preceding the branch references the program counter or is itself a branch. For instance, `LDR R2, [PC,#16]` in Figure 3 uses the current value of `pc` to load a pointer. Note that such instructions are not allowed on Intel x86. In such scenarios, we use an entirely different approach: upon initialization, we register an iOS exception handler for illegal instructions. The dispatcher instruction is then simply an arbitrary illegal instruction that will trigger our exception handler. Since this technique induces additional performance overhead, we only use it for exceptional cases. To further reduce the use of the exception handler, one could calculate the address from which `pc` is loaded in the static analysis phase and replace the relevant load instruction with a new memory load instruction which could be placed at the beginning of the trampoline.

Note that our exception handler forwards all exceptions not caused by *MoCFI*. Furthermore, by monitoring the exception handling API, we can ensure the position of our handler in the exception chain.

5.2.2. Runtime Module: CFI Enforcement

An abstract view of the runtime module is shown in Figure 4: it mainly consists of dedicated validation routines for each branch type, where each type is represented by a rectangle on the left side of Figure 4. The validation routines have to validate the target of every branch to prevent the application from targeting a BBL beyond the scope of the CFG and the current execution path. Obviously, each branch target requires a different type of validation, as we will describe in the following.

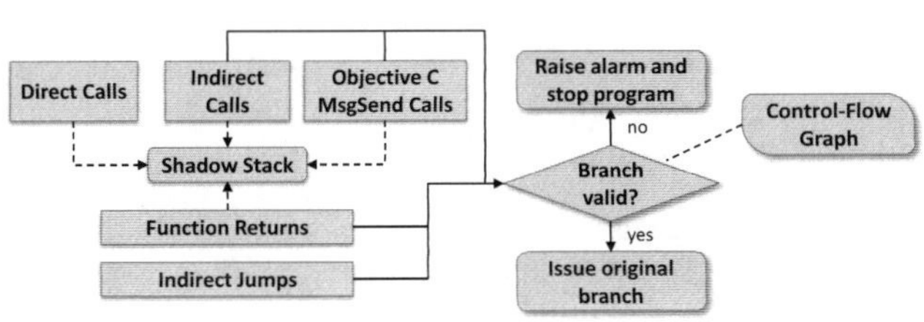

Figure 4. Overview of the runtime module

Function Calls and Returns. To prevent return-oriented attacks, we monitor all function calls and returns, and apply the *shadow stack paradigm* [12]: whenever the program invokes a subroutine (through a direct, indirect, or dispatcher call), we copy the return address on a dedicated shadow stack. Upon function return, we compare the return address the program wants to use to the address stored on our shadow stack. Since function calls (through `BL` or `BLX`) automatically store the return address in `lr`, we simply need to push `lr` onto the shadow stack. Further, we maintain a separate shadow stack for each execution thread to support multi-threaded programs. Upon function return, we determine the return address the program aims to use and retrieve the required stack pointer offset from the patchfile.

As mentioned in Section 3.3, return instructions can be implemented in many different ways on ARM, and often involve the loading of several general-purpose registers. We ensure that all side-effects are correctly handled by issuing the original return at the end of the trampoline (as described in Section 5.2.1).

Indirect Jumps and Calls. The possible jump targets for indirect jumps and calls have either been calculated during static analysis (see Section 5.1) or remain completely unknown. In the first case, the pre-calculated values have to be compared to the outcome of the instruction that *MoCFI* intercepted. In the most complex and versatile form, the instruction is of the form `LDR pc, [rX,rY,LSL#z]` which loads `pc` according to the given register values: $pc \leftarrow r_x + r_y \cdot 2^z$. Consequently, *MoCFI* checks the current value of the registers according to the above equation to match one of the saved, valid jump targets. The information which registers are used by the indirect jump is saved in our patchfile. However, for simpler indirect jumps such as `MOV pc,rX` and indirect calls (`BLX rX`) we simply have to check the content of `rX`. In case the required information cannot be calculated in advance during the static analysis phase, we use heuristics (see Section 5.1) to ensure that the jump targets reside inside the scope of the current function, or for indirect calls, target a valid function prologue.

Objective C MsgSend Calls. Dispatcher calls via the `objc_msgSend` function work like indirect calls. However, instead of a register, they use the function's name (*selector*) and *class instance* to refer to a function's implementation address (see Section 5.1). We trust the implementation of `objc_msgSend` and do not check whether it resolved the correct address. We rather check the supplied parameters *selector* and *class instance*. Both is necessary as the emitted code by GCC usually de-references a register and passes its de-referenced value to `objc_msgSend`. However, the referenced memory is writable and could be overwritten by an adversary. The selector is a simple zero-terminated C-string. Checking whether the selector is still correct can be verified by comparing the original string extracted during static analysis to the current string *selector* points to.

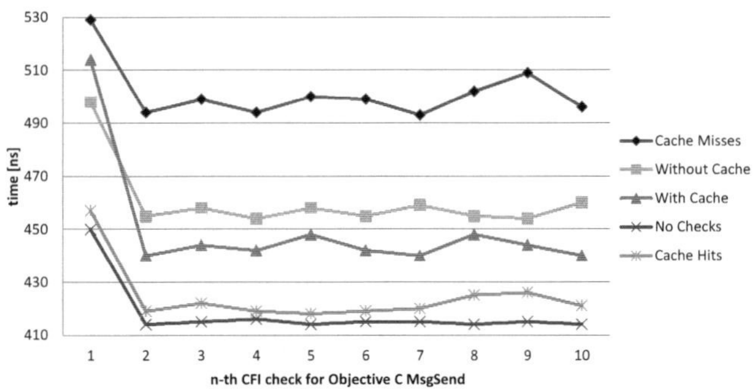

Figure 5. Objective C string comparison optimization using a Cache

We enhanced the performance by introducing a string cache (see Figure 5). This is possible as the strings themselves are write-protected. This enables us to cache the result of the comparison based on a pointer to that string.

For the class instance checking, the name of the class has been extracted by the static analysis. This name is of the form `_OBJC_CLASS_$_NSObject`, where `NSObject` is the class name. The *Runtime Module* obtains the load address of every symbol by using `dlsym()`. The class instance parameter supplied to `objc_msgSend` must then either directly point to that symbol address (static class) or is an instance of that class. For class instances, the first word (32 bit pointer) points to the symbol address of the corresponding class.

6. Discussion and Security Considerations

Our solution adheres to the goal of detecting deviations from the control-flow at runtime from the known-good control-flow. Since iOS enforces $W \oplus X$, a memory page cannot be writable and executable at the same time. Hence, it suffices to check branch targets that can be changed during runtime as they depend on the value of a variable. These include indirect branches and returns from function calls, as they use an address popped from a potentially tampered stack. As we check each such instruction, an adversary cannot subvert the control-flow without *MoCFI* noticing it. However, not all valid, known-good targets can be calculated in advance during the static analysis phase. If this is not the case, we need to apply heuristics to hinder (or at least minimize) their impact. Fortunately, for the majority of tested applications, the indirect branches are used in conjunction with jump tables (see Section 5.1), and can be resolved during the static analysis phase. Moreover, our static tools could be extended by enhanced backtracking techniques to limit the set of possible branch targets. However, the design of sophisticated static tools is not within the scope of this paper, instead our focus is a framework that provides the foundation for system-wide and efficient CFI enforcement on smartphone platforms with an underlying ARM processor.

Since *MoCFI* performs binary rewriting after the iOS loader has verified the application signature, our scheme is compatible to application signing. On the other hand, our load-time module is not directly compatible to the iOS CSE (code signing enforcement) runtime model (see Section 2.2). CSE prohibits any code generation at runtime on non-jailbroken devices, except if an application has been granted the *dynamic-signing* entitlement. To tackle this issue, one could assign the *dynamic-signing* entitlement to applications that should be executed under the protection of *MoCFI*. On the one hand, this is a reasonable approach, since the general security goal of CFI is to protect benign applications rather than malicious ones. Further, the *dynamic-signing* entitlement will not give an adversary the opportunity to circumvent *MoCFI* by overwriting existing control-flow checks in benign applications. In order to do so, he would have to mount a control-flow attack beforehand that would be detected by *MoCFI*. On the other hand, when *dynamic-signing* is in place, benign applications may unintentionally download new (potentially) malicious code, or malicious applications may be accidentally granted the *dynamic-signing* entitlement (since they should run under protection of *MoCFI*) and afterwards perform malicious actions. To address these problems, one could constrain binary rewriting to the load-time phase of an application, so that the *dynamic-signing* entitlement is not needed while the application is executing. Further, new sandbox policies can be specified that only allow the *MoCFI* library to issue the `mmap` call to replace existing code, e.g., the internal page flags of the affected memory page are not changed, or their values are correctly reset after *MoCFI* completed the binary rewriting process.

Finally, special care must be taken that an adversary cannot tamper with the *MoCFI* library and thus bypass *MoCFI*. Since our library is small in size, the probability for exploitable vulnerabilities is very low. Given the small code base, we could also apply code verification tools.

Limitations. Similar to CFI for Intel x86, our current implementation does not detect attacks exploiting exception handlers: an adversary can overwrite pointers to an exception handler and then deliberately cause an exception (e.g., by corrupting a pointer before it is de-referenced). This is possible because GCC pushes these pointers on the stack on demand. We stress that this is rather a shortcoming of the iOS operating system — similar problems have already been solved on other platforms, such as on Windows [31]. Therefore, we encourage Apple to port these techniques to iOS.

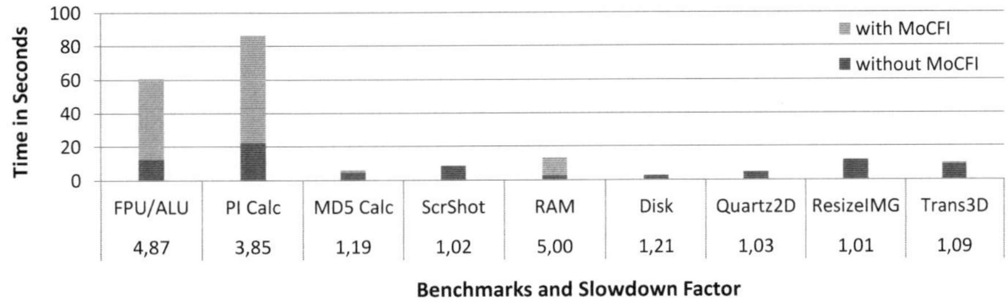

Figure 6. Gensystek Lite Benchmarks

As already mentioned in Section 5, *MoCFI* does currently not protect shared libraries, which an adversary may exploit to launch a control-flow attack. However, extending *MoCFI* accordingly is straightforward, because we already overcame the conceptional obstacles. Note that Apple also explicitly discourages developers to employ shared libraries. Hence, all loaded libraries are typically from the operating system and Objective C frameworks.

Consequently, we currently disable the return check if an external library calls a function that resides in the main application. Therefore, *MoCFI* registers when execution is redirected to a library and disables the return address check for functions that are directly invoked by the shared library. However, note that this can be easily fixed by either applying our trampoline approach to function prologues (i.e., pushing the return address on the shadow stack at function entry) or by applying *MoCFI* to shared libraries.

7. Evaluation

In order to evaluate the performance of *MoCFI*, we applied it to an iOS benchmark tool (called Gensystek Lite[2]), applied it to a full-recursive own developed quicksort algorithm, and performed micro benchmarks to measure the overhead for each type of branch. As we described in Section 6, we apply *MoCFI* to the main application code, and not to the libraries. However, the benchmark tools we apply perform most part of the computation within the application.

Figure 6 shows the results for the Gensystek Lite application, where the slowdown factor for each individual benchmark is shown at bottom of the x-axis. Remarkably, the FPU/ALU, PI calculation, and the RAM (memory read-/write) benchmarks add the highest overhead. However, their slowdown is still reasonable (3.85x and 5x, respectively) considering that FPU/ALU and PI calculations are computationally intensive tasks. The overhead (slowdown greater than factor 1) for the remaining benchmarks is very low and ranges between 1% to 21%.

[2]http://www.ooparts-universe.com/apps/app_gensystek.html

n	Without *MoCFI*	With *MoCFI*
100	0.047 ms	0.432 ms
1000	0.473 ms	6.186 ms
10000	6.725 ms	81.163 ms

Table 1. Quicksort

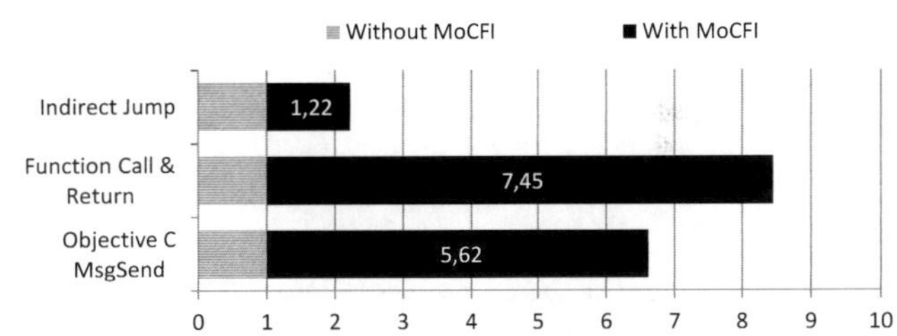

Figure 7. Overhead for each branch type

In order to approximate an upper boundary for performance penalties, we evaluated *MoCFI* by running a quicksort algorithm. Our implemented algorithm makes use of recursion and continuously calls a compare function which consists of only 4 instructions and one *return*. Therefore, *MoCFI* frequently performs a control-flow check in this worst-case scenario. Nevertheless it performs quite well and needs 81ms for $n = 10,000$ (see Table 1).

In order to evaluate the overhead of an instruction that has been replaced by a CFI check, we measured the execution time of three typical instructions and their replacement by *MoCFI* (see Figure 7). The calculation of the overhead per replaced instruction is depicted in Figure 8. For the exemplary case of *Function Calls and Returns*, the ac-

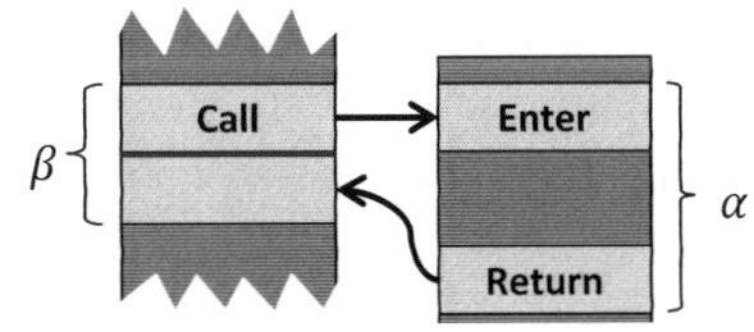

Figure 8. Overhead calculation

n	50	100	500
ψ **(Indirect Jump)**	2.4%	1.2%	0.2%
ψ **(Func. C. & R.)**	14.6%	7.4%	1.5%
ψ **(ObjC MsgSend)**	11.0%	5.6%	1.1%

Table 2. Total overhead ψ

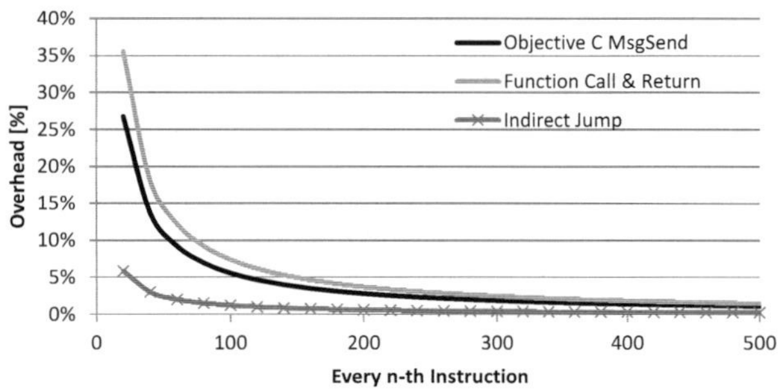

Figure 9. Average overhead

tual function bodies (α) are subtracted from the time measurement between *call* and *return* (β). The actual execution time is therefore $\beta - \alpha$. When running with *MoCFI*, the measurements (α' and β', respectively) are set in relation to the measurement without *MoCFI*. Hence, the instruction slowdown factor φ for one function replaced by *MoCFI* is $\varphi = \frac{\beta'-\alpha'}{\beta-\alpha}$. For our tests, all the measurements have been conducted $10,000$ times and averaged. However, in a typical program, instructions that have to be checked by *MoCFI* are surrounded by other instructions. For n instructions in between, *MoCFI* only has to be called every $(n+1)$-th instruction. The total slowdown ψ is therefore $\psi = \frac{n+\varphi}{n+1}$. The overhead ($\psi - 1$) as a function of n (instructions between CFI checks) is plotted in Figure 9. An exemplary table with exact values resulting from of $n = 50, n = 100$ and $n = 500$ instructions between CFI checks is depicted in Table 2.

Moreover, we applied *MoCFI* to several popular iOS applications, among others Facebook, Minesweeper, TexasHoldem, and Gowalla. Our experiments showed that *MoCFI* does not induce any notable overhead while the applications execute. Further, *MoCFI* induces an acceptable overhead at load-time: e.g., for the Facebook application (code size 2.3MB; 33,647 calls; 5,988 returns; 20 indirect jumps) and TexasHoldem (2.8MB; 62,576 calls; 4,864 returns; 1 indirect jump) our rewriting engine required less than half a second to rewrite the entire application.

On the other hand, our tests on iOS applications revealed that *MoCFI* raises certain false positives. A remarkable false positive occurs for large jump tables: For theses cases, the compiler calls dedicated switch functions that calculate the address to be used as jump target, where the particular function call is realized via a `BLX` instruction. However, these switch functions never return; instead they use the value of `lr` (loaded via `BLX`) as base pointer to the jump table, and use an indirect jump after the target has been calculated (i.e, a return to the initial call is missing). In order to avoid this false positive, *MoCFI* could be extended if the bytes succeeding the `BLX` are belonging to a jump table. If so, *MoCFI* could enforce a different check in the switch functions: rather than checking the return address, we check if the last indirect jump of the switch function targets an address that is used in the jump table. We aim to integrate additional handling of exceptional cases in our future. In general, one can apply similar policies as mentioned above, or exception handling rules as discussed in [16].

Mitigating Advanced Attacks. In order to demonstrate that *MoCFI* detects advanced attacks that hijack the control-flow of an application, we adopted a return-oriented programming (ROP) attack presented by Iozzo et al. [25] (developed for iOS v2.2.1) to iOS v4.3.1 and extended it in such a way that it bypasses memory randomization on iOS. Specifically, our sample attack exploits a buffer overflow vulnerability and forces the device to beep and vibrate. When protecting the vulnerable application with *MoCFI*, the attack fails and we successfully prevent an exploitation attempt. We implemented the exploit and used techniques similar to *GOT dereferencing* [45, 22] to bypass ASLR on iOS. Since constructing iOS exploits is not the main objective of this paper, we refer the interested reader to Appendix B where we describe our vulnerable program and the payload we used.

8. Related Work

Control-flow (runtime) attacks are a prevalent attack vector since about two decades and a lot of research has been performed to either exploit such vulnerabilities or to find ways to protect against them. In the following, we focus on defense strategies to prevent control-flow attacks and discuss how previous works relates to the approach presented in this paper.

Control-Flow Integrity. The basic principle of monitoring the control-flow of an application in order to enforce a specific security policy has been introduced by Kiriansky et al. in their seminal work on *program shepherding* [29]. This technique allows arbitrary restrictions to be placed on control transfers and code origins, and the authors showed how such an approach can be used to confine a given application. A more fine-grained analysis was presented by Abadi et al., who proposed *Control Flow Integrity* enforcement [1]. We use CFI as the basic technique and show that this principle can be applied on the ARM processor architecture to protect smartphones against control-flow attacks.

Several architectural differences and peculiarities of mobile operating systems complicate our approach and we had to overcome several obstacles. XFI [2] is an extension to CFI that adds further integrity constraints for example on memory and the stack at the cost of a higher performance overhead. The current prototype of *MoCFI* does not implement these additional constraints, but our framework could be extended in the future to also support such constraints.

In contrast to the original CFI work and our *MoCFI*, *Write Integrity Testing* (WIT) [3] also detects non-control-data attacks. This is achieved by interprocedural points-to analysis which outputs the CFG and computes the set of objects that can be written by each instruction in the program. Based on the result of the points-to analysis, WIT assigns a color to each object and each write instruction. WIT enforces write-integrity by only allowing the write operation if the originating instruction and the target object share the same color. As a second line of defense, it also enforces CFI to check if an indirect call targets a valid execution path in the CFG. However, WIT does not prevent return-oriented attacks, because it does not check function returns. Moreover, it requires access to source code. In contrast, *MoCFI* can protect an application against advanced attacks and our tool works directly on the binary level.

HyperSafe [42] protects x86 hypervisors by enforcing hypervisor code integrity and CFI. Similar to *MoCFI*, it instruments indirect branch instructions to validate if their branch target follows a valid execution path in the CFG. However, HyperSafe only validates if the return address is within a set of possible return addresses which has been calculated offline. In contrast to HyperSafe, *MoCFI* enforces fine-grained return address checks, and does not require source code. Moreover, the dynamic nature of smartphone applications, prevents us from calculating return addresses offline.

Native Client (NaCl) [46, 36] provides a sandbox for untrusted native code in web browsers. In particular, NaCl enforces software fault isolation (SFI [41]) and constraints branches to an aligned address. However, this still allows an adversary to subvert the control-flow (as long as the target address is aligned). Moreover, NaCl does not support THUMB code (which is main instruction set on smartphones) and requires recompilation of applications as well.

In a very recent work Zeng et al. [47] showed that CFI combined with static analysis enables the enforcement of efficient data sandboxing. In particular, the presented scheme provides confidentiality of critical memory regions by constraining memory reads to uncritical data regions. This is achieved by placing guard zones before and after the uncritical data area. The solution has been implemented in the LLVM compiler infrastructure (similar to the NaCl compiler [46, 36]) and targets the Intel x86 platform.

Orthogonal Defenses. Many techniques to detect or prevent control-flow attacks have been proposed in the last few years such as for example stack canaries [15], return address stacks [12, 21], and pointer encryption [14]. Such techniques are orthogonal to CFI and focus on specific aspects of exploits. As a result, an attacker might find novel ways to bypass them in order to exploit a given vulnerability.

9. Conclusion and Future Work

In this paper, we focus on the problem of mitigating runtime attacks on modern smartphone platforms. This class of attacks on software is still one of the major threats we need to deal with and we recently saw several runtime attacks against smartphones. We showed how the principle of *control-flow integrity* (CFI) enforcement can be applied on the ARM platform. Our solution tackles several unique challenges of ARM and smartphones operating systems, which we discussed in detail. We solved all challenges and implemented a complete CFI enforcement framework for Apple iOS. Our evaluation shows that we can successfully mitigate even advanced attacks. Moreover, our performance measurements show that *MoCFI* is efficient: it performs well in worst-case scenarios (e.g., computationally intensive algorithms such as quicksort) and does not induce any notable performance overhead when applied to popular iOS applications.

Our current prototype implementation protects the main application binary against control-flow attacks. Therefore, we aim to apply *MoCFI* to shared iOS libraries in our future work, which should be straightforward since there are no conceptional obstacles to overcome. Besides working on a formal analysis along the lines of the original CFI proposal [1], we are currently investigating the possibility of runtime attestation (a trusted computing mechanism to attest the software state of remote platforms) and enhanced application sandboxing based on CFI enforcement.

Acknowledgments

This work has been supported by the Ministry of Economic Affairs and Energy of the State of North Rhine-Westphalia (grant 315-43-02/2-005-WFBO-009), the Federal Ministry of Education and Research (grant 01BY1020 MobWorm), and by the European Union's Seventh Framework Programme (FP7/2007-2013) under grant agreement n°257243 (TClouds project: `http://www.tclouds-project.eu`). This work was also partially supported by the ONR under grant N000140911042 and by the National Science Foundation (NSF) under grants CNS-0845559, CNS-0905537, and CNS-0716095.

References

[1] M. Abadi, M. Budiu, U. Erlingsson, and J. Ligatti. Control-Flow Integrity: Principles, Implementations, and Applications. In *ACM Conference on Computer and Communications Security (CCS)*, 2005.

[2] M. Abadi, M. Budiu, U. Erlingsson, G. C. Necula, and M. Vrable. XFI: Software Guards for System Address Spaces. In *USENIX Symposium on Operating Systems Design and Implementation (OSDI)*, 2006.

[3] P. Akritidis, C. Cadar, C. Raiciu, M. Costa, and M. Castro. Preventing Memory Error Exploits with WIT. *IEEE Symposium on Security and Privacy*, 2008.

[4] Aleph One. Smashing the Stack for Fun and Profit. *Phrack Magazine*, 49(14), 1996.

[5] Anonymous. Once upon a free(). *Phrack Magazine*, 57(9), 2001.

[6] Apple Inc. Manual Page of `dyld` - the dynamic link editor. `http://developer.apple.com/library/mac/#documentation/Darwin/Reference/ManPages/man1/dyld.1.html`, 2011.

[7] Apple Inc. Manual Page of `mmap` - allocate memory, or map files or devices into memory. `http://developer.apple.com/library/mac/#documentation/Darwin/Reference/ManPages/man2/mmap.2.html`, 2011.

[8] ARM Limited. Procedure Call Standard for the ARM Architecture. `http://infocenter.arm.com/help/topic/com.arm.doc.ihi0042d/IHI0042D_aapcs.pdf`, 2009.

[9] blexim. Basic Integer Overflows. *Phrack Magazine*, 60(10), 2002.

[10] E. Buchanan, R. Roemer, H. Shacham, and S. Savage. When Good Instructions Go Bad: Generalizing Return-Oriented Programming to RISC. In *ACM Conference on Computer and Communications Security (CCS)*, 2008.

[11] S. Checkoway, L. Davi, A. Dmitrienko, A.-R. Sadeghi, H. Shacham, and M. Winandy. Return-oriented Programming Without Returns. In *ACM Conference on Computer and Communications Security (CCS)*, 2010.

[12] T. Chiueh and F.-H. Hsu. RAD: A Compile-Time Solution to Buffer Overflow Attacks. In *International Conference on Distributed Computing Systems (ICDCS)*, 2001.

[13] comex. `http://www.jailbreakme.com//#`.

[14] C. Cowan, S. Beattie, J. Johansen, and P. Wagle. Pointguard^{TM}: Protecting Pointers From Buffer Overflow Vulnerabilities. In *USENIX Security Symposium*, 2003.

[15] C. Cowan, C. Pu, D. Maier, H. Hintony, J. Walpole, P. Bakke, S. Beattie, A. Grier, P. Wagle, and Q. Zhang. StackGuard: Automatic Adaptive Detection and Prevention of Buffer-Overflow Attacks. In *USENIX Security Symposium*, 1998.

[16] L. Davi, A.-R. Sadeghi, and M. Winandy. ROPdefender: A Detection Tool to Defend Against Return-Oriented Programming Attacks. In *ACM Symposium on Information, Computer and Communications Security (ASIACCS)*, 2011.

[17] J. Duart. Objective-C helper script. `https://github.com/zynamics/objc-helper-plugin-ida`, 2010.

[18] A. Edwards, A. Srivastava, and H. Vo. Vulcan Binary Transformation in a Distributed Environment. Technical Report MSR-TR-2001-50, Microsoft Research, 2001.

[19] M. Egele, C. Kruegel, E. Kirda, and G. Vigna. PiOS: Detecting Privacy Leaks in iOS Applications. In *Symposium on Network and Distributed System Security (NDSS)*, 2011.

[20] A. Francillon and C. Castelluccia. Code Injection Attacks on Harvard-Architecture Devices. In *ACM Conference on Computer and Communications Security (CCS)*, 2008.

[21] M. Frantzen and M. Shuey. StackGhost: Hardware Facilitated Stack Protection. In *USENIX Security Symposium*, 2001.

[22] G. Fresi Roglia, L. Martignoni, R. Paleari, and D. Bruschi. Surgically Returning to Randomized lib(c). In *Annual Computer Security Applications Conference (ACSAC)*, 2009.

[23] gera. Advances in Format String Exploitation. *Phrack Magazine*, 59(12), 2002.

[24] R. Hund, T. Holz, and F. C. Freiling. Return-Oriented Rootkits: Bypassing Kernel Code Integrity Protection Mechanisms. In *USENIX Security Symposium*, 2009.

[25] V. Iozzo and C. Miller. Fun and Games with Mac OS X and iPhone Payloads. In *Black Hat Europe*, 2009.

[26] V. Iozzo and R.-P. Weinmann. PWN2OWN contest. `http://blog.zynamics.com/2010/03/24/ralf-philipp-weinmann-vincenzo-iozzo-own-the-iphone-at-pwn2own/`, 2010.

[27] M. Keith. Android 2.0-2.1 Reverse Shell Exploit, 2010. `http://www.exploit-db.com/exploits/15423/`.

[28] I. King. Will Intel finally crack smartphones? `http://www.businessweek.com/magazine/content/11_25/b4233041946230.htm`, 2011.

[29] V. Kiriansky, D. Bruening, and S. P. Amarasinghe. Secure Execution via Program Shepherding. In *USENIX Security Symposium*, 2002.

[30] T. Kornau. Return Oriented Programming for the ARM Architecture. Master's thesis, Ruhr-University Bochum, 2009.

[31] Microsoft. The `/SAFESEH` compiler flag. `http://msdn.microsoft.com/en-us/library/9a89h429%28v=vs.80%29.aspx`, 2011.

[32] C. Miller and D. D. Zovi. *The Mac Hacker's Handbook*. Wiley Publishing, 2009.

[33] C. Mulliner and C. Miller. Injecting SMS Messages Into Smart Phones for Security Analysis. In *USENIX Workshop on Offensive Technologies (WOOT)*, 2009.

[34] Nergal. The Advanced return-into-lib(c) Exploits: PaX Case Study. *Phrack Magazine*, 58(4), 2001.

[35] B. Prince. Security Expert Evades Apple's Mobile Security Measures via iOS Vulnerability. `http://s1.securityweek.com/apple-security-expert-evades-apples-mobile-security-measures-ios-vulnerability`, 2011.

[36] D. Sehr, R. Muth, C. Biffle, V. Khimenko, E. Pasko, K. Schimpf, B. Yee, and B. Chen. Adapting Software Fault Isolation to Contemporary CPU Architectures. In *USENIX Security Symposium*, 2010.

[37] H. Shacham. The Geometry of Innocent Flesh on the Bone: Return-into-libc Without Function Calls (on the x86). In *ACM Conference on Computer and Communications Security (CCS)*, 2007.

[38] H. Shacham, E. jin Goh, N. Modadugu, B. Pfaff, and D. Boneh. On the Effectiveness of Address-space Randomization. In *ACM Conference on Computer and Communications Security (CCS)*, 2004.

[39] Solar Designer. "return-to-libc" attack. Bugtraq, 1997.

[40] A. Sotirov and M. Dowd. Bypassing Browser Memory Protections in Windows Vista - Setting back browser security by 10 years. `http://www.phreedom.org/research/bypassing-browser-memory-protections/`, 2008.

[41] R. Wahbe, S. Lucco, T. E. Anderson, and S. L. Graham. Efficient Software-based Fault Isolation. *ACM SIGOPS Operating Systems Review*, 27(5), 1993.

[42] Z. Wang and X. Jiang. HyperSafe: A Lightweight Approach to Provide Lifetime Hypervisor Control-Flow Integrity. In *IEEE Symposium on Security and Privacy*, 2010.

[43] R.-P. Weinmann. All Your Baseband Are Belong To Us. hack.lu, 2010. `http://2010.hack.lu/archive/2010/Weinmann-All-Your-Baseband-Are-Belong-To-Us-slides.pdf`.

[44] S. Winwood and M. Chakravarty. Secure Untrusted Binaries – Provably! In *3rd international workshop on formal aspects in security and trust*, 2006.

[45] R. Wojtczuk. Defeating Solar Designer's Non-executable Stack Patch. `http://insecure.org/sploits/non-executable.stack.problems.html`, 1998.

[46] B. Yee, D. Sehr, G. Dardyk, J. B. Chen, R. Muth, T. Ormandy, S. Okasaka, N. Narula, and N. Fullagar. Native Client: A Sandbox for Portable, Untrusted x86 Native Code. *IEEE Symposium on Security and Privacy*, 2009.

[47] B. Zeng, G. Tan, and G. Morrisett. Combining control-flow integrity and static analysis for efficient and validated data sandboxing. In *ACM Conference on Computer and Communications Security (CCS)*. ACM, 2011.

[48] D. D. Zovi. Apple iOS Security Evaluation: Vulnerability Analysis and Data Encryption. In *Black Hat USA*, 2011.

APPENDIX

In the following, we describe the implementation of our trampolines, and present a return-oriented programming payload that ASLR on iOS.

A. Trampoline Implementation

Listing 2 and 3 show the implementation of our ARM and THUMB trampoline for all indirect branches (i.e., indirect calls / jumps, and returns). In contrast to the ARM trampoline, the instruction which precedes the (replaced) indirect branch is placed on the top of the THUMB trampoline. The subsequent instructions save the registers on the stack, load the pointer to the patch structure into `r1`, and the pointer to the specific validation routine in `r2`. Furthermore, `sp` is loaded into `r0` so that the invoked validation routine can access the register set of the current execution state. Afterwards, the `BLX` instruction is used to invoke the validation routine. Upon function return, all registers are reset to their original state. Finally, the original branch instruction is executed. Note that we avoid setting `lr` for indirect calls[3] by transforming it to an indirect `BX` jump. Otherwise, the called function would return to our trampoline, and not to the original caller.

```
char customThumbTrampoline[] = {
  0x00,0xbf,0x00,0xbf,  // prev. instruction
  0x2d,0xe9,0xff,0x5f,  // push.w {r0-r12,lr}
  0x68,0x46,            // mov r0,sp
  0x03,0x49,            // ldr.w r1,[pc,12]
  0x03,0x4a,            // ldr.w r2,[pc,12]
  0x90,0x47,            // blx r2
  0xbd,0xe8,0xff,0x5f,  // pop.w {r0-r12,lr}
  0x00,0x00,0x00,0x00,  // orig. instruction
  0x00,0x00,0x00,0x00,  // *patch structure
  0x00,0x00,0x00,0x00   // *validation routine
};
```

Listing 2. THUMB Trampoline

```
ulong customARMTrampoline[] = {
  0xe92d5fff, // stmfd sp!,{r0-r12,lr}
  0xe1a0000d, // mov r0,sp
  0xe59f1010, // ldr r1,[pc,16]
  0xe59f2010, // ldr r2,[pc,16]
  0xe12fff32, // blx r2
  0xe50d0004, // str r0,[sp,-4]
  0xe8bd5fff, // ldmfd sp!,{r0-r12,lr}
  0x00000000, // orig. instruction
  0x00000000, // *patch structure
  0x00000000, // *validation routine
};
```

Listing 3. ARM Trampoline

Our generic trampolines for direct calls are implemented in ARM (see Listing 4 and 5). Note that this does not raise an interworking problem since direct calls are overwritten with a `BLX` instruction.

```
long ExternalCallTrampoline[] = {
  0xe92d5fff, // stmfd sp!,{r0-r12,lr}
  0xe1a0000d, // mov r0,sp
  0xe59f1028, // ldr r1,[pc,#40] ; -> validate
  0xe12fff31, // blx r1
  0xe50d0004, // str r0,[sp,#-4]
  0xe8bd5fff, // ldmfd sp!,{r0-r12,lr}
  0xe1a0e00f, // mov lr,pc
  0xe51df03c, // ldr pc,[sp,#-60];
  0xe92d000f, // push {r0,r1,r2,r3}
  0xe59f1010, // ldr r1,[pc,#16] ; -> get_lr
  0xe12fff31, // blx r1
  0xe1a0e000, // mov lr,r0
  0xe8bd000f, // pop {r0,r1,r2,r3}
  0xe12fff1e, // bx lr
  0x00000000, // *validation routine
  0x00000000, // *get_lr
};
```

Listing 4. External Call Trampoline

[3] However, our validation routine correctly sets `lr` by changing the `lr` value that is stored on the stack (because it has been pushed by the second instruction of the THUMB trampoline).

```
ulong InternalCallTrampoline[] = {
   0xe92d5fff, // stmfd   sp!,{r0-r12,lr}
   0xe1a0000d, // mov     r0, sp
   0xe59f100c, // ldr     r1, [pc,#12]
   0xe12fff31, // blx     r1
   0xe50d0004, // str     r0, [sp,#-4]
   0xe8bd5fff, // ldmfd   sp!, {r0-r12,lr}
   0xe51df03c, // ldr     pc, [sp,#-60]
   0x00000000, // *validation routine
};
```

Listing 5. Internal Call Trampoline

The start of both trampolines is similar to the aforementioned custom trampolines: storing all registers, loading the required parameters, and the final call to the validation routine. Our validation routines for direct calls save the return address, check the parameters for Objective C `msgSend` calls, and finally provide the original branch target in `r0`. This value is stored on the stack, and after resetting all registers, loaded into `pc`. As mentioned in Section 6 calls to external (shared libraries) require in our current implementation specific handling: we store the return address on an external shadow stack and change `lr` so that it points to our trampoline. Hence, when the external function returns, it returns to our trampoline, where we invoke the *get_lr* to retrieve the original return address. Note that the *get_lr* function is also invoked when an external library function returns that has been originally invoked via an indirect call. Therefore our validation for indirect calls checks whether the branch target resides in the same code segment or targets a library function. For the latter one we change `lr` in such a way that *get_lr* is invoked after the library function returns.

B. Control-Flow Attacks Against iOS

In the following we describe how we constructed a sample iOS exploit that circumvents memory randomization and let the device beep and vibrate.

The vulnerable program is realized as follows:

```
FILE *sFile;
void foo(char *path, file_length) {
   char buf[8];
   sFile = fopen(path, ``r'');
   fgets(buf, file_length, sFile);
   fclose(sFile);
}
```

The shown *foo()* function simply opens a file, where the file path and length are provided as parameters to the function. Further, via *fgets()* it reads as many characters as specified by the `file_length` parameter, and finally copies them into the local buffer `buf`. However, *fgets()* does not check the bounds of the buffer `buf`. This in turn allows an adversary to divert the control-flow by overflowing the buffer. This can be achieved by providing a file which length's exceeds the buffer's size (here more than 8 Bytes). Hence, the adversary can overwrite the return address of *foo()*, and inject a ROP payload on the stack. In particular, our constructed ROP gadget chain invokes (1) *AudioServicesPlaySystemSound(0x3ea)* to play a sound and vibrate the phone, and (2) *exit(0)* to close the application. However, our ROP exploit will only succeed if it bypasses ASLR.

Bypassing ASLR on iOS. iOS offers two levels of ASLR protection [48]: (1) full ASLR, and (2) ASLR only for shared libraries and the program heap. The former one randomizes each code and data segment of the program. On the other hand, it can only be applied to applications that are compiled as position independent executables (PIE). While built-in applications such as the Safari Browser are compiled as PIEs, third-party applications typically do not support PIE [48]. Hence, for these applications, iOS only randomizes the base addresses of shared libraries, but omits the randomization of the program binary, and dynamic areas such as the stack. Moreover, the iOS linker `dyld` is always loaded at a fixed location. In the following, we focus on applications that do not support PIE. Nevertheless, control-flow attacks can be also launched against PIE applications, if an adversary finds and exploits a memory disclosure vulnerability.

Our target function *AudioServicesPlaySystemSound()* is from the `AudioToolbox` library that iOS randomizes after each device boot for PIE and non-PIE applications. We successfully adopted GOT dereferencing and GOT overwriting [22] techniques which have been recently deployed on Intel x86 (Linux) to resolve an absolute address of a function the adversary wants to execute. In the following, we briefly describe how principles of GOT dereferencing can be applied to ARM and iOS.

GOT dereferencing exploits a common data leakage problem of the *Global Offset Table* (GOT). Typically, the GOT contains references to library function addresses the program aims to use. iOS uses a very similar data structure called indirect symbol table. By dereferencing a single entry of the indirect symbol table, we can obtain an absolute (i.e., runtime) address of a function, which in turn allows us to calculate the randomization offset by subtracting the static address of the same function. For our specific attack, we read the absolute address of *fgets()* and subtract its static address. We store the calculated offset value into the indirect symbol table entry for *fgets()*, from where it can be loaded each time the offset is needed. We calculate the absolute address of *AudioServicesPlaySystemSound()* by adding the randomization offset to the static address of this function, and redirect the control-flow to the computed address. Note that we use the non-randomized code base of the static `dyld` library to compute the randomization offset and to resolve absolute addresses of functions (or instruction sequences) from randomized libraries.

Payload and Instruction Sequences. To construct our malicious program, we leverage six different instruction sequences, while several of them are used more than once. The execution order of the instructions sequences is shown in Listing 6.

```
0x2fe16a66: ldma sp!, {r7, lr}
0x2fe16a6a: add sp, #12
0x2fe16a6c: bx lr

0x2fe06528: pop {r1,r3,r5,r7,pc}

0x2fe1e4c8: pop {r0,r4,r5,r7,pc}

0x2fe0efc2: ldr r1, [r1, #0]
0x2fe0efc4: adds r0,r0,r1
0x2fe0efc6: bx lr

0x2fe06528: pop {r1,r3,r5,r7,pc}

0x2fe0f0e4: str r0, [r1, #20]
0x2fe0f0e6: bx lr

0x2fe06528: pop {r1,r3,r5,r7,pc}

0x2fe1e4c8: pop {r0,r4,r5,r7,pc}

0x2fe0efc2: ldr r1, [r1, #0]
0x2fe0efc4: adds r0,r0,r1
0x2fe0efc6: bx lr

0x2fe06528: pop {r1,r3,r5,r7,pc}

0x2fe0ec40: mov r12, r0
0x2fe0ec44: pop {r0,r1,r2,r3,r7,lr}
0x2fe0ec48: add sp, sp, #8
0x2fe0ec4c: bx r12

0x2fe1e4c8: pop {r0,r4,r5,r7,pc}
```

Listing 6. Instruction Sequences

```
0000: 41 41 41 41  41 41 41 41  30 30 30 30
000C: 67 ba e1 2f  30 30 30 30  29 65 e0 2f
0018: 41 41 41 41  41 41 41 41  41 41 41 41
0024: 10 30 00 00  41 41 41 41  41 41 41 41
0030: 30 30 30 30  c8 e4 e1 2f  1f 61 0c cc
003C: 41 41 41 41  41 41 41 41  30 30 30 30
0048: c3 ef e0 2f  fc 2f 00 00  41 41 41 41
0054: 41 41 41 41  30 30 30 30  e5 f0 e0 2f
0060: 10 30 00 00  41 41 41 41  41 41 41 41
006C: 30 30 30 30  c8 e4 e1 2f  cd ca 8a 33
0078: 41 41 41 41  41 41 41 41  30 30 30 30
0084: c3 ef e0 2f  41 41 41 41  41 41 41 41
0090: 41 41 41 41  30 30 30 30  40 ec e0 2f
009C: ea 03 00 00  41 41 41 41  41 41 41 41
00A8: 41 41 41 41  30 30 30 30  c8 e4 e1 2f
00B4: 30 30 30 30  41 41 41 41  00 00 00 00
00C0: 41 41 41 41  41 41 41 41  30 30 30 30
00CC: dc 2f 00 00  30 30 30 30
```

Listing 7. Payload

Our payload is shown in Listing 7. The first two words of the payload fill the buffer `buf`. The next two words are popped from the stack into `r7` and `pc` upon return of *foo()*. Specifically, our exploit overwrites the return address with `0x2fe16a67` to redirect execution to the first instruction sequence. The following five addresses point to the subsequent sequences: `0x2fe06529`, `0x2fe1e4c8`, `0x2fe0efc3`, `0x2fe0f0e5`, and `0x2fe0ec40`. Note that code sequences compiled in THUMB mode have to be addressed by an odd value (+1).

The address `0x33a8cacd` is the static address of *AudioServicesPlaySystemSound()*. Further, the address `0x3010` points to the absolute address of *fgets()* stored in the indirect symbol table of the vulnerable program. The value `0xcc0c611f` is an inversion of the static address of *fgets()* `0x33f39ee0`. `0x03ea` and `0x00` are parameters for the functions *AudioServicesPlaySystemSound()* and *exit()*, respectively. Finally, `0x2fdc` is the address of the indirect symbol table entry of *exit()*. We use `0x41414141` and `0x30303030` as pattern bytes to compensate the side effects of our invoked sequences.

19th Annual Network & Distributed System Security Symposium

Towards Taming Privilege Escalation Attacks on Android

Alexandra Dmitrienko
Fraunhofer Institute for Secure Information Technology, Darmstadt, Germany

Sven Bugiel, Lucas Davi
TU Darmstadt/CASED, Germany

Ahmad-Reza Sadeghi, Bhargava Shastry
Fraunhofer SIT/CASED, Darmstadt, Germany

Thomas Fischer
Ruhr-University Bochum

App Installation in Android

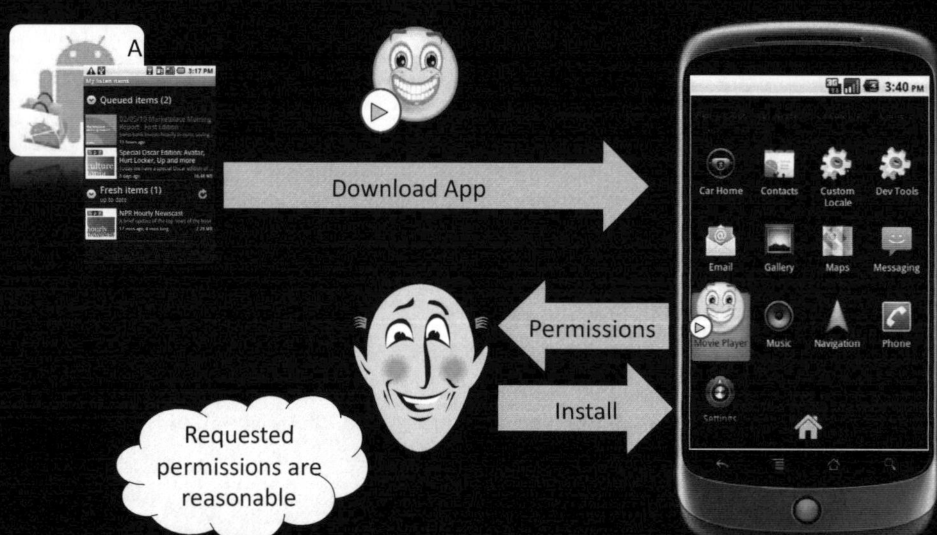

Can apps go beyond their privileges?

YES

Privilege escalation attacks

3

Confused Deputy Attack

Do not have a right permission? Ask your neighbor!

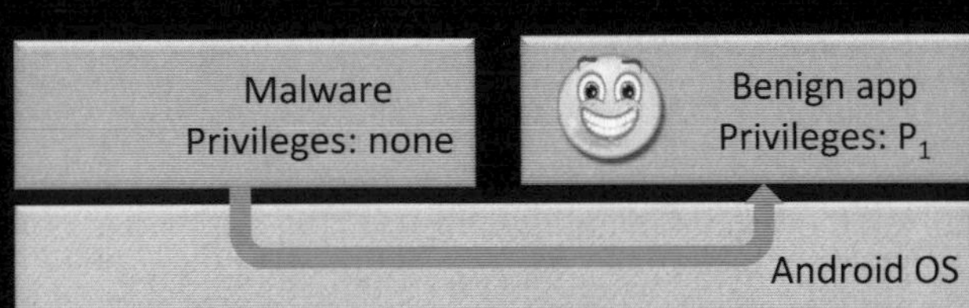

Examples:

1) Invoke browser to download malicious files (Lineberry et al., BlackHat 2010)
2) Invoke Phone app to perform a phone call (Enck et al., TechReport 2008)
3) Invoke Android Scripting Environment to send SMS messages (Davi et al., ISC'2010)

4

Collusion Attack

Two (or more) apps collude to launch the attack

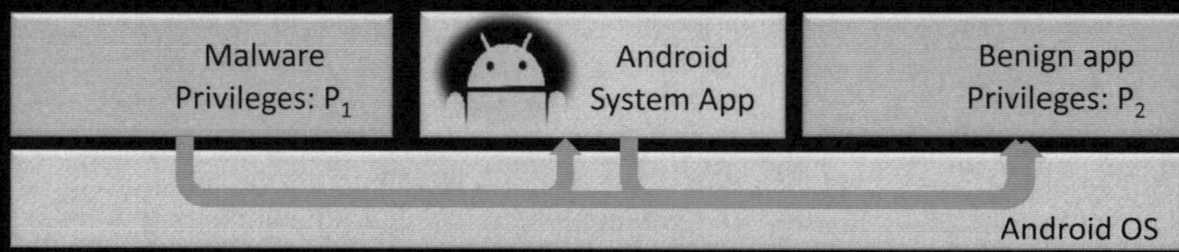

1) Apps communicate directly

Example: Claudio Marforio et. al, TechReport ETH Zurich

2) Apps communicate via covert (e.g., volume settings) or overt (e.g., content providers) channels in Android System components

Example: Soundcomber (Schlegel et al., NDSS'2011)

5

Inter-Application Communication

- Inter-process communication (IPC)
  - Intents and remote procedure calls
- File system (files, Unix domain sockets)
- Network sockets

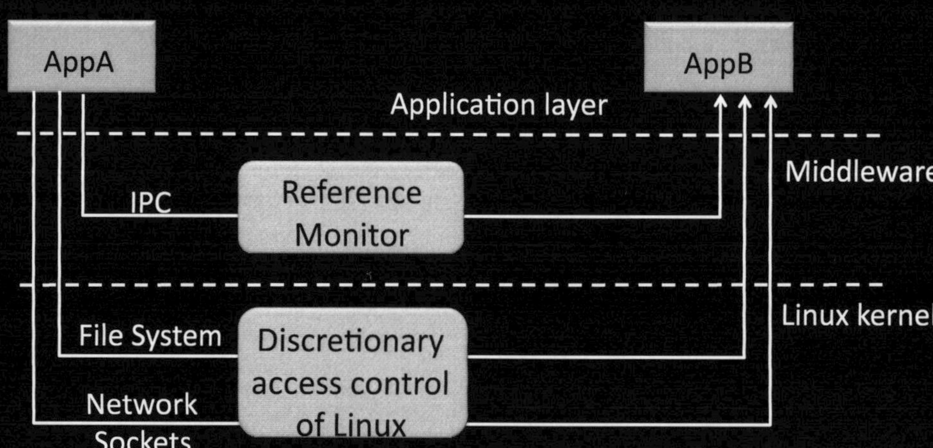

6

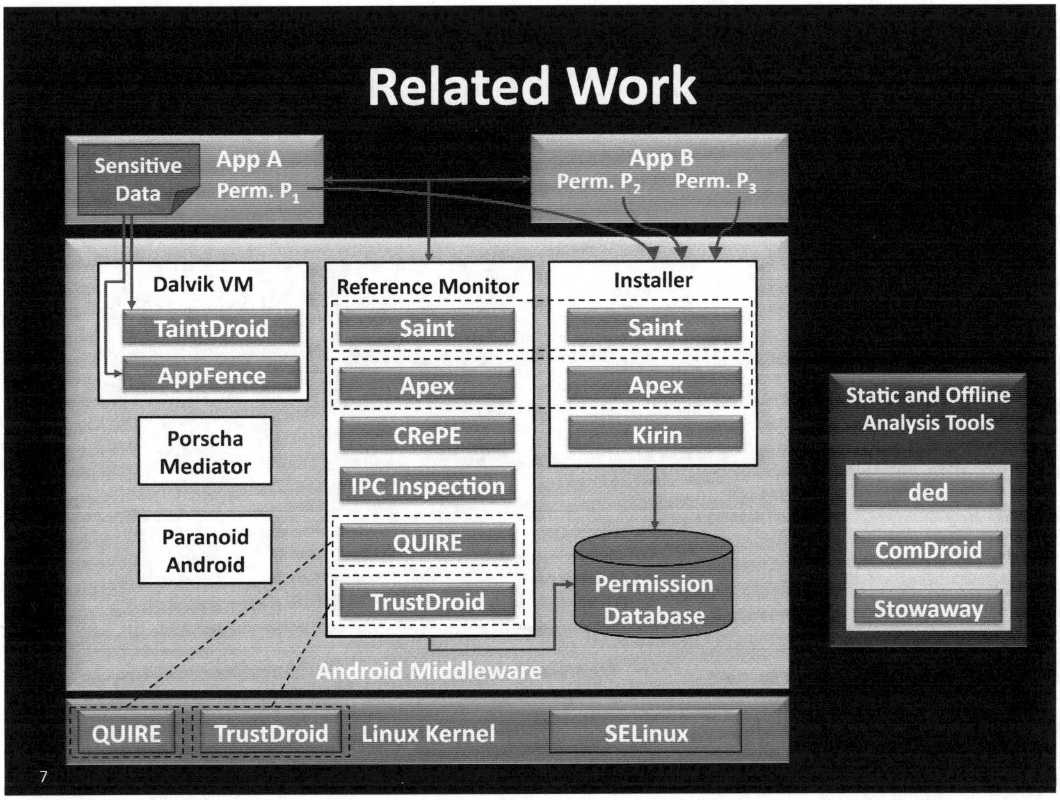
Related Work
Sensitive Data
App A
Perm. P1
App B
Perm. P2
Perm. P3
Dalvik VM
TaintDroid
AppFence
Reference Monitor
Saint
Apex
CRePE
IPC Inspection
QUIRE
TrustDroid
Installer
Saint
Apex
Kirin
Porscha Mediator
Paranoid Android
Permission Database
Android Middleware
Static and Offline Analysis Tools
ded
ComDroid
Stowaway
QUIRE
TrustDroid
Linux Kernel
SELinux
7

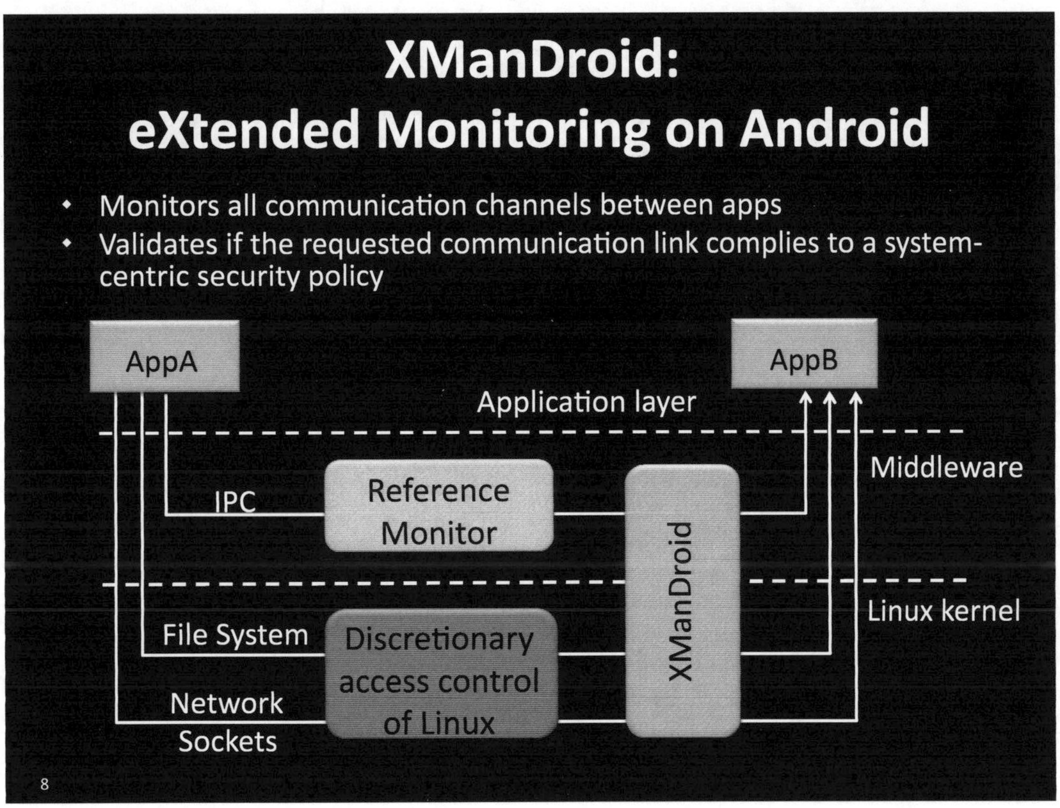
XManDroid:
eXtended Monitoring on Android
• Monitors all communication channels between apps
• Validates if the requested communication link complies to a system-centric security policy
AppA
AppB
Application layer
Middleware
IPC
Reference Monitor
XManDroid
Linux kernel
File System
Discretionary access control of Linux
Network Sockets
8

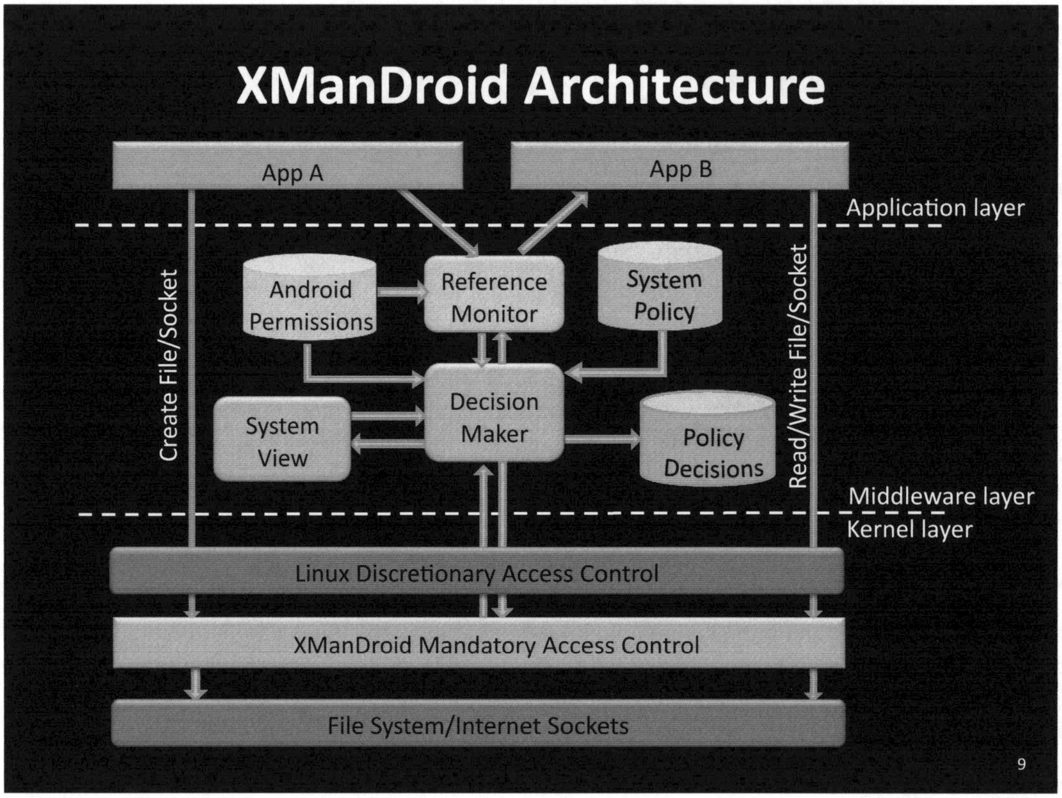
XManDroid Architecture
App A
App B
Application layer
Create File/Socket
Android Permissions
Reference Monitor
System Policy
Read/Write File/Socket
Decision Maker
System View
Policy Decisions
Middleware layer
Kernel layer
Linux Discretionary Access Control
XManDroid Mandatory Access Control
File System/Internet Sockets
9

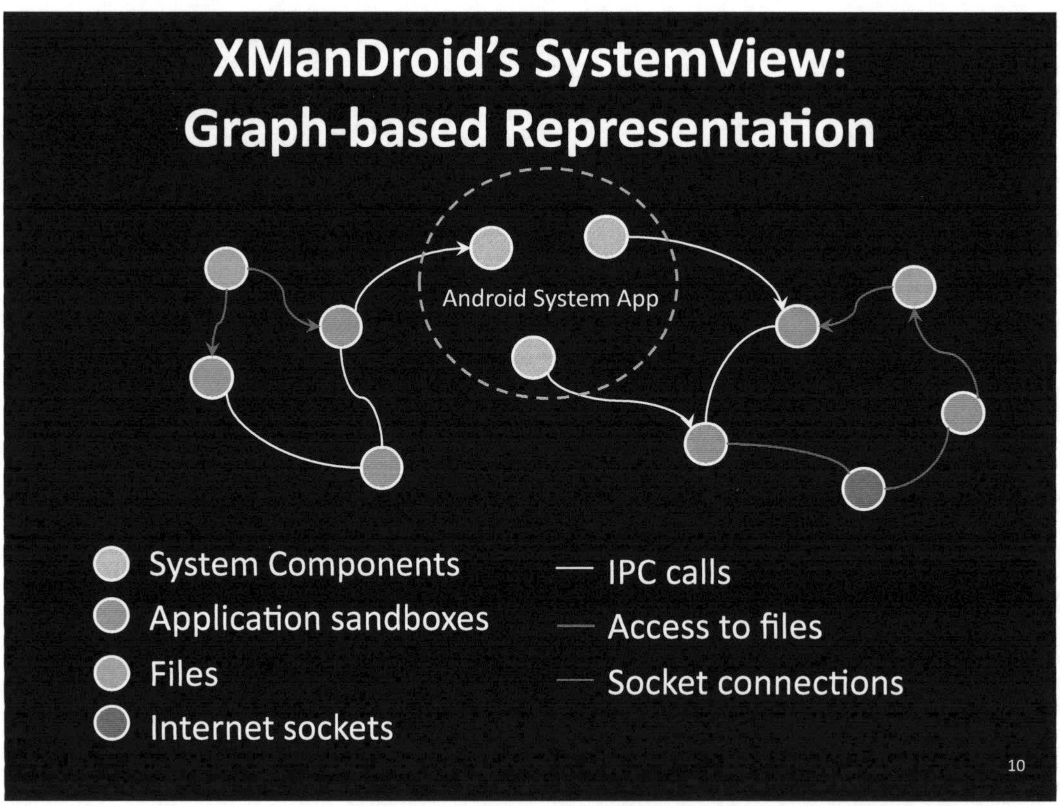
XManDroid's SystemView: Graph-based Representation
Android System App
System Components
Application sandboxes
Files
Internet sockets
IPC calls
Access to files
Socket connections
10

XManDroid: Simplified Example

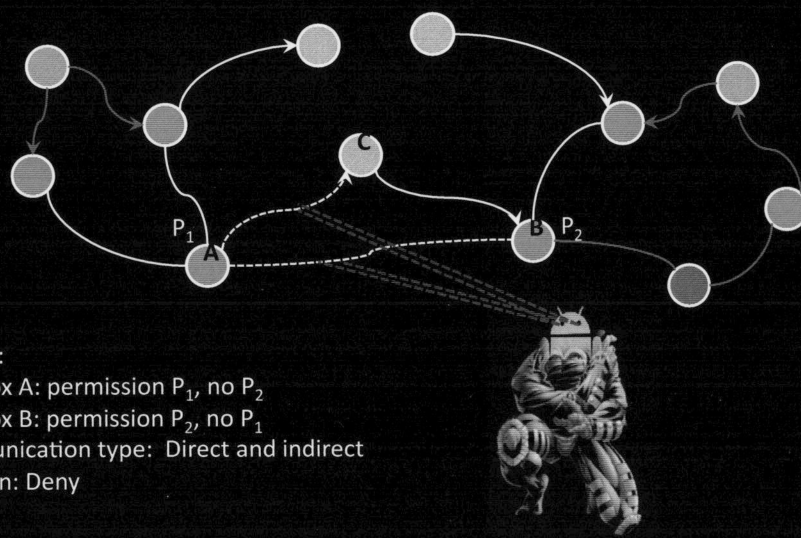

Policy Rule:

- Sandbox A: permission P_1, no P_2
- Sandbox B: permission P_2, no P_1
- Communication type: Direct and indirect
- Decision: Deny

11

Contributions

- **Design**
  - A general framework towards taming privilege escalation attacks
  - System-centric policy enforcement
- **Implementation**
  - Kernel-level mandatory access control based on TOMOYO
  - Callback channel between kernel-level and the middleware
  - System-centric IPC call chain tracking for Intents (inspired by QUIRE)
- **Tests**
  - Evaluation
  - Study on inter-application communication

12

Evaluation

1. Effectiveness (attack prevention)
2. Performance
3. Rate of falsely denied communications

13

Study on Application Communication Patterns

14

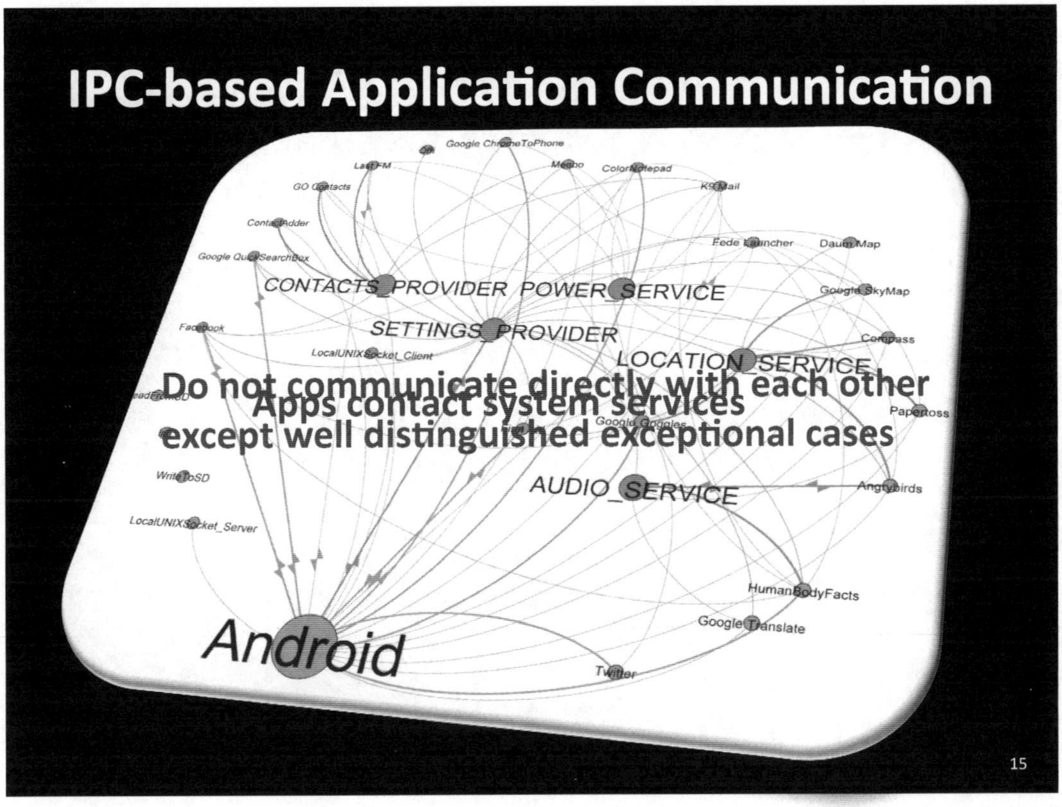
IPC-based Application Communication
Do not communicate directly with each other
except well distinguished exceptional cases
Apps contact system services
CONTACTS_PROVIDER
POWER_SERVICE
SETTINGS_PROVIDER
LOCATION_SERVICE
AUDIO_SERVICE
Android
Facebook
WriteToSD
LocalUNIXSocket_Server
LocalUNIXSocket_Client
Google QuickSearchBox
GO Contacts
ContactAdder
Google ChromeToPhone
Meebo
ColorNotepad
K9 Mail
Fede Launcher
Daum Map
Google SkyMap
Compass
Papertoss
Angrybirds
HumanBodyFacts
Google Translate
Twitter
15

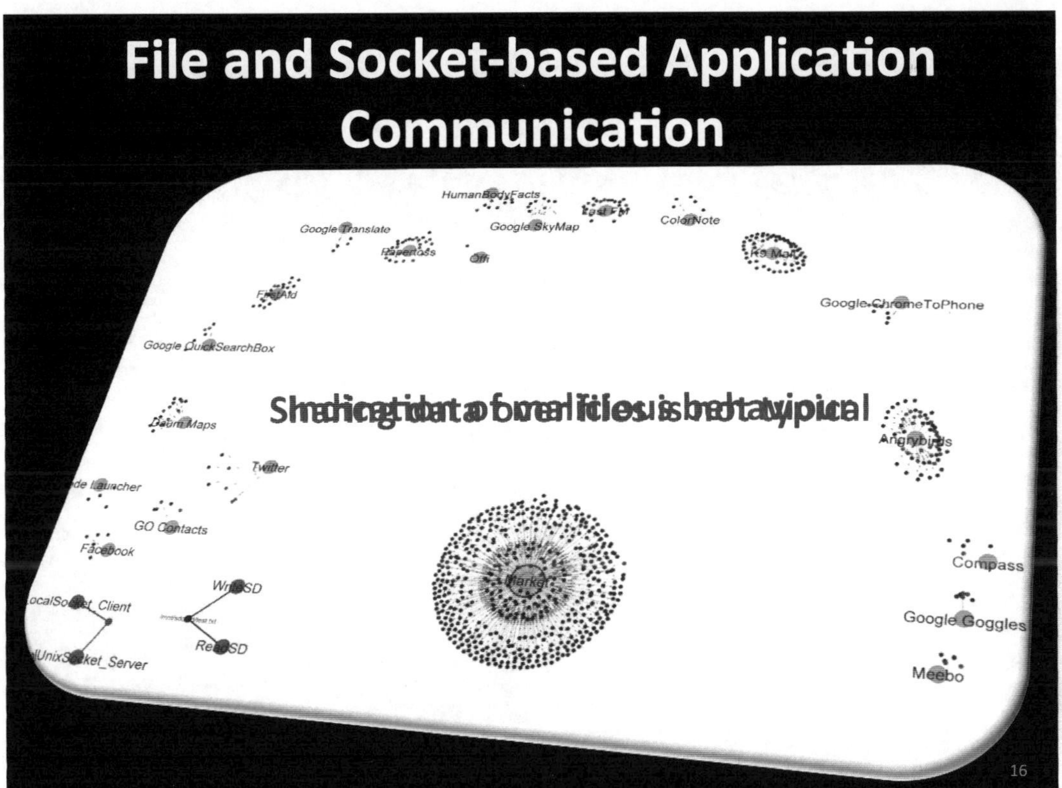
File and Socket-based Application Communication
HumanBodyFacts
Google Translate
Google SkyMap
ColorNote
Papertoss
Google ChromeToPhone
Google QuickSearchBox
Daum Maps
Twitter
GO Contacts
Facebook
Angrybirds
Compass
Google Goggles
Meebo
WriteSD
ReadSD
16

Conclusion and Future Work

- First general approach towards tackling privilege escalation attacks (at application level)
- Runtime monitoring, but quite efficient
- No false negatives
- No false positives, but conceptually they are possible

- Current work
  - Large scale evaluation
  - Automatic policy engineering
  - Full IPC call chain tracking
  - Applying XManDroid framework for domain isolation on Android

BizzTrust

17

Current Work: BizzTrust

- Special case of XManDroid
- Allows dual use of phone for Private and Enterprise usage

18

Thank you

alexandra.dmitrienko@sit.fraunhofer.de

19

Fine-grained Analysis of System Sandbox

System Services:
Extend API to enforce permission check between the last writer of a value and the reader upon reading of a value

System Content Provider:
Extend API to filter all data from the response to a read access whose reader-writer(s) pair violates the system policy

20

Privilege Escalation Attacks

Scenario 1:

Confused deputy attack

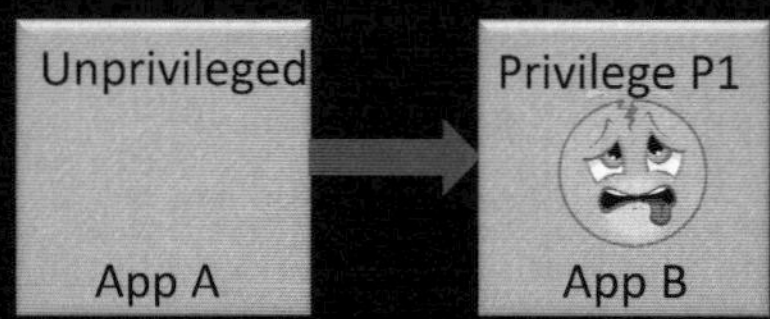

Examples:

1) Invoke browser to download malicious files (Lineberry et al., BlackHat 2010)
2) Unauthorized phone call (Enck et al., TechReport 2008)
3) Invoke Android Scripting Environment to send SMS messages (Davi et al., ISC'2010)

Scenario 2:

Collusion attack

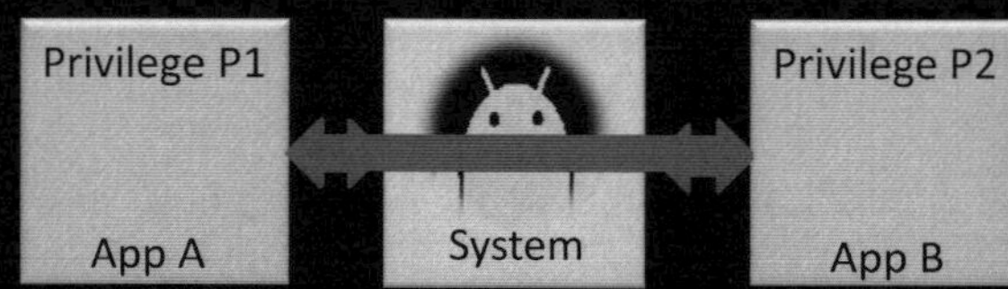

1) Apps communicate directly (Claudio Marforio et. al, TechReport ETH Zurich)
2) Apps communicate via covert (e.g., volume settings) or overt (e.g., content providers) channels in Android System components

   Example: Soundcomber (Schlegel et al., NDSS'2011)

21

Permission Framework

- Applications must be granted corresponding permissions to be able to access protected interfaces
- Permission assignments are monitored by middleware reference monitor
- Some exceptional cases: INTERNET and EXTERNAL_STORAGE permissions
  - Enforced by Linux kernel rather than middleware
  - These permissions are mapped to Linux groups (e.g., each app granted Internet permission is a member of a group which is allowed to access Internet driver)

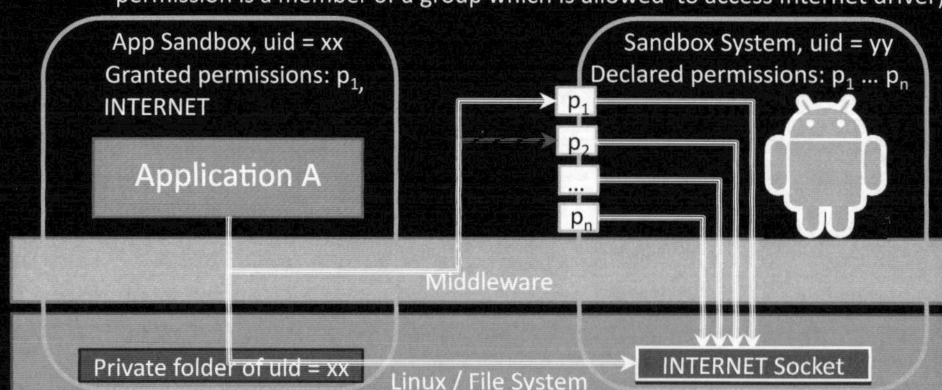

22

Policy Language

Based on VALID [Bleikertz et al., POLICY 2011] – a formal security assurance language for graph-based virtualized topologies

- Expresses properties of graph vertices and paths
- Defines high-level security goals in a form of attack states

<u>Policy rule for our simplified example:</u>

A,B – application sandboxes

L(A,B) – path

goal RuleName(deny) := A.hasPermission(p1) ^ ¬(A.hasPermission(p2) ^ B.hasPermission(p2) ^ ¬(B.hasPermission(p1)) ^ L.connects(A,B) ^ L.type(direct I indirect)

23

Challenges: False Positives

Problem: The same communication channels can be used for both, legitimate purposes and attacks

App invokes the browser to open the link to advertisements

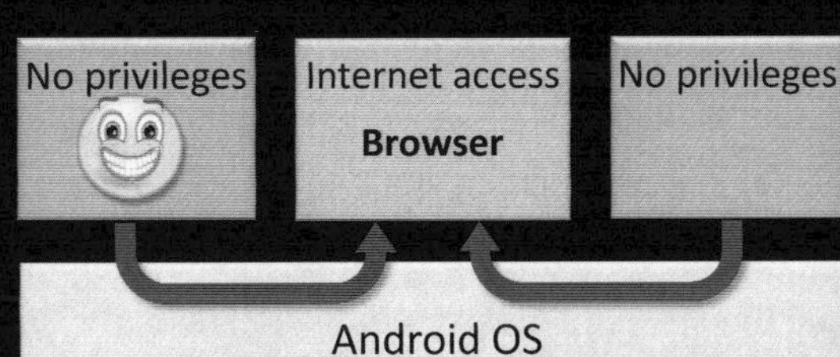

App invokes the browser to download malicious files

(Lineberry et al., BlackHat 2010)

Performed a study on third party application communication to discover possible sources of false positives

24

Tchnical Challenges to Mitigate Falselz Denied

1. Fine-grained analysis of communication links via system components
2. Directed edge representation upon file access and upon read/write access to system databases and system services
3. Establishment of the semantic links for IPC calls (inspired by QUIRE, (Dietz et al., USENIX Security 2011)
4. Deployment of exceptional policy rules to handle exceptional cases of application-to-application communication

25

System Sandbox: Fine-grained Analysis

- Extract System Services (SS) and Content Providers (CP) from monolithic Android System Sandbox as virtual nodes
- Distinguishing read/write access to SSs and CPs (directed edges)

SSs (e.g., location manager or audio manager):

- Check privileges of the last writer of a value and the current reader

CPs (SQL-like databases, e.g., user contacts):

- Coloring data
- Filtering query response

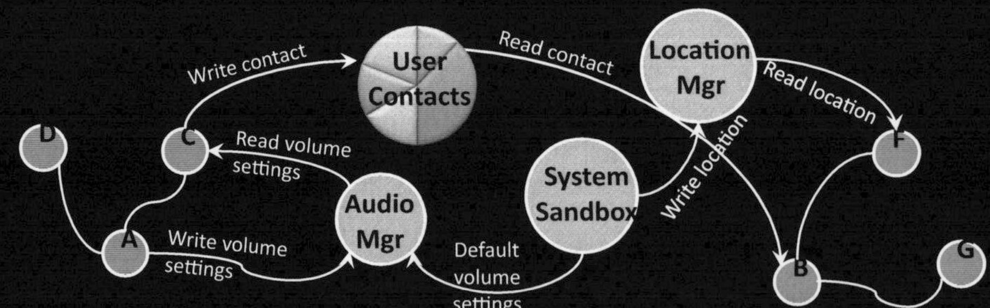

26

Contribution

- A general framework to prevent both classes of privilege escalation attacks
  - Middleware: Runtime monitoring of IPC calls, establishment of the semantic links for IPC calls (inspired by QUIRE [Dietz et al., USENIX Security 2011])
  - Kernel level: Mandatory access control on file system and Internet sockets (based on TOMOYO)
  - Runtime mapping of middleware policies to kernel level
- Policy
  - System-centric policy enforcement
  - Expressed on adopted VALID policy language [Bleikertz et al., POLICY 2011]
- Evaluation
  - Performance, effectiveness, rate of falsely denied communications

XManDroid Architecture

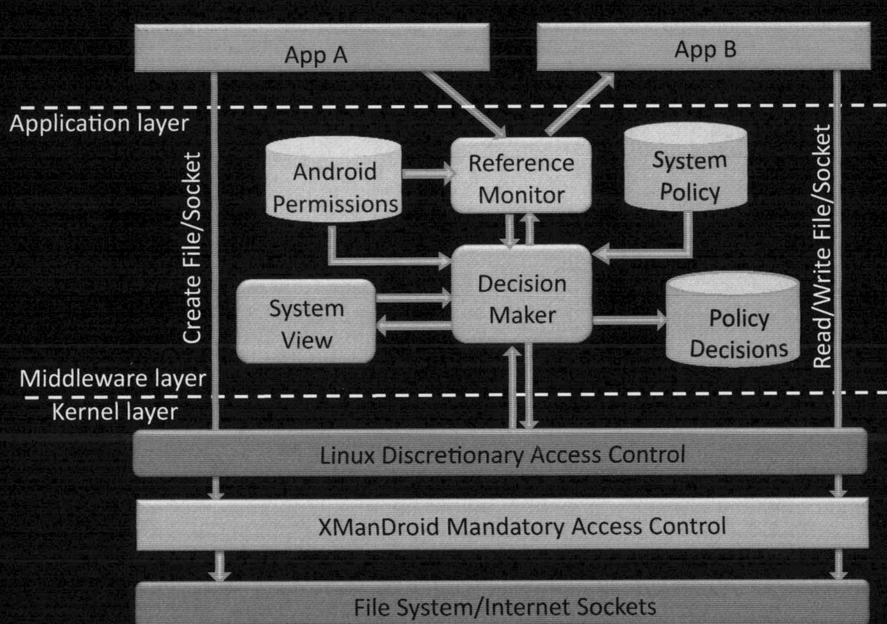

Confused Deputy Attack

Do not have a right permission? Ask your neighbor!

- Invoke browser to download malicious files (Lineberry et al., BlackHat 2010)

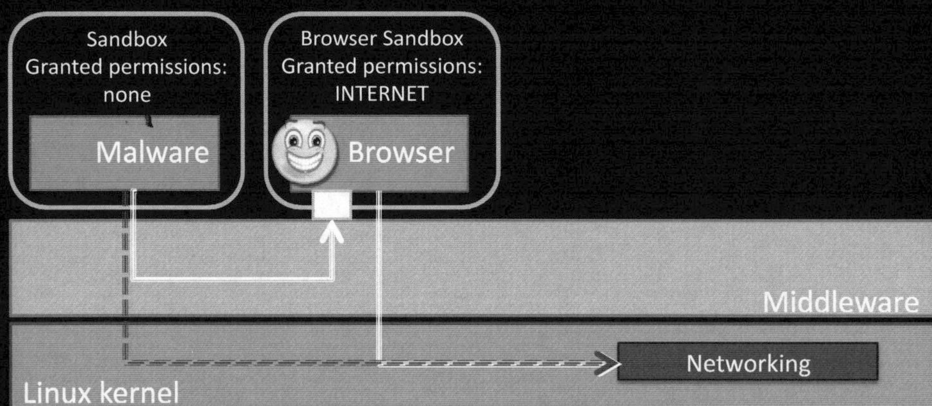

29

Confused Deputy Attack

Do not have a right permission? Ask your neighbor!

- Invoke browser to download malicious files (Lineberry et al., BlackHat 2010)
- Invoke Phone app to perform a phone call (Enck et al., TechReport 2008)

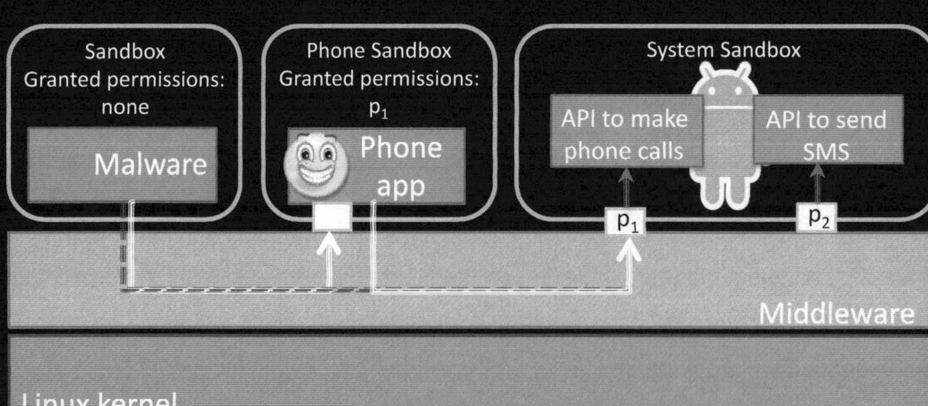

30

Confused Deputy Attack

Do not have a right permission? Ask your neighbor!

- Invoke browser to download malicious files (Lineberry et al., BlackHat 2010)
- Invoke Phone app to perform a phone call (Enck et al., TechReport 2008)
- Invoke Android Scripting Environment (ASE) to send SMS messages (Davi et al.,ISC 2010)

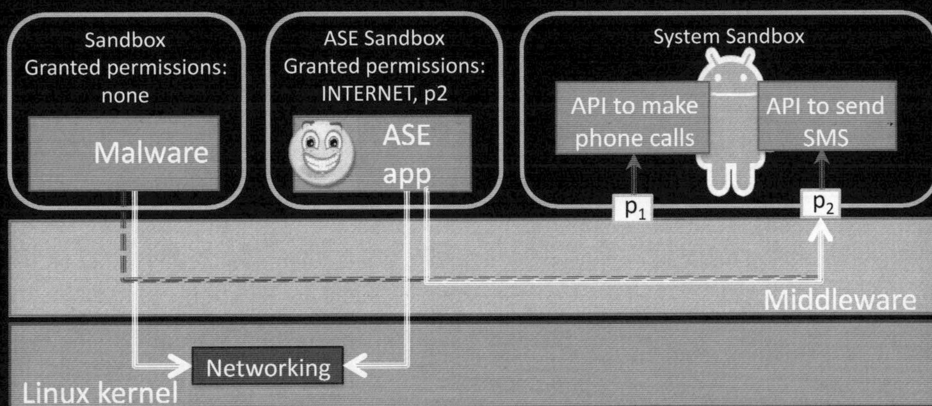

31

Collusion Attack

Divide necessary permissions among two (or more) apps

- 1st app has access to user location; 2nd is granted Internet access
  - Apps communicate directly
  - Apps communicate via overt/covert channels in a System Sandbox (e.g., write/read data to system databases, or write-read system settings) (Soundcomber, NDSS`2011)
  - Apps communicate via file sharing

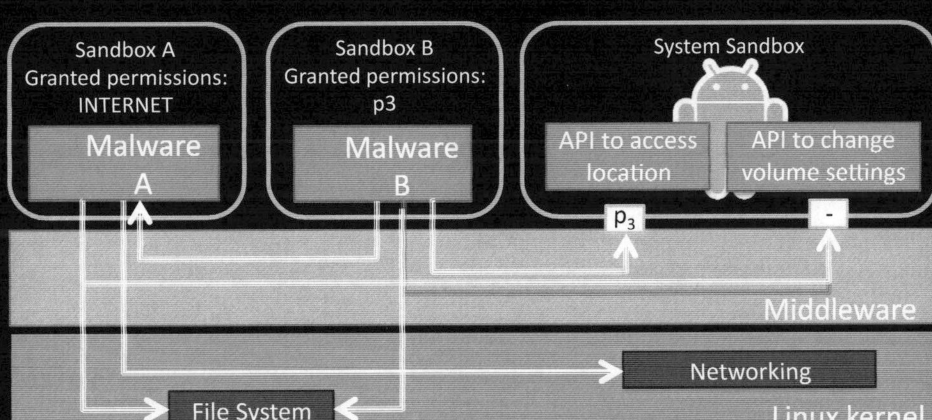

32

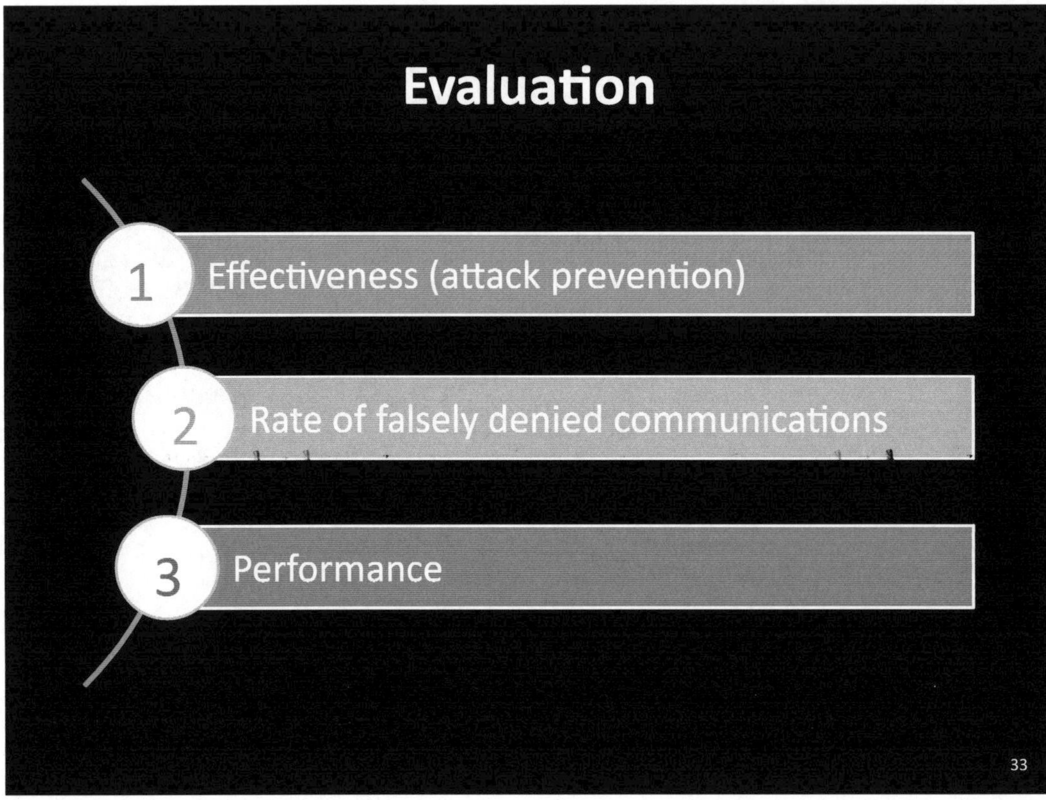
Evaluation
1
Effectiveness (attack prevention)
2
Rate of falsely denied communications
3
Performance
33

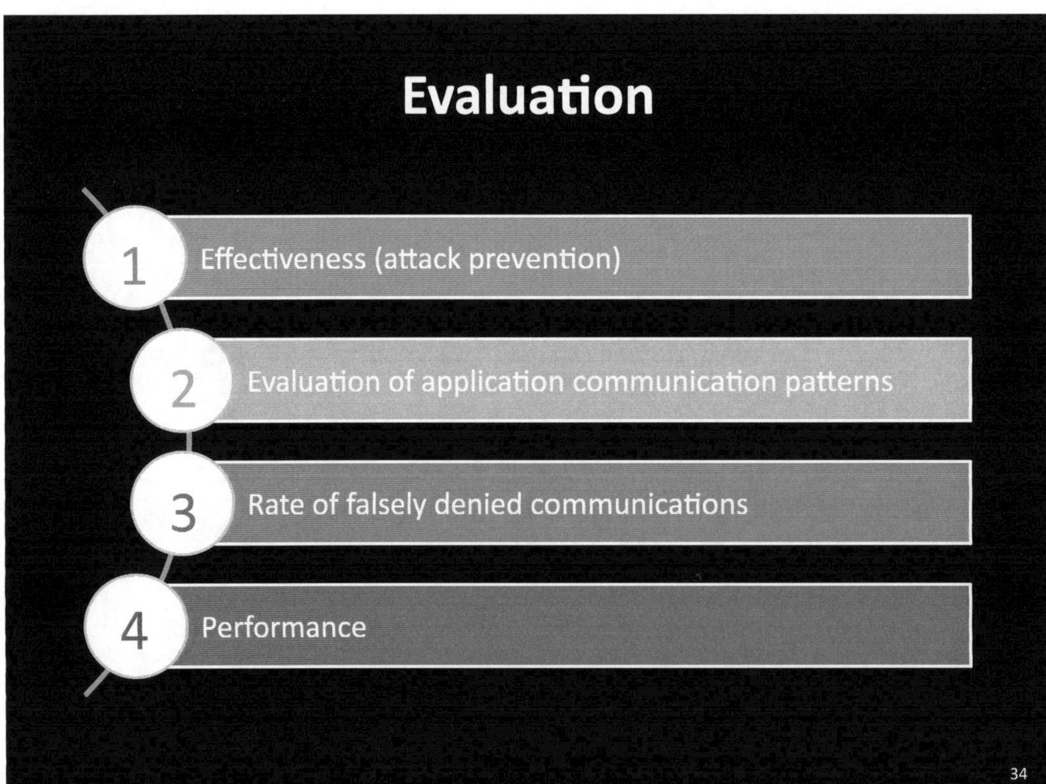
Evaluation
1
Effectiveness (attack prevention)
2
Evaluation of application communication patterns
3
Rate of falsely denied communications
4
Performance
34

Performance

- Small runtime overhead
  - Non-Intents: overhead is low, especially considering ratio for cached/uncached decisions, low standard deviation
  - Intents: overhead is higher due to analysis of data included into Intent

IPC Type	Number of Calls	Average	Std. Dev.
Runtime for IPC without XManDroid			
All types	11003	0.184 ms	2.490 ms
XManDroid overhead for IPC			
Uncached, except Intents	312	6.182 ms	9.703 ms
Cached, except Intents	10691	0.367 ms	1.930 ms
Intents (never cached)	1821	8.621 ms	29.011 ms
XManDroid overhead for file read			
File read	389	3.320 ms	4.088 ms

35

Performance (ctd.)

- Access to System Content Providers imposes higher overhead, because multiple reader-writer pairs have to be checked

	Number of Calls	Average	Std. Dev.
Access to System Content Provides			
Without XManDroid	591	10.317 ms	41.224 ms
Overhead of XManDroid	591	4.984 ms	36.441 ms
Access to System Services			
Without XManDroid	87	8.578 ms	20.241 ms
Overhead of XManDroid	87	0.307 ms	0.4318 ms

36

Evaluation: Attack Prevention

- Malware test suite
  - Misusing Phone app (Enck et al. [TechReport 2008])
  - Misusing Android Scripting Environment (Davi et al. [ISC'2010])
  - Collusion over covert channels (Schlegel et al. [NDSS 2011])

- Deployed policy
  - 7 rules target confused deputy attacks
  - 4 more general rules target collusion attacks

=> All attacks were successfully prevented

Expected result, as we had policy rules against all these attacks

37

Rate of Falsely Denied Communications

- Test setup
  - Manual tests by 25 users
  - 50 third party applications

- Policy
  - 7 rules targeting confused deputy attacks
  - 4 rules targeting collusion attacks
  - 1 exceptional policy rule to allow launching other apps by sending Intents which do not include any data

=> No false positives were detected

Result confirms our observations on inter-application communication patterns

38

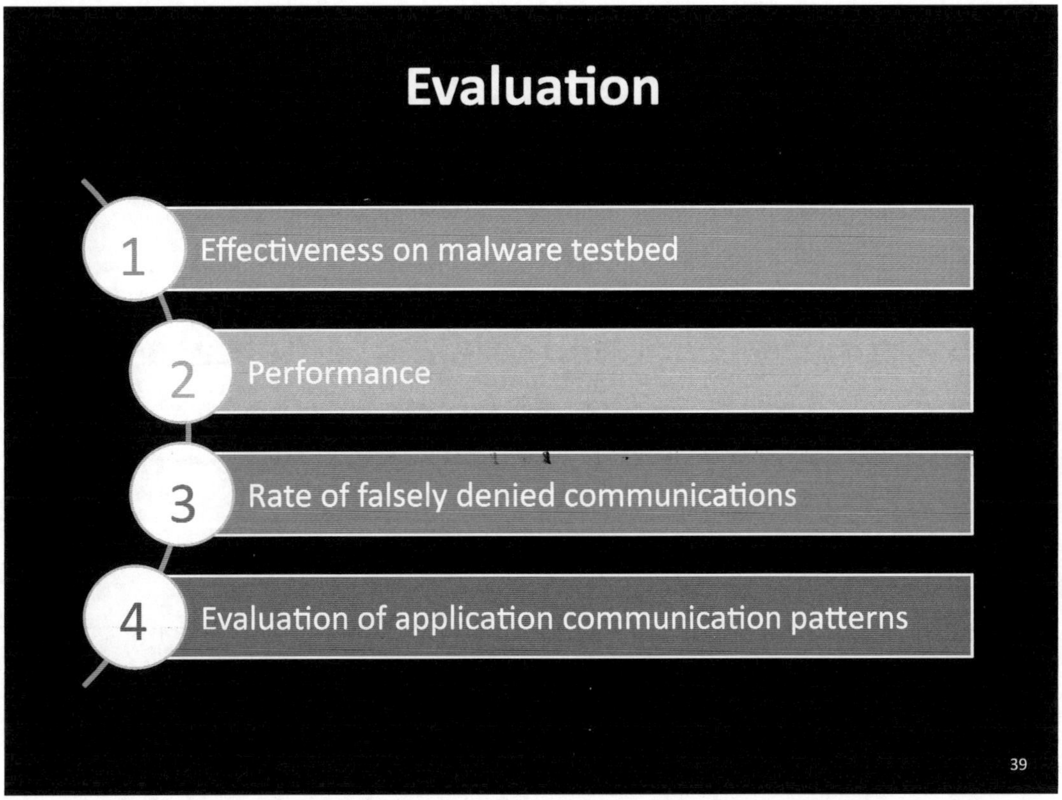
Evaluation
1
Effectiveness on malware testbed
2
Performance
3
Rate of falsely denied communications
4
Evaluation of application communication patterns
39

NDSS 2012, February 7th 2012, San Diego

NC STATE UNIVERSITY
Department of Computer Science

Systematic Detection of Capability Leaks in Stock Android Smartphones

Michael Grace Yajin Zhou Zhi Wang Xuxian Jiang

North Carolina State University

Phones and Computers

NC STATE UNIVERSITY

"I have always wished that my computer would be as easy to use as my telephone. My wish has come true. I no longer know how to use my telephone."

– Bjarne Stroustrup (designer of C++)

2

Phones: the PCs of the Future?

NC STATE UNIVERSITY

- Smartphone shipments increased 42% between 3Q 2010 and 3Q 2011 (Gartner, 11/15/2011)

- More smartphones shipping than personal computers (IDC, 2/7/2011)
  - New markets: first computer = smartphone

3

Smartphone ≠ Handheld PC

NC STATE UNIVERSITY

- Unique abilities specific to the form factor
  - Many sensors: "context-aware"
  - Dialup ➔ always on ➔ always with you

- Resource constrained

- Different vendor relationships and primacy

4

Related Work

NC STATE UNIVERSITY

- Problems with Permissions
  - e.g., **Kirin** [Enck *et al.*, CCS '09], **Soundcomber** [Schlegel *et al.*, NDSS '11], **Stowaway** [Felt *et al.*, CCS '11], **Guess Who's Texting You** [Schrittwieser *et al.*, NDSS '12]...
- Information Leak Detection
  - e.g., **PiOS** [Egele *et al.*, NDSS '11], **TaintDroid** [Enck *et al.*, OSDI '10]...
- Phone Defenses
  - e.g., **MockDroid** [Beresford *et al.*, HotMobile '11], **TISSA** [Zhou *et al.*, TRUST '11], **AppFence** [Hornyack *et al.*, CCS '11], **Permission Re-Delegation** [Felt *et al.*, USENIX Security '11], **QUIRE** [Dietz *et al.*, USENIX Security '11], **XManDroid** [Bugiel *et al.*, NDSS '12], **MoCFI** [Davi *et al.*, NDSS '12]...
- Market Issues
  - e.g., **DroidMOSS** [Zhou *et al.*, CODASPY '12], **DroidRanger** [Zhou *et al.*, NDSS '12]...

5

Firmware and Fragmentation

NC STATE UNIVERSITY

- A conspicuous gap in the body of work!
- Not like on desktops, or other smartphone platforms
- Research Goal: Determine the impact firmware customizations have on security and privacy

6

Android Capabilities

NC STATE UNIVERSITY

- Platform defines some APIs
- APIs *may* require capabilities (called permissions)
- Applications can define APIs the same way
- What happens when an application defines a new API based on a restricted old one?
  - That's up to the author!

7

Capability Leaks

NC STATE UNIVERSITY

- Capability Leak: A situation where an app can gain access to a restricted API without requesting proper permission
- Explicit Capability Leak: Broadening access to a restricted API by exposing it via another API
- Implicit Capability Leak: Inheriting permissions from other applications

8

Explicit Capability Leaks

NC STATE UNIVERSITY

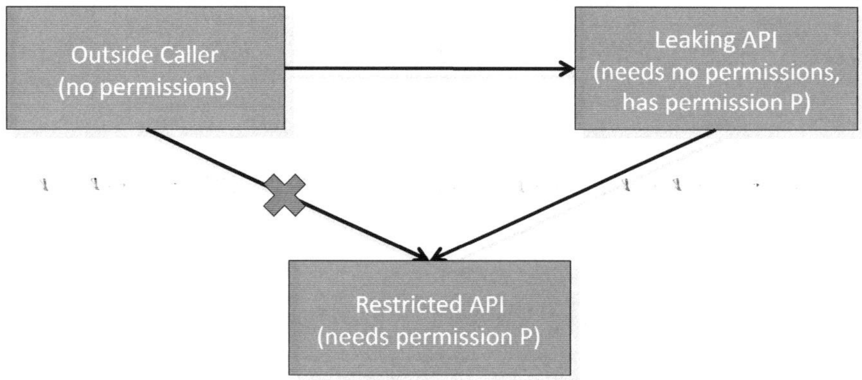

9

Detecting Capability Leaks

NC STATE UNIVERSITY

- Android SDK gives us no tools!
- Function composition
  - Capability leak: g(x) = f(x) + some other stuff
- Intuitive algorithm:
  1. Find interesting (dangerous) APIs (f(x))
  2. Find new API definitions (g(x))
  3. Link them!

10

System Overview

NC STATE UNIVERSITY

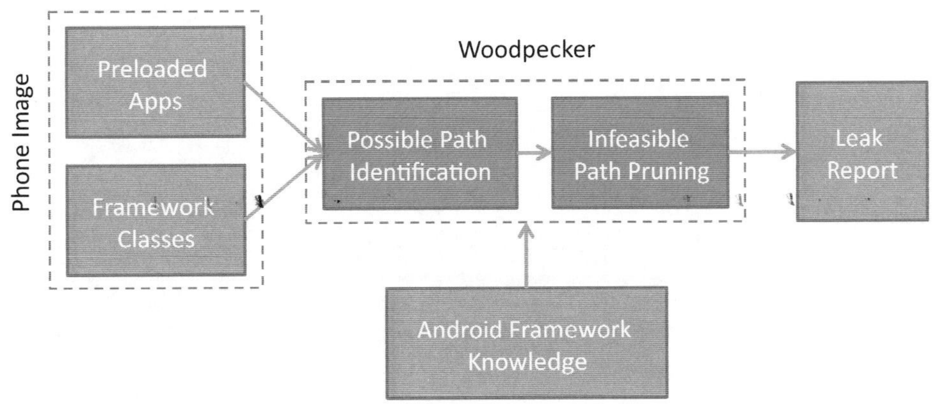

11

Possible Path Identification

NC STATE UNIVERSITY

1. Construct a control-flow graph

2. Find all paths from an IPC entry point to an API of interest

12

Possible Path Identification: Challenges

NC STATE UNIVERSITY

- Object references
  - Class hierarchy used to conservatively resolve references

- Extensive use of callbacks
  - Use framework knowledge to stitch together callbacks

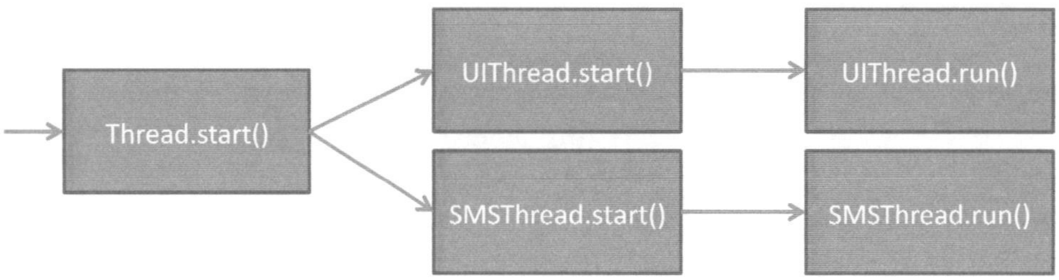

13

Infeasible Path Pruning

NC STATE UNIVERSITY

- *Many* potential paths exist
  - Most are either impossible or uninteresting

- Must prune these uninteresting paths
  - Branch conditions need an understanding of program data-flow
  - Explicit permission checks are "infeasible paths"

- Our approach: *Symbolic Path Simulation*

14

Symbolic Path Simulation

NC STATE UNIVERSITY

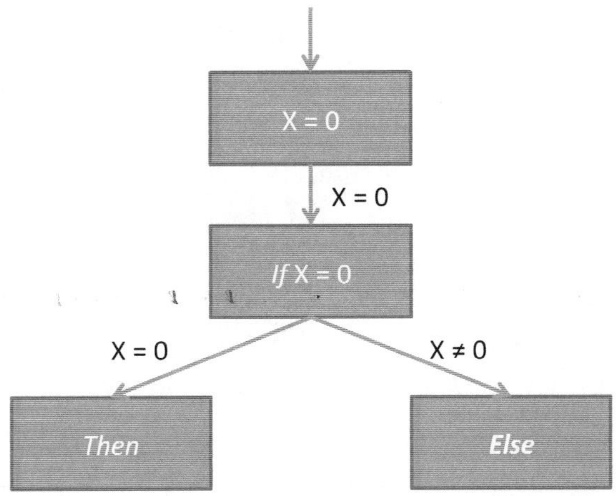

15

Implementation

NC STATE UNIVERSITY

- Based on the baksmali decompiler (1.2.6)
- Covers 13 permissions, controlling:
  - Phone information
  - Location API
  - Phone dialing
  - Sending text messages
  - Camera/microphone
  - Rebooting/shutting down the device
  - Installing/removing apps
  - Factory reset

16

Evaluation

NC STATE UNIVERSITY

17

Explicit Capability Leaks Found

NC STATE UNIVERSITY

	HTC			Motorola		Samsung	Google	
Permission	Legend	EVO 4G	Wildfire S	DROID	DROID X	Epic 4G	Nexus One	Nexus S
Coarse Location	✓	✓			✓			
Fine Location	✓	✓			✓			
Call Phone						✓		
Call Privileged								
Camera	✓	✓	✓					
Delete Packages	✓	✓	✓	✓	✓	✓	✓	✓
Install Packages								
Master Clear					✓			
Read Phone State				✓				
Reboot		✓						
Record Audio	✓	✓	✓					
Send SMS	✓	✓	✓					
Shutdown		✓						

18

Demo

NC STATE UNIVERSITY

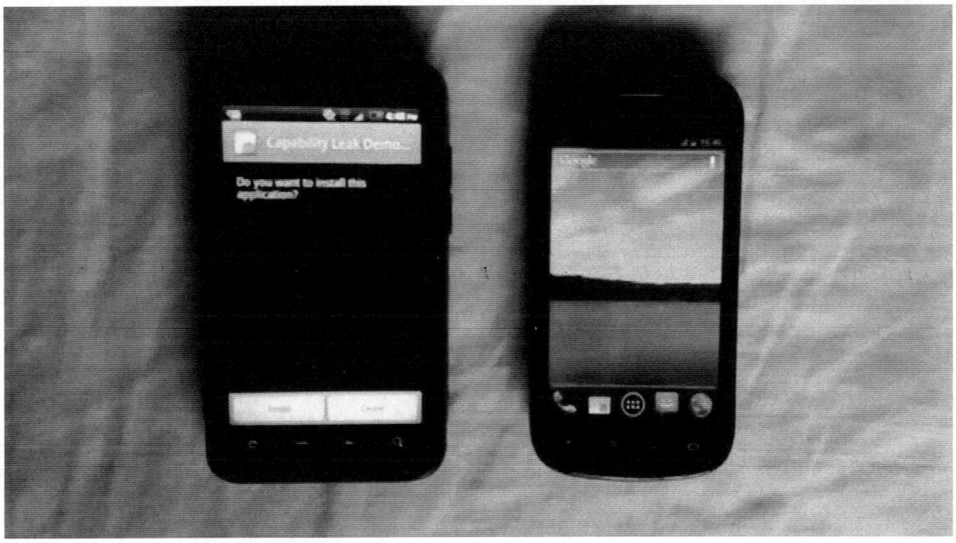

19

Implicit Capability Leaks Found

NC STATE UNIVERSITY

	HTC			Motorola		Samsung	Google	
Permission	Legend	EVO 4G	Wildfire S	DROID	DROID X	Epic 4G	Nexus One	Nexus S
Coarse Location	✓	✓	✓					
Fine Location			✓					
Call Phone						✓		
Call Privileged			✓					
Camera								
Delete Packages								
Install Packages								
Master Clear								
Read Phone State	✓	✓	✓			✓		
Reboot								
Record Audio								
Send SMS								
Shutdown								

20

Performance Measurement

NC STATE UNIVERSITY

Vendor	Model	Time	# Apps
HTC	Legend	3366.63s	125
	EVO 4G	4175.03s	160
	Wildfire S	3894.37s	144
Motorola	DROID	2138.38s	76
	DROID X	3311.94s	161
Samsung	Epic 4G	3732.56s	138
Google	Nexus One	2059.47s	76
	Nexus S	1815.71s	72

21

Discussion

NC STATE UNIVERSITY

- Accuracy
  - False negatives: native code, undocumented extensions
  - False positives: conservative analysis
- Threads and Time
  - Instruction interleaving, shared state
  - Example: callback handling

22

Conclusions

NC STATE UNIVERSITY

- Capability leaks present a tangible threat to security and privacy on existing Android smartphones

- We present a system, Woodpecker, to detect these capability leaks

23

NC STATE UNIVERSITY

Thank you!

24

Implicit Capability Leaks

NC STATE UNIVERSITY

- Applications don't have permissions, *user identifiers* (UIDs) do.

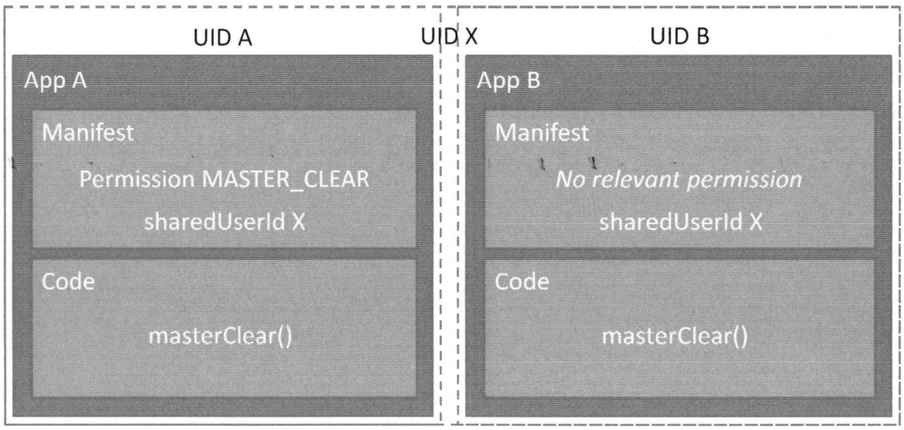

25

NDSS 2012, February 7th 2012, San Diego

NC STATE UNIVERSITY
Department of Computer Science

Hey, You, Get Off of My Market: Detecting Malicious Apps in Official and Alternative Android Markets

Yajin Zhou **Zhi Wang** Wu Zhou Xuxian Jiang

North Carolina State University

Motivation: Smartphones

NC STATE UNIVERSITY

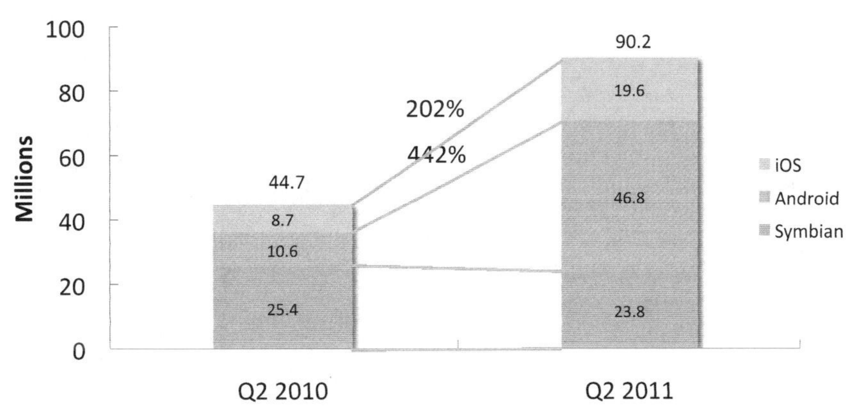

Worldwide Smartphone Sales [1]

[1]Data source: gartner.com

2

Motivation: Apps

NC STATE UNIVERSITY

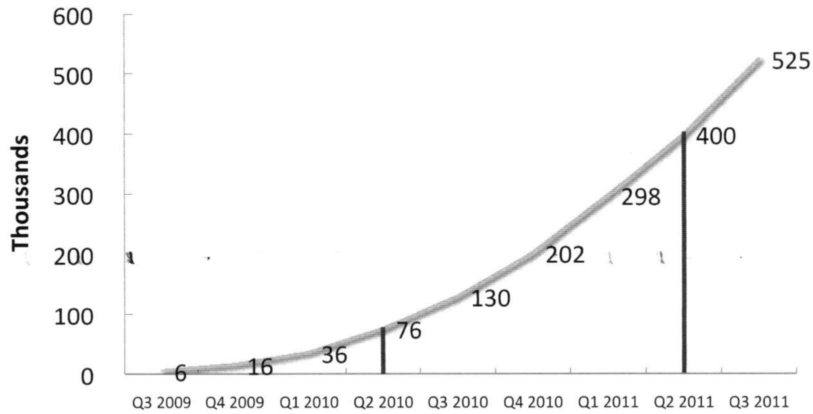

Number of Apps in Official Android Market[2]

[2]Data source: androlib.com

3

Motivation: Markets

NC STATE UNIVERSITY

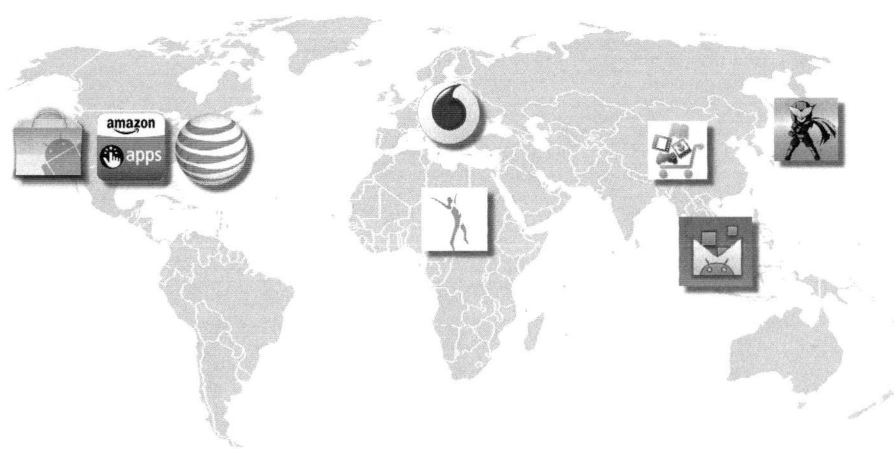

4

Motivation: Malware in Markets

NC STATE UNIVERSITY

What is the overall health of Android Markets?

5

Design Goals

NC STATE UNIVERSITY

- Accuracy
  - Detect malware with low false positives and negatives
- Scalability
  - Scale to hundreds of thousands apps
- Efficiency
  - Process all apps in a reasonable amount of time

6

DroidRanger Overview

NC STATE UNIVERSITY

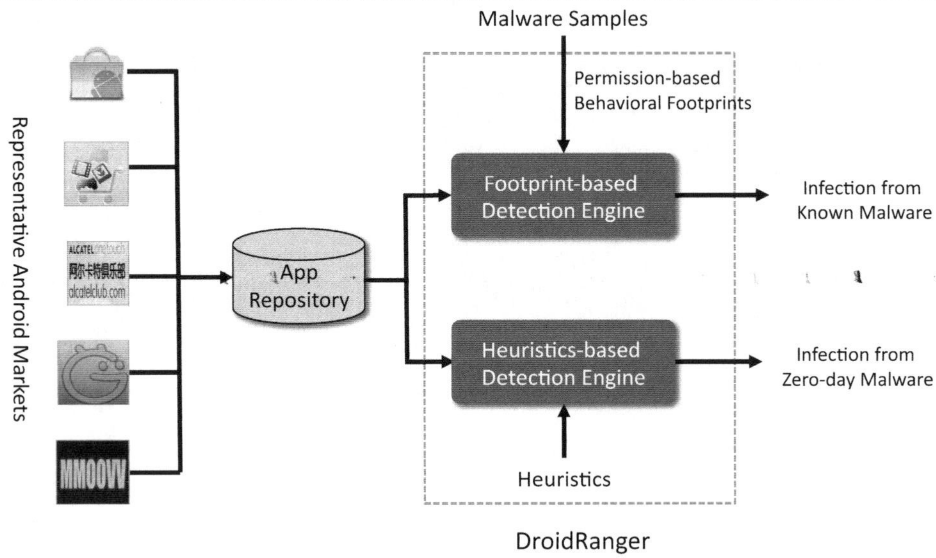

7

Footprint-based Detection Engine

NC STATE UNIVERSITY

- Filter apps with essential permissions

Malware	Essential Permissions	Apps
Geinimi	INTERNET, SEND_SMS	7, 620 (4.17%)
ADRD	INTERNET, ACCESS_NETWORK_STATE RECEIVE_BOOT_COMPLETED	10, 379 (5.68%)
Pjapps	INTERNET, RECEIVE_SMS	4, 637 (2.54%)
Bgserv	INTERNET, RECEIVE_SMS, SEND_SMS	2, 880 (1.58%)
DroidDream	CHANGE_WIFI_STATE	4, 096 (2.24%)
zHash	CHANGE_WIFI_STATE	4, 096 (2.24%)
jSMSHider	INSTALL_PACKAGES	[illegible]
Zsone	RECEIVE_SMS, SEND_SMS	[illegible]

Reduced to 0.64% when considering a broadcast receiver

8

Footprint-based Detection Engine

NC STATE UNIVERSITY

- Match apps to malware behavioral footprints in multiple dimensions
  - Information in manifest file
    - ➢Declare a receiver listening to SMS_RECEIVED
  - Semantics in the byte-code
    - ➢Register a receiver listening to SMS_RECEIVED
    - ➢Call *abortBroadcast* in the receiver
    - ➢Send SMS messages to premium numbers
  - Structural layout of the app

Behavioral footprint of Zsone

9

Heuristics-based Detection Engine

NC STATE UNIVERSITY

- Select apps with dynamic Java/native code loading
- Monitor their runtime behavior
  - Java code: permission-related framework APIs
  - Native code: system calls requiring root privileges

10

Evaluation: Overall

NC STATE UNIVERSITY

- Data set
  - Crawled the official & four alternative markets
  - Collected 204,040 free apps during 05/2011-06/2011
- Process time
  - Used four and half hours for all 204,040 apps

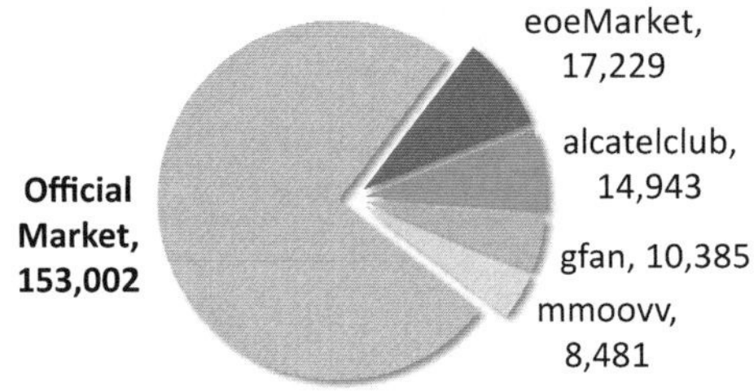

11

Evaluation: Overall

NC STATE UNIVERSITY

Malware	Official Market	eoeMarket	alcatelclub	gfan	mmoovv	Total
Known	21	51	48	20	31	171
Zero-day	11	9	10	1	9	40
Total	32 (0.02%)	60 (0.35%)	58 (0.39%)	21 (0.20%)	40 (0.47%)	211

Total infected apps detected by DroidRanger

12

Evaluation: Footprint-based Detection Engine

NC STATE UNIVERSITY

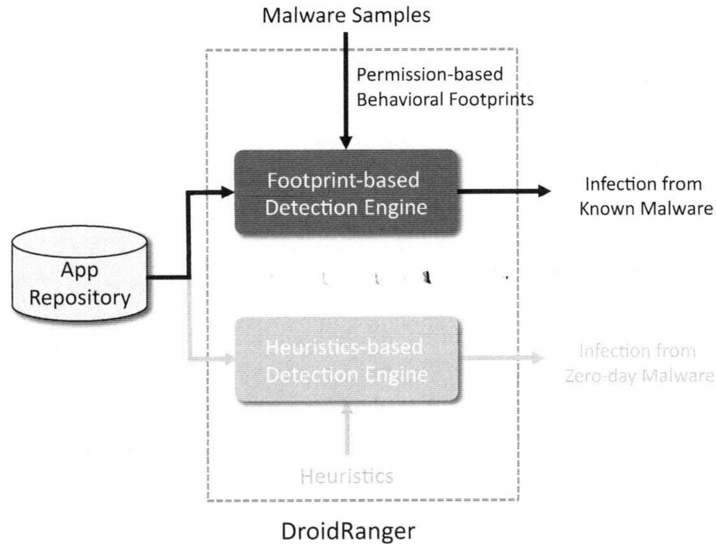

13

Evaluation: Infected Apps

NC STATE UNIVERSITY

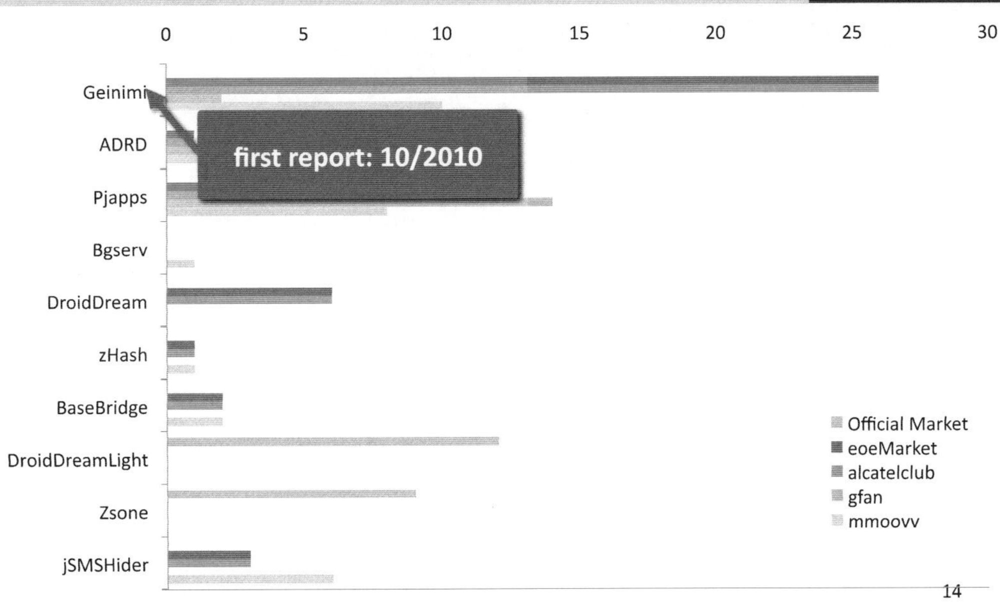

14

Evaluation: Accuracy

NC STATE UNIVERSITY

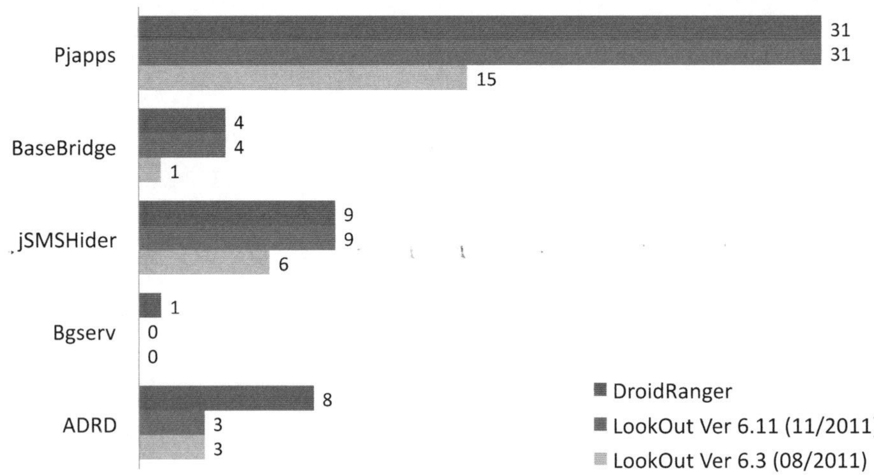

15

Evaluation: Accuracy

NC STATE UNIVERSITY

- 24 samples in 10 known families from *contagio*
- DroidRanger detected 23 samples (96%)
  - Missed a payload of DroidDream, not the malware itself
  - Found one mis-categorized sample for ADRD

16

Evaluation: Heuristics-based Detection Engine

NC STATE UNIVERSITY

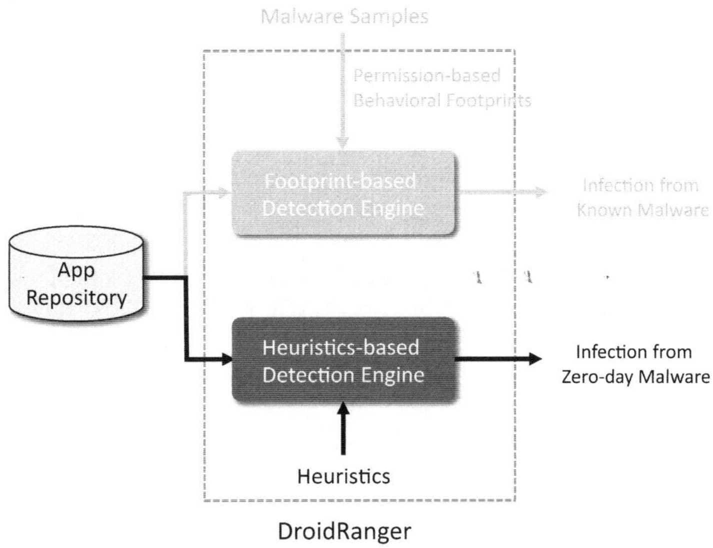

17

Evaluation: Infected Apps

NC STATE UNIVERSITY

- Detected two zero-day malware using heuristics
  - Plankton: dynamic loading of Java code
  - DroidKungFu: dynamic loading of native code
- Detected 40 samples using behavioral footprints
  - 11 samples from the official Android Market
  - 29 samples from alternative Android Markets

18

Evaluation: Malware Behaviors

NC STATE UNIVERSITY

- Plankton
  - Uploads a list of permissions before downloading a payload
  - Contains a bot-like command & control channel
- D

```
ACTIVATION         = new Commands("ACTIVATION", 1, "Activation", "/activate");
HOMEPAGE           = new Commands("HOMEPAGE", 2, "Homepage", "/homepage");
COMMANDS_STATUS    = new Commands("COMMANDS_STATUS", 3, "CommandsStatus", "/commandstatus");
BOOKMARKS          = new Commands("BOOKMARKS", 4, "Bookmarks", "/bookmarks");
SHORTCUTS          = new Commands("SHORTCUTS", 5, "Shortcuts", "/shortcuts");
HISTORY            = new Commands("HISTORY", 6, "History", "/history");
TERMINATE          = new Commands("TERMINATE", 7, "Terminate", "/terminate");
STATUS             = new Commands("STATUS", 8, "Status", "/status");
DUMP_LOG           = new Commands("DUMP_LOG", 9, "DumpLog", "/dumplog");
UNEXP_EXCEPTION    = new Commands("UNEXP_EXCEPTION", 10, "UnexpectedException", "/unexpectedexception");
UPGRADE            = new Commands("UPGRADE", 11, "Upgrade", "/installation");
INSTALLATION       = new Commands("INSTALLATION", 12, "Installation", "/installation");
```

19

Discussion

NC STATE UNIVERSITY

- Need more comprehensive heuristics
  - Background sending of unauthorized SMS messages?
  - Bot-like behavior controlled by SMS messages?
- A call for rigorous vetting processes
  - A large number of users can be infected
  - Malware remains in alternative markets for a long time
  - Zero-day malware exists in Android Markets

20

Related Work

NC STATE UNIVERSITY

- Smartphone platform security
  - TaintDroid (Enck et al., OSDI 10), PiOS (Egele et al., NDSS 11), Stowaway (Felt et al., CCS 11), Cells (Andrus et al., SOSP 11), AppFence (Hornyack et al., CCS 11), Quire (Dietz et al., USENIX Security 11), A Study of Android Application Security (Enck et al., USENIX Security 11), TISSA (Zhou et al., TRUST 11), Woodpecker (Grace et al., NDSS 12) ...
- Malware detection on mobile devices
  - pBMDS (Xie et al., WiSec 10), VirusMeter (Liu et al., RAID 09), Crowdroid (Burguera et al., CCS-SPSM 11) ...
- Other systematic security study
  - HoneyMonkey (Wang et al., NDSS 06), Systematic Web Spyware Study (Moshchuk et al., NDSS 06), All Your iFRAMEs Point to Us (Provos et al., USENIX Security 08) ...

21

Conclusion

NC STATE UNIVERSITY

- DroidRanger is a system to systematically study the overall health of existing Android Markets

Malware	Official Market	eoeMarket	alcatelclub	gfan	mmoovv	Total
Known	21	51	48	20	31	171
Zero-day	11	9	10	1	9	40
Total	32 (0.02%)	60 (0.35%)	58 (0.39%)	21 (0.20%)	40 (0.47%)	211

22

Thank You!

Evaluation: Known Malware Samples

- 20 samples from 10 malware families

Malware	First Report	Summary
Geinimi	10/2010	Trojan with bot-like capability
ADRD	02/2011	Trojan with bot-like capability
Pjapps	02/2011	Trojan with bot-like capability
Bgserv	03/2011	Trojan with bot-like capability
DroidDream	03/2011	Root exploit with Exploid, Rageagainstthecage
zHash	03/2011	Root exploit with Exploid
BaseBridge	05/2011	Root exploit with Rageagainstthecage
DroidDreamLight	05/2011	Trojan with information stealing capability
Zsone	05/2011	Trojan that sends premium-rate SMS
jSMSHider	06/2011	Trojan that target third-party firmware

Insights into User Behavior in Dealing with Internet Attacks

Northeastern University
Boston

Bilkent University
Ankara

Eurecom
Sophia Antipolis

Kaan Onarlioglu, Utku Ozan Yilmaz,
Engin Kirda, Davide Balzarotti

Problem

Exploit link	➡	Click
Risky file	➡	Download
Malware	➡	Run
Warning Message	➡	Dismiss

Interaction: "Human Aspect"

Previous Work

- How do attackers trick users?
- What techniques do they use?
- How successful are they?
  - [Dhamija, CHI '06]
  - [Sunshine, SSYM '09]
  - [Egelman, CHI' 08]
  - [Friedman, CHI '02]
  - ....and many more

- Usability of security solutions…

3 / 26

Our Questions

- How do users react to current threats?
  - XSS, session fixation, exploit links, file-sharing scams, malicious trick banners

- …evaluate security implications of actions?

- …assess the risk?

4 / 26

Experiment

- Online test system

- 44 security-related scenarios in 3 suites
  - Web attacks
  - Email attacks
  - File-sharing attacks

5 / 26

Contributions

- 164 participants
- Largest study on prevalent attacks

- Gain insights into 'Perception' & 'Security'
- Understand decision-making cues
- Identify attack vectors

6 / 26

Experiment Design

- Perception Score
  - "How dangerous or safe do you think clicking on this link is?"
- Security Score
  - "Would you click on this link?"
- "Please explain your reasoning."

Web Attacks

- XSS, session fixation, link manipulation tricks

Hey, check this article out, great stuff!

http://example.blog.com/show.php?title=%22%3E%3Cscript%3Edocument.location%3D%27http%3A%2F%2Fwww.cgisecurity.com%2Fcgi-bin%2Fcookie.cgi%3F%27+%2Bdocument.cookie%3C%2Fscript%3E

> **http://example.blog.com/show.php?title=%22%3E%3Cscript%3Edocument.location%3D%27http%3A%2F%2Fwww.cgi**
> example.blog.com

Web Attacks

- Benign URLs:
  - http://www.amazon.com/software-business-education-finance-childrens/b/ref=sa_menu_sw4/178-3182747-8297639?ie=UTF8&node=229534
- Raw IP address
- TinyURL
  - Destination?

Email Attacks

- .exe attachment, phishing, 419 scam, prize giveaway, newsletters, banking…

Look at this Inbox | X

Jane Doe

Hey,

Have you read this? I am sure you will find it interesting.

http://128.130.60.29/reading/?articleid=1376

File-Sharing Attacks

- BitTorrent
  - The Pirate Bay, Torrentz, isoHunt
- OCH:
  - Filesonic, Filestube, Megaupload/video, iFolder
- Cues:
  - Filename, download contents, size, date, uploader, comments, extensions, …

11 / 26

Nosferatu [Full DOWNLOAD]

Sponsored results

New! - How To Get One Access To ALL Download Sites?

Also try: **nosferatu** **nosferatu** eine symphonie des grauens **nosferatu** megaupload **nosferatu** rapidshare com **nosferatu** Movie **nosferatu** download

Nosferatu
filesonic.com ext: **.mp4** size: 699 MB date: 2010-08-30
☆☆☆☆☆ **Nosferatu**
http://www.filesonic.com - Download

Nosferatu
4shared.com ext: **.exe** size: 701 MB date: 2011-01-21
☆☆☆☆☆ **Nosferatu**
http://search.4shared.com/q/BFACAw/1/nosferatu - Download

Nosferatu 1922 F W Murnau
uploadbox.com ext: **.rar** parts: 6 size: 1.20 GB date: 2011-02-07
☆☆☆☆☆ **Nosferatu** 1922 F W Murnau
http://uploadbox.com - Download

Nosferatu 1922
4shared.com ext: **.rar** size: 790 KB date: 2010-08-31
☆☆☆☆☆ **Nosferatu** (1922)
http://search.4shared.com/q/AigCAw/1/nosferatu - Download

12 / 26

Trackers: (aggregated from BitTorrent sites everywhere for reliability and speed)

- tracker1.publicbt.com:80/announce: 19 seeds
- trfkad.tracker.prq.to:80/announce: 16 seeds
- tracker-torrentsbyrizzo.info:80/announce: 16 seeds
- t1.pow7.com:80/announce: 14 seeds
- torrentbay.to:6969/announce: 11 seeds
- tracker2.istole.it:80/announce: 9 seeds
- genesis.1337x.org:80/announce: 5 seeds
- 94.228.210.41:6969/announce: 4 seeds
- **inferno.demonoid.com:3408/announce**: ? seeds

Uploader's Comments:
[Find more at http://www.torrentportal.com]

Directory: Nosferatu.XviD

Files:

codecs.exe	1.2 MB
download_codecs.lnk	4.0 KB
download_free_movies.html	13.2 KB
Nosferatu.avi	700.24 MB
README.txt	550 bytes
subtitles.lnk	4.0 KB

***700.65 MB** in **6** files. Torrent created **187.2 weeks** ago.*

info_hash: 8a9a3be374c9af295ed7280acf18cc2f5cc36eff (?) | BTID: 119663733 | **Permalink**

13 / 26

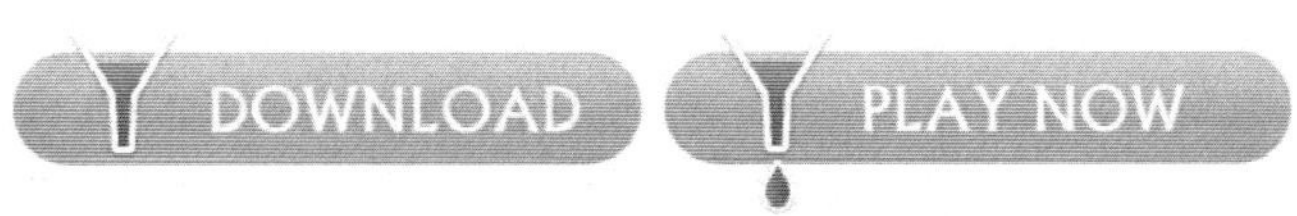

Nosferatu 1922 F W Murnau

Sponsored link: Nosferatu__1922__F.W._Murnau.rar [FAST DOWNLOAD]

Download now from uploadbox.com:

Nosferatu__1922__F.W._Murnau.rar 699 MB Download

Total size: 699.62 MB

New! - REGISTER FOR FREE and get ONE cheap ACCESS TO FILE SHARING SITES

Direct links:

```
http://uploadbox.com/files/64354de3d0?affil=1
```

Sponsored link: Nosferatu__1922__F.W._Murnau.rar [FAST DOWNLOAD]

Password recovery:	RAR Magic Password Cracker
Added:	2011-02-07 12:06:03
Link(s) source:	http://uploadbox.com

14 / 26

Participants

- 164 participants:
  - Facebook, Twitter, personal contacts
- Age: 19 to 69, Mean: 26.5
- 17 nationalities

- CS, Engineering, Law, Medicine, Geology…
- PhD, Master, Bachelor, High School

15 / 26

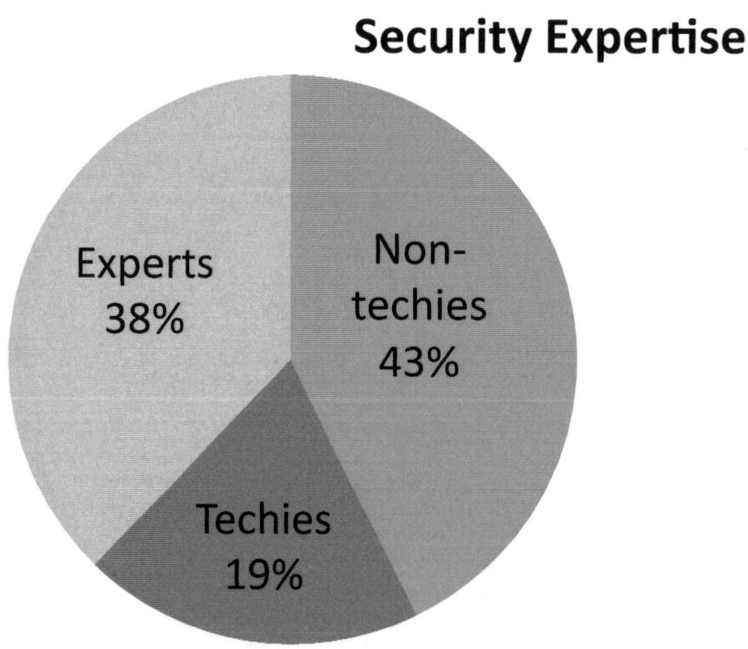

16 / 26

Total Scores

- Perception Score:
  - Experts > Techies > Non-techies
- Security Score:
  - Experts > Techies > Non-techies

[Kruskal-Wallis / Multiple comparison post-hoc tests]

- $H = 37.36$, $df = 2$, $p \ll 0.05$ for risk perception scores
- $H = 26.89$, $df = 2$, $p \ll 0.05$ for security scores

17 / 26

Individual Scores

- Perception Score: Experts > Non-techies
- Security Score:

  Web Attacks Suite: Experts > Non-techies

<u>No proof</u> that Experts > Non-techies

in Email and File-Sharing security scenarios

18 / 26

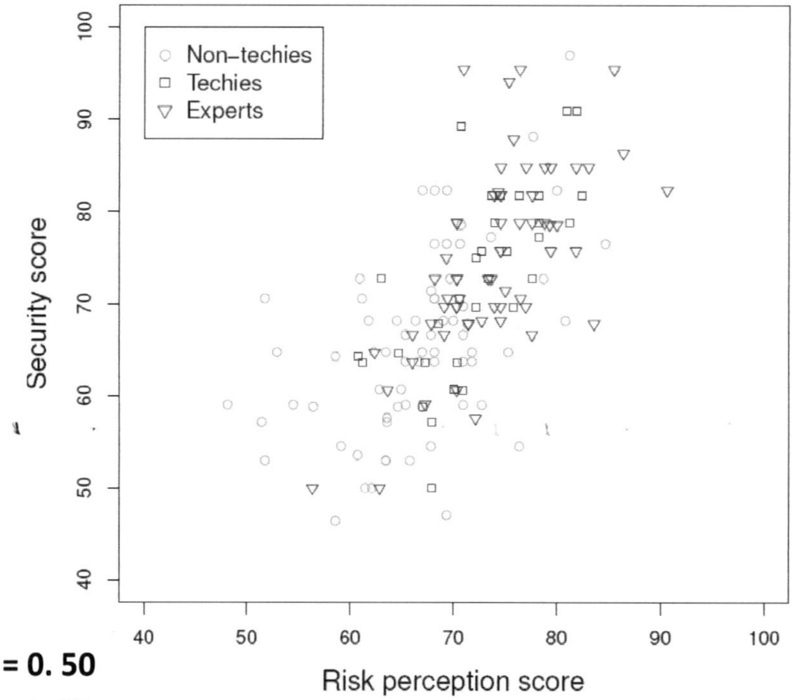

Non-techies: ρ = 0. 50

Rest: ρ = 0. 70

[Spearman's Rank Correlation]

Perception & Security

- Non-techies have bad perception
- …but still avert attacks!

- Exposure?
  - Spam: 95.7% Web attacks: 48.9%
  - Email attacks subverted: 97.1% by intuition
  - Can this be applied to more complex attacks?
    - Anti-Phishing Phil [Sheng, SOUPS '07]

Misleading Cues

- URL length & complexity:
  - "Too long and complicated"
  - "Many funny letters"
  - "Has a long name and unknown code in it"

- www.paypal.hostding.com:
  - "Easy to read"
  - "Clear obvious link"
  - "[Amazon link] was not like this"

21 / 26

Misleading Cues

- File size:
  - Movie.rar cannot be 700MB
  - 700KB movie from 1922: legit

- Informed decisions not possible
  - ➡ Rely on misleading cues

22 / 26

Shortened URL & IP Address

	Verify destination	Not familiar
TinyURL	0%	35.7%
IP address	0%	28.6%

- YouTube video
- Index of photographs
- Blog article
- Printer interface
- Proxy code
- Router configuration

23 / 26

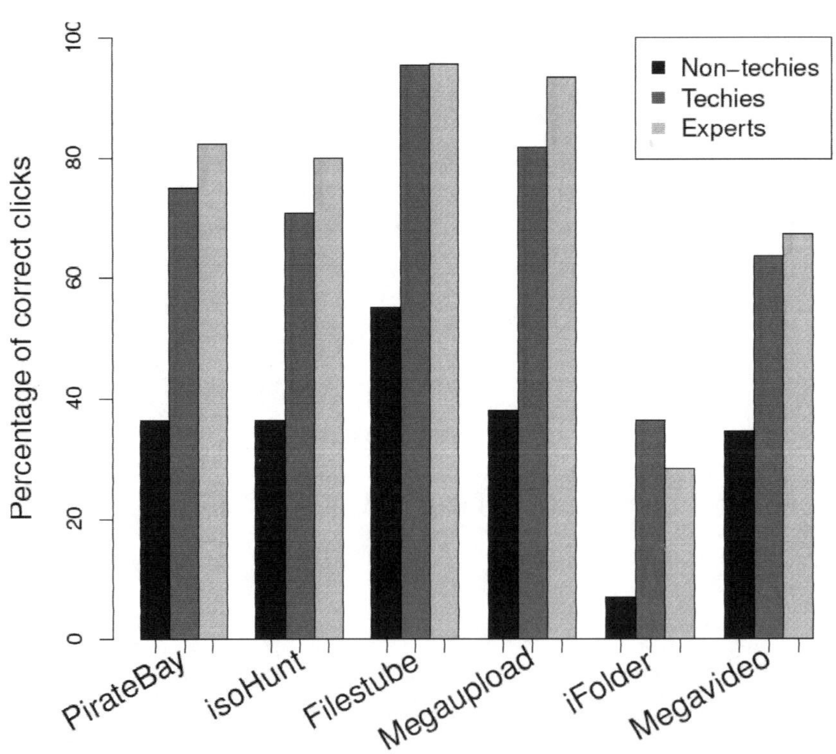

24 / 26

Conclusions

- Online test system, prevalent attacks
- 164 participants, largest study to date

- Perception ≠ Security
- Size and length: bad cues
- Shortened URLs: Tools, but no awareness
- Trick banners: Serious business

25 / 26

Thank you!

Q & A

26 / 26

PathCutter: Severing the Self-Propagation Path of XSS JavaScript Worms in Social Web Networks

Yinzhi Cao§, Vinod Yegneswaran†, Phillip Porras†, and Yan Chen§

§Northwestern Lab for Internet and Security Technology, Northwestern University, Evanston, IL

†SRI International, Menlo Park, CA

1

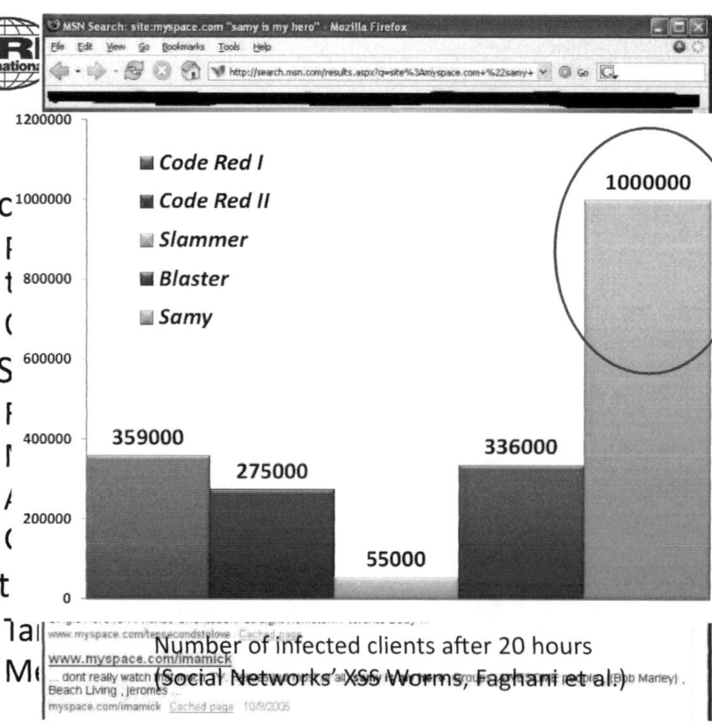

Number of infected clients after 20 hours (Social Networks' XSS Worms, Faghani et al.)

- Soc
  - I
    t ...inions,
  - (
- XSS
  - I
  - I
  - /
  - (
- In t
  - Ta
  - M ...n

2

Roadmap

- Introduction
- Background
  - Attack Steps
  - XSS Taxonomy
- Related Work
- Our Approach
- Implementation
- Evaluation

3

Background

- Step 1 – Enticement and Exploitation
- Step 2 – Privilege Escalation
- Step 3 – Replication
- Step 4 – Propagation

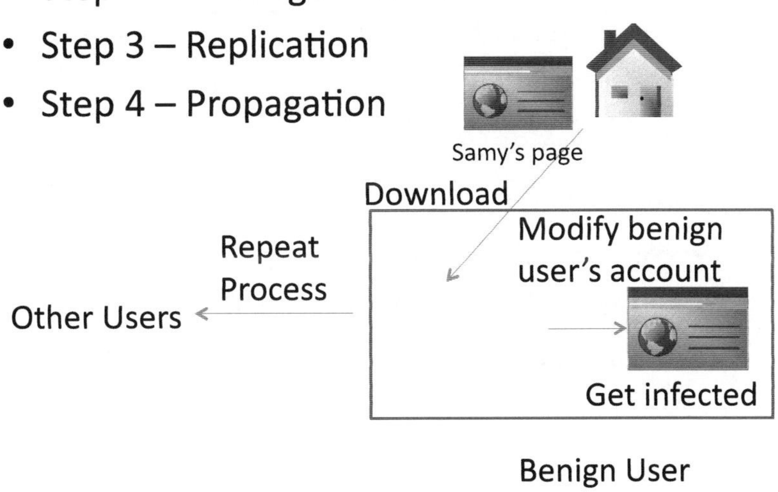

4

XSS Taxonomy

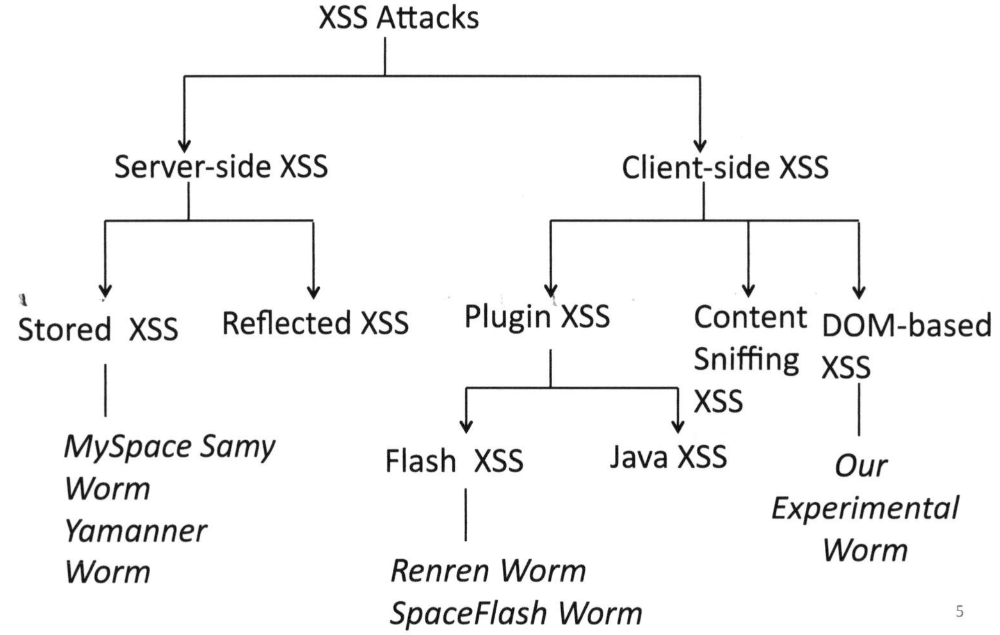

5

Related Work

- Group one: Prevent XSS vulnerabilities
  - Incomplete coverage (BluePrint, Plug-in Patches, Barth et al., and Saxena et al.)
- Group two: Prevent XSS worms
  - No early-stage prevention (Spectator and Xu et al.)
  - Not resistant to polymorphic worm (Sun et al.)
- Our goal: Prevent all the XSS worms with early-stage prevention and resistance to polymorphic worms

6

Our Approach

- Two key concepts: (1) request authentication and (2) view separation

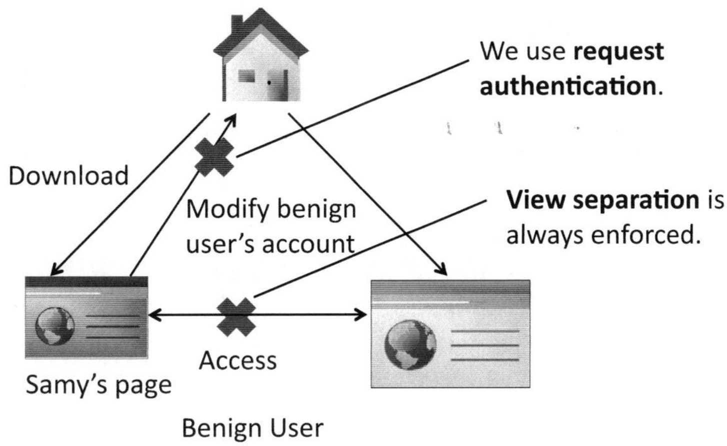

View Separation

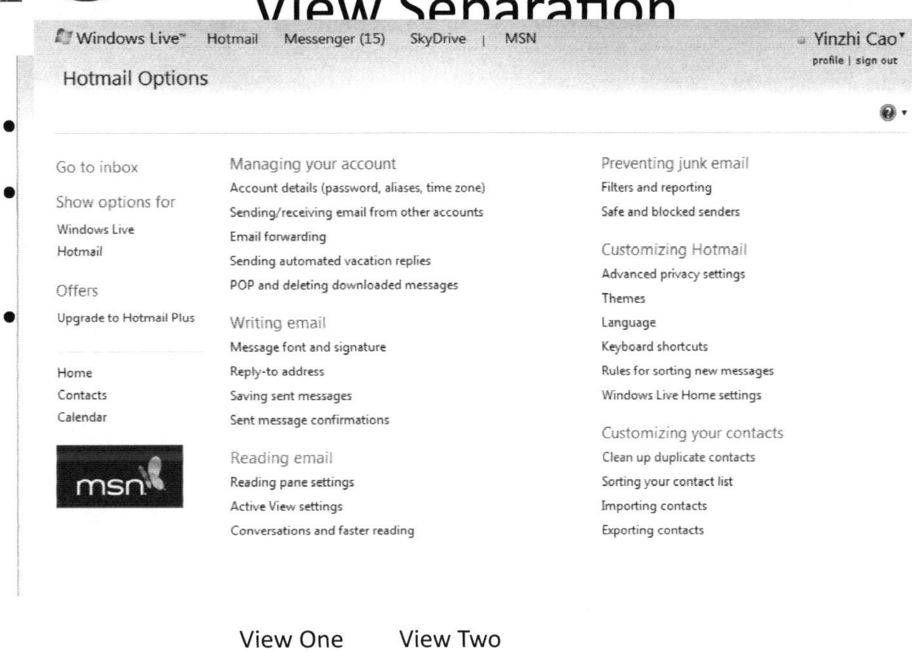

Request Authentication

- For example, requests from blog A does not have permissions to modify blog B
- Identifying which view a client-side request is from.
  - Secret token
  - Referer header
- Check if the view has the permission

9

Our Approach

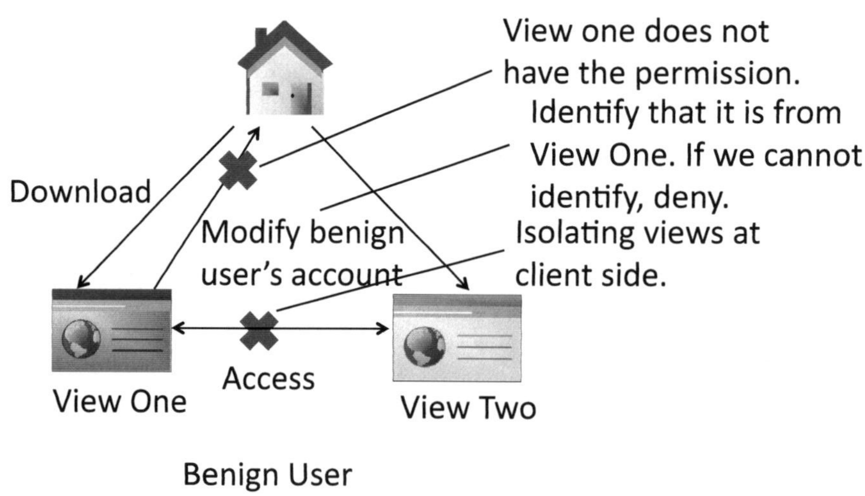

10

Roadmap

- Introduction
- Background
- Related Work
- Our Approach
- Implementation
  - Implementation One (Server Modification)
  - Implementation Two (Proxy)
- Evaluation
  - Case Study of Five Real-world Worms and Two Experimental Worms (only two covered in the talk)
  - Performance

11

Implementation One (Server Modification)

- Prototype examples: WordPress, Elgg
- Dividing views: by blogs
- Permissions for different views: can only modify its own blog.

12

View Isolation for Server Modification

- Isolating views at client side.
  - Pseudodomain encapsulation.

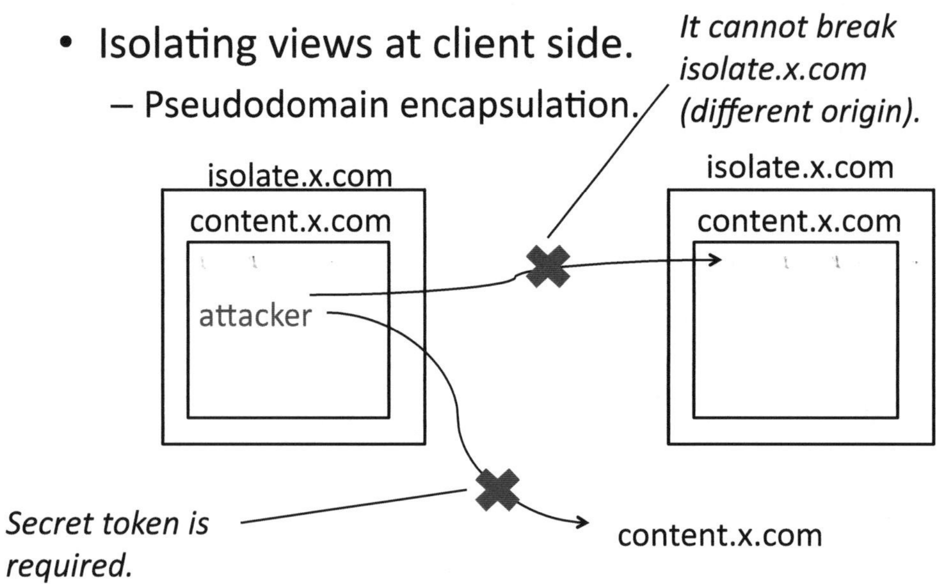

13

Request Authentication for Server Modification

- Identifying requests from client-side
  - Secret token
    - Insertion position: Each request that will modify server-side contents.
- Checking requests' permission
  - Checking position: Database operation. (A narrow interface that each modifying request will go through.)

14

Implementation Two (Proxy)

- Dividing views: by different client-side URLs.
- Permissions for different views:
  - Possible outgoing post URL from those URLs

15

View Isolation for Proxy

- Isolating views at client side
  - The same as implementation one.

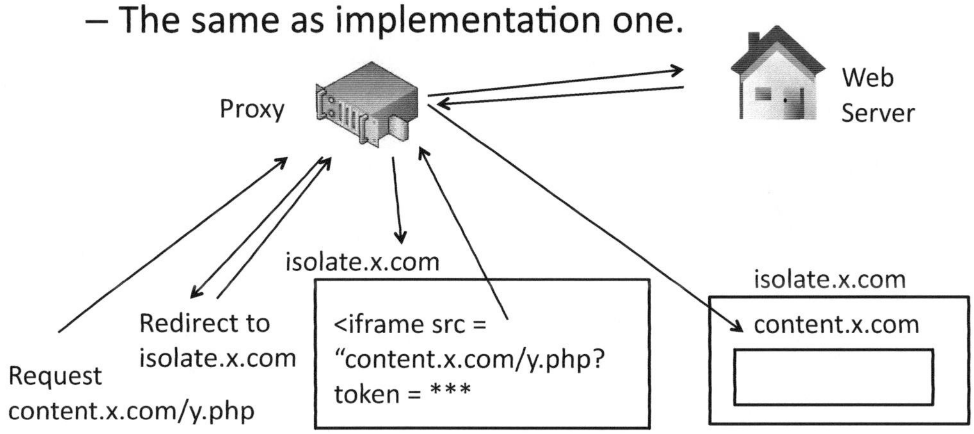

16

Request Authentication for Proxy

- Identifying requests from client-side
  - Referer header
    - Specified by the browser. Attackers cannot change it.
- Checking requests' permissions
  - Checking position: Proxy.
  - Method: See if the view has the permission to send the request.

17

Case Study for Real World Worms

- XSS Worm in Renren (Facebook in China)

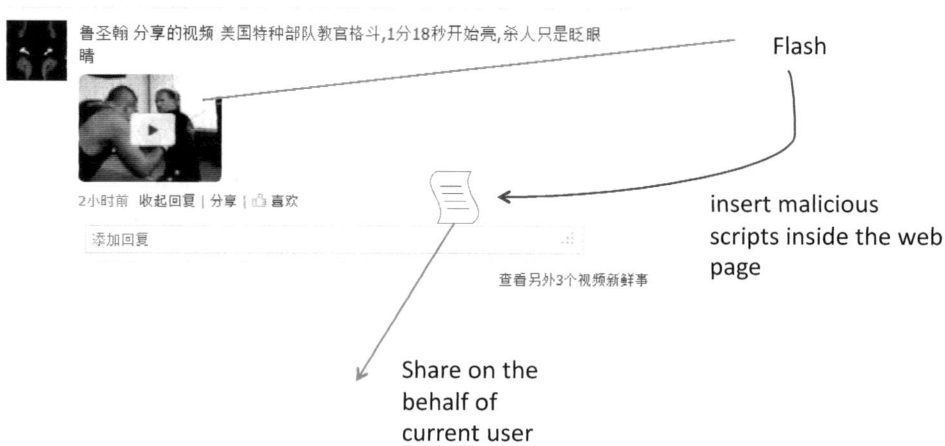

18

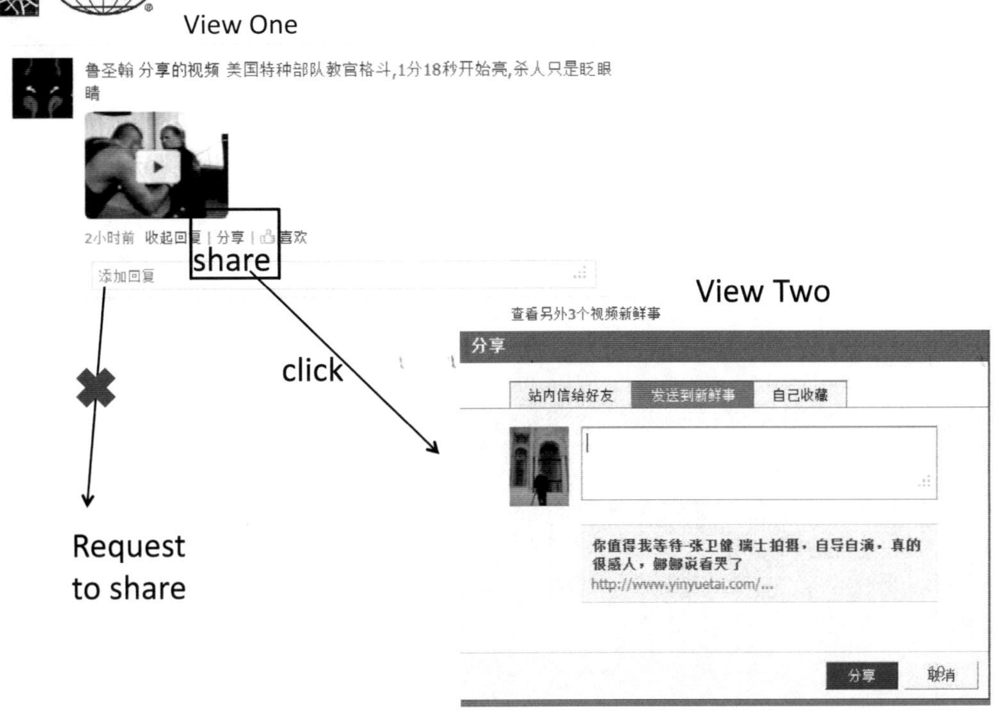

- Yamanner Worm

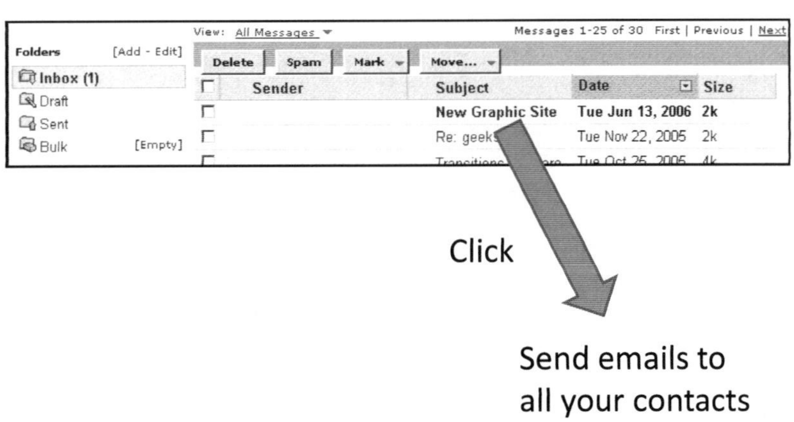

20

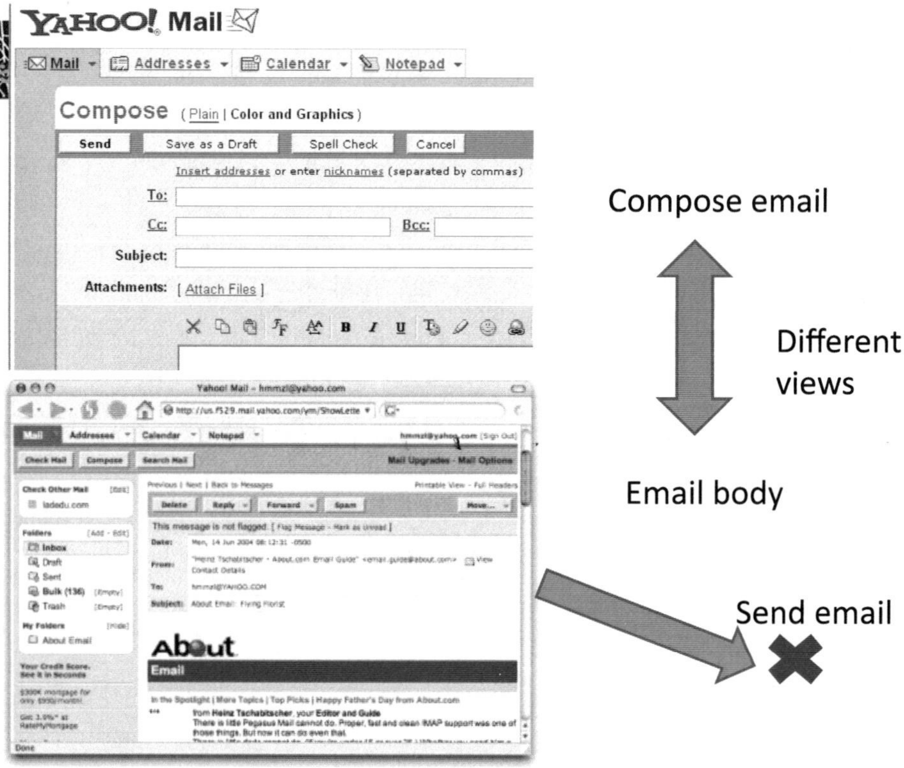

21

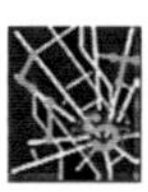

Evaluation

- N
  -
  ...ents
- R
  -

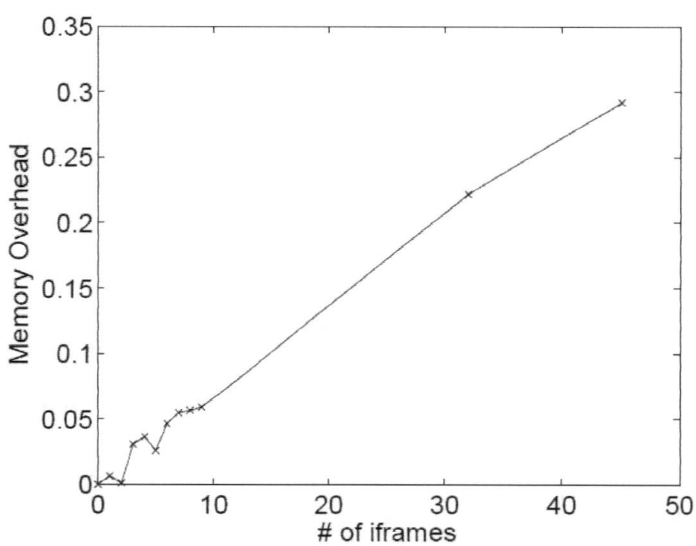

22

Conclusions

- We cut off the propagation path of XSS worms through view separation by psuedodomain encapsulation and request authentication.
- We implement PathCutter by proxy assistance and server modification.
- We evaluate PathCutter on 5 real-world worms and 2 proof-of-concept worms.

23

Thanks!

Questions?

24

Backup

25

Comparison with Existing Works

	Group Two: Worm prevention			Group One: Mitigating XSS				
	Spectator	Sun et al.	Xu et al.	BluePrint	Plug-in Patches	Barth et al.	Saxena et al.	PathCutter
Blocking Step	4	3	4	1	1	1	1	2
Polymorphic Worm	Yes	No	Yes	Yes	Yes	Yes	Yes	Yes
Early-Stage Prevention	No	Yes	No	Yes	Yes	Yes	Yes	Yes
Types of XSS that Can Be Defended	All	All	Passively Observable Worms	Traditional Server-side XSS Worms	Plug-in XSS Worms	Content Sniffing XSS Worms	DOM-Based XSS Worms	All
Deployment	Server or Proxy	Client	Server	Server	Client	Client	Client	Server or Proxy
Passive/Active Monitoring	Active	Passive	Passive	Active	Active	Active	Active	Active

26

Limitation

- Need to know the semantics of web application
- Only prevent worm behavior but not all the damages

27

Existing solutions

- Spectator

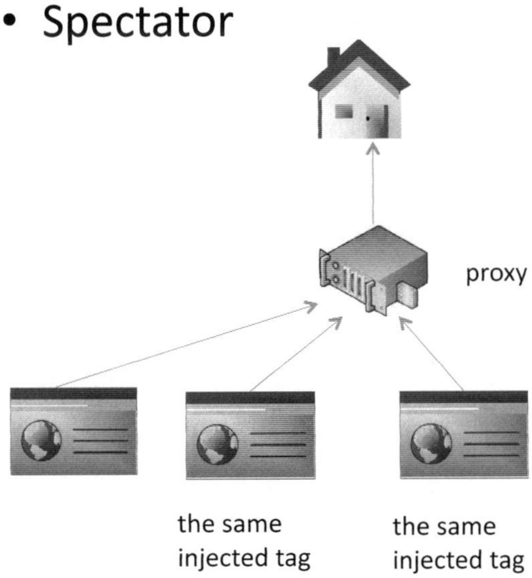

But it can only detect the worm when it spreads for a while!

... if it reaches a threshold, report it.

28

Existing solutions

- Esorics 09

But
(1) Payload may change.
(2) Pure client-side solution.

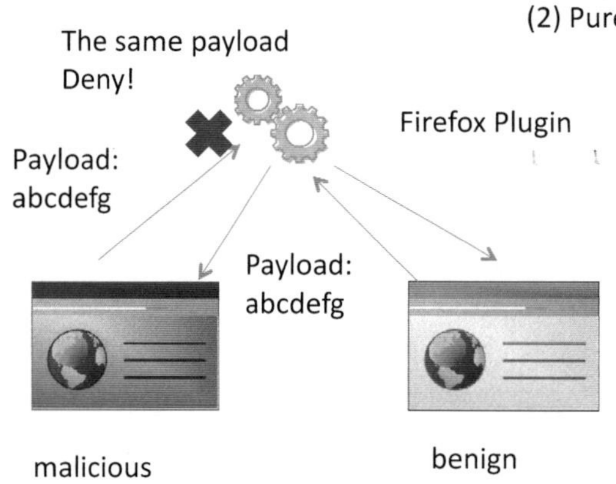

29

URL graph provided by the server or a third-party

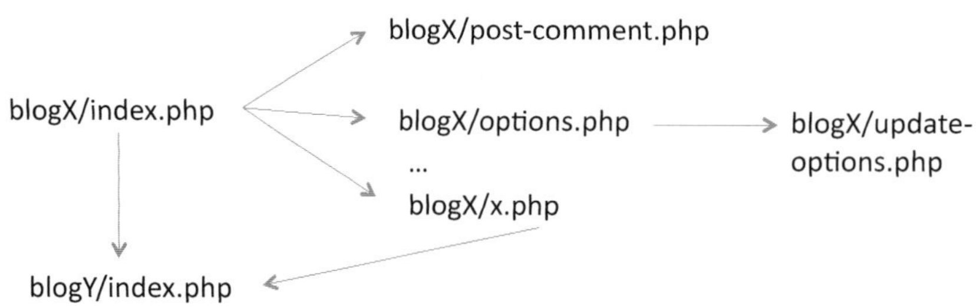

30

The Latent Community Model for Detecting Sybil Attacks

Zhuhua Cai, Christopher Jermaine
Rice University
{zc7, cmj4} @ rice.edu

Outline

I Sybil attack

II Current solutions

III Our approach

Sybil Attack

An attacker creates multiple fake identities (Sybils) to gain influence in the open system

… …

Examples

- Recommendation system, i.e., Drugstore …
- Email system, (spam email)
- Web spam
- Distributed Hash Table (DHT)
- Communication System (Tor)

… …

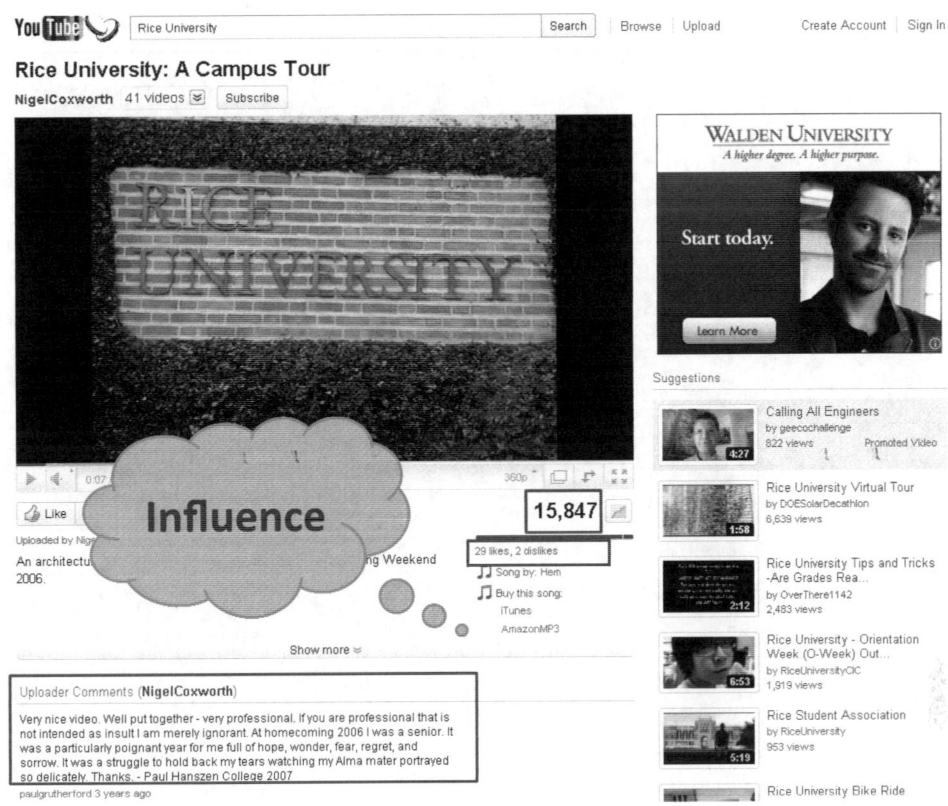

Outline

- I Sybil attack
- II Current solutions
- III Our approach

Database Group in Rice Zhuhua Cai 6

Current Solutions

- Prevention
- Detection

Solutions / Prevention

- Challenge/Response Mechanisms
  - Computational Puzzle or CAPTCHA
- Credentials
  - E.g., social security number, driver license, banking account

Solutions /Detection

- Trust/Reputation
  - Amazon's seller rating system
  - be subjected to Whitewashing attack
- IP/IP-Clustered
  - be subjected to Botnet
- Machine Learning
  - Features like invitation frequency, requests, etc
- PagePank and HITS
  - Trusted pages

Database Group in Rice Zhuhua Cai 9

Using Social networks

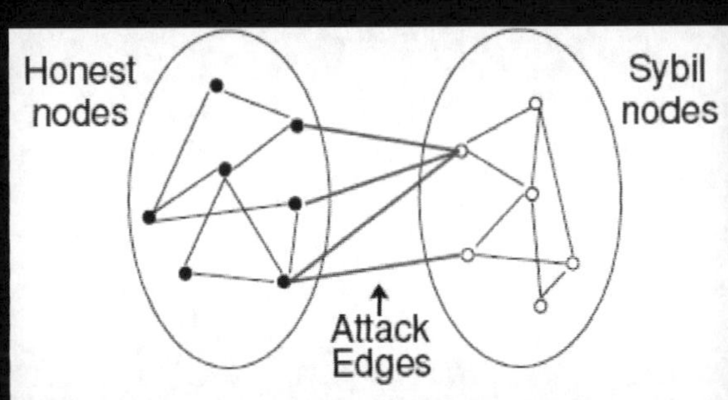

- Bottleneck Cut
- Fast Mixing Property

- SybilGuard [SIGCOMM'06], SybilLimit [Oakland'08], SybilInfer [NDSS'09], SumUp [NSDI'09], DSybil [Oakland '09], GateKeeper [Infocom' 10]

Database Group in Rice Zhuhua Cai 10

Outline

- I Sybil attack
- II Current solutions
- III Our approach

Database Group in Rice Zhuhua Cai 11

Our Approach

Rather than assuming the forms of attacks, we instead learn a statistical generative model for the underlying network, called the *latent community (LC) model.*

Database Group in Rice Zhuhua Cai 12

What is Generative Model ?

A generative model is a model that describes the sequence of distributions that generates our observable data.

Example

- Regression

  $y \sim Norm(a * x + b, \sigma^2)$

  - y: income, x : age
  - Given an x, you can estimate: y and its probability

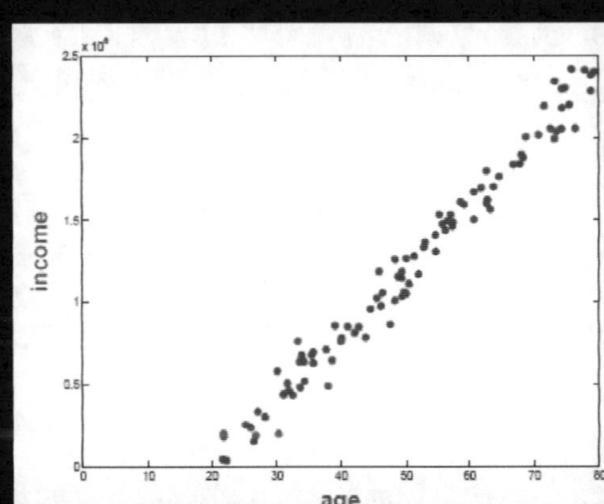

What is LC Model?

- LC is a Statistical generative model
  - Node
  - Edge
  - Community
  - Latent positions

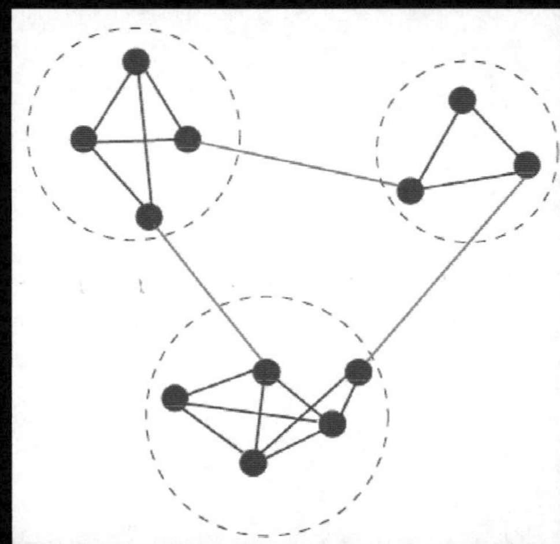

Database Group in Rice Zhuhua Cai 15

LC model

- Bayesian network of LC model
  - π: the fraction of nodes in each community.
  - δ: the internal edge density
  - μ: the positions in Euclidean space.
  - c: the membership of nodes
  - η: a scaling factor

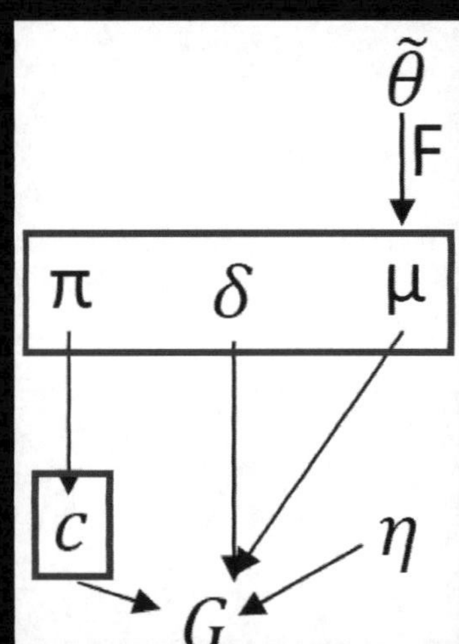

Database Group in Rice Zhuhua Cai 16

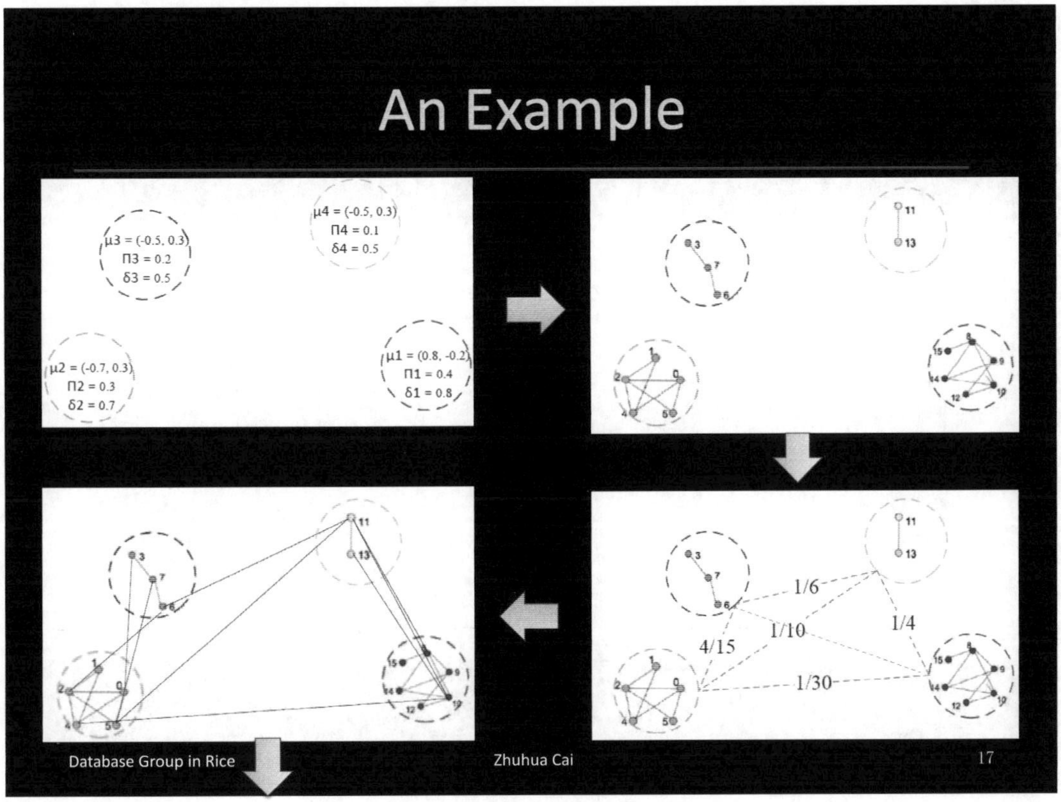
An Example
μ3 = (-0.5, 0.3)
Π3 = 0.2
δ3 = 0.5
μ4 = (-0.5, 0.3)
Π4 = 0.1
δ4 = 0.5
μ2 = (-0.7, 0.3)
Π2 = 0.3
δ2 = 0.7
μ1 = (0.8, -0.2)
Π1 = 0.4
δ1 = 0.8
1/6
1/10
1/4
4/15
1/30
Database Group in Rice
Zhuhua Cai
17

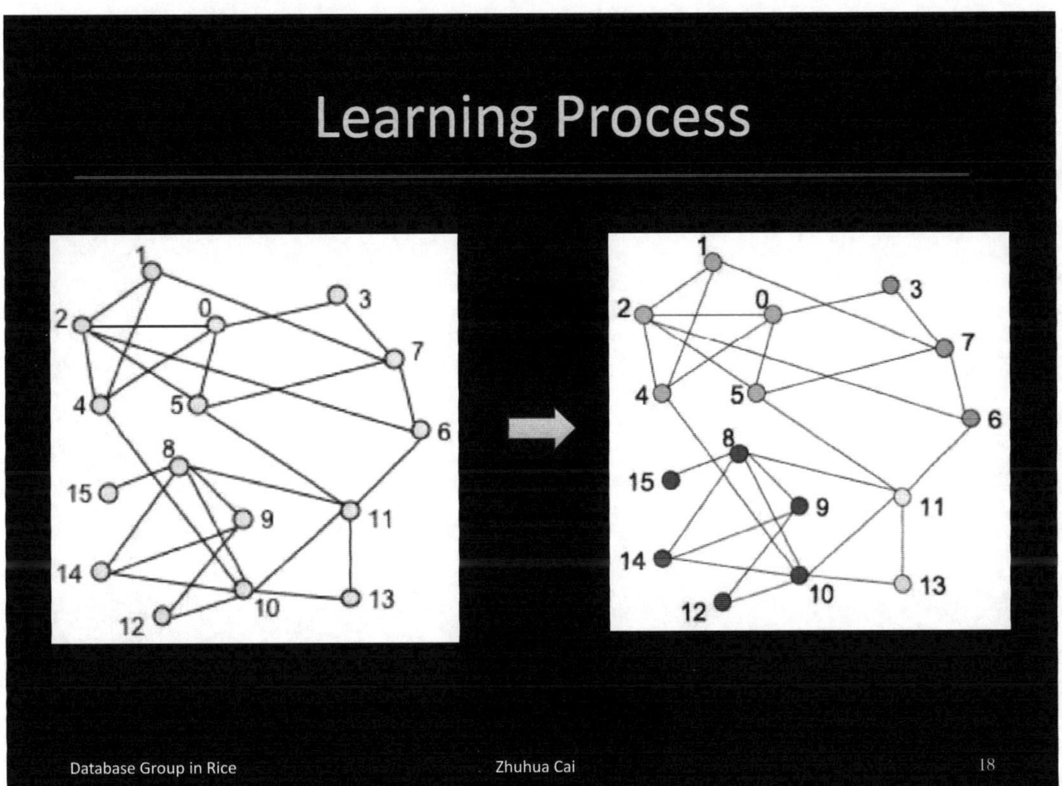
Learning Process
1
2
0
3
7
4
5
6
8
15
9
11
14
10
13
12
Database Group in Rice
Zhuhua Cai
18

Second Example

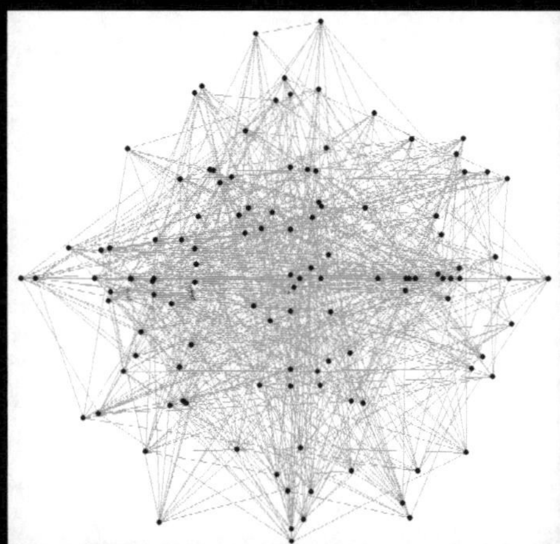

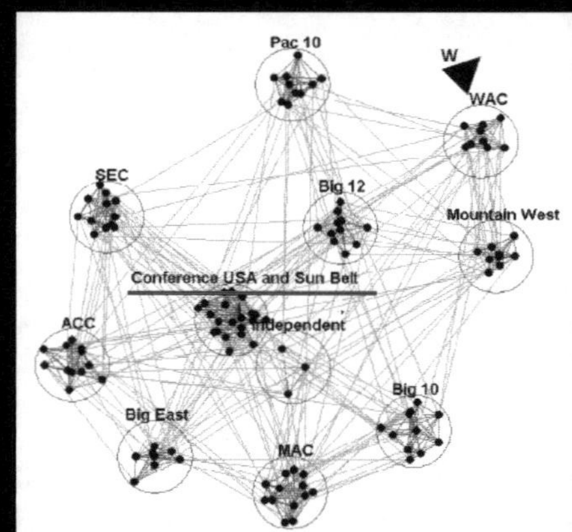

Figure 1: Learned model for the 2010 college football data set.

2010 American college football schedule

LC-based Sybil Detector (1/2)

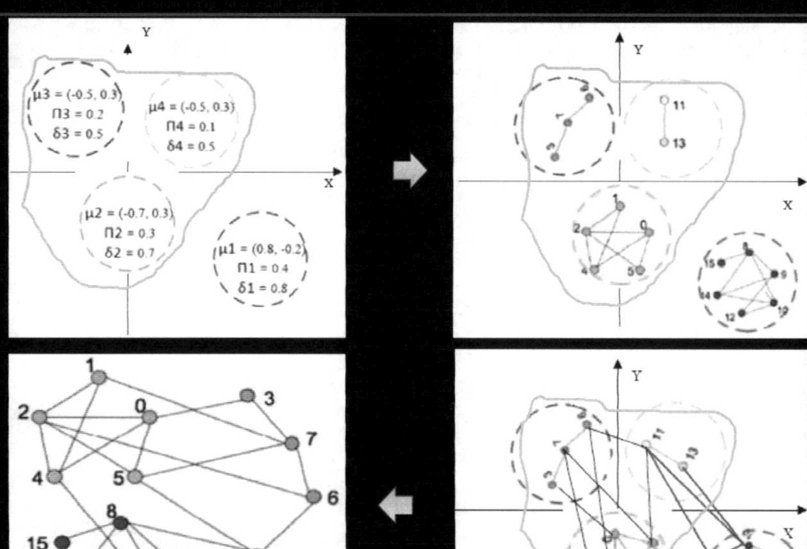

LC-based Sybil detector (2/2)

- Two kinds of communities
- Assumptions:
  - Seeds
  - Nodes in the same community have same properties.

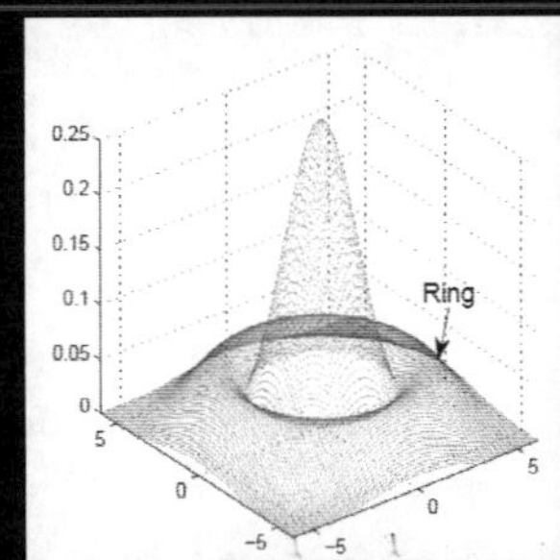

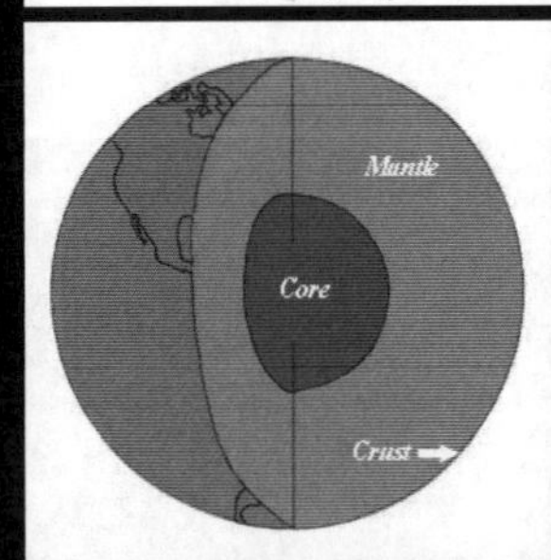

Bayesian Inference Engine for learning algorithm

- Learning Algorithm

$$P(\Theta|G) = \frac{P(G|\Theta)P(\Theta)}{P(G)}$$

- Gibbs Sampling
  1. Choose initial values.
  2. Iterate over each parameter, and sample values.
  3. Aggregate the distribution of target parameter.

LC Model on Digg (1/4)

- Digg
  - Following or being followed by others
  - Digg or Bury others
  - Motivation for Sybils
- Dataset
  - 594, 426 nodes
  - 5, 066, 988 edges

LC Model on Digg (2/4)

- Configurations
  - 100 clusters
  - "Kevin Rose" as a seed
  - 200 cycles
- Sybil communities
  - Community 3 and 4
  - δ: 0.40 and 0.55
  - n: 311 and 299

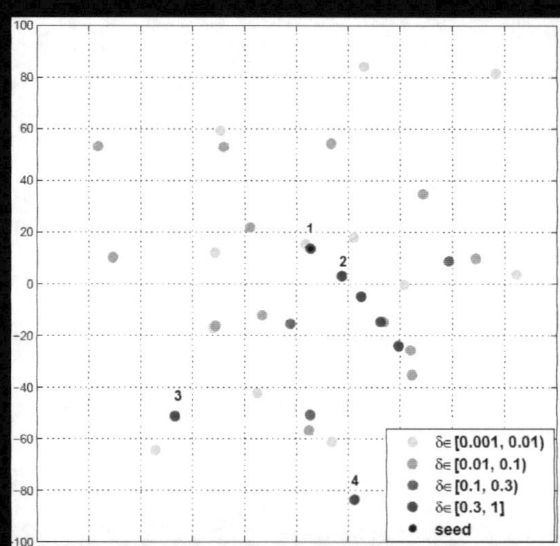

LC Model on Digg (3/4)

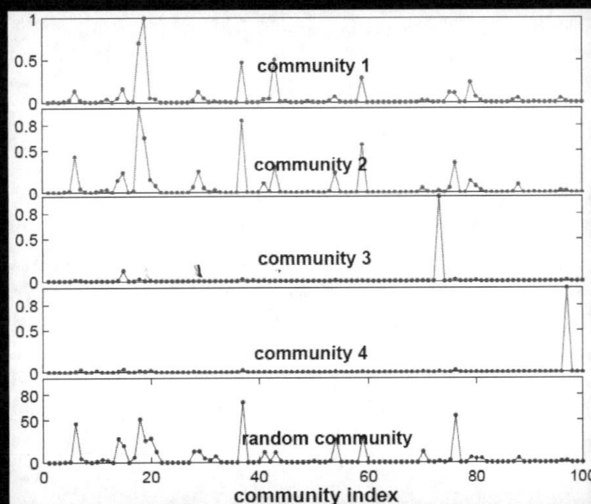

The relative edge density among Digg communities

LC Model on Digg (4/4)

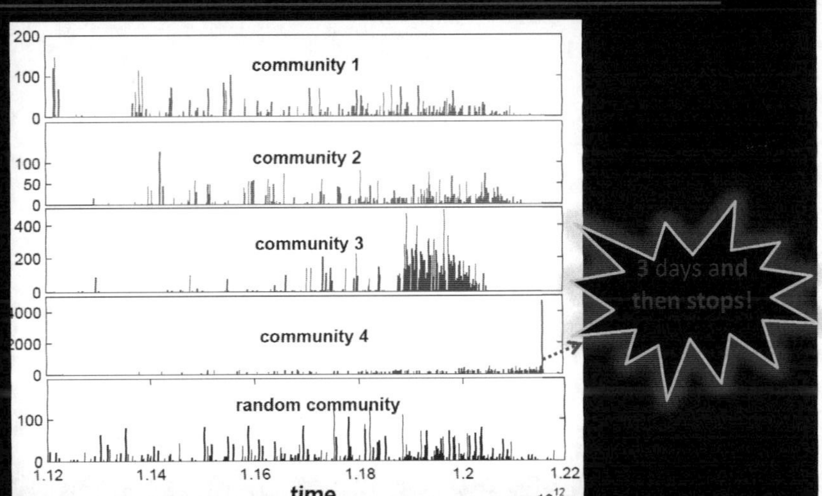

The creation time of edges in Digg communities

LC-based Sybil Detector (1/2)

- Compared Algorithm
  - SybilInfer and GateKeeper
- Simulate Sybil attacks
  - Attackers, victims, seeds, attack topologies
- Datasets

Dataset	Node	Edge	Directed
Irvine Community	1899	13, 820	True
Wikipedia Vote	7115	100, 762	True
Gnutella	8717	31, 525	False
Email-Enron	36, 692	367, 662	False

LC-based Automatic Sybil Detector (2/2)

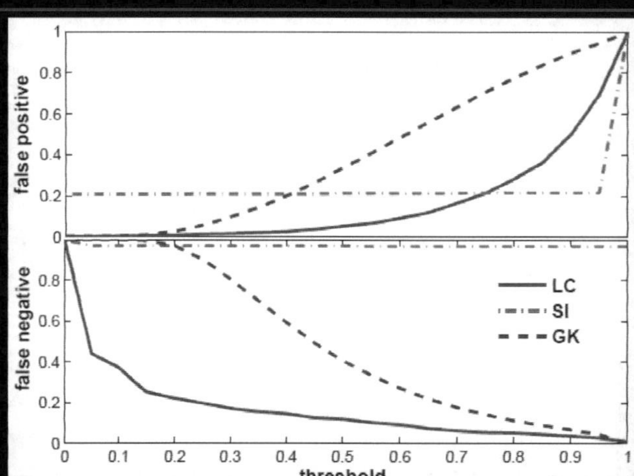

General result for comparison

Discussion

- Algorithm Complexity
  - O(k*n) (when the number of communities is k).
  - 200 cycles lead to result
- LC model in other literatures
  - Content distribution in clusters
  - Geographical applications
  - ……

Conclusion

- LC model shows good performance on the Sybil problem
- Weakness
  - Tree-topology attack or Sparse attack.
  - It is not a distributed algorithm.
  - It is not used in applications without social networks.

Q & A

Thank You !

Database Group in Rice | Zhuhua Cai | 31

BLACR: TTP-Free Blacklistable Anonymous Credentials with Reputation

Man Ho Au, Apu Kapadia, Willy Susilo
University of Wollongong &
Indiana University Bloomington

University of Wollongong   INDIANA UNIVERSITY

Anonymous access to services protects users' privacy

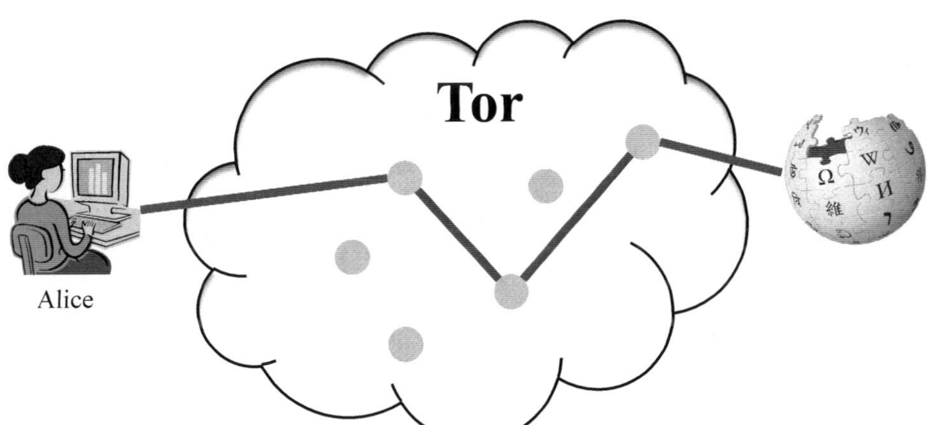

Tor prevents Wikipedia from learning Alice's location or browsing habits

Unfortunately, users can abuse their anonymity

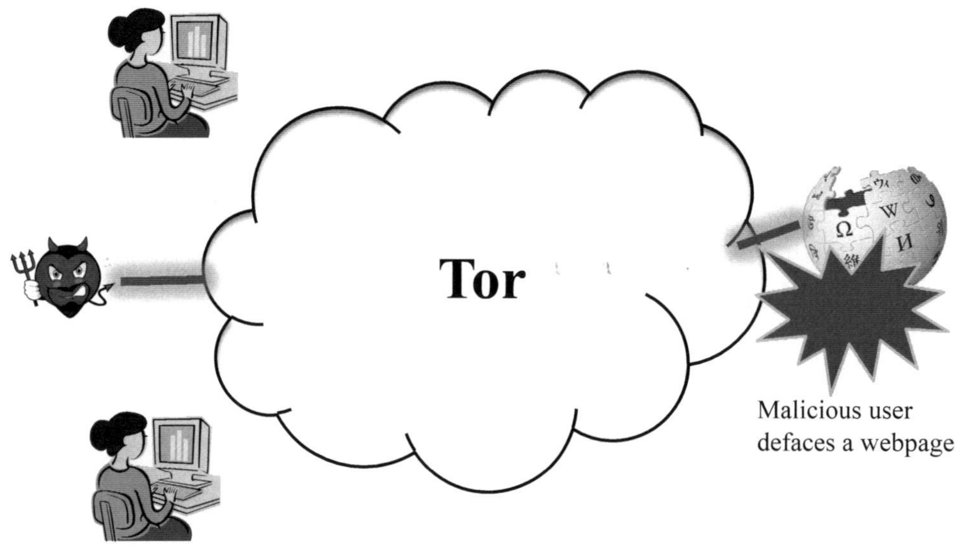

In response, some providers block anonymous access entirely

Revocable anonymous credentials can provide accountable anonymity

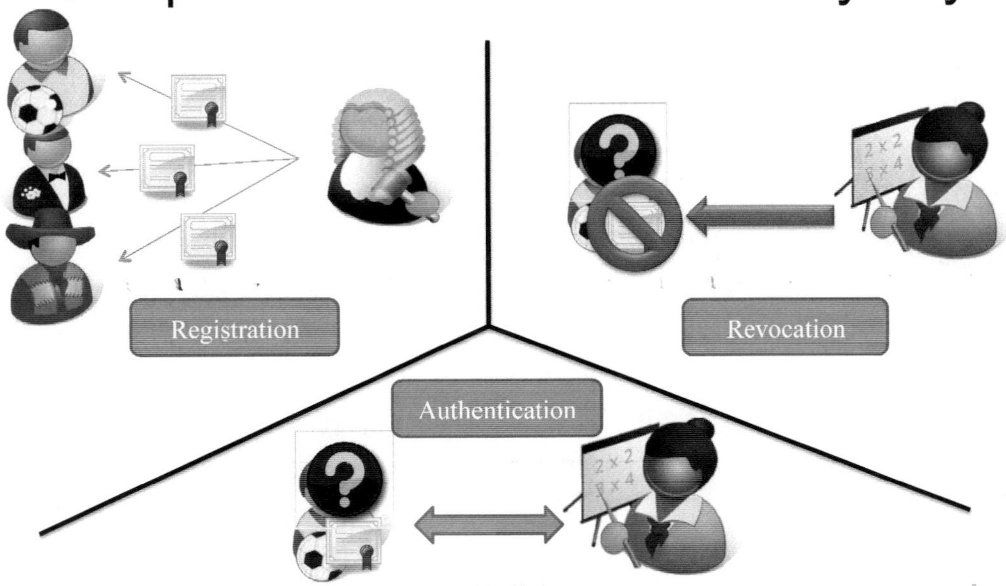

BLACR Man Ho Au 5

BLACR is TTP-free and provides the most general access policy

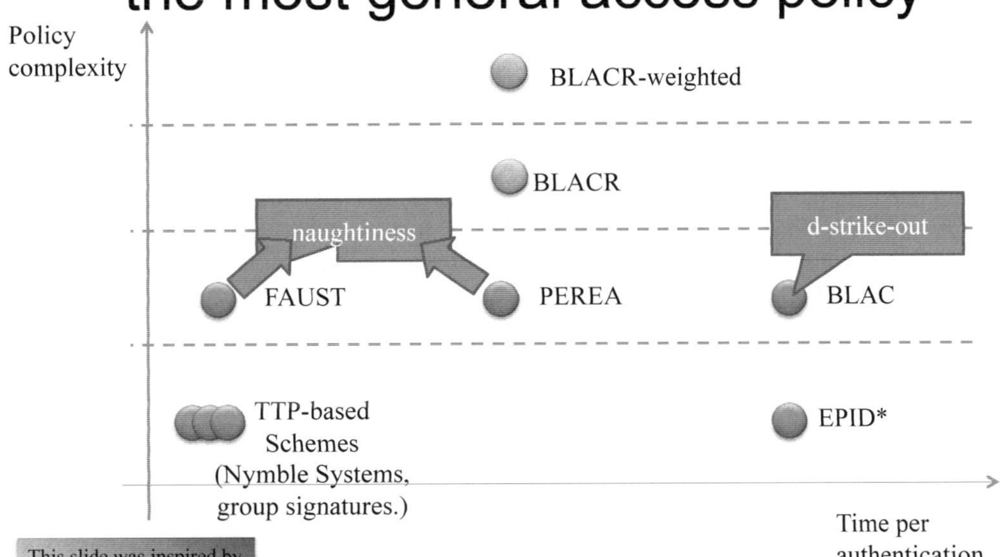

This slide was inspired by Nick Hopper's presentation on FAUST.

Man Ho Au 6

BLACR adds reputation to BLAC

Reputation = 5 – 10 = -5

Access Policy: User can authenticate if his/her reputation is above -10

Generalisation of naughtiness which supports positive score

BLACR scores reputation across different categories

A sever may maintain categories for
video content and **comments**

Video Content Rules:	
100 good karma	+ 5
Minor copyright violations	-2
Major copyright violations	-10

Comments Rules:	
Rated helpful by 100 users	+ 5
Use of offensive words	-2
Use of hate speech	-10

Access Policy: User can authenticate if his/her reputation in Video Content > -5 AND in Comments > -1

BLACR is similar to all anonymous credential systems in Registration

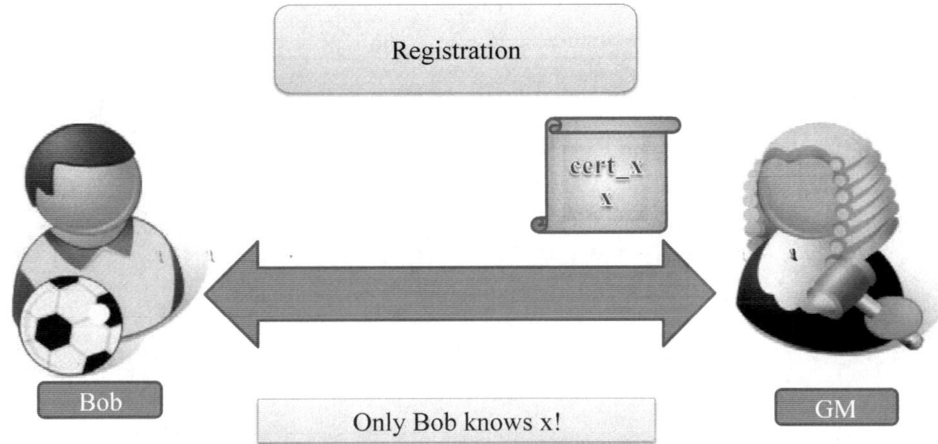

Anonymity is provided via a standard ZK Technique

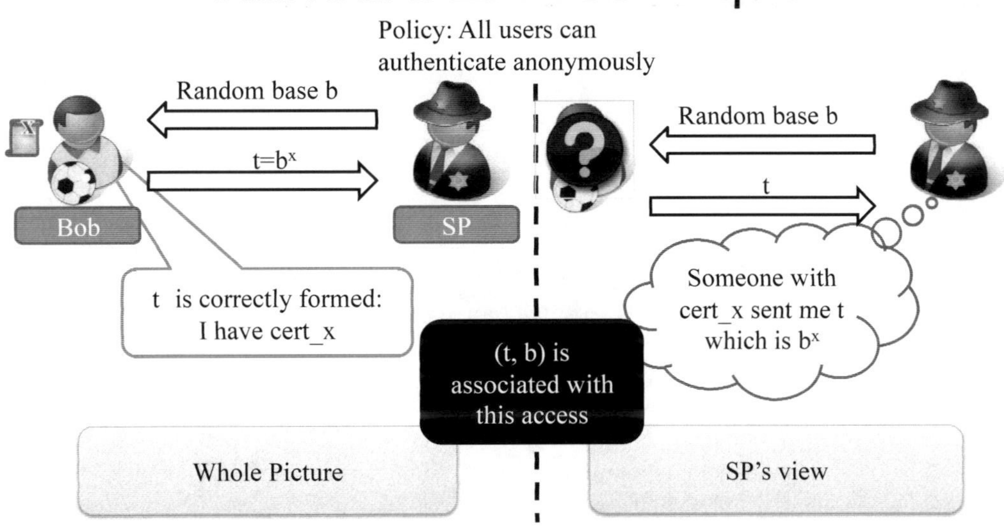

BLACR supports reputation via a novel use of ZK techniques

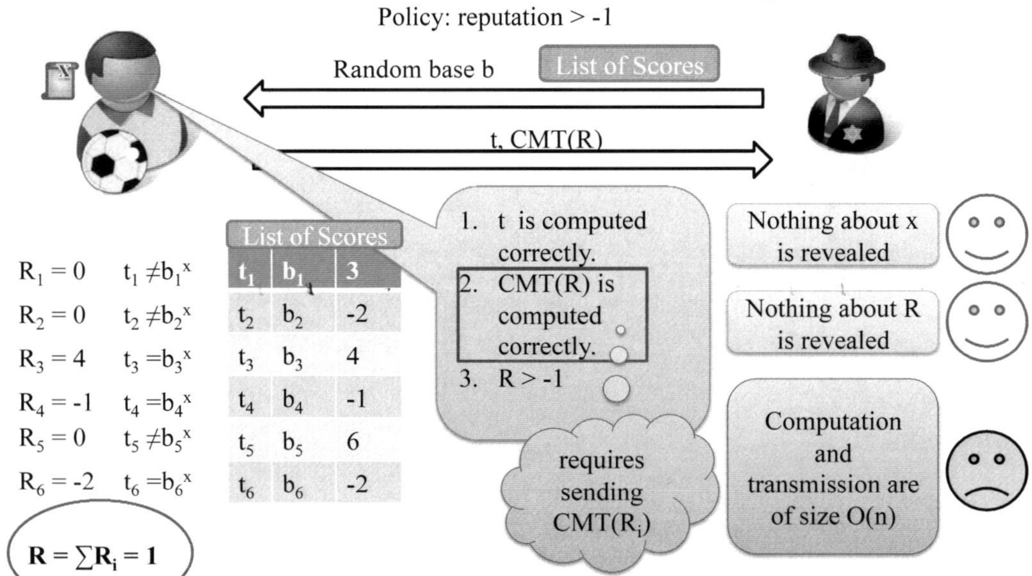

Only incremental work is needed in **express-lane authentication**

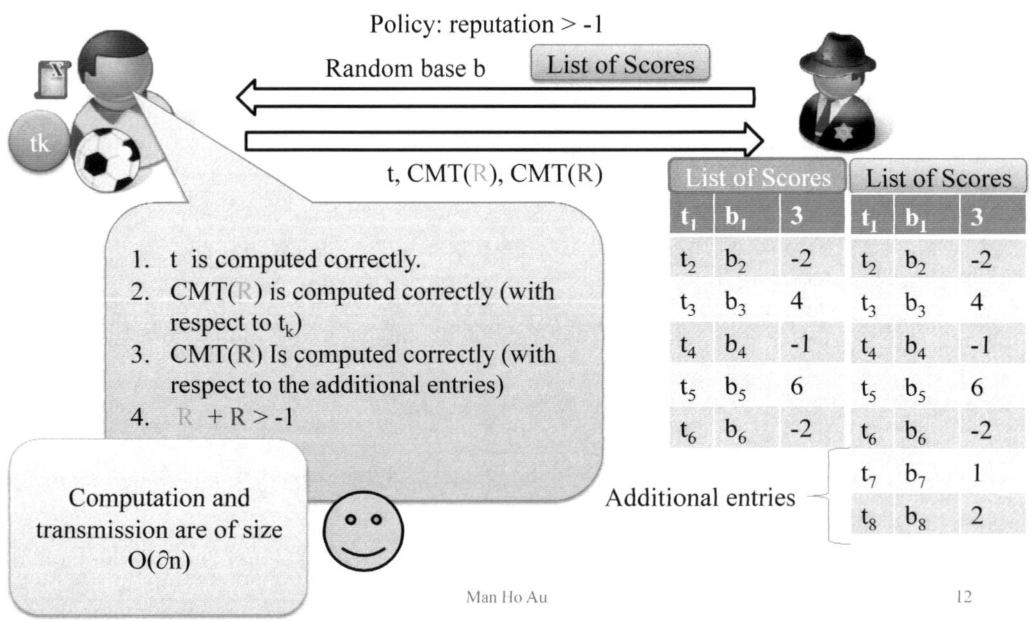

Express-lane tokens are tied to time periods to preserve anonymity

Authentication at T_8 results in a receipt t_k on list L

Authentication at T_9 involves:

1. List L
2. Additional entries ∂
3. Additional entries ∂^*

Obtain receipt t_k related to $L + \partial$

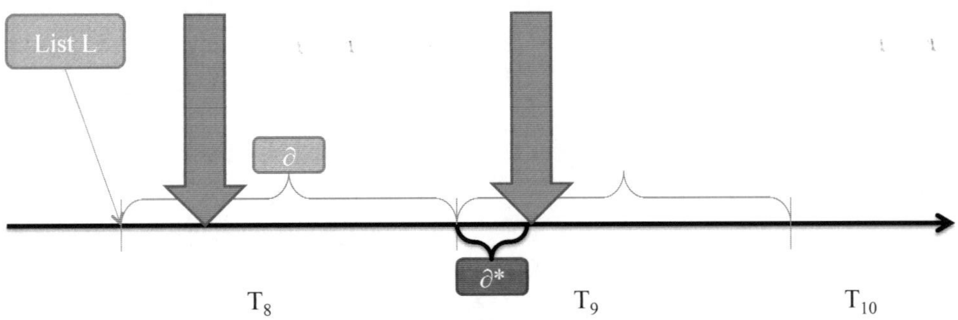

BLACR is fast at the server

Authentication time at the server vs. Blacklist size, 8 Cores

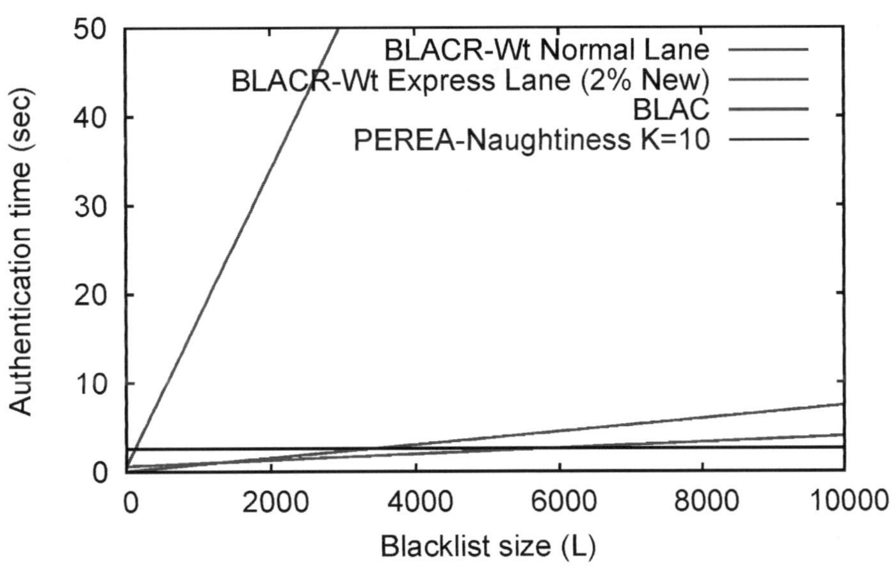

BLACR is fast at the user too

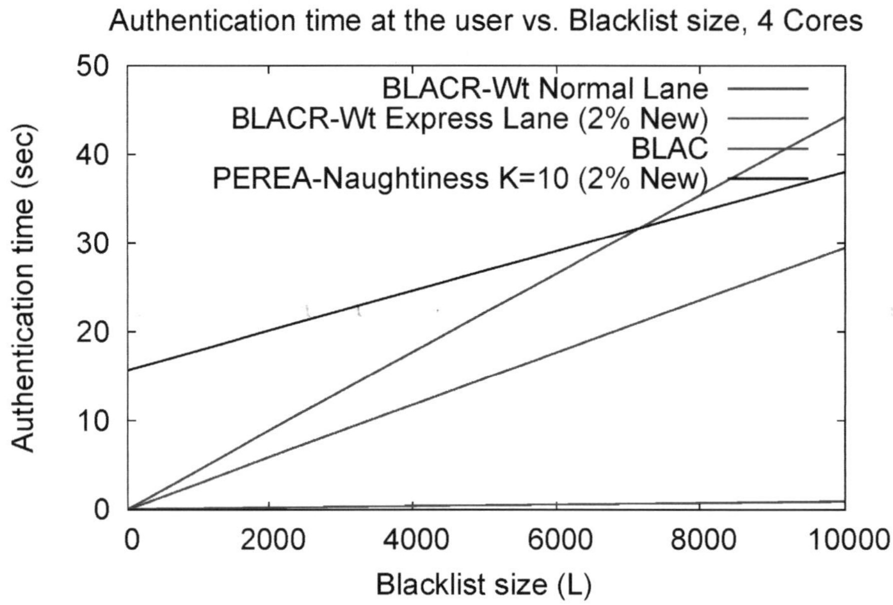

BLACR Man Ho Au 15

Conclusion: We make three contributions

We generalize the concept of **reputation based anonymous blacklisting**

We introduce **express-lane tokens** to greatly speed up authentication

We propose a **weighted extension** to penalize repeated misbehaviors

BLACR Man Ho Au 16

Punishing repeated misbehavior without affecting anonymity

List of Scores		
t_1	**b_1**	**-3**
t_2	b_2	-2
t_3	**b_3**	**-1**
t_4	b_4	-3
t_5	**b_5**	**-6**
t_6	b_6	-1

If t_1, t_3, t_5 belongs to Bob…

Reputation = -3 - 1 - 6 = -10

Weight	
1	1
2	2
3	4
4	10
5	20

In the weighted version:

Reputation = -3 + 2*(-1) + 4*(-6) = -29

BLACR improves the speed of authentication compared to BLAC

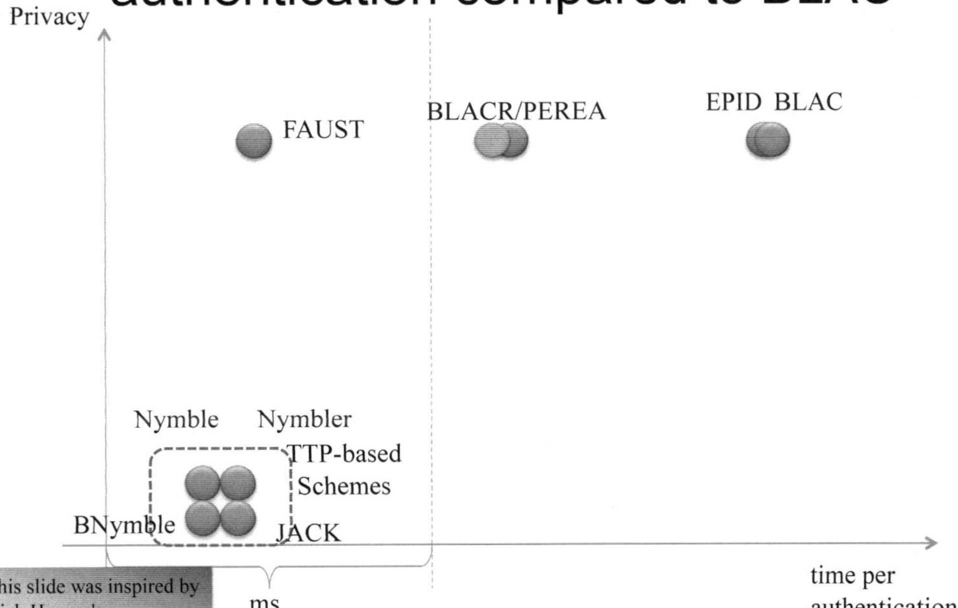

This slide was inspired by Nick Hopper's presentation on FAUST.

UNIVERSITY OF OREGON

Accountable Wiretapping

-or-

I know they can hear you now

Adam Bates
University of Oregon

Kevin Butler
University of Oregon

Micah Sherr
Georgetown University

Clay Shields
Georgetown University

Patrick Traynor
Georgia Institute of Technology

Dan Wallach
Rice University

NDSS'12, San Diego, CA, USA
7 February 2012

When wiretaps go bad...

UNIVERSITY OF OREGON

"Due to the improper minimization of calls, creating 'gaps' throughout the majority of calls, and preventing relevant conversations from being heard in their full context, Blagojevich requests that all wiretapped recordings be suppressed..."

Wiretapping, Unaccountably

UNIVERSITY OF OREGON

- United States wiretaps cannot demonstrate correct behavior or detect incorrect behavior.
- Wiretap targets can take active countermeasures to obscure communication or corrupt wiretap transcripts.
- Violation of wiretap laws could render transcripts inadmissible in federal trials.
- Citizens need stronger assurance that wiretaps were legally authorized and employed.

Oregon Systems Infrastructure Research and Information Security (OSIRIS) Lab 3

Accountable Wiretapping

UNIVERSITY OF OREGON

- Our work demonstrates that wiretap events can be safely logged in a privacy preserving manner.
- Our architecture assumes a potentially untrusted storage service that:

  (i) Never obtains access to plaintext wiretap records

  (ii) Cannot determine the number or scope of wiretaps orders
- In spite of this, our storage can prove to auditors that it has correctly recorded all encrypted data.

Oregon Systems Infrastructure Research and Information Security (OSIRIS) Lab 4

Background: Lawful Access

UNIVERSITY OF OREGON

- Modern United States wiretaps were established by the 1994 U.S. Communications Assistance for Law Enforcement Act (CALEA) and implemented via the 2003 ANSI J-STD-025 ("J-Standard") specification.
- Two forms of wiretap order: *pen registers* allow access to call metadata, *full audio interception* orders allow law enforcement to access call content.
- CALEA wiretaps lack audit features, complicating the process of generating the required annual wiretap report.

Background: CALEA Wiretapping

UNIVERSITY OF OREGON

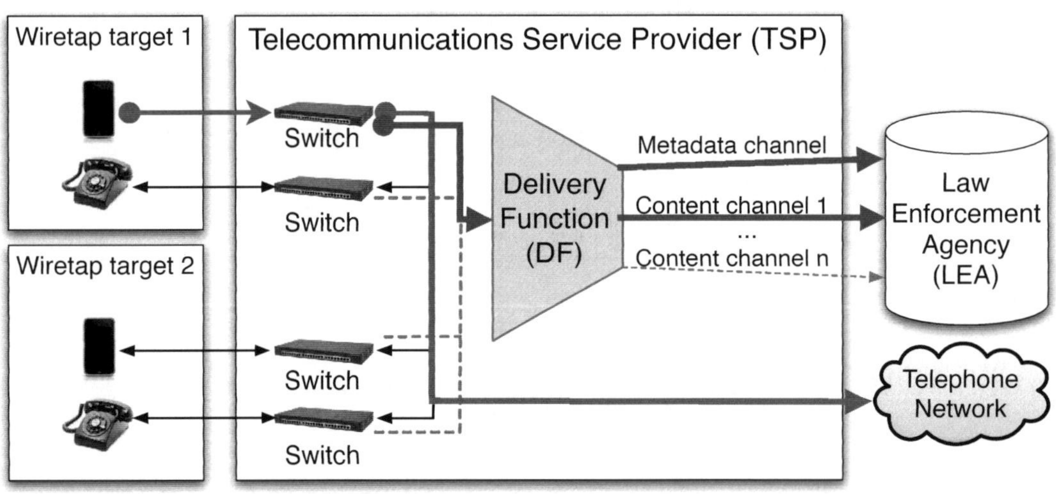

Background: Can They Hear Me Now?

UNIVERSITY OF OREGON

- Call Data Channel (CDC) Resource Exhaustion: wiretap targets can generate events at a rate that overwhelm the channel, preventing call data from being recorded.
- Injecting Confusion & Uncertainty: targets can deny reconstruction of traffic flows and craft packets that insert non-existent correspondence into wiretap transcripts.

Design: Overview

UNIVERSITY OF OREGON

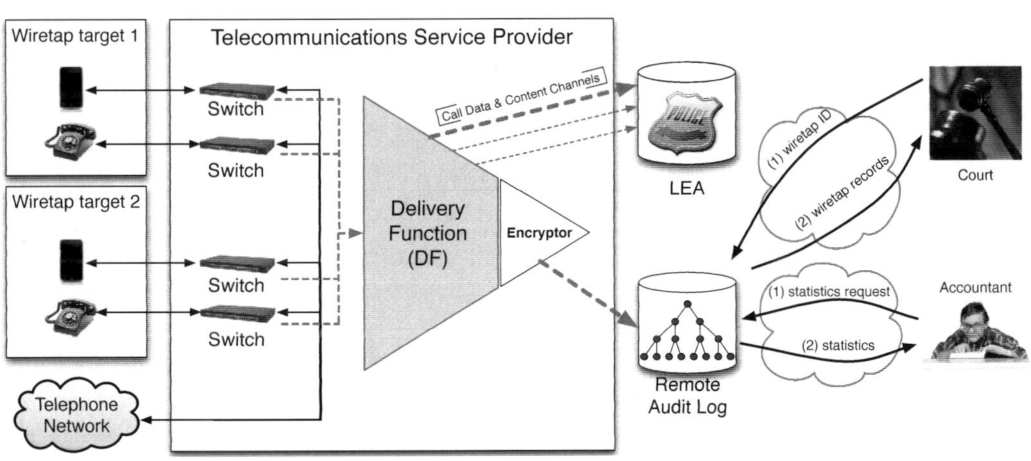

Oregon Systems Infrastructure Research and Information Security (OSIRIS) Lab 8

Design: Threat Model

- Wiretap Target: may attempt denial-of-service attacks (*Completeness*) on the wiretap resource channels.
- Unauthorized Wiretapper: may issue illegal wiretap orders (*Total Reporting*), or use a legal wiretap outside of the valid date range (*Date Compliance*).
- Dishonest Log: may attempt to read records (*Confidentiality*), discover the existence of a wiretap order (*Unlinkability*) or tamper with records (*Integrity*).

Protocol: Event Logging

Encryptor-to-Log Message (Signed)		Encryption
(1)	Wiretap Event	Record Key
(2)	Event Count (per wiretap)	Record Key
(3)	Hash of (1), (2)	Record Key
(4)	Aggregate Block	Accountant Public Key
(5)	Event Timestamp	Cleartext

Protocol: Court Audits

UNIVERSITY OF OREGON

Wishing to receive the records associated with wiretap order ω from time T_s to T_e, the court issues request:

$$Court\ Auditor\ \rightarrow\ Log:\ CourtAudit(T_s, T_e)$$

r_ω? ✓ r_ω? ✗ r_ω? ✗ r_ω? ✓ r_ω? ✓

Message	M_i	M_{i+1}	M_{i+2}	M_{i+3}	M_{i+4}
Time	t_s	t_{s+1}	t_{s+2}	t_{s+3}	t_e
Key	r_ω	r_ν	r_ν	r_ω	r_ω

Protocol: Accounting Audits

UNIVERSITY OF OREGON

The aggregation block is a set of counters encrypted with the Paillier system $\mathcal{E}_{G^+}(Q)$ such that for messages Q_1 and Q_2, $\mathcal{D}_{G^-}(\mathcal{E}_{G^+}(Q_1) \cdot \mathcal{E}_{G^+}(Q_2)) = Q_1 + Q_2$.

Aggregation Block Message Structure

Random seqno	Previous seqno	Pen Register, New	Audio Intercept, New	Pen Register, Expiring	Audio Intercept, Expiring

Protocol: Accounting Audits

UNIVERSITY OF OREGON

The accountant can use aggregate block sequence numbers to confirm that no records were omitted.

$$Accountant \rightarrow Log : AccountingAudit, T_1, T_4$$

$$Log \rightarrow Accountant : M_1, \sigma(M_1), M_4, \sigma(M_4), \sum_{1}^{4} B_i$$

The accountant subtracts the sequence numbers from the sum of the previous sequence numbers. Most cancel out, leaving the value $s_4 - s_0$.

Random seqno	Previous seqno
s_1	s_0
s_2	s_1
s_3	s_2
s_4	s_3

Oregon Systems Infrastructure Research and Information Security (OSIRIS) Lab 13

Protocol: Message Type Summary

UNIVERSITY OF OREGON

	Type	Description
(1)	Wiretap Event	Transmits legitimate wiretap data
(2)	Wiretap Start, Stop	Sets counters in aggregate block
(3)	Heartbeat Message	Bounds Log record omission
(4)	Noise	Thwarts timing analysis of channel

Oregon Systems Infrastructure Research and Information Security (OSIRIS) Lab 14

Security Analysis

UNIVERSITY OF OREGON

- Detecting Denial-of-Service: our architecture can detect lost messages through redundant storage and sequence numbering.
- Detecting Unauthorized Wiretaps: our architecture can detect unauthorized wiretaps whose data is relayed through the **Encryptor**.
- Handling a Malicious Log: wiretap records' confidentiality and privacy are handled through encryption of call and aggregation data. If the LOG attempts to modify or omit records, it will be evident in the accounting audit.

Evaluation: Microbenchmarks

UNIVERSITY OF OREGON

- We implemented our architecture using an Asterisk telephone softswitch.

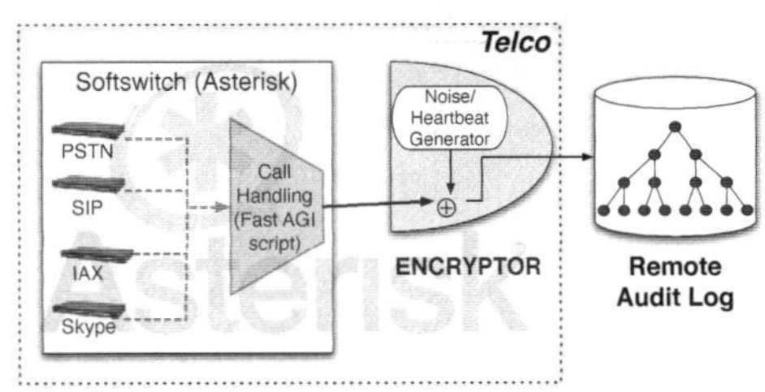

- Our Implementation's **Encryptor** throughput was 30.53 events per second with 1024-bit aggregate block size.

Operation	1024-bit Block	2048-bit Block
Encrypt Data	< 1%	< 1%
Hash Data	< 1%	< 1%
Encrypt Block	96%	99%
Sign Record	3%	< 1%
Transmission	< 1%	< 1%
Events per second:	30.53	4.98

Evaluation: University Traffic Test

UNIVERSITY OF OREGON

- Generated call events from the anonymized data of a major university (4/04/2011).

- Wiretapped call events from calls of the busiest 10 minute window of the day.

- On one desktop, our **Encryptor** accomplished this at less than 3.2% maximum throughput!

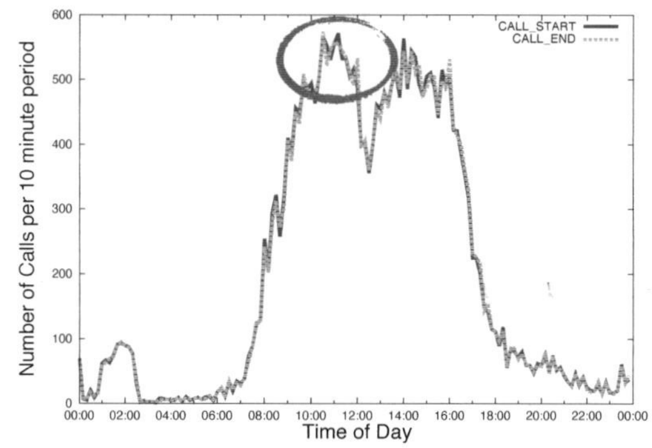

Evaluation: Additional Calculations

UNIVERSITY OF OREGON

- In 2008, there were 21,000 pen registers. Our implementation would require three commodity machines to handle this load.

- In 2003, ATT handled 3,500 calls per second. Our implementation could handle 10% of this traffic on a single multicore machine.

Conclusion

UNIVERSITY OF OREGON

In this work we have made the following contributions:

- Developed an attacker model for accountable wiretapping.
- Introduced new protocols to enable trustworthy wiretap auditing.
- Developed a minimal-impact retrofit for current interception systems.
- Demonstrated that all U.S. pen register traffic can be handled on a few commodity machines.

Oregon Systems Infrastructure Research and Information Security (OSIRIS) Lab 19

Questions?

UNIVERSITY OF OREGON

Adam Bates

amb@cs.uoregon.edu

Oregon Systems Infrastructure Research and Information Security (OSIRIS) Lab 20

Shadow: Running Tor in a Box for Accurate and Efficient Experimentation

Rob Jansen*
U.S. Naval Research Laboratory
rob.g.jansen@nrl.navy.mil

Nicholas Hopper
University of Minnesota
hopper@cs.umn.edu

Abstract

Tor is a large and popular overlay network providing both anonymity to its users and a platform for anonymous communication research. New design proposals and attacks on the system are challenging to test in the live network because of deployment issues and the risk of invading users' privacy, while alternative Tor experimentation techniques are limited in scale, are inaccurate, or create results that are difficult to reproduce or verify. We present the design and implementation of Shadow, an architecture for efficiently running accurate Tor experiments on a single machine. We validate Shadow's accuracy with a private Tor deployment on PlanetLab and a comparison to live network performance statistics. To demonstrate Shadow's powerful capabilities, we investigate circuit scheduling and find that the EWMA circuit scheduler reduces aggregate client performance under certain loads when deployed to the entire Tor network. Our software runs without root privileges, is open source, and is publicly available for download.

1 Introduction

Tor [8] is the most popular application providing anonymity for privacy-conscious Internet users. To achieve anonymity for its *clients*, Tor forwards communication between sources and destinations through a tunneled *circuit* of several volunteer *relays* located around the world. Data is encrypted using Onion Routing [11, 37] so that no single relay in the circuit can learn *both* the true source *and* the true destination of any forwarded message.

Tor's goal to provide *low-latency* anonymity for its clients has led to an enormous amount of research on topics including, but not limited to, anonymity attacks and defenses [3, 9, 13, 24, 32], system design, performance, and scalability improvements [2, 36, 40, 42, 47], and the economics of volunteering relays to the Tor network [1, 15, 28]. Most Tor research – whether implementing a new design approach or analyzing a potential attack – either requires or would benefit from access to the live Tor network and the data it generates. However, such access might invade clients' privacy or be infeasible to provide – testing a small design change in the real network requires propagating that change either to hundreds of thousands of Tor clients or to thousands of volunteer relays, and in some cases, both. Therefore researchers often use alternative strategies to experiment and test new research proposals.

Tor Experimentation. One approach for experimenting with Tor outside of the live public network is to configure a parallel private test network deployment [3, 42] either using machines at a university or a platform such as PlanetLab [7]. Since live deployments run real software over real hardware, the results are generally accepted. However, PlanetLab and other private deployments do not accurately reflect the same network conditions of the public Tor network, are difficult to manage, and do not scale well – PlanetLab has only around one thousand nodes of which roughly half are usable at any time. Therefore researchers often experiment through simulation [15, 25, 28, 33]. Simulating particular Tor mechanisms may increase scalability, but also harms accuracy: the Tor software and protocols are continuously updated by several Tor developers, causing simulators to become outdated and unmaintained. Moreover, since simulators tend not to be reused, the results of one group may be inconsistent with or can not be verified by other groups.

Tor in a Box. To increase consistency, accuracy, and scalability of Tor experiments, we design and develop a new and unique simulation architecture called Shadow. Shadow allows us to run a private Tor network on a single machine while controlling all aspects of an experiment. Results are repeatable and easily verifiable through independent analysis. Although Shadow *simulates* the network layer, it *links to and runs real Tor software*, allowing us to experiment with new designs by implementing them directly into the Tor source code. This strategy expedites the process of incorporating proposals into Tor since software patches can be submitted to the developers. Shadow is capable of simulating a *large* and *diverse* private Tor network, requiring little to no modification to the numerous supported Tor software

*Work partially performed at the University of Minnesota and the U.S. Naval Research Laboratory

versions. Shadow's focus on usability and commitment to open source software[1] improves accessibility and promotes community adoption.

Shadow is a discrete-event simulator that utilizes techniques allowing it to run real applications in a simulation environment. Real applications are encapsulated in a plug-in wrapper that contains functions necessary to allow Shadow to interact with the application. Although the application is only loaded into memory once, the plug-in registers memory addresses for all variable application state and Shadow manages a copy of these memory regions for each node in the simulation. Similar to a kernel context switch, Shadow swaps in the current node's version of this state before passing control to the application, and swaps out the state when control returns. Function interposition allows Shadow to intercept function calls, e.g. socket and event library calls, and redirect them to a simulated counterpart. As detailed in Section 3, we run Tor using these techniques and symbol table manipulations without modifying the source code.

Accurate Simulation. We validate Shadow's accuracy against a 402-node PlanetLab deployment, testing network performance using HTTP file transfers both directly and through a private Tor network deployment. Although private Tor networks on PlanetLab do not consistently represent the live Tor network well, they allow us to test our ability to model a real, diverse network (i.e. how well we can "shadow" PlanetLab conditions). We find that our results are within reason although PlanetLab exhibits highly variable behaviors because of overloaded CPUs caused by co-location and resource sharing.

To validate Shadow's ability to accurately and consistently represent the real, live Tor network, we simulate a 1051-node topology with bandwidth and relay characteristics taken from a live Tor network consensus. We model the Internet using network latency measurments taken between all PlanetLab nodes. We find that client performance in Shadow closely matches live statistics gathered by the Tor Project [45], with download time quartiles within 15 percent of the live statistics for various download sizes. Our results in Section 5 indicate that Shadow can accurately measure Tor client performance.

Improving Client Performance. Tor's popularity has lead to network congestion and performance problems. Tor's hundreds of thousands of clients [20] send data over a few thousand bandwidth limited relays, causing network bottlenecks that impair client performance. Using Shadow, we investigate scheduling as a technique to improve client performance. In Section 6 we explore the EWMA circuit scheduler [42] which prioritizes bursty circuits ahead of bulk circuits. We confirm previous results by re-evaluating EWMA when enabled on *small* bottleneck topologies consisting of three relays – similar to those tested by Tang and Goldberg. However, our results from a *network-wide* deployment of the scheduler in a scaled topology indicate that performance benefits are highly dependent on network load and a properly tuned half-life. We found that the scheduler *reduces* performance for Tor clients under certain network loads, a significant result since the EWMA scheduler is currently enabled by default for all sufficiently updated Tor relays.

2 Requirements

Accuracy. In order to produce results that are consistent and representative of the live Tor network, Shadow should run a minimally-modified version of the native Tor software. Running the Tor software in our simulator will ensure that Tor's behavior in our simulated Tor network will closely represent the behavior of Tor running on a real machine in the live network.

In addition to running the Tor software, Shadow should also have accurate models of system-level interactions. Tor is mostly concerned with buffering, encrypting/decrypting cells, and sending and receiving large amounts of network traffic with non-blocking I/O. Inaccurate models of these mechanisms would lead to inaccurate results and measurements of Tor's behavior. Therefore, we are required to model the system-level network stack of an operating system by simulating TCP and UDP, correctly managing network-level buffers and buffer sizes, and simulating non-blocking event-driven I/O. Since a large amount of Tor's run-time is spent performing cryptography and processing data, Shadow should avoid execution of expensive cryptographic operations while instead modeling the CPU delays that would have occurred had the cryptography actually been performed.

Finally, accurate software and an accurate system will not function correctly without an accurate network. First, Shadow requires models for network characteristics including latency and reliability of network links, complex AS-level topologies, and upstream/downstream capacities for end-hosts. Second, Shadow must accurately model the network characteristics of Tor, including relay-contributed bandwidth, faithful bandwidth distributions among entry, middle, and exit relays, and geographical distribution of relays. Shadow must also incorporate network traffic from Tor clients and model accurate distributions of that traffic from live Tor traffic patterns.

Usability and Accessibility. A simulator that produces accurate results characteristic of the live Tor network will be of little use to the community without a usable simulation framework. Shadow should therefore do the following to increase usability and promote community adoption.

First, Shadow should be simple to obtain, build, and configure to allow for rapid deployment. Users should be able to run a simulation with minimal overhead and little or no

[1]Shadow source code is publicly available under the GPLv3 [38, 39].

configuration. However, advanced users should be able to easily modify a simulation, generate new topologies, and configure network and system parameters. Simulation results should be easy to gather and parse to produce visualizations that allow the analysis of the network state. Second, Shadow should run completely as a user-level process on a single machine with inexpensive hardware to minimize overhead costs associated with obtaining, configuring, and managing multiple machines or clusters. Shadow should be accessible to anyone worldwide so results can be easily compared and verified.

3 Design

Shadow is a discrete event simulator that can run real applications as plug-ins while requiring minimal modifications to the application. Plug-ins containing applications link to Shadow libraries and Shadow dynamically loads and natively executes the application code while simulating the network communication layer. Shadow was originally a fork of Distributed Virtual Network (DVN) simulator [10], adding roughly 18,000 lines of code (including example plug-ins). An overview of Shadow's design is depicted in Figure 1 and details about Shadow's core simulation engine are given in Appendix A.

Shadow dynamically loads plug-ins and instantiates virtual nodes as specified in a simulation script. Communication between Shadow and the plug-in is done through a well-defined callback interface implemented by the plug-in. When the appropriate callback is executed, the plug-in may instantiate and run its non-blocking application(s). The application will cause events to be spooled to the scheduler by executing a system call that is intercepted by Shadow and redirected to a function in the node library. The interceptions allow integration of the application into the simulation environment without requiring modification of application code. Virtual nodes communicate with each other through a virtual network which spools packet and other network related events to the scheduler. Each virtual node stores only application-specific state and loads/unloads the state as necessary during simulation execution. We now describe the main architectural components that enable Shadow to realize the above functionality and fulfill our design requirements discussed in the previous section.

3.1 Simulation Script

Each simulation is bootstrapped with a simulation script written in a custom scripting language. This script gives the user access to commands that allow Shadow to dynamically load multiple plug-ins, create and connect networks, and create nodes. Valid plug-ins are loaded by supplying a filepath while parameters such as latency, upstream and downstream bandwidth, and CPU speed are specified by either loading a properly formatted CDF data file or generating a CDF using a built-in CDF generator. Hostnames may be specified for each node and are otherwise automatically generated to facilitate support for a Shadow name service. The script also specifies which plug-in to run and when to start each node.

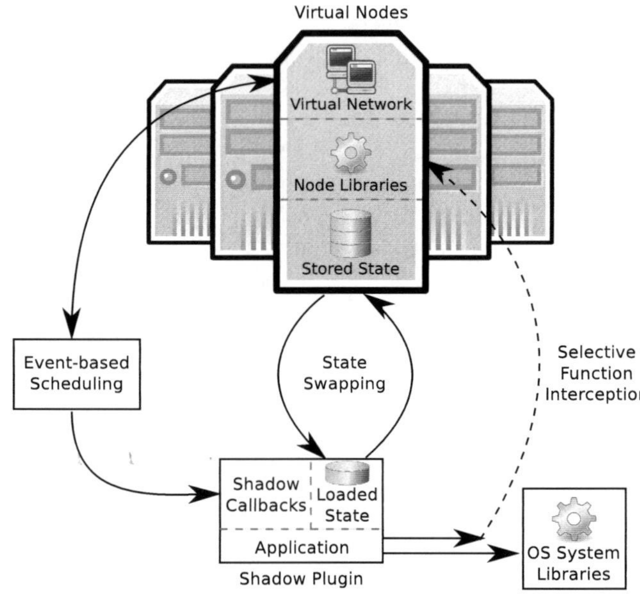

Figure 1: Shadow's architectural design. Using a plug-in wrapper, real-world applications are integrated into Shadow as virtual nodes while system and library calls are intercepted and replaced with Shadow-specific implementations.

Events are extracted from a properly formatted simulation script and spooled to the event scheduler using the times specified with each command. After the script is parsed, the simulation begins by executing the first extracted event and runs until either there are no events remaining in the scheduler or the end time specified in the script is reached. Each node creation event triggers the allocation of a virtual node and its network and culminates in a callback to a Shadow plug-in for application instantiation.

3.2 Shadow Plug-ins

A Shadow plug-in is an independent library that contains applications the user wishes to simulate and a wrapper around these applications allowing integration with the Shadow simulation environment. Each Shadow plug-in wrapper implements the plug-in interface – a set of callbacks that Shadow uses to communicate with the plug-in. Plug-ins may also link to a special Shadow plug-in utility libraries to, e.g. obtain an IP address or log messages.

Application. To run in Shadow, an application must be asynchronous, i.e. non-blocking, to prevent simulator deadlocks during the execution of application code. We note that asynchronicity may be achieved with a small amount of code in the plug-in wrapper that utilizes the built-in Shadow callbacks or by writing the application using the `libevent-2.0` asynchronous event library [17], as Shadow supports a subset of this library.

Next, the application must be run as a single process and in a single thread. Child processes or threads forked or spawned by an application will not be properly contained in the simulation environment and are therefore currently unsupported. In most cases forking or spawning children will lead to undefined behavior or undesirable results. We note that most multi-threaded applications have a single-threaded mode and the difficulty in porting those that do not is application-specific.

Finally, the plug-in must register all variable application state with Shadow to facilitate multiple virtual nodes running the same application. Plug-ins fulfill this requirement by passing pointers to node-specific allocated memory chunks and their sizes to a Shadow library function. Therefore each variable must be globally visible during the registration process. However, we note that a plug-in may use standard tools to scan and globalize symbols present in the binary after the linking process. As in our Tor plug-in (Section 4), this technique may be used to dynamically generate variable registration code and eliminates the requirement of modifying variable definitions inside the application.

Shadow Callbacks. The Shadow plug-in interface allows Shadow not only to notify the plug-in when it should allocate and deallocate resources for running the application(s) contained in the plug-in, but also to notify the plug-in when it may perform network I/O (reading and writing) on a file descriptor without blocking. The I/O callbacks are crucial for asynchronicity as they trigger application code execution and prevent applications from the need for polling a file descriptor. The Shadow plug-in library also offers support for a generic timer callback so plug-ins may create additional events throughout a simulation. Note that callbacks may also originate from the virtual event library, as described in Section 3.3.2 below, if the application uses the `libevent-2.0` library.

3.3 Virtual Nodes

In Shadow, a virtual node represents a single simulated host. A virtual node contains all state that is specific to a host, such as addressing and network information that allows it to communicate with other hosts in the network. Virtual nodes also contain Shadow-specific implementations of system libraries that promote homogeneity between existing interfaces. Function interposition allows for seamless integration of applications into Shadow by redirecting calls to system functions to our Shadow implementation. Virtual nodes store their own application-specific state and swap this state into the plug-in's address space before passing control of code execution to the plug-in.

3.3.1 Virtual Network

In Shadow, the virtual network is the main interface through which virtual nodes may communicate. Upon creation, each node's virtual network interface is assigned an IP address and receives upstream and downstream bandwidth rates as configured in the simulation script. Each virtual network contains a transport agent that implements a leaky bucket (i.e. token bucket) algorithm that allows small traffic bursts but ensures average data rates conform to the configured rate. The transport agent handles both incoming and outgoing packets, allowing for asymmetric bandwidth specifications. The agent provides traffic policing by dropping (and causing retransmission of) all non-conforming packets. Conforming incoming packets are passed to the virtual socket library (discussed below) for processing, while events are created for conforming outgoing packets and spooled to the scheduler for delivery to another node after incorporating network latency.

3.3.2 Node Libraries

Each virtual node implements several system functions as well as network, event, and cryptography libraries. *Function interposition* is used to redirect standard system and library functions calls made from the application to their Shadow-specific counterparts. Function interposition is achieved by creating a *preloaded* library with functions of the same name as the target functions, and setting the environment variable `LD_PRELOAD` to the path of the preload library. Every time a function is called, the preload library is first checked. If it contains the function, the preloaded function is called – otherwise the standard lookup mechanisms are used to find the function. No additional modifications are required to hook into Shadow.

Virtual System. The virtual system library implements standard system calls whose results must be modified due to the simulation environment. Functions for obtaining system time are implemented to return the simulation time rather than the wall time and functions for obtaining hostname and address information are intercepted to return the hostnames as defined in the simulation script configured by the user.

The virtual system also contains a virtual CPU module in an attempt to consider processing delays produced by an application. Using a virtual CPU and processing delays improves Shadow's accuracy since without it, all data is processed by the application at a single discrete instant in the simulation. When a virtual node reads or writes data between the application and Shadow, the virtual CPU produces a delay for processing that data. This delay is "absorbed" by the system by delaying the execution of every event that has already been scheduled for that virtual node. As virtual nodes read and write more data, the wait time until the next event increases.

We determine appropriate CPU processing speeds as follows. First, throughput is configured for each virtual CPU – the number of bytes the CPU can process per second. Modeling the speed of a target CPU is done by running an OpenSSL [31] speed test on a real CPU of that type. This provides us with the raw CPU processing rate, but we are also interested in the processing speed of an application. By running application benchmarks on the same CPU as the OpenSSL speed test, we can derive a ratio of CPU speed to application processing speed. The virtual CPU converts these speeds to a time per-byte-processed and delays its events appropriately.

Virtual Sockets. The Shadow virtual socket library, the heart of the node libraries, implements the most significant features for a Shadow simulation. The virtual socket library implements all system socket functionality which includes: creating, opening, and closing sockets; sending, buffering, and receiving data; network protocols like the *User Datagram Protocol* (UDP) [34] and the *Transmission Control Protocol* (TCP) [35]; and other socket-level functionalities. Shadow's tight integration of socket functionalities and strong adherence to the RFC specifications results in an extremely accurate network layer as we'll show in Section 5.

Shadow intercepts and redirects functions from the system socket interface to the Shadow-specific virtual socket library implementation. When the application sends data to the virtual socket library, the data is packaged into packet objects. The packaging process copies the user data only twice throughout the lifetime of the packet, meaning the same packet object is shared among nodes. Only pointers to the packet are copied as the packet travels through various socket and network buffers, although buffer sizes are computed using the full packet size.

Our virtual socket libraries implement socket-level buffering, data retransmission, congestion and flow control mechanisms, acknowledgments, and TCP auto-tuning. TCP auto-tuning is required to correctly match buffer sizes to connection speeds since neither high bandwidth connections with small network buffers nor low-bandwidth connections with large network buffers will achieve the expected performance. TCP auto-tuning allows network buffers to be dynamically computed on a per-connection basis, allowing for highly accurate transfer rates even when endpoints have asymmetric bandwidth.

Virtual Events. Shadow supports the use of `libevent-2.0` [17] to facilitate asynchronous applications while easing application integration. While applications are not required to use `libevent-2.0`, doing so will likely reduce the complexity of the integration process. Shadow intercepts and redirects functions from the `libevent-2.0` interface to the Shadow-specific virtual event library implementation. The virtual event library consists of two main components: an event manager and a virtual I/O monitor. The event manager creates and tracks events and executes event callbacks while the I/O monitor tracks the state of Shadow buffers, informing the manager when a state change may require an event callback to fire for a given file descriptor.

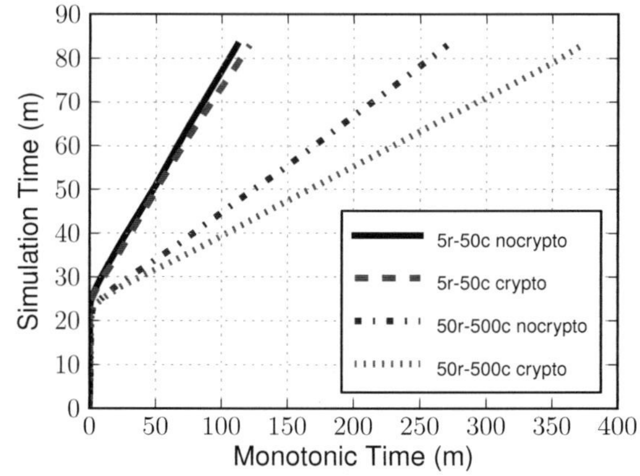

Figure 2: Simulation vs. wall clock time. Skipping expensive cryptographic operations results in a linear decrease in experiment run-time – nearly a one-third reduction in run-time for a small, 550-node Tor experiment.

Virtual Cryptography. Simulating an application that performs cryptography offers a chance for reducing simulation run-time. As data is passed from virtual node to virtual node during the simulation, in most cases it is not important that the data is encrypted: since we are not sending data out across a real network, confidentiality is not necessarily required. Therefore, applications need not perform expensive encryption and decryption operations during the simulation, saving CPU cycles on our simulation host machine.

Shadow removes cryptographic processing by preloading the main OpenSSL [31] functions used for data encryption. The `AES_encrypt` and `AES_decrypt` functions are used for bulk data encryption and the `EVP_Cipher` function is used to secure data on SSL/TLS connections. These functions only perform the low-level cipher operations: all other supporting cryptographic functionality is unmodified. When preloading these functions, Shadow will not perform the cipher operation during encryption and decryption. Our virtual CPU already models application processing delays, and skipping the cipher operations will not affect application functionality.

Figure 2 shows the time savings Shadow realizes using this technique with the Scallion plug-in (discussed below in Section 4) for various Tor network sizes. Larger savings in real running time are realized as experiment size increases.

3.3.3 Stored State

Multiple virtual nodes may run the same plug-in. Rather than duplicating the entire plug-in in memory for each virtual node, Shadow only duplicates the variable state – the state of an application that will change during execution. Registration of this variable state with Shadow happens once for each plug-in. The plug-in registration procedure allows Shadow to determine which memory regions (beginning address and length) in the current address space will be modified by each virtual node running the plug-in.

Following registration, Shadow possesses pointers to each memory region that may be changed by the plug-in or application. Multiple nodes for each plug-in are supported by allocating node-specific storage for each registered memory region and maintaining a copy of each plug-in's state. For transparency, Shadow loads a node's state before every context switch from Shadow to the plug-in, and saves state back to storage when the context switches back to Shadow. This process minimizes the total memory consumption of each plug-in, and results in significant memory savings for large simulations and large applications.

4 The Scallion Plug-in: Running Tor in Shadow

Shadow was designed especially for running simulations using the Tor application. Therefore, Shadow design choices were made in support of "Scallion"[2], a Tor plug-in implementation. Each virtual node running the Scallion plug-in represents a small piece of the Tor network. Since Shadow supports most functionality needed by Scallion, the plug-in implementation itself is minimal (roughly 1500 lines of code). Here we describe some of the specific components necessary for the Tor application plug-in.

State Registration. Recall that Shadow requires all variable application state to be registered for replication among virtual nodes. Scallion must find and register all Tor variables, including static and global variables. Unfortunately, static variables are not accessible outside the scope in which they were defined. Therefore, scallion uses standard binary utilities such as `objcopy`, `readelf`, and `nm` to dynamically scan, rename, and globalize Tor symbols. Registration code is then dynamically generated based on the symbols present in the Tor object files, and injected into the plug-in before compilation. Note that the size of each variable is also extracted with the binary utilities.

Bandwidth Measurements. TorFlow [44] is a set of scripts that run in the live Tor network, continuously measuring bandwidth of volunteer relays by downloading several files through each. TorFlow helps determine the bandwidth to advertise in the public consensus document. Scallion contains a component that approximates this functionality. However, Scallion need not perform actual measurements since the bandwidth of each virtual node is already configured in Shadow. Scallion queries for these bandwidth values through a Shadow plug-in library function and writes the appropriate file that is used by the directory authorities while computing a new consensus. The `V3Bandwidth` file is updated as new relays join the simulated Tor network.

Tor Preloaded Functions. In an effort to minimize the amount of changes to Tor, Scallion utilizes the same function interposition technique as Shadow. Scallion may intercept any Tor function for which it requires changes and implement a custom version. Changes in Tor are required only if the target function is static, in which case Tor can be modified to remove the static specifier. We now discuss some functional differences between Tor and Scallion.

The Tor socket function wrapper is one function that is intercepted by Scallion and modified to pass the `SOCK_NONBLOCK` flag to the socket call since Shadow requires non-blocking sockets. Another modification involves the Tor main function, which is not suitable for use in Scallion since it contains an infinite loop. This function is extracted to prevent the simulation from blocking, and Scallion instead relies on event callbacks from Shadow to implement Tor's main loop functionality.

Tor is a multi-threaded application, launching at least one CPU worker thread to handle onionskin tasks – peeling off or adding a layer of encryption – as they arrive from the network. Scallion implements an event-driven version of Tor's CPU worker since Shadow requires a single-threaded, single-process application. This is done by intercepting the Tor function that spawns a CPU worker and relying on the virtual event library to execute callbacks when the CPU worker has data ready for processing. The CPU worker performs its task as instructed by Tor, and communicates with Tor using a socket pair (a virtual pipe) as before. The virtual event library simplifies the implementation of the CPU worker functionality.

Finally, Scallion intercepts Tor's bandwidth reporting function. Each Tor relay reports its recent bandwidth history to the directory authorities to help balance bandwidth across all available relays. However, relays' reports are based on the amount of data it has recently transferred, and the reported value is updated every twenty minutes only if it has not changed significantly from the last reported value. This causes relays to be underutilized when first joining the network, and causes bootstrapping problems in new networks since every node's bandwidth will be zero for the first twenty minutes of the simulation. Without appropriate bandwidth values, clients no longer perform weighted relay selection and instead choose relays at random. To mitigate these problems, Scallion intercepts the bandwidth reporting function and returns its configured BandwidthRate no mat-

[2]Scallions are onion-like plants with underdeveloped bulbs.

ter how much data it has transferred. This improves bootstrapping and path selection for the simulated Tor network.

Configuration and Usability. There are several challenges in running accurate Tor network simulations with the Scallion plug-in and Shadow. Although Shadow minimizes the memory requirements, running several instances of Tor still requires an extremely large amount of memory. Therefore, simulations must generally run with scaled-down versions of Tor network topologies and client-imposed network load.

Correctly scaling available relay bandwidth and network load is complicated. For example, several relays with smaller bandwidth capacities will not result in the same network throughput as fewer relays with larger bandwidth capacities, even if the total capacities are equal. Further, correctly distributing this bandwidth among entry, middle, and exit nodes can be tricky. Although live Tor consensus documents may be used to assist in network scaling, two randomly generated consensus topologies can have drastically different network throughput measurements. Network throughput also depends on the number of configured clients and the load they induce on Tor. Published results about client-to-relay ratios [20] and protocol-level statistics [22] can only be used as a rough guide to creating clients and inducing the correct load. When generating a scaled topology, it is essential that performance measurements of simulations be compared to live Tor statistics for accuracy.

Due to these challenges, we implemented a script to generate and run simulations given a network consensus document. The script parses the consensus document and randomly selects relays based on configurable network sizes. Configurable parameters include the fraction of exit relays to normal relays, number of clients, and client type distributions. The script eases the generation of accurate scaled topologies and drastically improves simulator usability.

5 Verifying Simulation Accuracy

Many aspects of Shadow's design (discussed in Section 3) were chosen in order to produce accurate simulations. Therefore, we perform several experiments to verify Shadow's accuracy.

5.1 File Client and Server Plug-ins

HTTP client and server plug-ins were written for Shadow in order to provide a mechanism for transferring data through the Shadow virtual network. These plug-ins also include support for a minimal SOCKS client and proxy. The client may download any number of specified files with configurable wait times between downloads while the server supports buffering and multiple simultaneous connections. These plug-ins are used to test network performance during a simulation. Stand-alone executables using the same code as the plug-ins are also compiled so that client and server functionality on a live system and network is identical to Shadow plug-in functionality.

5.2 PlanetLab Private Tor Network

In order to verify Shadow's accuracy, we perform experiments on PlanetLab. Our experiments consist of file clients and servers running the software described above in Section 5.1. In our first PlanetLab experiment, each of 361 HTTP clients download files directly from one of 20 HTTP servers, choosing a new server at random for each download. 18 of the 361 clients approximate a bulk downloader, requesting a 5 MiB file immediately after finishing a download while the remaining 343 clients approximate a web downloader, pausing for a short time between 320 KiB file downloads. The length of the pause is drawn from the UNC think-time distribution [12] which represents the time between clicks for a user browsing the web (the median pause is 11 seconds). Clients track both the time to receive the first byte of the data payload and the time to receive the entire download. We selected the fastest PlanetLab nodes (according to the bandwidth tests described below) as our HTTP servers to minimize potential server bottlenecks, although we note that fine-grained control is complicated by PlanetLab's dynamic resource adjustment algorithms.

Our second PlanetLab experiment is run exactly like the first, except all downloads are performed through a private PlanetLab Tor network consisting of 16 exit relays, 24 non-exit relays, and one directory authority. All HTTP clients also run a Tor client and proxy their downloads through Tor using a local connection to the Tor SOCKS server.

Shadowing PlanetLab. To replicate the PlanetLab experiments discussed in Section 5 in Shadow, we require measurements of PlanetLab node bandwidth, latency between nodes, and an estimate of node CPU speed. These measurements allow us to configure virtual nodes and a virtual network that approximates PlanetLab and network conditions typical of the Internet. First, we estimate PlanetLab node bandwidth by performing Iperf [14] bandwidth tests from each node to every other node. We estimate a node's bandwidth as the maximum upload rate to any other node.

Figure 3a shows the results of our measurements compared with available bandwidth from Tor relays extracted from the Tor network status consensus. Notice the sharp increase in the number of nodes with 1.25 MiBps (10 Mbps) and 3.75 MiBps (30 Mbps) connections. PlanetLab rate-limiting is the likely reason: the most popular node-defined limit is 10 Mbps while PlanetLab also implements a fair-sharing algorithm by distributing opportunistic fractions of bandwidth to active slices. Also notice that our PlanetLab distribution does not approximate the live Tor distribution well, which means that our measurements in this experi-

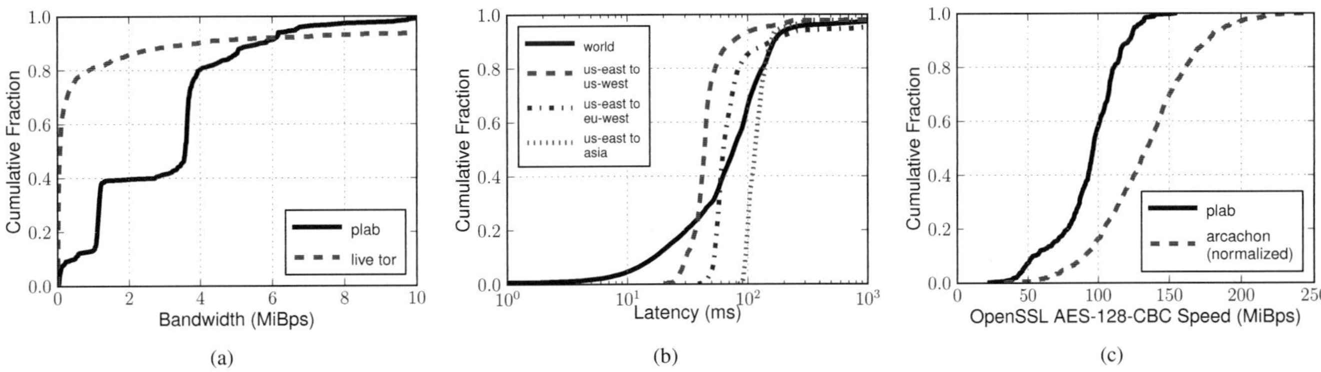

Figure 3: Network and CPU measurements used for Shadow experiments. (a) Bandwidth measurements of PlanetLab nodes and live Tor relays. Relay bandwidth values were taken from a live consensus. (b) Latency between PlanetLab nodes, shown as aggregate ("world") and inter-region latency measurements. (c) Measured CPU speeds for PlanetLab nodes and our Intel Core2 Duo lab machine *arcachon*. The results from arcachon were normalized to create a distribution usable in Shadow.

ment will not provide a good indication of the performance of the live Tor network. Recall, however, that our focus here is *accurately shadowing PlanetLab*: re-creating a network consistent with live Tor is explored below in Section 5.3.

To model network delays due to propogation and congestion, we perform latency estimates between all pairs of nodes using the Unix command `ping`. The aggregate results of world latencies are shown in Figure 3b. Deriving a network model and topology from the latency measurements is a bit more complex since it depends on the geographical location of the source and destination of a ping. We approximate a network model by creating nine geographical regions and placing each node in a region using a GeoIP lookup [21]. We then create a total of 81 CDFs representing all possible inter- and intra-region latencies. We configure nine virtual networks in Shadow and connect them into a complete graph topology, where latencies for packets traveling over each link are drawn from the corresponding CDF. Latencies for a few selected regions are also shown in Figure 3b.

Finally, we measure CPU speed of each node in order to accurately configure delays for Shadow's virtual CPU system described in Section 3.3.2. As in our previous description, `OpenSSL` speed tests are run to get raw CPU throughput for PlanetLab nodes. Since PlanetLab nodes are often constrained, we also created a normalized distribution based on the CPU speed of *arcachon* – a standard desktop machine in our lab. CPU throughput is shown in Figure 3c. Tor application throughput – measured by benchmarks in which the middle relay is configured with a bandwidth bottleneck – is combined with raw CPU throughput measurements to configure each node's virtual CPU delay.

Client Performance. Figure 4 shows the results of our PlanetLab and Shadow experiments. We are mainly interested in two metrics: the *time to receive the first byte* of the data payload (ttfb) and the *time to complete* a download (dt). The ttfb metric provides insight into the delays associated with sending a request through multiple hops and the responsiveness of a circuit, and also represents the minimum time a web user has to wait until anything is displayed in the browser. The dt metric captures overall performance.

Figures 4c and 4e show the ttfb metric for web and bulk clients with direct and Tor-proxied requests both in PlanetLab and Shadow. Downloads through Tor take longer than direct downloads, as expected, since data must be processed and forwarded by multiple relays. Shadow seems to closely approximate the *network conditions* in PlanetLab, as shown by the close correspondence between the lower half of each CDF. However, PlanetLab exhibits slightly higher variability in ttfb than Shadow as seen in the tail of the plab and shadow CDFs – a problem that is exacerbated when downloads are proxied through Tor. Higher variability in results is likely caused by increased PlanetLab node delay due to resource contention with other co-located experiments.

Figures 4d and 4f show similar conclusions for the dt metric. Shadow results appear off by a small factor while we again see higher variability in download completion times for PlanetLab. However, inaccuracies in download times appear somewhat independent of file size. As shown in Figure 4a, statistics gathered from Tor relays support our conclusions about higher variability in delays. Shown is the number of processed cells for each relay over the one hour experiment and the one-minute moving average. The moving average of processed cells is slightly higher for Shadow because of PlanetLab's resource sharing complexity while the individual relay measurements also show higher variability for PlanetLab. Figure 4b shows that Shadow queue times are very close to those measured on PlanetLab, and again shows PlanetLab's high variability. While we are optimistic about our conclusions, we emphasize that PlanetLab results should be analyzed with a careful eye due to the issues discussed above.

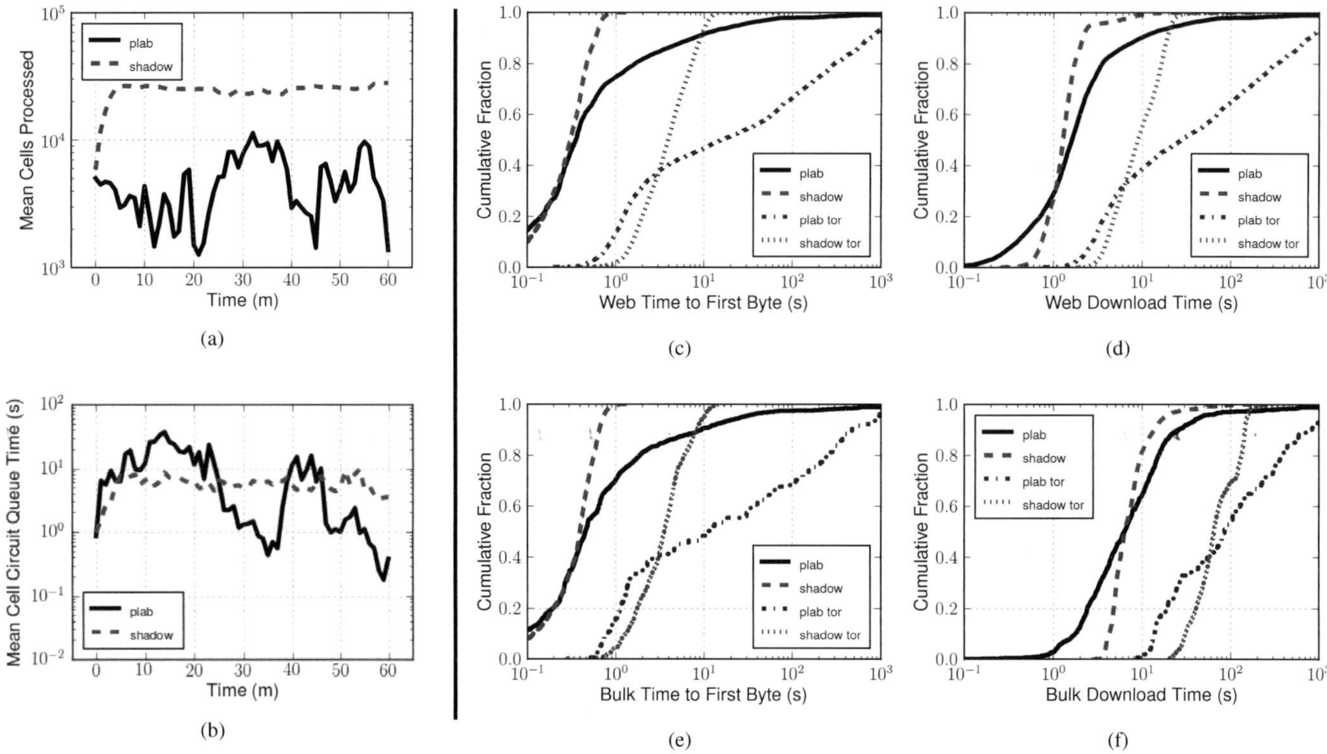

Figure 4: Shadow and PlanetLab network performance. PlanetLab download experiments were run with and without Tor and mirrored in Shadow. As shown in (a) and (b), Shadow approximates PlanetLab performance reasonably well while PlanetLab results show higher variability due to co-location and network/hardware interruptions. Also shown are CDFs of the number of elapsed seconds until the first byte of a 320 KiB file (c) and a 5 MiB file (e) is received, and the time to complete a download of the same files (d), (f).

5.3 Live Public Tor Network

Although the PlanetLab results show how Shadow performance compares to that achieved while running on PlanetLab and a *private* Tor network, they do not show how accurately Shadow can approximate the live *public* Tor network containing thousands of relays and hundreds of thousands of clients geographically distributed around the world. Therefore, we perform a separate set of experiments to test Shadow's ability to approximate live Tor network conditions as documented by The Tor Project [45]. Comparing results with statistics from Tor Metrics gives us much stronger evidence of Shadow's ability to accurately simulate the live Tor network.

The experiments are similar to those performed on PlanetLab: web and bulk clients download variable-sized files from servers through a private Tor network. However, file sizes are modified to 50 KiB, 1 MiB, and 5 MiB as used by TorPerf while configuration of Shadow nodes is also slightly modified to approximate resources available in live Tor. In these experiments, we use a directory authority, 50 relays, 950 web clients, 50 bulk clients, and 200 servers. We use a live Tor consensus[3] to obtain bandwidth limits for Tor relays and ensure that we correctly scale available bandwidth and network size, while client bandwidths are estimated with 1 MiB down-link and 3.5 MiB up-link speeds (not over-subscribed). Each relay is configured according to the live consensus: a `CircuitPriorityHalflife` of 30, a 40 KiB `PerConnBWRate`, and a 100 MiB `PerConnBWBurst`. Geographical location and latencies are configured using our PlanetLab dataset [39].

Figure 5 shows Shadow's accuracy while simulating a shadow of the live Tor network. CDFs of Shadow download completion times for each file size are compared with download times measured and collected by The Tor Project. The gray area represents the first-to-third quartile stretch and the dotted line shows the median download time extracted from live Tor network statistical data available at The Tor Metrics Portal [45] (gathered during April 2011 – the same month as our consensus). To maximize accuracy, the left edge of the gray area should intersect the CDF at 0.25, the right edge at 0.75, and the dotted line at 0.5. Our results show that the median download times are nearly identical for 50 KiB and 1 MiB downloads and within ten percent for 5 MiB downloads while the first and third quartiles are within 15 percent in all cases. We believe these results provide strong evi-

[3]The consensus was retrieved on 2011-04-27 and valid between 03:00:00 and 06:00:00.

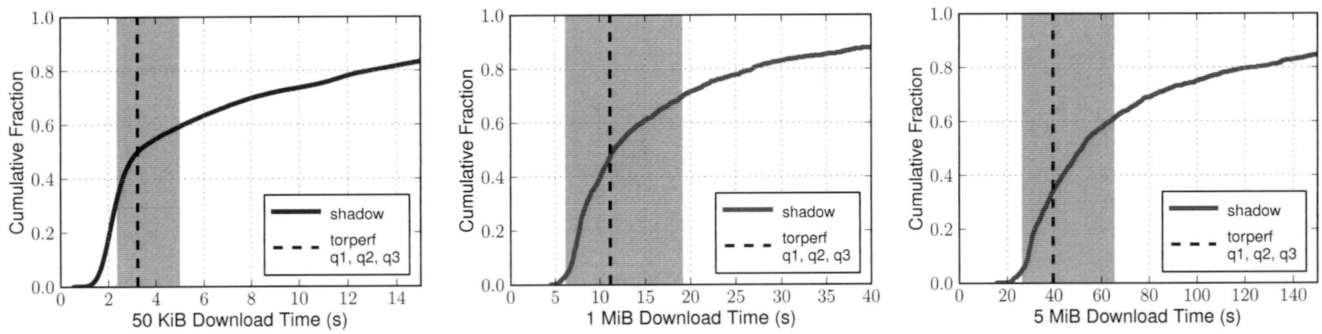

Figure 5: Shadow-Tor compared with live-Tor network performance. TorPerf represents live Tor network performance statistics available at `metrics.torproject.org`. The gray area shows TorPerf first to third quartile stretch while the dotted line represents the TorPerf median. Shadow closely approximates Tor performance for all file sizes.

dence of Shadow's ability to accurately simulate Tor. Further, we've shown that we can correctly scale down the Tor network in our simulations while maintaining the performance properties of the live Tor network.

6 Prioritizing Circuits

We now demonstrate Shadow's powerful capabilities by exploring a Tor circuit scheduling algorithm recently proposed and integrated into the Tor software. In Tor, whenever there is room in an output buffer, the circuit scheduler must make a decision about which circuit to flush. Tor's original design used a round-robin algorithm for making such decisions. Recently, an algorithm based on the Exponentially-Weighted Moving Average (EWMA) of cells sent in each circuit was proposed and incorporated into Tor, and has since become the default scheduling algorithm used by Tor relays. This section attempts to validate the results originally obtained by Tang and Goldberg [42].

EWMA in Bottleneck Topology. The EWMA scheduler chooses the circuit with the lowest cell count, effectively prioritizing bursty web connections over bulk transfers. Tang and Goldberg evaluated the EWMA algorithm by creating a congested circuit on a synthetic PlanetLab network and measuring performance of web downloads. Since the middle node was a circuit bottleneck, the benefits of EWMA for reducing web download times were clear. However, results for bulk downloads during this experiment were not given.

We perform a similar bottleneck experiment in Shadow. We configure a circuit consisting of a single entry, middle, and exit relay. Two bulk clients continuously download 5 MiB files to congest the circuit. Ten minutes after booting the "congestion" clients, two "measurement" clients are started and download for an hour: a third bulk client and a web client that waits 11 seconds (the median think-time for web browsers [12]) between 320 KiB file downloads. The middle relay is configured as a circuit bottleneck with a 1 MiBps connection while all other nodes (relays, clients, and server) have 10 MiBps connections.

We run the above experiment modifying only the scheduling algorithm. We test both the round-robin scheduler and the EWMA scheduler with a `CircuitPriorityHalfLife` of 66 as in [42]. Relay buffer statistics [43] are shown in Figures 6a and 6b. Notice a significant increase in traffic at the ten-minute mark, at which point the "measurement" clients start downloading. Figure 6a shows that the number of processed cells is similar for all relays, except occasionally the exit relay processes fewer cells due to middle relay congestion. Figure 6b shows that the circuit queues increase for the exit and middle relay while the entry relay's circuit queues are empty due to sufficient bandwidth to immediately forward data to the client.

Figures 6c and 6d show the performance results obtained from the web client for both schedulers. As expected, the time to the first byte of the data payload and the time to complete a download are both reduced for the web client, since bursty traffic gets prioritized ahead of the bulk traffic. The time to first byte for the "measurement" bulk downloader in Figure 6e also improves for a large fraction of the downloads because each new download originating from a new circuit will be prioritized ahead of the "congestion" bulk downloads. However, after downloading enough data, the "measurement" bulk client loses its priority over the "congestion" bulk clients and the time to first byte converges for each scheduler.

Tang and Goldberg claim that, according to Little's Law [19], bulk transfers will not be negatively affected while using the new circuit scheduler. While this may be theoretically true, it is not clear that it will hold in practice. The authors find that Little's Law holds when a single relay in the live Tor network uses the EWMA scheduler: their results show that bulk download times are not signifi-

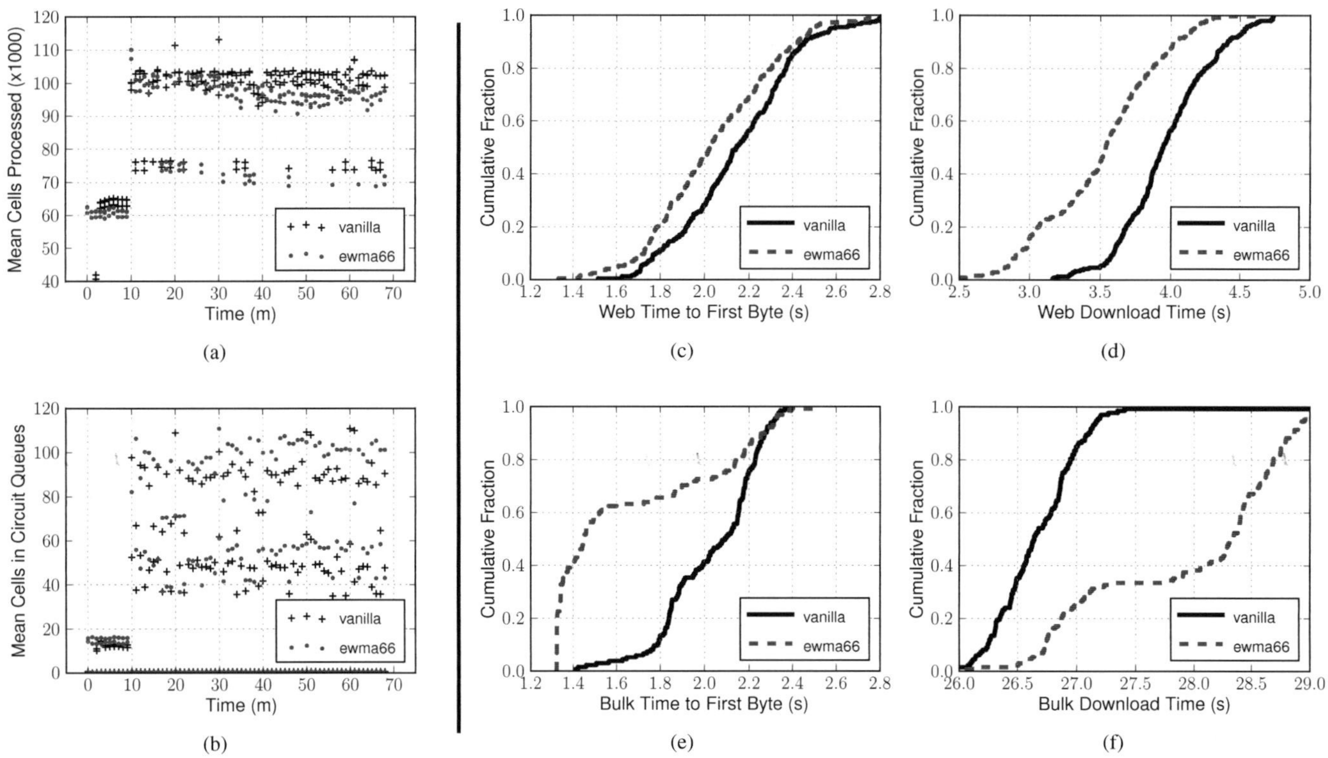

Figure 6: Seven-node bottleneck experiment similar to that performed by Tang and Goldberg [42]. The number of cells processed (a) and queued (b) increases at Time=10, when the measurement clients begin downloading. The EWMA scheduler improves responsiveness for bursty traffic (c), (d), and (e) but, contrary to the author's claims, decreases performance for bulk downloads (f).

cantly different for each scheduler. However, our results in Figure 6f indicate otherwise. Bulk download times are noticably worse for the EWMA scheduler, with a significant increase at around the 40th percentile. This increase again happens when the "measurement" bulk client loses its priority over the "congestion" bulk clients, suggesting a deeper analysis of the EWMA scheduling algorithm is appropriate.

EWMA in Network-wide Deployment. Tang and Goldberg's experiments suffer from a major limitation of scale: the experiments were run either on three-node PlanetLab topologies, or in the live Tor network with only a single relay scheduling with the EWMA algorithm. Although they provide results for what a single relay might expect when switching scheduling algorithms, they do not consider the network-wide effects of a full network deployment.

We explore the performance gains possible with the EWMA scheduler through a network-wide deployment in Shadow. We test the EWMA circuit scheduler with a range of half-life configurations and compare performance to the round-robin scheduler used in vanilla Tor. As in Section 5.3, we use 200 servers, 50 relays and 950 web clients for our experiments. To analyze the effects of various network loads on the scheduler, we run separate experiments configured with each of 25, 50, and 100 bulk clients. The adjusted load is significant since bulk clients account for a large fraction of network traffic. To reduce random variances, we run each experiment five times and show the cumulative results of each configuration by aggregating the results of all five experiments. Our results are shown in Figure 7.

Under a load of 25 bulk clients, Figures 7a–7c show that the EWMA circuit scheduler reduces performance over vanilla Tor for all clients, independent of the configured half-life. Bulk download times seem to be affected the most (7c), but our experiments indicate there is also a significant reduction in responsiveness for web clients (7a). As load increases to 50 bulk clients, Figures 7d–7f show that there are half-life configurations that still reduce performance when compared to vanilla Tor. The 30 and 90 second EWMA half-life configurations appear to improve performance for web clients (7d, 7e), but performance for bulk clients is either reduced or shows less improvement (7f). Performance is reduced for all clients when using a 3 second half-life. Finally, Figures 7g–7i show performance under the load of 100 bulk clients. Under heavy load, the EWMA scheduler appears to perform the best for web clients (7g, 7h) while bulk clients see no improvements over vanilla Tor and the round-robin scheduler (7i). Note that we also tested the schedulers under a lighter load than shown in Figure 7, but performance when the network is too lightly loaded is nearly identical regardless of the selected circuit scheduler.

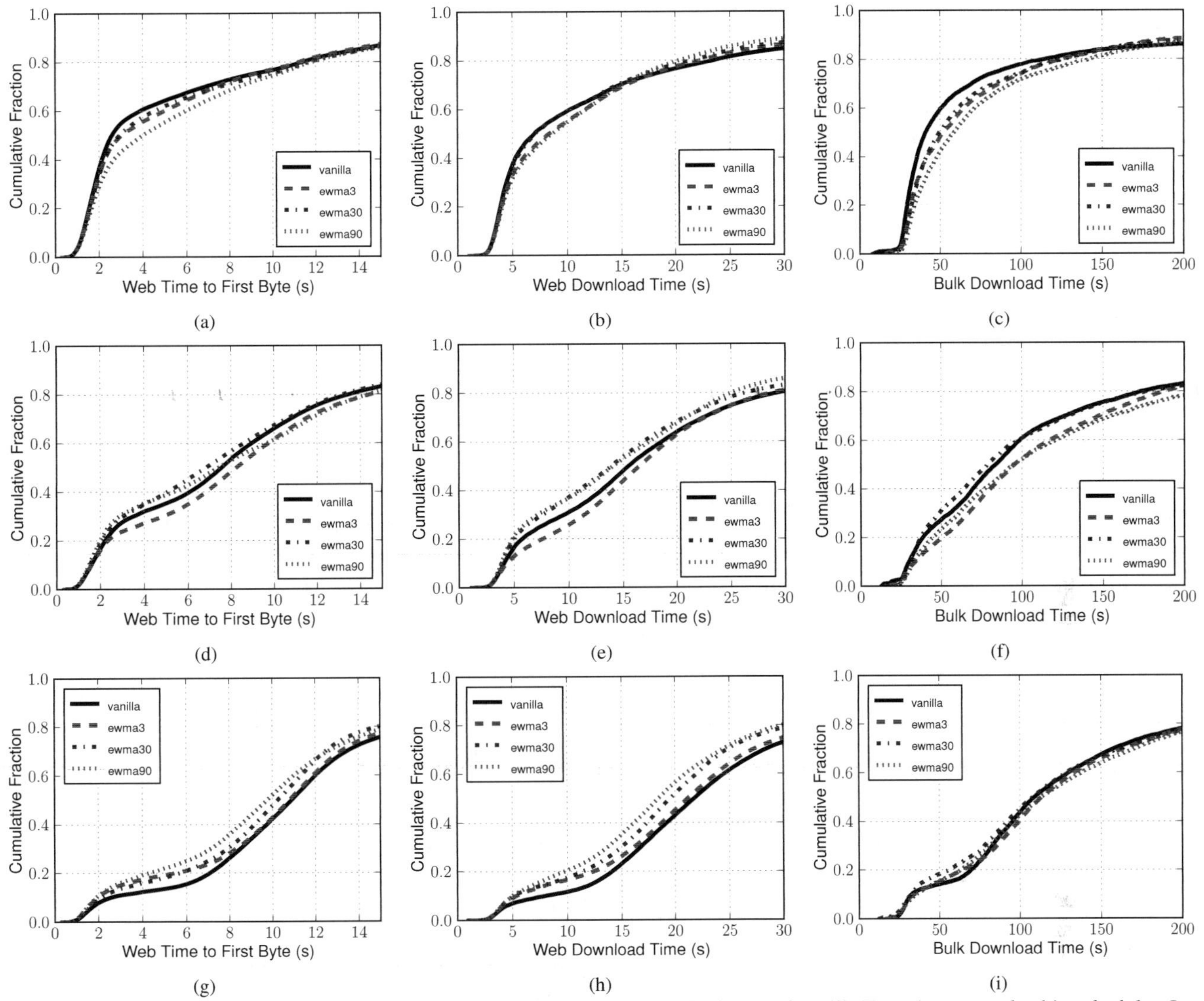

Figure 7: Performance of a full-network deployment of the EWMA circuit scheduler and vanilla Tor using a round-robin scheduler. Load is generated with 950 web clients and varied using (a)–(c) 25 bulk clients (d)–(f) 50 bulk clients, and (g)–(i) 100 bulk clients. While the EWMA circuit scheduler works best under heavily loaded networks, there are EWMA half-life configurations that lead to reduced client performance.

For these results, and responsiveness for bulk clients under the loads decribed above, please see Appendix B.

We conclude from our results that the EWMA scheduler should not necessarily be used under all network conditions since it is not clear that performance will always improve. When improvements over the round-robin scheduler are possible, they may be insignificant or depend on a correctly configured half-life. Tang and Goldberg find that low half-life values close to 0 and high values close to 100 result in little improvement when compared to unprioritized, vanilla Tor. We find this to be true under lighter loads, but Figure 7 shows that larger half-life values result in better performance for more heavily loaded networks. Our results illustrate that performance benefits are heavily dependent on network traffic patterns, and we stress the importance of frequently assessing the network to assist in determining appropriate half-life values over time. We suggest that more analysis is required to determine if the EWMA scheduler actually improves performance in the live Tor network, and if relays should enable it by default.

7 Related Work

This section reviews several experimentation techniques that have been used to test Tor's performance and resistance to various attacks. A test environment that accurately reflects Tor's behavior is crucial to produce meaningful results. We now briefly explore experimentation techniques chosen by researchers to evaluate Tor proposals. We note that: Kiddle [16] provides a comprehensive analysis and discussion of system simulation and emulation techniques; Naicken *et al.* [26, 27] provide details on several generic simulators; Bauer *et al.* [4] provide an in-depth survey of experimental approaches historically used in Tor-related research; and the EWMA circuit priority scheduler from Tang and Goldberg [42] is discussed in detail in Section 6.

Simulation. Simulation typically involves creating abstract models of system processes and running multiple nodes in a single unified framework. Experiment management is simplified since there are many fewer simulation host machines (typically one) than simulated nodes. By abstracting system processes, simulators can run much more efficiently and are not required to run in real time. However, the abstraction process has the potential to reduce accuracy since the simulator may not encompass complex procedures that may in fact be important to system interaction. Although generic simulation platforms exist [18, 29, 30, 41], they are not capable of running unmodified versions of the Tor software.

Simulation has often been employed for Tor research, but simulators tend to be written for a specific problem and may be difficult to apply to a generic context: Murdoch and Watson explore Tor path selection strategies and algorithms [25], O'Gorman and Blott simulate packet counting and stream correlation attacks [33], Ngan *et al.* study the effects of their gold-star priority scheme on Tor performance [28], and Jansen *et al.* simulate queuing models and traffic prioritization mechanisms [15]. These simulators have either become unmaintained or are not publicly available, making published results challenging to validate.

Emulation. A competing and fundamentally different experimentation approach involves emulation. An emulator "tricks" an application or operating system that it is running on its own physical machine, when in fact it is virtualized in software. Emulators require a large amount of overhead to ensure the emulated software runs in real time while providing the virtualization layers needed to emulate an entire system. Therefore, emulation is potentially more accurate than simulation, but *much less scalable*: emulators typically run hundreds of nodes while simulators run thousands.

Due to intensive resource requirements, emulation platforms often utilize a large testbed of geographically distributed physical hardware. PlanetLab [7] and DETER [5] are examples of whole-system emulation testbeds. Both of these frameworks only supply a few hundred nodes to a user. Several Tor studies have utilized the PlanetLab and DETER testbeds for experimenting with traffic analysis attacks [3, 6, 13], attacks on Tor bridges [23], and relay circuit scheduling [42]. Due to resource consumption and colocation of nodes on each physical machine, results on these testbeds often suffer from a reduced and false sense of accuracy. Further, distributed experiments like those run on PlanetLab are challenging to manage and control while results are difficult to recreate.

A Tor emulation testbed has recently been simultaneously and independently proposed by Bauer *et al.* [4] based on the ModelNet emulation platform [46]. The emulation testbed, called ExperimentTor, works by configuring multiple host machines with new operating system installations. Some of these host machines run a version of ModelNet link emulators while the remaining machines run Tor and other application instances. Tor nodes are given IP addresses from separate virtual interfaces to allow multiple nodes per machine while sending all traffic over the ModelNet hosts to emulate configured network properties.

Shadow has several advantages over ExperimenTor despite having similar goals and motivations. First, Shadow is more *usable* than ExperimenTor, which requires multiple physical machines, kernel modifications, and complex configuration. Shadow can be run as a stand-alone user application without root privledges and requires little configuration, leading to an extremely small barrier to entry and improving accessibility to students, developers, and researchers around the world. Second, Shadow is more *efficient* and *scalable* than ExperimenTor. Shadow implements a discrete-event simulator which allows full utilization of computational resources while eliminating the requirement of running in real time: experiments may run either faster or slower than real time without affecting accuracy. Conversely, ExperimenTor suffers from both CPU and bandwidth bottlenecks: the CPUs on the machines running the ExperimenTor testbed must run at far less than 100 percent utilization and the aggregate traffic load from all application instances must not exceed the capacity of the physical network connecting the host machines. Both requirements must be met to ensure the emulated applications do not lag, since lag would skew and invalidate results obtained in an experiment. Shadow also minimizes the memory overhead of running multiple applications on a single machine with its "state swapping" approach to memory management whereas ExperimenTor duplicates entire copies of the application in memory. Finally, Shadow allows for a richer *customization* of the experimental process, e.g. adversarial entities could easily be added to links between nodes to allow monitoring of network level traffic. Similar customizations would be difficult to add to an ExperimenTor testbed.

8 Conclusion

In this paper, we presented the design and implementation of a large scale discrete event simulator called Shadow, and a plug-in called Scallion that is capable of linking to and running the Tor software over a simulated network. In addition to an explanation of Shadow's non-trivial design, we performed an extensive experimental analysis to verify the accuracy of Tor simulations. We found that client performance for simulated Tor clients is surprisingly congruent to performance achieved through the live public Tor network. High accuracy is achieved by "shadowing" the Tor network, considering relay characteristics from a live Tor consensus and inter-node latency characteristics from PlanetLab ping measurements. As an example of the powerful capabilities of our simulation approach, we explore the EWMA circuit priority scheduler recently proposed and currently used in Tor to validate previous results and determine the effects of a network-wide deployment. We found that correct half-life configurations are highly network and load dependent, and that EWMA actually reduces performance for clients under certain network conditions. Although enabled by default, it is unclear if the scheduler improves performance in the live Tor network.

Limitations. Shadow is a discrete event simulator. By definition, Shadow imitates the behavior of system and network processes. These imitations were done by exploring and measuring real systems and real networks to produce models of real behaviors suitable for our study of performance in Tor. This modeling approach fundamentally limits the ability to adapt to highly dynamic environments, potentially reducing simulation accuracy. We now briefly discuss our modeling approaches in the context of their effects on simulations to emphasize the importance of analyzing and verifying results so that future researchers may make informed decisions regarding experimentation with their algorithms and protocols.

In addition to simulating TCP, Shadow models the Internet by utilizing real delays gathered from `ping` measurements on PlanetLab. The measurements give us a distribution of pairwise delays between nodes. We then categorize all nodes into geographical "regions" and aggregate node distributions between each region. This approximation forms our model of the Internet and is given as input to a simulation: when sending a packet from a node in one region to a node in another, we sample the distribution corresponding to the link between those regions. This model is based on specific measurements between specific points at a specific time. If Internet congestion at that time was uncharacteristically high or low, our model would skew results. Although this approach seemed to provide an adequate delay model in our simulations, future work should consider if their experiments could benefit from something more robust. In particular, experiments that depend on side-channels stemming from latency, throughput, or the inner workings of a specific TCP implementation may require more accurate simulations.

Scallion models system processing delays by gathering PlanetLab `OpenSSL` speed and application performance test measurements. Processing delays are then accumulated as the application reads and writes data, as this allows Shadow to quantify the amount of work the application is performing. Delays are incorporated into the event scheduling mechanism. This is a crude approximation of the real processing delays experienced on a system and is application specific: different applications may have very different processing delay models. For example, our processing delay model would be inadequate for an application that reads and writes data one percent of the time and spends the remaining time performing expensive operations. Inaccurate delay models would potentially skew results. Therefore, new application performance testing is required to appropriately model processing delays. Further, experiments that attempt to introduce variablilty in processing times as a key feature of an algorithm or as part of an attack will require more accurate simulations.

In our analysis of Tor performance, our modeling approaches were suitable to obtain realistic and consistent results. In particular, our Tor experiments were run using the same models while each experiment varied only a single configuration option. Therefore, each experiment was subject to the same system and network conditions and the same systematic biases that Shadow potentially introduces during simulation. As a result, we can be reasonably convinced that the *relative* differences between experimental results are due to our configured change and not to some systematic inaccuracy inherent to simulation, irrespective of how well the *absolute* simulation results match those obtained from real systems and networks.

Future Shadow users should be aware of the above limitations and recognize that adequate models are application dependent. It may be the case that more robust models are needed to effectively analyze particular algorithms or protocols. Future research should adapt models as appropriate to their work in order to draw meaningful conclusions, and validate results with other experimentation methods.

Future Work. Shadow may be used to explore a wide range of problems in Tor, including UDP transport mechanisms and alternative scheduling approaches. Shadow may also be used to validate previous work and analyze Tor attacks under various network configurations and client models. Finally, an exploration of more robust modeling techniques would reduce potential systematic biases introduced by our simulator and improve overall simulation accuracy.

There are several architectural modifications that can improve Shadow's run-time performance. The most significant improvement will enhance Shadow's ability to run in parallel environments, leading to faster experiments and better utilization of hardware resources. Shadow is open-source software that is available for download and includes useful tools for generating and running experiments. We feel Shadow is invaluable for understanding and evaluating Tor, hope that it will be useful to others in their research, and hope it will make a lasting impact on the community.

Acknowledgments. We thank John Geddes for assistance with Shadow plug-ins; Eric Chan-Tin, Denis Foo Kune, and Max Schuchard for discussions about Shadow's design; Chris Wacek for usability feedback; Roger Dingledine for insightful analysis of results; and Yongdae Kim, Nick Mathewson, and Paul Syverson for wisdom and encouragement. This research was supported by NFS grant CNS-0917154, ONR, and DARPA.

References

[1] A. Acquisti, R. Dingledine, and P. Syverson. On the economics of anonymity. In *Proceedings of the 7th International Conference on Financial Cryptography (FC'03)*, 2003.

[2] M. AlSabah, K. Bauer, I. Goldberg, D. Grunwald, D. McCoy, S. Savage, and G. Voelker. DefenestraTor: Throwing out Windows in Tor. In *Proceedings of the 11th International Symposium on Privacy Enhancing Technologies (PETS'11)*, 2011.

[3] K. Bauer, D. McCoy, D. Grunwald, T. Kohno, and D. Sicker. Low-resource routing attacks against Tor. In *Proceedings of the 6th ACM Workshop on Privacy in the Electronic Society (WPES'07)*, pages 11–20, 2007.

[4] K. Bauer, M. Sherr, D. McCoy, and D. Grunwald. Experimentor: A testbed for safe and realistic tor experimentation. In *the 4th Workshop on Cyber Security Experimentation and Test (CSET'11)*, 2011.

[5] T. Benzel, R. Braden, D. Kim, C. Neuman, A. Joseph, K. Sklower, R. Ostrenga, and S. Schwab. Design, deployment, and use of the DETER testbed. In *Proceedings of the DETER Community Workshop on Cyber Security Experimentation and Test*, 2007.

[6] S. Chakravarty, A. Stavrou, and A. Keromytis. Traffic analysis against low-latency anonymity networks using available bandwidth estimation. In *Computer Security – ESORICS*, pages 249–267, 2010.

[7] B. Chun, D. Culler, T. Roscoe, A. Bavier, L. Peterson, M. Wawrzoniak, and M. Bowman. Planetlab: an overlay testbed for broad-coverage services. *SIGCOMM Computer Communication Review*, 33:3–12, 2003.

[8] R. Dingledine, N. Mathewson, and P. Syverson. Tor: The second-generation onion router. In *Proceedings of the 13th USENIX Security Symposium*, 2004.

[9] N. Evans, R. Dingledine, and C. Grothoff. A practical congestion attack on Tor using long paths. In *Proceedings of the 18th USENIX Security Symposium*, pages 33–50, 2009.

[10] D. Foo Kune, T. Malchow, J. Tyra, N. Hopper, and Y. Kim. The Distributed Virtual Network for High Fidelity Large Scale Peer to Peer Network Simulation. Technical Report 10-029, University of Minnesota, 2010.

[11] D. M. Goldschlag, M. G. Reed, and P. F. Syverson. Hiding Routing Information. In *Proceedings of Information Hiding Workshop (IH'96)*, pages 137–150, 1996.

[12] F. Hernandez-Campos, K. Jeffay, and F. Smith. Tracking the evolution of web traffic: 1995-2003. In *The 11th IEEE/ACM International Symposium on Modeling, Analysis, and Simulation of Computer Telecommunications Systems (MASCOTS'03)*, pages 16–25, 2003.

[13] N. Hopper, E. Vasserman, and E. Chan-Tin. How much anonymity does network latency leak? *ACM Transactions on Information and System Security (TISSEC'10)*, 13(2):1–28, 2010.

[14] The Iperf bandwidth measurement tool. `http://iperf.sourceforge.net/`.

[15] R. Jansen, N. Hopper, and Y. Kim. Recruiting new Tor relays with BRAIDS. In *Proceedings of the 17th ACM Conference on Computer and Communications Security (CCS'10)*, pages 319–328, 2010.

[16] C. Kiddle. *Scalable network emulation*. PhD thesis, University of Calgary, 2004.

[17] The Libevent event notification library, version 2.0. `http://monkey.org/~provos/libevent/`.

[18] S. Lin, A. Pan, Z. Zhang, R. Guo, and Z. Guo. Wids: an integrated toolkit for distributed system development. In *Proceedings of the 10th conference on Hot Topics in Operating Systems (HOTOS'05)*, 2005.

[19] J. D. Little and S. C. Graves. Little's Law. `web.mit.edu/sgraves/www/papers/Little's%20Law-Published.pdf`, 2008. Accessed July, 2011.

[20] K. Loesing. Measuring the Tor network: Evaluation of client requests to directories. Technical report, Tor Project, 2009.

[21] The MaxMind GeoIP Lite country database. `http://www.maxmind.com/app/geolitecountry`.

[22] D. Mccoy, K. Bauer, D. Grunwald, T. Kohno, and D. Sicker. Shining light in dark places: Understanding the Tor network. In *Proceedings of the 8th International Symposium on Privacy Enhancing Technologies (PETS'08)*, pages 63–76, 2008.

[23] J. McLachlan and N. Hopper. On the risks of serving whenever you surf: vulnerabilities in Tor's blocking resistance design. In *Proceedings of the 8th ACM Workshop on Privacy in the Electronic Society (WPES'09)*, pages 31–40, 2009.

[24] S. Murdoch and G. Danezis. Low-cost traffic analysis of Tor. In *IEEE Symposium on Security and Privacy*, pages 183–195, 2005.

[25] S. Murdoch and R. Watson. Metrics for security and performance in low-latency anonymity systems. In *Proceedings of the 8th International Symposium on Privacy Enhancing Technologies (PETS'08)*, pages 115–132, 2008.

[26] S. Naicken, A. Basu, B. Livingston, S. Rodhetbhai, and I. Wakeman. Towards yet another peer-to-peer simulator. In *Proceedings of the 4th International Working Conference on Performance Modelling and Evaluation of Heterogeneous Networks (HET-NETs'06)*, 2006.

[27] S. Naicken, B. Livingston, A. Basu, S. Rodhetbhai, I. Wakeman, and D. Chalmers. The state of peer-to-peer simulators and simulations. *SIGCOMM Computer Communication Review*, 37(2):95–98, 2007.

[28] T.-W. J. Ngan, R. Dingledine, and D. S. Wallach. Building incentives into Tor. In *The Proceedings of Financial Cryptography (FC'10)*, 2010.

[29] The ns-2 Network Simulator. `http://www.isi.edu/nsnam/ns/`.

[30] The ns-3 Network Simulator. http://www.nsnam.org/.

[31] The OpenSSL cryptographic library. http://www.openssl.org/.

[32] L. Overlier and P. Syverson. Locating hidden servers. In *IEEE Symposium on Security and Privacy*, 2006.

[33] G. OGorman and S. Blott. Large scale simulation of Tor: Modelling a Global Passive Adversary. In *Proceedings of the 12th Conference on Advances in Computer Science – ASIAN*, pages 48–54, 2007.

[34] J. Postel. User Datagram Protocol. RFC 768, http://www.ietf.org/rfc/rfc768.txt, August 1980.

[35] J. Postel. Transmission Control Protocol. RFC 793, http://www.ietf.org/rfc/rfc793.txt, September 1981.

[36] J. Reardon and I. Goldberg. Improving Tor using a TCP-over-DTLS tunnel. In *Proceedings of the 18th USENIX Security Symposium*, 2009.

[37] M. Reed, P. Syverson, and D. Goldschlag. Anonymous connections and onion routing. *IEEE Journal on Selected Areas in Communications*, 16(4):482–494, 1998.

[38] Shadow Development Repositories. http://github.com/shadow/.

[39] Shadow Resources. http://shadow.cs.umn.edu/.

[40] R. Snader and N. Borisov. A tune-up for Tor: Improving security and performance in the Tor network. In *Proceedings of the 16th Network and Distributed Security Symposium (NDSS'08)*, 2008.

[41] Scalable Simulation Framework, SSFNet. http://www.cc.gatech.edu/computing/compass/pdns/index.html.

[42] C. Tang and I. Goldberg. An improved algorithm for Tor circuit scheduling. In *Proceedings of the 17th ACM Conference on Computer and Communications Security*, pages 329–339, 2010.

[43] Including network statistics in extra-info documents. https://gitweb.torproject.org/torspec.git/blob_plain?f=proposals/166-statistics-extra-info-docs.txt.

[44] The TorFlow measurement tools. https://gitweb.torproject.org/torflow.git/.

[45] The Tor Metrics Portal. http://metrics.torproject.org/.

[46] A. Vahdat, K. Yocum, K. Walsh, P. Mahadevan, D. Kostić, J. Chase, and D. Becker. Scalability and accuracy in a large-scale network emulator. *SIGOPS Operating Systems Review*, 36(SI):271–284, 2002.

[47] C. Viecco. UDP-OR: A fair onion transport design. In *Proceedings of Hot Topics in Privacy Enhancing Technologies (HOTPETS'08)*, 2008.

Appendices

A Core Simulation Engine

Shadow is a fork of the Distributed Virtual Network (DVN) Simulator [10]. DVN is a discrete event, multi-process, scalable UDP-based network simulator written in C that can simulate hundreds of thousands of nodes in a single experiment. DVN takes a unique approach to simulation by running UDP-based user applications as modules loaded at run-time. Among DVN's core components are the per-process event schedulers, a process synchronization algorithm, and a module subsystem. We describe the main components but note that Foo Kune *et al.* [10] provide details in much greater resolution.

Discrete-event Scheduler. DVN implements a conservative, distributed scheduling algorithm (see Figure 8) that utilizes message queues to transfer events between workers. The scheduling algorithm consists of three phases: importing events initiated from remote nodes, synchronizing worker processes, and executing local node events. During the import phase, workers process incoming messages containing events and store them in a custom local event priority queue. After all messages are imported, workers send synchronization messages (discussed below) to other workers and finally process local events in non-decreasing order. Incoming messages are buffered while processing local events and handled during the next import phase.

Multi-process Synchronization. Messages between the master and workers enable global time synchronization throughout the simulation. Synchronized time is vital to ensure events are executed in the correct order since a conservative scheduling algorithm can not revert events. By exchanging messages, each process tracks the local time of all other processes. A *barrier* is computed by taking the minimum local time of each process and adding the minimum network latency between any two network nodes in the simulation. The barrier represents the earliest possible time that an event from one process may affect another process. Each process may execute events in its local event queue as long as the event execution time is earlier than the barrier. This is called the *safe execution window*: any event in this window may be safely executed without compromising the order of events (i.e. time will never jump backwards to execute a past event). Barriers are dynamically updated as new synchronization messages update local times. Future events are allowed to execute as the barrier progresses through time. This synchronization approach allows the distribution of events to multiple processes.

Module Subsystem. DVN contains a subsystem for dynamically loading modules. Modules, pieces of code that are run by nodes, are generally created by porting application code to use DVN network calls and implementing special functions required by DVN. The special functions allow modules to receive event callback notifications from DVN. Although each module may be run by several nodes, module libraries are only loaded into memory once. In order to support multiple nodes running the same module, DVN requires each module to register all variable application state. Using the registered memory addresses, DVN may properly load variables before passing execution control to the module, and unload and save variables after regaining control.

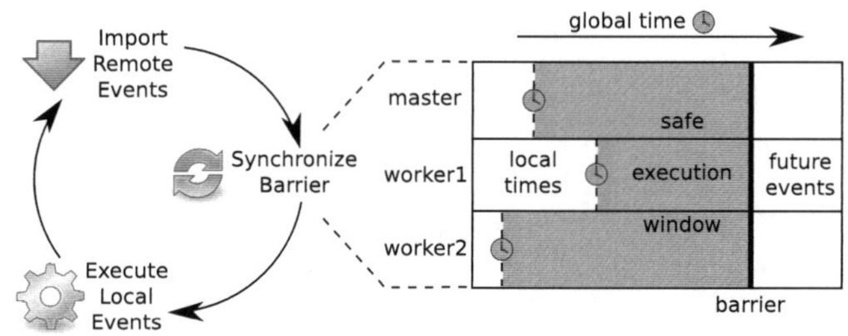

Figure 8: Main loop and conservative multi-process synchronization using dynamic barriers. Safe execution windows are calculated using the minimum local worker time plus the minimum simulated latency between nodes. The barrier is dynamically pushed as local times advance.

B Circuit Scheduler Performance

In Section 6, we showed results for web client responsiveness and overall performance for both web and bulk clients with different circuit schedulers under different network loads. In Figure 9 we show that responsiveness for bulk clients follow the same pattern as previously shown in Figure 7. (The results were obtained from the same experiments described in Section 6.) Although time to first byte is less important for bulk clients, the results support our conclusion that the EWMA circuit scheduling algorithm reduces performance both under lighter loads and when the half-life is not set correctly. Figure 10 shows performance under an extremely lightly loaded network of 475 web and 25 bulk clients. The results support our claims in Section 6 that choice of circuit scheduler is insignificant for client performance when the load on the network is too light.

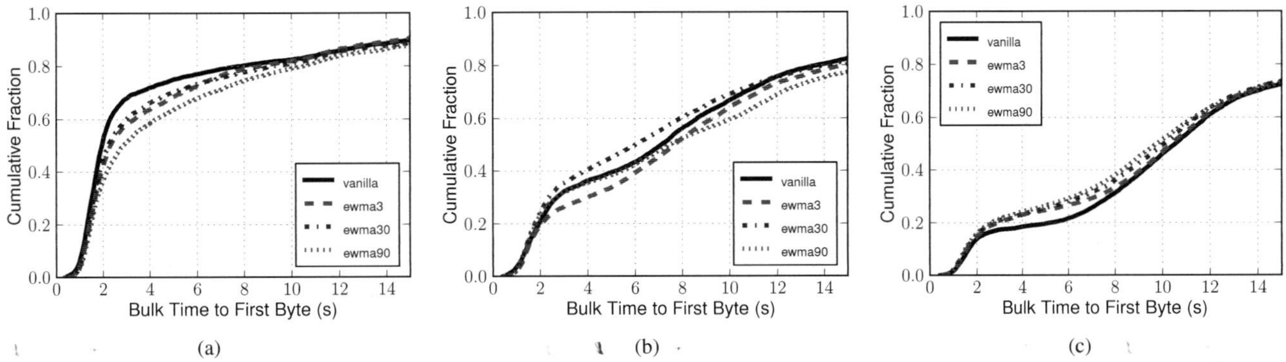

Figure 9: Responsiveness for bulk clients under a varying network load of 950 web clients and (a) 25 bulk clients, (b) 50 bulk clients, and (c) 100 bulk clients. As in Figure 7, the network is less responsive under lighter loads when using the EWMA circuit scheduler.

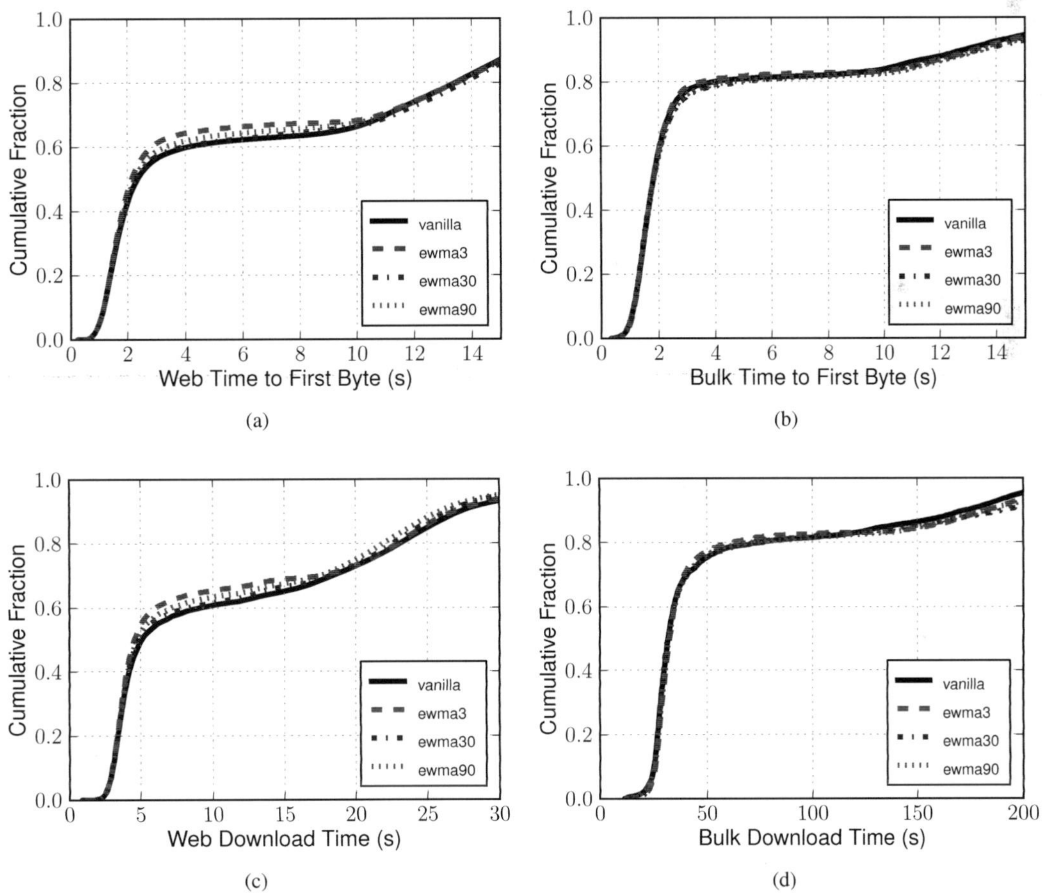

Figure 10: Network performance under an extremely light load of 475 web and 25 bulk clients. When the network load is too light, the circuit scheduling algorithm has an insignificant impact on performance.

DIMSUM: Discovering of Semantic Data of Interest from Un-mappable Memory with Confidence

Zhiqiang Lin[1] , Junghwan Rhee[2], Chao Wu[3], Xiangyu Zhang[3]
Dongyan Xu[3]

[1]University of Texas at Dallas
[2]NEC Laboratories America
[3]Purdue University

The Problem: Memory Forensics

- Given:
  - A set of memory pages
  - A data structure of interest (e.g., contact, cookie, chat history)
- Identifying:
  - Instances of that data structure in the memory pages
- Assuming:
  - No memory mapping information (e.g., page table)

Observation:
Dead Pages Left by Terminated Processes

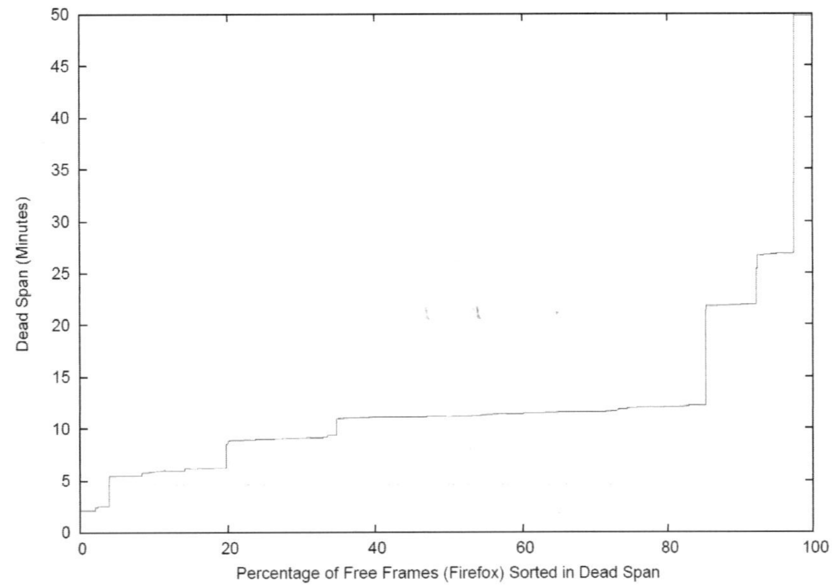

State of the Art

- Value invariant-based approaches
  - Klist [Rutkowska,2003]
  - GREPEXEC [bugcheck, 2006]
  - Volatility [Walters, 2006] [Schuster, 2006]
  - Robust signatures [Dolan-Gavitt et al., CCS'09]
- Pointer navigation-based approaches
  - KOP [Carbone et al.,CCS'09], CRASH [USENIX'05]
  - SigGraph [Lin et al., NDSS'11]

Use of Memory Mapping Information

```
000001f0: 08 80 04 08
```

Where is (0x08048008) pointing to?

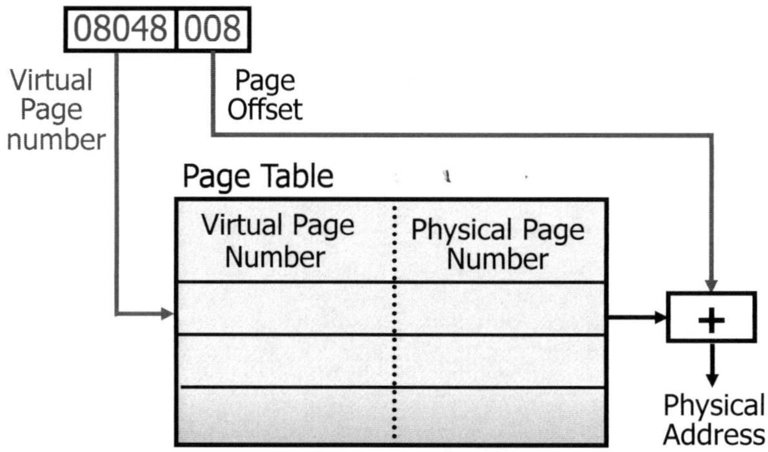

DIMSUM Overview

Discovering **I**nfor**M**ation with **S**emantics from **U**n-mappable **M**emory

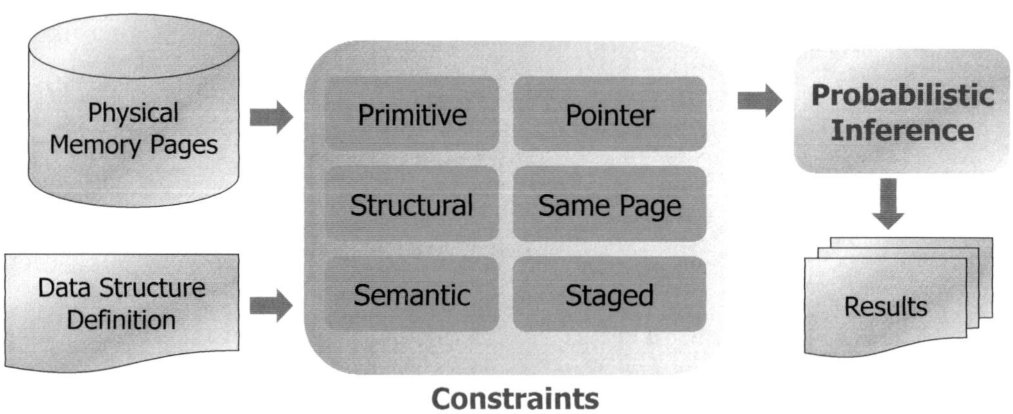

Structural Constraint

```
type = struct passwd {
     char *pw_name;       //00
     char *pw_passwd;     //04
     __uid_t pw_uid;      //08
     __gid_t pw_gid;      //12
     char *pw_gecos;      //16
     char *pw_dir;        //20
     char *pw_shell;      //24
}
```

p(pw_name) ∧ p(pw_passwd)
∧ I(pw_uid) ∧ I(pw_gid)
∧ p(pw_gecos) ∧ p(pw_dir)
∧ p(pw_shell)

Semantic Constraint

```
type = struct passwd {
     char *pw_name;       //00
     char *pw_passwd;     //04
     __uid_t pw_uid;      //08
     __gid_t pw_gid;      //12
     char *pw_gecos;      //16
     char *pw_dir;        //20
     char *pw_shell;      //24
}
```

p(pw_name) ∧ p(pw_passwd)
∧ I(pw_uid) ∧ I(pw_gid)
∧ p(pw_gecos) ∧ p(pw_dir)
∧ p(pw_shell)

(pw_uid >=0) ∧ (pw_gid >=0)

Same-Page (SP) Constraint

```
type = struct passwd {
     char *pw_name;         //00
     char *pw_passwd;       //04
     __uid_t pw_uid;        //08
     __gid_t pw_gid;        //12
     char *pw_gecos;        //16
     char *pw_dir;          //20
     char *pw_shell;        //24
}
```

p(pw_name) ∧ p(pw_passwd) ∧ I (pw_uid) ∧ I(pw_gid) ∧ p(pw_gecos) ∧ p(pw_dir) ∧ p(pw_shell)

(pw_uid >=0) ∧ (pw_gid >=0)

SP(*pw_name, *pw_passwd, *pw_gecos, *pw_dir, *pw_shell)

```
00000970  00 00 00 00 70 ac e6 08  75 ac e6 08 00 00 00 00
00000980  00 00 00 00 7b ac e6 08  80 ac e6 08 86 ac e6 08
00000990  00 04 00 00 00 00 00 00  00 00 00 00 00 00 00 00
```

```
00000c70  72 6f 6f 74 00 78 00 30  3a 30 3a 72 6f 6f 74 00
00000c80  2f 72 6f 6f 74 00 2f 62  69 6e 2f 62 61 73 68 00
00000c90  00 00 00 00 00 00 00 00  00 00 00 00 00 00 00 00
```

Probabilistic Inference Model

- Boolean variable x: type property of a memory location
  - x_1: There is an instance of passwd at offset 0 of page 100
  - x_2: There is a *char pointer at offset 0 of page 100
  - x_3: There is a *char pointer at offset 4 of page 100
- Constraint Cj: type/structural/semantic property for one or more memory locations
  - $C1: x_1 \rightarrow x_2 \wedge x_3 \wedge \ldots$
  - $C2: x_1 \rightarrow same\_page(*0^p \wedge *4^p \wedge \ldots)$

Probabilistic Inference Model (Cont.)

- Valuation function f_{Cj}: constraint Cj's evaluation with confidence
  - → $f_{C1} = \begin{cases} 1; if\ C1 = 1 \\ 0; otherwise \end{cases}$
  - → $f_{C2} = \begin{cases} \delta;\ if\ \exists p\ such\ that\ C2 = 1 \\ 1 - \delta; otherwise \end{cases}$

Probabilistic Inference Model (Cont.)

- Joint probability function:
  - → $p(x_1, x_2 \ldots x_n) = \frac{f_{C1} \times f_{C2} \times \ldots \times f_{Cm}}{Z}$
  - → $Z = \sum_{x_1, x_2 \ldots x_n} (f_{C1} \times f_{C2} \times \cdots \times f_{Cm})$
- Marginal probability:
  - → $p(x_i = 1) = \sum_{x_1, x_2 \ldots x_{i\_1} x_{i_+1} \ldots x_n} p(x_1, x_2 \ldots 1 \ldots x_n)$
  - → $p(x_1 = 1)$: probability of having an instance of passwd at offset 0 of page 100
- Implemented using *Infer.NET* engine

Evaluation Results with Linux-based Applications

Data Structure of Interest	% of Memory Pages	True Instances	SigGraph+		DIMSUM	
			FP%	FN%	FP%	FN%
Login record (`last`)	100.0	8	0.0	25.0	0.0	0.0
	66.7	6	0.0	66.7	0.0	0.0
	33.3	0	0.0	0.0	100.0*	0.0
Browser cookies (`chromium`)	100.0	25	69.5	0.0	44.4	0.0
	66.7	19	66.1	0.0	50.0	0.0
	33.3	9	79.1	0.0	43.8	0.0
Address book (`pine-4.64`)	100.0	124	48.5	4.8	0.0	18.5
	66.7	96	50.1	10.4	0.0	17.7
	33.3	63	56.8	39.7	0.0	33.3
Contact list (`pidgin`)	100.0	300	38.8	0.0	0.0	1.0
	66.7	198	22.8	0.0	0.0	1.0
	33.3	98	23.0	0.0	0.0	1.0

Case Study: Login Record `utmp` in `last`

```
struct utmplist {
00: short int ut_type;
04: pid_t ut_pid;
08: char ut_line[32];
40: char ut_id[4];
44: char ut_user[32];
76: char ut_host[256];
332: long int ut_etermination;
336: long int ut_session;
340: struct timeval ut_tv;
348: int32_t ut_addr_v6[4];
364: char __unused[20];
384: struct utmplist *next;
388: struct utmplist *prev;
}
```

All Dead Pages Available

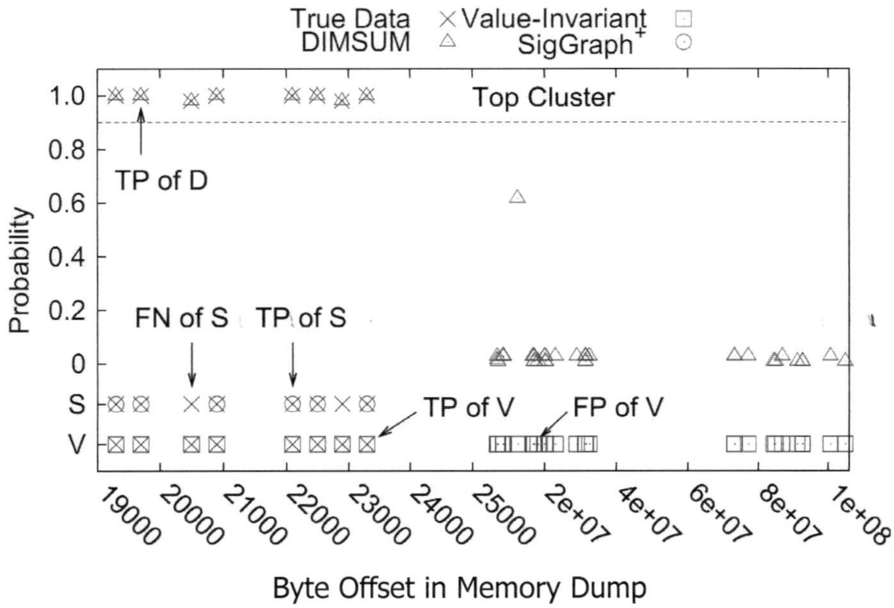

Results with Android 2.1 Applications

Data Structure of Interest	% of Mem. Pages	True Instances	SigGraph+		DIMSUM	
			FP%	FN%	FP%	FN%
`Cookie (Browser)`	100.0	31	77.0	0.0	0.0	0.0
	66.7	25	75.5	0.0	0.0	0.0
	33.3	6	85.8	16.7	0.0	0.0
`Phone Contact (Messaging)`	100.0	117	0.9	4.3	0.0	0.0
	66.7	79	0.0	3.8	0.0	0.0
	33.3	36	2.9	5.6	0.0	0.0
`Message Conversation (Messaging)`	100.0	101	0.0	2.0	0.0	0.0
	66.7	60	0.0	1.7	0.0	0.0
	33.3	40	0.0	2.5	0.0	0.0

Other Related Work

- ColdBoot [Halderman et al, USENIX Security'08]
- Laika [Cozzie et al, OSDI'08]
- DECODE [Walls et al, USENIX Security'11]

Conclusion

- DIMSUM recognizes data structure instances from memory pages
  - Without memory mapping information
  - Based on probabilistic inference
  - Solving constraints about type/structural/semantic properties
  - More accurate than non-probabilistic approaches

Thank you

67% of Dead Pages Available

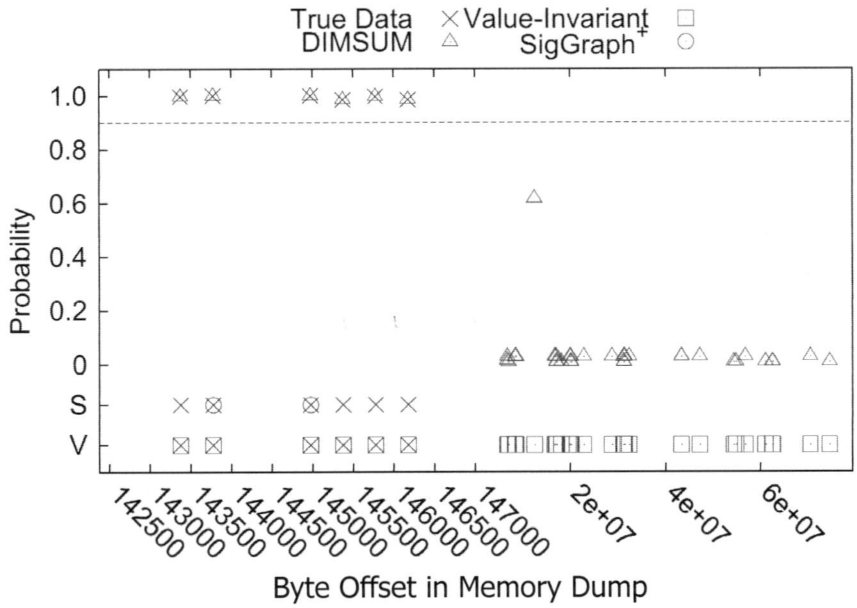

33% of Dead Pages Available

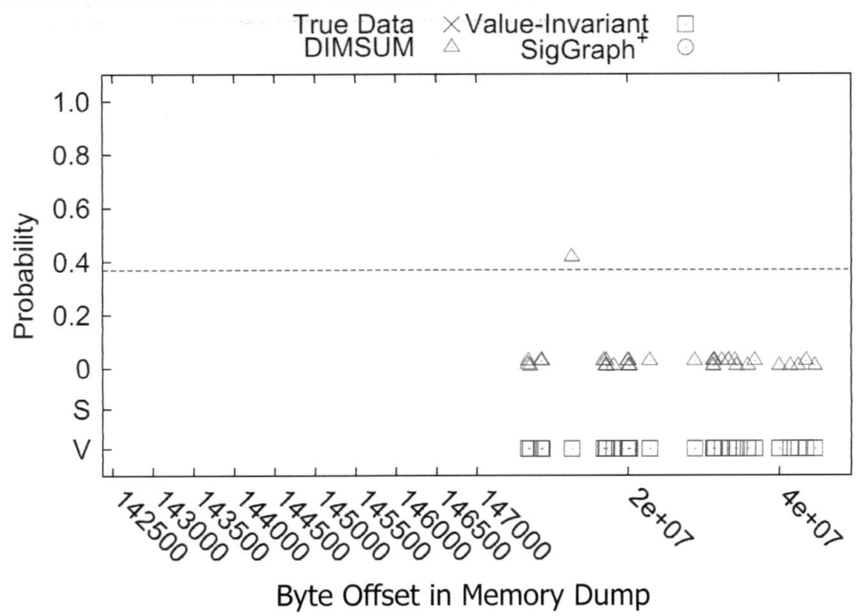

An Android-Specific Constraint

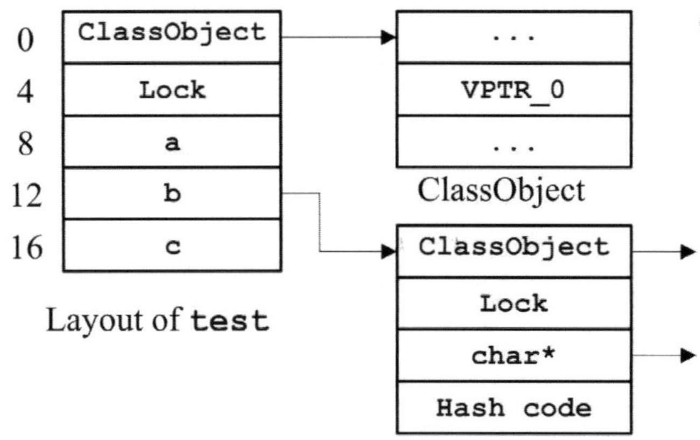


```
class test{
    int a;
    string b,
    float c;
}
```

SecureSwitch: BIOS-Assisted Isolation and Switch between Trusted and Untrusted Commodity OSes

Kun Sun, Jiang Wang, Fengwei Zhang, Angelos Stavrou
Center for Secure Information Systems
George Mason University

Outline

- Introduction
- Related Works
- Background Knowledge
- System Architecture
- Experimental Results
- Discussion
- Summary

Introduction

- Segregate personal communication and entertainment from business and government operations
  - In untrusted environment: Web browser, online gaming, social web portal
  - In trusted environment: Online banking, shopping, business email
- Trusted computing environment
  - Separate/isolate the trusted environment from the untrusted environment
  - Prevent data leakage even if the host has been previously infected with malware in the untrusted environment.
  - Enables secure transactions on demand with low context switching latency

GEORGE MASON UNIVERSITY

Outline

- Introduction
- Related Works
- Background Knowledge
- System Architecture
- Experimental Results
- Discussion
- Summary

GEORGE MASON UNIVERSITY

Lampson Red/Green System Separation

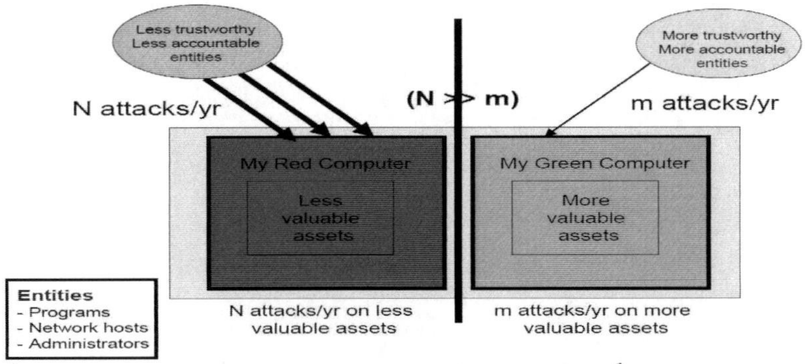

Red/Green system: Policy + Isolation + Accountability +Freedom
* Butler Lampson, Accountability and Freedom Slides, Microsoft, September 2005

- Our work focuses on isolation between two environments
  - Not on how the users decide what applications go into each OS
  - Not on how to give the user control over data exchanges between the two environments

GEORGE MASON UNIVERSITY

Software-based Isolation Solution

	VMM-based	OS-based	Browser-based
Isolation Level	OS level	User/Process level	Applet level
Examples	Xen, VMware, QEMU, UML	FreeBSD Jail, Linux OpenVZ, Solaris Container	Adobe Flash, Java applets, Silverlight
Security concerns	VMM vulnerabilities* Covert Channel	VMM vulnerabilities OS vulnerabilities Privilege escalation	VMM vulnerabilities OS vulnerabilities Browser vulnerabilities

* From 1999 to 2009, 373 vulnerabilities affecting virtualization solutions.
--- "IBM X-Force 2010 Mid-year trend and risk report"

GEORGE MASON UNIVERSITY

Hardware-based Isolation Solution

	Multiple Computers	Multi-boot	VT-x / SVM (DRTM)
Isolation Level	Whole physical computer	OS level;	Instruction level;
Examples		Bootloader: LILO, Grub	Flicker [1]; TrustVisor [2];
Problems	Cost, inflexible	Long switching time	Software compatibility

Our work provides an BIOS-assistant OS level isolation

- without using any mutable software layer (e.g., hypervisor)
- no changes of the OS source code
- no data leak between two OS environments
- fast switching time, around 6 seconds

GEORGE MASON UNIVERSITY

Outline

- Introduction
- Related Works
- Background Knowledge
- System Architecture
- Experimental Results
- Discussion
- Summary

GEORGE MASON UNIVERSITY

ACPI Sleeping States

- Advanced Configuration and Power Interface (ACPI)
  - OS-directed configuration; Power/thermal management
  - Industrial standard widely supported
- Global System States
  - G0 --- Working (System Operational)
  - G1---Sleeping (CPU stopped)
  - G2 ---Soft Off
  - G3 ---Mechanical off (Physical off switch)
- Sleeping States in G1: S1 – S4
  - S3: also *called Standby, Suspend to RAM*
    - DRAM still maintained
  - S4: also called *Hibernation or Suspend to Disk*
    - DRAM not maintained
- Device Power States: D0 – D3
  - D0 - Fully-On
  - D3 -- Power off to device

GEORGE MASON UNIVERSITY

BIOS, UEFI, and Coreboot

- Basic Input/Output System (BIOS)
  - Initializing hardware like processor, memory, chipset, hard disk, and other I/O devices.
  - Stored in non-volatile ROM chips.
- Unified Extensible Firmware Interface (UEFI)
  - Define a new software interface between OS and firmware.
  - Ease the development by switching into protected mode in early stage and writing code in C language.
  - Partially open source
- *Coreboot* (formerly as LinuxBIOS)
  - Similar functionality as UEFI
  - Open source
  - We use Coreboot V4

GEORGE MASON UNIVERSITY

DIMM Mask and DQS Setting

- A motherboard may have more than one Dual In-line Memory Module (DIMM) slot.
  - We assign one DIMM to one OS.
- BIOS uses "DIMM_MASK" variable to control which DIMMs to be enabled.
  - BIOS sets corresponding "data strobes"(DQS) parameters to enable DDR RAM memory access.
  - Require two sets of DQS setting to support the two DIMMs used by two OSes separately.

Outline

- Introduction
- Related Works
- Background Knowledge
- System Architecture
- Experimental Results
- Discussion
- Summary

System Architecture

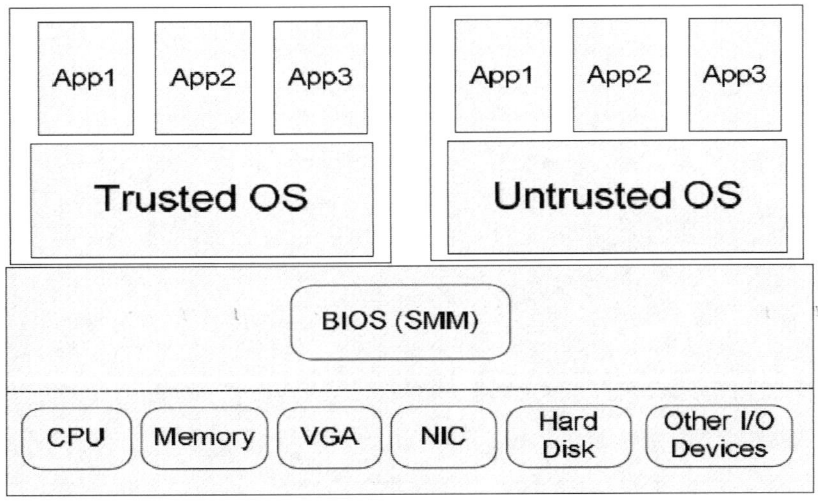

Attack Model

- Assumption
  - BIOS and option ROM on devices can be trusted.
  - No physical access to the protected machine
- Attacks from the untrusted OS
  - *Data exfiltration attacks*: stealing sensitive data from the trusted OS
  - *Spoofing Trusted OS attacks*: deceiving the user into a fake trusted OS to perform sensitive transactions.
  - *Cache-based side channel attacks*: extracting sensitive information
- Out of the scope
  - Denial of Service attacks
  - Network attacks on trusted OS
  - Malicious device firmware

Secure Switching State Machine

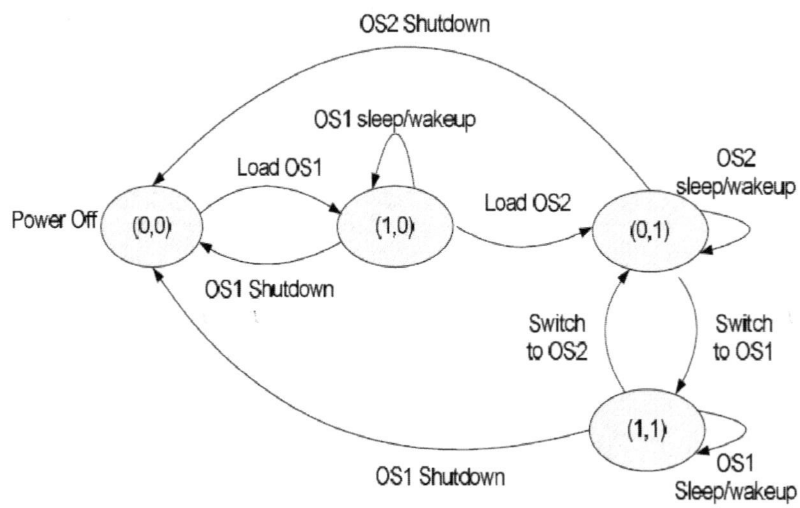

Trusted Path

- A trusted path assures users that they really are working with the operation system they intend to use.
- Prevent spoofing trusted OS attacks
  - Untrusted OS should be truly suspended.
    - Power LED lights up when system is powered on, and blinks in the sleep mode.
  - BIOS should be entered.
    - Press the power button.
  - Protecting system flags / variables
    - OS Flag: which OS should be woken next
    - Boot Flag: if untrusted OS has been loaded
    - Where to save these flags?

Boot Flag: in CMOS
OS Flag: physical jumper (e.g., pins in Parallel port connector)

Secure Switching Process

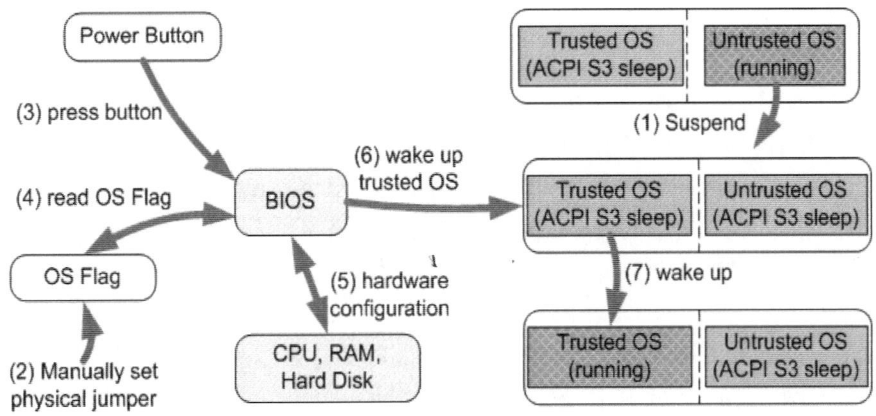

GEORGE MASON UNIVERSITY

System Isolation

- CPU Isolation: two OSes never run concurrently.
- Memory Isolation: physical-level isolation
- Hard disk isolation: encrypted hard disk + RAM disk
- Other I/O isolation: clean the buffers and states in devices.

- **Isolation Mechanisms:**

	CPU	Memory	Hard Disk	VGA	NIC
OS with ACPI S3	√	√	√	√	√
BIOS		√	√		

GEORGE MASON UNIVERSITY

Physical-level Memory Isolation

- OS environments run in separate Dual In-line Memory Modules (DIMMs).
- BIOS only enables and reports one DIMM for each OS.
  - Two DQS settings for two OSes
  - "DIMM_MASK" controlled by the physical jumper.
  - When the "DIMM_MASK" conflicts with DQS setting, the system crashes
- Only the BIOS can initialize and enable the DIMMs; software cannot initialize or enable DIMMs after the system boots up

GEORGE MASON UNIVERSITY

Hard Drive Isolation

- Hard disk encryption
  - Two hard disks, one for each OS.
  - Disk lock in ATA specification
- BIOS only enables one hard disk
  - Attacker may change the setting to enable all hard disks
  - We use SMM-based detection to check that the channel enable registers has not been changed
- RAM disk
  - For browser-based application, save a small amount of temporary data in the RAM

GEORGE MASON UNIVERSITY

Outline

- Introduction
- Related Works
- Background Knowledge
- System Architecture
- Experimental Results
- Discussion
- Summary

GEORGE MASON UNIVERSITY

Prototype

- **Hardware**
  - *Motherboard*: ASUS M2V-MX_SE
  - *CPU*: AMD Sempron 64 LE-1300
  - *DDR2*: Kingston HyperX 1GB
  - *HDD*: Seagate 500GB

- **Software**
  - *BIOS*: Coreboot + SeaBIOS
  - *Trusted OS*: Linux (Centos 5.5)
  - *Untrusted OS*: Windows XP

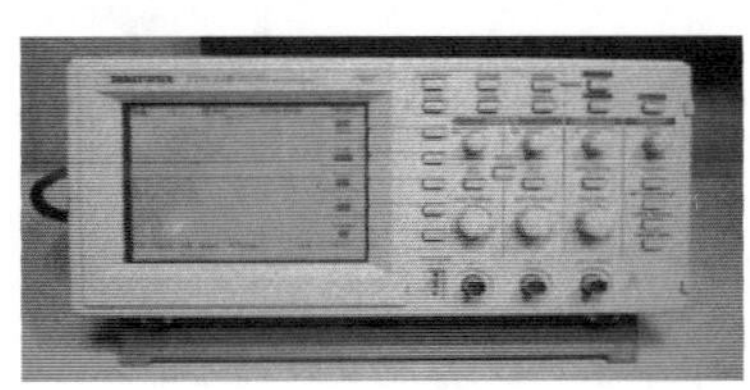

GEORGE MASON UNIVERSITY

Performance Analysis

Table 1: Switching Time

Switching Operation	Secure Switch(s)
Windows XP Suspend	4.41
CentOS Wakeup	1.96
Total	6.37
CentOS Suspend	2.24
Windows XP Wakeup	2.79
Total	5.03

GEORGE MASON UNIVERSITY

Linux Suspend Time Breakdown

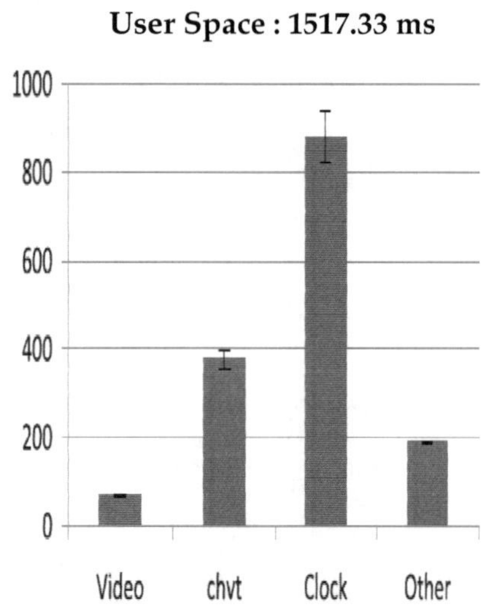

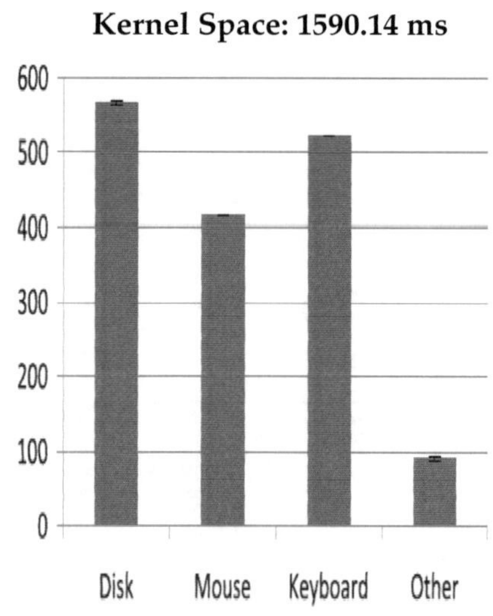

GEORGE MASON UNIVERSITY

Linux Wakeup Time Breakdown

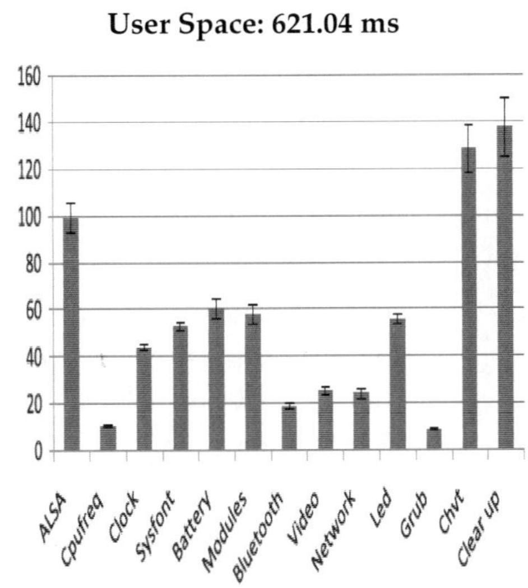

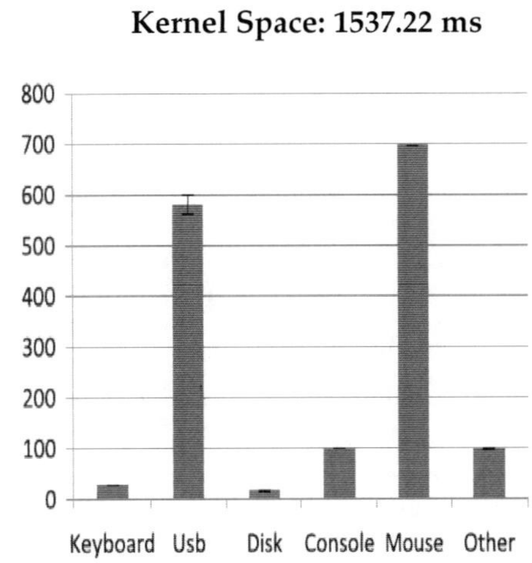

Outline

- Introduction
- Related Works
- Background Knowledge
- System Architecture
- Experimental Results
- Discussion
- Summary

Comparison with other systems

	SecureSwitch	Lockdown [41]	TrustVisor [29]	Flicker [28]	Xen [14]
Trusted Computing Base	BIOS	Hypervisor+BIOS	Hypervisor	250 LOC	Hypervisor
Switching Time (second)	≈6	40	<0.001	1	<0.001
Hardware Dependency	ACPI	ACPI+TPM+ VT-x/SVM	TPM+ VT-x/SVM	TPM+ VT-x/SVM	VT-x/SVM*
Software Compatibility	High	High	Low	Low	High
Memory Overhead	High	Low	Low	Low	Medium
OS Concurrency	No	No	Yes	No	Yes
Computation Overhead	Low	Medium	Medium	Low	Medium

* Xen requires VT-x/SVM to support full virtualization.

GEORGE MASON UNIVERSITY

Summary

- We develop a BIOS-based secure isolation and switching system to obtain a usable trusted workspace
  - Prevent data leakage
  - Without using hypervisor
  - No changes of OS source code
  - Low switching time

GEORGE MASON UNIVERSITY

Thank you.

- Questions?

Reference

- [1]. J. McCune, B. Parno, A. Perrig, M. Reiter, and H. Isozaki. Flicker: An execution infrastructure for TCB minimization. In Proceedings of the 3rd ACM SIGOPS/EuroSys European Conference on Computer Systems 2008, pages 315–328. ACM, 2008.
- [2]. J. M. McCune, Y. Li, N. Qu, Z. Zhou, A. Datta, V. Gligor, and A. Perrig. TrustVisor: Efficient TCB reduction and attestation. In Proceedings of the IEEE Symposium on Security and Privacy, 2010.

SMART: Secure and Minimal Architecture for Establishing a Dynamic Root of Trust

Karim El Defrawy, Aurelien Francillon, Daniele Perito, Gene Tsudik
UCI ETH INRIA UCI

Feb 8 2012

Low-end Embedded Devices

- Low cost, low power devices
- Built around a Micro-controller Unit (MCU)
- Limited:
  - Memory
    - 4 KB Data Memory (SRAM)
    - 128KB Program Memory (Flash)
  - Power
  - computation capabilities
- For example
  - MSP430
  - AVR

Critical Cyber-physical Systems

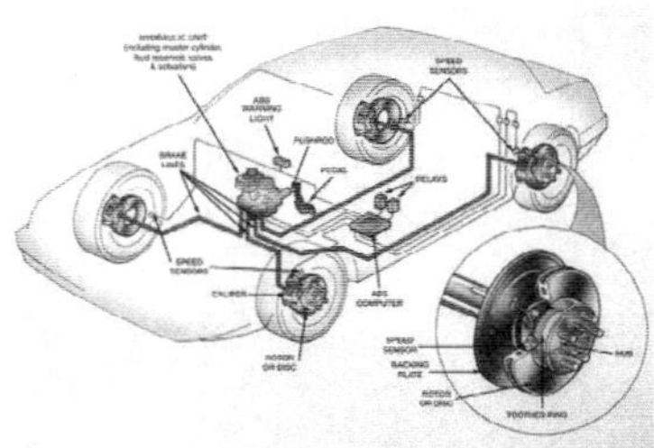

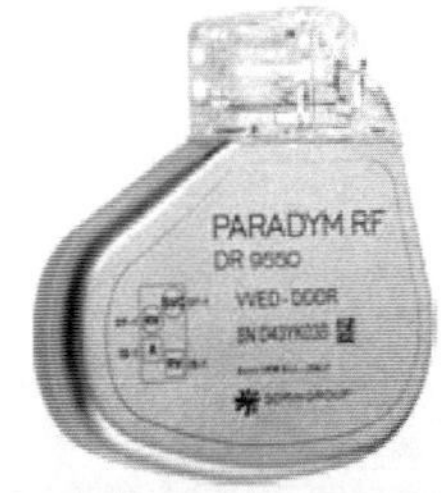

"A cyber-physical system (CPS) is a system where there is tight coordination of the system's computational and physical elements, though sensors and actuators"

3

Why Security Now?

- Cyber-physical systems are built to be reliable
- Security was treated as an afterthought
- Acceptable with very limited connectivity

And

- Ease of management is pushing wireless connectivity
  - Implantable medical devices can be accessed via home readers through an RF channel
  - In car systems are connected via wireless
- Indirectly connected to the Internet

4

Recent Attacks

- Stuxnet [1]
  - Infected controlling windows machines
  - Changed parameters of the PLC of the centrifuges of Iranian nuclear reactors
- Attacks against automotive controllers [2]
  - Internal controller-area network (CAN)
  - Exploiting one subsystem (e.g., bluetooth) allows access to critical subsystems (e.g., braking)

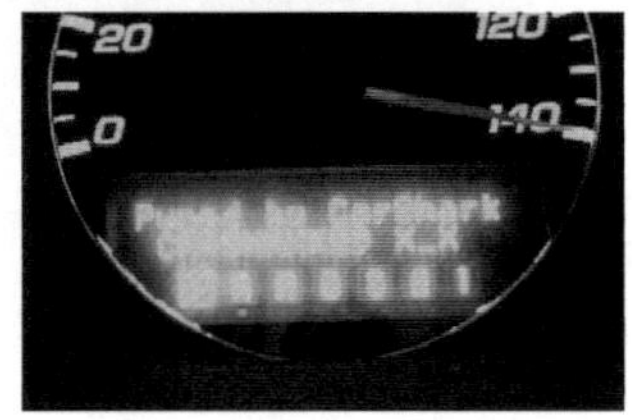

- Medical devices
  - Insulin pumps hack [3]
  - Implantable cardioverter defibrillator [4]

[1] W32.Stuxnet Dossier. Nicolas Falliere, Liam O Murchu and Eric Chien. Symantec 2011
[2] Comprehensive Experimental Analyses of Automotive Attack Surfaces. S. Checkoway et al. USENIX 2011
[3] Hacking Medical Devices for Fun and Insulin: Breaking the Human SCADA System. Jerome Radcliffe. Blackhat 2011
[4] Pacemakers and Implantable Cardiac Defibrillators: Software Radio Attacks and Zero-Power Defenses. S&P 2008

5

Remote Attestation

Definitions
- Two party protocol between trusted verifier and untrusted prover
- Remotely verify the internal state of the prover

Where
- Prover is the untrusted embedded device
- Verifier is the trusted reader/controller/base station
- Internal state is composed
  - Code
  - Registers
  - Data Memory
  - I/O

Two types of attestation:
- Secure Hardware supported (e.g., TPM)
- Software attestation
  - Does not support multi-hop communication

6

Remote attestation

- Malicious software will lie about the software state of the prover
- Need to have guarantees that the device is not lying

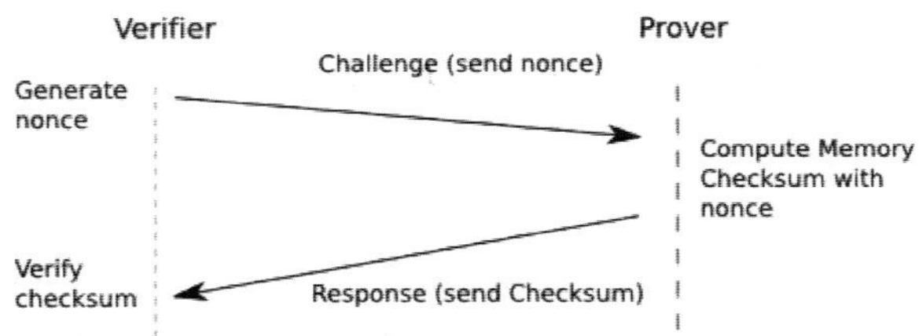

7

SMART: Secure and Minimal Architecture for a Root of Trust

Motivation:

- Existing solutions (TPM) are expensive for embedded devices
- What is a minimal set of architectural features to achieve remote attestation?

Desirable features:

- Minimal modifications to existing platforms
  - Fewest additional gates
- Security under a strong attacker model
- Portable to multiple platforms
  - Implemented on AVR and MSP430

8

Security Goals

Establish a dynamic root of trust on the prover

- "Guarantee untampered execution of a target piece of code, even in the presence of a corrupted platform"

In particular

- Prover authentication
  - Are we are talking with the right prover?
- External verification
  - Do we know the internal state of the prover?
- Guaranteed execution
  - Do we know the execution state?

No tamper resistance/no hardware attacks

9

Great. How do we do that?

10

Building Blocks

- Secure Key Storage
  - Required for multi-hop authentication
  - Provides prover authentication
- Trusted ROM code memory region
  - Read-only means integrity
  - Accesses and operates on key
- MCU access controls
  - Grants access to key to Trusted ROM

11

Key storage

- Provides remote prover authentication
- The key cannot be stored in normal memory
  - Malware would steal it
- Need to protect key access

Our approach

- Only a trusted code region can access the key

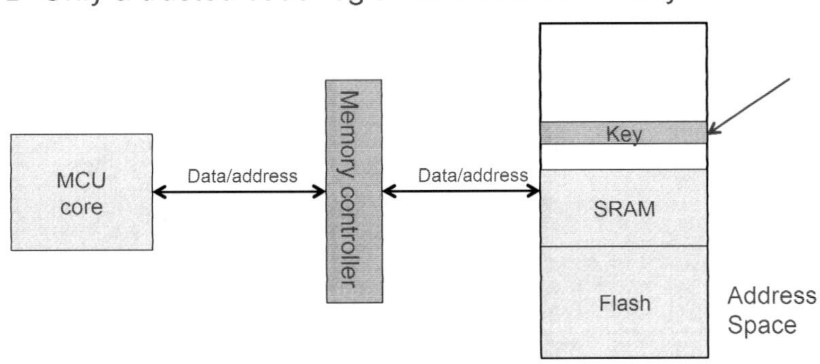

12

Trusted code region

- Low-end embedded devices do not have support for rings to restrict access to memory
- Adding those would require significant complexity

Our approach

- Restrict access to a read-only trusted code region
- Access control can be implemented easily

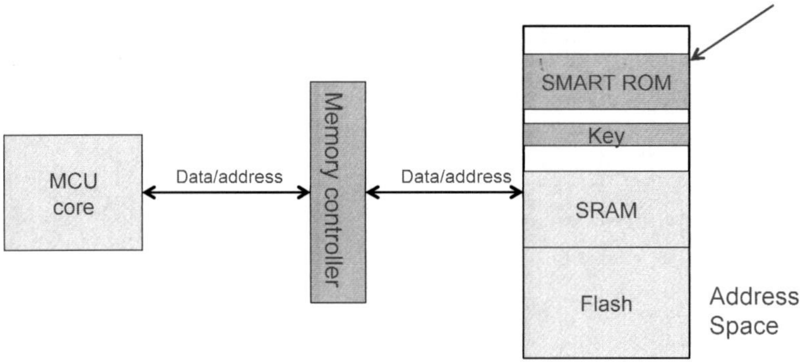

13

Memory access control

- Only ROM code must be able to access the key
- Control the program counter value

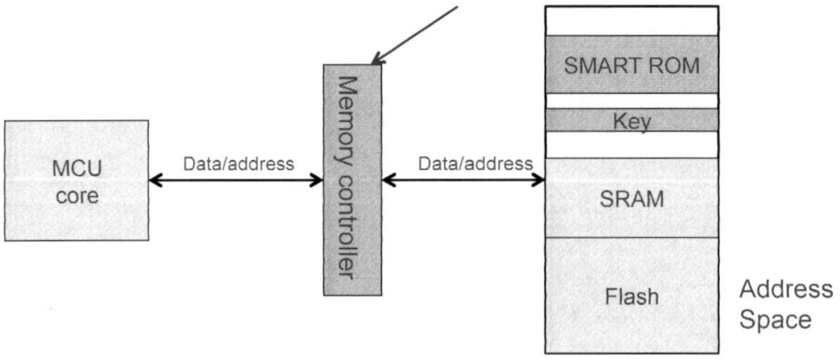

14

The complete protocol

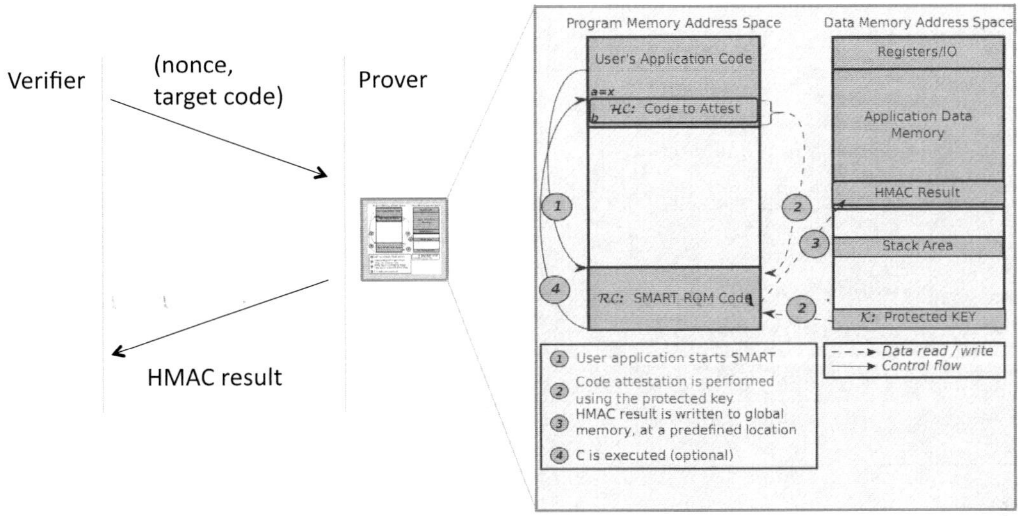

15

Problems to solve

Trusted ROM code and malware share the same resources

- Malware can set up the environment of the execution to compromise trusted code and extract the key
- Interrupts can asynchronously execute while a copy of the key is in main memory
- Malware can use code gadgets in ROM to access the key
  - Return oriented programming
- ROM code might leave traces of the key in memory after execution

16

Counter Measures

- Atomic ROM code execution
  - Enforce in hardware
  - Enter at first instruction
  - Exit at last instruction
- ROM code is instrumented to check for memory safety
  - Upon detecting error reboot and clean memory
- Interrupts are disabled immediately
  - Before key usage
- Erase key material before end of execution

17

Schematics

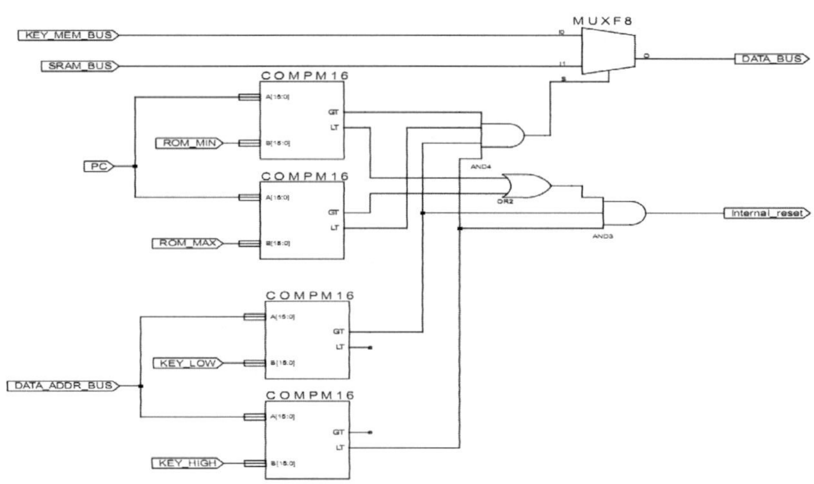

18

Cost of adding ROM and access control

- Implemented on two common MCU platforms
  - AVR
  - MSP430

Component		Original Size in kGE	Changed Size in kGE	Ratio
AVR MCU		103	113	10%
Core		11.3	11.6	2.6%
Sram	4 kB	26,6	26.6	0%
Flash	32 kB	65	65	0%
ROM	6 kB	-	10.3	-
MSP430 MCU		128	141	10%
Core		7.6	8.3	9.2%
Sram	10 kB	55.4	55.4	0%
Flash	32 kB	65	65	0%
ROM	4 kB	-	12.7	-

19

Considerations on SMART

- SMART provides an efficient hardware attestation solution for embedded devices
- Low additional gates required
- No run-time cost

20

Thanks for your time

Questions?

21

Low-end Embedded Devices

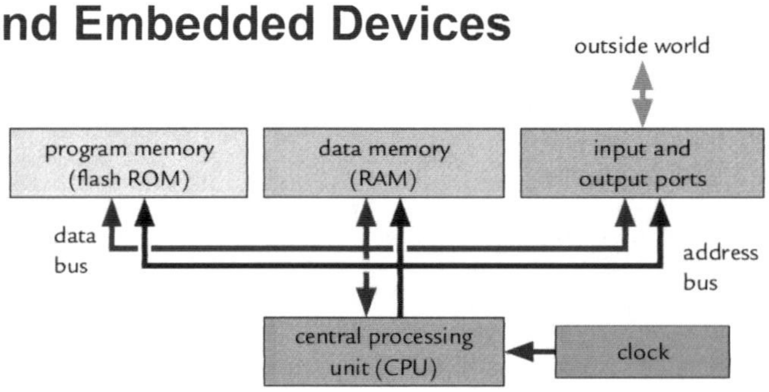

- Memory for program and data
- CPU
- Integrated clock
- In addition to
  - Communication interfaces (USB, CAN, Serial, Ethernet, etc.)
  - Analog to digital converters
  - ...

22

NDSS 2012

Kruiser: Semi-synchronized Non-blocking Concurrent Kernel Heap Buffer Overflow Monitoring

Donghai Tian[1,2], Qiang Zeng[2], Dinghao Wu[2], Peng Liu[2] and Changzhen Hu[1]

[1] Beijing Institute of Technology
[2] The Pennsylvania State University

1

Kernel Heap Buffer Overflow

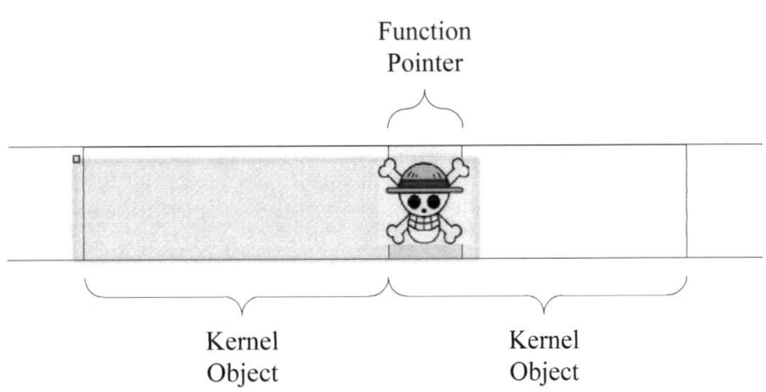

2

Motivation

- There are more and more kernel buffer overflow exploits.
- To our knowledge, there are no practical mechanisms that have been widely deployed detecting kernel heap buffer overflows.

3

Current Methods: Limitations 1 & 2

- Some approaches perform detection before each buffer write operation.
  [PLDI '04], [USENIX ATC '02], [NDSS '04]

  High overhead!

- Some approaches do not check heap buffer overflows until a buffer is de-allocated.
  [LISA '03], [BLACKHAT '11]

  Large detection delay!

4

Our Idea

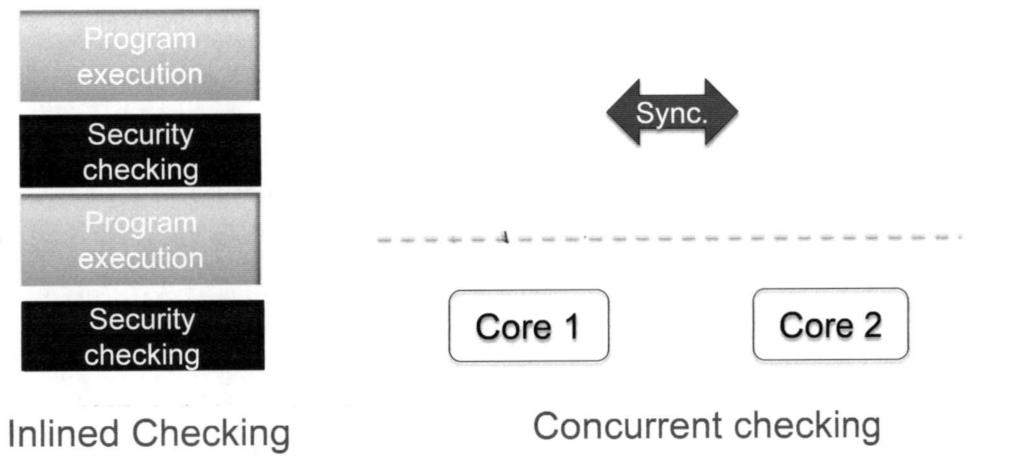

5

Basic Method

- Canary-based Concurrent Monitoring

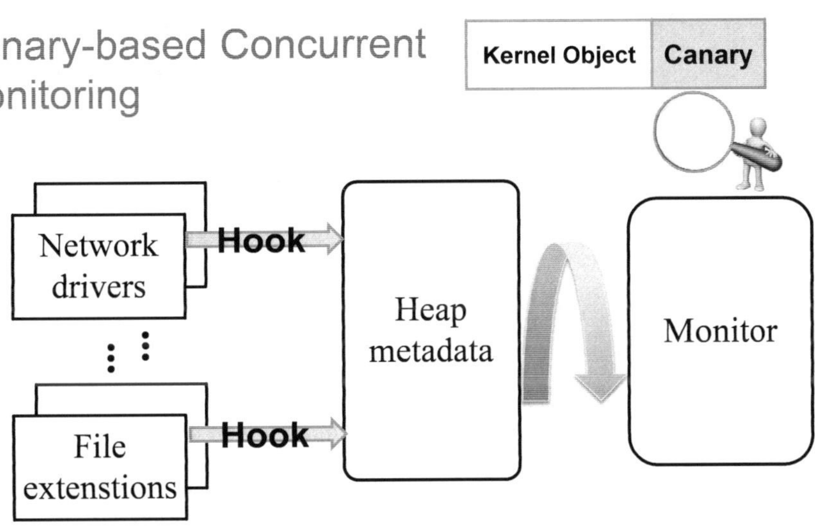

6

Challenges

- Self-protection.
  - Monitor and the metadata
- Synchronization.
  - Races between hooks and monitor
- Compatibility.
  - OS and hardware

7

Out-of-the-VM Architecture

(*Our previous CCS submission - **rejected***)

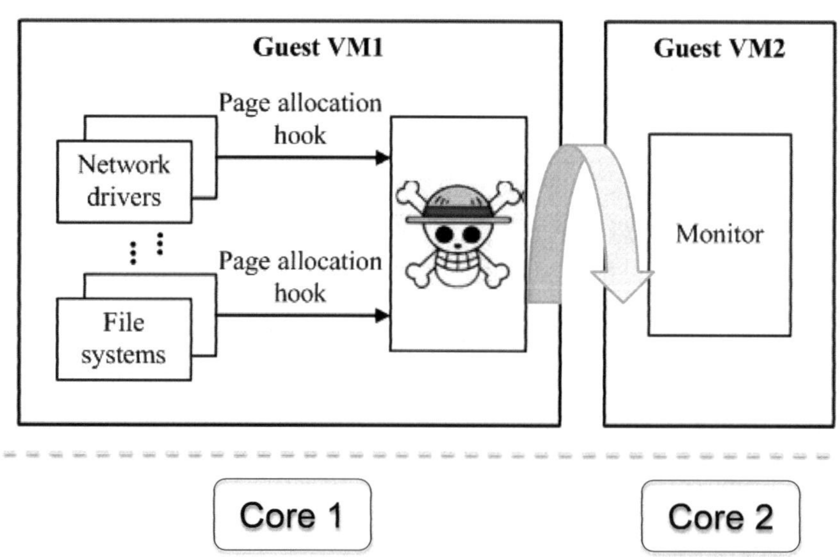

8

Hybrid VM monitoring Architecture

(NDSS submission - accepted)

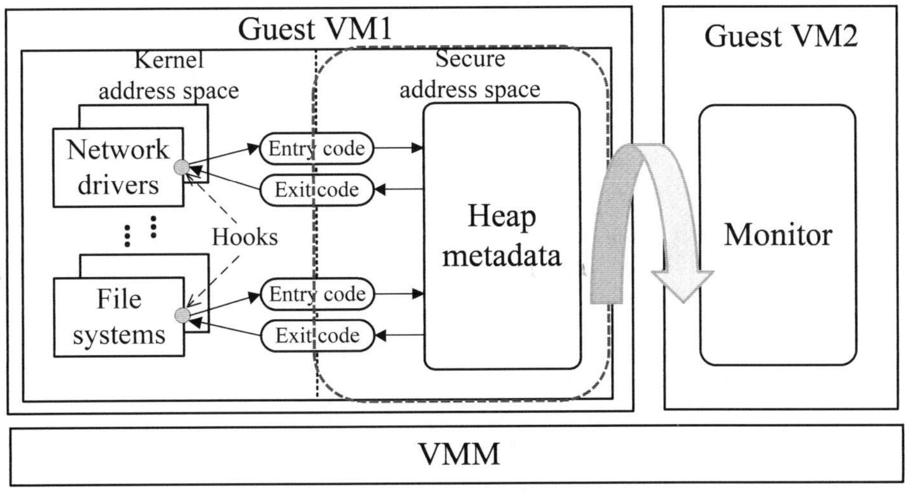

9

Now, Kernel Cruising

- How to gather canary location info?
- How to deal with the races between hooks and monitor?

10

Kernel Cruising

- Page Identity Array (PIA)
  - Heap buffer canary location information
  - Other information
- Race conditions
  - Concurrent updates by two hooks
  - Inconsistent reads by monitor
  - Time of check to time of use (TOCTTOU)

11

Semi-synchronized Non-blocking Cruising Algorithm

- Avoid Concurrent Entry Updates.
  - Put the PIA entry update operations into the critical section.

12

Resolve TOCTTOU

```
Hook:
if the page is moved to the heap page pool
        flag = true;
else if the page is removed from the heap
        flag = fal
```

true->false->true
A B A

```
Monitor:
if (the canary is te…ered) {
    if (flag == true) { // the page is still in heap
        report overflow!
    }
```

13

ABA Hazard Solution

```
if the page is moved to the heap page pool
        version++;
else if the page is removed from the heap
        version++;
...
if (the canary is tampered) {
        if (version == original version) {
            report overflow!
        }
}
```

14

Secure Canary Generation

- R1) The canaries are not predictable.
- R2) The canary generation and verification algorithms should be efficient.
- Generate unpredictable canaries using RC4 from a per-virtual-page random value.

15

Outline

- Idea
- Architecture
- Kernel Cruising
- **Evaluation**
- Related Work
- Summary

16

Effectiveness

- We exploited five heap buffer overflow vulnerabilities in Linux, including three synthetic bugs and two real world vulnerabilities .
- All the overflows are successfully detected by *Kruiser*.

17

Performance Overhead

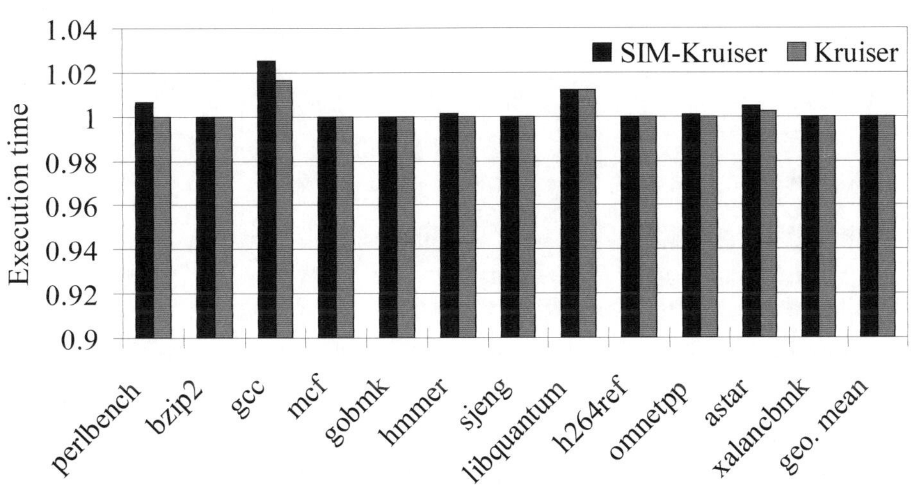

SPEC CPU2006 performance (normalized to the execution time of original Linux).

18

Scalability

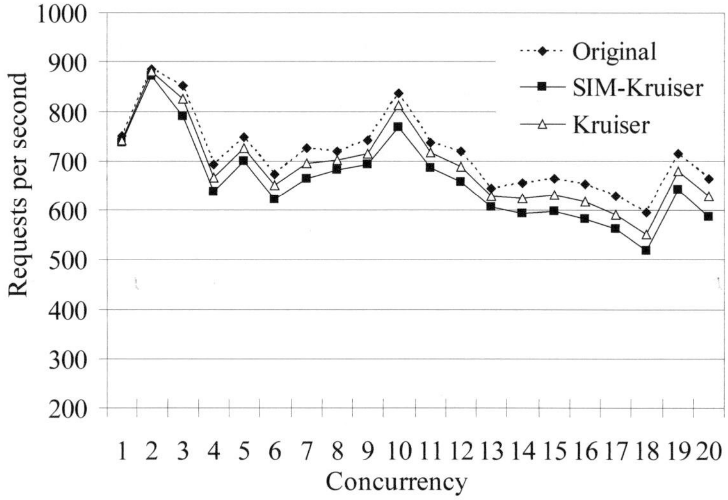

Throughput of the Apache web server for varying numbers of concurrent requests.

19

Detection Latency

Different cruising cycle for different applications in the SPEC CPU2006 benchmark

Benchmark	Maximum cruising number	Minimum cruising number	Average cruising number	Average cruising cycle(μs)
perlbench	107,824	105,145	106,378	39,259
bzip2	79,085	76,325	76,682	27,662
gcc	78,460	76,810	77,413	27,774
mcf	82,885	79,328	79,540	28,156
gobmk	80,761	80,345	80,519	28,606
hmmer	81,278	80,435	80,591	28,635
sjeng	81,437	80,259	80,535	28,610
libquantum	80,911	80,317	80,407	28,493
h264ref	80,756	80,337	80,480	28,572
omnetpp	82,109	80,796	81,088	28,836
astar	81,592	81,022	81,097	28,897
xalancbmk	99,436	82,747	88,454	30,190

10 of 12 applications have less than 29ms (for scanning the kernel heap).

20

Outline

- Idea
- Architecture
- Kernel Cruising
- Evaluation
- **Related work**
- Summary

21

Related Work

- Countermeasures Against Buffer Overflows
  - StackGuard [USENIX Security '98]
  - Heap Integrity Detection [LISA '03]
  - Cruiser [PLDI '11]
  - DieHard [PLDI '06] and DieHarder [CCS '10]
- VM-based Methods
  - SIM [CCS '09]
  - OSck [ASPLOS '11]

22

Summary

- *Kruiser* can achieve *concurrent monitoring* against kernel heap buffer overflows.
  - *Non-blocking*
  - *Semi-synchronized*
  - *NO false positive*
- The *hybrid VM monitoring* scheme provides high efficiency without sacrificing the security guarantees.

23

Thank you!

Questions?

24

Outline

- Background and Idea
- Architecture
- Kernel Cruising
- Evaluation
- Related Work
- Summary

25

Non-blocking Cruising Algorithm

```
Monitor(){
uint ver1, ver2;
for (int page = 0; page < ENTRY NUMBER; page++){
    ver1 = PIA[page].version;
    if (The page is non-heap page)
        continue; // Bypass non−heap page
    Read the metadata stored in PIA[page];
    ver2 = PIA[page].version;
    if (ver1 != ver2)
        continue; // Metadata was updated
    for (each canary within the page){
        if (the canary is tampered){
            DoubleCheckOnTamper(page, ver1);
        }
    }
}
```

Avoid Read Inconsistency!

Is the page still used by the heap?

27

WARNINGBIRD: Detecting Suspicious URLs in Twitter Stream *

Sangho Lee[†] and Jong Kim[‡]
[†]Department of Computer Science and Engineering
[‡]Division of IT Convergence Engineering
Pohang University of Science and Technology (POSTECH)
Pohang, Republic of Korea
{sangho2,jkim}@postech.ac.kr

Abstract

Twitter can suffer from malicious tweets containing suspicious URLs for spam, phishing, and malware distribution. Previous Twitter spam detection schemes have used account features such as the ratio of tweets containing URLs and the account creation date, or relation features in the Twitter graph. Malicious users, however, can easily fabricate account features. Moreover, extracting relation features from the Twitter graph is time and resource consuming. Previous suspicious URL detection schemes have classified URLs using several features including lexical features of URLs, URL redirection, HTML content, and dynamic behavior. However, evading techniques exist, such as time-based evasion and crawler evasion. In this paper, we propose WARNINGBIRD, *a suspicious URL detection system for Twitter. Instead of focusing on the landing pages of individual URLs in each tweet, we consider correlated redirect chains of URLs in a number of tweets. Because attackers have limited resources and thus have to reuse them, a portion of their redirect chains will be shared. We focus on these shared resources to detect suspicious URLs. We have collected a large number of tweets from the Twitter public timeline and trained a statistical classifier with features derived from correlated URLs and tweet context information. Our classifier has high accuracy and low false-positive and false-negative rates. We also present* WARNINGBIRD *as a real-time system for classifying suspicious URLs in the Twitter stream.*

*This research was supported by the MKE (The Ministry of Knowledge Economy), Korea, under the ITRC (Information Technology Research Center) support program supervised by the NIPA (National IT Industry Promotion Agency) (NIPA-2011-C1090-1131-0009) and World Class University program funded by the Ministry of Education, Science and Technology through the National Research Foundation of Korea(R31-10100).

1 Introduction

Twitter is a well-known social networking and information sharing service [15] that allows users to exchange messages of fewer than 140-character, also known as *tweets*, with their friends. When a user Alice updates (or sends) a tweet, this tweet will be distributed to all of her *followers*, who have registered Alice as one of their friends. Instead of distributing her tweets to all of her followers, Alice can send a tweet to a specific twitter user Bob by mentioning this user by including *@Bob* in the tweet. Unlike status updates, mentions can be sent to users who do not follow Alice. When Twitter users want to share URLs with friends via tweets, they usually use URL shortening services [1] to reduce the length of these URLs, because tweets can only contain a restricted number of characters. `bit.ly` and `tinyurl.com` are widely used services, and Twitter also provides its own shortening service `t.co`.

Owing to the popularity of Twitter, malicious users often try to find a way to attack it. Most common forms of Web attacks, including spam, scam, phishing, and malware distribution attacks, have appeared on Twitter. Because tweets are short in length, attackers use shortened malicious URLs that redirect Twitter users to external attack servers [6, 11, 19, 23].

To cope with malicious tweets, many Twitter spam detection schemes have been proposed. These schemes can be classified into account feature-based [2, 16, 23, 28] and relation feature-based [21, 31] schemes. Account feature-based schemes use the distinguishing features of spam accounts such as the ratio of tweets containing URLs, the account creation date, and the number of followers and friends. However, malicious users can easily fabricate these account features. The relation feature-based schemes rely on more robust features that malicious users cannot easily fabricate such as the distance and connectivity apparent in the Twitter graph. Extracting these relation features from the Twitter graph, however, requires a significant amount of time and resources, because the Twitter graph is tremendous in size.

A number of suspicious URL detection schemes [3, 17–19, 24, 30] have also been introduced. They use static or dynamic crawlers and may be executed in virtual machine honeypots, such as Capture-HPC [4], HoneyMonkey [29], and Wepawet [7], to investigate newly observed URLs. These schemes classify URLs according to several features including lexical features of URLs, DNS information, URL redirection, and the HTML content of the landing pages. Nonetheless, malicious servers can bypass investigation by selectively providing benign pages to crawlers. For instance, because static crawlers usually cannot handle JavaScript or Flash, malicious servers can use them to deliver malicious content only to normal browsers. Even if investigators use dynamic crawlers that have (almost) all the functionalities of real browsers, malicious servers may be able to distinguish them through IP address, user interaction, browser fingerprinting [8], or honeyclient detection techniques [14]. A recent technical report from Google has also discussed techniques for evading current Web malware detection systems [20]. Malicious servers can also employ temporal behaviors—providing different content at different times—to evade investigation [24].

In this paper, we propose WARNINGBIRD, a suspicious URL detection system for Twitter. Instead of investigating the landing pages of individual URLs in each tweet, which may not be successfully fetched, we considered correlated redirect chains of URLs included in a number of tweets. Because attackers' resources are limited and need to be reused, a portion of their redirect chains must be shared. We found a number of meaningful features of suspicious URLs derived from the correlated URL redirect chains and related tweet context information. We collected a large number of tweets from the Twitter public timeline and trained a statistical classifier with their features. The trained classifier has high accuracy and low false-positive and false-negative rates.

The contributions of this paper can be summarized as follows:

- We present a new suspicious URL detection system for Twitter that is based on correlations of URL redirect chains, which are difficult to fabricate. The system can classify suspicious URLs found in the Twitter stream in real time.
- We introduce new features of suspicious URLs: some of them are newly discovered and others are variations of previously discovered features.
- We present some investigation results regarding suspicious URLs that have been widely distributed through Twitter over the past several months and continue to remain active.

The remainder of this paper is organized as follows. In Section 2, we discuss case studies on suspicious URLs in Twitter. In Section 3, we introduce our system, WARNINGBIRD. In Section 4, we present the evaluation results. In Section 5, we discuss the limitations of the proposed system. In Section 6, we discuss related work. Finally, we conclude this paper in Section 7.

2 Case Study

2.1 blackraybansunglasses.com

We consider `blackraybansunglasses.com`, which is a suspicious site associated with spam tweets. We first encountered this site in April 2011 and it remains active. We use a one percent sample of tweets collected on July 11, 2011, to conduct an in-depth analysis of the site (see Figure 1). `blackraybansunglasses.com` has a page, `redirect.php`, that conditionally redirects users to random spam pages. It uses a number of different Twitter accounts and shortened URLs to distribute its URL to other Twitter users. According to our dataset, it uses $6,585$ different Twitter accounts and shortened URLs, and occupies about 2.83% of all the $232,333$ tweets with URLs that we sampled. When a user clicks on one of the shortened URLs, such as `bit.ly/raCz5i` distributed by `zarzuelavbafpv0`, he or she will be redirected to a private redirection site, such as `beginnersatlanta.tk`, which seems to be managed by the operator of `blackraybansunglasses.com`. The user will then be repeatedly redirected to `bestfreevideoonline.info` and `blackraybansunglasses.com`. The redirection site `blackraybansunglasses.com` evaluates whether its visitors are normal browsers or crawlers using several methods, including cookie or user-agent checking. When it is sure that a current visitor is a normal browser, it redirects the visitor to `forexstrategysite.com`, which then finally redirects him or her to random spam pages. When `blackraybansunglasses.com` determines that a current visitor is not a normal browser, it simply redirects the visitor to `google.com` to avoid investigation. Therefore, crawlers may not be able to see `forexstrategysite.com` or the further random spam pages.

Another interesting point about `blackraybansunglasses.com` is that it does not use Twitter APIs to distribute malicious tweets. Instead, it abuses the Twitter Web interface. Previous Twitter spam detection schemes usually assumed that many spammers would use Twitter APIs to distribute their spam tweets. Smart Twitter spammers, however, no longer rely on Twitter APIs, because they know that using APIs will

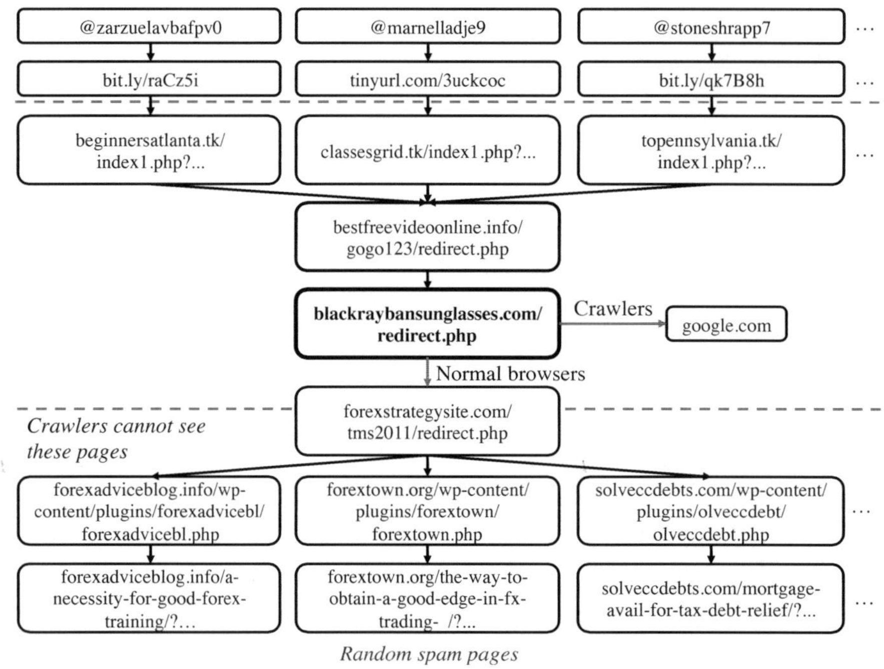

Figure 1. Redirect chains of blackraybansunglasses.com on July 11, 2011

distinguish their tweets from normal tweets. For instance, `tweetattacks.com` [26] sells a Twitter spam program that uses the Web interface instead of APIs to make spam receivers believe that the received tweets are not spam and to circumvent API limits.

2.2 24newspress.net

Let us also discuss `24newspress.net`, which is a suspicious site distributed via tweets. We first found this site at the end of June 2011 and it remains active. We use one percent of the tweet samples collected on July 23, 2011, to conduct an in-depth analysis of the page (see Figure 2). Unlike `blackraybansunglasses.com` `24newspress.net` does not perform conditional redirection to avoid investigation. Instead, it uses a number of IP addresses and domain names for cloaking like IP fast flux and domain flux methods [12, 22]. It has five other domain names: `24dailyreports.net`, `7reports.net`, `job365report.net`, `jobs-post.net`, and `week-job.net`. It also uses a number of different shortened URLs and different Twitter accounts to distribute tweets to Twitter users. In our dataset, we found 6,205 tweets related to `24newspress.net`, which represent about 2.41% of all the 257,329 tweets with URLs sampled. In addition, it abuses a mobile Twitter Web interface to distribute its spam tweets.

2.3 Frequent URL Redirect Chains

We performed a simple investigation on three days' worth of tweet samples culled from July 23 to 25, 2011. We extracted frequent URL redirect chains from the sample data and ranked them according to their frequency after removing whitelisted domain names. Many suspicious sites, such as `jbfollowme.com`, which attempts to attract Justin Bieber's fans, proved to be highly ranked (see Table 1).

2.4 Observations

From the previous examples, we can identify meaningful characteristics of suspicious URLs. They use a number of different Twitter accounts and shortened URLs, or a number of domain names and IP addresses to cloak the same suspicious URLs. They also use long redirect chains to avoid investigation. Moreover, they appear more frequently in the Twitter public timeline than benign URLs. These characteristics are the basis for the feature models we employ to classify suspicious URLs.

3 Proposed System

3.1 Motivation and Basic Idea

Our goal is to develop a suspicious URL detection system for Twitter that is robust enough to protect against con-

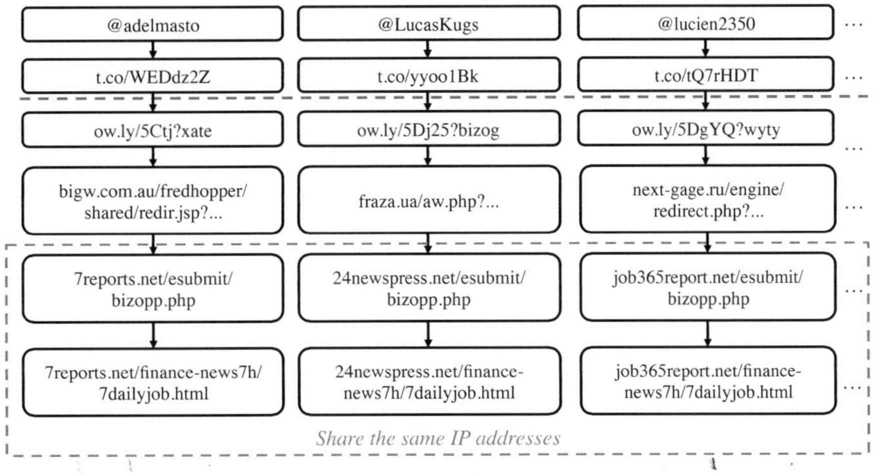

Figure 2. Redirect chains of 24newspress.net on July 23, 2011

Table 1. Domain names of frequent URL redirect chains from July 23 to 25, 2011

Rank	July 23	July 24	July 25
1	`24newpress.net`	`24newspress.net`	`24newpress.net`
2	`blackraybansunglasses.com`	`blackraybansunglasses.com`	`blackraybansunglasses.com`
3	`software-spot.com`	`cheapdomainname.info`	`bigfollow.net`
4	`ustream.tv`	`ustream.tv`	`twitmais.com`
5	`10bit.info`	`twitmais.com`	`jbfollowme.com`
6	`blackreferrer.com`	`bigfollow.net`	`addseguidores.com.br`
7	`tweetburner.com`	`jbfollowme.com`	`elitebrotherhood.net`
8	`livenation.com`	`10bit.info`	`livenation.com`
9	`twitmais.com`	`addseguidores.com.br`	`naturesoundcds.com`
10	`bigfollow.net`	`wayjump.com`	`all-about-legal.net`

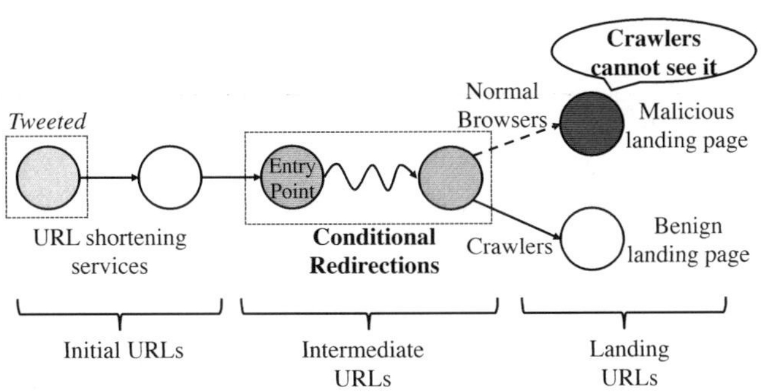

Figure 3. Conditional redirection

ditional redirections. Let us consider a simple example of conditional redirections (see Figure 3). In this example, an attacker creates a long URL redirect chain by using public URL shortening services, such as `bit.ly` and `t.co`, and his or her own private redirection servers to redirect visitors to a malicious landing page. The attacker then uploads a tweet including the initial URL of the redirect chain to Twitter. Later, when a user or a crawler visits the initial URL, he or she will be redirected to an *entry point* of intermediate URLs that are associated with private redirection servers. Some of these redirection servers will check whether the current visitor is a normal browser or a crawler. If the current visitor seems to be a normal browser, they will redirect the visitor to a malicious landing page. If not, they will redirect the visitor to a benign landing page. Therefore, the attacker can selectively attack normal users while deceiving investigators.

The above example shows us that, as investigators, we cannot fetch malicious landing URLs, because attackers do not reveal them to us. We also cannot rely on the initial URLs, because attackers can generate a large number of different initial URLs by abusing URL shortening services. Fortunately, the case study on `blackraybansunglasses.com` shows that attackers *reuse some of their redirection servers* when creating a number of redirect chains, because they do not have infinite redirection servers (see Section 2). Therefore, if we analyze a number of *correlated redirect chains* instead of an individual redirect chain, we can find an entry point of

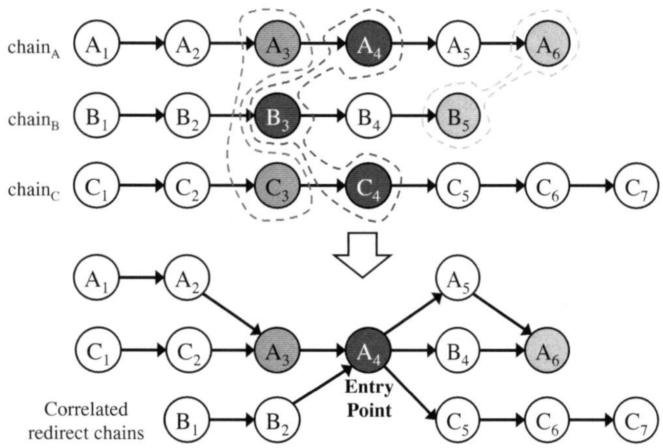

Figure 4. Redirect chains and their correlation

the intermediate URLs in the correlated redirect chains. Let us consider the three redirect chains shown in the top half of Figure 4. These three redirect chains share some URLs: A_3=C_3, A_4=B_3=C_4, and A_6=B_5. By combining the three redirect chains using these shared URLs, we can generate the correlated redirect chains (the bottom half of Figure 4) that share the same entry point URL, A_4 (because A_4 is the most frequent URL in the chains). The correlated redirect chains show that the entry point has three different initial URLs and two different landing URLs, and participates in redirect chains that are six to seven URLs long. These are the characteristics of the suspicious URLs that we considered in Section 2. Therefore, this correlation analysis can help to detect suspicious URLs even when they perform conditional redirections, because the suspiciousness of the two landing URLs is not important to the correlation analysis.

3.2 System Details

WARNINGBIRD is composed of four major components: data collection, feature extraction, training, and classification (see Figure 5).

Data collection: The data collection component has two subcomponents: the collection of tweets with URLs and crawling for URL redirections. To collect tweets with URLs and their context information from the Twitter public timeline, this component uses Twitter Streaming APIs [27]. Whenever this component receives a tweet with a URL from Twitter, it executes a crawling thread that follows all redirections of the URL and looks up the corresponding IP addresses. The crawling thread appends these retrieved URL and IP chains to the tweet information and pushes this extended tweet information into a tweet queue. As we have seen, our crawler cannot reach malicious landing URLs when they use conditional redirections to evade crawlers. However, because our detection system does not rely on the features of landing URLs, it works independently of such crawler evasions.

Feature extraction: The feature extraction component has three subcomponents: grouping identical domains, finding entry point URLs, and extracting feature vectors. This component monitors the tweet queue to check whether a sufficient number of tweets have been collected. Specifically, our system uses a tweet window instead of individual tweets. When more than w tweets are collected (w is $10,000$ in the current implementation), it pops w tweets from the tweet queue. First, for all URLs in the w tweets, this component checks whether they share the same IP addresses. If some URLs share at least one IP address, it replaces their domain names with a list of those with which they are grouped. For instance, when `http://123.com/hello.html` and `http://xyz.com/hi.html` share the same IP address, this component replaces these URLs with `http://['123.com','xyz.com']/hello.html` and `http://['123.com','xyz.com']/hi.html`, respectively. This grouping process allows the detection of suspicious URLs that use several domain names to bypass blacklisting.

Next, the component tries to find the entry point URL for each of the w tweets. First, it measures the frequency with which each URL appears in the w tweets. It then discovers the most frequent URL in each URL redirect chain in the w tweets. The URLs thus discovered become the entry points for their redirect chains. If two or more URLs share the highest frequency in a URL chain, this component selects the URL nearest to the beginning of the chain as the entry point URL.

Finally, for each entry point URL, this component finds URL redirect chains that contain the entry point URL, and extracts various features from these URL redirect chains and the related tweet information (details of these features will be given in Subsection 3.3). These feature values are then turned into real-valued feature vectors.

When we group domain names or find entry point URLs, we ignore whitelisted domains to reduce false-positive rates. Whitelisted domains are not grouped with other domains and are not selected as entry point URLs. Our whitelisted domain names include the Alexa Top 1000 sites, some famous URL shortening sites, and some domains that we have manually verified.

Training: The training component has two subcomponents: retrieval of account statuses and the training classifier. Because we use an offline supervised learning algorithm, the feature vectors for training are relatively old values than feature vectors for classification. To label the training vectors,

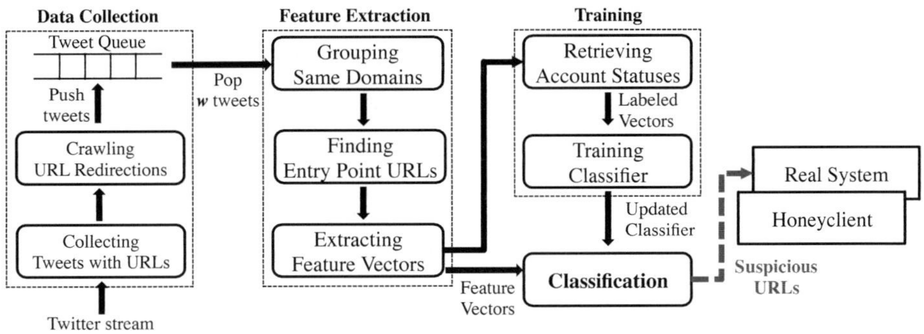

Figure 5. System overview

we use the Twitter account status; URLs from suspended accounts are considered malicious and URLs from active accounts are considered benign. We periodically update our classifier by using labeled training vectors.

Classification: The classification component executes our classifier using input feature vectors to classify suspicious URLs. When the classifier returns a number of malicious feature vectors, this component flags the corresponding URLs and their tweet information as suspicious. These URLs, detected as suspicious, will be delivered to security experts or more sophisticated dynamic analysis environments for in-depth investigation.

3.3 Features

We introduce 12 features for classifying suspicious URLs on Twitter. These features can be classified as features derived from correlated URL redirect chains and features derived from the related tweet context information. We also describe how we normalize these feature values to real values between zero and one.

3.3.1 Features Derived from Correlated URL Redirect Chains

URL redirect chain length: Attackers usually use long URL redirect chains to make investigations more difficult and avoid the dismantling of their servers. Therefore, when an entry point URL is malicious, its chain length may be longer than those of benign URLs. To normalize this feature, we choose an upper-bound value of 20, because most of the redirect chains we have seen over the four-month period have had fewer than 20 URLs in their chains. If the length of a redirect chain is l, this feature can be normalized as $\min(l, 20)/20$.

Frequency of entry point URL: The number of occurrences of the current entry point URL within a tweet window is important. Frequently appearing URLs that are not whitelisted are usually suspicious, as discussed in Section 2. When the window size is w and the number of occurrences is n, this feature can be normalized as n/w.

Position of entry point URL: Suspicious entry point URLs are not usually located at the end of a redirect chain, because they have to conditionally redirect visitors to different landing URLs. If the position of an entry point of a redirect chain of length l is p, this can be normalized as p/l.

Number of different initial URLs: The initial URL is the beginning URL that redirects visitors to the current entry point URL. Attackers usually use a large number of different initial URLs to make their malicious tweets, which redirect visitors to the same malicious URL, look different. If the number of different initial URLs redirecting visitors to an entry point URL that appears n times is i, this feature can be normalized as i/n.

Number of different landing URLs: If the current entry point URL redirects visitors to more than one landing URL, we can assume that the current entry point URL performs conditional redirection behaviors and may be suspicious. If an entry point URL that appears n times redirects visitors to λ different landing URLs, this feature can be normalized as λ/n.

3.3.2 Features Derived from Tweet Context Information

The features derived from the related tweet context information are variations of previously discovered features. Our variations focused on the similarity of tweets that share the same entry point URLs.

Number of different sources: Sources are applications that upload the current entry point URL to Twitter. Attackers usually use the same source application, because maintaining a number of different applications is difficult. Benign users, however, usually use various Twitter applications, such as TweetDeck and Echofon. Therefore, the number of different sources may be small when the current entry point URL is suspicious. If the number of different sources of an entry point URL that occurs n times is s, this feature can be normalized as s/n.

Number of different Twitter accounts: The number of different Twitter accounts that upload the current entry point URL can be used to detect injudicious attackers who use a small number of Twitter accounts to distribute their malicious URLs. If the number of Twitter accounts uploading an entry point URL that occurs n times is α, this feature can be normalized as α/n.

Standard deviation of account creation date: Attackers usually create a large number of Twitter accounts within a relatively short time period. Therefore, if the creation dates of the accounts that upload the same entry point URL are similar, it might indicate that the current entry point URL is suspicious. We use the standard deviation of account creation date as a similarity measure. To normalize the standard deviation, we assume that the time difference between any account creation dates is less than or equal to one year. Therefore, this feature can be normalized as

$$\min\left(\frac{\text{std(a set of account creation date)}}{(1\text{ year})\sqrt{n}}, 1\right).$$

Standard deviation of the number of followers and number of friends: The numbers of followers and friends of attackers' accounts are usually similar, because attackers use certain programs to increase their numbers of followers and friends. We again use standard deviations to check for similarities in the numbers of followers and friends. To normalize the standard deviations, we assume that the number of followers and friends is usually less than or equal to $2,000$, which is the restricted number of accounts Twitter allows one can to follow. Therefore, these features can be normalized as

$$\min\left(\frac{\text{std(\#followers or \#friends)}}{2000\sqrt{n}}, 1\right).$$

Standard deviation of the follower-friend ratio: We define the follower-friend ratio as below:

$$\frac{\text{min(\#followers, \#friends)}}{\text{max(\#followers, \#friends)}}.$$

Like the numbers of followers and friends, the follower-friend ratios of attackers' accounts are similar. We use a normalized standard deviation to check the similarity as

$$\min\left(\frac{\text{std(a set of follower-friend ratios)}}{\sqrt{n}}, 1\right).$$

Because attackers' accounts usually have more friends than followers, the follower-friend ratios of malicious accounts are usually different from the follower-friend ratios of benign accounts. Attackers, however, can fabricate this ratio, because they can use Sybil followers or buy followers. Therefore, instead of using an individual follower-friend ratio, we use the standard deviation of follower-friend ratios of accounts that post the same URLs and assume that fabricated ratios will be similar.

Tweet text similarity: The texts of tweets containing the same URL are usually similar (e.g., retweets). Therefore, if the texts are different, we can assume that those tweets are related to suspicious behaviors, because attackers usually want to change the appearance of malicious tweets that include the same malicious URL. We measure the similarity between tweet texts as

$$\sum_{t,u \in \text{a set of pairs in tweet texts}} \frac{J(t,u)}{|\text{a set of pairs in tweet texts}|},$$

where $J(t,u)$ is the Jaccard index [13], which is a famous measure that determines the similarity between two sets t and u, and is defined as below:

$$J(t,u) = \frac{|t \cap u|}{|t \cup u|}.$$

We remove mentions, hashtags, retweets, and URLs from the texts when we measure their similarity, so that we only consider the text features.

4 Evaluation

4.1 System Setup and Data Collection

Our system uses two Intel Quad Core Xeon E5530 2.40GHz CPUs and 24 GiB of main memory. To collect tweets, we use Twitter Streaming APIs [27]. Our accounts have the Spritzer access role; thus, we can collect about one percent of the tweets from the Twitter public timeline as samples. From April 8 to August 8, 2011 (122 days), we collected 27,895,714 tweet samples with URLs.

4.2 Feature Selection

To evaluate and compare the features of our scheme, we use the F-score [5]. The F-score of a feature represents the degree of discrimination of the feature. Features with large F-scores can split benign and malicious samples better than features with small F-scores. The F-score shows that the redirect chain length is the most important feature, followed by the number of different sources and the standard deviation of the account creation date (see Table 2). We also verify that the number of different Twitter accounts that upload an entry point URL is a less important feature.

Table 2. F-score of our features

Feature	F-score
URL redirect chain length	0.0963
Number of different sources	0.0798
Standard deviation of account creation date	0.0680
Frequency of entry point URL	0.0374
Position of entry point URL	0.0353
Standard deviation of friends-followers ratio	0.0321
Number of different landing URLs	0.0150
Number of different initial URLs	0.0117
Standard deviation of the number of followers	0.0085
Tweet text similarity	0.0060
Standard deviation of the number of friends	0.0050
Number of different Twitter accounts	0.0008

Table 3. Training and test datasets

Dataset	Period	Benign	Malicious	Total
Training	5/10–7/8	183, 113	41, 721	224, 834
$\text{Test}_{\text{past}}$	4/8–5/9	71, 220	6, 730	77, 950
$\text{Test}_{\text{future}}$	7/9–8/8	91, 888	4, 421	96, 309

This result implies that attackers use a large number of different Twitter accounts to distribute their malicious URLs. The similarity of tweet texts is also less important, because many attackers currently do not use different tweet texts to cloak their malicious tweets. In addition, the standard deviations of the number of followers and number of friends are less important, because benign users' numbers of followers and friends are also similar. Interestingly, the standard deviation of the number of followers has a higher F-score value than that of the number of friends, because fabricating the number of followers is more difficult than fabricating the number of friends.

4.3 Training and Testing Classifiers

We use 60 days of tweet samples from May 10–July 8 for training the classification models and 62 days of tweet samples from April 8–May 9 and July 9–August 8 to test the classifier with older and newer datasets, respectively. For training and testing, we need to label the datasets. Unfortunately, we cannot find suitable blacklists for labeling our datasets, because many URLs in our datasets, such as `blackraybansunglasses.com`, are still not listed on public URL blacklists such as the Google Safe Browsing API [10]. Therefore, instead of URL blacklists, we use Twitter account status information to label our datasets. Namely, if some URLs are from suspended accounts, we treat the URLs as malicious. If not, we treat the URLs as benign. Recently, Thomas *et al.* [25] figured out that most suspended accounts are spam accounts. Therefore, our treatment of URLs is valid. From the training dataset, we found 4, 686, 226 accounts that were active and 263, 289 accounts that were suspended as of August 11, 2011. We also found 224, 834 entry point URLs that appear *more than once* in some windows of 10, 000 sample tweets. Among them, 183, 113 entry point URLs are from active accounts and 41, 721 entry point URLs are from suspended accounts. Therefore, we designated the 183, 113 entry point URLs from active accounts as benign samples and the remaining 41, 721 entry point URLs as malicious samples. We also use the account status information to label the test datasets; the results are shown in Table 3.

Table 5. Comparing classifier accuracy while varying training weights of benign samples within a 10-fold cross validation (cost 1.6)

		%		
Weight	AUC	Accuracy	FP	FN
1.0	0.8312	87.66	1.67	10.67
1.2	0.8310	87.51	1.31	11.18
1.4	**0.8310**	**87.09**	**1.03**	**11.88**
1.6	0.8309	86.39	0.83	12.78
1.8	0.8310	86.15	0.71	13.14
2.0	0.8308	85.99	0.61	13.39

We used the LIBLINEAR library [9] to implement our classifier. We compared seven classification algorithms with our training dataset and selected an L2-regularized logistic regression algorithm with a primal function, because it shows the best accuracy values with our dataset (see Table 4). We also tested a number of learning cost values and chose a cost value of 1.6. Because our dataset is unbalanced—the number of benign samples is 4.4 times larger than that of malicious samples—we must choose a good weight value to give a penalty to benign samples. We compared six weight values and selected a weight value of 1.4 for benign samples, because this value produces good accuracy values and relatively low false-positive and false-negative rates (see Table 5). All the training and 10-fold cross validation can be done in less than three seconds in our evaluation environment. Therefore, the training time is negligible.

We use two test datasets that represent past and future values, to evaluate the accuracy of our classifier (see Table 3). Whether the test datasets regard the past or future ones, our classifier achieves high accuracy, and low false-positive and false-negative rates (see Table 6). Therefore, our features do not tightly depend on specific time periods and, hence, can be used generally.

Table 4. Comparing classifiers within a 10-fold cross validation (learning cost 1.0 and weight 1.0). Logistic regression (LR), support vector classification (SVC), area under the ROC curve (AUC), false positive (FP), false negative (FN), and Lagrange primal and dual maximal violation functions that determine termination of training.

Classifier	AUC	% Accuracy	% FP	% FN
L2-regularized LR (primal)	**0.8312**	**87.67**	**1.64**	**10.69**
L2-regularized L2-loss SVC (dual)	0.8267	86.93	1.40	11.67
L2-regularized L2-loss SVC (primal)	0.8268	86.95	1.38	11.67
L2-regularized L1-loss SVC (dual)	0.8279	87.50	1.38	11.67
L1-regularized L2-loss SVC (primal)	0.8269	86.74	1.40	11.86
L1-regularized LR (primal)	0.8312	87.64	1.68	10.67
L2-regularized LR (dual)	0.8310	87.63	1.69	10.67

Table 6. Classification accuracy of test datasets

Dataset	AUC	% Accuracy	% FP	% FN
$\text{Test}_{\text{past}}$	0.7113	91.10	1.32	7.57
$\text{Test}_{\text{future}}$	0.7889	93.11	3.67	3.21

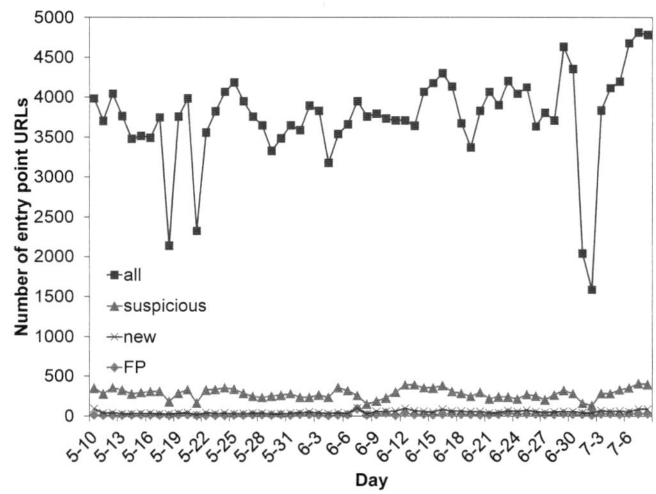

Figure 6. Daily analysis on training datasets (60 days: May 10–July 8)

4.4 Data Analysis

We performed a daily analysis on the training dataset. On average, 3756.38 entry point URLs appear more than once in each tweet window during a given day (with a window size of 10,000). Among them, on average, 282.93 suspicious URLs are detected, where 19.53 URLs are false positives and 30.15 URLs are newly discovered (see Figure 6). This relatively small number of new suspicious URLs implies that many suspicious URLs repeatedly detected by WARNINGBIRD are not detected or blocked by other existing detection systems. To verify the reoccurrence of suspicious URLs, we grabbed May 10's entry point URLs and checked how many times these URLs had appeared in the Twitter public timeline during the next two months (see Figure 7). On average, 17% of suspicious URLs and 5.1% of benign URLs of May 10 were observed during the two months; thus, suspicious URLs are more repeated than benign URLs. Interestingly, 38.9% of the suspicious URLs had appeared again on July 4, 55 days later. Therefore, existing detection schemes cannot detect or block a portion of suspicious URLs that can be detected by WARNINGBIRD.

We also determine whether the domain groupings allow us to detect a larger number of suspicious URLs. We compare grouped and ungrouped URLs by using 16 days of tweet samples from between July 23 and August 8 (except July 31 owing to a local power blackout). On average, we find 334.94 unique suspicious entry point URLs when we group URLs and 79.88 suspicious URLs when we do not group URLs (see Figure 8). Therefore, the domain groupings give us about 4.19 times better detection rates.

4.5 Running Time

We evaluated the running time of our system. First, we compared the running time of each component of our system—domain grouping; feature extraction, including the detection of entry points; and classification—in a single window of collected tweets that varies in size. Even if the

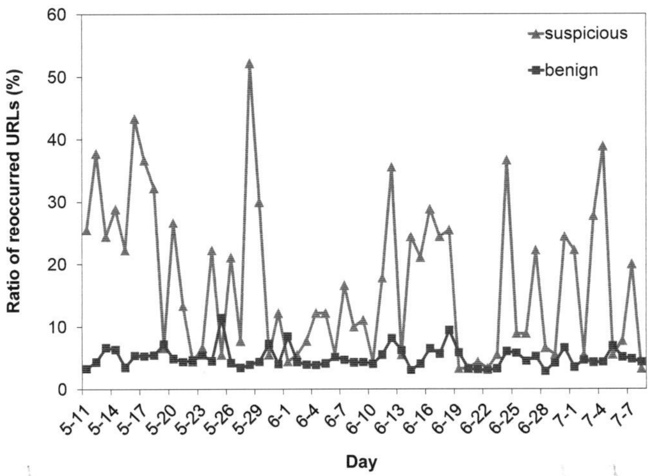

Figure 7. Reoccurrence of May 10's entry point URLs (59 days: May 11–July 8)

Table 7. Required time to classify a single URL when a window size is 100,000 and using 100 concurrent connections for crawling

Component	Avg. running time (ms)
Redirect chain crawling	24.202
Domain grouping	2.003
Feature extraction	1.618
Classification	0.484
Total	**28.307**

window size becomes $100,000$, which contains of about 10% of all tweets with URLs per hour, the running time is only 6.9 minutes (see Figure 9). Next, we estimate the time required to classify a single URL. Our system currently uses 100 crawling threads to *concurrently* visit URL redirect chains; on average, each thread requires 2.42 s to visit a single URL redirect chain. If the window size is $100,000$, we need 28.307 ms to process a single URL (see Table 7); thus, our system can process about $127,000$ URLs per hour. Therefore, our system can handle 10% of the tweet samples, the level provided by the Gardenhose access role, in real time. By increasing the number of crawling threads, we can process more than 10% of the tweet samples. For instance, if we use $1,000$ crawling threads, we can process about $576,000$ URLs per hour. Even if we do this, the current implementation cannot process all the tweets, because we would have to process a single URL in less than 3.6 ms to handle $1,000,000$ URLs per hour.

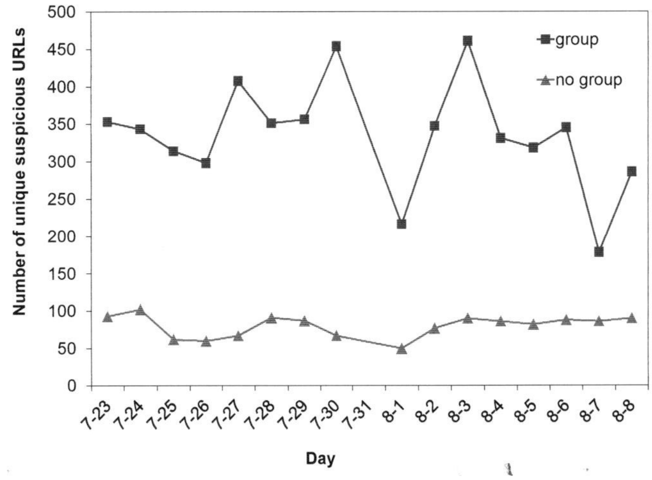

Figure 8. Comparing domain grouping results (16 days: July 23–August 8 excluding July 31)

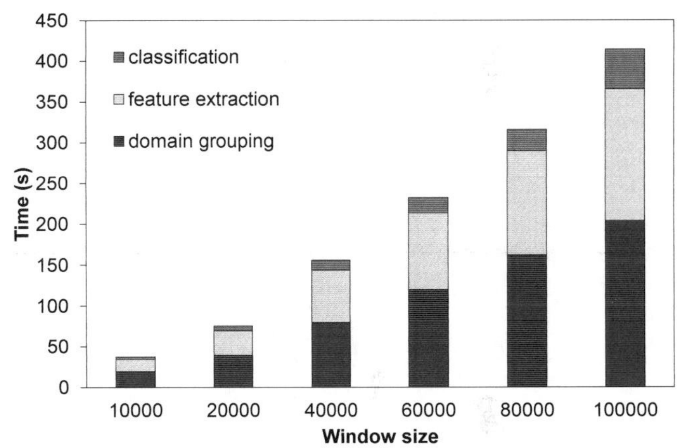

Figure 9. Running time for each component to process a tweet window

4.6 Real-time Detection and Sliding Window

The real-time version of WARNINGBIRD uses a sliding window technique for achieving good latency and detection coverage. A small window gives immediate results; however, it cannot catch suspicious URLs that repeat after long-time intervals. A large window has good detection coverage; however, its latency is bad. A sliding window is a well-known technique for taking advantage of both small and large windows. Let w denote the window size and s denote the sliding size ($s \leq w$). Whenever a sliding window system receives s new items, it processes the previous $w - s$ items and the s new items at the same time. Therefore, the latency of this method depends on s and its detection coverage depends on w. Currently, we have set w at

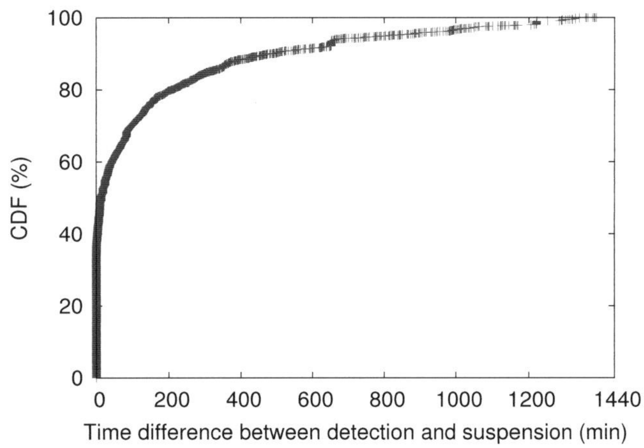

Figure 10. Time difference between WarningBird's detection of suspicious accounts and Twitter's suspension within a day

$10,000$ and s at $2,000$. Every 12 minutes, the real-time version of WARNINGBIRD returns suspicious URLs that have appeared in the previous hour. Because our system can process $10,000$ collected tweets in less than one minute (see Figure 9), we can detect suspicious URLs with only one-minute time lags. Between August 6 and August 18, 2011, the real-time WARNINGBIRD reported $4,336$ unique suspicious URLs without system errors.

4.7 Comparison with Twitter

We compare the efficiency of WARNINGBIRD with that of Twitter's detection system. For the comparison, we sampled $14,905$ accounts detected by the real-time WARNINGBIRD between September 1 and October 22, 2011. To compare their efficiencies, we measured the time difference between WARNINGBIRD's detection and Twitter's suspension of the accounts. We monitored the WARNINGBIRD to obtain newly detected suspicious accounts and then checked the status of each account every 15 s until it was suspended, within a day. Among the sampled accounts, $5,380$ accounts were suspended within a day; 37.3% of them was suspended within a minute, another 42.5% of them was suspended within 200 minutes, and the remaining 20.7% of them was suspended within a day (see Figure 10). The average time difference is 13.5 minutes; therefore, our detection system is more efficient than that of Twitter. We also checked the statuses of the sampled accounts on October 28, 2011 to verify the accuracy of our system. Among the $14,905$ accounts, $9,250$ accounts were suspended. We then randomly selected 500 accounts from the remaining $5,655$ active accounts to manually check their suspiciousness. Among the 500 accounts, 320 accounts were suspicious. Therefore, the detection accuracy of our system given the sample data is about 86.3%.

5 Discussion

In this section, we discuss some limitations of our system and possible evasion techniques.

Dynamic redirection: Currently, WARNINGBIRD uses a static crawler written in Python. Because it can handle only HTTP redirections, it will be ineffective on pages with embedded dynamic redirections such as JavaScript or Flash redirection. Therefore, WARNINGBIRD will designate pages with embedded dynamic redirection as entry point URLs. This determination causes inaccuracy in some of the feature values, including the redirect chain lengths, positions of the entry point URLs, and the number of different landing URLs. Therefore, in the future we will use customized Web browsers to retrieve redirect chains fully.

Multiple redirections: Web pages can embed several external pages and different content. Therefore, some pages can cause multiple redirections. Because our system currently only considers HTTP redirection and does not consider page-level redirection, it cannot catch multiple redirections. Therefore, we need customized browsers to catch and address multiple redirections.

Coverage and scalability: Currently, our system only monitors one percent of the samples from the Twitter public timeline, because our accounts have the Spritzer access role. As shown in Section 4, if our accounts were to take on the Gardenhose access role, which allows the processing of 10% of the samples, our system could handle this number of samples in real time. The current implementation, however, cannot handle 100% of the Twitter public timeline. Therefore, we must extend WARNINGBIRD to a distributed detection system, for instance, Monarch [24], to handle the entire Twitter public timeline.

Feature evasion methods: Attackers can fabricate the features of their attacks to evade our detection system. For instance, they could use short redirect chains, change the position of their entry point URLs, and reuse initial and landing URLs. These modifications, paradoxically, would allow previous detection systems to detect their malicious URLs. Attackers may also be able to reduce the frequency of their tweets to bypass our detection system. However, this will also reduce the number of visitors to their malicious pages. Features derived from tweet information, however, are relatively weak at protecting against forgery, as many researchers have already pointed out [21, 24, 31]. Attackers could use a large number of source applications and Twitter accounts, use similar tweet texts, and carefully adjust the numbers of followers and friends of their accounts to increase the standard deviation values. In addition, they could increase the standard deviation of their account creation date if they own or have compromised older accounts. Although these features are weak, attackers have to consume their resources and time to fabricate these features. Therefore, using these features is still meaningful. The strongest evasion method is definitely to increase the number of redirect servers. This method, however, would require many resources and large financial investment on the part of the attackers.

6 Related Work

6.1 Twitter Spam Detection

Many Twitter spam detection schemes have been introduced. Most have focused on how to collect a large number of spam and non-spam accounts and extract the features that can effectively distinguish spam from non-spam accounts. To detect spam accounts, some schemes investigate collected data manually [2, 28], some use *honey-profiles* to lure spammers [16, 23], some monitor the Twitter public timeline to detect accounts that post tweets with blacklisted URLs [11, 31], and some monitor Twitter's official account for spam reporting, *@spam* [21].

Much preliminary work [2, 11, 16, 23, 28] relies on account features including the numbers of followers and friends, account creation dates, URL ratios, and tweet text similarities, which can be efficiently collected but easily fabricated. To avoid feature fabrication, recent work [21,31] relies on more robust features extracted from the Twitter graph. Yang *et al.* [31] focused on relations between spam nodes and their neighboring nodes such as a bi-directional link ratio and betweenness centrality, because spam nodes usually cannot establish strong relationships with their neighboring nodes. They also introduced other features based on timing and automation. Song *et al.* [21] considered the relations between spam senders and receivers such as the shortest paths and minimum cut, because spam nodes usually cannot establish robust relationships with their victim nodes. The extraction of these robust features, however, is time and resource consuming.

6.2 Suspicious URL Detection

Many suspicious URL detection schemes have been proposed. They can be classified into either static or dynamic detection systems. Some lightweight static detection systems focus on the lexical features of a URL such as its length, the number of dots, or each token it has [19], and also consider underlying DNS and WHOIS information [17, 18]. More sophisticated static detection systems, such as Prophiler [3], additionally extract features from HTML content and JavaScript codes to detect drive-by download attacks. However, static detection systems cannot detect suspicious URLs with dynamic content such as obfuscated JavaScript, Flash, and ActiveX content. Therefore, we need dynamic detection systems [4, 7, 24, 29, 30] that use virtual machines and instrumented Web browsers for in-depth analysis of suspicious URLs. Nevertheless, all of these detection systems may still fail to detect suspicious sites with conditional behaviors.

6.3 ARROW: Generating Signatures to Detect Drive-by Downloads

Zhang *et al.* have developed ARROW [32], which also considers a number of correlated URL redirect chains to generate signatures of drive-by download attacks. It uses honeyclients to detect drive-by download attacks and collect logs of HTTP redirection traces from the compromised honeyclients. From these logs, it identifies central servers that are contained in a majority of the HTTP traces to the same binaries and generates regular expression signatures using the central servers' URLs. ARROW also groups domain names with the same IP addresses to avoid IP fast flux and domain flux [12, 22].

Although the methods for detecting central servers in ARROW and for detecting entry point URLs in WARNINGBIRD are similar, there are three important differences between these two systems. First, ARROW's HTTP traces are redirect chains between malicious landing pages and malware binaries. Therefore, ARROW cannot be applied to detect other Web attacks, such as spam, scam, and phishing attacks, which do not have such redirect chains to enable the downloading of malware binaries. Moreover, if honeyclients cannot access malicious landing pages owing to conditional redirections, ARROW cannot obtain any HTTP traces. Second, ARROW focuses on how to generate the signatures of central servers that redirect visitors to the same malware binaries, whereas WARNINGBIRD focuses on how to measure the suspiciousness of entry point URLs. Third, ARROW relies on logs of HTTP traces to detect central servers. Therefore, it cannot detect suspicious URLs in real time. In contrast, WARNINGBIRD is a real-time system.

7 Conclusion

Previous suspicious URL detection systems are weak at protecting against conditional redirection servers that distinguish investigators from normal browsers and redirect them to benign pages to cloak malicious landing pages. In this paper, we propose a new suspicious URL detection system for Twitter, WARNINGBIRD. Unlike the previous systems, WARNINGBIRD is robust when protecting against conditional redirection, because it does not rely on the features of malicious landing pages that may not be reachable. Instead, it focuses on the correlations of multiple redirect chains that share redirection servers. We introduced new features on the basis of these correlations, implemented a real-time classification system using these features, and evaluate the system's accuracy and performance. The evaluation results showed that our system is highly accurate and can be deployed as a real-time system to classify large samples of tweets from the Twitter public timeline. In the future, we will extend our system to address dynamic and multiple redirections. We will also implement a distributed version of WARNINGBIRD to process all tweets from the Twitter public timeline.

References

[1] D. Antoniades, I. Polakis, G. Kontaxis, E. Athanasopoulos, S. Ioannidis, E. P. Markatos, and T. Karagiannis. we.b: The web of short URLs. In *Int. World Wide Web Conf. (WWW)*, 2011.

[2] F. Benevenuto, G. Magno, T. Rodrigues, and V. Almeida. Detecting spammers on Twitter. In *Collaboration, Electronic messaging, Anti-Abuse and Spam Conf. (CEAS)*, 2010.

[3] D. Canali, M. Cova, G. Vigna, and C. Kruegel. Prophiler: A fast filter for the large-scale detection of malicious web pages. In *Int. World Wide Web Conf. (WWW)*, 2011.

[4] Capture-HPC. `https://projects.honeynet.org/capture-hpc`.

[5] Y.-W. Chen and C.-J. Lin. Combining SVMs with various feature selection strategies. In *Feature Extraction*, volume 207 of *Studies in Fuzziness and Soft Computing*, pages 315–324. 2006.

[6] Z. Chu, S. Gianvecchio, H. Wang, and S. Jajodia. Who is tweeting on Twitter: Human, bot, or cyborg? In *Annual Computer Security Applications Conf. (ACSAC)*, 2010.

[7] M. Cova, C. Kruegel, and G. Vigna. Detection and analysis of drive-by-download attacks and malicious JavaScript code. In *Int. World Wide Web Conf. (WWW)*, 2010.

[8] P. Eckersley. How unique is your web browser? In *Privacy Enhancing Technologies (PET)*, 2010.

[9] R.-E. Fan, K.-W. Chang, C.-J. Hsieh, X.-R. Wang, and C.-J. Lin. LIBLINEAR: A library for large linear classification. *Journal of Machine Learning Research*, 9:1871–1874, 2008.

[10] Google. Google safe browsing API. `http://code.google.com/apis/safebrowsing`.

[11] C. Grier, K. Thomas, V. Paxson, and M. Zhang. @spam: The underground on 140 characters or less. In *ACM Conf. Computer and Communications Security (CCS)*, 2010.

[12] T. Holz, C. Gorecki, K. Rieck, and F. C. Freiling. Measuring and detecting fast-flux service networks. In *Network and Distributed System Security Symp. (NDSS)*, 2008.

[13] P. Jaccard. The distribution of flora in the alpine zone. *The New Phytologist*, 11(2):37–50, 1912.

[14] A. Kapravelos, M. Cova, C. Kruegel, and G. Vigna. Escape from monkey island: Evading high-interaction honeyclients. In *SIG SIDAR Conf. Detection of Intrusions and Malware & Vulnerability Assessment (DIMVA)*, 2011.

[15] H. Kwak, C. Lee, H. Park, and S. Moon. What is Twitter, a social network or a news media? In *Int. World Wide Web Conf. (WWW)*, 2010.

[16] K. Lee, J. Caverlee, and S. Webb. Uncovering social spammers: Social honeypots + machine learning. In *ACM SIGIR Conf.*, 2010.

[17] J. Ma, L. K. Saul, S. Savage, and G. M. Voelker. Beyond blacklists: Learning to detect malicious web sites from suspicious URLs. In *ACM SIGKDD Int. Conf. Knowledge Discovery and Data Mining (KDD)*, 2009.

[18] J. Ma, L. K. Saul, S. Savage, and G. M. Voelker. Identifying suspicious URLs: An application of large-scale online learning. In *Int. Conf. Machine Learning (ICML)*, 2009.

[19] D. K. McGrath and M. Gupta. Behind phishing: An examination of phisher modi operandi. In *USENIX Workshop Large-Scale Exploits and Emergent Threats (LEET)*, 2008.

[20] M. A. Rajab, L. Ballard, N. Jagpal, P. Mavrommatis, D. Nojiri, N. Provos, and L. Schmidt. Trends in circumventing web-malware detection. Technical report, Google, 2011.

[21] J. Song, S. Lee, and J. Kim. Spam filtering in Twitter using sender-receiver relationship. In *Int. Symp. Recent Advances in Intrusion Detection (RAID)*, 2011.

[22] B. Stone-Gross, M. Cova, L. Cavallaro, B. Gilbert, M. Szydlowski, R. Kemmerer, C. Kruegel, and G. Vigna. Your botnet is my botnet: Analysis of a botnet takeover. In *ACM Conf. Computer and Communications Security (CCS)*, 2009.

[23] G. Stringhini, C. Kruegel, and G. Vigna. Detecting spammers on social networks. In *Annual Computer Security Applications Conf. (ACSAC)*, 2010.

[24] K. Thomas, C. Grier, J. Ma, V. Paxson, and D. Song. Design and evaluation of a real-time URL spam filtering system. In *IEEE Symp. Security and Privacy (Oakland)*, 2011.

[25] K. Thomas, C. Grier, V. Paxson, and D. Song. Suspended accounts in retrospect: An analysis of twitter spam. In *Internet Measurement Conf. (IMC)*, 2011.

[26] TweetAttacks. Twitter marketing software that breaks the limits. `http://tweetattacks.com`.

[27] Twitter Developers. Streaming API. `https://dev.twitter.com/docs/streaming-api`.

[28] A. Wang. Don't follow me: Spam detecting in Twitter. In *Int. Conf. Security and Cryptography (SECRYPT)*, 2010.

[29] Y.-M. Wang, D. Beck, X. Jiang, R. Roussev, C. Verbowski, S. Chen, and S. King. Automated web patrol with Strider HoneyMonkeys: Finding web sites that exploit browser vulnerabilities. In *Network and Distributed System Security Symp. (NDSS)*, 2006.

[30] C. Whittaker, B. Ryner, and M. Nazif. Large-scale automatic classification of phising pages. In *Network and Distributed System Security Symp. (NDSS)*, 2010.

[31] C. Yang, R. Harkreader, and G. Gu. Die free or live hard? empirical evaluation and new design for fighting evolving Twitter spammers. In *Int. Symp. Recent Advances in Intrusion Detection (RAID)*, 2011.

[32] J. Zhang, C. Seifert, J. W. Stokes, and W. Lee. ARROW: Generating signatures to detect drive-by downloads. In *Int. World Wide Web Conf. (WWW)*, 2011.

Using Replicated Execution for a More Secure and Reliable Browser

Hui Xue, Nathan Dautenhahn, Sam King
University of Illinois at Urbana Champaign

Browsers: Important App Platforms

- Email, Banking, Shopping, Social network...

2

Browsers Are Not Safe

- Browsers are plagued with vulnerabilities
  - Internet Explorer: 59 new vulnerabilities in 2010
  - Firefox: 100 new vulnerabilities in 2010
  - Safari: 119 new vulnerabilities in 2010
  - Chrome: 191 new vulnerabilities in 2010
- Attackers target browsers
  - Studies from Washington, Microsoft, and Google

3

Firefox Browser Exploit Example

- Firefox 3.0.x malicious popup by CVE-2009-3076

4

Opera: Exploit Fails

- Opera shows no popup

Reason: Browser Specific Vulnerabilities

- Different browsers different code bases
- The same bug often only in one browser

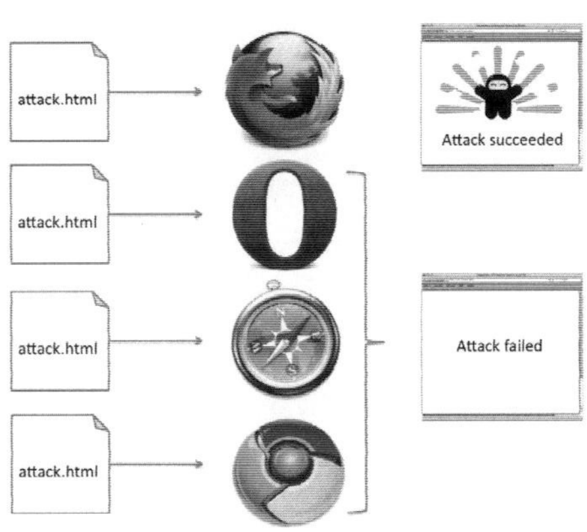

Cocktail: Mixing Browsers For Better Security

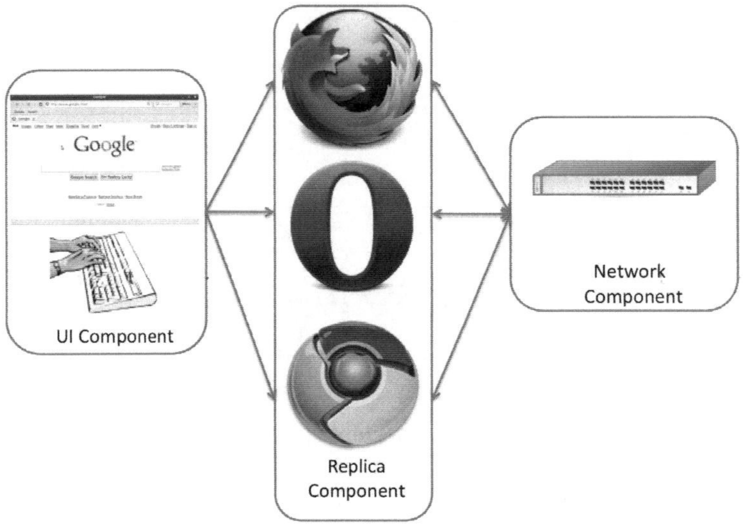

7

Overview

- Example
- Observation
- Design
  - Non-determinism
- Implementation
- Evaluation
- Conclusion

8

How Cocktail Works: Example

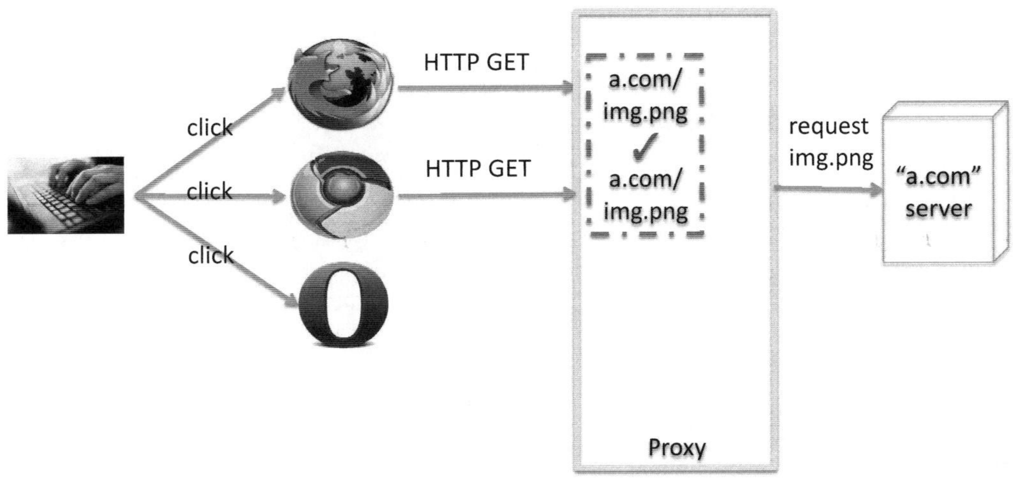

9

How Cocktail Works: Example

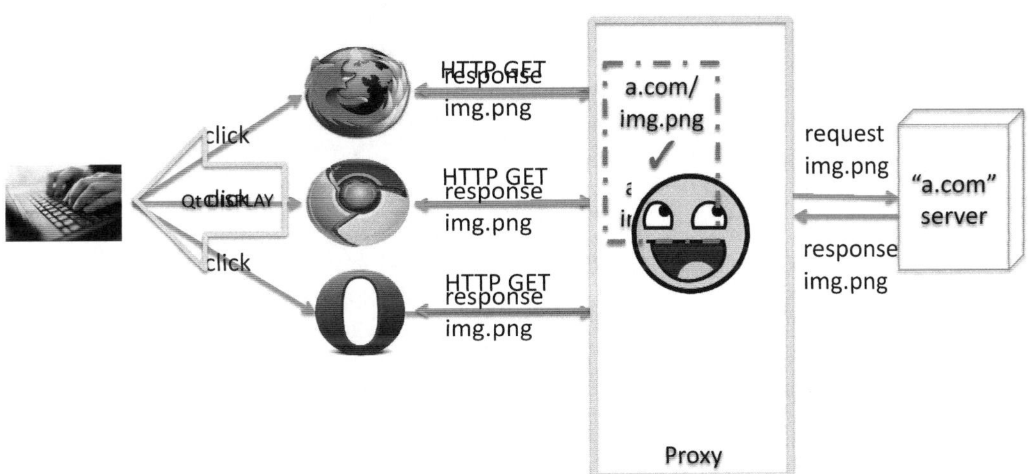

10

Withstanding False Positive/Attack

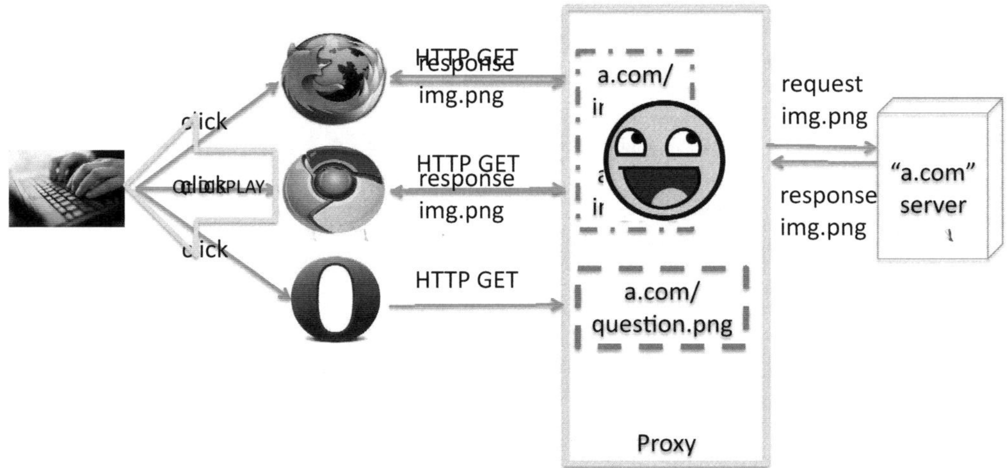

11

Observation : Opportunistic N-Version Programming

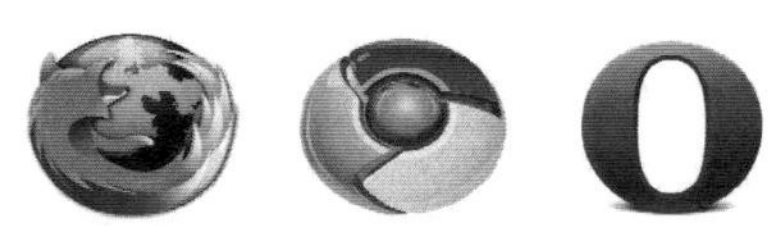

Different code base

+

DOM

Same specification "roughly" followed

12

How to Compare Different Browsers?

- States to compare: display + network
  - Display: vision based page layout abstraction
- Interaction with server
- Client side non-determinism

13

Challenge: Interaction with Server

- Pages from server can be different

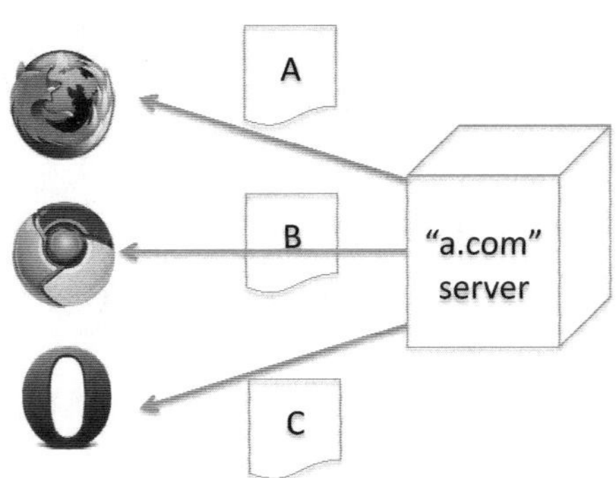

14

Request Duplication Is Bad

- Time difference
  - Page get updated
- Post requests
  - Output commit

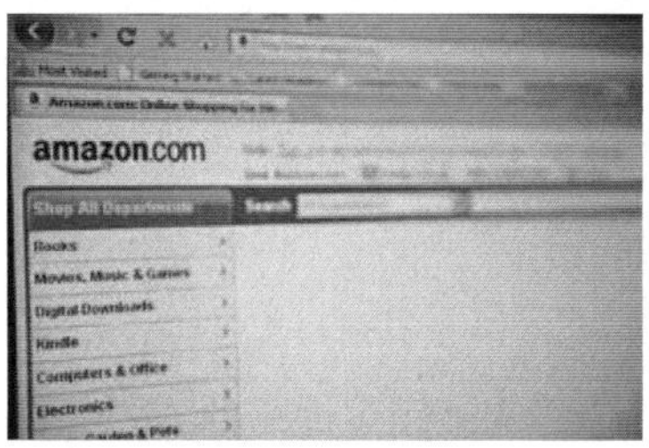

15

Solution

- Avoid major changes to browser
  - Browsers self-update is easy
  - Open source is not required
- Solution: proxy replication
  - Replicate incoming network data with proxy
    - HTTPS handling: Man-in-the-middle

16

Solution: Proxy Replication

- One browser as seen by server

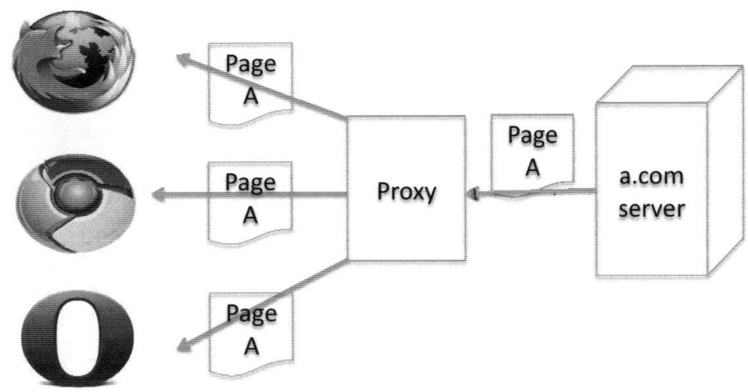

17

Challenge: Client Side Non-determinism

- Same page content, different execution result

```
<html>
...
<script>
randomId = Math.random();
url = "doubleclick.com?ad=" + randomId;
</script>
...
</html>
```

18

Client Non-determinism Summary

- Script related randomness

Random Number	Math.random()
Date and Time	new Date()
Browser Specific Value	window.opera; navigator.appName
Browser Locale	"en-us" VS "en-US"……….
…	…

- Browser specific behaviors
  - E.g., Opera community

19

Solution

- Extension modifies script execution
  - Overwrites Math, Date, window.opera

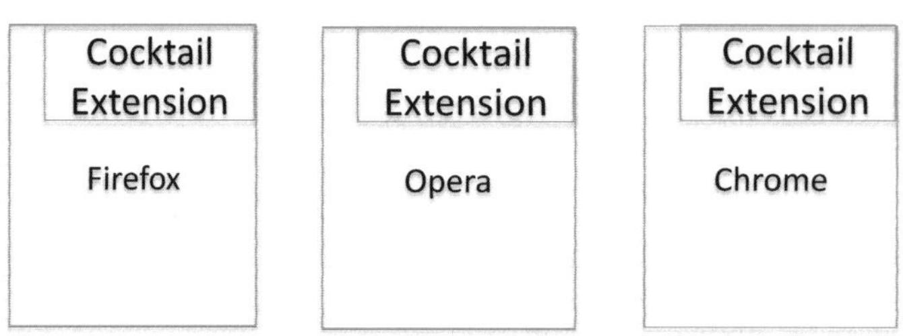

- Browser configuration change
  - Disable Opera community
  - Adjust browser locale

20

False Positive

- Browsers treat malformed URL differently

<iframe src="
http://www.adfusion.com/Adfusion.PartnerSite/ca
tegoryhtml.aspx?userfeedguid=948fbed8-69ae-4659
-b3c1-b9863e5ab24e&clicktag=http://ads.bluelith
ium.com/clk?2,13%...%2Flrec%2F,&CB={REQUES
TID}

"

width="300" height="250" scrolling="no"
frameborder="0" marginheight="0"
marginwidth="0"
></iframe>

21

Why Cocktail Is More Secure

- Voting == Security
- Withstand some F.P.
  - Only need 2 to proceed
- Ext. to eliminate non-determinism
- Looks like a good one
  Acts like a good one
  It *is* one uncompromised browser

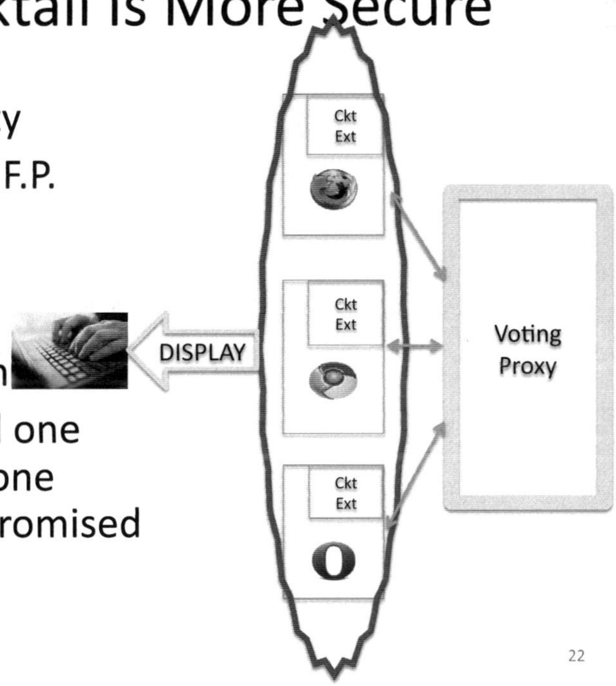

22

Implementation

- UI replication
  - Recorder and replayer: Extension
  - Passing UI events across browsers: Proxy
- UI Display capturing and voting
  - ImageMagick and OpenCV
- Proxy
  - OpenSSL for MITM

23

Evaluation

- Security analysis
  - User interaction: CVE-2009-3076
  - Heap overflow: CVE-2009-2477
  - DOS attack: Firefox 3.0.4 DOS, April 2009
  - Same origin policy bypassing: CVE-2007-0981
- Performance
  - 30% slower comparing to Firefox

24

Conclusion

- Mixing different browsers for better security
  - Practical N-Version programming for browsers
  - Solutions for design challenges
  - Security shifted to thin layer instead of big software

25

Thank you!

- Q/A
- Hui Xue (huixue2@uiuc.edu)
  https://netfiles.uiuc.edu/huixue2/www/

26

Window of Exposure

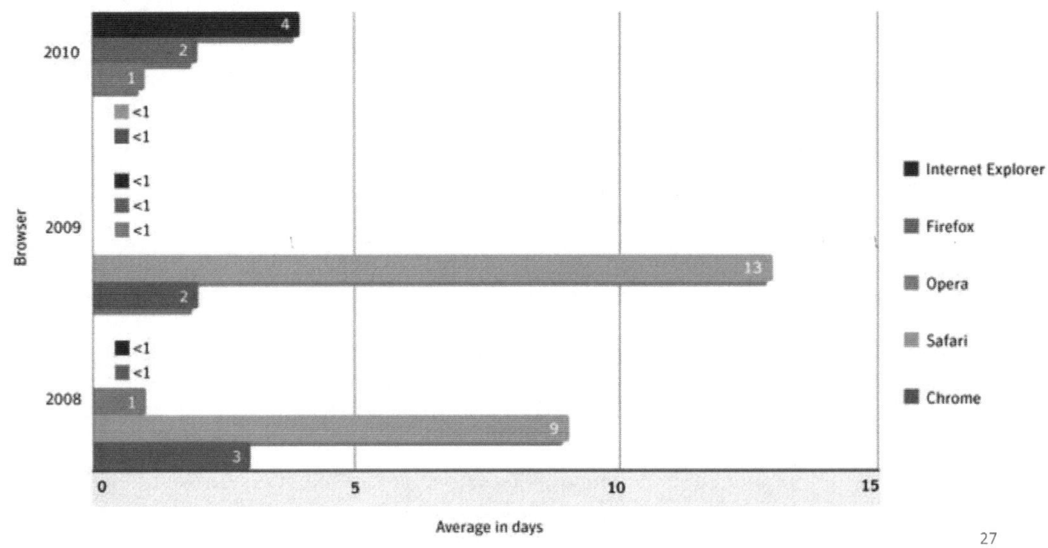

27

Host Fingerprinting and Tracking on the Web: Privacy and Security Implications

Ting-Fang Yen[1]*, Yinglian Xie[2], Fang Yu[2], Roger Peng Yu[3], Martín Abadi[2]†

[1]RSA Laboratories
[2]Microsoft Research Silicon Valley
[3]Microsoft Corporation
tingfang.yen@rsa.com, {yxie, fangyu, rogeryu, abadi@microsoft.com}

Abstract

Many web services aim to track clients as a basis for analyzing their behavior and providing personalized services. Despite much debate regarding the collection of client information, there have been few quantitative studies that analyze the effectiveness of host-tracking and the associated privacy risks.

In this paper, we perform a large-scale study to quantify the amount of information revealed by common host identifiers. We analyze month-long anonymized datasets collected by the Hotmail web-mail service and the Bing search engine, which include millions of hosts across the global IP address space. In this setting, we compare the use of multiple identifiers, including browser information, IP addresses, cookies, and user login IDs.

We further demonstrate the privacy and security implications of host-tracking in two contexts. In the first, we study the causes of cookie churn in web services, and show that many returning users can still be tracked even if they clear cookies or utilize private browsing. In the second, we show that host-tracking can be leveraged to improve security. Specifically, by aggregating information across hosts, we uncover a stealthy malicious attack associated with over 75,000 bot accounts that forward cookies to distributed locations.

*This work was done while Ting-Fang was an intern at Microsoft Research.

†Martín Abadi is also affiliated with the University of California, Santa Cruz.

1 Introduction

It is in the interest of web services and ISPs to track the mobility and usage patterns of client hosts. This tracking allows them to understand user behavior for supporting applications such as product suggestions, targeted advertising, and online fraud detection. However, clients may not wish that their activities be tracked, and can intentionally remove stored browser cookies or choose not to perform user logins. The growing awareness of privacy concerns is exemplified by the recent "do-not-track" initiative from the Federal Trade Commission [15], which outlines guidelines to which service providers must adhere in the collection and distribution of client information.

Several works aim to improve the accuracy of host-tracking by collecting detailed host information, such as installed browser plug-ins and system fonts [20, 31] or packet-level information that reveals subtle hardware differences [28]. By comparison, few studies exist on the effectiveness and privacy implications of host-tracking. Previous work tends to be qualitative in nature [29, 30] or limited to a single identifier [20].

In this paper, we attempt to facilitate the debate regarding host-tracking by performing a large-scale study to quantify the amount of identifying information revealed by common identifiers. Such analysis is critical to both service providers and end users. For example, service providers can determine where existing identifiers are insufficient and more sophisticated methods may be preferred. Users who do not wish to be tracked can learn the circumstances in which they can be identified accurately, so that they can take effective measures to protect privacy. Our analysis is based on month-long anonymized datasets from the Hotmail webmail service and the Bing search engine, including hundreds of millions of users across the global Internet IP address space. By characterizing hosts' activities across time using "binding windows", we show that common identifiers allow us to track hosts with high accuracy.

We further consider cases where users take initiatives to preserve privacy, e.g., by clearing cookies or switching to private browsing mode. Specifically, we analyze "one-time" cookies that do not return again in subsequent web requests, a phenomenon known as cookie churn. These cookies appear to be anonymous. However, by applying our host-tracking results, we show that a surprisingly large fraction can be recognized as belonging to returning users.

In addition to its privacy implications, we demonstrate that host-tracking can also be applied to improve security. We examine the mobility patterns of hosts traveling across multiple IP ranges, and establish normal user mobility profiles from aggregate host activities. In doing so, we are able to analyze unusual activities, e.g., the use of anonymous routing networks, and develop methods to detect attacks. In particular, our study uncovers previously unknown suspicious cookie-forwarding activities, which may have been adopted by attackers to evade spamming detection.

The key findings of this paper include:

- We show that 60%-70% of HTTP user-agent strings can accurately identify hosts in our datasets. When augmented with coarse-grained IP prefix information, the accuracy can be improved to 80%, similar to that obtained with cookies. User-agent strings combined with IP addresses have an entropy of 20.29 bits—higher than that of browser plug-ins, screen resolution, timezone, and system fonts combined [20].

- Applying our results to study cookie churn, we find that a service provider can recognize and track 88% of the "one-time" cookies as corresponding to users who later returned to the service. Among these users, 33% made an effort to preserve their privacy, either by clearing cookies through browser options or utilizing private browsing mode.

- Employing general mobility patterns derived by tracking hosts across network domains, we uncover malicious behaviors where cookies are forwarded from one IP address to distributed locations. In total, we identify over 75,000 bot Hotmail accounts in this relatively stealthy attack that has not been detected before.

Although our research relies on anonymized datasets from Hotmail and Bing, the analyses that we describe are a research effort only. Our goal is not to identify or study specific individual activities, but rather to understand the patterns of the aggregated activities and to explore their implications.

In the following, we first describe the identifiers that we study and our host-tracking methodology in Section 2, and present the evaluation of those identifiers in Section 3. We investigate the privacy and security implications of host-tracking in the context of cookie churn in Section 4 and of host mobility in Section 5. Finally, we describe related work in Section 6 and conclude in Section 7.

2 Exploring Common Identifiers

Given a log of application-level events collected over time, such as requests directed to a web server or user logins to a service, our goal is to quantify the amount of host-identifying information that is captured in identifiers within the log. Specifically, for an identifier I, which may take on a finite set $F_I = \{f_1, f_2, \ldots, f_n\}$ of possible values (called *fingerprints*), we are interested in whether a fingerprint f_i uniquely corresponds to a single host, among all hosts involved in the log. As we consider only client hosts in our scenario, we use *clients* or *hosts* interchangeably throughout the paper.

We assume the perspective of a passive observer of identifiers within application-level events. The common identifiers explored in this work include 1) user-agent string (UA), 2) IP address, 3) browser cookie, and 4) user login ID. We choose these identifiers because they are not particular to our datasets, and are available in a wide variety of service logs.

2.1 Host-tracking Graph

Our host-tracking approach attempts to infer the presence of a host at an IP address during a certain time interval. Upon observing a fingerprint f (and only f) that appears at an IP address A over a time interval Δt, we can infer a "binding window" for f. Events occurring within Δt at A can then be attributed to the host corresponding to f. (Hosts behind NATs/proxies can complicate matters; we quantify the occurrence of such hosts in our data in Section 3.3.)

Figure 1 illustrates how we infer the binding windows. In this example, user-agent strings (UA) are the identifiers, and the events are queries to a web search engine. A fingerprint UA_1 appears in two consecutive

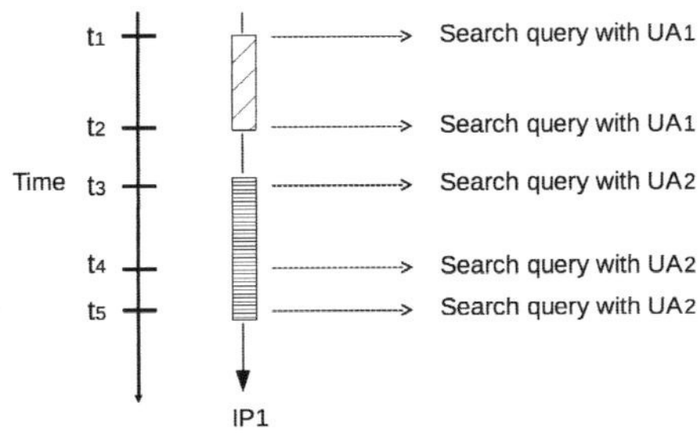

Figure 1. Binding windows identified on one IP.

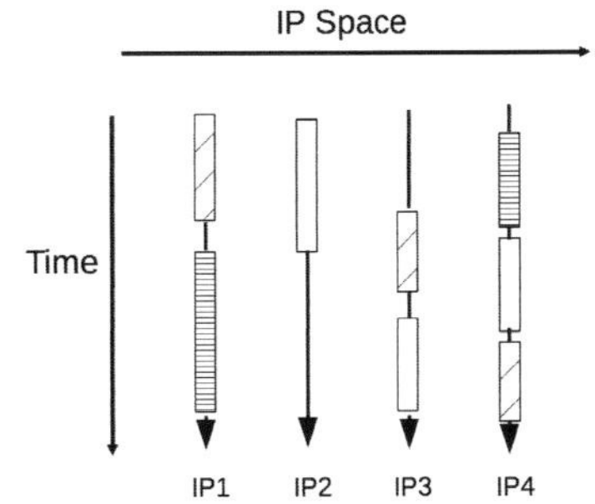

Figure 2. Example of a host-tracking graph. Bars with different patterns denote binding windows corresponding to different fingerprints.

search queries at time t_1 and t_2, followed by queries at time t_3, t_4, and t_5 with a different fingerprint UA_2. Thus we can identify binding windows corresponding to two different "hosts" on this IP: one spanning the time range $[t_1, t_2]$, and another spanning $[t_3, t_5]$. Having examined all search query events, we can construct a host-tracking graph as in Figure 2. Note that a fingerprint may be associated with multiple binding windows (since the host may not be up all the time) and across different IP addresses (e.g., because of DHCP). We refer to the host-tracking graph that represents hosts by identifier I as G_I.

A similar concept of host-tracking graph was also used by HostTracker [38] to support Internet accountability. HostTracker groups together user login IDs that are likely to be associated with the same host, e.g., family members that share a computer at home. It also filters events related to bots and large proxies. In contrast to this previous work, we make a broader use of the host-tracking graph (with a variety of common identifiers), and we apply host-tracking to the cookie-churn study (in Section 4) and the host-mobility analysis (in Section 5).

2.2 Datasets

The data for our study includes a month-long user login trace collected by the Hotmail web-mail service in August 2010. The trace contains coarse-grained information about the OS and browser type (e.g., Windows, Mozilla), the IP address from which the login was made, the time of the login event, and the anonymized user ID. In the following, we refer to this as the Webmail dataset.

We also obtained a month-long dataset consisting of search query events directed to the Bing search engine in August 2010. This data includes the fine-grained user-agent string from the HTTP header (anonymized via hashing), the IP address from which the query was issued, the time of the query, the anonymized cookie ID assigned by the search engine, and the date that the cookie ID was created. Specifically, the anonymized cookie ID is a persistent identifier that does not change over time, if users do not clear cookies or use private browsing. We refer to this as the Search dataset. As part of the processing performed by the Bing search engine, events generated by known bots are filtered in advance.

To validate our client-tracking approach, we leveraged a month-long sampled log of Windows Update events, also from August 2010. This data contains the time at which the update was performed, the IP address, and the anonymized hardware ID that is unique to the host. This is the Validation dataset.

Table 1 shows the fields and the total number of unique IPs observed in each dataset. All three datasets include tens to hundreds of millions of IP addresses, spanning a large IP address space.

The published privacy policies for Hotmail, Bing, and Windows Update address the storage, use, sharing, and retention of data collected in the course of the operation of these services. In particular, they indicate that Microsoft may employ this data for analyzing trends and for operating and improving its products and services, as we aim to do with this work. Since the datasets are sensitive, they are not publically available for further research.

2.3 Validation and Metrics

Without ground truth for the host-IP mappings, we evaluate a host-tracking graph G_I by overlapping it with the Validation dataset. If a fingerprint is able to correctly

Dataset	User-agent information	IP address	Timestamp	ID	Unique IP addresses
Webmail	OS and browser type	Yes	Yes	User ID	308 million
Search	User-agent string (UA)	Yes	Yes	Cookie ID	131 million
Validation	N/A	Yes	Yes	Hardware ID	74 million

Table 1. Fields in each dataset.

track a host, its bindings should overlap only with Windows Update events associated with a single hardware ID. Conversely, a hardware ID is also expected to overlap with bindings associated with only one fingerprint.

We quantify the accuracy of an identifier using *precision* and *recall.* Let $\mathsf{hidcount}(f)$ denote the number of hardware IDs to which a fingerprint f corresponds, and $\mathsf{fpcount}(m)$ the number of fingerprints to which a hardware ID m corresponds. Precision is defined as the percentage of fingerprints that correspond to one host (i.e., one hardware ID), while recall is the percentage of hosts that correspond to one fingerprint.

$$\mathsf{Precision}_I = \frac{|\{f : \mathsf{hidcount}(f) = 1, f \in F_I\}|}{|F_I|}$$

$$\mathsf{Recall}_I = \frac{|\{m : \mathsf{fpcount}(m) = 1, m \in M_I\}|}{|M_I|}$$

F_I is the finite set of values that identifier I takes in our dataset, i.e., the fingerprints (after some initial filtering, as described below). M_I is the set of hardware IDs that overlap with the host-tracking graph G_I. Roughly speaking, precision quantifies how accurate an identifier is at representing a host. Recall quantifies how well an identifier is able to track the events associated with the corresponding host in a log.

We also measure the *entropy* of an identifier, H_I, which is the amount of information identifier I contains that can distinguish hosts. The entropy is defined as

$$\mathsf{H}_I = -\sum_{f \in F_I} \mathsf{Pr}(f) \log_2(\mathsf{Pr}(f))$$

where $\mathsf{Pr}(f)$ is the probability of observing fingerprint f in the application log. A higher entropy indicates a smaller probability that any two clients are associated with the same fingerprint.

In our validation, we consider only those fingerprints that overlap with more than one Windows Update event, and only those hardware IDs that overlap with more than one application-level event pertaining to our identifiers. These restrictions allow us to focus on the portion of data that we can validate, though they can be biased to those clients that access the services consistently (i.e., multiple times and with the same identifiers). Similarly, because of the datasets available to us, our study is based on clients of Microsoft services. We acknowledge that any dataset will be incomplete and possibly biased.

3 Client-Tracking Results

In this section, we construct host-tracking graphs using the common identifiers user-agent string (UA), IP address, cookie ID, and user login ID, and evaluate their precision and recall. In particular, we explore the distinguishing power of UA by examining the browser anonymity sets. We also measure the impact of proxies and NATs in our study in Section 3.3, and describe the increased accuracy and confidence of tracking stable hosts in Appendix A.

Our analysis focuses on host-tracking within each network domain, derived using the BGP prefix entries obtained from RouteViews [9]. We investigate the occurrences of identifiers at multiple network locations in Section 5, in which we also study the security implications of host-tracking.

3.1 Precision and Recall

Table 2 presents our results on host-tracking. After overlapping the Validation dataset with the host-tracking graphs, the number of unique fingerprints and hardware IDs included in our evaluation is still large—on the order of millions.

Several observations are evident from Table 2. First, browser information (UA) alone can identify hosts quite well. Its 62.01% precision is perhaps surprising, as UA strings are commonly regarded as providing insufficient information to reveal host identities. Second, a combination of UA with the IP address (i.e., fingerprinting hosts by distinct (UA, IP) pairs) can boost the precision up to 80.62%. In fact, combining UA with only the IP prefix is sufficient to achieve approximately the same result as with UA+IP. This suggests that anonymization techniques that store the IP prefix may still retain distinguishing information. Third, cookie IDs offer only slightly better precision and recall than UA+IP. The inaccuracies of cookie IDs can be partly attributed to cookie churn, a phenomenon we study in more detail in Section 4.

Identifier I	Precision (%)	Recall (%)	Fingerprint count	Hardware ID count
UA	62.01%	72.11%	254,762	3,073,690
UA, IP address	80.62%	68.84%	1,685,416	1,771,907
UA, /24 IP prefix	79.33%	69.43%	1,652,546	1,772,104
Cookie ID	82.35%	68.64%	1,340,635	1,375,074
Cookie ID (with HostTracker)	79.74%	99.13%	713,110	1,001,450
User ID (with HostTracker)	92.82%	93.51%	4,608,980	4,820,116

Table 2. Common identifiers in host-tracking, evaluated using the Validation dataset.

As another method to make use of the identifiers, we also apply HostTracker [38] to the cookie IDs and user IDs from our Search and Webmail datasets, respectively. In the former case, the clients are now tracked by a group of correlated cookies, e.g., those belonging to two browsers running on a machine in parallel. In the latter case, user login IDs that frequently appear together, e.g., family members that share a computer at home, are used to track clients. We find user IDs achieving high precision and recall (over 92%), demonstrating that they are strongly tied to individual hosts.

Since HostTracker yields relatively high precision and recall with user IDs, we have also evaluated the other identifiers against user IDs (instead of hardware IDs). Even though hardware IDs and user IDs overlap with different portions of the datasets, we obtain results consistent with those of Table 2.

To summarize, we show that common identifiers can track hosts reasonably well, particularly when they are used in combination.

3.2 Browser Anonymity Set

Our evaluation suggests that a large fraction of browsers provide enough information to fingerprint hosts within each network domain. In this section, we examine in detail the anonymity set of browser fingerprints, defined as the set of hardware IDs that share the same fingerprint. Even though 62% of UAs map to unique hosts, popular UA strings still have large anonymity sets, i.e., additional examination shows that the most common fingerprint, `Mozilla/4.0(compatible;MSIE6.0;WindowsNT5.1;SV1)`, corresponds to 124,355 (4.05%) of the hardware IDs that overlap with the UA host-tracking graph.

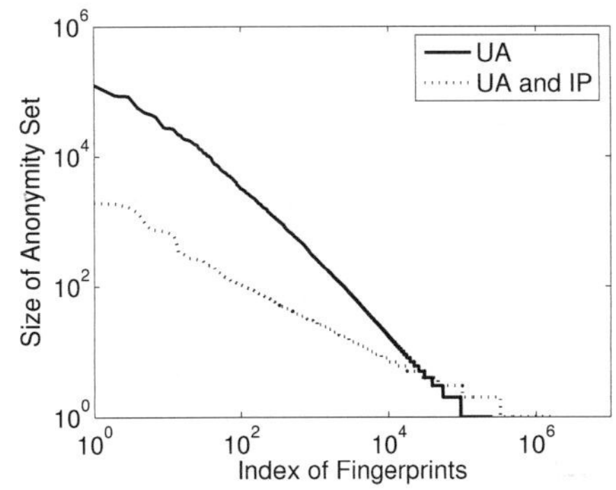

Figure 3. The distribution of the size of the browser anonymity sets, plotted in log-scale.

Figure 3 compares the size of the anonymity sets for UA and UA+IP. We find 98.92% of the UA+IP fingerprints to be relatively rare, with fewer than five hardware IDs, while this holds for only 89.69% of the UA fingerprints.

To quantify the amount of identifying information provided by browser fingerprints, we calculate their entropy. In our data, UA has an entropy of 11.59 bits, while the entropy of UA+IP is 20.29 bits. A study performed by Eckersley et al. [20] probed the remote client for installed plug-ins, screen resolution, timezone, system fonts, and user-agent strings, which altogether yielded an entropy of 18.1 bits. While this suggests that their detailed information provides more distinguishing power than UA alone, it is interesting to observe that such information may be less distinguishing than simply combining UA and IP address.

These results confirm our finding that UA strings augmented with IP addresses can identify hosts well. However, popular UA strings still have large anonymity sets. Changing the default UA string to one that corresponds to a popular browser version may hence allow a client to become less distinguishable.

3.3 Impacts of Proxies and NATs

Among the common identifiers we explored, none of them performs perfectly. Aside from their inherent ambiguity (e.g., some UAs are more common than others, cookies can be removed), proxies and NATs introduce fundamental difficulties in tracking hosts. The ability to detect and measure them allows us to understand precisely where such practical limitations will apply.

We first quantify the prevalence of large proxies and NATs that are typically configured by ISPs or enterprises. To do so, we examine "hosts" that correspond to a large number of user login IDs or cookie IDs. A small fraction of IP addresses in our datasets—31,874 and 2,151 from the Webmail and Search dataset, respectively—is each associated with more than 5,000 unique login IDs and cookie IDs. These are likely large proxies and we filter them in our evaluation.

Next, we examine small NAT devices that are often used by home networks. In this case, since it is relatively rare for a client to be running multiple operating systems in parallel, we leverage the coarse-grained OS type and IP address recorded for each user login event in the Webmail dataset. The majority (80.31%) of our login ID fingerprints are associated with only one unique user ID. When we observe multiple OS types, all from the same IP address, it indicates that the "host" may actually be a NAT device that masks multiple clients.

From this experiment, we find 10.60% hosts likely to be NATs. This number is a lower bound, since we cannot distinguish clients that are running the same OS behind a NAT device. Table 3 shows that while the large majority of NATed hosts include multiple Microsoft Windows OSes, hand-held devices also comprise a large fraction (about 16%). With the increasing popularity of multiple home devices and smart phones, we expect the percentage of NATs to grow further.

OS Types	NAT hosts (%)
Multiple Windows	81.32%
Windows and Hand-held device	15.62%
Windows and Mac OS/Unix	2.19%
Hand-held and Mac OS/Unix	0.55%
Windows, Hand-held, and Mac OS/Unix	0.31%
Multiple Mac OS/Unix	0.01%
Multiple Hand-held devices	0.01%

Table 3. Breakdown of the OS types found to be associated with hosts behind NATs.

4 Application: Cookie Churn Study

As the primary method for web sites to track returning users without requiring login-based authentication, browser cookies play an important role in customizing web services and maintaining user statistics. However, as shown in Section 3, using cookie IDs as client fingerprints can be unreliable. In particular, they have a relatively low recall rate—32% of the hardware IDs in our evaluation cannot be completely tracked by cookies.

A main source of the low recall rate is *cookie churn*, which we define as the phenomenon of cookies appearing at least once but *not* appearing again in subsequent web requests received by a server (within some observation time window). For service providers, being able to track hosts will allow them to quantify the underlying causes behind the cookie-churn phenomenon. In this section, we measure and analyze cookie churn in the Search dataset. (Among the datasets available to us, it is the only one that contains cookie IDs.) By applying our host-tracking methodology, we show that some client users may still be identified despite cookie churn.

4.1 Cookie Churn Measurement

Among cookie IDs that appear on the first day of our Search dataset, the rate of cookie churn, i.e., the fraction of cookie IDs that never returned again within our month-long observation, is 47.86%. On average, the daily cookie churn rate is around 45% across month-long sliding windows.

Furthermore, 81.98% of the new cookie IDs that are born on the first day of the Search dataset never returned within the month. For all cookie IDs observed on the first day of the month, Figure 4 shows cumulative distributions of the date that old and new cookies appear a second time. The churn rate of new cookies is significantly higher than that of old cookies—a difference of more than 40%.

4.2 Possible Reasons for Churn

Clearly, cookie churn can result from users quitting the service. As shown in Figure 4, engaged users that access the service multiple times (with old cookies) are more likely to return than new users.

Another reason for cookie churn is the removal of cookies from the client browser. This removal can happen in several cases, including when users manually clear cookies, when they set their browsers to automatically clear cookies on exit, or when users switch into or out of private browsing mode. Supported by all major web browsers today, private browsing takes a user's activities off records by removing caches, history, and in particular, cookies that are set during private mode.

To study how private browsing mode affects the cookie events observed by web services, we examine

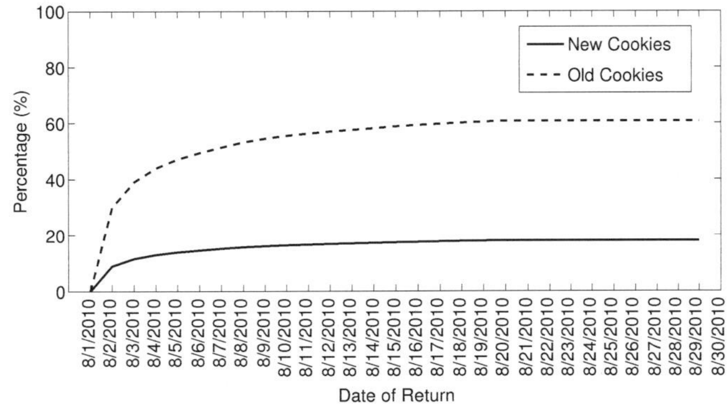

Figure 4. For cookie IDs observed on the first day of the month, the cumulative distribution of the date that old and new cookies appear again in our dataset.

Cookie Set	Cookie Accessed	Firefox	Safari	Chrome	IE
Public	Private	No	Yes	No	No
Private	Same private session	Yes	Yes	Yes	Yes
Private	Different private session	No	No	No	No
Private	Public	No	No	No	No

Table 4. Accessibility of cookies in different browsing modes.

four of the most popular browsers in use today: Firefox (version 3.6.11), Safari (version 5.0.2), Chrome (version 7.0.517.41), and Internet Explorer (version 8.0). Table 4 shows, for the browsing mode under which a cookie is set (the first column), whether the same cookie can be accessed under another browsing mode (the second column). In all cases, a cookie set in private mode can be accessed repeatedly in the same private browsing session, but not across different private browsing sessions. No cookies set in private mode can be accessed in public mode. Safari is the only browser that allows private mode to access cookies set in public mode.

In the next subsection, we perform fine-grained classification to quantify the above possible causes of cookie churn and characterize the corresponding users.

4.3 Understanding Cookie Churn

Applying the host-tracking results, we analyze cookie churn by identifying cookies that are associated with the same client host. In Section 3.1, we show that the host-tracking graph G_{UID} derived from user login IDs (with HostTracker) achieved over 92% precision and recall in tracking clients, which are represented by hardware IDs from the Validation dataset. Thus we use the hosts defined in G_{UID} to serve as ground truth for studying cookie churn. By overlapping G_{UID} with the Search dataset, we consider cookies whose query events fall into binding windows associated with the same host as corresponding to the same user (since user activity roughly approximates host activity).

We focus on studying new cookie churn, as it is more significant than that of old cookies (see Figure 4). We refer to the set of "one-time" cookie IDs (CIDs) that are born on the first day but do not return again in our dataset as the *churned new cookie IDs*. In total, there are 437,914 users (or hosts) that overlap with 847,196 churned new CIDs in the Search data. The number of hosts is only about half of the number of churned cookies IDs. We investigate the four cases that result in new cookie churn, as illustrated in Figure 5, where the breakdown of users belonging to each category is shown in Table 5. We elaborate on each of these cases separately below.

4.3.1 Case 1: Non-Returning Users

If a CID overlaps with one of host h's binding windows at time t, but no other CIDs overlap h's bindings from time t onwards, we consider this as corresponding to a user who does not return to the service (Figure 5(a)).

	Case 1	Case 2	Case 3	Case 4
Number of users	101,427	77,120	67,310	192,057
Percentage of users (%)	23.16%	17.61%	15.37%	43.86%
Number of churned new CIDs	101,427	77,147	123,757	544,865
Percentage of churned new CIDs (%)	11.97%	9.12%	14.60%	64.31%

Table 5. Breakdown of the churned new cookie IDs into four categories of users.

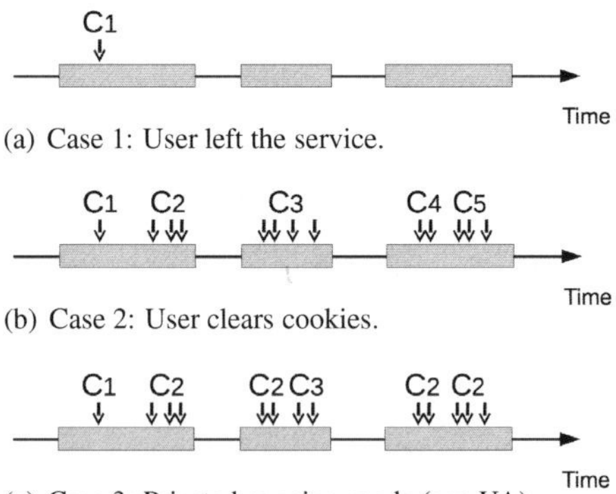

(a) Case 1: User left the service.

(b) Case 2: User clears cookies.

(c) Case 3: Private browsing mode (one UA). Case 4: Multiple browsers (multiple UAs).

Figure 5. Four cases of cookie churn. C_1 is the churned new cookie ID. Horizontal bars denote binding windows for a "host" defined by user IDs.

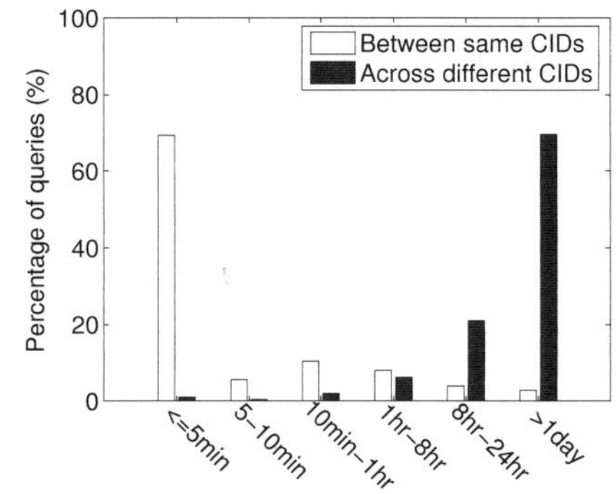

Figure 6. Distributions of query intervals.

We find that this case accounts for only 11.97% of the churned new CIDs. Thus, despite the high cookie churn rate, the majority (88.03%) of the churned new cookie IDs correspond to returning users who might still be tracked. The behaviors of the non-returning users are examined in detail in Appendix B.

4.3.2 Case 2: Users that Clear Cookies

Cookie churn can also result from users intentionally removing cookies. In this case, a host h's bindings should overlap with CIDs generated consecutively in time (Figure 5(b)). Each CID may be associated with multiple queries that typically belong to a session. Among hosts with new cookie churn, we find 77,120 (17.61%) in this category. Since we observe only cookies issued by the Bing search engine, we cannot distinguish between users who clear all cookies and those who selectively clear cookies from certain domains.

To find whether users clear cookies on exiting browsers, we examine the time intervals between consecutive queries associated with the same CID, and compare with those between consecutive queries associated with different CIDs. Figure 6 shows that the former is distinctly smaller, with 75% of them below 10 minutes and hence likely to belong to one session. By contrast, 90% of the query intervals between different CIDs are larger than 8 hours. This suggests that most users clear cookies *per session*, e.g., when they close the browser window.

We also find a small fraction (3.85%) of users whose cookies are cleared *per query*, i.e., each of their queries is associated with a different CID. These might be users who take extreme measures to clear cookies for each query to preserve privacy. However, such patterns can become a distinctive feature that makes tracking easier, despite the user's intention of remaining anonymous.

4.3.3 Case 3: Users with In-Private Browsing Mode

Another reason for cookie churn is the use of the browser's private browsing mode. As illustrated in Figure 5(c), upon entering private mode, the old cookie (C_2) set under public mode is replaced by a new cookie (C_3). Upon exiting the private mode, the old cookie (C_2) will continue to be used by the same user.

We focus on the hosts whose cookies appear interleaved in their binding windows, where an old cookie continues to appear after the user submit queries with a newer cookie. Since entering private browsing mode does not change the browser used by the host, we identify those associated with a single UA string as users who utilize private browsing mode, and 15.37% of users belong to this category.

Together with case 2, there are in total around 33%—a non-trivial fraction—of users who would like to preserve privacy by either clearing cookies or entering private browsing mode. These users may still be tracked when service providers combine the host-tracking results from other identifiers (e.g., login IDs) with cookie data.

4.3.4 Case 4: Users with Multiple Browsers

For the remaining users, we observe multiple cookies co-existing (as in Section 4.3.3), though they are associated with different UA strings. Upon examining these users more closely, we find around 67% associated with only two or three UAs. This observation suggests that these cases correspond to single hosts with multiple browsers or small home NATs. While it is more difficult to track hosts behind NATs, we note that the anonymity sets tend to be too small in such cases to protect user privacy.

A small fraction of these cases (3%) are associated with a large number of UA strings, which suggests that they are large proxies or NATs. Routing traffic through proxies thus provides better means for users who do not wish to be tracked.

Summary We study the cookie-churn phenomenon where privacy-aware users may clear cookies or switch to private browsing. We show that by applying host-tracking results with other identifiers, service providers may still be able to identify a large fraction (88%) of the "one-time", churned new cookie IDs as corresponding to users who return to the service.

5 Application: Host Mobility Study

In addition to switching between IP addresses within the same network (for instance, because of DHCP), a host may also travel across different IP ranges. This can occur if the host is a mobile device, or when a virtual private network (VPN) is used. Above, we track hosts within each IP prefix range separately, though it is also desirable to study clients that travel across domains, e.g., for traffic engineering or network management. More importantly, host mobility patterns can benefit security as well. We demonstrate this point by applying our host-tracking results to detect abnormal and malicious activities.

To understand the mobile behavior of hosts at a large scale, we make use of cookie IDs, since they are more closely tied to specific devices than other identifiers we studied in Section 3. We use the Search dataset for our study. Among cookie IDs in this dataset, 7.9 million appeared at more than one domain. While the majority of these cross-domain activities are associated with normal user travel patterns, there also exist unusual or suspicious activities, for example, cookie forwarding of the kind supported by CookieCooker [1].

In this section, we focus on detecting the following two abnormal host mobility patterns:

- Some cookie IDs move quickly between multiple domains, suggesting that they may not correspond to hosts who travel physically. In particular, we study those cookies that may be associated with anonymous routing, such as Tor routing [37].

- During an investigation into suspicious user email traffic that do not conform to the general host mobility profile, we uncover a stealthy type of malicious cookie-forwarding activity.

In the following, we first study patterns corresponding to users traveling across domains in general. We then use those patterns as baseline to identify abnormal activities.

5.1 Host Mobility Patterns

Our analysis yields a few key observations on general host mobility patterns. First, as shown in Table 6, ASes associated with cellular networks, i.e., Verizon Wireless and Carphone Warehouse Broadband Services, are ranked among the top domains with the largest number of traveling cookies. This fact reflects the proliferation of smart phones with mobile Internet access. In total, we find around 20% of the cookies among the top 500 AS pairs to be associated with cellular networks (Verizon Wireless, AT&T Wireless, Vodafone, Sprint, etc.).

AS pair	# Cookies	Affiliations
AS 17557, 45595	152871	Pakistan Telecom (PK)
AS 6167, 22394	70941	Verizon Wireless (US)
AS 13285, 43234	56600	Opal Telecom, Carphone Warehouse Broadband (GB)
AS 4134, 4837	52520	ChinaNet (CN)
AS 8228, 15557	36812	Neuf Cegetel (FR)

Table 6. Top five AS pairs associated with traveling cookies.

Second, we find traveling hosts to exhibit strong geographic locality. 83% of the cookies move between networks within the same country, and this number is even higher for the U.S. (95.44%). The strong geographic locality pattern can also be observed among cookies that travel across countries. Figure 7 shows the topology of international host travel, also drawn from the top 500 AS pairs. The node "EU" in the figure represents multi-regional networks in the European Union, which are not exclusively part of any European country. The size of each node in the figure is proportional to the number of cookies that originated from that country or region. The edges indicate the direction of travel. The figure shows that host mobility is largely bi-directional, and is commonly localized within the same general region (e.g., Europe).

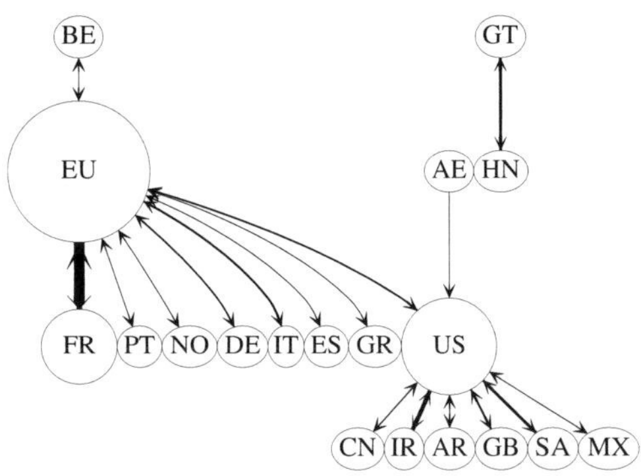

Figure 7. The topology of host mobility by country or region (e.g., "EU"), for top 500 AS pairs.

Third, a closer look at the AS topology of host mobility in the U.S. shows the existence of "hub" ASes that are connected to many smaller "leaf" ASes. The former are commonly associated with DSL broadband Internet services, while the latter include institutional and corporate networks. This star topology could result from clients' commuting patterns between home and work.

Finally, in addition to the source and sink domains, we are also interested in how far the hosts roam, i.e., how many ASes they travel through. Figure 8 plots the distribution of the number of ASes traveled by each host, with the Y-axis in log scale. The large majority (90%) of cookies are associated with only two domains.

These observations, based on aggregate information across the 7.9 million traveling hosts in the Search dataset, reflect general mobility patterns at a large scale. In the following, we investigate specific activities that fall outside this norm, including those that may involve suspicious behavior.

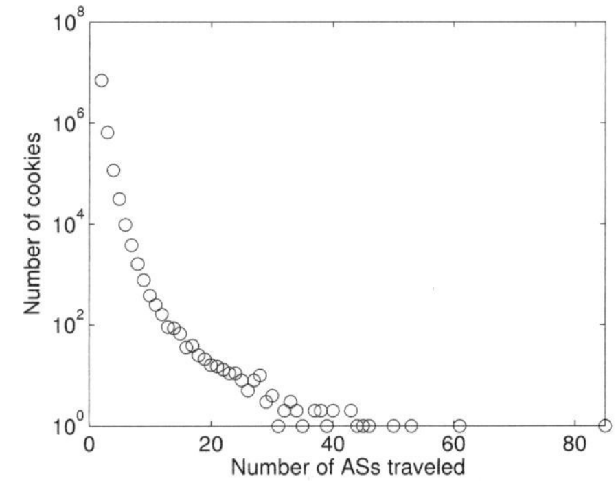

Figure 8. The distribution of the number of ASes traveled by each CID. Y-axis is in log scale.

5.2 Identifying Virtual Client Travel

Although the majority of traveling cookies correspond to physical host mobility, such as those associated with cellular networks, some switch between domains faster than seemingly possible for physical travel. Consecutively appearing from different ASes within a matter of minutes, the rapid movement of these cookies suggests the presence of some form of virtual client travel.

5.2.1 VPN Traffic Patterns

For the large majority of hosts that travel rapidly across only two or three domains, they likely have used VPNs or proxies. Virtual private networks (VPNs) allow traffic to be privately tunneled between two machines that are not in the same subnet. Creating an overlay network of clients that belong to the same organization, they are commonly used to provide corporate resources to remote employees. From the perspective of a web server, a user connecting to her company network from a DSL line at home can generate multiple requests with the same cookie, though they appear from two domains.

Specifically, we find a total 960,885 (12%) mobile cookies that travel between only two ASes, and that appear at the ASes consecutively within a short interval (i.e., 10 minutes). We call such cookies VPN-style cookies. Table 7 lists the top five AS pairs with the highest number of these cookies, which include institutional and corporate networks, e.g., City University of New York, NTT, and KDDI Corporation. VPN-style cookies comprise around 60% of all traveling cookies between a corporate network and a DSL broadband service provider. This observation indicates that VPNs can be a major explanation for host mobility.

AS pair	# Cookies	Affiliations
AS 6389, 35985	13249	BellSouth, One Ring Net. (US)
AS 702, 2856	8977	Verizon (US), BTnet UK Reg. Net. (GB)
AS 7018, 31822	7878	AT&T, City Univ. N.Y. (US)
AS 174, 701	6630	Cogent, MCI Comm.(US)
AS 4713, 4716	5770	NTT Comm., KDDI Corp. (JP)

Table 7. Top AS pairs associated with VPN cookies.

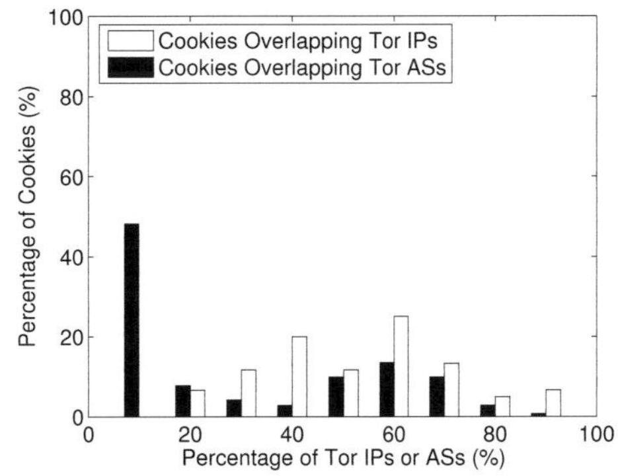

Figure 9. The percentage of Tor IPs or ASes on the path of wandering cookies.

5.2.2 The Use of Anonymous Routing

Examining the tail of the distribution in Figure 8, we also find a small fraction (0.02%) of cookies that migrate across more than 10 different domains. Stopping in each AS only for short durations, they do not return to a previously visited domain. Focusing on this behavior, we identify 309 cookies that travel across more than 10 ASes, and where the time between consecutive "jumps" to different ASes is less than 10 minutes (which is the default time to use a Tor circuit for new application connections). Compared to the AS peering relationship in Section 5.1, there does not appear to be any clear delineation of geographical regions.

The top ASes in this case are dominated by cable networks, with the previously top cellular networks disappearing completely from the list. Some university networks ranked significantly higher than before (AS 111, associated with Boston University, is on the path of 9% of these cookies). One explanation for the behavior of these cookies is the use of anonymous routing systems, such as Tor [37]. For a user that routes her traffic in this manner, if her traffic exits from different nodes in the mixing network, the same cookie may appear at different domains.

We obtained a list of active Tor nodes [8], including, for each node, its IP address, country, ISP, and whether it is an exit node. Among the 309 wandering cookies, 60 of them traverse through at least one Tor node, and 142 of them traverse through at least one AS that is also shared by a Tor node. We also examine ASes since some Tor nodes may already be assigned different IPs at the time of our lookup. Figure 9 plots the distribution of the percentage of Tor IP addresses or ASes that a cookie traverses. All of the cookies spend at least 12% of their time at a Tor IP address, with the maximum being 83%.

Using the Tor network hides the network origin of a user, addressing one aspect of online anonymity. However, the use of cookies may still reveal user activity patterns and potentially user network origins, e.g., if a user does not clear cookies prior to using the Tor network. To mitigate such privacy threats, users can install Torbutton [7] to manage their identifying information, for example.

5.3 Detecting Cookie-Forwarding Attacks

Based on the host mobility patterns derived from our analysis, we launch an investigation into abnormal user activities that include 28,208 unique user accounts, provided by the Hotmail web-mail service. These events are sampled over a 24-hour window in November 2010. In each event, a user submitted requests (e.g., checking new emails, listing contacts) from an IP range that was different from the one she used to log into her Hotmail account. One would imagine that this behavior can be attributed to the use of cellular networks, VPNs, or proxies. Surprisingly, we find many users exhibit quite different traveling patterns than those we learned in Sections 5.1 and 5.2.

5.3.1 Detection Methodology

We find two distinct patterns in these events that differ from those of general mobile hosts:

- One-third of the ASes associated with these events are exclusively sinks or sources. This is in contrast to normal host mobility, where the direction of travel is largely bi-directional. Table 8 lists the dominant sink ASes.

- Among the AS pairs with the largest number of these abnormal events, seven out of the top ten do not appear at all among those associated with normal hosts. These AS pairs are listed in Table 9.

Sink AS	# Cookies	Location
AS 34285	308	Seville, Spain
AS 40430	201	Miami, FL, USA
AS 14141	192	Atlanta, GA, USA
AS 19318	189	Jersey City, NJ, USA
AS 19194	174	Unknown (Satellite provider)

Table 8. Top ASes that are exclusively sinks in the abnormal events.

AS Pair	# Cookies	Affiliations
AS 766, 34285	308	RedIRIS AS (EU), SANDETEL (ES)
AS 30736, 25761	235	Easyspeedy Net. (DK), Staminus Comm. (US)
AS 30736, 40430	201	Colo4jax (US)
AS 30736, 1421	198	WANSecurity (US)
AS 30736, 14141	192	WireSix (US)
AS 30736, 29761	192	OC3 Net. & Web Solutions (US)
AS 30736, 19318	188	New Jersey Intl. Internet Exchange (US)

Table 9. Top AS pairs related to abnormal events.

Combining these two observations, we find that the dominant sinks in Table 8 significantly overlap with the sink ASes in Table 9. They share the common source AS 30736, located in Denmark. Upon examination, we find that there is a single IP address generating login events for a large number of users, who then submit subsequent requests from multiple ASes in the U.S., violating the geo-locality travel pattern observed in Figure 7 as well.

We find that the user login IDs associated with this particular source IP address contain more suspicious patterns. In particular, they are groups of bot-user accounts all registered on the same day in November 2010, with the same user age, location information (country, state), and scripted naming patterns. Among the top five dominantly sink ASes, four of them are used by these bot groups to submit requests.

Sink AS	# IP	# Req.	# Acct.	Location
AS 14141	12	262	192	Atlanta, GA
AS 19194	10	225	174	Unknown
AS 19318	11	242	189	Jersey City, NJ
AS 40430	12	269	201	Miami, FL
AS 25761	14	324	235	Fullerton, CA
AS 1421	10	265	198	Bordentown, NJ
AS 29761	10	244	192	Los Angeles, CA
AS 30058	10	261	180	Woodstock, IL
AS 18779	10	246	180	San Francisco, CA

Table 10. Statistics for detected bot-user groups.

By examining all the sink ASes with source AS 30736 in these events, we find a total of 9 bot-user groups, corresponding to 9 sink ASes geographically distributed over the U.S. The activities between some of these ASes are subtle, and would not have been detected without leveraging the normal host mobility patterns described in Section 5.1.

5.3.2 Cookie-Forwarding Bot Users

Table 10 lists the statistics for the 9 detected bot-user groups. Each of these groups includes around 190 users. A different /24 subnet is associated with each user group that submit requests without explicit login activities from the same subnet. For each /24, the sink IP rotates among 10 to 14 addresses.

From a more recent user login dataset collected by Hotmail in January 2011, we find over 75,000 email accounts associated with the suspicious source IP address in Denmark, all exhibiting similar patterns to the 9 groups we discovered. Manual investigation by Hotmail shows that these accounts were used by attackers for the purpose of receiving and testing spam. After these accounts are logged into from one machine (i.e., one IP address), their cookies are forwarded to multiple locations so that further requests can be submitted in a distributed fashion during the validity period of the cookies, which is 24 hours in our case.

There are at least two possible explanations for such malicious cookie-forwarding activities. First, some web-mail providers identify an account as suspicious if it performs logins from multiple geographic locations within a short time interval. By forwarding cookies to other locations through a private communication channel, attackers can successfully offload the requests to distributed hosts without them performing explicit user logins, hence reducing the likelihood of detection. Second, as a preparation step in launching session-hijacking attacks on real user accounts (e.g., [6]), attackers may be testing the effectiveness of forwarding cookies via stealthy communication channels.

Although the user accounts we identified were all newly created, it is possible that attackers can employ hijacked cookies stolen from actual users and forward them to botnet hosts in the future. Understanding normal host mobility patterns can help detect such stealthy attacks.

6 Related Work

Many efforts on tracking hosts focus on identifying specific hardware characteristics, such as radio frequency [23, 34, 18] or driver [21]. Identifiers such as network names or the IP addresses of frequently accessed services also enable host fingerprinting [32]. However, these approaches require the observer to be in close physical proximity to the target host.

Remote host fingerprinting can leverage packet-level information to identify the differences in software systems [2, 4, 5] or hardware devices [28]. Other works on tracking web clients require probing hosts' system configurations [20] or the installation order of browser plug-ins [31]. Persistent browser cookies [3, 36] have also been proposed; these systems store several copies of a cookie in different locations and formats, so that they cannot be removed by standard methods.

Compared with these efforts, our work focuses on studying the effectiveness and implications of tracking hosts using existing identifiers, without requiring new information or probes. Although the issue of privacy leakage has been repeatedly discussed, e.g., personally identifiable information in online social networks [29, 30], there has been limited study using large-scale datasets. Our work uses month-long datasets from a large search engine and a popular email provider to quantify the amount of host-identifying information revealed by a variety of common identifiers. To the best of our knowledge, we are also the first to demonstrate applications of host tracking to analyze cookie churn in web services and to detect suspicious cookie-forwarding activities.

Apart from its privacy implications, understanding cookie churn is an important topic for estimating web user population and personalization. Previous studies mostly rely on user surveys or active user participation (e.g., by installing a software on user machines) [12, 11, 16, 14]. Their findings show that 30% to 40% of users clear cookies monthly. A separate study by Yahoo! [13] find that 40% and 60% of users have empty browser caches, so they probably have cleared cookies as well. While our results are consistent with previous findings, the approach we take requires neither user cooperation nor special content setup.

Host mobility studies have been performed in the context of wireless [17, 27, 22, 25], ad hoc [24, 26], and cellular networks [19] to obtain more accurate device moving models or to predict user locations. Simler et al. [35] studied user mobility in terms of session characteristics based on login events to a university email server in order to generate synthetic traces. Recent work [33] proposed a technique for classifying IP addresses into home and travel categories to study host travel and relocation patterns in the U.S. By studying cross-domain cookies, our work focuses on normal host mobility patterns that enable us to observe uncommon phenomena and detect malicious activities.

7 Discussion and Conclusion

In this paper, we perform a large-scale exploration of common identifiers and quantify the amount of host-identifying information that they reveal. Using month-long datasets from Hotmail and Bing, we show that common identifiers can help track hosts with high precision and recall.

Our study also informs service providers of the potential information leakage when they anonymize datasets (e.g., replacing IP addresses with IP prefixes) and release data to third-party collaborators or to the public. For example, we show that hashes of browser information (i.e., the anonymized UA strings) alone can be quite revealing when examined in one network domain. Furthermore, coarse-grained IP prefixes achieve similar host-tracking accuracy to that of precise IP address information when they are combined with hashed UA strings.

Our analysis suggests that users who do not wish to be tracked should do much more than clear cookies. Uncommon behaviors such as clearing cookies for each request may instead distinguish a host from others who do not do so. Users should take notice of their user-agent strings (e.g., modify the default setting [10]), consider the use of proxies, and possibly resort to sophisticated techniques such as anonymous routing [37]. In some cases, several of these techniques should be combined to be effective, e.g., clearing cookies in addition to the use of proxies or Tor.

Finally, despite its privacy implications, we demonstrate the security benefit of host-tracking. Given the growing concerns over account hijacking and session hijacking, we expect host fingerprinting and tracking techniques can help defend against such attacks in the future.

Acknowledgments

We are grateful to Hotmail, Bing, and Windows Update for providing us with data access that makes this study possible. We thank Zijian Zheng for his guidance and insight on cookie-churn analysis. We thank Keiji Oenoki and Hersh Dangayach for providing us with data related with cookie-forwarding attacks and for the help in the subsequent investigation. We thank the reviewers, and in particular Paul Syverson, for their suggestions of improvements to this paper.

References

[1] CookieCooker. http://www.cookiecooker.de/.

[2] Nmap free security scanner. http://nmap.org.

[3] Project details for evercookie. http://samy.pl/evercookie/.

[4] Project details for p0f. http://lcamtuf.coredump.cx/p0f.shtml.

[5] Project details for xprobe. http://sourceforge.net/projects/xprobe/.

[6] Secure your PC and website from Firesheep session hijacking. http://www.pcworld.com/businesscenter/article/210028/secure_your_pc_and_website_from_firesheep_session_hijacking.html.

[7] Tor Project: Torbutton. https://www.torproject.org/torbutton/.

[8] Tor Proxy List. http://proxy.org/tor.shtml.

[9] U. Oregon Route Views Project. http://www.routeviews.org/.

[10] User-agent switcher. https://addons.mozilla.org/en-US/firefox/addon/59/?id=59.

[11] 40% of consumers zap cookies weekly. http://www.marketingsherpa.com/!newsletters/bestofweekly-4-22-04.htm#topic1, 2004.

[12] Measuring unique visitors: Addressing the dramatic decline in accuracy of cookie-based measurement. White paper, Jupiter Research, 2005.

[13] Yahoo! user interface blog: Performance research, part 2: Browser cache usage exposed! http://yuiblog.com/blog/2007/01/04/performance-research-part-2/, 2007.

[14] Cookie corrected audience data. White paper, Quantcast Corp., 2008.

[15] Protecting consumer privacy in an era of rapid change. Federal Trade Commission Staff Report, 2010.

[16] M. Abraham, C. Meierhoefer, and A. Lipsman. The impact of cookie deletion on the accuracy of site-server and ad-server metrics: an empirical comScore study. White paper, comScore, Inc., 2007.

[17] M. Balazinska and P. Castro. Characterizing mobility and network usage in a corporate wireless local-area network. In *Intl. Conf. Mobile Systems, Applications, Services*, 2003.

[18] V. Brik, S. Banerjee, M. Gruteser, and S. Oh. Wireless device identification with radiometric signatures. In *Intl. Conf. Mobile Computing and Networking*, 2006.

[19] I. Constandache, S. Gaonkar, M. Sayler, R. Choudhury, and L. Cox. Energy-efficient localization via personal mobility profiling. In *Intl. Conf. Mobile Computing, Applications, and Services*, 2009.

[20] P. Eckersley. How unique is your web browser? In *Privacy Enhancing Technologies Symp.*, 2010.

[21] J. Franklin, D. McCoy, P. Tabriz, V. Neagoe, J. V. Randwyk, and D. Sicker. Passive data link layer 802.11 wireless device driver fingerprinting. In *USENIX Security Symp.*, 2006.

[22] J. Ghosh, M. Beal, H. Ngo, and C. Qiao. On profiling mobility and predicting locations of wireless users. In *Intl. Workshop on Multi-hop ad hoc networks*, 2006.

[23] J. Hall, M. Barbeau, and E. Kranakis. Detection of transient in radio frequency fingerprinting using signal phase. In *Intl. Conf. Wireless and Optical Communications*, 2003.

[24] X. Hong, M. Gerla, G. Pei, and C. Chiang. A group mobility model for ad hoc wireless networks. In *ACM Intl. Workshop on Modeling, Analysis and Simulation of Wireless and Mobile Systems*, 1999.

[25] N. Husted and S. Myers. Mobile location tracking in metro areas: Malnets and others. In *ACM Conf. Computer and Communication Security*, 2010.

[26] A. Jardosh, E. Belding-Royer, K. Almeroth, and S. Suri. Towards realistic mobility models for mobile ad hoc networks. In *Intl. Conf. Mobile Computing and Networking*, 2003.

[27] M. Kim, D. Kotz, and S. Kim. Extracting a mobility model from real user traces. In *IEEE Infocom*, 2006.

[28] T. Kohno, A. Broido, and K. Claffy. Remote physical device fingerprinting. In *IEEE Symp. Security and Privacy*, 2005.

[29] B. Krishnamurthy and C. E. Wills. Characterizing privacy in online social networks. In *ACM Workshop on Online Social Networks*, 2008.

[30] B. Krishnamurthy and C. E. Wills. Privacy leakage in mobile online social networks. In *USENIX Conf. Online Social Networks*, 2010.

[31] J. R. Mayer. "Any person... a pamphleteer": Internet anonymity in the age of Web 2.0. Senior Thesis, Stanford University, 2009.

[32] J. Pang, B. Greenstein, R. Gummadi, S. Seshan, and D. Wetherall. 802.11 user fingerprinting. In *Intl. Conf. Mobile Computing and Networking*, 2007.

[33] A. Pitsillidis, Y. Xie, F. Yu, M. Abadi, G. Voelker, and S. Savage. How to tell an airport from a home: Techniques and applications. In *ACM Workshop on Hot Topics in Networks*, 2010.

[34] K. Rasmussen and S. Capkun. Implications of radio fingerprinting on the security of sensor networks. In *Intl. Conf. Security and Privacy in Comm. Networks*, 2007.

[35] K. Simler, S. Czerwinski, and A. Joseph. Analysis ofwide area user mobility patterns. In *IEEE Workshop on Mobile Computing Systems and Applications*, 2004.

[36] A. Soltani, S. Canty, Q. Mayo, L. Thomas, and C. Hoofnagle. Flash cookies and privacy. *SSRN preprint*, 2009.

[37] P. Syversion, D. Goldschlag, and M. Reed. Anonymous connections and onion routing. In *IEEE Symp. Security and Privacy*, 1997.

[38] Y. Xie, F. Yu, and M. Abadi. De-anonymizing the internet using unreliable IDs. In *ACM SIGCOMM*, 2009.

Appendix

A Tracking Stable Hosts

In the presence of NATs, proxies, and dynamic IP addresses, the mapping between a host and an IP address can be extremely volatile. Service providers that are interested in fingerprinting *stable* hosts may trade coverage for accuracy. We show that the binding window length can serve as a confidence measure for this purpose.

Intuitively, stable and active hosts should have longer binding windows that make them easier to track than hosts that appear infrequently or that change IP addresses often. Indeed, using UA+IP as an example, Figure 10(a) shows the increase in precision and recall with longer binding windows.

However, as we impose increasingly strict requirements on the binding window length, the percentage of fingerprints remaining decreases roughly proportionally, as shown in Figure 10(b). Half of the fingerprints have binding windows no longer than one week. We can thus explore a tradeoff between accuracy and coverage of tracking hosts using the binding window length as an adjustable parameter. In particular, Figure 10 suggests that using a binding window length of five days in practice can achieve both high precision and recall without losing significant coverage.

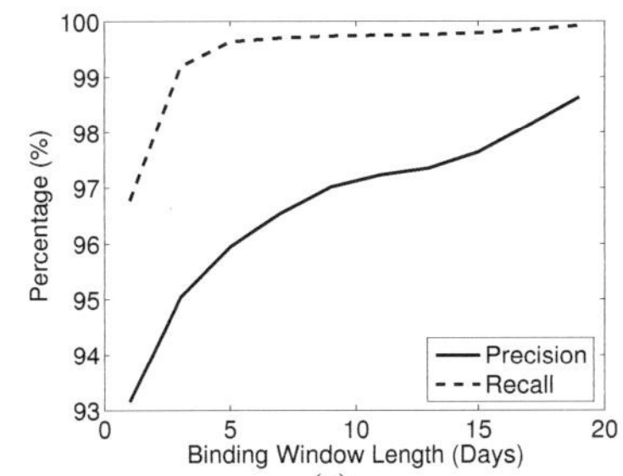

(a)

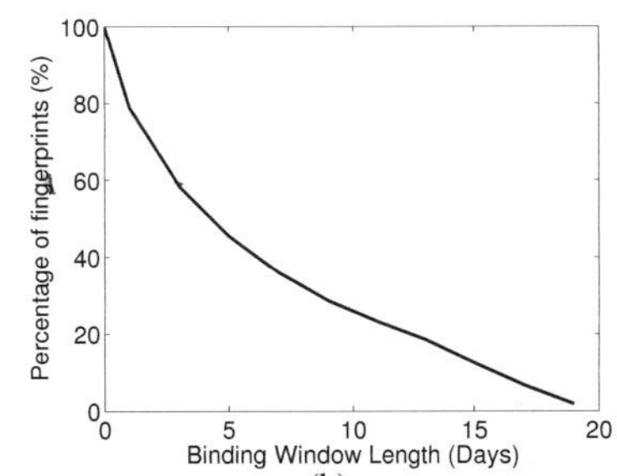

(b)

Figure 10. Binding length and accuracy tradeoff.

B Non-returning Users

For those 101,427 "one-time" non-returning users that were observed only on the first day of the Search dataset we are interested in whether this is because they stopped using the service or because they cannot be tracked. We expect users who leave the service to be less engaged than returning users. To test this hypothesis, we examine the average number of queries submitted by each CID and the percentage of CIDs that have clicked on the query results. We compare these two statistics between the set of returning users and the set of non-returning users. We consider only churned *new* CIDs in this comparison. For example, if a returning user has queries associated first with CID_1 and later with CID_2, we consider the subset of queries that correspond to CID_1 only, as they represent first-time user experience.

Table 11 shows that returning users indeed appear to

	Non-returning users	Returning users
Average number of queries per CID	4.7	7.0
Percentage of CIDs with clicks	60.73%	77.85%

Table 11. The query and click behaviors of returning and non-returning users from the first day of the log.

be more engaged in the service, generating more queries on average and are also more likely to make clicks. Overall, 77.85% of the churned new CIDs that belong to returning users have clicks, while only 60.73% of the churned new CIDs from non-returning users have clicks.

We further examine, for each CID, the percentage of search queries that resulted in clicks. For CIDs that belong to returning users, Figure 11 shows a larger percentage of queries have clicks than CIDs that belong to non-returning users. Half of the CIDs associated with returning users have clicks on 80% of their queries, while half of those associated with non-returning users have them on less than 50%.

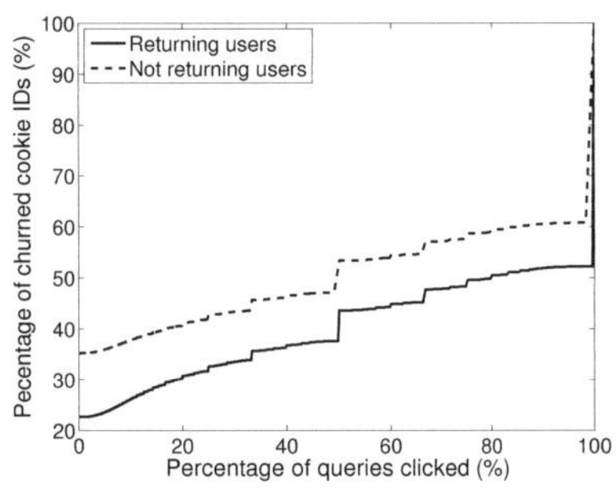

Figure 11. Cumulative distribution of the fraction of queries per CID that resulted in clicks.

Another question of interest is whether users stop using the service because they are less active and have infrequent online activities. To quantify the degree of activity of the non-returning users, we measure the time interval and the number of login events between the last Bing search query and the last Hotmail login event that fall within the host's binding windows, shown in Figure 12. We find that though users in our data may have left the search service, many of them have continued online activities. More than 80% of these users are active even after 25 days (Figure 12(a)), and around 60% of them logged in more than 40 times (Figure 12(b)).

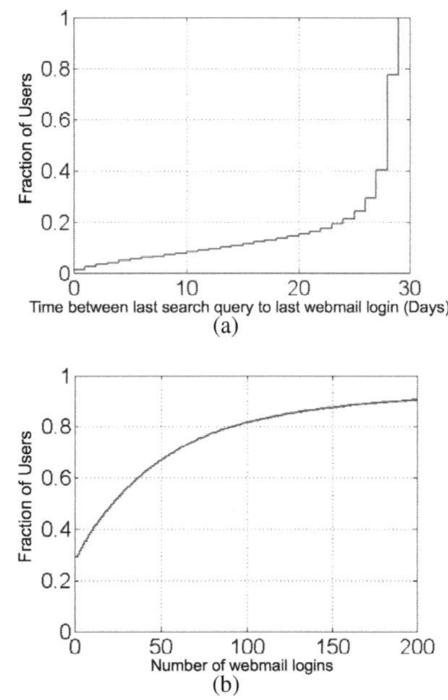

Figure 12. (a) The time between the last Bing search query and last Hotmail login. (b) The number of Hotmail logins after the last Bing search query.

Chrome Extensions: Threat Analysis and Countermeasures

Lei Liu, Xinwen Zhang*, Guanhua Yan*, and Songqing Chen

George Mason University
Huawei R&D Center
Los Alamos National Laboratory

NDSS'12

* Does not represent employer's opinion

Attacks via Extensions

- Extension is the vehicle for increasing attacks
- BHO/add-on is the one of the techniques used by many spyware writers in IE.
  - Kida et al'05, CERT'05, Egele'07, Li'07, Guha'11
- Abusing of Firefox extensions has been widely recognized and studied in literature
  - Defcon'09, Ter-Louw'08, Dhawan'09, Bandhakav'10, Djeric'10, Guha'11

Attacks via Chrome Extensions

- Buggy Chrome extensions have been identified recently
  - 27 out of 100 leak data
    - http://www.adrienneporterfelt.com/blog/?p=226

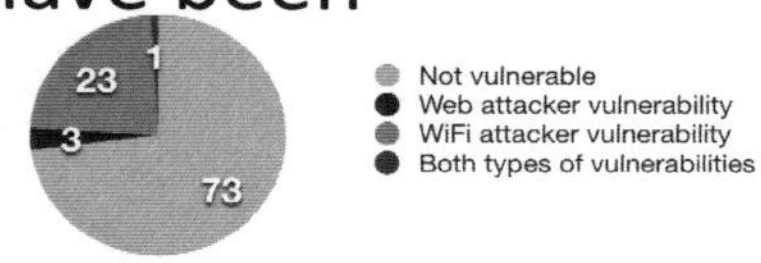

- Malicious extensions have appeared

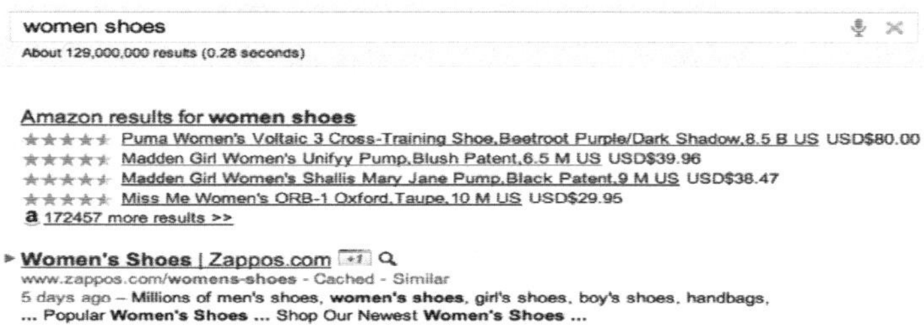

Problem Statement

- Why Chrome extension?
  - Chrome has built-in security model for browser architecture and extension
- Is current Chrome extension architecture good enough?
  - Particularly with the consideration of malicious extensions
- Easy to launch malicious extensions:
  - It is a difficult task to sanitize rapidly increasing extensions in Google Chrome Web Store with slow reviewing process
  - Users are free to download/install extensions from many (known/unknown) host servers
  - Strong incentive for attackers, e.g.,
    - harvest sensitive content in web pages
    - Modify web search content
- Google takes actions against malicious extension developers
  - singup fee for developers
  - Domain verification for developers
- Problem: Can we have a technical solution?
  - Or improvement of current permission model for better security with malware extension?

Contributions

- We demonstrate several attacks with malicious Chrome extensions through experimental implementation
- We do security analysis of the permission model of Chrome extension
  - With the assumption of malicious extensions
- We propose security enhanced extension permission model and enforcement mechanism
  - Following the principles of least privilege and separation of privilege in more strict way

Chrome Extension Architecture

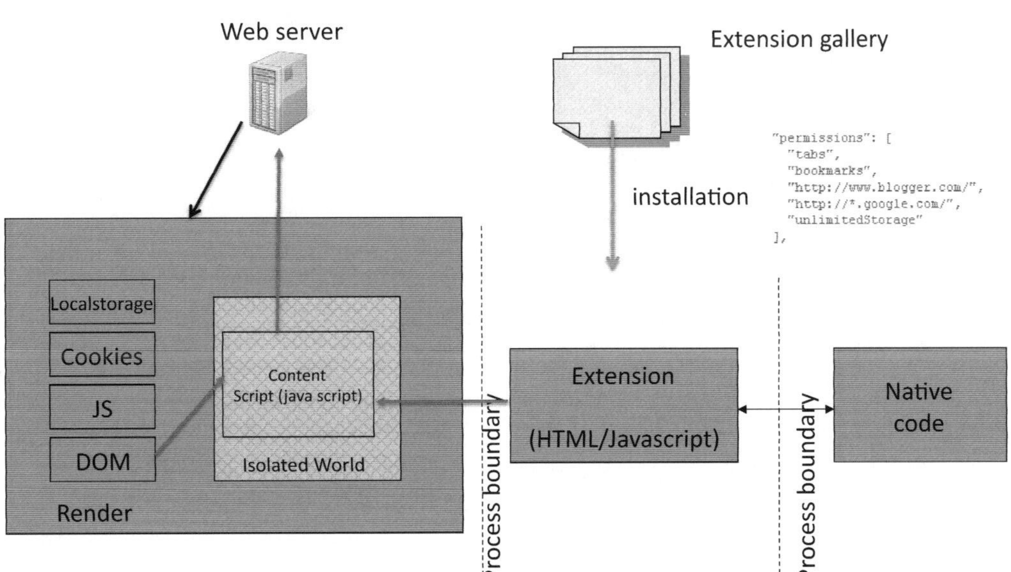

Chrome Extension Security Model

- Least Privilege
  - Pre-defined permission set (e.g.,. To access web sites, browser tab, bookmarks, history, ...)
  - Each extension declares permissions required
  - User authorizes permissions at installation time
- Privilege Separation
  - Different permissions for different components of extension
  - Content script can interact with web content, not browser modules
  - Extension core has more privileges, but insulated from web pages
- Strong isolation
  - Same origin policy
    - Each extension has unique origin
    - Accessing other origins requires cross-site permissions
    - Inject content script requires cross-site permissions
  - Process-level isolation: extension core runs in separated process from renderer and browser
  - Within a renderer process, content script runs in *isolated world* from Javascript of web page

Chrome Extension Trust Model

- The main trust model of Chrome extension assumes trusted but buggy extensions
- But malicious web pages
- Therefore the security objectives are mainly for restricting web pages to access browser resources via extensions
- And confine the damage propagation if possible

Experimental Attacks

- We develop a malicious extension as a bot
  - from Chrome 7 to the latest
  - does email spamming, DDoS, and phishing attacks easily
    - Through attacking web pages
  - Receive commands from bot master with built-in update mechanism of Chrome extension
    - No security check for update

Email Spamming

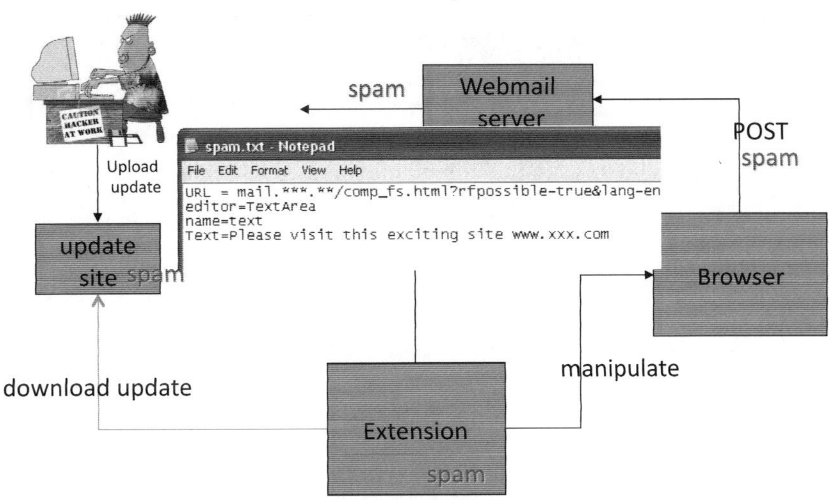


```
"permissions":  [
   "tabs", "http://*/*", "https://*/*"
]
```

Password Sniffing

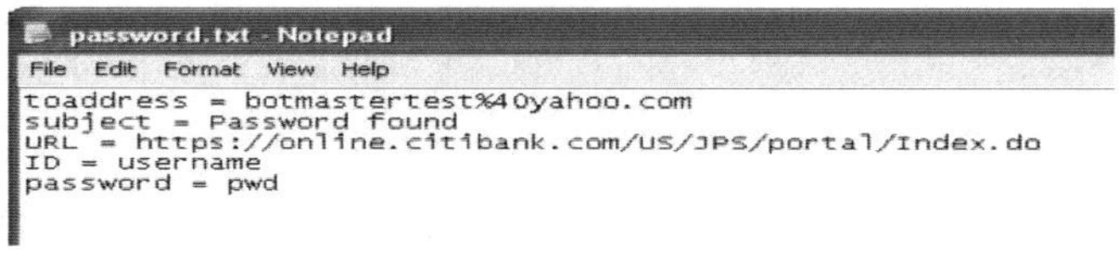

DDoS Attack

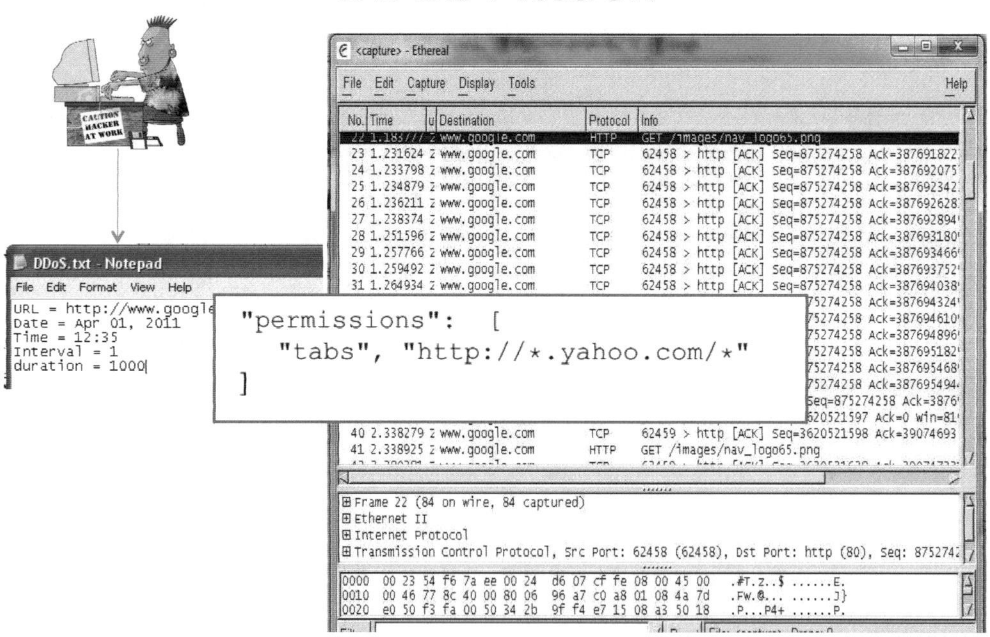

Security Analysis

- Trust Model:
  - We assume browser kernel and pulgins are trustworthy
  - Sandbox mechanism provided by OS works well
  - Native code for extensions is sandboxed
  - Web apps are trusted
- Threat model: malicious extensions
  - Extension core
  - Content scripts

Cross-site Forgery with Content Script

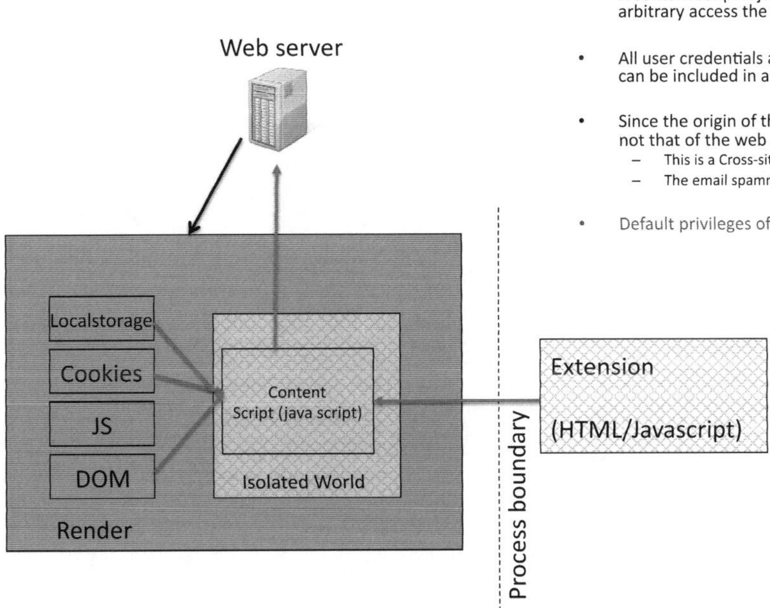

- A content script injected into web page can arbitrary access the origin of the page
- All user credentials associated with the origin can be included in an HTTP req
- Since the origin of the content script is usually not that of the web page
  - This is a Cross-site Forgery Req
  - The email spamming attack leverages this
- Default privileges of content script are not least

Cross-site Requests with Extension Core

- Cross-site reqs via content scripts through extension core
- The extension core can file cross-site HTTP reqs to multiple origins
  - Cross-site permissions are authorized in order to inject content scripts.

- Default privileges of extension core are not least
- No differentiated permission of extension core and content script
  - Inject scripts vs. cross-site reqs

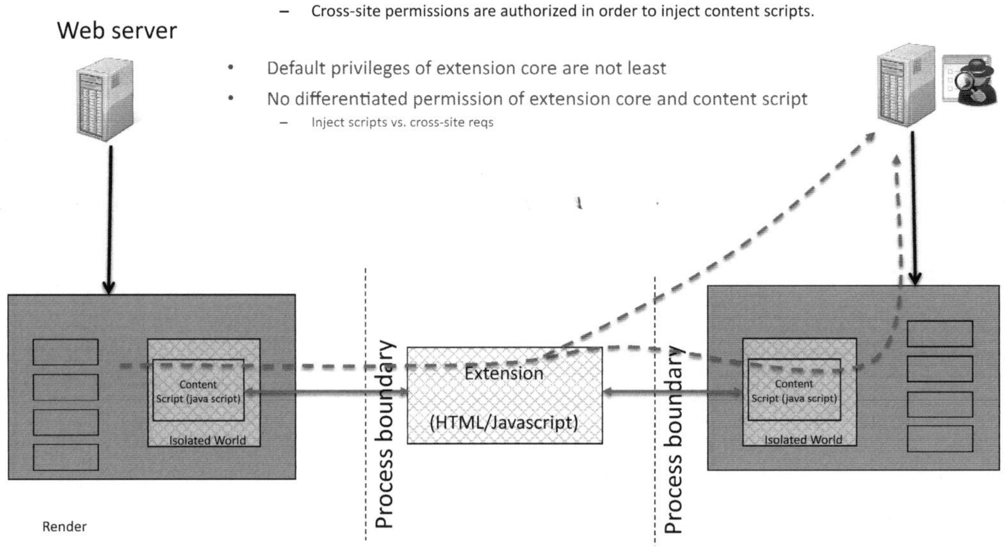

Cross-site Requests with Content Scripts

- Without cross-site permission, a running content script can only make HTTP reqs to the origin of the tab page

- However, since content script has full privileges of DOM, it can file unlimited cross-site HTTP reqs to arbitrary origin, e.g.,
  - Insert iframe
  - Load img
  - Modify src of DOM objects
  - With user credentials included in the req

- Loading of new DOM objects results in cross-site reqs

- Privilege to access DOM is not least for content script

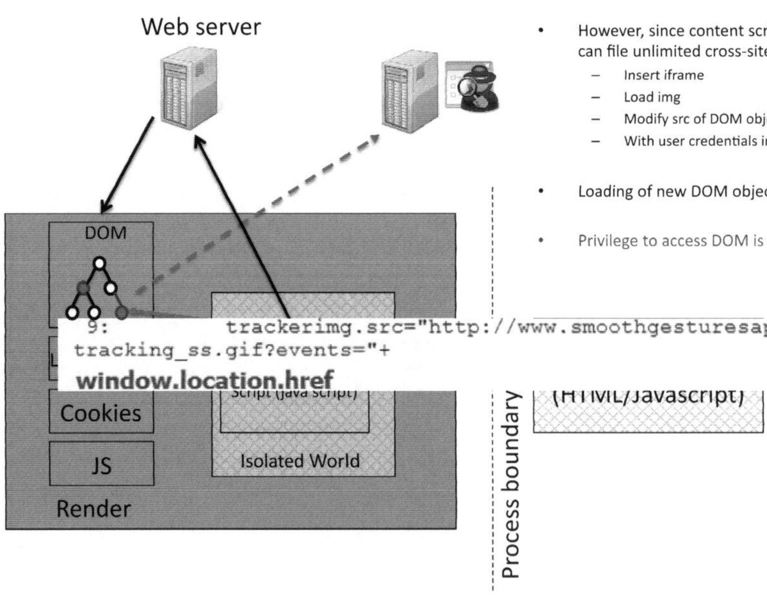

Undifferentiated Permissions

- An extension may inject content script to many origins
  - It does not need to file HTTP reqs to all origins
  - But only to a dedicated one, e.g., a translation web service
- When an origin is assigned to extension, all components get the full privileges
  - Extension core can file cross-site reqs freely
  - Content script can arbitrarily modify the DOM, and file cross-sit reqs
- Privilege separation is not fine-grained enough

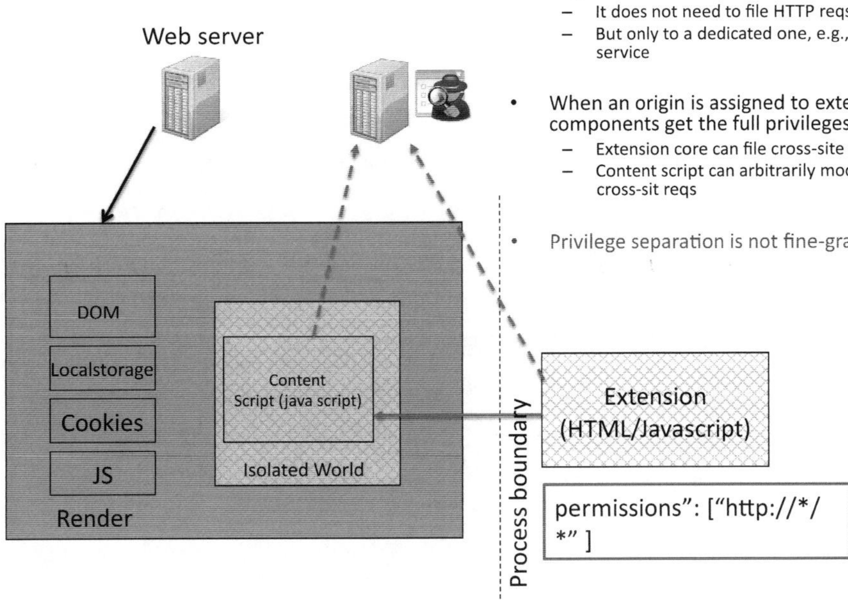

19 out of 30 most popular extensions have this type of over privileges

Security Enhanced Chrome Extensions

- Micro-privilege management
- Differentiate DOM elements with sensitivity

Micro-privilege Management

- More fine-grained permission definition and enforcement
- Fine-grained permission differentiation for extension core and content script
  - Permission specs are separated from different components
- Least default privileges
  - Content script cannot introduce new origin to DOM
  - no HTTP req to tab origin

	Permissions	Example Permission Spec
Extension core	inject_script cross_site	"http://*/*", "https://*/*" "http://www.translate.com"
Content script	sensitivity_level same_origin_request new_origin	"medium" "false" "http://www.translate.com"

Example Permission Spec

- Permissions for a translation extension:

```
"extension_core_permissions": [
  "inject_script":[
      "http://*/*", "https://*/*"
  ]
  "cross_site":[
      "tabs", "http://www.translate.com"
  ]
 ]
"content_script_permissions": [
  "sensitivity_level":[medium]
  "same_origin_request":[false]
  "new_origin":[
      "http://www.translate.com"
  ]
 ]
```

Differentiating DOM Elements

- To further reduce possible sensitive data leakage by content script, DOM elements can be differentiated with sensitivity levels
- A web app developer can identify sensitive information in a web page, e.g.,
  - High level data: only can flow to web origin
  - Medium level: may flow to authorized origins
  - Low level (default): can flow to any origin
- An extension developer can specify permissions accordingly:
  - E.g., HIGH for username/pw, MEDIUM for other user info

Implementation

- We have implemented the micro-privilege management and spec.
- For DOM sensitivity, we develop a helper extension (trusted):
  - To identify and label sensitive DOM elements
  - Re-write DOM element properties
    - According to configurable dictionary
  - Chrome enforces permission check based on extension manifest
  - Explicitly mark sensitive info by web app developer is not practical right now

Evaluations

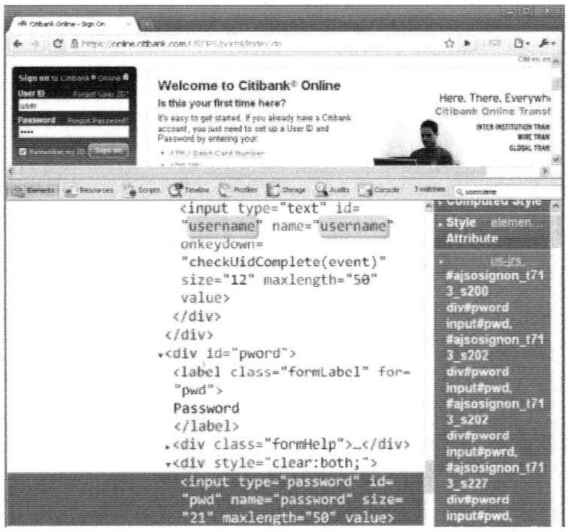

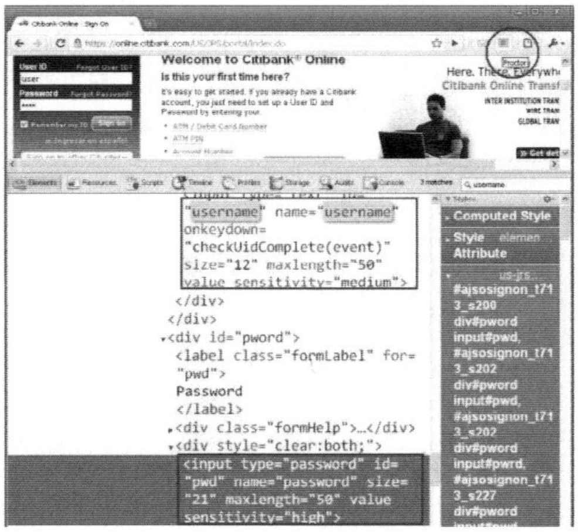

Evaluation

- We selected 30 most popular extensions from Google extension gallery
  - 24 of them have granted network access
  - 19 of them request higher privileges than necessary (http://*/*)
- Our implementation easily changes their spec to reduce privileges

TABLE II
SUMMARY OF TOP 30 CHROME EXTENSION PRIVILEGE ANALYSIS

rank	name	over-privileged?	rank	name	over-privileged?
1	AdBlock	✓	16	RSS Subscription Extension	✓
2	Google Mail Checker	✗	17	Clip to Evernote	✓
3	FastestChrome	✓	18	Google Chrome to Phone Extension	✓
4	IE Tab	✗	19	Webpage Screenshot	✓
5	Browser Button for AdBlock	✓	20	Xmarks Bookmark Sync	✓
6	DocsPDF/PowerPoint Viewer	✗	21	SmileyCentral	✗
7	Downloads	✗	22	SocialPlus!	✗
8	Google Translate	✓	23	Facebook for Google Chrome	✗
9	Facebook Photo Zoom	✗	24	Speed Dial	✓
10	Google Dictionary	✓	25	Google Voice	✗
11	Turn Off the Lights	✓	26	Cooliris	✓
12	Firebug Lite	✓	27	FlashBlock	✓
13	Download Master	✓	28	Smooth Gestures	✗
14	Google Mail Checker Plus	✓	29	Awesome Screenshot	✓
15	Adblock Plus	✓	30	WOT	✗

Evaluation

- Our implementation blocks all experimental attacks on the bot extension.

TABLE III
RE-EVALUATION OF BOT ATTACKS

attack	result	reason
spamming	✗	unauthorized cross-site requests are completely blocked
DDoS	✗	unauthorized cross-site requests are completely blocked
password sniffing	✗	Proctor forbids sensitive information access
cross-site forgery	✗	content scripts are not allowed to make same origin request
unlimited cross-site requests by content scripts	✗	content scripts cannot change the `src` property of DOM elements to unauthorized origins

Conclusions

- Demonstrated spamming, phishing, and DDoS attacks with implemented Chrome extensions
- Analyzed the permissions model that causes these problems
- Proposed security enhanced permission model and enforcement for Chrome extension architecture
  - Micro-privileged permission management and spec
  - Differentiate content script's permission with DOM sensitivity levels

Thank You!

Q&A

Ghost Domain Names: Revoked Yet Still Resolvable

Jian Jiang, Jinjin Liang
Network Research Center
Tsinghua University
{jiang-j08, liangjj09}@mails.tsinghua.edu.cn

Kang Li
Department of Computer Science
University of Georgia
kangli@cs.uga.edu

Jun Li
University of Oregon
Carlos III University of Madrid
Institute IMDEA Networks
lijun@cs.uoregon.edu

Haixin Duan*
Network Research Center
Tsinghua University
duanhx@tsinghua.edu.cn

Jianping Wu
Network Research Center
Tsinghua University
jianping@cernet.edu.cn

Abstract

Attackers often use domain names for various malicious purposes such as phishing, botnet command and control, and malware propagation. An obvious strategy for preventing these activities is deleting the malicious domain from the upper level DNS servers. In this paper, we show that this is insufficient. We demonstrate a vulnerability affecting the large majority of popular DNS implementations which allows a malicious domain name to stay resolvable long after it has been removed from the upper level servers. Our experiments with 19,045 open DNS servers show that even one week after a domain name has been revoked and its TTL expired, more than 70% of the servers will still resolve it. Finally, we discuss several strategies to prevent this attack.

1. Introduction

The Domain Name System (DNS), which provides a global mapping service between Internet domain names and IP addresses, is one of the most important components of the Internet. While primarily used for legitimate purposes, domain names have also been heavily leveraged by malicious activities such as phishing, malware propagation, and botnet command and control. A major endeavour in stopping these malicious activities has thus been identifying and deleting malicious domain names. For example, recent domain name takedown efforts have successfully shut down large scale botnets such as Waledac and Rustock [7].

While these successes have demonstrated that domain name revocation is effective in fighting against malicious activities, in this paper we show that removing malicious domains from domain registry is not enough to revoke the domain and IP mapping at the global scale. In fact, an attacker can keep their domain names continuously resolvable to attacker-controlled IP addresses—even after the original delegation data has been removed from the domain registry and the original time-to-live (TTL) period has expired. Because of the elusive nature of these domain names (i.e. revoked but still resolvable), we call them *ghost domain names*.

Ghost domain names are results of a vulnerability in the DNS cache update policy which prevents effective domain name revocation. The normal process of revoking a domain name from the global DNS system includes two steps: first the removal of the delegation data at the domain registry, and second the removal of all the cached copies throughout DNS resolvers. The first step is based on an explicit action, and the second one is implicitly governed by the TTL value associated with the delegation data. Although the TTL-based implicit revocation mechanism is not timely, it is still acceptable if a revoked domain name can be eventually cleared from every DNS resolver after the specified time according to the TTL value. Unfortunately, DNS allows a cached entry to be overwritten at a DNS resolver and the cache update logic is not strictly defined. An attacker can manipulate the cached delegation data and extend the TTL value. The attacker only needs to generate a recursive query to be resolved by the authoritative server (controlled by the attacker) before the TTL expires, and piggyback new delegation data in the crafted response from the authoritative server to the resolver (the victim). The new delegation data still resolves to an IP address controlled by the attacker but with new TTL value, and the attacker can continuously keep the delegation data alive in the resolver by repeating

*Corresponding author

the same attack.

This vulnerability is different from the notorious cache poisoning attacks [4]. While cache poisoning attacks compromise the integrity of DNS data by forging DNS responses, to exploit the ghost domain vulnerability, the attacker only needs to perform two legitimate actions: 1) querying the victim DNS resolver for a ghost domain to force the victim resolver to query the attacker's authoritative server before the delegation data expires, and 2) piggybacking new delegation data in the response from the authoritative server to the victim resolver. Because the two actions are seemingly legitimate, the vulnerability has not been addressed by the previous patches for cache poisoning.

Our study confirms that, until the writing of this paper, the majority of public DNS servers and up-to-date versions of popular DNS implementations, including the leading vendor BIND, are vulnerable. We believe that this vulnerability has not been suitably acknowledged by the networking and security community. Through experiments with 19,045 open DNS resolvers, we demonstrate that over 93% of experimental DNS resolvers are vulnerable and a large scale exploitation is practical. we have successfully created and kept ghost domain names in over 70% of experimental resolvers after one week of domain name revocation and TTL expiration.

This paper also discusses various approaches to addressing the problem of ghost domain names. Our study finds three DNS implementations, namely Unbound, MaraDNS and Microsoft DNS, have non-vulnerable versions. By comparing them, we find that although Unbound's strategy is simple in terms of implementation, MaraDNS's strategy is more fundamental — tightening the policy for delegation data update. We recommend that the DNS community adopt this defense strategy, and moreover consider a rigorous definition of DNS cache update policy.

The rest of this paper is organized as follows. We review necessary background of DNS in section 2. We then describe technical details of the vulnerability in section 3. In section 4 we present our exploitation experiments and analyze experimental results. We then discuss defenses and possible issues in section 5. Finally, we highlight the related work in section 6, and conclude the paper in section 7.

2. Background

In this section, we briefly summarize how DNS works. We focus on the concepts and details related to the vulnerability that we will present in the next section. Please refer to the DNS specifications for detailed descriptions [20] [21].

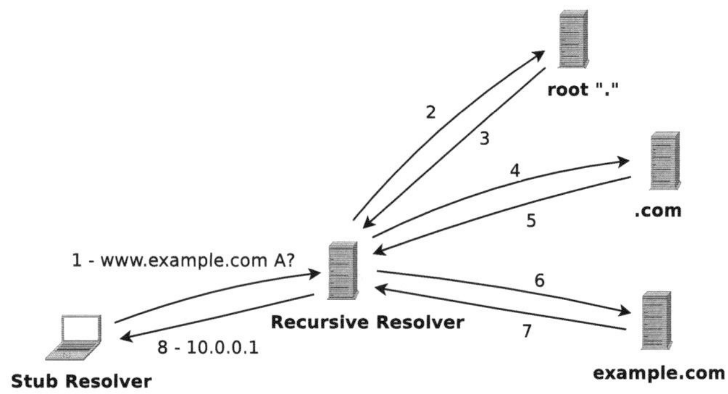

Figure 1. An example of DNS resolution process.

2.1. DNS Overview

DNS is organized around a hierarchical tree structure. Each domain name is composed of labels separated by dots. The domain name tree is divided into a series of *zones* based on the individual labels. Each zone represents a domain, and the server which holds the DNS data for all names under it is called the zone's *authoritative server*. An authoritative server may also delegate the authority of its sub-domains to other servers, which then serve as authoritative servers respectively for the sub-domains.

To a DNS client (*stub resolver*), a typical DNS name resolution process involves the client's local *recursive resolver* going through a series of queries to the authoritative servers of sub-domains along the tree of DNS. For example, Figure 1 shows a DNS resolution process of `www.example.com` through the three corresponding authoritative servers for the root zone, its child `.com`, and the next level sub-domain `example.com` respectively. Briefly, a stub resolver first requests a recursive resolver to resolve the domain `www.example.com`. Assuming the recursive resolver has no previous information about the domain, it will contact external servers in an iterative way. This iterative process includes a query to a root server (step 2) which redirects the recursive resolver to the `.com` authoritative server (step 3). Then the recursive resolver contacts the `.com` server (step 4), and from the reply it gets the information of authoritative server of `example.com` (step 5). The recursive resolver queries the authoritative server of `example.com` (step 6) which responds the IP addresses (step 7). The recursive resolver at the end forwards the response back to the stub resolver (step 8). During the process, the recursive resolver also caches received DNS data for further resolutions.

2.2. DNS Data Structure

Since the vulnerability we will present involves carefully crafted DNS responses, we also provide a brief summary about the DNS resource record and the DNS response format as background.

DNS data is stored using a basic data structure called *Resource Record* (RR). Every RR record is a five-tuple $< name, class, type, TTL, data >$, where $< name, class, type >$ serves as the key of *data*, *TTL* is a time-to-live value in seconds that limits the lifespan of cached copies. There are many *types* of RR records. Specifically, an `A` record gives the IP address of the name, and an `NS` record is another name that indicates the name of the server which has been delegated to serve as the domain's authoritative server. An `NS` record together with a corresponding `A` record are also known as *delegation data*. Delegation data points to the authoritative server of a sub-domain and provides its IP address as well.

When a DNS server receives a query that requests one or more types of RR records of a given name, it replies with a response that consists of three sections[1]: answer section, authority section and additional section. When the current DNS server cannot directly resolve the name in question, the authority section and the additional section, also known as referral sections, are used to carry an `NS` record and a corresponding `A` record. These records provide delegation data of a sub-domain that is closer to the name in question. The message below is a sample response of Step 5 in Figure 1.

```
;; ANSWER SECTION

;; AUTHORITY SECTION
example.com.    86400    IN  NS   ns.example.com.

;; ADDITIONAL SECTION
ns.example.com. 86400    IN  A    10.0.0.1
```

After a DNS resolver receives a DNS response, it then can cache the resource records contained in the response. Before the resource records expire based on the associated TTL value, the resolver does not need to go through the steps illustrated in Figure 1 to obtain the same records. For the sample response above, for example, the resolver can cache the delegation data of `example.com` for 86,400 seconds.

2.3. DNS Cache Update Policy

DNS cache is critical to its scalability and performance, and it can significantly reduce the overhead of authoritative servers and the response latency. However, it also poses many security threats. In the infamous *DNS cache poisoning* attack [4], an attacker can inject bogus RR records into DNS resolvers to redirect users to malicious addresses. For a number of reasons, DNS is inherently vulnerable to this type of attacks. For example, the connectionless nature of DNS protocol makes it vulnerable to spoofing attacks. An attacker can also use a compromised or malicious authoritative server to piggyback bogus records in referral sections of a DNS response.

The research and DNS communities have adopted several techniques to harden DNS against cache poisoning attacks. These techniques can be categorized into two classes: techniques for increasing forgery resistance and techniques for tightening cache update policy. Here we focus on the second class of techniques, specifically, the *bailiwick rule* [31] and the *credibility rule* [13]. The bailiwick rule checks referral sections in a DNS response to see if its contained RR records are in the authority range of the asked authoritative server. For example, if a DNS response comes from authoritative server of `.com` and contains a `NS` record of `.net`, then this record is considered as "out-of-bailiwick" and should be discarded. The credibility rule gives each RR record a different trust level according to where the response comes from and in which section the record is contained. Only when a new RR record has a higher or equal trust level should a cached RR record be overwritten.

Unfortunately, both the bailiwick rule and the credibility rule have limitations. The bailiwick rule does not have a standard specification and depends on implementation. While the credibility rule specifies when cached entries can be overwritten, it still could be exploited for malicious purposes. For example, Dan Kaminsky reported a novel cache poisoning attack [18] that leverages non-existent names to increase spoofing efficiency, and in particular, exploits the credibility rule to overwrite cached entries by piggybacked referral sections. Some DNS vendors have responded to this attack by enhancing the validation of any RR records included in the additional section. However, in the next section, we demonstrate that even with such validation, the DNS cache update policy is still insecure.

3. The DNS Name Revocation Vulnerability

We illustrate the DNS name revocation vulnerability in this section, focusing on how an attacker can generate and maintain a ghost domain name.

To completely revoke a domain name (e.g., `phishing.com`), the delegation data for the name must be deleted from the authoritative servers of the parent zone of the name (e.g., `.com`), and sufficient time must be allowed for every recursive resolver to remove the cached delegation data for the name when the data expires. However, the current bailiwick and credibility rules that govern the overwriting of cached DNS resource records do not prevent an attacker from illegally renewing

[1] A DNS response also contains a question section copied from the original request, which we ignored for simplicity.

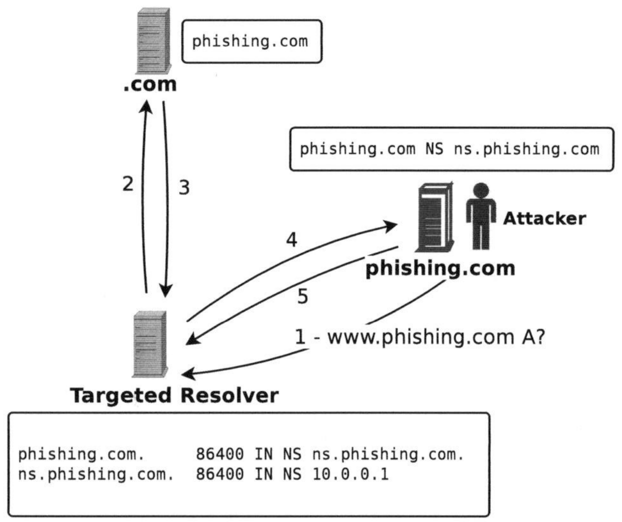

(a) Before phishing.com is deleted, the attacker pulls the delegation data for phishing.com into the victim DNS resolver.

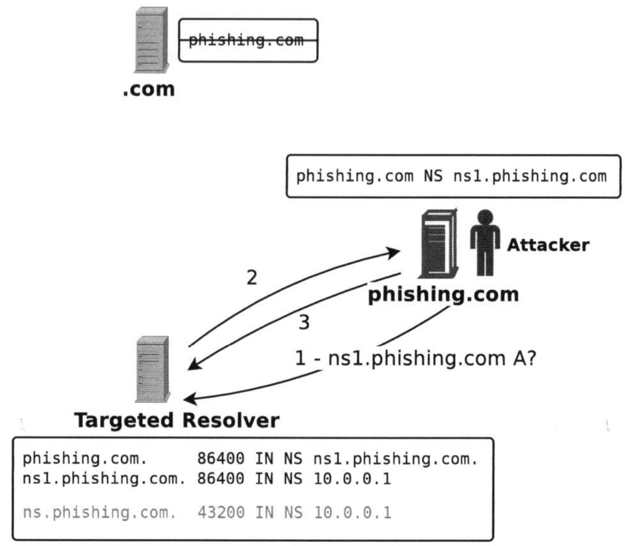

(b) After phishing.com is deleted, the attacker manipulates the victim resolver to keep the delegation data in its cache.

Figure 2. An example ghost domain name (phishing.com) attack.

cached delegation data, even after the data has been deleted from the parent zone. An attacker can extend the TTL (time-to-live) value of the cached delegation data, therefore keeping a malicious domain (such as phishing.com) continuously resolvable.

Figure 2 shows a typical ghost domain name scenario, where an attacker manages to keep the delegation data of phishing.com in a victim recursive resolver. We assume that the attacker has registered a domain name phishing.com at the authoritative server of .com. Although this server is out of the attacker's control, the attacker runs and controls the authoritative server of phishing.com.

Two phases of establishing a ghost domain name are involved:

- **Phase 1: Caching the delegation data of a domain name.** The attacker targets a DNS resolver and requests it to resolve a name under phishing.com, say www.phishing.com. During the resolution process, the authoritative server of .com provides the victim resolver with the delegation data of phishing.com, such as:

```
;; ANSWER SECTION

;; AUTHORITY SECTION
phishing.com.      86400   IN  NS   ns.phishing.com.

;; ADDITIONAL SECTION
ns.phishing.com. 86400     IN  A    10.0.0.1
```

  The victim resolver accepts and caches the delegation data above. After 43,200 seconds, as shown in Figure 2b, phishing.com is identified as a malicious domain and deleted from .com. At this moment, however, the victim resolver can still resolve phishing.com since it still caches the delegation data of phishing.com, which will not expire until another 43,200 seconds later.

- **Phase 2: Refreshing the cached delegation data of the ghost name.** At some point after phishing.com has been removed from .com but before the delegation data of phishing.com expires, the attacker manipulates the victim resolver to conduct a series of DNS operations in order to have it continue to cache the delegation data after the original expiration time. These operations follow the standard DNS protocol without violating any rules, and are as follows.

  The attacker first changes the NS record of phishing.com to a new name, say ns1.phishing.com, then queries the victim resolver for the A record of ns1.phishing.com. Based on the cached, non-expired delegation data of phishing.com, the victim resolver learns and contacts the authoritative server of phishing.com, and receives a response, such as:

```
;; ANSWER SECTION
ns1.phishing.com. 86400    IN  A    10.0.0.1

;; AUTHORITY SECTION
phishing.com.      86400   IN  NS   ns1.phishing.com.

;; ADDITIONAL SECTION
```

```
nsl.phishing.com. 86400   IN  A   10.0.0.1
```

Both the answer section and the authority section conform to the bailiwick rule. Also, according to the credibility rule, the new NS record in the authority section has the same trust level as the old NS record of phishing.com in the cache. The victim resolver will therefore overwrite the old NS record with the new one, and the A record in the answer section and the new NS record will form the complete delegation data of phishing.com, i.e.:

```
phishing.com.     86400   IN  NS nsl.phishing.com.
nsl.phishing.com. 86400   IN  A  10.0.0.1
```

Most importantly, the new delegation data has a fresh TTL value of 86,400, meaning the lifetime of phishing.com in the victim resolver starts over now for a new round of 86,400 seconds. In fact, the attacker can refresh the delegation data later again and again before the data expires, thus making phishing.com accessible from the victim resolver for a very long time. In another words, the resolver will be continuously haunted by this ghost domain name, so we also call this resolver a *haunted resolver*.

The attacker can target many other DNS resolvers and repeat the same cache-and-refresh manipulation operations as described above with these victims. As a result, the attacker can use phishing.com to host their malicious sites for a long time, and users throughout the Internet would continue to be able to resolve phishing.com to attacker-controlled IP addresses.

The success of the ghost domain name attack assumes the attacker is able to send regular DNS queries to DNS resolvers. This assumption is practical when the attacks target open resolvers; previous research [11] has shown that there are still a large number of open resolvers around the world. The assumption is also practical if the attacker is in the service range of a DNS resolver, or he can control a bot machine in that range thus can initiate DNS queries from the bot machine.

4. Experiments, Results, and Analysis

While theoretically feasible according to our discussion in Section 3, it is unclear if an attacker can indeed launch a large-scale exploitation in the real world based on the ghost domain vulnerability of DNS, and if so, to what extent and at what cost. We investigate this matter in this section, focusing on the following questions:

- How many deployed DNS resolvers and DNS implementations are vulnerable?
- What would be the cost for an attacker to maintain ghost domain names?
- For those vulnerable DNS resolvers, how long can an attacker keep their ghost domain names in these resolvers?

4.1. Experimental Setup

We collected 19,045 open DNS resolvers from the query log of a busy authoritative server, also with the help of the authors of [28]. Table 1 shows how these resolvers are distributed around different geographic regions and different autonomous systems (AS).

Region	Count	Percentage
Japan	2479	13.01
USA	2471	12.97
Russian	1987	10.43
China	1742	9.15
Taiwan	1093	5.74
Germany	1020	5.36
Poland	547	2.87
Britain	546	2.87
Italy	512	2.69
HK	348	1.93
Total 161 regions		

(a) Regions

AS number	Count	Percentage
3462	628	3.29
538	455	2.52
4713	384	2.38
4134	351	2.01
1659	261	1.84
4837	257	1.37
4732	200	1.34
17506	164	1.05
9600	115	0.86
2907	106	0.60
Total 5474 ASes		

(b) Autonomous Systems (ASes)

Table 1. Statistics of DNS resolvers used in our experiments.

We conducted several experiments using these resolvers. We registered a domain name ghostdomain.info, and created ten sub-domains ([1-10].ghostdomain.info). We then conducted the Phase-1 operations (as described in Section 3) with every resolver we collected, so that they all have a cached entry for every sub-domain of ghostdomain.info. After four hours, we simultaneously remove all sub-domains from the authoritative server of ghostdomain.info, except for one of the ten sub-domains, 1.ghostdomain.info. We then periodically conduct the Phase-2 operations (as described in Section 3) for *one* week on every resolver for the rest nine sub-domains, i.e., `[2-10].ghostdomain.info`. Each of these nine sub-domains has a different parameter setting for their domain names with regard to the original TTL value (1800, 3600, and 14400 seconds)[2] and the refreshing interval for Phase-2 operations (TTL/2, TTL/4, and TTL/8).

During the entire week, every ten minutes we probe every resolver to see if the cached entry of a sub-domain is still alive at every resolver, in order to learn the normal behavior after a domain name is revoked by testing `1.ghostdomain.info`, and how long a ghost domain name (`[2-10].ghostdomain.info`) can survive in every resolver. Every ten minutes we also check if every resolver can resolve `www.google.com` to make sure every resolver is still reachable and functioning.

4.2. Vulnerable Public DNS Servers and Popular DNS Implementations

Using `ghostdomain.info` under our control, we tested how public DNS servers and popular DNS implementations may be susceptible to the ghost domain name vulnerability. We discover that the distribution of the vulnerability is wide.

First, as shown in Table 2, we tested ten well-known public DNS servers from five service providers. Among tested servers, only the two from Google were not vulnerable. Since Google's DNS implementation was not open source, we could not know exactly how it avoided this vulnerability.

As shown in Table 3, we also chose six popular DNS vendors based on a recent DNS survey [30] and tested if they were vulnerable: *BIND, DJB dnscache, Unbound, PowerDNS, MaraDNS* and *Microsoft DNS*. For each vendor, we first tested its latest version. For those which were not vulnerable, we then tested their previous versions to see at which version the vulnerability got addressed. Five out of nine implementations, including the latest version from the leading vendor BIND, were vulnerable. We also found that three vendors had non-vulnerable versions, and we will discuss their defense strategies in Section 5.

[2]An attacker can set a very large TTL value for the delegation data of a malicious domain so that they can stay in cache for a very long time, even without launching the ghost domain name attack. But most DNS implementations have a maximum TTL limitation; they might force a DNS resolver to reset the TTL value of a cached entry, or even simply discard the entry if the original TTL exceeds the maximum TTL value allowed. We have made sure the TTL values we used here are less than the maximum TTL value allowed in DNS resolvers that we experiment with.

Service Provider	IP Address	Vulnerable?
Google	8.8.8.8	No
	8.8.4.4	No
DNS Advantage	156.154.70.1	Yes
	156.154.71.1	Yes
OpenDNS	208.67.222.222	Yes
	208.67.220.220	Yes
Norton	198.153.192.1	Yes
	198.153.194.1	Yes
GTEI DNS	4.2.2.1	Yes
	4.2.2.2	Yes

Table 2. Vulnerability testing of public DNS servers.

DNS Vendor	Version	Vulnerable?
BIND	9.8.0-P4	Yes
DJB dnscache	1.05	Yes
Unbound	1.4.11	No
	1.4.7	Yes
PowerDNS	Recursor 3.3	Yes
MaraDNS	Deadwood-3.0.03	No
	Deadwood-2.3.05	No
Microsoft DNS	Windows Server 2008 R2	No
	Windows Server 2008	Yes

Table 3. Vulnerability testing of popular DNS implementations.

4.3. Efficacy of Maintaining Ghost Domain Names

We measured how the 19,045 open DNS resolvers may continue to resolve a ghost domain name (`2.ghostdomain.info`). For comparison, we also measured (1) how every resolver may continue to resolve a continuously existent, legitimate domain name, for which we use `www.google.com`; and (2) how every resolver may continue to resolve a legitimate domain name that gets revoked without the ghost domain operations; we use `1.ghostdomain.info` for this purpose. We therefore have three types of domain names: ghost domain name, live legitimate domain name, and revoked legitimate domain name.

Figure 3a shows how the DNS resolvers in our experiments may continue to resolve the three different types of domain names. By probing a resolver for a particular type of domain name, we can identify whether it is resolvable or not. From Figure 3a, it is clear that the three different types of domain names present different behaviors. As expected, a live legitimate domain name (`www.google.com`) can be resolved by almost all resolvers continuously. The num-

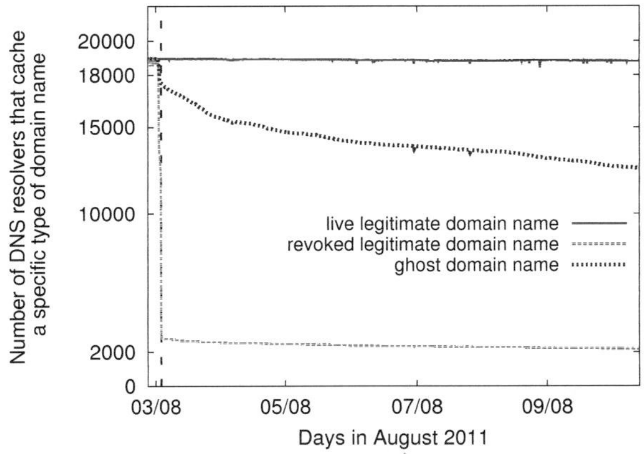

(a) Resolving of domain names at open DNS resolvers over time. The dashed vertical line indicates the original TTL expiration time for `[1-2].ghostdomain.info` after they are removed from domain registry.

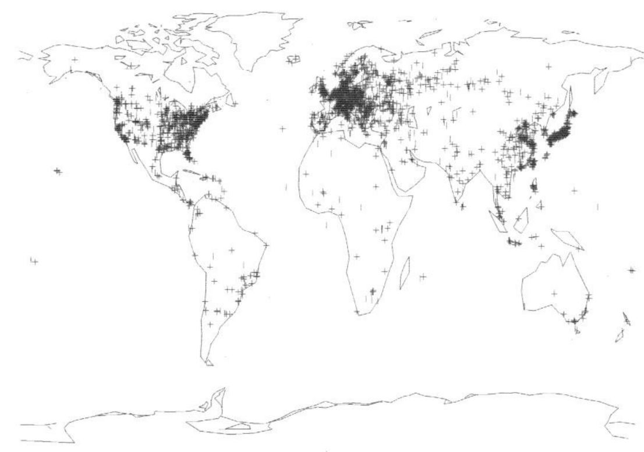

(b) Geographic view of open DNS resolvers that are still haunted by ghost domain names one week later.

Figure 3. Measurement of ghost domain names at open DNS resolvers.

ber of resolvers that can resolve a revoked legitimate domain name (`1.ghostdomain.info`), however, rapidly falls down after its TTL expires. In contrast, a ghost domain name (`2.ghostdomain.info`) can be resolved by most of DNS resolvers as time goes by, even after its TTL expiration time. More than 93% of DNS resolvers still reply with a positive response for resolving the ghost domain name after its TTL has expired, meaning all these resolvers are vulnerable to the ghost domain name attack. Even one week after TTL expiration, the ghost domain names are still resolvable by more than 70% of all DNS resolvers we collected. Figure 3b provides a geographic view of all the haunted DNS resolvers at this time point. (We discuss later why the number of DNS resolvers that resolve a ghost domain name, i.e. the number of haunted DNS resolvers, gradually declines as time goes by.)

We note that after TTL expiration, a revoked legitimate domain name can still be resolved by approximately 10% of DNS resolvers, rather than 0% as we might expect. This phenomenon is due to extremely loose enforcement of cache update policy at certain resolvers that still employ very old versions of DNS implementations. They accept all referral sections and overwrite cached entries without any validation. These resolvers can be haunted by a ghost domain name even without the sophisticated attack as described in Section 3, but simply with periodical queries of a ghost domain name.

4.4. Cost of Maintaining Ghost Domain Names

As we have shown the vulnerability of ghost domain in popular DNS implementations and widely deployed Internet DNS resolvers, a natural question is about the cost of launching and maintaining ghost domain names. Since the actions required by ghost domain attacks are sending queries to targeted resolvers, the main cost of maintaining a ghost domain name is network bandwidth consumption. An attacker needs to send plenty of DNS queries to refresh the cached entries of a ghost domain name, and the amount of such effort is proportional to the number of the targeted resolvers. For each individual targeted resolver, the bandwidth consumption of the ghost domain attack is mainly determined by the refreshing interval, which is related to two factors: the TTL value of the delegation data for the ghost domain and the refreshing interval per TTL. The refreshing interval relates to the TTL value because to keep the cached data alive, at least one refreshing operation is needed before a cached entry expires.

A naïve attacker might choose a very large TTL value of the delegation data with the hope of maintaining the ghost domain in a resolver's cache before refreshing it. This strategy saves bandwidth, but it is not practical since most of DNS resolvers enforce a maximum TTL limitation. We found empirically that most of our experimental resolvers have a maximum TTL limitation around one day (16.35%) or one week (79.81%), which means the TTL value of the ghost domain is limited.

For any given TTL value selected by the attacker, the bandwidth consumption is directly related to how often attackers refreshes in one TTL. Figure 4 shows the effects of ghost domain exploitation with different TTL values and refreshing intervals. From the results, we observe that if the attacker ensures that one refreshment is sent for each quarter of TTL, additional refreshing effort can increase the effec-

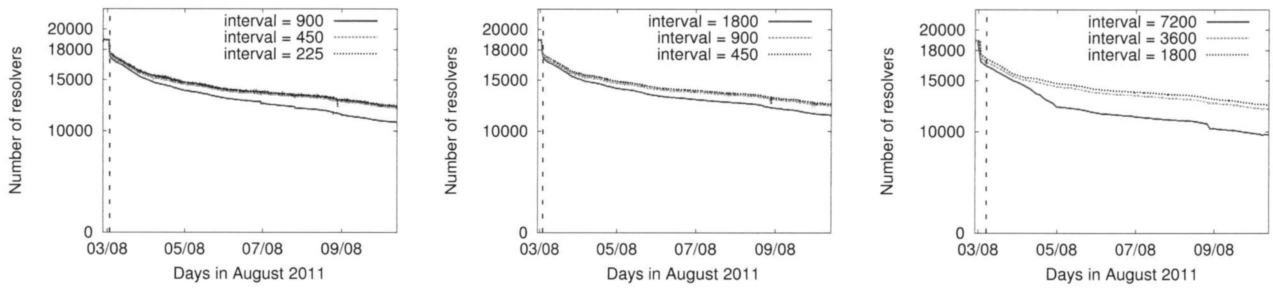

(a) TTL = 1800 (b) TTL = 3600 (c) TTL = 14400

Figure 4. Establishment of ghost domain names with different TTL values and refreshing intervals.

tiveness, but not significantly. This is reasonable because the attacker only needs to ensure one successful renewal before the ghost domain expires. refreshing more often is useful only to reduce the chance of packet losses. We also see that the curves of $TTL/2$ refreshing interval declines faster, since only one refresh within the TTL period might occasionally fail, so a timely renewal of the ghost domain cannot be ensured.

4.5. Other Factors that Affect The Lifetime of Ghost Domains

Through all our experiment results such as those shown in Figure 4 and Figure 3a, we observe that the numbers of exploited resolvers continuously decrease over time. Although this declining trend is affected by the attackers' actions (such as the refreshing frequency discussed above), the types of the recursive resolvers turn out to affect the lifetime of ghost domain as well.

To illustrate the impact of recursive resolver types, we analyze the experimental data of probing `www.google.com` to study when and how frequently a cached entry (in this case, the `CNAME` record of `www.google.com` as it has a large original TTL) gets evicted. Knowing how a cache record could be evicted in a resolver helps us to infer why a ghost domain could be lost. By tracking the TTL variations of the objective entry, we find that the experimental resolvers can be sorted into four types based on the different TTL variations of the objective entry.

- *Stable resolvers* (Figure 5a). As expected, the TTL value monotonically decreases to zero, then go back to the original value.
- *Resolvers that occasionally become unreachable* (Figure 5b). Unreachable periods derive the gap in the middle of the line. Ghost domains could fail to be renewed during such periods.
- *Proxies* (Figure 5c). The TTL values form multiple lines, which means there are multiple cache servers in the backend. Ghost domains are easy to be lost after churn of backend servers.
- *Resolvers that occasionally lose cached entries* (Figure 5d). This may be caused by several factors: cache replacement, cache flushing, or even reset of resolvers. These factors also could cause the loss of ghost domains.

In our experiments, we find that over 85% of resolvers that fail to keep ghost domains belong to the last two types, which are inherently easy to lose cached entries. Less than 10% of failed resolvers come from the set of stable resolvers, which means stable resolvers are less likely lose cached entries, including ghost domains. Since over 65% of our experimental resolvers are stable from current observation of the TTL variations, we infer that a ghost domain can stay alive for a long time. In fact, after one week, over 70% of experimental resolvers still keep the ghost domains we created and the decline trend is slow. We are currently exploring methods to identify the types of resolvers and study their individual reaction to different ghost domain exploitations.

5. Discussion

In this section, we discuss a few possible solutions to fix the problem of ghost domain names. We also discuss the current practices in some of the implementations that are not vulnerable to this problem. Finally, we conclude the section with a discussion of DNSSEC [2], which avoids this problem implicitly through its strict delegation requirements.

5.1. Defense Approaches

The ghost domain exploitation needs to launch a query to the target resolver. Thus a basic defense strategy is to

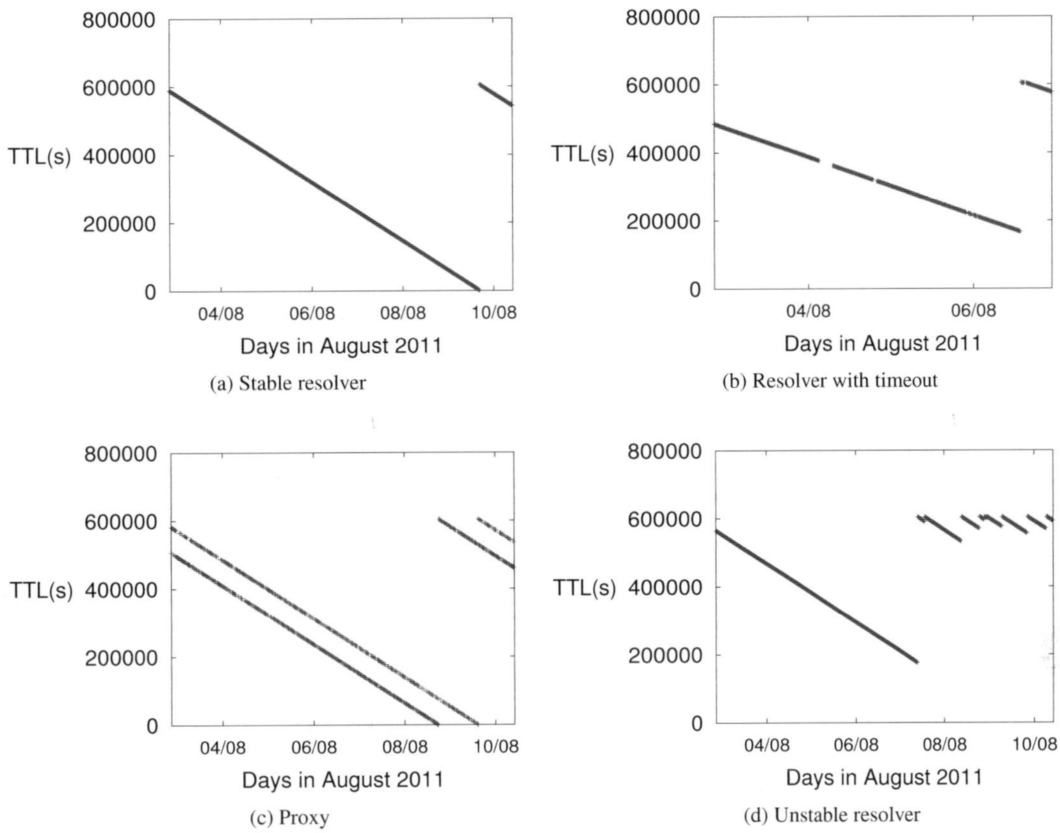

Figure 5. TTL variations in different types of resolvers

have DNS administrators restrict the service range of the DNS resolver. Also, administrators can routinely flush DNS cache to purge possible ghost domains.

These strategies however are not fundamental solutions. The root cause of the ghost domain problem is that the current DNS cache update policy allows authoritative servers to continuously renew their own delegation data in resolvers by themselves. Then once a domain delegates a sub-domain, there is no guarantee that the delegation can be revoked.

Intuitively, there are several approaches for correcting this problem, and we consider the following three:

1. *Strengthening the bailiwick rule* – DNS resolver implementation should tighten the bailiwick rule so that a recursive resolver only accepts a zone's delegation data from authoritative server of its parent zone.

2. *Refining the credibility rule* – Another possible solution is to refine credibility to disallow cache overwriting when received records have the same trust level as cached data.

3. *Allowing updates with the exception of the TTL value* – Since the ghost domain attack achieves the goal of preserving revoked domain by refreshing the delegation data with a new authoritative server name and thus a new TTL, one possible solution is to allow the cache update with exception of the TTL value.

The first solution derives from the semantics of the bailiwick rule. The purpose of bailiwick rule is to restrict authoritative servers so that they can only give records in their own range. From this point of view, an authoritative server has no right to change delegation data of itself since the delegation should be dominated by its parent zone.

However, applying the strict bailiwick rule might cause performance and management issues. One such issue is resilience to authority mismatches. Authority mismatch is a type of DNS misconfiguration in which the delegation data is different in the parent zone than in the child zone. Although the DNS specification [20] requires that delegation data must be consistent, previous studies [30] [27] show this configuration error is common in practice. While the current cache update policy is resilient to such error, the strict bailiwick rule will ignore delegation data from the child zone, and thus might make some of authoritative servers unusable.

Another issue is about authoritative server migration. Allowing cached NS records to be overwritten can speed up legitimate migration of an authoritative server. However, with the strict bailiwick rule and current DNS protocol, resolvers will not be aware of the migration until cached delegation data expires. What's even worse, DNS administrators tend to give large TTL values to delegation data. We measured the TTL values of the delegation data of the top one million Internet domains (ranked by alexa.com), and we found that the TTL values of most popular domains are one (12.04%) or two days (78.41%). This study indicates that with the strict bailiwick rule, legitimate authority changes would take days to complete.

The second approach can thwart the ghost domain problem since all self-issued delegation data has the same trust level [13]. Also, this approach remains resilient to the authority mismatch problem, as the self-issued delegation data from the child zone has higher trust levels than those from the parent. This approach has the additional benefit of eliminating some of the attack vectors that could be exploited by cache poisoning attacks [31]. But it still suffers from the authority migration problem.

The third approach (limiting TTL updates) does not have penalties for the legitimate changes of authoritative servers. This approach also remains resilient to authority mismatch, and it is the simplest one in terms of implementation. However, we only consider this approach as a temporary solution — it does not actively address the issue of the loosely defined update policy.

Although the second approach has more advantages in practice, we prefer the first one as the recommended solution. A strict bailiwick rule that rejects self-issued delegation data is semantically correct. More importantly, the DNS standard must clarify and formally define the cache update policy. We hope our work will promote such efforts in the DNS standards community.

5.2. Current Defense Implementations

As we have shown in the section 3, although the very popular DNS implementation (BIND) and most of the public DNS servers we tested are vulnerable, three implementations: MaraDNS (version Deadwood-3.0.03), Microsoft DNS (version Windows Sever 2008 R2) and Unbound (version 1.4.11), are immune to the ghost domain attack. The immunity of the latest version of Microsoft DNS derives from a new feature called DNS cache locking [12], but we cannot know the details of this feature because of its proprietary implementation. We reviewed the other two implementations and it turns out that each of them implemented one of the above proposed solutions. Since there is no prior public disclosure of the ghost domain behavior, we do not know whether these two versions of DNS implementation intentionally address the ghost domain name problems or not. Nevertheless, we summarize our findings on these implementations as follows: MaraDNS, has already applied the first solution listed in the above section. It only accepts a zone's delegation data from its parent zone. The Unbound DNS server adopts the 3rd solution that allows overwriting of delegated data but keeps its old TTL value in the cache.

5.3. Delegation Semantics in DNSSEC

We also consider the implication of the ghost domain attack on the DNSSEC system, and we believe a fully deployed DNSSEC is immune to the ghost domain problem. The immunity does not come from the initial intention of DNSSEC using cryptographic signatures to protect the integrity of DNS data. Instead, the immunity is an outcome of a strictly defined delegation behavior. In short, DNSSEC defines a new RR type, DS (Delegation Signer), to form a chain of trust between parent and child zone. In the DNSSEC standard, the specification [3] explicitly states that DS record can only be obtained from the parent zone. Therefore a ghost domain attacker cannot renew DS record of the ghost domain by himself. Without a valid DS record, the trust chain will be broken, so haunted security-aware resolvers will only resolve the ghost domain as non-authentic data.

However, in an environment of partial DNSSEC deployment, a security-aware resolver could still be haunted to resolve a ghost domain as authentic results. The reason is that partial deployment DNSSEC raises a trust anchor management issue called "isolated DNSSEC islands" [26]. Without fully DNSSEC deployment, A security-aware resolver cannot validate DNS data from isolated DNSSEC-enabled zones with one single trust anchor from the root. Instead, it needs to be configured with third-party trust anchor providers, such as DNSSEC Look-aside Validation (DLV) providers [33] [34] or public trust anchor lists [24], in order to obtain DNSKEY records of isolated DNSSEC-enabled zones to be able to authenticate their DNS data. The attacker can register DNSKEY records of the ghost domain to DLV providers and public trust anchor lists, so that DNS data of the ghost domain could still be validated by those trust anchors, even though the DS record is deleted from the parent zone. To prevent this, DLV providers and public trust anchor lists need to sync their database with DNS registries in a timely manner. In other words, a malicious domain not only needs to be revoked from the DNS registry, it also should be revoked simultaneously from third-party trust anchor providers. We are currently investigating revocation behaviors of several third-party trust anchor providers.

6. Related Work

Study of Malicious Domain Names. Our work is led by an initial motivation of understanding the lifetime of malicious domains and the effects of domain takedown. In previous studies [22] [23], Moore et. al. showed that most of phishing domains stay alive for several tens of hours before being taken down. The ghost domain problem could make the effect of takedown unpredictable.

Malicious domains must be identified first before being taken down. Recent research has proposed many approaches to distinguish malicious domain names from benign DNS usage. These approaches include extracting various features of malicious domain names from the usage of RR records [15], leveraging registration information [14], passive access logging [29] [1] [6] and lexical construction [19] [35]. From an intrusion detection perspective, the ghost domain exploitation is detectable as it has unusual usage of DNS records.

Cache Poisoning Attacks and Countermeasures. The ghost domain vulnerability comes from the loosely defined sanity check of DNS cache. This weakness is also being exploited by DNS cache poisoning attacks. As early as 1990, Steve Bellovin had indicated that a malicious DNS server can pollute cache resolvers by piggybacking arbitrary records in referral sections [5]. In response, the credibility rule and the bailiwick rule were proposed [32], and then adopted by most of DNS implementations. However, these rules are still insecure and recently have been exploited by the Kaminsky-class cache poisoning attack[18]. After disclosure of the Kaminsky-class attack, a number of approaches were proposed to increase DNS forgery resistance [10] [9] [16] [28], but only a few studies were concerned about the weakness of the DNS cache update policy. Son et. al. [31] gave a formal study of the bailiwick rule and the credibility rule; this work helped us to clarify some details of these rules.

DNS Cache Inconsistency. To some extent, the ghost domain problem is a form of DNS cache inconsistency. As DNS only supports a weak cache consistency by using TTL to limit the lifetime of cached copies, authoritative servers cannot propagate data changes to resolvers in a timely way, failing completely in the ghost domain case. Previous DNS studies have proposed a few approaches to address this problem. DNScup [8] proactively pushes data changes from authoritative server to cache resolvers. Osterwail et. al. proposed Zone State Revocation [25], which embedded `DNSKEY` revocation in DNS response to notify resolvers. Such cache consistency mechanisms could potentially avoid the ghost domain problem. However, considering the critical role of DNS, such a change needs to be carefully evaluated.

DNS Misconfiguration. In [17], Kalafut et. al. presented an interesting phenomenon named *orphan DNS server*. An orphan DNS server is a DNS server which has an address record in the DNS, even though its parent domain does not exist. Orphan DNS servers and ghost domains are superficially similar as both of them resolve domain names that should not exist. But they are substantially different. While orphan DNS servers come from typographical errors and misconfiguration in top level domain zone files, ghost domains are more fundamentally derived from the ambiguously defined DNS cache update policy.

7. Conclusion

In this paper, we present a vulnerability in DNS cache update policy, which prevents effective domain name revocation. Attackers could cause a malicious domain name to be continuously resolvable even after the delegated data has been deleted from the domain registry and after the TTL associated with entry supposed expires. These deleted but resolvable domains are called ghost domain names.

Although we have not found evidence that the vulnerability has been used by previous malicious attacks or botnets, our test results show that the majority of public DNS servers and implementations are vulnerable. Our experiments have also demonstrated that a large scale exploitation of this vulnerability is practical. This vulnerability can potentially allow a botnet to continuously use malicious domains which have been identified and removed from the domain registry. The same vulnerability also potentially allows attackers to make a malicious domain appeared to be deleted at most of the DNS servers but still resolvable at specifically targeted DNS resolvers. This makes the detection of ghost domains even more difficult.

We recommend that the DNS community apply a strict bailiwick rule to fix this vulnerability. Several DNS implementations have adopted various defense mechanisms, but many popular implementations are still vulnerable. Our ongoing work includes implementing patches for open source DNS implementations and addressing possible performance and management issues related to the implementation of a strict DNS cache update policy.

Acknowledgments

We would like to especially thank Jason Gustafson for valuable discussions and thoughtfully proofreading this material, as well as Roberto Perdisci and Zhankao Wen for assistance with experimental resource. We also gratefully thank the anonymous reviewers for their valuable comments, and Jianwei Zhuge, Meng Hu, Zongxu Zhao, Pengfei Xu, Xun Lu and Kevin Warrick for their suggestions and feedback. This work was supported in part by the National Basic Research Program of China (973 Project) grant 2009CB320505. Kang Li's research on this work was partially supported by the USA National Science Foundation (NSF) CISE grant 1127195 and a gift from Cisco systems. Jun Li was partially supported by the 2010 Chair of Excellence award from the University Carlos III of Madrid (UC3M), Spain, and the NSF CAREER award under award no. CNS-0644434. Any opinions, findings, and conclusions or recommendations expressed in this material are those of the authors and do not necessarily reflect the views of the funding agencies.

References

[1] M. Antonakakis, R. Perdisci, D. Dagon, W. Lee, and N. Feamster. Building a Dynamic Reputation System for DNS. In *19th Usenix Security Symposium*, 2010.

[2] R. Arends, R. Austein, M. Larson, D. Massey, and S. Rose. DNS Security Introduction and Requirement. *RFC4033*, 2005.

[3] R. Arends, R. Austein, M. Larson, D. Massey, and S. Rose. Resource Records for the DNS Security Extensions. *RFC4034*, 2005.

[4] D. Atkins and R. Austein. Threat Analysis of the Domain Name System (DNS). *RFC3833*, 2004.

[5] S. M. Bellovin. Using the Domain Name System for System Break-ins. In *Proceedings of the 5th conference on USENIX UNIX Security Symposium - Volume 5*, pages 18–18, Berkeley, CA, USA, 1995. USENIX Association.

[6] L. Bilge, E. Kirda, C. Kruegel, and M. Balduzzi. EXPOSURE: Finding Malicious Domains Using Passive DNS Analysis. *Proceedings of Network and Distributed Security Symposium (NDSS'11)*, 2008.

[7] R. Boscovich. Taking Down Botnets: Microsoft and the Rustock Botnet. `http://blogs.technet.com/b/microsoft_on_the_issues/archive/2011/03/18/taking-down-botnets-microsoft-and-the-rustock-botnet.aspx`, 2011.

[8] X. Chen, H. Wang, S. Ren, and X. Zhang. Maintaining Strong Cache Consistency for the Domain Name System. *IEEE Transactions on Knowledge and Data Engineering*, 19:1057–1071, 2007.

[9] D. Dagon, M. Antonakakis, K. Day, X. Luo, C. Lee, and W. Lee. Recursive DNS Architectures and Vulnerability Implications. In *Proceedings of Network and Distributed System Security Symposium (NDSS'09)*, 2009.

[10] D. Dagon, M. Antonakakis, P. Vixie, T. Jinmei, and W. Lee. Increased DNS Forgery Resistance Through 0x20-bit Encoding: security via leet queries. In *Proceedings of the 15th ACM conference on Computer and communications security*, pages 211–222. ACM, 2008.

[11] D. Dagon, N. Provos, C. Lee, and W. Lee. Corrupted DNS Resolution Paths: The Rise of a Malicious Resolution Authority. In *Proceedings of Network and Distributed Security Symposium (NDSS'08)*, 2008.

[12] M. DNS. DNS Cache Locking. `http://technet.microsoft.com/en-us/library/ee683892(WS.10).aspx`.

[13] R. Elz and R. Bush. Clarifications to the DNS specification. *RFC2181*, 1997.

[14] M. Felegyhazi, C. Kreibich, and V. Paxson. On the Potential of Proactive Domain Blacklisting. In *Proceedings of the 3rd USENIX conference on Large-scale exploits and emergent threats: botnets, spyware, worms, and more*, LEET'10, pages 6–6, Berkeley, CA, USA, 2010. USENIX Association.

[15] T. Holz, C. Gorecki, K. Rieck, and F. Freiling. Measuring and Detecting Fast-Flux Service Networks. In *Proceedings of Network and Distributed Security Symposium (NDSS'08)*, 2008.

[16] J. G. Hy. Anti DNS Spoofing-Extended Query ID (XQID). `http://www.jhsoft.com/dns-xqid.htm`, 2008.

[17] A. J. Kalafut, M. Gupta, C. A. Cole, L. Chen, and N. E. Myers. An Empirical Study of Orphan DNS Servers in the Internet. In *Proceedings of the 10th annual conference on Internet measurement*, IMC '10, pages 308–314, New York, NY, USA, 2010. ACM.

[18] D. Kaminsky. Its the end of the cache as we know it. *Black-Hat USA*, 2008.

[19] J. Ma, L. Saul, S. Savage, and G. Voelker. Beyond Blacklists: Learning to Detect Malicious Web Sites from Suspicious URLs. In *Proceedings of the 15th ACM SIGKDD international conference on Knowledge discovery and data mining*, pages 1245–1254. ACM, 2009.

[20] P. Mockapetris. Domain Names - Concepts and Facilities. *RFC1034*, 1987.

[21] P. Mockapetris. Domain Names - Implementation and Specification. *RFC1035*, 1987.

[22] T. Moore and R. Clayton. Examining the Impact of Website Take-Down on Phishing. In *Proceedings of the anti-phishing working groups 2nd annual eCrime researchers summit*, eCrime '07, pages 1–13, New York, NY, USA, 2007. ACM.

[23] T. Moore and R. Clayton. The Consequence of Non-Cooperation in the Fight against Phishing. In *eCrime Researchers Summit, 2008*, pages 1–14. IEEE, 2008.

[24] E. Osterweil, D. Massey, and L. Zhang. Deploying and monitoring dns security (dnssec). *Computer Security Applications Conference, Annual*, 0:429–438, 2009.

[25] E. Osterweil, V. Pappas, D. Massey, and L. Zhang. Zone State Revocation for DNSSEC. In *Proceedings of the 2007 workshop on Large scale attack defense*, LSAD '07, pages 153–160, New York, NY, USA, 2007. ACM.

[26] E. Osterweil, M. Ryan, D. Massey, and L. Zhang. Quantifying the Operational Status of the DNSSEC Deployment. In *Proceedings of the 8th ACM SIGCOMM conference on Internet measurement*, IMC '08, pages 231–242, New York, NY, USA, 2008. ACM.

[27] V. Pappas, Z. Xu, S. Lu, D. Massey, A. Terzis, and L. Zhang. Impact of Configuration Errors on DNS Robustness. In *ACM SIGCOMM Computer Communication Review*, volume 34, pages 319–330. ACM, 2004.

[28] R. Perdisci, M. Antonakakis, X. Luo, and W. Lee. WSEC DNS: Protecting Recursive DNS Resolvers from Poisoning

Attacks. In *IEEE/IFIP International Conference on Dependable Systems & Networks, DSN'09.*, pages 3–12. IEEE, 2009.

[29] R. Perdisci, I. Corona, D. Dagon, and W. Lee. Detecting Malicious Flux Service Networks through Passive Analysis of Recursive DNS Traces. In *Annual Computer Security Applications Conference*, volume 0, pages 311–320, Los Alamitos, CA, USA, 2009. IEEE Computer Society.

[30] G. Sisson. DNS SURVEY. `http://dns.measurement-factory.com/surveys/201010/`, 2010.

[31] S. Son and V. Shmatikov. The Hitchhikers Guide to DNS Cache Poisoning. In *Security and Privacy in Communication Networks*, volume 50 of *Lecture Notes of the Institute for Computer Sciences, Social Informatics and Telecommunications Engineering*, pages 466–483. Springer Berlin Heidelberg, 2010.

[32] P. Vixie. DNS and BIND Security Issues. In *Proceedings of the 5th conference on USENIX UNIX Security Symposium - Volume 5*, pages 19–19, Berkeley, CA, USA, 1995. USENIX Association.

[33] P. Vixie. Preventing Child Neglect in DNSSECbis Using Lookaside Validation(DLV). *IEICE Transactions on Communications*, pages 1326–1330, 2005.

[34] S. Weiler. DNSSEC Lookaside Validation (DLV). *RFC5074*, 2007.

[35] S. Yadav, A. Reddy, A. Reddy, and S. Ranjan. Detecting Algorithmically Generated Malicious Domain Names. In *Proceedings of the 10th annual conference on Internet measurement*, pages 48–61. ACM, 2010.

Carnegie Mellon
CyLab
CONFIDENCE FOR A NETWORKED WORLD

Carnegie Mellon CyLab
4616 HENRY STREET
PITTSBURGH, PA 15213
PH: (412) 268-7195
FX: (412) 268-7196
www.cylab.cmu.edu

ShortMAC:
Efficient Data-plane Fault Localization

Xin Zhang, Zongwei Zhou, Hsu-Chun Hsiao, Tiffany Hyun-Jin Kim
Adrian Perrig and Patrick Tague

What is Fault Localization?

- Problem definition
  - Identify faulty links during packet forwarding
- Attacker Model
  - Drop, modify, misroute, or inject packets at data plane
- Challenges
  - Selective attack: break ping, traceroute, etc
  - High overhead
  - Slander & framing

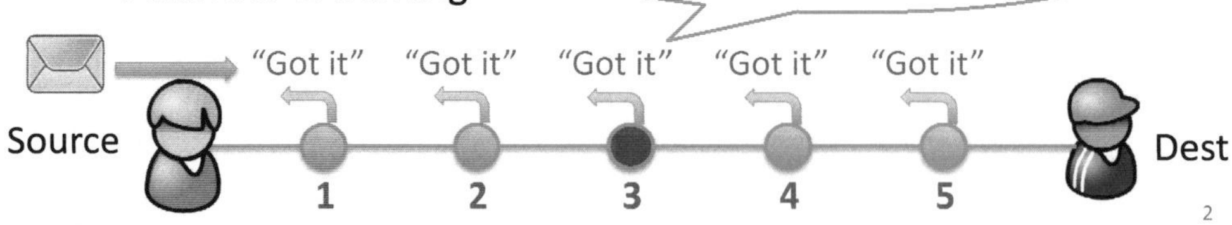

2

CyLab
www.cylab.cmu.edu

Carnegie Mellon

What is Fault Localization?

- Challenges (cont'd)
  - Attacks against sampling
  - Forgery attack: break Netflow, Bloom Filter, etc
  - Natural packet loss

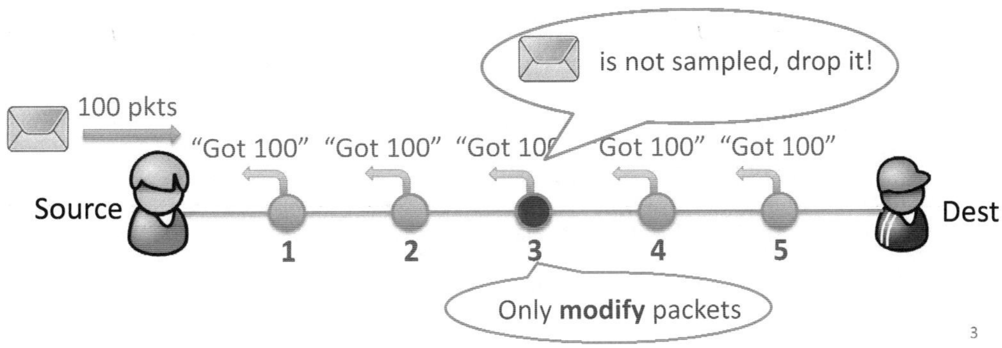

3

CyLab
www.cylab.cmu.edu

Carnegie Mellon

Why is Fault Localization Important?

- The current Internet
  - Best effort, purely end-to-end
- Fault localization enables:
  - Data-plane accountability
  - Intelligent path selection
  - Linear path trial

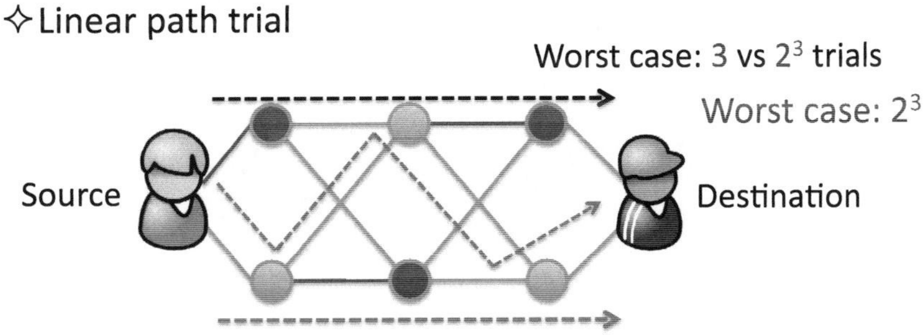

4

CyLab
www.cylab.cmu.edu
Carnegie Mellon

Design Goals

- Security
  - Against drop, modify, inject, and replay packets
  - Against multiple colluding nodes
- Efficiency
  - Low detection delay
  - Low storage, communication and computation overhead
- Provable guarantees
  - Upper bound of damage without being detected
  - Lower bound of forwarding correctness if no fault detected

5

CyLab
www.cylab.cmu.edu
Carnegie Mellon

ShortMAC Key Insight #1

- Fault Localization → Packet authentication
  - Fault Localization → monitor packet *count* and *content*
  - W/ pkt authen, content → count
  - Only counts → small state, low bandwidth cost

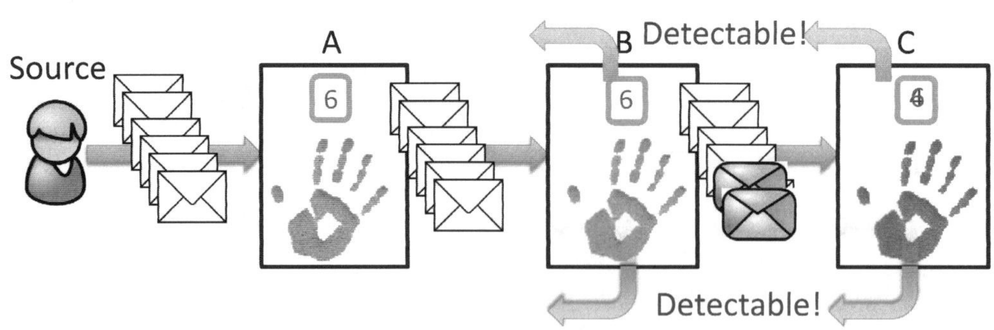

6

CyLab
www.cylab.cmu.edu
Carnegie Mellon

ShortMAC Key Insight #2

- *Limiting* attacks instead of perfect detection
  - Detect every misbehavior? Costly! Error-prone!
  - Absorb low-impact attack: tolerance threshold
  - Trap the attacker into a *dilemma*
  - Enable probabilistic algorithms with provable bounds

7

CyLab
www.cylab.cmu.edu
Carnegie Mellon

ShortMAC Key Ideas

k-bit MAC, e.g., k = 1

- The ShortMAC packet marking
  - Limiting instead of perfectly detecting fake packets
  - Source marks each packet with k bits (with keyed PRF)

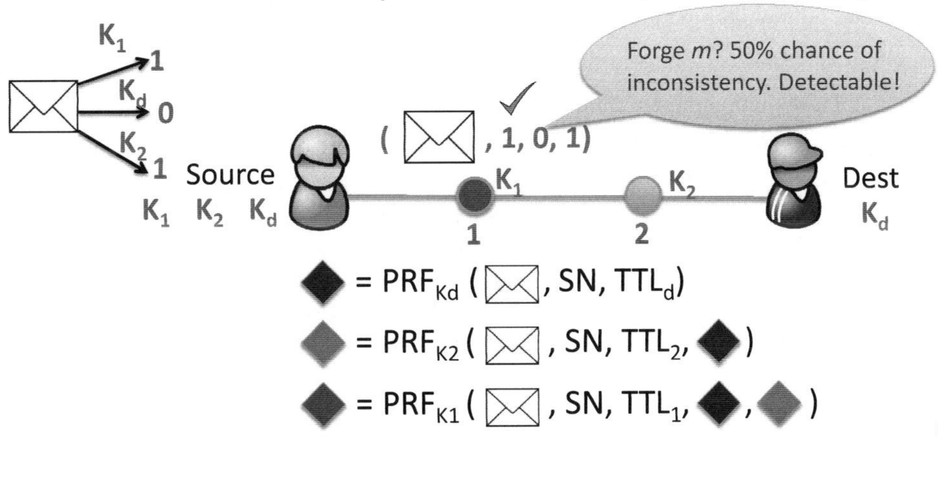

8

ShortMAC Key Ideas

- High-level steps
  - Each node maintains two counters (*counter only*!)
  - *Secure* reporting
  - Threshold-based detection robust to *natural errors*

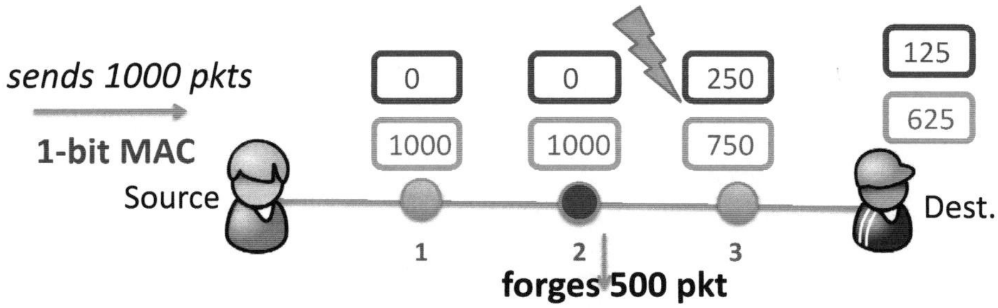

  - More details: Onion ACK for reporting, threshold-based detection, etc

Theoretical Bounds

- The math

$$\alpha = 1 - (1 - T_{dr})^2 + \frac{\beta}{N(1-T_{dr})^d} \qquad \beta = \frac{T_{in}}{q} + \frac{\sqrt{\left(\ln \frac{2}{\delta}\right)^2 + 8qT_{in} \ln \frac{2}{\delta}} + \ln \frac{2}{\delta}}{4q^2}$$

$$\theta = (1 - T_{dr})^d - \frac{\beta}{N} \qquad N = \frac{\ln(\frac{2d}{\delta})}{2\left(T_{dr}-\rho\right)^2\left(1-T_{dr}\right)^d}$$

- The numbers

Protocol	ShortMAC	PAAI-1	SSS	Sketch
Delay (pkt)	3.8×10^4	7.1×10^5	1.6×10^8	$\approx10^6$
State (bytes)	21	2×10^5	4×10^3	≈500

CyLab
www.cylab.cmu.edu
Carnegie Mellon

Experimental Evaluation

- Average-case performance, proof of concept
- Simulation + Prototyping
  - Simulation: large-scale, security properties
  - Prototype: computational overhead
- SSF-net based simulation
  - Single 6-hop path
  - Malicious node in the middle
  - Independently dropping/injecting packets

11

CyLab
www.cylab.cmu.edu
Carnegie Mellon

Simulation Results

- False rates, detection delay, and comparison
  - 2-bit-MAC

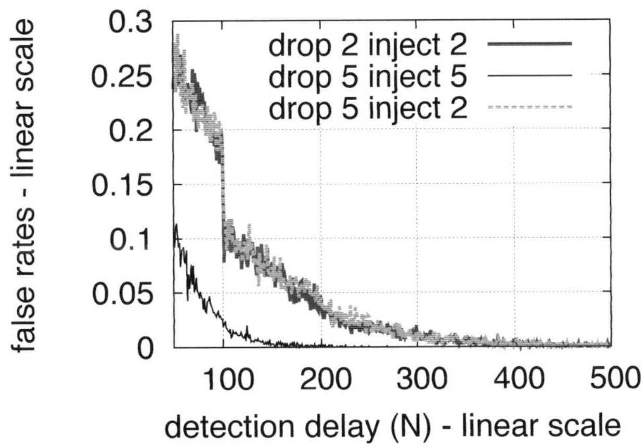

12

CyLab
www.cylab.cmu.edu

Carnegie Mellon

Prototyping Results

- ❖ Pure-software router prototype in Linux/Click
- ❖ Evaluation of fast path performance
  - ✧ Per-packet PRF computation
  - ✧ Different MACs with AES-ni
- ❖ Computational overhead
  - ✧ Throughput and latency
  - ✧ Linear path topology
  - ✧ Netperf benchmark

CyLab
www.cylab.cmu.edu

Carnegie Mellon

Prototyping Results

- ❖ Throughput and latency

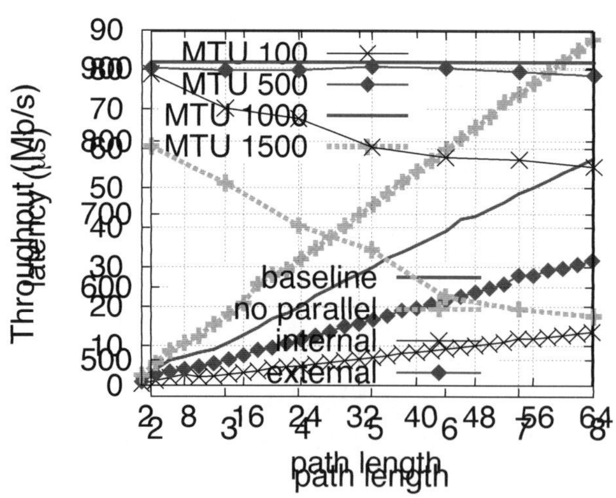

CyLab
www.cylab.cmu.edu

Carnegie Mellon

Phew… the end

- *Limiting* instead of perfectly detecting
  - Enables efficient algorithms
- *Provable* security guarantee
  - Theoretical bounds, against strong adversaries
- *High* efficiency
  - Low detection delay, router state, comm. overhead
- *Probabilistic* packet authentication
  - Building block for other applications

15

CyLab
www.cylab.cmu.edu

Carnegie Mellon

Thank you!

Questions?

Xin Zhang <xzhang1@cmu.edu>

Bypassing Space Explosion in Regular Expression Matching for Network Intrusion Detection and Prevention Systems

Jignesh Patel, Alex Liu and Eric Torng

Dept. of Computer Science and Engineering
Michigan State University

Problem Statement

- Core operation in IDS/IPS is Deep Packet Inspection
  - Past DPI: string matching
  - Current DPI: regular expression (RE) matching
    - Example: SNORT, Bro
- Problem: given a set of REs, how to quickly scan packet payload to determine which REs are matched?

Solution using Automata

- Common solution is to build an equivalent Finite State Automata based on DFA.
- DFA size grows exponentially with number of REs.
- Several alternate automata have been proposed D^2FA, XFA, δFA etc.

Limitations of Prior Work

- Prior solution: **Union then Minimize** framework.
  - First combined DFA for the whole RE set is built.
  - Compression technique is applied to the combined DFA to get the alternate automata.

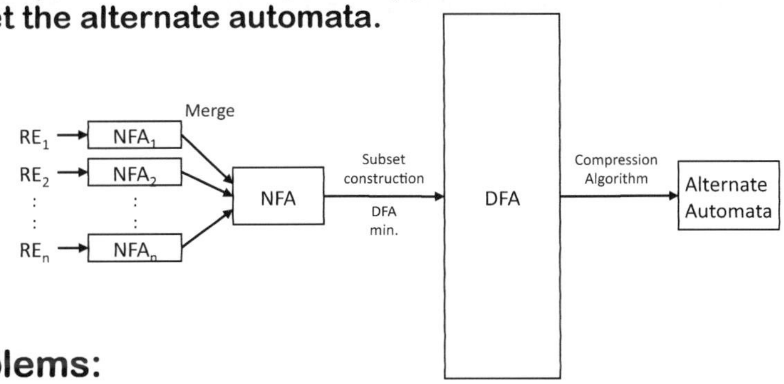

- Problems:
  - The minimization/compression is applied on large combined automata, hence requires too much time and memory.
  - The intermediate DFA might be too large to fit in memory.
  - Whole automata needs to be rebuilt if new RE is added to set.

Our Approach

- Our approach: **Minimize then Union** framework.
  - Build individual DFAs for each RE in the RE set.
  - Compress each DFA to get individual alternate automata.
  - Merge the all compressed alternate automata together.

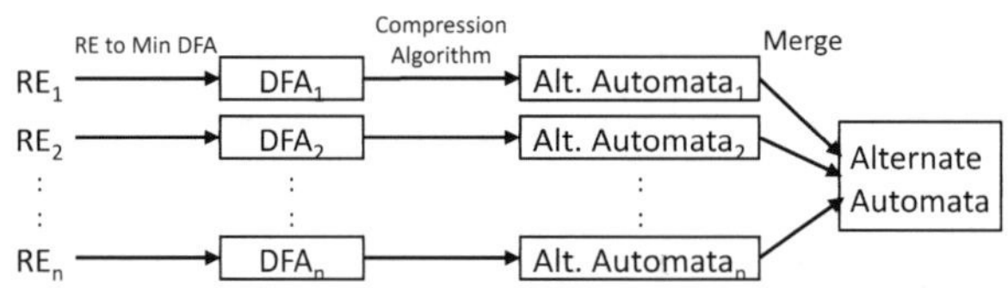

- Advantages
  - The compression algorithm is applied to small DFAs.
  - Large intermediate DFA does not need to be built.
  - Easy to add new RE to the set with one merge.
- In this work we focus on the D2FA.

D2FA Overview

- D2FA [Kumar et al., 2006] uses common transitions between states to reduce the number of transitions.

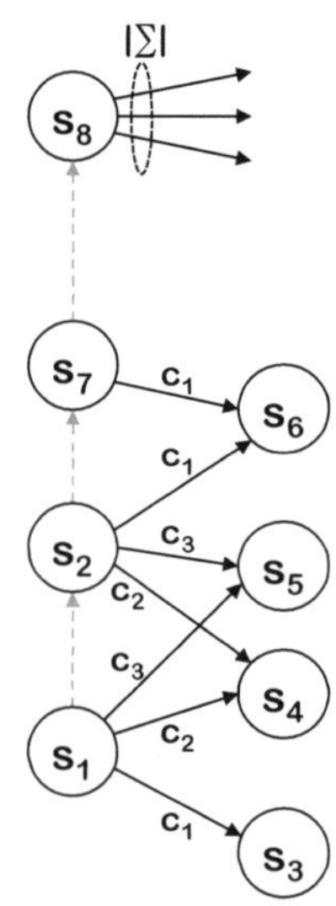

- To build a D2FA:
  1. We choose a deferred state for each state in the DFA.
  2. For each state, remove transitions that are common with its deferred state.

D²FA Construction

- **Build Space Reduction Graph (SRG)**
- **Find maximum spanning tree (MST) in SRG.**
- **Use the MST to set deferred states.**

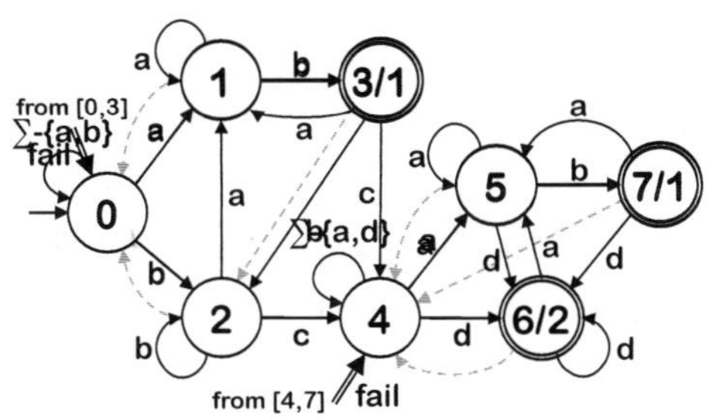

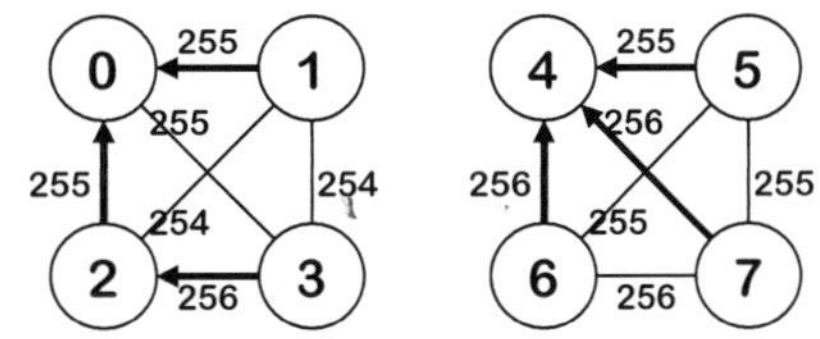

SRG

D²FA for RE set {ab, bc.*d}   2048 Transitions

DFA for RE Matching in DPI

- **Traditional DFA defined as**
$$(Q, \Sigma, \delta, q_0, A),$$
where $A \subseteq Q$ is the set of accepting states.
- **For RE matching in DPI, we redefine DFA as**
$$(Q, \Sigma, \delta, q_0, M),$$
where $M: Q \to 2^R$ gives, for each state, the subset of REs matched from RE set R.

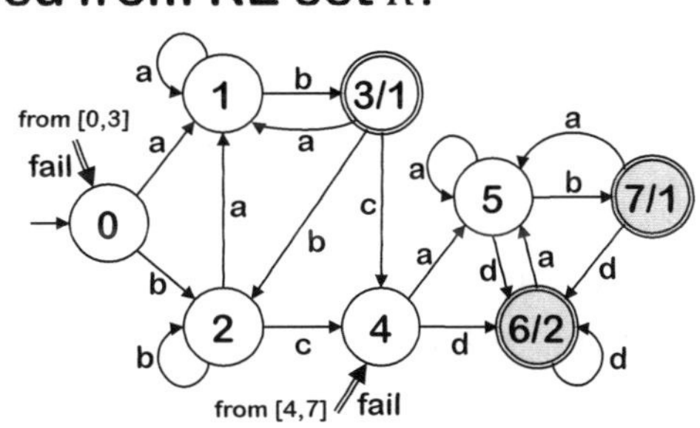

DFA for RE set {ab, bc.*d}

Merging DFAs (1)

- Input: Min. state DFAs D_1 and D_2 equivalent to RE sets R_1 and R_2.
- Output: Min. state DFA D_3 equivalent to RE set $R_1 \cup R_2$.
- Solution: Use the standard Union Cross Product (UCP) construction, $D_3 = UCP(D_1, D_2)$
- Each state in D_3 corresponds to a pair of states in D_1 and D_2. $Q3 = Q1 \times Q2$.

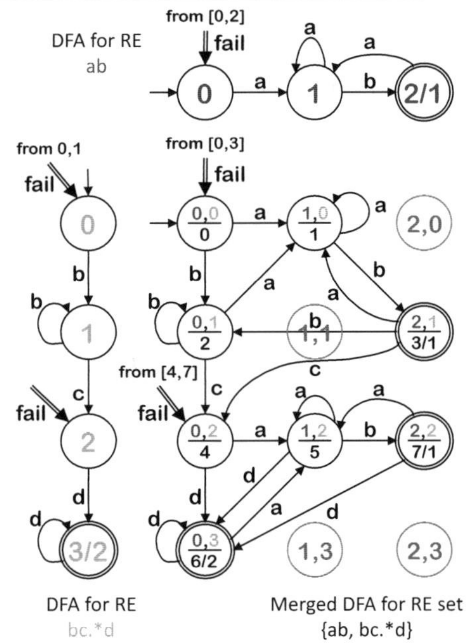

Merging DFAs (2)

- For traditional DFA, $D_3 = UCP(D_1, D_2)$ is not guaranteed to be minimum state.
- We prove that for redefined DFA for DPI, D_3 is guaranteed to be minimum state if:
  - Only reachable state pairs are generated, and
  - $R_1 \cap R_2 = \emptyset$.
- To create the DFA for the entire RE set:
  - First create DFA for each RE
  - Merge DFAs together in a binary fashion to get the final DFA.
- Merge method much faster than direct method
  - Time to build largest DFA in our experiments:
    - Direct method: 386 seconds
    - Merge method: 0.66 seconds.

Merging D^2FA

- We extend the UCP construction for merging DFAs to merge D^2FAs.
- To generate D^2FA, we need to set deferred state for each state.

- Set the deferred state as soon as new state is created.
- Since deferred state is set when a state is created, we only need to store the non-deferred transitions for the state.
- The whole DFA is never built since we always store the D^2FA.

Setting Deferred State

- Idea: Use deferment relation from the input D^2FAs to set the deferment in the merged D^2FA.

- To choose deferred state for new state, $u = \langle v, w \rangle$, in D_3, we use deferment of v in D_1 and w in D_2.

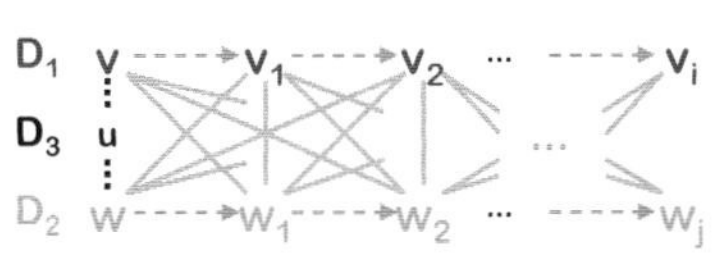

- Among all the (i+1)x(j+1)-1 possible state pairs, choose the one which has most common transitions with $\langle v, w \rangle$.

Merging D²FA Example

- For most states, one of the first pair is the best pair.
- In our experiments, average number of comparisons needed < 1.5

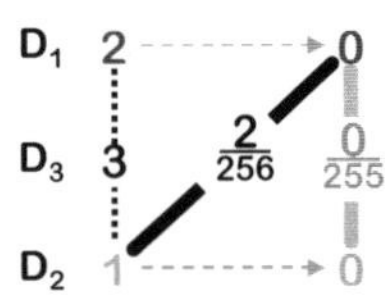

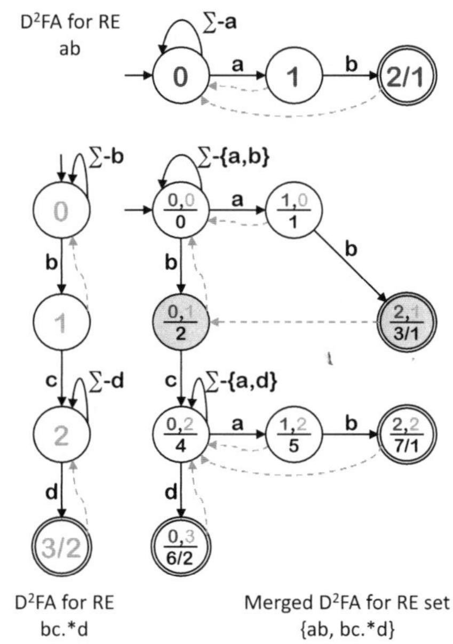

Experimental Results: Main

- We used real world 8 RE sets that were used in prior work for our experiments.
- We group the 8 RE sets into three groups according to type of REs in the sets: STRING, WILDCARD, SNORT
- We compare D²FA Merge algorithm with the Original D²FA algorithm.

RE set group	# States / ASCII len.	Trans increase	Def. depth ratio		Space ratio	Speedup factor
			Avg.	Max.		
All	17.7	20.10%	7.3	4.8	1390	301.6
STRING	0.7	44.00%	1.8	1.6	2672.8	99.5
WILDCARD	36	3.00%	12	8.2	42.7	338.2
SNORT	10.7	21.30%	6.3	3.6	1882.1	399.7

Experimental Results: Scale

- To test scalability we use a synthetic RE set with REs of the form $/c_1c_2c_3c_4.*c_5c_6c_7c_8/$
- We add one RE at a time until memory estimate goes over 1GB.

- Original D²FA algorithm:
  - # REs added: 12
  - # states in final D²FA: 397,312
  - Time to build D²FA: 71 hours

- D²FA Merge algorithm:
  - # REs added: 19
  - # states in final D²FA: 80,216,064
  - Time to build D²FA: 1.2 hours

- For 12 REs, D²FA Merge only needs 10 seconds to build.
- D²FA Merge results in same D²FA size as the original algorithm.

Questions?

- Thank you for listening!

The Case for Prefetching and Prevalidating TLS Server Certificates

Emily Stark, Lin-Shung Huang, Dinesh Israni, Collin Jackson, Dan Boneh

February 8, 2012

Transport Layer Security

- Want to secure traffic between web browsers and servers
- One problem is latency from TLS handshake

The TLS handshake

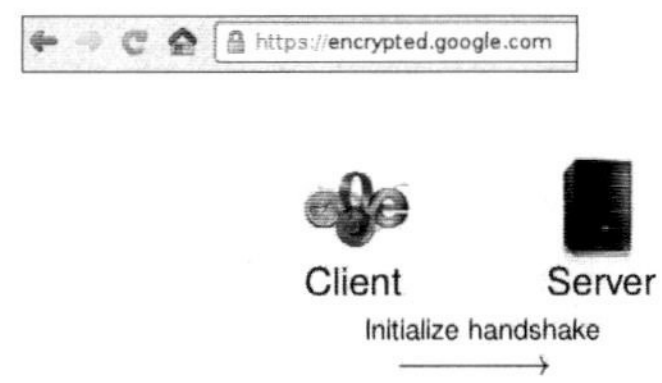

The TLS handshake

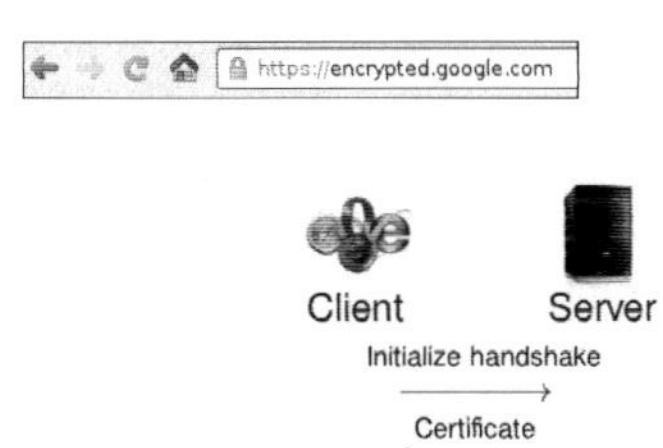

The TLS handshake

The TLS handshake

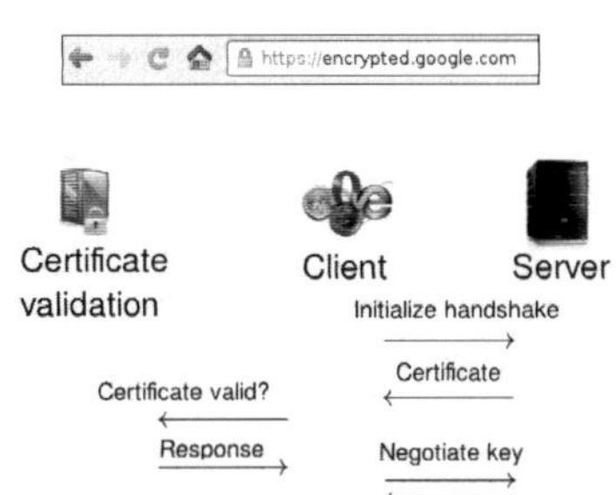

The TLS handshake

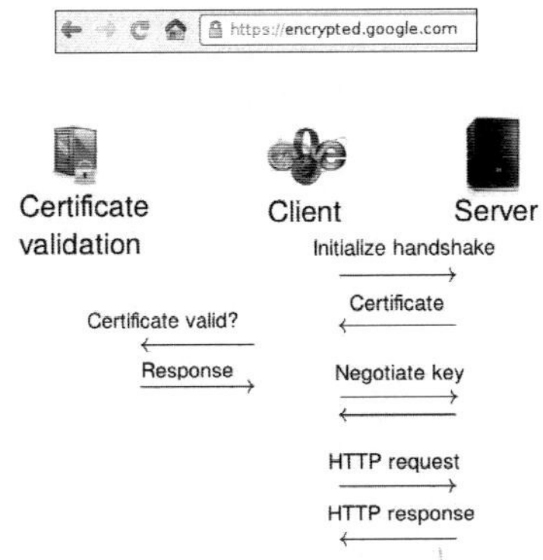

The TLS handshake

Certificate validation: OCSP

- Online certificate status protocol

Certificate validation: OCSP

- Online certificate status protocol
- Server certificate specifies OCSP responder

Certificate validation: OCSP

- Online certificate status protocol
- Server certificate specifies OCSP responder
- Clients asks responder whether cert is valid

Certificate validation: OCSP

- Online certificate status protocol
- Server certificate specifies OCSP responder
- Clients asks responder whether cert is valid
- Responder specifies how long response is valid for

The TLS handshake

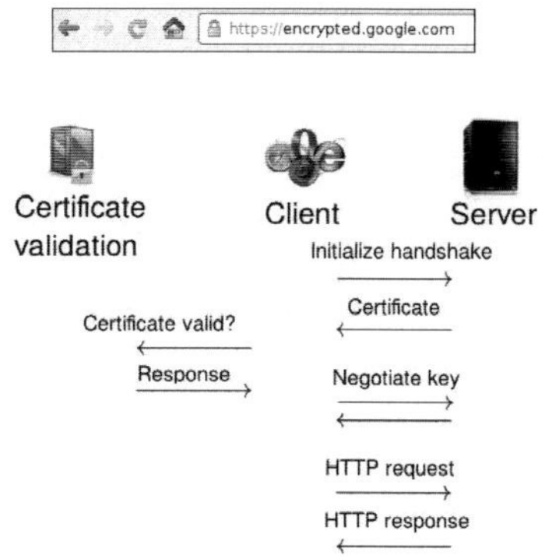

The TLS handshake

Removing round trips

Previous proposal, TLS Snap Start

- Zero round trip handshake

Removing round trips

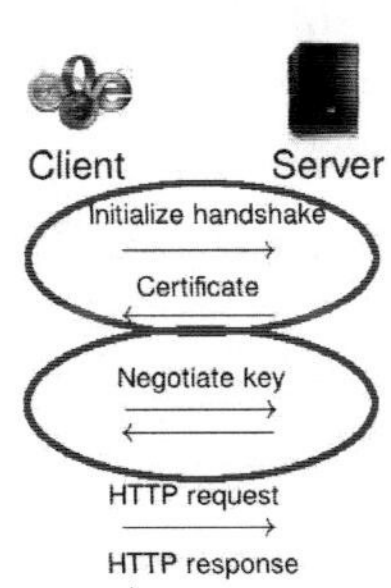

Removing round trips

Snap Start challenges

- Client must know server certificate
    - Cached from previous visit

Snap Start challenges

- Client must know server certificate
  - Cached from previous visit
- Revocation checking is still slow

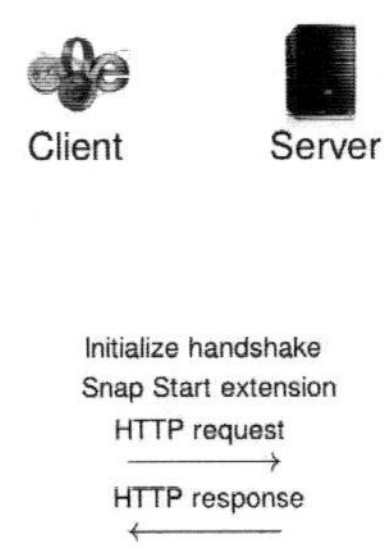

Snap Start challenges

- Client must know server certificate
  - Cached from previous visit
- Revocation checking is still slow

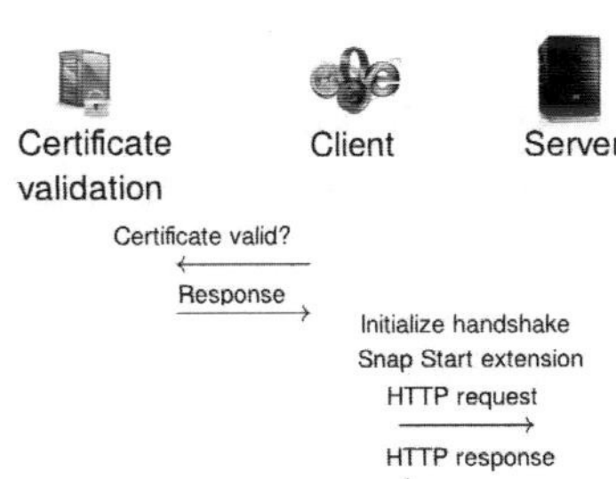

Problem

- TLS imposes extra latency due to retrieving and validating server certificate
  - How to obtain certificate to do Snap Start handshake?
  - How to validate without extra latency?

Contribution

- Real world study of OCSP response times
- Certificate prefetching and prevalidation
  - Propose four prefetching strategies
  - Analysis of effectiveness
  - Prototype implementation

How long does OCSP take in the real world?

- Experimental setup
  - OCSP response times collected from users running Perspectives browser extensions
  - 242 clients, 4474 certificates, 24 responders

OCSP in the wild

CDF of OCSP response time:

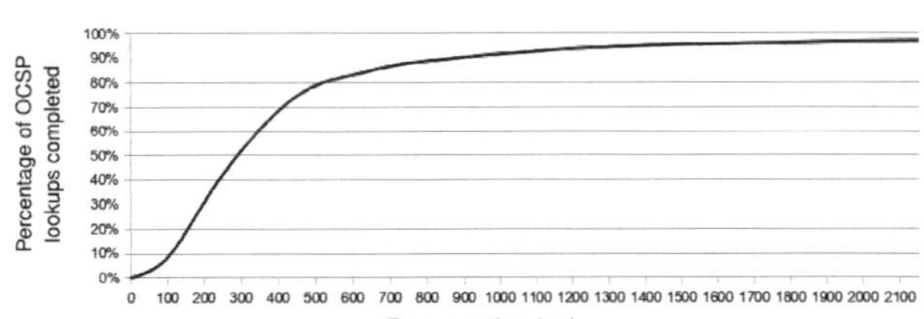

Median: 291 ms, **mean:** 498 ms

OCSP in the wild

CDF of OCSP response time:

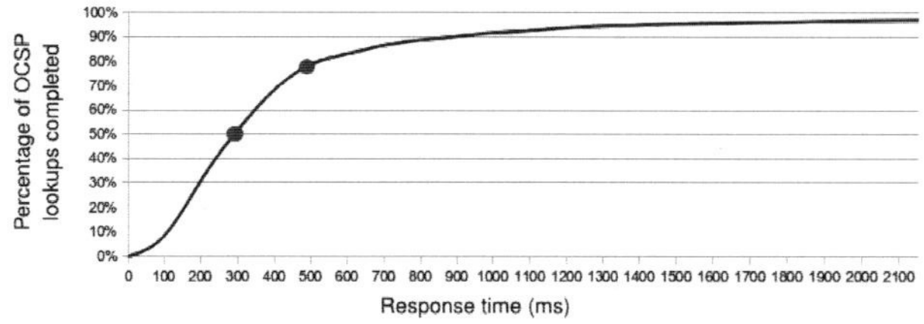

Median: 291 ms, **mean:** 498 ms

OCSP in the wild

CDF of OCSP response time:

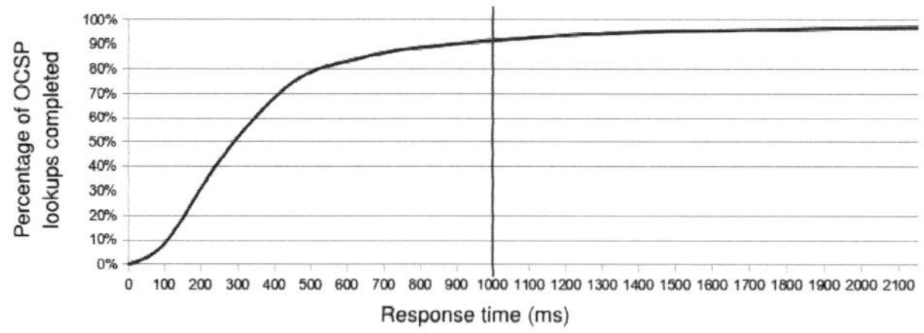

Median: 291 ms, **mean:** 498 ms

OCSP in the wild

CDF of OCSP response time:

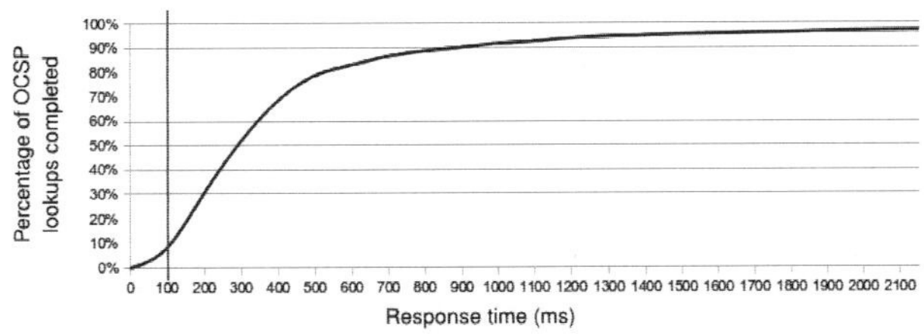

Median: 291 ms, **mean:** 498 ms

Design

- Prefetch certificates
  - Enables Snap Start handshakes more frequently
- Prevalidate certificates
  - Removes OCSP lookup from critical path

Design questions

- When to prefetch? When to prevalidate?
- How to obtain certificate?

When to prefetch

Ideas borrowed from DNS prefetching:

- DNS prefetching triggers are effective for certs

When to prefetch

Ideas borrowed from DNS prefetching:

- DNS prefetching triggers are effective for certs
- Could be deployed with HTML hints for effective prefetching

How to prefetch

- Goal: Obtain server certificate
- Challenge: Full TLS handshake is expensive
- Four proposed methods that are more efficient

Prefetching methods

Option 1: Truncated handshake

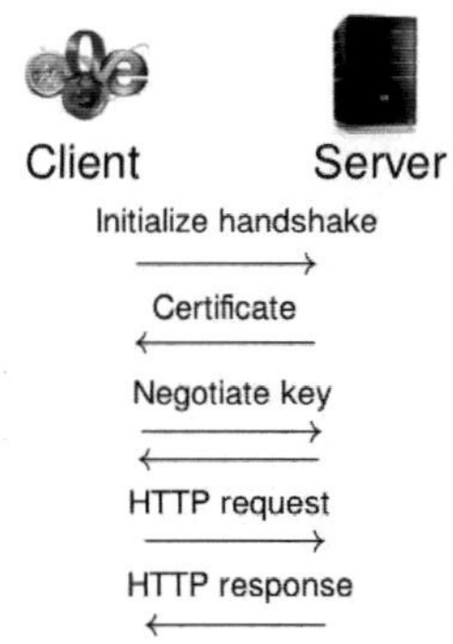

Prefetching methods

Option 1: Truncated handshake

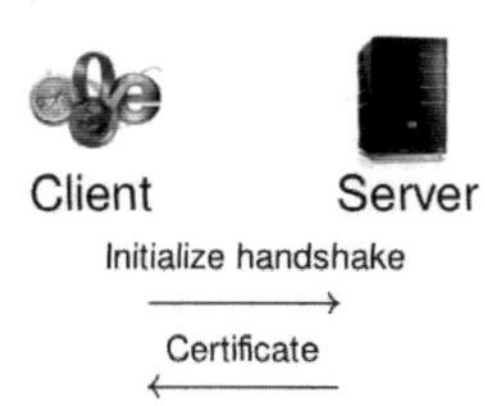

Prefetching methods

Option 1: Truncated handshake

- No public key crypto!
- Server admin does nothing
- But implementation requires new API in TLS layer

Prefetching methods

Option 2: HTTP GET request

e.g., to `http://www.domain.com/cert`

- Much less load than full TLS handshake, but still impacts the server

Prefetching methods

What if we want no additional load on server?

Prefetching methods

What if we want no additional load on server?
Option 3: Retrieve from CDN

- HTTP GET request, avoid hitting web server

Prefetching methods

What if we want no additional load on server?
Option 4: Retrieve from DNS

- DNS TXT record can store certificate
- No impact on web server

Prevalidation

- After prefetching cert, prevalidate it
  - Normal OCSP lookup

Prototype

- Prefetching and prevalidating in Chromium
- Piggyback on DNS prefetching architecture
- DNS and HTTP GET prefetching

Analysis

- How much does prefetching and prevalidating affect handshake latency?

Handshake latency

- Normal TLS handshake: **122 ms**

  ↓ Remove round trips by prefetching cert and using Snap Start

- Snap Start, unvalidated cert: **83 ms**

  ↓ Remove OCSP validation by prevalidating cert

- Snap Start, prevalidated cert: **30 ms**

Server: Ubuntu 10.04, 256MB, Apache 2.2.17, Client: Ubuntu 10.04, 1GB RAM

HTTP GET request: 16 ms

Conclusions

- OCSP latency matters, especially when handshakes have fewer RTTs
- Need prefetched certificate to **enable Snap Start** and for **OCSP prevalidation**
- 4 proposed strategies for prefetching certs
- Reduce TLS handshake by two RTTs and OCSP response time (factor of 4 in our experiments)

Gatling: Automatic Attack Discovery in Large-Scale Distributed Systems

Hyojeong Lee, Jeff Seibert, Charles Killian and Cristina Nita-Rotaru
Department of Computer Science
Purdue University
{hyojlee, jcseiber, ckillian, crisn}@purdue.edu

Abstract

In this paper, we propose Gatling, a framework that automatically finds performance attacks caused by insider attackers in large-scale message-passing distributed systems. In performance attacks, malicious nodes deviate from the protocol when sending or creating messages, with the goal of degrading system performance. We identify a representative set of basic malicious message delivery and lying actions and design a greedy search algorithm that finds effective attacks consisting of a subset of these actions. While lying malicious actions are protocol dependent, requiring the format and meaning of messages, Gatling captures them without needing to modify the target system, by using a type-aware compiler. We have implemented and used Gatling on six systems, a virtual coordinate system, a distributed hash table lookup service and application, two multicast systems and one file sharing application, and found a total of 41 attacks, ranging from a few minutes to a few hours to find each attack.

1 Introduction

Building robust, high-performance, large scale distributed systems is a challenging task given the complexity of designing, testing, and debugging such systems. Programming environments [27, 33, 35, 36, 38], execution logging and replay tools [20, 39], test case generation tools [13], and a variety of testbeds [4, 7, 44], emulations [1, 2, 52], and simulation platforms [3, 5, 6] were created to ease code development and testing.

Given the difficulty of finding bugs manually, several techniques have been applied to find them automatically. Model checking using static analysis [25, 34] has been used to verify that the design of a system is correct. Given the model of the system, this approach proves that some invariants hold for every reachable state in the system. Model checking has limited applicability for complex designs due to the intractable number of states that must be checked. Checking the design is not a guarantee that the actual code is free from bugs because models do not capture all the intricacies of real implementations and additional bugs can be introduced during implementation.

Finding bugs in distributed systems implementation has been done with the use of symbolic execution, fault injection, and model checking. Symbolic execution [13] has been used to generate test cases that are capable of covering many control flow branches. This technique also suffers from a state-space explosion when applied to more complex implementations. Fault injection [24] has been used to discover unknown bugs by testing fault handling code that would not normally be tested. Fault injection is often limited in scope because it is difficult to apply to an implementation in a systematic manner. Finally, model checking using a systematic state-space exploration [25,26,41,56,57] has been used on system implementations to find bugs that violate specified invariants. To mitigate the effect of state-space explosion, the state exploration uses an iterative search, bounding some aspect of the execution. These heuristics do not prove bug absence, but rather help pinpoint where bugs do exist.

More recently, debugging techniques have been applied to automatically find attacks. Many works have been focused on finding or preventing vulnerabilities that either cause the victim to crash or allow the attacker to gain escalated privileges [16, 22, 37, 43, 54]. Dynamic taint analysis [37, 43, 54] has been used to protect implementations from well-defined attacks, such as buffer overflow attacks. Taint analysis is limited in that it is a *detection* mechanism, not a search mechanism. Fault injection with an iterative parameter space search [11] has also been used to find vulnerabilities in distributed systems. However, this approach requires a costly parameter optimization limiting the size of the system it can be used to analyze.

Most distributed systems are designed to meet application-prescribed metrics that ensure availability and high-performance. However, attacks can significantly degrade performance, limiting the practical utility of these systems in adversarial environments. In particular, compromised participants can manipulate protocol semantics through attacks that target the messages exchanged with honest nodes. To date, finding attacks against performance has been primarily a manual task due to both the difficulty of expressing performance as an invariant in the system and the state-space explosion that occurs as attackers are more realistically modeled. The only works we are aware of that focused on automatically finding performance attacks are the works in [50] which considers lying in headers of packets in two-party protocols, and [32] which assumes the user supplies a suspect line of code, indicating that it should not be executed many times. The method in [50] explores all states and does not scale for a distributed system. The method used in [32] has better scalability by combining static with runtime testing, but focuses only on attacks that exploit control flow and where attackers know the state of the benign nodes.

In this work we focus on how to automatically detect performance attacks on *implementations of large-scale message passing distributed systems*. We consider insider attacks that have a global impact on system performance and which are conducted through message manipulation. We focus on these attacks given they have received limited attention, they can cause significant disruption on the system, and they are applicable to many distributed systems. Our goal is to provide a list of effective attacks to the user in a timely manner, requiring the user to provide only one or several metrics measuring system progress. Our contributions are:

- We propose Gatling, a framework that combines a model checker and simulator environment with a fault injector to find performance attacks in event-based message passing distributed systems. We identify basic malicious message delivery and message lying actions that insider attackers can use to create attacks. We design an attack discovery algorithm that uses a greedy search approach based on an impact score that measures attack effectiveness. Gatling works for a large class of distributed systems and does not require the user to write a malicious implementation. While Gatling does not fix attacks nor prove their absence, it provides the user with protocol-level semantic meaning about the discovered attacks.

- We provide a concrete implementation of Gatling for the Mace [27] toolkit. Mace provides a compiler and runtime environment for building high performance, modular distributed systems. Our changes include: (1) adding an interposition layer between Mace services and the networking services to implement malicious message delivery actions, (2) modifying the Mace compiler to include a message serialization code injector to implement message lying actions, and (3) modifying the simulator to implement our attack discovery algorithm. The user provides an implementation of the distributed system in Mace and specifies an impact score in a simulation driver that allows the system to run in the simulator.

- We demonstrate with a case study how to use Gatling to find attacks on a real system implementation, the BulletPrime peer-to-peer file distribution system. Our goal is not to criticize BulletPrime's design, but to explore its behavior in an adversarial environment. While some of the attacks found on BulletPrime were expected, such as delaying or dropping data messages, others were more surprising. Specifically, BulletPrime's reliance on services that provide improved download times led to a number of vulnerabilities.

- We further validate Gatling by applying it to five additional systems having different application goals and designs: the Vivaldi [19] virtual coordinate system, the Chord lookup service and distributed hash table (DHT) [51], and two multicast systems: ESM [17] and Scribe [49]. Gatling found a total of 41 performance attacks across the systems tested, 17 attacks based on message lying actions and 24 attacks based on message delivery actions. Finding each attack took a few minutes to a few hours.

Roadmap. Sections 2 and 3 describe the design and implementation of Gatling. Section 4 provides an example of how to use Gatling to find attacks in a well-known distributed file sharing system, BulletPrime [28]. Section 5 presents results on using our tool on five representative distributed systems: Vivaldi [19], Chord, DHT [51], ESM [17], and Scribe [49]. Section 6 presents related work and Section 7 concludes our paper.

2 Gatling Design

The design goal of Gatling is to automatically find insider attacks in distributed systems. We focus on attacks against system performance where compromised participants running malicious implementations try to degrade the overall performance of the system through their actions. Such attacks require that the system has a performance metric, that when evaluated gives an indication of the progress it has in completing its goals. For example, for an overlay multicast system throughput is an indication of the performance of the system. Specifically, we define:

Performance attack A set of actions that deviate from the protocol, taken by a group of malicious nodes, that results in performance that is worse than in benign scenarios by some Δ.

Next, we describe the system model we consider, identify malicious actions which represent building blocks for an attack, and describe our algorithm that searches and discovers attacks consisting of multiple malicious actions.

2.1 Design Overview

Model checking event-driven state machines. Many distributed systems [27, 29–31, 36, 40, 46–48, 55] are designed following event-based state machines that communicate through messages. Also several other systems use RPCs [35, 51], continuations [33], or data flow [38], which are *compatible* with this approach. Thus, we focus on distributed systems implementations that are conceptually message passing event-driven state machines, and we will refer to this as the *message-event model.*

A well-known approach to find bugs in distributed systems is to use model checking which allows a user to explore the set of all possible behaviors. This approach, when applied to systems implementations, results in a systematic state-space exploration through carefully controlled execution to determine all reachable system states. The state of a distributed system is conceptually the combination of the state maintained at each node, in conjunction with the state of the network connecting distributed nodes.

The message-event model provides opportunities for reducing the state space. First, it avoids the complexity of simulating networking and routing layers by abstracting the network to be a basic service which either provides FIFO reliable message passing (such as TCP), or best-effort message passing (such as UDP). As a result, the network state is given by the set of messages in-flight, and the corresponding service guarantees for each message. Second, it limits the complexity model of concurrency by maintaining the event queue, and systematically executing each possible event sequence. Events may be network events (e.g. delivery of a message), scheduled events (e.g. expiration of a timer), or application events (e.g. user request for an action).

Several prior model checker designs [21, 26, 41, 42] have explored the capabilities of event-driven state machines to find bugs in systems implementations. Each of these designs provide mechanisms to explore complex interactions between nodes which would normally be infeasible for a user to exhaustively explore. However, due to the exponential state space explosion as the search depth increases, these systems settle for heuristically exploring the state space and locating correctness bugs only in an execution with benign participants.

Our approach. Finding performance problems is very challenging in an exhaustive approach because often these bugs are the result of specific timings, for which finding would require searching on the space of possible timings of events, a far less practical approach. On the other hand, simulating performance of a system is straightforward - as the simulator keeps an ordered list of outstanding events, including the time at which they are scheduled to occur. Each time an event executes, the clock of that node advances, allowing the system to conduct a time-based event driven simulation. However, it does not systematically explore all the possible executions.

Our design, Gatling, overcomes these limitations by using a hybrid approach. Specifically, Gatling uses a time-based simulation model to provide support for detecting performance attacks, and integrates a search algorithm into the time-based simulation model to find in a practical way such attacks. The resulting architecture is illustrated in Fig. 1. Gatling constructs a set of nodes, with a fraction of them flagged as being malicious. Gatling maintains an event queue sorted by event start time, and simulates the event queue normally. However, when an event is executing on a node selected to be malicious, Gatling uses a model-checking exploration approach to test the set of different possibilities for what new events are scheduled by the malicious node; in particular, the set of messages sent by the malicious node. Note, Gatling does not require the developer to provide a malicious implementation. Instead, Gatling requires type-awareness of the messaging protocol, and applies the basic actions described in the next section to the *outputs* of a non-malicious node implementation. To measure the impact of the malicious action, Gatling executes an impact score function, considering only the nodes not flagged as malicious.

2.2 Malicious Actions

An insider attacker can globally influence the performance of the system by misleading other honest participants through exchanged messages. We classify all malicious actions on messages into two categories, message delivery actions and message lying actions. Message delivery actions refer to *how* a message is sent, while message lying actions refer to *what* a message contains. The list we present is not an exhaustive list and can be easily extended by adding additional delivery or lying strategies. Below we describe the specific malicious actions we consider.

Message delivery actions. Performing message delivery actions does not require knowledge of the messaging protocol, because the actions are being applied to where and when the message is delivered, rather than modifying the message contents. We define the following types of malicious message delivery actions.

- *Dropping*: A malicious node drops a message instead of sending it to its intended destination.
- *Delaying*: A malicious node does not immediately send a message and injects a delay.

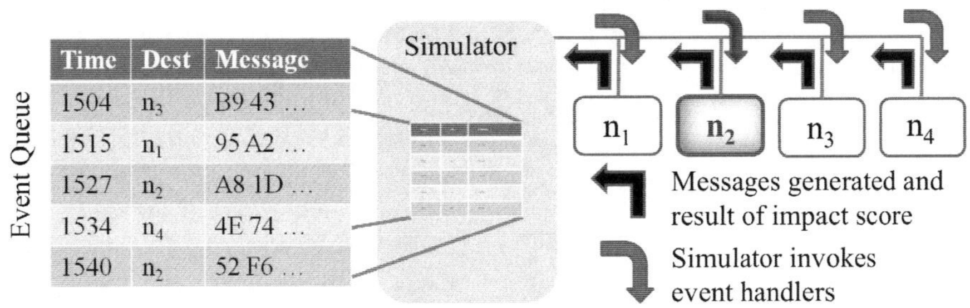

Figure 1. Gatling simulator model

- *Diverting*: A malicious node does not send the message to its destination as intended by the protocol, and instead enqueues the message for delivery to a node other than the original destination. The destination is randomly chosen from the set of nodes in the system.

- *Duplicating*: A malicious node sends a message twice instead of sending only one copy, applying delay to the second copy. We consider two versions of message duplication. One is to send the duplicated message to the original destination again, and the other is to divert the duplicated message to another random destination in the system.

Message lying actions. We define message lying actions as actions where malicious participants modify the content of the message they are sending to another participant. An effective lying action involves intelligently modifying fields of messages to contain contents likely to cause different behaviors, which is more sophisticated than random bit-flipping. Gatling makes data-type-specific changes to message contents by being dependent on the messaging protocol. As the number of possible values that the message field could contain may be extremely large, we define a few general strategies for field types that stress the system in different ways based on general experience on the kind of error cases or hand-crafted attacks observed in practice previously. We provide the following strategies for numeric types.

- *Min or Max*: A malicious node can change the value to be the minimum or maximum value for the type.

- *Zero*: For signed types, a malicious node can additionally change the value of the field to be the number 0.

- *Scaling*: A malicious node could increase or decrease the numeric value by a percentage.

- *Spanning*: A malicious node can select specific values from a set which spans the range of the data type. Spanning values are important because protocols sometimes use only a subset of legal values, apply sanity checks to inputs, or fail to apply sanity checks when necessary to avoid *e.g.* overflow/underflow. Spanning values can be chosen assisted by static analysis or developer insight; we find that a range of values orders of magnitude apart are sufficient to find attacks in many systems.

- *Random*: A malicious node can select a random value from the range of the type.

In addition to the above choices, boolean values have an additional option: toggling the value between true and false. The list can be easily extended, for example using a "complement" strategy for integral values (a generalization of the boolean flipping).

Node identifiers, such as an IPv4 address or a hash key, are integral aspects of distributed systems. Thus, we treat them as a native type and allow lying on them as well. Malicious nodes can lie about node identifiers, where lying values are selected randomly from the identifiers of all nodes, malicious nodes, or benign nodes.

We also have special handling for non-numeric types. For simplicity, collections (e.g. list, set, map, etc.) are treated as applying one of the above strategies to all of the elements within the collection. Users can further extend Gatling as needed to provide lying strategies for additional types, as we have done for node identifiers.

2.3 Discovering Attacks

A naive approach to discovering attacks is executing all possible sequences of actions (malicious and benign) in the system and then finding the sequences that cause performance to degrade below the benign case scenario. However, this approach becomes intractable because of the size of the search space considering the number of possible sequences of actions. Specifically, at every time step, any benign event could execute based on timings, but additionally, any malicious node could generate any message defined by the system, performing any combination of malicious actions on it and send it to any node. Considering all possible attack values for a message containing a single 32-bit integer entails an exploration branching at the impractical rate of at least 2^{32}. Benign state-space exploration is shielded from this problem by the fact that while the message field could theoretically contain any of the 2^{32} values, at any point in time only a small subset of those values would be sent by a non-malicious node.

Attack properties. As a first step toward practical automated search of attacks, we focus on a class of performance attacks that have several properties that reduce the state space exploration needed to discover them:

1) Single-behavior: We define a single-behavior attack as a list which describes, for each type of message, what malicious or benign action all malicious nodes will take whenever sending a message of that type. Intuitively, this attack definition is based on the principle that in some cases, past success is an indication of future success. Thus, every time a malicious node must decide how to behave when sending a message, it can choose the same action that succeeded before, and expect success again. This allows us to reduce the search space of malicious actions substantially, because once we have discovered a successful malicious action for a message type, we no longer explore other possibilities for the same type of message sent by any malicious node.

2) Easily reproducible: We assume attacks that are not largely dependent on the specific state of the distributed system and thus can be easily reproduced. Intuitively, the attacks we discover are those to which the system is generally vulnerable, rather than having only a small vulnerability window. Easily reproducible attacks allow us to safely ignore the particular sequence of benign actions that occur alongside the malicious actions and focus our search solely on malicious actions.

3) Near-immediate measurable effects: We consider attacks that do not have a large time-lag between when they occur and when the performance of the system is actually affected. Intuitively, focusing on near-immediate effective attacks will be ideal for finding direct attacks on system performance, but it will not allow Gatling to discover stealth attacks, where the goal is to obtain control without affecting the performance of the system under attack. The near-immediate impact on the system performance of the attacks creates the opportunity to find attacks by only executing a smaller sequence of actions for a relatively short window of time. We decide if a malicious action is a possible attack by using an impact score I_s function that is based on a performance metric of the system and is provided by the user. We require two properties of the impact score. One, that it can be evaluated at any time during the execution. Two, that when comparing scores, a larger score implies that the performance is worse.

4) Most effective minimal combination: While Gatling will discover single-behavior attacks that contain basic behaviors for many message types, some behaviors will have only a nominal impact on the performance of the system, and other behaviors may be quite effective as stand-alone attacks. To allow the developer to discern these cases, Gatling automatically determines the relative contribution of each attack action to the overall performance degradation, allowing the developer to further reduce the attack to their minimal portions that have the most significant impact.

Gatling builds up an attack by finding several instances where applying a malicious action on a message results in an increase in the impact score, then building up the maximally effective single-behavior attack across message types. Once it has found the maximally effective single-behavior attack, it determines the contribution of each malicious action of the attack, and then can be repeated to find additional attacks.

Greedy action selection procedure. To find an instance where a single malicious action results in an increase in the impact score, we use the procedure depicted in Fig. 2. The main idea is to execute the program normally until a malicious node attempts to send a message. At this point we branch the execution and run on each branch the malicious version of the sending of the message (try all malicious actions described in Section 2.2) and then continue running the branch for a window of time t_w. By measuring the impact score at the end of each window of execution, we can determine whether any of the malicious actions degraded the performance relative to the baseline without a malicious action. Since we measure the impact of only a single malicious action instance, we consider any increase in the impact score to suggest that the particular malicious action could be a part of a successful attack. We greedily select the strongest such malicious action and update a tally for that message type and malicious action.

Building up the single-behavior attack. The greedy action selection procedure finds the most effective malicious action for a single instance of sending a message. We report a malicious action as part of an attack once it has been selected in n_a *different instances* for the same message type. The n_a threshold allows us to avoid cases in which the impact was a random variation, and provides a balance between attacks which are more frequently successful but with a lower impact, and attacks which are less frequently successful but with a higher impact.

If we only wished to find attacks incorporating a single message type at a time, we could at this point simply iterate through the set of message types, and perform the greedy procedure each time that message type is sent. While suc-

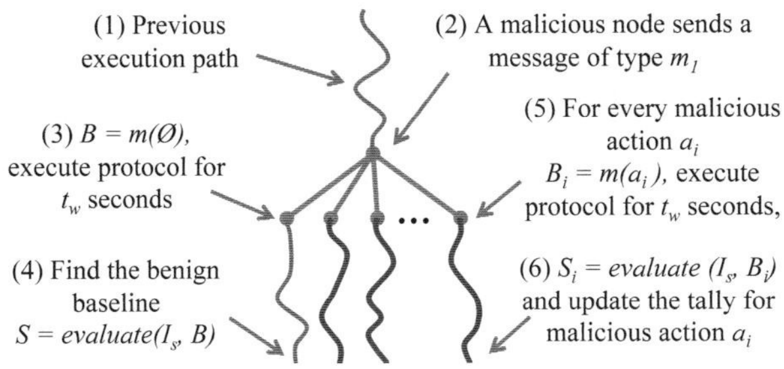

Figure 2. Greedy action selection procedure for one instance of sending message type m_1

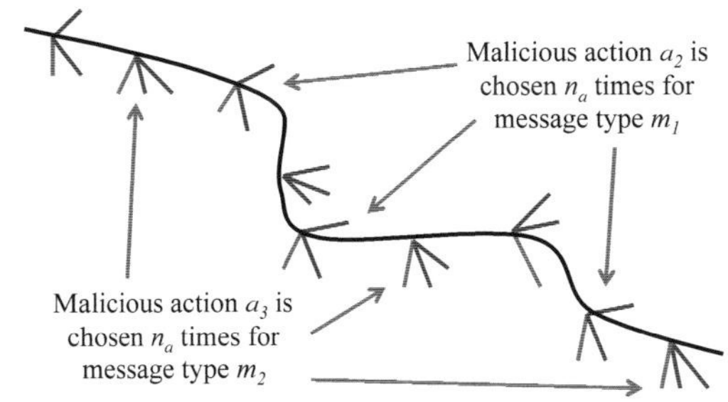

Figure 3. Greedy procedure applied for several instances of message types m_1 and m_2

cessful in finding single-behavior, single-message attacks, this approach would not find *dependent* attacks, where the success of an attack is conditional on a prior malicious action choice. Consider for example the case of a malicious node which lies to increase the number of children it has in a tree overlay. If the malicious node does not also perform an action on application data, then this kind of attack would not be discovered using single-message attacks.

To discover dependent attacks, Gatling simultaneously searches across all message types, allowing it to find combination attacks, where individual malicious actions work together to build stronger overall attacks. By applying the greedy action selection procedure to the instances as they are encountered, rather than iterating through message types, our algorithm can locate amplifying stealth attacks without prior knowledge of the order in which malicious actions must occur. Specifically, the system is simulated normally until a malicious node attempts to send a message of a type for which an attack has not been identified. The greedy selection procedure is used to determine the best action to take for this instance, and a tally is kept of the times each malicious action was chosen. The number of times no malicious action is selected in a row is also tallied, as a means to halt the search. We show in Fig. 3 the greedy procedure being applied to several instances for two different types of messages.

Once the search halts, the contribution of each of the actions is computed, and if the attack impact is greater than some Δ, the user is notified, and the algorithm repeats but does not search on previously used malicious actions. Computing the action contribution involves running the system again for an extended period both with and without the determined attack. This allows Gatling to verify that the attack satisfies the requirement that its impact is greater than Δ. Gatling then determines the relative contribution of each component by running additional tests, subtracting out the least effective contributor until it is no longer an attack. This computation and sorting procedure is important for

variables:
  vector $Attack$: Learned behaviors for most effective attack for each message type
  map $AttackAndContribution$: Attack listing relative contribution of actions
  matrix $AttackTally$: Count, for each message type, the times the attack is determined most effective
  $IneffectiveTally$: The number of times no malicious action is chosen consecutively
while $IneffectiveTally < HaltingThreshold$ **do**
  Continue simulating system until malicious node sends a message m;
  $msgType \leftarrow typeof(m)$;
  $MostEffectiveAction \leftarrow Attack[msgType]$;
  if $MostEffectiveAction = \emptyset$ **then**
    Find behavior $MostEffectiveAction \in \{\emptyset, A(msgType)\}$ according to selection procedure (Fig. 2)
    if $MostEffectiveAction \neq \emptyset$ **then**
      $AttackTally[msgType][MostEffectiveAction]$++;
      $IneffectiveTally \leftarrow 0$;
      if $AttackTally[msgType][MostEffectiveAction] = n_a$ **then**
        $Attack[msgType] \leftarrow MostEffectiveAction$;
      end
    else
      $IneffectiveTally$++;
    end
  end
  execute behavior $m(MostEffectiveAction)$;
end
$AttackAndContribution, \delta$ = computeActionContribution($Attack$);
if $\delta > \Delta$ **then**
  output $AttackAndContribution$;
  Repeat, ignoring prior Attack actions
end

Algorithm 1: Attack discovery algorithm

three reasons. First, as a greedy approach, it is possible that Gatling finds a local maximum, but that the order in which malicious actions were selected diminished the overall impact (e.g. an attack may later be found which by itself is more potent than when combined with the earlier attack). Second, some malicious actions may depend on other malicious actions for success, this search will order them accordingly. Third, some malicious actions may have only a minor impact, or a strong enough impact to be used in isolation, this post processing can provide this information. In fact, we often find multiple attacks from a single run of the Gatling search algorithm. We present our algorithm in details in Algorithm 1.

Impact score and parameter selection. The user must specify an impact score. As stated, the impact score must be able to be executed at any time, rather than only at the completion of an execution, and must let greater values indicate a greater impact. Consider, for example, an impact score for a file download system. Using total download time as an impact score would satisfy the requirement that bigger numbers indicate more impact (slower download times), but fails the requirement that it can be evaluated at any time (it can only be evaluated once the file is downloaded). The current average goodput of the file download satisfies the requirement that it can be evaluated at any time, but in the case of goodput, bigger numbers actually mean less impact. An alternative might include an inversion of the goodput, or instead it could simply be a measure of how much of the file is left to download.

Gatling requires the setup of two parameters, t_w and n_a. Larger values of t_w increase the search time while smaller values may not capture the effects of the malicious action on performance. In the case of n_a, its setup should take into account the normal variability of performance in the system that is evaluated.

3 Implementation

We created a concrete implementation of Gatling for the Mace [27] toolkit. Mace is publicly available and was designed for building large-scale, high-performance distributed systems implementations based on C++. It consists of a source-to-source compiler, a set of runtime libraries, as well as a model checker and time-based simulator. The release also includes several distributed systems implementations. The Mace compiler enforces the *message-event model* and generates implementations of message serialization, both useful for Gatling. Specifically, the message event-model allows us to influence message delivery, while message serialization allows us to implement message lying without modifying the target system code, but just by defining specific lying actions for different types.

To implement Gatling we made the following changes to Mace. We added an interposition layer between Mace services and the networking services, we modified the Mace compiler to include a message serialization code injector, we added supporting serialization code in the Mace runtime library, and we modified the simulator to implement our attack discovery algorithm. The user provides an implementation of the distributed system in Mace and specifies an impact score in a simulation driver that allows the system to run in the simulator. The Mace compiler will generate the message serialization injected code in the user code.

This modular design allows code reuse and allows Gatling to focus attacks on modules independently. The interposition layer implements *malicious message delivery actions*. When a node requests sending a message, before providing the message to the network messaging services, Gatling consults the attack discovery algorithm to decide whether to take any message delivery action. Message dropping, delaying, diverting, and duplicating are provided by either not making the call to the messaging services, queueing the message for sending 0.5 to 2 seconds later, calling into the messaging services multiple times, or passing a different destination to the messaging services. To support diverting messages, the simulator provides lists of malicious and benign node identifiers.

The injected serialization code component implements *malicious message lying actions*. The injected code similarly consults the attack discovery algorithm to determine if a lying action should be taken. As we are searching for single-behavior attacks, the simulator directs only a single field in a message to be lied about during one branch of the greedy selection procedure. If any lying does occur, when serializing the appropriate field of the message a simulator chosen value is used instead of the one provided. The user-written code is not modified, nor are any user-visible variables. Simulator-provided lists are similarly used to lie about node identifiers.

Fig. 4 shows the Mace+Gatling architectural design when testing a layered DHT application. The parts noted with G represent the Gatling additions and modifications. The user provides each DHT component layer in the Mace language (shown at left): a simulation driver (*SimDriver*), containing the impact score function; the storage layer (DHT); a recursive overlay routing layer (ROR); and the Chord lookup service layer. The Mace compiler then translates each layer into C++ code, injecting message lying actions into each layer tailored to the messages that layer defines. Standard C++ tools then compile and link the generated code with the Gatling interposition layer, Mace runtime library, simulated TCP and UDP messaging services, and the Mace simulator application. *SimDriver* allows the application to run in the simulator; to deploy the DHT application, the C++ code need only be re-linked with the real TCP and UDP messaging services, and a C++ user applica-

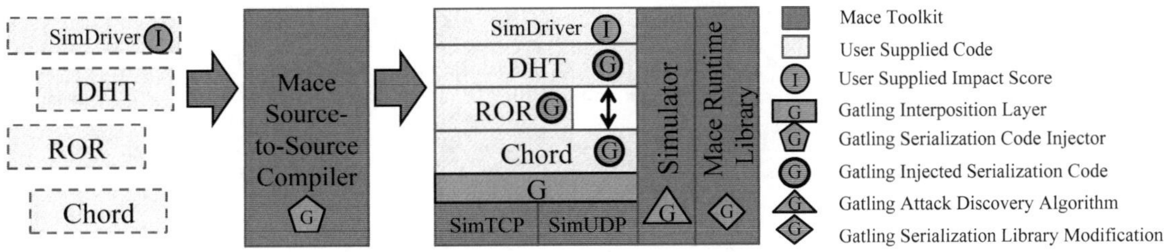

Figure 4. Gatling implementation for one node: DHT example

tion in lieu of *SimDriver*.

4 Case Study: BulletPrime

In this section we demonstrate how to use Gatling to find attacks on a real system implementation. For our case study we apply Gatling to an implementation of the BulletPrime peer-to-peer file distribution protocol [28, 31] that we received from the authors of the system. We selected BulletPrime as a case study because it uses a more complex design involving several services. While we illustrate how a developer might use Gatling to find attacks arising from a malicious or simply misconfigured node, our intention is not to criticize BulletPrime's design. Instead we explore its behavior in an adversarial environment that many practical uses might require.

BulletPrime is a file distribution system similar to BitTorrent [18]. However, where BitTorrent focuses on local optimizations that greedily benefit each node individually, BulletPrime uses a more collaborative set of algorithms that are geared towards global optimization. For example, while both BitTorrent and BulletPrime implement mesh-based strategies for peering, and use rarity as a mechanism for increasing block diversity, BulletPrime learns about new peers by using a gossip protocol that guarantees each node receives a uniformly random distribution of peers and their current download status. BulletPrime also searches independently for peers that can provide maximal download or upload bandwidth, as opposed to BitTorrent's symmetric block exchange algorithm.

The BulletPrime component design is illustrated in Fig. 5. The BulletPrime service manages the state of the file download, implements sending Diff messages to connected peers with information of newly available blocks of the file; and tracks the performance of the peers. It utilizes the Distributor service to manage the queued Data messages to each peer, keeping the network buffers full without sending excess data. BulletPrime uses the Mesh service to learn of new peers and maintain active connection to upload and download peers. The Mesh service sends Join and JoinReply messages, and uses the RanSub [30] service to discover potential peers. RanSub, meanwhile, uses an overlay tree to perform a specialized type of aggregation, proceeding in periodic phases that Collect candidate sets of information to the root, and then Distribute uniformly randomized candidate sets to all peers.

To run Gatling on BulletPrime, we first had to prepare it to run in the simulator and implement an impact score. We wrote an 85 line simulated application driver that provides the basic functionality of having the source node distribute data to others and having the client nodes download and participate in the file-sharing protocol. We chose for the impact score a performance metric which captures the progress of node downloads; namely the number of blocks of the file downloaded. To satisfy the requirement that a higher score indicates more attack impact, we instead use the total number of blocks *remaining* before completion. We had to modify BulletPrime slightly, adding the 8-line impact score function, because it did not expose enough information to the simulated driver to compute the score. We simulated BulletPrime with 100 nodes disseminating a 50MB file. We use a small 5 sec t_w as nodes download blocks quickly, starting nearly at the beginning of the simulation. Due to some variable system performance, we set n_a to 5, allowing Gatling to explore a few instances per message type. We set Δ to be zero for all our experiments to find as many attacks as possible.

Assertions and segmentation faults: As we began to use Gatling on the BulletPrime implementation, we encountered nodes crashing due to the fact that BulletPrime assumes peers to act correctly. For example, we found nodes crashing due to assertions and segmentation faults when receiving a malicious FileInfo message. This message defines the file and block size and is created by the source. Intermediate nodes that forward the message can lie about its contents when passing it along. We found another crash scenario when a malicious node requests a non-existing block, causing the recipient to crash by assertion attempting to retrieve the block. We implemented checks in the code to prevent crashing and we disabled any attack on FileInfo for

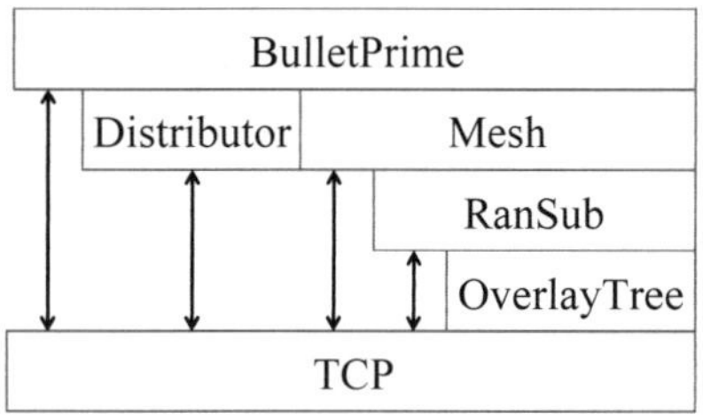

Figure 5. BulletPrime design

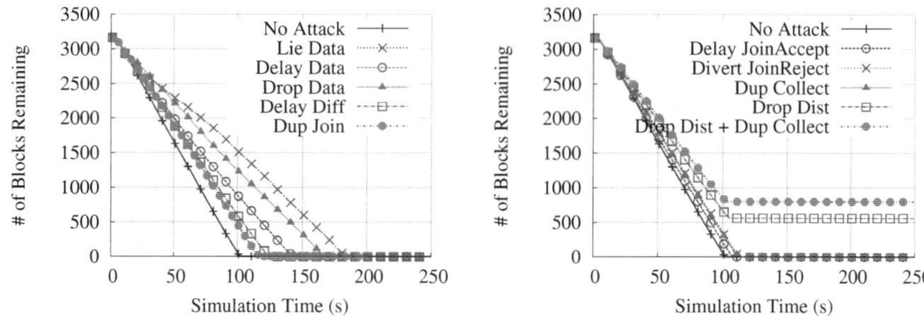

Figure 6. Remaining blocks for the attacks found on BulletPrime

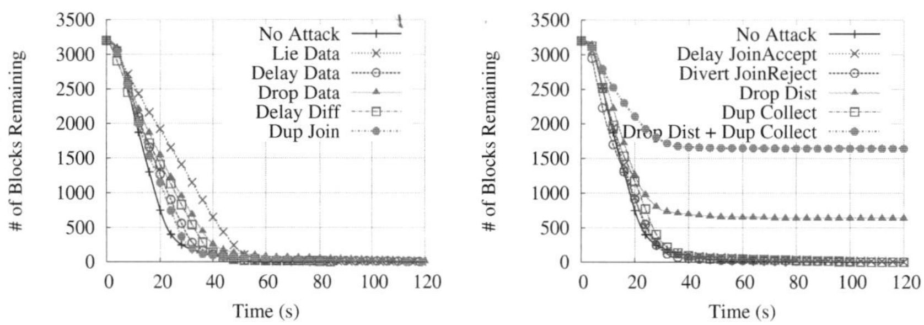

Figure 7. Remaining blocks for the attacks found on BulletPrime on PlanetLab

further Gatling simulations.

Fig. 6 shows the performance of the system under the attacks we discover. To give a baseline comparison, we also show the benign scenario when there is no attack. We have found attacks against four of the five services.

Distributor service: We found several attacks on Data messages. Lying on the id field of a Data message degrades the performance significantly. We also found dropping or delaying Data causes performance degradation.

BulletPrime service: Furthermore, Gatling found a delaying attack on the Diff message which causes a performance penalty, since peers cannot request the block until receiving the Diff message.

Mesh service: Gatling also reported an attack vector that is a combination of 1) duplicate Join message and divert the second copy to a random destination, 2) delay JoinAccepted message for 0.5s, and 3) divert JoinRejected message to a random destination. Gatling computed the most effective minimal combination found that all actions are effective even when they are used alone, however the combination of the three was the most effective. We show the individual attacks in Fig. 6.

RanSub service: Gatling found an attack which was a combination of dropping Distribute messages that are disseminated from the root toward the leaves over the control tree and also duplicating Collect messages that are collected from leaves towards the root. Gatling found that both actions alone degrade performance and furthermore dropping Distribute messages causes nodes to never be able to download a number of blocks.

While some of the attacks found on BulletPrime were expected, such as delaying or dropping data messages, less obvious was the impact of the attacks on the Mesh and RanSub services. Although BulletPrime gains nice mathematical properties by using RanSub, it seems that a BulletPrime implementation robust to insider attacks may be better served by a gossip service re-design. As an extra benefit, Gatling also identified several cases where insiders can crash system nodes due to a lack of input validity checking.

To validate that the attacks are not a result of lack of fidelity in the simulator we ran real-world experiments with the discovered attacks on the PlanetLab testbed, with the same number of nodes and file size. We confirmed that all attacks have a similar effect as in the simulator and we show graphs in Fig. 7.

5 Results

We further validate the Gatling design by applying it to five systems with different application goals and designs. Specifically, we evaluate the Vivaldi [19] virtual coordinate system, the Chord lookup service and distributed hash table (DHT) [51], and two multicast systems: ESM [17] and Scribe [49]. Chord, DHT, and Scribe were previously implemented for Mace; we implemented Vivaldi and ESM according to published papers. We set the number of malicious nodes to be 20% and we select malicious nodes randomly.

Gatling found performance attacks in each system tested, taking from a few minutes to a few hours to find each attack. Gatling was run on a 2GHz Intel Xeon CPU with 16GB of RAM. Gatling processes are CPU bound, so parallelizing the search could further reduce the search time. We discovered 41 attacks in total, however due to lack of space we only present in detail a subset of attacks that illustrate the capabilities of Gatling. In Table 1, we summarize all the attacks.

5.1 Vivaldi

System description. Vivaldi [19] is a distributed system that provides an accurate and efficient service that allows hosts on the Internet to estimate the latency to arbitrary hosts without actively monitoring all of the nodes in the network. The system maps these latencies to a set of coordinates based on a distance function. Each node measures the round trip time (RTT) to a set of neighbor nodes, and then determines the distance between any two nodes. The main protocol consists of Probe messages sent by a node to measure their neighbors RTTs and then a Response message from these neighbors is sent back with their current coordinates and local error value.

Impact score. We use the *prediction error* [19] which describes how well the system predicts the actual RTT between nodes. Prediction error is defined as $median(|RTT^{i,j}_{Est} - RTT^{i,j}_{Act}|)$, where $RTT^{i,j}_{Est}$ is node i's estimated RTT for node j given by the resulting coordinates and $RTT^{i,j}_{Act}$ is the most recently measured RTT.

Experimental setup. We simulated 400 nodes and randomly assign RTT values for each node from the KING data set [23] which contains pair-wise RTT measurements of 1740 nodes on the Internet. Malicious nodes start their attacks from the beginning of the simulation. We set t_w to be 5 sec and n_a to be 5.

Attacks found using prediction error. We found five attacks using the prediction error impact score. In Fig. 8 we show how each attack affects Vivaldi prediction error over time. The Overflow attack is omitted because the prediction error was *NaN* (not a number). As a baseline we also present Vivaldi when there are no attacks, which we find converges to a stable set of coordinates with 17 ms of error.

Overflow. We first found two variations of an attack where malicious nodes lie and report DBL_MAX for their coordinate and their local error, respectively. In both cases the result is that honest nodes compute their coordinates as *NaN*. We implemented safeguards to address the overflow.

Inflation, oscillation, deflation. We then found three previously reported attacks against Vivaldi [58]. First, known as inflation is a lying attack where malicious nodes lie about their coordinates, providing larger than normal values from the spanning set without causing overflow. Second, known as deflation attack, occurs when where malicious nodes drop outgoing probes, thereby never updating their own coordinates. The third, known as the oscillation attack, occurs where attackers set their coordinates to random values. This is a very effective attack in which nodes cannot converge and the prediction error remains high, about 250,000 ms.

5.2 Chord

System description. Chord [51] is an overlay routing protocol that provides an efficient lookup service. Each node has an identifier that is based on consistent hashing, and is responsible for a range of keys that make up that space. Nodes in Chord construct a ring and maintain a set of pointers to adjacent nodes, called predecessors and successors. When a node i wants to join the ring, it will ask a node already in the ring to identify the correct predecessor and successor for i. i then contacts these nodes and tells them to update their information. Later, a stabilization procedure will update global information to make sure i is known by others in the ring.

Impact score. We use an impact score which measures the progress of forming a correct ring. Since Chord correctness depends on being able to reach every node by following the successor reference around the ring, we use as the impact score the average number of nodes each node can reach by following each node's successor. For a benign case, the impact score should be equal to the total number of nodes.

Experimental setup. We simulate Chord with 100 nodes. Malicious actions start immediately as the goal of Chord is to construct a properly functioning ring and thus we want to find attacks on that construction process. We set t_w to be 2 sec as ring construction takes only 10 sec in the benign case and set n_a to 5.

Attacks found using number of reachable nodes. We found six attacks against the Chord protocol. In Fig. 9 we show the effects of the attacks and illustrate the resulting ring for one attack. As a baseline we verify that when there is no attack all 100 nodes are able to form a ring in less than 10 sec.

Dropping attacks. We found three attacks where malicious nodes drop responses or do not forward replies to requests for predecessor and successor information. The attacks prevent a correct ring from forming. We show in Fig. 9(a) (*Drop Find Pred*, *Drop Get Pred*, and *Drop Get Pred Reply*) that when malicious nodes drop predecessor related messages, less than half the nodes are reachable.

Lying attacks. We found three lying attacks that prevent a

System	Metric Used	Attack Name	Attack Description	Known Attack
BulletPrime	Number of Blocks Remaining	Lie Data	Lie data message distribution	
		Delay Data	Delay data message distribution	
		Drop Data	Drop data message distribution	
		Delay Diff	Delay diff information	
		Dup Join	Duplicate join message and send copy to another	
		Delay JoinAccept	Delay join accepted	
		Divert JoinReply	Send join rejected to another node	
		Drop Dist	Drop information distributed	
		Dup Collect	Dup information collected	
Vivaldi	Prediction Error	Overflow	Lie about coordinates, setting them to maximum value	
		Inflation	Lie about coordinates, setting them to large values	[58]
		Oscillation	Lie about coordinates, setting them to random values	[58]
		Delay	Delay probe reply messages 2s	[58]
		Deflation	Do not initiate request (Drop probes)	[58]
Chord	Number of Reachable Nodes	Drop Find Pred	Drop query to find predecessor	[45]
		Drop Get Pred	Drop query to get predecessor and successor	[45]
		Drop Get Pred Reply	Drop the answer to find predecssor	[14]
		Lie Find Pred	Lie about key that is in query while forwarding queries	[14]
		Lie Predecessor	Lie about predecessor in response while forwarding	[14]
		Lie Successor	Lie about successor candidates in response while forwarding	[14]
DHT	Lookup Latency	Drop Msg	Drop recursive route messages	[14]
		Delay Msg	Delay recursive route messages	
		Dup Msg	Delay recursive route messages and divert second message	[14]
		Lie Msg Src	Lie about the source of recursive route messages	[14]
		Lie Msg Dest	Lie about the destination of recursive route messages	[14]
		Lie SetKeyRange	Lie about what keys are stored	
		Lie Reply Key	Lie about the key in get reply messages	[14]
		Lie Reply Found	Lie about finding the value in get reply messages	[14]
		Lie Reply Get	Lie about the request wanting the value in get reply messages	[14]
ESM	Throughput	Drop Data	Drop data messages	[53]
		Dup Parent	Duplicate parent reply messages, drop data	
		Lie Latency	Lie about measured latency, duplicate probe messages, drop data	[53]
		Lie Bandwidth	Lie about received bandwidth, duplicate probe messages, drop data	[53]
	Latency	Drop Parent	Drop parent reply messages	
Scribe	Throughput	Drop Data	Drop data messages	
		Drop Join	Drop join messages	
		Dup Join	Duplicate join messages	
		Dup Data	Duplicate data messages, sending second message to random node	
		Drop HB	Drop heartbeat message	
		Lie GroupId HB	Lie about the group identifier in a heartbeat message	
		Lie GroupId Join	Lie about the group identifier in a join message	

Table 1. Attacks found using Gatling: 41 attacks in total (17 lie, 12 drop, 6 delay, 5 duplicate, 1 divert)

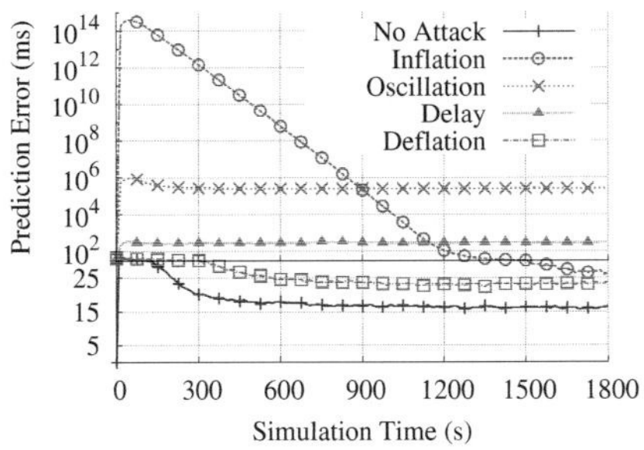

Figure 8. Prediction error for the attacks found on Vivaldi

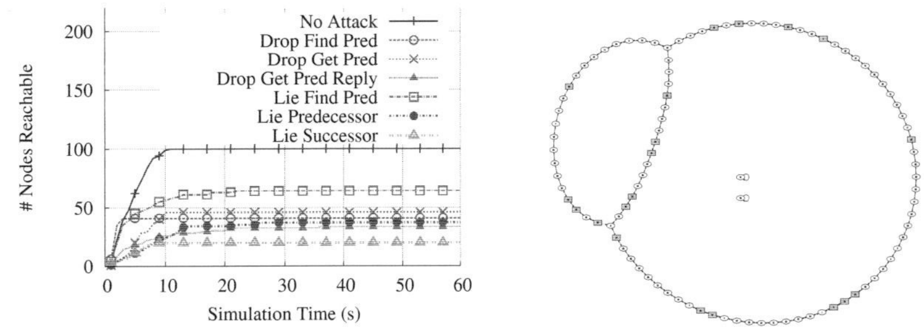

(a) No. of reachable nodes for the attacks found on Chord

(b) *Chord ring under Lie Predecessor attack*

Figure 9. Attack impact on Chord

correct ring from forming. The join protocol first locates the predecessor of a given address i by forwarding a FindPred message through the Chord overlay. If a malicious node modifies the address i in the message, it effectively redirects the node joining to an incorrect place in the ring, and can cause inconsistent state in the nodes, which can lead to a failure to properly join (*Lie Find Pred*). We found similar attacks when a malicious node, during stabilization, queried as to who are its predecessors and successors, lies and gives incorrect information (*Lie Predecessor*, *Lie Successor*). We show impact scores of these attacks in Fig. 9(a). The effect of *Lie Predecessor* on the ring can be seen visually in Fig. 9(b), where some nodes failed to join, and others are confused about their relationships to adjacent nodes.

5.3 Distributed Hash Table

System description. A Distributed Hash Table (DHT) provides a scalable key-value storage service, where nodes self-organize so that each node is responsible for storage of a portion of the key-space. DHTs expose at least two operations to the user, a put operation that stores a value based on its key in the overlay and a get operation that retrieves key-values that are previously stored. The DHT implementation used is a basic one based on the outline in the Chord paper [51], structured as the example described in Figure 4. When an application node requests an operation (get or put), the storage layer routes the operation to the responsible node using the recursive routing layer. The recursive overlay routing layer forwards any message to the destination by forwarding it hop-by-hop along the Chord overlay links. The DHT also responds to changes in the responsible address space by sending a SetKeyRange message to the new owner to notify it of the keys it should now manage.

Impact score. For an impact score we use *lookup latency*, which measures the amount of time passed between a node issuing a get request on a key and when it actually receives the corresponding value. Formally, the impact score is the average time spent on lookups that either completed in the last t_w or elapsed time of pending lookups.

Experimental setup. We simulated 100 nodes and each one randomly generates 100 key-value pairs which it puts around the DHT, thus we expect that each node stores one of its values on every node. Each node then tries to retrieve 2 values every second, and tries to retrieve the whole set of values 10 times. A request is timed-out if no response is received before the next retrieval attempt. Most experiments allow Chord 10 sec to form the overlay before beginning to put data. It then uses 50 sec to put data, putting only 2 values every second, before beginning to lookup data. The remaining lookups take 500 sec. We set t_w to be 70 sec, which allows Gatling to find attacks during the Chord setup and DHT put phase; n_a was set to 5.

Attacks found using lookup latency. We show lookup latency over time for each attack in Fig. 10. As a baseline we show DHT with no attack and find it converges to 215 ms. We found a total of seven attacks (and several variants) against DHT and rediscovered some attacks against Chord.

Recursive Overlay Routing Attacks. We first run Gatling on the recursive message routing layer that routes all DHT messages. We begin malicious actions after 10 sec, after the Chord ring converges. We found two attacks where delaying or dropping messages causes an increase in lookup latency (*Drop Msg, Delay Msg*). We also found a third attack where duplicating the message and diverting the second copy to a random node causes network flooding and congestion due to malicious nodes repeatedly replicating the same messages (*Dup Msg*). Finally, we found an attack where in forwarding messages, an attacker provides a false destination key for the message, causing the *next hop* of the message to forward it incorrectly (*Lie Msg Dest*).

Storage Attacks. We found two lying attacks. The first one, *Lie Reply Key* occurs when a node responds to a DHT get request and it lies about the key it is responding about. The second one, *Lie Set Key Range* occurs during the setup phase of the DHT, considering a scenario where nodes start putting data into the DHT at the beginning of the simulation, before the Chord ring can stabilize. We found that attackers can subvert the process of load-balancing and cause many key-value pairs to go missing. This occurred when an attacker notified another node of what key-value pairs it had. The attacker lied about what keys it was responsible for, then when another node takes over a part of that key-range, he will not know the real values that it should store, thus losing them.

5.4 ESM

System description. ESM [17] is a multicast system that efficiently disseminates video streaming data broadcast by a single source. ESM accomplishes this by building up a tree, rooted at the source, where each child node forwards on the data to its own children. Each node maintains a set of neighbors periodically reporting their throughput and latency. With this information, a node can change parents to maintain desired performance.

Impact score. We use two scores [17]: *throughput* and *latency*. Throughput as described in [17], is the amount of data received over the last 5 sec, so the impact score is the streaming rate minus the throughput, to satisfy requirements that larger means more impact. Latency is the amount of time it takes for data to reach each node after being initially sent by the source, and the impact score is the average latency of data in the last t_w.

Experimental setup. We simulated ESM with 100 nodes and one source streaming data at 1 Mbps. As the goal of ESM is both to form an efficient tree and to stream data to all participants, we use two different settings for the time (i.e., 0 sec and 10 sec) when attackers start their malicious actions. Thus we can find attacks both against tree formation and data delivery. We use a t_w of 5 sec and n_a of 5.

Attacks found using throughput. We found four attacks using throughput as an impact score. Fig. 11(a) shows the results of how each attack affects ESM where we plot the throughput over time. For a baseline we also have ESM in the benign case when there is no attack, delivering average throughput near 900 kbps.

Drop Data. First we delay malicious actions until 10 sec into the execution, to allow ESM to build a tree first, and test the steady state. Despite ESM using an adaptation mechanism to switch to parents that give them good performance, dropping data was an effective attack.

Dup Parent. We then examined attacks that targeted the tree formation and adaptation process. We increased the window size t_w to 10 sec, and had attackers immediately start trying malicious actions once the simulation started. Gatling again added dropping data as an attack action, then proceeded to amplify that attack with another malicious action—duplicating messages that tell a node they are accepted as a child, sending the duplicate message to a random node. With this amplification, the throughput is usually below 200 kbps.

Attraction attacks. In these attacks malicious nodes amplify dropping streaming data by lying about their performance metrics, making them look better than what they actually are. This causes benign nodes to continually ask malicious nodes to be their parents. The first attraction attack found is where nodes lie about their latency (*Lie Latency*), setting it to zero. This causes nodes to think the attacker is close to the source. The second attraction attack is when malicious nodes lie about their bandwidth using scaling (*Lie Bandwidth*), increasing it to appear they are receiving much of the streaming data. To further amplify the attack the attackers also duplicate probe messages, diverting the second message to random nodes, causing the attackers to be more well-known in the overlay, thus more likely to be asked to be a parent. These two attacks are very effective, causing all nodes to have a very low throughput of less than 100 kbps when lying about latency and 300 kbps when lying about bandwidth.

Attacks found using latency. We found one attack using latency as an impact score function. We compare in Fig. 11(b) the latency when there is no attack with the attack we found.

Drop Parent. We found an attack where malicious nodes drop replies to parent request messages. This results in increased latency due to malicious nodes gaining spots high up in the tree over time by simply following the adaptation protocol, and then never allowing the tree to grow beyond them. Furthermore, as benign nodes never get a response, the protocol dictates that they wait 1 sec to send another parent request to a different node, further slowing down their attempt to find or change parents.

5.5 Scribe

System description. Scribe [49] is an application-level multicast system that organizes each group into an overlay tree to efficiently disseminate data. To send data, a node sends the message toward the root, and each node forwards it to its parent and children. Scribe is built on top of Pastry [48], an overlay routing protocol with similar functionality to Chord. Scribe trees are built based on reverse-path forwarding combined with load balancing: the multicast tree is the reverse of the routes Join messages take when routed from tree participants to the Pastry node managing the group identifier, except that nodes whose out-degree is too high will push children down in the tree.

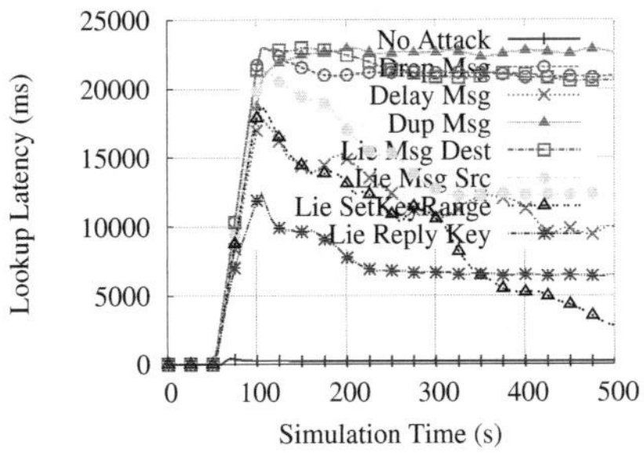

Figure 10. Lookup latency for the attacks found on DHT

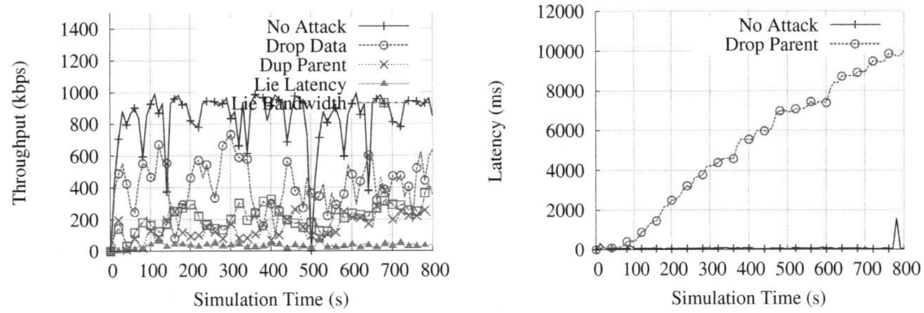

(a) Throughput impact score

(b) Latency impact score

Figure 11. Throughtput and latency for the attacks found on ESM

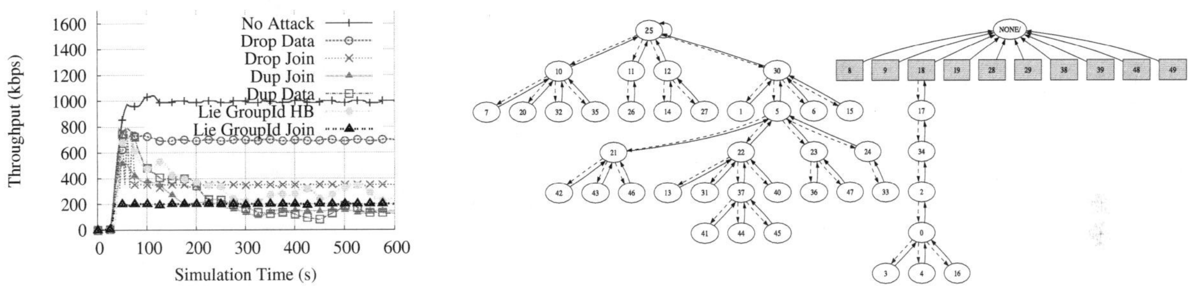

(a) Throughput for the attacks found on Scribe

(b) Scribe tree under Lie GroupId Join attack

Figure 12. Attack impact on Scribe

Impact score. We use *throughput*, which measures the average amount of data received over time. As with ESM, the impact score is the streaming rate minus the average throughput over the last t_w seconds.

Experimental setup. We simulated Scribe with 50 nodes and test it under the scenario where a source node creates a group, publishes streaming data at a rate of 1 Mbps, and all other nodes subscribe to that group. We start malicious actions immediately after the experiment starts so we can attack tree construction, however as we find the tree takes up to 30 sec to form in our test environment, we set t_w to be 35 sec. We also find malicious actions have a high probability of being effective the first time tried and thus set n_a to be 1.

Attacks found using throughput. We found seven attacks using throughput as an impact score. Fig. 12(a) shows the effects of the different attacks. As a baseline we run the system with no attack and find that nodes are able to consistently receive 1 Mbps of data.

Drop Data and Dup Data. First we found two obvious attacks where nodes do not forward the data or they duplicate data messages and send the second message to a random node. In the latter case, loops can occur, causing significant system load as data is increasingly replicated, resulting in throughput to decrease below 200 kbps.

Dup Join, Lie GroupID Join, Drop Join. We found that when malicious nodes duplicate Join messages and divert the second message to a random node this causes the throughput to drop below 200 kbps. This drop is due to temporary forwarding loops when a tree node is a child of multiple parent nodes. This temporary error will be corrected by a heartbeat protocol, but only after a period of time in which forwarding loops can cause damage. Gatling found two additional attacks that cause the tree to not be formed properly. If malicious nodes lie about the group identifier in the Join message, then effectively the malicious nodes are joining a different group, while believing they are joining the requested group. Malicious nodes still respond normally to other nodes' requests to join the correct group. This lie led the system to a situation that all malicious nodes fail to join, and some benign nodes build a tree under malicious nodes as seen in Fig. 12(b). Since the tree is split, only nodes in the tree that have the source node inside can receive data and nodes in other tree(s) can not receive any data. Gatling also finds an attack of dropping Join messages, causing the same effect, but in the explored simulation, more benign nodes happened to be a part of the tree with the source, allowing better throughput.

6 Related Work

Automated debugging techniques, such as model checking, have been in use for many years. Most similar to our work is CrystalBall [56], where Yabandeh *et al.* utilize state exploration to predict safety violations and steer the execution path away from them and into safe states in the deployed system. Nodes predict consequences of their actions by executing a limited state exploration on a recently taken snapshot, which they take continuously. Since a violation is predicted beforehand, it is possible to avoid actions that will cause the violation. The Mace model checker is utilized for safety properties and state exploration. However, they do not consider performance metrics and thus can only find bugs or vulnerabilities that cause safety violations but not performance degradation.

Many previous works have also used debugging techniques for the purpose of automating the process of discovering or preventing attacks. Proving the absence of particular attacks have also been explored in the context of limited models and environments [9, 10, 12]. These debugging techniques include static and dynamic analysis [16, 22, 32, 37, 43, 54], modelchecking [9, 10, 12], and fault injection [8, 11, 50]. Below we summarize the works that are focused on discovering attacks and are most similar to our own.

Finding vulnerabilities in distributed systems has recently been explored by Banabic *et al.* [11]. They employ a fault injection technique on PBFT [15] to find combinations of MAC corruptions that cause nodes to crash. Our work is more general, as Gatling does not focus on finding all possible inputs that cause a single kind of vulnerability, but rather searches on basic malicious actions to find new attacks.

Stanojevic *et al.* [50] develop a fault injection technique for automatically searching for gullibility in protocols. They experiment on the two-party protocol ECN to find attacks that cause a malicious receiver to speed up and slow down the sending of data. Their technique uses a brute force search and considers lying about the fields in the headers of packets and also drops packets. As they also utilize Mace they are able to conduct protocol dependent attacks. Our work differs in that we focus on large-scale distributed systems, incorporate a fault injector that includes more diverse message delivery and lying actions, and use a greedy approach to avoid brute forcing.

Kothari *et al.* [32] explore how to automatically find lying attacks that manipulate control flow in implementations of protocols written in C. Their technique focuses on searching for a sequence of values that causes a particular statement in the code to be executed many times, thus potentially causing an attack. Their method first utilizes static analysis of the code to reduce the search space of possible attack actions and then uses concrete execution to verify the attack. However, to utilize the technique the user must know ahead of time what parts of the code, if executed many times, would cause an attack, which may not always be obvious. Gatling, on the other hand, utilizes an impact score to direct its search. Furthermore, some distributed systems, such as Vivaldi, do not have attacks on them that manipulate control flow, but only attacks that involve lying about state. Such attacks would go undiscovered by this technique.

7 Conclusion

Securing distributed systems against performance attacks has previously been a manual process of finding attacks and then patching or redesigning the system. In a first step towards automating this process, we presented Gatling, a framework for automatically discovering performance attacks in distributed systems. Gatling uses a model-checking exploration approach on malicious actions to find behaviors that result in degraded performance. We provide a concrete implementation of Gatling for the Mace toolkit. Once the system is implemented in Mace the user needs to specify an impact score in a simulation driver that allows the system to run in the simulator.

To show the generality and effectiveness of Gatling, we have applied it to six distributed systems that have a diverse set of system goals. We were able to discover 41 attacks in total, and for each system we were able to automatically discover attacks that either stopped the system from achieving its goals or slowed down progress significantly. While some of the attacks have been previously found manually through the cleverness of developers and researchers, we show that the amount of time Gatling needs to find such attacks is small. Therefore, we conclude that Gatling can help speed up the process of developing secure distributed systems.

References

[1] Cyber-DEfense Technology Experimental Research laboratory Testbed. http://www.isi.edu/deter/.

[2] Emulab - Network Emulation. http://www.emulab.net/.

[3] Georgia Tech Network Simulator. http://www.ece.gatech.edu/research/labs/MANIACS/GTNetS/.

[4] Global Environment for Network Innovation. http://www.geni.net.

[5] Network Simulator 3. http://www.nsnam.org/.

[6] p2psim: A simulator for peer-to-peer protocols. http://pdos.csail.mit.edu/p2psim/.

[7] Resilient Overlay Networks. http://nms.csail.mit.edu/ron/.

[8] J. Antunes, N. Neves, M. Correia, P. Verissimo, and R. Neves. Vulnerability Discovery with Attack Injection. *IEEE Transactions on Software Engineering*, 36:357–370, 2010.

[9] A. Armando, D. Basin, Y. Boichut, Y. Chevalier, L. Compagna, J. Cuellar, P. H. Drielsma, P. Hem, O. Kouchnarenko, J. Mantovani, S. Mdersheim, D. von Oheimb, M. Rusinowitch, J. Santiago, M. Turuani, L. Vigan, and L. Vigneron. The AVISPA Tool for the Automated Validation of Internet Security Protocols and Applications. In *Proceedings of Computer Aided Verification*, 2005.

[10] A. Armando and L. Compagna. SAT-based model-checking for security protocols analysis. *International Journal of Information Security*, 7:3–32, January 2008.

[11] R. Banabic, G. Candea, and R. Guerraoui. Automated Vulnerability Discovery in Distributed Systems. In *Proceedings of HotDep*, 2011.

[12] B. Blanchet. From Secrecy to Authenticity in Security Protocols. In *Proceedings of International Static Analysis Symposium*. Springer, 2002.

[13] C. Cadar, D. Dunbar, and D. Engler. KLEE: Unassisted and automatic generation of high-coverage tests for complex systems programs. In *Proceedings of OSDI*, 2008.

[14] M. Castro, P. Drushel, A. Ganesh, A. Rowstron, and D. Wallach. Secure routing for structured peer-to-peer overlay networks. In *Proceedings of OSDI*, 2002.

[15] M. Castro and B. Liskov. Practical Byzantine fault tolerance. In *Proceedings of OSDI*, 1999.

[16] C. Y. Cho, D. Babi, P. Poosankam, K. Z. Chen, E. X. Wu, and D. Song. MACE: Model-inference-assisted concolic exploration for protocol and vulnerability discovery. In *Proceedings of USENIX Security*, 2011.

[17] Y.-H. Chu, A. Ganjam, T. S. E. Ng, S. Rao, K. Sripanidkulchai, J. Zhan, and H. Zhang. Early Experience with an Internet Broadcast System Based on Overlay Multicast. In *Proceedings of USENIX ATC*, 2004.

[18] B. Cohen. Incentives build robustness in BitTorrent. In *Proceedings of P2P Economics*, 2003.

[19] F. Dabek, R. Cox, F. Kaashoek, and R. Morris. Vivaldi: a decentralized network coordinate system. In *Proceedings of SIGCOMM*, 2004.

[20] D. Geels, G. Altekar, P. Maniatis, T. Roscoe, and I. Stoica. Friday: global comprehension for distributed replay. In *Proceedings of NSDI*, 2007.

[21] P. Godefroid. Model checking for programming languages using Verisoft. In *Proceedings of POPL*, 1997.

[22] P. Godefroid, M. Y. Levin, and D. Molnar. Automated Whitebox Fuzz Testing. In *Proceedings of NDSS*, 2008.

[23] K. P. Gummadi, S. Saroiu, and S. D. Gribble. King: Estimating Latency between Arbitrary Internet End Hosts. In *Proceedings of ACM SIGCOMM-IMW*, 2002.

[24] H. S. Gunawi, T. Do, P. Joshi, P. Alvaro, J. M. Hellerstein, A. C. Arpaci-Dusseau, R. H. Arpaci-Dusseau, K. Sen, and D. Borthakur. FATE and DESTINI: a framework for cloud recovery testing. In *Proceedings of NSDI*, 2011.

[25] G. J. Holzmann. The Model Checker SPIN. *IEEE Transactions on Software Engineering*, 23:279–295, May 1997.

[26] C. Killian, J. W. Anderson, R. Jhala, and A. Vahdat. Life, Death, and the Critical Transition: Detecting Liveness Bugs in Systems Code. In *Proceedings of NSDI*, 2007.

[27] C. E. Killian, J. W. Anderson, R. Braud, R. Jhala, and A. M. Vahdat. Mace: language support for building distributed systems. In *Proceedings of PLDI*, 2007.

[28] D. Kostić, R. Braud, C. Killian, E. Vandekieft, J. W. Anderson, A. C. Snoeren, and A. Vahdat. Maintaining high bandwidth under dynamic network conditions. In *Proceedings of USENIX ATC*, 2005.

[29] D. Kostic, A. Rodriguez, J. Albrecht, , and A. Vahdat. Bullet: High Bandwidth Data Dissemination Using an Overlay Mesh. In *Proceedings of SOSP*, 2003.

[30] D. Kostic, A. Rodriguez, J. Albrecht, A. Bhirud, and A. Vahdat. Using random subsets to build scalable network services. In *Proceedings of USENIX-USITS*, 2003.

[31] D. Kostić, A. C. Snoeren, A. Vahdat, R. Braud, C. Killian, J. W. Anderson, J. Albrecht, A. Rodriguez, and E. Vandekieft. High-bandwidth data dissemination for large-scale distributed systems. *ACM Transactions on Computer Systems*, 26(1):1–61, 2008.

[32] N. Kothari, R. Mahajan, T. Millstein, R. Govindan, and M. Musuvathi. Finding Protocol Manipulation Attacks. In *Proceedings of SIGCOMM*, 2011.

[33] M. Krohn, E. Kohler, and M. F. Kaashoek. Events can make sense. In *Proceedings of USENIX ATC*, 2007.

[34] L. Lamport. *Specifying Systems: The TLA+ Language and Tools for Hardware and Software Engineers*. Addison-Wesley Longman Publishing Co., Inc., Boston, MA, USA, 2002.

[35] L. Leonini, E. Rivière, and P. Felber. SPLAY: distributed systems evaluation made simple (or how to turn ideas into live systems in a breeze). In *Proceedings of NSDI*, 2009.

[36] S. Lin, A. Pan, Z. Zhang, R. Guo, and Z. Guo. WiDS: an Integrated Toolkit for Distributed Systems Deveopment. In *Proceedigs of HotOS*, 2005.

[37] Z. Lin, X. Zhang, and D. Xu. Convicting exploitable software vulnerabilities: An efficient input provenance based approach. In *Proceedings of DSN*, 2008.

[38] B. T. Loo, T. Condie, J. M. Hellerstein, P. Maniatis, T. Roscoe, and I. Stoica. Implementing Declarative Overlays. In *Proceedings of SOSP*, Brighton, United Kingdom, October 2005.

[39] X. Lui, W. Lin, A. Pan, and Z. Zhang. WiDS Checker: Combating Bugs In Distributed Systems. In *Proceedings of NSDI*, Cambridge, Massachusetts, April 2007.

[40] N. Lynch. *Distributed Algorithms*. Morgan Kaufmann, 1996.

[41] M. Musuvathi, D. Park, A. Chou, D. Engler, and D. Dill. CMC: A pragmatic approach to model checking real code. In *Proceedings of OSDI*, 2002.

[42] M. Musuvathi, S. Qadeer, T. Ball, G. Basler, P. A. Nainar, and I. Neamtiu. Finding and Reproducing Heisenbugs in Concurrent Programs. In *Proceedings of OSDI*, 2008.

[43] J. Newsome and D. Song. Dynamic Taint Analysis for Automatic Detection, Analysis, and Signature Generation of Exploits on Commodity Software. In *Proceedings of NDSS*, 2005.

[44] PlanetLab. http://www.planetlab.org.

[45] S. Ratnasamy, P. Francis, M. Handley, R. Karp, and S. Shenker. A scalable content-addressable network. In *Proceedings of SIGCOMM*. ACM, 2001.

[46] S. Rhea, D. Geels, T. Roscoe, and J. Kubiatowicz. Handling churn in a DHT. In *Proceedings of USENIX ATC*, 2004.

[47] A. Rodriguez, D. Kostić, Dejan, and A. Vahdat. Scalability in Adaptive Multi-Metric Overlays. In *Proceedings of IEEE ICDCS*, 2004.

[48] A. Rowstron and P. Druschel. Pastry: Scalable, Decentralized Object Location, and Routing for Large-Scale Peer-to-Peer Systems. In *Proceedings of IFIP/ACM Middleware*, 2001.

[49] A. Rowstron, A.-M. Kermarrec, M. Castro, and P. Druschel. SCRIBE: The design of a large-scale event notification infrastructure. In *Proceedings of NGC*, 2001.

[50] M. Stanojevic, R. Mahajan, T. Millstein, and M. Musuvathi. Can You Fool Me? Towards Automatically Checking Protocol Gullibility. In *Proceedings of HotNets*, 2008.

[51] I. Stoica, R. Morris, D. Karger, M. F. Kaashoek, and H. Balakrishnan. Chord: A Scalable Peer-to-Peer Lookup Service for Internet Applications. In *Proceedings of SIGCOMM*, 2001.

[52] A. Vahdat, K. Yocum, K. Walsh, P. Mahadevan, D. Kostić, J. Chase, and D. Becker. Scalability and accuracy in a large-scale network emulator. In *Proceedings of OSDI*, 2002.

[53] A. Walters, D. Zage, and C. Nita-Rotaru. A Framework for Mitigating Attacks Against Measurement-Based Adaptation Mechanisms in Unstructured Multicast Overlay Networks. *IEEE/ACM Transactions on Networking*, 16:1434–1446, 2008.

[54] W. Wang, Y. Lei, D. Liu, D. Kung, C. Csallner, D. Zhang, R. Kacker, and R. Kuhn. A Combinatorial Approach to Detecting Buffer Overflow Vulnerabilities. In *Proceedings of DSN*, 2011.

[55] M. Welsh, D. E. Culler, and E. A. Brewer. SEDA: An Architecture For Well-conditioned, Scalable Internet Services. In *Proceedings of SOSP*, 2001.

[56] M. Yabandeh, N. Knezevic, D. Kostic, and V. Kuncak. CrystalBall: Predicting and Preventing Inconsistencies in Deployed Distributed Systems. In *Proceedings of NSDI*, 2009.

[57] J. Yang, T. Chen, M. Wu, Z. Xu, X. Liu, H. Lin, M. Yang, F. Long, L. Zhang, and L. Zhou. MODIST: transparent model checking of unmodified distributed systems. In *Proceedings of NSDI*, 2009.

[58] D. J. Zage and C. Nita-Rotaru. On the accuracy of decentralized virtual coordinate systems in adversarial networks. In *Proceedings of CCS*, 2007.

Automated Synthesis of Privacy-Preserving Distributed Applications

Michael Backes
Saarland University and MPI-SWS
Germany
backes@mpi-sws.org

Matteo Maffei
Saarland University
Germany
maffei@cs.uni-saarland.de

Kim Pecina
Saarland University
Germany
pecina@cs.uni-saarland.de

Abstract

We introduce a framework for the automated synthesis of security-sensitive distributed applications. The central idea is to provide the programmer with a high-level declarative language *for specifying the system and the intended security properties, abstracting away from any cryptographic details. A* compiler *takes as input such high-level specifications and automatically produces the corresponding* cryptographic implementations *(i.e., cryptographic library, cryptographic protocols, and F# source code).*

In this work, we focus on two important, and seemingly contradictory, security properties, namely, authorization and privacy. On the one hand, the access to sensitive resources should be granted only to authorized users; on the other hand, these users would like to share as little personal information as possible with third parties. These opposing goals make it challenging to enforce privacy-aware authorization policies in a distributed setting.

The high-level declarative language builds on Evidential DKAL, a logic for authorization polices of decentralized systems, which we extend to reason about privacy policies. Specifically, the traditional says modality from authorization logics is accompanied by existential quantification in order to express the secrecy of sensitive information. The cryptographic realization of privacy-aware authorization policies is obtained by a powerful combination of digital signatures and zero-knowledge proofs. This approach is general and can be seen as a privacy-enabling plugin for existing authorization languages and proof-carrying authorization architectures.

We proved that the implementations output by the compiler enforce the intended authorization policies and we conducted an experimental evaluation to demonstrate the feasibility of our approach.

1. Introduction

One of the central challenges in the development of distributed systems is the design of cryptographic protocols that meet the desired functional requirements and enforce the intended security properties. There is a common understanding that basic security properties such as secrecy and authentication can easily be enforced via encryption and digital signatures, respectively. Modern applications, however, exhibit more sophisticated and heterogeneous security requirements: for example, social networks, e-health systems, and reviewing systems must fulfill sophisticated access control, privacy, and anonymity constraints. Devising a cryptographic infrastructure for the enforcement of these properties is challenging and highly error-prone for security experts, and even prohibitive for regular programmers, which do not have the required background and expertise in cryptography. Currently, many popular applications rely on trusted third parties to collect and process sensitive information (e.g., conference reviewing systems like Easychair or social networks like Facebook). The presence of trusted parties simplifies the system design but gives rise to a number of privacy concerns related to the deliberate or accidental disclosure of sensitive information. Other applications are fully decentralized but employ ad-hoc cryptographic protocols that are not always flawless and, due to their diversity, break any form of interoperability.

We believe that the design of security-sensitive distributed applications should be driven by rigorous, formally certified, and possibly automated, techniques, as opposed to best practices and informal guidelines. Specifically, developers should be given the possibility to specify the functional behavior of the system and the intended security properties using convenient, security-oriented, programming abstractions that conceal cryptographic details. A compiler should automatically turn user-provided, high-level system descriptions into executable cryptographic implementations. Ideally, these implementations should be open-ended and interoperable, i.e., it should be possible to extend the system with new functionalities and to share information among different, independently developed, applications.

This work introduces such a framework, focusing on two important, and seemingly contradictory, security properties, namely, authorization and privacy. Authorization is a key ingredient in virtually any security infrastructure. The fundamental idea is to let the *resource provider* define a security policy that constraints the operations on sensitive resources and to let a *reference monitor* filter access requests in a way that an operation is allowed only if the *requester* has sufficient permissions according to the security policy. For instance, let us consider a simple university management system in which, at the end of each semester, students are given a certificate of the form Uni says $Stud(id, program, grd)$, reporting their id, the program they are enrolled in, and their grades. Such a certificate is typically implemented as a digital signature of the form $\mathsf{sig}(Stud(id, program, grd))_{Uni}$, issued by the university administration on (a bit string encoding of) the predicate $Stud(id, program, grd)$. The system under consideration is *open-ended* in that the student certificate may be employed in a number of different services: scholarship assignment, discounted museum entrances, access to university buildings (as in the Grey system [17] for device-enabled authorization), and so on. For instance, the policy for scholarship assignments may be of the form $\forall x, y, z.\ Uni$ says $Stud(x, y, z) \wedge \mathsf{average}(z) \geq X \Rightarrow GetScholarship(x)$, where X is the minimum average grade that is required to get the scholarship. Systems and authorization policies of this form can be conveniently described in a variety of logic-based authorization languages, such as DCC [3, 2], Aura [43], PCML$_5$ [9], and Evidential DKAL [7].

The combination of authorization and privacy, however, is challenging, even more so in the context of open-ended applications, in which it is not known in advance how sensitive information is used by other applications (for instance, the university does not necessarily know all services that make usage of student credentials). Let us consider, for instance, the entrance to university buildings: students might not want their movements within the university to be tracked. Let us suppose that one of the authorization policies ruling the entrance to the computer science laboratory is of the form

$$\begin{aligned}&\forall x, y.\\ &\quad Uni \text{ says } Stud(x, cs, y) \ \wedge\ x \text{ says } Acc(lab)\\ &\quad \Rightarrow OkAcc(lab)\end{aligned} \qquad (1)$$

Ideally, students would like to prove to be enrolled in the computer science program, without disclosing their identity. From a logical point of view, we propose to capture privacy constraints via existential quantification, i.e., privacy-relevant values are hidden by existentially quantified variables. For instance, students can provide the following piece of information:

$$\exists x, y.\ Uni \text{ says } Stud(x, cs, y) \wedge x \text{ says } Acc(lab) \qquad (2)$$

This logical characterization of privacy and authorization is simple and elegant, but providing a faithful cryptographic evidence thereof turns out to be quite challenging: digital signatures do not offer any sort of privacy and standard cryptographic solutions like encryptions and MACs are not suitable for open-ended applications. This is the reason why existing authorization languages do not allow for such a usage of existential quantification and fall short of supporting privacy properties. We present a general and automated procedure to implement privacy-aware authorization policies by means of a powerful combination of digital signatures and zero-knowledge proofs.[1] The idea is to use signatures to justify the validity of logical formulas, as previously shown, and zero-knowledge proofs of knowledge of such signatures to justify the validity of variants of these formulas – variants in which the sensitive arguments are existentially quantified. The unique properties of zero-knowledge proofs assure the verifier of the validity of these formulas, without revealing any sensitive data that the prover wishes to keep secret. For instance, the cryptographic realization of the formula (2) is a zero-knowledge proof of knowledge of two signatures of the form $\mathsf{sig}(Stud(x, cs, y))_{Uni}$ and $\mathsf{sig}(Acc(lab))_x$, for some student x and grades y that are not revealed to the verifier. This approach is flexible and, depending on what information is kept secret, can be used to express a variety of privacy properties, such as data secrecy and user anonymity. Furthermore, this approach is well suited for open-ended applications, since each party can prove any statement of which she knows a cryptographic evidence and, while doing so, autonomously hide any information considered sensitive for the specific application.

Our contributions. To summarize, this work presents:

- a generally applicable and efficient cryptographic implementation of privacy-aware authorization policies, which builds on automorphic signatures [5] and the Groth-Sahai zero-knowledge proof system [40] (cf. § 2);
- a high-level, declarative language for distributed systems, which extends Evidential DKAL [7] to deal with privacy properties (cf. § 3);

[1] A zero-knowledge proof combines two seemingly contradictory properties. First, it is a proof of a statement that cannot be forged, i.e., infeasible, to produce a zero-knowledge proof of a wrong statement. Second, a zero-knowledge proof does not reveal any information besides the bare fact that the statement is valid [39]. A non-interactive zero-knowledge proof is a zero-knowledge protocol consisting of one message sent by the prover to the verifier. A zero-knowledge proof of knowledge additionally ensures that the prover knows the witnesses to the given statement.

- a compiler that turns high-level descriptions into executable implementations, comprising cryptographic libraries, cryptographic protocols, and F$^{\#}$ source code (cf. § 4);
- a correctness result, which ensures that the implementations output by the compiler enforce the authorization policies specified by the user (cf. § 5);
- two case studies, consisting of a distributed reviewing system and a distributed social network, which demonstrate the possibility to specify relatively complex decentralized systems in a simple and elegant manner, without requiring any cryptographic expertise on the part of the users (cf. § 6);
- and an experimental evaluation, which demonstrates the feasibility of our approach (cf. § 7).

Due to space constraints, we postpone the proofs, the details of the cryptographic realization, and further case studies to the long version, which is available online [12].

Related Work. The seminal works by Abadi et al. [44, 4] on access control in distributed systems paved the way for the development of a number of authorization logics and languages [32, 19, 43, 38, 29, 9]. In the literature it is well-known that logical formulas based on a says modality can be implemented in a distributed setting via digital signatures, but the problem of ensuring the privacy of data employed in authorization proofs has not been tackled thus far. A noticeable exception is AuraConf [54], a confidentiality extension of the Aura [43] programming language based on public-key encryption and a monadic constructor. In AuraConf, the programmer has to specify the intended recipient of each data and the compiler is in charge of encrypting such data with the appropriate public key. In our approach, the programmer does not need to know in advance all the intended usages and recipients of the digital signatures issued in the protocol run, which is crucial to deal with open-ended systems. In fact, principals can use received signatures to construct arbitrary authorization proofs, using zero-knowledge proofs to selectively hide sensitive data.

Digital signatures and zero-knowledge schemes proved to be salient tools for achieving fine-grained anonymity properties in a number of applications, such as trusted computing [26], digital credentials [20], trust protocols [47, 10], and social networks [13]. The relationship between privacy-preserving cryptographic constructions and authorization logics, however, has been investigated only partially and in specialized settings. For instance, Li et al. [45] developed a framework for Automated Trust Negotiation using anonymous credentials, which is tailored to RT, a family of Trust-management languages [46]. Frikken et al. used a combination of hidden credentials, homomorphic encryption, and oblivious transfer to enforce access control policies while keeping both policies and credentials secret [37]. Our framework is not tailored to a specific language and can be seen as a generally applicable privacy-preserving plugin for authorization logics: in the long version, we report on a privacy-oriented extension of the Proof Carrying Authorization framework [8, 18] and we envision the usage of our framework within several other authorization languages, such as Aura [43], $PCML_5$ [9], F* [52], and SecPal [19]. Some preliminary ideas on privacy-aware proof-carrying authorization were anticipated in a position paper by Maffei and Pecina [48].

Backes et al. have recently presented G2C [14], a goal-driven specification language for distributed applications. This language supports secrecy, access control, and anonymity, which are enforced by means of broadcast encryption and group signatures. Similarly to our approach, G2C conceals cryptographic details and lets a compiler generate the cryptographic implementation. G2C, however, does not support open-ended applications (i.e., it is not possible to extend the system in order to provide new functionalities without generating the whole protocol from scratch). Furthermore, the G2C compiler yields cryptographic protocols as opposed to executable implementations and it does not provide security by construction guarantees.

The proof of correctness for our compiler builds on the type theory for zero-knowledge proofs by Backes et al. [11] and, in particular, on their compiler from zero-knowledge statements to symbolic cryptographic libraries. These libraries model the ideal behavior of cryptographic schemes using standard language constructs and are thus suitable for verification but cannot be used for deployment. Our compiler, instead, converts a DKAL derivation of the intended protocol run into an executable implementation, which includes concrete, executable cryptographic libraries. Devising an efficient, yet expressive and flexible cryptographic realization of privacy-aware authorization proofs is one of the challenges faced in this work.

Recently, Meiklejohn et al. [49] and Almeida et al. [6] have independently presented two compilers for zero-knowledge proofs, which take as input a specification of the cryptographic statement to be proved. The cryptographic realization of such specifications is based on Σ-protocols [30]. Our compiler builds on the Groth-Sahai zero-knowledge proof scheme [40], which is based on pairing-based cryptography and is, in general, more efficient and more expressive. Furthermore, our compiler provides a higher level of abstraction, since it takes as input logical formulas as opposed to cryptographic statements.

Table 1 Cryptographic evidence of authorization formulas.

$$
\begin{array}{rcll}
ap & := & \mathsf{ver_{sig}}(u_s, u_A, F) \mid E & \text{(atomic predicates)} \\
S & := & ap \mid S_1 \wedge S_2 \mid S_1 \vee S_2 \mid \exists x.\, S & \text{(statements)}
\end{array}
$$

$$
[M] = \begin{cases} vk_A \ \mathsf{says}\ F & \text{if } \mathsf{ver_{sig}}(M, vk_A, F) \\ [S]_{\mathsf{zk}} & \text{if } \mathsf{ver_{zk}}(M, S) \end{cases}
\qquad
[S]_{\mathsf{zk}} = \begin{cases} u_k \ \mathsf{says}\ F & \text{if } S = \mathsf{ver_{sig}}(u_s, u_k, F) \\ [S_1]_{\mathsf{zk}} \wedge [S_2]_{\mathsf{zk}} & \text{if } S = S_1 \wedge S_2 \\ [S_1]_{\mathsf{zk}} \vee [S_2]_{\mathsf{zk}} & \text{if } S = S_1 \vee S_2 \\ \exists x.\, [S']_{\mathsf{zk}} & \text{if } S = \exists x.\, S' \end{cases}
$$

2. Privacy-aware Evidential Authorization

This section gives an intuitive overview of our framework (§ 2.1), establishes the binding between authorization formulas and cryptographic messages (§ 2.2), describes the class of statements that can be proved in zero-knowledge (§ 2.3), and characterizes which of them provide meaningful security guarantees (§ 2.4).

2.1. Overview

Let us consider the example discussed in § 1. The student's goal is to provide evidence of the validity of the predicate *OkAcc*(lab). The validity of this predicate is ruled by the authorization policy (1) and the minimal amount of information the student has to reveal is captured by formula (2). The key insight is that the student does not need to reveal her identity nor her grades, since they do not occur in the predicate *OkAcc*(lab) and can thus be existentially quantified. The student has two signatures at her disposal, namely, $\mathsf{sig}(\mathit{Stud}(\mathsf{vk}_{id}, cs, grd))_{Uni}$ and $\mathsf{sig}(\mathit{Acc}(lab))_{id}$. Our idea is to let the student create a proof of the following statement:

$$
\begin{array}{l}
\exists x_1, x_2, x_{id}, x_{grd}. \\
\quad \mathsf{ver_{sig}}(x_1, \mathsf{vk}_{Uni}, \mathit{Stud}(x_{id}, cs, x_{grd})) \\
\quad \wedge\ \mathsf{ver_{sig}}(x_2, x_{id}, \mathit{Acc}(lab))
\end{array} \tag{3}
$$

This statement says that there exist two signatures x_1 and x_2, a verification key x_{id} (which constitutes the student's id), and grades x_{grd} such that (i) x_1 is a signature on the predicate $\mathit{Stud}(x_{id}, cs, x_{grd})$ that can be successfully verified with the university administration's verification key vk_{Uni} and (ii) x_2 is a signature on the predicate $\mathit{Acc}(lab)$ that can be successfully verified with the student's verification key x_{id}. Since we use zero-knowledge proofs of knowledge, the above statement actually implies that the prover knows the signatures and the verification key. Upon reception and verification of this proof, the verifier can safely derive the logical formula (2), which in turn allows *OkAcc*(lab) to be derived as previously described.

2.2. Mapping Cryptographic Messages to Logical Formulas

Here and throughout this paper, we let M range over cryptographic messages (digital signatures and zero-knowledge proofs), a, b, m over names (i.e., bit strings), x, y, z over variables, u over names and variables, F over authorization formulas,[2] and E over quadratic equations in $\mathbb{Z}_n$ [40], which are used to express arithmetic properties (e.g., $\mathsf{average}(z) \geq X$ from § 1). The predicate $\mathsf{ver_{sig}}(\mathsf{sig}, \mathsf{vk}, m)$ denotes the successful verification of signature sig on message m with verification key vk, and the predicate $\mathsf{ver_{zk}}(\mathsf{ZK}, S)$ denotes the successful verification of the zero-knowledge proof ZK for statement S.

Predicates of the form $\mathsf{ver_{sig}}(u_s, u_k, F)$ and quadratic equations in $\mathbb{Z}_n$ form the class of *atomic predicates*, which are ranged over by ap (cf. Table 1). Zero-knowledge statements, ranged over by S, are built on atomic predicates using conjunction, disjunction, and existential quantification.

The function $[\cdot] : M \mapsto F$ establishes the logical interpretation of cryptographic messages. The logical interpretation of a signature on (the bit-string encoding of) the predicate F, verifiable with key vk_A, is vk_A says F. The logical interpretation of a zero-knowledge proof is similarly defined by induction on the structure of the statement.

2.3. Construction of Zero-Knowledge Proofs

The deduction system in Table 2 characterizes what kind of statements a principal can prove in zero-knowledge starting from a database Γ of signatures and zero-knowledge proofs at her disposal. Intuitively, these statements may regard properties of digital signatures, as formalized by the judgment $\Gamma \vdash_{\mathsf{S}} S$, or be obtained by combining the statements of existing zero-knowledge proofs, as formalized by the judgment $\Gamma \vdash_{\mathsf{ZK}} S$.

The statements proved by the judgment $\Gamma \vdash_{\mathsf{S}} S$ are obtained by combining statements of the form $\mathsf{ver_{sig}}(s, vk, F)$ (I-S-VER) in conjunctive (I-S-$\wedge$) and disjunctive (I-S-$\vee$-1

[2] Our framework is independent of the underlying authorization logic: we just assume the presence of conjunction, disjunction, and existential quantification operators.

Table 2 Zero-knowledge deduction system.

$$\text{I-S-VER}\quad \frac{M \in \Gamma \qquad \mathsf{ver}_{\mathsf{sig}}(M, vk, F)}{\Gamma \vdash_{\mathsf{S}} \mathsf{ver}_{\mathsf{sig}}(M, vk, F)} \qquad \text{I-S-}\wedge\quad \frac{\Gamma \vdash_{\mathsf{S}} S_1 \qquad \Gamma \vdash_{\mathsf{S}} S_2}{\Gamma \vdash_{\mathsf{S}} S_1 \wedge S_2} \qquad \text{I-S-}\vee\text{-1}\quad \frac{\Gamma \vdash_{\mathsf{S}} S_1}{\Gamma \vdash_{\mathsf{S}} S_1 \vee S_2} \qquad \text{I-S-}\vee\text{-2}\quad \frac{\Gamma \vdash_{\mathsf{S}} S_2}{\Gamma \vdash_{\mathsf{S}} S_1 \vee S_2}$$

$$\text{I-ZK-S}\quad \frac{\Gamma \vdash_{\mathsf{S}} S}{\Gamma \vdash_{\mathsf{ZK}} S} \qquad \text{I-ZK-VER}\quad \frac{M \in \Gamma \qquad \mathsf{ver}_{\mathsf{zk}}(M, S) \qquad S \text{ well-formed}}{\Gamma \vdash_{\mathsf{ZK}} S} \qquad \text{I-ZK-}\exists\quad \frac{\Gamma \vdash_{\mathsf{ZK}} S\{u/x\}}{\Gamma \vdash_{\mathsf{ZK}} \exists x.\ S} \qquad \text{E-ZK-}\wedge\text{-1}\quad \frac{\Gamma \vdash_{\mathsf{ZK}} \exists \widetilde{x}.\ S_1 \wedge S_2}{\Gamma \vdash_{\mathsf{ZK}} \exists \widetilde{x}.\ S_1} \qquad \text{E-ZK-}\wedge\text{-2}\quad \frac{\Gamma \vdash_{\mathsf{ZK}} \exists \widetilde{x}.\ S_1 \wedge S_2}{\Gamma \vdash_{\mathsf{ZK}} \exists \widetilde{x}.\ S_2}$$

$$\text{I-ZK-}\wedge\quad \frac{\Gamma \vdash_{\mathsf{ZK}} \exists \widetilde{x}.\ S_1 \qquad \Gamma \vdash_{\mathsf{ZK}} \exists \widetilde{y}.\ S_2 \qquad \widetilde{x} \cap \widetilde{y} = \emptyset}{\Gamma \vdash_{\mathsf{ZK}} \exists \widetilde{x}, \widetilde{y}.\ S_1 \wedge S_2}$$

and I-S-$\vee$-2) form. Notice that logical conjunctions reveal more information than each of the two individual conjuncts, while logical disjunctions reveal less information in that it is not possible to determine which of the two disjuncts holds true.

The statements proved by the judgment $\Gamma \vdash_{\mathsf{ZK}} S$ build on the aforementioned statements (I-ZK-S) and on the statements of the zero-knowledge proofs in Γ (I-ZK-VER). Such statements can be refined by existential quantification (I-ZK-$\exists$) and conjunction elimination (E-ZK-$\wedge$-1 and E-ZK-$\wedge$-2) to hide information. It is also possible to combine the statements of two zero-knowledge proofs in conjunctive form (I-ZK-$\wedge$).

Notice that logical disjunctions are introduced by judgment $\Gamma \vdash_{\mathsf{S}} S$ and not by judgment $\Gamma \vdash_{\mathsf{ZK}} S$, since we are not aware of efficient cryptographic constructions that allow the prover to create a zero-knowledge proof of $S \vee S'$ from a zero-knowledge proof of S.

Example 1. Let us consider again the example from § 2.1. We let $M_1 = \mathsf{sig}(\mathit{Stud}(\mathsf{vk}_{id}, cs, grd))_{Uni}$, $M_2 = \mathsf{sig}(\mathit{Acc}(lab))_{id}$, $V_1 = \mathsf{ver}_{\mathsf{sig}}(M_1, \mathsf{vk}_{Uni}, \mathit{Stud}(\mathsf{vk}_{id}, cs, grd))$, $V_2 = \mathsf{ver}_{\mathsf{sig}}(M_2, \mathsf{vk}_{id}, \mathit{Acc}(lab))$, and $\Gamma = M_1, M_2$. The creation of the zero-knowledge proof of statement (3) is specified in Table 3.

Example 2. It is worth to mention that I-ZK-$\exists$ may also be used to hide equality relations among secret values: for instance, one can derive $\exists x, y.\ A \text{ says } p(x, y)$ from $\exists x.\ A \text{ says } p(x, x)$.

2.4. Validity of Zero-Knowledge Statements

It is interesting to observe that not all zero-knowledge statements are meaningful. For instance, suppose that a principal receives a zero-knowledge proof of the following statement:

$$\exists y_s, y_I.\ \mathsf{ver}_{\mathsf{sig}}(y_s, y_I, \mathit{Stud}(\mathsf{vk}_{id}, cs, grd)) \tag{4}$$

We would be tempted to let this principal entail $\exists y_I.\ y_I \text{ says } \mathit{Stud}(\mathsf{vk}_{id}, cs, grd)$. This zero-knowledge proof, however, does not reveal the identity of the person issuing the signature, nor is there any evidence that this person is a principal of the system. In fact, this zero-knowledge proof might have been constructed by an attacker, using a fresh key-pair and, therefore, the formula $\exists y_I.\ y_I \text{ says } \mathit{Stud}(\mathsf{vk}_{id}, cs, grd)$ is not necessarily entailed by the formulas proved by the principals of the system. Notice that we assume that the principals of the system are honest, i.e., they issue signatures to witness the validity of the corresponding logical predicates. We cannot, of course, assume the same for the attacker.

We stipulate that principals only sign verification keys that belong to principals of the system (as opposed to attacker's keys).[3] We call these keys *trustworthy*. Checking whether a verification key that occurs in a zero-knowledge proof is trustworthy is subtle. The idea is that a key is considered trustworthy if either it is revealed by the proof and known to belong to a principal of the system, or, recursively, it is endorsed by a trustworthy key. For instance, the statement (4) does not guarantee that the existentially quantified verification key y_I is trustworthy. Conversely, the verification key x_{id} that is existentially quantified in the statement (3) is signed by Uni and, therefore, is trustworthy. Hence, this statement justifies formula (2).

In other words, a statement is well-formed if it ensures that all verification keys are trustworthy. Despite the simplicity of this intuition, the formal definition has to take into account a number of complications, including the presence of logical disjunctions in the statement. For instance, the statement $\exists y_s, y_I.\ \mathsf{ver}_{\mathsf{sig}}(y_s, y_I, F) \vee \mathsf{ver}_{\mathsf{sig}}(y_s, \mathsf{vk}_{Uni}, F)$ is not well-formed, since we do not know which of the two disjuncts holds true. The idea is to transform a statement

[3] We assume a public-key infrastructure that binds public keys to their owner in a publicly-verifiable manner. Such a PKI may be centralized (e.g., Verisign) or decentralized (e.g., Webs of Trust). In the example from § 2.1, the university serves as a (centralized) PKI.

Table 3 Deduction of the zero-knoweldge proof for Example 1.

$$T_{\mathsf{ZK}} := \dfrac{\dfrac{\dfrac{\dfrac{M_1 \in \Gamma \quad V_1}{\Gamma \vdash_{\mathsf{S}} V_1}\text{I-S-VER}}{\Gamma \vdash_{\mathsf{ZK}} V_1}\text{I-ZK-S} \quad \dfrac{\dfrac{M_2 \in \Gamma \quad V_2}{\Gamma \vdash_{\mathsf{S}} V_2}\text{I-S-VER}}{\Gamma \vdash_{\mathsf{ZK}} V_2}\text{I-ZK-S}}{\Gamma \vdash_{\mathsf{ZK}} V_1 \wedge V_2}\text{I-ZK-}\wedge}{\Gamma \vdash_{\mathsf{ZK}} \exists x_1, x_2, x_{id}, x_{grd}.\ \mathsf{ver}_{\mathsf{sig}}(x_1, \mathsf{vk}_{Uni}, \mathit{Stud}(x_{id}, cs, x_{grd})) \wedge \mathsf{ver}_{\mathsf{sig}}(x_2, x_{id}, \mathit{Acc}(lab))}\text{I-ZK-}\exists\text{ (x4)}$$

Table 4 Verification rules.

VER-SIG
$$\dfrac{M \in \Gamma \quad \mathsf{ver}_{\mathsf{sig}}(M, vk_A, F)}{\Gamma \vdash vk_A \text{ says } F}$$

VER-ZK
$$\dfrac{M \in \Gamma \quad \mathsf{ver}_{\mathsf{zk}}(M, S) \quad S \text{ well-formed}}{\Gamma \vdash [S]_{\mathsf{zk}}}$$

in disjunctive form and then to check that all keys in each sequence of conjunctions are registered. We formalize the notion of trustworthiness for keys below. Here and throughout this paper, we write $\widetilde{u}$ to denote the sequence $u_1, \ldots, u_\ell$ for some ℓ.

Definition 1 (Trustworthiness of keys). *A key u is* trustworthy *in a monomial $\mathcal{M} = \bigwedge_{i=1}^{m} ap_i$ iff one of the following conditions holds:*

- *$u = vk$ is registered*
- *there exists $ap_j = \mathsf{ver}_{\mathsf{sig}}(u_s, u_k, F)$ such that u is a variable occurring free in F and u_k is trustworthy in $\mathcal{M}$*

Definition 2 (Disjunctive form). *We say a statement S is in* disjunctive form *iff $S = \exists\widetilde{x}.\ \bigvee_{i=1}^{m} \mathcal{M}_i$, where $\mathcal{M}_i = \bigwedge_{j=1}^{n} ap_j$.*

It is clear that each statement can be rewritten in disjunctive form. In the following, we assume a disjunctive normal form[4] for each statement S, written as $dnf(S)$.

Definition 3 (Well-formedness of statements). *A monomial $\mathcal{M} = \bigwedge_{i=1}^{m} ap_i$ is* well-formed *iff for every $ap_i = \mathsf{ver}_{\mathsf{sig}}(u_s, u_k, F)$, u_k is trustworthy in $\mathcal{M}$.*

A statement S such that $dnf(S) = \exists\widetilde{x}.\ \bigvee_{i=1}^{m} \mathcal{M}_i$ is well-formed if each $\mathcal{M}_i$ is well-formed.

We are now ready to characterize the logical formulas that are justified by the digital signatures and zero-knowledge proofs in Γ, as formalized in Table 4. The rules are self-explanatory: we just point out that the statements of zero-knowledge proofs are required to be well-formed.

[4]The disjunctive normal form can be obtained, for instance, by lexicographical order.

3. Specification Language: Privacy-aware Evidential DKAL

The Distributed Knowledge Authorization Language (DKAL) [41, 42] is a logic-based language for modeling and analyzing decentralized polices. A distinctive feature of DKAL is the possibility to explicitly describe the exchange of information among principals. Recently, Blass et al. introduced Evidential DKAL [7], an extension of DKAL in which the formulas exchanged by principals are justified by digital signatures, which allows for more expressive logical derivations. In this section, we extend Evidential DKAL with existential quantification, in order to express privacy constraints, and with zero-knowledge proofs, in order to justify logical formulas in which sensitive values are existentially quantified.

3.1. Overview of Evidential DKAL

Authorization languages such as PCA or SecPAL [19] often rely on fragments of first-order or higher-order logic to describe and enforce authorization policies. The logic underlying DKAL, called infon logic, is fundamentally different: instead of dealing with the validity of statements, this logic focuses on the notion of information. A statement represents a piece of information, as opposed to a truth value, that a specific principal has obtained, and access control is decided by deriving certain information, as opposed to proving a formula valid.

Table 5 reports some fundamental rules of Evidential DKAL. Here and throughout this paper, we let Γ denote a set of pieces of information, i.e., logical formulas and cryptographic messages. ENSUE says that if A knows Γ, then A knows also the information derivable from Γ. The initial knowledge of principal A is given in terms of knowledge assertions of the form $A : F$, which can be seen as axioms in the system. Rule P-A says that given the knowledge assertion $A : F$, A knows F. For easing the presentation, we deviate from the original presentation [7], which does

Table 5 Selection of rules from Evidential DKAL.

$$\textsc{Ensue}\ \frac{A \text{ knows } \Gamma \quad \Gamma \vdash F}{A \text{ knows } F} \qquad \textsc{P-A}\ \frac{A : F}{A \text{ knows } F} \qquad \textsc{P-S}\ \frac{A : \mathsf{vk}_A \text{ says } F \quad \mathsf{ver}_{\mathsf{sig}}(M, vk_A, F)}{A \text{ knows } M}$$

$$\textsc{Comm-J}\ \frac{\begin{array}{c}\text{if } F_B \text{ then } B \text{ sends } F \text{ to } p \\ \text{if } F_A \text{ then } A \text{ receives } F' \text{ from } q \\ B \text{ knows } F_B\,\eta \quad B \text{ knows } M \quad A \text{ knows } F_A\,\theta \\ p\,\eta = A \quad q\,\theta = B \quad [M] = F \quad F'\,\theta = F\end{array}}{A \text{ knows } M}$$

not precisely specify how principals acquire the knowledge of signatures. We introduce rule P-S to express that given the knowledge assertion $A : A$ says F, A can produce a self-generated signature M on F.

Example 3. Let us consider the example from § 2.1. The generation of student certificates is modeled by knowledge assertions of the form

$$Uni : \mathsf{vk}_{Uni} \text{ says } Stud(\mathsf{vk}_{id}, cs, grd) \qquad (5)$$

One can derive Uni knows $Stud(\mathsf{vk}_{id}, cs, grd)$ by P-A and Uni knows M by P-S, where M is a signature issued by Uni on $Stud(\mathsf{vk}_{id}, cs, grd)$.

The communication rule Comm-J describes the exchange of cryptographic messages that justify (i.e., provide evidence of) a certain statement. This rule is used to synchronize a communication assertion of the form if F_B then B sends F to p with a communication assertion of the form if F_A then A receives F' from q. In order to fire this rule, B must know $F_A\eta$ and A must know $F_B\theta$, for some substitutions η and θ mapping variables[5] to messages in the knowledge of A and B, respectively. Furthermore, conditional guards may be omitted, obtaining communication assertions of the form A sends F to B and A receives F from B. In order to fire Comm-J, we additionally require the sender and the receiver to coincide on both sides, i.e., $p\,\eta = A$ and $q\,\theta = B$. Finally, B must know a cryptographic evidence M for the statement F sent to A and the statement F' expected from A has to be unifiable with F by substitution θ. Once Comm-J is fired, A knows the cryptographic evidence M of F.

Example 4. The issue of student certificates can be specified via the following assertions:

$$Uni \text{ sends } \mathsf{vk}_{Uni} \text{ says } Stud(\mathsf{vk}_{id}, cs, grd) \text{ to } id \qquad (6)$$

$$id \text{ receives } \mathsf{vk}_{Uni} \text{ says } Stud(\mathsf{vk}_{id}, cs, y) \text{ from } Uni \qquad (7)$$

[5]The variables occurring in communication assertions are implicitly universally quantified.

Table 6 Core Rules of Privacy-aware Evidential DKAL.

$$\textsc{P-ZK}\ \frac{A \text{ knows } \Gamma \quad \Gamma \vdash_{\mathsf{ZK}} S \quad \mathsf{ver}_{\mathsf{zk}}(M, S)}{A \text{ knows } M}$$

$$\textsc{Comm-A}\ \frac{\begin{array}{c}\text{if } F_B \text{ then } ? \text{ sends } F \text{ to } p \\ \text{if } F_A \text{ then } A \text{ receives } F' \text{ from } ? \\ B \text{ knows } F_B\,\eta \quad B \text{ knows } M \quad A \text{ knows } F_A\,\theta \\ p\,\eta = A \quad [M] = F \quad F'\,\theta = F\end{array}}{A \text{ knows } M}$$

The intended communication protocols is modeled by the DKAL derivation below (for the sake of readability, we omit some trivial hypotheses and use the abbreviations defined in Example 1):

$$T_C := \frac{(6) \quad (7) \quad \dfrac{(5) \quad V_1}{Uni \text{ knows } M_1}\ \textsc{P-S}}{id \text{ knows } M_1}\ \textsc{Comm-J}$$

We finally derive id knows vk_{Uni} says $Stud(\mathsf{vk}_{id}, cs, grd)$ as follows:

$$T_S := \frac{T_C \quad \dfrac{V_1}{M_1 \vdash \mathsf{vk}_{Uni} \text{ says } Stud(\mathsf{vk}_{id}, cs, grd)}\ \textsc{Ver-Sig}}{id \text{ knows } \mathsf{vk}_{Uni} \text{ says } Stud(\mathsf{vk}_{id}, cs, grd)}\ \textsc{Ensue}$$

3.2. Privacy-Aware Evidential DKAL

Evidential DKAL does not feature any mechanism to enforce the privacy of sensitive information. We solve this problem by integrating our zero-knowledge deduction system and by refining the syntax of statements in order to support existential quantification.

Formally, we extend evidential DKAL with the rules from Table 2, Table 4, and Table 6. P-ZK bridges between DKAL and the zero-knowledge deduction system, bringing the zero-knowledge proofs derived by A into A's knowledge. Comm-A is a variant of Comm-J that is introduced for modeling anonymous communication: In this variant, the identity of the sender is replaced by the special symbol '?' and is not known to the receiver.

Example 5. We describe the anonymous entrance to the laboratory by means of the following assertions, where AS denotes the access control system:

$$id : \mathsf{vk}_{id} \text{ says } Acc(lab) \quad (8) \qquad ? \text{ sends } (2) \text{ to } AS \quad (9)$$

$$AS \text{ receives } (2) \text{ from } ? \quad (10)$$

Table 7 Derivation tree modeling the communication protocol from Example 5

$$T_A := \dfrac{(9) \qquad (10) \qquad \dfrac{\dfrac{T_C \qquad \dfrac{(8) \qquad V_2}{id \;\mathsf{knows}\; M_2}\;\text{P-S}}{id \;\mathsf{knows}\; M_1, M_2}\;\text{MSG-U} \qquad \mathsf{ver}_{\mathsf{zk}}(M_{\mathsf{ZK}}, (3)) \qquad T_{\mathsf{ZK}}}{id \;\mathsf{knows}\; M_{\mathsf{ZK}}}\;\text{P-ZK}}{AS \;\mathsf{knows}\; M_{\mathsf{ZK}}}\;\text{COMM-A}$$

The communication protocol is modeled by the derivation tree displayed in Table 7.

The student creates the zero-knowledge proof of statement (3) using the signature M_1 received from the university and the signature M_2 from the knowledge assertion (8) as witnesses. Using ENSUE, we can eventually derive AS knows $\exists x, y.\ Uni$ says $Stud(x, cs, y) \ \wedge$ x says $Acc(lab)$.

4. Compiler

We developed a compiler $\mathcal{C}[\cdot] : \mathcal{T}_{\mathsf{dkal}} \rightarrow C_{\mathrm{F}\#}$ that takes as input the Privacy-aware Evidential DKAL derivation capturing the intended system behavior and produces the $\mathrm{F}^{\#}$ executable code for each of the principals in the system. In this section, we overview the algorithm and state the soundness results.

Intuitively, the compiler builds on a translation function $\mathcal{T} : \mathcal{R}_{\mathsf{dkal}} \rightarrow C_{\mathrm{F}\#}$ from DKAL rules to $\mathrm{F}^{\#}$ code. Each rule of the zero-knowledge deduction system (cf. Table 2) is translated into a sequence of calls to functions of the zero-knowledge library. Communication rules (namely, COMM-J and COMM-A) are translated by extending the current code of the sender and the receiver with the output and input of the cryptographic message, respectively. In order to protect the secrecy of exchanged information, the communication is always encrypted with the public key of the receiver. The code of the receiver is further extended to verify the signature or the zero-knowledge proof received from the network.

The compiler produces the code of each principal by scanning the DKAL derivation top-down (i.e., from the outermost hypotheses until the thesis) and, for each rule R, by appending the code $\mathcal{T}(R)$ to the current code for the corresponding principal.

Example 6. Let us describe the compiler in more detail by illustrating the code produced by translating the T_A derivation tree from Example 5 (cf. Table 8). The compiler generates three functions, one for each role (i.e., university, student, and access control system). These functions are meant to be integrated in the code of the respective application and are consequently parameterized by a number of values, including the cryptographic keys of the running principal, the ones of the intended communication partners, network addresses, and so on. On the right-hand side of each line of code, we indicate the rule application (i.e., the rule name and the derivation tree) that has been processed by the compiler. For the moment, we invite the reader to ignore the annotations between square brackets, which play a role in the formalization of the correctness result (cf. § 5) but do not have any computational significance.

The T_A tree is scanned top-down. The first rule that is processed is the application of P-S in T_C, which introduces the signature issued by the university on the predicate $Stud(\mathsf{vk}_{id}, cs, grd)$ into the derivation tree: this rule is translated into a call to the signature creation function in the university's code. The next rule is COMM-J from T_C, which describes the transmission of the student's certificate: the signature is first encrypted with the recipient's encryption key and then sent to the address of the recipient, who receives the message, decrypts the ciphertext, and finally verifies the signature. The application of P-S in T_A leads to a call to the signature creation function in the student's code. The rules in T_{ZK} model the creation of the zero-knowledge proof and are translated into a sequence of calls to the corresponding functions in the zero-knowledge library. Finally, the application of COMM-A in T_A models the transmission of the zero-knowledge proof and is translated similarly to COMM-J.

5. Formal Verification

We verify the correctness of our compiler using the security type system for $\mathrm{F}^{\#}$ developed by Bengtson et al. [21] and recently extended by Backes et al. in order to support zero-knowledge proofs [11]. The semantics of $\mathrm{F}^{\#}$ is formalized using RCF, a concurrent lambda calculus that has successfully been used to encode and verify the security of $\mathrm{F}^{\#}$ protocol implementations [22]. Authorization policies are expressed in code by means of annotations: *assumptions* introduce new hypotheses (i.e., formulas that are assumed to

Table 8 Source code for the running example

```
Uni(sk_Uni, ek_id, vk_Uni, vk_id, ad, cs, grd) ≜
  [[ assume F_Uni ; ]]                          } T_C
  let s = sig sk_Uni                            } (P-S)
    (pickle Stud(vk_id, cs, grd)) in            }
  let msg = enc ek_id s in                      } T_C
  let c = connect ad in                         } (COMM-J)
  send c msg                                    }

AccSys(dk_AS, vk_Uni, vk_id, ad, cs, lab) ≜
  let c = listen ad in                          }
  let msg = recv c in                           } T_C
  let x_zk = dec dk_AS msg in                   } (COMM-A)
  let x = unpickle (ver_zk(3) x_zk) in          }
  [[ assert (2) ]] ;                            }

where  F_Uni = vk_Uni says Stud(vk_id, cs, grd)
       F_id = vk_id says Acc(lab)
```

```
Stud(sk_id, dk_id, ek_AS, vk_Uni, vk_id, ad_id, ad_AS, cs, lab) ≜
  let c = listen ad in                          }
  let msg = recv c in                           }
  let s = dec dk_id msg in                      } T_C
  let x = unpickle(ver_sig vk_Uni s) in         } (COMM-J)
  match x with Stud(vk_id, cs, grd) ⇒           }
  [[ assert F_Uni ]] ;
  [[ assume F_id ]] ;                           } T_A(P-S)
  let s' = sig sk_id (pickle Acc(lab)) in       }
  let x = create_zk-s s vk_Uni in               } T_ZK(I-ZK-S)
  let x' = create_zk-s s vk_id in               } T_ZK(I-ZK-S)
  let x_zk = create_zk-∧ x x' in                } T_ZK(I-ZK-∧)
  let y_zk = create_zk-∃ (3) x_zk in            } T_ZK(I-ZK-∃)
  [[ assert( (2) ) ]] ;                         } T_A(P-ZK)
  let msg = enc ek_AS y_zk in                   } T_A
  let c = connect ad_AS in                      } (COMM-A)
  send c msg                                    }
```

hold) and *assertions*[6] declare formulas that are expected to logically follow from the previously introduced hypotheses.

Definition 4 (Safety [21]). *A program P is safe if and only if, in all executions of P, all assertions are entailed by the current assumptions.*

In general, we are interested in the safety of programs that are executed in parallel with the attacker. The attacker is modeled as some arbitrary (untyped) expression that has access to the functions exported by the program. The idea is to let the attacker create arbitrary parallel instances of the protocol roles and to let him send and receive messages on the network channels. If the attacker cannot break the safety property, then the program is robustly safe. In the following, we write $P\ Q$ to denote the application of program P to program Q (i.e., P can access the functions exported by Q).

Definition 5 (Formal threat model [21]). *A program A is an attacker if and only if A contains no occurrence of* assert *and each type annotation within A is* unit.

A program P is robustly safe if and only if the application $A\ P$ is safe for all attackers A.

The compiler automatically generates assumptions and assertions that capture the logical formulas that are introduced and derived in the DKAL derivation, respectively. In particular, the translation of a knowledge assertion of the form $A : F$ (rules P-A and P-S) introduces an assumption of the form assume F into A's code. The translation of any other rule with a thesis of the form A knows F (e.g., ENSUE) or A knows M (e.g., COMM-J) introduces an assertion of the form assert F in A's code, where F is the logical interpretation of M (i.e., $[M] = F$), thereby ensuring that the formula F is indeed derivable at run-time.

[6] RCF assertions are not to be confused with DKAL assertions.

Example 7. Let us consider the annotations in Table 8. The P-S rule in T_C introduces the formula vk_{Uni} says $Stud(\mathsf{vk}_{id}, cs, grd)$ in the DKAL derivation and therefore the compiler inserts assume vk_{Uni} says $Stud(\mathsf{vk}_{id}, cs, grd)$ into the university's code. The COMM-J rule in T_C models the transmission of the information vk_{Uni} says $Stud(\mathsf{vk}_{id}, cs, grd)$ from the university to the student. Consequently, the compiler inserts assert vk_{Uni} says $Stud(\mathsf{vk}_{id}, cs, grd)$ into the student's code after the signature verification, which ensures that vk_{Uni} says $Stud(\mathsf{vk}_{id}, cs, grd)$ is indeed derivable from the current assumptions at run-time.

For verification purposes, $F^{\#}$ programs are linked to a symbolic cryptographic library, comprising functions for public-key encryption, digital signatures, and zero-knowledge proofs. This library models the ideal behavior of cryptographic primitives using standard language constructs. We programmed the symbolic zero-knowledge library making usage of the tool developed by Backes et al. [11], which takes as input a zero-knowledge statement and produces methods for the construction and verification of the corresponding zero-knowledge proof. For protocols based on digital signatures and public-key encryption, safety carries over to programs linked to concrete cryptographic libraries [15, 36]. Preliminary results for the computational soundness of symbolic abstractions of zero-knowledge proofs have been proved in [16]. The soundness of the type system ensures that well-typed programs are safe.

Theorem 1 (Safety by typing [21]). *If* $\emptyset \vdash P : U$, *then* P *is safe.*

For verifying the security of the F# code that is generated by our compiler, it is in principle enough to run the type-checker. This *compilation validation* approach has the advantage of smoothly supporting optimizations of the result of the compilation and of the compiler itself. Nevertheless, we additionally prove that all programs output by the compiler are well-typed. This *security by construction* approach has the advantage of making the type-checking of the result of the compilation unnecessary, unless the code is modified, and gives stronger guarantees about the correctness of the compiler.

Theorem 2 (Soundness of the compilation). *For all logical derivations* $T \in \mathcal{T}_{\mathsf{dkal}}$, *there exists a type* U *such that* $\emptyset \vdash \mathcal{C}[\mathcal{T}] : U$.

Our main theorem states that well-typed programs that use the cryptographic library and the functions produced by the compiler are safe. In the following, we write $\mathcal{I}_{\mathcal{C}[\mathcal{T}]}$ to denote the typed interface of the library produced by the compiler and $P \cdot \mathcal{C}[\mathcal{T}]$ to denote the program obtained by linking P to such a library.

Theorem 3 (Robust safety of the compilation). *If* $\mathcal{I}_{\mathcal{C}[\mathcal{T}]} \vdash P : U$, *then* $P \cdot \mathcal{C}[\mathcal{T}]$ *is robustly safe.*

6. Case studies

In this section, we utilize our framework to specify a distributed reviewing system and a distributed social network. Given these logical specifications, the compiler automatically produces the corresponding cryptographic implementations. The goal is to demonstrate the possibility to specify relatively complex decentralized systems in a simple and elegant manner, without requiring any cryptographic expertise on the part of the users.

6.1. Distributed Reviewing System

Current reviewing systems (e.g., Easychair and EDAS) are designed around a trusted party that serves as custodian of a huge amount of data about the submission and reviewing behavior of thousands of researchers, aggregated across multiple conferences. The deliberate or accidental disclosure of such information is a recognized privacy problem [51]. In this section, we design a decentralized reviewing system that offers strong privacy guarantees.

The first functionality that a reviewing system should offer is paper assignment. This functionality is realized by the following protocol (for the sake of readability, we depict the protocol and omit the corresponding knowledge and communication assertions):

$$Chair \quad \xrightarrow[]{\text{COMM-J}}\; Chair \text{ says } RevAssign(id, paper) \longrightarrow \quad id$$

The authorization policy for reviews is as follows:

$$\begin{aligned} &\forall x_{id}, y_p, z_{rev}.\\ &\quad Chair \text{ says } RevAssign(x_{id}, y_p)\\ &\quad \wedge\, x_{id} \text{ says } Rev(y_p, z_{rev}) \Rightarrow Rev(y_p, z_{rev}) \end{aligned} \tag{11}$$

Ideally, reviewers should upload the minimal amount of information required to show that the review was submitted by an authorized reviewer. This can be achieved as follows:

$$Chair \longleftarrow \begin{array}{l} \exists x_{id}.\\ \quad Chair \text{ says } RevAssign(x_{id}, paper)\\ \quad \wedge\, x_{id} \text{ says } Rev(paper, rev) \end{array} \xrightarrow{\text{COMM-A}} \quad id$$

The information transmitted to the PC chair does not reveal the identity of the reviewer, which may be desirable, for instance, if the paper's author is a colleague of the PC chair or the reviewer does not want to reveal her identity to the whole PC. The long version of this paper reports the complete formalization and describes additional features, such as the management of rebuttals.

6.2. Distributed Social Network

The users of social networks have to face a surprisingly vast range of privacy issues. Well-understood problems, such as the centralized management and sharing of personal information, are accompanied by novel threats: for example, the Italian police is reported to have stipulated agreements with Facebook to get unfettered access to user profiles [35] and, in other countries, people that used social networks to organize protest activities were subject of repercussions, censorship, and coercion [34, 50, 1, 55, 28]. We used our framework to design a distributed social network that provides access control and, at the same time, user anonymity. This social network is close in spirit to the one that was recently developed by Backes et al. [13]. The cryptographic implementation that we obtain by compilation, however, is substantially different, being based on pairing-based zero-knowledge protocols as opposed to traditional Σ-protocols [30], arguably simpler, and open-ended. Users may establish social relations as follows:

$$\begin{array}{lcr} A & \longleftarrow B \text{ says } FriendReq(A) \xrightarrow{\text{COMM-J}} & B\\ & \xrightarrow[]{\text{COMM-J}} A \text{ says } Friend(B) \longrightarrow & \end{array}$$

The predicate B says *FriendReq*(A) represents a friendship request from B to A (social relations are unidirectional); the predicate A says *Friend*(B) represents the corresponding friendship confirmation. B can use this information to engage in a number of activities. Suppose, for instance, that the access to A's wall is limited to friends: B can anonymously post messages on A's wall by existentially quantifying his identity, as shown below:

$$A \xleftarrow{\exists x.\ A \text{ says } \mathit{Friend}(x) \wedge x \text{ says } \mathit{Wallpost}(m) \quad \textsc{Comm-A}} B$$

We additionally provide a method for downloading resources anonymously. Realizing this functionality is challenging since B does not want to reveal her identity to A, who has to know, however, to whom to send the response. We solve this problem by introducing into our framework the notion of anonymous identifiers, which are locally generated and distributed to other principals, who can then use them as intended recipients in communication assertions. Anonymous identifiers are cryptographically implemented by fresh public keys and can be realized at the network layer via rendezvouz-points [33]. Suppose B is interested in a picture that can only be seen by A's friends. Similarly to the previous protocol, B can prove to be a friend without revealing his identity and, in addition, give A a fresh anonymous identifier B^1, which she can use as intended recipient in the following communication assertion, as shown below:

$$A \xleftarrow{\exists x.\ A \text{ says } \mathit{Friend}(x) \wedge x \text{ says } \mathsf{getResource}(B^1, \mathit{pic\text{-}id}) \quad \textsc{Comm-A}} B$$

$$\xrightarrow{\textsc{Comm-J} \quad \mathit{Resource}(\mathit{pic})}$$

The long version gives a formal account of anonymous identifiers and illustrates other interesting features of the social network, such as friend-of-a-friend relationships and pseudonyms.

7. Implementation and Experimental Evaluation

We conducted an experimental evaluation to demonstrate the feasibility of our approach. This section overviews the cryptographic setup (§ 7.1) and discusses the experimental results (§ 7.2).

7.1. Cryptographic Setup

Devising a cryptographic realization for our logical framework turned out to be quite challenging. The cryptographic scheme has to be efficient and, at the same time, flexible enough to support the different usages of existential quantification, namely, the hiding of predicate arguments, principal identities, and equality relations among secret values (cf. Example 2).

Σ-protocols constitute a particularly efficient and widely deployed class of zero-knowledge protocols. Existing solutions, however, are not flexible enough to implement arbitrary existential quantification: for instance, existentially quantifying verification keys that are both signed and used to verify signatures (e.g., the key vk_{id} in statement (3)) is impractically slow [10].

A general solution to this problem was discovered only recently by Abe et al. [5], who introduced the notion of automorphic signatures. The distinctive feature of this signature scheme is that verification keys lie in the message space. Since messages and signatures consist of elements of a bilinear group and verication is done by evaluating a set of pairing-product equations, automorphic signatures make a perfect counterpart to the powerful zero-knowledge proof system by Groth and Sahai [40], which supports a large class of statements over bilinear groups. Our cryptographic implementation builds on a combination of these two cryptographic schemes. An other advantage of the Groth-Sahai scheme over Σ-protocols is the possibility (i) to re-randomize proofs without knowing their witnesses [20] and (ii) to existentially quantify information in existing proofs. We exploit the first property to hide the equality relations among secret values, while the second property is crucial for open-ended applications. We implemented the cryptographic library in Java and we relied on the jPBC library [31] for the computation of mathematical operations. A detailed description of our cryptographic implementation is reported in the long version.

7.2. Experimental evaluation

We conducted our experimental evaluation on a standard notebook with a 2.5 GHz dual-core processor[7] and 8 GB of main memory. We measured the time required to create and verify various proofs and studied how these are influenced by the length of the security parameter, the size of the statement, and the number of existentially quantified values. In our experiments, the elliptic curves are such that the key length equals twice the security parameter [53], e.g., we use 160 bit keys to obtain a security parameter of 80 bits.

As illustrated in Figure 1, time and size grow linearly in the size of the statement, although increasing the number of conjuncts (and disjuncts) is more expensive than increasing the number of predicate arguments. The reason lies buried within the automorphic signature scheme for vectors of messages. Intuitively, setting up such a vector is computationally more expensive than filling it with elements [5]. An exact analysis shows that adding one argument to a predicate costs roughly 5 seconds of proof generation time for a security parameter of 80 bits, while a zero-knowledge proof of a statement composed of one predicate with four arguments is computationally as expensive as a zero-knowledge proof for a statement composed of two predicates with one argument each.

[7] The full model description is "Intel Core i5-2520M"

The graphs in Figure 2, Figure 3, Figure 4, and Figure 5 (cf. Appendix A) depict the results obtained for some of the proofs illustrated in this paper for various security parameters. Time and size grow linearly in the length of the security parameter. The results for a security parameter of 80 bits vary from 31 seconds for anonymously posting messages on a friend's wall up to 41 seconds for anonymously accessing a university lab. The reason for the small time and size differences is that the zero-knowledge statements are structurally very similar: they all comprise two signature verifications and the number of predicate arguments is only marginally different.

As previously discussed, existential quantification is very expensive in Σ-protocols [10] and the protocols themselves change depending on which and how many values are existentially quantified. The Groth-Sahai proof system combined with our encoding of predicates, instead, allows for a very efficient and arbitrary existential quantification. As a matter of fact, existential quantification comes at *no costs at all* in our implementation, as illustrated in Figure 6 (cf. Appendix A). Actually, the more information is existentially quantified, the shorter the zero-knowledge proof is. This is explained by the fact that we implement existential quantification by deleting certain information (specifically, the opening information for the corresponding commitment) from the proof and the performed computations are always the same.

We remark that our proof-of-concept implementation is not optimized in any way. In particular, we do not yet exploit readily available optimizations such as the multi-core architecture of today's processors and batch verification techniques [24]. As the computations are largely independent, multi-core architectures yields a great performance gain. Batch verification techniques significantly speed up the verification process; the verification performance gains can be well above 50% [24]. We are working on the integration of such optimizations in our implementation.

8. Conclusion and Future Work

Ensuring the privacy of sensitive data is crucial for the widespread deployment of authorization infrastructures. In this paper, we show how to enforce privacy-aware evidential authorization using a powerful and efficient combination of digital signatures and zero-knowledge proofs. We developed a high-level declarative language that lets the user conveniently specify the system and the desired security properties, and a compiler that automatically produces executable cryptographic implementations. Although we studied the theoretical properties of our framework in the context of Evidential DKAL, our cryptographic construction is language-independent and generally applicable: in the long version, we report on a privacy-oriented extension of the Proof Carrying Authorization framework [8, 18] and we envision the usage of our framework in several other authorization languages, such as Aura [43], $PCML_5$ [9], F^* [52], and SecPal [19].

We are currently implementing our framework on top of JXTA and JGroups, two open-source development platforms for distributed systems. These platforms provide high-level communication primitives that conceal the network layer and allow the designer to focus on the functional behavior of the system; our framework provides security-oriented data abstractions that hide the cryptographic layer as well.

We have formally proved that the implementations produced by the compiler enforce the intended authorization policies. Local privacy properties expressed via existential quantification are directly guaranteed by the zero-knowledge property of the employed proofs. Global privacy properties, such as strong secrecy and anonymity, are harder to enforce by construction, since they are not closed by composition and depend on the system as a whole. They can, however, be verified directly on the protocols produced by the compiler using off-the-shelf cryptographic protocol verifiers (e.g., ProVerif [23]). As a future work, it would be interesting to develop techniques to quantitatively measure global privacy properties (e.g., in terms of information flow, k-anonymity, etc.).

Finally, we intend to extend our framework in a number of directions. For example, we would like to develop primitives to share and process distributed data structures, yet preserving the privacy of sensitive information; this could be achieved by a combination of homomorphic encryptions and secure multiparty computations. It would also be interesting to offer support for other security properties, such as linear authorization policies [25] and trust properties [27].

Acknowledgments
This work was partially supported by the initiative for excellence and the Emmy Noether program of the German federal government.

References

[1] C. Abadi. Iran, Facebook, and the Limits of Online Activism. *Foreign Policy*, 2010. `http://www.foreignpolicy.com/articles/2010/02/12/irans_failed_facebook_revolution`.

[2] M. Abadi. Access Control in a Core Calculus of Dependency. *SIGPLAN Notices*, 41:263–273, 2006.

[3] M. Abadi, A. Banerjee, N. Heintze, and J. G. Riecke. A Core Calculus of Dependency. In *Proc. Symposium on Principles of Programming Languages (POPL'99)*, pages 147–160. ACM Press, 1999.

[4] M. Abadi, M. Burrows, B. Lampson, and G. Plotkin. A Calculus for Access Control in Distributed Systems. *ACM*

Transactions on Programming Languages and Systems, 15:706–734, September 1993.

[5] M. Abe, G. Fuchsbauer, J. Groth, K. Haralambiev, and M. Ohkubo. Structure-Preserving Signatures and Commitments to Group Elements. In *Proc. Advances in Cryptology (CRYPTO'10)*, volume 6223 of *Lecture Notes in Computer Science*, pages 209–236. Springer-Verlag, 2010.

[6] J. B. Almeida, E. Bangerter, M. Barbosa, S. Krenn, A.-R. Sadeghi, and T. Schneider. A Certifying Compiler for Zero-Knowledge Proofs of Knowledge Based on Sigma-Protocols. In *ESORICS'10*, pages 151–167, 2010.

[7] M. M. Andreas Blass, Yuri Gurevich and I. Neeman. Evidential Authorization. *The Future of Software Engineering*, pages 77–99, 2011.

[8] A. W. Appel and E. W. Felten. Proof-Carrying Authentication. In *Proc. ACM Conference on Computer and Communications Security (CCS'99)*, pages 52–62. ACM Press, 1999.

[9] K. Avijit, A. Datta, and R. Harper. Distributed Programming with Distributed Authorization. In *Proc. ACM SIGPLAN workshop on Types in language design and implementation (TLDI'10)*, pages 27–38. ACM Press, 2010.

[10] M. Backes, S. Lorenz, M. Maffei, and K. Pecina. Anonymous Webs of Trust. In *Proc. Privacy Enhancing Technologies Symposium (PETS'10)*, volume 6205 of *Lecture Notes in Computer Science*, pages 130–148. Springer-Verlag, 2010.

[11] M. Backes, M. Maffei, and C. Hriţcu. Union and Intersection Types for Secure Protocol Implementations. In *Proc. Conference on Theory of Security and Applications (TOSCA'11)*, Lecture Notes in Computer Science. Springer-Verlag, 2011.

[12] M. Backes, M. Maffei, and K. Pecina. Automated Synthesis of Secure Distributed Application. Long version available at `http://lbs.cs.uni-saarland.de/asosda`.

[13] M. Backes, M. Maffei, and K. Pecina. A Security API for Distributed Social Networks. In *Proc. Network and Distributed System Security Symposium (NDSS'11)*, 2011.

[14] M. Backes, M. Maffei, K. Pecina, and R. M. Reischuk. G2C: Cryptographic Protocols from Goal-Driven Specifications. In *Proc. Conference on Theory of Security and Applications (TOSCA'11)*, Lecture Notes in Computer Science, Saarbrücken, Germany, 2011. Springer-Verlag.

[15] M. Backes, M. Maffei, and D. Unruh. Computationally Sound Verification of Source Code. In *CCS '10*, pages 387–398. ACM, 2010.

[16] M. Backes and D. Unruh. Computational Soundness of Symbolic Zero-Knowledge Proofs Against Active Attackers. In *CSF'08*, pages 255–269. IEEE, 2008.

[17] L. Bauer, S. Garriss, J. M. McCune, M. K. Reiter, J. Rouse, and P. Rutenbar. Device-Enabled Authorization in the Grey System. In *Proc. Information Security Conference (ISC'05)*, Lecture Notes in Computer Science, pages 431–445. Springer-Verlag, 2005.

[18] L. Bauer, M. Schneider, E. Felten, and A. Appel. Access Control on the Web Using Proof-Carrying Authorization. In *Proc. DARPA Conference on Information Survivability Conference and Exposition (DISCEX'03)*, volume 2, pages 117–119, 2003.

[19] M. Y. Becker, C. Fournet, and A. D. Gordon. Design and Semantics of a Decentralized Authorization Language. In *Proc. IEEE Symposium on Computer Security Foundations (CSF'07)*, pages 3–15. IEEE Computer Society Press, 2007.

[20] M. Belenkiy, J. Camenisch, M. Chase, M. Kohlweiss, A. Lysyanskaya, and H. Shacham. Randomizable Proofs and Delegatable Anonymous Credentials. In *Proc. Advances in Cryptology (CRYPTO'09)*, volume 5677 of *Lecture Notes in Computer Science*, pages 108–125. Springer-Verlag, 2009.

[21] J. Bengtson, K. Bhargavan, C. Fournet, A. D. Gordon, and S. Maffeis. Refinement Types for Secure Implementations. In *Proc. IEEE Symposium on Computer Security Foundations (CSF'08)*, pages 17–32, 2008.

[22] K. Bhargavan, C. Fournet, and A. Gordon. Modular Verification of Security Protocol Code by Typing. *ACM SIGPLAN Notices*, 45(1):445–456, 2010.

[23] B. Blanchet, M. Abadi, and C. Fournet. Automated Cerification of Selected Equivalences for Security Protocols. *Journal of Logic and Algebraic Programming*, 75(1):3–51, 2008.

[24] O. Blazy, G. Fuchsbauer, M. Izabachène, A. Jambert, H. Sibert, and D. Vergnaud. Batch Groth-Sahai. In *Proc. International Conference on Applied Cryptography and Network Security (ACNS'10)*, volume 6123 of *Lecture Notes in Computer Science*, pages 218–235. Springer-Verlag, 2010.

[25] K. D. Bowers, L. Bauer, D. Garg, F. Pfenning, and M. K. Reiter. Consumable Credentials in Linear-Logic-Based Access-Control Systems. In *Proc. Network and Distributed System Security Symposium (NDSS'07)*. Internet Society, 2007.

[26] E. Brickell, J. Camenisch, and L. Chen. Direct Anonymous Attestation. In *CCS'04*, pages 132–145. ACM Press, 2004.

[27] G. Caronni. Walking the Web of Trust. In *Proc. IEEE International Workshops on Enabling Technologies: Infrastructure for Collaborative Enterprises (WETICE'00)*, pages 153–158. IEEE Computer Society Press, 2000.

[28] H. Carter. England Riots: Pair Jailed for Four Years for Using Facebook to Incite Disorder. *Guardian*, 2011. `http://www.guardian.co.uk/uk/2011/aug/16/uk-riots-four-years-disorder-facebook`.

[29] A. Chaudhuri and D. Garg. PCAL: Language Support for Proof-Carrying Authorization Systems. In *Proc. European Symposium on Research in Computer Security (ESORICS'09)*, Lecture Notes in Computer Science, pages 184–199. Springer-Verlag, 2009.

[30] R. Cramer, I. Damgård, and B. Schoenmakers. Proofs of Partial Knowledge and Simplified Design of Witness Hiding Protocols. In *Proc. Advances in Cryptology (CRYPTO'94)*, volume 839 of *Lecture Notes in Computer Science*, pages 174–187. Springer-Verlag, 1994.

[31] A. De Caro. jPBC Library. `http://libeccio.dia.unisa.it/projects/jpbc/download.html`.

[32] J. DeTreville. Binder, a Logic-Based Security Language. In *Proc. IEEE Symposium on Security & Privacy (S&P'02)*, pages 105–113. IEEE Computer Society Press, 2002.

[33] R. Dingledine, N. Mathewson, and P. F. Syverson. Tor: The Second-Generation Onion Router. In *Proc. USENIX Security Symposium (USENIX'04)*, pages 303–320. USENIX Association, 2004.

[34] F. Fassihi. Iranian Crackdown Goes Global. *The Wall Street Journal*, 2009. http://online.wsj.com/article/SB125978649644673331.html.

[35] G. Florian. La Polizia ci Spia su Facebook. *L'Espresso*, 2010. http://espresso.repubblica.it/dettaglio/<div>la-polizia-ci-spia-su-facebook<div>/2137277.

[36] C. Fournet. Cryptographic Soundness for Program Verification by Typechecking. Unpublished draft, 2011.

[37] K. Frikken, M. Atallah, and J. Li. Attribute-Based Access Control with Hidden Policies and Hidden Credentials. *IEEE Transactions on Computers*, 55(10):1259 –1270, 2006.

[38] D. Garg and F. Pfenning. A Proof-Carrying File System. In *Proc. IEEE Symposium on Security & Privacy (S&P'10)*, pages 349–364. IEEE Computer Society Press, 2010.

[39] O. Goldreich, S. Micali, and A. Wigderson. Proofs that yield nothing but their validity or all languages in NP have zero-knowledge proof systems. *JACM*, 38(3):690–728, 1991.

[40] J. Groth and A. Sahai. Efficient Non-interactive Proof Systems for Bilinear Groups. In *Proc. Advances in Cryptology (EUROCRYPT'08)*, volume 4965 of *Lecture Notes in Computer Science*, pages 415–432. Springer-Verlag, 2008.

[41] Y. Gurevich and I. Neeman. DKAL: Distributed-Knowledge Authorization Language. In *CSF'08*. IEEE, 2008.

[42] Y. Gurevich and I. Neeman. DKAL 2 – A Simplified and Improved Authorization Language. Microsoft Research Technical Report, 2009.

[43] L. Jia, J. A. Vaughan, K. Mazurak, J. Zhao, L. Zarko, J. Schorr, and S. Zdancewic. AURA: A Programming Language for Authorization and Audit. *ACM SIGPLAN Notices*, 43(9):27–38, 2008.

[44] B. Lampson, M. Abadi, M. Burrows, and E. Wobber. Authentication in Distributed Systems: Theory and Practice. *ACM Transactions on Computer Systems*, 10:265–310, November 1992.

[45] J. Li, N. Li, and W. H. Winsborough. Automated trust negotiation using cryptographic credentials. In *Proceedings of the 12th ACM conference on Computer and communications security*, CCS'05, pages 46–57. ACM Press, 2005.

[46] N. Li, J. C. Mitchell, and W. H. Winsborough. Design of a Role-Based Trust-Management Framework. In *Proc. IEEE Symposium on Security & Privacy (S&P'02)*, pages 114–130. IEEE, 2002.

[47] L. Lu, J. Han, Y. Liu, L. Hu, J.-P. Huai, L. Ni, and J. Ma. Pseudo Trust: Zero-Knowledge Authentication in Anonymous P2Ps. *IEEE Trans. on Parallel Distributed Systems*, 19(10):1325–1337, 2008.

[48] M. Maffei and K. Pecina. Position Paper: Privacy-Aware Proof-Carrying Authorization. In *Proc. ACM SIGPLAN Workshop on Programming Languages and Analysis for Security (PLAS'11)*, 2011.

[49] S. Meiklejohn, C. C. Erway, A. Küpçü, T. Hinkle, and A. Lysyanskaya. ZKPDL: A Language-Based System for Efficient Zero-Knowledge Proofs and Electronic Cash. In *Proc. USENIX Security Symposium (USENIX'10)*, pages 193–206, 2010.

[50] E. Morozov. Foreign Policy: Iran's Terrifying Facebook Police. *National Public Radio*, 2009. http://www.npr.org/templates/story/story.php?storyId=106535773.

[51] M. D. Ryan. Cloud computing privacy concerns on our doorstep. *Communications of the ACM*, 54:36–38, 2011.

[52] N. Swamy, J. Chen, C. Fournet, K. Bharagavan, and J. Yang. Security Programming with Refinement Types and Mobile Proofs. Technical Report MSR-TR-2010-149, Microsoft Research, 2010.

[53] The National Institute of Standards and Technology. Recommendataion for Key Management – Part 1: General (Revised). *NIST SP*, 800–57, 2011. http://csrc.nist.gov/groups/ST/toolkit/key_management.html.

[54] J. A. Vaughan. A Confidentiality Extension to the Aura Programming Language. In *Proc. ACM SIGPLAN workshop on Types in language design and implementation (TLDI'11)*. ACM Press, 2011.

[55] D. Wolman. Cairo Activists Use Facebook to Rattle Regime. *WIRED Magazine*, 2008. http://www.wired.com/techbiz/startups/magazine/16-11/ff_facebookegypt.

A. Experimental results

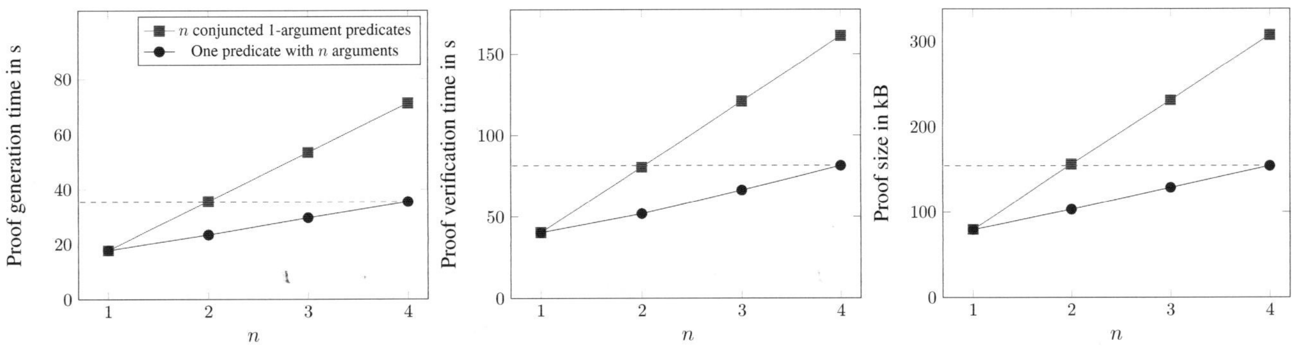

Figure 1. Comparison of the experimental evaluation of zero-knowledge proofs for predicates with various argument lengths against the conjunction of zero-knowledge proofs for predicates with only one argument. The security parameter is fixed to 80 bits.

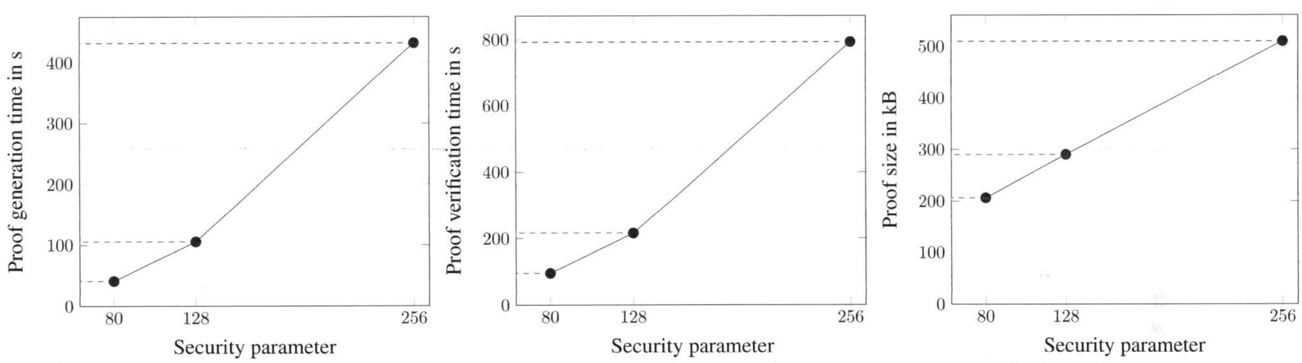

Figure 2. Experimental evaluation on the zero-knowledge proof corresponding to formula (3) (a computer science student requesting access to a lab) for various security parameters.

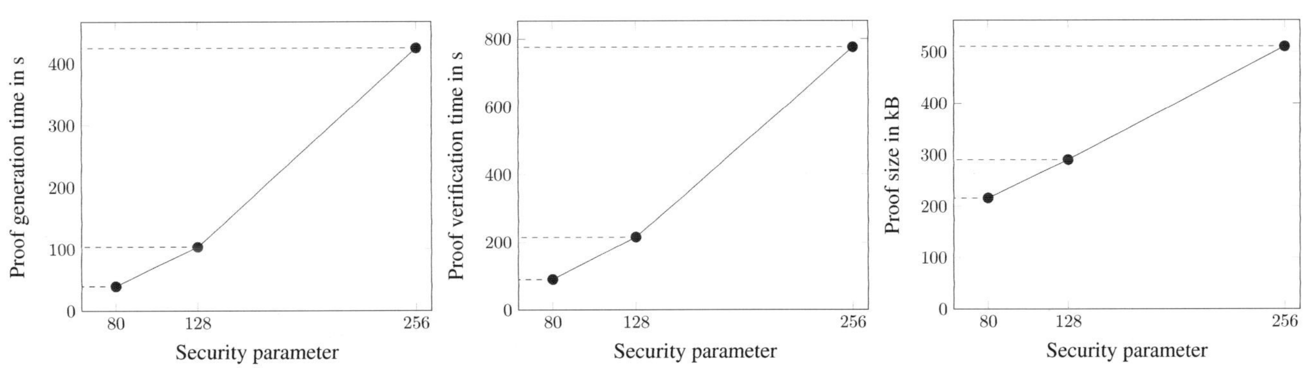

Figure 3. Experimental evaluation on the zero-knowledge proof sent by the reviewer in the example in § 6.1 for various security parameters.

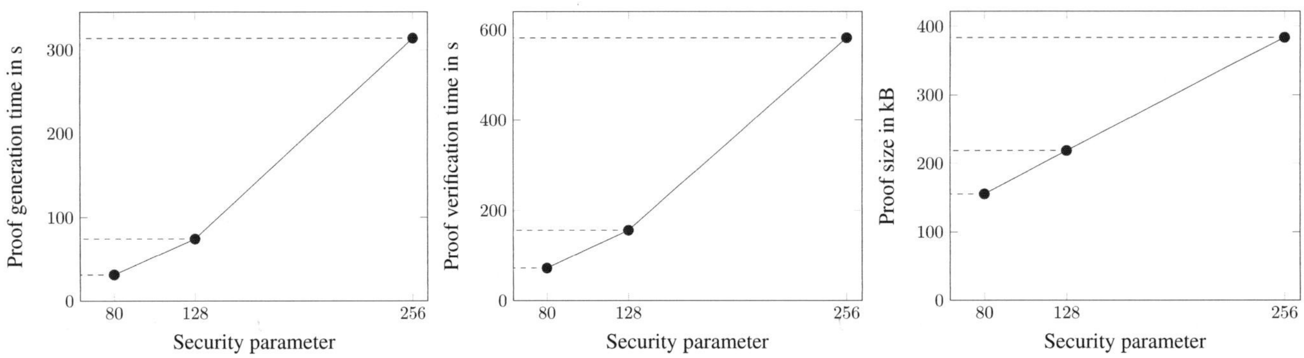

Figure 4. Experimental evaluation on the zero-knowledge proof for posting a message on a friend's wall from § 6.2 for various security parameters.

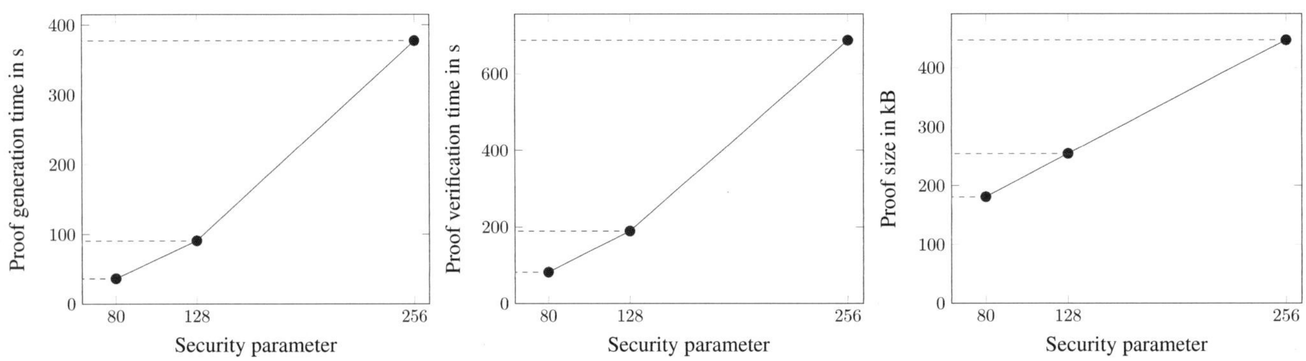

Figure 5. Experimental evaluation on the zero-knowledge proof for retrieving a resource from a friend from § 6.2 for various security parameters.

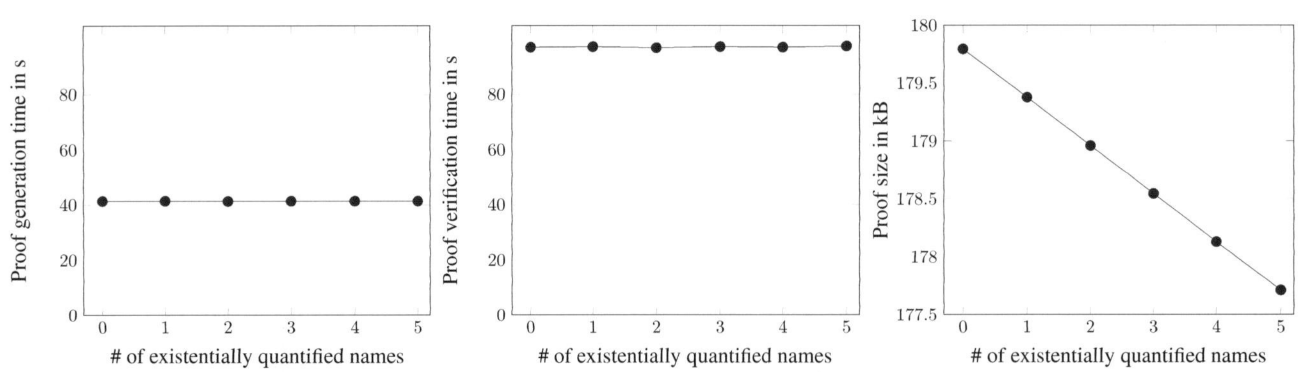

Figure 6. Experimental evaluation on the computational and spacial impact of existential quantification for a predicate with 5 arguments and fixed security parameter of 80 bits.

A General Approach for Efficiently Accelerating Software-based Dynamic Data Flow Tracking on Commodity Hardware

Kangkook Jee
Columbia University

Joint work with
Georgios Portokalidis[1] , Vasileios Kemerlis[1] ,
Soumyadeep Ghosh[2], David August[2], Angelos Keromytis[1]

[1]Columbia University, [2]Princeton University

1

Data Flow Tracking (DFT)

- A great security tool with many applications
  - Tag input data and track them
  - Software exploits, Information misuse or leakage malware analysis ...
- Implementation approaches
  - Hardware assisted: Raksha, RIFLE ...
  - Source code based: GIFT ...
  - Binary only: TaintCheck, Dytan, Minemu, Libdft ...

<u>Binary only DFT</u>: Most promising, but too slow!

2

This Talk Is About

- New optimization approach for
  - Currently sub-optimal binary only DFT
  - Performance gain up to x2.23 (on average x1.77)
  - Real-world applications: Firefox, Chrome ...
- Segregation of tracking logic from execution
  - Taint Flow Algebra (TFA): IR for DFT
  - Compiler optimization + DFT specific optimization

3

DFT: Basic Aspects

- DFT is characterized by *three* aspects
  - **(1) Data Sources**: program or memory locations where data of interest enter the system and is subsequently tagged
  - **(2) Data tracking**: process of propagating data tags according to the program's semantics
  - **(3) Data Sinks**: program or memory locations where checks for "tagged" data can be made

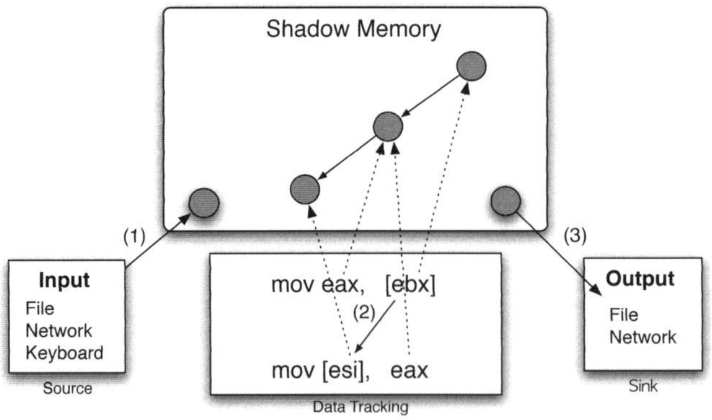

4

DFT Operation

- Real Memory = Address space + register context

5

DFT Operation

- Real Memory = Address space + register context
- Shadow memory to track metadata update

6

DFT Operation

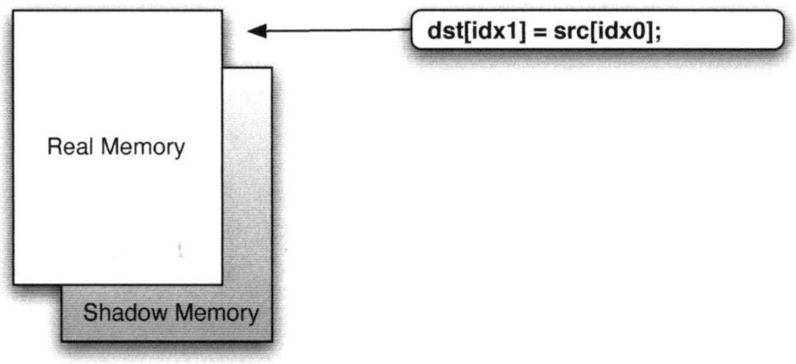

- Memory copy statement from the original execution

7

DFT Operation

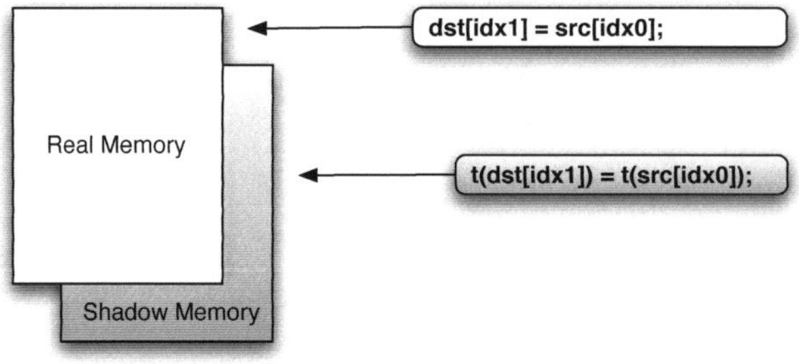

- Memory copy statement from the original execution
- Corresponding shadow memory update

8

DFT Operation

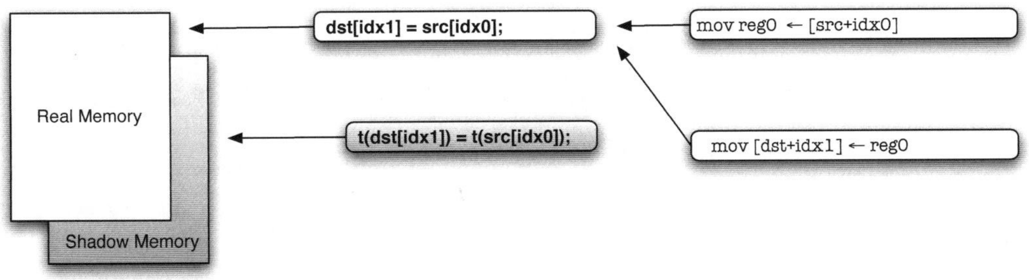

- Original operation translated into machine code
- It requires intermediate register repository (reg0)

9

DFT Operation

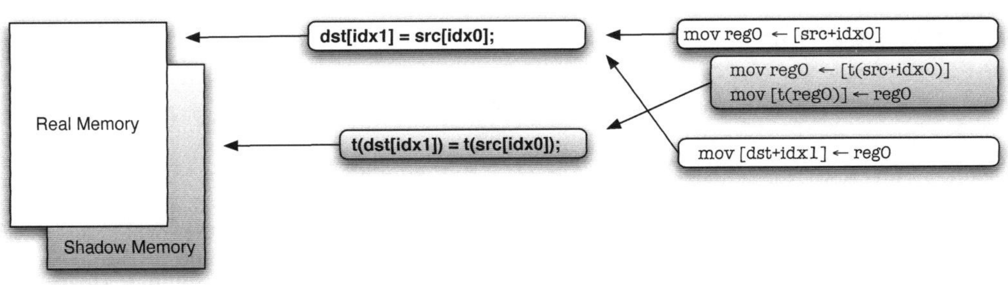

- Instruction level instrumentation to implement shadow update

10

DFT Operation

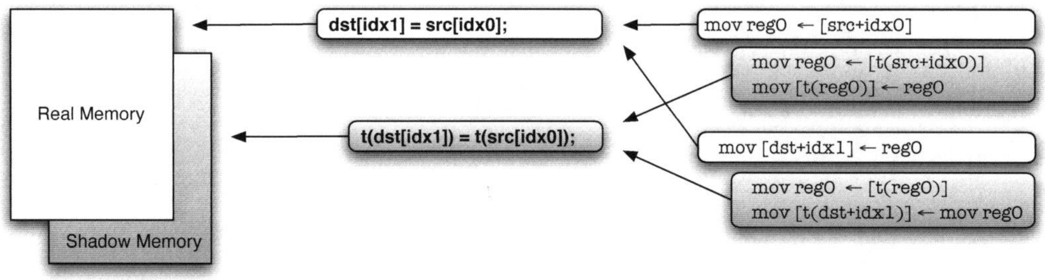

- 2 original instructions + 4 tracking instructions
- 2 instrumentation units

11

Why So Slow?

- Framework cost
  - DBI, Hypervisor instrumentation
- DFT cost
  - Accesses to shadow storage
- Naïve Implementation
  - No understanding of global context
  - No understanding of DFT semantics

12

Our Approach

- Application specific analysis
- DFT specific analysis
- Integrated with *libdft*
  - High performance DFT tool [VEE 2012]
    - 1.46x ~ 8x slowdown (over native execution)
  - Designed for use with *Pin DBI framework*
  - Open source
    - http://www.cs.columbia.edu/~vpk/research/libdft

13

Optimizing DFT

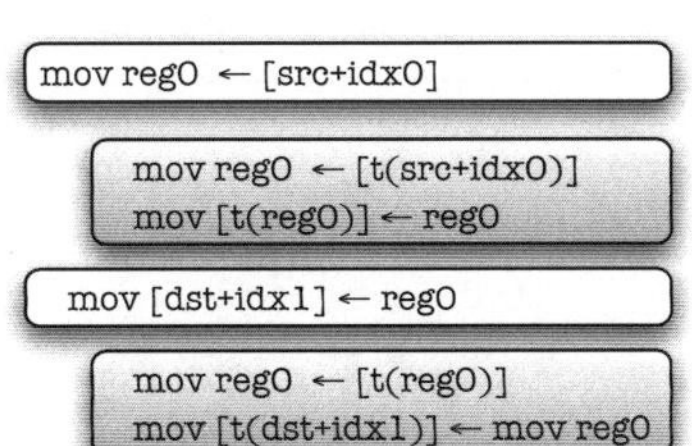

- Each Instrumentation unit requires head/tail instructions
- *t( )* : shadow memory access cost

14

Optimizing DFT

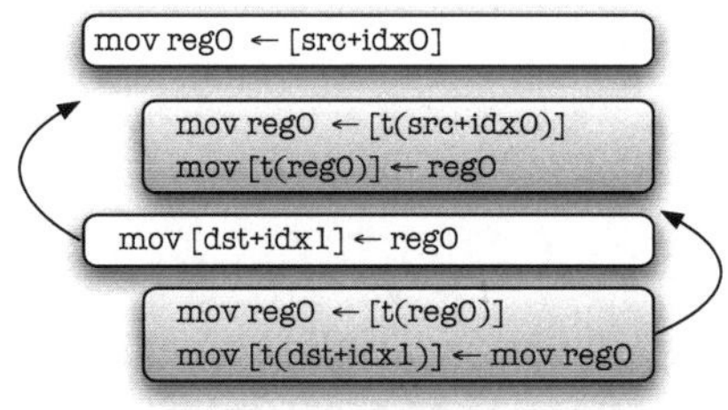

- Re-locatable

15

Optimizing DFT

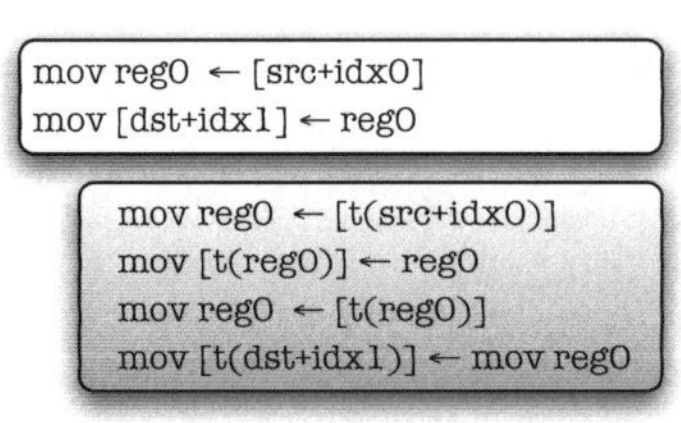

- Less instrumentation units (2→1)

16

Optimizing DFT

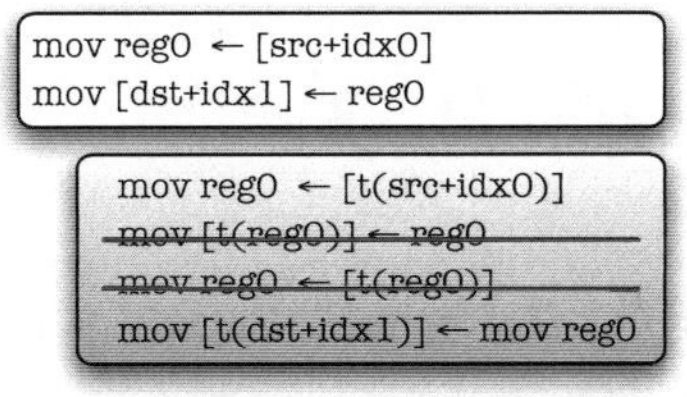

- Less instrumentation units (2→1)
- Less tracking instructions (4→2)

17

Execution Model

- 3 Components
  - Profiler, Analyzer, DFT Runtime
- Static/offline analysis + Dynamic runtime
  - Feedback loop

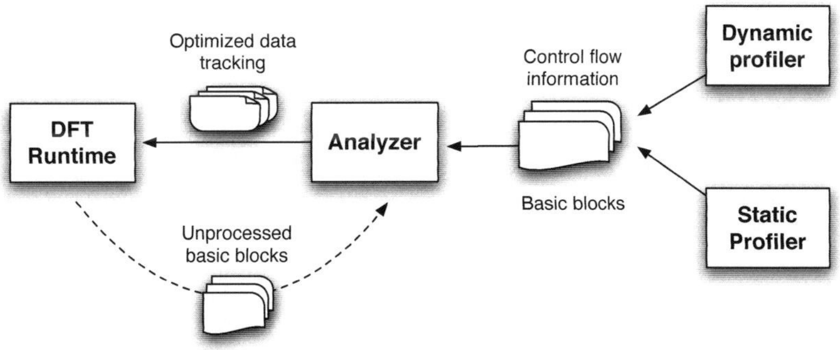

18

Analyzer

- Taint Flow Algebra
  - Represent binary analysis result
  - IR tailored to capture DFT semantics
- Compiler optimization to TFA
  - Inner (intra) basic block:
    Dead code elimination, Algebraic simplification, ...
  - Outer (inter) basic block:
    Data flow analysis
- DFT specific considerations
  - Valid location for each instrumentation unit
  - Number of instrumentation units

19

TFA Optimization

```
1: mov ecx, esi
2: movzxb eax, al
3: shl ecx, 0x5
4: add edx,0x1
5: lea esi, ptr [ecx+esi]
6: lea esi, ptr [eax+esi]
7: movzxb eax, ptr [edx+esi]
8: testb al, al
9: jnzb 0xb7890200
```

(a) x86 instruction

- Per basic block analysis
- Gray instructions: non-tracking instructions

20

TFA Optimization

(a) x86 instruction	(b) TFA transformation
1: mov ecx, esi	1: ecx1 := esi0
2: movzxb eax, al	2: eax1 := 0x1 & eax0
3: shl ecx, 0x5	3:
4: add edx,0x1	4:
5: lea esi, ptr [ecx+esi]	5: esi1 := ecx1 | esi0
6: lea esi, ptr [eax+esi]	6: esi2 := eax1 | esi1
7: movzxb eax, ptr [edx+esi]	7: eax2 := 0x1 & [edx0+esi2]
8: testb al, al	8:
9: jnzb 0xb7890200	9:

- Translated into TFA
- Input operands, output operands

TFA Optimization

(a) x86 instruction	(b) TFA transformation	(c) TFA optimization
1: mov ecx, esi	1: ecx1 := esi0	1: ecx1 := esi0
2: movzxb eax, al	2: eax1 := 0x1 & eax0	2:
3: shl ecx, 0x5	3:	3:
4: add edx,0x1	4:	4:
5: lea esi, ptr [ecx+esi]	5: esi1 := ecx1 | esi0	5:
6: lea esi, ptr [eax+esi]	6: esi2 := eax1 | esi1	6: esi2 := 0x1 & eax0 |esi0
7: movzxb eax, ptr [edx+esi]	7: eax2 := 0x1 & [edx0+esi2]	7: eax2 := 0x1 & [edx0+esi2]
8: testb al, al	8:	8:
9: jnzb 0xb7890200	9:	9:

- Output operands are expressed in terms of input operands
- Data flow analysis to remove irrelevant outputs

TFA Optimization

1: mov ecx, esi
2: movzxb eax, al
3: shl ecx, 0x5
4: add edx,0x1
5: lea esi, ptr [ecx+esi]
6: lea esi, ptr [eax+esi]
7: movzxb eax, ptr [edx+esi]
8: testb al, al
9: jnzb 0xb7890200

(a) x86 instruction

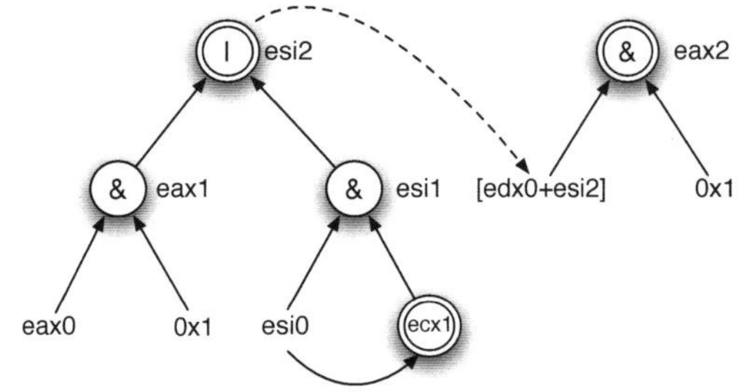

DAG Representation

- DAG Representation
- Express root nodes in terms of leaf nodes

23

DFT Runtime

- Generate/Inject optimized tracking code to the baseline DFT platform
  - Translate optimized TFA
- Our prototype extends libdft
- Code generation of libdft/PIN-aware C code
  - A function per each instrumentation unit
  - e.g., Firefox: 50K customized functions

24

Evaluation

- Optimization schemes
  - Code reduction: Simple dead code eliminations
    - Inner, Outer
  - Code generation: Optimized tracking codes
  - TFA Scatter, TFA Aggregation

Category	Optimization schemes	CFG Consideration	TFA Optimization	Aggregation
Code reduction	Inner	No	No	No
	Outer	Yes	No	No
Code generation	Scatter	Yes	Yes	No
	Aggregation	Yes	Yes	Yes

25

Evaluation: SPEC CPU2000

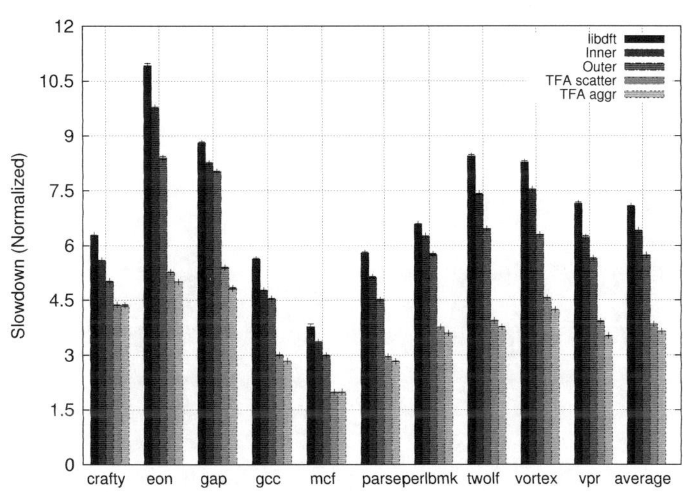

- CPU intensive workloads
- TFA's speedup over libdft: on average 1.90x (the largest 2.23x)
- ~3x slowdown over the native execution

26

Evaluation: Server applications

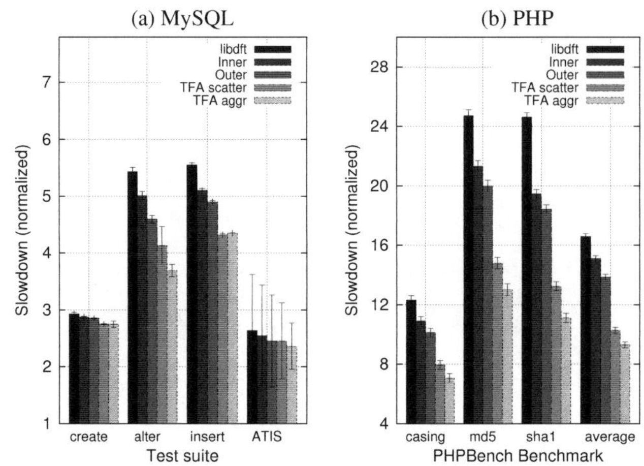

- Mysql's own benchmark suite (sql-bench) and PHP micro benchmark suite (PHPBench)
  - Plotted representative subsets

27

Evaluation: Client Applications

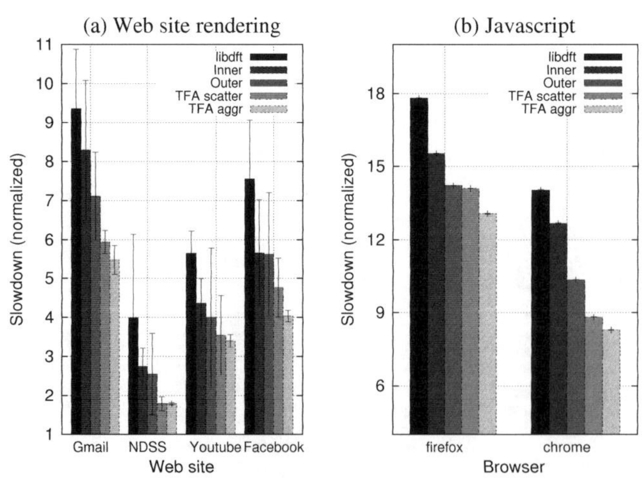

- Rendering measurement for Alexa's Top 500 sites and NDSS 2012 site
  - For Firefox web-browser
- Dromaeo (http://www.dromaeo.com) Javascript benchmark suite
  - For Firefox and Google Chrome web-browser

28

Discussion

- TFA for other DFT solutions
  - For most binary DFT implementations e.g., TaintCheck, Dytan, Minemu ...
  - Orthogonal to existing optimization schemes e.g., LIFT
- Tools with memory shadowing
  - Memcheck (Valgrind), Dr. Memory (DynamoRIO)
- Higher perspective
  - Offline analysis to improve expensive dynamic monitors

29

Conclusion

- Current binary-only DFT implementations are sub optimal
  - No consideration for DFT semantics
  - No consideration for global context
- Proposed a novel optimization scheme that
  - Combines static and dynamic analysis
  - Segregates execution and tracking logic
- ~2x Speedup for real-world applications

30

Backup slides

31

DFT Operation

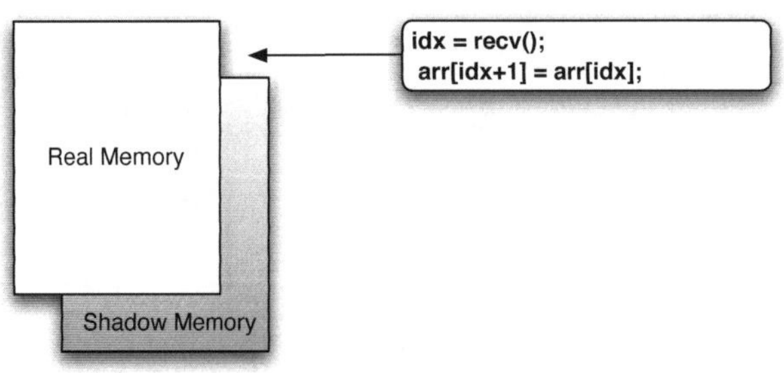

- Memory copy statement from the original execution

DFT Operation

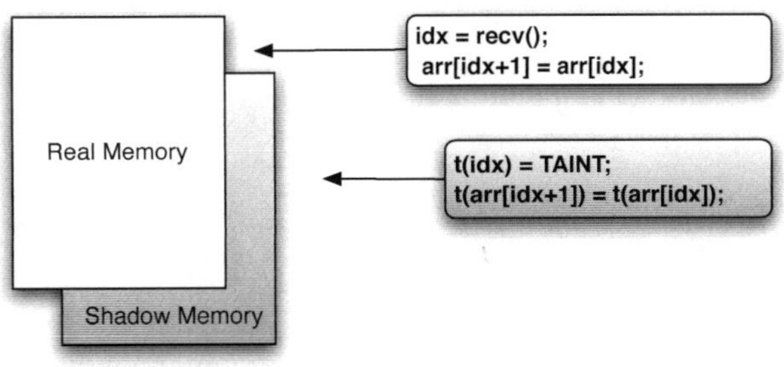

- Memory copy statement from the original execution

DFT Operation

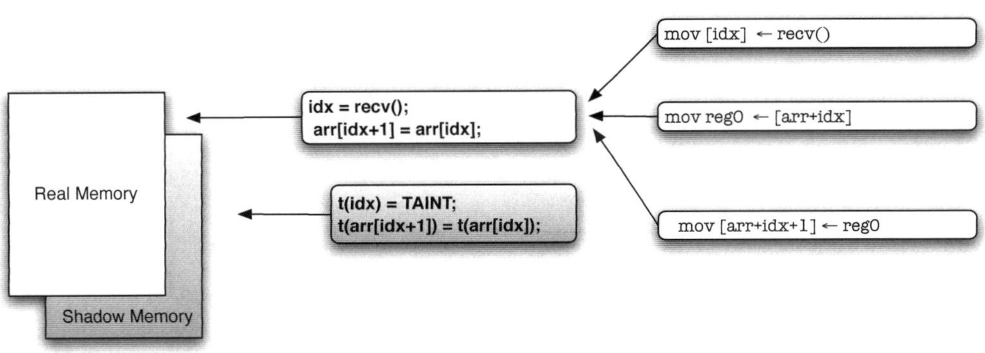

- Memory copy statement from the original execution

DFT Operation

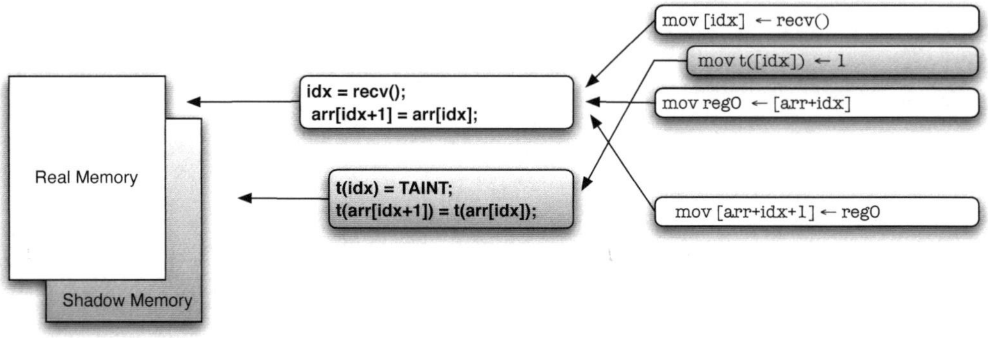

- Memory copy statement from the original execution

DFT Operation

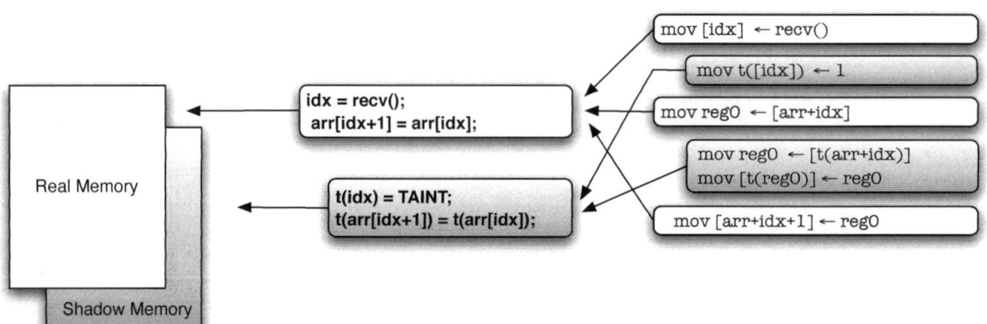

- Memory copy statement from the original execution

DFT Operation

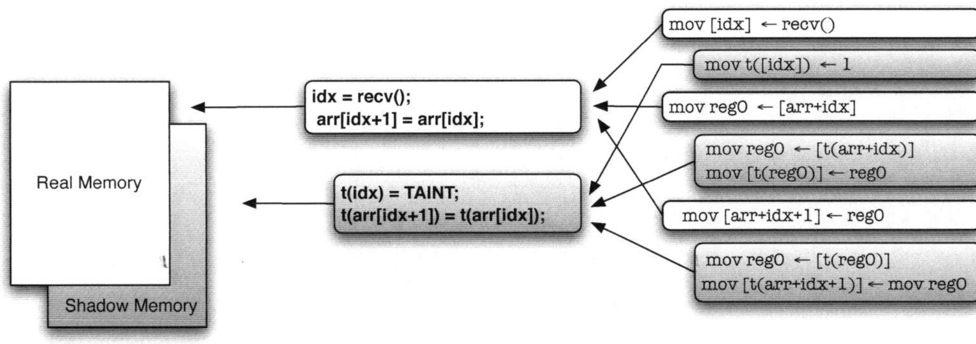

- Memory copy statement from the original execution

Optimizing DFT

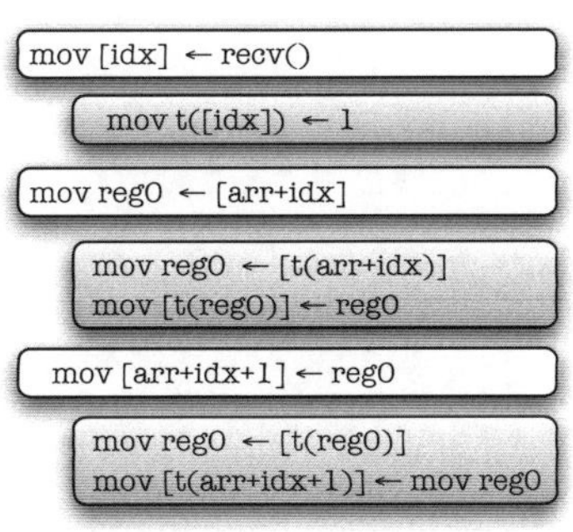

- Each Instrumentation unit require head/tail instructions
- t( ): shadow memory access cost

Optimizing DFT

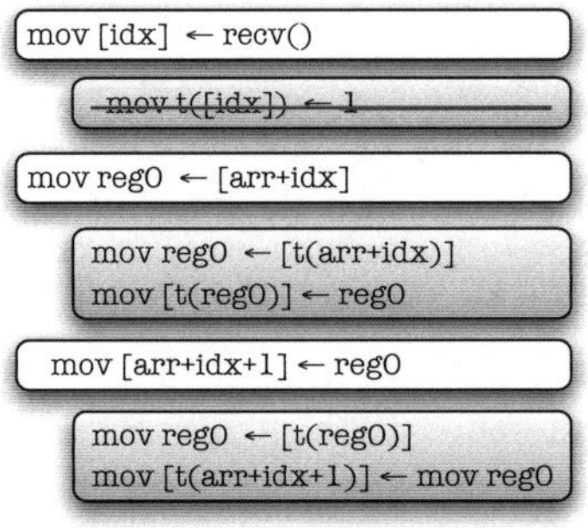

- Each Instrumentation unit require head/tail instructions
- t( ): shadow memory access cost

Optimizing DFT

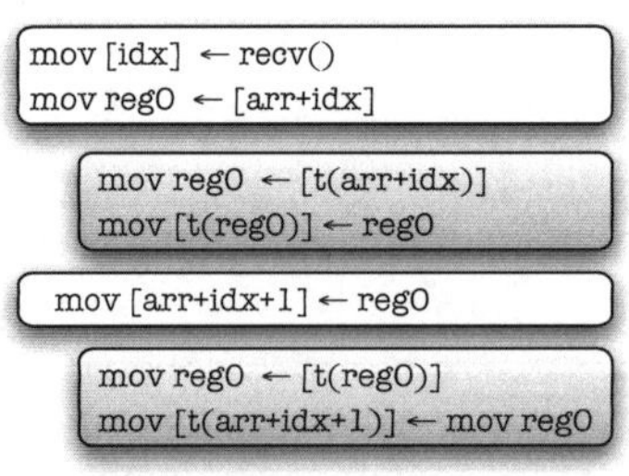

- Each Instrumentation unit require head/tail instructions
- t( ): shadow memory access cost

Optimizing DFT

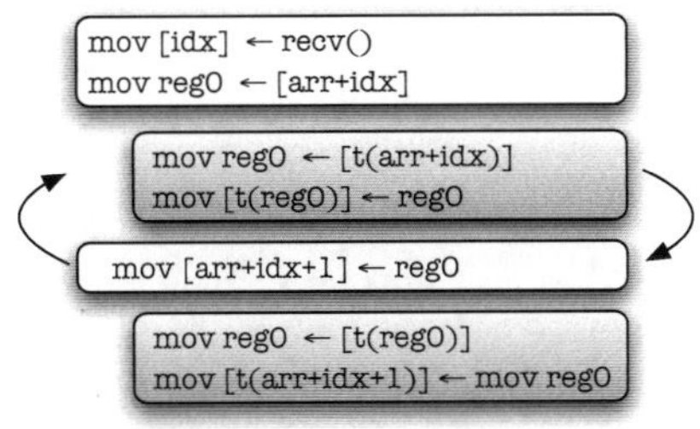

- Each Instrumentation unit require head/tail instructions
- t( ): shadow memory access cost

Optimizing DFT

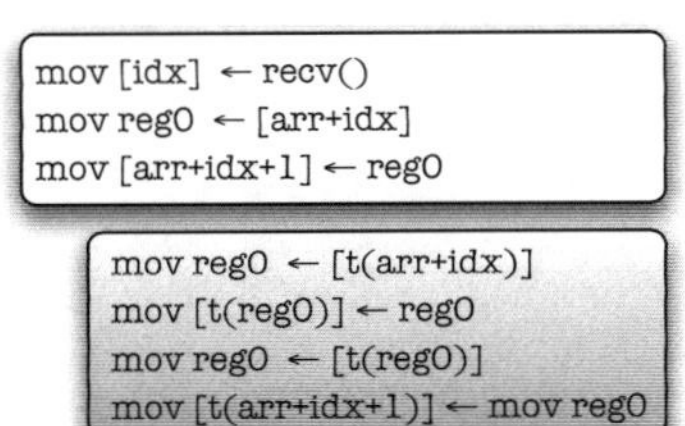

- Each Instrumentation unit require head/tail instructions
- t( ): shadow memory access cost

Optimizing DFT

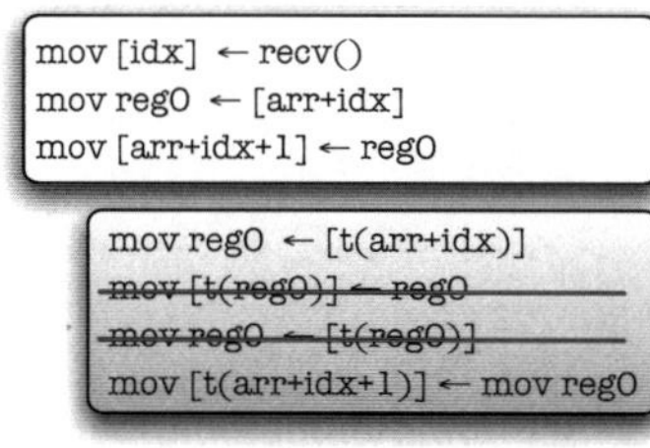

- Less instrumentation units (2→1)
- Less tracking instructions (4→2)

Static detection of C++ vtable escape vulnerabilities in binary code

David Dewey Jonathon Giffin
School of Computer Science
Georgia Institute of Technology
{ddewey, giffin}@gatech.edu

Common problem in C++

In C++ specifically, how does one convert and instance of an object into an instance of another object?

"...use `static_cast` in all cases and see what the compiler says."

B. Stroustrup. The Design and Evolution of C++. Pearson Education, 1994.

C++ Type confusion vulnerabilities

Adobe Flash Player SharedObject Type Confusion Vulnerability

CVE-2011-0611

Microsoft ATL/MFC ActiveX Type Confusion Vulnerability

CVE-2009-2494

Microsoft Office Excel Conditional Expression Ptg Type Confusion Vulnerability

CVE-2011-1989

The list goes on… and on… and on…

Reverse engineering C++ binaries is hard

```
; END OF FUNCTION CHUNK FOR ?_SendRequestWithDrainComplete@HTTP_USER_REQUEST@@AAEKPAVPENDING_
; ---------------------------------------------------------------------------
; START OF FUNCTION CHUNK FOR ?SendRequest@HTTP_USER_REQUEST@@QAEKQAEK_KHP6GXPAXKK2K@ZKKH@Z

loc_EAFB93D:                            ; CODE XREF: HTTP_USER_REQUEST::SendRequest(uchar *
                mov     eax, [ecx]
                call    dword ptr [eax+4]
                mov     [esi+14h], edi
                jmp     loc_EAE7DFD
; END OF FUNCTION CHUNK FOR ?SendRequest@HTTP_USER_REQUEST@@QAEKQAEK_KHP6GXPAXKK2K@ZKKH@Z
; ---------------------------------------------------------------------------
; START OF FUNCTION CHUNK FOR ?OnIoComplete@WEBIO_REQUEST@@UAEXKKPAVHTTP_ASYNC_OVERLAPPED@@@

loc_EAFB94A:                            ; CODE XREF: WEBIO_REQUEST::OnIoComplete(ulong,ulong
                mov     ecx, [ebp+arg_8]
                mov     eax, [ecx]
                inc     ebx
                call    dword ptr [eax]
; ---------------------------------------------------------------------------

loc_EAFB957:                            ; CODE XREF: WEBIO_REQUEST::OnIoComplete(ulong,ulong
                                        ; WEBIO_REQUEST::OnIoComplete(ulong,ulong,HTTP_ASYNC_
                mov     esi, [esi+20h]
                mov     eax, [esi]
                push    edi
                mov     ecx, esi
                call    dword ptr [eax+10h]
; ---------------------------------------------------------------------------
```

As it turns out, these are all the same problem…

- Recently, many software-level vulnerabilities caused by C++ type confusion
- Compiled C++ code can be very difficult to analyze
  - IDS/IPS vendor wanted to provide signature coverage
  - Software consumer concerned with application security
  - Third-party interoperation
- Software developers regularly incorrectly use the `static_cast` operator
  - No compiler warning from most modern compilers
  - C++ standard only requires "cv-check"

Root of the problem

- This code compiles without warning with Visual Studio and g++ (< 4.6)
- Running this code causes a call to arbitrary memory

```
class class1 {
public:
     class1();
     ~class1();
     virtual void addRef();
     virtual void print();
};

class class2 : public class1 {
public:
     class2();
     ~class2();
     virtual void voidFunc1() {};
     virtual void debug();
};

int tmain(int argc, TCHAR* argv[])
{
     class1 C1;
     C1.addRef();
     C1.print();
     static cast<class2*>(&C1)->debug();
     return 0;
}
```

Same problem

- In the previous slide, the problem should be obvious to a developer
- Consider this code. `_tmain()` and `internalFunction()` may be “miles apart”
  - Separate libraries
    - Not caught by g++ 4.6
- Very common code construct in MS COM

```
int internalFunction(void *pv)
{
  static_cast<class1*>(pv)->addRef();
  static_cast<class1*>(pv)->print();
  static_cast<class1*>(pv)->debug();
  return 0;
}

int _tmain(int argc, _TCHAR* argv[])
{
  class1 *C1 = new class1;
  class2 *C2 = new class2;
  internalFunction((void *)C1);
  internalFunction((void *)C2);
  return 0;
}
```


Structure of a C++ object after compilation

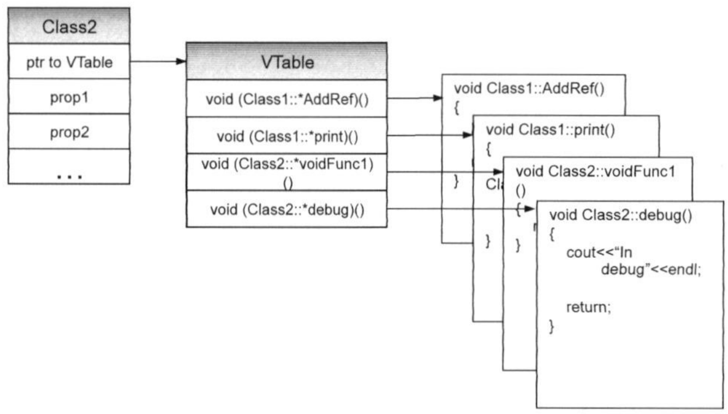


```
00402138 off 402138 dd offset sub 4010D0
0040213C dd offset sub 4010A0
00402140 dd offset nullsub 1
00402144 dd offset sub 4010B0
00402148 dd offset dword 402274
0040214C off 40214C dd offset sub 4010D0
00402150 dd offset sub 4010A0
00402154 align 8
00402158 db 48h ; H
00402159 db 0
0040215A db 0
0040215B db 0
0040215C db 0
```

RECALL

- Reconstruct C++ objects from binary code
- Perform reaching definition analysis on object definitions to determine which object is being referenced at a given use point (make reverse engineering easier)
- Perform a "congruence check" to determine the safety of the use of a given object (detects vtable escape vulnerabilities)

High-level architecture of RECALL

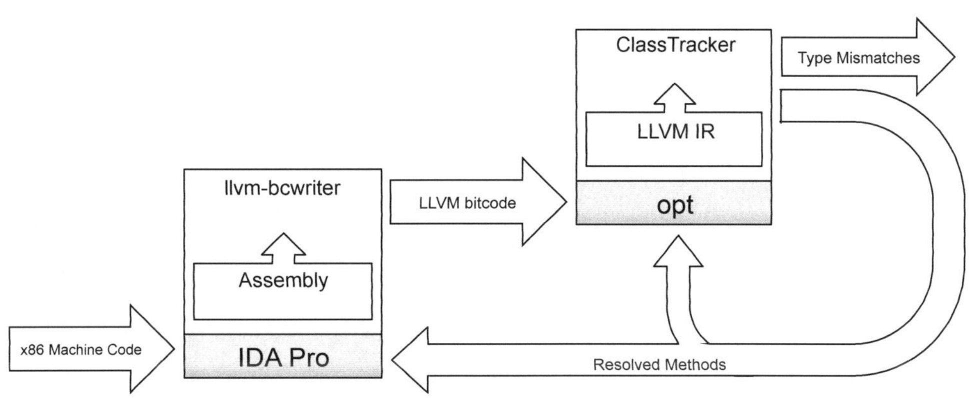

x86 to SSA

- First, we translate x86 machine code into an SSA-based IR
- We chose an SSA-based IR to make translation simpler
  - x86 assembly is mostly triple-based
  - Use-def chains are implicit (core requirement for reaching definitions)
  - Problems with going to higher-level IR
- Chose the LLVM IR due to the robustness of the LLVM analysis framework
- LLVM is attractive from a licensing perspective

Object reaching definition analysis

$$REACH_{IN}[S] = \bigcup_{p \in pred[S]} REACH_{OUT}[p]$$

$$REACH_{OUT}[S] = GEN[S] \cup (REACH_{IN}[S] - KILL[S])$$

Where:

GEN is the set of objects that are instantiated in a given basic block

KILL is the set of objects that are deleted in a given basic block

For interprocedural analysis, $REACH_{IN}$ at the entry of a function F is equal to REACH[c] at the call to F from a call site c

Indentifying object instantiation

- Stack-allocated

  Implement object structure heuristics
  - Inline constructor
  - Explicit constructor

- Heap-allocated – new() operator

  Call to `YAPAXI(uint size)`
  - Inline constructor
  - Explicit constructor

Tracking object types

- For each object, create a structure mapping the structure of the object
- Tag each object type with the virtual address of the constructor

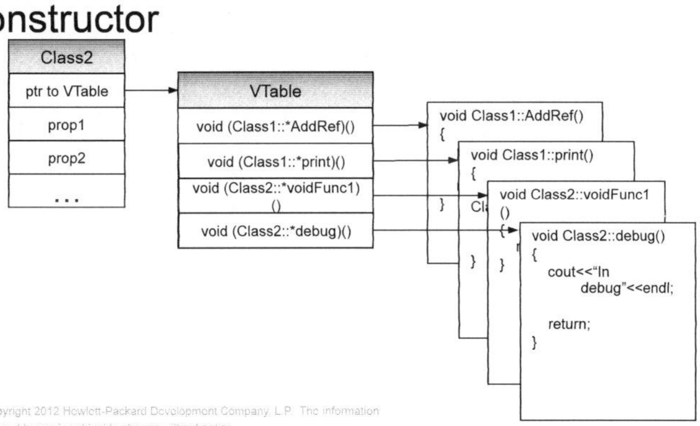

Congruence Check

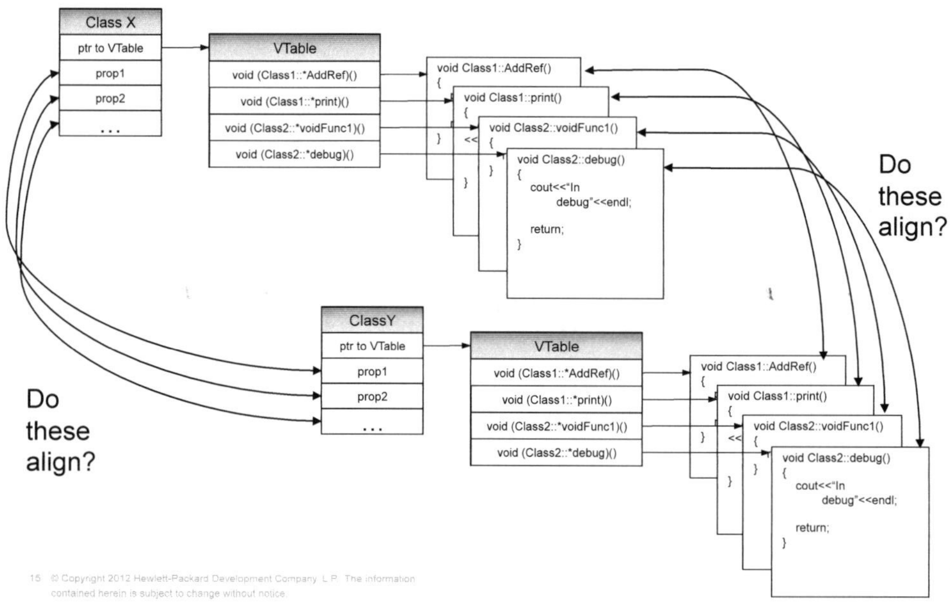

Caveats

- Not designed for the analysis of malware or obfuscated code
- Does not require RTTI or debug symbols
- Focus is on code compiled with Visual Studio, but techniques can be generalized to other compilers
- If an object is allocated and the class pointer is stored in a collection, when the pointer is retrieved, we cannot track the type (future work)

Results

- Able to reconstruct and analyze objects from sample code that models:

  [stack-allocated, heap-allocated] x [inlined ctor, explicit ctor]

- Able to identify vulnerabilities in microbenchmarks designed to simulate real vulnerabilities:
  - Simulated CVE-2011-0611(Adobe Reader)
  - Simulated CVE-2010-0258 (Microsoft Excel)

Why microbenchmarks?

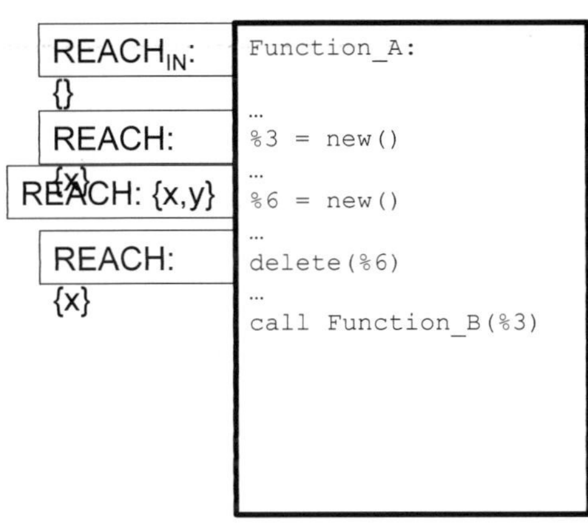

- Analysis is performed interprocedurally
- Procedures can be analyzed independent of their location in the binary
- "Moving" procedures does not impact the correctness of the analysis

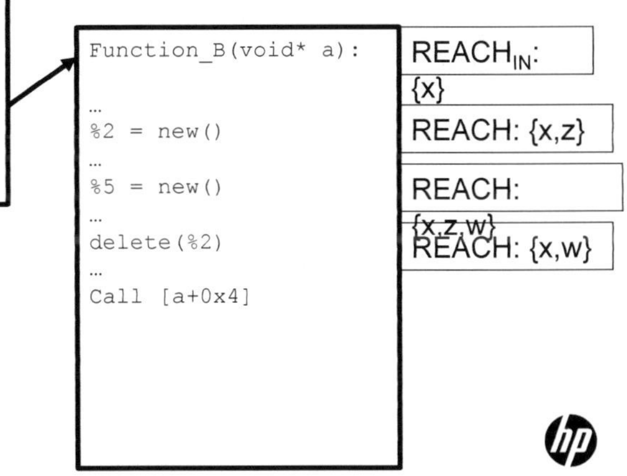

Select Related Work

D. F. Bacon and P. F. Sweeney. Fast static analysis of C++ virtual function calls. In Proceedings of the ACM SIGPLAN Conference on Object-Oriented Programming, Systems, Languages, and Applications (OOPSLA), 1996.

B. Calder and D. Grunwald. Reducing indirect function call overhead in C++ programs. In Proceedings of the ACM SIGPLAN-SIGACT Symposium on Principles of Programming Languages (POPL), Portland, Oregon, 1994.

C. Meadows. A procedure for verifying security against type confusion attacks. In IEEE Computer Security Foundations Workshop (CSFW), Pacific Grove, California, June 2003.

H. Pande and B. Ryder. Data-flow-based virtual function resolution. In Proceedings of the Third International Symposium on Static Analysis (SAS), 1996.

H. D. Pande and B. G. Ryder. Static type determination for C++. In Proceedings of the 6th USENIX C++ Technical Conference, 1994.

A. Slowinska, T. Stancescu, and H. Bos. Howard: A dynamic excavator for reverse engineering data structures. In Proceedings of the Network and Distributed Systems Security Symposium (NDSS), 2011.

D. Song, D. Brumley, H. Yin, J. Caballero, I. Jager, M. Kang, Z. Liang, J. Newsome, P. Poosankam, and P. Saxena. BitBlaze: A new approach to computer security via binary analysis. In International Conference on Information Systems Security, 2008.

J. Viega, J. T. Bloch, Y. Kohno, and G. McGraw. ITS4: A static vulnerability scanner for C and C++ code. In Proceedings of the 16th Annual Computer Security Applications Conference (ACSAC), 2000.

Conclusion

- In our paper, we make the following contributions:
  - Resolve vtable dispatch calls in compiled binaries
  - Programmatically identify vtable escape vulnerabilities introduced by C++ developers
  - Construct a general C++ decompilation framework for use in other analyses

Questions?

ddewey@gatech.edu
giffin@gatech.edu

Identifying and Analyzing Pointer Misuses for Sophisticated Memory-corruption Exploit Diagnosis

Mingwei Zhang (†)
Aravind Prakash (§)
Xiaolei Li (†)
Zhenkai Liang (†)
Heng Yin (§)

(†) School of Computing, National University of Singapore
(§) Department of Electrical Engineering and Computer Science, Syracuse University

Simple Stack Buffer Overflow

- An attacker overwrites vulnerable function return address, which points to shellcode on stack.

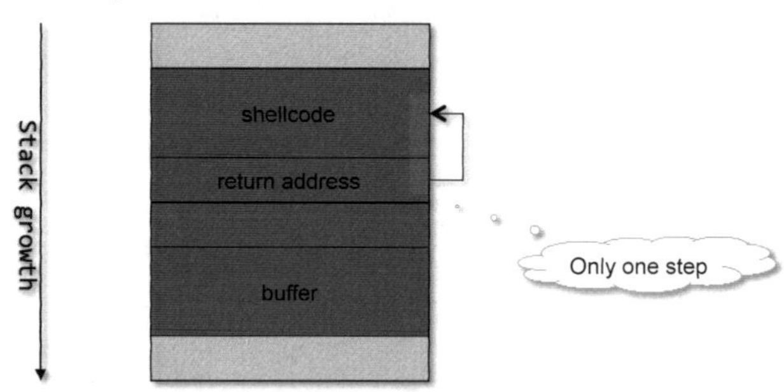

- These single step attacks don't work anymore thanks to:
  - ASLR, DEP, NX, etc.

2

Exploiting SEH Mechanism

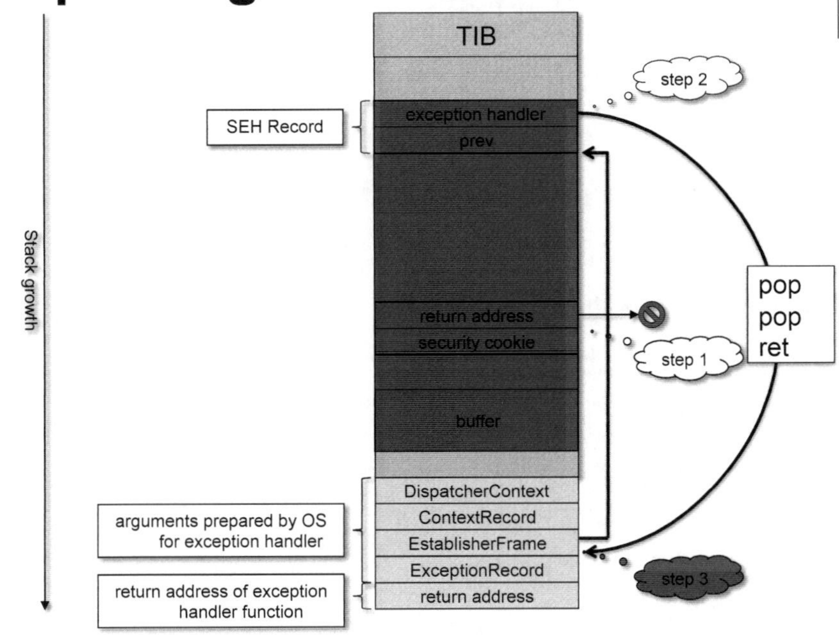

3

Insights

- Recent attacks employ **multiple steps**.
- **Pointer misuse** is very prominent in sophisticated attacks.
- Key steps constitute pointer misuses.

Our Goal:
Diagnosing pointer misuses in a multi-step attack.

4

Pointerscope – Attack Diagnosis Engine

- **Type System** tailored to diagnose pointer misuse.
- **Eager type inference** system to detect pointer misuses.
- Provide **big picture** of the misuse through *key steps* graph.

5

Overview

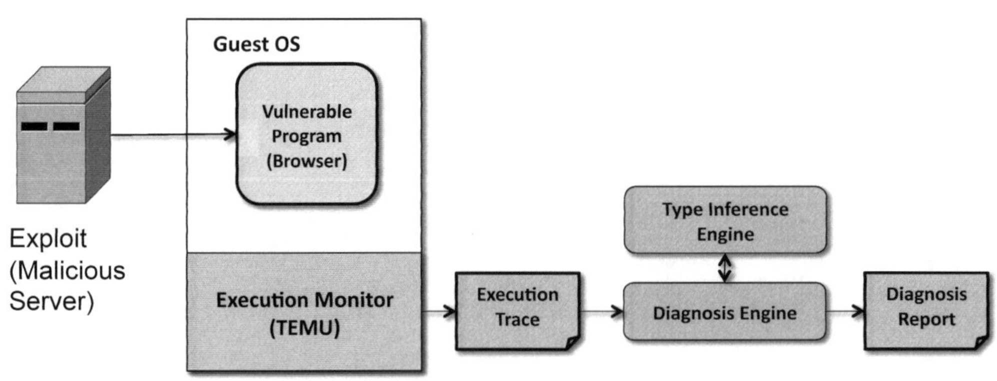

6

Variable And Variable Type

- A variable is a memory location or a register.
- Simple primitive variable types:
  - Integer
  - Control Pointer (or code pointer)
  - Data Pointer
  - Other. (The rest of the types)

7

Type Lattice

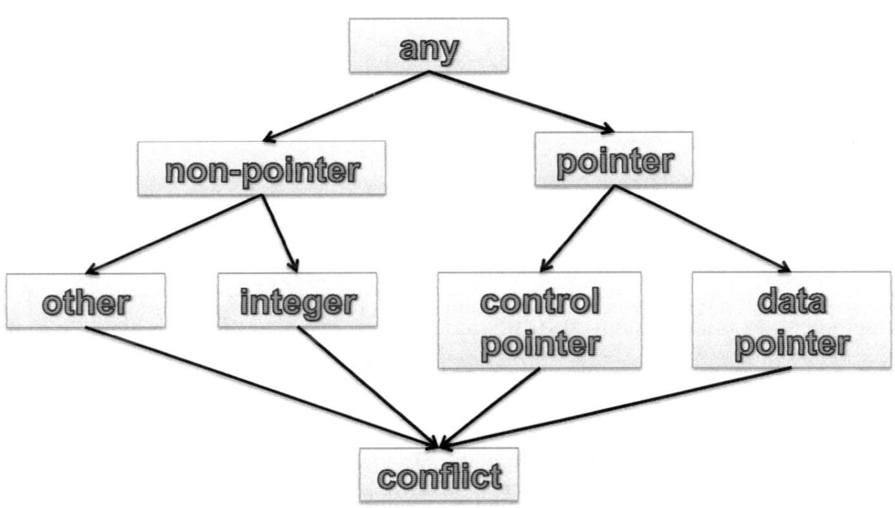

8

Eager Dynamic Type Inference

- Type Propagation:
  - mov %eax, %ebx
    - Inference: eax and ebx have same type
- Type Constraints:
  - call %eax
    - Inference: %eax contains Control Pointer

9

Example – Type Inference

{eax, ebx} : **ANY**	mov %eax, %ebx
{eax, ebx, ecx} : **ANY**	mov %ebx, %ecx
ecx is an INT {eax, ebx, ecx}: **Integer**	imul $0x05, %ecx, %ecx
{eax, ebx, ecx, edx} : **Integer**	mov %ecx, %edx
Used as a pointer. **Conflict**	call *%ecx

Harder than it seems!

10

Challenges

- X86 supports base-index with displacement – Problem: Compilers don't follow convention.

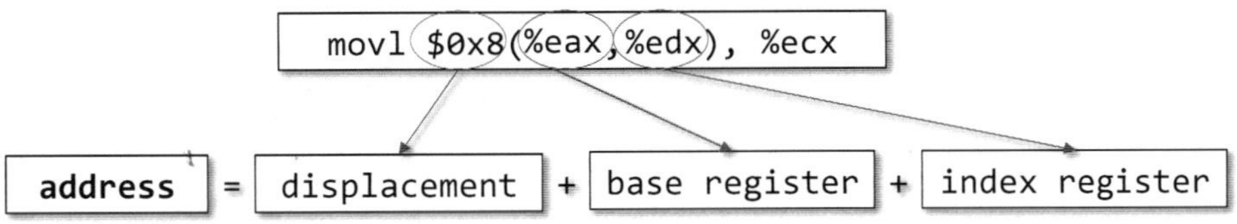

Solution: Register closest to result is the base.

11

Challenges… contd.

- Individual instructions not always lead to accurate type inferences.
  - Eg:

```
not %ebp
or  $0x3,%ebp
not %ebp
```

⇔

```
and $0xfffffffc,%ebp
```

  - Solution: recognizing the common patterns and treat them as special cases

12

Challenges… contd.

- LEA designed to load effective address, but often used in arithmetic.

lea \$0x8(%eax,%edx,4), %ecx ⇨ %ecx = %eax + %edx×4 + \$0x8

Solution: Treat lea as an arithmetic operation.

13

Challenges…

- More challenges discussed in the paper!

14

Key Steps Graph – Example

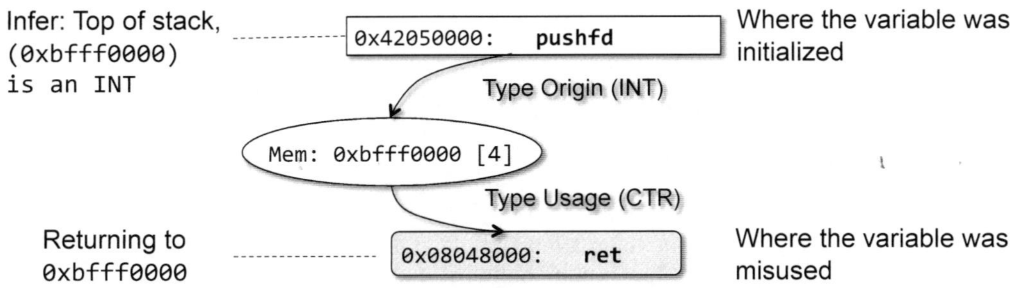

15

Evaluation

- Implementation
  - Execution monitor on TEMU.
  - 3.6K lines of C code.
- Experimental setup
  - Evaluated against real world exploits from Metasploit framework.

16

Summary of Effectiveness

CVE	Attack Technique	Runtime*	Pointer Misuses	Trace Size	Slice Size
CVE-2010-0249	Uninitialized memory; heap spray	18m23s, 8m30s	11	307,987,560	48,404,242
CVE-2009-3672	Incorrect variable initialization; heap-spray	3m10s, 31s	2	22,759,299	955,325
CVE-2009-0075	Uninitialized memory; heap spray	25m, 21m16s	6	411,323,083	44,792,770
CVE-2006-0295	Heap overflow; heap spray	3m5s, 1s	3	808,392	34,883
CVE-2006-1016	Stack overflow; SEH exploit	4m59s, 1m33s	3	64,355,691	1,334,253
CVE-2006-4777	Integer overflow; heap spray	1m45s, 40s	3	2,632,241	1,669,751
CVE-2006-1359	Incorrect variable initialization; heap spray	11m58s, 13s	2	8,336,193	29,520
CVE-2010-3333	Stack overflow vulnerability; SEH exploit	18m53s, 7m24s	1	236,331,307	814,305
CVE-2010-3962	Incorrect variable initialization; heap spray	10m36, 15s	2	9,281,019	78,704

*Time taken to generate trace, time taken to generate key steps

Case Study: CVE-2009-3672

- This is a real world exploit for vulnerable version of IE Browser
- This attack is caused by a vulnerability in the class `CDispNode`'s member function `SetExpandedClipRect`

The First Type Conflict

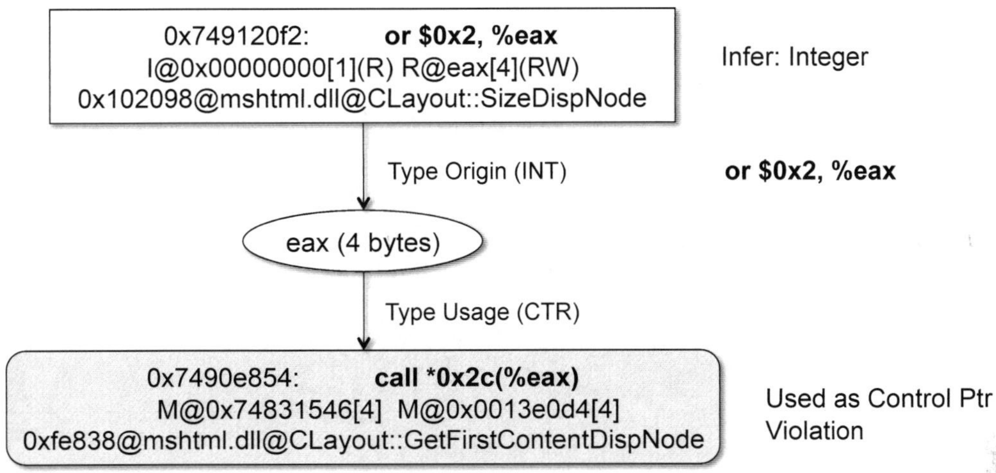

19

The Second Type Conflict

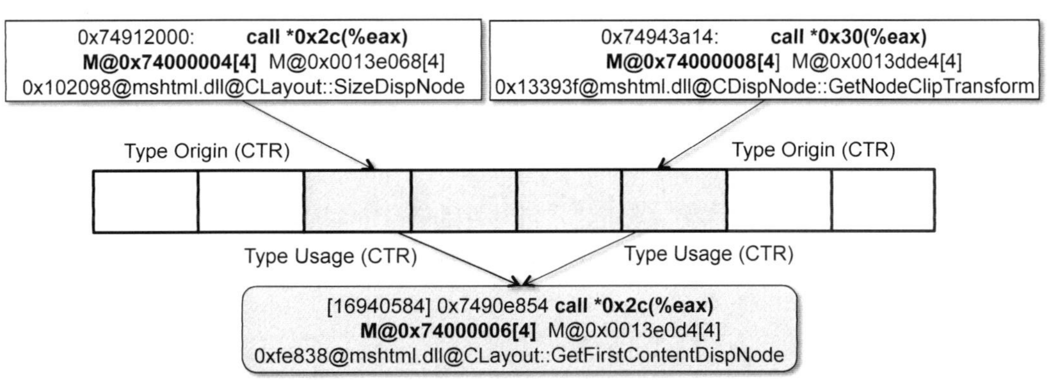

20

Final Result

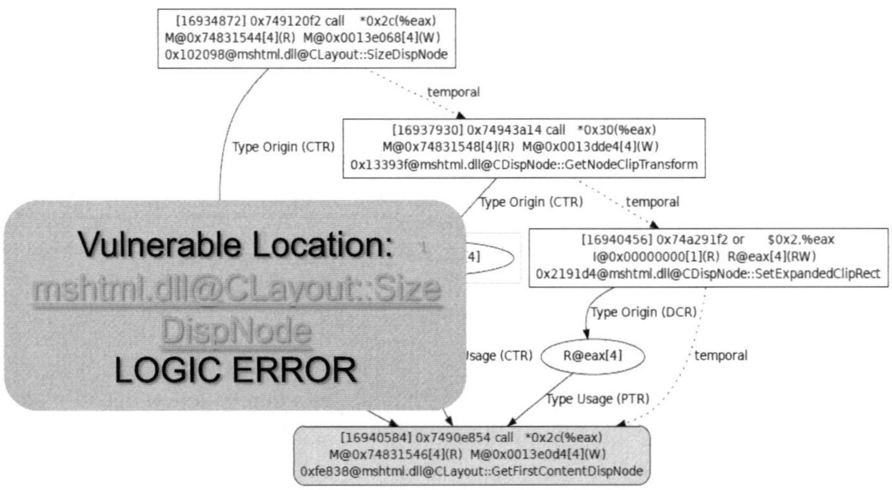

21

Reducing False Positives

- What makes it hard?
  - Compiler optimizations
  - Code obfuscation – even by proprietary code.

- Note: Our goal is NOT to eliminate False Positives.

22

Related Work

- Attack Diagnosis Techniques
  - BackTracker [King, et. al, SOSP'03], Dynamic Taint Analysis [Newsome, et. al, NDSS'05]
- Type and Data Structure recovery from binary
  - Rewards [Zin, et.al, NDSS'10], Howard [Slowinska, NDSS'11], Tie [Lee, et.al, NDSS'11]
- Defense and evasion techniques
  - CFI [Abadi, et.al, CCS'05], DFI [Castro, et.al, OSDI'06], WIT [Akritidis, et.al, IEEE S&P'08]

23

Conclusion

- We define a **pointer centric type system** to track pointers.
- We design a **type inference system** to detect pointer misuses.
- We **generate the key steps graph** to identify key steps.
- We evaluate our work by testing our system on real-world exploits from metasploit.

24

Questions?

25

Challenges… contd.

- Handling memory copy operations
  - Memory copy operations may break the integrity of variables

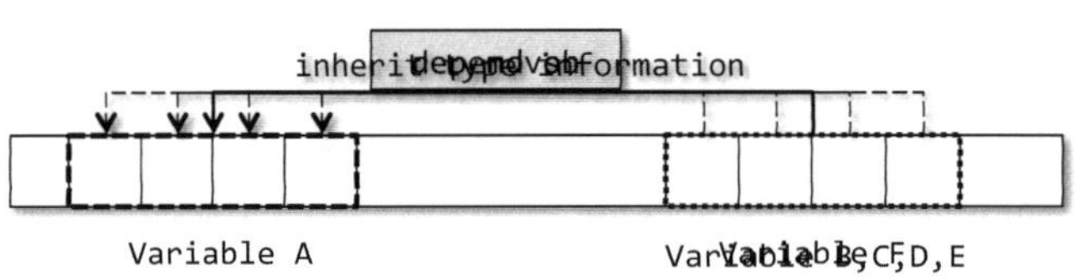

Solution: Aggregation.

26

Case Study: SEH Attack

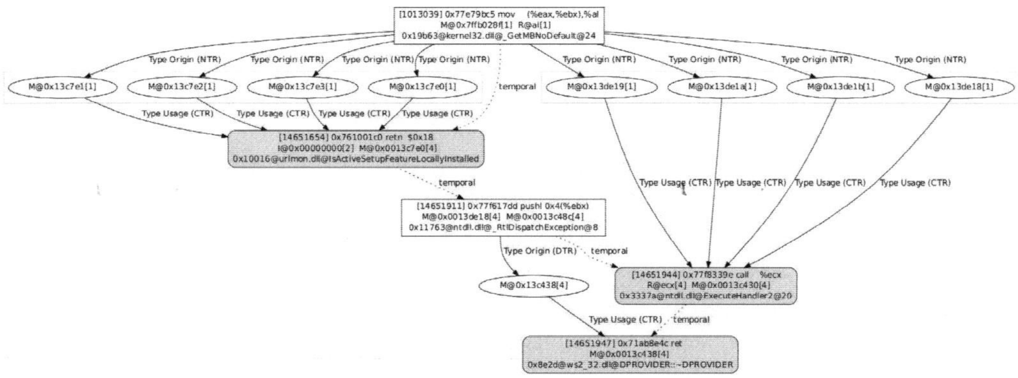

AUTHOR INDEX